## Praise for Whitney Balliett and *Collected Works:* A Journal of Jazz 1954–2001

*Winner of the ASCAP-Deems Taylor Award*

"*Collected Works* stands alongside Gary Giddins's similar book, *Visions of Jazz: The First Century,* as an invaluably cogent and forthright, self-assuredly individualistic history of jazz." —David Hajdu, *The New York Review of Books*

"Not only does Whitney Balliett know and love jazz, but he also possesses the poetic genius to champion it, riffing on language with all the fluency of the musicians whose praises he sings." —*San Francisco Chronicle*

"Whitney Balliett's words are magic. His descriptions of the music and musicians are very affecting and his love for jazz shines through with every elegant phrase." —Marian McPartland

"Balliett is a master of language." —Philip Larkin

"Few people can write as well about anything as Balliett writes about jazz." —*Los Angeles Times Book Review*

"I am not really generous enough to tell you what I really think about how good you are. Let's say I'm flabbergasted. And that I think you are extremely important." —Harold Brodkey

## Books by Whitney Balliett

*For the paints-poet and the pianist (Mr. and Mrs. Richard Mills), with love, Whitney Balliett*

# Whitney Balliett

*N.Y.C. May 1, 2002*

# COLLECTED WORKS

## A journal of jazz 1954-2001

St. Martin's Griffin ≈ New York

For Nancy
with admiration and love

www.stmartins.com

ISBN 0-312-20288-1 (hc)
ISBN 0-312-27008-9 (pbk)

Book designed by Victoria Kuskowski

First St. Martin's Griffin Edition: April 2002

10 9 8 7 6 5 4 3 2 1

# Contents

# An Introduction

This book is a distillation of many of the reviews and critical pieces that I have written about jazz from the early fifties to 2000. (I have also included three reporter pieces—a trip to New Orleans, in 1966, to gauge the health of the music in that haunted city; a visit, in 1969, to one of Dick Gibson's early jazz parties, in Aspen, Colorado; and a trip to Mobile, Alabama, in 1970, to hear a festival of high school and college players.) The pieces first appeared in the *Saturday Review*, *The Reporter*, a new quarterly, *Brilliant Corners*, and *The New Yorker*, and they were published in *The Sound of Surprise* (1959), *Dinosaurs in the Morning* (1962), *Such Sweet Thunder* (1966), *Ecstasy at the Onion* (1971), *New York Notes* (1976), *Night Creature* (1981), and *Goodbyes and Other Messages* (1990). Those pieces written between 1991 and 2000 have never been in book form. In effect, this book rounds out my *American Singers* (1988) and *American Musicians* II (1996), which contain the rest of my work—that is, the hundred-odd biographical essays I have done on jazz performers, many of the essays being natural outgrowths of pieces included here. I chose my title, *Collected Works*, because I like its ring, and in hopes that all three volumes of my work will one day be issued side by side as my true *C. W.*

In this memoir-ridden time, several paragraphs of autobiography: I first wrote about jazz at Exeter, and was probably influenced by Barry Ulanov in *Metronome*, a music magazine. I continued at Cornell, doing pieces for the *Widow* and the *Cornell Daily Sun*, where I printed my first timely review—of a concert given on December 10, 1948, by Duke Ellington, and run the next day. The head was simply "MUSIC" and beneath that "By Balliet" (sic). Here it is, a frazzled mixture of nerves, haste, and budding taste:

> Edward Kennedy "Duke" Ellington presented his second Cornell concert in Bailey Hall last night under the auspices of the worthy Rhythm Club. His music was little short of impeccable. Twenty years' leadership in the field of jazz has not faded the Duke, nor his great love of jazz.
>
> Due to limited space, unfortunately, the hunt and pick method will have to be employed. The first half of the concert was notable for "Reminiscing in Tempo," a piece written in 1935, that will be suitable in 1955. It is a study in moods that is delightful in its warmth and humor. The Duke's new bass player, Wendell Marshall, showed fine technique and imagination in the cute "She Wouldn't Be Moved." Billy Strayhorn, the

Duke's erstwhile arranger, presented Harry Carney's baritone in Paradise; one can do no less than marvel at this man's command of his instrument. A two-part satiric rendition, "Symphomaniac," lampooned the "King of Jazz," Paul Whiteman in his heydays of '29, closing with sharp consideration of the music of Dizzy Gillespie; Dizzy would have smiled grimly. . . .

And on for two more game paragraphs. (The concert was recorded and listening to it now I was pleased to find that I was not too far off the mark. I should have mentioned Sonny Greer's majestic and swinging drumming and the many beautiful background chordal hums that Ellington invariably posed his soloists against. Also Duke's penchant for show-biz tricks—here the blaring five-man trumpet section and the ridiculous up-tempos.)

I graduated from Cornell in 1951, and two or three years later I started writing regularly about jazz for the *Saturday Review*. (I was already at *The New Yorker*.) William Shawn, *The New Yorker*'s omniscient editor, eventually read some of the pieces and in 1957 he asked me if I'd like to try a jazz column for the magazine. (He was, of course, a jazz fan and an enthusiastic Fats Waller pianist.) The piece on Cecil Taylor and Gerry Mulligan in "The Fifties" was the first column, and it ran on April 13. In 1962, I wrote my first Profile, on Pee Wee Russell.

Guided by Edmund Wilson's precept that a critic must first describe what he is going to criticize, I began trying to describe what jazz sounded like. Music is transparent and bodiless and evanescent, so I was forced to use metaphor and simile and other such circumambulatory devices, all of which caused the musicology boys to deride me as an "impressionist." They were right. I was and am an impressionist, and as such have been told that I come closer to delineating the music than any notator, that, anyway, jazz, with its odd non-notes and strange tones and timbres, is almost impossible to translate into notes on paper.

*Collected Works* is also an indirect and cumulative history of the music, which has moved like lightning since its turn-of-the-century New Orleans beginnings, when it was a heedless, primitive, inward-leaning collective music. Since then, in its multifarious guises—swing, Dixieland, boogie-woogie, bebop, hard-bop, the "new thing," free jazz, abstract jazz, atonal jazz—it has rocketed through the world. The music will persist as long as it radiates its unique emotional energy and catches us by surprise with an untoward phrase or sound. The music is, as I pointed out in the title of my first book, the sound of surprise.

I made a startling discovery when I reread the pieces from the fifties and the early sixties: I was learning on the job. How fine of William Shawn to let a still-shapeless critic and writer loose in his pages so that he could finish growing up, and then, hopefully, turn to and pay *The New Yorker* back! Anyway, I thank my first editor Rogers Whitaker, who snickeed at the jejune and cosseted the good and such later helpmeets as Susan Moritz and Adam Gopnik. (And I thank Tim Bent and Julia Pastore at St. Martin's. Their memories and sharp eyes have had much to do with shaking this book into shape.)

What this country's strange love-hate attitude toward its own music comes down to, I guess, is a brief, indelible conversation I had with my Philharmonic-going mother some thirty years ago:

ME: "Ma, I have a new book out. Would you like a copy?"

SHE: "Is it about that jazz?"

ME: "Yes."

SHE: "No, thank you."

# THE FIFTIES

# 1954

## First Festival

The first Newport Jazz Festival started in many places, and one of them was in front of Local 802 of the A. F. of M., on West Fifty-second Street in New York when twelve musicians, a lady novelist, a jazz promoter, a jazz record executive, and I boarded a Greyhound bus. It was one P.M. on a Saturday in mid-July. The bus, headed for Rhode Island, was an hour late in getting off, and only three musicians, who had stepped around the corner for a beer, were left behind. (As jazz musicians will, they materialized like genii at the proper time at the concert.) The musicians on board included two distinct camps. On one side of the aisle were Eddie Condon, the lizard-tongued guardian of the remnants of the Austin High School gang, Pee Wee Russell, whose incomparable face and clarinet have been around since Prohibition, and Wild Bill Davison. On the other side were several members of Dizzy Gillespie's band, and the Modern Jazz Quartet, consisting of Horace Silver, Percy Heath, Milt Jackson, and Kenny Clarke who, with Gillespie and Charlie Parker, was one of the founders of bebop. It was a jovial ride until the bus was held up at eight P.M. at the Jamestown Ferry, which is just across Narragansett Bay from Newport, by an inscrutable official who said, come hell or high water, the bus would take its turn, in spite of the fact that Eddie Condon and his boys were scheduled to begin the festival at 8:30.

An hour later, the crossing finally achieved, the first concert was opened in the elegant tennis Casino by the festival's master of ceremonies, Stan Kenton. He began to read a kind of history of jazz prepared by Nat Hentoff of *down beat* magazine, then introduced Eddie Condon who, in company with Wild Bill Davison, Ralph Sutton, Peanuts Hucko, Lou McCarthy, Jack Lesberg, and Cliff Leeman, got things off to an ebullient start. A second, and better band, numbering Bobby Hackett, Pee Wee Russell, Vic Dickenson, Sutton, Milt Hinton, and Buzzy Drootin, followed. Pee Wee was eloquent and almost forthright, and Vic Dickenson, who plays the trombone with genius, was in excellent form. While the group was sailing through "Royal Garden Blues," a sprite dressed in dungarees suddenly appeared on the sharply peaked roof of a nearby Casino outbuilding, and burst into a wild, spidery dance against the moonlit sky. The evening was crystalline, the music warm and meaningful, and it seemed as if the spirit of jazz itself had materialized in appreciation of the celebration being held in its honor. A few minutes later, the figure had vanished, but the image—black arms and legs spinning in the light blue air—stuck. Lee Wiley sang five songs accompanied by Hackett and his rhythm section. Three numbers would have been enough; it was growing chilly, and the crowd was restive. But after Miss

Wiley a jam-session group, which involved most of the members of the two Dixieland groups, ran through the "Bugle Call Rag" and "Ole Miss" with verve and economy in just six minutes.

The intermission was forgone, and the Modern Jazz Quartet appeared. Due to the fortunate handling of microphones, and the advantageous half-shell in which the musicians performed, none of its subtleties, innuendoes, or quiet humor was lost. Dizzy Gillespie, playing his new trumpet, which has a bell that points directly toward Heaven, brought on a quintet, and for the first time in the evening the crowd of 7,000, which had had a tendency to sit on its hands, erupted. Lee Konitz and his quartet were called out, played with its customary coolness, and things settled down again. Oscar Peterson and his trio appeared, and the lid blew off again, for Peterson, who is the Man Mountain Dean of modern pianists both in figure and ability, seemed to fill the arena completely. Gerry Mulligan's quartet displayed the flowing lines that have been its remarkably successful trademarks in the past year. They were followed by a lady considered by many as nonpareil among female jazz vocalists, Ella Fitzgerald, who aroused the audience to a frenzy. The finale was an extraordinary jam session, suspended from "I Got Rhythm." By this time the air was blue with cold, the moon was directly overhead, and it was time for bed.

The second evening got off to an earlier start, in spite of a heavy shower. Stan Kenton again acted as MC, and 5,000 souls were present. A "tribute" to Count Basie, nicely performed by Lester Young, Buck Clayton, Vic Dickenson, Jo Jones, Ray Brown, and Oscar Peterson, all of whom (with the exception of Brown and Peterson) have played with the Count, opened the evening, and gave way to Peterson and his trio, augmented by guitarist Johnny Smith; Dizzy Gillespie, who was unquenchable both evenings; and George Shearing's quintet, which seemed with its blandly controlled fusions, to be spreading oil over swinging waters. After the intermission, Gil Melle, one of the most promising of the young West Coast arranger–composer–tenor saxophonists, made a surprise appearance. Next came a booting sextet composed of Teddy Wilson, Jo Jones, Milt Hinton, Bill Harris, Gerry Mulligan, and Ruby Braff. Lennie Tristano, creating more than a passing murmur in the audience because of his almost complete seclusion in the past two years, appeared with a quartet that included Billy Bauer, Warne Marsh, and Lee Konitz. His playing was as brilliant as ever. Gene Krupa and his trio bombarded the Casino with rim-shots, and was followed by Billie Holiday, who is considered by many as their choice for the first lady vocalist of jazz. She was accompanied by Wilson, Dickenson, Young, Jones, Clayton, and Hinton, who were often with her in the late thirties when she made her monumental sides for Columbia. This was the peak of the festival.

An hour later (after a final outsized melee by the evening's participating musicians) buses and cars were pouring out of Newport, which contracted visibly, and the first Newport Festival of Jazz was over. It will be good to see a second festival next year, for jazz goes well with sea air, trees, history, and the *haut monde*.

*The spasmodic quality of this review is largely the result of its having been written on the night train from Providence to New York and turned in, for timeliness, at the* Saturday Review *office at eight A.M. that morning. I have tried to calm it by adding the description of the rooftop sprite, actually written a week later.*

## Pandemonium Pays Off

**N**orman Granz, a lean, fast-talking, sandy-haired man of thirty-six, with bullying eyebrows, sends out single-handedly over a good part of the Western world a yearly series of jazz concert tours known as "Jazz at the Philharmonic," owns and operates a record company that has mushroomed so quickly in its first year that it has had to be split into two companies to accommodate overworked distribution facilities and, as a canny businessman, is generally regarded as the first person who has ever been able to successfully mass-produce jazz. The total worth of these enterprises is estimated by Granz at five million dollars. Of this, a million accrues from JATP, and the rest from his record firm. These sums—staggering for jazz, since it was not long ago that jazzmen were dying of malnutrition and exposure—are easily accounted for, if not easily explained. Last year JATP included eleven jazz musicians and a singer, who played in fifty American and Canadian cities where seventy-five concerts were held; in Japan where twenty-four concerts were given; in Honolulu; and in twenty-five cities in Europe, where some fifty concerts occurred. The group appeared before approximately four hundred thousand persons, who paid from $2 to $4.80 for their seats. Granz's recording activities, which are sandwiched in between tours and business trips abroad, were equally cornucopic. Over two hundred ten- and twelve-inch jazz LP albums were released on the Clef and Norgran labels, and in a recent month twenty-one new Granz records flowed into record stores across the country. Columbia and Victor, who are again marketing jazz in a big way, released about forty albums apiece. In fact, perhaps 50 percent of all the jazz records produced last year came from Granz factories, a development that has become somewhat of an uneasy joke in the industry. Granz's recording efforts are also encyclopedic. At present his catalogue lists seven LPs devoted to the work of Lester Young. Art Tatum is represented by five twelve-inch LPs, with seven more promised. Charlie Parker has eight. Johnny Hodges has five. And Oscar Peterson, the twenty-nine-year-old Canadian pianist, who has virtually been handmaidened into fame by Granz and has since become the Granz house pianist, now has sixteen titles to his credit.

Granz was born in Los Angeles, and attended UCLA, where, as a part-time quotation clerk with the Los Angeles Stock Exchange, he picked up some useful rudiments about money. After college and a stint in the Army, which was followed by a film editor's job at MGM, Granz, who was a jazz fan and a strong liberal, decided that jazz should be listened to in the pleasantest possible surroundings by the largest possible number of people of all races, creeds, and colors. The non-segregated concert hall was the answer. Late in 1945, after running a series of successful informal concerts at the Los Angeles Philharmonic Auditorium, he took a handpicked group of musicians on a limited tour of the western United States and Canada.

Unfortunately, the public, unlike Barkis, was not willing, and the tour collapsed in Canada after working its way up the West Coast. A few years later, with the assistance of names on the Granz payroll like Gene Krupa, Coleman Hawkins, Bill Harris, Flip Phillips, and Buddy Rich, and with the release of the first of fifteen on-the-spot recordings of JATP concerts, the public changed its mind. In the meantime, Granz had not forgotten his liberal instincts. He succeeded in taking his groups, which have been a consistent mixture of Negro and white, into those parts of the country where racial bias still persists, and two years ago had a rider put in certain of his contracts with theater owners to the effect that if any discrimination is practiced against his audiences, the concert may immediately be canceled.

Since the shaky days of 1945, Granz's acquaintances have been continually astonished by his drive and durability in a notoriously unsympathetic business. He works without any regular assistants, outside of a few harassed secretaries and a publicity agent. Granz books almost all his own concerts, an accomplishment that was of some proportions in his pioneering days and that has since been partially alleviated by arranging future concerts in a city while his men are playing it. In line with his recent efforts to give his enterprises a single, well-honed edge, Granz now schedules concerts in new cities on the strength of his record sales in that area; for the roster of his recording artists, which numbers over a hundred, is a fairly accurate mirror, past and present, of the personnel he has had in his various JATP groups.

Granz attends every concert JATP gives, acting as both MC and stage manager. Out front, he seems an almost timid figure, for he is distinguished in neither voice nor presence. Backstage, however, Granz is highly inflammable. "I go crazy at concerts," he said recently. "I lose my temper every five minutes. I yell at everybody. I'm rude to people who pester me. Every concert has to go perfectly. If somebody goofs, he pays for it." But if Granz is touchy under pressure he is generally of temperate mien. Most of his musicians like working for him, and return to JATP year after year. There are occasional familial eruptions, of course, such as a falling out about a year ago that Granz had with Buddy Rich, the drummer. Rich announced in the pages of *down beat* magazine that he was through with JATP because Granz made his musicians play nothing but "junk." Granz answered hotly that he never told his musicians what to play, and that Rich was a "liar" and an "adolescent." A short time later Rich was contentedly thumping away on a new Granz recording date, and appeared, as usual, in last year's JATP lineup.

Granz the businessman has occasionally made profitable room for Granz the jazz lover. In 1944, for instance, he supervised one of the few honest motion pictures ever made about jazz. A short, photographed in color by Gjon Mili, and called *Jammin' the Blues*, it won an Academy Award nomination for the best short feature of the year. (Many of the musicians involved were drawn from the Granz-sponsored concert group then appearing in Los Angeles.) In 1949, when he was using the facilities of the Mercury record company, he issued a deluxe twelve-inch 78-rpm album which featured such oddities as Harry Carney, the baritone saxophone player, backed by strings, the unorthodox arrangements of George Handy and Ralph Burns, an unaccompanied saxophone solo by Coleman Hawkins, and generous quantities of Bud Powell and Charlie Parker. The album had, in addition, a folio of handsome life-size Gjon Mili photographs, and the whole package, five thousand of which were printed, was priced at a cool twenty-five dollars. It was sold out in a year.

Granz was the first person to experiment widely with on-the-spot recordings, and with studio recordings that took advantage of the longer playing time of the LP. Record stores have been reordering them ever since. Two years ago he released four twelve-inch LPs, titled *The Astaire Story*, which showed off Fred Astaire's singing and dancing before a small Granz-picked jazz unit. The set was panned by the critics, but has been just as widely accepted by the public, which tends to ignore critics, a fact that Granz is well aware of.

Granz the businessman, who has become increasingly dominant in recent years, is most aggressive when he is near the concert stage. Here he believes that a small group, working within a loose framework, is the surest means of producing satisfying, freewheeling jazz. He chooses musicians who, he feels, are the best or the near best on their instruments, regardless of school or style. This does not mean that Granz would be apt to hire an excellent but largely unknown musician, for he is never unconscious of the drawing power of a name. (If Granz decides, though, that a certain unknown musician should become a member of a future JATP tour, he carefully builds his name during the preceding year by releasing several of his LPs. The most recent example of this technique has been his promotion of Buddy de Franco, the clarinettist, and Louis Bellson, the drummer, both of whom will join JATP for the first time this year.)

The result of these policies is a nervous jazz that is somewhere between small-band swing and bebop. It is also a purely solo jazz, where collective improvisation or teamwork is left to other, more pedestrian schools. This concentration on the solo has brought off some weird musical acrobatics. One is a regularly featured trumpet battle—Roy Eldridge and his old pupil Dizzy Gillespie will be the participants this year—in which two trumpeters squeal at each other for chorus after chorus. Another is a deafening drum battle that invariably jellies the stoutest audience. In still another, two tenor saxophonists shriek and roar at each other. Most of the musical materials employed are banal, being restricted to the commonest type of blues, and to such evergreens as "How High the Moon" and a handful of Gershwin tunes.

Granz feels that the average age level of his audiences has increased in the past nine years, and that it is now somewhere between twenty-one and twenty-eight, a rather casual statistic, judging by the oceans of heated teenage faces found at any Granz concert. One might at first describe these audiences as the spiritual offspring of the sprites who jitterbugged in the aisles and on the stage of the Paramount Theatre in New York in the late thirties when Benny Goodman first came to town. But at second glance these present-day audiences are different, and more warlike. They rarely move from their seats, yet they manage to give off through a series of screams (the word "go" repeated like the successive slams of the cars on a fast freight), blood-stopping whistles, and stamping feet a mass intensity that would have made Benny Goodman pale.

Granz the jazz lover is predominantly visible through his studio recording sessions. In these he has been responsible for a certain amount of excellent jazz, as well as for a great deal of mediocrity. Granz officiates at every recording date, and announces this fact on his record labels and sleeves with, respectively, the words "Recorded Under the Personal Supervision of Norman Granz" and "Supervised by Norman Granz." He also composes many of the liner notes for his albums, which have become noted for their superlatives and lack of information. Although Granz claims that he never dictates to his musicians, much of what emanates from his recording studios has come to have a distinct flavor. For, in spite of the fact that his personnels are often laundry lists of jazz royalty, many Granz records are luxurious wastes. One reason for this is that many of the musicians on Granz recordings are members of JATP, and, because of the nature of the music they play seven months out of the year on the concert stage, their musical batteries have gone dead. And if a touring job with Granz often makes his musicians artistically laconic, it has also not advanced the musical growth of such men as Flip Phillips, Oscar Peterson, Charlie Shavers, and Buddy Rich.

When Granz inaugurated this year's JATP tour on September 17, in Hartford, he had eleven of the best jazz musicians money can buy. He is paying them salaries that start at several hundred dollars a week, and range up to $6,000 a week for Ella Fitzgerald and $5,000 for Peterson. In addition to the European tour in the spring, and the fall tour of the United States and Canada, JATP will swing through Australia, as well as Japan and Honolulu. Granz has also promised a minimum of 120 LP albums in the next twelve months. To at least half a million potential customers around the world Granz may well be doing for jazz what another prestidigitator, P. T. Barnum, did for midgets.

*A parody of the way Granz often ended his monosyllabic album lines notes goes:* "This, then, is this, then."

*I wonder how much the instrumental histrionics at the JATP concerts had to do with the animal and traffic noises made in the early sixties by such avant-gardists as Albert Ayler, Archie Shepp, and John Coltrane.*

# 1955

## Artistry in Limbo

Stan Kenton got started officially as a band leader on Memorial Day, 1940, when he opened with a thirteen-piece group at the Rendezvous Ballroom in Balboa, California. The music, already indicative of things to come, was relentless and heavy-booted, with a staccato two-beat attack that resembled in intent, if not execution, the style of the Jimmy Lunceford band of the time. Perhaps it was persuasive because it was rhythmically overpowering, for by the summer's end, Kenton had built a staunch following on the West Coast and considerable speculation about his "new music" in the East. Kenton's second period began in 1944 after he had been East, and, although the band was defter and less aggressive, it was not much different. The third era, 1945–46, illustrated what is now known as the band's principal style—a big reed section securely rooted with a baritone saxophone, an inflexible, metallic-sounding rhythm section, and ear-bursting brass teams. The next two periods extended from 1947 to 1951, years in which Kenton turned restlessly to his "progressive jazz" and "innovations in modern music," using, in addition to his own works, the compositions and arrangements of Bob Graettinger, Pete Rugulo, Ken Hanna, Neil Hefti, and Shorty Rogers. Here the music moved ceaselessly and cumbersomely between the funereal orchestrations of Graettinger, mood music performed by a forty-piece band with strings that was perilously close to movie music, and immense jazzlike frameworks constructed about scintillating section work and occasional soloists. The last era, which brings the band up through 1953, was more or less of a deflation to the mid-forties period, and reveals a clearer jazz feeling than the band had ever before had.

It is impossible not to be impressed by Kenton's aural bulk, by the sheer sinew and muscle that have gone into his music. It is not impossible, however, to remain almost completely unmoved. Kenton's bands, in spite of all the organlike talk that has surrounded their "progressivism" in the past ten years, fit roughly into the tradition of the silvery semi-jazz groups of Larry Clinton, Glen Gray, Glenn Miller, the Dorseys, and Ray Anthony. This tradition, although aereated from time to time by Bunny Berigans and Bobby Hacketts, is quite different from the genuine big jazz bands cradled by Fletcher Henderson and Duke Ellington, and maintained since by Goodman, Lunceford, Calloway, Basie, and Woody Herman. Kenton does not fit easily into the white-collar music of the former tradition, however, for he tried to combine the two movements, with the help of extracurricular seasonings, into something new. This he did, in part, by allowing ample solo space within glistening limousines of sound that, in the end, tended only to stifle whatever potentialities for jazz there were on hand. He also created, as a result of purposely and confusedly trying to be a musical refractor of his times, a self-conscious music that was caught—strident and humorless—somewhere between the pseudo-classical, jazz, and popular music.

Nevertheless, Kenton's sounds and furies have, partly through accident, had certain positive effects within jazz. His various bands have been rigorous training grounds for many younger musicians, particularly those who have gone on to fashion in the past few years, in probable revolt, the small-band parlor jazz of the West Coast. His pelting about of words like "progressive" and "innovation," together with the uncompromisingly modernistic tenor of his music, has helped prepare the public for true futurists like Gillespie, Parker, Monk, Powell, and John Lewis. And, finally, he has inadvertently defined the possible wastelands of his own medium, thus performing the negative service of showing many jazzmen where not to tread.

Kenton says in the epilogue to a recent album called *The Kenton Era* that "It is too early yet to attempt to ascertain whether our efforts over the years have contributed to the development of the world's music." It isn't, of course, for—as is apparent in this album—his music has come just about full circle. Indeed, it deserves a prominent place in that fascinating museum where the curiosities of music are stored.

*We shouldn't forget Eddie Condon's mot about Kenton: "Every Kenton record sounds to me as though Stan signed on three hundred men for the date and they were all on time."*

# 1956

## The Bibulous Aunt

It has become customary, during the thirty-five or so years in which a body of critical writing has sprung up around jazz, for its authors to preface their remarks with indignant statements about all the "nonsense" written on the subject, and then sit down and write some more. There are, of course, good reasons for this. Until the past five or so years, jazz has been widely regarded in this country as a kind of queer Victorian aunt who laces her tea, belches in public, and uses improper amounts of rouge. As a result, its defenders, or better, apologists have often been guilty of a harmful immoderation—gassy prose, provincialism, inaccuracy, and condescension—originally born of a fervent desire to help. But now jazz is played in concert halls and colleges around the world, as well as taught in accredited university courses. It is sent abroad under the sponsorship of the U.S. State Department as a benevolent cultural ambassador. Heavily attended summer festivals of jazz are sprouting around the country. The *New York Times* has a jazz critic. And lastly, jazz has become, with the combined help of the long-playing record and an economic boom, a big business—perhaps the most heartfelt blessing Americans can bestow on a native endeavor.

Europeans have loved, if not always understood, jazz almost since its inception. In 1919, Ernest Ansermet, the Swiss conductor, wrote with perception about Sidney Bechet, whom he had heard in London. A few years later, a German published a short book with the engaging title *Jazz und Shimmy*, which was followed by *Das Jazz-Buch*. (There is something about the German language that is all elbows and belly when it comes to jazz; in the 1930s, another German wrote a paper called "Was Ist mit der Jazzmusik?") Then in 1932 Robert Goffin, a Belgian, wrote what amounts to the first real book about jazz. In the meantime, American magazines like the *Ladies' Home Journal*, *Literary Digest*, and *Etude* were boiling over with pieces called "Is Jazz the Pilot of Disaster?," "The Doctor Looks at Jazz," "Unspeakable Jazz Must Go!," and "Does Jazz Put the Sin in Syncopation?" And in 1926 a man named Henry O. Osgood wrote a solemn, seemingly official book, *So This Is Jazz*, which didn't mention a single jazz musician, but pored reverently over the works of "jazz" composers like Gershwin and Ferde Grofé. In fact, it was not until 1938, when Winthrop Sargeant and Wilder Hobson produced their still-valuable books, *Jazz: Hot and Hybrid* and *American Jazz Music*, that the first full-dress American analytical works were written on the subject. Since then, books on jazz by Americans have been piling up on remainder counters like politicians' diaries, and in some sort of mid-century ecstasy there have recently appeared a discography of LP records, a couple of histories, several autobiographies, a biography, an encyclopedia, and two bibliographies, one of which has well over three thousand entries.

Possibly because zealots have a weakness for the convenient half of any truth, many books on jazz have been highly personalized histories, full of myth, sentimentality, and blowzy writing. Witness *The Real Jazz Old and New*, by Stephen Longstreet. The author, who is perhaps best known as a screenwriter, has compiled, in the form of a history, a great many supposed quotes taken down from nameless jazz musicians, and has packed them in between a whimsy of his own. He explains, for example, that Buddy Bolden, the legendary New Orleans cornetist, was committed to a state institution for the insane in 1907 (he was), and then declares later on that Bolden "may have made the first jazz recordings around 1912." (It has been fairly well proved that Bolden did record, but it was probably around the turn of the century; if the cylinders are ever found, they'll be roughly equivalent to the Rosetta stone.) Charlie "Big" Green, a trombonist, who is supposed to have frozen to death one night on a Harlem doorstep, becomes Charlie Long Green. The first bebop recordings, made in 1944 under Coleman Hawkins' name, are reported to have been released on the "Bluebird" label, instead of the Apollo label. And in his introduction Mr. Longstreet says, "I don't know of another book like [mine]—that lets the jazzmen tell their own story in their own words." Such a book was published well over a year ago—*Hear Me Talkin' to Ya*, edited by Nat Shapiro and Nat Hentoff.

Hugues Panassié, a prejudiced but good-hearted French critic who published one of the pioneering books on jazz, *Le Jazz Hot*, in 1934, and who, through some mysterious chemistry, was chosen to write the entry on jazz for the recently issued fifth edition of *Grove's Dictionary of Music and Musicians*, is far guiltier of uncinching his ego than Longstreet, who at least makes no pretense at being more than an amateur. For Panassié's new book, *Guide to Jazz*, done with Madeleine Gautier, which Louis Armstrong describes in a short preface as "the musicians' Bible" (Panassié later retaliates by calling Armstrong "a genius comparable with the greatest names in the history of music"), is a collection of opinions, peppered with facts, on jazz musicians, songs, jazz categories, and musical terms. It is also very entertaining reading, for Panassié is a jubilantly wrongheaded critic who champions his unwillingness to understand all jazz produced since 1940. Thus, bebop is a disease, and any musician who has become contaminated is either unmentionable or is straight-armed, like Charlie Parker: "An extremely gifted musician, Parker gradually gave up jazz in favor of bop . . ." Panassié's book does, however, provide a distinct, if sometimes abortive, service by listing dozens of obscure or dead rural and urban blues musicians and singers. The fact that some of these entries are all but useless (JENKINS, MYRTLE Piano. Very good in blues, and has made a number of records accompanying blues singers, notably: with Bumble Bee Slim, "New Bricks in My Pillow," "When I Get My Money," 1936), is, of course, partly due to a genuine dearth of information on the subject, as well as, one suspects, to the casualness that elsewhere leads Panassié to label Snooky Young, the trumpeter, as a trombonist.

*The Heart of Jazz*, by William L. Grossman (an associate professor at the New York University School of Commerce) and Jack W. Farrell (a jazz collector), is similar—at least so far as raw prejudice is concerned—to the efforts of Longstreet and Panassié. Written in a bearded drone punctuated with footnotes and phrases like "the nonsensicality of content" (inherent in the trumpet playing of Dizzy Gillespie), the book is by far the canniest and most subtle defense of the moldy-fig school of jazz appreciation that we have yet had.

Grossman puts his shoulder to the moldy-fig dogma with tortoiselike deliberation. Gradually he builds a fustian image of the old New Orleans musician as a carefree, humble, and saintly Uncle Tom who somehow crystallized in his music both the reason and freedom of the humanist and the selfless dignity of the Christian. (Grossman plants this theory squarely on the nonsensical supposition that the "contents" of any music can be unalterably fixed.) Then, he says, along came Louis Armstrong and in 1925 began destroying the religious content in New Orleans jazz through an act of "apostasy," by becoming a self-serving soloist rather than an integrated part of the traditional New Orleans ensemble structure, which has few if any solos. Grossman heaps most of the evils he finds in swing, bebop, and progressive jazz on Armstrong, describing him as playing with "an expertly controlled barbaric yawp," "frenzy," "an undisciplined emotional expansiveness," and "wildness." (A contemporary of Armstrong's, Jabbo Smith, who fits these phrases to a "T," is not mentioned in the book.) The remedy for this unfortunate heresy, Grossman eventually tells us, is that jazz musicians must rediscover the original "Judeo-Christian content" of New Orleans jazz—the origins of which, of course, are now as remote as Chellean man simply because the environment in New Orleans sixty and more years ago will never again exist.

Fortunately, neither André Hodeir, in his *Jazz: Its Evolution and Essence* (Grove Press), nor Marshall Stearns in *The Story of Jazz* (Oxford University Press) has to labor along under this blarney advanced by Grossman early in his argument: "It would indeed be curious if, upon careful critical examination, two very different directions in a creative art were found equally desirable." Hodeir, a cool-minded young French composer and critic, has written a dry and difficult semi-musicological study of jazz that seeks—and often finds—profound insights into the methods of musicians, ranging from the New Orleans clarinettist Johnny Dodds to Charlie Parker. (Dodds is unstintingly praised by Messrs. Grossman and Farrell and is both praised and sharply criticized by Hodeir for his obvious musical waywardness.) If the book has a fault, it is a hyper-intensity that leads Mr. Hodeir into the hushed zones of French theoretical criticism, where, in searching for the very "essence" of jazz, he strips it of its two fundamentals, improvisation and the blues.

Stearns is an associate professor of medieval history at Hunter College, and his book is a smooth and often witty attempt to trace jazz from the cultures current in West Africa two hundred years ago to the enormously complicated mixture it has become. He has been criticized for having produced a disappointingly incomplete history of jazz, but it seems fairly certain that he had little intention of writing a complete work, which would be premature and even impossible. What he has done, however, is give a broad indication, largely gathered from the research of social scientists, as to where many of the religious and secular sources that went into jazz—the English hymn, the spiritual, the blues, African rhythms, the French quadrille, European band music, and the like—came from and how they reacted on one another. There is also, among other things, a sensitive chapter on the tricky attitudes of the Negro toward the white and vice versa, as well as a rather confusing section, in which he tries, with a kind of cinematic transition technique, to map out what was happening simultaneously in jazz in the 1920s and 1930s from Florida to Oregon.

One of the smaller but more durable mysteries of the past twenty years has been the almost total lack of success that novelists and short-story writers have had in dealing with jazz. Jazz is notably unsentimental, as are, in the main, the people who play it. Yet countless bleary novels and stories have appeared in which jazz musicians, postured in various awkward attitudes, produce a cathartic, semi-divine music. At the same time, jazz seems to provide a safety valve for these writers, who invariably let loose a thick spray of metaphor and simile that forms a distracting counterpoint to the subject matter. Here is a paragraph from *The Horn*, a new novel about a saxophonist named Edgar Pool, by John Clellon Holmes, one of the pioneer chroniclers of the world Jack Kerouac presides over:

> [Pool] fled down the immemorial Big River of his music, wanting to follow moving water because it went somewhere, and all complexities and attitudes and wraths were swept away before it. And so he fled down the Great Brown Snake that made the entire continent one vast watershed to it, and that from deepest, woodsy north at its trickling beginnings over smooth Canadian pebbles, to its final, timeless spending in the Gulf, drained out of the heart of America, melling Pittsburgh slag from the Monongahela with dust that blew across the faceless Badlands to the Milk . . . until in huge, instinctive death beyond the last bayous, it joined the other waters of the world.

In the rare moments when Holmes pauses for breath, he tells with considerable authenticity of the last twenty-four hours in the life of Pool, who suggests a combination of Lester Young and Charlie Parker (incidents in Pool's life seem to be lifted directly from Young's and Parker's careers). But then the rhapsody shuts down again, and after a couple of hundred pages one's sense of pity for, or even understanding of, Pool's misery is hopelessly dampened. Holmes says, in a note, that his book, "like the music that it celebrates, is a collective improvisation on an American theme; and if there are truths here, they are poetic truths." What he probably means—if he means anything—is poetical truths. There are plenty of those.

*Literally thousands of books on jazz have appeared since these relatively concise pioneer days. See my reviews later on of some of the rare successes.*

*A "moldy fig" was any jazz lover whose appreciation of the music stopped somewhere between 1930 and 1945. For the moldy fig, small- and big-band swing was anathema, as was bebop. In the forties, there was even a rather synthetic "war" between the figs and the modernists, in which Eddie Condon–type bands were pitted against bebop groups. Neither group ever won, of course, and the tempest soon died.*

# 1957

## Progress and Prudence

Transition, a small and apparently fearless firm in Cambridge, Massachusetts, has issued a brilliant, uncompromising record on which the principal performer is a twenty-three-year-old pianist named Cecil Taylor. *Jazz Advance: The Cecil Taylor Quartet*, the record in question, offers two possibilities. It could have the same revolutionary impact upon modern jazz as the recordings of Charlie Parker, or, because it rejects both the listener and standard jazz procedure with an almost vindictive vigor, it could go the ineffectual way of the big-brass-band works of Stan Kenton. Taylor is a graduate of the New England Conservatory of Music, and his technique and knowledge of music are, like those of most young jazz pianists, more than adequate. But, unlike many of his colleagues, he has a musical imagination that is, within its chosen limits, astonishing. In the six selections on the disc (one apiece by Thelonious Monk, Duke Ellington, and Cole Porter, and the rest by Taylor), he plunges—usually backed by two or three sidemen—into a type of daring jazz improvisation that has been tried occasionally by men like Sonny Rollins, Lennie Tristano, and Charlie Mingus. Heretofore, a classic jazz solo has often been regarded as the creation, from a melody or a set of chords, of a heightened alter-melody that can, in the hands of such a master as Coleman Hawkins, be a far more complex composition than the original. Taylor goes one step further; in, for example, "Charge 'Em Blues" and "Azure" he replaces all the original melodic content with a seemingly disconnected series of hard, jagged, and at times even ugly atonal structures that are jerked back and forth by rhythmic patterns that shift with bewildering speed and frequency. It is exhausting music; in addition to its demanding harmonic and rhythmic complexities, it has considerable power and emotion. Taylor batters us one second with moody, Monklike dissonances, the next second with a nervous run that would be Debussyan were it not so slyly stated, and then with a rush of grinding, staccato chords. This is followed by a short, jolting pause before he races off again. Despite all this strutting activity, there is an overweening muddiness that is due in part to the density of Taylor's style and in part to his habit of mixing in bits and pieces of, apparently, every one of the musical traditions he has ever been in contact with. Under the circumstances, Taylor's drummer, Dennis Charles, and his bass player, Buell Neidlinger, are remarkable. Charles is uncanny at divining just which tortuous rhythmic path his leader is about to explore. The addition, in two numbers, of the keening soprano saxophone of Steve Lacy is, in the face of the fireworks it must contend with, rather unfortunate.

———

Although Gerry Mulligan, composer, arranger, and baritone saxophonist, has never shied at the experimental, his new record, *Mainstream of Jazz*, sounds after Taylor's effusions, like a Louis Armstrong Hot Five. Taylor stuns us with the curious; Mulligan beguiles us by refining the accepted with unflagging warmth and intelligence. In fact, the sextet he employs for this record—Jon Eardley or Don Ferrara, trumpet; Zoot Sims, tenor saxophone; Bobby Brookmeyer, valve trombone; Bill Crow, bass; and Dave Bailey, drums—becomes a self-charging unit that can be traced directly to Jelly Roll Morton's Red Hot Peppers and the early Duke Ellington. There are six numbers, three of them written by Mulligan, and in every one he uses the devices that worked so well with his pioneer quartet (trumpet, baritone saxophone, bass, and drums) of several years ago—casual, baggy counterpoint, subtle dynamics, sensitive exploration of instrumental timbres, and again the absence of a piano (except in "Blue at the Roots," for which Mulligan sits down at the keyboard, with original results). For example, Mulligan inserts, usually after the solos, patches of loose yet thickly textured counterpoint, in which all or some of the melody instruments noodle around for several choruses at a time with contrasting figures—in "Igloo" with a plaintive humming effect, in "Elevation" with an irresistible intensity. This refreshing polyphony spills over into the solos, which are often framed by softly stated chords or counter-melodies that throw the soloist into even bolder relief, while discreetly reminding him that he is still part of a group. The result is a relaxed, intricate busyness that is a pleasing contrast to the widespread practice among modern jazz musicians of allowing soloist after soloist to perform at excessive—and generally vacuous—length, supported by an inevitably metronomic rhythm section.

*Taylor, staying within his own unique borders, has not become a revolutionary force. You visit him, borrow what you can understand, and leave.*

*This was the first jazz column I wrote for* The New Yorker. *It ran on April 13, 1957.*

## The Duke at Play

Duke Ellington, the ingenious composer, arranger, and band leader, is reportedly staging a comeback—the mysterious, often imaginary trek that almost every American artist who has a press agent worth his salt makes at least once in his career. Ellington, whose music continues to color nearly every corner of jazz, and whose songs and serious works rank with any produced in this country, has, of course, been suffering not from oblivion but from a combination of personnel problems within his band and the watery economic condition of the big-band business. In its resurgence, his outfit is playing with more punch and persuasiveness than it has in a decade, and Ellington himself, who has always used his orchestra as a proving ground for his compositions, has begun to write large, ambitious pieces again. In the past year or so—in addition to bringing the Newport Jazz Festival to a memorably ringing climax—he has composed and performed a suite based on Shakespeare's plays, and has concocted a musical and dramatic fantasy, *A Drum Is a Woman*, which was presented last week as an hour-long show on C.B.S. television. The show marked the first time that a full-length musical-dramatic creation written by Ellington (and Billy Strayhorn, his musical right hand) had been presented anywhere, but, aside from its inspired title, it was an almost embarrassingly flimsy affair, which failed both as a piece of light nonsense and as a true indication of Ellington's abilities.

The work was adapted for television, with only minor changes, from a recently recorded version, and is, loosely, a symbolic, tongue-in-cheek retelling of the history of jazz. It revolves around two figures—Carribee Joe, a jungle drummer, who represents the African origins of jazz, and Madam Zajj, who is the music that has evolved. Madam Zajj, at first a drum, metamorphoses into a flashy, snaky woman, who travels by hurtling through the sky on the trade winds or by driving an eighty-eight-cylinder car at four hundred and forty miles an hour. She and Carribee Joe sing and dance heatedly to express their love for one another, in a series of episodes, introduced and commented on by Ellington, that are set in Barbados, in New Orleans, at Mardi Gras time, in a Chicago night club, in a Fifty-second Street night club, and on a spot near the moon. The rest of the work, for the purposes of television, was filled, rather desperately, by an extraordinary amount of sinewy, perspiring modern ballet, which was choreographed by Paul Godkin and executed, with a lot more gesture than meaning, by a sizable group. Margaret Tynes, a dramatic soprano, and Joya Sherrill, a singer who has worked with Ellington in the past, shared the role of Madam Zajj (she was danced by Carmen de Lavallade) and sang it with ease and clarity, and Carribee Joe (danced by Talley Beatty) was handled more than adequately by Ozzie Bailey. Unfortunately, the Ellington band was seen and heard only fitfully, but there were brief, spirited solo passages by nearly everyone, including Clark Terry and Ray Nance, trumpets; Russell Procope, clarinet; Johnny Hodges, alto saxophone; and Sam Woodyard, drums. The music, which consisted of thirteen numbers, some of them instrumentals, seemed incidental at times. It ranged from a calypso ("What Else Can You Do with a Drum?"), which had a good deal of melodic charm, to a couple of dramatic, almost operatic laments (the title song and "Carribee Joe"). Ellington appeared half a dozen times or so, resplendent in white tie and tails, and delivered such Technicolor periods as "The Mississippi River, a puddle of Pekin blue pudding, pistachio and indigo" and "His heartbeat was like bongos" with so much conviction and charm that they seemed almost possible.

On Saturday evening, a new big band, led by Johnny Richards, gave a concert, along with the Horace Silver. Quintet, at Town Hall. Richards' group, which played for roughly two-thirds of the time, was a seventeen-piece organization that demonstrated much of the polish and all of the alarming volume of Stan Kenton. (Richards has worked for Kenton as an arranger and composer off and on for the past ten years.) In addition to piano, bass, and drums, its brassy, basso-profundo instrumentation included four trumpets, three trombones, a French horn, a tuba, a bass saxophone, a baritone saxophone, timpani, and an alto and a tenor saxophone. All but two of the dozen-odd pieces heard were by Richards. Top-heavy structures, full of tight, convoluted scoring that was frequently punctuated or underlined by the timpani and bongo drums, they seemed to keep toppling over on the many soloists, who could be heard only in bursts, like voices shouting into the wind. Among these all but submerged performers were Burt Collins, a pleasant, neo-bop trumpeter; Doug Met-tome, a restless trumpeter who favors generous, legato swoops; Jimmy Cleveland, a masterly trombonist, who ripped off phenomenally rapid, burr-like strings of notes; and Gene Quill, an alto saxophonist, who emulated all the worst tonal aspects of Charlie Parker's style.

Although the Silver Quintet—Art Farmer, trumpet; Hank Mobley, tenor saxophone; Teddy Kotick, bass; Louis Hayes, drums; and the leader, piano—played with considerable heat, in the manner of many small modern-jazz groups, it sounded, in contrast to Richard's aggregation, somewhat like the Camp Fire Girls in song. Of its four extended compositions—all of them by Silver—perhaps the most striking was a rollicking blues, "Señor Blues," played in six-eight time, in which Silver, a dissonant and engagingly earthy pianist, and Farmer, a forceful, highly lyrical performer, produced an eloquence that seemed—partly, at least—the result of their restricting themselves to blessed everyday volume.

## Pastoral

Jimmy Giuffre, the gifted clarinettist, arranger, and composer, has made a new recording. "The Jimmy Giuffre 3," that is a delightful jelling of many of his recent bold experiments with jazz rhythms and jazz themes. Although revolutionary, these experiments have had far less than an electric effect on modern jazz. For Giuffre's dulcet style of playing and the subtle, leafy structure of his writing have a deceptively timid, almost insulated quality, which is often ignored or shrugged off by the exponents of the beefier jazz experimentalism of Charlie Mingus and Teo Macero. Giuffre's work is also elusive because of a characteristic he shares with an increasing number of his colleagues: he comes in two differ-ent parts—the highly inventive arranger-composer, and the accomplished instrumentalist. (Although he also plays the tenor and baritone saxophones, he has been concentrating in the past couple of years on a unique clarinet style. It is notable for its delicate vibrato, its simple legato phrasing, and the exclusive use of the lower and middle registers of the instrument, all of which produce a limpid, mahogany sound.) This duality is, in some respects, even more marked in Giuffre than it is in other musicians; his instrumental style frequently seems a direct organic outgrowth of his compositions, and vice versa.

Giuffre, who is thirty-six years old and holds a degree in music, was one of the founders of the now declining West Coast school of modern jazz, a suave splinter movement that got started five years ago around Los Angeles and San Francisco. It produced, in the main, a glazed small-band jazz, which nevertheless brought to the fore excellent musicians like Giuffre, Shorty Rogers, Gerry Mulligan, and Shelly Manne. The movement developed, in addition to a sleek compositional approach—smooth unison ensembles, hushed dynamics, and sliding rhythm—an instrumental style very close to that of the cool school. At first, Giuffre's work seems the epitome of the West Coast method. Yet his playing has an urgent, if constantly veiled, lyric quality that suggests, rather than the bland variations of Shorty Rogers, the liquid but muscular work of such men as Jimmy Noone, Irving Fazola, and Pee Wee Russell. His arranging and composing have been equally independent of the West Coast school. In, for example, *Tangents in Jazz: The Jimmy Giuffre Four*, a remarkable recording produced two years ago, Giuffre—in company with Jack Sheldon, trumpet; Ralph Peña, bass; and Artie Anton, drums—dropped the customary steady sounded beat and employed the rhythm instruments as semi-melodic, almost harmonic devices that underscore and liberate the melody instruments. As Giuffre says in his notes for this record:

I've come to feel increasingly inhibited and frustrated by the insistent pounding of the rhythm section. With it, it's impossible for the listener or the soloist to hear the horn's true sound . . . or fully concentrate on the solo line. . . . The essence of jazz is in the phrasing and notes, and these needn't change when the beat is silent. Since the beat is implicit, this music retains traditional feeling; not having it explicit allows freer thinking.

So the horns coast effortlessly in and out of the written and improvised passages, which are broken by rests that are filled by the bass and drums with contrasting or imitative figures. (Giuffre often breaks up the standard thirty-two-bar chorus this way, and sometimes he abandons it for his own forms, of whatever length.) Although the implied beat occasionally seems more compelling than the steady thump of a bass drum, these rhythmic dalliances create a magic, free-ballooning setting for a second but equally important quality: the injection into much of the music of an elusive pastoral dimension. Two of the tunes, "The Leprechaun" and "Chirpin' Time," which are blues and folk in origin, have, because of Giuffre's clarinet and Sheldon's soft trumpet, a kind of evening, piper-in-the-meadow quality.

All this is buoyantly and intricately present in "The Jimmy Giuffre 3." Giuffre is accompanied by Jim Hall, guitar, and again by Ralph Peña. There are nine selections, seven of them by Giuffre. These are, nearly without exception, either unadorned blues or derived from blues. They are effectively broadened by the addition, here and there, of folk-song and spiritual elements that appear both in the arranged passages, notably in "That's the Way It Is," and in the ad-lib playing, notably in "The Crawdad Suite," a tune in which Hall lets loose clusters of ringing chords that could easily have come from Leadbelly. "The Crawdad Suite" is a seven-minute composition built around two themes—an ingratiating blues and a haunting minor figure. The blues is played in a slow, steady rhythm, while the minor theme—which is stated sotto voce from time to time by the various players, as in a series of asides—has no rhythm at all. Both the blues and the minor theme are improvised upon (about half of the entire recording is written, though), and they are connected by short, lyrical passages, usually played by the guitar, that allow the two to logically follow one another. "The Train and the River" is a little descriptive piece, a refreshing idea that—except for rarities like Ellington's "Harlem Air Shaft" and Meade Lux Lewis' "Honky Tonk Train Blues"—has largely been ignored in jazz. Giuffre embellishes the lively melody successively on the clarinet and two saxophones, while Peña and Hall work out train-like rhythms, which add to Giuffre's suggestion, on his tenor saxophone, of the melancholy wail of the steam whistle. Although there are never more than three instruments at work simultaneously, Giuffre manages—through the deft use of such devices as the constant varying of instrumental combinations (clarinet with bass, baritone saxophone with guitar, and so on), a fragile, intense counterpoint, and the occasional insertion of bits of fugue—to develop a multiplicity of sounds that suggests a ten-piece group. Hall is a young, no-nonsense guitarist who has much of the spare deliberation of Charlie Christian, and Peña is a forceful, big-toned performer. Giuffre matches their combined strengths with gentlemanly ease.

*O tricky taste! The Giuffre trio sides have recently been reissued, and they now seem pallid and a little cute—children attempting to take the blues down.*

## Hot

**R**oy Eldridge, fiery and indefatigable, makes it plain in a new recording, "Swing Goes Dixie," that he has lost none of the crackling excitement that has distinguished his work for the past twenty years. Few jazz trumpeters—even the young Louis Armstrong—have achieved Eldridge's pure, electric hotness. Yet he is often academically dismissed as being merely the connecting link between Armstrong, who formed the style of almost every trumpeter of the twenties and thirties, and Dizzy Gillespie, who influenced (after a brief period as an admirer of Eldridge) almost every trumpeter of the forties and fifties. Eldridge is, however, far more than a transitional agent. His style is wild and dancing and nervous, he bites at, instead of merely blows, his notes, which rise in sudden, breathtaking swoops to the upper registers of his instrument or plummet to the low registers, where he achieves a bleary, loving sound. Eldridge also possesses a gift that is rare among jazz musicians; at his best—his unruly imagination now and then outruns his sizable technique—his solos are marvels of spontaneous construction, which march with a steady, unbreakable logic from sometimes offhand beginnings to soaring, hats-off climaxes. When this happens, one gets the impression that Eldridge has exhausted for all time the melodic potential of the material at hand.

The congenial group he works with on this recording includes Benny Morton, trombone; Eddie Barefield, clarinet; Dick Wellstood, piano; Walter Page, bass; and Jo Jones, drums. The title of the album is misleading, for, rather than being Dixieland, this is an informal, unclassifiable type of jazz that prevailed before and during the Second World War at occasional recording dates and at legendary after-hours jam sessions. Eldridge is most eloquent in "Tin Roof Blues" and "Jada," in which he solos with a majesty that one expects not in jazz but in opera. Morton, Barefield, and Page are competent, and so is Wellstood, but Jones is superb, for he performs with a stomping exhilaration he has rarely revealed on records. His work behind Eldridge's first solo chorus in "Royal Garden Blues" is classic, rocketing jazz drumming.

Jimmy Rushing, the huge, suave blues shouter, has always sounded as if he were wearing spats and a morning coat and had just had a good laugh. His supple, rich voice and his elegant accent have the curious effect of making the typical roughhouse blues lyric seem like a song by Noel Coward. In his most recent recording, "The Jazz Odyssey of James Rushing Esq.", he is accompanied by four groups, all headed by Buck Clayton, a trumpeter who worked with Rushing for many years in the Count Basie band. The personnel also includes Vic Dickenson and Dickie Wells, trombones; Buddy Tate, tenor saxophone; Hank Jones, piano; and, again, Jo Jones. Four of the twelve numbers are blues, and it is on these that Rushing, who pauses for wonderful solos by Clayton, Tate, and Dickenson, is in his gracious, and occasionally mournful, prime. There is also an ingratiating piece of Americana, "Tricks Ain't Walkin' No More," in which Rushing, accompanying himself on the piano, delivers a funny monologue on the waywardness of urban low life. The album cover, done in tempera by Thomas Allen, showing Rushing, in a red shirt, black suit, and battered panama, hustling off to New York, is perfect.

The baritone saxophone can be an obtuse instrument. But both Harry Carney, who has been the foundation of the Ellington reed section since the

Coolidge administration, and Gerry Mulligan have mastered its thick sonorities, and Serge Chaloff, a contemporary of Mulligan's, handles the instrument with an equal and almost alarming agility. He exudes an unashamedly broad lyricism, based on a rich tone and a vibrato that matches the celebrated vibrations of Sidney Bechet, the New Orleans clarinettist and soprano saxophonist. A restless player, Chaloff darts from bumptious bass notes to breathy high ones that barely get out of the loudspeaker. "Blue Serge," made with an extraordinary pickup group—Sonny Clark, piano; Leroy Vinnegar, bass; and Philly Joe Jones, drums—is a classic recording. Clark and Jones are particularly stimulating, and a refreshing structural device is used here and there that adds a light, surprised air to the proceedings: all the four-bar breaks are *a cappella*. There are seven selections, ranging from a medium blues to "Thanks for the Memory," "Stairway to the Stars," and "I've Got the World on a String," all of which Chaloff converts into fervent arabesques.

*Chaloff died of cancer in July of 1957 at the age of twenty-four, and this was his last recording. He was, I think, the most eloquent of all the baritone saxophonists.*

## Avant

Teddy Charles is a militant and talented twenty-nine-year-old arranger, composer, and vibraphonist, who has been chiefly responsible in the past couple of years for an illuminating series of experimental recordings and concerts that have dealt largely with the problem of making jazz composition as interesting as jazz improvisation. Although most of the compositions Charles has played call for standard jazz instrumentation, they depend on such classical devices as atonality, polytonality, and frameworks of varied length. These innovations sometimes tend to bury the customary emotional content of jazz beneath a variety of formidable intellectual superstructures. As a result, Charles' music often has a juiceless air—cool, dry, and tense. This is the result, as well, of Charles' precise, metallic playing and the inevitable difficulty the musicians who work with him have in remaining relaxed when confronted by unwieldy materials. A few evenings ago, Charles took part in a concert in the Contemporary Jazz/Composers' Series, at the Carnegie Recital Hall, and it was, in comparison with earlier recitals he has been involved with, a brittle affair, distinguished by its mechanical enthusiasm and by the arch manner of many of the compositions.

The musicians—Idrees Sulieman, trumpet; Teo Macero, alto and tenor saxophone; Mal Waldron or Hall Overton, piano; Bob Prince or Charles himself, vibraphone; Addison Farmer, bass; and Jerry Segal, drums—performed in varying combinations, and all but Farmer and Segal contributed one or two of the eleven new pieces heard, which included a couple by a non-performer, John Ross. They ran, on the average, ten minutes, and they sounded, with three notable exceptions, pretty much alike—as if, in fact, they were all part of one huge composition that had been arbitrarily cut into sections. The exceptions, however, were completely engrossing—a slow ballad by Ross, "Ted's Twist," which had an extremely long chorus and an attractive melodic line; "Take Three Parts Jazz," an ambitious venture by Charles, with a complex structure full of abrupt shifts from idyllic passages to sharply rhythmic ones; and "Tension," by Waldron, which used explosive, contrasting introductory figures, played alternately by trumpet and drums, and a taut contrapuntal ensemble, filled with effective dissonances. The other pieces ranged from "Threnody," by John Ross, that balanced brief solo flights against discordant ensembles, to Macero's heated "Conference with D.B.," which ended with lacy, upper-register piano notes pitched against the tinkling of Egyptian finger cymbals.

Charles, who carried the weight of the solo work, performed with his usual taste and fleetness. Waldron kept running up big, dark chordal structures that, perhaps because of the generally oblique turn of the music, never seemed conclusive. Sulieman, a flaring, rapid-fire trumpeter, fluffed a good many notes, and Segal, though an invariably steady performer, made his drums sound as resonant as hatboxes. Macero, an emotional musician who emits a variety of gasps and screeches, played with gusto, which occasionally lent the proceedings a fractious atmosphere, as if something exciting were about to happen.

## Djinni

When Art Tatum, the miraculous, almost totally blind pianist, died last fall, at the age of forty-six, he was widely considered the greatest of all jazz pianists. This universal regard, however, has been at least partly created by the ballooning powers of a legend that confused his massive technique with his somewhat average abilities as a jazz improviser, and that got its start when Tatum appeared in the early thirties as one of the first full-fledged virtuosos in jazz. The astonishment at his style—smooth, whipping arpeggios that seemed to be blown up and down the keyboard; impossibly agile bass figures; and furious tempos played with perfect touch—was deep and apparently permanent. For the rest of his life, Tatum continued to receive more attention than the average jazz musician, perhaps because he worked largely as a bravura solo pianist, whose surging orchestral approach rarely fitted into the collaborative confines of a jazz band. When he played with other musicians, an embarrassing thing happened: no matter how resolute his cohorts, he inevitably overran them; even while supplying accompaniment, he never seemed able to keep himself from swelling up, like an enormous djinni, alongside the soloist. Thus, Tatum was practically forced to establish his own medium of expression. His technique was, of course, based in jazz, but it so overshadowed the standard popular songs he invariably used—peculiarly, Tatum never wrote a single tune—that it often took on a life of its own. A fantastic embellisher, Tatum used the melody at hand not as a basis for improvisation but as an outline, which he would clothe with unique rococo rhapsodies of runs, breaks, and chords that at times seemed—because of their essential similarity—as if they could be transplanted intact from number to number with identical results.

Some of Tatum's brilliant cavorting is evident in a new recording—"The Art Tatum Trio," made not long before his death, with Red Callender, bass, and Jo Jones—which is, compared to some of his other late work, a fairly docile effort. (A few years ago, in a set of a dozen or so Clef records, called "The Genius of Art Tatum," the pianist, unaccompanied, set down his ruminations on more than a hundred standard selections, in which he developed, again and again, elaborate clouds of sound that departed completely from an explicit beat and lasted for minutes at a time.) Tatum's bustling attack can, however, be heard here in "Just One of Those Things" and "Trio Blues," the latter of which he converts into a sly, though always gracious, parody of the blues. While Callender plays with aplomb throughout (there are ten selections in all), Jones fearlessly provides—in addition to a couple of stunning solos with the wire brushes that override Tatum's creeping, vine-like background figures—an almost governing support, which suggests that if Tatum had played with more musicians of Jones' strength, he might in time have pocketed some of his insuperable fireworks.

Another new recording, "The RCA Victor Jazz Workshop: George Russell and His Smalltet," is one of the most articulate and uncompromising offerings to date by the steadily growing school of modern jazz composers. The record presents twelve of Russell's compositions. They are played faultlessly by Art Farmer; Hal McKusick, alto saxophone and flute; Bill Evans, piano; Barry Galbraith, guitar; Milt Hinton or Teddy Kotick, bass; and Joe Harris, Paul Motian, or Osie Johnson, drums. The result is a series of dry, tight, and intricate pieces—two of them appear to be completely written and the rest both written and improvised—that use such devices as 6/4 rhythm, shifting tonal centers, dissonant counterpoint, and a soloist improvising in one key against a background written in another. Although there are a good many excellent solos squeezed in between the written passages—Farmer and Evans, a young pianist who plays with exhilarating clarity, are the most rewarding—the overall effect is starchy and convoluted. Often enough the writing, with its abruptness and its crackling discords (in "Round Johnny Rondo" there are a couple of arranged sections in which the trumpet and alto saxophone engage in a jarring and disconcerting counterpoint), doesn't seem to have much relation to the improvisation, and at times it even comes close to a skilled travesty of jazz that might have been cooked up by someone who despised the music.

Even in the best of hands, the French horn is apt to emit a kind of strangled, mauve sound. An exception is the adroit work of a thirty-five-year-old musician named Julius Watkins, who appears in a recent recording, "Four French Horns Plus Rhythm," in company with three other horn players (David Amram, Fred Klein, and Tony Miranda), an accordionist (Mat Mathews), and a rhythm section (Joe Puma, guitar, Milt Hinton, and Osie Johnson). The record, which consists of three standard tunes and six original ones, is full of admirable things—a pinging Spanish guitar pitted against the four horns; muted ensemble choirs that produce far-off, bovine sounds; and the soaring solos of Watkins, who often darts restlessly and easily into the highest register of his instrument and plays at all times with a compelling and unfailing rhythmic sense. Fortunately, Mathews, a Dutch accordionist, avoids all the beery sounds usually associated with his instrument, and is, in fact, capable (in "Come Rain or Come Shine") of constructing solos that have both wit and considerable emotional weight.

The celebrated Dave Brubeck is a melodramatic pianist who sometimes tops even the magniloquence of Wagner. On a new and surprisingly restful recording, "Jazz Impressions of the U.S.A.: The Dave Brubeck Quartet," made with Paul Desmond, alto saxophone, Norman Bates, bass, and Joe Morello, drums—he plays eight discreet and hummable compositions (one is an unaccompanied piano solo) that he wrote as evocations of various phases of a recent nationwide tour. In the notes on the record cover, Brubeck says of a tune called "History of a Boy Scout": "It is a mixture of humor and reverence that is so typical of the American G.I. It contains some of the skyrocket spirits of a Fourth of July parade, but there is an undercurrent of hallowed respect for the men of Valley Forge, Gettysburg, Ardennes, Wake, the Bulge, and Korea." As if that weren't enough, Morello, an exceptional young drummer who lately joined Brubeck, contributes masterly support, and, in "Sounds of the Loop," takes a four-minute solo that should not be missed.

## Mammoth

The most impressive thing about the four-day Newport Jazz Festival, which was held over the Fourth of July weekend in a lake-sized sports arena in Rhode Island, was its bulging proportions. There were seven long concerts (four in the evening and three in the afternoon), at which forty groups of performers—plus a couple of discussion groups—held forth before forty-odd thousand people. Yet in all this vast and steamy musical circus, perhaps only a dozen musicians and singers performed with any impetus and inspiration—a situation that quite possibly came about because most of the extraordinary number of musicians who appeared had to play at a dead run in order to avoid being trampled by the next group. The rest of the Festival was occupied by such things as a long and vapid performance by Louis Armstrong and his small band, which delivered, in a manner that was close to unintentional self-caricature, a program that has become as unalterable as the calendar; a series of interpretive jazz dances by Eartha Kitt and three members of the New York City Ballet, with accompaniment by Dizzy Gillespie's big band, that were, in addition to being disjointedly executed, without taste or point; and a confused and disrupted hour and a half by the Count Basie band, haphazardly augmented from time to time by such of its alumni and non-alumni as Jo Jones, Illinois Jacquet, Roy Eldridge, Sarah Vaughan, Lester Young, and Jimmy Rushing, the last of whom, nevertheless, outlasted sloppy and blatant support.

The opening concert, on the evening of July 4th, purportedly a fifty-seventh-birthday celebration for Armstrong, was saved by the unassuming presence of George Lewis' band, an admirable seven-piece group that is one of the few genuine New Orleans–style bands still in existence. Although largely made up of near-octogenarians, it played with a sturdy and lively dignity that was most apparent in the long but continually absorbing ensemble passages and in the brief solos by Jack Willis, a trumpeter whose simple, classic playing had much of the orderly lyricism of Tommy Ladnier. Jack Teagarden also propped the evening up by performing in several numbers with an uneven group led by Red Allen, which included Buster Bailey and J. C. Higginbotham, and in doing so proved that he has retained all his calm, lissome ways of singing and playing. Then Kid Ory, the great New Orleans trombonist, joined the group, and, though seventy now, puffed his way through "Muskrat Ramble" and "High Society" as if he were merely cooling his soup.

The other evenings were equally fitful. On Friday, Bobby Hackett conducted a six-piece organization that used, in varying combinations, such instruments as the alto horn, tuba, baritone saxophone, clarinet, and vibraphone, and that attempted, largely through rich, arranged ensemble passages, to chart an intrepid course between small-band swing and the early cool recordings by Miles Davis and Gerry Mulligan. Their playing was impeccable, but the result was damaged by the amplification system, which not only added an otherworldly humming sound to the instruments but tended to magnify them individually in the ensemble parts instead of reproducing the ensemble collectively. The indomitable Erroll Garner gave a spirited, professional performance, with rhythm accompaniment, and a unit composed of, among others, Roy Eldridge, Coleman Hawkins, Jo Jones, and Pete Brown, an alto saxophonist, was notable for the ringing, declarative work of Hawkins. They were succeeded by Stan Kenton's newest big band, which brayed at the moon for at least an hour. On Saturday night, after a sparkling, if glancing, appearance by Teddy Wilson's trio, the Gerry Mulligan Quartet (Bob Brookmeyer, Joe Benjamin, and Dave Bailey) put on a performance that paled in comparison with the efforts of his recent and ingenious sextet. After its struggles with Miss Kitt and several inconclusive selections in which Mary Lou Williams, a masterly and semi-legendary pianist, was the soloist, Dizzy Gillespie's band roared raggedly on by itself and, at least in "School Days," sounded as if it really meant business. The final evening began—and to all intents and purposes ended—with the remarkable Jimmy Giuffre 3 (Giuffre, Jim Hall, Ralph Peña), which on top of absurdly having to provide quieting-down music for the late-arriving audience, was given just twenty minutes onstage.

The afternoon sessions, though longer and even more heavily populated by musicians, were delightful. On Friday, Ruby Braff, the trumpeter, led an octet that included Pee Wee Russell, the trombonist Jimmy Welsh, and the pianist Nat Pierce through four selections that offered exceptional solos by Braff and Russell; in "Nobody Else but You," Russell took a gentle, barely audible low-register solo that matched any improvisation during the whole weekend. The following afternoon included short but characteristically impassioned performances by Eddie Costa, a young pianist who hammered out, with the help of a rhythm section, an exhilarating version of "Get Happy," and the Cecil Taylor Quartet (Taylor, Steve Lacy, Buell Neidlinger, and Dennis Charles), whose dissonances seemed less cloistered and academic in the hot sun. The Farmingdale High School Dance Band, from Long Island, a fourteen-piece group whose average age was fourteen, ran through eight numbers that ranged from Basie's "Taps Miller" to an intricate modern piece, and did them all with a precision and barefoot bounce. The principal soloist, an alto saxophonist named Andy Marsala, who is not related to the Marsala brothers, played—with a stone face—exactly as if he were Charlie Parker.

Sunday afternoon was given over wonderfully to gospel singing. The first half involved the Clara Ward Singers, a lively but somewhat affected group; the Back Home Choir, a fifty-voice group that performed with volume and conviction; and the Drinkards, most of whose numbers were built around the swooping shouting—and fascinating bodily contortions—of Judy Guions, who sang with hair-raising fervor. Then, Mahalia Jackson delivered over a dozen selections, accompanied by piano and organ, with an eloquence that led a swaying, front-row spectator to moan repeatedly, "Say it, 'Halia! That's right, say it now!"

*Pee Wee Russell's solo on "Nobody Else but You" remains in the head; such was his genius.*

## The M.J.Q.

**I**n the three years since its formation, the Modern Jazz Quartet, which has settled into what appears to be its permanent makeup of John Lewis, piano; Milt Jackson, vibraphone; Percy Heath, bass; and Connie Kay, drums, has become one of the most intelligent and moving of all modern-jazz groups. Most contemporary small-band jazz depends on dull unison ensemble passages, which are used as terminal points for long strings of solos. But the Modern Jazz Quartet, although it occasionally fritters away its subtle, intense inventions in a tangle of structural devices like the fugue and the rondo, has rejuvenated, in a sometimes brilliant manner, one of the earliest and most valuable ingredients in jazz—collective improvisation, which was prematurely swamped in the 1930s by the arrival of the big jazz bands and great individualists, like Louis Armstrong and Coleman Hawkins. The quartet's soloists, who are most often Jackson and Lewis, usually perform—because of the sensitive, close-knit nature of the group—more as temporary offshoots from tight, central frameworks than as independent improvisers stepping off into space. When Jackson, who gets a rich, belling tone from his instrument, solos, Lewis works out a clear secondary melodic line behind him that is sometimes so provocative it unintentionally upstages Jackson. (Lewis has the rare gift among jazz pianists of being able to act both as a sympathetic and agreeably distorted echo of the soloist he is supporting and as a convenient source of choice phrases that the soloist, if flagging, can lean on.) Thus the group is always in a state of easy counterpoint, where, in the busiest passages, all the performers seem to jostle each other graciously, like the occupants of a crowded royal box.

Aside from the consistent excellence of its playing, much of the success of the group is due to its leader, Lewis, who is also an exceptional composer and arranger. Although his playing—simple, single-note melodic lines that have a dogged, crystalline quality—has a deceptive, amateur air, he often puts together, from combinations of nearly childish figures, solos that take on the ring of classic improvisations. In addition, Lewis, who is thirty-seven, has few equals in contemporary jazz as a melodic composer. His melodies have a graceful melancholy that sticks in the mind, much in the manner of such simpler pioneering jazz compositions as "Royal Garden Blues" and "That's a Plenty." Two of them—"Django," written as a requiem for the late French guitarist Django Reinhardt, and "Two Degrees East, Three Degrees West"—have already become indestructible.

In addition to Lewis' "La Ronde," a two-minute piece that offers some solo wire-brush work by Kay, and "Baden-Baden," a fast blues by Jackson and bassist Ray Brown, the quartet's new recording, "The Modern Jazz Quartet," consists of nine standard tunes, five of which form a ballad medley played as a single unit. "Bags' Groove" and "Baden-Baden" have simple structures and straightforward solos, while Kay, a superior drummer who generally uses the wire brushes, shifts forcibly to sticks. The quartet's collective approach is particularly apparent in "Between the Devil and the Deep Blue Sea." During Jackson's second solo, Lewis drifts in behind him with a series of queer, limping tremolo phrases that nudge Jackson quietly and firmly along.

Modern jazz drumming appears to have become permanently set in the narrow, florid, and often insensitive patterns of Max Roach, who, in the past seven or eight years, has had as much influence on his instrument as Charlie Parker on his. A new recording, "Orgy in Rhythm: Art Blakey," though a sometimes unruly, tobogganing affair, is a stirring exception to the staccato, typewriter insistence of the

Roach school. Blakey, whose style is full of mushrooming cymbal sounds and tidal snare-drum rolls, is joined on the trap drums by Arthur Taylor, Specs Wright, and Jo Jones, the last two of whom occasionally take turns on the timpani. Also present are Ray Bryant, piano; Herbie Mann, flute; Wendell Marshall, bass; and a steaming Afro-Cuban rhythm section, made up of Sabu on the bongos and timbales, and four others, who rattle away on conga drums, timbales, maracas, the cencerro, and the tree log. Of the four numbers on the record, three are largely Afro-Cuban, and have opening and closing sections, which are chanted by Sabu and Blakey. In between, Jones rackets along against a conga-drum background; sharp, rifle-like bongo drums are pitted against the subterranean rumbling of the timpani; and, in a couple of places, three trap drummers playing vigorous unison figures. Blakey takes a stunning solo in a number called "Toffi," and in "Split Skins" the Afro-Cuban drummers rest while Blakey, Taylor, and Jones work out intricate supporting and solo figures, not to mention a solo that is probably the best one Jones has recorded. Although the notes on the record designate which soloist is which, it might be of help to know that Taylor and Wright produce identical heavy, clipped, rather wooden sounds, Jones a lighter, crisper, almost startled sound, and Blakey a muzzy, booming sound.

Prestige has reissued on one side of a twelve-inch long-playing record called "Walkin': Miles Davis All Stars," a recording made about three years ago, with Davis, trumpet; J. J. Johnson, trombone; Lucky Thompson, tenor saxophone; Horace Silver; Percy Heath; and Kenny Clarke, all of whom play, in two extended blues— "Walkin' " and "Blue 'N Boogie"—some of the best jazz improvisation set down in the past decade. On the second side, Davey Schildkraut, alto saxophone, replaces Johnson and Thompson, and the results (there are three standard tunes) are only slightly inferior.

*Davis rarely equalled the spare, annunciatory quality he achieved on these recordings.*

## The Olden Days

The first Great South Bay Jazz Festival, which was held late in July in a spacious, open-sided tent in Great River, Long Island, was, almost without exception, a miraculously sustained event. Many of the dozen groups appeared at least twice during the three evening and two afternoon concerts, and, after a time, the music took on a kind of unity that allowed Coleman Hawkins, for one, to be heard every day in every conceivable sort of tune and mood, ranging from an impassioned "Body and Soul" to a loose, stampeding, up-tempo "Rosetta." Moreover, the tent helped establish an often exhilarating bond between performers and audience; Sunday night, Charlie Mingus suddenly burst

into a breathtaking, half-shouted, half-sung accompaniment to his solo on
"Woody 'n' You," and in answer to an exclamation from the audience, the
venerable clarinettist Garvin Bushell broke off in the middle of one of his
solos, bellowed "Yes!," and resumed playing with even greater fervor.

The Festival was opened on Friday night by a seven-piece group led by
cornetist Rex Stewart and including such men as Bushell, Hawkins, Benny
Morton, and Bill Pemberton, bass. Although its ensembles tended to be
patchy, the soloists displayed an invention that reached notable proportions
in a gentle, almost carved passage by Stewart in "Lazy River," in a long, slow
"Tin Roof Blues" with a muted, from-afar solo by Stewart that seemed to be
seized and shaken by an angry, rolling counter-statement by Hawkins, and
in the closing ensemble of "Basin Street," when Hawkins came up with a
couple of abrupt, yearning figures that had the effect of a gospel shouter letting loose. The Horace Silver Quintet (Art Farmer, Cliff Jordan, tenor saxophone, Silver, Teddy Kotick, and Louis Hayes) played with its usual
decisiveness, and a half-dozen extended numbers by the Jimmy Giuffre 3
were capped by "The Train and the River," which evoked the melancholy of
steam-engine whistles.

Saturday afternoon, a downy performance by the Billy Taylor Trio,
which included Earl May, bass, and Ed Thigpen, drums, was saved by the
taut, expert work of Thigpen. The Lawson-Haggart Dixieland Band (Yank
Lawson, trumpet; Cutty Cutshall, trombone; Peanuts Hucko, clarinet; Bob
Haggart, bass; George Barnes, guitar; Cliff Leeman, drums) pumped
through six numbers, including a loping, twelve-minute "Jeepers Creepers"
that was enhanced by the unscheduled appearance of Gerry Mulligan, who
played with a gusto not always apparent with his own groups. In between,
there was an absorbing hour by the Charlie Mingus Jazz Workshop, in
which such musicians as Bill Triglia (piano), Curtis Porter (alto and tenor
saxophones), and Jimmy Knepper offered three labyrinthine selections that
included a blues played simultaneously in two keys; "Tia Juana Table
Dancer," which rose, in its ensemble sections, to a dissonant, volcanic din;
and "Dizzy's Mood," with a tricky passage during which the rhythm section
slid into a kind of double-time waltz tempo.

Saturday evening was memorable. Aside from two satisfying appearances
by a sextet that included Buck Clayton, Vic Dickenson, Hank Jones, and the
indomitable and gracious Jimmy Rushing, it was devoted to a reunion of the
Fletcher Henderson band, pieced out (where necessary) with a few ringers.
Seventeen strong, the band—which was under the direction of Rex Stewart,
and offered, among others, J. C. Higginbotham and Benny Morton, trombones; Joe Thomas, Emmett Berry, and Paul Webster, trumpets; Bushell,
Edgar Sampson, and Hilton Jefferson, saxophones; Bernard Addison, guitar;
and Jimmy Crawford (an alumnus of the Lunceford band), drums—surged
through more than a dozen numbers. In addition to superior solos by Stewart, Hawkins, and Berry, the drumming of Crawford, and the nostalgic

pleasure of hearing, straight from the horse's mouth, Henderson arrangements of "Down South Camp Meeting," "King Porter Stomp," and "Wrappin' It Up," there was the pleasure of listening to the singing way the band attacked its material.

Sunday afternoon was run through meditatively by the Marian McPartland Trio, augmented by Bud Freeman, Vic Dickenson, and Jimmy McPartland, and the Miles Davis Quintet, which included Sonny Rollins and Paul Chambers, and which included a languishing rendition by Davis, playing a tightly muted trumpet, of "It Never Entered My Mind." That night the Lawson-Haggart band and Rex Stewart's septet, joined at times by Roy Eldridge, Jimmy Rushing, and Sammy Price (piano), reappeared, and so did Mingus, now as a soloist accompanied by rhythm. Much of the concert was given over to the blues. Two priceless things occurred: Mingus put so much overweening emotion into a blues called "The Haitian Fight Song" that his instrument became an inadequate medium for all it was forced to do; and immediately after Rushing's first choruses of "Good Morning, Blues," Eldridge, who had been playing unevenly until then, slipped into a triple-time tempo and, sotto voce, in the highest register of his instruments, delivered a solo chorus quite possibly as exhilarating as any he has ever played.

## Cootie

Unhappily, most admirers of jazz still appear to be governed either by a faddism that selects its youthful heroes on a musician-of-the-month basis or by an academic approach that sets up in bronze and stone musicians who haven't played a fresh, honest note in fifteen years. As a result, a steadily diminishing number of middle-aged men, such as Ben Webster, Jimmy Rushing, Coleman Hawkins, Ike Quebec, and Jimmy Crawford, have, caught in the vacuum between these two groups, gone largely unnoticed since the mid-forties, although their faculties and inspiration remain demonstrably unimpaired. (Crawford, one of the ablest of all big-jazz-band drummers, has been pumping away in Broadway pit bands for years.) These thoughts have been touched off by a valuable new release, "Cootie & Rex in the Big Challenge," which features Cootie Williams, the masterly, forty-nine-year-old trumpeter, in the first jazz recordings he has made in nearly a decade. Williams, of course, was one of the principal reasons for the success, in the thirties, of Duke Ellington and, in the early forties, of Benny Goodman. He perfected, under the influence of Bubber Miley, a trumpeter whom he replaced in Ellington's band, a still-unsurpassed handling of the plunger mute (the plain old plumbing utensil, minus its handle) that results in some of the unique sounds in music. Williams generally plays in the middle registers and uses simple phrases, but when he applies the plunger, he produces an inexhaustible variety of sounds: aching growls, yearning, ghostly wahoos, and tight, intimate effects that suggest a wordless language of sharp consonants and drawn-out vowels. By comparison, hearing his open-horn style is like emerging from a dense wood into a bright meadow, for with it he gets a pushing, majestic tone that moves with ease from a gentle urgency to a kind of shouting savagery.

In addition to Rex Stewart, who has his own battery of tricks—half-valvings, bent, slippery open-horn phrases that start and end in mid-air, distant fog-bound muted sounds—the ensemble includes Bud Freeman, Coleman Hawkins, Lawrence Brown, J. C. Higginbotham, and a rhythm section made up of Hank Jones, Billy Bauer on guitar, Milt Hinton, and Gus Johnson on drums. They play five standard tunes, a composition by Stewart, and a blues. There is a good deal of unevenness in the record—the choice of tempos occasionally seems inept and both Higginbotham and Free-man are somewhat uncertain—but there are memorable things, too. One is "Alphonse and Gaston," in which Williams, in alternating choruses with Stewart, plays a muted chorus, a growl chorus, and a plunging open-horn chorus. Another is the two eloquent duets between Hawkins and Williams—in the opening and closing sections of "Do Nothing Till You Hear from Me," and in the first chorus of "I Got a Right to Sing the Blues"—in which Hawkins noodles ferociously in the background while Williams, muted, plays the melody. Another is a sheet-tearing growl chorus by Williams in "I'm Beginning to See the Light."

"Back Country Suite" is a graceful and original first recording by Mose Allison, a pianist, singer, and composer who is just twenty-nine. It includes, in addition to five unrelated selections, a long suite that celebrates the innumerable moods of the blues. Allison, who is competently accompanied by Taylor La Fargue on bass and Frank Isola on drums, has a direct, clean manner of playing that suggests Nat Cole. The suite contains ten brief descriptive sketches ("Train," "Warm Night," "Saturday," and so forth), all of them straight blues or derived from blues and all of them apparently almost completely arranged rather than improvised. In the course of the work, Allison moves from the deep-dish blues piano associated with Jimmy Yancey to several light, jigging up-tempo dances. He even sings once, in a piping, skinny fashion. The suite is, however, more successful as a whole than in its parts; some of the pieces ("Spring Song" and "Highway 49") seem unfinished, and others ("Blues" and "January") might, if enlarged, allow Allison some room for improvisation. Nonetheless, this is an honest distillation of an ageless jazz form.

A fascinating new tour de force from the Coast, "Sonny Rollins Way Out West," involves Rollins, the bass of Ray Brown, and the drums of Shelly Manne. Although all six numbers run five minutes or more (one runs over ten), Rollins performs with a consistent resourcefulness and vigor that leave most of his contemporaries far behind. On such numbers as "I'm an Old Cowhand" and "Wagon Wheels," Rollins plays choruses that are—regardless of his hard tone and abrupt, cantankerous phrasing—a clear indication of a striving toward an improvisational approach that is revolutionary, for it is based on remarkable polyrhythms and a new, elastic phrasing that reshapes the accepted measure-by-measure patterns of the thirty-two-bar chorus, which Charlie Parker and Lester Young first broke down. Rollins will, for example, concoct a simple six-note figure, repeat it insistently, then catch the listener up with a long moment of silence before sliding off into a soft, dizzying run that may be capped by a raucous bass note. Manne and Brown more than fill the holes opened up by such inspirations, and, in their brief solos, come close to equaling Rollins' freshness and agility.

## Hot Night, Little Light

**N**orman Granz's current Jazz at the Philharmonic tour opened last Saturday night at Carnegie Hall, and, in view of earlier JATP appearances, the concert was surprisingly tepid. It was of little help that midway in the evening the hall suddenly seemed to run out of air, leaving a hot, sticky vacuum, which was intensified by the melancholy lighting. For the most part, this was restricted to one large, soft spotlight, which focused on each of the soloists in turn and left the other musicians stumbling inkily around. The proceedings were begun by an uneven eight-piece group made up of four tenor saxophonists (Lester Young, Sonny Stitt, Illinois Jacquet, and Flip Phillips) and a rhythm section that included Oscar Peterson, Herb Ellis, guitar, Ray Brown, and Jo Jones. Stitt, who was the first, and is still the best, of Charlie Parker's countless followers, played with spirit and assurance, matched only by Lester Young's initial eight bars of "These Foolish Things Remind Me of You," in which he created a memorable set of coasting, oblique variations. Most of the group's final selection, an extremely fast version of "Indiana," was given over to a long drum solo by Jones, a hypnotically graceful performer, who used both sticks and bare hands. Toward the end of it, while hitting a pair of flanking tom-toms, he began crossing and recrossing his arms with such rapidity that the ensuing blur gave the startling impression that he was casually waving a large, transparent fan.

The gloom in the hall seemed to thicken during four numbers performed by the Modern Jazz Quartet. It played with a delicate limpness, which was briefly relieved by a slow blues, "Now's the Time," with distinguished solos from Jackson and Lewis, and by a nimble tune of Lewis' called "The Golden Striker." The first half of the concert was brought to a close by a group consisting of the M.J.Q. minus Jackson but augmented by Roy Eldridge and Coleman Hawkins. Although Hawkins played with a stirring doggedness, his solos tended to come out in an unaccustomed series of lumpy, strained phrases. Eldridge, who was equally ill at ease for the first few numbers, warmed up, however, and during his last tune he was bowling irresistibly along, top down and throttle open. During all this, the M.J.Q. rhythm section, falling into its customary subtle intricacies, sounded as if it were performing by itself in an adjacent room.

After the intermission, the Oscar Peterson Trio (Peterson, Ellis, and Brown) rumbled through four tunes, and, joined by Jo Jones, played on as a rhythm section for Stan Getz and J. J. Johnson with such ardor that the two horns, operating in a cool, glacéed manner, nearly sank out of hearing. Eldridge and Hawkins swelled the group for one number, and balance was restored until Jones abruptly allowed the tempo to sag. Ella Fitzgerald, whose clear, scrubbed voice often takes on a blank perfection, sang half a dozen songs backed by the same rhythm section, and afterward was joined in a fast "Stompin' at the Savoy" by the entire cast, which riffed ponderously away behind her. The last of her accompanists to reach the stage was Stan Getz, who, just as he was emerging from the Stygian backstage area, executed a quick, ghostly buck-and-wing before strolling demurely up to join his colleagues. It was the most spontaneous act of the night.

## The Three Louis

Decca has issued a hefty album, "Satchmo: A Musical Autobiography of Louis Armstrong," done up like a box of Christmas chocolates, that includes—in addition to some enormous photographs (Armstrong in his stocking feet, Armstrong fondling a cat), a plodding account of his career (Louis Untermeyer), and an oblique appreciation (Gilbert Millstein)—no fewer than forty-eight pieces of music. Forty-one were recorded within the past nine months, and the rest in the past decade. All but two are replayings of numbers he first recorded between 1923 and 1934. Each one is introduced by Armstrong himself, who reads from an implausible script. There are mediocre pieces, but the album also contains some of his most durable work. It comes at a fortunate time. A celebrated figure, Armstrong has recently begun offering in his public appearances little more than a round of vaudeville antics—clowning, bad jokes—and a steadily narrowing repertory.

Armstrong comes in several parts—the trumpeter, the singer, and the showman. As a trumpeter, he is one of the few jazz musicians whose careers have had the length and variety to be divided into distinct periods. The first began in the early twenties and ended around 1930. Playing in small New Orleans–style ensembles, he had an uncluttered, deceptively matter-of-fact manner that was marked by a brassy tone and a tendency to fluff notes. But his basic style—a lyrical hugging of the melody and a rich, fervent texture— was already unmistakable. In the late twenties, he abandoned the New Orleans style, and became the first of the great primitive jazz soloists, and for the next three or four years was a soloist with raggedy big bands. Despite the backgrounds they generally gave him, he produced a series of solos, on such tunes as "Basin Street Blues," "That's My Home," and "I Gotta Right to Sing the Blues," in which, moving into the upper register, he perfected a soaring lyricism, full of swoops and falls and stately long notes. Since the mid-thirties, his style, hampered by an inevitable lessening of physical power, has become a mixture of his first two periods—short, simple, declamatory phrases placed end to end with uncertain, empurpling sorties into the high register.

Although Armstrong has for twenty-five years been regarded, because of his influence over his contemporaries, as a supernal figure, he has, at the same time, rarely seemed to extend himself beyond a straightforward use of his unique gifts. Never in recent years an energetic improviser, he has limited himself to direct, if sometimes unforgettable, embellishments. He even plays certain solos nearly note for note year after year. And his emotional vigor has often peculiarly just missed getting through the broad assurance of his playing. For all that, he has managed, as the purest of all jazz musicians, to be an infallible definition of just what jazz is.

Armstrong has always been a seminal jazz singer. His baritone sounds as if it had been irreparably frayed from overuse, yet he handles a song with a matchless sensitivity. In fact, the agile warmth of his voice has, in the long run, surpassed, in its imaginativeness and flexibility, his trumpet playing. It is quite possible, too, that Armstrong's stage presence—a heady and steadily revolving mixture of thousand-watt teeth, marbling eyes, rumbling asides, infectious laughter, and barreling gait—is as endearing a spectacle as we have had on the American stage.

Armstrong is accompanied for much of the first half of the album by his regular group (Edmond Hall, clarinet; Trummy Young, trombone; Billy Kyle, piano; Squire Gersh, bass; and Barrett Deems, drums), which plays a tenuous New Orleans style and is augmented here and there by George Barnes and Everett Barksdale, guitar, and Yank Lawson. It is spelled on several occasions by a couple of other groups, including such men as Jack Teagarden, Barney Bigard, Earl Hines, and Sidney Catlett. Among the tunes are many of the ones that Armstrong previously recorded with King Oliver's Creole Jazz Band and with his own Hot Five and Hot Seven. The present recordings—not counting an exceptional version of "King of the Zulus," a raucous "Snag It" (which he has never recorded before), and an intense "All the Wrongs You've Done to Me"—are inferior to the earlier ones. There are also, however, four blues, sung with earnest monotony by Velma Middleton, in which Armstrong acts as an accompanist, as he often did in the twenties for such singers as Ma Rainey and Bessie Smith. In two of them, "Reckless Blues" and "Court House Blues," he plays shaded, casual obbligatos—some so soft they can barely be heard—that are as moving as anything he has ever recorded.

The final half of the album concentrates on the years between 1929 and

1934, and, again, is mostly given over to Armstrong's present group, enlarged by a saxophone section. On tunes like "Lazy River," "Song of the Islands," "If I Could Be with You," and "I Surrender, Dear," Armstrong plays and sings with a lift and ease that at times remind one of his greatest period. Edmond Hall, throaty and granular, is flawless throughout, and Young, an alumnus of the old Lunceford band, plays with more thought than he has shown recently. Both Kyle and Gersh are satisfactory, but Deems remains a soggy performer.

## Stress and Strain

One of the leaders of an increasingly fashionable school of modern jazz called "hard bop" or "funky" is Horace Silver, a thin, hard-working pianist, composer, and arranger of twenty-nine, who resembles an inverted, jiggling fishhook when he plays. In an ambitious new recording, "The Stylings of Silver," the leader, in company with Art Farmer, Hank Mobley, Teddy Kotick, and Louis Hayes, demonstrates a good many of the rules and regulations of the movement. Its firmest is the homage it gives the blues. Many of the compositions they play are straight blues or are based on the blues, and they usually sound as if they were attempting to resurrect old blues singers and pianists like Blind Lemon Jefferson and Jack Dupree. To this end, the hard boppers employ a heavy or sharply accented beat, a florid, staccato attack, and a hardness of timbre that is in direct contrast to the soft sounds of the cool school. (Few of Silver's cohorts, though, have rejected one habit of the cool school—an affected boredom that is sometimes more noticeable than the music itself.) The instrumentation of the funky school is generally the one Silver employs, and its structure is time-honored—opening and closing unison ensembles that form a container for the solos, which are occasionally of great length. In fast tempos, these methods are apt to produce a metronomic feverishness that reminds one of the early Lunceford band. In slow tempos, curious things happen: the rhythm section, apparently unable to keep a relaxed beat, frequently slips into a disconcerting, ticlike double time behind the soloists, while the horns, seemingly incapable of developing the logical melodic flow of, say, Coleman Hawkins, tend to blurt and stagger. These peculiarities, combined with a sameness of dynamics and voicings, can result in a queer paradox—the anxiety and energy the musicians devote to their work flattens the very aggressiveness they seek.

One of the six selections on the record is a standard tune. The others, by Silver, are the most arresting pieces, melodically and structurally, that he has written. The complex and ingratiating melodic figure of "Soulville," a minor-key blues, is spun out over a chorus of three twelve-bar sections, which is broken by an eight-bar bridge. Another blues, "Metamorphosis," has an extremely long chorus (sixty-one bars) and a sixteen-bar bridge. Several of the tunes slip in and out of two-beat and beguine rhythms. Silver is a gifted pianist. His style, a first cousin to Thelonious Monk's, involves spare, reiterated, single-note right-hand figures that sometimes have the woodpecker tenacity of certain boogie-woogie patterns. They are offset by cautious off-beat figures in the left hand. All the musicians play with their customary zest, except perhaps Farmer, who sounds out of sync in "No Smokin'."

Farmer can be heard to better advantage in the "Hal McKusick Quintet," which contains the best work he has yet recorded. In the past year, Farmer has become one of the few genuinely individual modern trumpeters. (Nine out of ten modern trumpeters are true copies of Dizzy Gillespie or Miles Davis.) His playing is an offshoot of Davis as well of the great Ellington cornettist Rex Stewart, and offers a round, chamois tone that stiffens only slightly in fast tempos, highly selective notes, each given equal thought. Together with McKusick, an alto saxophonist and clarinettist who bears a refreshing resemblance to Benny Carter (nine out of ten modern alto saxophonists are true copies of Charlie Parker), he plays ten selections, four of them new tunes and the rest standards. In most of them, Farmer and McKusick, accompanied by an excellent rhythm section (Eddie Costa, Milt Hinton, and Gus Johnson), move easily through partly contrapuntal ensembles that are most effective in "For Art's Sake," in which Farmer uses a mute and McKusick the bass clarinet, a deep, soothing instrument that has an irresistible lowing quality. All the solos are creditable, but Farmer takes an unforgettably poignant break at the start of his solo in "Gone with the Wind," first pausing for a couple of beats and then launching into a gentle, seven-note figure that resembles a slow, graceful dance.

Capitol has released "Gotham Jazz Scene: Bobby Hackett and His Jazz Band," by a group that offers the unusual instrumentation of cornet (Hackett), E-flat horn (Dick Cary), clarinet and baritone saxophone (Ernie Caceres), vibraphone and clarinet (Tom Gwaltney), and a rhythm section of piano, bass, tuba, and drums. The group handles Cary's ingenious arrangements with unflagging wit and vigor. Half of the eleven tunes are Dixieland numbers whose partly arranged ensembles give them a taut and tidy air. Two numbers—slow, richly textured pieces, full of dark voicings—are similar to some of the work done eight years ago by the Miles Davis–Gerry Mulligan group. "In a Little Spanish Town" is a cheerful, stomping spoof, in which the principal ensemble figure, a souped-up version of the original, is delivered jointly by the tuba and a clarinet. It is punctuated several times by a wild bebop figure—from "Salt Peanuts"—played by the rest of the band. All the numbers are demonstrations of the way inspired ensemble passages, no matter how tightly structured, can send a soloist flying into space. Hackett has never before displayed such fire and bounce on records, and Cary, who has become a first-rate practitioner on his horn—a muffled cross between a French horn and a trombone—does a solo in a long and rambling rendition of "Tin Roof Blues" that is a model combination of lazy, soaring figures and nimble runs. Everyone else follows close behind.

*I wonder where my comparison of Art Farmer—so cool, so recherché—to Rex Stewart—so rambunctious and unyielding—came from. It's like comparing the Luminists to J.M.W. Turner.*

## Mingus Breaks Through

The Clown," a recent recording by Charlie Mingus, the redoubtable bassist and composer, is, despite its occasional freakishness, an even more exhilarating effort than "Pithecanthropus Erectus," made a year ago. It is one of the few recordings in which a modern jazz composer has successfully produced, through the blending of complex compositional devices with improvisation, that indispensable and ingenuous lyricism on which jazz has floated for the past fifty years. Most experimental jazz has been governed by newness for newness's sake, and much of it has been little more than an agglomeration of classical technique pasted onto standard jazz contents. Mingus has allowed his forms to be primarily ordered by the original content of his music, and, unlike a lot of his contemporaries, he performs with an exuberant, sometimes unruly urgency that ignites both his compositions and the musicians who work with him.

Mingus, a large, shapeless man of thirty-five, belongs to no school of jazz. He has appeared with an extraordinary variety of musicians, including Kid Ory, Louis Armstrong, Duke Ellington, Red Norvo, and Charlie Parker. His playing has always reflected the easy lyricism of these men, and he is blessed with a superlative technique. He has an enormous tone, and a dexterity that enables him, for example, to repeatedly pluck one note so rapidly that it sounds like a sustained note, or to impart to a note the clarity and resonance of a drumbeat. In ensemble, he unreels unbroken countermelodic lines—most bassists simply supply the basic chords of the tune—while maintaining a thumping beat that leans slightly ahead of itself (like the drumming of Sidney Catlett), so that his cohorts are forcibly shunted along, both melodically and rhythmically. His solos are never displays of virtuosity. Occasionally, Mingus tends to belabor his instrument, as if it had attacked *him*, but at their best his solos contain a poignance that is unmistakable despite the essentially fuzzy, low-pitched properties of the pizzicato bass. Mingus' composing is often built around the particular talents of the musicians on hand—in the manner of Duke Ellington, whose methods appear in various shades throughout Mingus' work. It uses forms that grow directly out of his melodic ideas. In the notes for his new recording, Mingus says of the title piece, "The Clown": "I was playing a little tune on the piano that sounded happy. Then I hit a dissonance that sounded sad, and realized the

song had to have two parts." Despite such haphazard and elementary beginnings, Mingus shapes his melodic inventions into an intricate harmonic system, which he describes in the notes to "Pithecanthropus Erectus":

I "write" compositions—but only on mental scorepaper—then I lay out
the composition part by part to the musicians. I play them the "framework" on piano so that they are all familiar with my interpretation and
feeling and with the scale and chord progressions to be used.

Later, he says of a number called "Love Chant":

This is an extended form version on a more or less standard set of chord
changes. This form challenges the musician to create a line of long-held
notes for the first chorus, to develop it on one or two chords (or rhythm
patterns, scales, etc.) and then redevelop the line on the out chorus. This
is done using only one or two chords per phrase so the lines must be
developed for a much longer period of time than is usually taken before
the chord change. . . . The whole success of extended form depends on
the ability of the musicians to do this in soloing and also in playing
counter or accompanying lines.

Thus Mingus, as a jazz composer, daringly asks of his musicians even more
than the classical composer asks of his—that they carry both the letter and the
spirit of the basic patterns of his composition over into their improvisations
instead of conventionally using them as a trigger for their own ruminations.
Still another characteristic of Mingus' writing is his peculiar preoccupation
with program music. It is here that the experimentalist slides over into the
showoff. In "A Foggy Day," which is in "Pithecanthropus Erectus," the Gershwin melody, though handled in a fairly straightforward manner, is delivered
against a barrage of police whistles, simulated taxi horns, sirens, foghorns, and
the sound of a docking ferry, done by Mingus on the bowed bass.

Mingus really lets go in his new record. There are four numbers, all by
Mingus, who is joined by Curtis Porter, Jimmy Knepper, Wade Legge,
piano, and Dannie Richmond, drums. Most of the tune called "The Clown,"
which lasts over twelve minutes, is an "improvised" narration, spoken with
custardlike emphasis by Jean Shepherd, that deals with a symbolic clown
who wants only "to make people laugh" but who gets the biggest laugh of his
career when he is accidentally hit by a backdrop and killed. Fortunately, the
narration is accompanied by and interspersed with some marvelous musical
antics—comic trombone slurs, oompah rhythms, a waltz section, and a short,
lovely melodic theme. The most striking number on the record, however, is
a very long blues, "Haitian Fight Song." Mingus introduces it on his bass
with two clarion choruses that rival Louis Armstrong's opening of "West
End Blues." He then shifts into a medium tempo and plays a brief, impelling

rhythmic figure, which is gradually built upon by the rest of the musicians, who play with an increasing intensity and volume that reach a heads-off climax in a series of dissonant shrieks, an effect that is almost unendurably heightened by a weird whooping sound, like a wild, if muted, trumpet growl, presumably delivered, at the top of his lungs, by Mingus. The passage dissolves abruptly into the first solo, which, like many of the succeeding ones, is restlessly broken into four sections—medium tempo, double-time tempo, stop-time tempo, and again medium tempo. "Blue Cee," another blues, revolves around an attractive melody and is capped by a weird ooh-wah figure, played partly in unison, partly in counterpoint, by the two horns. This starts off at a whisper, quickly reaches a howl, and then suddenly—when one is prepared for a demonic ending—subsides into a mournful lyric call.

Porter is an adept, if somewhat conventional, student of Charlie Parker and Sonny Rollins. But Knepper, unlike most modern trombonists, who skate around on the glassy surface of J. J. Johnson's style, achieves here and there a rough, hustling invention reminiscent of the work, twenty years ago, of J. C. Higginbotham. Mingus is superb. His long solos in "Haitian Fight Song" and "Blue Cee" are—full of lightning combinations of fluttering, high notes, spacious intervals, and stentorian single notes broken by reverberative silences.

## The Resurgence of Red Allen

It has been nearly thirty years since Red Allen, the tireless, sad-faced trumpeter, became one of the first practitioners of the instrument to move away from the blanketing influence of Louis Armstrong. Today, at the age of forty-nine, he is, astonishingly, still widening his style. Allen left an identifiable mark on the early work of Roy Eldridge, who, in turn, influenced Dizzy Gillespie. Allen is erratic, restless, and highly lyrical. Sustained legato phrases that undulate like a calming sea are linked by jumpy connective passages full of seven-league intervals and slightly flatted notes. His coppery tone occasionally softens, but more often it pierces straight to the bone. Once in a while, he ascends wildly into the upper register or relies on technical tricks, such as a rapid, birdlike tremolo, achieved by fluttering two valves up and down, that sound more difficult than they are. Allen's melodic feeling is governed almost completely by the blues; he infuses just about every tune with broadly played blue notes. But a remarkable thing has happened to Allen's playing in the past few years. Unlike many of his contemporaries, who tend to ignore what has come after them musically, he appears to have been listening to modern jazz. The unsteady, staccato blare that has characterized his work now frequently gives way to a thoughtful, more generous tone and a myriad of soft glancing notes that resemble nothing so much as a nervous, vigorous Miles Davis.

Allen's rejuvenation is apparent in the recent "Ride, Red, Ride in Hi-Fi," which contains nine numbers. Also on hand, among others, are Buster Bailey, J. C. Higginbotham, Coleman Hawkins, and Cozy Cole. The recording is exasperatingly uneven. The barely skeletal arrangements are climaxed a couple of times by meaningless grandstand codas, and a desperate, semi-burlesque number, "Ride, Red, Ride," is done at a flag-waving tempo full of boiling trumpet and a chorus of voices that chants the title. Both Bailey and Higginbotham are in uncertain form, and Cole, who usually combines a faultless technique with sensitive support, indulges in a door-slamming afterbeat that continually joggles the melodic flow. Nonetheless, in "Sweet Lorraine," "I've Got the World on a String," and "I Cover the Waterfront," all taken at slow speeds, Allen produces long and memorable solos, in which he alternates judicious high notes with soft, lush low notes. He does not, however, top Hawkins, who has recently begun to use a heated, angry style that suggests the work of a young, uninhibited imitator.

"Traditionalism Revisited" is a relaxed recording in which Bob Brookmeyer and Jimmy Giuffre unpretentiously ease into their own idiom some of the numbers that Allen and Hawkins grew up with. (Their companions are Jim Hall, two alternating bassists, and a drummer.) There is, though, one pleasant bit of imitation; in the opening section of "Sweet Like This," Brookmeyer and Giuffre copy, almost note for note, two solos in the original King Oliver recording. Several of the tunes are associated with other musicians—"Louisiana" with Count Basie, "Some Sweet Day" with Louis Armstrong, "Truckin' " with Fats Waller—and are successful attempts to capture their melodic rather than their improvisatory possibilities. Thus, "Don't Be That Way" is turned into a slow, swaying number that contrasts sharply with the foundry treatment usually accorded it by Benny Goodman's big band; "Sweet Like This," a plaintive blues, becomes a short, poetic idyll; "Ja-Da" is played in an oblique way, free of the bounce generally given it by Dixieland groups. In half of the eight tunes Brookmeyer switches to the piano, which he plays like a sleepy Thelonious Monk, while Giuffre shuttles back and forth between the clarinet and the tenor and baritone saxophones. The musicians' total immersion in their materials may be responsible for an accidental resurrection; during his solo in "Honeysuckle Rose," Hall slips in some chunky figures straight from the late Charlie Christian, and Brookmeyer immediately adds some rumbling, striding left-hand Basie figures. It is precisely the sort of collaboration Basie and Christian so often achieved on several of the old Goodman small-band records.

Victor has issued a puzzling record, "Dave Garroway: Some of My Favorites," on which Matt Dennis, a gifted songwriter and cabaret singer, does four pleasant selections, which surround four nearly perfect numbers by a Red Norvo group that includes (in addition to the celebrated vibraphonist) Ben Webster on tenor saxophone, Harry Edison on trumpet, Jimmy Rowles on piano, and bass and drums. All of their selections are slow, suave blues, one of them a first-rate re-creation of "Just a

Mood," a languorous milestone first recorded in 1937 by Norvo, Harry James, Teddy Wilson, and bassist John Simmons.

*Two notes: Red Allen's Victor record was reissued under a different title in 1992. See my much longer review and summary of his career in "The Nineties" section of this book.*

*It is highly unlikely that Jim Hall's Charlie Christian figures on "Honeysuckle Rose" in the "Traditionalism" album were "accidental resurrections." Hall revered Christian then and reveres him still. Hall and Brookmeyer knew exactly what they were doing.*

# 1958

## Epitaph

The withering of the big-band era in the late forties left a permanent hole in jazz. The big bands provided not only finishing schools for young musicians but the sort of excitement that the small jazz group, for sheer want of power, rarely matches. There were at least three distinct types of big band—the milky, unabashed dance band (Guy Lombardo, Charlie Spivak), the semi-jazz dance band (Tommy Dorsey, Artie Shaw), and the out-and-out jazz band (Duke Ellington, Fletcher Henderson). The demise of this lively industry was due largely to economics; it is also true that the big jazz band had just about run dry. It ended as it had begun—as a highly regimented expansion of the traditional New Orleans instrumentation of cornet, clarinet, trombone, and rhythm section. There was not really much difference, for example, between the Goodman band of 1936 and the Woody Herman band of a decade later. Goodman had fourteen pieces and a mechanized style, and Herman had four or five more sidemen and a loose, flag-waving approach, but both groups depended on the same basic practices—elementary harmonies, short solos framed by opening and closing ensembles, brass and saxophone sections that stated (sometimes in mild counterpoint) simple riffs, often written to be played in unison, and a clocklike four-four beat. Indeed, the riff became the identifying badge of the big band. The exception was Duke Ellington, whose music of the period still sounds almost avant-garde. Ellington, in fact, had begun replacing conventional big-band devices in the mid-thirties with new harmonies and instrumental combinations, his own brilliant melodies, and concerto-type structures usually built around one soloist. These departures gave his band the sound of a unified instrument, rather than that of several determined platoons marching in the same general direction. Some of his inventions rubbed off in the mid-forties on such quixotic, short-lived organizations as those of Boyd Raeburn, Elliot

Lawrence, Raymond Scott, and Billy Eckstine, while Stan Kenton was testing various experiments in his laboratory. Today, however, there are just
four or five big jazz bands—Kenton, Gillespie, Basie, Ellington, and Herman—and they are, in the main, only heavier versions of their earlier selves.

In the face of this situation, Columbia has released a new big-band
record, "Miles Ahead: Miles Davis + 19," that is the most adventurous effort
of its kind in a decade. All the ten selections, by a variety of hands, have been
shaped by the gifted arranger Gil Evans into small concertos centered on
Miles Davis, who plays the flügelhorn instead of the trumpet. Evans came
into prominence in the early forties, when he wrote for the Claude Thornhill band a number of gliding, richly textured pieces that made use of such
unorthodox instruments as the French horn. He reappeared as a collaborator
with Davis and Gerry Mulligan in some of the suave, contrapuntal small-
band recordings made for Capitol in 1949 and 1950. For "Miles Ahead,"
Evans' choice of instrumentation—five trumpets, three trombones, bass
trombone, two French horns, tuba, alto saxophone, clarinet, bass clarinet,
flute, bass, and drums—is an expansion of the ensemble involved in most of
the Davis-Mulligan records. Plush, subtle sounds predominate, and the tempos, with two exceptions, are slow or medium. All the solos are by Davis.
Buried in all this port and velvet is Evans' revolutionary use of structure,
dynamics, and harmony. Reeds and woodwinds mix gracefully with the
brass and then withdraw; trombones play countermelodies against sustained
French-horn chords; a distant, undulating basso-profundo figure is part of
the background for a stark Davis solo; another background figure, played in
stop time, is repeated with slightly different harmonies and by slightly different combinations of instruments; trumpet shouts disappear abruptly into
mutes. Evans continually "improvises" on the melodies in the ensemble passages and rarely presents them anywhere in straightforward fashion. For all
this, none of the pieces, except for parts of "Springsville" and "I Don't
Wanna Be Kissed," ever get free from a chanting, hymnlike quality. There
is, in fact, too much port and velvet, and Davis, having set aside the belling
style he used in "Walkin'," backslides into a moony, dirgelike approach.
(The use of the varying textures of other soloists might have relieved this.)
Despite its technical innovations, "Miles Ahead" seems almost an epitaph
for the cool school, whose beginnings are often dated by the brilliant Davis
"Birth of the Cool" records. The playing throughout is impeccable.

Duke Ellington's newest record, "Such Sweet Thunder," seems uncomfortably thin beside the work of Evans, who learned much from Ellington.
The twelve numbers, all by Ellington and/or Billy Strayhorn, are supposedly
based on incidents and characters in Shakespeare. Ellington says, in the
album notes about a tune called "Lady Mac," which begins in waltz time,
"Though (Lady Macbeth) was a lady of noble birth, we suspect there was a little ragtime in her soul." "Lady Mac," "The Telecasters," "Up and Down, Up
and Down," and "Half the Fun" are witty and lively pieces, but they are no

more than casual sketches that depend largely on the soloists involved and not on the ensemble-solo development one expects from Ellington. The band, nevertheless, sounds almost as confident, precise, and full-bodied (in "Sister Kate," for example) as the great Ellington organization of 1940. It has few soloists the equal of Tricky Sam Nanton, Cootie Williams, Ben Webster, or Jimmy Blanton (Harry Carney and Johnny Hodges, though, are still on hand), but both Clark Terry and Quentin Jackson are not far behind.

*See another estimation of the Davis-Evans sides in "The Nineties" section. Done on the occasion of their reissue in 1996, it is, I hope, both kinder and more penetrating.*

# Melee

Fifteen years ago, "Dixieland" defined any small band made up of white musicians who depended on the high-heeled collective improvisation performed around the time of World War I by the Original Dixieland Jazz Band. It didn't include "New Orleans" jazz, which was usually played by Negroes and was predominantly given over to complex crocheted ensembles, and it didn't include "Chicago" jazz, which was originated in the late twenties by such men as Dave Tough, Jimmy McPartland, Bud Freeman, and Frank Teschemacher as a perfervid solo music that foreshadowed the swing era. Dixieland now embodies all these distinct types—or what is left of them—as well as the various new "revivalist" groups, which, to compound the confusion, are generally scarecrow imitations of such early New Orleans–style groups as those of King Oliver and Jelly Roll Morton. Nonetheless, at a concert titled "Dody in Dixieland," which was presented last Saturday night at eight-thirty and again at midnight in Carnegie Hall, the term was expanded still further.

The forty-odd musicians who appeared on the program included a gospel singer, a bassist from the early days of bebop (Tommy Potter), half a dozen or so big swing-band musicians (Charlie Shavers, Tyree Glenn, Cozy Cole, and Roy Eldridge), some of the boys from the Chicago-style school (George Wettling, Jimmy McPartland, Bud Freeman), a Harlem stride pianist (Willie the Lion Smith), a couple of New Orleans–style musicians (Zutty Singleton and Tony Parenti), a vaudeville performer (John W. Bubbles), a trombonist who began in the twenties on the fringes of Dixieland but soon moved into a condensed streamlined version of Chicago jazz (Miff Mole), and one Dixieland musician (the pianist Gene Schroeder). Three of the eight or so groups present had the look and instrumentation of Dixieland groups—those led by Stan Rubin, McPartland, and Wild Bill Davison— while the rest resembled everything from a chamber group to a Sousa band. There were motleys made up of three clarinets plus rhythm, five trumpets plus rhythm, and three trombones plus rhythm; a group composed of a vibraphonist, a bassist, and two drummers, one of whom sat in the dark off to one side of the stage and never touched his drums; and, at the opening of the second half of the concert, a swollen aggregation consisting of a pianist, two bassists, four drummers, and at least ten horns. The only real music of the evening occurred just after this display, when Bobby Hackett's flexible, highly imaginative six-piece group appeared and, after a nod in the direction of what has come to be a Dixieland standard, "Muskrat Ramble" (which was written by a New Orleans–style trombonist), performed three smooth, witty pieces that resembled the sound of the small Ellington groups of the forties and employed an almost endless variety of instruments, including cornet, tuba, bass saxophone, piano, baritone saxophone, tenor saxophone, alto trumpet, vibraphone, clarinet, and bass clarinet. Dody Goodman, an attractive comedienne who lent her name to the festivities, came onstage sporadically to trade quips with the MC ("I used to think the 'Jelly Roll Blues' was some kind of dessert"). She also did a brief soft-shoe routine with Mr. Bubbles that was announced as a "Cavalcade of the Dance."

*New York City overflowed with jazz concerts in the fifties and sixties. Rarely a weekend went by without a concert at Carnegie Hall or Town Hall or Merkin Hall, and they were of every school. Many, like the above, were dispensable, and even silly. But they helped to keep the music up front.*

## Vic Dickenson and the P.J.Q.

**V**ic Dickenson, a lean, forty-nine-year-old trombonist has, in the past twenty years, perfected a combination of sly, prodding humor, graceful lyricism, and easy technical mastery that is unique on an instrument that has had very few able practitioners. Its career as a solo instrument has been comparatively brief. Until the big-band era of the early thirties, the trombone was largely either an ensemble instrument in small bands—in which, in a stertorous, down-in-the-cellar way, it filled in harmonic chinks—or, in the hands of men like Miff Mole and Kid Ory, a whiplash to keep things rolling. By the late thirties, however, it had become, with the help of Jimmy Harrison, J. C. Higginbotham, Dickie Wells, Jack Teagarden, and Dickenson, a first-rate solo vehicle. Only a handful of persuasive trombonists have turned up since (the difficult mechanics of bebop and hard bop offer the trombonist technical problems that often make him sound like a fat man trying to run uphill), while of the older men only Teagarden, Benny Morton, and Dickenson have retained the push they started with.

A recent recording, "Vic's Boston Story," provides a generally satisfying demonstration of Dickenson's abilities. He is accompanied in the twelve selections by George Wein on piano, Jimmy Woode or Arvell Shaw on bass, and Buzzy Drootin on drums. Dickenson has a smooth, generous tone, and approaches a tune not as a full-dress improviser but as a funny and seemingly casual embellisher. Bleary glissandos appear side by side with stuttering triplets that often give way to guttural sounds, full of a slapstick grace. In such slow numbers as "Yesterdays" and "All Too Soon," which he plays with and without a mute, he uses a near-whisper that matches the celebrated chromium utterances of the late Tommy Dorsey, but it also has a smoky blue air that Dorsey never captured. In such up-tempo selections as "Lover Come Back to Me," his smears and snorts, occasionally broken by shouting phrases, are projected by an intense, unceasing rhythm. The more than ample solo space given Wein, a mediocre but sometimes rather moving pianist, unfortunately prevents Dickenson from ever really stretching his legs, as he did, say, in a Commodore recording made in the mid-forties called "Bottom Blues," on which he constructed two slow choruses—a mixture of groans, subterranean asides, and stately motion—that remain indestructible.

Dickenson is in excellent form on another recent record, "Buckin' the Blues," performed by a group led by Buck Clayton and including Earl Warren on alto saxophone, Kenny Burrell on guitar, Aaron Bell on bass, Hank Jones, and Jo Jones. Most of the eight numbers are extended treatments of the blues and are built around Clayton, who plays with a gentle, garrulous lyricism—quick, glancing phrases, sustained blue notes, and a delicate, nervous vibrato. The rhythm section, with the exception of Hank Jones, a precise, nimble performer, tends to lumber, but Dickenson compensates for this by acting as a springy foil for the lighter-than-air ruminations of Clayton.

A recently formed group made up of vibraphone, piano, bass, and drums provides on its first release, "The Prestige Jazz Quartet," a refreshing contrast to the Modern Jazz Quartet, which has the same instrumentation and which shows signs of becoming fixed in a state of frozen fragility. The P.J.Q.—Teddy Charles, Mal Waldron, Addison Farmer, and Jerry Segal—plays with as much subtlety and intramural support as the M.J.Q., but, unlike the M.J.Q., which often submerges its content in spidery, complex forms borrowed from classical music, it handles its materials with a brisk expressiveness that makes secondary whatever forms are being used. Almost half of the recording is occupied by "Take Three Parts Jazz," an accomplished work by Charles. The piece, built around a couple of simple, appealing themes (one of them used as the basic idea for both the opening and closing parts), is actually a study of rhythms. Part 1 jockeys between an out-of-rhythm section and a brief fast section before settling into a pleasant medium tempo. Part 2 is a slow, romantic movement that slips in and out of tempo, and the final part is performed at a sturdy, flying tempo, ending in a delicate but hammering climax. The three other selections are of nearly equal interest—two adept numbers by Waldron ("Meta-Waltz," which moves back and forth between waltz and four-four time, and "Dear Elaine," a slow, deliberate ballad number), and a Thelonious Monk tune, "Friday the Thirteenth," which sets up an uncluttered platform for the soloists. Charles is a subdued, almost droning performer whose playing sometimes suggests the click of knitting needles and whose total lack of accent demands the listener's complete attention. Waldron offers a relaxed intensity that is full of rhythmic variations; series of elementary, highly melodic phrases are examined again and again, each time in slightly altered rhythmic patterns that generally build toward powerful climaxes (clusters of clean, ringing high notes in "Dear Elaine," and a long run of woodpecker notes in "Friday the Thirteenth").

Waldron and Charles appear in another recording, "Olio," a thoughtful effort that reveals the methodical control of Charles, who directed the session as well as contributed two of the six numbers. (Two are by Waldron, one is a standard, one is a blues.) Also on hand are Thad Jones on trumpet, Frank Wess on flute and tenor saxophone, Doug Watkins on bass, and Elvin Jones on drums. Thad Jones is a brassy, sure-footed trumpeter whose solos are now and then so perfectly structured they appear to have been carefully written out beforehand, and Wess, in contrast to the hardpan approach of most contemporary flutists and tenor saxophonists, achieves a soft and purposeful eloquence. Waldron's solos again attain a direct poignance.

## Monk

The vinegary, dissonant, Gothic music that Thelonious Monk has been producing since his arrival fifteen years ago as a pianist and composer has been steadily reshaping, rather than rejecting, the traditions that preceded him. His playing, though camouflaged by the occasional use of an elbow and by dodging, jabbing rhythms, still reveals a stride pianist not at all dissimilar to two other former stride men, Duke Ellington and Count Basie. His compositions—with their bristling discords, unexpected notes, and coded titles ("Crepuscule with Nellie," "Epistrophy")—are often no more than old blues, harmonically remodeled and infused with a melodic sense as original and lyric as Ellington's. A diffident, evasive performer, whose feet sometimes flap about like fish while he plays, Monk invariably manages either to thoroughly imbue his co-workers with his rambunctious iconoclasm or, once in a while, to make them as awkward as wallflowers at their first dance.

Monk, who is now thirty-seven, helped to found bebop, along with Charlie Parker, Dizzy Gillespie, Charlie Christian, and Kenny Clarke. His playing has not changed appreciably since then. His runs are apt to sound stringy, his chords as if they were compounded of wrong notes. His touch always seems startled; scurrying, barely struck notes alternate with sudden, heavy chords that surprise the listeners as sharply as a thump on the back. But this apparent disarray is held together by its unfailing consistency, which, in turn, is dictated by an extraordinary rhythmic sense. If Monk plays a raggedy run, it is usually because he is trying either to retard the rhythm (sometimes this antic is simply an unabashed breathing space), or, if a banging discord comes next, to lift the rhythm, to force his colleagues to get up and go. The result is a rare and superb unpredictability. Monk's composing is less disordered. Although his songs ripple with dissonances and rhythms that often give one the sensation of missing the bottom step in the dark, they are generally written in simple figures that rarely stray from the accepted chorus structures. The best of them display minor, brooding melodies that, in their most intense moments, suggest lullabies.

Monk is in matchless form in three recent recordings—"Monk's Music: Thelonious Monk Septet," "Mulligan Meets Monk," and "Thelonious Himself." In the first of these, Monk is joined by Ray Copeland on trumpet, Gigi Gryce on alto saxophone, Coleman Hawkins, John Coltrane, Wilbur Ware on bass, and Art Blakey. The six numbers—five by Monk, and one a nineteenth-century hymn—reflect the familiar prickly-pear Monk, as well as a remarkable, and heretofore largely undemonstrated, talent as an arranger. His scores for seven instruments have the depth of a seventeen-piece group. The saxophones may work in unison for a few bars in the ensemble and then suddenly dissolve into counterpoint, while Monk plays a separate melodic line in company with the trumpet. This is abruptly broken by a series of harsh piano chords rhythmically and harmonically counter to everything else that is going on. The total effect, perfectly exemplified by "Well, You Needn't," is of a controlled unsteadiness that gives the impression—in contrast to the mannered ensemble writing in so much modern jazz—of being composed as it is played.

The first number, the hymn "Abide with Me," is played by the four horns in a pleasant, rasping, barbershop-quartet style. They deliver just a single chorus and—when one is prepared for the entrance of the rhythm section and the first solo—simply stop. "Well, You Needn't," "Off Minor," and "Epistrophy" are long, fervent, medium-tempo exercises set in the conventional ensemble-solo-ensemble framework, and include satisfactory solos from everyone, despite the occasional scuffling brought about in "Epistrophy" by two players trying to start their solos at once. "Ruby, My Dear," one of Monk's casual but inimitable ballads, is divided up between his piano and Hawkins, who, as is his custom these days, manages, in both his fairly straightforward statements of the melody and his improvisations, to convert his materials into an impassioned music that seems almost visible. The final number, "Crepuscule with Nellie," is a slow, blueslike piece. The first half is played by Monk, with and without rhythm accompaniment; then the band enters to underscore the melody in such a way that it achieves Monk's lullaby quality.

"Mulligan Meets Monk" is unsettling. On hand, in addition to Gerry Mulligan, are Ware and Shadow Wilson. Four of the six numbers are by Monk, one is by Mulligan, and one is a standard. Monk's playing is as sprightly as anything he has recorded in years, but Mulligan sounds crabbed and stilted; even his ensemble work is uncertain and labored. The difficulty, perhaps, is the hopelessly different rhythmic approaches of the two men; Monk's is staccato, jumpy, sometimes almost arrhythmic, and Mulligan's is legato and flowing, in the manner of Miles Davis and Stan Getz. Some of the wreckage is cleared away by Ware, who, both in this case and in "Monk's Music," demonstrates an attack that is as startling as that of the late Jimmy Blanton. Although Ware often unfashionably plays his solos directly on the beat, they are varied by meditative pauses and repetitions of a single note. These produce gliding, declarative melodic lines that, combined with a distinct yet soft tone, make a good many of his colleagues (who are apt to handle their instrument as if it were a horn) sound incessant.

On *Thelonious Himself*, Monk plays seven unaccompanied piano solos (he is joined in the eighth by Coltrane and Ware), three of them his own pieces and all of them in slow tempos that would be lackadaisical if it were not for the oblique, needling restlessness, the getting-through-to-the-other-side of the melody, that invariably drives the most aimless-seeming passage.

## This Whiskey Is Lovely

Riverside Records has reissued a unique and invaluable chunk of jazz archaeology, "Jelly Roll Morton: The Library of Congress Recordings," in twelve records, wherein Morton, the New Orleans pianist, arranger, and composer, reminisces, plays and sings several dozen songs, expounds his musical theories ("Vibrato . . . was nothing at the beginning but an imitation of a jackass hollering"), lies, brags ("I didn't name the 'Jelly Roll Blues' myself; it was named by the people of the city of Chicago"), and cavorts ("Oh, this whiskey is lovely") his way through some of the best performances he ever gave. The recordings were made for the Folk Music Division of the Library of Congress by Alan Lomax early in 1938, and they were a minor stroke of genius on his part, for Morton—old, tired, down-at-the-heels, and completely out of fashion—died just three years later. In the mid-forties, a limited edition of 78-rpm recordings, a hodgepodge arrangement of most of what Lomax had taken down, was put on the market. It reappeared a few years later as a set of LPs, which soon went out of print. The present edition, which is pleasingly designed, includes an admirable fifteen-thousand-word essay on Morton by Martin Williams. At the same time, Riverside has perpetuated many technical deficiencies in the recordings. One is forced to battle the sharp gavel sound of Morton's shoe tapping out the beat, a volume that goes precipitously up and down, an endless series of squeaks, thumps, and rattles (the faulty equipment Lomax had to use), an unsteady recording speed that makes Morton's voice slide back and forth between a foghorn and an Irish tenor, and a system of collating that results, for example, in beginning the "Original Jelly Roll Blues" in Volume I and concluding it in Volume X. Fortunately, Morton was a forceful player and a clear speaker, and if one has decent sound equipment and does some athletic knob-twirling, nine-tenths of the material is intelligible.

Morton was an indelible figure. A handsome, intelligent, sensitive-faced man with an aquiline nose and a high forehead, he was born Ferdinand La Menthe of Creole parents in New Orleans around 1885, and by his mid-teens had become a proficient pianist, dandy, and gambler. He left the city for good about 1907, and for fifteen years roamed the country (he turned up in New York in 1911) as a vaudeville performer, gambler, patent-medicine man (Coca-Cola mixed with salt, at a dollar a bottle), cabaret owner, procurer, tailor, and occasional pianist and band leader. In time, he acquired a hundred and fifty suits, a diamond in a front tooth, and a diamond stickpin, watch, ring, and belt buckle, and he took to carrying a thousand-dollar bill. He also perfected a highly vocal vision of himself as a witty, adroit boulevardier. He became a full-time pianist, composer, and band leader in the early twenties in Chicago, and between 1926 and 1930 was responsible for some imperishable small-band recordings. (Inexplicably, only half-a-dozen reissues are now available, in Victor, Camden, Folkways, and Jazztone anthologies, but many of the old 78-rpm discs are still around.) Then his luck ran out; he blamed a spell a West Indian had put on him. The early swing musicians considered him old-fashioned, jobs were infrequent, and he spent most of his last years as manager of a shabby night club in Washington, D.C.

Morton ranks with Louis Armstrong, Duke Ellington, and Charlie Parker as a great jazz innovator. His best small-band records are buoyant, fresh, and ingenious works full of revolutionary devices that are only now being rediscovered by modern musicians. Although they have all of the roomy spontaneity of New Orleans jazz, they were, with the exception of the solos, largely written out. Each horn in the invariably rampaging final ensembles loosely follows a brilliantly sketched-out melodic line, in the fashion of the semi-arranged polyphonic exercises in Gerry Mulligan's recent sextet recordings. Such devices as the following gave structure, clarity, and variety to a music that was often accidental: three clarinets delivering a soft, engaging riff in unison against a trombone counter-melody; an orchestral passage led by a tuba, and another played without rhythm accompaniment (a recent "discovery" of the West Coast school of jazz); a Basielike rhythm-section passage that is started off by a booming trombone figure; a continual web of counter rhythms; graceful and extended melodic lines; and an uncommon attention to instrumental timbres and orchestral textures. Morton wrote perhaps a hundred compositions, many of whose titles have an eccentric motion of their own—"Tanktown Bump," "Pep," "Boogaboo," "Fickle Fay Creep." In contrast to the thirty-two-bar structure that became a confining fixture in the swing era, most of Morton's pieces were constructed, in the manner of ragtime, of carefully complementary parts of varying length. His melodies lack the subtle languor of Ellington's, but they have an attractive, straightforward lyricism. Today, Morton's piano often sounds romantic and old-fashioned, and it is difficult to say why. It is true that his touch was undistinguished, that he used a lot of overweight, blurred chords in the right hand, and that his rhythmic approach tended toward the heavy ump-cha. Not only that, he favored rich, sweet, melodic figures that at times become downright lacy. Nonetheless, he was an accomplished technician whose left hand could slip deftly back and forth between intricate counter-rhythms and whose right could reel off impressive arpeggios. Beneath the predominantly decorative air of his style—even at fast tempos he seems to be bowing to the right and left—one finds complex, inspired, and thoughtful variations that match anything of their sort in jazz.

Half of the Library of Congress recordings are given over to talk, most of which is the core of *Mister Jelly Roll*, Lomax's book about Morton. Morton's soft, clear voice and easy rhythmic manner of speech are an unfailing pleasure. He was a magnificent tale-spinner who could make a New Orleans funeral or Memphis barroom brawl unforgettable. The rest of the recordings are a compact history of all the ingredients that went into the creation of jazz. Morton had a wonderful memory, and he effortlessly resurrects quadrilles, tangos, marches, spirituals, blues, boogie-woogie, stomps, rags, jazzed-up bits of opera, and an Indian Mardi Gras song. He even does some first-rate takeoffs, including a subtle and mischievous one on the blues, one on a popular song of the period (which he sings in a way that is strikingly like the whispers of Gene Austin and Rudy Vallée), and a delightful one on a bad honky-tonk pianist. Morton sang on only a handful of other records, which is a pity, for he belongs with Bessie Smith and Louis Armstrong as a jazz singer. His light, perfectly controlled baritone reveals a direct emotion that, in the half-dozen blues in these albums, results in some of the most affecting jazz vocals ever recorded. And, with few exceptions, he surpasses himself at the piano. "Creepy Feeling," one of his own pieces, which lasts eight minutes and is played at a slow tango tempo, is a hypnotic series of variations, each a development of the last. But it has, like much of the other music in the albums, a sad, ruminative quality, too. The bragging, spirited front of talk, talk, talk that sustained Morton suddenly makes perfect sense.

## Chameleon

Almost everything about Miles Davis seems ambiguous. A short, thin, retiring man, now thirty-one years old, who often stands motionless and slightly hunched when he plays, his horn pointed at the floor, like a crane poised on a mud flat, he is generally considered a founder of cool jazz. Davis' debut, some twelve years ago, with such musicians as Charlie Parker and Max Roach, was wobbly. His approach consisted largely of an awkward blotting-up of the work of Dizzy Gillespie. He had a mousy tone, he hit a lot of clams, and he always sounded as if he were playing in a monotone. Since then, his technique has improved steadily; his style, in fact, now comes in several shades. In slow numbers, he often uses a tight mute and, by playing directly into a microphone, achieves a hollow but penetrating sound not unlike blowing into the neck of an empty bottle. At the same time, he employs economical, melodic phrases decorated with off notes, which give the effect of his casually twisting the melody as if it were soft metal. Davis frequently plays open horn in middle tempos, and the change is startling. Fat, delicate phrases, reminiscent of a man slowly and rhythmically beating a soft punching bag, round it off. Fast numbers appear to unsettle him, though, for he often relies on a fretwork of empty runs and unsteady spurts into the upper register. But in a medium-tempo blues, say, Davis is capable of creating a pushing, middle-of-the-road lyricism that is a remarkable distillation, rather than a one-two-three outlining of the melodic possibilities; indeed, what comes out of his horn sounds like an instantaneous editing of a far more diffuse melodic line being carried in his head.

Two recent releases—"Relaxin' with the Miles Davis Quintet" and "Bags' Groove: Miles Davis and the Modern Jazz Giants"—give a complete picture of Davis' virtues and faults. In the first, which was made not long ago and is the less satisfactory of the two, he appears with John Coltrane, Red Garland, Paul Chambers, and Philly Joe Jones. There are six numbers, four of them standard tunes and one apiece by Dizzy Gillespie and Sonny Rollins. Davis uses a mute in five of them. There are occasional sketchy ensemble figures, and a string of rather haphazard solos. The most impressive moments occur in "If I Were a Bell," played at a pleasant up-tempo, and "Oleo," done slightly faster, in which Davis gets a balsa quality by using just bass accompaniment, except in the bridge, during which the rest of the rhythm section falls in. Garland, a bright, dandyish pianist, also takes a surprisingly incisive solo in the lower register. "You're My Everything," which is slow-paced, is an excellent example of Davis the bottle blower; "Woody 'n' You," delivered at a fast clip, displays his nervous, squeaky style. Coltrane has a dry, unplaned tone that sets Davis off, while Jones, who can be rambunctious, behaves throughout with restraint and sensitivity.

"Bags' Groove," on the other hand, contains some of Davis' most inspired work. The first side is given over to two versions of the title piece, a medium-tempo blues recorded late in 1954 with Milt Jackson, Thelonious Monk, Percy Heath, and Kenny Clarke. In both versions, Davis' solos, which are played open horn, have an oblique relentlessness and are full of perfectly executed variations. Monk is superb. In the first version, his solo is broken by such long pauses that it appears he has left the studio; then he suddenly resumes, with clumps of clattering, offbeat dissonances. In the second version, his pressure up, he engages in a dizzy series of jagged runs. An indispensable record.

Vanguard has reissued two other indispensable efforts—"The Vic Dickenson Showcase," in two volumes, and "Buck Meets Ruby," made four years ago. These include some classic examples of an arbitrary type of small-band jazz that flourished between 1935 and 1945, and generally consisted of simple arrangements or improvised ensembles—the New Orleans type of ensemble, but with its tangles and intensities laid aside. The musicians involved were generally members of big bands and, temporarily freed of the strictures of their parent organizations, they usually reacted as if on holiday. Many of their records—particularly the Lionel Hampton Victors, the Teddy Wilson–Billie Holiday collaborations, the small Ellington units, and various Sidney Bechet "Feetwarmer" sessions—have an undying freshness. The Dickenson records Vanguard has reissued involve Ruby Braff; Shad Collins; Dickenson; Edmond Hall; Sir Charles Thompson, piano; Steve Jordan, guitar; Walter Page; and Les Erskine or Jo Jones. There are extended versions of ten standards and a couple of blues. Among them are strolling renditions of "Jeepers Creepers," "Russian Lullaby," and "I Cover the Waterfront" (which are, however, not lifted by the thump-thump-thump monotony of the Thompson-Page-Jordan-Erskine rhythm section), as well as slow, graceful interpretations of "Old Fashioned Love" and "When You and I Were Young, Maggie." "Old Fashioned Love" ends with a swaying, jostling ensemble in which Braff and Collins engage in slow-motion leapfrog, Hall slides discreetly around in the middle register, and Dickenson lays down a memorable floor of smears, growls, and rumbles.

"Buck Meets Ruby" concerns two groups, one under the leadership of the pianist Mel Powell (Buck Clayton, Henderson Chambers, trombone, Jimmy Crawford, Hall, Jordan, and Page) and the other under the leadership of Clayton (Braff, Buddy Tate, Benny Morton, Jimmy Jones, Jordan, Aaron Bell, bass, and Bobby Donaldson, drums). The Powell numbers (four, all standards) alternate between taut, jubilant ensembles and arranged passages, and they reach perfection in a long "I Must Have That Man," which gradually develops an extraordinary, ascending lyricism. Hall produces a sorrowing, practically trembling solo in the lower register that is unlike anything else he has recorded. The Clayton-Braff numbers (two standards and two originals) have a Basie sound, and there is notable work from everyone. Clayton is a performer whose emotions are always on view, while Braff, a well-stirred mixture of Armstrong and Bunny Berigan, plays with an almost overbearing legato attack that is frequently punctured by short connecting phrases and fleeting runs.

## The M.J.Q. (Continued)

Monte Kay presents an Evening with the Modern Jazz Quartet," given a week or so ago at Town Hall, marked the first time that a jazz concert has been served up—greaseless and perfectly cooked—under glass. There were none of the Katzenjammer aspects of the usual jazz concert. John Lewis, the Quartet's leader, briefly described all the numbers, which appeared in the order given in the program, which in turn expatiated on the selections in no-nonsense terms ("'Angel Eyes,' by Matt Dennis. A lyrical American song popularized by Ella Fitzgerald"). The group, arranged in a neat semicircle on the stage, was dressed in tuxedos, and bowed in effortless unison to the applause. The concert, which was neither too long nor too short, was carefully worked out in both choice of materials and change of pace. Not a whistle or a catcall eddied the air. Indeed, the audience seemed to be holding its breath, a band of bird watchers who had suddenly stumbled on an unknown species. Part of this general decorum was the result of the staging, and the rest was due to the Quartet, which, poker-faced and never fluffing a note or missing a beat, went at its instruments like jewelers intently at their work. After a time, one longed for a good sneeze or a rude shout to soften the unremitting industry.

The M.J.Q. has made invaluable contributions to jazz. It has resuscitated, in quiet fashion, the art of collective improvising. It has reintroduced, through Lewis' compositions, the delicate, lyrical element of jazz that was brushed aside in the bop era. It has pointed the way toward the use of classical forms—the fugue, the rondo, and the episode—while maintaining, through some memorable improvisations and a frequent use of the blues, direct contact with the fundamentals of jazz. In the past year, however, the M.J.Q.—whether because of restlessness or too much conscientiousness—has tended to over-refine these approaches. Many of the numbers it played at Town Hall seemed like distillations of earlier versions of the same pieces. The solos were tentative and restrained, and the tonal qualities of the group appeared to rise higher and higher. Lewis stuck largely to the middle and upper registers, in both solos and accompaniment; Kay spent much of his time tiddling with his cymbals, which had a hard, high-pitched sound, or with a variety of tambourines, triangles, and finger cymbals (the few times he struck his snare drum, it sounded like thunder); and Jackson's vibraphone, an instrument that in the most skilled of hands has a light metallic timbre, reflected Lewis and Kay. This steady shrillness was particularly noticeable because of the absence of microphones, which made Heath's bass, which normally provides a respectable basso balance, barely audible.

There were seven pieces by Lewis, three by Charlie Parker, one by Dizzy Gillespie, and three standards. "Willow Weep for Me" was done as a solo by Jackson, who, though the best of the modern vibraphonists, revealed the limitations that always threaten his work. He does get a round, vibrating tone from his instrument, but at Town Hall he relied heavily on devices—a complex, seesawing figure; the rapid hammering of a single note; a four-note phrase not unlike a traditional trumpet flourish—that after a while made every solo seem like a variation on his previous one, instead of on a new melody. Two examples of the M.J.Q. as distillers occurred in "Two Degrees East Three Degrees West" and "A Night in Tunisia." The first is a simple, charming blues by Lewis, yet the Quartet peeled off all the outer melodic wrappings, delivering in its ensembles a series of clandestine chords that only implied the melody. "A Night in Tunisia," whose repeated descending phrases build gradually to a breathtaking break and the entrance of the first soloist, received the same treatment. Moreover, the break was eliminated, and so was much of the excitement of the piece. The first half of the concert was closed by a flowing but tenuous fifteen-minute work by Lewis, "Fontessa" (described as "a little suite inspired by the Renaissance Comedia Dell'arte"), which involved a series of improvisations on a blues, a ballad, and a boplike number.

Four of the numbers in the second half were from a score by Lewis for a recent French motion picture, and though they consisted of such things as a triple fugue, funeral music, a blues, and some heated triangle work by Kay, they sounded much like "Fontessa." The rest were by Charlie Parker, and in them the Quartet finally began to loosen its galluses. This continued during the three encores, when it really got down to business by playing with a lightness and fervor that made the audience sit up and pay attention.

## Ben Webster

Ben Webster, the forty-nine-year-old tenor saxophonist from Kansas City, has for almost twenty years played with a subtle poignancy matched only by Coleman Hawkins and Johnny Hodges (from both of whom he learned a good deal). A heavy, sedate man, with wide, boxlike shoulders, who holds his instrument stiffly in front of him, as if it were a figurehead, Webster played in various big bands before the four-year tour of duty with Duke Ellington that began in 1939. Since then, he has worked with small units and his style, which came to fruition during his stay with Ellington, has become increasingly purified and refined. Like the work of many sensitive jazz musicians, it varies a good deal according to tempo. In a slow ballad number, Webster's tone is soft and enormous, and he is apt to start his phrases with whooshing smears that give one the impression of being suddenly picked up by a breaker and carried smoothly to shore. Whereas Hawkins tends to reshape a ballad into endless, short, busy phrases, Webster employs long, serene figures that often (particularly in the blues, which he approaches much as he might a ballad) achieve a fluttering, keening quality—his wide vibrato frequently dissolves into echoing, ghost-like breaths. His tone abruptly shrinks in middle tempos and, as if it were too bulky to carry at such a pace, becomes an oblique yet urgent and highly rhythmic whispering. In fast tempos a curious thing frequently happens. He will play one clean, rolling chorus and then—whether from uneasiness, excitement, or an attempt to express the inexpressible—adopt a sharp, growling tone that, used sparingly, can be extremely effective, or, if sustained for several choruses, takes on a disagreeable, monotonous sound. At his best, though, Webster creates, out of an equal mixture of embellishment and improvisation, loose poetic melodies that have a generous air rare in jazz.

Webster is in rare condition in two recent recordings, "Bill Harris and Friends" and "Gee, Baby, Ain't I Good to You: Harry Edison." In the first, he is given as much space as Harris, a trombonist who delivers dogged, vibratoless notes that seem to perforate rather than transform the melody. The contrast to Webster's style is striking. There are seven numbers, all of them standards, including a spoofing of sweet music—"Just One More Chance"—that is more energetic than funny. (Jazz and slapstick rarely mix.) Webster gives a classic five-and-a-half-minute treatment to a slow ballad, "Where Are You?"; plays a memorable solo in "I Surrender, Dear," again at a slow tempo; and then in Ellington's "In a Mellotone," which is done at a relaxed jog and lasts almost ten minutes, puts together a long, perfectly sustained set of variations. The rhythm section (Jimmy Rowles on piano, Red Mitchell on bass, and Stan Levey on drums) is precise but reserved. It brings to mind the handful of records Webster made in the mid-forties with Sidney Catlett, who brushed aside Webster's occasional tendency to coast by ceaselessly pushing him with sharp, perfectly timed rimshots and bass-drum accents. Webster has never played with quite the same intensity since.

On the second record, Webster appears with Harry Edison, Oscar Peterson, Barney Kessel, Ray Brown, and Alvin Stoller (drums). There are seven standards, including three extremely pleasant blues. Edison, a casual repetitive soloist, shares a good deal of space with Kessel and Peterson, who are intense but equally repetitive performers. The rhythm section, indeed, has an airless sound that seems to hobble Edison, if not Webster, who, particularly in the opening of his solo in "Taste on the Place," lines along like a gull.

"Trav'lin' Light: The Jimmy Giuffre 3" is a peculiarly static series of embellishments on the techniques—intricate, partly written contrapuntal ensembles; short solos; the absence of a sounded beat—evident in Giuffre's one previous trio recording, which, even in its more mournful moments, had a buoyant, Panlike quality. One reason for this deliberateness is a change in instrumentation; the bassist has been replaced by the valve trombonist, Bob Brookmeyer, whose work recalls that of the late Brad Gowans. (Jim Hall, the guitarist, remains, and Giuffre, as usual, alternates between the clarinet and the tenor and baritone saxophones.) At the same time, the tonal qualities of Brookmeyer's instrument both fill in and blur the outlines of the original trio, which had a pleasant clarity. Another reason is Giuffre's predominant use of ensembles—there are almost no solos—in which the three voices wind heavily around one another, like garrulous people gossiping away a hot summer evening. There is, however, excitement in such numbers as "Forty-second Street," "Show Me the Way to Go Home," and "The Swamp People" (there are, in all, four numbers by Giuffre and four standards), but it evaporates in the slow, lyrical pieces, in which Giuffre sticks to the clarinet, playing it in a pale, gloved manner, as if he were trying to imply rather than state his music.

## Big Sid

**D**ecca has reissued, on two LPs, "Louis Armstrong Jazz Classics" and "Satchmo's Collectors' Items," twenty-four records made by Armstrong with groups of various size, between 1935 and 1941, that are valuable not only for the presence of Armstrong—at the time, the taut directness of his earliest style had reappeared and become a kind of ballast for the Alpine lyricism he developed in the early thirties—but for the presence, on two-thirds of them, of Sidney (Big Sid) Catlett, the irreplaceable drummer who died seven years ago. Born in Evansville, Indiana, in 1910, Catlett came into prominence in New York with, among others, the bands of Elmer Snowden (a remarkable kindergarten that included such other beginners as Roy Eldridge, Chu Berry, and Dickie Wells), Benny Carter, Fletcher Henderson, and, finally, Armstrong. He stayed with Armstrong until 1942, except for a brief period in 1941 with Benny Goodman, who, though Catlett contributed immeasurably to some of Goodman's most relaxed big-band efforts ("Pound Ridge," "The Count," "I Got It Bad and That Ain't Good"), abruptly let him go, reportedly because Catlett, a superb showman, was upstaging him. Then Catlett won a couple of magazine awards, and celebration seemed at hand. He worked at Café Society Uptown in New York with a memorable Teddy Wilson group (Emmett Berry, Joe Thomas, or Bill Coleman on trumpet, Edmond Hall on clarinet, and Benny Morton on trombone), and then with his own excellent quartet, which included Ben Webster and the pianist Marlowe Marris and which made a handful of records. In 1947, he rejoined Armstrong, who then had Earl Hines, Barney Bigard, and Jack Teagarden, a wonderfully limber band that was recorded during several concerts and whose recordings are still available from Victor and Decca. But in 1949, Catlett's heart acted up, and he quit the band, spending his last two years doing pickup work and shuttling between Chicago and New York and Boston. He died at the worst possible time. The LP recording had just come in, opening all sorts of possibilities, jazz drumming was being overhauled and needed guidance, and good taste—Catlett's taste—was low in the music.

Coleman Hawkins is perhaps the only jazz musician, who approaches Catlett's extraordinary adaptability, for Catlett worked successfully with such disparate jazz musicians as Sidney Bechet, Eddie Condon, Hot Lips Page, Goodman, and Ellington, as well as Dizzy Gillespie and Charlie Parker. His style appears to have been almost totally his own. (His use, particularly with Bechet and Armstrong, of several types of press roll, for both accompaniment and solos, suggests Zutty Singleton, and the way he employed the wire brushes and the high-hat and other cymbals is reminiscent of Chick Webb.) Its main characteristics were an intense, buoyant, metronomic beat (it is surprising how many good drummers cannot keep time), which he would now and then hurry very slightly to give the effect of urgency; a light, forceful touch; a sensitivity to what was going on elsewhere in a group that sometimes uncannily resulted in the anticipation of what a soloist was about to do; a technique that was always sufficient for what he had in mind (as opposed to the remarkable technique of Buddy Rich, which has long existed for the sake of itself); and consummate taste.

Catlett was an inspired accompanist. Always conscious of dynamics (a fundamental largely foreign to modern drummers), he would use a light, clear cymbal behind a clarinet solo; half-closed high-hat cymbals, which produce a heavier, treading-water effect, behind a trumpet; a Chinese cymbal (whose edges are perforated with holes through which naillike pieces of metal are loosely hung, making a shushing sound, or the full high-hat, played in a clipped, flowing manner, behind a trombone; a closed high-hat, which gives a ticking effect, like a rubber eraser being tapped on metal, behind a bass or piano. At the same time, Catlett's left hand would work out inimitable accents on the snare-drum head, on the head and rim simultaneously (a rimshot), or by hitting one stick, held firmly against the snare head, with the other, which resulted in a thick chonking sound. Catlett's left-hand rhythms were wholly unpredictable, yet always right, and they created a tension off which the most sluggish soloist could rebound. His work on the bass drum, which until then was used by most drummers to emulate the tread of a giant, alternated between soft but solid beats, complete pauses, and sudden offbeats, which paralleled the work of Jo Jones and foreshadowed the bop drummers. And his use of wire brushes (a rapidly vanishing art) varied between a rich, distinct padding sound at fast tempos and, at slower speeds, a crystalline sound, like fingernails on wood.

Most drum solos are fountains of noise. Catlett was an exception. He was, after Baby Dodds, the first of the melodic drummers. He might, in a five-minute excursion, begin (using the sticks) with a series of quiet, delicate, sharp figures on the snare head, release the snares (so that a tom-tom effect was produced), move rapidly between the head and the rims (tickety-thump tick-tack-tick-thump-thump), and then (switching to mallets) move over to the tom-toms, while gradually intensifying his patterns and volume. Then he would suddenly break the flow with a perfectly placed silence, move back to the snare drum (using sticks again), return to a whisper, and with the snares on once more, start working toward a crescendo, which generally would incorporate a series of abrupt, stunning explosions, carried out on every part of his set with a speed and definition that even Rich, who drums faster than light, has never topped. Catlett the showman often appeared in his solos. Well over six feet tall, with enormous shoulders and slender fingers the length of dinner knives, Catlett sat at his drums with Prussian erectness, his trunk motionless and his arms (weighted by hands that made drumsticks look like matches) moving so fast that they seemed to be lazily spinning in slow motion. It was an unforgettable ballet. Once in a while he would twirl his sticks over his head or throw them in the air, allowing their motions to silently measure off several beats. The effect was louder than any shout.

There are tantalizing glimpses of Catlett's work in the Decca reissues. In the final choruses of "Bye and Bye," one can hear how Catlett, using tight, powerful rimshots on the afterbeat, could drive a big band to a climax. His left hand is in excellent evidence all through "Hear Me Talkin' to Ya" and "Savoy Blues," in which he lays down a thick carpet of press rolls. Toward the end of "Save It Pretty Mama," he slips into a soft afterbeat behind Armstrong, subtly shifting the rhythm from an even glide to a slow, irresistible rock. In "You Rascal You," he ticks the snare-drum rims every four measures behind Armstrong's vocal, as though he were counting telegraph poles from a slow train—an invention used, in a slightly different fashion, by most modern drummers, and generally credited to Art Blakey. Perhaps the best example of Catlett's precision and excitement occurs in "Baby, Won't You Please Come Home," when he closes Higginbotham's trombone solo with an emphatic rimshot, followed by a pause, and, a split second after Armstrong's horn enters, another emphatic rimshot, which sends Armstrong rolling down the road. It's an electric moment.

## Mammoth (*Continued*)

Since its beginnings, in 1954, the Newport Jazz Festival has slowly grown sleeker and rounder. The first Festival consisted of two modest concerts attended by some fifteen thousand people. The latest Festival, held over the Fourth of July weekend in an arena called Freebody Park, was a statistician's dream: There were seven concerts (afternoon and evening) and two musically illustrated morning lectures, all of which amounted to over thirty-five solid hours of music and talk; approximately two hundred and fifty musicians, including five big bands, sixteen singers, and a welter of small groups; and a total attendance of sixty thousand. But bigness is partial to flabbiness, and the bigger the Newport convention has grown, the softer it has got. Aside from such superficially discomfiting trivia—the sort of trivia that when multiplied can seem mountainous—as asking an audience tightly packed on wooden camp chairs to remain attentive for six hours at a time, introductory Capitol Hill remarks by Senator Green (R.I.), the public presentation to musicians of several awards by *Playboy* magazine, the ceaseless churring of movie cameras that surrounded the bandstand, and a C.B.S. broadcast that, because of the demands of sponsored radio, got all the evening concerts off to a shambling start, there were such misfires as an interminable Benny Goodman evening, in which Goodman, heading a dispirited big band, played nervously and off pitch; the International Youth Band, a theoretically heartening aggregation made up of eighteen of the leading players from sixteen nations, which, because of the largely pompous arrangements it was forced through, sounded heavy and listless; a small modern group, including flute, oboe, tuba, timpani, xylophone, and vibraphone, that produced a half hour of tinkling, be-boom, and oompah; several enormous female singers, who sang with a resolute, ringing monotony; the big, whumping Maynard Ferguson band; and an amorphous small group, made up of Urbie Green, Terry Gibbs (vibraphone), Dinah Washington, Don Elliott (mellophone and vibraphone), and Max Roach, that went on forever, particularly in a vibraphone duet.

But there were exceptions. On Friday morning, during a lecture by Professor S. I. Hayakawa, a semanticist from San Francisco State College, on "The Origin and Nature of the Blues," Jimmy Rushing, who provided the accompanying demonstrations, sang—backed by a six-piece Dixieland band, Eli's Chosen Six—eight numbers with an easy, shouting articulateness (he has a way of rounding off every word, like a man polishing an apple to a gleam) that included "Careless Love," "Goin' to Chicago," and "St. Louis Blues." On Saturday morning, Marshall Stearns gave an informed and amusing rundown on jazz dancing, which was illustrated with two dozen interludes by two remarkable dancers, Leon James and Al Minns, who seemed in motion even while standing stock-still, and who did the Cakewalk, the Shake Dance, the Camel Walk, the Eagle Rock, the Shimmy, the Charleston (seven variations), the Jig Walk, the Lindy Hop, Trucking, the Suzy-Q (the Arthur Murray version, as taught in 1936, and the legitimate version), the Shorty George, the Big Apple, and a good many more. During the Big Apple (1938), a dance with sixteen separate steps, Minns executed a section in exquisitely slow slow motion, moving his arms and legs in a series of spare swoops and wide steps, which sustained, for perhaps a minute, a liquid tension that was extraordinarily poignant and graceful. This was balanced by a dance called the Shag (1938), which consists of extremely fast, short steps, delivered while the dancer—stiff as a ramrod, his arms at a forty-five-degree angle over his head—moves directly up and down like a pile driver, and by the Apple Jack (1945), a dance done to bebop by James, who gave the impression of creating a casual, contrapuntal offsetting melody. Minns and James closed the morning with a two-part sketch—a man asking a woman to dance in the days of the Big Apple and in the present time of cool music— that was a masterpiece of exact, funny, understated satire. And on Sunday morning, just after midnight, at the end of a long evening devoted to the blues and including a superior performance by the Gerry Mulligan Quartet, Mahalia Jackson, accompanied by a pianist, organist, and bass player, sang a dozen spirituals and gospel songs. Miss Jackson's presence on a stage is a hypnotic lesson in graciousness and poise, and this, combined with a rich alto voice that effortlessly bends and slides around her materials, made her performance perfection, particularly in a soft, nearly tempoless rendition of the Lord's Prayer, which had a melodic delicacy that brought tears to the eyes.

There were other good things. On Thursday evening, Joe Morello, the drummer of the Dave Brubeck Quartet, displayed—in a long series of four-bar exchanges with his cohorts—a fresh, decisive imaginativeness, a sense of rhythm, and quick, shifting emphases that recalled some of the snap, pop, and crackle of Sidney Catlett. On the same night, Duke Ellington, in the course of fifteen numbers, a good many of them pleasant new compositions, again and again pushed his band until it became one large, floating collective voice—a momentarily realized dream of what a big jazz band should be. On Friday afternoon, the Jimmy Giuffre 3, a group that hasn't been successfully recorded yet, performed five numbers, including a medium-tempo version of Giuffre's "That's the Way It Is." It was centered on a short blues-spiritual theme that was bandied about in brief solos and ensemble passages full of counterpoint, echoing fugal bits, and nicely jarring timbres. It was an irresistible performance. The next afternoon, Herb Pomeroy and his big band played half a dozen blazing Kentonish-Basielike arrangements and then—in its final number, "The Lunceford Touch," done in the manner of the Lunceford band—got off some brass figures that were so loud and so brilliantly executed that the air in the park seemed to be rolled right back to the bleachers. On Sunday afternoon, Thelonious Monk, accompanied by bass and drums, was, in an almost perversely quiet way, matchless. Sonny Rollins, who appeared just before (also with bass and drums), was allowed exactly two numbers (Anita O'Day was allowed seven selections earlier in the afternoon), but managed to suggest forcibly his skill at masterly improvisations compounded of fast runs, lazy, sway-backed melodic phrases, and jolting off-rhythms. Jimmy Knepper, the trombonist, with a small group led by Tony Scott, who played with a fervency bordering on desperation, proved again that he is the first trombonist since J. J. Johnson with his own style—one that is a mixture of the directness of Benny Morton and the obliquity of Johnson. The Festival was closed that night by Louis Armstrong's small band (which includes Peanuts Hucko, Trummy Young, and Billy Kyle), whose past Newport performances have been mostly vaudeville in nature. There was still plenty of vaudeville in evidence—off-color jokes and words, facial contortions, and the like—but in at least half of his twenty numbers Armstrong played with a controlled, feverish lyricism (in such numbers as "Sunny Side of the Street," "Mack the Knife," and "The Star-Spangled Banner") that suddenly dispelled the chromium-and-tail-fins pall that had hung over most of the weekend.

## The Olden Days (Continued)

**A**lmost without exception, the second annual Great South Bay Jazz Festival, which consisted of five evening concerts, held in an open-sided sailing ship of a tent in Great River, Long Island, over the last weekend of July and the first of August, was, for a combination of who knows what reasons—fitful production, bad weather, the doldrums of a gray, wet summer, a general lack of musical inspiration—a desultory affair that made last year's Festival, which included extraordinarily sustained work by Coleman Hawkins, Yank Lawson, Jimmy Giuffre, and Charlie Mingus, seem a legendary event. This year, performance after performance turned out to be either uncooked or exasperatingly dull.

The South Bay Seven (with Rex Stewart, Benny Morton, and Jerome Richardson on flute and baritone saxophone), which opened the Festival, played eight numbers that alternated between vague Ellingtonish selections and rackety free-for-alls (all of them weighed down by a spiritless rhythm section) that were briefly improved by Richardson, who, making his way vigorously upstream, contributed to a slow "Tin Roof Blues," a solo with a stunning, hallooing climax. The following weekend, a quartet led by the baritone saxophonist Pepper Adams (Kenny Burrell was on guitar, George Duvivier on bass, and Elvin Jones on drums) did half a dozen numbers that went on and on in a heated monotone. Adams has a curiously muffled, oblique tone, as if his notes evaporate when they hit open air, and he plays in the manner of the hard-boppers (fast, skidding runs, thick staccato phrases, and an almost indiscernible rhythm), who are apt to float around for twenty choruses whether they have something in mind or not. The Fletcher Henderson All-Stars (eighteen strong, and including Joe Thomas and Taft Jordan on trumpets, Morton, Dickie Wells, Hilton Jefferson, Buddy Tate, and Stewart as leader) was loud and ragged. The saxophones stepped on each other, the trumpet section wavered, and the rest of the rhythm section was inaudible beneath the slamming, abrasive drumming of Mousie Alexander.

On the final night of the Festival, Charlie Mingus, heading a group made up of Shafi Hadi on alto and tenor saxophones, Horace Parlan on piano, Jimmie Knepper, and Danny Richmond, performed three superior numbers, which included a blues with an extremely attractive melody, several rhythms, breaks, and some first-rate solos. (A fourth number was centered on an actor, Melvin Stewart, who, accompanied by Mingus on piano, read some bad poems.) And then, the pot on the lip of boiling, the group packed up and left. The evening was closed by Duke Ellington, who delivered a new four-part piece, "The Great South Bay Jazz Festival Suite," consisting of an Afro-Cuban number, a reshaping of "Rosetta," and a long blues in two sections. This had some flowing trombone figures pitted against the solo horn of Harry Carney, two excellent choruses of muted wah-wah trombone by Quentin Jackson, and a solo by Paul Gonsalves. Gonsalves, like Pepper Adams, got caught in his own momentum, but he was eventually carried along by the band, which developed a series of arch, tight brass figures, and an irresistible rocking motion. For the next dozen numbers, Ellington fell back on such things as an absurd Spanish pirouette featuring the trumpet of Cat Anderson; a couple of numbers from his "A Drum Is a Woman"; a number called "Hi Fi Fo Fum" and built around an interminable tom-tom solo by Sam Woodward; and, finally, in the fashion of Guy Lombardo, a long medley of Ellington numbers, all of them celebrated and lovely songs that were barely stated before being swept aside to make way for the next number. The band, undismayed as always, played impeccably.

The major exceptions during the two weekends were forceful. On the opening night, Al Minns and Leon James strutted, slid, stomped, and spun their way through eighteen jazz numbers, accompanied by recordings that included a Fletcher Henderson side, dating back to the thirties, with a piercing, majestic Roy Eldridge solo that was the best thing of its kind during the whole Festival. They were followed by the Modern Jazz Quartet, which during half of its ten numbers battled a thunderstorm that pushed the rain right through the canvas. The results were tonic, for the group performed with a brashness and lift that brought each of its pieces—particularly the "D & E. Blues," "I'll Remember April," "The Golden Striker," and the new "Festival Sketch"—into perfect balance, so that Connie Kay, Milt Jackson, and John Lewis formed a liquid moving counterpoint that in time seemed to effortlessly still the din. On the second night of the final weekend, the pianist Cecil Taylor, accompanied by Sylvester Candy on bass and Dennis Charles on drums, played four of his own compositions. Taylor's music is, in the main, unclassifiable. It is an improvised atonal music that has jazz rhythms more often implied than stated, and elusive forms that appear to be strictly his own. An expert, classically trained pianist, he plays with a hammering intensity. The result is a passionate, often grinding mixture of sounds, which range from graceful, lyric Debussy arpeggios to angry staccato chords that leap back and forth two or three octaves at a time. Yet his work invariably *suggests* jazz through its rhythms and attack, and appears, excitingly and furiously, to be trying to force its way to a level that has only been hinted at before.

## One Step Forward, Two Steps Back

T he nerviest, most tenacious movement to emerge from all the bewildering backing and filling in the jazz of the past decade—which includes the birth of hard bop; the rise and fall of the cool school; the resurgence of such swing musicians as Coleman Hawkins, Ben Webster, Roy Eldridge, Vic Dickenson, Edmond Hall, and Jo Jones; the effort to revive New Orleans jazz; and the fitful activity of the few remaining big jazz bands—has been the intense laboratory work of the small but steadily increasing group of experimental composers and arrangers, that includes Charlie Mingus, Jimmy Giuffre, John Lewis, Gerry Mulligan, Teddy Charles, Gil Evans, and George Russell. Starting with the basic belief that jazz can be composed—an assumption long ago proved by Jelly Roll Morton and Duke Ellington—these men have attempted, in compositions that often have no improvisation at all, to broaden its harmonic, rhythmic, and structural boundaries, as well as to widen its content. At the same time many of them have resurrected, in new and vigorous ways, collective improvisation, a kind of jazz that began going under in the late twenties, when the first great soloists appeared.

In the forties, many young jazz musicians plunged into formal musical training. Within the framework of the Modern Jazz Quartet, John Lewis has gone in for interplay and such devices as the rondo and the fugue; Giuffre has experimented with an implied rather than a sounded beat, with (like Mulligan) a careful, almost bemused counterpoint, and with lyrical blues-folk themes largely foreign to jazz; Mingus' preoccupation with the content of his music, which is often satiric and bitter, has resulted in his abandoning (like Charles) conventional chorus structures for his own patterns, the invention of weird chord sequences upon which to improvise, and the use, for certain effects, of the human voice, foghorns, taxi horns, and so on; Evans has developed new instrumentations and tonal colors; and Russell has employed atonality, broken rhythms, and solos as organic outgrowths—rather than battling opposites—of the ensemble. Some of this has been exciting, and some of it has been depressing.

That is pretty much the case with a new Columbia record, "Modern Jazz Concert," an exasperating, but occasionally brilliant and always ambitious collection of six compositions commissioned by Brandeis University, and played last year at its Festival of the Arts. Of the six composers, three are classical (Gunther Schuller, Milton Babbitt, Harold Shapero) and three jazz (Mingus, Russell, Giuffre). All the pieces are played by a fourteen-piece group that includes two saxophones (John La Porta and Hal McKusick), two trumpets (Art Farmer and Louis Mucci), a trombone (Jimmy Knepper), a flute, a bassoon, a French horn, a harp, a vibraphone (Teddy Charles), a piano (Bill Evans), a guitar, a bass, and drums. Although the album notes, by Schuller, include an admirable map of what goes on, they also state, as in a vision, "Perhaps this is jazz or perhaps it is not. Perhaps it is a new kind of music not yet named." Perhaps, on the other hand (with a little boiling and scraping), it is this: one fairly successful jazz composition (Russell's "All About Rosie"); an obtuse atonal contrapuntal classical piece (Babbitt's "All Set"); a concoction in which, through sheer cleverness and compositional strength, jazz and classical music are forced together (Schuller's "Transformation"); a watery work that never, except in one brief instance, makes up its mind where it belongs (Shapero's "On Green Mountain"); and a couple of pieces (Giuffre's "Suspensions" and Mingus' "Revelations, First Movement") that are variations on jazz material that their composers have handled better elsewhere.

"All About Rosie" is, though at times a peculiarly cold work (much of Russell's composing has the same detached air), a frequently exhilarating effort. The first of its three movements is an up-tempo, semi-contrapuntal development, by the ensemble, of an Alabama folk song. The second is a sort of slow blues, with an attractive introduction that has several of the horns skating slowly through an atonal section, which, when finally resolved, turns into a slowly building pattern of riffs delivered in a dragging round, with a sharp afterbeat by the drummer, that eventually reaches a relentless conclusion. (The orchestration, however, is as colorless as it is throughout the record.) In the final movement, the folk theme is taken up again at a faster tempo by the ensemble until—bang!—in comes Evans for an improvised solo, which is a fascinating stomping effort, with fresh blues figures and a couple of sparkling single-note passages.

The best part of Shapero's rather dandyish "On Green Mountain," which is based on a chaconne by Monteverdi, is also its brief improvised section. Art Farmer, in the course of four choruses on the eight-bar theme, states the melody, embellishes it, then turns to a half-tempo improvisation and, in his last go-round, lets loose a full set of up-tempo improvisations.

Schuller's "Transformation" begins as an unadorned classical piece in which a short, simple melody is repeated individually, as a slightly varied ground, by the horns, while the piano and drums inject clumps of jazz rhythms. By the time the theme is fully stated by the ensemble, the rhythm section has broken into a four-four gallop, which, in turn, dissolves into another first-rate Evans solo. This is overpowered by a lunging, shimmying riff that comes gradually out of the background. Then the rhythm slowly breaks into pieces, and there is a shift back to a classical design. It is a perfect, through totally unconvincing, tour de force.

*Evans' solo on "All About Rosie" put him on the map, and was the beginning of his pervasive influence on jazz piano.*

## M. Bechet

Although Sidney Bechet, the high-domed, slightly Oriental-looking clarinettist and soprano saxophonist from New Orleans, has been in France for a decade (where he has successfully launched, at the age of nearly seventy, a new career as a music-hall performer), the gap he has left on this side of the ocean has never quite closed. By the early forties, Bechet had been elevated to the aerie occupied by Louis Armstrong, Bunny Berigan, Art Tatum, and Coleman Hawkins. This was brought about by a swarm of praise (from the moldy figs) and scorn (from the modernists), which appeared to enlarge him, the way a fog seems to swell a house or a ship. As a result, when Bechet left for Europe there was general agreement on at least one thing: no matter what else, he was big. Part of this distortion has been Bechet's own unintentional doing. More than any other major soloist in jazz, he has made a basically unsentimental music come extremely close to the romantic—a magnetic, invariably troubling conversion, which usually draws either slings or hugs. Primarily, Bechet's style has a jumpy, passionate, skating quality. On the soprano saxophone he has an impenetrable, almost teeming tone. An embellisher more than an improviser, he may, at fast and medium tempos, pour out straight melody, or stretch it into a series of commanding, sometimes shouting, legato phrases, or break it up into tight staccato bits that occasionally turn into dirty, coruscating growls. What gives Bechet's lyricism its unique accents, while also appearing to shake it into one piece, is his vibrato, an astonishing device that, in its width and intensity, often resembles the phrase endings of an aging diva. Bechet's clarinet playing, on the other hand, is a kind of antidote. Because of the compressing tonal limitations of the instrument, he is reduced to warm, eloquent pools of sound that, particularly in the blues, result in an inescapable melancholy. (Bechet is one of the great blues soloists; he seems almost magisterially at home within its one-two-three chord structure.) But this restraint never lasts long; his tone on the instrument eventually turns querulous and sharp, as if, unbearably impatient, he were trying to escape from its cramped instrumental confines.

Bechet has almost always been regarded as a New Orleans performer, despite the brilliant recordings he made in the thirties and forties, with such swing musicians as Sidney Catlett, Sandy Williams, Sidney de Paris, Charlie Shavers, and J. C. Higginbotham, playing in the loose, collective style then fashionable for small-band recordings. Such baggy surroundings suit Bechet perfectly. For when he is playing the saxophone, either in ensemble or in solos, he generally flattens everyone else on hand, through sheer volume and aggression. (The most conspicuous exception is a recording he made for Victor of "I Found a New Baby," in 1932, in which the terse, almost timid trumpeter Tommy Ladnier, apparently exercised beyond endurance by Bechet, loudly and alarmingly roars again and again into the upper register).

Bechet is first-rate in a recording made not long ago in Paris and called "Sidney Bechet Has Young Ideas." On hand, at Bechet's wish, is a mixed bag of modern musicians—the French pianist Martial Solal, Pierre Michelot or Lloyd Thompson on bass, and Kenny Clarke or Al Levitt on drums. The balance between Bechet's old lyrical flourishes and the chopped, boppish accents of his accompaniments is ideal; both parties seem to be continually and jovially correcting each other. There are fourteen tunes, all of them compactly handled standards done largely in medium tempos. (Bechet's choosing standards, rather than Dixieland tunes, is true to form; many of his earlier records are refashionings of numbers like "Rose Room," "Lady Be Good," and "Sweet Lorraine." It is a pity, though, that there are no blues on the record.) Bechet plays only the soprano, and in a thoughtful, rather subdued way floats lazily through most of his material, varying puffs of melody with gently pressing variations. The most successful moments occur in "The Man I Love," which Bechet drives down as if it were a blues, and "These Foolish Things Remind Me of You," which, taken at a slightly faster tempo than it usually is, has a Bechet solo that booms along and then drains away in a series of rude, growling two-bar exchanges with Solal, who supplies a surprising combination of suspended tremolos, fleeing runs, and stark bass chords. Solal, indeed, is a constant delight. The rest of the rhythm section is lively, if jagged, with the exception of Clarke, whose accompaniments always resemble a steady, admiring stream of whispers. In fact it was Clarke who, with Bechet in 1940, first recorded in the style that, a year or two later, produced the quicksands of bebop drumming.

## The Best Medicine

When Big Bill Broonzy, the dean of the old-time blues singers, died last summer, at the age of sixty-five, the *Times* printed a short notice near the middle of its obituary page, the area generally reserved for passé novelists and upstate businessmen. A few years ago, the late Art Tatum was given a resounding top-of-the-page two-column photograph and a statesman-length notice. The *Times* was right; the obituaries were accurate reflections of where the two men stood at the end of their lives. Thirty years ago, their positions would have been reversed. For although blues singing has been slowly and steadily declining ever since, it was regarded in the twenties with much the same enthusiasm as rock-and-roll, a corruption of the blues, now is. Nonetheless, Broonzy, who made hundreds of often obscure records, was widely recorded before his death. Three of the efforts—"Big Bill Broonzy Sings Country Blues", "Big Bill Broonzy: The Blues", and "Big Bill's Blues: Big Bill Broonzy"—all first-rate demonstrations of his later style, were set down in the past seven years but have only lately been released. They are a remarkable celebration of the blues.

Perhaps the best thing to do with our sporadically threatened national anthem, whose manhandling melody resembles a plain with a butte in the middle, would be to replace it with a good blues. The blues are indisputably American, they can be sung with ease, and they just about cover the register of human emotions. Washington Irving is credited with having first used the term "the blues" in 1807, as a synonym for melancholy: "He conducted his harangue with a sigh, and I saw he was still under the influence of a whole legion of the blues." His usage was a shortening of "the blue devils" (Robert Burns: "In my bitter hours of blue-devilism"; Thomas Jefferson: "We have something of the blue devils at times"), a synonym for a baleful presence that goes back at least to Elizabethan times, when blue apparently became associated with being down in the dumps. By the third quarter of the nineteenth century, both the non-musical term and the still nameless music derived from Negro spirituals, work songs, field hollers, and the like were in full swing, and since frequent characteristics of this music are slow rhythms and a seemingly minor harmonic cast, someone inevitably pasted them together. Although the blues can express total gloom, as in

Blues, blues, blues, why did you bring trouble to me?
Blues, blues, blues, why did you bring trouble to me?
Oh, death, please sting me, and take me out of my misery,

they can also, as in many of the vocal and instrumental blues that began coming out of Kansas City in the early thirties, communicate an equally expressive buoyancy and abandon. Unlike the typical Anglo-American folk song, which has become largely picturesque and ornamental, the blues are still a functional music that is used both as elementary autobiography or confession (like all vital folk music) and/or as an emotional safety valve—for both the performer and the listener. At the same time, the blues can represent a kind of unspecified ill, which assumes a nearly visible shape, like the old blue devils themselves. The late Leadbelly once prefaced a song by saying:

When you lay down at night, turn from one side of the bed all night to the other and can't sleep, what's the matter? Blues got you. Or when you get up in the mornin', and sit on the side of the bed—may have a mother or father, sister or brother, boy friend or girl friend, or husband or wife around—you don't want no talk out of um. They ain't done you nothin', and you ain't done them nothin'—but what's the matter? Blues got you. Well, you get up and shove your feet down under the table and look down in your place—may have chicken and rice, take my advice, you walk away and shake your head, you say, "Lord have mercy. I can't sleep, what's the matter?" Why, the blues still got you.

This process of catharsis is achieved in many ways. In vocal blues, anger can be got rid of with anger ("I can't eat the marriage license 'cause I ain't no billy goat [repeat] / I can laugh in your face and cut your doggone throat"); cruelty with satire or ridicule; disaster with humor ("If your house catch on fire, Lord, and there ain't no water around [repeat] / Throw your trunk out the window and let the shack burn down"); bereavement with selflessness ("That was the last time I saw my daddy's face [repeat] / Mama loves you sweet papa, wish I could take your place"); fear by disguising it in fable. Instrumental blues are an abstraction of vocal blues. With the comparative limitations of words, meanings, and the human voice removed (but with its image exaggerated by the horn), a good blues instrumentalist, like Louis Armstrong or Vic Dickenson, can, with delicate inflections, a wide range, and an inexhaustible variety of timbres—the growl, the mute, the thin, high-pitched note—seemingly revel in the ache at the center of the blues. More-over, the more elaborate, repetitive structure of blues singing, with its substructure of instrumental accompaniment, occasionally tends to become blurred and top-heavy, while a classic blues solo, like Armstrong's at the close of "Knockin' a Jug," a Columbia recording made in 1929, retains all its sharpness. The most astonishing thing about the blues, that all-purpose medicine, is their ingenuity and simplicity.

The blues, which predate instrumental jazz, seem to have been specifically designed for jazz improvisation. Stripped to the essentials, the blues, which are a highly malleable form, have no set melody. A fairly common type developed in the thirties is most often twelve bars long and consists basically of three chords. In the key of B flat, a common one for blues, these chords are B flat, E flat seventh, and F seventh. They are arranged in a rough rondo form: B flat (four measures), E flat seventh (two measures), B flat (two measures), F seventh (two measures), and B flat (two measures.) The form moves toward a subtle climax with the F chord, and then slopes satisfactorily away to where it began. This pattern may be varied by all kinds of sub-chords, breaks, and ornamental notes. It is repeated again and again during a performance, so that the climatic chord in each chorus is picked up and slightly heightened by the same chord in the next. But the mysterious emotional pull of the blues also resides in the so-called "blue notes," slightly flattened ones that frequently occur in the second and fourth chords; they may, however, appear in any of the chords. At slow tempos, these notes, in combination with the continually revolving tonic-subdominant-dominant form, can pleasurably evoke just about anything—a black-and-white November twilight, the longing bound up in the steam whistle, wind coming up in the trees. This air of melancholy, however, is sublimated at fast tempos, so that the harmonic structure becomes only a short, brisk, but still highly flexible form upon which to improvise.

Good lyrics rarely read well, just as good poetry is rarely set successfully to music. Despite their frequently being celebrated as a unique and beautiful folk poetry, blues lyrics are not often an exception. They are occasionally in a rough iambic pentameter, which is set in queer couplets whose first line is repeated twice. Broonzy had a disarmingly logical explanation for this:

> There's a lot of people can understand English, but you gotta talk very slow. So, the blues singers, they sing the same thing over twice. The same thing. Over and over again. No matter 'cause you're dumb, but simply to give you a chance to catch it the next time when they come around.

Blues lyrics usually don't scan, have faulty, strained rhymes, are repetitive and ungrammatical, and abound in non sequiturs. Yet they sometimes come close to the concision of rhythms, words, and imagery of genuine poetry. There is a kind of one-armed poetry in this graceful brevity:

> If you see me comin', hoist your window high.
> Oh, if you see me comin', hoist your window high.
> And if you see me goin', hang your head and cry.

This terseness is intensified, in the following stanza, by the words "rail-road iron" and "pacify" and by the insistent, almost stuttering middle-of-the-line breaks:

I'm gonna lay, lay my head—yes,
On some sou-, southern railroad iron,
I'm gonna let that two, two-nineteen, dear,
Pacify my mind.

Through a Biblical foreshortening of space and time, parts of Bessie Smith's "Backwater Blues" achieve a rough majesty:

When it thunders and lightnin's, and the wind begin to blow,
When it thunders and lightnin's, and the wind begin to blow,
There's thousands of people ain't got no place to go.
Then I went and stood up on some high old lonesome hill,
Then I went and stood up on some high old lonesome hill,
Then I looked down on the house where I used to live.

Totally different is Muddy Waters' "Honey Bee," with its possibly unconscious parody of a poem that used to be drummed into every fifth-grader in America:

Sail on, sail on, my little honey bee, sail on,
Sail on, sail on, my little honey bee, sail on.
You gonna keep on sailin' till you lose your happy home.

Thus, the real lyricism of vocal blues is a careful balance of the quality of the words, the particular melody hit upon, and the mood and technique of the performer. As in any fine mechanism, the parts are inseparable.

The first of the two great blues periods began around the turn of the century and ended about 1930. It involved two quite different groups. The earlier was the "country" blues singers, who, like Broonzy, worked their way all over the country as laborers, and, like genuine troubadours, recorded their adventures in their blues. (Parallel with them are the pioneer blues pianists, like Montana Taylor, Romeo Nelson, Pinetop Smith, Jimmy Yancey, and Cripple Clarence Lofton, who, though they occasionally sang, were primarily instrumentalists whose work, ironically, became well known only because of their best pupils—Albert Ammons, Pete Johnson, and Meade Lux Lewis.) They were, in the main, rough-and-ready singers. Operating on the fringe of show business, they frequently adopted pseudonyms—the Yas Yas Girl, Speckled Red, Sunny Land Slim, Memphis Minnie, and Washboard Sam. Paradoxically, their blues were far more complex in structure and meaning than those of the "city" blues singers, who form the second group.

For some reason, the best of the early "city" blues singers were women, among them Chippie Hill, Ida Cox, Sara Martin, Ma Rainey, and the unrelated Smith girls (Bessie, Clara, Trixie, Mamie, and Laura). All in all, Bessie Smith has never been equaled. A monument of a woman, with a hard, handsome face, she had a heavy contralto voice that seemed to threaten almost everything she sang. At the same time, her deliberation had a serenity and majesty that can be approximated only in opera. By 1930 many of these singers were dead or in obscurity, and the second blues period began. In one of its two groups are such singers as Jimmy Rushing, Joe Turner, Hot Lips Page, Teddy Bunn, Muddy Waters, and Jack Teagarden. They are, for the most part, more adept technicians, but they also have less of the brimstone quality of their predecessors. The second group includes the great blues instrumentalists, who, curiously, are also the great jazz musicians, the spirit of the blues having become the cornerstone of jazz. New blues singers have simply stopped appearing. (An indirectly related form, gospel singing, appears, however, to be booming.) Perhaps the principal reason is that blues singing—passed orally from generation to generation—once filled a gap that, even in the remote backlands of the South, is now taken up by jukeboxes, radio, and television. In comparison, some of the old blues sound as archaic and unwieldy as Chaucerian English.

During the forty years that Broonzy sang the blues, he composed three hundred songs and provided a model for countless singers, the best known of whom is Josh White. He made his living not from singing or composing but by working as everything from a farmhand to a janitor, a necessity commemorated in such pieces as "Plough-Hand Blues" and "Mopper's Blues." Although his uncut baritone lost some of its resilience and lightness before he died, the outlines of his spacious technique are clearly visible in the three dozen selections on the Folkways, Columbia, and EmArcy records. "Trouble in Mind," an eight-bar blues on the Folkways record, is a superb example. Most blues singers rely on an unvarying method of attack, the boisterous shout. Broonzy, however, has a continual awareness of dynamics, dramatics, and shifting rhythm that is faultless. Here is the first stanza of "Trouble in Mind":

I'm troubled in mind, baby, I'm so blue,
Yes, but I won't won't be blue always,
You know the sun, sun gonna shine
In my back door someday.

Singing at a very slow tempo, Broonzy delivers the first line almost as an aside, neatly squeezing all the syllables into about a measure, with a vague emphasis on the word "mind." Then, abruptly, he shouts the "yes" at the start of the next line, sustaining it on one note for two measures. He cuts off the shout as suddenly as it begins (Broonzy used almost no vibrato) and eases through the rest of the line in a rapid, plaintive, gradually melting way. His voice continues to sink until the last line, which he half shouts in such a way that the emphasis curves up to the words "back door," and then subsides. The total effect of the stanza is of slow, deliberate, slightly irregular hammer strokes. Broonzy's own "I Wonder When I'll Get to Be Called a Man," a social-protest blues, on the same record, which goes, in part,

When I got back from overseas,
That night we had a ball,
Next day I met the old boss,
He said, "Boy, you get some over-hauls!"

is sung at a rolling medium tempo, but in a delicate, offhand way that inescapably points up the meaning of the lyrics. In "Texas Tornado" (on the Columbia record), he reverts to the classic blues-singing style—a sustained shout, with a slight dropping of the voice at the end of each of the first two lines, followed by the quieter, resolving third line. His treatment fits the words nicely:

My baby is a Texas tornado, and she howls just like the wind.
My baby is a Texas tornado, and she howls just like the wind.
She'll blow the house down, Lord, if I ask her where she been.

Broonzy is incomparable in "Southbound Train." It is sung slowly and gently all the way through, each word sliding into the next, as if being hummed. (Broonzy backs himself on guitar on all three records, except for five numbers in which he is accompanied by a small blues band.) The melancholy in his voice never varies, but because of the inexorable blues pattern it seems to deepen steadily. The last two stanzas, though unashamedly emotional, are not, as is true of all blues, the least sentimental:

Standin' at the station, tears was in my eye.
Standin' at the station, tears was in my eye.
Now that I've lost my best friend, how can I be satisfied?

I hear a whistle, wonderin' where is that train.
I hear a whistle, wonderin' where is that train.
Now that I've lost my baby, I've got all red brain.

Broonzy fills in the pauses between lines with quiet staccato strummings that provide a fine contrast to the fiber of his voice. Indeed, the balance between voice and guitar, form and content, and emotion and restraint is perfect.

# 1959

## Mingus Among The Unicorns

Last Friday Night, in the Nonagon Art Gallery, on lower Second Avenue—a long, narrow, second-floor room whose fireplace, brooding beams, heavy chandeliers, and dark woodwork carved with unicorns, lions rampant, and medieval heads give it the air of a Hohenzollern hunting lodge—the third in a superior series of monthly modern-jazz concerts was devoted to the Charlie Mingus Quintet. In addition to being a reaffirmation of the passionate intelligence Mingus has for several years been pouring into his work, it was perhaps the only first-rate affair of its kind held in New York since the Modern Jazz Quartet's Town Hall appearance last year. Fortunately, Mingus usually bears down with equal weight on his talents as composer, arranger, and bassist. He excels at fresh, poignant blues melodies and leisurely, almost ornate ballad numbers spelled out in long, graceful melodic lines that move as if they were being played in slow motion. He is an arranger who experiments continually with rhythm by supercharging his pieces with different but always related tempos, stop-time choruses, and complex double-time or staccato background effects whose near frenzy seems to endow whatever else is going on with a tranquillity and stateliness rare in modern jazz. He has also developed various raucous, rasping contrapuntal ensemble methods that, by persistently rubbing its melody the wrong way, fill the cheeks of the palest tune with color. Finally, Mingus gives the impression of accomplishing on his bass what the instrument was never intended for, and yet it is not his virtuosity that one is hypnotized by but the daring melodic and rhythmic content that is the result of it.

All of Mingus' sizable achievements—and his bulk, which is approaching that of the late Sydney Greenstreet—were in evidence at the concert. On hand with him were Booker Erwin, tenor saxophone; John Handy, alto saxophone; Richard Wyands, piano; and Danny Richmond, drums. The first of the eight numbers, which ranged from seven to seventeen minutes, was a rather perfunctory medium up-tempo version of "Take the 'A' Train." It was followed by Mingus' attempt to capture the essence of Jelly Roll Morton in a number called "Jelly Roll Jellies." Instead of being a celebration, the number turned into a clumsy takeoff; the saxophones mooed out a dolorous melody reminiscent not of Morton but of Art Hickman, and gave way to similarly parodying solos, which in turn evaporated into the various instrumentalists' own styles. The foolhardiest effort came from Richmond, who, before slipping into his own manner of playing, played several solo choruses, presumably modeled on Zutty Singleton and Baby Dodds. "Alice's Wonderland," a slow ballad by Mingus, with a wandering melody, followed, and it was, in contrast, a delight from beginning to end. After stating the melody, the horns, swelled abruptly by Mingus' humming in falsetto at the top of his lungs, slid into a weird, wavering descending figure, which was cut off by a short arrhythmic interlude, with the piano fashioning porous, impressionistic chords, the drummer pinging on finger cymbals, and Mingus playing rapid strumming phrases. There was a swaggering, exaggerated melodic restatement by the horns, then some good solos, and, finally, a repetition by the ensemble of the patterns used at the outset. Handy was particularly striking. A young musician from San Francisco, he played with flawless control, and though the work of Charlie Parker forms a broad dais for his style, he used, unlike most of his colleagues on the saxophone, a highly selective number of notes, a warm tone, and a couple of devices—a frequently prolonged trill astonishingly like that of the old New Orleans clarinettist George Baquet, and ivorylike sorties into the upper register reminiscent of Benny Carter's smooth ascents—that set him several paces away from his first model. "Billie's Bounce," done at a brisk tempo broken by stop-time rhythms and double-time effects in the background, disintegrated halfway through into a drum solo, which was long, lurid, and loud.

After the intermission, a ten-minute rendition of "I Can't Get Started" was built around Handy and Mingus, who produced an extraordinary solo three or four choruses long and full of quick, two-steps-at-a-time clambering around the scale, lightning strummings, sometimes carried out with both hands, and slow, low booming notes. The concert closed, after another Mingus ballad, with "Wednesday Night Prayer Meeting," a rocking blues founded on the accents and rhythms of gospel music, which were pulled back and forth by a variety of rhythms.

*Two years before, Mingus, never famous for his humility, wrote me a letter, ending it by saying, "Thanks for your kind words—I'll try to continue to justify them and, who knows, maybe even improve." He probably reached his brilliant peak around 1960.*

## The Last of the Mohicans

Erroll Garner is already a legend. During the past fifteen years, he has made more solo records than any other jazz pianist, alive or dead (between five hundred and a thousand for well over seventy labels, some of which, it is said, stay in existence by simply pirating his records back and forth), including a recent release, "Concert by the Sea," that is reported to be one of the four or five most popular jazz records ever put out. (Garner is phenomenal in a recording studio; in a few hours he sometimes sets down, without pause or retakes, a dozen or more numbers, some of them eight or ten minutes in length.) Garner's appeal stems from his style, which is rococo and eccentric, and from the easily accessible flash, geniality, and warmth that continually propel it. A short, ebullient, parrot-nosed man who invariably accompanies himself with an infectious and appreciative series of grunts, hums, buzzes, and exclamations ("Uh-huh," "Yahhm," "Oho"), which seem to double the already high emotional level of his music, Garner is a totally untutored musician who cannot read a note of music. Basically, his plush, pumping orchestral style is divided into two quite different approaches—the rhapsodic and the stomping. When Garner rhapsodizes, he floods the keyboard, producing, with frequent use of the pedal, vaporous waves of sound, full of vague chords and trailing, blurred strings of notes. It takes a steady beat to marshal his peculiar characteristics. These involve an extraordinary, almost melodramatic sense of dynamics that no other jazz musician has used, and a shifting, highly distinctive rhythmic attack.

Garner's introductions, which sometimes last eight bars, are often complete compositions in themselves. In a typical medium-tempo number, he may start with heavy, seesawing chords in the left hand that, pitted against his right hand, produces the tantalizing effect of rapid backing and filling. When the listener has been bullied into a cliff-hanging frame of mind (on top of all this, Garner's introductions never indicate what they are introducing), Garner abruptly lowers his volume and drops lightly and offhandedly into the first chorus. Staying close to the melody, his right hand may play barely struck chords that lag just behind the beat, while his left hand settles into metronomic dum-dum-dum chords, each dropped precisely on the beat. Before the end of the chorus, he will slip back into jockeying, arrhythmic figures, increase his volume, drop it again, and slide into the next chorus, where his left hand begins frequently interrupting its strumming with sharp, perfectly spotted offbeats and his right hand starts dancing off marvelous single-note patterns that leap through several octaves, continually circling the beat but never quite landing on it. Carrying an increased volume intact into the following chorus, he will shift into a complex of tremolo chords (right hand) and blocklike thumpings (left hand), which, when he reaches the bridge of the tune, he abruptly abandons for warring contrapuntal single-note lines, played by both hands. The final chorus, though often a simmering-down version of the first, often dissolves into a wandering coda, which is suddenly clapped shut with a heavy chord.

For all its wonders, Garner's style, which has changed very little during the past decade, has become so rapidly perfect within its own terms that it borders on monotony. The nimble, devious single-note passages begin, after a time, to sound much alike, as do the jumbled, chorded interludes, and the this-way, that-way rhythmic approach. The enormous vitality in his work seems, because it can find no new outlets, to be ceaselessly turning back on itself or getting out through variations of variations of the same old figures. Like any Mandarin stylist, Garner should be sampled, not swallowed.

That, in fact, is the best approach to his new album, "Paris Impressions:

Erroll Garner," which contains eighteen numbers, two-thirds of them his own celebration of a recent tour of France. He is accompanied throughout by bass and drums. The tempos are restricted to slow and medium, and in only a handful ("Left Bank Swing," "La Petite Mambo," and "The French Touch"), which include, in addition to some spirited singlenote passages, several of his inimitable bridges (complete with assorted grunts), does he get down to business. This also happens when, for four selections, he shifts for the first time to the harpsichord. The results are memorable, especially in a slow, blueslike number of his own, "Don't Look for Me," in which, by using rapidly changing combinations of watery tremolos, he states the melody in the left hand while banging out wild, spindly figures in the right, and generally revels in the sonorities of the instrument.

## P. W. Russell, Poet

The clarinettist Pee Wee Russell has long been regarded a loveable freak. One reason is his physical makeup. Thin and tallish, he has a parenthesis-like stoop, spidery fingers, and a long, wry, gentle face governed by a generous, wandering nose. When he plays, this already striking facial arrangement, which is overlaid with an endless grille of wrinkles and furrows, becomes knotted into grimaces of pain, as if the music were pulling unbearably tight an inner drawstring. (At rest or in motion, Russell has one of the classic physiognomies of the century; C. Aubrey Smith's and John L. Lewis' seem barely finished beside it.) The other reason is his style, which is often considered hopelessly eccentric because of its deceptive coating of squeaks, coppery tone, querulousness, growls, and overall hesitancy. For almost two decades Russell has been chiefly identified with innumerable Eddie Condon groups, which over the years have created a sallow and mechanical tradition, compounded of Chicago jazz and small-band swing. This association has done more good than harm to Russell, for many of the men in these groups have been indifferent musicians who, like the inepts so often surrounding Bix Beiderbecke, have, as unintentional reflectors for Russell, emphasized that he is one of the most original stylists in all jazz.

Russell can be devastating in a slow blues. Sidling softly into the lower register, he will issue, after some preliminary blinking and squinting (as if he had just entered a dark room from a bright street), a series of irregularly staccato phrases, each shaken by a worrying vibrato and each pressed tightly against its predecessor. After this, he may rocket up an octave and adopt a quavery manner, or he may introduce dark, stuttering growls which seem to lacerate what he is playing so severely that one is invariably surprised that there is any sound at all left at the close of the solo. In faster tempos, Russell often assumes a jaunty, hat-tilted-over-the-ears manner, full of trills, sudden drops behind the beat, nervous vaultings around the scale, and a gasping, old-womanish tone just this side of a shriek. Russell is also a great ensemble performer. One moment he will be idle dispiritedly along in the middle register, as if he were trapped between the other horns, and the next, breaking free, he will rear back into a retarding, soaring wail that runs along the outermost edge of pitch—an area Russell frequently inhabits—until, with superb navigation, he lands unerringly on the note he began reaching for several measures before.

Russell is in all of his myriad forms in five recent releases. Three of them—"Portrait of Pee Wee", "Pee Wee Russell Plays Pee Wee", and "52nd Street Scene: Tony Scott and the All Stars"—were made not along ago, and the rest—"Mild and Wild: Wild Bill Davison" and "Condon a la Carte"—are taken from a series of Commodore recordings set down in the early forties. Russell appears on sixteen of the twenty-four Commodores in half a dozen groups, which include such men as Max Kaminsky, Davison, Brad Gowans, George Brunis, Fats Waller, George Wettling, and Sid Catlett. Aside from the generally tattered, hurrying ensembles, there are often surprisingly eloquent solos, the best of them by Davison, Kaminsky, Gowans, Waller, and Russell, who moves from hoarse, snuffling low-register work, in "Panama" and "Save Your Sorrow," to excited gesticulations in the upper ranges in "Ballin' the Jack" and "That's a Plenty."

The Russell on the newer records is startlingly different. The frameworks are roughly those of small-band Kansas City jazz, and the materials include blues and standards and no Dixieland tunes. "Portrait of Pee Wee" includes Ruby Braff, Bud Freeman, Vic Dickenson, and Nat Pierce; "Pee Wee Russell Plays Pee Wee" has only a rhythm section made up of Pierce, Steve Jordan, Walter Page, and George Wettling; and the "52nd St. Scene"—an attempt to re-create some of the types of music that could be heard up to ten or twelve years ago on the Street—has several groups, one of which is allotted two numbers and is made up of, among others, Russell, Tony Scott, Joe Thomas, J. C. Higginbotham, Wilbur de Paris, Al Casey, and Denzil Best. Of the nineteen selections, the "Blues for 'the Street,' " on the "52nd St. Scene" is the best. A long, marvelously relaxed blues, terminating in one of those remarkable loafing-in-the-sun ensembles, the piece reaches its climax after de Paris's statement, when Russell puts on his slippers, shuffles into the lower register, and produces, in his first chorus, a tight, ruminative series of phrases—some so soft they are no more than tissues of breath—that resemble an inner monologue. Even in the standard tunes, he plays with a softness of tone and inflection that makes his Commodore work appear rather feverish, and although he displays his growl on the "The Lady's in Love," it doesn't have the emery quality it had fifteen years ago but seems only good-humored self-mimicry. Dickenson is the steadiest of his associates, and in "That Old Feeling," plays a snorting, stamping solo, while throughout the record Freeman emits further variations on the solo he has been at work on for several decades.

## Roach, Blakey & P. J. Jones, Inc.

The drummers Max Roach, Art Blakey, and Philly Joe Jones (no relation to Jo Jones) have almost completed a drum revolution that represents possibly the broadest technical change ever to affect a jazz instrument, and three of their recent records—"Deeds, Not Words: Max Roach New Quintet," "Art Blakey's Jazz Messengers with Thelonious Monk," and "Blues for Dracula: Philly Joe Jones Sextet"—provide ample and occasionally brilliant demonstrations of their various gospels. (There is another and quite different school of modern drummers, headed by such men as Shelly Manne, Joe Morello, Ed Shaughnessy, and Louis Bellson, who are, by and large, no less accomplished than Blakey, Roach, and Jones. But they fall between the great swing drummers and the avant-gardists. Though under the spell of Roach, Manne is fundamentally an extremely sensitive swing drummer, with overtones of Jo Jones and Dave Tough in his work; Morello, a crackling performer, owes much to Buddy Rich; Shaughnessy, an expert wire-brush performer, has listened to both Jo Jones and Sid Catlett; and Bellson, an extraordinary technician, resembles both Rich and Gene Krupa.)

The rebellion has gradually altered every piece of drum equipment. In the thirties, the average set of drums recalled a late-Victorian parlor. It included a parade-size bass drum that emitted subterranean tones; a thick, sonorous snare drum; two or three tom-toms that were lesser versions of the bass drum; several cymbals, often hung from looped metal stands like those once used to support bird cages, and including the high-hat, a crash cymbal, a Chinese cymbal, and a couple of ride cymbals, similar to the invincible cymbals used by nineteenth-century German brass bands; a variety of bric-a-brac, consisting of tuned hollow gourds (called temple blocks), chimes, wood blocks, timpani, and at least one cowbell; and, finally, drumsticks that frequently approached billy clubs in size and heft. Modern drummers have whittled away about fifty pounds of that equipment. The bass drum has shrunk in some cases, to half its old size, and gives off a pinched sound. The snare drum, now the thickness of a frying pan, produces—partly because of its shallowness and partly because it is usually tightly snared and muffled—a thin, clapping sound, as of palm fronds in a strong breeze. There is generally one tom-tom, again a diminutive version of the bass drum, while the cymbals, which are uniformly lighter, now number only the high-hat cymbals, a slightly heavier crash cymbal, and a thin, tremulous ride cymbal the size of a hoop. The drumsticks, more often than not, are elongated toothpicks. (For some reason, the Roach-Blakey-Jones division of modern drummers has just about given up wire brushes, which is too bad; in the hands of men like Jo Jones, Catlett, O'Neil Spencer and Tough, the brushes, with their subtle, needling delicacy, could be even more exhilarating than sticks.) The total effect, which is nearly the direct opposite of the earlier drum sets, is falsetto, chattery and nervous.

Indeed, an aggressive nervousness is the secret of the new drumming. While the older men, with all their equipment, filled a fairly unobtrusive supporting role, setting off ensembles and soloists with relaxed, comparatively simple highlights—rimshots, the swimming sound of the high-hat, the pad-pad of brushes—performers like Roach, Blakey, and Jones, with practically no equipment at all, have pushed themselves steadily into a semi-independent position in the ensemble almost level with that of the melody instruments. (As a result, they are frequently and confusingly termed "melodic" drummers, which apparently means that they are melodic in that they use, like the great drummers of the past, a fairly wide degree of shading and timbre, or that they are melodic because they are attempting, through the use of overbearing, frequently uninterrupted rhythmic patterns, to raise the drum from the role of a supporting instrument to that of a melody instrument.) This invasion has been brought about by some radical technical departures. The modern drummer has shifted the basic marking of the beat from the bass drum, which he uses only for accents, to the ride cymbal and the high-hat, on the last of which he relentlessly sounds the afterbeat by metronomically clapping its cymbals shut with a choshing effect. Most important, this drummer worships the rhythmically oblique. Except when he is concerned with the ride cymbal and the high-hat, almost every motion the drummer makes, whether in the background or in solos, goes toward a collection of purposely disjointed out-of-metre patterns, which, carried to their farthest limits (Roach) result in a totally separate, arrhythmic wall of sound. As a result, three essentials of background jazz drumming—taste, variety, and control—have been practically lost sight of. Unlike the older drummers, who valued silence, dynamics, and the emphasizing coloring effects of using different parts of their set behind different instruments—sticks on a closed high-hat (the ticking of a large clock) behind a clarinet, wire brushes on cymbals (rustling silk) behind a piano, sticks on a ride cymbal (a cheerful belling sound) behind a trumpet—many modern drummers rely loudly and exclusively on the ride cymbal, an addiction that, after a time, creates an aggravating monotone that seems to drain all individual color out of the melodic instruments. In addition, many of these drummers have not yet mastered the complexities of out-of-rhythm playing, particularly in their solos, so the conflicting arrhythmic patterns they build tend simply to cancel each other out.

Roach is an excellent example. A first-rate technician, he has an intense touch on his instrument. In his backing up, he fills in every chink with an unbroken succession of dum-de-da strokes, triplets, rolls, and staccato accents scattered on every part of his set (he is, however, never far from the ride cymbal), and punctuated from time to time with bass-drum "bombs," which unlike true punctuation, are not pauses but only dislocate the din.

Consequently, when Roach takes a solo he is like a non-stop talker who finally forces the group around him into silence while he rattles on and on. And, though perfectly executed, his solos are made up of so many contradicting rhythms and disconnected, rapidly rising and falling pyramids of sound that the beat, which they are supposed to be embroidering, disappears. Indeed, it is not unusual to find oneself hypnotized by the lightning concatenation of sounds in a Roach solo, and then to discover that it has been managed without ever making you tap your foot.

Blakey, five years older than Roach, who is thirty-four, has learned from both Roach and Catlett. He is a raucous, uneven, and sometimes primitive performer who gets a dense, rattly tone and who plays, now and then, with such nervous power that he is apt to drown his musicians under streaming cymbal work and circuslike snare-drum rolls. After a spell of plain timekeeping, he will suddenly slip into a crooked, seemingly palsied series of staccato or double-time beats, snicked off on rims, cymbals, and drums, which introduce a wild, impatient air. Blakey is an extremely dramatic, and occasionally melodramatic, soloist. He may begin a statement with a silence that is broken only by the sound of the high-hat on the afterbeat (which immediately creates a Chinese-water-torture tension), introduce some clicking sounds on the snare rims, abruptly spaced here and there with offbeats on the tom-tom or snare, fall silent again, resume his knickety-knacking, this time hitting one stick against the other in the air, and then without warning launch into a fusillade of sounds between the snare and tom-tom. He will then resort entirely to the snare, playing a hard, on-the-beat pattern, as if he were travelling very fast over a bumpy road, before departing on a second roundelay, which dissolves into beats on the bass drum, executed with such rapidity that they blur into one prolonged beat, and climaxed by a crescendo snare-drum roll that calls the horns back from lunch.

Jones, who is thirty-six, is, like any good revolutionist, both a development of the best of Roach and Blakey and a throwback to earlier methods. Obviously an admirer of Roach and Blakey, he is also an admitted student of Tough, Catlett and Rich. He achieves a neat, clipped sound, which also has much of the richer resilience of the swing drummers. When Jones is in balance, he is a master of silence, dynamics, and surprise. He will keep a steady, unobtrusive beat on the ride cymbal, repeatedly dotting it with flickering snare-drum accents, and, like Blakey, occasionally heighten it with double-time excursions, which, however, do not expunge the original beat but, instead, set up a fascinating undertow beneath the basic rhythm. Jones is becoming an increasingly formidable soloist. Close to Blakey and Catlett in this respect, he will open a medium-tempo solo with heavy, on-the-beat strokes that move inexorably back and forth, like seven-league strides, between the snare drum and the tom-tom. Gradually, he will complicate this boom-boom-boom sequence by sliding in and out of double time and, after settling into full double time, with the listener running at top speed to keep up, he will abruptly fall back to the original beat, drop his volume, and begin soft, shuffling snare-drum rolls tamped down by a rhythmic pattern of rimshots that goes directly back to the work of Zutty Singleton. He will then rear up again and, like Catlett in his most inspired moments, rumble around his set, frequently bringing himself up short with explosive silences or hammering offbeat bass-drum beats. Carrying this tension into the final ensemble, he will dart in and out of the holes in the melody with quick cymbal splashes (Tough) and fast, rounded double-time effects, and then close with a giant, simmering cymbal stroke.

The LPs mentioned above are striking evidence of the power of Roach, Blakey, and Jones, for, with the exception of the one in which Monk appears, the records would be worthless without their leaders. In fact, Roach's record (with him are trumpet, tenor saxophone, tuba, and bass) is chiefly interesting for an unaccompanied medium-tempo drum solo (there are six other numbers) called "Conversation," which displays all of Roach's tendencies toward intricate, overlapping, rhythmless crosscurrents of sound that are, nonetheless, absorbing simply because they are carried out with such precision and authority. "Art Blakey's Jazz Messengers with Thelonious Monk," on the other hand, is a superb rhythmic exercise from start to finish, largely because of the unique combination of Monk and Blakey. (Also on hand for the six numbers—five of them Monk's—are trumpet, tenor saxophone, and bass.) Monk is his own devious, irrepressible, built-in rhythm section, and Blakey is the only drummer around who knows how to supplement it without getting in its way. Blakey is a wonder behind Monk. On "In Walked Bud," a medium-tempo number, Monk begins with irregular, offbeat chords (Blakey counters with a long string of seemingly irrelevant tappings, as if he were a mason tunking bricks into place); Monk continues with expanded variations on the same figures (Blakey dodges lightly back and forth between the snare and tom-tom, planting quick, skidding sounds); Monk loafs (Blakey loafs and then starts knocking his sticks against each other, as though baiting Monk); Monk, baited, resumes (Blakey joins him and closes the chorus with a swooshing roll that picks Monk up and drops him neatly into his second chorus). Jones' record would collapse without him. Working, in its five numbers, with cornet, trombone, tenor saxophone, piano, and bass, all of them rather diffuse performers, he employs every supporting mechanism in the book, including hushed, quick-breathing double-time figures on the high-hat at the start of the piano solo in "Blues for Dracula," pushing snare and tom-tom work behind the tenor saxophone in "Ow!," and, at the end of the same number, some stunning ensemble accompaniment that recalls the best of Tough and Catlett. His solos, particularly a long one in "Ow!," are remarkably graduated structures, full of surprises, varied timbres and old-fashioned emotion. Jones, practically single-handed, is winding up the insurrection.

## Daddy-O

Kenneth Rexroth, the fifty-two-year-old poet, translator (modern Greek, ancient Greek, Latin, Spanish, Chinese, Japanese), anthologist, painter (abstract), and critic (literary, music), who has also been a hobo, range cook, horse wrangler, cab driver, and sheepherder, was born in South Bend, Indiana, but has lived for much of the past thirty years in San Francisco, where he has become a leader of that city's ongoing poetry revival. He has also helped found a poetry-read-to-jazz movement there, and the other day he opened in New York at the Five Spot Café, a Saroyan bar-and-grill at the south end of Cooper Square, for a couple of weeks of readings with the Pepper Adams Quintet. I had lunch with him on the day of his début, and found him a nervous, medium-sized man with short gray hair, a mustache, a towering forehead, and eyes that slope like a sharply peaked roof when his face is in repose. He has a voice that is apt to move in mid-syllable from a whisper to a roar, and he often erupts into machine-gun laughter, delivered in a low monotone. He was dressed in a gray-black suit, a transparent white silk shirt, and a blue-and-white polka-dot string tie. After he had ordered oysters, shad roe, vegetables ("Waiter, I don't care *which* vegetables, so long as they're *fresh*"), salad, and dark beer, he looked down at the table and said, "I've been supporting myself since I was thirteen. I've only had five years of school. In fact, I've *lived* in the kind of world that Jack Kerouac *imagines* he has lived in." His eyes shot up, and he sprayed a dozen rounds of laughter about the room. "A good many people, including the musicians I work with, think of jazz poetry at first as something only a weedhead would do. Not long ago, I worked with a symphony bassist, and he told me afterward, 'You know, I was really scared, but it's been one of the greatest musical experiences of my life.' I didn't start this thing. Renegade monks were doing it in the Middle Ages. Charles Cros, a nineteenth-century poet, read his stuff (things like '*Le Hareng Saur*': 'There was a great white wall, bare, bare, bare'—ha-ha-ha-ha-ha-ha) to *bal-musette* bands. There have been countless talking-blues singers in the South. Maxwell Bodenheim did it in the twenties and Langston Hughes in the thirties, and even I did it in the twenties, at the Green Mask, in Chicago, with Frank Melrose, a K.C. pianist. I've been reading poetry to jazz for two years now, starting in The Cellar, in San Francisco, with a quintet. Since then, I've done all of the West Coast, St. Louis, Chicago, Minneapolis. The most important instrument in my accompaniment is the bass. The bass goes right up your leg and sends out the voice. Modern jazz has outgrown everything. The audience can't get into the music without verbal contact. The poetry gives you that, and the jazz gets the poetry out of those seminars taught by aging poets for budding poets in corn-belt colleges. I plan a good deal of the musical accompaniment, which isn't all jazz by any means. I use bits of Satie, Webern, Boccherini. Each musician has a copy of what I'm reciting, with cues and musical notations on it. I read

Ruthven Todd, Larry Durrell, Ferlinghetti, and some of my own stuff, including a lot of translations. A friend warned me about New York. 'You've got to be careful, man,' he said. 'They've been having meetings to keep Rexroth out.' Ha-ha-ha-ha-ha-ha-ha!"

Rexroth asked me to stop in at the Five Spot before his first show that night, and I was met there by Ivan Black, a stocky, black-mustached representative of the Five Spot, who ushered me to a table near the bandstand, a raised platform roughly the size of a large window seat. "I've got to go and wake Rexroth up," he told us. "He's sleeping at a friend's, over on Second Avenue. I'll be right back." The Five Spot is long and narrow, with a bar, sheltered by a fringed canopy, running down most of one wall; three gold-colored macelike objects suspended from a maroon ceiling; and the rest of the wall space spattered with posters and programs of various sorts. "He wasn't asleep at all," Black's voice said after a while, in a relieved way, and Rexroth, wearing impenetrable dark glasses, sat down beside me. "These shades protect you in a club," he said. "I've decided they relax you. I read my stuff. You can't do it out of your head. You get swinging, and you don't know what you're talking about."

Rexroth then said it was time to begin. Black excused himself and, while squeezing onto the platform to introduce Rexroth, accidentally brushed a thick sheaf of manuscripts off a wobbly music stand.

"Damn it, Ivan! What are you doing?" Rexroth bellowed as Black backed and filled on the manuscripts.

The manuscripts were replaced, a drum roll crashed out, and Black introduced Rexroth as a horse wrangler and the Daddy-O of the jazz-poetry movement.

Rexroth got up on the platform, plunged his left hand into his left coat pocket, took as wide a stance as space permitted, stuck his stomach out, and read, in a strong singsong voice, a Ruthven Todd poem; Carl Sandburg's "Mag," accompanied by an Ellington blues; a poem by Pablo Neruda; a poem of his own; and a twelfth-century Chinese poem, accompanied only by the bass, which played long passages between such lines as "But why do the birds all hate me?," "Why do the flowers betray me?," "Why do the peach and cherry blossoms prostrate me?"

# The Great Gillespie

Of all the uncommunicative, secret-society terms that jazz has surrounded itself with, few are more misleading than "bebop." Originally a casual onomatopoeic word used to describe the continually shifting rhythmic accents in the early work of Charlie Parker, Dizzy Gillespie, Kenny Clarke, and Thelonious Monk, it soon became a generic term, whose tight, rude sound implied something harsh and unattractive. (Jazz scholars, who are nonpareil at unearthing irrelevancies, have discovered that the two syllables first appeared in jazz as a bit of mumbo-jumbo in a vocal recorded in the late twenties.) Although many admirers of Parker and Gillespie—and occasionally Parker and Gillespie themselves—helped this misapprehension along in the mid-forties through their playing, bebop was, in the main, a graceful explosion. It replaced the old chunky Republican phrasing with long, teeming melodic lines, broke the insouciant flow of the four-four beat into chattering pockets of rhythm, and added fresh harmonies, the combination producing an arabesque music that had an irreverent beauty suggested in jazz up to that time only by such soloists, as Pee Wee Russell, Dickie Wells, Jabbo Smith, and Roy Eldridge. Bebop was an upheaval in jazz that matched the arrival of Louis Armstrong, Duke Ellington, Coleman Hawkins, and Lester Young, but it was not, as it is frequently taken to be, a total musical revolution. (The most usable elements of the movement have long since been absorbed into jazz, and the term itself has fallen into disuse, but a variation, known as "hard bop," persists.) To be sure, it introduced radical techniques, but it stuck close to the blues, which it dressed up in flatted chords and various rhythmic furbelows. The chord structures of popular standards, which provided the rest of its diet, were slightly altered, and were given new titles and often barefacedly copyrighted by their "composers." This renovating process, begun in the mid-thirties by men like Duke Ellington and Count Basie, proliferated in the bebop era. Thus, "Indiana" reappeared as "Donna Lee" and "Ice Freezes Red"; "How High the Moon" became "Bean at the Met," "Ornithology," and "Bird Lore"; and "Just You, Just Me" turned into "Evidence," "Spotlite," and "Mad Bebop." The music made little attempt at fresh ensemble voicings, but relied instead on complex unison figures—in the manner of the John Kirby band—that sometimes sounded like fattened-up extensions of the solos they enclosed. A final confusing peculiarity of bebop is that although Parker, Gillespie, and Monk, each of whom possessed enormous talent, emerged at about the same time, they never enjoyed the spotlight simultaneously, as did such slightly older men as Hawkins, Eldridge, Art Tatum, and Sidney Catlett. Gillespie had become celebrated by the late forties; Parker was at the height of his fame when he died, in 1955; and it is only recently that Monk has slid wholly into view.

When Gillespie appeared on the first bebop recordings, in 1944, he gave the impression—largely because a long recording ban had just ended—of springing up full-blown. He had, however, been slowly developing his style for some seven or eight years. Although Gillespie was for a time an unashamed copy of Eldridge, the records he made in the late thirties with Cab Calloway—in which he tossed off strange, wrong-sounding notes and bony phrases that seemed to begin and end in arbitrary places—prove that his own bent, mixed perhaps with dashes of Lester Young and Charlie Christian, was already in view. By 1944, the transformation was complete, and Gillespie had entered his second phase.

Gillespie never merely started a solo—he erupted into it. A good many bebop solos began with four-bar breaks, and Gillespie, taking full advantage of this device (a somewhat similar technique had been used, to great effect, in much New Orleans jazz, but had largely fallen into disuse), would hurl himself into the break, after a split-second pause, with a hundred notes that danced through a couple of octaves, sometimes in triple time, and that were carried, usually in one breath, past the end of the break and well into the solo itself. The result, in such early Gillespie efforts as "One-Bass Hit" and "Night in Tunisia," were complex, exuberant, and well-designed. (Several of Gillespie's flights were transcribed note for note into ensemble passages for various contemporary big bands, an honor previously granted to the likes of Bix Beiderbecke.) Gillespie's style at the time gave the impression—with its sharp, slightly acid tone, its abrupt phrase endings, its efflorescence of notes, and its brandishings about in the upper register—of being constantly on the verge of flying apart. However, his playing was held together by his extraordinary rhythmic sense, which he shared with the other founders of bebop. When one pinned down the melodic lines of his solos, they revealed a flow of notes that was not so much a melody, in the conventional sense, as a series of glancing but articulate sounds arranged in sensible rhythmic blocks that alternated from on-the-beat playing to offbeat punctuation, from double and triple time to half time. One felt that Gillespie first spelled out his rhythmic patterns in his head and then filled in their spaces with appropriate notes. A hard, brilliant, flag-waving style, in which emotion was frequently hidden in floridity, it persisted until four or five years ago, when Gillespie popped, again seemingly full-blown, into his third, and present, period.

A mild-mannered, roundish man, who wears thick-rimmed spectacles and a small goatee, and has a new-moon smile and a muffled, potatoey way of speaking, Gillespie is apt, when playing, to puff out his cheeks and neck into an enormous balloon, as if he were preparing himself for an ascent into the ionosphere. He has a habit, while his associates play, of performing jigs or slow, swaying shufflings, accented by occasional shouts of encouragement— bits of foolishness that he discards, like a mask, when he takes up his own horn, an odd-shaped instrument whose specially designed bell points in the direction of the upper bleachers. Gillespie, at forty-two, an age at which a good many jazz musicians begin falling back on a card file of phrases—their own and others'—built up through the years, is playing with more subtlety and invention than at any time in his past. He has learned one of the oldest and best tricks in art—how to give the effect of power by *implying* untapped energy. This method is opposed to the dump-everything approach, which swamps, rather than whets, the listener's appetite. His tone has taken on a middle-age spread; his baroque flow of notes has been judiciously edited; his phrase endings seem less abrupt; and he now cunningly employs a sense of dynamics that mixes blasts with whispers, upper-register shrieks with plaintive asides. However, his intensity, together with his rhythmic governor, which still sets the basic course of his solos, remains unchanged. Provided a solo does not open with a break, which he will attack with the same old ferocity, Gillespie may now begin with a simple phrase, executed in an unobtrusive double time and repeated in rifflike fashion. Then he will lean back into half time and deliver a bellowing upper-register figure, which may be topped with a triple-time descending arpeggio composed of innumerable notes that dodge and dodge and then lunge ahead again. These continue without pause for several measures, terminating in a series of sidling half-valved notes, which have a bland complacency. In the next chorus, he may reverse the procedure by opening with a couple of shouts, and then subside into a blinding run, seemingly made up of hundred-and-twenty-eighth notes, that will end in high scalar exercises. And so it goes. Gillespie rarely repeats himself in the course of a solo. In fact, he is able to construct half a dozen or more choruses in which the element of surprise never falters.

Gillespie is in good form on three fairly recent records—"Crosscurrents," "Sonny Side Up," and "Have Trumpet, Will Excite!" Of the three, "Crosscurrents" is the most satisfactory. On hand with Gillespie, for two originals, a blues, and four standards (three of them done as a short medley of solos), are Sonny Stitt, John Lewis, Percy Heath, the guitarist Skeeter Best, and the drummer Charlie Persip. In long solos in "Tour de Force" (medium tempo) and "Dizzy Meets Sonny" (very fast), Gillespie gives his all—particularly in the latter, where he ranges from sotto-voce figures, at the start of the first chorus, to upper-register harum-scarum in the third, bumblebee fluctuations in the fourth, and staggering runs, which dissolve into a thumb-twiddling phrase, in the fifth. In "How Deep Is the Ocean," Gillespie takes just one chorus, at a slow tempo, and, winding closely around the melody, plays with a gentle poignancy, achieved by moving precisely back and forth between loud phrases and furtive ones. The record closes with a slow blues, "Blues for Bird," in which Gillespie constructs three choruses proving that one needn't, in the manner of many of his students, add curlicues to the blues to make them effective. (Almost all of Gillespie's admirers fall short of him in another way, too; they are unable to sustain a persuasive melodic line on slow ballads.)

Although much of "Sonny Side Up" is given over to Stitt (on tenor saxophone here) and Sonny Rollins, Gillespie comes through with three consummate choruses in "After Hours," the Avery Parrish–Erskine Hawkins blues. Using a mute, Gillespie darts from a level first chorus to a red-faced high note, opening the second chorus, that falls away to sly, disconnected notes, each one on the beat, and into a final chorus, where, stretching out, he strikingly recalls, probably on purpose, Roy Eldridge. He plays almost as well in the three remaining numbers (two standards and an original), and in "Sunny Side of the Street" he sings the vocal, delivering the first sixteen bars in a nasal monotone that seems, in its perversity, more melodic than the tune's real melody.

For some reason, Gillespie loafs through much of his own record, "Have Trumpet, Will Excite!" He is accompanied by an adequate rhythm section, whose guitarist, Les Spann, occasionally doubles on flute. All eight numbers are standards, the best of which are a wry "My Heart Belongs to Daddy" (much of Gillespie's work has a forthright mocking quality), a brisk "St. Louis Blues," and a slow, almost back-scratching "There Is No Greater Love." There isn't an unforgettable moment on the record, but there aren't many passages that could be surpassed by Gillespie's contemporaries, most of whom would be in other lines of work if it weren't for him.

## Toshiko

None of the foreign jazz musicians who occasionally land on our shores has been more comely, modest, or accomplished than Toshiko Akiyoshi, a twenty-seven-year-old Japanese pianist. Much of the time since her arrival, Toshiko, as she is known, has been in Boston, where, by day, she has been studying musical composition and theory at the Berklee School of Music and, by night, filling a night club named Storyville. Last week, Toshiko opened at the Hickory House with her trio, a handful of appropriate kimonos, and a gorgeous scarlet, gold, and white ceremonial *obi* (a broad, heavy silk sash worn about the middle). I went to see her at the Park Sheraton on the afternoon of her début, and she was a vision in black: neat black dress, black patent-leather shoes, wide black eyes, and glistening black hair that fell in a dancing ponytail to her waist. Stocky and quick-moving, Toshiko gave a shy, brilliant smile and lit on the edge of a chair. I asked her how she had become a jazz pianist. "Oh, was by accident," she said. "In '46, I decide to go to medical school. My father very much want me to become doctor. Before school begin, I visit cousin in Beppu. She hear of Japanese dance band there that need piano player. I take piano lessons since seven years old and my cousin say, 'Do you play jazz?' I say, 'I never hear of jazz.' At audition, I play a German tango called 'Blue Sky.' The leader, Mr. Yamada, say, 'Oh, she can play piano.' So I join the band. One week later, my father find out. He was very mad. Seventeen-year-old daughter playing piano in a dance palace. Toof! But I told my mother, who is very, very understandable person, that I will quit when school starts. But I didn't. A big fourteen-piece Japanese orchestra want me, then later an Argentine tango band, then another Japanese band. In '49, I went to Tokyo and joined Mr. Ikoma and his orchestra. All this time, I play no solos, just umpcha-umpcha behind band. Then, one time, I wrote out all the notes in solo on Teddy Wilson record of 'Sweet Lorraine' and put his notes beside straight melody to compare. I study difference hard and then write down new figures of my own, learn them by heart, and play them in solo next day with band. Great success."

For the next few years, Toshiko worked in Tokyo with such indigenous groups as the Blue Coast Orchestra, the Gay Stars Orchestra, the Tokyo Jive Combo, and the Six Lemons. After that, equipped with a style akin to that of Bud Powell, she formed her own group, the Coy Quartet. "One night," she said, "Oscar Peterson, in Tokyo with Norman Granz and the Jazz at the Philharmonic group, heard me play. Of course, he was idol, and when he came to speak to me, I was shaking all over. He introduce me to Mr. Granz, and Mr. Granz say, 'Would you like to make record?' He gave me Oscar Peterson rhythm section, and two weeks later I make my first record." Three years later, after the proper amount of complicated correspondence, she was offered a four-year scholarship at the Berklee School.

Toshiko was born of Japanese parents in Dairen, a seaport in Manchuria, the youngest of four girls. The family lived in Dairen until 1946, when they were exiled to Japan by the Chinese Nationalists. From 1945 on, Dairen was occupied by the Russians, the Red Chinese, and the Chinese Nationalists. "When Russians come, my father make my sister and I cut off all our hair to look like boys. All day long, Russian soldiers come into our house and take things. They sell them in the park in front of our house to Manchurian merchants. My sisters and I get up about four–five o'clock every morning to make many rice balls, and hide all day up on veranda and eat them. When Red Chinese come, a Communist officer and his wife—how do you say?—requisition upstairs in our house. Then the Nationalist Chinese come, and a general move in upstairs. He was very funny man. Every night, he bring young officers home to play games like chess with me and my sisters. He say to my father many times, 'Don't sell anything in your house, please. If you need money, I will give you all you want.' He want everything in house for himself after we leave. We could take only what we could carry and three dollars apiece. The general came to the station, and gave us a case of soda, like ginger ale, for going-away present."

What are Toshiko's plans for the future? "If possible, if I good enough," she said, "I would like to finish four years at Berklee early, and play a year for experience. Maybe go to Europe, too. Then I will go home and teach young Japanese jazz musicians. There are two, three with very good potential. I have learned many things from musicians here, but I will finish my life in Japan. Here is too fast. I am more or less enjoying type, slow-motion type. In Tokyo are many tiny coffeehouses, hold eight, ten people. Each have hi-fi sets and enormous collection of American jazz records. You buy one cup coffee only and sit four, five hours listening to records. Is nothing like that here."

*In 2000, Toshiko is still very much here. She lives in New York, is married to the tenor saxophonist Lew Tabackin, has a big band that appears periodically, and has become a passionate wine collector.*

# Bean

Improvisation, the seat of jazz, is a remorseless art that demands of the performer no less than this: that, night after night, he spontaneously invent original music by balancing emotion and intelligence, form and content, and tone and attack, all of which must both charge and entertain the spirit of the listener. Improvisation comes in various hues and weights. There is the melodic embellishment of Louis Armstrong and Vic Dickenson; the similar but more complex thematic improvisation of Lester Young; the improvisation upon chords, as practiced by Coleman Hawkins and Charlie Parker; and the rhythmic-thematic convolutions now being put forward by Thelonious Monk and Sonny Rollins. Great improvisation is rare; bad improvisation, which is really not improvisation at all but a rerun or imitation of old ideas, is common. No art is more precarious or domineering. Thus, such consummate veteran improvisers as Armstrong, Dickenson, Hawkins, Buck Clayton, and Monk are, in addition to being master craftsmen, remarkable endurance runners. One of the hardiest of these is Hawkins, who, now fifty-four, continues to play with all the vitality and authority that he demonstrated during the Harding administration as a member of Mamie Smith's Jazz Hounds.

Hawkins is a kind of super jazz musician, for he has been a bold originator, a masterly improviser, a shepherd of new movements, and a steadily developing performer. A trim, contained man, whose rare smiles have the effect of a lamp suddenly going on within, he was the first to demonstrate that jazz could be played on the saxophone, which had long been a mainstay of brass bands. He did this with such conviction and imagination that by the early thirties he had founded one of the two great schools of saxophone playing. Then, in 1939, Hawkins set down, as an afterthought at a recording session, a version of "Body and Soul" that achieves the impossible—perfect art. A few years later, he came close to repeating this success with "Sweet Lorraine" and "The Man I Love." Unlike those jazz musicians who regard anything new with suspicion, Hawkins has always kept an ear to the ground for originality, and as a result he led the first official bebop recording session, which involved Dizzy Gillespie, Max Roach, and the late Clyde Hart. Soon afterward, he used the largely unknown Thelonious Monk in some important recordings. Then his playing inexplicably began to falter and he went into semi-eclipse, from which he rocketed up, without warning, in the early fifties, landing on his feet with a brand-new style (his third), whose occasional febrility suggests a man several decades younger.

Hawkins's early style was rough and aggressive, and he used a great many staccato, slap-tongued notes. But these mannerisms eventually vanished, and by the mid-thirties he had entered his second and most famous phase. His heavy vibrato suggested the wingbeats of a big bird and his tone halls hung with dark velvet and lit by huge fires. His technique had become infallible.

He never fluffed a note, his tone never shrank or overflowed—as did Chu Berry's, say—and he gave the impression that he had enough equipment to state in half a dozen different and finished ways what was in his head. This proved to be remarkable, particularly in his handling of slow ballads.

Hawkins would often begin such a number by playing one chorus of the melody, as if he were testing it. He would fill its fabric with tone to see how much it would take, eliminate certain notes, sustain others, slur still others, and add new ones. Then, satisfied, he would shut his eyes, as if blinded by what he was about to play, and launch into improvisation with a concentration that pinned one down. (Hawkins' total lack of tentativeness—the exhilarating, blindman tentativeness of Pee Wee Russell or Roy Eldridge—suggested that he had written out and memorized his solos long before playing them.) He would construct—out of phrases crowded with single notes, glissandos, abrupt stops, and his corrugated vibrato—long, hilly figures that sometimes lasted until his breath gave out. Refilling his lungs with wind-tunnel ferocity, he would be off again—bending notes, dropping in little runs like steep, crooked staircases, adding decorative, almost calligraphic flourishes, emphasizing an occasional phrase by allowing it to escape into puffs of breath. He often closed these solos with roomy codas, into which he would squeeze fresh and frequently fancy ideas that had simply been crowded out of his earlier ruminations. If another soloist followed him, he might terminate his own statement with an abrupt ascending figure that neatly catapulted his successor. When Hawkins had finished, his solo, anchored directly and emphatically to the beat, had been worked into an elaborate version of the original melody, as though he had fitted a Victorian mansion over a ranch house. At fast tempos, Hawkins forced the same amount of music into a smaller space. There seemed to be no pause between phrases or choruses, and this produced an intensity that thickened the beat and whose vehemence was occasionally indicated by sustained growls. Yet for all this enthusiasm, Hawkins' playing during this period often left the listener vaguely dissatisfied. Perhaps it was because his style had an unceasing—and, for that time, unusual—intellectual quality, with the glint of perfection and a viselike unwillingness to let any emotion out, lest it spoil the finish on his work. One kept waiting for the passion beneath the surface to burst through, but it never did—until five years ago.

Hawkins can now be volcanic. His present style is marked primarily by a slight tightening of tone, which sometimes resembles the sound he achieved at the outset of his career; the use of certain harsh notes and phrases that, not surprisingly, suggest Charlie Parker and Sonny Rollins; and an almost dismaying display of emotion. This exuberance has been costly. In his pursuit of pure flame, Hawkins sometimes misses notes or plays them badly, and he falls back, perhaps out of fatigue, on stock phrases of his own, such as a series of abrupt, descending triplets. When everything is in mesh, however, the results are formidable.

This happens more than once in two recent Hawkins recordings—"The High and Mighty Hawk" and "Coleman Hawkins/Soul." Despite a few flat spots, the first recording, in which Hawkins is joined by Buck Clayton, Hank Jones, Ray Brown, and the drummer Mickey Sheen, is one of his superior efforts. There are a blues, three originals, and two standards. The blues, taken at a medium tempo, is a tour de force in the best sense. After the opening ensemble, Hawkins slides, with another-day, another-dollar casualness, into a soliloquy that lasts for no less than seventeen choruses, each of them totally different and each perfectly placed. The best qualities of his present work are evident—the unremittingly logical development of a three- or four-note figure (the first five choruses), the near-parodying reflections of John Coltrane (tenth chorus), the tremendous bustle (eleventh and twelfth choruses), and the emotion (fifteenth and sixteenth choruses). Hawkins matches this in "You've Changed," a slow ballad, which, however, does not receive the glossy treatment he might have offered it a decade ago. Instead, for only a chorus and a half, he approaches the melody in a cautious, exploratory way, savoring its pleasant design, making minor improvements here and there, and infusing it with warmth and lyricism. Clayton and Brown play with considerable beauty. Brown's long solo in the blues number, with its darting runs, exaggerated pauses, and half-time retarding phrases, is ingenious.

The second record is aptly named. Hawkins is accompanied by Kenny Burrell, Ray Bryant, Wendell Marshall, and Osie Johnson. There are seven numbers, most of them blues. The longest is a very slow one, which is so blue—it is filled with tremolos, gospel rhythms, rock-and-roll, and screaming blue notes—that it becomes at once the epitome of all slow blues and a caricature of all slow blues. Hawkins takes a short, plaintive solo near the opening and returns later for a chorus, in which, after some moody chanting, he emits a wail that sounds like an exhalation from Hell. The shortest number on the record is totally dissimilar—a revitalization of "Greensleeves." Hawkins simply plays embellishments on the melody, but with such pathos that one fears he will break down before it is finished. Instead, plumbing his three and a half decades of playing, Hawkins turns it into a kind of Gettysburg Address on improvisation.

## Buck Clayton and Emmett Berry

Graduates of the Basie school (an institution that has settled, in recent years, into a ponderous bureaucracy), Buck Clayton and Emmett Berry are part of a small group of trumpet players who appeared in the wake of Louis Armstrong and who developed a singular and subtle lyricism. Clayton, a handsome man of medium height, whose face tends to float upward at the corners when he plays, giving him a Mephistophelean appearance, performs in a style whose imperturbable continuity is based on a flawless set of balances. Unlike Coleman Hawkins or Dizzy Gillespie, he is, though a consummate musician, not a great improviser; completely aware of his own limitations, he restricts himself to an agile, ceaseless form of embellishment. In a medium-tempo blues, Clayton, whose tone has a hammered-gold quality, is apt to state, in a hushed, placating fashion, a short riff, which he may repeat or alter with added notes and short, skipping runs. This gives way to a lagging behind the beat, which he achieves by hitting the same note four or five times a split second after the beat. He then returns to the beat and finishes the chorus by linking related melodic figures that suggest a man humming an improvised tune to himself. In the space of several choruses, Clayton will gradually and logically work toward a climax by slightly increasing his volume, incorporating high, probing notes, and, in general, momentarily allowing his passionate qualities to catch the sun. But Clayton's style is remarkable not so much for the notes he plays as for its urgency and sweetness, which are accented by his vibrato—a vibrato whose light earnestness gives each phrase a stirring, now-I-really-mean-it air. Clayton frequently employs a mute. As opposed to Cootie Williams, who, by constantly waggling his mute about with his hand, emits vowel sounds and windy growls, Clayton keeps his mute tightly in place, producing a distilled version of his open-horn style, in the manner of a man trying to carry on a conversation with his mouth closed.

Berry, on the other hand, has a hustling style, which is, however, no less controlled. Short, round-faced, and wearing the expression of a man peering through a venetian blind, Berry, despite his restlessness, is even more sparing of notes than Clayton. Berry, who has a hoarse, congested tone, frequently gives the impression of putting the shot, for he delivers his often vibratoless phrases in a heave-ho way that makes him seem far louder than he is. Marvelously adroit at juxtaposing the expected and the unexpected, Berry may play the first half of a chorus in a jabbing, reiterative way, and then, just as one is prepared for a repetition or a slight variation (like Clayton, Berry is primarily an extremely skilled embellisher), he will slip into phrases that leap through a couple of octaves before coming to rest. Nonetheless, Berry has a stubborn, introverted quality, which stems from his mostly seeming to play in a minor key—an effect gained by his frequent use of slightly flatted notes. Berry, too, often employs a mute, and with tantalizing results. Whereas a mute seems to compound Clayton's lyricism, it conceals Berry's, reducing him to metallic asides.

Clayton and Berry play well in a couple of neo-Basie efforts—"Basie Reunion" and "Songs for Swingers: Buck Clayton with His All-Stars." The first includes such ex-Basie men as Clayton (Berry does not appear in this one), Shad Collins, Paul Quinichette, Jack Washington, and Jo Jones, together with Basie's present bassist, Eddie Jones, and Basie's indefatigable pupil, Nat Pierce. The five numbers, all of them extended, are Basie reruns. The performances, with the exception of Clayton and Jo Jones, are mixed. Collins is a loose player, who always seems like the auxiliary member of the band; Quinichette is an eerily close copy of Lester Young; and Washington, a baritone saxophonist who has apparently played only the alto saxophone in late years, sounds impassioned but inexact. Clayton more than makes up for these deficiencies. In the medium-slow "Blues I Like to Hear," he begins in his familiar sidestepping way, pulls himself into the second chorus with a brief growl, and ends up by sailing through the third chorus with perfectly spaced high notes and an inescapable beat. He takes three comparable choruses in an up-tempo version of "John's Idea." These begin with a break, in which, by fluttering rapidly up and down through a cluster of three notes, like a bird bathing, he sets up an unfaltering tension. During the opening and closing ensembles of "Baby Don't Tell on Me," a slow, rocking blues, Clayton, muted, plays alternately dancing and musing obbligatos behind the other horns, recalling his work behind Paul Robeson in "King Joe," a blues recorded in the early forties with the Basie band, in which Clayton's distant, hollering, phrases managed to both deflate Robeson's pretentiousness and emphasize the booming, Grand Central Station quality of his voice.

Clayton is joined in the second recording by Berry and such former Basie associates as Dickie Wells, Earl Warren, and Buddy Tate. (The rhythm section, which is adequate, is made up of three men, two of them non-Basie graduates.) There are eight numbers—three blues, three standards, and a couple of Clayton originals. It is Berry, and not the leader, who steals the show, as if Clayton had, out of politeness, deferred to his guest or had simply been bowled over by him. In three numbers—"Swinging at the Copper Rail," "Outer Drive," and "Night Train"—Berry, playing open-horn, performs with an assurance that he has rarely shown on records. Indeed, his two choruses in "Outer Drive," a medium-tempo blues, are close to classic blues improvisations. Tate, a tenor saxophonist who has been celebrating Herschel Evans for a couple of decades, and Warren, an alto saxophonist who switches profitably to clarinet for two numbers, are in good form.

## Humph

**H**umphrey Lyttelton, a thirty-eight-year-old English trumpet player, is his country's most celebrated hot musician. Lyttelton and his eight-man band were in town a week or so ago, preparing for a seventeen-day concert tour through fifteen Eastern cities, to be undertaken with Anita O'Day, and groups headed by George Shearing, Thelonious Monk, Lennie Tristano, and an English colleague, Ronnie Ross. I talked with him on the eve of the tour in a friend's midtown apartment, and discovered him to be a tall (six feet three), ample-waisted man with a high forehead, unruly hair, long sideburns, and a sad-eyed mien that strikingly resembled Claude Rains'. He was wearing a brilliant-blue tie, a gray shirt, and a shapeless gray suit, and he looked tired. "I'm dead," Lyttelton said, reading my thoughts. "I finished being interviewed on the radio by Bea Kalmus at 2 A.M. this morning, and then I ran into Ronnie Ross, and he said, 'Come on, let's go to Eddie Condon's,' and we did, and I had a good long sit-in with the band. It's been that way ever since I arrived, a few days ago. This is my first American visit, and there's so much jazz here that I feel rather like a starving man suddenly confronted with a nine-course meal. I've been to Condon's, the Metropole, and Basie's bar in Harlem, and had an excellent Italian dinner at the Arpeggio with Roy Eldridge blowing in my ear."

How had Lyttelton happened to become a jazz musician? "I had to break the family mold to do it," he replied. "We go back to the twelfth century, and aside from such renegades as myself and the last Humphrey Lyttelton, who got himself hanged, drawn, and quartered for his part in the Gunpowder Plot, we've had nothing but judges, generals, schoolmasters, bishops, and the like. My father, who's seventy-six now, was a professor of English literature at Eton for twenty-five years, and that's where I was raised. I took up the trumpet at fifteen, after hearing Louis Armstrong's first recording of 'Basin Street,' which hit me with terrible force. My mother gave me the money for the trumpet during the annual Eton-Harrow cricket match, which takes place over a weekend in London. I was attending the match in the full school uniform of top hat, colored waistcoat, black-and-white checked trousers, and pale-blue carnation, but after the first few hours I couldn't stand it any longer and took off, top hat and all, for Charing Cross, London's Tin Pan Alley and musical-instrument center. I created quite a stir in the shops. A year later, I had a four-piece band, and for six months we practiced every Sunday afternoon in a room directly beneath my father's study. The only tune we knew was 'Whispering,' and it's the only pop tune my father has ever learned. Then came six years in the Grenadier Guards. I landed at Salerno with a pistol in one hand and my trumpet, wrapped in a sandbag, in the other. After the war, I played the trumpet by night and worked as a cartoonist on the London *Daily Mail* by day. Part of my job was to fill in the dialogue in the balloons of another cartoonist's drawings, which my family regarded as the first serious step in my decline. In 1948, I hit bottom by forming my own band. We've played at the same place in London ever since, and everybody there, waiters included, calls me Humph. We used to play Dixieland, which was very popular. Even the mums and dads liked it, probably because they felt that in any deeper kind of jazz there might be something going on that they'd just as soon not know about. Now we resemble the old Basie band, and we're not as popular any more, but we're happier. I do a lot of writing. I have two music columns in London papers, in which I act as a kind of counter-jazz critic by salving down all the harsh things that other critics say. I've written two books, both autobiographies, and I do a lot of television work."

Lyttleton interrupted himself with a cavernous yawn, slowly stood up, and said he'd like some tomato juice. He fetched a pail-sized glass, fell back into his chair, and resumed talking. "What English jazz musicians need more than anything else is to hear and play with American musicians. When Armstrong came to England a while back, I heard him twenty-two times. I went to eleven Ellington concerts and twenty-five Basie concerts not long afterward. I regard this tour as the peak of my career. My father, though, regards it philosophically. 'Do what you want, but do it *well*,' he's always told me. Not long ago, he dropped into the night club in London to look around, and the only comment he made was that he'd never seen so many beautiful girls under one roof at one time before. A fine gentleman.''

## Dinosaurs in the Morning

Te best thing that ever happened to jazz is the recording machine. Without this means of preservation, the music might simply have bumbled on awhile as a minor facet of American life and then vanished. At that, the countless jazz records made since 1917 represent only a tiny fraction of all the jazz that has been played. Gone forever are such unrecorded events as the Kansas City saxophone bees between Lester Young, Coleman Hawkins, and Ben Webster; the trumpet playing of Buddy Petit, Chris Kelly, and Emmett Hardy; the Chick Webb–Benny Goodman duels at the Savoy Ballroom, in Harlem; the Sunday-afternoon jam sessions at Jimmy Ryan's, at any one of which could be heard Hot Lips Page, Roy Eldridge, Sidney Catlett, James P. Johnson, Frankie Newton, Coleman Hawkins, and Sidney Bechet; the Earl Hines band of 1943, in which Dizzy Gillespie and Charlie Parker were busy fashioning the cornerstone of bebop; and the monumental unaccompanied ten-minute drum solo Catlett took one night at Café Society Uptown just to pass the time until the floor show got under way. Moreover, very little of the enormous amount of jazz that *has* been recorded is satisfactory. The blank, now-or-never atmosphere of the recording studio has unbalanced more than one jazz musician; indeed, such resolute performers as Fletcher Henderson, Bix Beidebecke, and Art Tatum reportedly never came through whole on records.

All this is by way of saying that when one hears the album "Spirituals to Swing," which contains thirty-one numbers recorded at the two legendary Carnegie Hall concerts presented by John Hammond in 1938 and 1939, it is like getting up one morning, going to the window, and seeing a dinosaur walk by. Landmarks in more ways than one, these concerts helped, because they were played largely by Negroes, to loosen the bars that still prevented Negro jazz musicians from performing in the nation's major entertainment outlets. They brought to wide attention such obscure and valuable performers as Albert Ammons, Pete Johnson, Meade Lux Lewis, Joe Turner, Ida Cox, Big Bill Broonzy, Sidney Bechet, Tommy Ladnier, James P. Johnson, Lester Young, and Charlie Christian. They amounted to a miniature history of jazz that was played, often as not, by its very creators, many of whom are now dead. Finally, they produced some extraordinary music. The selections from the two evenings have been adroitly chosen and arranged; there are few dull spots, and the continuity is full of invigorating changes of pace. Thus, we hear, on the second side, a couple of selections by the Kansas City Six (Buck Clayton, Lester Young, Freddie Greene, Walter Page, and Jo Jones, with Charlie Christian sitting in); a Count Basie piano solo accompanied by Page and Jones; the Kansas City Six again, with Basie instead of Christian; a pair of unaccompanied piano solos by James P. Johnson; and two numbers by Sidney Bechet's New Orleans Feetwarmers, with Ladnier, Johnson, and part of the Basie rhythm section included.

It's almost impossible to single out any person or group from all the delights that occur. Near the head of the list is Christian, who, at the age of twenty, had just joined Benny Goodman, and who, during the two years before his death, was to help put bebop on its feet. Plucked out of Oklahoma by Hammond, who has singlehandedly changed the course of jazz by similarly boosting Count Basie, Goodman, and Billie Holiday, Christian had a revolutionary style. He was, after Lonnie Johnson, Eddie Lang, Eddie Durham, and Dick McDonough, the first guitarist to explore fully the use of single-string rather than chorded solos. His almost orchestral tone fell between the singsong effect of his predecessors (most of whom, of course, had used the unamplified guitar) and the projectile smoothness of his successors. Although he invariably managed to transmit the emotional fervor behind his work—a difficult accomplishment on a semi-percussive instrument—Christian's playing was utterly relaxed. In a solo, he would often develop a simple, arresting riff figure (many of these riffs eventually reappeared as the melodies of the tunes recorded by the Goodman sextet and septet) for a couple of measures, drop in a short connecting phrase, and, after holding its last note for several beats, tip into a long single-note melodic line that elbowed the limits of conventional jazz harmony and that might continue for eight or more measures and then be capped by another sustained note, which seemed to leave the solo hanging peaceably in midair. Not one of Christian's half-dozen solos is mediocre, and some are stunning. These last occur in "Memories of You," played with the Goodman sextet (Goodman, Christian, Lionel Hampton, Fletcher Henderson, Artie Bernstein, Nick Fatool), and in a slow, affecting blues, "Paging the Devil," done with the Kansas City Six, in which Christian takes two choruses, replete with those stopped-motion notes, lanky explorations into the lower registers of the instrument, and graceful in-one-breath melodic lines.

Lester Young, who appears with Christian in three numbers, is in equally good form, particularly in "Blues with Helen," where he delivers two choruses on the clarinet. In "Good Morning Blues" and "Pagin' the Devil," he switches to the tenor saxophone and plays so softly he seems to be merely thinking his notes, and in "Don't Be That Way" he takes a remarkable chorus that challenges all his recorded work in the late thirties. Next in line after Young are Pete Johnson and Joe Turner, who do a variation of "Roll 'Em Pete" called

"It's All Right, Baby." In addition to playing two solo choruses, Johnson provides bustling accompaniment for Turner, who has never, at least on records, been in better voice. There are many more sweets—a rousing solo by James P. Johnson, "Carolina Shout," in which he pits cannonlike left-hand chords against filigreed right-hand figures; another piano solo, "I Ain't Got Nobody," in which Count Basie explicitly and charmingly spells out his debt to Johnson and Fats Waller for two choruses and then slips into two double-time choruses of his own style; Sidney Bechet and Tommy Ladnier attempting to outshout each other (as they had done on their original Feetwarmer sides six years before); a couple of blues by Sonny Terry, who shifts back and forth so rapidly between eerie falsetto singing and his harmonica that the two sounds sometimes seem simultaneous; and Mitchell's Christian Singers, a gospel group, composed of two tenors, a baritone, and a bass, whose subtle and ingenious ensemble singing is full of brownish, grating harmonies and counterpoint. There is one major disappointment on the records. The Count Basie band, at the peak of its powers, appears in only two and a half numbers—a blues, in which it accompanies the trumpet of Hot Lips Page, who was a better blues singer than a trumpeter; a fast, ragged rendition of "Rhythm Man"; and the last three ensemble choruses of "One O'Clock Jump."

*In 1999, Vanguard released what purports to be the complete 1938 and 1939 concerts, adding over twenty "new" selections, among them two roaring Basie big-band numbers, "Swingin' the Blues" and "Every Tub"; Meade Lux Lewis' great "Honky Tonky Train Blues" and Albert Ammons' "Boogie Woogie"; two Kansas City Five 1938 studio sessions with Lester Young, Buck Clayton, and Basie; and wonderful, though glancingly recorded, vocals by Sonny Terry, Big Bill Broonzy, Joe Turner, Ida Cox, Sister Rosetta Tharpe, Jimmy Rushing (listen to Clayton's muted far-away solo in the second chorus of Rushing's "Stealin' Blues"), and the mellifluous Helen Humes.*

# Introducing Ornette

It is quite possible that the encomiums that appear in the liner notes for two new records by Ornette Coleman, an amazing twenty-nine-year-old alto saxophonist from Texas, might repel as many listeners as they attract. Charlie Parker supplies the central heating for Coleman's style, which is both heretical and traditional. As a radical, Coleman has moved abreast of Charlie Mingus and Cecil Taylor, using a method of nearly free improvisation, in which the chord structure and melody of a tune are only nodded at in his effort to create unfettered rhythmic and harmonic excursions. Thus, after a series of deceptively simple phrases, played in a kind of alter-rhythm to the established beat and colored here and there with brief atonal sallies, he will suddenly shoot into a couple of ascending yelps—incredibly swift runs whose notes actually seem to be

vibrated out of the instrument. This device leads to the other side of Coleman's style, which is almost archaic. For Coleman's most adventurous tonal
flights appear to be attempts to reproduce on his horn the more passionate
inflections of the human voice, which, of course, provided the first model for
instrumental jazz. These weird emulations come off best at slow tempos and
they are a peculiar and wrenching music.

The two records under consideration, "Ornette Coleman: 'Tomorrow is
the Question!' " and "Ornette Coleman: The Shape of Jazz to Come," are
uneven. Possibly because of a conventional rhythm team, made up of Percy
Heath or Red Mitchell and Shelly Manne, Coleman is in comparatively
restrained form on the first record. (Don Cherry, his exact counterpart on
cornet, is also on hand.) The best of the nine numbers, all of them by Coleman, are "Lorraine," a slow, chanting dirge, complete with a long, mercurial
human-voice run by Coleman that raises the hair on one's neck, and "Turn-
around," a comfortable medium-tempo blues. (Coleman's and Cherry's
ensembles, which are not unlike Coleman's solos, often make it difficult to
make out just what the melody is, if, indeed, it is a melody at all.) On the second record, a different drummer and bassist come closer to Coleman's own
tastes (Cherry is again present), and the results are even more otherworldly.
The "tempos" tend to be faster and the rhythmic foundations are full of
steadily shifting twists and turns, with the drums and bass performing deco-
rative-melodic rather than purely percussive roles. These deviations,
together with Coleman's bare-ganglion playing, give most of the six numbers, all of them again Coleman's, a harum-scarum air. Listen to Coleman;
he is unique, he is new.

# THE SIXTIES

# 1960

## Jo Jones, dms.

One of the minor legends of jazz, which has a mythology as busy as the Greeks', credits Jo Jones, the forty-eight-year-old Chicago-born drummer, with single-handedly setting off, in the late thirties, the revolution in drumming since blown forward by Kenny Clarke, Max Roach, Art Blakey, Philly Joe Jones, and Elvin Jones. This theory holds that Jo Jones was the first drummer to use his bass drum for accents as well as for a timekeeper, the first to shift his other accompanying effects to his cymbals, and, all in all, the first to develop a whistling-in-the-morning attack that made most previous drumming resemble coal rattling down a chute. Nonetheless, several contemporary drummers were doing many of the same things, and not necessarily because they knew Jones's work. (A highly regarded legendizing process in jazz is the device of linking musicians with similar styles. Thus, John Lewis was once told that he resembled the late Clyde Hart, an economical and original pianist who was an indirect founder of bebop. Lewis replied that he had never heard Hart, in the flesh or on records.) Among these drummers were Chick Webb, whose work on the high-hat and the brushes is among the permanent ornaments of jazz; Alvin Burroughs, an adept, clean, nervous performer, who played as if on springs; O'Neil Spencer, who had much in common with Burroughs; Sidney Catlett, whose cymbal patterns, singular snare accents, and free-floating foot pedal were neater and snappier than Jones'; and Dave Tough, who often implied even more than Jones and whose cymbals, in particular, had a splashing beauty. But any disagreement with the theory about Jones's supposed pioneering is leveled not at him but at his admirers, who, like all jazz appreciators, are full of imagination. One of the handful of irreplaceable drummers, he stands—since Webb, Catlett, Burroughs, Spencer, and Tough are dead and most of the rest of his contemporaries are either inferior or in decline—as the last of a great breed.

One reason for Jones' glorification as a pioneer was his membership, from 1936 to 1948, in the Count Basie rhythm section, which included—in addition to Basie and Jones—Freddie Greene and Walter Page. This Basie rhythm section was classic proof of the powers of implication, for it achieved its ball-bearing motion through an almost Oriental casualness and indirection, as if the last thing in the world it wanted was to supply rhythm for a jazz band. The result was a deceptive sailing-through-life quality that was, like most magic, the product of hard work and a multi-layered complexity that offered the listener two delightful possibilities: the jointless sound of the unit as a whole, or, if one cared to move in for a close-up, the always audible timbre of each of its components. And what marvelously varied timbres they were! At the top was Basie's piano, which, though most often celebrated for its raindrop qualities, attained its relaxed drive from a skillful pitting of loose right-hand figures against heavy left-hand chords. On the next rung came Greene, a peerless rhythm guitarist, whose Prussian beat, guidepost chords, and aeolian-harp delicacy formed a transparent but unbreakable net beneath Basie. Page, who had a generous tone on the bass, gave the group much of its resonance, which was either echoed by Jones's foot pedal and snare or diluted by his cymbal work. The Basie rhythm section dedicated itself to the proposition that each beat is equal, and, knee-actioned, seemed to automatically erase both its own occasional lapses (Jones' loss of tempo; Page's bushy-sounding bass), as well as those of every vulnerable rhythm section in history. Although the group broke up more than a decade ago (only Greene remains with Basie), its low-key drive continues to seep into the four corners of jazz. And Jones, who has since worked with all types of jazz musicians, has been particularly pervasive.

Jones' style, which has not changed appreciably in the past twenty-five years, except for some sporadic, and pardonable, middle-aged heaviness, is elegant and subtle. As an accompanist, he provides a cushion of air for his associates to ride on. Primarily, this is achieved by his high-hat technique. His oarlocks muffled, he avoids the deliberate chunt chunt-chunt effect of most drummers by never allowing the sound of his stick striking the cymbals to be audible, and instead of ceaselessly clapping his cymbals shut on the traditionally accented beats he frequently keeps them open for several beats, producing a shooshing, drifting-downstream quality. Jones' high-hat seems alternately to push a soloist along, to play tag with him, and—in the brief, sustained shooshes—to glide along beside him. His high-hat also varies a good deal according to tempo. At low speeds the cymbals sound like water ebbing. At fast tempos they project an intensity that is the result of precision rather than the increase in volume displayed by most drummers. The rest of the time, Jones carries the beat on a couple of ride cymbals, on which—as opposed to the tinsmith's tink tink-tink of many drummers—he gets a clean, pushing ring. All of Jones' cymbal-playing is contained by spare and irregular accents on the bass drum and the snare, the latter of which he employs for rim shots that give the effect of being fired at the soloist's feet to keep him dancing. On top of all this, these devices form an unbroken flow; each number—pneumatically supported—comes through free of the cracks and breaks that drummers often inflict in the belief that they are providing support. Jones' brushes have been equaled by only a few drummers. They are neat, dry, and full of suggestive snare-drum accents, and when used on cymbals often seem an embellishment of silence rather than a full-blooded sound.

Jones is the embodiment of his own playing. A handsome, partly bald man whose physique resembles a tightly packed cigar and who moves in a quick, restless way, he smiles continually when he is at work, in a radiant, everything-is-fine-at-home fashion. Although he sits very still behind his drums (remember the demonic posturing of Gene Krupa?), his hands, attached to waving undersea arms, flicker about his set and his head snaps disdainfully from side to side, like a flamenco dancer's. His solos, which have recently increased in length and variety but without losing any of their structure, sometimes begin with the brushes, which tick and polish their way between his snare drum and his tom-toms in patterns frequently broken by punching pauses. (Jones' solo brushwork—stinging and nimble—suggests, in sound and figure, that ideal of all tap-dancing, which great tap-dancers always seem headed for but never quite reach.) After a while Jones may joggle his high-hat cymbals up and down with his foot, while switching to drumsticks, and launch into riffling, clicking beats on the rim of a tom-tom as well as on its head (he may muffle it with one hand, achieving the sound produced by kicking a full suitcase), interspersed with sudden free tom-tom booms. He will then drop his sticks, under cover of more high-hat joggling, and go at the tom-toms with his hands, hitting them with a finger-breaking crispness. More high-hat, and he will fall into half time and, sticks in hand again, tackle the snare drum, at which he is masterly, starting with a roll as smooth as hot fudge being poured over marble. Gradually loosening the roll with stuttering accents, he will introduce rim shots—a flow of rolling still intact beneath—spacing them with a breath-catching unevenness, and then, in a boomlay-boom fashion, begin mixing in tom-tom strokes until the tom-toms take over and, in turn, are broken by snippets of snare-drum beats. Jones will slowly subside after returning to the snare for a stream of rapid on-beat strokes, and—an eight-day clock running down—end with a quiet bass-drum thump. There have been no cymbal explosions, repetitions, or dizzying, narcissistic technical displays. One has the feeling of having heard distilled rhythm.

Three of Jones' recent efforts—"The Jo Jones Special," "Jo Jones Trio," and "Jo Jones Plus Two"—are sufficient samplers of his work. The first record is valuable largely for two takes of "Shoe Shine Boy," in which the old Basie rhythm section is reassembled, along with Emmett Berry, Lucky Thompson, and Benny Green. (Nat Pierce is on piano in four of the five other numbers, and for the last there is an entirely different group, composed of—among others—Pete Johnson, Lawrence Brown, and Buddy Tate.) The two versions are done at medium–up-tempos, and are just about equal in quality. Thompson and Berry are in commendable form, but the rhythm section is priceless. Listen, in the first take, to the way Jones switches from joyous high-hat work behind Basie's solo to plunging, out-in-the-open patterns on his ride cymbal when the first horn enters; to Basie's down-the-mountainside left hand near the end of Thompson's first chorus; and to Jones' four-bar break on his snare drum at the close of the number, done with sharply uneven dynamics that make the prominent beats split the air. There is also a rendition of "Caravan," by the alternate group, in which Jones takes a tidy solo, complete with mallets on the tom-toms, hands on the tom-toms (here, a plopping sound like that achieved by hooking a finger into one's mouth, closing the lips, and drawing the finger abruptly out), and oil-and-water patterns on the snare with sticks.

Jones is accompanied on the trio records by Ray and Tommy Bryant. Although the first record is crowded with twelve numbers, which seem, because of their brevity (the kind of brevity that smacks of the nervous A&R man), more like suggestions than complete numbers, there are brilliant instances of Jones' brush work. These occur in a fast blues, "Philadelphia Bound," into which Jones injects some fine high-hat work, particularly behind the bass solo; in the slower "Close Your Eyes," in which his first four-bar break is taken in a startling and absolutely precise double time that conveys to the listener that sense of pleasant astonishment unique to good jazz drumming; and in the leisurely "Embraceable You," in which Jones washes discreetly and ceaselessly back and forth on his snare. On the second trio record, Jones develops his "Caravan" solo, in a hundred-miles-an-hour version of "Old Man River," by taking a four-minute excursion in which he uses the brushes, sticks on muffled tom-toms, sticks on open tom-toms, hands on tom-toms, sticks on snare and tom-toms, and a soft ending with sticks on the snare. Jones is exemplary in the remaining eight numbers, both in briefer solos and in his accompaniment. He also allows a good deal of space to Ray Bryant, lending him the same heedless, sparkling force he grants everyone.

## Catching Trout

There is an unbroken Olympian lineage at the top of jazz—Jelly Roll Morton, Duke Ellington, Count Basie, Thelonious Monk, and John Lewis—which has been distinguished by the curious fact that all its members are composers, arrangers, leaders, and pianists. Monk, however, has added an authentic dimension to the qualities he shares with his colleagues, for he is an almost unparalleled *performer*. Monk is not a vaudevillian in the sense that Louis Armstrong, Dizzy Gillespie, and Gene Krupa are. Instead, he offers the rare spectacle of a man pleasantly and unself-consciously obsessed by his art. He is, in fact, a transparent, pliable vessel that takes on the shapes, colors, and movements that his emotions, washing against each other within, may dictate on a particular night. A bearish, densely assembled man, with a square head and an oblique face that emits a veiled but unmistakable light, Monk never merely sits at a keyboard. He will hunch his shoulders, elbows akimbo, and knead the keys, bend backward, bring his elbows in, shoot out his forearms, and pluck notes from either end of the keyboard, as if he were catching trout with his bare hands. Then, a giant hammer, he will hit several closely grouped chords, simultaneously jerking his torso. If he is accompanying he may abruptly "lay out" and unconcernedly mop his head, neck, and hands with a flag-size handkerchief, or he may wind his body sinuously from side to side in half time to the beat and, his arms horizontally crooked, slowly snap his fingers—a dancer grace-fully illustrating a step in delayed motion. Monk's feet carry on a steady counterpoint. Flattish and nimble, they alternately rustle about beneath the piano, flap convulsively, and dig heel-first into the floor. All of this is by way of saying that Monk's five selves were in notable balance early last week, at the most recent of the "Jazz Profiles" concerts.

The affair, held at the Circle in the Square, was given over entirely to Monk's present quartet, which includes Charlie Rouse, Ron Carter, and Art Taylor. There were eleven numbers, all by Monk, including "Straight, No Chaser," "Crepuscule with Nellie," "Well, You Needn't," "Blue Monk," and "Ruby, My Dear," as well as less familiar pieces like "Hackensack," "Epistro-phy," and "Ask Me Now." Two infrequently-heard Monk compositions— "Monk's Dream" and "Criss-Cross"—were scheduled but never rose to the surface. There were surprises in almost every number. " 'Round Midnight," a ballad with a purplish melody that gives the impression of being too fin-ished for the meddling of improvisation (Monk himself generally sticks close to its melody in his solos), was taken at a jogging double time, which stripped it of some of its subtlety. In "Well, You Needn't," done in a medium tempo, Monk offered an exceptional display of his accompanying technique behind Rouse. He started with offbeat melodic chords, changed to dissonant chords that climbed steadily and slowly up and down the key-board, released acrid single notes in the upper registers, splattered a chord with his right elbow, and then, falling silent, began one of his Balinese dances. His backing here suggested that he was using Rouse's work as a soft clay on which to record his thoughts; elsewhere, he seemed to be rubbing pleasurably against the grain of Rouse's playing. "Crepuscule with Nellie," a slow hymn-lullaby, received tantalizing treatment. The first chorus was played straight by the group, and then, with the audience prepared for improvisation, the number ended. "Blue Monk" was taken at a medium-fast tempo instead of its usual slow rock, and paved the way for the closing num-bers, "Hackensack" and "Rhythm-n-ing," two steam baths that left the audi-ence at that exquisite point between satisfaction and wanting more at which all audiences should be left. Monk is a master of this art—in the way he measures his solos, his numbers, and even whole concerts.

## Something Else

A singular event took place last week, when Baby Laurence, the semi-legendary jazz tap-dancer, opened at the Showplace, a second-story cave on West Fourth Street. Indeed, Lau-rence's opening set was one of those claps of brilliance that are seemingly over before they have begun. Working on a stage the size of a billiard table Laurence danced only two numbers, which, taken together, lasted well under ten minutes, but which were of such intensity that they appeared to be a telescoping of all tap-dancing. Laurence was discreetly backed in the first number by Charlie Mingus, Roland Hanna (piano), and Danny Richmond. After some purposely heavy, flatfooted introductory steps in medium tempo, Laurence shot into double time, pausing repeatedly and suddenly for short triple-time passages, done as breaks, that were compounded of a startling variety of accents, not one of which was missed, and that invariably came out just right. These seesaw patterns were followed by abrupt slow shufflings, which gave way to offbeats against a backboard, and then to irregular, out-of-rhythm scrapings carried out on three shallow steps on one side of the stage. More breaks, a few crackling spins, and the dance was over. The shorter second number was a solo. It consisted of half a dozen rhythms—including a military beat—that, flawlessly juxtaposed, proved that what Laurence is, essentially, is a great drummer.

Later in the evening, I asked Laurence how his engagement had come about. "Marshall Stearns, the jazz writer, helped me get the job," Laurence, a short, slim, dapper man with gray-streaked hair, told me. "He'd interviewed me for a book he's doing on jazz dancing, and he suggested I come here to the Showplace, where Mingus puts on informal dance sessions on Thursday nights. So I did, I danced, and Mingus said, 'Baby, you want a job, I'll fire my piano player who's always late anyway and hire you.' I'm very lucky, you know. Between the entertainment tax and the Hollywood and Broadway producers, who use nothing but what we call choreography dancing, there just aren't many jobs for jazz dancers.

"Dancing was an accident I fell into. I started as a Bobby Breen–type singer in Baltimore late in 1932, when I was twelve. I worked with McKinney's Cotton Pickers over at College Park, and one day Don Redman's band come to town, and he heard me sing and asked my mama could he hire me and take me on the road. My mama told him, 'Get him a tutor, provide him an education, and he can go.' Well, Redman did, and I was on the road with him for about a year. Then my mother died, and I went home and joined my brother in a vocal group, the Four Buds, and we went up to New York. We accompanied ourselves on the ukulele and did some dancing, too, and that's when I started to learn. We worked at Dickie Wells' place in Harlem, and he kind of adopted me. I was born Laurence Donald Jackson, and he gave me my professional name. Then I started going over to the Hoofer's Club, where all the dancers hung out. Harold Mablin began teaching me there. He gave me the devil because I turned all his steps around, and pretty soon he just gave me ideas and I went on from there. In a year, I was really dancing. I don't know how I did it. It was just one of those things. I jobbed around Harlem and Cincinnati and Washington, and in the late thirties I joined a group called the Three Gobs. We got on the bill at the Apollo, but the manager didn't want us in sailor suits, so he dressed us up in kilts and called us the Merry Scotchmen. We stopped the show. Then we went into Kelly's Stable, downtown. We accompanied ourselves and sang Jimmie Lunceford arrangements in five-part harmony, and it was something else. Around 1940, I started doing a single—just dancing. I worked with Rochester at the Apollo. I opened the show, and I broke it up. Nobody wanted to come on after me—the band, which was the Savoy Sultans, Rochester—no one; so they put me at the end of the bill. I did a couple of coffee concerts at the Museum of Modern Art, and traveled with Count Basie and Duke Ellington until the entertainment tax came along and things got hard." Laurence sighed, pulled a long face, and fell silent. "After that, I began running with a fast crowd and got sick. I pretty much stopped dancing. I learned the guitar and started singing again, and I even wrote poetry. I got married in 1953, and my wife kept after me and started me dancing again."

I asked Laurence who had taught him most.

"I've learned from everybody," he said. "Dancers like John Bubbles and Teddy Hale. Hale got a sound—Lord, what a sound! He died last year. And dancers like Eddie Rector and Pete Nugent and Honi Coles and Toots Davis and Jack Wiggins. I learned from Art Tatum, too. I worked with him on Fifty-second Street, and I tried to duplicate his sound with my feet. I did the same thing rhythmically when Charlie Parker came along. Maybe I've learned most from drummers, though. One time I was on the television show Eddie Condon had in the forties. There was Buddy Rich, Teddy Hale, Milt Buckner, and me, and we each took a chorus, then we started swapping eight-bar breaks, then four-bar breaks, then two. It was something else. I've worked with Max Roach, and we trade ideas. I'm learning right now from Mingus. I'm also inventing new solo routines. Last week, I stumbled onto something I call 'An Afternoon in Percussion,' which is supposed to sound like a jazz drummer practicing at home in the afternoon and driving his neighbors wild. But I have a dream. I'd like to give a concert in Carnegie Hall and get all the great jazz tap-dancers and let the people see what they've been missing these past ten, twelve years. People should know. It's a beautiful art. I'd get everybody from uptown—Bubbles and Nugent and Coles—and a boy works in Cincinnati who's never been to New York named Ground Hog. He's a little, short, homely-looking stud, but when he dances you forget that. The people should know about Ground Hog and all the rest. They should see what they've been missing all these years."

## Miss Holiday

Toward the end of her life, Billie Holiday, who died last summer, at the age of forty-four, had become inextricably caught in a tangle of notoriety and fame. It was compounded of an endless series of skirmishes with the police and the courts (she was shamelessly arrested on her deathbed for the alleged possession of narcotics); the bitter, vindictive, self-pitying image of herself established in her autobiography, published in 1956—a to-hell-with-you image that tended to repel rather than attract compassion; and the fervent adulation still granted her by a diminishing but ferocious band of admirers. Her new listeners must have been puzzled by all this turmoil, for she sang during much of the fifties with a heavy, unsteady voice that sometimes gave the impression of being pushed painfully in front of her, like a medicine ball. She seemed, in fact, to be embattled with every song she tackled. Nonetheless, her admirers were not mad. Between 1935, when she popped out of nowhere, and 1940, Holiday had knocked a good portion of the jazz world on its ear with a hundred or so recordings, several dozen of which rank with the greatest of non-classical vocal efforts. Part of the success of these recordings, which have an uncanny balance of ease, control, unself-consciousness, emotion, and humor, is due to the accompaniment provided by small bands made up of men like Lester Young, Buck Clayton, Roy Eldridge, Benny Goodman, and Teddy Wilson. Though their work—in obbligatos that underline the grace of her voice, in exemplary solos, and in tumbling, laughing ensembles—often takes up as much space as the vocals, it is Miss Holiday who continues to astonish.

Until she appeared, genuine jazz singing had been practiced largely by a myriad of often obscure blues singers led by Bessie Smith, and by a handful of instrumentalists led by Louis Armstrong. Bessie Smith leveled a massive lyricism at limited materials, while Armstrong's coalyard rumblings, though irresistible in themselves, occasionally seemed to have little to do with singing. Distilling and mixing the best of her predecessors with her own high talents, Billie Holiday became the first full-fledged female jazz singer. She could sing anything, and her style was completely her own. She appeared to *play* her voice rather than sing with it. In addition to a hornlike control of melody and rhythm, she had an affecting contralto that took on innumerable timbres: a dark-brown sound, sometimes fretted by growls or hoarseness, in the lower register; a pliable oboe tone in the high register; and a clear, pushing, little-girl alto in between. Her style came in three subtle different parts. There was one for ephemeral popular songs, one for the more durable efforts of George Gershwin and his peers, and one for the blues. Since she was primarily an improviser, not an interpreter, she was often most striking when handling pop songs, like "Yankee Doodle Never Went to Town," "It's Too Hot for Words," and "What a Little Moonlight Can Do," which she spattered with a mocking, let's-have-some-fun-with-this air. Thus, at a fast tempo, she might loll back in half time, and not only elongate each word, so that it seemed nothing but vowels, but flatten the melody into a near-monotone of four or five notes. Then, in the last eight bars or so, she would suddenly pounce on the beat, pick up the melody, and close in a here-I-am rush. (If the evil was in her she might stomp such a number all the way through, rocking it relentlessly back and forth and coating it with dead-serious growls.) At slow tempos, she would use the full range of her voice, adding exaggerated smears to her phrases or dotting them with series of laughlike staccato notes. At the same time, she was busy fashioning a deceptively simple and thorough melodic variation on the tune, smoothing its wrinkles, toughening up its soft spots, and lending it far more lyricism than it usually deserved. This was accomplished not by superimposing melodic candelabra on her material, in the manner of Sarah Vaughan, but by unobtrusively altering its melodic and rhythmic structure with a flow of marvelously placed phrases that might wander around behind the beat, and then suddenly push ahead of it (each syllable urgently pinned to a staccato note) or slide through legato curves full of blue notes and generous vibratos. Holiday's rhythmic sense had much in common with Lester Young's. Moreover, her enunciation of pop songs was a mixture of clarity and caricature, bringing into action that rule of ridicule that the victim be reproduced perfectly before being destroyed. Her "moon"s and "June"s rang like bells, and one didn't hear their cracks until the sound began to die away. The composers of the pop songs she sang should be grateful; her renditions ("Ooo-ooo-ooo / What a lil' moonlaight can do-oo-oo"), and not the songs, are what we remember.

Her approach to Gershwin and such was almost reverent in comparison. In a number like "Summertime," she allowed the emotion that she had spent on lesser materials in sarcasm or near-flippancy to come through undisguised. Ceaselessly inventive, she would still shape the melody to fit her voice and mood, but in such a way that its beauties—and not hers—were pointed up. "Summertime" became a lullaby, "But Not for Me" a self-joshing lament, and "Porgy" a prayer. When there were superior lyrics on hand she underlined them with a diction and an understanding that pushed the meaning of each word forward. More than that, she would, at her best, lend a first-rate song a new and peculiarly heightened emotion that, one suddenly realized, its composer had only been reaching for. And the effort never showed.

Holiday simply let go when she sang the blues. She was never, however, a loud singer, nor did she depend on the big whisper of most of her microphone-reared successors; instead, she projected her voice firmly, keeping in steady balance her enunciation, timbre, and phrasing. She was, in fact, a model elocutionist. Free of the more complex structures of the standard popular song, she moved through the innumerable emotional pastures of the form, ranging from the down-and-out to the joyous, to the nasty and biting, to quiet, almost loving blues.

Then, in 1944, when Holiday started recording again (after the recording ban), the magic had begun to vanish. Perhaps it was the increasing strain of her private life, or the mysterious rigor mortis that so often freezes highly talented but untrained and basically intuitive performers. At any rate, she had become self-conscious. Although her voice had improved in resonance and control, her style had grown mannered. She ended her phrases with disconcerting, lachrymose dips. She struggled with her words instead of batting them about or savoring them. The melodic twists and turns lost their spontaneity. One could accurately predict her rhythmic patterns. Even her beauty—the huge gardenia clamped to the side of her head; the high, flashing cheekbones; the almost motionless body, the snapping fingers; and the thrown-back head; the mobile mouth, which seemed to measure the emotional shape and texture of each word—implied careful calculation. From time to time, some of this stylization lifted—she never, of course, lost her *presence*, which became more and more melancholy—and there were glimpses of her old naturalness. After 1950, her voice grew deeper and coarser, and her sense of pitch and phrasing eluded her, and finally she became that most rending of spectacles—a once great performer doing a parody of herself. Her still devoted partisans clamored on; they would have done her greater service by doffing their hats and remaining silent.

Holiday's most recent records chronicle her work from 1944 until a year or two before her death. Among them are "An Evening with Eddie Heywood and Billie Holiday," "The Billie Holiday Story," and "The Unforgettable Lady Day." By and large, they proceed steadily and sadly downward. The first record includes four Holiday numbers—three standards and a blues—that were done in 1944. (The rest are instrumentals by Eddie Heywood's small band, which also provides her accompaniment.) The best of them is a slow blues, "I Love My Man," in which, dropping her mannerisms, she nearly equals her classic rendition of another blues, "Fine and Mellow," recorded five years before. The Decca collection brings together twenty-four numbers—most of them standards—recorded between 1944 and 1950, and it varies sharply in quality. The accompaniment runs from the indifferent to the stifling. Nevertheless, in numbers like "Lover Man," "I'll Look Around," "Deep Song," "My Man," "Good Morning, Heartache," and "Solitude," she sings in her best forties style.

The Verve album, which consists of twenty-three standards recorded between 1949 and 1957 with a variety of small groups made up of Ben Webster, Harry Edison, Charlie Shavers, Oscar Peterson, and Benny Carter, begins—give or take a little overlapping—where the Decca set stops. There are some valuable things. Six of the numbers were set down at a concert in 1949 on the West Coast, and Holiday sings throughout with an ease and confidence that result in two first-rate efforts—a medium-slow "Man I Love," which ranks with any of her work in the forties, and a fresh, peaceful "All of Me." The eleven numbers from 1952 are not far behind; the notable ones are slow versions of "I Can't Face the Music" and "These Foolish Things." The cracks begin to show in the two 1954 numbers, and then, amazingly, there is a medium-tempo "Please Don't Talk About Me When I'm Gone," done a year later, in which Holiday magically reverts to the late thirties, delivering the first chorus in a light, bantering, husky voice that is memorable. ("When Your Lover Has Gone," apparently made at the same session, is, nevertheless, curiously heavy and uncertain.) With the exception of the last chorus of a 1957 "Gee Baby, Ain't I Good to You," in which she virtually rocks herself into effective shape, the rest of the album is rewarding only for the accompaniment of Webster and Edison. But one is cheered by the recent news that Columbia is considering reissuing the best of the 1935–40 Holiday sides hidden away in its vaults.

## R.I.P.

The appearance of "The Real Boogie Woogie: Memphis Slim, Piano Solos" is a surprise. It is the first new boogie-woogie record to be released in nearly a decade, and, more than that, its title tells the truth. An all-but-vanished art, boogie-woogie remains, in recordings and in the memory, one of the milestones of jazz. A complex, incandescent solo-piano music whose thematic material was restricted almost wholly to the twelve-bar blues, it embraced, because of its variety and power, all the emotional shades of the blues. Its obvious features have been widely celebrated and widely misunderstood. Unlike the rest of jazz piano, which depends largely on the right hand, boogie-woogie was a two-part, two-handed contrapuntal music that suffered if either hand was undeveloped. It was also a basically rhythmic and harmonic form that only nodded at melodic invention. The left hand was chiefly characterized by the *ostinato* bass. This bass was often composed of dotted eighth or dotted sixteenth notes, and it included "walking" basses, "rolling" basses, heavy staccato basses, and spare four-four basses often tinged with Spanish rhythms. (Contrary to general belief, only a few boogie-woogie basses had eight beats to the bar.) A boogie-woogie pianist might use the same bass through an entire chorus or a succession of choruses, but more often he changed basses, and sometimes even registers, in each solo. The monotonous rumble popularly associated with boogie-woogie was an illusion; close attention revealed a constant flow of new colors. The right hand was even freer. The pianist might use arpeggios, a single note struck lackadaisically throughout a whole chorus, tremolos of various speeds, chorded or single-note riffs, simple, fragmentary melodic lines, and clusters of chords that frequently absorbed single-note melodies or dissolved into them. Occasionally one rhythm popped up, simultaneously in the bass and treble, but generally the right hand went its own way, setting up a welter of cross-rhythms that sometimes shifted from measure to measure. Added to all this was an intuitive harmonic sense that ranged from single or multivoiced melodies to dissonances. Boogie-woogie was a polyphonic, polyrhythmic, and at times even polytonal music.

It is often regarded primarily as a stomp music. Nonetheless, it was played at every speed. There were tempos that were so slow they were tempoless. Numbers played this way became a collection of sorrowful, introverted reflections on the blues that have rarely been surpassed for unadulterated sadness. The brighter the tempo, the more effulgent the music; at medium-slow or medium speeds, the lyrical content was perfectly balanced by its rhythmic aspects. Many of the "train" pieces—Meade Lux

Lewis's "Honky Tonk Train Blues" is the most famous—were played in these tempos, and they provided extended musical images that caught perfectly the concatenation of sounds, motion, and force of steam-hauled trains. They also caught the emotions of transition that trains so peculiarly symbolize. Fast boogie-woogie was a rock-breaking wonder. A distillation of hurry and strength, it was one of the few forms of jazz with a climactic structure. In a fast number, melodic repetition and the compounding of various rhythms gradually took on a solidity that had no breathing spaces and that reached an impressive intensity in the closing choruses. Not many other types of music have offered such a sense of rampage. And yet, despite its turbine quality, fast boogie-woogie never lost the essential plaintiveness of the blues. Slow boogie-woogie was a carefully arranged array of still shots; fast boogie-woogie transposed those stills into a motion picture.

The history of boogie-woogie is blurred, romantic, and short. So far as is known, the form was invented around the turn of the century in the Midwest and scattered areas of the South by itinerant laborer-musicians. Its singular percussiveness was probably the result of attempts by its pioneers to overcome, through sheer volume, both inferior instruments and the noisy environment—dances, lumber camps, rent parties, and the like—in which they played. Its repetitiveness and wayward harmonies, which were eventually handled with considerable intelligence, grew out of plain ineptitude. The music was largely unknown until the late thirties, when it suddenly became a national fad. Every swing band had at least one boogie-woogie arrangement, while one band—Will Bradley's—made a career out of it. Correspondence-course pianists played it at parties. José Iturbi made an unbelievable two-sided 78-rpm boogie-woogie record. The term became widely and genially mispronounced. (Both words rhyme, more or less, with "bookie," rather than "bootie.") The results were ironic and disastrous. The unwieldy complexities and fire of the form, untouched by this imitative army, settled to the bottom, leaving a vapid, colorless liquid. At the same time, the handful of genuine boogie-woogie pianists who abruptly achieved fame and fortune were forced by overexposure to mechanize a fundamentally instinctive music. The craze had vanished by the end of the Second World War, and so, to all intents and purposes, had boogie-woogie itself. Two of its leading exponents, Albert Ammons and Jimmy Yancey, died not long after, while two others, Meade Lux Lewis and Pete Johnson, dropped into obscurity.

Although there must have been dozens of proficient boogie-woogie pianists in the twenties and thirties, only Yancey, Ammons, Lewis, and Johnson left a sizable and first-rate body of work behind them. Jimmy Yancey, who died in 1951, at the age of fifty-seven, was, in addition to being a model for Ammons and Lewis, possibly the greatest of all blues pianists. A small, lean, shy man who gave up music professionally in the twenties and took a job as a groundkeeper for the Chicago White Sox, Yancey had a style of classic simplicity. He invented a wide selection of discreet, almost tentative basses that were often set in four-to-the-bar or Spanish-tinged rhythms. His right hand was similarly understated. It rarely left the middle registers, and was limited to elementary chords, loose tremolos, and, principally, to lucid, reiterated melodic figures grouped around or below middle C. He had a sure sense of dynamics, and never went above brisk medium tempos, favoring slow speeds, which gave him the time to wring the maximum amount of emotion from his notes. Indeed, the best of his slow blues—"Death Letter Blues," "Five O'Clock Blues," and "35th and Dearborn"—are indelible. Ammons, Lewis, and Johnson were altogether different from Yancey. In their heyday, in the early forties, all three swelled to tremendous girths, and all three played with a rococo fury that made Yancey seem schoolmasterish. Lewis was the most accomplished of the three. He was adept at all speeds and was perhaps the most complex of all boogie-woogie pianists. His variety of basses was limitless, and so were his right-hand figures. Yancey's influence was clear, but it had been transformed into a nimbler, more intense approach. Ammons was at once a looser and even more driving pianist. At leisurely tempos, he seemed to spread slowly, occasionally slipping out of the confines of boogie-woogie altogether to play a straight stride bass and heavily pedaled right-hand chords. At up-tempos, though, he generated a passion that was bent wholly to the rhythmic characteristics of the music. Johnson was a Kansas City–trained pianist who frequently used a walking bass. His slow pieces often resembled Ammons's, but at fast tempos—despite his mountainous walking basses and his agile staccato right-hand chords—he achieved only a tight, dispassionate quality. Johnson's work had more bark than bite. Both Lewis and Johnson have recorded in the past decade, but, sadly, their inventiveness is gone. One hears only repetitions of old phrases, mixed here and there with intimations of their old ingenuity.

Memphis Slim, a forty-five-year-old performer whose real name is Peter Chatman, stands within and without the Yancey tradition. He has obviously listened to Yancey, Ammons, and Lewis, but there are also distinct overtones of lesser-known and less-adept pianists like Roosevelt Sykes, Speckled Red, and Cow Cow Davenport. The jostling of these influences is absorbing, notwithstanding Slim's fluffed notes, uncertain time and tonality, and choruses of carelessly varied lengths. The record includes fourteen blues, three of them outstanding. (Slim sings the two vocals on the record in a rich, liquid voice.) The first, ".44 Blues," has a slurred, delayed-action bass that suggests Spanish rhythms, while the right hand plays a stream of staccato chords. "Down Home Blues" is the essence of slow blues. It is so slow it has no beat, and is largely a mass of sonorous sounds that creep back and forth between an attenuated Yanceylike bass and right-hand chords broken by wild arpeggios. The Spanish rhythms reappear in "Roll and Tumble," which is in a medium-slow tempo and has a rolling bass that here and there is replaced by on-the-beat chords that lend the piece a mock-martial air. The rest of the numbers, though valuable, are uneven.

Nonetheless, Memphis Slim comes close to persuading us that he is not, after all, merely vestigial.

## Historic

Through jazz and classical music have been living side by side for forty years, until recently it was classical music—in the form of Stravinsky, Milhaud, Ravel, Satie, Křenek, and Copland—that did all the running across the yard to borrow a cup of this and a pinch of that. These borrowings included rhythms, minor structural devices, improvisation, the blue note, and the all-but-inimitable timbres of jazz. During the past ten years or so the practice has become two-way, for jazz has begun adopting the forms, the harmonies, and the instrumentation of classical music, and even its discipline. This neighborliness has grown out of distinct needs. Much modern classical music has dry rot, and the exuberance and fearlessness of the best contemporary jazz offer a possible cure—on the presupposition, of course, that improvisation is a defensible musical form. (Perhaps the chief appeal of genuine jazz improvisation lies in its ability to supply the listener in a matter of moments with an emotional and aesthetic sustenance comparable to that provided by the heavier arts—a peculiarly valuable ability in this split-second age.) At the same time, the finished techniques of many modern jazz musicians have forced them to look abroad for more challenging forms, harmonies, and rhythms. Nevertheless, it is obvious that the set designs of classical music cannot swallow the fluidity of jazz, and vice versa, or each will simply turn into the other. But there is a possible compromise—a new music consisting of the most durable elements of both—and it already has its first prophet. He is Gunther Schuller, a young classical composer and French-horn player with wide experience in modern jazz. For the past three or four years, Schuller has been vigorously stumping for his vision, and last week, at the final "Jazz Profiles" concert, held at the Circle in the Square, he presented the first program devoted entirely to this new music.

There were seven compositions, all by Schuller, who conducted. The music was played jointly by three groups, which, give or take a few musicians, remained onstage throughout. Present were the Contemporary String Quartet (Charles Treger, Joseph Schor, John Garvey, and Joseph Tekula), the Bill Evans Trio (Bill Evans; Scott LaFaro, bass; and Paul Cohen or Sticks Evans, drums), and six ringers (Ornette Coleman; Eric Dolphy alto saxophone, flute, clarinet, or bass clarinet; Buell Neidlinger, bass; Barry Galbraith, guitar; Eddie Costa, vibraphone; and Robert DiDomenica, flute). The opening number, "Little Blue Devil"—part of a symphonic work that was given its première earlier this year—was hardly more than a cough-quieter, in which patches of strings, a flute solo, and a regular beat were bandied about. But it readied one for the next piece, the new "Variants on a Theme of Thelonious Monk," which Schuller introduced as a set of four variations on Monk's "Criss-Cross." In the first part, taken at a medium tempo, Coleman and Dolphy, on alto saxophone, stated the melody, and then Coleman soloed, immediately delivering two fluttering, whimpering downward runs that dissolved into squeaks, freshly coined notes, and rhythmic displacements. Dolphy, a young West Coast musician and one of Coleman's first apostles, chimed in with his bass clarinet, producing a tone that alternated between moos and a hubble-bubble, and for several measures the two jostled each other, dissonantly and marvelously, providing a singular example of dual improvisation. The brief second section, which displayed some tempoless impressionistic spinach that was rudely swept aside by a yawp from Coleman, gave way to a medium-tempo sequence in which LaFaro, an extraordinary bassist, and Dolphy, on bass clarinet again, played a double cadenza set off by the strings. The textural contrasts alone were memorable—high, rapid, spinsterish notes from the bass, the deep-blue-sea sounds of Dolphy in his lowest register, and the background breezes of the quartet. The last section was a kind of decompression period. Then came "Conversations," in which written and improvised sections succeed each other. This rendition, which included a remarkable solo by Bill Evans, was followed by the most striking effort of the evening—the atonal "Abstraction No. 1," written recently for Coleman. The composition, one of those rare artless pieces that seem to fashion themselves on the spot, had a resiliency that was the result of the written and improvised interplay between the string quartet and Coleman. The strings first struck off follow-the-leader chips of sound that appeared to have been extracted from old Coleman solos. Coleman jousted appreciatively with the strings, joined them briefly, and abruptly sailed into a bucking solo that was underlined by the strings with an ecstasy of pushing, chanting sounds. Then Coleman sedately re-entered the ensemble for a further exchange of compliments, and the piece ended. Composition and improvisation had been organically and inextricably linked.

After the intermission, the number was refreshingly performed again, complete with a new segment of the Coleman canon, and next there was an impressive tour de force, "Transformation," which was originally unveiled a few years back. Here a "classical" passage is gradually coupled with a regular beat, diminishes, and is supplanted by an improvised section, which in this performance was played by Evans. A groundswell, in the form of a riff, appears, and then two parts—written and improvised—pump away neck and neck to the finish line. A new work, "Variants on a Theme of John Lewis," followed, and it had much of the coherence of "Abstraction No. 1." Based on Lewis's lovely "Django"—a tribute to Django Reinhardt—it began with Galbraith, who played the melody in a sorrowing, bareheaded fashion. The rhythm section and the vibraphone entered; LaFaro soloed and then joined forces with Galbraith; Dolphy, on flute, and LaFaro collaborated handsomely; the quartet slipped in some Reinhardt tremolos; and the piece slowly assumed a glistening, spidery air. The closing section trailed off, pressing the last drops from Lewis's melody. The finale was another fresh composition, "Progression in Tempo," a blues done as a rhythmic experiment, in which the tempo was gradually speeded up and then abruptly doubled. Fortunately, the number was anticlimactic, allowing one to settle peacefully back to earth.

This concert engraved on my mind, I had dinner with Coleman soon after at a restaurant on West Eleventh Street. He arrived carrying an instrument case, a navel orange, and a tightly furled umbrella, which swung easily from his left arm. A handsome man of medium height, dressed in an impeccable dark-green suit and a black tie, and wearing a beard, Coleman checked his case and umbrella, placed the orange carefully beside his butter plate, shook hands in a self-deprecating way, sat down and, without hesitation, began a concentrated, nonstop monologue that had a lot in common with one of his solos: "I'm not very hungry. I just ate a little while ago, but I'll have a small Salisbury steak and a salad, maybe with some Thousand Island dressing. I haven't heard one person yet who can explain what I'm doing. People laugh at me, shake their heads. But I won't let any of that affect me. There's but one thing you can do—play the true essence of yourself. Talent and appearances have nothing to do with each other. Look at Van Gogh. He cut off his ear; it didn't hurt his talent. Most people fail to hear what is being played at the *moment* it is played. They pay more attention to behavior and what they see than to what is happening musically. I know exactly what I'm doing. I'm beginning where Charlie Parker stopped. Parker's melodic lines were placed across ordinary chord progressions. My melodic approach is based on phrasing, and my phrasing is an extension of how I hear the intervals and pitch of the tunes I play. There is no end to pitch. You can play flat in tune and sharp in tune. It's a question of vibration. My phrasing is spontaneous, not a style. A style happens when your phrasing hardens. Jazz music is the only music in which the same note can be played night after night but differently each time. It's the hidden things, the subconscious that lies in the body and lets you know: you feel this, you play this. Do you understand that? After all, *music* is harmless. It all depends on which way a person is using it. I give my musicians one of my tunes and tell them, 'You play that your way. You add to it what you can. Enlarge it. Extend it.' But this isn't easy, I know. The other night, at a rehearsal for the concert I played in of Gunther Schuller's music, Schuller made me play a little four-measure thing he'd written six or seven times before I got it right. I could read it, see the notes on the paper. But I heard those notes in my head, heard their pitch, and what I heard was different from what Schuller heard. Then I got it right. I got it his way. It was as simple as that."

Coleman paused abruptly, picked up the orange, hefted it, and rolled it around reflectively in his hands. I asked him to tell me about his early career. "I started playing the alto when I was about fourteen," he said, replacing the orange and attacking his Salisbury steak. "My family couldn't afford to give me lessons, so I bought an instruction book and taught myself, but I taught myself wrong. I thought the low C on my horn was the A in the book, and when I joined a church band the leader said, 'Look at this boy. Playing the instrument wrong for two years. He'll never be a saxophone player.' You can't live down your mistakes, but if you keep thinking about them you can't emerge from them, either. I hooked up with a carnival band, then a rhythm-and-blues group, which stranded me in California in 1950. They kept telling me in that band I was doing this wrong, doing that wrong. In the next six, seven years, I traveled back and forth between Fort Worth and California, playing once in a while but doing day work mostly—stockboy, houseboy, freight-elevator operator. By 1957, I had got very depressed in California, and I wired my ma would she send me a bus ticket home, and on the day the ticket arrived, Les Koenig, of Contemporary Records, asked me to audition some of my tunes for him. I did, and he gave me my first record session. I began playing around California, and in 1959 John Lewis heard me in Frisco and asked me to come to the School of Jazz, at Lenox, Massachusetts, that summer, and after that, since I felt I'd never got a chance to exist properly, to know what I truly am, I migrated to New York. Now I'm set. Or anyway, set to be set. What I'd like most now is a vacation, but I've got three musicians depending on me. I'm tired. Six hours a night, six nights a week. Sometimes I go to the club and I can't understand what I feel. 'Am I here? How will I make it through tonight?' I say to myself. I'd like to play a couple of nights a week is all. I'd have more to say. I'd get closer to harnessing my feelings, to getting down to the true essence. Well, it's time to work."

Coleman yawned, picked up his orange, and tossed it into the air.

"What are you going to do with that orange?" I asked.

"Why, eat it, man," he said, laughing. "What else? An orange is very pleasant one–two o'clock in the morning."

## Mingus

Until 1939, when Jimmy Blanton appeared, the bass fiddle had occupied the position in jazz of a reliable tackle. It had, a decade before, replaced the tuba in the rhythm section, and its best practitioners—Pops Foster, Al Morgan, Wellman Braud, Milt Hinton, Walter Page, and John Kirby—had become adept at rigid time-keeping and at itemizing the chords of each tune. These bassists also boasted tones that could be felt and even heard in the biggest groups. But they rarely soloed, and, when they did, restricted themselves to on-the-beat statements that were mostly extensions of their ensemble playing. Blanton, who died in 1942, at the age of twenty-one, abruptly changed all this by converting the bass into a hornlike instrument that could be used both rhythmically and melodically. Since then, the bass has taken over the rhythmic burdens once carried by the pianist's left hand and by the bass drum, and it has added a new melodic voice to the ensemble. At the same time, a group of Blanton-inspired bassists have sprung up to meet these new duties, and have included such remarkable performers as Oscar Pettiford, Ray Brown, Red Mitchell, Wilbur Ware, Paul Chambers, Scott LaFaro, and Charlie Mingus. All are first-rate accompanists and soloists, and all possess exceptional techniques. The youngest have even begun to wander toward the fenceless meadows of atonality. Mingus is the first modern jazz musician who has success-fully combined virtuosity, the revolutions brought about by Charlie Parker, and the lyricism of such pre-bebop performers as Ben Webster, the boogie-woogie pianists, and Billie Holiday.

Like many contemporary jazz musicians, Mingus is far more than an instrumentalist. He is a formidable composer-arranger and a beneficent mar-tinet who invariably finds, hires, and trains talented but unknown men. A big, loosely packed man of thirty-eight, with a handsome face and wary, intelli-gent eyes, Mingus is an indefatigable iconoclast. He is a member of no move-ment and vociferously abhors musical cant. He denounces rude audiences to their faces. (A recent scolding, administered in a New York night club, was tape-recorded on the spot, and has been printed in an anthology of jazz pieces. It is a heartening piece of hortatory Americana.) He unabashedly points out his colleagues' shams and weaknesses in his album-liner notes or in crackling letters to magazines like *down beat*. When tongue and pen fail him, he uses his fists. Mingus compresses all this dedication into his playing. Despite the blurred tonal properties of the bass, Mingus forces a kaleidoscope of sounds from it. However, much of the time he uses a penetrating tone that recalls such men as Foster and Braud, and that is especially effective in his accompanying, where it shines through the loudest collective passages. (It sometimes shines so brightly that Mingus, in the manner of Sidney Bechet, unintentionally becomes the lead instrument.) Mingus's supporting work is an indissoluble mixture of the rhythmic and the melodic. By seemingly play-ing hob with the beat—restlessly pulling it forward with double-time inserts, rapid tremolos, or staccato patterns, reining it in with whoa-babe legato fig-ures, or jumping stoutly up and down on it—he achieves the rhythmic loco-motion of drummers like Sid Catlett and Jo Jones. Yet he carefully fits these devices to each soloist, lying low when a musician is carrying his own weight, and coming forward brusquely and cheerfully to aid the lame and the halt. It is almost impossible to absorb all of Mingus at a single hearing. In addition to carrying out his rhythmic tasks, he simultaneously constructs attractive and frequently beautiful melodic lines. These may shadow a soloist, or they may be fashioned into counterlines that either plump the soloist up or accidentally upstage him. Mingus is a dangerous man to play with.

He is also an exhilarating soloist. The pizzicato bass was not designed for the timbres Mingus extracts from it. He may hit a note as if it were a piece of wood, getting a clipped thup. He may make a note reverberate or, rubbing his left hand quickly down the fingerboard, turn it into an abrasive glissando. Sometimes he fingers with the nails of his left hand, achieving a rattling sound. Or he may uncoop a string of whispered notes that barely stir the air. He will start a solo in a medium-tempo blues with a staccato, deck-clearing phrase, cut his volume in half, play an appealing blues melody that suggests the 1928 Louis Armstrong, step up his volume, line out a complex, whirring phrase that may climb and fall with a cicadalike insistency for a couple of measures, develop another plaintive a-b-c figure, improvise on it rhythmically, insert a couple of sweeping smears, and go into an arpeggio that may cover several octaves and that, along the way, will be decorated with unexpected accents. In ballad numbers, Mingus often plays the first chorus almost straight, hovering behind, over, and in front of the melody—italicizing a note here, adding a few notes there, falling silent now and then to let a figure expand—and finishing up with an embossed now-listen-to-this air. There are only half a dozen jazz soloists skilled enough for such complacency.

Mingus the bassist is indivisible from Mingus the leader. He conducts with his bass, setting the tempos and emotional level of each tune with his introductory phrases, toning the ensemble up or down with his volume or simply with sharp stares, and injecting his soloists with countless c.c.s of his own energy. His methods of composition are equally dictatorial and are a fascinating variation of Duke Ellington's. Mingus has explained them in a liner note:

> My present working methods use very little written material. I "write" compositions on mental score paper, then I lay out the composition part by part to the musicians. I play them the "framework" on piano so that they are all familiar with my interpretation and feeling and with the scale and chord progressions. . . . Each man's particular style is taken into consideration. They are given different rows of notes to use against each chord but they choose their own notes and play them in their own style, from scales as well as chords, except where a particular mood is indicated. In this way I can keep my own compositional flavor . . . and yet allow the musicians more individual freedom in the creation of their group lines and solos.

Most of his recent work can be divided into three parts—the eccentric, the lyrical, and the hot. His eccentric efforts have included experiments with poetry and prose readings and attempts to fold non-musical sounds (whistles, ferryboats docking, foghorns, and the like) into his instrumental timbres. The results have been amusing but uneasy; one tends to automatically weed out the extracurricular effects in order to get at the underlying music. The lyrical Mingus is a different matter. His best ballad-type melodies are constructed in wide, curving lines that form small, complete études rather than mere tunes. Their content dictates their form, which resembles the rag-time structures of Jelly Roll Morton or the miniature concertos of Duke Ellington, both of whom Mingus has learned from. But Mingus has been most successful with the blues and with gospel or church-type music. The pretensions that becloud some of his other efforts lift, leaving intense, single-minded pieces. More important than the use of different tempos and rhythms in these compositions, which repeatedly pick the music up and put it down, are their contrapuntal, semi-improvised ensembles, in which each instrument loosely follows a melodic line previously sketched out by Mingus. The results are raucous and unplaned, and they raise a brave flag for a new and genuine collective improvisation.

Mingus's most recent records—"Mingus Ah Um," "Blues & Roots," and "Mingus Dynasty"—offer some spectacular things. Most of the compositions are by Mingus and are played by nine- or ten-piece groups (a size beyond the budgets of most of the offbeat night clubs in which Mingus generally performs), which employ his collective techniques with considerable aplomb, thus pointing a way out of the box that the big band built itself into before its decline. Mingus delivers a fireside chat on the problem in the notes to the second record:

> The same big bands with four or five trumpets, four or five trombones, five or six saxophones, and a rhythm section . . . still [play] arrangements as though there were only three instruments in the band: a trumpet, a trombone, and a saxophone, with the other . . . trumpets . . . trombones . . . and saxophones there just to make the arrangement sound louder by playing harmonic support. . . . What would you call this? A big band? A loud band? A jazz band? A creative band?
>
> I'd write for a big sound (and with fewer musicians) by thinking out the form that each instrument *as an individual* is going to play in relation to *all* the others in the composition. This would replace the old-hat system of passing the melody from section to section . . . while the trombones run through their routine of French-horn chordal sounds. . . . I think it's time to discard these tired arrangements and save only the big Hollywood production introduction and ending which uses a ten-, or more, note chord. If these ten notes were used as a starting point for several melodies and finished as a linear composition—with parallel or simultaneous juxtaposed melodic thoughts—we might come up with some creative big-band jazz.

"Blues & Roots" provides several first-rate demonstrations of this approach. On hand with Mingus are Jackie McLean and John Handy, alto saxophones; Booker Ervin, tenor saxophone; Pepper Adams, baritone saxophone; Jimmy Knepper and Willie Dennis, trombones; Horace Parlan or Mal Waldron, piano; and Dannie Richmond, drums. There are six numbers, all blues by Mingus. One of the best is the fast "E's Flat Ah's Flat Too." The baritone saxophone opens by itself with a choppy *ostinato* figure, and is joined, in madrigal fashion, by the trombones, which deliver a graceful, slightly out-of-harmony riff. The drums, bass, and piano slide into view. The trombones pursue a new melody, the baritone continues its subterranean figure, and the tenor saxophone enters, carrying still another line. Several choruses have elapsed. Then one of the alto saxophones slowly climbs into a solo above the entire ensemble, which, with all its voices spinning, becomes even more intense when Mingus starts shouting at the top of his voice, like a growl trumpet. Solos follow, giving way to the closing ensemble, which pumps off into twelve straight choruses of rough, continually evolving improvisations on the shorter opening ensemble. Near the end, Mingus starts bellowing again, and then everything abruptly grows sottovoce. The trombones dip into a brief melodic aside, and the piece closes in a maelstrom, with each instrument heading in a different direction. New tissues of sound emerge in this number and all the others at each hearing—a shift in tempo, a subtle theme being carried far in the background by a saxophone, a riff by the trombones that is a minor variation on one used in the preceding chorus.

The remaining two records, which include eighteen numbers (all but two by Mingus) and pretty much the same personnel, are not as headlong. "Mingus Ah Um" has a couple of ballads, more blues, and, most important, generous amounts of the satire that is present in almost everything Mingus writes. This quality is most noticeable in "Fables of Faubus," which concentrates on two themes—an appealing and rather melancholy lament, and a sarcastic, smeared figure, played by the trombones in a pompous, puppetlike rhythm. At one point, the two melodies—one bent-backed, the other swaggering—are played side by side; the effect is singular. Mingus's needling is more subdued in pieces on Lester Young ("Goodbye Pork Pie Hat"), Ellington ("Open Letter to Duke"), and Charlie Parker ("Bird Calls"). "Mingus Dynasty" has pleasant, reverent reworkings of a couple of Ellington numbers; a somewhat attenuated selection called "Far Wells, Mill Valley," written in three sections for piano, vibraphone, flute, four saxophones, trumpet, trombone, bass, and drums; and a fresh version of one of Mingus's gospel numbers, "Wednesday Night Prayer Meeting," this one called "Slop."

Mingus has never had a substantial following, and it is easy to see why: he courts only himself and his own genius. A one-man clique, he invents his own fashions and discards them when they are discovered by others. The content of his compositions is often repellent; it can be ornery, sarcastic, and bad-tempered. His own overbearing, high-tension playing pinions its listeners, often demanding more than they can give. In earlier days, Mingus's music might have caused riots.

## The Ragtime Game

Ragtime is by no means dead and gone. Indeed, it flickers bravely on, and the principal keeper of the flame is Joseph F. Lamb, who, at seventy-two, is the last of the big three among ragtime composers, the other two being Scott Joplin (1868–1917) and James Scott (1886–1938). After I'd heard "Joseph Lamb: A Study in Classic Ragtime," a collection of ten Lamb rags, played by him and recorded last summer at his home, in Brooklyn, I called him to ask if I could pay him a visit. "Be delighted!" he shouted over the telephone. "I'm a little hard of hearing, if that doesn't bother you. Take the B.M.T. Brighton local and get off at Avenue U. I'm five short blocks away. Any time after two."

First I did some homework on Lamb, and discovered that his reputation rests on just twelve rags, published between 1908 and 1919; that he has as many or more unpublished rags, some of them written in the last couple of years; that he had known Scott Joplin; and that he was rediscovered by Rudi Blesh in 1950, when Blesh, who was doing research for his book *They All Played Ragtime*, found that "Joseph Lamb" was not, as had long been believed, a pseudonym of Scott Joplin's but that Joseph Lamb was a once-celebrated contemporary of Joplin's and was still very much alive. Thus equipped, I arrived at a little past two at Lamb's house, a small brown shingled one not too far from Coney Island.

I was greeted by both Lamb, a slight, jovial, big-voiced, bespectacled, gray-haired man with a thin face and a long, generous nose, and Mrs. Lamb, a short, pretty woman, and they ushered me into a small front room furnished with two television sets, three bamboo chairs, and a mahogany secretary. When I was seated, I asked Lamb if he had had much response to his record. "Well, it's pretty hard to fathom!" he boomed. "I've got letters from all over, and Rudi Blesh called up immediately after he'd heard the record, and said, 'It's wonderful, Joe, wonderful.' It's no fault of mine that I'm still alive, and I guess the fact I am means a lot to these people. I'm not a conceited man, but I can't say I'm not pleased about it. It's got me playing once more, even though I don't catch everything I play, because of my hearing. Since Blesh's book, I've started writing rags again, which isn't easy, either. I can hear in my head what I want to put on paper, but I can't tell if it sounds right on the piano. That record was a hell of an experience. I was all out of practice and didn't much want to do it, but Sam Charters, who made it, pestered me and pestered me, and finally he came out here on a hot day and we did it. Who ever knew that stuff was going to come back?" Lamb shook his head in bewilderment, and Mrs. Lamb, who had slipped out of the room, returned and set down a glass of apricot juice and a plate of Lorna Doones next to him.

"Something to wet your whistle!" she shouted at him.

"Well, good," Lamb said, and took a sip. "I was born in Montclair, New

Jersey, and taught myself the piano. My sisters used to tell each other, 'That Joe will be a composer. You watch.' Pretty soon I was writing two-steps, waltzes, and intermezzos—the 'Florentine Waltz,' 'I Love You Just the Same,' and 'My Fairy Iceberg Queen,' which started out as a cowboy song. In 1904, after I'd graduated from St. Jerome's College, near Toronto, I went to work in New York in a wholesale dry-goods place, and I was buying a lot of sheet music. Gimbel's and Macy's used to have seven- and eight-cent sales on it Saturdays. I found I was partial to rags, particularly the harder kind, and then Scott Joplin's 'Maple Leaf Rag' hit me good and proper. Ninety-five percent of the best rags were written by Negroes, you know, and I seemed to fall right in with their things. In 1907, I wrote my first rag, the 'Sensation Rag.' One day around then, I was in the office of John Stark, the music publisher, where I bought most of my rags. There was a colored man sitting in a corner, his foot gouty and wrapped up, and crutches beside him. I was telling Mrs. Stark how much I admired Scott Joplin and how I'd like to meet him, and she said, 'Is that so? Well, here's your man,' and pointed to the colored fellow. I don't know what I said, I was so worked up. He was my pattern in the ragtime game. We left together, and he said did I mind if he walked along with me? I was tickled to death, you can imagine. Later, I went up to his boarding house, in Harlem, and played 'Sensation' for him, and he suggested a few changes. I had a chromatic scale going up the keyboard in both hands in one place, and he said, 'Make that left-hand scale go down instead of up.' He persuaded Stark to publish 'Sensation,' and Stark gave me twenty-five dollars for it, and twenty-five more after the first thousand copies were sold. After that, Stark published the 'Excelsior Rag,' the 'Ethiopia Rag,' the 'American Beauty Rag,' and all the rest. I stopped writing rags around 1920, when ragtime went out. The stimulation was gone. I've never made any money from my rags. The satisfaction of getting them published and on the counters is what mattered to me, and still matters. I've got seventeen rags right here, unpublished, some of them fifty years old."

"If you sell them all, you'll be a millionaire, Joe," Mrs. Lamb said, and laughed.

" 'Bird-Brain Rag' is one of them," Lamb said. "Nobody likes the title. What's the matter with them? The first strain starts like a bird. Listen."

Lamb hopped up, disappeared into his living room, sat down at an upright, and played a quick five-note bird phrase.

"That doesn't sound like a bird, it sounds like a bugle call, Joe," Mrs. Lamb said, and laughed again.

Lamb returned to his chair, puffing a little, and said, "I've got all the time I need now. I retired in 1957, after forty-four years with a factoring concern in the import-export line. Who knows about ragtime? A fellow was here from N.B.C. last week and said they might do a ragtime program in the fall, and Burl Ives is helping me join A.S.C.A.P. I'm writing rags again after forty years. I get these seventeen published, I'll do seventeen more."

# David and Goliath

t is not common knowledge that *two* jazz festivals were held in Newport over the Fourth of July weekend—the multi-engined Newport Festival (seventh model) and a far
smaller wind-driven affair, Jazz at Cliff Walk Manor. Nor is it generally
known that when the dust from the crash of the big festival, which was
abruptly closed on Sunday afternoon, had subsided, the rump festival was
still going strong. Suffice it to say that the riot that destroyed the Newport
Festival was the work of amusical yahoos of college age, many of them barefoot, loutish, and overvitamined. No one involved was badly damaged,
which is miraculous when one considers this item from a long, detailed
story in next morning's Providence *Sunday Journal*: "State Police Cpl. Peter
J. O'Connell was giving orders to half a dozen uniformed state police when
he suddenly fell unconscious, struck on the nose by a flying full beer can.
He later regained consciousness and appeared not seriously hurt." Moreover, the outcome of the unofficial contest between the two festivals produced an unavoidable state of irony. The Cliff Walk Manor festival, hastily
organized a couple of weeks before by Charlie Mingus and Max Roach,
constituted a rebellion against what they claimed was the small pay the
Newport Festival accorded its lesser-known attractions, as well as against its
mastodon ways.

The Cliff Walk Manor festival was held on the football-field-size lawn of
the Cliff Walk Manor Hotel, a stucco-and-red-brick mansion high above
Easton's Beach and just three or four city blocks east of Freebody Park, the
site of the other festival, which, as long as it lasted, overlaid this one with a
steady flow of sounds. The C.W.M. festival was virtually handmade by the
musicians involved, who constructed a bandstand, decorated it in a fire-
engine red, enclosed the lawn with snow fencing, erected half a dozen tents
to sleep in, procured five hundred undertakers' chairs, issued handbills, and,
after the weekend was in progress, collected contributions from onlookers
outside of the fence. The lawn sloped accommodatingly toward the bandstand, where the musicians, silhouetted against distant Middletown, resembled figures in a vast diorama. Gulls, swallows, and an occasional helicopter
circled their heads, and the shumm-shumm-shumm of the waves below provided—especially during bass solos—a majestic background. When it
rained, as it did on Friday and Sunday nights, the proceedings were moved
into a square, airy room in the hotel. (By Sunday night, Freebody Park stood
empty and silent, and the wrangling thunderstorm that took place had an
unnerving Jehovah air.)

The C.W.M. festival had its own private ironies. Free to play as they
wished, the musicians involved—on hand all weekend, along with various
ringers, were the Max Roach quintet, the Charlie Mingus Jazz Workshop,
the Ornette Coleman quartet, the Coleman Hawkins–Jo Jones quartet, and

a six-piece pickup outfit led by Kenny Dorham—performed mainly as if the assembly-line procedures of the Newport Festival, at which most of them had appeared at one time or another, had been stamped on their souls. Sets were often limited to three or four numbers, the concerts (afternoons excepted) were too long, and the same tunes were offered over and over again. Roach's quintet played a slow, lengthy, bagpipe dirge, built chiefly around his drumming, no less than four times. The first hearing was delightful; the second was absorbing for the improvisational contrasts it afforded; the third was abrasive; and the fourth was torture. But there were corrective moments. These came when personnels were temporarily shuffled or pared down for such things as a duet by Mingus and Roach; a lengthy free improvisation by Mingus, Roach, Coleman, and Dorham; a collaboration by Dorham, Hawkins, and Jones; and a couple of Near Eastern love songs performed by Ahmed Abdul-Malik, the Roach bassist, on the oud, a large Egyptian stringed instrument.

Four notable things occurred during the opening concert, on Thursday evening. Wilbur Ware, the bassist in Dorham's group (Allen Eager on alto saxophone, Teddy Charles, Kenny Drew, and Arthur Taylor), fashioned a solo in "Lover Man" that was a masterpiece. Ware stands alone among modern bass players. His work is not patterned on that of Jimmy Blanton, but is restricted to an on-the-beat attack and singsong harmonic investigations that give the impression of someone striding purposefully over uneven ground. Later, Coleman Hawkins, accompanied by Drew, Ware, and Jones, played half a dozen choruses in "Lover Come Back to Me" (fast) and "September Song" (slow), which insinuated their way into one's marrow. In the fast number, Jones took a long solo with his hands, scraping the drumheads, snapping them disdainfully with his fingernails, and cleaving them with the edges of his palms. Baby Laurence did two numbers, backed by Mingus's group, that, with the help of a couple of microphones tilted against the front edge of the platform on which he danced, went off like machine guns.

The next afternoon was parceled among reshuffled groups, which huddled beneath two enormous yellow-and-green beach umbrellas when it began drizzling. The evening performance, which had more first-rate Hawkins and Ware, as well as a rampaging rendition by the Mingus group (Booker Ervin, Eric Dolphy, Ted Curson, and Danny Richmond) of a Mingus gospel number, "Better Git It in Your Soul," dissolved into a jam session that continued until four in the morning. (The C.W.M.'s only yahoos arrived around three, and, half a dozen strong, stood beerily about for ten minutes or so, bare feet matting the floor, peacock-colored shirts hanging out, pedal-pushers tight and wrinkled.) Abdul-Malik conversed with his oud, Roach performed a ten-minute drum solo, and Mingus and Roach engaged in a duet. This was followed by a free-for-all by Mingus, Roach, Dorham, Julian Priester (Roach's trombonist), and Coleman. It provoked Mingus into one of the best solos he has ever played, while Roach softly tapped his drumsticks together in the background. The same group, minus Priester, appeared the next afternoon, and, taking advantage of the preliminaries of the previous night, developed a totally free improvisation that lasted for nearly three-quarters of an hour. Each man soloed several times, tempos rose and fell, sea-swell interludes came and went, and the piece was closed by a long, zigzagging collective atonal ensemble. The Saturday-evening concert was embellished by the presence of Roy Eldridge, who worked with the Hawkins-Jones group, and by Ornette Coleman, who when all was said and done, emerged as the champion of the weekend. All the twenty or so numbers performed during the festival by Coleman's band, which included Don Cherry, Charlie Haden and Eddie Blackwell (drums), were by the leader and all were different. Coleman reached his peak on Saturday night in a new and lovely medium-slow number. His solo, free of the commotion he often raises in his relentless search for unknown sounds, had an affecting directness and simplicity.

The Thursday concert at Cliff Walk Manor had an attendance of ten. By Sunday hundreds were on hand. Throughout there was a catching bonhomie between all present, and this, together with Roach's emceeing, gave the event an unfailing smoothness and graciousness. Best of all, there wasn't an impresario in sight.

*Before the first (afternoon) concert, Mingus collected contributions from the still tiny audience in a derby hat he had been wearing.*

## Walpurgis Night

A lithe, compact, nervous, temperamental man with close-cropped hair and a gladiator handsomeness, the drummer Buddy Rich has had an explosive history that began on the vaudeville stage when he was eighteen months old and that has carried him through the bands of Bunny Berigan, Artie Shaw, Tommy Dorsey, Count Basie, and Harry James, through Norman Granz's "Jazz at the Philharmonic," through recording sessions with everyone from Art Tatum to Charlie Parker, and through innumerable groups of his own. Rich came into prominence in the early forties with Dorsey, ran neck and neck for several years with his principal model, Gene Krupa, eclipsed him, and in turn was set aside by the tumultuous arrival of bebop and the new school of jazz drumming led by Max Roach. Nonetheless, Rich's influence is still considerable. (Virtuosos occupy their own niches, and are rarely affected by fad and fashion.) Among others, Louis Bellson, Ed Shaughnessy, and Shelly Manne have admired him, and so have latecomers like Joe Morello, Philly Joe Jones, and Frank Butler.

Aside from his debt to Krupa, Rich's style is his own. Monolithic and commanding, Rich has an infallible beat, and the exuberance to make that beat catching. His playing is clean and decisive, and he never misses a stroke. He is a proficient ensemble man and a frequently stunning soloist. But those qualities are not enough—or, rather, they are too much. Overpowered by his astonishing gifts, Rich has become a captive of his own virtuosity. As a result, the felicities that have made less well-equipped drummers, such as Sid Catlett and Jo Jones, his superiors have been almost completely crowded out. He has little sense of taste, dynamics, and shading, and none of the elasticity essential to great drumming. His playing never changes, his solos are often militaristic and far too long, and in general he projects an uncompromising rigidity that tends to flatten rather than inspire his cohorts.

For all of Rich's energy and steadiness, he is a peculiarly dull accompanist. One reason lies in the way he tunes his drums. They give off a dry, stale sound that never blends tonally with the other instruments. Another reason is plain unimaginativeness. Instead of sympathetic timbres behind a soloist (the ocean motion of Jo Jones's high-hat cymbals, Catlett's rimshots, the sleigh-bell tintinnabulations of Connie Kay's ride-cymbal figures), one is conscious only of a metronomic deliberation. His cymbal work is light and clear, but it evaporates before it has taken effect, while his accents on the bass drum and snare are limited to thuds and implacable rimshots, fired exactly where expected. All of Rich's accompanying has, in sum, a now-is-it-my-turn-yet? air. When his turn does come, his face exhibits agony, his body contracts, taking on a ball shape, his arms blur, his drumsticks break and rocket about. For many years, there was no selectivity in Rich's solos, no chance for the listener to sort out what was happening. Recently, though, he has begun to construct them instead of merely spawning them. His best ones occur in middle tempos. He may begin on his snare with a series of I.B.M. beats arranged intensely on or near the beat (from which he never wanders far), insert cracked-knuckle rimshots and short rolls, drop Big Ben offbeats on the bass drum, intensify his snare-and-rimshot patterns, and, bringing his auxiliary arms into action, overlay these patterns with staccato cymbal strokes. Gradually, this duplex figure grows increasingly solid as he forces more and more beats into spaces seemingly already filled. By this time, his virtuosity has begun to devour him. Casting aside all that has come before, he rotates, crisscrosses, and trampolines around his set, moving with incredible speed from snare to tom-tom to cymbals to snare to cymbals to tom-tom snare cymbals cymbals snare tomtomsnaretomtomtom. . . . Walpurgis Night. High winds. Thunder and lightning. And even though what he is playing has ceased to make any musical sense, it has become the sort of high-wire exhibitionism that compels the listener to jump up and make foolish sounds. Then, a hypercrescendo is reached, and suddenly it is over. The roar drifts smartly away, the ball unfurls, the arms slip back into focus, the face smiles, and the ovation—a kind of coda to the solo itself—begins.

All that need be known about Rich can be found on two records, "Buddy and Sweets" and "Rich versus Roach." "Buddy and Sweets," made with

Harry Edison, Jimmy Rowles, and John Simmons, contains two of the best and most conservative solos Rich has recorded. (There are seven numbers in all.) These occur in "Yellow Rose of Brooklyn," which is taken at a very fast tempo, and in the medium "Barney's Bugle." In the second solo, which Rich holds down to five minutes, he pauses now and then before falling into his customary trance, and there are even a few round-the-set explosions, topped with silence, that suggest the timing of Catlett—a comparison that might not please Rich. Here is the pianist Billy Taylor reminiscing, in the oral history *Hear Me Talkin' to Ya*, about Rich versus Catlett: "Sid was a great soloist and a great showman. He was completely at home musically in whatever he was doing. I remember once on the Coast, when Buddy Rich, Dodo Marmarosa, and Buddy De Franco were all with Tommy Dorsey, they used to come into the clubs and cut everybody. [Rich] was cutting all the drummers, but not Sid. It used to annoy Buddy so much. He'd play all over his head—play fantastically—and then Sid would gently get back on the stand, and play his simple, melodic lines—on drums—and he'd make his point."

"Rich versus Roach" is rewarding for the way in which Rich's rigidity and Roach's limpidity offset each other. There are eight numbers, in which two small groups led by Rich and Roach collaborate, giving way frequently for short exchanges and full-length excursions between the drummers. Rich comes through best in the medium "Sing, Sing, Sing (With a Swing)," where he is in a nervous rimshot mood, and in the slower "Big Foot," a blues in which he matches double-time breaks with Roach. "Figure Eights" consists of four and one-half minutes of Rich and Roach trading breaks at a tempo faster than the ordinary mortal can tap his foot to. The inevitable happens. After Rich's third break, a sensational bit of broken-field running, the two men attempt to quell one another by falling into a series of buzzes—Rich: zzzzzzzzzzz; Roach: zzZzzZZZzzZ; Rich: ZZZZZZZzzZZ, and so forth. But there has been no contest; a sundial doesn't stand a chance with a clock.

# 1961

## The Rabbit Returns

The celebrated fickleness indulged in by admirers of the arts, most of whom resemble housewives selecting cantaloupes, reaches epic proportions among jazz audiences. Thus, the Original Dixieland Jazz Band, flourishing in 1920, had been largely forgotten by 1930. In 1935, King Oliver, famous less than a decade earlier, was in total obscurity. The *nouvelle vague* of Charlie Parker, Dizzy Gillespie, and Stan Kenton had, by the late forties, replaced almost completely such recent landmarks as Count Basie, Benny Goodman, Ben Webster, Art Tatum, and even Duke Ellington. This capriciousness increased in the fifties. Gillespie was abruptly set aside for Miles Davis. Basie reappeared and Kenton went under. Woody Herman, pumping furiously in the forties, became largely a memory, while a West Coast movement made up of musicians like Shorty Rogers, Shelly Manne, and Jimmy Giuffre rose and fell. Sonny Rollins burst briefly into view, then was overtaken by John Coltrane, and early in 1960 Ornette Coleman blanked everyone out. The reasons for these lightning love-hate cycles are fairly clear. Jazz thrives both artistically and socially on rebellion; indeed, it is the most liberal of musics. Until recently, its audiences have been composed mainly of the young, who relish such hot sauces. And these audiences, more unskilled than not, often train their ears only on what they are told is worthy by the jazz press, which tends to confuse newness with progress and progress with quality. One of the most striking victims of this fickleness has been the fifty-four-year-old alto saxophonist Johnny Hodges. Unlike many other swing musicians, Hodges was toppled by a double whammy. He suffered, along with his colleagues, from the rise of bebop, but he also suffered because the leader of that movement, Charlie Parker, played the same instrument. When Parker died, in 1955, Hodges had become an out-of-fashion leader of a small semi-rock-and-roll group. However, the tastemakers were at work, and by 1959 Parker's enormous ghost had been sufficiently laid to allow Hodges to win the *down beat* critics' poll, an award that paid a considerable compliment to Hodges' staying powers and none at all to the fitful perceptions of those who had voted it.

A short, taciturn man with a beak nose, heavily lidded eyes, and an impassive Oriental air, Hodges, who is known as Rabbit, has been almost perpetually bound up with Duke Ellington since 1928. (He left the Ellington band in 1951 but rejoined it, apparently for good, in 1955.) Unlike most Ellington musicians, who have unwittingly come to depend on Ellington for balance and inspiration and who generally lose their bearings when they leave the band, Hodges functions well with and without Ellington. He is most comfortable in a small band, which became plain in the late thirties and early forties on those invaluable records made by chamber groups from the Ellington band. Nearly nonpareil among Ellingtonians, Hodges has become one of the big five among saxophonists, the rest of whom are Coleman Hawkins, Ben Webster, Lester Young, and Parker. Even more important, he belongs in that small collection of jazz musicians who, lyric poets all, function closest to the heart of the music—such men as Webster, Herschel Evans, Sidney Bechet, Buck Clayton, Bill Coleman, Vic Dickenson, Red Allen, Pee Wee Russell, Charlie Mingus, and John Lewis. And within *that* collection, he has joined Bechet—who tutored him on the soprano saxophone in the early thirties, and who had a good deal to do with his ultimate style—in bringing jazz perilously close to a sentimental music.

Hodges' bent toward sweetness did not emerge until the mid-thirties, when he began recording, with Ellington, a series of slow ballad solos. On such occasions, which he still indulges in, Hodges employs a tone that seems to be draped over the notes like a lap robe. Hodges does little improvising in these ballads. Instead, he issues languorous statements of the melody and long glissandi topped by an almost unctuous vibrato. Hodges' Edgar Guest strain is generally well concealed, though, and it is nowhere in sight when he plays the blues, which have long provided his basic materials. His tone shrinks, occasionally even becoming dry and sharp, he uses more notes, his vibrato steadies, and his impeccable sense of rhythmic placement—how long to tarry on this or that note, just where to break a pause, which notes (if any) should be emphasized in a run—is put to work. In a medium-tempo blues—the speed at which Hodges most often jells—the result is a mixture of lullaby delicacy and gentlemanly emotion. Suggesting but never commanding, Hodges may start such a solo by sounding four descending notes, which are placed on successive beats and connected by an almost inaudible threadlike hum, as if he were two instrumentalists in one— the first playing the four notes and the second providing background choir chords. After a short pause, he will applaud his own natty lightness by repeating the pattern, adding a single offbeat note and increasing his volume. Then he will double his volume and deliver a soaring exclamation, which he will sustain only long enough to make it ring, and end it with an unexpectedly soft blue note. He may start this cry once more, break it off with a complex descending-ascending-descending run, and, all delicacy gone, launch into a second chorus with a short, heavy riff, which will either be repeated, with variations, or give way to several rapid staccato phrases. He will close his solo by returning to a whispered three- or four-note passage, which floats serenely at one, slips past, and offhandedly disappears. Hodges' blues solos are classic balancings of tone, dynamics, rhythm, and choice of notes. There is no extraneous matter, and no thinness. There is no opacity. It is *mot-juste* improvising, and because of its basic understatement it illuminates completely the elegance and purity of the blues. At faster tempos, Hodges relies almost entirely on his rhythmic capacities. The solos he thus achieves are often the quintessence of "jump" playing. They move on and sometimes ahead of the beat, and there is a good deal of tasteful repetition. At the same time, Hodges' rhythmic attack is mainly implied; he rolls rather than tramps toward his destination, which, in contrast to the majority of jazz soloists, he always reaches.

Hodges is in tonic condition in "Side by Side: Duke Ellington and Johnny Hodges" and "Blues A-Plenty: Johnny Hodges and His Orchestra." Of the nine titles on the first record (four blues, four standards, and an Ellington original), three were recorded by Hodges, Ellington, Harry Edison, and a rhythm section including Jo Jones. These three are notable for Hodges' strict jump choruses in "Stompy Jones" and for all of Ellington's solos, which are given uncommon lift by Jones, particularly in "Stompy Jones." Edison, despite similar assists, remains Johnny-one-note throughout, and it is difficult to see why he was matched with Ellington and Hodges. On hand with Hodges on the rest of the record are Roy Eldridge, Ben Webster, Lawrence Brown, Wendell Marshall, Billy Strayhorn, and Jones. "Big Shoe" is similar to those attractive medium-tempo blues that made up most of Hodges' small-band recordings in the forties. Eldridge, in his Sunday-best, delivers two perfect choruses bracketed between exhilarating but controlled dashes into the upper register and deep-down growls. Hodges' second chorus is largely smears. "Just a Memory" and "Let's Fall in Love," which are done in medium tempo, include gentle statements from all the horns, who demonstrate precisely how to construct solos with a beginning, a middle, and a climactic end.

Four of the nine numbers in "Blues A-Plenty," which is played by the leader plus Eldridge, Webster, Vic Dickenson, Strayhorn, Jimmy Woode, and Sam Woodyard, are better-than-average Hodges rhapsodies. He neither weeps nor moans, and in "Satin Doll" he delivers much of the melody in a blunt lower-register manner that suggests Webster. (Hodges gave Webster a graduate course in how to play lyric poetry on the tenor saxophone while he was with Ellington.) The rest of the numbers are excellent blues. Most remarkable of all is the long medium-tempo "Reeling and Rocking," which, after the ensemble, is given over to a succession of choruses by Hodges, Dickenson (following by a restatement of the melody), Webster, Eldridge, and Hodges again that are consummate lyrical jazz improvisations. Each soloist, his clichés left at home, is in peak shape, and the results are five studies in the blues that are singular for Hodges' way of seemingly attacking his notes from behind (first solo) and then for his landing on them in an almost soundless slow motion (second solo); for Dickenson's jumble of smears, growls, knucklings, and swaggers at the outset of his second chorus; for Webster's sliding, hymnlike statement; and for Eldridge's reined-in fury. This is one of those rare jazz performances that defy all faddishness, fickleness, and foolishness.

## Yes Yes Yes Yes

When I heard that Ida Cox, the legendary seventy-year-old blues singer, had been located in Knoxville after a long search, that she was still in excellent voice, and that she had been persuaded by Chris Albertson, of Riverside Records, to come to New York and make her first recording in over twenty years, I arranged to have a talk with Miss Cox before the recording session and to drop in at the studio and witness the start of her new career. On the appointed day, I went over to the Paramount Hotel, on West Forty-sixth Street, where Riverside has its offices and where Miss Cox was staying, and was ushered up to her room by Albertson, who introduced us. Tallish, straight-backed, gray-haired, and handsomely proportioned, Ida Cox was wearing schoolmarm spectacles, a smart brown dress, and red bedroom slippers, and looked at least a decade younger than her age.

"Take that nice chair in the corner, honey," she told me firmly. "And put your feet up on the bed and be comfortable."

I asked Ida Cox if she was uneasy about the recording.

"Lord, I haven't thought about it since I finally decided to do it," she replied. "At first, I felt I just couldn't. My health haven't been so good since I had a stroke in Buffalo in 1944. I walked out on a night-club floor there and it look like everything left me, everything went black. I haven't sung a note since, and I do thank God for sparing me this long. Of course, I'm here now, and I mean to do the best I can, but then I'm going back home—*whoom*, like that. I'll record some of my own blues—' 'Fore Day Creep,' 'Moanin' Groanin' Blues,' 'Cherry Pickin' Blues,' 'Graveyard Dream Blues.' I remember the words pretty well, even if most everything else—people and all what I've done in my life—it vanishes away.

"I was born in Cedartown, Georgia. When I was fourteen, I ran away and joined a minstrel show, the Black and Tan. I sang blues and ragtime songs, like 'Put Your Arms Around Me, Honey' and an old, old one I learned from my brother, 'Hard, Oh Lord.' Oh, how does that go?" Ida Cox put her hand to her forehead, sat silent for several moments, and then sang, in a quiet, clear voice, "Hard, hard, ain't it hard, Oh Lord, / To love and can't be loved. / Hard, hard, ain't it hard, Oh Lord, / To love and can't be loved." She stopped and laughed. "Now, I mean that's been *years* ago. Then I went with the Rabbit Foot Minstrels and the Florida Blossom Minstrels and into vaudeville. Jelly Roll Morton—he was a good-lookin' light-skinned boy—played for me at the Eight One Theatre, on Decatur Street, in Atlanta, and one of his tunes, 'Jelly Roll Blues,' was my first big success. I worked at the Plantation, in Chicago, with King Oliver and Louis Armstrong. Oliver was fat and plain, and almost as homely as I am. After that, I sang in every state in the Union. I had one of the most lovely colored shows on the road—a beautiful chorus line. I got to know everybody, and worked with the biggest portion of them. Bessie Smith was an old, old friend and everybody loved her, which was why they was so shocked when she died in that accident. Of course, she *did* have enemies. Who don't? She was a very high-tempered person, and she didn't take anything from anybody. But she was a good girl, on the whole. Billie Holiday, she was a fine person, too. Always smiling. But her ways were her own. That's a girl's life, it seemed to me, was just snapped away from foolishness. She was a deserving person. Ethel Waters is another dear friend, and Duke Ellington. One time, I was playing Houston, and Ellington and his band was sitting around a table out front. I went out after I was done and kissed him—just fooling, you know. When I got home, my husband like to all but knock my block off. Some crazy little things happen in your life."

There was a rap on the door, and Albertson told Ida Cox it was time for rehearsals.

I thanked her and said I'd see her at the recording studio.

"That would be nice, honey," she said. "You come, please."

The studio, on the eighth floor of Radio City Music Hall, turned out to be a spacious buff-colored room filled with microphones, timpani, bass drums, tom-toms, chimes, vibraphones, a small Wurlitzer organ, a grand piano, musicians, and interested observers. Miss Cox, a white sweater drawn around her shoulders, was seated near the piano, her hands folded placidly in her lap and a benign expression on her face, while a handful of photographers hovered about her. "Coleman Hawkins overslept," Albertson said. "We're waiting on him, and we've substituted Sammy Price on piano for Jesse Crump, who couldn't make it from the Coast." On the opposite side of the room, a loud argument was going on between Price and the rest of Ida Cox's accompanists—Roy Eldridge, Milt Hinton, and Jo Jones—about the whereabouts of Jabbo Smith.

"I saw him two years ago in Newark," Eldridge said to Price. "And he was playing trombone, too!"

"Jabbo Smith?" Price exclaimed. "Why, he's dead, man! Here, I'll bet you a hundred dollars."

"Dead? He lives in Milwaukee," Jones said. "I've got his address right in my book."

"Put up your money," Price said to Eldridge.

At this point, the studio door opened, and Hawkins, his eyes puffy with sleep, a black felt hat low on his head, walked quickly in. One of Ida Cox's blues, "Hard Times," was chosen for the first number, and after the arrangement had been sketched out, Ida Cox walked up to a microphone, tilted her head slightly back, bent her shoulders, and dropped her hands to her sides. Price played the introduction, and she began to sing, in a round, serene, low voice, while Eldridge growled distantly in the background:

"I never seen such real hard times before.
No, I never seen such real hard times before.
The wolf keeps walkin' all around my door.

"They howl all night long, and they moan till the break of day.
They howl all night long, and they moan till the break of day.
They seem to know my good man gone away."

After two more choruses of singing, Hawkins soloed and Miss Cox exclaimed, in double time, "Yes yes yes yes yes, talk to me, talk to me," and then returned to the lyric: "I'm a big fat momma, got the meat shakin' on my bones . . ."

## Sonny Greer

At work, most modern jazz musicians appear to be suffering from shock. They adopt blank, masklike faces, stand rigidly still, and rarely speak to one another, let alone the audience. The only proof they are not hallucinations is the sound that comes from their instruments, and even this isn't always conclusive. Twenty years ago jazz musicians usually mirrored every emotion they were undergoing. Drummers, in particular, went further by adding the icing of guileless showmanship. They twirled their sticks or tossed them into the air, generally in time to the music, smiled expansively or grimaced (Kansas Fields always looked on the verge of tears), snapped their heads about militaristically, and manipulated the wire brushes like skilled house painters. The three consummate showmen-drummers were Sidney Catlett, Jo Jones, and Sonny Greer. (Gene Krupa and Buddy Rich were show-offs.) Now that Catlett is dead and Greer in partial obscurity, only Jones remains consistently on view. A week ago, however, Greer, who is sixty, appeared in full bloom at a Duke Ellington Society concert given in the Carnegie Recital Hall.

Greer quit Ellington in 1951, after thirty-odd years—a departure that has left a permanent gap in the band. A flattish, dapper man with a thin, tongue-in-cheek face and a patent-leather air, Greer epitomized the easy elegance of the Ellington band. He was generally enthroned slightly above and to the rear of his colleagues, amid a resplendent array of equipment that included a couple of timpani, chimes, and a J. Arthur Rank gong. For all his outward grace and polish, though, Greer's style was and is strictly homemade. He is only a fair technician (his time is uneven, sometimes he is overbearing, and he misses strokes) and he has never been much of a soloist. Indeed, he often gives the impression that he is *testing* rather than playing his drums. He moves ceaselessly back and forth between his cymbals, sampling their centers, drops in sudden experimental offbeats on the cowbell (an unfortunately outmoded bit of drum paraphernalia), rustles his high-hat cymbals ominously and then clamps them shut with a *whussht*, inserts crescendo snare-drum rolls, sounds jumbo beats on his bass drum or settles into steady lackadaisical afterbeats on the snare rims. Greer's showmanship accents all this. A mock-serious look will dissolve into a broad smile, a wide-eyed expression into a sleepy one. An eyes-right-or-left head motion punctuates every number. After twirling a stick faster than a propeller, he may rear back in amazement at his prowess. Greer is sound and motion in miraculous counterpoint.

With Greer were Clark Terry on trumpet and flügelhorn, Hilton Jefferson, Wendell Marshall, and a ringer, Jimmy Jones, on piano. Greer's solo number was an up-tempo version of "Caravan," in which he started softly with his hands on the tom-toms, gradually increased the volume, picked up two sticks in his right hand, pitted this hand against his still-empty left hand (much rattling and whapping), tucked his sticks nonchalantly under his right arm, returned to his hands, reduced his volume, and closed with a jarring bass-drum *frump*. During the rest of the afternoon, Greer ticked off all of his tricks—wire brushes on a large tom-tom behind Jones, mallet crescendos during the ensembles, spinning sticks, and casual, offbeat rimshots. In fact, Greer managed to convey the notion that he was still supporting the entire Ellington band—insouciance, white jackets, the Duke, and all.

## Young Werther

**B**arring the blues and Duke Ellington, jazz has never bothered its head much about content. It has been far more concerned with such technical matters as improvisation, timbre, tone, attack, and, lately, form. Thus, the outstanding thing about Miles Davis is not his style but its genuine, though elusive, content. This style consists largely of carefully modulated mannerisms. In the slow ballads, Davis, using a mute, buzzes rhythmically and persistently at the melody, like a bluebottle. In the easy medium-tempo numbers, often blues played open-horn, he irregularly issues long, thick-voiced single notes that are neither quite on nor quite off pitch, brief, stabbed notes, and little broken-off runs that suggest unfinished staircases. In the fast uphill tempos, his come-as-you-are technique races along just behind his ideas, never quite catching up. The results are feminine forays into the upper registers, curiously heavy arpeggios, and a nutant melodic line. Of late, Davis has added to these approaches an almost funereal legato style in the middle and lower registers. These young-Werther ruminations most clearly reveal the content of Davis's music—a view of things that is brooding, melancholy, perhaps self-pitying, and extremely close to the sentimental. It is, except for certain aspects of Johnny Hodges and Sidney Bechet, a new flavor in jazz.

Davis's recent recordings as a soloist with various big bands led by the arranger-composer Gil Evans have had a good deal to do with this revelation. Evans is an ingenious orchestrator whose often unique and not necessarily jazzlike instrumental combinations give off a moody, caressive air. Unavoidably, Davis has taken on some of the colors and shapes of Evans' work. This was strikingly evident last Friday in Carnegie Hall, when Davis and Evans offered their first concert collaboration. The concert was something of a jumble. Five numbers were played by Davis's quintet (Hank Mobley, Wynton Kelly, Paul Chambers, and Jimmy Cobb), two were joint efforts by the quintet and Evans's twenty-piece group, and four were by Davis and the group, with Evans conducting. Davis the stylist was brilliantly visible in the quintet numbers, which included a slow muted ballad, a leisurely middle-tempo open-horn blues, and a couple of agitated up-tempo pieces, none of them identified. (A laconic, weedlike figure, Davis never lets his audiences know that he knows they're there; he neither speaks to them nor looks at them nor even plays to them.) Davis the philosopher emerged in two of his numbers with Evans. These were Evans' reworking of part of Joaquín Rodrigo's "Concierto de Aranjuez," for guitar and orchestra, and Evans' variations on a *saeta*, or Spanish folk song. In the first, which lasted better than fifteen minutes, Davis, backed by Evans's mistiest palette, improvised on the guitar part, reveling in declamatory phrases, low, round-shouldered notes, and simple embellishments of the melody, which drips with flamencan dolor. Indeed, Davis was misery distilled. The *saeta* was a short, delightful piece in which Davis, framed by marching drums, tambourines, a harp, and trumpets, issued a series of prolonged, fluttering muezzin calls with bent-note endings. Although Evans' men occasionally stumbled, they managed to sustain much of the silken roll of his music.

## Trove

There's no gainsaying that Hollywood's cheerful desecration of the arts has been all but impartial. Literature, music, and the dance—let alone the film itself—have been sterilized with equal vigor and concentration. But jazz, which didn't reach Hollywood until the late twenties, is an exception. To be sure, countless full-length burlesques of the music exist, among them those oleaginous biographies in which Danny Kaye appears as Red Nichols and Kirk Douglas as Bix Beiderbecke. Nonetheless, while Hollywood's right hand was fashioning such vaudeville items, its left hand was turning out untold numbers of invaluable jazz shorts. Though almost invariably hoked up with dancers, Uncle Toms, precious photography, and costumes ranging from bellhops' uniforms to leopard-skin togas, these films often contain excellent jazz—some of it, in fact, by groups that were never recorded elsewhere. One celebrated example is Elmer Snowden's 1932 Small's Paradise band. A disheartening number of these shorts have been lost or have simply disintegrated, but a good many others have been rescued by collectors. Recently, one of these collectors, Ernest R. Smith, a fast-talking, thirty-seven-year-old advertising executive, exhibited, as the first of three programs, eleven jazz shorts (all but two from his collection) in a small auditorium in Freedom House.

The program was opened and closed by two extraordinary films—*St. Louis Blues*, a short made in 1929 with Bessie Smith, and *Jammin' the Blues*, photographed in 1944 by Gjon Mili. Miss Smith plays what appears to be a lady of the night who is knocked down and robbed by her man. Most of her picture, which is an odd mixture of realism and soap opera, is given over to a scene in a night club, where Miss Smith, propped drunkenly but magisterially against the bar, sings a monumental version of the title song, accompanied by part of Fletcher Henderson's band and the Hall-Johnson choir—a combination that lends an operatic atmosphere to the number. (Joe Smith, Henderson's great, ruby-toned cornetist, is also visible and audible.) Parts of

*Jammin' the Blues* are arty, but the picture is largely a straightforward record of such men as Lester Young, Harry Edison, Jo Jones, and Sid Catlett playing a couple of blues and a standard. Included are superb shots of Young's lidded, moonlike face, a bassist's bony, concave fingers, and Catlett obliquely from the rear, his sequoia self swaying slowly from side to side, his left arm hanging limp, wire brush in hand.

In between these pictures, Smith ran off two Ellington shorts—*Black and Tan Fantasy* (1929) and *Symphony in Black* (1935)—that are, despite their theatrics, filled with commendable solos by Bubber Miley, Johnny Hodges, Tricky Sam Nanton, Cootie Williams, and Lawrence Brown. Moreover, in the second one, Billie Holiday sings a couple of choruses of the blues. The Ellington shorts were almost matched by a Louis Armstrong film, *Rhapsody in Black and Blue* (1932), in which Armstrong, at the height of his powers and dressed in a leopard skin, gets off a fast "I'll Be Glad When You're Dead You Rascal You" and a fascinating "Shine," sung and played in both middle and up-tempos. The rest of the evening was more absorbing sociologically than musically. Armstrong reappeared, both live and animated, in a Betty Boop cartoon, also entitled *I'll Be Glad When You're Dead You Rascal You*, which is so tasteless it is funny. (At one point, Armstrong's huge, mugging, disembodied head chases a tiny animated missionary across an endless plain.) The program was completed by five so-called "soundies," which were three-minute films made in the early forties for jukeboxlike machines equipped with small screens. Two were by Gene Krupa's band (1941–42), with Roy Eldridge and Anita O'Day, and three by Fats Waller (1941 and 1942), who, surrounded by a gaggle of beauties, rubbers and jowls his way through "Ain't Misbehavin'," "Honeysuckle Rose," and "The Joint is Jumpin'."

All but two of the fifteen or so films in Smith's second showing, which included shorts, sequences from shorts and full-length pictures, and soundies, were from his collection. The best things were often the most tantalizing. In an excerpt from *After Seven*, a short done in 1928 with Chick Webb's band, there was a single, fleeting glimpse of Webb himself—peering, tiny and spidery, over the top of his drums—and a great deal of James Barton, singing and dancing in blackface. A Count Basie short, made in 1939 by the greatest of the Basie bands, was centered on the Delta Rhythm Boys and on let's-get-it-over-with footage of the band doing three lightning numbers that included solos—and good shots—of Harry Edison, Buck Clayton, Jo Jones, Walter Page, Don Byas, and Basie, dressed in a Glen-plaid horse blanket. *Bundle of Blues*, a 1933 Ellington short, was less frustrating. Although most of the film was taken up with poetic shots of a rain-streaked window, an axe stuck in a wet stump, a slave cabin in the rain, rain on leaves, and rain on a pond, while an invisible Ivie Anderson sang "Stormy Weather" (what a good singer she was!), there were satisfying close-ups and statements from Cootie Williams, Tricky Sam Nanton, Freddy Guy, and Sonny Greer. Best of all was a 1940 short, filmed in the vanished Café Society Uptown.

Albert Ammons and Pete Johnson buffaloed their way through "Boogie Woogie Dream," Lena Horne sang a blues, exhibiting the finest teeth ever owned by a human being, and Teddy Wilson's small band (Emmett Berry, Benny Morton, Jimmy Hamilton, and J. C. Heard) played an exemplary medium-tempo blues.

The rest of the evening was either square and funny or given over to maddening snippets. The squarest moments came during shorts by Artie Shaw (1939) and Stan Kenton (1945). In the first a commentator anatomized swing ("a pounding, ensenuating rhythm") while Shaw and Buddy Rich, looking barely hatched, did a duet, and in the second a leviathan Kenton ensemble (six trumpets, four trombones, five saxophones, four rhythm) demonstrated how to play for the millennium. The snippets were sometimes dazzling: Cab Calloway shouting and shimmying "Minnie the Moocher" while Cozy Cole, Jonah Jones, Mousie Randolph, and Danny Barker graced the background; Jack Teagarden singing and playing "Basin Street Blues" in 1938 (shots of the Mississippi and the Mardi Gras); part of a 1946 "March of Time," showing the Art Tatum Trio on Fifty-second Street and an Eddie Condon group with Dave Tough, his face cavernous and haunted, his arms like thongs; and another Basie short, made by his sextet in 1950, that included two superb selections by Billie Holiday ("God Bless the Child" and a blues), and half a dozen boogie-woogie numbers by a ten-year-old prodigy named Sugar Chile Robinson.

The final showing numbered two dozen shorts, snippets from shorts, brief films done around 1950 for television, and soundies. Since Smith's collection, like all treasure-troves, has a bottom, the program was pretty raggle-taggle. There were lots of vocals by Louis Jordan, Peggy Lee, Sarah Vaughan, June Christy, Billy Eckstine (with his 1946 big band, which had Gene Ammons and Art Blakey, both of them visible), and Fats Waller, as well as instrumentals by the clean-cut, 4-H bands of Glen Gray, Buddy Rich, Larry Clinton, and Stan Kenton. But the scattered exceptions were wonderful. In a couple of 1942 Louis Armstrong soundies, done with the last of his big bands, Armstrong sang "Shine" and played a fine short solo, and the late Velma Middleton, straining the joists, sang and danced "Swingin' on Nothin'." The high points of the Armstrong selections, though, were several fleeting shots of Sid Catlett, who was between jobs with Benny Goodman and Teddy Wilson's Café Society Uptown band. A monumentlike figure behind his drums, his eyes revealing the slightly malevolent expression they sometimes assumed when he was concentrating, he could be seen, in a last glimpse, casually spinning a drumstick through the air (a blurred-moon effect) with his right hand while his left descended like an enormous fly swatter on his hi-hat cymbals. Of equal value were a number by Al Cooper and his Savoy Sultans, a semi-legendary and very hot Harlem band from the late thirties, and two short television films by Jack Teagarden (made in company with Ray Bauduc and Charlie Teagarden), who fashioned first-rate solos in

"That's A-Plenty" and "The Jack Armstrong Blues." Three kick-the-can Lionel Hampton big-band numbers (1950–52) were saved by the spectacle of Milt Buckner, a round, bespectacled frog, who played the up-tempo "Cobb's Idea" with such fervor that he cleared both the piano stool and the floor on each beat. The usual Uncle Tom effects were visible during the evening (Armstrong's "Shine" opened with two Negroes shining a huge shoe—an unpardonable visual pun, since the title of the song is simply a pejorative term for a Negro) and reached an apogee in "Sophisticated Lady," a 1951 Duke Ellington short, in which the alto saxophonist Willie Smith, who is a nearly white Negro, was shown not in the band but as a soloist standing well in front of it, his chair in the saxophone section remaining resoundingly empty throughout the picture.

Not long after Smith's film showings, I had a talk with him at his apartment, at Lexington Avenue and Eighty-ninth Street.

Once I was settled in Smith's workroom, a small, immaculate box filled with reels of film, cardboard files, huge loose-leaf notebooks, and film reference books, I asked him how he had become involved with a television show called *Chicago and All That Jazz*. Smith, who is a short, amiable, firmly built man with a soft aquiline nose and dark hair, told me that N.B.C. had approached him late in June, and that he had worked closely with an admirable woman named Helen Kiok, who was the show's film researcher. "They asked me if I knew of anything on Eddie Lang or Bix Beiderbecke or Mamie Smith," Smith said, putting out a cigarette and taking a brownie from a dish at his elbow. "I didn't, but things got started when Len Kunstadt, a jazz-collector friend of mine who lives in Brooklyn, told Helen that Tony Parenti, the clarinettist, had a home movie of Lang, with Tommy and Jimmy Dorsey, taken in a recording studio. Helen reached Parenti, but unfortunately the film wasn't used, even though it's great—Lang standing by a piano with the Dorseys off to one side. More important, Parenti said that the twenties bandleader Boyd Senter—Boyd Senter and His Senterpedes he was known as—might have some film or stills. But where was Senter? As it happened, on my way to Kalamazoo by train early last summer I had got off in Detroit and bought an apple and all the local papers—a research habit I've gotten into. This was before I'd even heard of the television show. I found a tiny ad in one of the papers: Boyd Senter and His Orchestra. When the matter of Senter came up, I told Helen about this, and she called the place in the ad, and they said Senter had just closed and gone home to Mio, Michigan. She left a message with the sheriff in Mio—Senter has no phone—and Senter called back. He didn't have anything, but suggested she contact Doc Cennardo, in California, who was a drummer with Jean Goldkette, and who had a home movie with Bix Beiderbecke on it. I flipped; I'd never heard of Bix on a film. Helen reached Cennardo, and he pooh-poohed the film, saying it was a bad print, made in 1927, in Massachusetts, and that Bix was only visible for seconds. But we looked at it, and there's Bix, in a natty suit and white socks, his cornet in the side of his mouth, playing with a bunch of Goldkette musicians. All I had on Mamie Smith was a note that mentioned a 1929 short, *Jail House Blues*. Helen looked up the copyright material in the Library of Congress and discovered that Columbia Pictures had made the film. However, Columbia, it turned out, had sold TV rights to all its early shorts to a California distributor. Helen tracked down the distributor, and, miraculously, he still had a copy of the short. But there wasn't any soundtrack. Before soundtracks were perfected, they sometimes used regular discs that were synced with the lip movements, and when John Baker heard about the film, he said he had an acetate disc that might fit it. And, astonishingly, it did. Baker mailed the record, a twelve-incher, to Helen. When she opened the package, Lord, there it was—in six perfect pie-shaped pieces! A technician at N.B.C. stuck them back together. Then they put the record onto tape, edited out the cracked sounds—over two hundred of them—and the awful surface noise, and matched the edited tape to Mamie's lip movements, with the help of the original continuity sheets, which Columbia provided in New York. The results are fantastically clear."

I asked Smith how he had started his collection.

"I've been both a jazz fan and a film fan for years. But the idea of collecting jazz films only occurred to me about five years ago, when I was helping Marshall Stearns, down at the Institute of Jazz Studies, on Waverly Place. How to start? I went to Irving Klaw's old-photographs place, on Fourteenth Street, and sifted through thousands of stills dealing with all aspects of showbiz. Then I read every issue of *Variety* from 1926 on up. In the early days, *Variety* had a column, 'Talking Shorts,' in which each new short was reviewed in detail. When I came to a mention of, say, a 'darkie jazz band' or 'dancers hotfooting it,' I had photostats made. I went through *down beat* and *Metronome*. I also went through periodicals like *Film Fun* and *Billboard*, which were even more helpful than the music magazines. I began indexing all this material, and now I have three or four thousand pages of references. I've discovered that there have been countless films made by all-Negro casts strictly for Negro audiences, and that a lot of them, terrible as they are, have jazz in them. Lena Horne was in something called *Bronze Venus* long before anyone heard of her, and Ruby Dee was in *Love and Syncopation*. I bought my first film—a Fats Waller short—three years ago, and in the last year or two I've accelerated. I spent nearly two thousand dollars last year alone on films, stills, and the like. I've begun writing a history of jazz in films, but I have so much more research to do—the Negro newspapers, the Library of Congress, the Schomberg Collection, on West 135th Street. I belong to all the film societies in New York, and every Saturday I tour all over the city, stopping at places like the Memory Shop, on Fourth Avenue, where they keep a file in my name. I look at all of the Late Late Shows on television, where things are always turning up, like *Girl Without a Room*, a Charles Ruggles picture, a while ago, in which there was a Paris night-club scene showing a

Negro band dressed in Zouave uniforms. I'm positive one of the musicians was Lionel Hampton. I've been going without much sleep since I was sixteen, and it doesn't seem to bother me."

Smith told me that he was born in Los Angeles. "My parents were on the Hungarian stage circuit that existed in this country until the Depression almost knocked it out," he went on. "In fact, my father was a kind of Hungarian Orson Welles. I didn't go to college, but I studied art in Pittsburgh and on the Coast. I joined the advertising firm of Sudler & Hennessey, where I work, in 1951. I'm an art director and a vice-president. When I first came to New York, I still wanted to paint, and I used to hang around the Cedar Street Tavern, hoping to run into De Kooning and people like that. I don't paint too much anymore. This jazz-film thing has become all-consuming. I wish it could be my whole life, but that would take more bread than I'm making now from a full-time job."

## The Call

If heaven does induce the final cooling of those fleshy turbines the emotions, then all great religious music, which is distinctly fleshy and highly emotional, is basically secular. (Most Protestant hymns, with their Babbittlike rhythms and oaken melodies, *are* religious.) Indeed, some religious music shines with evil. Consider the ominous chants and down-there brass choirs in Berlioz' *Requiem*, which reverberate through the vaults not of heaven but of hell. And consider one of the newest of religious musics, the American Negro's gospel songs. Though there is probably no more aspiring religious music being composed or performed anywhere today, gospel music, which has mushroomed in the past couple of decades, is infused by its secular relative—jazz. It is largely a vocal music, whose waltzlike rhythms, simple form and harmonies, complex phrasing, and blue notes have almost all been borrowed from jazz—an odd situation, for the Negro church abhors jazz. Bessie Smith was the progenitor of Mahalia Jackson, the supreme gospel singer. Other gospel singers unmistakably echo certain jazz instrumentalists, among them Bubber Miley and Red Allen. At the same time, modern jazz has recently reached out and tapped gospel music, and is absorbing the gospel variations of jazz devices invented a generation or two ago. Gospel music is two-way in other respects. A church music, it is now enjoyed—through recordings, the radio, and concerts—by an enormous secular audience, which includes a good many whites. Its melodies (all cut from the same charming, loosely woven cloth) and its lyrics, though often banal and even lachrymose, can be majestic in the right improvisatory hands. African in origin, it celebrates a Protestant God. Its performers, a generally devout people, are given to all sorts of ejaculatory motions, frequently behaving like vaudevillians.

Most of these crosscurrents were visible at the Museum of Modern Art a week or so ago in a concert given by Marion Williams and the Stars of Faith (Frances Steadman, Catherine Parham, Henrietta Waddy, and Mattie Williams). Marion Williams, an agile, Victorian-shaped woman, was dressed in the traditional semi-bouffant Greek robes and Germanic bun of the gospel singer (she was in white, her cohorts in green), and she spent most of the evening swaying about, marching from one side of the stage to the other, clapping her hands, presenting her profile—chin stabbing heavenward, eyes shut, and hands outstretched. Her singing, equally physical, seemed an exact reflection of her movements. Each syllable was fixed to a different note, some of the notes registers apart. In fact, Miss Williams is gifted with the irrepress-ible ambition (but not the equipment) to slip gracefully from the coloratura range down through the contralto. (Mahalia Jackson has greater technique and less ambition.) As a result, Miss Williams' high-register statements were encased in growls or tubular moans. She sang several of the twelve selections solo, four or five with her group, which chanted contrapuntally in the back-ground, and then allowed each of her singers a solo number. The best of these was "My Lord and I," sung by Frances Steadman, who has a camel's-hair contralto, a startling contrast to her background music, which resembled a treeful of starlings. The group's vaudeville bent reached a climax in the final number, when Miss Williams introduced her son, a two- or three-year-old got up in a blue suit and white shoes. While he executed bits and pieces of soft-shoe and the chorus rocked back and forth, Miss Williams marched off into the audience, arms up, chin reared, and singing at peak power. It was an exhilarating and even proselytizing moment, and if the chance had been offered, I would have answered the call on the spot.

## The Other Cheek

Legendary figures are blessed properties. They enliven us by defying life and death. They are what, one morning, we hope to see in the glass. They are imaginary pied pipers for-ever summoning us from the crown of the next hill. Yet the best legendary figures are not legends at all; they *are* what they seem. Such is Bix Beider-becke, the great cornetist, who died in 1931, at the age of twenty-eight. Archetypical, the Beiderbecke legend tells of a gifted small-town boy (Dav-enport, Iowa) who makes the big time in his early twenties, starts drinking, becomes frustrated by the chromium surroundings he must endure to make a living, drinks more heavily, loses his health, and dies, broke, of pneumonia in a baking August room in Queens. But this lugubrious chronicle, true though it is, soft-pedals the very thing that gives it backbone—Beiderbecke's extraordinary skills. For he was, unlike the majority of short-lived "geniuses," already just about complete. Had he lived, he would probably—in the manner of his close friend and peer Pee Wee Russell, who is only now reaching a serene perfection—have simply refined his playing past reproach.

The adulation that encases Beiderbecke began soon after the start of his career. (Professional adulation, that is; it has been estimated that Beiderbecke was praised in print just twice during his life. Nowadays, musicians are fitted out with a full set of adjectives before making their first record.) Beiderbecke was the sort of jazz musician who provokes vigorous imitation. Andy Secrest, Sterling Bose, Leo McConville, Jimmy McPartland, Red Nichols, and Bobby Hackett were or are faithful copies, while Rex Stewart, Frankie Newton, Buck Clayton, Joe Thomas, and Roy Eldridge appear to have divided their formative years between Louis Armstrong and Beiderbecke, who also studied each other. (Why certain jazz styles are imitable and certain are not is altogether mysterious. Lester Young, Charlie Parker, and Charlie Christian have countless facsimiles, who, in turn, have *their* facsimiles. At the same time Thelonious Monk, Pee Wee Russell, Sidney Catlett, Billie Holiday, Vic Dickenson, and Django Reinhardt appear inimitable, and not because they are any more individualistic. But good musicians do not copy their elders; they use them only as primers. Thus, Count Basie out of Fats Waller, Dizzy Gillespie out of Roy Eldridge, and Teddy Wilson out of Earl Hines.) Despite their assiduousness, none of Beiderbecke's disciples have matched his unique *purity*. They have approximated his tone, his phrasing, and his lyricism, but his mixture of these ingredients remain secret. Ample proof of this freshness is provided in a new set of reissues, "The Bix Beiderbecke Legend," which brings together fourteen numbers (two of them alternate takes) made by Beiderbecke between 1924 and 1930 with Jean Goldkette, Paul Whiteman, Hoagy Carmichael, and a group of his own.

Beiderbecke's recordings were generally made with second-rate Dixieland bands, or with small, tightly regulated oompah groups, or with the full Goldkette or Whiteman ensemble. For the most part, the musicians involved are his inferiors. The arrangements are starchy and overdressed. The rhythm sections suffer from stasis. The materials include offensive Uncle Tomming and items like "There Ain't No Sweet Man That's Worth the Salt of My Tears" and "I'll Be a Friend (with Pleasure)." Indeed, these recordings have a dumfounding insularity when one considers the contemporary output of King Oliver, Jelly Roll Morton, Fletcher Henderson, and Duke Ellington. Beiderbecke's failure to record with his peers (there are a few exceptions) was apparently due to the rigid color line that prevented mixed sessions, as well as to his own celebrated waywardness; other people generally set up his recording dates, which he simply attended. Too bad, for Beiderbecke and other white musicians often jammed with the great Negro musicians, and the results, reportedly, were awesome. (The supreme cabaret singer Mabel Mercer has said that she once heard Django Reinhardt and Louis Armstrong jamming in Paris; and Armstrong and Beiderbecke are known to have played together.) On the other hand, the desultory groups that Beiderbecke trailed into recording studios have taken on a backhanded value. They obviously made him work. In many of his Dixieland recordings, he single-handedly plumps the ensembles into shape, covers up for the rhythm sections, and solos brilliantly. Moreover, his accompanists set him off in an exhilarating fashion. The effeminate vocals, the fudgelike saxophones, the trick-dog muted trumpets, and the glacial drummers all point up and magnify his solos. He is the jewel in the cabbage. Some Beiderbecke aficionados hold that the ideal Beiderbecke record date would have included the likes of Frank Teschemacher, Eddie Condon, Joe Sullivan, and Gene Krupa. But what of a Beiderbecke session attended by, say, Armstrong, Jack Teagarden, Coleman Hawkins, Earl Hines, and Chick Webb?

Not once did Beiderbecke's uncanny tone—a carillon playing on a dry morning, an August moon over the water—go soft or sour: it shines right through the cramped, tinny recordings of the time. Beiderbecke did not *play* his notes; he struck them, as Hoagy Carmichael has pointed out. Each note hung three-dimensional in the air before being replaced by the next. He had almost no vibrato, and often used the whole-tone scale. Despite this affection for the hearty, all-American notes, he usually conveyed a minor, blues-like feeling. The dominant impression of Beiderbecke's work, in fact, was a paradoxical combination of the legato and the clenched, of the lackadaisical and the on-time, of calm and exuberance. In the way that winter summons up summer and summer winter, his hottest attack implied coolness, and vice versa. He might start a solo by sounding several clipped on-the-beat notes, allowing the tones from each note to wash at the next one. Then he would float into an air-current phrase and hang motionless for a second or two, like a dragonfly; abruptly start pumping again with a pattern of declamatory notes, each behind the beat; slide into a brief, side-of-the-mouth run, executed with such nimbleness that it seemed made up of three or four closely related notes instead of an octave-jumping dozen; and fashion an abrupt concluding upward gliss—troops being ordered to pop to. His short solos have a teasing preview quality, while his immaculately structured long statements ("Singin' the Blues" and "I'm Coming Virginia") offer overwhelming repletion—a *compositional* repletion, at that. Primarily a melodist, Beiderbecke moved steadily toward the kind of improvisation that was later achieved by Lester Young, who also liked to linger over melodic fragments, switching them this way and that to see how much light they would catch. But Beiderbecke lacked Young's rhythmic tricks and simply pushed the beat before him. (Whenever Krupa worked behind him, Beiderbecke's rhythmic stiffness disappeared, and he gained some of the flow of his Negro colleagues.) Beiderbecke's most successful recorded solos invite immediate and unerasable committing to heart. Best of all, they have a jaunty, sun's-up quality—a declaration of fun—that is not an accident of technique. Many jazz musicians use their instruments to repay life's lumps; Beiderbecke always seemed to be turning the other cheek. Although the content of Beiderbecke's cornet work remained constant, it was increasingly overshadowed by his dabbling on the piano. Somewhere along the line, Debussy and Holst, among others, had infected him, and he began composing and playing—on piano—cloudy impressionistic pieces that he supposedly felt were his most important work.

Three of the numbers on the Victor reissue are from Goldkette period, and are notable mainly for the long-lost "I Didn't Know," made in 1924, in which Beiderbecke plays a brief and inconclusive solo. In the other selections, he can be heard in the ensembles, beckoning the sheep after him. The seven items from Beiderbecke's Whiteman days are considerably more interesting. There are two takes of "Changes" (muted) and two of "Lonely Melody" (open-horn). Beiderbecke is gorgeous in all four, flashing out of the mire like a snowy egret. He demonstrates his hot-coolness in the brisk "From Monday On," as well as in "San," both of them made with Whiteman splinter groups. The last two sides, though, are invaluable. In "Barnacle Bill the Sailor" Beiderbecke is accompanied by a curious pickup band that includes Bubber Miley (not heard), the Dorsey brothers, Benny Goodman, Bud Freeman, Eddie Lang, and Krupa. There is some novelty singing, but in between Beiderbecke delivers a short, furious up-tempo explosion that reveals what he must have sounded like in the flesh. The second record, "I'll Be a Friend," has many of the same men and some equally sappy singing. However, it suddenly slips into gear when Beiderbecke appears—a derby over his horn—for a short, superbly built solo full of legato windings, gong-like notes, and casual harmonic inversions. There is a new subtlety in the solo, along with an unmistakable sense of melancholy. But this isn't surprising; eleven months later he was dead.

## Joe Thomas

The last of this season's Museum of Modern Art outdoor concerts, given by the Buster Bailey sextet, began cheerlessly. Fall was everywhere—in the escaping leaves, in the breeze, in the huddled, hooded look of the audience, which only half filled the garden. It even got into the music, a limping Dixieland played by swing musicians who have lived long enough to see their own music go out of fashion. But the evening was saved by the performances of two of Bailey's sidemen—Vic Dickenson and the renascent Joe Thomas (the trumpeter, and no relation to the tenor saxophonist). Thomas, a short man with a broad, downcast face, is one of the ghosts of jazz. Now fifty-two, he has spent the past decade in dispirited obscurity. But, even before that, Thomas, though possessed of a consummate style, was far from renowned. During the late thirties he worked with Fletcher Henderson and Benny Carter, and in the early forties with Teddy Wilson's Café Society Uptown band. From 1941 to 1946, he made several dozen often magic small-band pickup recordings. (His 1941 sessons with Art Tatum, Edmond Hall, and Joe Turner are indelible in themselves. And in 1944 he made four sides with Roy Eldridge and Emmett Berry, plus a rhythm section; Thomas effortlessly cut his two competitors.) However, bebop had arrived, and soon Thomas had vanished.

Thomas's style is an uncanny blend of Louis Armstrong and Bix Beiderbecke, with a dash of Henry Allen. His tone, darker than Beiderbecke's, is no less marvelous. It rings, it sings, it celebrates itself. It is smooth marble and empty skies. Like all flawless-toned trumpeters, Thomas is primarily a legato performer. (His many-noted opposites, Roy Eldridge and Dizzy Gillespie, have always been short on tone; they rarely stay on one note long enough for its sound to crystallize.) He often plays in half time, loafing along near the beat or well behind it. A superb melodic embellisher, Thomas uses almost no vibrato and has an unrivaled grasp of dynamics on the trumpet. He frequently *announces* the opening notes of a phrase—this is *me*, and *these* are important notes, he seems to say—and while they are still echoing, he tucks in a short, rapid *piano* run, so that loud and soft notes sound simultaneous. The *piano* phrase is followed by another, which gives way to a second announcement, and so on. The most striking aspect of Thomas's playing is its spareness and detachment. Each solo has the perfect number of notes, as well as the perfect notes. And each, while immensely warm, gives the impression of being an aloof melodic distillation. In this sort of classicism, a muffed note is as disastrous as a slightly off-pitch glissando; indeed, one clam can sink a Thomas solo. Unfortunately, this has happened more than once in the increasingly frequent recordings that Thomas has made in the past year or so, and it happened at the Museum. Nonetheless, Thomas played with an assurance that he has not shown since the forties.

Nine of the thirteen selections were Dixieland standards. Thomas was his lucent self in "High Society," "Beale Street," "Struttin' with Some Barbecue," and "Royal Garden Blues," each of which he put definitively in its place. But his best moments occurred in a slow "Don't Blame Me." His solo, splintered notes and all, was full of calm, declaratory phrases, shaded volume changes, and that tone, which made the sculptures themselves glance up in surprise. Dickenson, perhaps nerved by Thomas's efforts, was memorable, mocking his way through "Tenderly" and then settling down for a lyrical and straight—well, almost straight—version of "Basin Street" that was knotted together with a couple of spectacular breaks. Buster Bailey has long been a puzzle. Though he is technically as gifted as such contemporaries as Benny Goodman and Artie Shaw, his work has never seemed more than a flow of handsome arabesques, and in recent years this lack of content has been emphasized by pitch difficulties. The rest of the group—Red Richards, piano; Leonard Gaskin, bass; and Jackie Williams, drums—were steady.

# Abstract

Folk music is a practical art. The great body of European balladry both carried and ornamented the news. The American blues chronicle the sorrows of the Negro. The Indian *ragas* (the most refined and complex of all folk musics) celebrate certain seasons or times of day. Until the mid-forties, jazz, which since then has more or less been forced into the fine arts, was primarily a dance music. However, there's a winsome notion, which can be neither proved nor disproved, that it was also, and is, a handy reflector of its times. New Orleans and Chicago jazz embody the cheerful ingenuousness of the First World War and the twenties. The post-Depression era can be found in miniature in the bureaucratic big bands of the late thirties. (Only the blues had the stamina to record the Depression.) Bebop—lyric, nervous, *furioso*—symbolizes the Second World War, while its first cousin, cool jazz, mirrors the fake euphoria that set in soon after. The newest revolution in jazz—the music of Ornette Coleman, Cecil Taylor, Charlie Mingus, and George Russell—is uncannily topical. A largely free atonal music, it eerily reflects the mad, undecided temper of the present. This is clear in two momentous new recordings—"The World of Cecil Taylor" and "Free Jazz: A Collective Improvisation by the Ornette Coleman Double Quartet." Despite their occasional shortcomings, these recordings indicate the direction in which jazz is to go.

"The World of Cecil Taylor" is the best of the handful of utopian records that Taylor has made. It also displays a considerable advance over his first recording, a revolutionary effort set down in 1957. Taylor occupies an odd place in jazz. Leagues ahead of most of his contemporaries, he has, unlike the customary prophet, no followers, even distant ones. At the same time, he is roughly neck and neck with Coleman, Mingus, Eric Dolphy, and Russell. He is, in short, an accidental co-leader of the first great upheaval in jazz since the arrival, in the early forties, of Charlie Parker, Dizzy Gillespie, and Thelonious Monk. This movement is still nameless. It has inaccurately been called "third-stream" music. It has also been termed "space music," and, with a sigh of desperation, "the new thing." Since this music is highly abstract, why not "abstract jazz"? Anyway, abstract jazz is as far removed from bebop as bebop is from swing. An attempt to free jazz of the arbitrary rules and regulations hit upon in its earliest days (and adhered to even by bebop musicians), it sets aside tonality, the unwavering beat, the conventional chorus structure, and improvisation that is based chiefly on chord progressions. Discarded shackles are invariably replaced by new, if at first invisible, ones, and in abstract jazz these paradoxically take the form of absolute freedom. Every conceivable rhythm is used, and the tempos may be halved, doubled, tripled, or slowly accelerated or decelerated. Sometimes, in cadenza fashion, there isn't any beat at all. (The soloists in one number of a recent recording by Don Ellis simply chose their own tempos.) Improvisation is often built around a brief motif, an arbitrary row of notes, or the twelve-tone scale. Or it may be wholly free and off the top of the head. The soloists' melodic lines (usually not melodic at all) tend to be extremely long, altogether ignoring bar divisions and the standard chorus measure. The new musicians are also experimenting tonally with a variety of emanations that fall between anguished human and electronic sounds. Yet for all these neoteric methods, abstract jazz is not aimless and amoebic. The lyricism of the blues colors it, the tension-and-release patterns of older jazz are its skeleton, and it possesses the unified non-unity of all abstract art. Most important, it challenges—almost for the first time in jazz—the emotions *and* the intellect.

In 1957, Taylor's work approximated what might have happened if a gifted modern classical pianist had sat down at the keyboard and attempted to improvise whole compositions in the combined manners of Debussy, Stravinsky, and Bartók. Though this music was worked out against jazz rhythms, it rarely stated the beat, and its largely atonal substance seemed foreign, and even inimical, to jazz. Dense and dark, it offered an on-the-spot survey of contemporary classical music. Since then, Taylor has begun to digest his classical training and turn more firmly toward jazz. His playing now has breathing room, and is ten or twenty pounds lighter. Its buttonholing urgency is often transmuted into a subtle but unmistakable lyricism; some of Taylor's chords are even unabashedly blueslike. (Like all great rebels, Taylor has sniffed at the past before moving on, for his work also demonstrates a knowledge of ragtime, boogie-woogie, and stride piano.) Moreover, his present approach, as opposed to his shapeless earlier one, is a visionary attempt to fashion *each number* into an indivisible whole, just as older jazz musicians constructed an indivisible *chorus*. Taylor uses every sort of device to achieve this enlarged structure. He rarely plays in a tempo; he implies one, he nods at it, he rides slightly to one side of it. For minutes at a time, he may invent bitter, unbroken series of single right-hand notes, which fall like acid on powerful, irregular chaconnes in the left hand. He may then slightly increase his volume and play a formidable two-handed tremolo, and, lowering his voice again, issue shocking, painful dissonances, which may give way to a resounding rest and then impeccably struck chords that leap through most of the registers on the keyboard. (Taylor's technique is stunning.) Non-climactic music is flatfooted, and Taylor knows this. Each of his numbers is a true orchestral composition pivoted on one or more climaxes, which may occur at the end, in the middle, or even at the start. Indeed, his work makes Art Tatum's greatest pyramids appear hollow. Taylor is never euphoric. Each step of the way is an equal mixture of passion and thought, which, in catharsis fashion, is virtually *forced* on the listener—an exhilarating if bone-trying experience.

There are five pieces in Taylor's new recording. Three are his and two are standards. He is accompanied by a couple of holdovers from his first record—Buell Neidlinger, bass, and Dennis Charles, drums. Also present for two numbers is Archie Shepp, on tenor saxophone. Taylor has used horn players before, in recordings and in the flesh, and the results have been uneasy. Like Tatum, Taylor swallows them. Ornette Coleman has unconsciously come closest to Taylor's orchestral approach, but the two have played together just once, and briefly at that. Perhaps the only way for predominantly single-voiced instruments to match Taylor is through the kind of ensemble combinations invented by Coleman, Mingus, and George Russell. Be that as it may, Shepp is surprisingly successful. The most fascinating number on the record is an unearthly rendition by Taylor—with rhythm section only—of Richard Rodgers's "This Nearly Was Mine." Ten minutes long, it is, aside from a few ominous discords, an ephemeral series of blues-derived variations—done first arrhythmically and then with a beat—in which the melody keeps rising into view just beneath the surface and then falling away. The number swells and subsides, swells and subsides, and the lovely, inexhaustible single-note passages practically lilt, while the chordal sections are full of blue notes and Monkish dissonances. It is the sort of rare jazz performance that is constructed in layers, each more delicate and finely tempered than the last. "Lazy Afternoon," four minutes longer, is another standard, with much of the same quality, which is intensified by Shepp's two anthracite-toned solos. The number reaches a distinct climax in the middle and then gradually melts away through a long and intricately textured duologue between Taylor and Shepp. "Air," "E.B.," and "Port of Call" are more typical up-tempo excursions, full of atonal explosions, bits of ragtime, ice-breaking dissonances, and racking tensions.

An appreciable part of the success of the record is due to Charles' support. Most drummers these days either obstruct the proceedings or wander off by themselves. But Charles creates a steady, listening foundation for Taylor, whether Taylor chooses to use it or not. He even predicts some of Taylor's moves. In "E.B." he underscores perfectly a couple of Taylor phrases with the snare and bass drum, although there is no indication that Taylor is going to play those particular phrases. And at the end of "Air" there is a marvelous exchange of breaks between the two; Taylor improvises on Charles' patterns, which, in turn, are enlarged upon by Charles, and so on. Neidlinger is one of the handful of skilled young bassists who have appeared in the past several years, and he plays with a sympathy and inventiveness that seem to radiate Taylor's work.

Ornette Coleman is working toward the same goal as Taylor but from the opposite quarter. Taylor is a well-schooled classical pianist whose use of atonality and free improvisation is conscious and academic; Coleman is a self-taught musician whose methods are mostly intuitive. In fact, Coleman considers such devices as the thirty-two-bar chorus, the old-fashioned beat, and chord-based improvisation artificial. He does not merely improvise on a tune, he improvises on what he regards as its essence—rhythmic, melodic, tonal, or lyric. He writes most of his materials (they begin roughly where Thelonious Monk's stop), and, putting the cart before the horse, designs each number to provoke a specific attack. Some of Coleman's works are pure rhythmic exercises, constructed of many-noted figures that move rapidly up and down the scale. In performance, Coleman may handle one of these by exaggerating its rhythmic structure, by playing it backward, by distilling it within a single phrase, or by pressing the entire composition into a rhythmless legato statement. Other Coleman numbers consist of long, graceful melodic lines based on the blues. He will rummage mercilessly through the emotions inherent in such numbers, so that we get a lament on loneliness or racial injustice or plain Sunday melancholy. Still other Coleman compositions are hinged on tonal aberrations or peculiarities of pitch, which he investigates—no matter how unearthly the sounds—to their limits. In short, Coleman thinks of a number not as a melody sewn to a set of chords but as a specific musical state of mind. At first hearing, he sounds inflexible, crude, and even brutish. His tone appears thick-thumbed and heavy. He plays insane and seemingly purposeless runs. His intensity is apoplectic. But once Coleman's ground rules have been absorbed, the strange timbres and dervish rhythms become less imperious and even tend to point up the blueslike passages and snatches of often beautiful melody that occur more frequently than one had first thought. Most important, Coleman's work is bound tightly together by a passion associated more with the Romantic composers than with jazz. However, his music is not Lisztian; rather, it falls in that zone where compassion is levelheaded and sound of heart.

Unlike the great prima donnas of swing and bebop, who are basically soloists, Coleman belongs with Mingus, John Lewis, Jimmy Giuffre, and George Russell, all of whom place equal emphasis on collective interplay and soloing. As a result, Coleman has made his various quartets (himself, a trumpeter, a bassist, and a drummer) into seamless units that nonetheless sport an individual daring comparable to that of most Mingus groups. His dissonant "unison" ensemble figures are treated with aplomb, and during the solos the accompanists simultaneously counterpoise and interpret what the soloist does. "Free Jazz" is an attempt to magnify these achievements. Its instrumentation includes two trumpeters (Don Cherry and Freddie Hubbard), two reeds (Coleman and Eric Dolphy on bass clarinet), two bassists (Charlie Haden and the late Scott LaFaro), and two drummers (Billy Higgins and Eddie Blackwell). Moreover, it consists entirely of a single, unbroken free improvisation (no key, no chords, no theme, no time limits) that lasts just over thirty-six minutes. The astonishing result is the longest jazz recording ever made. Like Cecil Taylor's improvisations the number is an unbroken whole, and it goes like this: brief introductory ensemble; Dolphy's solo (five minutes); ensemble; Hubbard (five minutes); ensemble; Coleman (ten minutes); ensemble; Cherry (five minutes); ensemble; Haden (two and a half minutes); ensemble; LaFaro (two and a half minutes); ensemble; Blackwell (two and a half minutes); ensemble; Higgins (two and a half minutes); closing ensemble. The tempo is roughly medium—roughly because Blackwell and Higgins, who, like the bassists, play together throughout, do not keep a level four-four beat but revolve arbitrarily around a kind of rolling, overlapping de-dat-de-dat-de-dat-de-dat shuffle rhythm. The only written parts of the number are the ensembles, which vary from typical Coleman patterns to short bursts. But there are other collective passages. During the solos, the remaining horns occasionally move in behind for group improvisations that may increase in intensity and volume until the soloist becomes totally enmeshed, or that may simply reach a loud mutter and fade away, returning the soloist to the rhythm section. These collective outbursts operate both as help-meets for the faltering (Cherry is the only one who gets into difficulty, and the resulting assistance is so warm it almost sends him under for good) and as celebrations for the superior (these occur half a dozen times during Coleman's memorable statement). They also go directly back to King Oliver's Creole Jazz Band, and in places they even bear a nightmarish resemblance to the neolithic brass-band recordings made in Alabama in the fifties by Frederic Ramsey.

The contour of "Free Jazz," though largely accidental, is just about right. The first ensemble opens with an avalanche of scales, which are quickly ironed out into a soaring legato figure, which, in turn, is followed by Dolphy's solo. Dolphy maintains this uplands feeling remarkably well; Hubbard, pretending here and there that he is Miles Davis, dissipates it somewhat; and Coleman gradually and casually brings it to the highest point on the record. Cherry follows, rather fumblingly, and the elevation slowly decreases through the bass and drum solos before being momentarily heightened in the brief final ensemble. (A longer and more complex closing ensemble, which might have been improvised rather than written, would have tied the entire number together more satisfactorily; its present ending has a disquieting midair quality.) Coleman's solo is the best he has recorded. Barring a few dicey arpeggios and "Night on Bald Mountain" screeches, it is mainly a series of blues phrases, some of them reminiscent of the plow-and-mule alto-saxophone playing you used to hear in the thirties on "city" blues records. These phrases disarmingly develop an emotional momentum that becomes nearly unbearable by the time the releasing connective ensemble comes along. But the bassists come close to Coleman, and together attain remarkable lyricism. (LaFaro, a brilliant bassist, was killed in an automobile accident in 1961, at the age of twenty-five. His solo, and Haden's, are perfect epitaphs.) Haden begins with half-time single notes (LaFaro runs up and down in the high register behind him), to which he adds a sitarlike vibrato. He pauses, and, strumming his instrument like a guitar, shifts into flowing tremolo chords (the drummers hustle into a kind of oblique double time, with brushes on their snares), which gradually separate until the chords fall on the beat, behind the beat, and finally are barely sounded, while LaFaro and the drummers imperceptibly allow *their* lines to dissolve. An abrupt ensemble discord restores order, and LaFaro opens his solo with high, rapid single notes (Haden plays harplike figures behind), which are slowly transposed into beautiful flamenco chords. A poignant Django Reinhardt single-note passage follows (Haden is now in a straight four-four beat, and the contrast is stunning), culminating in fast, ascending runs that are so explicit they take your breath away. The drummers' solos (each man backs the other) are almost as good, and Higgins is particularly impressive in a statement made up wholly of rising and falling cymbal splashes dotted with snare offbeats.

"Free Jazz" causes earache the first time through, especially for those new to Coleman's music. The second time, its cacophony lessens and its complex balances and counter-balances begin to take effect. The third time, layer upon layer of pleasing configurations—rhythmic, melodic, contrapuntal, tonal—becomes visible. The fourth or fifth listening, one swims readily along, about ten feet down, breathing the music like air.

## Sabbatical

When life becomes nothing but a bowl of clichés, how many young and successful people of non-independent means have the resilience and backbone to withdraw completely from the world and reorganize, refuel, retool, and refurbish themselves? Well, there is one such heroic monk—Sonny Rollins, the thirty-one-year-old tenor saxophonist. In the summer of 1959, Rollins, finding himself trapped between burgeoning success and burgeoning displeasure with his playing, dropped abruptly and voluntarily into oblivion, where he remained until recently, when he momentously reappeared at the Jazz Gallery, with a quartet. At the time of his self-banishment, Rollins was, among other things, the most influential tenor saxophonist to come along since Lester Young and Coleman Hawkins; the unofficial head of the hard-bop school; and one of the first of the now plentiful semi-abstract jazz improvisers. As a result, his Return—rumored for months—took on a kind of millennial air, which I got caught up in several days before the event by interviewing the Master himself. A tall, broad-shouldered, thin-waisted man who resembles a genie, Rollins has a shaved head, a long, lemon-shaped face, slightly Oriental eyes, a generous nose, and a full, non-pointed goatee. He was wearing, from the skin outward, a gray turtleneck sweater, a blue-and-white-striped button-down shirt, open at the neck, and a handsome blue-gray V-neck sweater, above gray slacks. This ensemble was rounded out with shined black space shoes, a black porkpie hat with a medium brim, and a gabardine overcoat.

I asked Rollins why he had decided to retire and whether his sabbatical had been a success. "People are not doing things as well as they can do them anymore," he replied. "The par of products is not high enough, and in 1959 I felt that way about my playing. The extraneous things had gotten in the way of it. I didn't have time to practice, and I wanted to study more. I was playing before more and more people, and not being able to do my best. There was no doubt that I had to leave the scene, and it was just a matter of when I could bring it about. I'd lost the ability to play what I *wanted* to play every night without the interference of emotionalism. I was filled with question marks. Also, as a leader, you have to keep the audience. You have to think about those people, and you have to fill the image the critics make of you. At the same time, you have to maintain your product. There is an almost invisible line there. But I'm no longer nervous about those things. I don't read the critics anymore. Something I want to know, I go and ask a musician I respect. I'm bringing a whole new understanding to the scene. If no one comes to the opening, if they don't like me, if they rush out—I'm prepared for all those contingencies, and they would not influence me adversely."

Rollins looked at a white handkerchief he was holding in his right hand. "I've been practicing and practicing," he continued. "When I quit working, I tried to revise the way I played the horn. Completely. But then I amended that. Instead, I have made an exploration of the horn. I practiced at home all day at first, but I was conscious of bothering people. There's a law that allows me to play from seven to eleven, if I don't overdo it. But I was very loud. There was a girl next door who was having a baby, and I was anxious to see if my playing would give that baby bad ears. I was anxious to see how it would be born, what effect my playing would have. But it turned out a very beautiful child. You go near it, it laughs. It listens. Then I discovered the Williamsburg Bridge, which is near where I live, and I stopped practicing at home. I started walking over the bridge, and I found it's a superb place to practice. Night or day. You're up over the whole world. You can look down on the whole scene. There is the skyline, the water, the harbor. It's a beautiful scene, a panoramic scene. The bridge offers certain advantages that can't be duplicated indoors. You can blow as loud as you want. It makes you think. The grandeur gives you perspective. And people never bother you. I saw the same people almost every day. Sometimes they stopped and listened, sometimes they just went by. New Yorkers are very sophisticated. When I wasn't on the bridge, I studied piano, harmony, and counterpoint with Max Hughes, who's from Frisco. I've also tried to improve my health. I've quit smoking. Every now and then I goof off for short periods, but by and large I've licked the habit. I've cut down on drinking, and I lift barbells every day. I walk and walk. I have to have good lungs and quick fingers. The whole country needs exercise, and I feel if I keep in shape other people will see me and they'll do it. My wife and I have gotten along all right. We have a very modest apartment, and she's been working, and I've received royalties from records and tunes. I even taught a little at the end—after I got to where the question marks stopped."

Rollins wrapped the handkerchief tightly around his right hand. "I was born right here, and I was forced to take piano lessons at eight, or around there. I didn't like it. But I had a musical ear, and I used to hear my brother practicing violin. And my sister played the piano. Later on, a friend of mine who had a tenor sax had his picture taken with it. It all looked *so* nice. It inspired me to get a horn—an alto. I listened to Louis Jordan a lot. I mean he gassed me. He had the first of the little blues bands, like what Ray Charles has now. Coleman Hawkins influenced me after that, and I started playing the alto like a tenor, using a tenor reed. Then I switched to tenor, and people said I sounded like an alto. I started jobbing around, and made my first records in 1948. I worked with Charlie Parker—he solidified things, the linear approach and the chord approach—and later with Max Roach and my own groups. My new group will have Jim Hall on guitar. I want to do more things with harmony, and he'll give me the framework. He's an excellent soloist. But it's most important he's willing to do things for the good of the group. He has an attitude to work *for* the group. I'll also have Bob Cranshaw, who's very, very good, on bass, and Walter Perkins on drums."

Rollins stood up, folded his handkerchief carefully, put it in his pocket, and shook hands with me. "I've got to walk my dog, and then we practice at two o'clock. I'll miss the bridge, but I've got to begin to get this group tight."

Rollins' opening at the Jazz Gallery made it clear that the only differences between the old Sonny Rollins and the new one are that he is even better now and that he suddenly sounds— and this isn't meant pejoratively—rather old-fashioned. The self-criticism that led to Rollins' sabbatical without pay was pretty rarefied, for his playing appeared, if anything, to be steadily improving. His once mannered and querulous tone had become larger and freer, his singular thematic-rhythmic approach to improvisation was a constantly changing delight, and he had perfected an awesome authoritativeness that permitted him to hypnotically play entire numbers a cappella. These virtues have simply been intensified in the renascent Rollins. His playing, edged with even more wit and sarcasm, has become almost unbearably personal. This is not to say that Rollins, in the sentimental catchphrase, "tells his story" through his horn. Instead, he creates sounds that mirror precisely his formidable personality and that are played in such a way as to be well-nigh evangelistically stamped on the listener. Whether one is willing or not, one becomes Rollins' follower each time he picks up his horn. Rollins' new, seeming old-fashionedness is not his doing. During his absence, Ornette Coleman and Eric Dolphy arrived with an attack that goes a step or two beyond Rollins' semi-abstract one. Rollins, however, understands Coleman and Dolphy (he once played early-morning duets with Dolphy on a Pacific beach), and perhaps in time he will beat them at their own game—if, that is, he decides it is worth playing at all.

Rollins' tone is hard when compared to that of Chu Berry, Ben Webster, or Coleman Hawkins. But it is the hardness of muscle, not stone—a warm hardness. Like those of Ornette Coleman and Cecil Taylor, Rollins's solos, free of the rule-sticks of measures and choruses, are in each case an attempt to fashion an indivisible composition. They are also free of dependence on chord structures and ordinary four-four time. Rollins, however, is kinder to his listeners than Coleman and Taylor. In the course of a solo, he will return repeatedly to the theme or rhythmic motif on which it is based, placing signposts in the snows of his variations. But he is never straightforward. Frequently, the theme he improvises on is itself a variation on the original melody, and whenever he goes back to this theme he varies it still further, though always leaving it recognizable. As he delights, he teaches. Rollins' favorite materials are usually standards done in medium tempos. He will play one chorus of the melody, and the amount of pressure he applies to it may depend on his attitude toward the tune or toward life in general. If the world appears askew or the tune in need of improvement, Rollins will slyly and sardonically slur certain phrases, end others with abominating smears, and inject ridiculing rhythms. After this introductory chorus, which forces the listener to hear the original melody in a curiously objective way, he will invent a short variation on it and devote several choruses to taking this variation painstakingly apart, rebuilding it, taking it apart again, rebuilding it differently, and so forth. Often he will do this with series of single notes separated by speaking silences and suspended in an almost rhythmless void. He will sound some notes experimentally, barely touching them, hold others expressionlessly for several measures (Rollins' vibrato is sparing), and cut the rest off abruptly. Here and there, he will stir in fast, urgent runs. Or he may play whole swatches of the melody, stretching them, contracting them, and turning them over and over in whatever inner winds possess him. All this is done with unflagging wit, with the parodist's sense of corrective admiration. At the same time, Rollins' personality dominates the musical aspects of these displays, filling each note or fragment or phrase with a distinctive, almost moral flavor. Rollins, in short, is the true stylist—form and content handsomely locked in each other's embrace.

Last week, Rollins gave the second "Jazz Profiles" concert of the season at the Museum of Modern Art. His group consisted of Jim Hall, Bob Cranshaw (bass), and Albert Heath (drums), and the program, not unexpectedly, included five standards and two Rollins originals, one a blues. For the first half of the concert, something—worries, the weather, the surroundings—was too much with Rollins, and he sounded strained and apprehensive. The tempos themselves were indicative. "Oleo" and "Will You Still Be Mine" were recklessly fast, and Rollins largely slid over them, using more notes than there was space for, and never allowing any of them to settle to the bottom of the listener's mind. There were exceptions in the medium-tempo "Gone with the Wind," which Rollins opened with a long and marvelous ad-lib passage and closed with a parody of one of those swelling, periwigged Coleman Hawkins

codas. And in a slow "Sentimental Mood" he bent Ellington's melody affectionately out of shape, using low, nearly derisive notes and lemony smears. But
it was an unsettling hour or so; the dampers were shut, the lights too bright.

Knute Rockne must have been backstage during intermission, because
the second half of the evening was exultant. The first number, "Love Letters," was taken at a medium-slow tempo, and had a classic, mocking first
chorus by Rollins, who, through exaggeratedly legato half-time phrases and
heavy choke-toned notes, seemed to drag the melody out of its very shell.
His solo was full of double-stops and breathless figures that moved from the
highest register to the lowest. "I'm Old-Fashioned" was given over to Hall,
and then the group played a twenty-minute fast blues, "Sonnymoon." After
a brief ensemble riff, Rollins arranged a sparse, severe tableau of notes,
allowed these to gradually multiply and grow swaggering (Rollins paying his
particular brand of respects to Hawkins, Lester Young, and Charlie Parker),
and then passed into chorus after chorus of semi-atonal passages, possibly
aimed at Ornette Coleman. He must have put together thirty choruses—different, startling, and funny. Hall, whose background chords were brilliant,
followed manfully, and the piece ended with a brisk round of four-bar
exchanges. Once a placid, timid, and somewhat academic guitarist, Hall has
perfected his rhythmic and harmonic sense, and, unlike his contemporaries,
he never glosses over his notes. Two-thirds of his solos were good, and the
rest exceptional. Cranshaw is a Wilbur Ware student, and Health an attentive, if nervous, drummer.

## Cheers for Red Allen

The preeminence of Louis Armstrong from 1925 to 1935 had one unfortunate effect: it tended to blot out
the originality and skill of several contemporary trumpeters who, though
they listened to Armstrong, had pretty much gone their own way by 1930.
These included, among others, Bobby Stark, Joe Smith, Jabbo Smith (no
relation), Bill Coleman, and Henry (Red) Allen. Stark and Joe Smith are
dead. Jabbo Smith, a scarifying musician, lives in Milwaukee and performs
rarely. Coleman, in Europe, still displays much of his grace. But Allen, the
most steadfast of the three, and a distinct influence on Roy Eldridge, who
taught Dizzy Gillespie, who taught Miles Davis, and so forth, is playing
(usually in New York) with more subtlety and warmth than at any other time
in his career. This is abundantly evident in two fairly recent and rather odd
releases, "Red Allen Meets Kid Ory" and "We've Got Rhythm: Kid Ory and
Red Allen," in which Allen, lumped with second- and third-class musicians,
plays with a beauty and a let's-get-this-on-the-road obstinacy that transform
both records into superior material.

A tall, comfortably oval-shaped man of fifty-four, with a deceptively sad
basset-hound face, Allen, born in Algiers, Louisiana, has had a spirited

career, despite the shadows he has been forced to work in. He played briefly with King Oliver in 1927, and two years later he joined Luis Russell, another Oliver alumnus. Russell's band was possibly the neatest, hottest, and most imaginative group of its time. It was also, thanks to Russell's arrangements and rhythmic innovations and to Allen's already exploratory solos, a considerably advanced one. In 1933, Allen joined Fletcher Henderson, with whom he continued his avant-garde ways, and after a period with the Blue Rhythm Band he came face-to-face in 1937 with Goliath himself when he became a practically silent member of Louis Armstrong's you-go-your-way, I'll-go-mine big band, a group kept afloat by Sid Catlett, J. C. Higginbotham, Charlie Holmes, and the leader. Since 1940, Allen has led a succession of often excellent small groups, which have included Higginbotham, Edmond Hall, Don Stovall (alto saxophone), and Alvin Burroughs. Allen's recording activity has been prolific; he was particularly active during the thirties, when he set down fifty or sixty numbers with small groups, some of which were unabashed attempts to make money ("The Miller's Daughter Marianne," "The Merry-Go-Round Broke Down," "When My Dream Boat Comes Home") and some of which were, and are, first-rate jazz records ("Why Don't You Practice What You Preach," "There's a House in Harlem for Sale," "Rug Cutter's Swing," "Body and Soul," and "Rosetta").

Allen's style had just about set by the time he joined Russell. There were traces in it of Oliver and Armstrong, but more apparent were its careless tone, its agility, and a startling tendency to use unprecedentedly long legato phrases and strange notes and chords that jazz musicians hadn't, for the most part, had the technique or courage to use before. Allen's playing also revealed an emotion and a partiality to the blues that often seemed to convert everything he touched into the blues. But his adventurousness and technique weren't always in balance; he hit bad notes, he blared, and he was ostentatious. Once in a while he would start a solo commandingly and then, his mind presumably going blank, would suddenly falter, ending his statement in a totally different mood and tenor, as if he were attempting to glue parts of two unmatchable solos together. By the mid-forties, Allen's work had, in fact, turned increasingly hard and showy—he fluttered his valves, used meaningless runs, and affected a a stony tone—and this peculiar shrillness continued into the fifties. Then, six or so years ago, Allen made a pickup recording with Tony Parenti, the clarinettist, and, not long after, one with Higginbotham, Coleman Hawkins, and Cozy Cole, and a remarkable new Allen broke into view. Perhaps sheer middle-aged physical wear—a reluctance to *blow* so hard, a reluctance to try and *prove* so much—was the reason. Or perhaps he had been listening to younger and milder trumpeters like Miles Davis and Art Farmer. For his tone has become softer and fuller, he shies away from the upper register (he spends a good deal of time inflating sumptuous balloons in the lowest register), his customarily long figures are even longer, his sensuous, mid-thirties affection for the blues has again become dominant, and he often employs harmonies that would please Thelonious Monk. In short, he gives the impression not of hammering at his materials from the outside but, in the manner of Lester Young and Pee Wee Russell, of transforming them insistently if imperceptibly from the inside. The results, particularly in slower tempos (the old shrillness sometimes recurs at faster speeds), can be unbelievably stirring. An Allen solo in a slow blues may go like this: He will start with a broad, quiet, shushing note, pause, repeat the note, and, using almost no vibrato, fasten two more notes onto it, one slightly higher and one slightly lower, pause again (Allen's frequent use of silences is another new aspect of his work, as is his more expert use of dynamics), repeat and enlarge the second phrase a little way down the scale, and, without a rest, get off a legato phrase, with big intervals, that may shatter into a rapid run and then be re-formed into a dissonant blue note, which he will delightfully hold several beats longer than one expects; he then finishes this with a full vibrato and tumbles into a quick, low, almost under-the-breath flourish of half a dozen notes. Such a solo bears constant re-examination; it is restless, oblique, surprising, lyrical, and demanding. It seizes the listener's emotions, recharges them, and sends them fortified on their way.

The pairing of Allen with the venerable Kid Ory is curious, to say the least. Allen is a modernish swing musician, and Ory is one of the last representatives of genuine New Orleans style. His solos are gruff paraphrases of the melody, while Allen's are intricate temples of sound. Moreover, Allen's leisurely, independent melodic lines are far too spacious to fit within the limitations of the New Orleans ensemble. But perhaps all this is to the good. Ory's sandpaper tone and elementary patterns tend to set off Allen's house-top-to-housetop swoops, and since Allen can't, or won't, adapt himself to the ensemble, he simply solos throughout most of the recordings, which gives us twice as much of him. By and large, the first of the Verve records is the better. Of the seven numbers, all standards, three—"Blues for Jimmy," "Ain't Misbehavin'," and "Tishomingo Blues"—present Allen at his peak. In fact, his single-chorus solo in the slow "Blues for Jimmy" is faultless. This is nearly true of his work on the Waller tune, which is full of blue notes and wind-borne figures. (Puzzlingly, neither of the two vocals is by Allen, who, in addition to his other merits, is one of the handful of true jazz singers. His voice is in between Armstrong's and Jelly Roll Morton's, and because of its almost feline, back-of-the-beat phrasing it has long foretold his playing of today.) The second session contains seven more standards, which are notable for Allen's playing in "Some of These Days," in which he tries a few teetering but generally successful auld-lang-syne upper-register handstands; for, in "Christopher Columbus," his muted chorus, which is followed by an open-horn one that begins in his lowest, or trombone, register; and for his three remarkably sustained choruses in the medium-tempo "Lazy River."

The rest of the band stands around and watches, so to speak, and only the drummer, Alton Redd, gets in the way.

# 1962

## Problem

Unfortunately, philosophers and theologians, while urging the pursuit of perfection, do not tell us where to turn once that state is reached. Consider the Modern Jazz Quartet, which is ten years old and, to all intents and purposes, perfect. Collectively, the group has no peers, past or present. It exudes tact, understanding, sympathy, and a loyalty that conceals all inward friction, if any. Indeed, its members, having attained a utopian selflessness, listen to each other more than to themselves. When they serve as soloists—Milt Jackson and John Lewis are the principal ones—the M.J.Q. exhibits the same checks and balances. Lewis, an epigrammatic pianist, balances Jackson's Byronic ways, while Jackson softens Lewis's spareness. Percy Heath and Connie Kay offset or buoy up Jackson and Lewis, as the need may be, while keeping one another in full play. But the M.J.Q. is not merely a performing group. Like the old Ellington band, it is an extension of its repertory, much of which has been contributed by Lewis. This repertory includes fugues, rondos, miniature concertos, thirty-two-bar standards, waltzes, blues, laments, program pieces, little suites, and even carols. It also changes continually. Certain pieces, as old as the group itself, now bear almost no resemblance to their original form. Some have been expanded, many more have been endlessly refined and polished. Others, not up to such pressure, have been replaced by new and often superior material. But this admirable compositional and improvisational elasticity may not save the group from its technical proficiency. New blood, not blue blood, preserves old families.

A week or so ago, at a concert in Town Hall, the M.J.Q. made a tentative and unfruitful attempt to solve what may be unsolvable. In three of the numbers, a trumpet (Freddie Hubbard), a tenor saxophone (Jimmy Heath), and a trombone (Curtis Fuller) were added to the group. (The M.J.Q. has taken on occasional single ringers in the past, and with mixed results. Jimmy Giuffre dissolved into the group, while Sonny Rollins, at his most sarcastic, came close to demolishing it. The group's infrequent experiments with the enlarged instrumentation demanded by third-stream music have been more successful.) The outcome was curious. The quartet—Kay in particular—seemed oppressed by the visitors, and the visitors appeared frightened by their hosts. The added horns, none of them first-rate, obscured the delicate ensemble interplay of the group, and were outshone in their solos by

Lewis and Jackson. To be sure, it was pleasant to hear such Lewis melodies as "Odds Against Tomorrow," "Django," and "Two Degrees East, Three Degrees West" spelled out loud and clear by horns. But this much was only superficial; part of the appeal of Lewis's work, as we have come to expect, is to hear what the M.J.Q. will do with it. There was a second, if lesser, innovation during the evening. The group played, in addition to its customary selection of Lewis pieces and standards, two originals by outsiders—"Lonely Woman," by Ornette Coleman, and "Why Are You Blue?," by a young West Coast composer-arranger named Gary McFarland. Coleman's melody has an opaque, keening quality, and the M.J.Q., perhaps out of sheer awe, tended to be smothered by it. Or perhaps the group, accustomed to trimming and sharpening its materials over a period of years, has not yet digested it. The group displayed, rather than played, the number. McFarland's tune, an attractive, more accessible affair, was given a sure, relaxed rendition. It was the sort of thing, indeed, that might have been written for the M.J.Q.

The rest of the concert, undiluted and unalloyed, was flawless. There were a very fast "How High the Moon," which has slowly grown into a solo vehicle for Jackson; several of Lewis's *commedia dell'arte* pieces, performed with a lot more gristle than is usual (a couple of them were intricate and outright rhythmic studies, and to hell with the gentle melodies); some ingratiating Lewis ballet music, done with equal push; several blues; "God Rest Ye Merry, Gentlemen"; and a ballad. Lewis coined fresh aphorisms in nearly every number, and Jackson, a passionate and romantic performer whose chosen instrument is just not up to transmitting his vigor and inspiration, was especially orotund. Heath has become the M.J.Q.'s All-American center. And Kay got about as much color and dynamics out of his drums as is possible. He shifted constantly between his four exquisitely pitched ride cymbals. (Most young drummers have one or two, and they generally sound alike.) He used finger cymbals, his hands, and the metal loops on his wire brushes in place of sticks. He was never obtrusive, never retiring. In short, he provided the sort of infectious, steadily expanding beat that his model, Sidney Catlett, is still celebrated for.

*It turns out that Kay's exquisitely pitched ride cymbals were chosen by Lewis, who imparted this information some years later, after Connie Kay's death. It's not surprising that Kay rarely answered his telephone until it had rung at least twenty times—probably because he feared it might be John Lewis suggesting still another shopping trip to the Zildjian cymbal factory up in Quincy, Mass.*

## Masterly Milquetoast

Two of the most elusive and fascinating jazz pianists are Count Basie and Duke Ellington. Though dissimilar stylistically, they have much in common. They are the last of the great graduates of the school of Harlem stride pianists founded by James P. Johnson, furthered by Fats Waller, and presided over now by such elders as "Willie the Lion" Smith and Luckey Roberts. They are, like most stride pianists, irresistible ensemble pianists, who with their left hands alone can make any band pick up its bed and run. Despite their proved skill as soloists, they are outrageously modest and have steadfastly refused to consider themselves first-rate solo performers. Accordingly, each has recorded just one album of piano solos (with rhythm accompaniment), and once every blue moon has been persuaded to sit in with recording groups, generally with excellent effect. Finally, each is a witty and original stylist. But here the similarities cease. Basie's style is a rhythmic study in rests, occasionally broken by simple right-hand chords or single notes so judiciously placed and sparingly chosen that they suggest impeccably worn jewels. It is stride piano edited, honed, and rubbed into a laconic, semi-comic shape one never tires of. It is Hemingway minus the "truly"s, "and"s, and "good"s. Ellington is twice as adventurous. He has taken the Harlem style apart and rebuilt it, with Gothic flourishes, into an infinitely more imposing structure. He has replaced the ump-chump ump-chump of the left hand with startling offbeat chords and generous basso profundo booms. He has added populous dissonances and far-out chords. And into these he has worked crooked arpeggios—directionless, seemingly drunken ones—and handsome upper-register necklaces of notes that poke harmless fun at James P.'s often lacy right-hand garlands. As such, Ellington's piano style has had a good deal of subtle influence, particularly on Thelonious Monk and Cecil Taylor; it takes iconoclasts to hear one.

It was, then, a pleasant shock when it was announced that Ellington would appear for the first time in a concert as a solo pianist, an event that took place in the Museum of Modern Art last week. Regrettably, Ellington hid for most of the evening—behind his unfailing graciousness, behind his compositions, and behind his accompanists, Aaron Bell and Sam Woodyard, who appeared in the second half of the concert. In the first half, Ellington set forth, in perfect cocktail-piano fashion, six of his more unfamiliar pieces—"New York City Blues," "Blue Belles of Harlem," "The Clothèd Woman," "Reflections in D," a selection from the "Deep South Suite," and "New World A'Comin'." It was a swooning, impressionistic performance that magnified the numbers' virtues and blurred Ellington. After the intermission, Ellington at last gave the impression that he was about to let go. He played several inspiriting choruses of "Take the 'A' Train" (this part of the program was mainly given over to the works of Billy Strayhorn), and then, changing his mind, gradually handed over the proceedings to Bell and Woodyard, who were allotted a number apiece. (Bell is an accomplished, tonally uncertain Blanton admirer; however, Woodyard, a handsome man who sings a steady song of appreciative grunts and exclamations while he plays, sometimes tends to be a caricature of a drummer.) Ellington raced through his customary medley of old pieces, and, again hinting at concealed riches, closed with a delightful "Dancers in Love" that was full of sly, uppity stride-piano figures. After this he retired into his stage presence, disarmingly stating that he was no match for Waller, Tatum, Johnson, etc., and left the stage.

*Of course, Ellington the pianist emerged brilliantly when he accompanied his own band—prodding soloists with disconcerting, far-out chords, rumbling behind a lazy trombone section, out-Monking Monk when the spirit was on him.*

# Mechanic

The Fletcher Henderson Story: A Study in Frustration," which contains sixty-four numbers recorded between 1923 and 1938, is somewhat like reissuing Dr. Johnson's *Dictionary*. Both Henderson's band and Johnson's work were seminal affairs, both were training schools, both were widely copied, both had serious faults, and both, despite their considerable period appeal, are outdated. At the same time, the Henderson album unintentionally reaffirms the theory that the most lasting music of the big-band era, which began around 1925 and ended during the Second World War, was provided not by the big bands but by countless small swing groups. Though obscured by the bluster of the larger groups, these thrived in the thirties and early forties. A few were permanent or nearly permanent groups, others were drawn from the big bands for informal recording sessions. The full-time small bands were led by Red Norvo, Joe Marsala, Roy Eldridge, Bunny Berigan, Stuff Smith, John Kirby, Adrian Rollini, Frankie Newton, and Fats Waller. The best of the myriad recording groups were organized by Teddy Wilson, Mezz Mezzrow, Red Allen, Lionel Hampton, Sidney Bechet, and various Ellington sidemen, or appeared under names like the Kansas City Six, the Chocolate Dandies, and the Varsity Seven. The small Goodman and Artie Shaw combinations were both in-the-flesh and recording groups. The recordings made by all these bands generally followed these patterns: arranged ensembles–solos–arranged ensembles, or solos–arranged ensembles, or solos–jammed ensembles, or unadorned solos. Some groups were miniature big bands, others were purely improvisatory. Most important, the recordings were relaxed and impromptu; they abound in clams, exhilaration, and sterling solos. There are two ever-lasting exceptions to this small-swing-group theory—the big bands of Duke Ellington and Count Basie. Both resembled small groups, though in different ways. Ellington used massed instruments only to set the tone or melody of a piece, and tightly blended his instrumental sections, or parts of them, with his soloists. One was conscious not of size but of continually shifting play of melodies, textures, and colors, in which the soloists and ensembles had a kind of familial relationship. There was no military display, no bunched redcoats potting away at the soloists. The Basie band achieved its lightness and seeming smallness through simple, often poignantly played ensemble riffs, which were handed around with a casualness and lack of emphasis that buoyed up the frequent solos. Moreover, the Ellington and Basie bands had unique, easily identifiable styles. Henderson's band, on the other hand, was big, noisy, imitable, and peculiarly flavorless. It was the sort of thick-waisted assemblage that invites weighing and measuring. Indeed, Henderson, along with Don Redman and Benny Carter, who wrote his arrangements before he himself took over, invented the big band, and was more or less responsible for designing the pantheon later inhabited by—among countless others—Goodman, Shaw, Cab Calloway, Glen Gray, the Dorsey brothers, Charlie Barnet, Woody Herman, and Stan Kenton. But Henderson also invented a problem—successfully skirted by Ellington and Basie, and presently under consideration by Charlie Mingus—that neither he nor any of his imitators solved before the big-band era collapsed: how to squeeze ten to fifteen jazz musicians into a wasteless and flexible jazz unit.

A calm, tall, poised man with a pleasant, bland face, Henderson was born in Cuthbert, Georgia, in 1898, of parents who were teachers, and died in New York in 1952. He attended Atlanta University, where he majored in chemistry, and in 1920 headed for Columbia and post-graduate work. (Many of the Negro bandleaders of the late twenties and early thirties came from similar backgrounds; fortunately for jazz, it wasn't as easy for even educated Negroes to find jobs as bus drivers and the like as it is now.) Henderson, an easygoing follow-your-nose soul who had been taught piano by his mother, fell into music, and formed his first band in 1923. The rest of his career was equally rudderless. He was a fair-to-poor businessman, a spotty disciplinarian (his often great and ingeniously chosen sidemen eventually became a collection of prima donnas who were frequently tardy, heavy-drinking, and quarrelsome), and the kind of man who regards opportunities as insults. Toward the end of the twenties, Henderson suffered severe injuries in an automobile accident, which apparently converted him from a relaxed man into a lazy one. As a result, he never quite reached the top, and after a fitful decade and a half as a bandleader, he went into semi-retirement. However, Henderson did succeed, in an ironic fashion. In 1935, he began writing arrangements for Goodman. It was an indenture that lasted well over a decade and that had much to do with Goodman's fame. For Goodman's band was largely a popularization of Henderson's, down to the very solos. It is hard, in fact, not to think of Goodman's band as the Benny Goodman–Fletcher Henderson Orchestra.

Henderson was more of a talented accidentalist than an originator. His first band had, like the large white dance bands that had preceded it, nine or ten men and an instrumentation of two trumpets, one trombone, two or three reeds, piano, banjo, tuba, and drums. It employed brief solos and arrangements that alternately sighed and bumped along on fashionable clarinet trios and two-beat now-you-hear-us, now-you-don't rhythm sections. Then, in 1924, Louis Armstrong joined the band and Don Redman began to take hold. Redman's arrangements sidestepped New Orleans polyphony and served up smooth, melodic variations written for specific sections of the band and often set in call-and-response patterns. And Armstrong's imaginativeness completed the shift from an imitation white dance orchestra to a jazz band. Between 1925, when Armstrong departed, and 1930, the band began collecting superior soloists like Joe Smith, Rex Stewart, Benny Morton, Jimmy Harrison, Tommy Ladnier, and Bobby Stark. It also collected Benny Carter, as an arranger, alto saxophonist, and clarinetist. Carter's arrangements were in many ways the most accomplished ones Henderson ever used. Carter wrote limber, seemingly improvised passages for the reeds and light, complementary brass figures, all of which were immeasurably helped by a steady four-four beat and the substitution of the guitar and string bass for the banjo and tuba. Henderson's own arrangements, which began coming off the presses in quantity after Carter left, were far more formal. The sections shouted stubbornly at one another or were mixed in colorless voicings. They called for more instruments, and those instruments called for even more instruments. But Henderson's arrangements, along with those of his younger brother Horace, achieved considerable polish (though also predictability) and served as the latticework for the magnificent soloists who continued to file in and out of the band—Claude Jones, Cootie Williams, Red Allen, J. C. Higginbotham, Dickie Wells, and (in the last years) Roy Eldridge, Chu Berry, Sid Catlett, Emmett Berry, and Ben Webster. Stark stayed on until 1933 and Coleman Hawkins until 1934, and Walter Johnson, who—Chick Webb excepted—was the first of the big-band drummers, was with Henderson almost continually from 1928 until the end. The band reached two peaks—between 1932 and 1934, and briefly in 1936.

But even in these years something was missing. The foursquare arrangements, though adept, were dull and gray, and were often executed accordingly. Unlike those used by Ellington and Basie, they seemed unrelated to the soloists; they filled the ears and they filled space. The puzzle of what to do with the twelve and more instruments slowly accumulated through the years was met simply by pressing them into four regiments, which exchanged riffs and fragmentary melodic variations or marched stoutly together, parting here and there to let a soloist through. Yet the soloists *were* the Henderson band, and it is Red Allen, Eldridge, Hawkins, Benny Morton, Claude Jones, Benny Carter, Rex Stewart, Joe Smith, J. C. Higginbotham, and Bobby Stark who provide the excitement in Henderson's recordings. To be sure, it has frequently been pointed out that Henderson's band almost never came through properly on records. And barring the solos, many of the numbers in the album do have a stale, time-clock air. Some are even pallid. But there are exceptions—a very fast "Chinatown" (1930); Carter's arrangement of "Sweet and Hot" (1931); Horace Henderson's "Hot and Anxious" (1931), in which some of the riffs that became "In the Mood," "Swingin' the Blues," and "One O'Clock Jump" are three-dimensionally on view (Henderson *was* a star-crossed man); Horace Henderson's "Comin' and Goin' " (1931), with exemplary Stark and Morton solos; the various "King Porter Stomp"s (1932, 1933), which are—some of the solos included—the Goodman band to come, and which reveal Hawkins entering his great middle period; Horace Henderson's arrangement of Hawkins's "Queer Notions" (1933), a fascinating, semi-atonal avant-garde piece, with solos to match by the composer and Red Allen; and the celebrated 1936 "Christopher Columbus," "Stealin' Apples," and "Blue Lou," all of them brilliantly dominated by Roy Eldridge and Chu Berry.

Most of the drawbacks in the reissue are unavoidable. The sound of the pre-1930 records is generally sandy and remote, though it is better than on the original 78s, and there is a complete blank between 1933 and 1936, and for a good reason: five celebrated sides, made under Horace Henderson's name for English Parlophone in 1933, were unavailable for the album, as were the sixteen or so superior numbers set down the following year for Decca and Victor. Accordingly, the accent in the album falls rather heavily on the early academically-interesting-only years. (However, none of the first-rate small-band efforts made in 1930 by the Chocolate Dandies, who were drawn from the band, are included.) The set is rounded off with a sizable booklet, which has good photographs and an excellent account of Henderson's career by Frank Driggs. There is also a brief memoir by John Hammond, who, as Henderson's friend and as the head of Columbia's current reissue program, deserves high commendation for restoring the master machine that produced the machines that eventually ate it.

## Slow Sleeper

Until the late twenties, the trombone was the clown of jazz. In the ensembles it was used to plug holes, provide comic smears and asides (Kid Ory's "Muskrat Ramble" celebrated these functions), and anchor the trumpet and clarinet. It was an infrequent and unsteady solo instrument, and was limited to whiskey-baritone paraphrasings of the melody. Then the big bands, two or three trombones strong, came along, and by 1930 first-rate trombonists who could both read and improvise were everywhere. Among them were Miff Mole (largely a small-band performer), J. C. Higginbotham, Dickie Wells, Benny Morton, Jimmy Harrison, Claude Jones, Sandy Williams, and Jack Teagarden. Harrison, who died in 1931, is generally thought of as the first swing trombonist. To be sure, he helped shape Williams, Morton, and possibly Jones, but Higginbotham and Wells were already on their respective trapezes (if Higginbotham listened to anybody, it was to Mole), and when a fully formed Teagarden arrived in New York, in 1927, he astonished everyone, including

Harrison. The big bands began to disappear in the mid-forties, and Bill Harris and Trummy Young became the bridge between the older men and bebop, which produced J. J. Johnson and Kai Winding, fine technicians who figure-skate rather than improvise. Among the younger men, who are faced with the mists of abstract jazz, only Willie Dennis, an apoplectic performer, and Jimmy Knepper, who has learned from Johnson and the likes of Higginbotham, are attempting to expand the possibilities of their instrument. (Bob Brookmeyer, like Ruby Braff and Gerry Mulligan, is an accomplished neo-swing musician.) As a result, when one wants to hear a *trombone*, one turns to Vic Dickenson, who emerged in the late thirties, or to Ellington's Lawrence Brown, to Morton, and particularly to Teagarden, who is fifty-six, and who reached perfection before the present generation was born. (Wells and Higginbotham are waning. Williams has retired, and Mole and Jones are dead.)

Teagarden's career has been a marathon scramble. From 1921 until his arrival in New York, he jobbed around the Southwest with the pianist Peck Kelley and the songwriter Willard Robison, and then existed largely on recording dates before he joined Ben Pollack, in 1928. He left Pollack in 1933, starved briefly, and was hired by Paul Whiteman, who housed him for four or five years. Teagarden then formed his own big band, a talented and unsuccessful group that moved back and forth across the country until its leader, weary of nursemaiding fifteen-odd people around, gave it up, in 1947, and joined Louis Armstrong's All Stars. He stayed for four years with this disheveled, bejeweled group, which also included Barney Bigard, Earl Hines, and Sidney Catlett. Since then, he has led an adept small band of his own. Teagarden is often lumped with Eddie Condon and the Chicago boys, but he is really a lone wolf who has worked with dance bands and swing bands of all sizes as well as with neo–New Orleans and –Dixieland groups. His style, equally unclannish, apparently sprouted whole out of the Southwestern soil. (He was born in Vernon, Texas.) For Teagarden has said that his influences, if any, were Bessie Smith, Negro church singers, and Indian music he heard as a boy in Nebraska.

A tall, handsomely constructed man, Teagarden has a square, rocky, Indian face (he is of Germanic descent), topped by black, patent-leather hair, and a casual, smiling demeanor. (Once, asked why he slept so much, he replied that, like most Southerners, he was a slow sleeper.) His trombone style is chiefly marked by a nasal, bright-gray tone and an apparent insouciance which conceals iron principles. It is a unique style, which has not changed, except for steady but microscopic refinements, for nearly three decades. Indeed, it is impossible to think of a poor Teagarden vocal or solo. Teagarden has developed a sustaining set of mannerisms—lazy glissandos, abrupt, change-of-pace triplets and runs, and an occasional hoarseness of tone—that offer a seemingly bland façade. But Teagarden demands close listening, for he uses these devices in oblique, shifting combinations that invariably catch one off balance. In short, he seems to have in mind a sort of

Platonic master solo, from which he adapts the solo he actually plays—a subtly accented variation. He will open a slow blues in the low register, hold the note just long enough to snare the listener, slide quietly into the middle register (while blending in a few up-and-down configurations), then, increasing his volume slightly, move even higher, and fall away into a hoarse blue note. Then he may shift into a rapid, soft-shoe series of triplets, pause for the first time, and shape a declamatory phrase, reach swiftly upward again, and drop softly back to his starting point. It is a poured rather than a played solo, done so offhandedly that one doesn't realize its technical wizardry until a second or third hearing. His ballad numbers receive the same gentle reshufflings, and so do his up-tempo statements, which come closest to letting the constant emotion inside his work into the open. His reluctance to rant and weep in public has made Teagarden one of the few genuinely cool jazz musicians. When he leaves the middle range, uses a vibrato, alters his volume, or fashions a coda, he does these things in a gloved way. The results are painless, graceful, and never slick.

Teagarden's superlative singing is a direct extension of this coolness. Although his baritone voice, which has deepened considerably in the past ten years, is strikingly close to his trombone, it is smoother and almost completely legato in style. Indeed, Teagarden's slurred, rubbing delivery of lyrics suggests that he is trying to abolish consonants in favor of a new, vowels-only language. At the same time, his singing has both the unobtrusive amiability of a Bing Crosby and a singular behind-the-beat jazz intensity. He neither moans nor shouts; instead, he undersings, flattering the ear and forcing one to listen.

Teagarden's recent recordings have done him little justice. He has been laced into tight Dixieland bands and plastered down with strings. He has used exhausted materials and appeared with exhausted musicians. Some of these things are true of his newest efforts—"Chicago and All That Jazz!" (done just before the television show of the same name) and "Mis'ry and the Blues: Jack Teagarden and His Sextet." Teagarden is weighted down in the first recording with Joe Sullivan, Eddie Condon, Jimmy McPartland, Bud Freeman, and Gene Krupa. But he rises easily. On the first half of the record (he is heard only briefly on the second side), he plays marvelously in a slow blues, "Logan Square," and sings three classic choruses in it; solos well in "Chicago"; sings another classic chorus in "After You've Gone"; and begins a magnificent chorus of "China Boy," then is abruptly replaced by another soloist.

The second record, done with Teagarden's own group, is a far sweeter affair. Aside from King Oliver's "Froggie Moore Blues," the "Dixieland One-Step," and the "Basin Street Blues," which Teagarden sings and plays as if he had just discovered it (he and Glenn Miller wrote the lyrics in 1929, and Teagarden has probably sung them five days a week ever since), the record consists of a couple of charming Willard Robison tunes, "Don't Tell a Man About His Woman" and "Peaceful Valley," and out-of-the-way numbers by Seger Ellis and Charlie La Vere. Teagarden sings in six of the ten numbers and solos in all but one. He is effortless, inspired, and technically perfect. His restrained and helpful accompanists include Don Goldie (a Charlie Shavers admirer whose father played trumpet with Teagarden in Whiteman's band), Don Ewell, and Barrett Deems.

## Third-Stream Music

I recently talked with Gunther Schuller, the thirty-six-year-old Castiglione, who is, among other things, composer and chief prophet of "third-stream" music (six compositions); composer of atonal classical works (over thirty of them, including orchestral, chamber, and vocal compositions); French-horn player (two years with the Cincinnati Symphony, fourteen with the Metropolitan Opera, eventually as its first horn); teacher (horn and composition, for both classical and jazz students); editor (M.J.Q. Music, Inc., a music-publishing firm); music critic (jazz, classical music); lecturer; conductor; author (*Horn Technique*, a book on the art of playing the French horn, and an untitled, unfinished analytical history of jazz); and music commentator on radio (a weekly program on WBAI-FM). When I arrived at Schuller's apartment, on West Ninetieth Street, I was greeted by my host, who is tall and slightly stooped, and resembles a kindly, unself-conscious John Barrymore. He said that he was finishing a session with a student, and showed me into the living room, which was filled with music manuscripts, records, rolls of tape, books, heaps of papers, music stands, musical instruments, and a couple of barn-door-size loudspeakers. When the student, a pretty Negro girl horn player, had left, Schuller, who looked somewhat haggard and was dressed in a bright checked shirt, olive-drab corduroy trousers, and moccasins (no socks), sat down and leaned intently forward, and I asked him how he managed his nonagonal existence.

"Oh, it's hell in terms of my private life," he said, and laughed. "I used to teach twenty-five hours a week, and now I've cut down to ten. I have just four horn students left, but jazz musicians come to me a good deal for advanced training and I seldom have the guts to turn them down. There aren't many teachers who know both jazz and advanced techniques of classical music. I've just come back from a three-week trip to Europe, and, God, it was marvelous! Seven countries! A new piece of mine, 'Contrasts,' was given its world première at the Donaueschingen Festival, in West Germany. The whole German music scene is outrageously chauvinistic and outrageously avant-garde, and I guess I'm the first American ever commissioned by Donaueschingen. I also lined up outlets for M.J.Q. Music and hunted all over for European jazz musicians for the International Jazz Festival, which is being sponsored by the President's Music Committee in Washington in the spring. I didn't get into Poland, where a big festival was going on, and where Friedrich Gulda was appearing as a jazz baritone saxophonist. But I found a superb Yugoslavian trumpeter in the Dixieland tradition and a good Miles Davis–type Swedish trumpeter." Schuller leaned back and laughed again.

"What about the third stream?" I asked.

"I coined the term as an *adjective*, not a noun," he replied, hunching forward excitedly. "I never thought it would become a slogan, a catchword. I hit upon the term simply as a handle, and it has achieved a kind of pompousness and finality that are totally inaccurate. This music is only *beginning*. I conceive of it as the result of two tributaries—one from the stream of classical music and one from the other stream, jazz—that have recently flowed out toward each other in the space between the two main streams. The two main streams are left undisturbed, or mostly so. I'm often criticized for trying to *force* classical music and jazz together. But this is nonsense. There will always be jazz musicians who have absolutely no knowledge of classical music, and classical musicians and composers who abhor jazz. But if a person has been exposed to both streams honestly and thoroughly, it's bound to show up in his creative products, and those of us who see this possible alignment have the great privilege of working toward it. I conceive that sooner or later the musical public will have more awareness of this situation. I see it beginning everywhere. Kids in universities where I speak think nothing of playing a Charlie Parker record right after *Eine Kleine Nachtmusik*. Third-stream music is a stylistic question more than anything else. The main differences between jazz and non-jazz are the improvisation and the naturally based and intuitive inflections of jazz. The new music is, in part, a process of joining jazz inflections and phrasing to the more set phrases and techniques of non-jazz. The point is, though, to have the two approaches occur *simultaneously*. Up to now, they have usually been linked *alternately*. There are many other problems. The improviser has to fit himself to the composer, and the composer to the improviser. When Ornette Coleman performed my 'Abstraction,' he already knew my non-jazz music, and I had listened closely to him. He had given me a wonderful sense of freedom, because his horizons are so wide. I hope that classical music will get from jazz a spontaneity and naturalness of phrasing that it no longer has. Of course, contemporary classical music *is* becoming more improvisational. It's different from the kind of improvisation you get in jazz, though—less melodic, and more concentrated on ensemble textures and the like. But then ninety-eight percent of the classical musicians simply don't have the sense of timing that jazz musicians have. All those ragged ensembles and sloppy notes! When I write a run of eighth notes for a violin section, I generally get back in performance about a tenth of what I've written. Centuries of abuse have brought this about. I'm convinced that in baroque music the performers had good timing. They had to have it."

I asked Schuller to tell me how his career had got started.

"My father has been a violinist with the New York Philharmonic for thirty-eight years," he said. "I heard music from the day I was born. I absorbed a fantastic amount of music. I remember sitting in the bathtub with my brother when I was only six and the two of us singing the whole *Tannhäuser* Overture together and imitating all the instruments. I started school in Germany, and when I came back, at eleven, I had a good boy soprano's voice, and was sent to the St. Thomas Church Choir School. They discovered there that I could sight-read like a whiz. When I started studying music, it was a process not of learning the cold and new but of recognizing things that I had known subconsciously all along. My first instrument was the flute, which I took up in my early teens. My father, who never pushed me, said whatever you do, don't play the violin. Violinists were starving to death in New York then. One of his friends in the orchestra suggested he try me on the French horn. Wind players—particularly American ones—were still terribly scarce. So I studied horn for two years, and at sixteen I quit school and got a job with the Ballet Theatre Orchestra, at a hundred and twenty-five dollars a week. I never went back to school, and have no diploma of any kind. I joined the Cincinnati Symphony the next year, and made my début as a soloist and a composer with my Concerto for Horn and Orchestra. I was nineteen. I was hired by the Met in 1945 and left in 1959. I got interested in jazz in Cincinnati, when I first heard Duke Ellington. It was a stunning experience. I made entire scores of Ellington recordings—things that had never been completely annotated before. If I could work full-time on my book on jazz, I'd finish it in three or four months; as it is, I turn down quite a few commissions for composing. We know all about *who* made jazz but not *how* and *why*. My first chapter is an investigation of what happened here in the nineteenth century, and I hope it will blast things wide open. I studied A. M. Jones' extraordinary two-volume work on African music, and I've used his findings—he's made complete scores of pieces that go on for hours—in examining, say, the slave songs first published in America in 1863. The results are quite astonishing. African music is the most complex and sophisticated music in the world, and jazz is—or was, in its primitive stages—a simplification of its polyrhythmic structure. Jazz is now heading back toward this complexity. I've gone through the Folkways Records catalogue and found things like three girls down South singing a strange little song that is practically identical with one recorded about ten years ago in equatorial Africa. I'm on the track of the origin of the blues, which may have started in India and traveled through the Arab countries, and then to Spain and/or to Africa and on to the Caribbean and New Orleans. I've got masses of material all ready to put on the page, but the time—where is the time?"

## Non-Spectrum

The First International Jazz Festival, sponsored by the Music Committee of the President's People-to-People Program, and recently held in Washington, was one of those paternal-visionary affairs designed, according to the official program, "to provide national recognition of jazz through the creation of a Festival in the nation's capital which will explore the full spectrum of jazz and indicate its influence throughout the world." Of the ten main events six were peripheral—a program of symphonic jazz, a jazz liturgical service, a gospel-music program, a jazz ballet, a program of "jazz for a young audience," and a chamber concert showing the supposed influence of jazz on classical music. Three of the rest were, aside from other faults, largely inaudible; straight jazz programs, they were held in the Washington Coliseum, a small, barrel-vaulted Madison Square Garden with the acoustics of the Penn Station concourse. And the last, devoted to small groups, was, give or take a few performances, merely dull. Woven throughout these ten were incidental appearances by the remarkable Eureka Brass Band, of New Orleans; a continuous showing of jazz films at the National Gallery (including Gjon Mili's "Jammin' the Blues" and Bessie Smith's "St. Louis Blues"); and a display at the Smithsonian of jazz memorabilia—photographs, old records, books, posters, paintings, drawings, one of Lester Young's tenor saxophones, and the prehistoric cornet that Louis Armstrong played in the Colored Waifs' Home, in New Orleans.

What this cornucopia failed to produce was good journeyman jazz, of whatever school. Thus, the Dave Brubeck quartet and the Charlie Bell ensemble were present, but the Modern Jazz Quartet was not; George Russell and a Dadaist named John Benson Brooks were there, but Ornette Coleman, Cecil Taylor, and Charlie Mingus were not; the jazz ballet, performed by Lee Becker and a group of ten or twelve dancers, with the great Baby Laurence tacked gratuitously on, was chosen in place of Al Minns, Leon James, John Bubbles, Honi Coles, and Pete Nugent; swing was represented by Lawrence Brown, Harry Carney, and Johnny Hodges (present as members of the Ellington band), and, in just four numbers, by Ben Webster and Roy Eldridge, but Pee Wee Russell, Red Allen, Coleman Hawkins, Benny Carter, Jo Jones, Vic Dickenson, Jack Teagarden, Benny Morton, Buddy Tate, and Doc Cheatham were absent; Dinah Washington and the Clara Ward Singers were on hand, but Jimmy Rushing, Mahalia Jackson, and Joe Turner were not; the international note was struck by Chris Barber (from England) and the Wreckers (from Warsaw), instead of by Martial Solal (from France). In short, almost every performer had superior ghosts peering over his shoulder.

Probably the most contrived spectacles were the jazz ballet and the evening of symphonic jazz. The ballet, which consisted largely of decorous bumps-and-grinds, was accompanied partly by musicians and partly by records, and now and then an Abstract Expressionist painter, Paris Theodore, appeared and whipped off an inspirational work on a huge canvas with black paint and a ten-foot brush. Baby Laurence, in trim condition, thankfully danced by himself to two Charlie Parker records and again, for twenty seconds or so, in the finale. The symphonic-jazz evening was sweltering (Constitution Hall) and often pompous. The National Symphony Orchestra was onstage, and so, at various times, were the Duke Ellington band and such instrumentalists as Don Ellis, Ron Carter, Eddie Costa, Charlie Persip, and J. J. Johnson. Ellington and the N.S.O. played his "Night Creature" (1955), a three-part descriptive piece, notable principally for the marvellous caricatured boogie-woogie bass at the beginning and end of the second movement. Costa, on vibraphone, read his way through a short, metallic concerto for the instrument by André Hodeir, and the program closed with J. J. Johnson's "Scenario for Trombone and Orchestra," a porous jumble of Tchaikovsky effects, Spanish melodies, Gil Evans orchestrations, and brief rhythmic passages. The single worthwhile event during the evening was a shortened version of James P. Johnson's "Yamekraw," written as a piano work in 1927 and newly orchestrated by Gunther Schuller, who also conducted. A charming period piece, based largely on the blues and full of lullaby string passages, "Yamekraw" in many ways captures what ultimately escaped Gershwin in the "Rhapsody in Blue." Schuller was also on hand, as composer and conductor, during the young folks' jazz program, when the première of his "Journey Into Jazz"—a "Peter and the Wolf" piece, with fragmentary, elusive music and a Golden Book narration written by Nat Hentoff—was presented. (Music cannot be raised or lowered to fit certain ages; the audience itself must fall short of, match, or outgrow what it hears.)

Some of the rare exceptions to this non-spectrum occurred during the small-ensemble program, where Sonny Rollins, in company with Jim Hall, played two long ballads, in which he soloed brilliantly and at length. Gerry Mulligan offered six creditable numbers with Bob Brookmeyer. And the pianist-composer John Benson Brooks, along with an alto saxophonist and a drummer (equipped only with a snare drum and cymbal), performed a couple of atonal pieces in which moans and thumps were endlessly exchanged. The remaining exceptions were buried in the Luxor-steam-bath atmosphere of the Coliseum concerts. An excellent Mississippi blues singer, Howlin' Wolf, was submerged by the amplification system. The Oscar Peterson trio accompanied Roy Eldridge and Ben Webster, who were nervous but rewarding, and Thelonious Monk, accompanied by Charlie Rouse, Art Davis, and Billy Higgins, played three superb numbers. (Higgins took two exceptional drum solos.) The Ellington band tired after five excited and exciting instrumentals.

On Sunday morning, four groups of gospel singers appeared at the Coliseum and demonstrated that gospel singing is sliding rapidly from an irresistible amateurism down to a glossy professionalism of noisy hand-clapping, self-conscious growl-singing, dancing, and racing up and down the aisles. Several members of the audience worked hard at hearing the call, but it never quite reached them—a shorting-out in keeping with the rest of the weekend.

## The Inheritors

F rom the audience's point of view, the ideal for a jazz festival runs in threes—three concerts, each limited to around three hours and to three stylistically different groups, and held in a place that affords intimacy between the performers and the three-thousand-only listeners. This ideal materialized stirringly at the first Great South Bay Festival, in 1957, but, inexplicably, not enough customers did, and after a second, equally idealistic attempt the next year, the G.S.B. went under. The Newport Jazz Festival courted this ideal in its first couple of years (1954–55), and then abandoned it for Growth. As a result, it died in its seventh year, of overweight and social pressure—the now celebrated Newport Riot. Last year, a popular-music festival was substituted in Newport. Law and order prevailed, and the town fathers, nudged by the local merchants, who are said to clear upward of a million dollars on festival weekends, asked George Wein, the founder of the Newport Jazz Festival, to resurrect it, and he did, over the Fourth of July weekend. There were five concerts, most of them too long; there was dross; and the audiences, sometimes twelve thousand strong, were again herded into Freebody Park, a corral the size of Yankee Stadium. But the festival was trimmer, purer, and more light-footed than it has been since its opening years. Indeed, it had one concert of the kind that becomes legendary the next day and that is described with firsthand relish years later to children and grandchildren by people who were not even there.

This graceful and affecting event, on Saturday afternoon, was given over largely to jazz tap-dancing, a classic American art long obscured by the belly-and-bottom modern dance beloved by Broadway, Hollywood, and television. The dancers were Baby Laurence, Bunny Briggs, Pete Nugent, Charlie Atkins, and Honi Coles, and there was a loose narration by Marshall Stearns, who was responsible several years back for reviving Al Minns and Leon James, the masters of "ballroom" jazz dancing. Stearns pointed out, among other things, that tap-dancing resulted from the slow fusion of Irish jigs and clogs and various soft-shoe dances, like the Sand, invented by American Negroes. The dancers demonstrated—singly, in pairs, in trios, and all together—the formidable intricacies of "time" steps, the many "wing" steps (saw wings, pump wings, double-back wings), and "flash" steps, such dances as the trenches-and-over-the-top and the soft-shoe "class" acts, and the styles of originators like Eddie Rector, John W. Bubbles, and Bill Robinson. Coles and Atkins performed a delicious class act. At a slow, slow tempo, they slid across, around, and up and down the stage, mixing in offhand gull turns, polite double toe-taps, hip wiggles, and arm movements ranging from cold-engine propeller motions to weighty pumping. The afternoon came to a climax in two dances—one by Briggs and one by Laurence. Briggs, short, slim, and shaggy-headed, is a fey, airborne dancer whose steps and motions are an exquisite balance of comic exaggeration and almost fussy precision. In the Paddle-and-Roll (a Midwestern dance that arrived in New York in the forties), he began with a long sequence of abrupt, irregular heel beats, punctuated by silences and quick, stiff head-and-arm motions, broke into a barrage of military-type flam strokes, and settled into soft, dizzying heel-and-toe beats (his torso and head now motionless) that carried him smoothly all over the seemingly ice-coated stage. Gradually, he brought his body into action with swaying motions, high-kneed walking (the clickclickclickclick of his feet never ceasing), and drawn-out slides, and then released loud, fast staccato beats, sometimes with both feet and sometimes with first one and then the other, and returned suddenly to his opening pattern. Laurence unenviably followed with a bop dance, and, though exceptional, did not quite match Briggs. (Laurence's style—intense, direct, overbearing—is the opposite of Briggs'.) At the close of the afternoon, all five men did an uproarious takeoff on rock-and-roll and the Twist. The program was helped immeasurably by the accompaniment of Jo Jones and Roy Eldridge (plus bass and piano), both of whom equalled what they were watching. Saturday evening, before a far larger audience, Briggs and Laurence, accompanied by the Duke Ellington band, did variations of their afternoon performances and then danced together and *at* each other; this time, it was a draw.

There were other delights during the weekend. Sunday night, Wein, crowning his managerial functions, sat down at the piano and, in an engaging Jess Stacy–Fats Waller–Teddy Wilson fashion, led a group consisting of Ruby Braff, Pee Wee Russell, Marshall Brown, Bud Freeman, John Neves, and Buzzy Drootin through six numbers. These included a relaxed rendition of Waller's "Crazy 'Bout My Baby"; a "Blue and Sentimental" notable for its tempo (molasses dripping) and for Braff's gorgeous playing; and a slow blues in which Russell tunneled through four lower-register choruses. Wein's group, which has worked together off and on for several years, represents a type of jazz that is rapidly disappearing. Relaxed, emotional, unpretentious, and of no school, it firms the heart and brightens the eye, and it will be a gloomy day when it is gone. Still other beauties were scattered about. Eldridge, accompanied by a rhythm section including Jo Jones, opened the festival, on Friday evening, with three exemplary numbers, and, later in the evening, Coleman Hawkins joined Gerry Mulligan's quartet for "Sunday" and a remarkable "Body and Soul," complete with a leonine coda. Mulligan never worked harder. The next evening, Charlie Mingus set forth six or so strange, congested numbers, and unpardonably took no solos. Sonny Rollins appeared on Sunday afternoon with Jim Hall,

Bob Cranshaw, and Ben Riley, and played two long and imaginative numbers, and that evening Thelonious Monk sat in with the Ellington band,
which hummed "Monk's Dream" and a blues. Monk, who learned much
from Ellington, suggested a witty, kindly, and ingenious parody of his master. Monk then led his quartet through four numbers, soloed brilliantly, and,
during his colleagues' contributions, stood up and worked out a series of
slow, breezy dances that were, in their way, as fresh as the Briggs-Laurence
displays. The last of the weekend's blessings was startlingly funny. It was
offered by Roland Kirk, a blind tenor saxophonist and flutist who doubles on
a number of horns, some of his own design (he occasionally plays three
instruments at once). They are the manzello and the stritch, early forebears
of the saxophone; a pocket-sized nose flute; the poor man's piano, or melod-
ica, a kind of accordion that is blown, not pumped; and the swarellophone, a
small trombone with a horizontal bell and a vertical slide. Kirk produces a
hellish combination of sounds from these instruments, but his clowning,
which is embellished by comic introductory remarks and a physical intensity
that threatens to hurl him from the stage, disguises a first-rate musician.

The rest of the weekend was mechanical and/or silly, and included Oscar
Peterson, Dave Brubeck, and Max Roach, who appeared with a sextet and an
eight-voice choir plus conductor, which sounded like a theremin.

## Pure

I have just spent several illuminating days getting reacquainted with Benny Carter's recordings, which run
from 1928 to now, and they offer indisputable evidence that few of his
contemporaries continue to play or arrange or compose as well as he does,
and none of them plays as many instruments *and* arranges *and* composes with
such aplomb. His work is an unfailing balance of technique, emotion, freshness, and taste. Carter knows, within his own terms, exactly what to play and
how to play it. This is not to say that such pure-jazz musicians as Bix Beiderbecke, Nat Cole, Sidney Catlett, Joe Thomas, Lester Young, and John
Lewis are unrivalled. Some of the greatest jazz musicians have been *im*pure,
and have made virtues of being excessive, eccentric, or even erratic. But they
flare up and flicker out, leaving the Carters to carry the music from decade
to decade.

Carter, a man for all seasons, has had an oddly unattended career. Born in
New York in 1907, he began his second-banana life with Fletcher Henderson. During the time (1928–31) Carter played and arranged for Henderson,
he turned out possibly the best arrangements the Henderson band ever used.
But it was Don Redman's and Fletcher and Horace Henderson's more ordinary scores that gave the band its stamp. In 1932, after fleeting appearances
with Charlie Johnson, McKinney's Cotton Pickers, and Chick Webb,
Carter formed his own big band, and it became law among New York musi-

cians that you had arrived if you were hired by Carter. But the depression was on, and Carter's band soon went under. For the next couple of years, he subsisted as a freelance arranger and by doing pickup recordings. In 1935, he left for Europe, and recorded in London, Stockholm, Amsterdam, Copenhagen, and Paris. He returned to America in 1938 and put together a big band that included Joe Thomas, Vic Dickenson, Coleman Hawkins, Bill Coleman, Sandy Williams, Jonah Jones, Sidney de Paris, Doc Cheatham, Emmett Berry, J. C. Heard, J. J. Johnson, and Max Roach. It was a first-rate band, but Carter's luck was still out; Benny Goodman and Artie Shaw had the public by its lapels, and two other bands—Duke Ellington's and Count Basie's—were just reaching apogees. Carter drifted into Hollywood studio work in the mid-forties, big bands disappeared, bebop caught up, and it wasn't until five or six years ago that he began edging back toward jazz.

At one time or another, Carter has played the alto saxophone, the trumpet, the clarinet, and the trombone, but he has concentrated on the alto and the trumpet. Carter has an unstudied middle-of-the-road tone on the alto; in fact, his sound is as close to the ideal one as any alto saxophonist has come; smooth and almost transparent, it has a light, slightly remote quality. Tonally, Carter's contemporaries and descendants fall neatly on one side or the other of him. Hilton Jefferson is decorous and waxy, and Paul Desmond is ethereal. The heavier-toned men include Willie Smith, whose sound is sharp and gesticulating; Tab Smith (no relation), who suggests butterballs and cherubim; Pete Brown, a fat man with a fat, jumping tone; Johnny Hodges, who is Bristol Cream; and Charlie Parker, who was simply careless, sometimes allowing his tone to slip halfway to the tenor saxophone's. In many ways, Carter's approach to improvisation forms a link between Coleman Hawkins and Lester Young. At slow and medium tempos, Carter is apt, in Young fashion, to hover around the melody, or ghosts of the melody, using legato sliding phrases, frequently fitted into lazy descending patterns, and a vibrato that is not really a vibrato but a nod toward one. The effect is a succession of orderly arabesques in slow motion. At faster speeds, Carter folds this method into a more rhythmic, Hawkinslike attack. (Carter is not an imitator of Hawkins or Young; he and Hawkins, self-taught rookies; went their own ways in the Henderson band, and in the early thirties, when Carter's style was pretty well set, Young was still an unknown sideman in King Oliver's last, disaster-ridden band. Carter has mentioned learning from Bubber Miley, Cuban Bennett [a trumpeter], Beiderbecke, and Frankie Trumbauer, the last two of whom are just beginning to be credited with the wide influence they had on Negro musicians in the late twenties.) He will open an up-tempo improvisation by constructing a fleeing quasi-melodic line, which he breaks only to catch his breath, and which is full of intervals, riff figures, and pitching runs. Then, abruptly going languorous, he fashions a series of brief descending planes, each of which pours over into the next plane, lulling listeners into a calm that he will shatter by picking up fistfuls of notes and returning to a near-staccato rhythm-bound approach. Whether Carter rides his notes or barely touches them, he tints each one with his presence, his special touch; any two, or perhaps three, Carter notes make him immediately identifiable. But the singular things about his most energetic alto solos are their seemingly prearranged unity and their steady undercurrent of emotion. He is like a deer; one is first struck by his grace and lightness, then by the tensions that govern such beauty.

Carter's trumpet playing, which he began recording in the mid-thirties, is a delight. It has much in common with the spare and melodious style developed by such men as Joe Thomas, Shorty Baker, and Doc Cheatham. Since it is not his chief instrument, Carter approaches it the way Babe Ruth played golf—proficiently, but largely for kicks. His legato style, parcelled out among short, easy phrases, is tinged with a nice vibrato, and his tone is bright and direct. Carter displays more emotion on the trumpet than he does on the saxophone; perhaps it is because he can ignore his "p"s and "q"s—a relaxed attitude that also occasionally leads him into mild and attractive disarrays of fluffed notes. Carter has played trumpet sparingly in his recent recordings. But the results are as of old, and this is especially agreeable at a time when such laissez-faire trumpet playing has all but vanished.

One of the persistent sorrows of jazz is Carter's abandonment of the clarinet, which he played through the thirties. (Lester Young, equally lamented, quit the instrument before 1940.) Carter's clarinet on the celebrated Chocolate Dandies sides made in 1930 has a timeless air, and so have the bits and pieces of it that pop to the surface of his big-band records of ten years later. His tone was new. It had none of the unctuous liquidity of the New Orleans men and none of the manly woodenness of the later white clarinettists. It fell handsomely between, and—like his saxophone—it offered the ideal sound for the instrument. His attack was close to his saxophone one. Fertile double-time runs dominated his saxophone and trumpet plane phrases, but there was never any urgency. (There is nothing more racking than a clarinettist playing beyond his means.) The clarinet is a demanding instrument, but Carter handled it with an assured looseness.

Carter's songs often have a blue, minor cast, but his arranging is an extension of his instrumental buoyancy. His arrangements for Henderson were in a sense done for the wrong band. They demand a flowing rhythm section and precise execution by the horns, neither of which the Henderson band had until the mid-thirties. Nonetheless, the spareness of these Carter arrangements suggested for the first time how a big jazz band could get around its Prussian tendencies. Unlike Ellington, who often blends all his instruments, Carter regards a big band as made up chiefly of saxophones, with trumpets-trombones-and-rhythm in attendance. He doesn't pit the sections against one another; instead, he often uses them in pastel sequences whose colors and timbres are homogeneous. Carter insinuates with a big band rather than startles. He builds his arrangements around his saxophones, which he supplies with resilient passages, and these, perhaps unwittingly, are generally close approximations of his alto-saxophone solos. These leavening figures are enclosed or underlined by salutary trumpet accents or riffs, frequently muted, and occasional trombone choir effects. His arrangements, particularly for his second big band, have an improvised air; the writing is as spontaneous as the solos. Unfortunately, Carter's arranging methods have never caught on. The long-prevalent Henderson vein was finally worked out by Stan Kenton, while Ellington's ingenuity has resulted largely in the lugubrious chants of Gil Evans. For a time, Basie reflected some of Carter's tricks (there was considerable similarity between the two bands in the late thirties), but he has given them up, leaving the big band in general pretty much where it was in 1940.

Carter almost always sounds at ease on records. This is true on his "Further Definitions: Benny Carter and His Orchestra" (Coleman Hawkins, Phil Woods, Charlie Rouse, Dick Katz, John Collins, Jimmy Garrison, and Jo Jones). Indeed, Carter's solos (alto saxophone) are perhaps the freest, most jubilant ones he has recorded. Listen to him in "Honeysuckle Rose," "Cherry," and "Doozy." And listen to his longest, most sustained written passage on the record, which comes at the end of his "Blue Star" and which is a distillation of all his solos. Indeed, "Blue Star" is, a few blank spots notwithstanding, close to a classic performance. It is a lovely tune, and Hawkins, well pulled together (as he is in his magnificent coda in "Body and Soul"), plays the melody against handsome Carter ensemble figures in that bravura, intense, frontal way he uses these days. And Carter's solo matches Hawkins'. Rouse and Woods also have their moments, mainly in "Doozy," an infectious Carter medium-tempo blues. Carter's written and improvised contributions to the record have a *beginning* air, and the only things that are missing are his trumpet and clarinet.

# 1963

## The Street

During the thirty years that New York has been the headquarters of jazz, the music has been played in ballrooms, theatres, supper clubs, night clubs, hotels, Macy's, museums, concert halls, stadiums, Madison Square Garden, classrooms, school and college auditoriums, Central Park, churches, subways, radio and television studios, in the street, and on the floor of the Stock Exchange. It has, though, centered on three areas—Harlem, Broadway and the Fifties, and Greenwich Village. In the twenties, it could be found in the Harlem and Broadway ballrooms and behind the floor shows in night clubs like Connie's Inn, the Kentucky Club, and the Cotton Club. After Prohibition, the focus shifted gradually to Fifty-second Street, between Fifth and Seventh Avenues, where the music was almost entirely for listening. (The Savoy, the Apollo, Minton's, and Monroe's remained essential outposts in Harlem.) Fifty-second Street, or The Street, as it came to be known, was filled with office buildings after the Second World War, and the music began a retreat to the Village, where a few jazz night clubs had existed since the late thirties, and to a handful of places in the East Fifties.

Fifty-second Street was the best of the communes. The first club on it was the Onyx, an upstairs speakeasy, which later moved downstairs and across the street, and the only remaining one is Hickory House. The Street was in its glory between 1940 and 1945. Its clubs—the Onyx, the Three Deuces, the Club Downbeat, Jimmy Ryan's, the Spotlite, and the Famous Door—were clustered toward the west end of the block between Fifth and Sixth (Kelly's Stable was, and Hickory House still is, in the next block), and they frequently changed hands and names and swapped locations. The clubs occupied the ground floors of indifferent brownstones and had interchangeable interiors. There was a small vestibule, with a coffin-sized coatroom, and, beyond, a bar along one wall. This gave onto a forest of postage-stamp tables, and at the end of the room, flanked by rest rooms and a nominal kitchen, was a tiny bandstand on which four men were comfortable and five a crowd. The décor ran to stamped-tin ceilings, tinted mirrors, maroon velours hangings, and water-stained plaster. The clubs were dark and smoky, they smelled like caves, and the liquor was bad but cheap. But they were good places to hear jazz. Although sheer human density sometimes muffled the music, you could see the performers from anywhere in the house, even at the bar, and there was an intimate give-and-take between the audience and the musicians. (A front table might be three feet from Art Tatum's right elbow.) Even better, the musicians flowed from club to club, so that you'd hear in three or four places the same two or three musicians in three or four bands. Visiting musicians also sat in frequently, as did nonprofessionals without union cards. (This fertile crossbreeding has just about disappeared in New York. The esoteric, coded manner of much modern jazz doesn't encourage sitting in, and neither does the union, which feels that musicians should not play without pay—even for pleasure.)

The music on Fifty-second Street included New Orleans and Chicago jazz, small- and big-band swing, bebop, and the early cool groups, and, because of competition, crossbreeding, variety, and the intense atmosphere of the place and the times, it was often uncannily good. Between December and February of 1944–45, for example, The Street displayed Hot Lips Page, Ben Webster, Barney Bigard, Stuff Smith, Wingy Manone, Art Tatum, Joe Marsala, Coleman Hawkins, Trummy Young, Benny Morton, Art Hodes, Oscar Pettiford, Dizzy Gillespie, Max Roach, Don Byas, Tiny Grimes, Charlie Shavers, and Billie Holiday. Best of all were the sometimes classic Sunday-afternoon jam sessions at Jimmy Ryan's. Musicians of every persuasion sat in with two basic bands, and during an afternoon the parade might include Bill Coleman, Pee Wee Russell, James P. Johnson, Edmond Hall, Vic Dickenson, Sid Catlett, Frankie Newton, Morton, Pete Brown, Jack Teagarden, Sidney Bechet, J. C. Higginbotham, Red Allen, Hawkins, Claude Jones, and Roy Eldridge. Unfortunately, none of the Ryan's sessions were recorded, although similar ones in Harlem were. At the close, every musician in the house squeezed onto the bandstand for the "Bugle Call Rag." The results, though untidy (there might be fifteen men on the stand), were often stunning.

Columbia has seen fit to celebrate Fifty-second Street in a four-record set, "Swing Street." The album contains sixty-four titles (sixty-three, actually, since one record, Bobby Hackett's "Bugle Call Rag," is inadvertently repeated), recorded between 1931 and 1947. It is, however, a lopsided celebration, for only eighteen numbers were recorded after 1939. During the war, Columbia, discouraged by the unfashionableness of jazz and by two long union bans on recording, went pretty much off the jazz standard. The slack was taken up by small labels—Blue Note, Commodore, H.R.S., Keynote, Dial, Savoy, Manor, Guild, Apollo, Signature, Session, Delta, Continental, and many others. Because of apathy and procedural complications, only a few of these recordings, many of which were superb, have been reissued. Nonetheless, the Epic album, despite some odd choices from what *is* available to Columbia, contains pleasant and even valuable material and is a reasonably accurate picture of the warming-up days on The Street. There are four selections by the Spirits of Rhythm, a guitar-tipples-bass-and-drums group, notable for the guitarist Teddy Bunn and the Surrealistic scat singing of Leo Watson; all of a 1933 Eddie Condon session, played by Sid Catlett, Pee Wee Russell, Floyd O'Brien, and Max Kaminsky; two good small-band Henry Allen sides, "Every Minute of the Hour" and "Lost"; two good numbers by Frankie Newton's Uptown Serenaders (which contained the nucleus of the John Kirby band) that have snatches of Newton's irreplaceable legato trumpet; Fats Waller, Art Tatum, and Teddy Wilson piano solos; three average John Kirby sides (why not the un-reissued "Blue Skies" and "Royal Garden Blues"—the band minus its customary veil and gloves?); a couple of fine Billie Holidays, "I Hear Music" and "Practice Makes Perfect"; two welcome 1940 Basie numbers, "Love Jumped Out" and "Five O'Clock Whistle"; Roy Eldridge's "That Thing"; and two Dizzy Gillespie dates from the Manor label (Columbia now owns the masters), "I Can't Get Started" and "Good Bait," the second of which contains a shouting, jolting bridge by Gillespie that is the most exhilarating moment in the album. The rest of the material, which ranges from the academic to the poor, is by—among others—Mildred Bailey, Red Norvo, Frankie Froeba, Wingy Manone, Toy Wilson, Sidney Bechet, Clarence Profit, Louis Prima, Hot Lips Page, Stuff Smith, and Red McKenzie. There is a lengthy booklet, with excellent photographs and a memoir by Charles Edward Smith. There is also a short note by John Hammond, who points out that The Street was Jim Crow for many years (the Columbia album is proof) and that the salaries paid the performers were often minimal.

The sound reproduction, by the way, is poor—inexplicably, since many of the original 78 rpm's were well recorded.

Hickory House, on the first floor of a twelve-story loft-and-office building on West Fifty-second Street, opposite the Americana Hotel, is celebrating its thirtieth anniversary, and is, since the recent defection of Small's Paradise, in Harlem, the oldest non-stop jazz club in the city. One icy day I stopped in at Hickory House around lunchtime to talk with John Popkin, its owner and founder, and discovered that it hadn't changed a bit since my last visit, six or seven years before. A deep, high-ceilinged room with stained-glass windows and panelled walls, broken here and there by heroic oil paintings of such as Babe Ruth, Jack Dempsey, Red Grange, and Bobby Jones, Hickory House is built chiefly around an oval bar, some forty feet long, which contains a bandstand and is covered by an oval wooden canopy. A dozen or so wrought-iron chandeliers frame the canopy, and at the back of the room are several open grills, where steaks and chops are broiled. Booths line one wall, and the rest of the floor is taken up by large, indifferently arranged tables. John Popkin, an amiable, medium-sized man with thinning hair and a crinkled, pleasantly worn face, greeted me and introduced me to Joe Morgen, his publicity agent.

Morgen, who is short and melancholy-looking, pulled a thick sheaf of newspaper clippings from an envelope and dumped them on the table. "Duke Ellington sent these from England, John," he said. "He's on tour, you know. In fact, I spoke to him this morning. On the phone."

"You spoke to him in *England*?" Popkin asked, raising his eyebrows. "A call like that costs! I've known Duke thirty or thirty-five years. He's been coming in here since I opened. That man works too hard, but he eats nothing but proteins."

Morgen nodded solemnly, and said, "He spends hundreds of dollars a month here feeding himself and his family and friends."

Popkin nodded with equal solemnity, and turned to me. "I haven't had breakfast yet, so all I'm going to have is a medium egg and orange juice," he said.

I asked Popkin about the early days of the Hickory House.

"I rented the place with three other men in 1933 and rebuilt it," he said. "It was a secondhand-car salesroom, and the idea to make it a steakhouse was mine, and so the name, which is based on the fact that we cook our steaks entirely over hickory logs—two-foot hickory logs shipped special from a farmer up at Cornwall on the Hudson, and another man, up in Durham, Connecticut. In November, 1934, after I'd bought out my partners, I got the idea to bring in jazz, so I hired Wingy Manone, who had the Marsala brothers with him and Eddie Condon. Not long after that, the Three Ts—Jack and Charlie Teagarden and Frankie Trumbauer—came in from Paul White-man's band, and when they left, Joe Marsala formed his own group. Marsala was in and out of here right into the early forties, and had people like Adele Girard, the harpist, who became his wife; Joe Bushkin; Flip Phillips; George Wettling; Bobby Hackett, on guitar and cornet; and Buddy Rich. I brought Rich in from Brooklyn myself. He was playing in a little place right on the edge of Washington Cemetery, facing Ocean Parkway. Right on the edge, surrounded by stones. I heard music coming out of there one night—it was eerie—and went in, and this kid was playing. He was sensational. 'How old are you, sonny?' I asked him during the intermission, and he said, 'Seventeen, but I'll be eighteen soon.' I told him I wanted to hire him, but he wouldn't believe me, so later I drove him home and we woke up his father at four in the morning, and he *did* believe me. Then it took me a week to persuade Marsala to use him. I can't tell you, in order, all the rest of the bands I had in the thir-ties. My memory used to be like a telephone book, but it skips on me now. Anyway, there was Red Norvo and Mildred Bailey; Red McKenzie; Bud Freeman; Red Allen; the Adrian Rollini Trio; John Kirby; Louis Prima; Riley and Farley, who wrote 'The Music Goes 'Round and Around'; Bunny Beri-gan; and all sorts of intermission pianists—Hazel Scott, Frances Faye, Irving Fields, Toy Wilson, Pearl Williams, and Frankie Froeba. Fats Waller, who was in a floor show next door at the Yacht Club, came in every evening just to play what he wanted to play, and they'd have to send somebody over to get him when his next set began. Around 1935, I started Sunday-afternoon jam sessions. Everybody dropped in—Basie, Teddy Wilson, Art Tatum, Hot Lips Page, Chu Berry, Roy Eldridge, the Dorseys, Artie Shaw, Goodman, and Nat Cole, who was across the street at Kelly's Stable. Frank Sinatra and Frankie Laine used to hang around in that back booth, waiting for a chance to sing. Beer was thirty-five cents and whiskey fifty, and the customers would be three-deep around the bar, some of them nursing one drink for the entire afternoon. I stopped hiring horns in the late forties. The food side had become very important, and the horns made too much noise. Since then, I've had small, quiet groups, a lot of them led by women, like Mary Osborne, the guitarist; Jutta Hipp and Toshiko; Marjorie Hyams, the vibraphonist; and, of course, Marian McPartland, who's a fixture, and who gave Joe Morello his start. George Shearing started here, too, and so did Peter Nero, in 1959. He was Bernie Nierow then, and an intermission pianist."

Popkin finished his egg and took a sip of coffee. What had he done in his pre–Hickory House days? "I was born—real name of Pupko—in Vilna, Rus-sia, in 1895, and came over in 1907 on a cattle boat from Latvia," he said. "My father had been in New York three or four years, and owned a fish cart. I didn't go to school; I started right away as a newsboy. Then I worked for Postal Telegraph and became Eva Tanguay's personal messenger boy. At seventeen, I took a job as a salesman with United Cigar, and after that as a men's-clothing model in a store on Fourteenth Street. My father and I had a fish market down on Ludlow for a while, and at twenty-one I went into the auction business. On Lispenard Street. I made a little money and bought a duck ranch in Yardley, Pennsylvania. I was the only Jewish duck-raiser at that time, and I lived in an old house that George Washington had had as his headquarters. The keys to the doors were all a foot long. I got married in that house. A very historical wedding. I gave up the ranch after I lost most of my ducks in an epidemic, and worked for the Commission for Relief in Belgium, under Herbert Hoover, during the First World War. Then I opened the Little Club, a speakeasy on Forty-fourth between Broadway and Eighth Avenue. I always wanted to be in the theatrical and musical line. I quit the Little Club in 1925 and went into perfumes. I was very successful until 1929, when I went broke on Wall Street. I didn't want to go back with my father, and I was having a hard time when I started this place. I can't retire. If I do, I'm afraid I'll die. I'm here fourteen, fifteen hours a day. I meet people and talk. Time flies. There are always problems to occupy my mind. People keep telling me, 'Modernize the place, John. Pep it up.' Maybe I'll do some fixing this spring, but I won't change it much. I'm too old-fashioned."

## His Master's Voice

The arts have long come in two grades—the original and its popularization. Jazz is no exception. Almost every poll-winning big band, group, instrumentalist, or singer is a loose copy, adaptation, or even mockery of a lesser-known and often pioneering big band, group, instrumentalist, or singer. (Jazz is often called "popular music." It isn't. Popular music is Frank Sinatra and Doris Day, vocal groups, dance bands, hotel bands, and rock-and-roll. Some of these are remotely related to jazz, some are not.) Popularized jazz is more popular than jazz but not as popular as popular music. There are a good many jazz popularizers. Here are some of them—the originals on the left, their adapters on the right:

Fletcher Henderson = Benny Goodman
Chick Webb = Buddy Rich
Jimmy Lunceford = Stan Kenton
Billie Holiday = Anita O'Day and Peggy Lee
Lester Young = Stan Getz
Albert Ammons, Meade Lux Lewis, and Pete Johnson = Freddie Slack
Bix Beiderbecke = Red Nichols and Bobby Hackett
Art Tatum = Oscar Peterson and André Previn
Charlie Parker = Cannonball Adderley
Bud Powell = Barry Harris

There are odd twists here. A few jazz pioneers have popularized themselves—that is, they have, because of wear and tear, perfected easily prepared, easily digested versions of their original selves. These include Louis Armstrong, whose many imitators, however, have never become popular; Ella Fitzgerald; Count Basie; and Erroll Garner, whose popular form—another odd twist—is identical with his original form. The most obvious difference between the pioneers and their adapters is racial. The Negro invents, the white man takes. The other differences are subtler. The popularizers tend to be better technicians and steadier performers (read: mechanical). At the same time, they are less inventive, less high-minded about their work, more ostentatious, and perhaps because they are borrowers, less sure of themselves. A few of these popularizers have come extremely close to equalling their models. One of them is the celebrated Stan Getz, the thirty-six-year-old tenor saxophonist form Philadelphia.

Getz is the poll winners' poll winner. He won the *Metronome* poll eleven years in a row and would probably still be winning if the magazine hadn't gone out of business. He won the *down beat* readers' poll eleven times and its critics' poll six times. He topped the *Playboy* poll seven years and is one of *Playboy*'s All Stars' All Stars. (Getz's chief model, Lester Young, pulled down just two *Esquire* polls, one *down beat* readers' poll, and a posthumous election to *down beat*'s Hall of Fame.) Continuous poll winners breed admirers, and Getz's are legion and often interchangeable. Some of them are Zoot Sims, Allen Eager, Brew Moore, Herbie Steward, Al Cohn, Dick Hafer, and Bill Perkins. Lester Young, late in life, was therefore in the lamentable position of being unable to turn around without hearing a Getz-filtered facsimile of himself, and the less knowledgeable among his audiences frequently mistook him for just another Getz admirer.

Getz looks like a country boy. He is of medium build, with the bland, homogeneous handsomeness that belongs with plenty of milk and regular sleep. Like many other white musicians, he shows the strain of trying to keep up with the Joneses when he plays. He clamps his eyes shut, contorts his face, stoops and stands up, stoops and stands up. His style is romantic, and this makes him an alien in jazz, where softness and sentiment have little honor. His tone is a moist, primped version of Lester Young's, which was dry and nasal. It is, at first, a lovely tone, the kind of tone one would want to go home to. But after repeated hearings one notices a whining quality, a note of self-pity. Coleman Hawkins and Ben Webster, by comparison, are dark, tough, and intense; they are affecting because they express what they feel, not what they think they ought to feel. Getz's tone is at the mercy of his romanticism, which is a yearning after those blues emotions natural to Webster, Hawkins, and Young. In a slow blues or a ballad, he exhibits all the paraphernalia jazz musicians use to convey emotion. He grows husky, he plays blue notes, he goes soft and sinuous, and he preaches. But his effects come through as genteel and falsetto, particularly when he ascends into the upper register, which he does frequently in heated moments. The exterior is flawless, but the guts are missing. This emotional anemia is to an extent disguised, for Getz is a formidable technician. In fast tempos, he uses many-noted lines that gallop around the scale (and sometimes off it), short, peremptory riffs, a trim vibrato, complex staccato intervals, and down-low honks. He becomes liquid, and he hounds the beat—until, that is, he runs out of patterns, when he slips behind the beat into a legato refuelling passage. But many of these thousands of notes, though well chosen, accented, and joined, are merely excited and compulsive. (Getz made an absorbing record five or six years ago with Dizzy Gillespie; on it, he is largely rhetorical, while Gillespie is witty and passionate.) Getz approaches fulfillment in slow ballads. He has an unmistakable gift for inventing sweet and graceful melodies, which, though stated fulsomely, are original. One or two close hearings of these lyric flights do them justice; after that they grow transparent.

Getz's career has been divided between being a sideman in big bands (the forties) and the leader of small groups (the fifties, the sixties), both here and in Scandinavia. In 1957, though, he toured with a black-tie Jazz at the Philharmonic group that was recorded in action at the Chicago Opera House. Getz's portion of the concert, "Stan Getz and J. J. Johnson at the Opera House," has now been reissued by Verve. It is well recorded, the crowd sounds are not objectionable, and, all in all, it is probably the best record Getz has made. (He has recorded prolifically, and at the moment is hip-deep in *bossa nova*. Some of his *bossa-nova* efforts are best-sellers, and they may suitably shape him, after all these years, into a purely popular musician.) Oscar Peterson, Herb Ellis, Ray Brown, and Connie Kay accompany Getz and Johnson. There are two blues and four standards. "Billie's Bounce," a Charlie Parker blues, is in a medium-fast tempo, and is an excellent example of Paganini-Getz, who takes a dozen choruses, each more heated and hollow than the last. Getz is nearer his peak in the medium-tempo "My Funny Valentine," in which he controls his moony tendencies and displays a firmness of tone and an invention that come close to Ben Webster's. "Crazy Rhythm" is a very fast and predictable flag waver, and the slow "Yesterdays" is given over to Johnson. In "It Never Entered My Mind," Getz plays just one chorus, in an ad-lib tempo. It is a saintly demonstration of how to woo fragile embellishments from an even more fragile melody. "Blues in the Closet," which takes the tempo up again, is notable for Getz's tribute to Lester Young. Toward the end of a dozen, choruses, he discards all pretense and plays a couple of choruses straight from the Master's mouth. The rhythm section, with Connie Kay in command and Oscar Peterson heard only as an accompanist, is first-rate.

*For an estimation of the other Getz, the bad Getz, see p. 845.*

## Hear Today, Gone Tomorrow

J azz has always been bedevilled by certain audiences—the social-protesters, the Beats, and the hard thinkers who use the music as a weapon or smoke screen, and the eccentrics who spend lifetimes squabbling over the merits of spent musicians and unearthing the matrix numbers of forgotten, third-rate recordings. The chatty illiteracy of the occasional bulletins published by these archaeologists calls to mind the nudist magazines whose editorials are apt to lead off, "Hi ya, skinfolks!" One reason for this condition, though, is the music itself, which changes too much and too fast. No sooner has a style or school begun to attract an audience (this usually takes two or three years) than a new style or school overtakes it. First came the primitives (the rural singers and instrumentalists). They were followed by the classicists (New Orleans and Dixieland), who were toppled by the romantics (the first great soloists). These were supplanted by the neo-classicists (the big swing bands), who went down before the neo-romantics, or first moderns (bebop). Out of the moderns grew the avant-garde (abstract jazz) and, indirectly from that, the—well, neo-avantgarde (third-stream music). One trouble with these changes of skirt length is their increasing frequency. In the past fifteen years, jazz has suffered two thorough revolutions (bebop, abstract jazz). Apprentice musicians, watching idol after idol diminish, are left with half-formed, polyglot styles, and the often gifted idols are unemployable at the advanced age of thirty-five. Record companies, trying to keep up, concentrate on the New, and so force the very thing they pursue to accelerate. Thus the jazz student who grew up in the relatively stable days of 1940 has had, since his first enthusiasms, to absorb Charlie Parker and Dizzy Gillespie, then Lennie Tristano, then the Modern Jazz Quartet, then Charlie Mingus and Sonny Rollins, then John Coltrane and Cecil Taylor and Ornette Coleman. And while the rug is repeatedly pulled from under him, he is asked to be alert, broadminded, judicious, sympathetic, and eager.

Consider the concert given at the Carnegie Recital Hall under the title of "Recent Developments in Jazz." Organized by Gunther Schuller, who conducted, the evening was a *potage* of third-stream compositions (André Hodeir and Lalo Schifrin), atonal jazz (George Russell), and Duke Ellington, plus three numbers by the Eric Dolphy quartet that fell between hard bop and abstract jazz. One of Hodeir's four pieces, "Jazz Cantata," has seven movements, and it shuttles between written solos, fairly conventional ensemble scoring, and passages of up-tempo scat singing, which were read with aplomb by a soprano, Susan Belink. Schifrin's "The Ritual of Sound" is a jumpy study of timbres, and employs staccato clumps of sound and passages in which a bass clarinet, playing a ground, is pitted against a flute and French horn, then against a tuba and unison trumpets, and so on. Schifrin's program notes, written in Sanskrit, explain: "The thirteen-piece instrumental ensemble is used so as to achieve textures which are determined by seri-ally derived degrees of density and timbral associations, both singly and in combination. In order to locate this sound material in sound space, registral displacement was determined on the basis of a numerical series derived from the original pitch series." After Schifrin's serially derived density, George Russell's "Lydian M 1," seven years old, sounded old-fashioned. The last composition of the evening was a transcription, by Schuller, of Ellington's pioneering "Reminiscin' in Tempo," a twelve-minute tone poem written in 1935. Ellington's piece is—for me, anyway—an almost static work, and it suggests the probable fate of the works of Hodeir, Schifrin, and Russell.

The selections by Dolphy's quartet (the leader on alto saxophone, flute, and bass clarinet, with Edward Armour on trumpet, Richard Davis on bass, and J. C. Moses on drums) were notable for Dolphy's arpeggio flute (his work on the bass clarinet, though, was rough on that instrument's deep-pile tone). Charlie Parker's "Donna Lee" ("Indiana") was then performed in a straightforward ensemble-solos-ensemble fashion by ten of the eighteen musicians on hand during the concert. As they neared the final chorus, how-ever, all the horns, improvising collectively, stumbled on a marvellous, shat-tering chord that had the Furies in it and a moment-of-truth intensity that had been missing all evening.

## Supreme Tickler

I t has become clear only in the past decade that the up—the—river—from—New Orleans story is merely a rib or two of jazz history. Long before this overcelebrated migration, itinerant blues guitarists and pianists washed back and forth across the Southwest, the Southeast, and the Midwest. Jelly Roll Morton, a one-man vanguard, had travelled from coast to coast, sowing as he went, and by the time the New Orleans-to-Chicago migration was complete, independent and equally important jazz movements were entrenched in Kansas City, the Southwest, Baltimore, and New York. Perhaps the most influential and undervalued of these movements involved the Harlem "stride" pianists, who began to appear during the First World War and flourished in the twenties and thir-ties. Stride piano is characterized chiefly by an oompah left hand (a two-beat seesaw, whose ends are a powerful mid-keyboard chord and a weaker single note played an octave or a tenth below) and by an arabesque of right-hand chords and arpeggios, fashioned in counter rhythms. Stride piano, unlike New Orleans jazz, did not pop from one mythical man's forehead. It grew slowly out of ragtime, a unique piano form that lasted from about 1900 to about 1920. Though ragtime had similar features, it was not jazz. It was a complex, rococo *composed* music that evolved, as far as anyone knows, from the music used in the eighties and nineties to accompany Southern dances like the cakewalk. It employed the oompah left hand, syncopation, and elaborate treble figures, and each number was built on three or four distinct themes, arranged in *a-b-a-c-d*, *a-b-c-d*, or rondo form. It was a brittle, spirited, elegant music which had considerable lyric charm, and in its highest form (the work of Scott Joplin, James Scott, and Joseph Lamb) it demanded a Lisztian technique. Recorded on widely bought piano rolls, it was the first machine-fostered musical fad. It was also the first musical fad to be destroyed by over-exposure. (Its lack of development helped cause its death, too; the late rags, though often fancier, do not differ much from those written in 1900.) The stride pianists, however, were busy remodelling ragtime long before it sank, and by the time it did they had perfected a full-bodied replacement—an improvised music, at once telescoped and loosened. The multiple themes of the typical ragtime composition gave way to the *a-a-b-a* structure of the thirty-two-bar chorus; the oompah left hand was supplemented by four-four chords, broken-rhythm chords, and single-note melodic lines; the right-hand figures became less garrulous; longer rests and behind-the-beat legato phrases were added; and there were fewer tremolos and trills, although the arpeggios and sudden breaks persisted. Like the ragtime pianists, the stride men were orchestral pianists, and they most often played by themselves or in "cutting" contests, which took place in cabarets, in back rooms, and at rent parties. At their height, the stride pianists formed a glittering, ritualistic duchy. James P. Johnson, the dean of the Harlem "ticklers" (one of those *mots justes* that only jazz musicians seem able to fashion about their music), recalled several of its rules of etiquette a couple of years before his death, in 1955:

When a real smart tickler would enter a place, say in winter, he'd leave his overcoat on and keep his hat on, too. We used to wear military overcoats or what was called a Peddock Coat, like a coachman's; a blue double-breasted, fitted to the waist and with long skirts. We'd wear a light pearl-gray Fulton or Homburg hat with three buttons or eyelets on the side, set at a rakish angle. . . . Then a white silk muffler and a white silk handker-chief in the overcoat's breast pocket. Some carried a gold-headed cane, or if they were wearing a cutaway, a silver-headed cane. A couple of fellows used to wear Inverness capes, which were in style in white society then. . . .

When you came into a place you had a three-way play. You never took your overcoat or hat off until you were at the piano. First you laid your cane on the music rack. Then you took off your overcoat, folded it and put it on the piano, with the lining showing.

You then took off your hat before the audience. Each tickler had his own gesture for removing his hat with a little flourish; that was part of his attitude, too. You took out your silk handkerchief, shook it out and dusted off the piano stool.

Now, with your coat off, the audience could admire your full-back, or box-back, suit, cut with very square shoulders. The pants had about fourteen-inch cuffs and broidered clocks.

Full-back coats were always single-breasted, to show your gold watch fob and chain. Some ticklers wore a horseshoe tiepin in a strong single-colored tie and a gray shirt with black pencil stripes.

We all wore French, Shriner and Urner or Hanan straight or French last shoes with very pointed toes, or patent-leather turnup toes, in very narrow sizes. . . . They cost from twelve to eighteen dollars a pair. . . . [Fred Tunstall] was a real dandy. I remember he had a Norfolk coat with eighty-two pleats in the back. When he sat down to the piano, he'd slump a little in a half hunch, and those pleats would fan out real pretty. That coat was long and flared at the waist. It had a very short belt sewn on the back. His pants were very tight.

He had a long neck, so he wore a high, stiff collar that came up under his chin with a purple tie. A silk handkerchief was always draped very carefully in his breast pocket. His side view was very striking.

Johnson stands with Duke Ellington, Count Basie, and Jelly Roll Morton among the seminal jazz figures. Johnson's principal admirers and pupils in the early twenties were Ellington and Fats Waller. Ellington is now an institution, and as both pianist and composer he has affected Thelonious Monk, who in turn has spawned a host of lesser pianist-composers. Waller, an ironic master of self-parody, taught Count Basie, who became head of the Kansas City school as well as an unmistakable influence on John Lewis, another institution. Waller also made a lasting imprint on Art Tatum, a genuine virtuoso, and Tatum inspired—among countless others—Bud Powell and Charlie Parker. For all this, Johnson was passé when he died. Seventy-five people attended his funeral. His career was a string of quick successes and slow-burning failures. Born in 1894, in New Brunswick, New Jersey, of a poor but solid family, Johnson picked up the piano from his mother and other informal teachers, and in his early teens became a reasonably good tickler. By the mid-twenties, he was a master pianist, songwriter ("If I Could Be with You One Hour Tonight," "Charleston," "Carolina Shout," "Old Fashioned Love"), and piano-roll maker. He was also writing music for revues and Hollywood shorts, playing in pit bands and onstage, making records as a bandleader and soloist, and performing in vaudeville. But Johnson, in the manner of the comedian lusting after the role of Hamlet, had dreams, and around 1930 he retired to a house he had bought in Jamaica, Long Island. There he composed a couple of symphonies, an orchestral suite based on the "St. Louis Blues," and a one-act opera with a libretto by Langston Hughes. Some of these were performed, but none were recorded. In the late thirties, John Hammond's Carnegie Hall "From Spirituals to Swing" concerts brought Johnson out of retirement, and he made a fine series of solo and small-band jazz recordings. In 1940, he suffered a stroke. Several years later, he was back again, appearing on some classic Blue Note recordings, as well as with desultory Dixieland groups. In 1951, a second stroke permanently disabled him.

Although Johnson metamorphosed from a slim, dapper man with a long, narrow head into a bear with a profusion of lips and double chins, his style—give or take a little elaboration—remained much the same. All in all, he was the steadiest and most refined Harlem stride pianist. Luckey Roberts, who taught Johnson, was and is more showy, and there is a Fragonard quality in his slow playing. Willie the Lion Smith, a contemporary of Johnson, has a frightening rhythmic bark but not much melodic bite, which was generally true of Waller, a first-rate second-rate pianist. Many of Johnson's compositions reflect the Old South church-meeting atmosphere of his home when he was a child. His "Carolina Shout" and "The Mule Walk" are *dances*, and they have an exuberant, extrovert air. This cheerful openness flowed into Johnson's playing, which has little of the dark, in-turning concentration of Southern jazz musicians. Indeed, his piano often suggests the bounce of polkas and schottishes. In contrast to Jimmy Yancey, who wore his soul on his sleeve, Johnson played *at* the blues; he never seemed to take them seriously—an attitude shared by Waller and Art Tatum, both Northerners. But the emotional caution of Johnson's composing and playing was balanced by the glistening architecture of his style. When necessary, his left hand produced oompah patterns equalled only by Waller and Smith. These figures, though, were constantly relieved by offbeat chords, rests, and little melodic lines, all of which gave his oompah twice as much force. His right hand was brilliantly casual. He liked broken arpeggios (Monk, Bud Powell), and generously spaced chords (Tatum) that outlined the melody and then floated off. He liked to decorate the melody with a furze of staccato, single-note lines, and he liked the ring of the upper registers and the boom of the deepest octave. But he was never predictable. His chords were oddly placed (Monk again), and, just at the right moment, they dissolved into single notes or runs that in turn fell before brief, virtuoso breaks and arrhythmic interludes (Tatum again). No matter how fast the tempo, Johnson never hurried (John Lewis). And no matter how slow the tempo, he never dragged (Basie). Most important, Johnson's solos, of whatever length, were not bound by measures and bridges and reprises but were wholes—an improvisational skill only recently rediscovered by the young abstract performers.

Two welcome sets of Johnson reissues have now been put out—"Backwater Blues: The Stride Piano of James P. Johnson" and "James P. Johnson: Father of the Stride Piano." They stretch from 1920 to 1939, forming a nearly complete picture of Johnson's career. The twelve numbers on the first record were done between 1920 and 1927 as piano rolls. Four ("Charleston," "Daintiness Rag," "It Takes Love to Cure the Heart's Disease," and "Caprice Rag") are by Johnson. By and large, the record reveals the flashy, stylized Johnson of the rent parties. Ragtime influences are still strong, particularly in "Daintiness Rag," "Caprice Rag," and "Baltimore Buzz." More impressive, though, are Johnson's left hand in "Vampin' Liza Jane," when he matches runs and single notes against right-hand slurs; his left-hand tremolos and right-hand staccato figures in "Don't Tell Your Monkey Man"; and, in "Gypsy Blues," his heavy right-hand chords and the plopping left-hand single notes. "Backwater Blues," made in 1927, has a boogie-woogie bass, tremolos, and the porous stride attack that Albert Ammons and Pete Johnson sometimes used a decade later. It is an excellent example of Johnson balancing a blues on one finger and saying, in a mock-melancholy way, "Ah, yes, those *sad, sad* blues."

There are sixteen selections on the second record. Five are piano solos from the twenties; one is a funny 1930 duet with Clarence Williams; five are 1939 piano solos; and five are small-band sides from the same year. The 1939 solos show Johnson at his peak. He is less mannered and fussy than he was in the twenties, and he uses more pronounced dynamics and rhythms. "If Dreams Come True," the best of the lot, has glassy out-of-tempo interludes and irresistible oompah passages, and "The Mule Walk" rolls with polyrhythms. "Blueberry Rhyme" has a rhapsodic Tatum quality. The small-band sides, made with Red Allen, J. C. Higginbotham, Gene Sedric, Al Casey, Johnny Williams or Pops Foster, and Sidney Catlett, fall below the small-band efforts Johnson made with Frankie Newton for Victor and with Sidney De Paris and Ben Webster for Blue Note. But there are good moments from Allen and Higginbotham and Catlett, the last of whom adopted an attack when he played with Johnson that was a delicate mixture of spoofing and respect. The piano solos from the twenties are creditable, though poorly recorded. Fortunately, Ellington's short eulogy of Johnson in the liner notes has none of the customary lollipop flavor of his public effusions. James P., a disciplined man, would be pleased.

## The Well

Sometimes the best place to hear jazz is outdoors, beneath trees or in the sun. Sometimes it is under a circus tent during a thunderstorm. Sometimes it is in a classroom. (Thelonious Monk, with Louis Bellson on drums and Jimmy Hamilton on clarinet, demonstrating how "Tea for Two" sounds as written and in Monk fashion), and sometimes it is in an abandoned Elks hall or a living room (Pee Wee Russell, sitting in a curved-back Pennsylvania Dutch rocker—his profile to his listeners—and playing the blues, with George Wein on the piano). Once in a great while it is in a concert hall, which tends to separate the musicians and the audience and which inflicts echoing amounts of space on the musicians. It is never in a recording studio, whose clinical confines and now-or-never pressures cage the musician. And sometimes it is in the night club, which, for better or worse, has nurtured the music for many years.

Since the disappearance of the ideal, longhouse-shaped clubs on West Fifty-second Street, the downtown New York jazz clubs have sprouted in cavernous basements (some of them like swimming pools and some of them like old-fashioned hotel lobbies), in reconverted stores, in old dance halls, in bars, and in cafeterias. One of the most satisfactory of these was the Five Spot, a plain Third Avenue bar, at the foot of Cooper Square, that took on jazz in the mid-fifties simply by adding a piano and a small bandstand. It was small and unpretentious and you could see and hear from anywhere in the room. As a result, it was intricately awash with music and reaction, reaction and music. Then the building it occupied was torn down and it vanished. But in March a new Five Spot opened, three blocks north, on Third Avenue and Eighth Street, in a reconverted cafeteria.

The new one comes in three sections. Behind its glass front is a kind of arcade filled with small tables. This is separated from the main room by a wall punctuated with four archways, and the main room, which is about thirty by fifty and has a long bar down one side, is partly divided by a row of mirror-encased pillars. The bandstand is at right angles to the bar. The tables are cafeteria tables, the walls are a heavy red, and the ceiling is literally carpeted in matching red. It is a spacious room, with good sound and little atmosphere. Thelonious Monk, fresh from a tour of Japan, was at the new Five Spot recently with his quartet (Charlie Rouse on tenor saxophone, Butch Warren on bass, and Frankie Dunlop on drums). During the past three or four years, Monk has gone through a curious transformation: he has retreated physically from the world while his music has grown increasingly aggressive and explicit. He now generally performs in a disguise that consists of a hat (the other night, he was wearing a narrow-brimmed Tyrolean model, its crown pushed out in a sawed-off stovepipe effect), dark glasses, two blunderbuss-sized rings, one on each hand, and his beard, which is slowly increasing in length. He never speaks to his audiences, nor does he face them when, at least once in every number, he gets up from the piano and—his arms outspread and groping, his torso erect, his feet flapping—performs a unique soft-shoe. Thus, even though he is unmistakably there, it is difficult to *see* him. At the same time, his playing, once an equal mixture of sound and silence, has become extraordinarily busy. Savory dissonant chords dwindle abruptly into stiff, purposely crooked arpeggios. Repeated single-note figures end in crossed-hands chords or in upper-register splats effected with his right elbow. Stride-piano basses appear and disappear. And his backing-up, which includes his dancing and is both a fun-house mirror of and a prod for the soloist, is just as busy. All this was apparent at the Five Spot, particularly in a slow solo version of "Don't Blame Me"; "Crisscross"; a fine, lingering "I'm Getting Sentimental Over You," in which he played, almost note for note, Tommy Dorsey's celebrated solo, and then—after a quick, tantalizing pause—parodied it; "Well, You Needn't"; "Epistrophy"; and "Blue Monk," in which he stayed close to the melody, while repeatedly reorganizing its rhythmic structure. (Monk's sets are at least an hour long, and usually contain half a dozen numbers.) His quartet is satisfactory. Rouse is an intense, often affecting saxophonist whose hard-bop outlines have gradually softened, and Butch Warren is another of the gifted bassists who have appeared in the wake of Charlie Mingus. Dunlop is a measured, careful soloist and a measured, careful accompanist (Monk, though, loves a drummer who will occasionally war with him). But his accompanists matter little; his music is a well, and at its bottom—alone and furiously digging—is Monk himself.

## The Ladies

By releasing "Billie Holiday: The Golden Years" and "Mildred Bailey: Her Greatest Performances," three-record sets, each containing forty-eight selections, the first made between 1933 and 1941 and the second between 1929 and 1946, Columbia is doing a public service. So it is an apt time to ponder again the miraculous work of Billie Holiday, which has not dated, and to ponder Mildred Bailey, who was just about unclassifiable.

In spite of their differences, the two women had strikingly similar careers and even personalities. Both attracted and held small, vociferous coteries, and both were unsuccessful commercially. Both had appearances that went against them—Mildred Bailey was fat and plain, and Billie Holiday was a Negro. Partly for these reasons, both were emotional cripples. Mildred Bailey was addicted to food and Billie Holiday to drugs. Both made good money at times and died poor. Both had unsatisfactory relations with men and lavished their affections on pets. Both had sharp tongues and sharp tempers. Both had a sense of humor and delighted in kidding inferior material into superior material. Both lived to the age of forty-four, and both died puzzled, bitter women.

Mildred Bailey's singing had set by the late twenties, and it never changed. She was already a sizable woman, and, like many fat people, she had a little voice, a trapped voice. It gave the impression of being a miniature one, with everything in scale. It was also pure and neat. She used her vibrato (which was quite pronounced in the twenties) sparingly, her diction was absolutely clear, and she never went off pitch. She generally placed her notes on or a trifle behind the beat, and she always placed them perfectly. She never growled or allowed any huskiness in her voice, and she rarely indulged in blue notes. She had a finished, sweet, china-doll voice, and she sang as well at the end of her career as she did at the beginning. But Mildred Bailey had no real style. Her *voice* was unmistakable, but the conscious imbalances and flourishes and original colorations that are the marks of style were missing. She might have become a good comic singer. This is suggested by the Betty Boop scat passages she sometimes slipped into and by her funny, bouncy handling of ridiculous lyrics. She sang the blues the way she sang "There's a Cabin in the Pines"—directly, discreetly, assuredly, and with small emotion. Indeed, the emotional content of her singing was turned inward. One had the feeling that if she let it out, she knew it would shake her to pieces. So she was not emotional and she was not sentimental; a good jazz singer must be the first and a good popular singer the second. She was caught between.

This plight is clear all through the Columbia album. Again and again, on the fine sides made in 1935 with Bunny Berigan and Johnny Hodges, and on those made later with Mary Lou Williams, she inches up to the verge and seems about to tip over into jazz singing, but then she retreats into what she *knows* she can do. And there are many instances, in numbers like "Thanks for the Memory," "Heaven Help This Heart of Mine," and " 'Tain't What You Do," when she just misses a plain, rousing popular vocal. After a time the no-man's-land in which Mildred Bailey ran continually and hopelessly from side to side palls. Each vocal sounds like the last; not even material and tempo make a difference. One turns for relief to her accompanists, among them Red Norvo, Benny Goodman, the John Kirby band, a Basie contingent, Coleman Hawkins, Chu Berry, Roy Eldridge, and Teddy Wilson, but they, too, never rise past a predictable level.

Billie Holiday had everything Mildred Bailey lacked. In fact, it was a superabundance, and when she discovered this she tried to control it, but with disastrous results. She simply hardened a marvellously intuitive style and almost overnight turned it into mannered torch singing, and when her voice gave out, around 1950, there was nothing left but a stylized skeleton. But it is always astonishing to return to the records she made before 1939. They are superb jazz recordings, and a few—"I Must Have That Man," "What a Night, What a Moon, What a Girl," "It's Too Hot for Words," "Miss Brown to You"—are possibly without peer. No matter how many times they are heard, they remain fresh, and even when one hums her melodic lines from memory they magically retain their surprise. This surprise comes from her effortless refashioning of the melody; her remarkable simultaneous stretching and reshaping of the lyrics, which nonetheless are never garbled (listen to the way she makes one long, bumpy word out of the first twelve words of "Them There Eyes" in the Columbia album: "IfellinlovewithyouthefirsttimeIlookedinto—them there eyes"; once heard, never forgotten); her wit and humor; the continually changing colors in her voice, effected through her use of vibrato, huskiness, and bent notes, and by playing hob with the beat; and her steady, enclosing warmth. All these qualities are apparent on the first two records of the Columbia set, which begin with her extremely creditable 1933 début and which end in 1939. And the accompaniment, particularly when Teddy Wilson, Lester Young, and Buck Clayton are on hand, is as good as she is. (Such is not the case on three previously unreleased air shots made in 1937 at the Savoy Ballroom, when she was with the Basie band, which sounds like the rabble marching off to Quebec.) The rest of the album distinctly falls off. Self-consciousness had set in, and many of the post-1938 numbers are strained. The tempos drag and the brilliant fun of the early sides is gone. Numbers like "Gloomy Sunday," "I Cover the Waterfront," "Time on My Hands," and "Body and Soul" are depressing.

Both the Bailey and Holiday albums come with booklets that have good photographs, complete discographies, and varyingly fulsome appreciations. The Bailey booklet, though, includes three sentences by Irving Townsend that amount to an epitaph: "I remember watching her late one night at her farm in upstate New York while she listened to a record of Duke Ellington's 'Black Butterfly.' She sat at the kitchen table with a single candle blowing in the wind from the open door. The shadows of the leaves on the maples outside the door danced all over the kitchen walls, and Mildred played the record over and over again as if afraid the trees might stop blowing if the band did."

## Evans vs. Evans

The most impressive of modern pianists is Bill Evans, a pale, shy, emaciated figure who wears glasses and long hair combed flat, and who, when he plays, hunches like an S over the keyboard, his face generally turned away from his audience, as if the struggle of improvisation were altogether too personal to be practiced in public. For Evans, improvisation is obviously a constant contest—a contest between his intense wish to practice a wholly private, inner-ear music and an equally intense wish to express his jubilation at having found such a music within himself. When Evans edged into sight five years ago, as a sideman in experimental and modern-jazz groups (one was led by Miles Davis, who has long waged a war similar to Evans'), his extrovert tendencies were uppermost. Already a finished pianist, with a sure touch, perfect rhythm, and a superb dynamic sense, Evans was marked by Bud Powell and Lennie Tristano. At medium and fast tempos, he played long, uniquely shaped single-note phrases that were distinguished by staccato figures, sudden on-the-beat or double-time clusters, and short, purposeful arpeggios. (Most jazz pianists exude arpeggios the way a squid exudes ink; by the time the clouds of sound clear, a new idea has been found and the danger is over.) These three attacks were rhythmically and melodically exciting because they were beautifully juxtaposed, and they were the means of building within each solo a series of bright climaxes. That is, Evans would play six or seven close-together, ascending, on-the-beat notes, abruptly accenting the last one, and perhaps repeating it several times; he would then quickly fall into a little run, would pause, and would begin climbing another slope of the hill, this time in a staccato onetwothreefourfive manner, until he again reached the top note, which he would again accent before lightly rolling away through both soft and loud notes. These undulations had a windblown sound, and their most insistent sections pulled tenaciously at his listeners, making them strain to hear what surely came from Evans' depths. At slow tempos, he turned inward, playing pedalled Debussy chords, and his single notes were filigree. It was a wistful, aeolian-harp music.

When Evans formed a trio, late in 1959, with Scott La Faro on bass and Paul Motian on drums, a peculiar thing happened: The burden of being *the* soloist instead of *a* soloist appeared too much for him, and he became increasingly ruminative and withdrawn. He experimented endlessly with slow, cloudy numbers, and the singing climaxes all but vanished. Then, in the spring of 1961, La Faro, a stunning musician who tried to draw Evans out by working contrapuntally with him and by playing daringly executed solos, was killed in an accident, and Evans' work became even more closeted and gloomy. The irony was uncomfortably plain: Evans, shy to the point of pain, had become a young Werther. But in the past year Evans has unexpectedly made three quite different recordings—a duet with Jim Hall, a trio effort with Shelly Manne and Monty Budwig, and a small-band date with Freddie Hubbard, Hall, Percy Heath, and Philly Joe Jones—which suggest that he is again doing battle with himself.

"Undercurrent," which he recorded with Hall, resembles two close friends talking quietly late at night. There are six standards, one of them Hall's "Romain," and each consists of gentle ensemble passages, sometimes with and sometimes without a lead voice, and brief solos in which the accompanist moves into the background. Nobody bothers about steady tempos, but if one seems appropriate, it is sounded and then abandoned before it becomes assertive. "Romain" and John Lewis's "Skating in Central Park" work out best; the two men are in clearest accord, and Evans even goes through the motions of setting up and knocking down several climaxes. These moments invigorate Hall, who in turn cheers Evans.

Unlike Elvin Jones and Philly Joe Jones and Billy Higgins, who use the drums as polyrhythmic engines, Shelly Manne accomplishes his infinite colorations through implication. His work, particularly behind pianists and bassists, abounds in odd, pleasant, oblique sounds—fingers and hands on cymbals, a silver dollar spinning on a drumhead, ruffling wire brushes, and occasional tom-tom or cymbal-top pongs. In four of the six numbers (all standards) in "Shelly Manne/Bill Evans with Monty Budwig: Empathy," Evans responds to these touches with vigorous solos, full of up-and-down figures, startling rhythmic and harmonic turns, and an iron concentration. Manne takes a couple of delightful solos ("The Washington Twist" and "With a Song in My Heart"), which, as is usual with him, are partly contrapuntal exercises with either piano or bass and partly pure solo. Indeed, they are refreshing offshoots of the ensemble rather than look-Ma exhibitions. Budwig is a skilled bassist and a sufficient soloist. And, near the end of "With a Song in My Heart," Evans reveals a new side by dropping in a heavy, mock-pompous statement of the melody that comically evokes everything from Victor Herbert baritones to Erroll Garner.

Evans responds almost as well to Philly Joe Jones in "Interplay: Bill Evans

Quintet" (Riverside) as he does to Manne. Jones can be overweening, but he restricts himself here to precise pushing. (His loudness is caused by recording imbalance.) Listen to his worrying but exact ride-cymbal patterns behind Hall in "Interplay," an ingenious medium-tempo blues by Evans (the five other numbers are standards), and to his pumping hi-hat work during the ensembles. Hall is in good form, and Heath, as always, is safe and polished. Unfortunately, Hubbard, who is still an overblowing admirer of Miles Davis and Art Farmer, tends to jar the easy communion of the rhythm section. His presence, in fact, induces wishful thinking. Had either Davis or Farmer been on hand, Evans, who has made some of his best recordings with them, might have shaken off the last of his melancholia.

Since the release of these recordings, Evans' new trio (Gary Peacock on bass and Paul Motian on drums) has been taken on as the house band at the Village Vanguard. On the basis of its showing one night recently, it is an intense, welling-up group. It works contrapuntally a great deal of the time, with both Peacock, a superb bassist in the tradition of La Faro, and Motion developing their own "melodic" lines instead of acting as mere timekeepers. Evans, more of a ghostly figure than ever, seems freer and has perhaps found the median between his Werther musings and open, selfless playing. In a long, medium-slow rendition of Monk's " 'Round Midnight," which has the sort of imperious melody that almost commands note-for-note repetition, he attacked from every point—with loose chords, rising and falling single-note clusters, and excited rhythmic turns. The tune gradually softened under these pressures, and became a perfectly harmonious composition by Monk *and* Evans. Similar happy collaborations took place during the evening, giving the impression, all in all, that Evans' celebration of himself has resumed.

## Herd After Herd

One of the oddest contagions in jazz was the outpouring of big quasi-jazz bands that proliferated from 1935 to 1950. The most celebrated of the countless dozens that could be found in every ballroom, movie house, hotel, and college gym in the country in the late thirties and early forties were led by Glen Gray, Benny Goodman, Artie Shaw, Jan Savitt, Bob Crosby, Glenn Miller, Will Bradley, the Dorsey brothers, Harry James, Les Brown, Charlie Barnet, Bob Chester, Woody Herman, and Stan Kenton. These bands crowded the sizable gap between, on the left, the genuine jazz bands led by Duke Ellington, Count Basie, Jimmie Lunceford, and Benny Carter and, on the right, the out-and-out dance bands of Shep Fields, Russ Morgan, Guy Lombardo, and Alvino Rey. Indeed, it is difficult not to think of them in political terms. Their leaders, in the main, were smiling, affable businessmen, bent on pleasing all of the people all of the time. Their organizations were polished, predictable, and popular, and were capable of rabble-rousing and speaking softly. They were dead center musically, avoiding the heresies of the left and the Mickey Mouse tendencies of the right. Sometimes they were grandiloquent (Artie Shaw) and sometimes they were just folks (Glenn Miller). In short, they were paragons of conservatism, and while they were in office they ruled with a becalming moderation. The most agile and durable of these all-but-extinct bands is Woody Herman's, now in its twenty-eighth year of public service. Herman has tried to please not only his fellow-conservatives but also impressionable listeners on both flanks. He has done this by discreetly adapting the more accessible experiments of the left and mixing them with the least gluey ones from the right. As a result, the various Herman bands, or Herds, as they are called, have always sounded fresh and up-to-date. But, like the insistently *au courant*, the Herds tend to falter under a hard contemporary stare, and even worse things happen when they are subjected to hindsight.

Such is the case with the First and Second Herds, many of whose records have been reissued in an album titled "Woody Herman: 'The Thundering Herds.' " Its three LPs contain forty-five numbers, and the years covered are 1945 to 1948. The First Herd evolved from the Infant Herd, an almost forgotten group that, in 1936, grew out of the Isham Jones orchestra. In the manner of the early bands of Tommy Dorsey, Bob Crosby, and Artie Shaw, the Infant Herd tried to inflate Dixieland to big-band proportions. It used two-beat rhythms, and its arrangements suggested the collective interplay of the Dixieland ensemble. It played pop songs and novelty numbers, and a lot of blues, which it handled in the self-conscious gut-bucket fashion of Dixieland bands. Aside from Cappy Lewis, an estimable Bunny Berigan student, and Neal Reid, a Jack Teagarden–flavored trombonist with an enormous range, its soloists were unprepossessing. Herman, a thin, short, pleasant-faced man from Milwaukee, played the clarinet like Jimmy Noone and the alto saxophone like Johnny Hodges. The band sank during the early years of the war, and then, in 1944, made a handful of records for Decca that showed a sudden fondness for Duke Ellington. (Hal McIntyre and Charlie Barnet had been seized by similar enthusiasms.) Ben Webster and Johnny Hodges and Juan Tizol sat in on some of these recordings, illuminating otherwise gray efforts. Another quiet period followed; then, early in 1945, the First Herd roared over the horizon. It was a nineteen-piece band made up of a lot of fledglings (Sonny Berman, Pete Candoli, Ralph Burns, Billy Bauer, Chubby Jackson) and a few veterans (Flip Phillips, Bill Harris, Dave Tough), and at first it appeared to be travelling fast. It was noisy and excited and determined, and everyone pointed out how much it *swung*. Those good old Goodman days were back, people said. Then it became clear that the band's repertory consisted of just two basic patterns—one fast and one slow. The fast numbers, or flag-wavers, were based on blues and standards, and were played in loose, on-the-spot (or "head") arrangements, which went something like this: a riff, repeated for sixteen bars by the saxophones and supported only by the rhythm section, followed by an eight-bar piano solo on the bridge; return of the riff, with background trumpet punctuations, and the first chorus ends; next, a broken-rhythm interlude, introducing trombonist Bill Harris, who plays one chorus, backed by a saxophone figure; another interlude, introducing Flip Phillips, who plays two tenor-saxophone choruses, backed by a trombone figure; a gathering of wind and steam; and two final, overheated ensemble riff choruses, which include a bridge played by Herman on clarinet, a bridge played by a high-noted trumpeter, whose effects are echoed, in floor-show fashion, by the drummer, and a rum-te-dum coda by the bassist or drummer. After a time, the flag-wavers ("Northwest Passage," "Apple Honey," "Caldonia," "Blowin' Up a Storm") became interchangeable, and only their tempos varied. However, Charlie Parker and Dizzy Gillespie, busy elsewhere, helped by continually putting forward new patterns, and so did Basie and Jimmie Lunceford. The slow numbers, adapted mostly from the right, were ballads and novelties and were built around vocals by Herman ("Put That Ring on My Finger") or Frances Wayne ("Happiness Is a Thing Called Joe") or around fulsome solos by Bill Harris ("Everywhere") or Flip Phillips ("With Someone New"). Harris specialized in staccato, circus-band phrases, and Phillips swam back and forth between Ben Webster and Lester Young. The First Herd was also rife with humorists. There were funny vocals, mostly by Herman ("Caldonia"), cute trumpet licks ("Goosey Gander"), a lot of *in-medias-res* shouting, and catchy codas. Like the Shriners, the First Herd had a lot of harmless fun.

Late in 1946, however, it grew serious and recorded a three-part suite by Ralph Burns called "Summer Sequence," which was full of dappled guitar passages (Chuck Wayne) and lacy piano fills (Burns). It was the sort of impressionistic, finger-bowl piece that Billy Strayhorn sometimes exudes. The effort proved fatal, and not long afterward the First Herd disbanded. In 1947, the Second Herd galloped into view. The new band had digested bebop, and it also had a new saxophone section, made up of three tenors and a baritone. Lester Young, in the person of such admirers as Herbie Steward, Stan Getz, and Zoot Sims, was everywhere, and there was a drummer, Don Lamond, who dropped bass-drum bombs and accented each phrase with stop-the-music rimshots. (The one ornament of the First Herd, Dave Tough, had been responsible for whatever grace the band had. Using ingenious, liquid, perfectly pitched cymbal work and beautifully placed accents, he tricked more than one listener into believing it was the band, and not he, that was swinging so.) The slow-or-fast pattern of the repertory remained unchanged, but it was now coated with the multi-note melodic lines of bebop. Moreover, the flag-wavers ("Keen and Peachy," "The Goof and I," "Four Brothers") were more nonchalant, and the slow tunes were jazzier and often taken up by Herman vocals delivered in a husky, low-down buzz.

This is roughly where the album ends, but the Second Herd went on, with occasional personnel refuelling, until 1949. A year or so later, the Third

Herd an even cooler version of the Second, crossed the prairies, alternating between well-combed flag-wavers and sotto-voce riff numbers that recalled Lunceford's "Organ Grinder's Swing." For the rest of the fifties, the Third Herd continued, in reincarnation after reincarnation, in the same direction, although at one point it was reduced to a distilled but recognizable octet. In its present reincarnation, the band, which has lots of new young soloists, displays considerable affection for the high points of the Second and even the First Herd, as well as for Ellington, the blues, and the fashionable accents of gospel music. All the Herds have now been conveniently rolled into one, which should please the voters a good deal.

*I don't agree with this rather sour piece. The First Herd, with Dave Tough performing rhythm miracles, sometimes rose right off the ground, it swung so hard. Harris was a good trombonist and Phillips was more than adequate. And the Second Herd had the Four Brothers saxophone section, which gave it an unmistakable texture and swing, an originality.*

## A Burning Desire

A few weeks ago, I got a letter from Vance Bourjaily, the novelist and an assistant professor of English at the State University of Iowa, telling me that Lou Black, the original banjoist with the New Orleans Rhythm Kings, a seven-piece white group that set Chicago on its ear in 1921, was considering a part-time comeback. He went on to say that Black, who is a hunting and fishing companion of his, had retired from music in 1931 and had become a successful Midwestern businessman as well as a "legendary shotgun shooter and fly-caster"; that he had bought a new thousand-dollar banjo nearly a year ago and had been practicing ever since; and that the results were astonishingly good. He closed by saying that he and Black would be in New York soon, and suggested that I call Black at the Gramercy Park Hotel. I did, and arranged to meet him at the hotel. He sounded big and hearty on the phone, and before he hung up, he uttered these cautionary words: "One thing I want to make absolutely clear, sir. I wouldn't go back into the music business full-time for all the tea in China. I'm sixty-two and have too much sense."

I found that Black *is* big and hearty—tall, bald, and ample-waisted, with an open, generous face and a wide smile. He was dressed in a short-sleeved white shirt, a brown tie, black slacks, and black shoes. "You know, I don't understand it," he said. "I went out this morning for breakfast in this shirt and a summer jacket, and people were wearing hats and overcoats up to their ears. This is some place! I can go fishing on North Wind Lake in the big woods way up north in Ontario and not get turned around for a second. Here, I never know where I'm at or what's going to happen next. Last night, Vance and Jim Silberman, an editor, and I went over to Bourbon Street. I took my banjo and they asked me to play, and, by golly, we were there until four o'clock. I'm a small-town boy likes to go to bed early. Dick Wellstood was on piano and Ahmed Abdul-Malik was on bass, and Malik told me he'd never heard things like that on the banjo. I can tell you I was pleased. I hadn't touched the instrument for thirty years when one day, around last Christmas, my daughter Joyce—she's an accomplished pianist—said, 'I want you to teach me the banjo.' I said, 'You're crazy, a beautiful girl like you playing banjo.' My wife, Natalie, who's a darn good Dixieland pianist, said, 'Nonsense, Dad. Go ahead and teach her.' We were at it two or three weeks, and then I said, 'What we need is another banjo.' I went to Chicago and bought this Vega, and we played duets, and suddenly I discovered I'd been lonely for playing. Of course, I'm not completely happy with it yet. Some things I used to do on the instrument are still quite impossible. As soon as I get this new banjo working, I may try a recording, but there's no rush. If there's anything more pitiful than a has-been trying to make a comeback who isn't ready, I don't know it."

I asked Black when he had first taken up the instrument.

"When I was about seven," he replied. "I was born in Rock Island, Illinois, where I still live. My dad was a conductor on the Chicago, Rock Island & Pacific, and he played banjo, and he and my mother used to sing old songs like 'Nelly Gray.' I had a burning desire to play the banjo, and it was my brother started me on it. Oh, my, he was good! When I was around twelve, I met a banjoist named Homer Garber in Des Moines, through relatives, and he showed me some things. He was a clerk in a cigar store, and he was the best banjo player I've ever heard. I started professionally in 1917, with a dentist named Wrixon. He had a four- or five-piece outfit, and we played the Rock Island society parties, the country club, and a dance hall named the Coliseum, which is still going. My schooling—I'd been through twelve years in nine—was already over, and in 1919 I joined Carlisle Evans, a pianist and good, solid orchestra man. Evans' Original Jazz Band, his group was called. In 1920, we worked on the riverboat *Capitol* between St. Louis and St. Paul in the summer, and around New Orleans in the winter. Leon Roppolo, the clarinettist, was in the band, and so were Emmet Hardy, a marvelous cornetist who never recorded, and Leon Prima, Louie's brother. I left Evans in 1921 and went over to the New Orleans Rhythm Kings, which already had Roppolo, Jack Pettis on saxophone, Frank Snyder on drums, George Brunies on trombone, Paul Mares on cornet, and Elmer Schoebel on piano. Steve Brown, the bassist, joined after me. We were at the Friar's Inn for a couple of years, and when we'd finish work, or when there were no more customers to play for, we'd go over to the Dreamland and sit in with Pop Oliver and Louis Armstrong. You know why he was called Pop? When he played, his right eye came almost out of the socket from the force of his blowing. It was the damnedest sight I've ever seen. He had enormous lips, too, and his cornet mouthpiece would disappear right inside them. Once in a while, he'd stand up there in front of the band, cradle the cornet on its valves on a handkerchief in his left hand, put his right hand in his pocket, and play ten or eleven choruses of 'Tiger Rag' or 'Dippermouth Blues' without ever touching the valves with his right hand and without repeating himself. Nobody ever matched Pop Oliver, except Bix Beiderbecke, who sat in with us when he was in town. Once, someone wrote out one of Bix's solos note for note and, without letting on, put the transcription in front of him and asked him to play it. Bix, who was a grand kid, looked at the music and looked at him, and said, 'Hell, I can't play that fancy stuff!' Dave Tough and Jimmy McPartland and Bud Freeman used to hang around, and Jelly Roll Morton did too. Well, the Rhythm Kings broke up in 1923—largely for personal reasons—and some of us joined the Memphis Melody Boys. It was a dance band—an eight-forty-five–to–eleven-forty-five band. In 1925, I rejoined Carlisle Evans, and a few years later I began jobbing around, and then, because things were already beginning to fall apart, I took a job as a staff man with Station WHO, in Des Moines, where I stayed until 1931. Then I quit music and went to work for a roofing company, and in 1940 I joined John Deere, the farm-implement manufacturers. After the war, I was hired by the Moline Consumers Company, where I'm an outdoor-building-materials man. I'm never going to retire, and I've made my boss sign a statement saying he'll never make me. I'll retire when I fall right flat dead on my face."

Black got up, stretched, walked easily up and down the room several times, and sat down. "I said my playing again would be a part-time thing, and that's just what it is. Since last August, I've been working two nights a week at the Arabian Room of the Holiday Inn, in Moline, with a trio. There wasn't anybody around those parts who remembered who Lou Black the banjoist was, but now the place is packed. The banjo has been maligned, and I'd like to help set that right. Brian Rust, the English jazz critic, has been writing me, and he'd like me to come over to England and play. An English friend of Vance's says that in England everyone knows who Lou Black is."

## Uncharted

For purposes of orientation, I sometimes travel by mental helicopter over an imaginary relief map of Western music, which looks like this: On the right is a broad, old river, its many sources buried deep in Appalachian-type mountains. It is marked "Classical," and it has countless tributaries, some generally identified (Hungarian-Folk, Indian-Folk), some specifically (Monteverdi, Palestrina, Gluck). On the left of the map is a shorter, far narrower river, originating in a peak-encircled lake. These are the river Jazz and Lake European-African. The river courses through canyons and over dangerous rapids until it comes out on the same plateau as the Classical. It, too, has tributaries, some generally named (Spirituals, Field Cries, Blues), some specifically (Scott Joplin, Louis

Armstrong, James P. Johnson). On the plateau separating the rivers, however, is a sizable stream fed by trickles from the rivers and called the Third Stream, or Schuller's Brook, after its discoverer, Gunther Schuller. This stream heads toward and perhaps feeds into—I am not always sure—a swampy, unexplored area. At any rate, during much of a third-stream concert given by the Orchestra U.S.A. at Hunter College, I found myself hovering between the brook and the swamp.

The Orchestra U.S.A. is a twenty-nine-piece coöperative group made up about half and half of jazz and classical musicians, and directed by John Lewis, the musical director of the Modern Jazz Quartet. Lewis and Gunther Schuller act as conductors. According to an inclusive program note, the orchestra was "organized for the purpose of exploring fully the possibilities of the wide repertoire which the modern musician of all-around ability and understanding can perform." Last week, this repertoire consisted of a Bach fugue; two pieces by Miljenko Prohaska, a Yugoslavian jazz-and-classical musician; and six by Lewis. The Bach was the jazz counterpart of a Stokowski transcription, and used a light, ineffectual echoing of themes, supported by an occasionally sounded four-four beat. The rest of the repertoire had dimmer origins. Most had jazz rhythms, and most had solos of varying lengths by Gerry Mulligan (a guest), Eric Dolphy, Jerome Richardson, Joe Newman, and Lewis. The orchestrations suggested Gil Evans and Schuller and Jimmy Lunceford (Prohaska's "Intima"), and were overlaid here and there by strands of Debussy, Bartók, and Stravinsky. But, unlike some of the earlier and frequently exciting third-stream investigations by Schuller and Lewis, usually performed by less unwieldy groups, the selections played by the orchestra lacked the obvious qualities both of classical music (majesty, variety, complexity, passion) and of jazz (tone, timbre, improvisation, emotion).

The remainder of the evening was given over to seven straight jazz numbers played by Mulligan and such orchestra members as Jim Hall, Richard Davis, Connie Kay, and Lewis. All but one were standards, and all were distinguished by the work of Kay, Lewis, and Hall. Kay was comfortable with both groups, and his cymbal work demonstrated that it is, with the exception of Sid Catlett's and Dave Tough's, unprecedented in jazz. He uses thin, gorgeously toned cymbals, from which he gets a triangle-like ring, and he varies his patterns continually, often condensing the customary *da de-da* beat into a quick *da-da*. He never uses the expected cymbal, and he never plays at conventional volumes (thus his beautiful soft drumstick strokes behind the beginning of Mulligan's solo in "Poor Butterfly"; most drummers would have jumped in). Lewis was his succinct, impassioned self, and Hall played with a delicacy and thought that suggest he abandon the electric amplifier— a now superfluous device (guitarists adopted it during the big-band era simply to be heard) that distorts and cheapens the natural guitar sound. Mulligan was flawless and, for reasons beyond me, totally unaffecting. Perhaps the baritone saxophone, with its heavy tone, should not be played so *well*; Harry Carney and Serge Chaloff, though equally expert, purposely manhandle the instrument, breaking down its pomp and solemnity. Davis took a witty walking-bass solo in "The Way You Look Tonight," but elsewhere he used too many upper-register notes, which tended to jostle Kay's basically high-toned attack.

## Fortieth

The lot of the long-lived artist in this country is hazardous. He may be fulsomely praised too soon, and then suffer from the inevitable swing of the pendulum. Or he is ignored during his life, and canonized when he is dead. Or he is encircled by cultists, and abruptly seized upon by the public and sentimentalized. Or he is teasingly paid middling compliments, and then, the gears skipping a couple of speeds, is taken for granted. The last of these alternatives has long since been thrust upon Duke Ellington, who, now sixty-four, is celebrating his fortieth anniversary as a composer-orchestrator-bandleader-pianist. There are explanations of this suspended status. Ellington is unique, and he has usually been praised by the wrong people for the wrong reasons. The world of classical music has compared him favorably (and condescendingly) to Ravel and Delius and Debussy, although the two musics cannot be compared. The world of jazz—when it has not downgraded him out of jealousy or ignorance—has deified him solely as a jazz musician, though he is far more. The Broadway musical world has nervously clapped him on the back but has rarely sought him out for a form that, given the chance, he might well revolutionize.

But his originality, grace, durability, and variety demand that he be considered in relation to all American music. When that critical readjustment is made, it is immediately clear that Ellington, in his iconoclastic way, has constructed a musical organism without counterpart. This organism—built sometimes accidentally, sometimes consciously, but always painstakingly over the past four decades—functions something like this: Ellington composes a number, which may be a blues, a capsule concerto, a ballad, a program piece, a tone poem, a sly bit of portraiture, an up-tempo celebration of nothing in particular, or a reworking of a standard. It is tried out by the band, which makes suggestions, and an arrangement is developed. This arrangement is orchestrated and played over and over and, if it is found not wanting, passes into the band's repertory. Once there, it is far from static, for each time it is performed it is improvised upon, to different degrees, by both the ensemble and the soloists, among them the composer himself. Finally, a kind of composite rendition emerges, and a "Solitude" or "Mood Indigo" or "Never No Lament" takes permanent, though always malleable, shape. Thus Ellington is at once a classical and a popular-music composer, an interpretive classical musician, a conductor, and a jazz improviser.

How beautifully this organism functions at its best! Ellington is an extremely gifted melodist (he is comparable, in this respect, to Tchaikovsky). Moreover, unlike Gershwin and Berlin and Kern and Rodgers, whose finest tunes are discreet displays of subjective emotions, Ellington writes numbers that objectively suggest, with wit and poetry and subtlety and great taste, the *only* way to feel about a local train in the South, melancholy, the clatter in a Harlem air shaft, a beautiful woman, racism, a celebrated vaudevillian, a happy party, or a three-cent stamp, the last of which was immortalized in a number written in the forties and titled, naturally, "Three Cent Stomp." But Ellington is also a *composer*, whose miniature concertos are substantial in form and content as well as inimitable, and whose orchestrations, continually ruffled by the individualities of his sidemen, delight the ear and refresh the mind. The Ellington band, as the inseparable second half of this organism, is a remarkable democracy. Each member is a hero, yet each is beholden to the whole. The reason is brilliantly simple: Ellington, in shying away from such one-man bands as Armstrong and Lester Young and Charlie Parker, has chosen musicians whose originality stops at the eccentric rather than the iconoclastic. And yet these eccentrics—consider the varieties of sound and attack of such men as Cootie Williams, Jimmy Blanton, Lawrence Brown, Johnny Hodges, and Tricky Sam Nanton—have become a unit which is always a degree or two ahead of its marvelous parts.

These fortieth-anniversary thoughts have been provoked by Columbia's fitting release of "The Ellington Era: 1927–40." Although the album ends on the eve of Ellington's superb 1940–42 period (the property of Victor), it demonstrates, in many of its forty-eight numbers, just how Ellington readied himself and his band for that miraculous musical explosion. This preparation was accomplished in three bursts. The first, and faintest, lasted from 1925, when Ellington made his first records, to around 1928. The band was only on a par with Fletcher Henderson's and perhaps slightly below Jelly Roll Morton's various groups. It was distinguished by just two things— Ellington's already unmistakable talents as a composer ("Black and Tan Fantasy," "The Mooche," and "East St. Louis Toodleoo"), and the presence of Bubber Miley, Tricky Sam Nanton, Barney Bigard, Harry Carney, and Johnny Hodges. From 1927 to 1932, the band played for dancing and the floor show at Cotton Club, and these functions are reflected in its sassy fast tempos ("Jubilee Stomp"), its occasionally duddish saxophone-section work, and Ellington's showy ragtime stride piano. Miley and his pupil, Nanton, were already imposing soloists who, with their plunger mutes and growling, were contributing wholly new musical sounds, and Hodges, Carney, and Bigard forcefully suggested their later selves.

The second period opened in 1929, with the departure of Miley and the arrival of Cootie Williams and Juan Tizol, and it ended in 1935, when the band had swelled to fourteen men, among them Rex Stewart and Lawrence Brown. Ellington's tunes in these years became virtual compositions—such things as "Rockin' in Rhythm," "Mood Indigo," "It Don't Mean a Thing," and "Drop Me Off in Harlem." These used varying chorus lengths, simultaneous solos, new harmonies (especially in the background saxophone figures, as in "Blue Tune"), the human voice as an instrument, swelling and subsiding brass-section chords ("Bundle of Blues"), and such rhythmic devices as unexpected breaks, double-time passages, and Afro-Cuban beats. Ellington's soloists developed with remarkable speed, and by 1935 Williams, Brown, Hodges (on soprano and alto saxophones), Nanton, and Stewart were first-rate improvisers, while the band, by virtue of Ellington's scoring and the originality of its ensemble sound, had a new texture and consistency. It could play anything and play it uniquely—a mock-mournful blues ("Saddest Tale"), fast blues, descriptive stomps ("Lightnin'," "Old Man Blues"), mood pieces ("Solitude," "Lazy Rhapsody"), and standards ("Sheik of Araby").

In 1936, the band blossomed into the marvel it has been ever since. The rhythm section, long bedevilled by inadequate bassists and a general four-square approach, suddenly started to swing. Ellington began fashioning his perfect concertos around his sidemen ("Clarinet Lament" for Bigard, "Echoes of Harlem" for Williams, "Boy Meets Horn" for Stewart), and, in so doing, developed ensemble passages that were really collective alter-solos, often worthy of being expanded into whole numbers ("The Sergeant Was Shy"). Now and again, the entire band played together, in unison or in harmony—a rending, incredibly rich sound that is one of the delights of Western orchestral music. (Here is the nub of Ellington's success. Any proficient musician could transcribe such a passage and any proficient group of musicians could play it. But the results would not be the same, for no musician, regardless of his skill, could reproduce the timbre, tone, and inflections of Ellington's musicians. In short, their styles—massed into a single voice or heard alone—are as important to Ellington's music as his compositions.) In the six minutes of "Diminuendo in Blue" and "Crescendo in Blue," he proved once and for all that jazz can be a composed music, by letting the band roll through almost two dozen medium-tempo ensemble choruses of the blues, each completely different (an ingenious two-note saxophone riff, echoed by Cootie Williams—one chorus; a ripe-on-the-bough clarinet trio pitted against booming trombones—one chorus; and so forth). He went on writing gorgeous melodies—"I Let a Song Go Out of My Heart," "Prelude to a Kiss," "Subtle Lament," "Sophisticated Lady"—and his portraits of people took on an oblique and irresistible wittiness. The band, stimulated by these innovations, surpassed itself individually and collectively, and in turn stimulated Ellington. In 1939, when Billy Strayhorn, Ben Webster, and Jimmy Blanton were hired, the band reached perfection. One looked—and looks—for its match in jazz, on Broadway, and in the music of Copland and Virgil Thomson and Charles Ives. That this achievement—together with Ellington's sporadic echoes of it—should be taken for granted must distress him considerably. But gentlemen of genius never let on; they just keep working.

# Cootie

Duke Ellington's band has something in common with the Supreme Court: its members tend to stay put for life. Harry Carney has been with him since the Coolidge administration; Johnny Hodges, except for a five-year stint of iconoclasm, has played for him since 1928; Lawrence Brown, another temporary individualist, has occupied his chair most of the time since 1932; Jimmy Hamilton has been with Ellington for twenty-one straight years; and Ray Nance has, with the exception of a year or so, been around for twenty-two years. Thus, when one of Ellington's sidemen quits, seismographs pick up the tremors. At least, that happened in 1940, when Cootie Williams left Ellington, after twelve years of service, to join Benny Goodman. Williams received hundreds of how-could-you-you-traitor letters, there were half-mast editorials, and the bandleader Raymond Scott wrote and recorded a lament called "When Cootie Left the Duke."

Well, Williams, after an absence of twenty-two years, has rejoined Ellington. I recently caught up with him and asked him how it felt to be back in the fold.

"It feels good," Williams said, in a deep, laconic voice. "My name is still on some of the parts in the arrangements, and that makes me feel specially good. Oh, the band have changed some. Jimmy Blanton, he's gone, and Sonny Greer and Ben Webster and Tricky Sam Nanton, and I think Duke builds the band more around arrangements now than around soloists. Of course, he had a lot of soloists to work with when I left. One reason I came back with Duke is he's the greatest man I ever knew. Everybody thought when I left I just jumped up and out. That's not true. When Benny Goodman wanted me, I told Duke, and he said, 'Let me handle everything. Let me see how much I can get for you. You deserve to make some money.' So he did—he handled the contract. And when I left, I said 'You have my job open when the contract is up?' and he said 'Your chair's always open.' "

A medium-sized, barrel-chested man with a square, imperious face, Williams was wearing a dark-blue suit, a pale-blue shirt, and a tie with broad red and black stripes. "I was born in Mobile, Alabama, in 1910—not 1908, like the history books say. My mother was a church organist, and my father ran a gambling house along with a man named Son Coin. When I was around three or four, my parents took me to a band concert in the park, and on the way home they asked me what did I hear. I said, 'Cootie cootie cootie.' It stuck. I took up drums when I was about five, and later, in the school band, I wanted to switch to trombone. But my arms were too short to reach the lowest position on the slide, so the bandmaster told me, 'You play trumpet.' I said I didn't like the trumpet, so he gave me a whooping, and I played the trumpet. Louis Armstrong has always been my idol, and I saw him first one summer when the school band went up to Chicago. A little kid,

I stood outside the fence of the Oriental Garden, I think it was, and listened to Louis in King Oliver's band. When I got back that night, I got a whooping for that." Williams chuckled in a slow, easy way. "I worked around Mobile with Holman's jazz band and Johnny Pope's band, and then Edmond Hall, who was with Eagle-Eye Shields' band in Jacksonville, Florida, told Shields about me. Shields wanted to hire me, and Hall got hold of my father to see if it was all right. Well, Son Coin have relatives in Jacksonville, so my father say OK and put me in their care. Hall and I left Shields after two years and joined Alonzo Ross's band and toured all over Florida and Georgia. I believe we were the first colored band to play Miami. I was making two hundred and fifty or three hundred dollars a week and I was only seventeen. I sent it home to my father. Then a ballroom in Brooklyn sent for Ross's band, and after the engagement Hall and I stayed on. We got a job playing at a dancing school in midtown, and after-hours we used to jam at the Band Box, up at 131st Street. They specialized in certain instruments on certain nights, and on the night of the trumpet I always went there. One time, somebody got Chick Webb out of bed, and he came and listened to me and asked me to join him. He was at the Savoy Ballroom, and this would have been about 1928. I worked with Chick a month, and then the union delegate came around, and since I didn't have my union card, he and Chick got in a big argument. We went down to union headquarters, and this union man said, 'All right, I'll tell you what I'll do, young fellow. Until you get your card, I'll let you work with anyone in New York *but* Chick Webb.' Chick didn't want me with anyone else, so he paid me a salary. Then Fletcher Henderson asked Chick could I come with him on a six-week road trip, and Chick said yes. It was rough at first. Big Green, Henderson's trombonist, used to sit right behind me in the band, and he'd lean over and say, 'Boy, I'm going to kill you, kill you, kill you,' and Bobby Stark, the trumpeter, sat next to me, and he'd say, 'Big, leave this boy alone. What's the matter with you?' Big Green scared me to death. I worked with Henderson for a while at the Roseland Ballroom when we got back, and then Johnny Hodges told Duke Ellington about me and I joined him at the Cotton Club. It was quite a different sound in music. I laughed out loud at first when I heard those weird wa-wa-wa jungle sounds. Then it seemed to me since I'd been hired to take Bubber Miley's place, I better learn to play the mute like him. I never heard Bubber in person, so I learned from Tricky Sam Nanton. Duke didn't tell me I had to learn. I just did, and it didn't take very long."

Williams leaned back, smoothed his shirt with his hand, expanded his chest, and exhaled slowly. "When my contract with Benny Goodman was up in 1941, I asked Duke for my job back, and he told me, 'You're too big for the job. You're bigger than you think you are. Go on your own.' So I did. I organized a big band, and for a while things were bad. But in 1943 I made two hundred and fifty thousand dollars. Half of that went to my backers. Everybody had backers in those days, or they would have sunk. Then I quit my backers and *I* sunk, and in 1948 I gave up the big band and took on a small one. In the fifties, we worked the Savoy Ballroom for seven years, until it closed. Then I toured as a single, and that was the hardest musical experience I ever had. Once, in Toronto, I played with a local group that had other jobs during the day, and we'd play 'Do Nothin' Till You Hear from Me'— that's what they called Duke's old 'Concerto for Cootie' after they put lyrics to it—and that group sound like they was playing something else. I had to learn to close my ears. I couldn't take it after that, so I got my own quartet, and then I was a musical director for a singer, and then I played for a month so with Goodman, and finally I came back with Duke. And that's where I'll stay. My nerves are not good enough to go along with the crowd of musicians that are coming up. I went in Small's, in Harlem, a while back. A young tenor man—you'd know his name if you heard it—happened to be playing there. I listened. I thought, This can't be true. I left, and I came back and listened again, and it *was* true. I thought, He sound like a be*ginn*er to me." Williams chuckled. "Now, Charlie Parker and Bud Powell, they were *musicians*. Oh, they could play! I had both of them in my big band. But Charlie Parker was a bad influence on jazz. There never was a musician before that influenced all the instruments—saxophones, drums, trumpets, piano. Everybody had his own style in those days. Now everybody's Charlie Parker. Maybe in three or four months I'll write a book on the trumpet. I see so many young musicians don't even stand properly, don't know how to breathe. My power comes from breathing properly, from using my chest and my abdomen. Tomorrow we go to Newark, and then to Lowell, Massachusetts, and then to Europe. A musician have to travel to work."

Almost a year after I had interviewed Williams, Ellington, with Williams in striking evidence, gave a magnificent concert at Carnegie Hall. My report follows:

None of the trumpeters who replaced Williams in the Ellington band matched him, for he is—like such colleagues as Johnny Hodges, Lawrence Brown, and Harry Carney—unique. When he first joined Ellington, his style was already statuesque. He had a curiously dense tone, and he played with a deliberation and poise still new in jazz. He rarely left the middle register, he used few notes, and he conveyed an almost bullying emotion. This style, though, was soon overshadowed by his adoption of the plunger mute. By 1940, Williams' plunger-mute playing had become one of the wonders of music. Its sounds seemed to bridge the twilight between thought and speech. There were crescendo growls (anger, happiness, jubilation), half-sounded sighs (sorrow, serenity), stuttering figures (surprise, laughter), and legato wa-wa's (compassion). He mixed these devices continually, forcing into them the same power that distinguished his open-horn work. Occasionally he put his mute aside, and with great effect. His tone swelled and rang, producing sounds that suggested anthems and whipping flags. Williams' abilities have diminished little since then. His tone has deepened and he uses even fewer notes. The dancing, tongued figures have slowed down and sometimes give way to rests or long-held notes, the last of which are literally pushed from his horn. His open-horn work remains proclamatory and final.

Williams is a fervent performer. At Carnegie Hall, he played throughout "Caravan" and a medium blues, exhibiting a singular mixture of shyness and bold professionalism. Standing stage front, he seemed to lift out his notes with his shoulders, which rose steadily during every phrase. At the same time, he listed slowly to port, and rocked easily back and forth, his face an intense whorl. During the interludes between his solos in the blues number, he went into a bearlike dance in which he spun, bowed, and shuffled, all the while mumbling loudly to himself. When the number ended, he clapped his horn to his side as if he were saluting, did an about-face, and was back in his seat before the applause began.

Williams appeared to ignite the whole band. Ellington himself, got up in Edwardian style, looked buoyant. Aside from half a dozen throwaway numbers built around Paul Gonsalves, Hodges, Rolf Ericson (flügelhorn), and Cat Anderson, the program, in contrast to Ellington's recent wont, was varied and surprising. He introduced a five-part suite, "Impressions of the Far East," that was full of wit, Oriental harmonies and rhythms, and resplendent solos by Harry Carney and Lawrence Brown. There were several short new numbers, one written by Williams. He played "Harlem—A Tone Parallel," a first-rate program piece from the early fifties that has been rescored and is dominated by rubato effects and stunning crescendos. And there were gentle, mocking reworkings of "Rockin' in Rhythm," "Satin Doll," "Black and Tan Fantasy," "Creole Love Call," and "The Mooche," the last three done as a medley.

## Praise

Duke Ellington has had a bullish year. The Pulitzer Prize Advisory Committee's refusal to honor him with a special long-term achievement award in music has brought him twice the attention the award would have. He has produced three well-received albums—witty reshapings of the "Mary Poppins" score, of some of the Beatles' music, and of old big-band hits—and last month he appeared at the Newport Jazz Festival; a week or so ago he conducted the New York Philharmonic in the world première of his "The Golden Broom and the Green Apple," and a few days later he was awarded the Bronze Medal of the City of New York. I was on hand at City Hall Plaza for the medal presentation. It was a hot, sunny day, and when I arrived, a five-piece Department of Sanitation band, stationed at one side of the platform, was doing wonders with Ellington's theme song, "Take the 'A' Train." I found an aisle seat on the platform beside a pleasant, bright-haired woman who introduced herself as Mrs. Wallace Lomoe, of Milwaukee, and as an old friend and fervent admirer of Ellington's. On her left was Willis Conover, of the Voice of America, and, on *his* left, Nesuhi Ertegun, vice-president of Atlantic Records.

"I'm staying at Delmonico's, and I'm having a fantastic week in New York altogether," Mrs. Lomoe told me. "On Friday night, I was at Philharmonic Hall for the première of 'The Golden Broom.' Duke made the Philharmonic *swing*. There were even some good solos, although the strings had trouble with a longish blues passage. And now I'm here at this marvellous ceremony. These are things that should happen often but do only rarely."

"There's Clark Terry and Billy Taylor and Bunny Briggs," Conover said. "And Jerome Richardson and Ben Tucker and Joe Benjamin. All the bass players in New York must be here. And there's Constance Baker Motley, the Manhattan Borough President, and Supreme Court Judge Edward Dudley."

Mrs. Motley and Judge Dudley took seats at the front of the platform.

"There's John Popkin, of the Hickory House," Conover said. "Hi, John!"

Popkin sat down across the aisle, and the Sanitation Department band broke into "Perdido." It stopped abruptly and started "Take the 'A' Train" again. Ellington, accompanied by his wife and by his sister Ruth and his nephew Stephen, had arrived and was approaching the platform. Shaking well-wishers' hands, he mounted the platform, where he shook more hands, delivered several embraces, and made his way over to Mrs. Lomoe and Conover. "I've got to get out of this sun," he said, looking at the sky and shutting his eyes. "It will give me a sunstroke." He leaned over and kissed Mrs. Lomoe, and waved at Conover. "Sweet kisses on you both," he said. "This scene is a complete shock to me. I thought they were calling me down here to some office to give me a certificate or something." Then he descended from the platform and, his family in tow, disappeared into City Hall. The Sanitation Department band took up "Perdido" again. It was hot and getting hotter. An elderly man with a kindly face, steel-rimmed glasses, and a wide-brimmed hat sat down in the front row.

"That's Arthur Spingarn, the president of the N.A.A.C.P.," Conover said, leaning across Mrs. Lomoe. "And the big man with white hair next to him is Dr. Arthur Logan, Duke's personal physician and the chairman of the city's Council Against Poverty. Over there is Robert F. Wagner, Jr."

The music stopped, there was a cheer from the audience in the Plaza, which was a sizable one, and Ellington appeared at the top of the City Hall steps and posed with Mrs. Ellington for pictures. "Take the 'A' Train" started again. Ellington conducted the Sanitation Department band briefly and shook each member's hand. Then he mounted the platform with Acting Mayor Paul Screvane and sat down between Screvane and Mrs. Motley. He was dressed in a dark blue-green suit with soft black stripes, a subtle blue-green shirt, a black tie, and black socks and moccasins.

"Have you noticed the cuffs on Duke's pants?" Mrs. Lomoe whispered to me. "They're at least four inches high. He's starting a new fashion."

Robert Dowling, the city's cultural executive, who was the MC for the
occasion, took his place at the lectern and introduced Dr. Logan, who
quoted a biological definition of the word "sport" as "a sudden spontaneous
deviation or variation from type" and went on to say that Ellington was a
biological sport, a psychological sport, a physiological sport, and a sport in
human relations. Ellington, shielding his head from the sun with a square,
flat, gold-wrapped package, beamed. Mr. Dowling introduced Billy Taylor,
pianist and Station WLIB disc jockey, who linked Ellington with all generations and with Beethoven and Debussy. Ellington looked quizzical.

Taylor then introduced Clark Terry, Jerome Richardson, Benny Powell,
Ben Tucker, and Grady Tate, who took over from the Sanitation Department band and immediately began "Take the 'A' Train." At the end of the
number, Ellington gave them a short standing ovation and sat down and put
up his sunshade again. Joe Williams sang "Come Sunday," from Ellington's
"Black, Brown and Beige," and was given another standing Ellington ovation.
This was followed by "Satin Doll" and still another s.E.o. Dowling took
the microphone and said, "You have just heard the sound heard around the
world. It makes us proud of our American musicality," and introduced the
Reverend John Gensel, a Lutheran missionary to the New York jazz commu-
nity. The Reverend Mr. Gensel closed some remarks on Ellington by saying,
"All of us want him to know that we love him gladly." Dowling read a con-
gratulatory telegram from the president of A.S.C.A.P. and introduced Acting
Mayor Screvane, who closed his remarks, addressed to Ellington by intoning,
"Through the years of your eminence, you have avoided being misled by that
which was merely popular. You survived the Charleston; you will outlast the
Watusi. You have remained unaffected by passing fads and fancies. You built
your repute and your work on the deep musical tastes of a people. You captured the spirit of a time and of a whole nation. You were able to do this by
demanding of yourself and your associates the highest professional performance. Your standard was perfection." Screvane then rummaged around in the
lectern, found the medal, which was the size of a small pancake, and read the
inscription on its back: "Presented in appreciation to Edward Kennedy
Ellington, Known as Duke—'Musician of Every Year'—distinguished composer and worldwide Ambassador of Good Will—by Robert F. Wagner,
Mayor of the City of New York." Mr. Screvane handed the medal to Ellington, shook his hand warmly, and said "God bless you."

Ellington's remarks were brief and gracious. He thanked Screvane and all
the others present, explained that he needed a sunshade because he was "a
night creature," explained the meaning of the title "The Golden Broom and
the Green Apple," brought Billy Strayhorn, his alter ego, onto the platform
and announced that Strayhorn—*not* Ellington—was the composer of "Take
the 'A' Train" (Strayhorn's response: "Well, all I can say is 'Take the "A"
Train' " ), embraced Strayhorn, and somewhat hesitantly presented copies of

Ellington albums to Screvane and Robert F. Wagner, Jr., apologizing for them as "a sort of understated commercial."

"What a marvellous man!" Mrs. Lomoe said.

# 1964

## Triumph

The curse of the originator is that his inventions, diffused and sullied by admiring hands, will disappear behind a skein of imitations. But some originators, through sheer inventiveness, outwit their apostles; no matter how often their work is emulated, it remains indestructible. One such figure is the pianist Earl Hines, who, visible in New York just once in the past decade, recently gave a stunning concert at the Little Theatre.

Hines founded one of the three schools of jazz piano playing. The earliest, made up mainly of blues pianists, flourished under Jimmy Yancey and his disciples Meade Lux Lewis and Albert Ammons. The second, an outgrowth of ragtime, was established by James P. Johnson and others. Hines, drawing in small part from these traditions and in large part from himself, came to prominence in 1928. The effect was startling; no one had ever played the piano that way before. Like Bix Beiderbecke and Jack Teagarden and Louis Armstrong, Hines seemed to spring up unique and fully grown. Before Hines, jazz pianists had been orchestral and baroque (the stride men), or one-track primitive (the blues men). The ground between was bare. Hines retained the orchestral quality and skimmed the cream from the blues, but he subordinated these to remarkable innovations. His style, which has changed little, is marked by enormous rhythmic impetus, rich harmonies, total unpredictability, and a singular joyousness. Hines did not—despite the critical cliché—invent the single-note melodic line in the right hand. He did, however, compound usually incidental methods of earlier pianists with knifelike arpeggios, on-time and double-time runs that disregarded bar measures, and octave doublings. He frequently added tremolos to the last in an attempt to shake a vibrato from a vibratoless instrument. (He is celebrated for his hornlike approach, and in this sense he should be.) At the same time, he set off his single-note patterns with chords played a little behind the beat or in rapid staccato ladders. In his equally important left hand, he occasionally commemorates the stride pianists' oompah bass, but more frequently he uses tenths, trills, isolated chords placed everywhere around the beat, and percussive single notes. His hands seem at war. A right-hand run races ahead of a fragment of stride bass; a left-hand trill rumbles while the right hand rallies irregular octave doublings; staccato right-hand chords are poised, like an inverted pyramid, on a simple legato left-hand melody; sustained right-hand tremolos cascade toward ascending left-hand block chords. These devices constantly advance and retreat, and now and then dissolve into brief arhythmic interludes in which the beat gives way to a whirling, suspended mass of chords and single notes. (This exciting, treading-water invention was carried to great lengths by Art Tatum, and has been abandoned by modern pianists, which is too bad.) Hines was the first pianist to make full use of dynamics. With an infallible sense of emphasis, his volume may swell in mid-phrase or at the outset of a new idea and then fall away, before cresting again a few measures later. He makes sound flash. The epitome of the solo pianist, Hines is freest without a rhythm section. He is, though, a masterly accompanist who, with a discreet tremolo or seemingly wandering melodic figure, immeasurably heightens the greatest and the meanest soloists. Hines has sporadically let down in the past decade or so, and in slow tempos he may even turn rhapsodic, as if all that muscle were going to fat.

Hines—tall and quick-moving, with a square, noble face—is a hypnotic performer. His almost steady smile is an unconscious, transparent mask. When he is most affected, the smile freezes—indeed, his whole face clenches. Then the smile falters, revealing a desolate, piercing expression, which melts into another smile. He tosses his head back and opens his mouth, hunches over, sways from side to side, and, rumbling to himself, clenches his face again, tears of sweat pouring down his cheeks. His face and his manner are his music—the sort of perfect, non-showman showmanship that stops the heart. And time and again at the Little Theatre, Hines did just that. Each of his thirty-odd numbers—about half were medleys devoted to such as Fats Waller and Duke Ellington—was done as if nothing had come before and nothing would come after. He exhibited arpeggios that made Tatum sound electronic and Monk scraggly; shocking dynamic shifts; melancholy, turned-in chords; an unbelievable rhythmic drive; lyricism upon lyricism; and a juxtaposition of moods that made one laugh with delight. "Love Is Just Around the Corner," "I Ain't Got Nobody," and "Rosetta" were done without his fine but expendable accompanists—Ahmed Abdul-Malik (bass) and Oliver Jackson (drums)—and they were awash with stride passages, staccato chords, hide-and-seek runs, quick double-time accelerations, and arrhythmic interludes, one of them (in "Love Is Just") done in the upper registers, and giving the impression of chiming crystal. "Tea for Two," a tune surely beyond rescue, was converted into an impressionistic lullaby, as well as an extraordinary display of dynamics; after several measures of floating half-time chords that appeared to be leading up to a brassy stride or block-chords passage, Hines, pausing a split second, slid into an even softer roundabout, on-the-beat run. Similar wonders occurred in "Stealin' Apples"; "Sweet Lorraine," in which he sang in a way reminiscent of Jelly Roll Morton; and "St. Louis Blues," a bravura performance topped with a right-hand, two-note tremolo that he held for six choruses while his left hand played casual middle-register melodies and accompaniment for bass and drum solos. Poised on the lip of melodrama, he never slipped. He was joined in three numbers by Budd Johnson, a tenor saxophonist, former colleague, and sturdy eclectic who admires Coleman Hawkins, Lester Young, and Stan Getz. Hines, whose face was a study in pleased concentration, provided backing that italicized Johnson at nearly every turn. Early in the evening, Hines suggested that he was not giving a concert but was simply playing in his living room for friends.

## Sweet Tedium and Crippled Crabs

I invariably feel when I hear the likes of the New Christy Minstrels or Peter, Paul, and Mary or the Serendipity Singers that I'm foundering in milk. Not since the days of the barbershop quartet has a popular music been so bland and cherubic. Its performers exude health and bonhomie. The girls, in flyaway hairdos, are pretty and wholesome and amply constructed, and the boys are handsome and short-haired and flat of stomach. Onstage, all wear crisp, casual clothes and gleaming shoes, and all have wide white smiles. They display the easy presence of good swimmers and tennis players, and were they to appear with snorkels and rackets instead of guitars and banjos nothing would seem amiss. Their "John Henry"s and "Frankie and Johnny"s and "Barbara Allen"s would take on tone and color, and their emotional content would swell to at least that of Doris Day. As it is, they offer sweet tedium (their occasional mouthings of deep-country blues recall children doing a deathbed scene), and it is hard to believe that they are the progeny of Leadbelly and Big Bill Broonzy and Josh White.

Luckily, a large and attentive collection of prospective Peters, Pauls, and Marys were at Hunter College for a concert by such elders and betters as Brownie McGhee and Sonny Terry, Muddy Waters, and Sister Rosetta Tharpe. Two folk-music fads have been under way in recent years—the Kingston Trio, or white-shoe, fad and the one instigated by John and Alan Lomax and dedicated to finding blues singers who went underground twenty or thirty years ago. This second movement has brought back Roosevelt Sykes, Sunnyland Slim, Lightnin' Hopkins, and Speckled Red, and it was responsible for the presence the other night of Mississippi John Hurt. Most country-blues singers sound like courting seals, but Hurt, dressed in work clothes and a wide-brimmed brown derby, sang with a singular softness and unself-consciousness. (When the audience shouted requests, he would raise his head, make a half-moon with his mouth, look bemused, lower his head, and get on with what he was doing.) Although poor microphone placement made mush of his words, his remarkable guitar playing came through beautifully. His singing was full of open spaces, into which he poured spidery silver figures, many of them made up of *ostinato* basses supporting light, single-note treble lines. The contrast between Hurt and another country singer, the Reverend Gary Davis, was instructive. Davis, a member of the seal persuasion, started each line with a roar, dwindled to a guttural moan, and ended in a mutter. His guitar playing merely lapped at the rocks. Still another totally different singer was Cousin Joe, or Pleasant Joe, a wiry, fox-faced man from New Orleans, who in the course of five numbers (he accompanied himself on the piano) managed to parody most schools of blues singing—genuine and imitative. His sad blues were so sad they dissolved, his up-tempo blues had a mischievous Stepin Fetchit air, and he sang a blues that began with this champion verse:

> I wouldn't give a blind sow an
>     acorn, a crippled crab a crutch,
> No, wouldn't give a blind sow an
>     acorn, a crippled crab a crutch,
> 'Cause I found out that the woman
>     I love, she ain't so such a much.

The better-known singers at the concert were surprisingly uneven. They tended to cavort nervously and to Uncle Tom, as if such theatrics would help them match the wild success of their juniors. Sister Rosetta Tharpe, who is reminiscent of Mahalia Jackson and Julia Lee, strutted and bounced and drowned herself out with a roaring electric guitar, and Sonny Terry (harmonica) and Brownie McGhee (guitar) issued a combination of arch jokes and barnyard sounds that occasionally made way for Terry's eerie harmonica. Unfortunately, the last and best performers on an overcrowded program were Muddy Waters and his first-rate pianist-accompanist, Otis Spann. Caught between the clock and a sated audience, they simply never got a chance.

## Drummin' Man

Gene Krupa, who is fifty-five, is one of the handful of universally known jazz musicians, and he remains the most famous jazz drummer. He records frequently, and he draws sizable crowds wherever he plays. And he is credited with putting jazz drumming on the map and with showing the public the way to such lesser-known drummers as Baby Dodds, Jo Jones, and Sidney Catlett.

Krupa came to prominence in 1935, after being hired away from Buddy Rogers by Goodman. Not much later, Goodman boomed, and Krupa boomed with him. In the seven or eight years before that, Krupa had recorded frequently with such jazz groups as the McKenzie-Condon Chicagoans and the Mound City Blue Blowers, and with Adrian Rollini, Goodman, Red Nichols, and Bix Beiderbecke; he had made his living, though, with the dance bands of Russ Columbo, Irving Aaronson, Mal Hallett, and Rogers. He stayed with Goodman until 1938 and then, shooting out of the Goodman canon, formed his own band, which was a commercial success. He gave it up for a time in the early forties, re-formed it, and abandoned it for good in 1951. He has since toured with Jazz at the Philharmonic and with small groups, which have included the likes of Charlie Ventura, Eddie Shu, and Teddy Napoleon.

Krupa the drummer is difficult to isolate from Krupa the showman. Short, handsome, dark-haired, and smiling, he established the image of the drummer as madman. It was an image—calculated or not—that hypnotized the eye and stopped the ears. When he played, his hair fell over his eyes; he chewed gum; he hunched over his drums or reared back, arms straight in the air, like a politician at a rally; he sweated; in his climactic moments he converted his arms and hands and drumsticks into sculptured blurs. The mania for speed had begun to take hold by the late thirties, and Krupa was its epitome. Sorting out the components of the thunder underlying this spectacle was not easy at the time, because it was a new thunder. Before Krupa, drummers had largely been timekeepers. Their rare solos were limited by their technique, and their showmanship was homely. Krupa, however, was the first book-learned drummer. He started, in the twenties, as an admirer of Baby Dodds and Zutty Singleton, and slowly expanded their styles by keeping a four-four beat on the bass drum, by relying on cymbals rather than on wood blocks and temple blocks, and by instituting the crackling rimshot. He sometimes rushed the tempo, and he was heavy. Then he began studying his instrument and, before he joined Goodman, fell under the sway of Chick Webb.

When all this had settled, Krupa's style went something like this: As an accompanist, he was busy and unselective. He got a low-thyroid sound from his drums, and he depended a good deal on the high-hat, on which he achieved a fair imitation of Webb's clean, imperious *shoo shi-shah*. His ride-cymbal work was straightforward and largely inaudible (light, small cymbals were in vogue until the mid-fifties), and he sometimes punctuated breaks with a sock cymbal the size of a cookie. He occasionally marked the afterbeat on the partly closed high-hat or on the tom-toms. He used rimshots continually—on afterbeats and offbeats, and for double on-the-beat blams. His solos had a good deal in common with Singleton and Webb, but they were more academic. He might start with rapidly swelling and subsiding rolls on the snare (accented here and there on the rims), break into an irregular pattern of rimshots mixed with tom-tom beats, press into an even, multi-stroked roll, pass, with greater and greater speed, through half a dozen drum rudiments, and close with staccato rimshots. He didn't bother to adjust his volume, and he rarely paused, not realizing that unexpected silences in drum solos are twice as stunning as a mounting roar. His brush solos were fast and crowded. Through the years, Krupa has grafted a few of the innovations of modern drumming onto his approach, but in the main his playing has not changed. What he started has been carried forward, in different ways, by Buddy Rich and Louis Bellson.

These reflections have been caused by "Drummin' Man: Gene Krupa," which consists of thirty-one reissues and one unissued number made between 1938 and 1949. Thirty are by Krupa's big band and two by his trio. Aside from several decent semi-bop numbers from the late forties (Gerry Mulligan arranged one) and a fine 1939 Leo Watson scat vocal ("Tutti Frutti"), the album is valuable only for eight selections done between late 1941 and early 1942, when Roy Eldridge was with the band. (In many ways, these recall the Paul Whiteman–Bix Beiderbecke recordings.) Indeed, "After You've Gone," "Rockin' Chair," and "Let Me Off Uptown" are almost all Eldridge. "After You've Gone," which Eldridge had recorded several years before with his own band, is taken at a machine-gun tempo, and it includes three matchless Eldridge breaks. In the slow "Rockin' Chair," Eldridge is at the height of his powers. His tone is brilliant and edgy, but he plays softly, alternating dancing middle-range notes with high, surreptitious jabs, and he closes many of his phrases with a loose vibrato. The opening of his solo in "Let Me Off Uptown," which includes cheering-crowd sounds from the rest of the band, is an idiotic and priceless moment. He solos briefly and well on the other sides, and in "Knock Me a Kiss" he delivers a classic, funny, low-down vocal. Krupa's backing in the album is instructive, and his solos are short and restrained. He was a formulator, and without his bullying we would not have learned so soon that the secret of jazz is rhythm.

## Mingus Regained

There are many Minguses: Mingus the exhorter, who lectures his audiences on their inattentiveness or rudeness and writes steaming letters to the editor; Mingus the organizer, who, with Max Roach, put together, ran, and played in the wonderful rump jazz festival at Newport in 1960; Mingus the bandleader who took a superlative thirty-piece band into Town Hall, then devoted most of his time to explaining to the audience why he wasn't playing more and talking less; and Mingus the autobiographer, who has completed a long and controversial book to be published soon. All the while, Mingus, in addition to growing a beard, had been steadily swelling in size, as if he needed more room to house his many selves. Then it became clear that the inevitable struggle was at last shaping up between Mingus the bassist and his offshoots. For a time, it looked dark for Mingus the bassist; he quit the instrument altogether and tried the piano, on which he resembled a watery Thelonious Monk. But the balance of power abruptly and mysteriously shifted, and Mingus the bassist floored his usurpers. He took up his instrument again, lost seventy or eighty pounds, cut off his whiskers, shackled his extraneous selves, and opened at the Five Spot with a brand-new quartet. I had forgotten, I discovered a night or two after his return, what a marvel the old Mingus is.

Mingus's music is ruthlessly honest. He is incapable of giving a performance for the sake of a performance. When he feels right, his music is exhilarating; when he is angry, his music is angry; when he is dispirited, his music is dispirited. The other night, Mingus was reportedly in a fury, and his music showed it. (The day before his opening at the Five Spot, an acquaintance of his told me, he had wound up an engagement on the West Coast and hadn't been paid what he had hoped.) It was raw and loud and exhausting. Each of the five numbers I heard lasted upward of half an hour. No rhythm or tempo appeared to satisfy him. In rapid succession, he used waltz time, four-four, six-eight, and Oriental rhythms. He doubled and tripled tempos, used curved tempos (slowly accelerating and decelerating), and played without tempo of any sort. He used stop-time and shuffle rhythms. There were some noble moments. In "Meditations," he played a long bowed solo that was beautiful despite its sounding somewhat flat. (He had complained to the management at the outset of the number that the piano was out of tune and had apparently then perversely tuned his bass to match the piano.) In "The Fables of Faubus," which has a sly, sarcastic melody, he took the subtlest bass solo I've ever heard. No note was accented beyond its time value; there were runs of bewildering speed and precision; there were ringing pauses and dense sprays of notes that dissolved when they hit the air. Best of all, in an untitled medium-tempo blues, was a series of four-bar exchanges with Danny Richmond, his drummer. Mingus was all over Richmond, parodying his breaks, suggesting new ones, and capping Richmond's answers. Richmond's ensuing solo reflected the fervor that his leader had worked him into. The rest of the quartet was swept along by the tide. Jane Getz, a new pianist, and no relation to the tenor saxophonist, kept her head above water, and Clifford Jordan, an easygoing hard-bop tenor saxophonist, did even better. At one point in the evening, Mingus the exhorter appeared briefly, trading insults with a heckler in the audience. The exchange went no further than that (at its conclusion Mingus, in the manner of a pitcher disgusted with an umpire's call, turned his back squarely on his antagonist and went on with his work), but it suggested that Mingus the bassist must be on guard.

## Slow Motion

At his best, in the forties, Bud Powell was a wonder. He converted the left hand, which had been a timekeeper since the days of ragtime, into a levering, pushing agent for the right hand. (The bass and drums quickly filled the ensuing rhythmic vacuum.) He fashioned in the right hand long, lean single-note melodic lines that were apt to start and break off in odd places and that followed one another so rapidly they sometimes appeared to overlap. The jaggedness, rhythmic complexity, and plethora of flatted notes in these melodic lines gave them a sharp, dry, hard aspect; they seemed to be all bone and metal. Powell and Monk had started off in the same direction in the mid-forties, but Monk went Gothic, while Powell remained spare and classical. Such a style as his, with its delicate balance of speed and melodic originality, moves on a tightrope, and in the early fifties Powell slipped. The melodic lines blurred and grew introverted, he slowed down, and many of his pieces had an incomplete, bewildered air. His health, it was soon clear, was hobbling him. Nonetheless, he has continued to play between his withdrawals from music—sometimes inchoately, sometimes with all his early invention.

With all this in mind, I stopped in at Birdland to hear Powell, who had just returned from six years in Paris. It was a strange and affecting evening. He has gained weight, which adds to his impassive Oriental look, and between numbers and during his accompanists' solos he sat large and still, eyes hooded, slowly twiddling his thumbs. It was a stony inertia, and his playing reflected it. The old mastery was there, but it was caught in an eerie slow-motion. The long, barbed melodic lines hung together, but they flowed somewhere below the beat, like the delayed-action timing in a dream. Occasionally he caught up and held tight, only to fall below again, with a flurry of missed notes. Entire passages went by in a monotone, but they were relieved by abrupt, articulate, flashing figures. These good moments cropped up in the blues—three of the twelve numbers I heard—and in "Shaw-Nuff," "I Know That You Know," and "52nd Street Theme," all taken at high tempos that seemed to sustain rather than outdistance him. Most important, Powell invariably gave the impression of being wholly confident about his ideas; one could almost *see* them start bright and bold from his mind and then, more often than not, twist away before reaching his fingers. His accompanists— John Ore on bass and Horace Arnold on drums—were models of steadiness.

## Basie

Decca has released "The Best of Count Basie," which reissues twenty-four recordings made between 1937 and 1939, and which contains as much original, subtle, and poetic music as any jazz album that comes to mind. Basie should not be mentioned without out Duke Ellington, and vice versa; in the late thirties the two bands, though they were never popular, ruled the spectrum of big jazz bands. Because of surface dissimilarities, they were often considered direct opposites, but they were really kissing cousins, and it is surprising that they eventually diverged as much as they did. Both leaders were from the East and were tutored by James P. Johnson and Fats Waller. Both attracted sidemen influenced by Louis Armstrong and Coleman Hawkins and New Orleans jazz, and both had absorbed the early experiments of Don Redman and Fletcher Henderson. Both bands had superlative soloists (who were sometimes stylistically similar), superlative-sounding sections, and the ability to swing. (Basie, though, learned first.) Despite their size—fourteen or so men—both groups achieved a unified, small-band sound; their sections were never used for display but were strictly melody or riff-carrying vehicles or marvellously colored backdrops for the soloists, all of whom seemed to drift out of and melt back into their sections like ghosts. (Some soloists war constantly with the bands they work in.) But Basie and Ellington were totally original, and this virtue finally sent them down their separate pikes. Ellington was primarily a composer, who used his band to explore and exhibit his ideas, and after a time it became inextricably linked with him; neither could have existed without the other. Basie was first and last a *jazz* musician who early in his career became fascinated by the blues, the rhythmic possibilities of stride piano, and the value of true improvisation. All his efforts were bent toward raising these aspects of jazz to their highest denominations. He became an expert borrower and distiller of the best that was around him. He shaped the blues of the Southwest—where he spent seven years before forming his own band, in 1935—into a sporting, cheerful form that made all other blues sound mulish. Even his slow blues, though often elegiac, were invariably relieved by the Oxford accents of Jimmy Rushing or the mocking obbligatos of Dickie Wells. He thinned his stride piano by rationing the oompah left hand and reducing the right hand to widely spaced beginner's chords and single notes. He did this for lightening purposes and to allow his champion rhythm section (Freddie Green, Walter Page, Jo Jones) to shine through. This rhythm section diverted jazz rhythms into lighter-than-air channels that are still being explored. Basie had such a rhythm section, as well as soloists who were fresh improvisers, because of his uncanny knack for hiring original musicians. His soloists, in addition to possessing varied styles, rarely repeated themselves and often surpassed themselves. Only Ellington and Fletcher Henderson made equally homogeneous collections out of such iconoclasts. Basie's reed and brass sections found that pleasant middle ground between the slapdash and the immaculate. The results were suppleness and clarity. Beyond that, his sidemen handled their section parts with affection and even excitement; some of the riffs and melodic passages, particularly among the trombones, assumed a personal semi-improvised quality.

At least eight first-rate soloists passed through the Basie band in the late thirties. The most notable, because of the space they were given, were the tenor saxophonists Lester Young and Herschel Evans. Their styles were in most ways antithetical. Young had a dry Boston tone, he often played behind the beat, and he based his variations on melodic rather than harmonic ideas. His solos were frequently witty and represented spare *new* melodies. His relation to the band in a solo was that of a migrating bird to a tree: he circled, perched briefly, preened, and moved on; he enhanced the band, but it did not alter him. He founded a new school of tenor-saxophone playing. Evans, on the other hand, grew directly out of Coleman Hawkins. He had a rich tone, a pronounced vibrato, hovered on or near the beat, and was unstinting with his emotions. For some reason, most saxophonists have tended to avoid blue notes, leaving those illegitimate notes to trumpeters and trombonists. Evans used them continually, and they gave his style an urgency and appeal that were in striking contrast to Lester Young's seeming casualness. He seemed, especially in those fast numbers in which he was allowed a full chorus, to engage in hand-to-hand combat with the rest of the band; sometimes he disappeared in the sound of the accompanying sections, and sometimes he rode triumphantly over them. Basie's brass soloists were equally imposing. Buck Clayton was liquid and lyrical, in the manner of Bill Coleman and the Louis Armstrong of the middle thirties, while the younger Harry Edison was staccato and pushing. Until the arrival of Benny Morton and Vic Dickenson, Dickie Wells *was* the trombone section. He had been a great trombonist for almost a decade before he joined Basie, and his high notes, smears, off notes, complex introversions, and rambunctiousness offset the sweetness of Clayton and Evans and the detachment of Young. Dickenson learned something from Wells, but his fine wit was always his own, and Morton had been a polished, stately performer since his Fletcher Henderson days. Perhaps the most remarkable thing about Basie's stable was that it fell into place so soon; Ellington's great 1940 band had taken well over a decade to find its stride.

Basie, born in Red Bank, New Jersey, is a medium-sized, solidly set-up man who affects a mustache and a quiet, smiling manner and who looks as if the last thing he would ever want to do would be to lead a band. So he remains seated at his piano and leads with his keyboard (a chord here, a single note there, a following silence), his chin (raised, lowered, jutting), and with his eyes (open wide, half-shut, smiling). His band grew out of one that had been led by Bennie Moten in the Southwest in the mid-twenties. From time to time, Moten's band swapped personnel with Walter Page's Blue Devils, an equally renowned Southwest group that included Buster Smith, Eddie Durham, Lips Page, Lester Young, and Basie himself. Basie took over after Moten's death. When the band was discovered by John Hammond in a small Kansas City night club, it had just nine pieces and was, from all reports, perfectly proportioned. Its bookers thought it advisable to add four or five men—a bit of meddling that was for a time disastrous. It was as if a trim man had suddenly gained twenty-five pounds. By 1937, when the band did its first recording, the extra weight had been converted to muscle, and it remained that way. Toward the end of the forties, the intuition and homegrown inspiration that had sustained the group had hardened, and this, together with the departure of his best soloists and dwindling business, forced Basie to disband. From 1949 to 1952 he led a bright small group, and then he formed his present band—a smooth, heavyset machine that never falters and never surprises.

With the exception of occasional ballads and up-tempo standards, the old Basie band played just three kinds of numbers—slow, medium, and fast blues. Its slow blues were generally distinguished by a delicate, muted Buck

Clayton solo, backed by dreaming organ chords or distant wa-wa brass figures; a Jimmy Rushing vocal, with Dickie Wells or Lester Young obbligatos
and a brief full-band climax. Sometimes Basie soloed, using perhaps six or
eight notes, which only deepened the misterioso atmosphere. The medium-
tempo numbers had rich trombone figures, casual riffs that were lobbed back
and forth between the sections, and solos that seemed extensions of or inspirations for these riffs. At this speed, the band suggested that it was barely
tapping its reserves. It generously dipped into them at fast tempos, achieving
a drive and exuberance matched only by Ellington and Jimmy Lunceford.
The soloists blew themselves red, the riffs took on an irresistible momentum, and Basie himself often fell back on his stride piano. In Leadbelly's
words, the band rocked church.

The Decca set reveals all these delights. "Swinging at the Daisy Chain"
has that eerie quality, and it is also notable for Basie's sidestepping stride
solo, a muted, faraway Clayton, and a mourning Evans. "Panassie Stomp"
and "Every Tub" are monuments of heat and power, as is "Doggin'
Around," in which Evans battles his peers with classic results. "Swinging the
Blues," an irresistibly attractive riff number, has an Edison solo that shoots
like a branch from the main trunk. "Topsy," "Sent for You Yesterday," and
"Jive at Five" are medium-tempo swims and have peerless Young and Evans
solos. Evans is at the center of "Blue and Sentimental," which explains once
and for all how a big jazz band should handle pretty material. (Listen to the
perfect, freakish contrast between Evans' billowing periods and Young's
clarinet.) Basie himself is everywhere in the album—introducing numbers
with plunging left-hand chords or helium right-hand notes, pushing and
pushing his soloists, and coasting through those moment-for-meditation
bridges in the last chorus. Nostalgia feeds on the dated; this Basie band is
still brand-new.

## A Creative Thing

The flute, one of the most ancient and most lyrical of instruments, has long occupied a second-best, decorative position in jazz. This injustice, however, may soon be righted single-
handed by an extraordinary twenty-two-year-old flutist named Jeremy
Steig. I began to suspect this after hearing Steig's first recording, a Columbia
offering called "Flute Fever," in which he demonstrates—on a notably fragile instrument—a technique and tone and fervency as bold and easy as those
of Sonny Rollins and Ornette Coleman. Steig's talents are displayed on the
record cover as well as inside it. The front of the cover is taken up by a Steig
painting of a green-clad flutist dancing his way across a riotous jungle under
a Van Gogh sun, and on its back are four funny Steig caricatures of the musicians on the record, including a self-portrait that shows the artist, flute in
mouth, sitting cross-legged atop a grand piano.

I recently called on Steig at his small Greenwich Village apartment, and found a slim, brown-haired man with a gentle face and a gentle voice. He led me into a room looking out on a garden and containing a low bed, books, a tape recorder, and a work-table on which two flutes stood like rockets at the ready. I asked him if he was pleased with the record. "Yes, I am," he said. "I wanted to do 'Lover Man' over, and on 'Willow Weep for Me' I mixed up the last two notes on the bridge. But 'Oleo' and 'So What' are pretty much what I had in mind. The session was tough. I didn't sleep for two days, I was so nervous, and the studio was this great big dully-lit room that made me feel like a dot. Then the A&R man and Denny Zeitlin, the pianist he brought in for the record, got this thing going, and it was Denny this and Denny that between the studio floor and the control room until I began to wonder whose session it was. I was on the verge of tears a couple of times. But I'm seeing Columbia next week about another recording. I want to do one of children's songs—'Go Tell Aunt Rhodie' and 'Dark as a Dungeon' and 'What Shall We Do with the Drunken Sailor?' and a great Greek song my mother just brought back on a record from Greece. I play every chance I get, but when I'm out of work, my father, who's the artist William Steig, helps me. Last week, I sat in for a set with Bill Evans at the Café au Go Go. I didn't ask him. I wouldn't have dared. He asked me, and he even paid me. He just reached in his pocket and said he had some old money and gave it to me. Bill Evans can do everything, including play a good game of golf. But he can't play the flute. He kept asking me how I did this or did that. It really boosted me up playing with him. What a great thing to happen!

"I took up the flute when I was eleven. My mother suggested it. I knew I could play it, just from blowing on Coke bottles. I've been improvising ever since I started, but I studied three years with Page Brook, of the Philharmonic. I went to the High School of Music and Art, and I started playing jazz when I was sixteen, and started that humming I do when I'm playing—parallel fifths or holding a single note—the next year. The best things about my playing I learned by myself or from records by Thelonious Monk and Rollins and Gerry Mulligan and Miles Davis. I used to sit in at jam sessions around town, but the other horns drowned me out, and who wants a five-foot-two kid with a flute hanging around anyway? Then two years ago I busted my head in a motor-bike accident down in Bermuda. It paralyzed the left side of my face, and my left ear is deaf. I had to learn how to talk and walk again. I had to *start* again. The doctors said I'd never be able to play, but I re-learned, and a funny thing happened. Before the accident, I played very melodic, very strict flute, and afterward it all came out atonal and wild. I couldn't understand Ornette Coleman before, and afterward I understood him perfectly. I can control only half my mouth, so I invented this gadget." Steig held up a two-inch square of what appeared to be matted adhesive tape. "It goes inside my left cheek and it keeps the air from escaping. The tendency is for the right half of my mouth to get stronger and stronger, and I have to keep pushing my food over to the other side, where there's no taste anymore, to try and keep things even."

Steig paused and rubbed the left side of his face. "Would you like some tea? I'll fix it, and you go in the bathroom—just there around the corner— and look at my murals."

I obliged, and was confronted by two large murals painted on adjacent walls and lit by a high skylight. Both are in the spirit of Steig's album cover, depicting tropical scenes awash with flutists, naked women, big, heavy birds, palm trees, and shouting colors. "When I'm painting or drawing," Steig said, coming up behind me, "my playing is better, and the other way around. I think of my flute as a kind of soundtrack for my art and my art as an illustration of my flute. I take a sketchbook to clubs with me and draw before I start to play. It's as good as a warm-up set. And I draw between sets. Everything works together. You should keep your whole life that way—improvising. Improvise all the time, no matter what you're doing—lighting a pipe, washing your face. It makes a creative thing out of life."

Steig picked up a flute and began fingering it. "I can take a flute and sit in with Greek musicians and Oriental musicians and Indian musicians and jazz musicians. It fills a gap among the instruments. It can make every sort of sound. Here's how a Villa-Lobos flute piece ends." He slipped his adhesive square inside his cheek, put the flute to his mouth, squinted his left eye, and stared balefully at me with his right one. Out came two startling banshee wails. Then, pulling the flute apart, he blew across the top of the lower section, producing heavy moans, which gradually melted into a melody. "That's good for a certain kind of accompaniment," he said as he reassembled the instrument. Then he played a fast blues, and suddenly began humming what he was playing. He hummed a single note, held it, and worked out a succession of trills on the instrument that hovered around the hum like a bee around a flower. He stopped and smiled. "It's a fantasy thing," he said. "But it's got to mean something. I try to get the wind or colors or the motion of a swing moving through the air into my playing. I used to do a piece called 'Tantrum'—all screams and moans and groans. I want to play way-out flute that's not so way out it gives somebody a headache. I'm long after Charlie Parker. I get a bigger kick from John Coltrane and Rollins and Bill Evans. But I like Leadbelly and Robert Johnson, the old blues singer, and Mitchell's Christian Singers. I've studied those falsetto notes and wails of Johnson's, but I didn't realize how great he was until I tried to *play* him. I want to experiment with an echo chamber, a reverberator that's attached to the microphone. It will help me hear myself, and if I'm fast enough I'll get a double vibrato. And it would work fine with a bass flute, which is so soft it's hard to hear. I'd use this electronic stuff with a really good rock-and-roll group I have in mind—two guitars, an electric bass, and drums, with the drummer using a maraca on a tambourine fastened to his big tom-tom. I want to do a Happening, but with *good* painters, my music, and maybe people climbing a tree and playing instruments—all on a big stage and so that everything works together. And I want a modern group, but I'm not up to it yet. There are things—Coltrane's 'Giant Steps' is one—that I just can't do yet. Every year, people stop expanding and drop off and are gone. You have to stay with it, and I will, because I can do anything."

## Chicago, Chicago

Some of Chicago's finest musical moments occurred between 1920 and 1930, when it was a way station (Kansas City was another) on the grand twenty-five-year peregrination of jazz from the South to New York, where it settled for good in the early thirties. Advance guards had been arriving in Chicago from New Orleans and elsewhere since before the First World War, and by 1925 one could find there such eminences as King Oliver, the Dodds brothers, Jelly Roll Morton, Kid Ory, and Louis Armstrong. These men, who represented the second generation of New Orleans jazz, were playing a highly stylized form of their forebears' invention, and Armstrong's Hot Five and Morton's Red Hot Peppers recordings caught its last, superb gasps. But astonishing things grew out of the ruins. Armstrong and Earl Hines, who worked together for a time, became the first great jazz soloists, abandoning the constricting New Orleans ensemble. At the same time, a number of young white musicians from the Chicago area suddenly coalesced and produced a new ensemble-solo music that is generally known as Chicago jazz. (A third kind of jazz in Chicago, fostered by a host of Negro blues pianists and singers, continued its homespun ways, and exists to this day.) These men worshipped Oliver and Armstrong and Hines, and they had listened to an earlier white band, the New Orleans Rhythm Kings, but their music was their own. It seemed, next to the tattered New Orleans banners, very snappy and very modern. Much of the small-band Negro jazz in Chicago in the twenties had a legato manner; the trumpeters used trembling vibratos, the clarinettists were baroque, the trombonists lumbered, and the drummers slid along on endless snare-drum rolls. It was a patient, lyrical music whose fires were hot but low. The white Chicagoans had the new-broom quality that bebop offered fifteen years later. They used charging four-four rhythms, rapid shuffle rhythms, and unexpected breaks and stops. The drummers experimented with rimshots and afterbeats, and for the first time the bass drum became a fixture in recording studios. The horn men, who had no time for vibratos, adopted—in contrast to Armstrong's barn-swallow motions—short, quickly turning phrases that had a throwaway sound. The staccato gallop replaced the legato glide. And fresh ensemble devices were constructed. The collective passages were distinguished by odd harmonic interludes and by end-of-the-chorus explosions that were approached sotto-voce or abruptly dropped in, like a burst of applause. Since the soloists were not at first distinguished, it was the total impression of crackle and hurry that counted.

The nucleus of Chicago jazz came out of Austin High School as the Blue Friars—the brothers Jimmy and Dick McPartland (trumpet and guitar), Bud Freeman (saxophone), Frank Teschemacher (clarinet), Dave North (piano), Jim Lannigan (bass), and Dave Tough (drums); Floyd O'Brien (trombone) was a ringer. They were soon joined by Eddie Condon, Mezz Mezzrow, Joe Sullivan, George Wettling, Muggsy Spanier, and Gene Krupa. The godly Bix Beiderbecke visited with them, and so did Benny Goodman. By 1930, the Depression had driven most of the Chicagoans hopefully on to New York, where, continuing to starve, they were exposed to the wonders of Fletcher Henderson and Chick Webb and Duke Ellington. New recruits appeared—Brad Gowans, George Brunies, Pee Wee Russell, Jess Stacy, Wild Bill Davison, the Marsala brothers, Bobby Hackett, and Jack Teagarden, the last of whom remained only a visiting fireman. It was less a school now than a free-floating group of individuals who made their livings from recordings, with hotel and society bands, and with the early swing bands. Indeed, men like Krupa, Goodman, Stacy, and Tough never formally returned to the fold. Then, in 1938, Commodore Records began recording the survivors, and they had a renaissance—or, better, they reached the fruition the depression had blocked. For the next six or seven years, a steering committee made up of Max Kaminsky, Davison, Hackett, Russell, Brunies and Gowans, Sullivan and Stacy, Wettling and Tough and Condon, and assisted now and then by Teagarden, Fats Waller, and the Marsalas, produced countless records that were often superior to the pioneer 1927 Chicago sessions. Russell, Gowans, Teagarden, Hackett, Stacy, and Davison were first-rate soloists, and the ensembles retained their fire-brigade quality. Then bebop, the Joyce of jazz, arrived, and the Chicago school, which had mysteriously never become more than a highly proficient mutual-admiration society, went under. A remarkable number of its charter members are still active, but they are usually heard as soloists backed by rhythm sections or as members of hybrid groups. (Not long ago, a band at the Metropole consisted of Buck Clayton, Russell, Kaminsky, J. C. Higginbotham, Freeman, and Ben Webster; the music was Babelian.) On the few occasions when the Chicagoans have been brought together for "reunion" recordings and the like, the results have been fitful.

By and large, the best numbers in Columbia's recently released "The Sound of Chicago (1923–1940)" are by 1927 and 1928 Austin High School groups. Their efforts include the celebrated "Liza," "Nobody's Sweetheart," and "China Boy," by Red McKenzie's and Condon's Chicagoans, two Condon quartet numbers, and two Freeman small-band selections. There is a lickety-split atmosphere and a general authority that sweeps over the sporadic raggedness. The most interesting soloist is Jimmy McPartland, an assiduous Beiderbecke admirer. Frank Teschemacher, whose early death

called forth a small cult, now seems only a juiceless Russell. The jazz geneal-
ogists notwithstanding, Freeman *does* suggest the Lester Young of a decade
later, and all of Gene Krupa is there, including the razzle-dazzle.

The rest of the forty-eight numbers in the album are often academic, for
Columbia long ago reissued the Armstrong Hot Five and Hot Seven
records, Victor owns the Jelly Roll Morton Red Hot Peppers, and Decca the
weird 1929 Jabbo Smith sessions. But the atmosphere is lightened by several
Armstrong offerings, by some fair blues and piano selections, and by scattered after-the-fact records made in the thirties—among them a couple of
Earl Hines big-band numbers, two first-rate Jimmy Noones, and three
superlative 1937 Roy Eldridge small-band efforts, the best of which, "Heckler's Hop," has a classic trumpet solo.

## Ground Hog

**M**arshall Stearns, the jazz historian, is writing a pioneering study of American dancing, and the other day
he called up to say: "You should know about the tap exhibition at the
Village Gate tonight. I've organized it with the help of Art D'Lugoff, the
owner of the Gate, and it's a one-shot affair. It will be built around Ground
Hog, a legendary dancer from Cincinnati whom I've been trying to locate
for the past ten or eleven years. Charlie Atkins, who has danced at the Newport Jazz Festival, says that Ground Hog is better than Baby Laurence.
Then I heard, a week ago, that Ground Hog was in New York. He's been
here only twice—in 1938, with Count Basie, and in 1951. And briefly both
times." Ground Hog, Stearns went on, began dancing in 1928, when he was
six, with four dancers named the Whitman Sisters. He was a "pic," the term
for small Negro children hired off the streets of Southern towns on the Theatre Owners' Booking Association circuit by entertainers and incorporated
into their acts. "Rhythm Red, Ground Hog's sidekick, will be at the Gate,
too," Stearns said. "He claims that Ground Hog has avoided New York
because he is disdainful of it, but Ground Hog says he has been waiting for
tonight for twenty years. Lon Chaney and Chuck Green will be there.
Green is a disciple of John W. Bubbles. Jo Jones will head up the backing.
We'll kick off at ten-thirty, and we'll only have about half an hour, so don't
be late. Ground Hog may disappear tomorrow."

When I arrived at the Village Gate, I was greeted by Stearns, who is tall
and large-headed and bespectacled. "There are now six dancers instead of
four," he said. "Gentleman Pepe and Tommy Powell have been added.
Nipsey Russell, a comedian who is a fine dancer himself, is here. I'm trying
to persuade Max Roach, who's coming, to accompany Ground Hog on
drums in one number. He's told me he has learned more from tap-dancers
than he can say. There's Roach now." Stearns deposited me at a table under
the brow of the bandstand and excused himself.

A pianist and a bassist appeared above me, followed by Jo Jones, who was wearing a dark suit and white socks, and by Stearns, who sat on a stool beside Jones at the back of the bandstand. Stearns pulled a microphone over to him, cleared his throat, and made some remarks about tap-dancing as a "lost art" and about Ground Hog as a "lost dancer."

Suddenly, five of the six dancers bounded onto the bandstand, accompanied by a medium-tempo "Tea for Two," the tap-dancers' national anthem. Tapping and spinning and bowing in unison, they worked one chorus and departed, eyes right and smiles fixed.

Stearns introduced Gentleman Pepe, formerly of the team of Brown & Beige. Pepe, thin and fox-faced, was wearing a dark suit and a red vest, and he began with a medium-tempo "Lullaby of Birdland." Swinging his arms, he slipped from on-the-beat to double-time steps, walked backward tapping, stopped, leaned forward, and, his hands flat and low over the floor, rattled his way to the front of the stage. He straightened up, caught his breath, and announced, "This will be a little impromptu thing, a Sunday punch of music." Turning to the musicians, he said, "Give me a chorus of 'Laura' after my solo thirty-two-bar tap." Pepe's feet moved so fast they almost buzzed, and when the music started, he loosed some thundering steps.

The next dancer, Tommy Powell, was described as the sparkplug of the Hi-De-Ho Boys. The musicians played "Fly Me to the Moon," and Powell, in a gray suit and a matching hat, started a Raggedy Andy dance, his arms floppy, his legs bent, his head lolling from side to side. Then he tightened up and spun around, releasing a spray of serious steps, and at the last minute became a doll again. Powell went into a fast "How High the Moon," tapped half a chorus or so, executed a couple of admirable splits and broke into rapid steps on one leg, his other leg held above the floor at a forty-five-degree angle. Then he took off his hat, tossed it onto the toe of his lifted foot, tapped in a one-legged circle, kicked the hat in the air, and caught it on his head.

Powell almost collided with the next entry, a heavy man dressed in a blue suit and identified as Lon Chaney, a one-time prizefighter. Chaney announced a dance called the Paddle and Roll, which was full of slow, gliding, jumping-rope steps. Despite his relaxed air, he was clearly working harder than his predecessors, and Nipsey Russell, seated by the bandstand, shouted "Ha-ah!" Chaney returned the compliment with intricate, nibbling steps and ricocheting handclaps, which made him sound like several dancers instead of one, and after a stop-time chorus, marked every four beats by Jones on the bass drum, he bowed to Russell, his face streaming.

Chaney was followed by Rhythm Red, an equally large man, in white shoes and a pearl-gray suit. Rhythm Red looked shy and, standing near the rear of the stage, said, "It's a pleasure to be here this afternoon. I don't have anything to say about myself. I do the best I can and get off." He edged into floating, almost pottering patterns, which caused Russell to shout, "You're a racehorse on the curve! Go now!" Rhythm Red obliged, urging himself on with a string of soft "Yeh"s. "Get it proper!" Russell shouted. Rhythm Red responded with a long sequence of sliding-tapping steps, and at the end of it Russell was graced with another bow.

A tall, flat cardboard figure in a baggy suit—Chuck Green, of Chuck & Chuckles—appeared. He began *a cappella*, shifting quickly back and forth between medium and fast tempos. His concentration was complete and his steps were offhandedly perfect, and the room seemed to sit up and lean forward. Jones broke in on the drums, and Green worked out an astonishing series of counter-rhythms, which flowed in and out of Jones's beat. Stearns reared back in amazement. Russell shouted unintelligibly. Green's patterns, now on the beat, grew increasingly fervent, and when he suddenly finished, he was swamped with cries of "One more!"

Stearns said, "And now the Lochinvar from the West—Ground Hog!" Nothing happened. Then a short, mischievous-faced man with a gap-toothed smile and new patent-leather shoes appeared. He was already dancing, and he was talking, too: "Let's do it à la Charlie Parker. [Machine-gun steps.] Now watch this one. [Heels clicking rapidly together and on the floor.] Chuck, Chuck Green was up here. That's the challenge. [More heel-work.] Now, I wonder where *these* belong. [Triple-time steps at the front of the stage.]" Ground Hog flung open his arms, made pigeon toes, and scraped his feet toward each other, ending each scrape with a flutter of beats. Max Roach, who had slipped onto the bandstand, sat down at Jones's drums and began a furious tempo. Ground Hog jumped, assumed a mock expression of surprise, and began dancing in a jiggling half time. Chuck Green reappeared and joined him. Roach cut the tempo in half and relinquished his seat to Jones. Ground Hog nodded at Jones, smiled, and said, "He's an old-ster, he's an oldster." Ground Hog and Green exchanged steps, alternately copying and parodying each other. Roach, standing near Jones, tapped two drumsticks together, and Ground Hog, his head forward, looked hard at Green and said, "I'm going to *put* something on you." Ground Hog's light-ning taps were flawlessly returned by Green. Ground Hog improvised on the same pattern, and said, "I *know* you can do better than that." Green came back with a new pattern and Ground Hog, aping it, shouted "Oh, you want to play showbiz!" and, flying into the air, landed smack on his knees, his legs crossed behind. Then he sprang up and into a bewildering, straight-faced volley of fast steps, and, abruptly laughing, threw his arms around Green. The two men rocked back and forth together. Ground Hog pushed Green away and raised his arms over his head. "Finale! Finale!" he cried. "Let these guys dance!" The remaining dancers poured onto the bandstand and into an easy "Lady Be Good." Ground Hog danced apart from them and, at the sound of an ear-splitting rimshot from Jones, froze to attention, then slowly bowed. The lights went out.

# 1965

## The New Thing

I t is not proper for the founder of a revolutionary movement to set the engines of rebellion in motion and then disappear. He not only leaves his disciples still recovering from the wounds inflicted by his ideas but leaves them leaning on memory. The ghostly rebel I have in mind is Ornette Coleman, who all but derailed jazz— to say nothing of its admirers—when he first appeared, five years ago. Like the best revolutionists, he was a highbrow disguised as a primitive. He was a largely untutored musician who, with one leap, passed directly from the past (Charlie Parker, country blues, rock-and-roll) into the unknown. He offered a formless improvisation that ignored melody, chords, keys, and fixed rhythms, and that flowed from the rhythmic patterns or the mood or the sense of pitch and timbre that a particular number inspired in him. He seemed, in effect, to improvise on *himself*. At the same time, he rendered this free music, which has come to be called "the new thing," with an extraordinary force and emotion. Coleman's explorations had chaotic results. Brilliant musicians like John Lewis buried him with praise, while brilliant musicians like Dizzy Gillespie threw their hands in the air. Nonetheless, a group of young and unknown performers began to gather under Coleman's banner—and then, the air still churning, he went underground. No one seemed to know why he had turned his back. Rumor had it that he felt he was underpaid, that he couldn't find satisfactory accompanists, that he had quit to learn the trumpet and the violin. Then, not long ago, he abruptly materialized at the Village Vanguard.

One batch of rumors was right: Coleman, looking leaner and more unassailable than ever, appeared with a couple of alto saxophones, a trumpet, and a violin. His accompanists were Dave Izenzohn on bass and Charles Moffett on drums. Coleman played the saxophone in his first number, a beseeching dirge whose melodic line moved in huge atonal steps, and he proved that he has compressed his style even more since his 1963 Town Hall concert. His phrases, though still wrapped around off-notes and off-rhythms, are shorter, and his tone is more controlled. He has largely abandoned the animal shrieks that characterized his early work for soft, almost honeyed passages. At one point, he even unrolled a straight melody, with Izenzohn bowing in unison, that recalled Schubert lieder. Coleman's second number—I heard three, each of them close to half an hour in length—was "fast." (Actually, there are no fast or slow or medium tempos in Coleman's music; the beat, or suggested beat, changes from measure to measure and sometimes from note to note, becoming a cyclical rhythm.) He again played the saxophone and he again employed a quiet tone and short phrases, freshly spiked by freakish but always startlingly *right* notes. The violin suddenly appeared at the outset of the third number. Coleman plays it left-handed, and he is trying to force as much through it as he once jammed through the saxophone. He flattened three and even four strings at once with his bow, achieving a weird, steamboat-whistle chords; he sawed away on off-notes with the speed of a hummingbird's wings; he got unique grinding effects. It was nightmarish; the inanimate violin seemed to rise up against the animate Coleman. Midway in the number, Coleman took up his trumpet, which he played in a high-pitched, almost electronic manner. Occasionally, though, he sank into low, tail-switching figures; the instrument instantly stopped rebelling, and the effect was lovely. Moffett went around and around on his circular rhythms, and Izenzohn released a dazzling variety of bowed and pizzicato figures. Indeed, both men worked so closely with Coleman that after a time the trio virtually became one instrument. (At one point, they were meshing in this fashion: Coleman had slipped into a casual riff, Izenzohn was playing rapid offbeat double stops, and Moffett was pushing out broken snare-drum rolls. Each was audible and sovereign, and yet the effect was harmonious.) May the inventor of this instrument again point the way.

The inevitable lag between the start of an artistic revolution and public awareness offers several blessings: it gives the rebels time to test and tighten their dream, it allows disciples to gather and be screened, and it lets the public, without whose support any artistic upheaval is meaningless, absorb the shock and tune in. The waves Louis Armstrong set off around 1925 began lapping at the public ear in the early thirties, and those set off by Charlie Parker and Dizzy Gillespie in the early forties were felt a year or two after the last war. The new thing, the third great revolution in jazz, has suddenly found its audience. This revolution is an attempt to free jazz of its metronomic rhythms and its reliance on chordal or melodic improvisation, set keys, and choruses of specific length. At its loosest, the new thing is semi-atonal and almost wholly free rhythmically. Its audience first appeared last fall, at a series of successful new-thing concerts given by largely unknown musicians in an uptown club called the Cellar. Then, late in December, the Jazz Composers Guild, formed by such Cellar men as Cecil Taylor, and the trumpeter Bill Dixon, the tenor saxophonist Archie Shepp, the trombonist Roswell Rudd, and the alto saxophonist John Tchicai, gave four heavily attended concerts at Judson Hall, and since then it has been putting on a weekly series of concerts in a small dance studio above the Village Vanguard.

Not long ago, I attended a Guild concert given by the New York Art Quartet, one of the Guild's five or six regular groups. The quartet was made up of Tchicai, Rudd, Al Dodson on bass, and Lowell Davison on drums. Dodson and Davison, who is also a pianist, were sitting in for bassist Eddie Gomez and the drummer Milford Graves. The seven long numbers included a Coleman blues, a Parker blues, and pieces by Rudd and Tchicai. For the most part, they recalled the celebrated free-improvisation double-quartet recording made several years ago by Ornette Coleman. Fairly straightforward ensembles bracketed long stretches of collective improvising and long solos that were both supported and interrupted by one or more of the other instruments. Aside from these ensembles, both the collective and the solo improvisations appeared to be completely free. Tonality and measures and choruses were abandoned, and all the while the drummer, who literally convulsed his way around his equipment, maintained the slippery, chattering, beatless rhythm of the new thing. The bassist made complex echoes. Rudd, a former Dixieland trombonist, is the most revolutionary member of the quartet. He is clearly familiar with Dickie Wells and J. C. Higginbotham, but he has reshaped their best-known devices—long, high-register wails, growls, and a pushing emotion—into wild atonal patterns full of staccato runs and wide, off-note smears. He uses the plunger mute effectively, and during a drum solo he vanished behind the backdrop and emitted a series of elephantine roars that toned up the solo considerably. Tchicai, a Dane, lies between Sonny Rollins and Coleman. He was at his best during the Parker blues, which he converted into an atonal, tongue-in-cheek exercise. But the total effect of the quartet was puzzling. Its ease and dedication made Thelonious Monk and even Charlie Mingus sound old hat for the first time, yet within its own free-for-all terms it seemed rather safe and conventional. It drove fast, with seat belts.

The next night, I went to Judson Hall to hear Giuseppi Logan, a Guild sympathizer who plays the alto and tenor saxophones, the trumpet, the trombone, the violin, the vibraphone, and the Pakistani oboe, which looks like a child's tin horn. He was assisted by a pianist (Don Pullen), a bassist (Gomez), two drummers (Graves and Raleigh Sahumba), and a string quartet. Five of the numbers were by Logan, one was by Graves, and one was a collaboration by Logan and Graves. All were of a piece with what I had heard the night before, despite the different instrumentation and the presence of the strings, which were restricted largely to ill-wind sounds or furious pizzicato effects. Atonality reigned, there was a lot of collective improvisation, the rhythmic base went around and around, and everything—solos, collective interplay, ensembles—was self-indulgently long. I suspect, though, that Graves will become the modern counterpart of such pioneering drummers as Sidney Catlett and Max Roach. Even his set of drums was unorthodox, for he used—in addition to the traditional apparatus—a second snare drum (set on a muffling piano stool), a couple of conga drums, a heavy piece of wood shaped like a new moon, and an old bass drum tilted on its side and loosely tuned. Moreover, he had removed the snares on both snare drums, and he used—in place of the customary pair of drumsticks or mallets or wire brushes—a stick and a mallet, a mallet and a wire brush, or a stick and a wire brush. His style is a cascade of strokes placed everywhere in what amounts to a small drum shop. Some were deafening and some were sandpiper snickerings that moved with incredible speed from cymbal to cymbal or from cymbals to drums or from drum to drum. He never sounded a regular beat; instead, he used his ride cymbal for irregular patterns and pumped his high-hat cymbals with such speed and ferocity that he finally turned the top cymbal inside out. Such chaos can make sense in only two ways—tonally, and in relation to what the rest of the musicians are doing. Graves succeeded on the first count, repeatedly developing a welter of booms and rifle shots and clicks and tinklings, but he seemed to have little connection with the horns and strings. His playing needs no one to accompany and no accompaniment; he is a one-man drum corps.

Logan's sheer dexterity masks sly sins. His violin work, made up of a million short, scratchy notes, was demonic; his trombone was equally congested; his trumpet playing was high and strangled; his alto and tenor saxophones—he dangled each instrument from his mouth like a cigarette—were a mockery of Ornette Coleman; his Pakistani oboe was a Pakistani oboe; and his vibraphone sounded as if he were pouring loose change into it. Pullen revealed admiration for the ladderlike atonal chords of Cecil Taylor, and Gomez, when audible, was competent. That the string quartet read and played its wan scores with such composure was to its credit. Next to Graves, the most impressive aspect of the evening was its solemnity. The New York Art Quartet had displayed a good deal of humor the night before, but Logan and his associates—to say nothing of the furrowed, rapt audience—had the air of mediums possessed.

Before the arrival of the new thing, jazz offered a soft-sell array of emotions that ranged easily from mourning to exhilaration. It didn't matter much to the musician whether or not the listeners reacted, for he knew when he was good and when he was bad, and he also knew that audiences tend to appreciate or ignore the wrong things; poor drum solos are cheered just as heartily as good ones, which are very rare. But the new thing is hard-sell music. It depends not on mere emotion but on an armored passion. It grits its teeth, seizes the listener, shakes him, and hisses, "Damn you, *listen* to this!" This belligerence is behind most of the movement's confusions and shortcomings. The "new-thing" musicians play too loudly and appear never to have heard of dynamics (some of the most affecting moments of the likes of Ben Webster and Red Allen have been delivered at a whisper), they play too long (time and again, good solos or good collective passages are ruined by repetition or sheer, wearing length), and they often become so caught up in their own musical gales that they completely forget their compatriots (good jazz rests on collective individualism). At its worst, then, the new thing is long-winded, dull, and almost physically abrasive. At its best—in the hands of Ornette Coleman or Cecil Taylor—it howls through the mind and heart, filling them with an honest ferocity that is new in jazz and perhaps in any music. (Some observers have suggested that the new thing is primarily a social-protest music, that its sledging is still another anti-white Negro shout. If that is so, it will date as quickly as the proletarian novel.) Both the best and the worst of the new thing were in evidence at Town Hall in a concert given by Cecil Taylor, the nominal head of the movement, and four aides.

Taylor is a hammer and the keyboard is an anvil. His single notes and chords and runs ring and clang and thunder. At Town Hall, his exertions forced him to strip down to a sweatshirt, through which one could see his biceps working and bulging. His solos are virtually forged. Part of one might go like this: A legato passage, made up of well-spaced, high-register single notes, struck all around the beat and chosen to form a discordant lyricism, will idle by, and then, after a pause during which one can just about hear Taylor's computer whirring, he will leap to the bottom of the keyboard and let loose a two-handed tremolo, which swells into a volcanic shudder, and then start a series of irregular, pounding left-hand chords while his right hand shoots through a descending-ascending run that may end in a skidding glissando. Abrupt silence. He may then fire a salvo of staccato chords in the middle register, allow his hands to move apart and into different rhythms and dissonant chords, drop his volume, and, after another silence, float back into another legato pool. The intensity in each Taylor solo is unbelievable; it scales peak after peak and then, reaching an impossibly high point, simply passes on to another peak, and still another. He knocks the wind out of the piano and he knocks the wind out of the listener. This happened at least twice at Town Hall—in his first solo in his fast waltz called "Live," in which his frenzy seemed to freeze, like rapidly spinning spokes, and in his "Soft Shoe," an unaccompanied solo that was notable for its mixture of oblique lyricism and operatic crescendos. The three remaining numbers, also by Taylor, exhibited, at least in their opening and closing sections, the sort of stubborn melodic irregularity that appears in Ornette Coleman's composing. They also included endless solos by Mike Mantler on trumpet and Jimmy Lyons on alto saxophone. Mantler is another adherent of the choked, anti-brass style introduced by Don Cherry, and Lyons, when he was audible, moved around on the plains that stretch between Charlie Parker and Coleman. The rhythm section—Andrew Cyrille on drums and Reggie Workman on bass—assiduously pursued Taylor through his labyrinth. Taylor's own accompanying is, in general, an extension of his solos, and it is puzzling that he uses any other performers at all. He is not merely a pianist but a whole rocketing musical world.

## Northern Lights

J azz musicians tend to be provincial. The great players often do not know one another or even hear one another. They rarely buy records, even their own, and they generally depend on radio and television for their musical news. They are, by and large, workaday stay-at-homes who avoid all-star get-togethers and who keep the sources of their magic close to their chests. Thus, the recent six-day collaboration of Earl Hines and Coleman Hawkins at the Village Vanguard (they were accompanied by George Tucker on bass and Oliver Jackson on drums) was surprising: It *happened*. Summit meetings, though, tend to start at a shamble. The opening night was reportedly indifferent, and the next night was disastrous. Hines and Hawkins were unavoidably late, and Charlie Mingus, the leader of the alternate group, was asked to begin the evening. But Mingus demurred, telling the audience that he resented being second banana to Hines and Hawkins, that the audience was transparent because it was mostly white, that it didn't know music and would applaud when he purposely played wrong notes, and on and on. During the next hour, he punctuated reluctant bursts of his own music by storming off the stand because the audience, he said, was too noisy, and by firing his pianist, Jaki Byard, when he refused to let a pianist Mingus had invited sit in. By this time, Hines and Hawkins had arrived and witnessed some of Mingus's calisthenics. Hines, an old-school musician who wears a tie when he works, smiles at and speaks kindly to the audience, and obeys show-business codes, apparently was troubled by all this, for he was noticeably uneven during the evening. And this, in turn, upset Hawkins, who turned his back on the audience in his closing number and ambled dispiritedly into the far corner of the bandstand to play to himself.

But two nights later, the planets were miraculously in harmony. Mingus held his tongue, and Hines and Hawkins worked as one. (They had met just once before their Vanguard stint—at a fine 1944 Keynote recording session.) Their first set was notable for Hines' fast solo version of "But Not for Me," which had a rampaging broken-rhythm passage, and for a Hines-Hawkins "Just One More Chance." Hines' judicious use of the loud pedal and of broad, come-to-me tremolos turned the number into a rolling lullaby, which sent Hawkins into a chorus of soft, dreaming phrases. Between phrases, he seemed to accent his feelings by lightly touching the bell of his horn with the outspread fingers of his left hand; the motion suggested a butterfly landing on a flower. Hines worked even harder behind Hawkins in "Perdido," feeding him offbeat chords, echoing phrases, and monument-building riffs. Hawkins was impassioned in return, and then Hines played a solo, full of characteristic hide-and-seek runs and breathtaking broken rhythms. Their second set was even better. Hines did a grab bag of tunes that ranged from "Tangerine" to "Lullaby of Birdland," and then performed a Fats Waller medley that reached its climax in a "Honeysuckle Rose" that sounded—curiously—as if George Gershwin were playing it. Hines and Hawkins converted "It's the Talk of the Town" into another lullaby, and Hawkins complimented Hines with a booming version of Hines' "Rosetta." Hines, with his customary sense of nicety, didn't solo. Both Jackson and Tucker hurried after the masters, whose mutual respect and inspiration seemed to dance in the air like northern lights.

Mingus apparently grasped this vision, for his set was equally exhilarating. A fast "Groovin' High" included a long series of exchanges between Mingus and Danny Richmond (Jaki Byard, rehired, was also on hand, as were a trumpeter and an alto saxophonist), after which they played a volcanic walking-rhythm duet. This was capped by an Ellington medley that ended with a furious "Take the 'A' Train," in which Byard applauded Hines with several measures of flawless 1928 Hines piano, Richmond took a fine solo full of Jo Jones dynamics, and Mingus played some lightning shuffle rhythm. The audience rounded out the evening perfectly by being one of the most cosmopolitan ever assembled; Wilt (The Stilt) Chamberlain was on hand and so was Robert Graves. It wouldn't have seemed odd if they had sat in.

## Zeus

The noble tradition in jazz of the trumpet as a brass instrument began to falter in the early fifties with the rise of such angora-toned performers as Miles Davis, Chet Baker, and Art Farmer. Before that, when a trumpeter stood up to solo one expected the windows to shiver, and they did. But the Davis-Baker-Farmer method now marches on in the persons of the new-thing trumpeters, all of whom heedlessly pinch off their myriad notes—most of them high and most of them barely sounded—and ignore such regimental customs as tone and attack and vibrato. Better indeed if they simply traded in their trumpets for saxophones, their swords for ploughshares, and be done with it. So it was a tonic to go down to the Village Vanguard and hear Roy Eldridge, who has been hidden for the past couple of years behind the skirts of Ella Fitzgerald as her accompanist.

Eldridge remains—with his diamond smile, his short, tidy stature, his small, important bay window, and his limitless energy—an irresistible performer. And his style is as of old. His tone at slow tempos still supplicates and enfolds and at fast speeds hums and threatens. In a slow blues chorus, he will begin with two or three long-held notes, shaped into a simple melody and played behind the beat. The last of these notes may end in a whiskey-baritone growl kept low to the ground by a brief, waddling vibrato. He may repeat the phrase, adding several notes, an octave or so higher, that sound almost falsetto because of their suddenness, and then he will pause and—making you hold your breath, since you suspect what may come next—tear into the highest register, seize a high note, hold it briefly, pause again, fall through a wild sotto-voce run, and close the phrase with a mock-pompous growl. High notes are pep pills to Eldridge, and he may shoot back up and blast out two or three more, drop an octave or two for a soughing blue note, and sink peacefully to earth for the end of the chorus. He played four or five such choruses in the slow "Have You Ever Loved a Woman" in his second set; and he sang as many choruses in a voice that was a perfect miniature of his horn playing. (He was accompanied well by Barry Harris on piano and Bob Cranshaw on bass, but Oliver Jackson, his drummer, had time trouble all evening.) "In a Mellotone," which followed, was as exhilarating for its mistakes (a couple of overshot high notes) as for its successes (several more of those Niagara runs). He began his first set with "I Remember Harlem," in a low, muted mood, abruptly shifted into double time and took out his mute, releasing an engulfing tone and flow of notes (he clearly considers a chorus wasted if he doesn't startle the listener—and himself—at least once), and, after a sunny coda, passed on to an easy "Caravan" type of number that was a welter of high notes, swollen growls, and arching blue notes. This was followed by an extraordinary fast "Undecided." He started with the mute, playing a hundred notes to the measure without a fluff, stepped aside to let Harris and Cranshaw solo, and exchanged eight-bar breaks with Jackson. Then he settled into a riff and, suddenly abandoning it for a gorgeous ad-lib passage full of oblique runs and bellying single notes, sauntered into a slow, rocking half time. Lucky Thompson, who preceded him on the soprano and tenor saxophones in both sets, played Mercury, while Charlie Mingus, who led the alternate band, played Zephyr. Eldridge was Zeus.

## Bird

There are two kinds of apprentices—those who borrow from their master the bones upon which to hang their own vision, and those who, fatally mistaking imitation for an art, become perpetual mimics. The mimics have always outnumbered the borrowers and this is particularly true in jazz, where the apprentice faces special problems. His model is almost schizoid, for it comes in two disparate parts— live and recorded. The live model makes it hard for the student. The musician may be in bad form, which is confusing, or he may be brilliant, which is even more trying, since it is nearly impossible to relish *and* remember more than the brightest patches in a fine solo. (The excitement induced by first-rate improvisation also produces interfering static.) And recordings often provide only glimpses of a musician's work, yet these glimpses tend, simply because they are frozen, to eventually seem complete and even perfect. One of the most widely admired jazz musicians was Charlie Parker, and he made it relatively easy for his emulators. He recorded prolifically and he was on nearly constant view. But highly gifted jazz musicians have a presence, a mantle of steady, animating accomplishment, that cannot be transferred to a record, and when Parker died, ten years ago, at the age of thirty-four, his students were left with only memories and the tableau of his recordings. Their loss condensed into self-pity and sentimentality (those *graffiti* that appeared all over New York after his death, announcing that "Bird lives"); the mimics, deprived of their sustenance, fed on themselves, and the borrowers wandered into styleless, uncertain meadows. This was plain at a concert given at Carnegie Hall in Parker's memory by his old helpmeet Dizzy Gillespie and by a dozen of their most assiduous students.

Gillespie opened the concert with his quintet, and he was in top form. His style is now governed by a matchless sense of dynamics, by unfailingly swift and subtle rhythmic changes, and by an implied power-in-reserve. His tone has mellowed, his agility increased. In a medium blues, he played several muted choruses that ranged from an easy whisper to excited multi-noted chatter, and several open-horn choruses that began with an oceanic blast and ended with soft, skipping high notes linked by dodging, Roy Eldridge runs. Of equal merit was a very slow "My Funny Valentine," in which Gillespie used a mute, first playing the melody with offhand delicacy and then employing it as a tailwind for an exultant stream of swoops and climbs and glides.

By and large, second-team men controlled the rest of the evening. The exceptions were Roy Eldridge and Coleman Hawkins, who blew the skin of a Charlie Parker blues very tight, and Bud Powell, whose old self was slowed, in " 'Round Midnight," to a tortured, determined walk. Another exception was the alto saxophonist Lee Konitz, who now appears to have survived Parker very well. Indeed, he pulled off a remarkable tour de force in a long unaccompanied blues that was a history of jazz saxophone playing from Parker to the present and that was infused with the old-time, hard-knocks emotion Parker released in every solo. The second team at least sweated. J. J. Johnson let loose some blazing choruses of the blues that didn't contain an original phrase, and Benny Green, an occasionally witty trombonist, went on, in another Parker blues, for twenty uneven choruses. Sonny Stitt, perhaps Parker's most faithful admirer, sounded pale and irresolute, and Kenny Dorham and Howard McGhee, both out of Gillespie, sang their creator's praises. Roy Haynes was on drums throughout, and his accompanying was vigorous hen-party. In the final number, a blues by Billy Taylor, Gillespie reappeared for several more faultless choruses. The evening soared again.

## The Fat and the Lean

The big-band arranger was the most eminent of the middlemen who have fed on jazz for the past forty years. When, in the late twenties, the big band replaced the play-as-you-go New Orleans and Chicago ensembles, its members, in general, had to be told what to do; only one soloist could play at a time, and collective improvisation for more than four or five horns was rabblesome. A tables-of-organization man was needed, and that was what the conventional arranger became. He divided the big band into four platoons—trumpets, trombones, reeds, and rhythm—and assigned three or four men to each. The trumpets were used to decorate, punctuate, or simply make noise; the trombones did smears and rumbles; the saxophones toted the melody; and the rhythm section provided wheels. At first, these platoons were subservient to the soloists, but in time the arranger became so powerful that the soloist considered himself fortunate when he was given eight bars. The arranger reached his heart's desire with the sololess score; in a protean, vicarious way, *he* became the chief soloist. The first of the big-band arrangers were Don Redman and Fletcher Henderson, and the last were the tank commanders who kept the Stan Kenton band in dictatorial roar. Not all these arrangers were tabulators. Mary Lou Williams turned the Andy Kirk band into a graceful group, and Benny Carter made his sections sound as if they were improvising. When the big bands went down, in the mid-forties, they took their arrangers with them, and jazz was once again dominated by autonomous small groups.

In the early fifties, a seemingly new breed of arranger—the *composer-arranger*—arrived to meet the increasing need in jazz for new and more flexible forms. (The pioneering arrangers often wrote their own materials, but these were either elementary riff tunes or simple variations on standard tunes or the blues.) The new arrangers generally played in the groups they wrote for, and, more important, they allowed their materials to define their form. The first of them was probably John Lewis, the director of the Modern Jazz Quartet. Lewis, a highly gifted melodist, found his tunes flowing into rondo or fugue forms and even into collective improvisation. Charlie Mingus forced eight or ten pieces through semi-improvised ensembles that paralleled the New Orleans ensemble. George Russell resembled Mingus, but his effects depended on dissonance and atonality. All three of these men restored the soloist to a place of honor. Then, in the late fifties, it became clear that this second generation of arrangers was not wholly original but was simply the late-arriving offspring of Duke Ellington, who for thirty years had been letting every sort of musical form evolve from the content of his compositions. The newest of these Ellington-inspired composer-arrangers are the diametrically opposed Gil Evans and Gary McFarland. Evans grew up during the big-band days, as an arranger for Claude Thornhill, and McFarland is in his early thirties. Evans is a sensualist, McFarland is an ascetic. Evans uses soloists sparingly and only if they suit his writing in tone and style. McFarland favors soloists to the point of allowing two or three to improvise at once.

Evans loves sounds that suggest being smothered in a heavily brocaded bosom. He loves sounds that insinuate and flatter and cozen. He loves the lower regions of the scale. He loves hums and chants and choirs. His passion for these effects has led him to favor woodwinds, French horns, trombones, tubas, and bass violins, most of which can be found in large and luxuriant numbers in his recordings. It has also turned him into an ingenious Berlioz orchestrator who pits muted trumpets against French horns and trombones, working in a muffled shuffle rhythm; a tuba against a heavy reed background; a bass solo against guitar chords, French horns, and muted trumpets. Moreover, these combinations—some of which are unique—change ceaselessly. Evans ignores measures and channels and choruses, and accordingly his music is molten. But it is also impossible to listen to as *music*. It induces metaphors; instead of melody and harmony and rhythm, one is steadily put in mind of colors (russets, mauves, charcoals) and shapes (elephants, hippos) and materials (velvets, satins, silks). Listening to Evans is like eating hallucinatory mushrooms.

Evans' newest effort, "The Individualism of Gil Evans," is all plush and Aubusson carpets, and it becomes suffocating in a twelve-minute blues called "Hotel Me." The instrumentation consists of a piano (Evans), two basses, a guitar, drums, a tuba, a French horn, two trombones, and two trumpets. The entire piece is balanced on a ponderous backbeat and is given over to a simple descending tremolo figure strikingly akin to one in a 1941 Joe Marsala recording called "Lower Register." Not much else happens. Evans appears and disappears and reappears; the rhythm section bulges and subsides; a flute becomes briefly entangled with the piano; the brass rises up and sinks; and then the number, caught in its own tedium, fades away rather than ends—an escapist device used elsewhere on the record.

Evans' scores trap his musicians; McFarland's serve as lubricants. No matter how many instruments McFarland uses, the results are light and economical. There is no stuffing and there is no narcissism. There is, though, plenty of wit and elegance. Just six musicians appear in "Point of Departure"—Willie Dennis on trombone, Richie Kamuca on tenor saxophone and oboe, Jimmy Raney on guitar, Steve Swallow on bass, Mel Lewis on drums, and McFarland on vibraphone. The McFarland recordings by large groups suggest small bands; this one suggests a big band. His combination of instruments shifts continually. The vibraphone works first in unison with the oboe and is then echoed by the trombone; the vibraphone carries a melody over offbeat guitar chords, and vibraphone and guitar are in turn bolstered by a trombone–tenor saxophone smear; the oboe and the trombone play a theme *a cappella* and ad-lib, and are then pursued by guitar chords and soft wire brushes. Although McFarland's rhythms are full of stop-times, double-time passages, six-eight time, and shuffle rhythms, they form an unbroken flow. There is a good deal of simultaneous improvisation on the record—a welcome idea that arrangers are inexplicably only beginning to experiment with. In "Sandpiper," McFarland and Swallow solo together and are then joined by Lewis. McFarland drops out, leaving Swallow and Lewis to their ruminations. In "I Love to Say Her Name," McFarland and Raney work together, and there are brief ensemble passages throughout that may or may not be improvised. McFarland always ignites his musicians in both ensemble and solo passages, and "Point of Departure" is no exception. Raney, Lewis, and Swallow are in good form, and so is McFarland. Most vibraphonists—possibly because of the tintinnabulous nature of their instrument—sound very much alike. McFarland is unique. He places his notes sparingly and even hesitantly; each solo thinks as it goes along.

"Essence: John Lewis Plays the Compositions and Arrangements of Gary McFarland" offers six graceful settings for John Lewis's piano. They reveal McFarland as an inventive melodist. His ballads have an elusive, almost fey quality. (This odd strain has appeared before in McFarland's composing.) His blues are fresh and free of the old-timey loam that covers so many contemporary blues pieces. And there is an up-tempo number with a witty flamencan tinge. McFarland uses three groups—an Evanslike ensemble with trumpets, a trombone, French horns, and a tuba; a woodwind-and-saxophone group; and a conventional trumpet-and-saxophone small band. The brass passages—in particular the trumpets—contain the best writing on the record. His trumpets blast discreetly; they play difficult melodic lines with swoop and lightness; they move in behind soloists for sunny organ chords. Moreover, McFarland's brass writing tends here to have a reedlike quality, while his woodwinds and reeds are brassy. Lewis solos at length and is in rare form, especially in the blues "Tillamook Two," for which he produces—at the opening of the fifth chorus of his solo—a descending, at once sure and hesitant single-note figure that carries the sort of emotion that only Bill Evans, among the younger pianists, knows how to convey. Jim Hall solos admirably in a couple of pieces, and Connie Kay appears with all three groups.

McFarland's handful of recordings are studio efforts. Would that present conditions allowed him a full-time group. He could then develop what he has so brilliantly begun.

*But he never had a chance. Not long after he had recorded his witty, original, swinging version of the Burrows-Loesser musical,* How To Succeed in Business Without Really Trying, *someone—so the story goes—dropped a pill into his drink in a Greenwich Village bar, and he died, not yet thirty. He would have supplied a lot of badly needed additives to the jazz world—humor, swing, lyricism, and his special arranging originality.*


## Frankie ex Machina

The eleventh Newport Jazz Festival was leviathan (seven concerts, thirty groups, forty-five thousand customers), bland, banal, occasionally original, never exciting, and—a new note this year—unintentionally funny. This comedy made the general mediocrity of the weekend bearable. The first burst came on Thursday evening when Pete Seeger, accompanied by his own banjo and by a George Wein group that resembled a *bar-mitzvah* band, sang "Summertime" in spindly shouts. A little later on, Les McCann, a middling West Coast pianist who has grown sleek and plump on a diet of fake blues and gospel music, offered four such imitations, topping them with a Liberace version of "Yours Is My Heart Alone." At the close of the evening, Joe Williams, another melodramatist, began by announcing that both he and McCann, his accompanist, loved "Yours Is My Heart Alone," and then sang it. McCann smiled like someone being told his own joke twenty minutes later. The comic pickings on Friday afternoon came largely from Archie Shepp, a new-thing tenor saxophonist who unwittingly parodies Ben Webster and Johnny Hodges and Ornette Coleman. Saturday evening was enlivened by a Japanese girl who belted out her songs as if she were an electronic machine set for Ella Fitzgerald and Dinah Washington and Judy Garland. But Sunday evening was a circus. Frank Sinatra appeared with Count Basie. Sinatra's stint was carried out with commando precision. Late Sunday afternoon, during a Stan Getz *bossa-nova* number, a couple of helicopters scouting the area for Sinatra fell out of the sky with a roar and touched down briefly just behind the bandstand. At exactly seven-forty-five, they returned, carrying Sinatra and his entourage, and at nine, after half a dozen desultory Count Basie numbers, Sinatra paraded onstage with his own drummer, his own trumpet player—Harry (One-Note) Edison—and his own arrangements. Basie put on a pair of glasses and started reading his part, and Sinatra sang "Get Me to the Church on Time." Seven or eight vocals later, Sinatra paused, got himself a cup of tea from the piano, and, sipping it stage center, delivered a monologue made up of Bob Hope gags larded with plugs for a Las Vegas hotel that Sinatra has an interest in, recent and forthcoming Sinatra movies, and Dean Martin and Sammy Davis. Then he replaced his teacup, sang ten more songs, and waved goodbye. He was airborne before the Basie band had finished a concluding "One O'Clock Jump." The tab was reportedly thirty-five thousand dollars.

But there was intentional humor, too. Dizzy Gillespie was on hand with his quintet on Thursday and Friday evenings, and although his playing was first-rate, his comportment was even better—particularly on Friday. Working his way through half a dozen south-of-the-border selections, he danced (a series of motions in which his shoulders, hips, and arms became an uninterrupted flow), spent part of a number conducting his drummer, carried on a shoving match with his saxophonist James Moody that ended with a warm embrace, sang a funny calypso tune in a macramé voice and announced that he would like to introduce the members of his band (handshakes all around among the musicians). Earlier on Friday, Thelonious Monk and his quartet strolled through a handful of numbers, each of them full of sly, affectionate pokes at stride piano and of the steady inner pleasure that Monk rests all his music on. Jo Jones aerated Saturday afternoon. Appearing in a so-called drum workshop with Buddy Rich, Elvin Jones, Roy Haynes, Louis Bellson, and Art Blakey, each of whom fired off Judgment Day solos, he restricted himself to brief, toying statements swathed in mischievous grins and eye-poppings. But despite his subtlety and despite Rich's jet stream, Bellson's automation, and an all-nerves Haynes solo, Elvin Jones was the winner. It is his way to manipulate two or three different rhythms at once, and after a time these rhythms seemed to become disembodied and self-sufficient; the fact that they were emerging from a set of drums was almost incidental.

The tedium of the groups led by Carmen McRae and Dave Brubeck and Stan Getz and Billy Taylor and Art Blakey and Oscar Peterson was relieved by the Modern Jazz Quartet, which on Thursday evening delivered seven numbers, all perfect, all affecting, and all demonstrating that Milt Jackson, with his energy and ululating vibrato, is the Sidney Bechet of the present. On Saturday night, Earl Hines, backed by Earl May and Louis Bellson, played four numbers (one a long medley) that were climaxed, in "Boogie Woogie on the St. Louis Blues," by a couple of brilliant high-register bird-song choruses. Hines was followed by Duke Ellington, whose misdemeanors outshine most men's excellences. The solos were predictable, the brass section was exhilarating but deafening, and Ellington himself seemed preoccupied, both in his manner and in his playing. The young pianist Denny Zeitlin appeared on Sunday afternoon with a good drummer, Jerry Granelli, and the extraordinary bassist Charlie Haden, who, except in a fine flamencan passage, was largely inaudible. They were followed by the Wynton Kelly trio (Paul Chambers on bass and Jimmy Cobb on drums), which was the best rhythm section of the weekend, and by Wes Montgomery, a guitarist who gets off his clichés with cannonic force.

Friday afternoon was given over to the new thing. The Jazz Composers Guild Orchestra, which included Mike Mantler on trumpet, Roswell Rudd on trombone, a reed section (John Tchicai, Charles Davis, and Ken McIntyre), Carla Bley on piano, Steve Swallow on bass, and Milford Graves on drums, shambled through two long numbers—one by Mantler and one by Carla Bley. They were notable for a slow lyrical interlude in Mantler's piece, in which Bley, typing out a solo with one finger, was backed by congested organ chords and some marvelous sleight-of-hand cymbal work from Graves, and for a calypso passage in Bley's composition, in which the melody was handled as if the band were on the verge of inventing the fugue. Cecil Taylor finished the afternoon, and, as is his wont, constructed in each solo an immense tower of notes that withstood the great winds his playing generated. There was a lot of *thinking* onstage that afternoon.

The festival was held this year on the side of a gently sloping hill just north of Newport Harbor. The only changes from Freebody Park, which had been the festival site for nine years, were the fine amplifying system and a new, Expressionistic bandstand ringed by myriad multicolored spotlights and resembling a woman in curlers on a Saturday night.

## Evans to Tate to . . .

Until recently, jazz has been an unschooled, homemade music. Its inventors have served as its textbooks and teachers, and around each has gathered a host of pupils, the best of whom have attracted their own admirers. The effect has occasionally been of a handful of strong voices drowning in their echoes. By and large, though, this neophyte clamor has been beneficial, and when great originators have died young it has been a blessing. Thus we can still hear Bix Beiderbecke in

Bobby Hackett and Jimmy McPartland, Jimmy Harrison in Benny Morton, and Herschel Evans in Buddy Tate. The case of Evans and Tate is a little ghostly. When Evans died, in 1939, at the age of thirty, Tate replaced him almost immediately in Count Basie's band. Tate's closeness to his friend was and is uncanny. He resembles him facially (particularly when he wears spectacles) and in his courtly, attractive manner, and his playing is a direct extension. Evans' career was not cut short; it simply changed hands. But Tate, who is fifty, is more than a living memorial. He invents, moves himself, and in turn moves us—a split-second chain reaction that reveals not so much how he plays as why: to make something utterly new. Tate's solos do not depend simply on improvisation, or even on design, but on burst after burst of emotion. These are shaped into long, falling blue notes, crooning phrases that end in fluttering vibratos, and cries that arch across the upper register. Tate's emotions, which are blue and sorrowing, have none of the self-pity and boohooing that leak from the work of some of his contemporaries. He seems to say, Damn, my heart aches; hear it. He has Herschel Evans' tone, fine rhythmic agility, and a neat harmonic sense. For the past fifteen years, Tate has camped largely at the Celebrity Club in Harlem, and his recent appearance with an eleven-piece band at the Museum of Modern Art was a bracing surprise.

Four of the band's members—Tate himself, Emmett Berry, Dickie Wells, and Eli Robinson (trombone)—constituted a reunion of part of the old Basie band, and one had to continually dispel the illusion of hearing that band; in "One O'Clock Jump" and a fast "Sent for You Yesterday," the group handled its riffs and swung with the same passionate ease. Tate was in good form throughout and was memorable in a slow ballad, "Born to Be Blue," in which he hung out a series of fat, Japanese-lantern notes, and in "Every Day," in which he released a descending, terraced wail that caused an outbreak of goose pimples. Berry was a slow starter, but in the last couple of numbers he played handsome solos, full of his studied, rocklike notes and muscular legato phrases. At the end of the evening, Jimmy Rushing, another alumnus of the old Basie band, appeared and sang six superb numbers. He shouts the blues as if he were leafing through the "Social Register." In the next-to-last number, one could almost hear the audience supply the final line of his most celebrated blues couplet. It begins

> Anybody ask you, baby, who was it
>     sang this song,
> Anybody ask you, baby, who was it
>     sang this song,

and ends

> Tell him little Jimmy Rushing, he's
>     been here and gone.

## The Road to Big Sur

In recent years, most of the reports about and the recordings of the annual Monterey Jazz Festival, which began in 1958, have indicated that it has taken up where the lamented Great South Bay Festival (1957–58) left off. Primed with expectation and hope, I attended the eighth edition of the Festival. Like the turtle, most travellers take their houses with them, and I was no exception. The moment I arrived in Monterey, after a three-hour drive down the Coast from San Francisco, the past and present collided. Monterey's houses and buildings seemed a polyglot of Florida Spanish, Long Island motel, and 1910 Frank Lloyd Wright. Its restaurants are vaguely New York "Continental" and are apt to feature Green Goddess salads and sour cream–loaded baked potatoes that look like galleons under full sail. (Artichokes, which grow in superabundance in nearby Castroville and sell for twenty-five cents a dozen at roadside stands, are not to be had.) Even the air and light in Monterey, loosed now of the dogging summer fogs, rang a bell—the crystalline atmosphere of Maine. But this traveller's game suddenly became pointless when, on the morning after I arrived, I drove south through Carmel (an old artists' colony turned genteel tourist trap) to Big Sur. For forty miles, I followed a narrow road strung between imperious hills and precipitous seven-hundred-foot cliffs. Each turn unlocked a more magnificent spectacle than the last. At first, stung by such beauty (sea lions decked the rocks far below, and above me cows, their seaward legs seemingly longer than their landward legs, grazed on steep smooth tan hills), I mentally trotted out the great gorges of upper New York State and the rocky drops on the south shore of Bermuda. But after a few miles none of these props helped. They were oranges and this was a spectacular, brand-new apple; my disbelief was suspended.

It took a little longer to adjust my sights at the Festival, which consisted of two afternoon and three evening concerts. Odd associations kept blurring them. The site, a small, rectangular amphitheatre in the Monterey Fair Grounds, suggested a kind of corral. The wide, shallow bandstand recalled, with its plush red colors and Pop Art décor, a stage setting for an Off Broadway musical. Oddest of all, the audience tended to behave in the celebrated chattering-guffawing manner of the pit at the Globe Theatre; the most affecting music was overlaid by talk and laughter. Then, as the concerts rolled by, it became plain that the Monterey Festival, which is financially *and* artistically in the black, is what the Great South Bay Festival might have become and what the Newport Festival ought to be. Like the road to Big Sur, it is an original. The Newport Festival enjoys a love-hate relationship with its host town, which abhors it socially and loves it financially; everybody in Monterey—with the chamber of commerce carrying the flag—champions the Festival. Newport seats twelve to fifteen thousand; Monterey seats half as many. An afternoon concert at Newport may include as many as five or six groups that practically jostle one another to gain playing time; there were three groups at the Sunday-afternoon proceedings at Monterey this year. Newport is held in a sprawling arena that precludes any audience-performer intimacy; one could see the musicians' eyes from the back row at Monterey. The ever-increasing bigness and glossiness of Newport reflect a fat-man insecurity; the highly selective, tightly run Monterey Festival exudes confidence. The very size of Newport breeds dullness; the Monterey I attended was never less than professional.

I suspect, though, that the weekend was a couple of notches below those of past years, for there were tedious patches and there was even some out-and-out musical conning. The tedium was contributed largely by the half-dozen vocalists, among them the hipper-than-thou Jon Hendricks, who seemed to appear with every group, and by an ambitious twenty-piece band, which, recruited especially for the Festival and made up of the likes of Harry Edison and Clark Terry, never freed itself of its star-studded specialness, to say nothing of the ironbound arrangements of its leader, Gil Fuller. The not-surprising musical conning was perpetrated by Louis Armstrong, who appeared Friday evening with a group consisting of Buster Bailey, Tyree Glenn, Billy Kyle, and bass and drums. Armstrong restricted himself to interminable vocals of "Hello, Dolly!" and "Mack the Knife" and to a handful of solos, none of them distinguished. (Armstrong is sixty-five, but his recent recordings sporadically prove that he can still play as he did in the thirties. Why, before it is too late, doesn't someone put him in a studio with his peers rather than with his own indifferent band?) Bailey played a couple of good choruses of "Memphis Blues," and then, in "Night Train," used his clarinet to make vaudeville chuffing noises. Tyree Glenn offered variations on the patent-leather solo he invented twenty-five years ago, larding them with funny-trombone antics. One kept expecting a tiny car to drive onstage and disgorge a dozen clowns. But such mistakes tend to be rapidly forgotten at jazz festivals, and by Saturday evening it was hard to believe that Armstrong had even been there.

Saturday was Local Talent Day at the Fair Grounds. The Festival big band opened the afternoon concert with a fifteen-minute Festival-commissioned composition by Hollywood's Russ Garcia. It belonged in that castle of musical horrors long presided over by another West Coaster, Stan Kenton. Earsplitting brass figures gave way to timpani drums, which paused for Debussy piano passages, which sank into dissonant dying-fall ensemble chords. But things brightened when Denny Zeitlin, a pianist–psychiatrist resident in San Francisco, appeared with Charlie Haden on bass and Jerry Granelli on drums. Zeitlin has caused a lot of excited chatter in the past year, and it is easy to see why. He is an expert and flashy pianist who draws heavily on Lennie Tristano and Bill Evans, he writes readily identifiable program pieces ("The Carnival," "Mirage"), and he runs a taut trio. Indeed, Haden and Granelli are so good that they outclass their leader. Haden is an alumnus of the original Ornette Coleman quartet as well as a prominent member of the new school of bassists who consider their instrument a Full Orchestra. He took three brilliant solos, one of them spelled out in great, booting single notes and another in luxurious flamencan strumming passages. Granelli is a remarkably prescient accompanist; his accents almost seem to foretell what they are accompanying. He is an equally skilled soloist, and he took an exemplary mallet solo in the slow "Mirage" and a superb solo with sticks in "At Sixes and Sevens," a Zeitlin piece based on 7/4 and 6/4 time signatures. San Francisco was also represented by the alto saxophonist John Handy. Handy has caused—on the West Coast, anyway—as much of a flutter as Zeitlin, and he brought a singular quartet with him, made up of a violin (Mike White), a guitar (Gerry Hahn), and bass and drums. When Handy first appeared, in the late fifties, with Charlie Mingus, he sounded like Benny Carter trying to sound like Charlie Parker. He has since developed a handsome and original style. He plays his instrument perfectly, achieving a tone that is just about the purest ever got by a jazz saxophonist. But Handy puts this conventionality to radical uses, for, ignoring the new thing and John Coltrane's hunt for the lost chord and Sonny Rollins' sarcasm, he concentrates on Melody. His solos are composed of an unfaltering succession of lyrical, few-noted melodies, each set out in long, curving lines, which reach into every register and which are often played at ad-lib or half-time tempos. He is not afraid of a vibrato, and he will enliven these leisurely inventions—his unaccompanied, ad-lib solo in "If We Only Knew" lasted at least ten minutes—by choking his tone and getting a trumpet sound, by fluttering up and down the scales, by growling politely, and by delivering wails that are repeated over and over until they are simonpure. White, who is an accomplished ensemble foil to Handy, is a well-ordered Ornette Coleman, and Hahn is an amazing guitarist who uses double-stop effects and single-note passages that have an undersea sound. Handy's ensemble techniques—momentum playing leapfrog with momentum—are derived from Charlie Mingus, and they brought the audience to its feet. And then—stern irony!—who should round out the afternoon but Mingus himself, with a brand-new septet, made up of three trumpets, a trombone, a French horn, a tuba, and drums. When Mingus is upstaged—which is extremely rare—he generally reacts with heroic retaliatory roars or by going comatose. He chose the latter course on Saturday. The only lively number of the four he played was a mock-pomp version of "When the Saints Go Marching In," and even that limped. There were also glimpses of wonderful brass sonorities, a couple of good solos, and occasional stirrings of the extraordinary musical tensions indigenous to Mingus. (The word "indigenous" puts me in mind of the helpful answer I got from a native of Monterey when I asked him the name of a tall, Oriental-looking fir in the Fair Grounds—"It's a fir, indigenous to the region.") But only great teachers are upstaged by their own pupils.

More local talent appeared Saturday night when Earl Hines came onstage with a bassist and a still-flawless Jerry Granelli. Since his recent resurgence, Hines has perfected a bill of fare generally made up of whatever he has just recorded, a medley of Ellington or Waller or Erroll Garner tunes, "Memories of You," and a long blues capped by a two-note tremolo that he may hold for a dozen choruses. But he was surprising in "Body and Soul," which was done first as a rhapsody and then in a medium tempo notable for a fine, upper-register chorus. Hines was followed by Duke Ellington, who was deep in a three-month Western trip. Ellington was off stride at Newport, but he was in excellent form at Monterey. The reason, I think, was his singular performance, the night before the Festival, at Grace Cathedral, in San Francisco, where he offered a program composed for the occasion. I was lucky enough to be there, and it was a stirring event. Although it was uneven and the acoustics were poor, the band matched in sound and demeanor the majesty of its surroundings. One extraordinary Ellington number, "David Danced Before the Lord with All His Might," included a passage during which Bunny Briggs executed a series of rapid soft-shoe steps, backed by soft organ chords, a muted trumpet, and a children's choir. The effect was eerie and unique and enchanting. At Monterey, Ellington played upward of twenty tunes, which were climaxed by a repeat of Briggs' "David Danced" and by "The Applejack," in which Briggs both tap-danced and went through a series of feints and slides and bobbings designed to match visually the sounds behind him.

Barring a late and unexpected explosion, Sunday was a day of ease. In the afternoon, Dizzy Gillespie, Rex Stewart, Clark Terry, and Red Allen, backed by a rhythm section, offered five affable exercises that included a lush, virtuoso "Stardust," played by Terry; an aching slow blues, in which Allen played and sang; and a funny "Don't Get Around Much Anymore," played and sung, in a husky beer-barrel voice, by Stewart. Next came "St. Martin de Porres," a short oratorio by Mary Lou Williams that was sung admirably by a local choir and that displayed an almost—so ingenuous and pleasing was it—saintly melody. She then sailed into three first-rate standards. The explosion went off Sunday evening, when Harry James' big band, which, as an observer put it, "resembles Basie's, only it's white," played the "Two O'Clock Jump." Buddy Rich, who has worked with James off and on through the years, was on drums, and his accompanying was the finest I have ever heard from a big-band drummer. He punctuated breaks and shaded melodic passages and underlined crescendos with such pinpointed verve that the musicians were nearly lifted out of their seats, and then he took a breathtaking solo. It had dynamics (a powerful snare-drum roll that sank to a whisper and ended with rapid, clocklike ticking on the snare rims), unbelievable speed (a three-drum section, involving two different rhythms, that was watched with glassy-eyed fascination by the drummers who happened to be in the wings), and a whirling inventiveness. It was a mad, magnificent performance.

The Festival was virtually shepherded by Dizzy Gillespie, who performed at every concert, either with his quintet or as a guest. He also danced, played the piano and the conga drums, sang, and acted as MC. He was effortless and delightful at every turn. Indeed, without putting his mind to it at all, Gillespie could stage a consummate one-man festival.

I drove back to San Francisco through the olive country, the wine country, the artichoke country, and the prune country. I passed under trees so dense they made little nights on the road, and by hilly green pastures smooth enough to shoot marbles on. It was a perfect coda.

## Zutty

A chill has crept into jazz in the past decade. One feels it in the glittering younger pianists, in the crushing sarcasm of Sonny Rollins and the autonomous frenzy of John Coltrane, in the vapid musings of Miles Davis, and, most depressingly, in the drummers shaped by Max Roach. Sounding their shrill, high-pitched sets, these drummers create—with their insistent mono-method of accompaniment—a hard, false background. They are bric-a-brac performers who clutter the air. (Max Roach plays with passion? Rather with a frightening, cold anger. He is the first *social* drummer.) In an effort to ease these damp humors, I stopped at Jimmy Ryan's to hear Zutty Singleton, the sixty-seven-year-old New Orleans drummer. I confess that I hadn't really listened to Singleton since the days when he was a fixture at the old Ryan's, and hearing him again was a lovely experience. He is, of course, seminal. Big Sid Catlett drank of him deeply, and it would profit every drummer under fifty to do the same. The warmth and drive and pleasure that flow out of Singleton and his drums are irresistible. He is a sun.

Singleton's style—to say nothing of his appearance: a gentle, Teddy-bear face, with a high forehead and heavily lidded eyes and a generous mouth, sits easily on a short, solid figure—probably hasn't changed much since 1915. It grew directly out of parade-band drumming, and is centered on the snare and bass drums. Covering these foundations is a steadily changing layer of embellishments, carried out on the cymbals (in addition to a high-hat, which he rarely pedals, he has three cymbals, one shaped like a floppy garden-party hat and sounding like a sharp intake of breath), on three tom-toms, on three cowbells and a wood block, and on the rims of his drums. In the course of an ensemble chorus, Singleton's accompaniment goes like this: He will start with a heavy, accented snare-drum roll, which bulldozes the horns, and a two-beat rhythm on the bass drum. Then he will break the roll, silence the bass drum, and sprinkle his cymbals with fairy beats, shift his sticks to the high-hat, which he leaves agape, and pile into four bass-drum beats to the bar. The high-hat work will be accented with lightly struck eighth notes on the tom-toms, and at the end of the bridge he will circulate between the snare and the cowbells and the wood block and the bass drum, the last of which he smacks with his sticks. Back to the snare for a series of press rolls and rimshots, a couple of tom-tom beats and bass-drum accents, and the chorus ends. Singleton's backgrounds are a continually revolving dream of carefully pitched sounds (his drums are tuned to an almost basso-profundo level), which both nourish the horns and move on a private, self-sufficient course. His brief solos are simply extensions of his accompanying, and usually consist of massed rolls topped by a rattling, around-the-set explosion. These solos rear up and burst genially. He exudes delight when he plays. Emotions chase and flicker through him, appearing when he drops his eyelids and hoists his eyebrows, when, abruptly lunging at a cymbal, his stick a truncheon, he clamps his lips shut, and when, delivering a mighty roll, he shakes his head from side to side with a fury that compounds his rhythms. But just his arms and head really move; his trunk is a rigid, stately pivot. Singleton is an elegant primitive. His technique is probably no better than Ringo Starr's. He is apt to speed up or drag the tempo, and he can be punishingly ponderous. But, oddly, his wayward cymbal work, his constant broken rushes around his set, and his always surprising rhythmic deviations are not in the least old-fashioned. In fact, they are strikingly similar to the heretic experiments of Milford Graves, the best of the new-thing drummers. Singleton, who has surely never even heard of Graves, would shock him.

# 1966

## Mecca, La.

The first jazz I heard—recordings by Louis Armstrong's Hot Five and Jelly Roll Morton's Red Hot Peppers— hurt my ears. Then I read *Jazzmen*, a pioneering history published in the late thirties, and the pain vanished. Like Thomas Wolfe, *Jazzmen* should be read at sixteen or seventeen. A collection of articles by nine enthusiasts, it offers an irresistible all-American myth of New Orleans as a wild, dark pantheon, roamed by gods like Buddy Bolden, the first celebrated jazz musician, who achieved immortality by going mad during a parade in 1907. Then I discovered that New Orleans jazz was out of fashion, and it was an atavistic shock when the current New Orleans revival began a few years ago. I had thought that jazz had pretty much died out in New Orleans after Storyville, its notorious red-light district, was closed in 1917, forcing the musicians it helped support to migrate North. But the present revival, it appears, is being carried forward by musicians who have been playing in New Orleans ever since. Many of them are in their sixties or seventies, some are in their eighties, and a few have passed ninety. As the number of new New Orleans recordings swelled, I suspected that the old myth was simply being dusted off and revised. The liner notes on these recordings revere unfamiliar musicians like Sweet Emma Barrett, Kid Thomas, and De De Pierce, new brass bands, and upstart musical temples like Preservation Hall and Dixieland Hall, but their hyperbole is familiar, and with good reason—it is often the work of the surviving contributors to *Jazzmen*. Most indicative, the music on the records, though almost always honest-sounding, is rough and halting and frequently out of tune. It could have been recorded in 1925, or even in 1915.

I went to New Orleans not long ago to find out whether this new edition of the myth is as good as the old one. I had written to Richard Allen, the curator of the Archive of New Orleans Jazz, at Tulane University, and asked if he would shepherd me around, and he had replied that he would be delighted to. His letter continued, "I am afraid that I do not spend too much time around Preservation Hall or Dixieland Hall, but since a new hall, Southland Jazz Club, has recently opened, I have attempted to give it some of my support until it becomes established. You are fortunate that you are arriving on Saturday, as there is to be a concert on Sunday in the Grand Salon of the Royal Orleans Hotel. A parade will precede it. I hope that we will be able to find some jazz in less commercial surroundings. I frankly have grown allergic to tourists by this time, and enjoy getting away from the French Quarter to brass-band functions, rehearsals, and dance halls."

A few minutes after I had checked into my motel, in the Quarter, Allen telephoned and asked if I was too tired to hear some music. I said I wasn't, and he told me, in a measured Southern drawl, that a band led by a white trumpet player named Tony Fougerat was playing a one-night stand in Munster's. "Munster's is near the riverfront, in a section we call the Irish Channel, about sixty blocks from the Quarter," he said. "It's a workingman's neighborhood, and it might be a little rough, but it should have a lot of the atmosphere of the cabarets Buddy Bolden and Joe Oliver worked in."

Allen picked me up in a cab. He is short, round, and bullet-headed, and has thick, graying hair. His face is placid and intelligent. "Hello and good evening, as we say in New Orleans," he said, shaking hands. He had two umbrellas with him, and he handed me one. "The rainy season is upon us," he said. "You'll need this every day."

The French Quarter, with its decaying, shuttered houses, its spooky wrought-iron balconies, its secret alleys, and its ancient smell, has the peculiar density and air of resignation common to all old cities. But the Garden District, which we drove through on our way to Munster's, is full of trees and grass and big, ornate houses, and it smelled green and fresh. Allen pointed out the window at a white blur and said, "I think either that house or the one just around the corner is where Joe Oliver worked as a butler before he went to Chicago in 1918. But I really don't care. It's not the places here that interest me as much as the people. Fougerat, who is sixty-six, is something of a rarity. He played with Papa Jack Laine, who is in his nineties, and who probably had the first white jazz band. He also recorded with Jimmie Rodgers, the old hillbilly singer. Fougerat is an insurance man by trade, but he still plays a lot. He might have a white trombonist with him named Red Margiotta, who's about the same age. Margiotta's right arm is amputated just below the elbow, but that doesn't bother his playing. Munster's is a white bar, and Negroes aren't welcome. But desegregation is better here than most people think. There never *have* been any truly segregated neighborhoods, and the big hotels, like the Royal Orleans, have been open to Negroes for four or five years. Dizzy Gillespie stayed there a little while ago. The first Negro to eat in the Rib Room in the Orleans is supposed to have left a fifty-dollar tip, and there hasn't been any trouble since. The public swimming pools will be reopened this summer, but the schools are still a problem."

Our cabdriver, who was a Negro, said, "There's a white private school established here in the Garden District after the Supreme Court decision, and it's so crowded it's spread between two residences about a mile apart." He laughed. "Man, there's a lot of bussing goes on."

Munster's Bar proved to be in a low cement-block building. The air inside was rigid with smoke and the smell of beer. A bar stretched along one wall, and plastic-topped tables were ranged loosely around the three other walls. Large coat hooks stuck out from the walls like elephant ears. The room, which had a cement floor, was jammed with stolid-faced dancers of every age. A tall, red-haired girl hung over an old Brueghel type. A thin elderly lady was with a stocky young man. Some of the dancers were in work clothes, and some were in their Sunday best. Allen led the way to the rear of the room. Fougerat, who has a pleasant, angular face, was seated against the wall, and was deep in "Margie." Margiotta had his trombone tucked deftly under his stump, and his bald head and red face glistened as he played. A beefy drummer with a big Roman nose was drawn up to a historic set of traps made up entirely of a small bass drum, a cymbal, and a snare drum. A bassist and a guitarist, both of them weathered and lanky, rounded out the group. All were in shirtsleeves. Fougerat nodded to Allen and indicated a table near the bandstand. The band broke into "Lazy River."

A lean, brown-faced man with a shock of beautiful white hair bumped against our table. He reared back and smiled widely at us and at a tiny old woman with him. "I'm only seventy-five," he said, and swayed away. A fat-armed, round-shouldered woman in a silk dress and harlequin glasses stood in front of the band, alternately singing and conducting. Her voice was sweet and quavery. "I used to have my own band!" she shouted at Allen. "I could sing like Helen Morgan then, but who cares now?" She shifted into a heavy, one-footed dance, her arms held out like a gull's wings, her fingers snapping. A young man with flat black hair unpacked an accordion and joined the band. The band and the dancers were matched in a way I had never seen before; each group seemed an extension of the other. The music was primitive, unhurried, and perfectly executed. The improvisation was limited to gentle variations and formal flourishes. The tempos were medium, and the tunes ranged from "Girl of My Dreams" to "Hello, Dolly." Fougerat is a blunt, homemade trumpeter. His phrases are short, and his tone is heavy and dark. Like most New Orleans trumpeters, he doesn't solo much. Margiotta does, however, and he delights in melody. His tone is pure and plaintive, and he sounds like a mannerly Kid Ory. The accordionist comfortably plugged the chinks in the ensemble, and the rhythm section kept strict two-beat time.

Allen, who had been rocking discreetly back and forth in his chair, suddenly excused himself and asked Helen Morgan to dance. They moved off to the middle of the floor, and Allen began a slow-motion Twist. The drummer, relinquishing his seat to an intense young man, sat down with me, and mopped his forehead. He was chewing tobacco. "That snare drum, the strings they come loose on it," he said, in a curious French-Italian accent. "So I have a tom-tom instead of a snare. I ask the bartender for a little piece string. No string. I ask Fougerat. No string." He shrugged. "I live fifty miles from here, in Raceland, up Bayou Lafourche way. Raceland, she has the longest main street in the world—thirty-seven miles. I go home tonight, sleep two hours, go to choich, and in the evening show a quarter horse." He shrugged again, got up, and cut in on a plump woman.

Allen sat down. He was beaming. "This is it, isn't it? This is how it all began. A classic atmosphere."

When we left, around one o'clock, the dance floor was crowded and the band sounded fresh. Helen Morgan was singing "Bye Bye Blackbird."

I got to the junction of Basin Street and Canal Street, where the parade was forming, at two o'clock Sunday afternoon. It was warm and sunny, and there were two brass bands—the Onward and the Eureka. I found Allen in a swarm of musicians and onlookers. He had on dark glasses and was carrying a clipboard. "Hello and good day," he said. "I'm one of the sponsors of this affair—it's a Heart Fund benefit—and I have to show Danny Barker, who's the marshal of the Onward Brass Band, the route we are taking to the Royal Orleans. He's a little out of practice. He only moved back to New Orleans six or seven months ago."

Barker, a Negro, has spent most of his career in the North—as a big-band guitarist (Benny Carter and Cab Calloway) and a small-band banjoist (Wilbur de Paris). He has also spent a good part of it writing an enormous autobiography, which, though unpublished, has long been regarded by students of jazz as an invaluable lode of New Orleania. I hadn't seen him for ten years, but he looked about the same—lean, stooped, his smile crooked and mischievous. He had on a Madras jacket, dark pants, and dark glasses, and he was holding a straw hat. A heavy multicolored sash across his chest seemed to increase his stoop.

"The Eureka Brass Band has Fats Houston as grand marshal," Allen said. "Both bands are running a little large—ten or eleven men. Louis Cottrell and Willie Humphrey are on clarinets and Louis Nelson and Jim Robinson on trombones. Louis Barbarin, Danny Barker's uncle, is on snare with the Onward, and Peter Bocage, who played with Bolden, is on trumpet with the Eureka. He's in his late seventies. The youngest men are Milton Batiste, trumpeter, and Keith Smith, an English trumpeter who's been here several weeks. English musicians come to New Orleans by the drove and support themselves however they can, and when they've had their fill they go home. It's their Mecca."

Each band fell into rough ranks. The trombonists were first, and the drummers brought up the rear, behind the trumpeters. The two groups had identical uniforms—dark caps, white shirts and dark ties, and dark pants. Allen stationed himself near Barker, and the Onward burst into "Bye and Bye" and started down Canal Street. The Eureka marched in silence not far behind. The second line—a name given to the dancers who appear from the woodwork for every parade in New Orleans, and whose agility and beauty are barometers of the quality of the music—had already collected in front of the Onward. Most of its members were young Negro men. They were dressed in singlets and shorts and sneakers, and half a dozen of them were carrying the traditional open umbrellas. The Onward gathered steam slowly, and so did the dancers. They shuffled along the pavement pigeon-toed, their arms bent and held close to their sides, their umbrellas at shoulder arms. Then the band found its groove, and the dancers obliged. Their knees shot up like those of broken-field runners, and some of them spun around, their hips rotating. They moved up onto their toes, came together in an undulating, umbrella-bumping mass, flew apart, and came together again. A stream of onlookers moved along on each side of the street, carrying with it a matron who jiggled like a truck, and an aristocratic New Orleanian who let loose a skip every ten feet or so.

The Onward fell silent, and the Eureka took up "Bye and Bye." The second line split in two, raced back up the street, and re-formed in front of the Eureka. Two tiny Negro boys in gray business suits joined the dancers, and so did two women. One was fat and gray and had an enormous bust, which moved oceanically. The other was tall and hawk-nosed and rodlike. The large woman rolled and swayed, the thin one moved as if she were on a pogo stick. A beautiful young Negro woman in a close-fitting blue dress danced up to the gray-haired woman, laughed, and said, "They always ask who taught me to dance—ho, ho." Her name, I learned later, is Ellyna Tatum, and she is a breathtaking dancer. Leaning backward, she did a steady, rolling shimmy, her knees bent and her toes curling down. Her arms crooked and uncrooked, and her head, tilted slightly forward, snapped gently from side to side. All the while, she sang in a fine, clear voice. Now and then a couple of men would dance up to her and around her, making mock bows. She would flow between them, and they would peel away, very low to the ground.

Allen held up his left hand, and Barker, who was slippering along backward with a bemused expression, turned into Royal Street, which is narrow and was filled with parked cars. The parade poured into the street like lava. Natives clapped in time on their wrought-iron balconies, and tourists, clustered in the doorways of antique shops, blinked. Royal Street had a miraculous effect on the music. (The Onward was playing "When the Saints Go Marching In.") The walls of the houses collected and compressed it, and the volume doubled. The musicians, probably hearing themselves clearly for the first time, reacted accordingly. The trumpeters let loose a series of high, glistening notes, and the drummers took up the tempo. The second line, squeezed into a space roughly ten feet square, danced perpendicularly, umbrellas chopping up and down. At Toulouse Street, Allen halted the parade, glanced at his watch, and consulted his clipboard. He looked like an official at a track meet. The Onward was playing "Victory Walk," an engaging stop-time number, which, like every number played during the parade, was an extraordinary collective scramble. The nearest thing to a solo was a snare-and-bass-drum duet by Louis Barbarin and Chester Jones. Barbarin played loose, galloping, marching figures while Jones dropped in jarring single and double offbeats. It was superb counterpoint in which the two men at once challenged and supported each other. The rest of the number was given over to intricate, heaving polyphony that suggested Charlie Mingus's more ambitious ensemble ventures. With the exception of several choruses of plunging, bowsprit riffs, each horn went its own way. The trombones snaked ceaselessly around each other, staying just above the sousaphone. The tenor saxophone provided a central monotone, and the trumpeters took turns carrying the lead. Occasionally, one of them would lean back and fire directly at the sky. The clarinet fluttered and swooped and dived. It was a gorgeous rug of sound.

Allen gave a Teddy Roosevelt charge signal, and the parade oozed around the block, paused briefly in front of the Royal Orleans, and suddenly turned into a flood. The second line swept into the hotel, laughing and whirling and dancing. I caught a glimpse of Allen and Barker sailing through the doorway. Dancers, musicians, and onlookers shot through the dark, cool lobby, leaped like salmon up a couple of flights of stairs, and flowed down a luxuriously carpeted hallway to the door of the Grand Salon, where the whole mass broke over a couple of ladies who were shouting, "No one allowed in without a ticket! No one allowed in without a ticket!" Most of the second line couldn't meet the tab, which was two dollars and fifty cents, and, slowly subsiding, it washed casually down the stairs and onto the street. The bands marched into the Grand Salon—a large, mirrored room full of pillars, draperies, chandeliers, and blue-haired women—and formed a long line in front of the bandstand occupied by a sedate-looking group that included George Lewis (clarinet), Punch Miller and Kid Thomas (trumpets), Cie Frazier (drums), and De De and Billie Pierce (cornet and piano). All three bands roared through a short "St. Louis Blues," which visibly shook the watching cheeks and jowls. Then the Onward and the Eureka blew their way out of the Grand Salon, and the concert began. After the brass and the sun and the dancing, it was a letdown. The music sounded thin and mossy, and it seemed to get entangled in the chandeliers, which repeatedly changed color, and in the massed blue hair. Things toned up considerably when the Onward marched back in, played "When the Saints," and marched out again. I marched out after them, and found Allen by the door.

"Enjoy yourself?" he asked me.

I said the parade had been magnificent and the concert disconsolate.

"But I was glad to see Punch Miller," he said. "Punch is seventy-two, and he hasn't been well. He came to talk and play at my Wednesday-evening lecture last week, and during a number that reminded him of his childhood he got so sad he broke down and cried right in class. It was pretty upsetting, and I'm worried about him."

Allen had told me that New Orleanians in general don't care about jazz. I stopped in at the New Orleans Tourist Commission on the way back to my motel and asked a pigeon-shaped woman behind a desk where I might hear some good jazz. She looked startled. "I'm sorry, but we can't help you. We don't have anything on jazz."

I had asked Allen on Saturday if he knew someone who could show me what was left of the New Orleans of *Jazzmen*, and he had suggested Manuel Manetta. Manetta, he told me, is at least seventy-eight and is a Creole of color, as they say in New Orleans. Manetta plays several instruments, but he is primarily a teacher; his pupils have included Wingy Manone, Red Allen, Kid Rena, and Emmett Hardy, the last of whom is said to have influenced Bix Beiderbecke. He played with Buddy Bolden in 1904, with Frankie Dusen's Eagle Band in 1909, for Lulu White, the celebrated octoroon who ran Lulu White's Mahogany Hall, on Basin Street, in 1910, and with Kid Ory and King Oliver in 1916. "I don't know if Manetta—or Professor Manetta, as I call him—will take you," Allen had said. "But we'll go and see him across the river in Algiers anyway. Negroes haven't been riding in cabs with white people all that long, and he might feel uneasy about it. But he might ride with his old friend Louis Kohlman, a Negro who runs a cab in Algiers."

Manetta's house is small and gray, and beside it stands his studio, a high, oblong structure on stilts. He was in the studio, sitting on a piano stool and smoking a cigarette. A tan fedora with a brim as wide as a running board rested on the keys of a yellow-and-black upright, and he was dressed in a brown business suit and a green sports shirt. Allen and I sat down, and Manetta handed me his card, which read:

"FESS" M. MANETTA'S
MASTER OF ALL INSTRUMENTS

He has a hound-dog face, with a pendulous lower lip that folds up like a drawbridge. His voice is low, and he speaks slowly. He obviously delights in keeping his fire carefully damped. He and Allen exchanged pleasantries for about ten minutes, and then he told Allen, "I don't take but three or four pupils a week now. I stopped regular teaching about four years ago. When I was young, the piano was considered a lady's instrument, a sissy job. I wanted to play the piano, but I didn't have the spunk. Then, one night, my brother took me to the Ping Pong Club, near here, on Brooklyn Street, to hear Gussie Neil. He was playing in the back room, and I couldn't get over it. My eyes were popping. I'd seen a man *could* play the piano and not be made fun of, and when I got home I took a big old lantern and crept into the parlor to the piano and sat there picking out tunes until my brother got home, and said, 'Hey, it's five o'clock. What you doin', Fess?' Well, I been doing it ever since." Manetta gave a soundless chuckle and lit another cigarette. "It's still there, the Ping Pong Club."

I asked Manetta what he remembered about Buddy Bolden, who died in an insane asylum in 1931.

"The first time I saw Bolden was at the Odd Fellows Hall, on Seguin Street. That's gone now. Frank Lewis was Bolden's regular clarinettist, but he took sick, and Alphonse Picou, who passed just a little while back, came in for the night. He was just about white, and it caused a stir. 'Oh, say, Buddy's got a white man playing with him' was all they could say. Bolden was a ragtime player. Very powerful, but he could play those little trills and runs, too. He was a very nice, fine gentleman, and the ladies' favorite of nights."

Allen laughed, and said, "That reminds me of when I had my record shop on Baronne Street in the fifties, not long after I came down here. The bass player Albert Glenny, who also played with Bolden, came in one day, and I said, 'You must be about the last surviving member of Buddy Bolden's band.' Glenny turned and pointed at the street. 'See that man standing over there at the bus stop? *He* play with Bolden, too.' And he was right. Glenny was a funny man. Another time, a woman asked him for his autograph, and he thanked her and said no, he couldn't do that. 'When I went to school,' he told her, 'they didn't teach us to read and write.' Of course, that would have been in the eighteen-seventies."

There was a knock, and a short man of about fifty with a big paunch and an amiable face came in. "Hey, Fess, how are you feeling?" he said. His voice went falsetto. "Teacher, I'm a little late for my lesson and I forgot my clarinet." He and Manetta laughed and embraced. He turned out to be a former pupil of Manetta's—Freddie Kohlman, a drummer, who has worked in Chicago for the past ten years or so. He is Louis Kohlman's son.

Allen mentioned the tour to Manetta for the first time, and then explained to Kohlman what we had in mind.

Manetta looked guarded, and Kohlman said he'd drive us to his father's house. "I don't know where he's at, but maybe he's left word. Anyway, Fess and I got to arrange about a get-together Thursday."

When we reached the Kohlman house, Freddie Kohlman's mother, who is handsome and bespectacled, offered us a drink in her parlor.

"I'll have just a tall glass of water with a taste of that good stuff in it, and a little sugar," Manetta said. "Freddie knows what I take."

"Fess, you got to hear Mama play her new electric organ," Kohlman said.

Mrs. Kohlman giggled, sat down at a small organ, and played "I'm Getting Sentimental Over You" in a dirge tempo. Manetta stood behind her and coached: "Get at those quarter notes, now. Get at those quarter notes."

"Now, that's what I'm having trouble with," Mrs. Kohlman replied as she played. "My time. I can't seem to get my time right."

When she finished, Kohlman said, "Fess, you know who came by my place in Chicago the other night and sat in? Lil Armstrong. She still plays very powerful piano."

"I first got acquainted with Lil in 1931," Manetta said. "She was married to Louis Armstrong then. Louis had a contract uptown here. I went to see him backstage, and he was shut up in this little bathroom trying to play two trumpets at once, like I used to do." Manetta dropped his voice and growled like Armstrong. " 'Hey, Fess. Hey, Fess. How you do that? Show me how you do that. How you play those two horns at once?' He put the horns back to his mouth and blew, and nothing happened. 'Show me, Fess. Show me.' Well, I tried, but he never learned." Manetta laughed, and finished his drink.

Kohlman senior arrived, a medium-sized man with short, grizzled hair, and ten minutes later he and Allen and I were waiting in his cab for Manetta, who was standing on the sidewalk talking to Freddie Kohlman.

"They're still setting up their Thursday meeting," Allen said.

"What'll they have left to talk about?" I asked.

"Oh, no trouble. They'll talk about today and the old days and tomorrow."

Manetta heaved himself into the back seat. We passed the Ping Pong Club, a dishevelled one-story building that looked deserted, and recrossed the Mississippi. Kohlman is a cautious driver, and he threaded his way through the tollgate at the bridge as if it were the eye of a needle. We turned off the Pontchartrain Expressway and found Simon Bolivar Avenue. "It's pronounced Salmon Boulevard hereabouts," Allen said. "Just as Socrates Street, in Algiers, is pronounced So-crate-eez, and Tchoupitoulas Street, where Frank Lewis lived, is Chapatoola. Turn into First Street, Mr. Kohlman."

The houses on First Street were low and scattered and dilapidated. The dirt sidewalks were crowded with telephone poles and children. Shaking his head, Kohlman said, "This place ain't changed a bit. Not one bit in fifty, sixty years."

Manetta, who had had a second taste before leaving Kohlman's house, looked shrunken and sleepy beneath his enormous hat.

"There's where Buddy Bolden lived," Allen said, motioning toward a squat brown house. A woman was standing dimly behind a screen door. "This was his address in the city directory for 1902." The screen door opened, and for a second I expected Bolden, who would be in his late eighties, to step out. But it was the woman, carrying a basket of clothes.

We passed Nelson Joseph's Shaving Parlor, where musicians had often been hired. On Danneel Street, which was the old Rampart Street, Kohlman pointed out the Joseph P. Geddes Funeral Home. "That's been there as long as I can remember," he said.

We stopped in front of a big two-story building with a stucco Spanish façade. "This was the Bulls' Club," Allen said. "It now belongs to the Elks. We call that three-story rise sticking up at its rear a camel's back."

Manetta opened his eyes and sat forward. "I played here with Chris Kelly, the trumpeter," he said. "He never recorded, but he was a great blues player. One night, he hired this boy Earl Humphrey on trombone. He still around, ain't he, Mr. Allen?"

"He played in the Heart Fund parade on Sunday," Allen said.

"Humphrey and Kelly were gettin' at each other that evening, I guess over money, and they came out in front right there, and Humphrey was full of wine and lost his mind and picked up a brick from the banquette, which is what we called the old raised sidewalks, and hit Kelly right on the side of his eye. Kelly fell down, and there was a lot of blood, but he was a tough fellow and he went back and finished the night, bandages and all."

We came to a three-story stone building. "Isn't that Masonic Hall, once the Eagle Saloon?" Allen asked Manetta.

Manetta grunted. "Frankie Dusen, Bolden's trombonist, played here every Saturday night, after he'd taken over Bolden's band and it became the Eagle Band. Fellow called Smith ran the hall. He had a floorwalker named Bob Foots, who wore size-fourteen shoes. Foots was a stick-beater, carried a police nightstick to keep down the fights. And over behind those new buildings—that's the Civic Center now—over there was the Battlefield. A very tough area. Ma Rainey, the blues singer, used to go back in there and work. And right on the edge of it was Louis Armstrong's stamping ground, and the parish prison."

"And that was Chinatown," Allen said, waving toward a group of buildings near Masonic Hall. "Kid Sheik, the trumpet player, told me the sidewalks would be covered with Chinamen, stretched out in the sun like alligators, smoking hop."

We turned into Iberville Street, which had been the northern boundary of Storyville. A raw-looking housing development covers it now.

"Oh, man, I like to see all these demolishings," Manetta said, and sighed. "It's a *new* world."

Allen asked Manetta if any cribs were left. Cribs were rows of small rooms, giving directly off the sidewalk, where the low-priced prostitutes worked.

"No, they all gone," Manetta said. "They was mostly over on Gravier Street. A short-time trick was fifty cents, and rolling around was a dollar a shot. Right down there, on St. Peter Street, in that old building, was my headquarters, where all my musicians hung out." He pointed into the housing development. "And I had a girl, she lived right about there."

We came to the intersection of Basin Street and St. Peter Street. A partly dismantled brick building stands on one corner. "That's what's left of Lulu White's saloon," Allen said. "Her Mahogany Hall was right next to it, where you see the Krauss department store's garage. It didn't come down too long ago. That park over there is Beauregard Square. A hundred years ago, it was Congo Square, and the slaves danced there on Saturday nights. George Washington Cable has written about it."

Manetta yawned.

"You getting tired, Professor Manetta?" Allen asked.

Manetta nodded.

"Mr. Kohlman, please leave us off at Chartres and St. Philip, in the Quarter," Allen said.

I paid Kohlman and thanked Manetta. He smiled, and the two men drove away. Only Manetta's hat was visible through the rear window.

After dinner, I persuaded Allen to show me Preservation Hall. It is on St. Peter Street, just below Bourbon Street, in a typical gravy-colored, two-story Quarter house, complete with tall, shuttered windows, a wrought-iron balcony, and a carriageway leading to a back garden. An old trombone case with the word "Preservation" on it in brass letters hangs above the carriageway entrance, and suspended from it is a smaller case, lettered "Hall." The hall, which we looked into from the carriageway, has a high ceiling and is roughly fifty feet square. A bandstand on the street side faces half a dozen rows of benches. There are cushions on the floor between the benches and the stand. The walls are grimy and the floorboards give. Gloomy paintings of musicians hang just below the ceiling. A tubby, stubbled man with wild hair and sleepy eyes joined us in the carriageway. Allen introduced him as Allan Jaffe, the operator of the hall, and then excused himself and said he was going home to bed. I told Allen I would stop by Tulane in the morning to see him.

Jaffe and I sat down on an ornate wooden bench set against one wall of the carriageway. It had three or four gracefully curved armrests. "I bought this beauty, which is a pew, along with a lot of others, from the Church of the Good Shepherd, uptown, before it was torn down," he told me. "It's cypress. I was going to furnish the hall with them, but I was afraid they'd get carved up. We've got a good band tonight—Kid Thomas on trumpet, and George Lewis and Louis Nelson. They start around eight-thirty and finish around midnight. We take contributions at the door—a dollar a head minimum. And we don't serve liquor."

I asked Jaffee how long he had run the hall.

"My wife and I quit our jobs in Philadelphia and moved to New Orleans in 1961," he said. "Sam Charters' New Orleans recordings gave us hope that things were coming to life. We lived next door to Dick Allen, and he suggested to Larry Borenstein, who owns this building, that we take over the informal sessions that were being given here. The hall was an art gallery then. We didn't have any big bang at first. New Orleans doesn't support its own music. It took two years to get the place going even on a month-to-month basis. In the early days, a sideman got thirteen-fifty a night and the leader twenty-six. Now the leader gets thirty dollars and a sideman twenty-fifty."

A tall man with a fringe of white hair, taped-up glasses, and a book in his hand came and sat down beside Jaffe. Jaffe introduced him as Bill Russell, and then said he had to leave us and start taking contributions.

Russell was one of the authors of *Jazzmen*. He is a composer, musicologist, and critic, and some of his early jazz criticism is definitive. He was largely responsible for the Bunk Johnson revival, and he has been a kind of amanuensis to Mahalia Jackson. Since 1942, he has spent most of his time in New Orleans, where, in addition to making and selling records, he has amassed an enormous amount of research material on the early musicians. He has biographies of Manetta and Johnson under way. By reputation, he is a lone wolf, an ascetic, and a mild anarchist. He has a gentle, caved-in face, and is a nonstop professorial talker.

"I often open up the Hall at night," he said, taking off his glasses. "I do it to pay back Jaffe, who takes care of Pretty Baby, my parakeet, when I'm away. Pretty Baby—he's named after a Tony Jackson tune—is ten, and if he's lucky he'll live to be twenty. I feed him nothing but vegetables and greens. I live upstairs, and pay Larry Borenstein rent by giving his wife and kid violin lessons."

I asked Russell if the musicians involved in the current New Orleans revival had been simply unable to make the grade up North.

"Yes, by and large they were. But there were a lot of others who just wouldn't leave the city or who died before they got the chance. Joe Oliver tried to get Bunk to join him in Chicago, but Bunk wouldn't go. The music has never died out in New Orleans—even in 1959 and 1960, when Kid Thomas, who's one of my particular favorites, had the only regular band here. During the Depression, there was a one-hundred-piece W.P.A. band. It had twenty trumpeters alone in it. It would break into groups, and they'd play. Most of the musicians had day jobs, too, and many still do. On my second visit to New Orleans, in the early forties, I ran all over the city on trolleys and buses looking for old musicians I'd heard were playing in out-of-the-way places, but I missed a lot of them. Papa Celestin was alive then, and so were Alphonse Picou and Big Eye Louis Nelson, the clarinettists, and Charlie Love, the trumpeter. Tom Brown, who took the first jazz band North, in 1915, was, too. Between 1900 and 1910, New Orleans was twenty years ahead of its time musically. The city was filled with music.

When you opened a store or restaurant, you hired a band. When you had a birthday party, you hired a band. Bands advertised their own dances in the streets and then played at them. There was music between the rounds at prizefights. Bands would be made up on the spot out of musicians who rode the old Smoky Mary, a train that ran from near the French Market to Lake Pontchartrain, where there was always a great demand for music."

"I've always wondered if Buddy Bolden had a first-rate predecessor—a kind of Essenic teacher," I said.

"Well, I've looked into that, and all I can find out is that there might have been a guitar player named Happy Galloway. Mutt Carey, the trumpeter, and Bud Scott, the banjoist, mentioned him when I was in California in 1939. Bolden *is* a legend, but sheer massed opinion among the musicians I've talked to who heard him makes it certain that he was good. The tales of his sexual prowess probably stem from the peculiar legend that all trumpet players are oversexed. Bolden may have learned a lot of his music in church, but I don't think it was instrumental music. I once asked the late Baby Dodds about music in the churches here, and he said, 'There was no music, no music, just singing.' Dodds was a purist. He often said the main job of the snare drummer in a brass band is to shade the band—make it play soft or loud, as the need arises. He considered it neurotic to have your name on your bass drum, and he would never use a snare drum that even had paint on it, because he thought the paint would affect the tone." Russell paused for a few moments, and then went on, "Lately, I have been getting disgusted with the way the bands play in the streets. Bunk Johnson played eight-hour parades almost up to the time of his death, in 1949, and he never put his horn down once. Now one or another of the trumpet players is always resting, and sometimes the drums stop altogether. And there are strings of solos, like an Eddie Condon jam session. And what business has a saxophone in a brass band? I can't believe that anyone would be that insensitive. In the old days, the leader never wanted to be a star. In the old days, it was always '*our* band.' "

The music had begun, and Russell and I went in and stood at the back of the hall. The cushions and the benches were all occupied, and the standees were three-deep. The audience was middle-aged, white, and easy to please. When Kid Thomas managed a triplet, it clapped; when Emmanuel Paul, the tenor saxophonist, held a single note for four measures, it clapped (I wondered how it would react to the twelve-chorus tremolo that Earl Hines tosses in at the end of his "St. Louis Blues"); when George Lewis interpolated the melody of "Oh, They Don't Wear Pants in the Southern Part of France" in a solo, it laughed uproariously. It was hard to see the musicians. Their color and their everyday clothes made them seem part of the décor. The most frequent soloists were Lewis, who is a thin, sweet embellisher, and Paul, who veered continually between the young Coleman Hawkins and a country-club saxophonist. Thomas is a rough, steady performer whose occasional solos reminded me of Yank Lawson, and Louis Nelson is a plank-by-plank melodist. The drummer's time suggested a roller coaster. The band sounded best collectively, when, leaning together like the old houses in the Quarter, it achieved a dense, hymnlike texture that reached affecting heights in soft versions of "Bye Bye Blackbird" and "Just a Closer Walk with Thee."

Most of the audience left at the end of the set. About half bought records at a rack in the carriageway and asked the musicians to autograph them. In five minutes, the hall filled again. Russell had slipped away, but I found Jaffe by the door, and said good night. He held a basket on his lap, like a woman shelling peas. It was brimming with money.

Outside, I was hit by a blast of music from across the street. It was coming from the new Southland Jazz Club. I gave a donation at the door to a peppy blonde in sneakers who resembled a gym teacher. She told me that George Finola was on cornet and Raymond Burke on clarinet. She also told me that Finola worshipped Bix Beiderbecke, that he was only twenty, and that he was from Chicago. She said that Danny Barker was a regular performer, but that he was home ill. The differences between Preservation Hall and the Southland were startling. The band was mixed (Finola and Burke white, and the trombonist, the pianist, and the drummer Negro), the audience was skimpy but mixed, and the room, about two-thirds as big as Preservation Hall, was full of fresh paint and good cheer. So was the music. Finola, who is thin and intense, is surprising. He has Beiderbecke's blessed tone, but he is freer rhythmically. His solos *rush* out of him, and are highly inventive. Burke, who has a reputation that is partly the result of his refusing to leave New Orleans, fits perfectly with Finola, for he resembles Beiderbecke's old friend Pee Wee Russell, minus Russell's stylistic kinks.

Deciding to finish off the big three in one swat, I worked my way several blocks up Bourbon Street, through knots of glass-carrying tourists, to Dixieland Hall. I was greeted there by the Southland gym teacher, who said she liked to help out wherever she could. She gave me a personnel list, and also a folder which stated that Dixieland Hall was founded in 1962, that "numerous television and movie stars flocked to hear its music and enjoy its fantastic 'good-time' atmosphere," and that it is "the only place on Bourbon Street where children may be brought to see and hear in person the old-time bands of New Orleans." Its décor—wooden benches, a peeling ceiling, and an out-of-tune upright—was Preservation Hall, but the band, led by the drummer Paul Barbarin, played with style and verve. Barbarin, who worked with Luis Russell in the early thirties and Louis Armstrong in the later thirties is compact and fierce-looking, and he blew the band along. New Orleans drummers tend to become hypnotized by their snare drums, lavishing on them endless press rolls and barn-door rimshots. But Barbarin, in addition to a marvellous press roll, in which his sticks come at one another low from opposite edges of the snare in fat blurs, like gulls after the same clam, uses a high-hat and ride cymbals to excellent effect. He also flashes about between his snare and his tom-toms, and during a brief ensemble pause in "Bill Bailey, Won't You Please Come Home" he got off a lightning multi-drum *poo-rum* that left him nodding with satisfaction. Louis Cottrell, his clarinettist, is a liquid performer who bastes his melodies, and Ernie Caglanatti, his trumpeter, is a tiny, contented-looking man who admires Red Allen.

The music was still charging around my mind as a taxi took me to Tulane the next morning, and so was a brief conversation I'd had at Dixieland Hall with a sociologist from Minnesota who told me he had been listening to jazz for forty years. "New Orleans jazz has never got over its marching-band origins," he said during an intermission. "It's still a communal music. And since communal projects, in order to remain communal, abhor the star system, it is also a mediocre music. Of course, this can be comforting, for mediocrity en masse often fools itself as well as its audience. But a superior talent wrecks this cozy ménage, which is why Armstrong and Red Allen and Jelly Roll Morton broke so quickly with their collective origins and became one-man bands. None of them were communal types, and none of them returned to New Orleans." He paused at this point and lit a small cigar. "I've noticed another striking, or diminishing, thing about New Orleans jazz. Its blues have as much color and life as lard. They have none of that old train-whistle keening you hear in Kansas City and New York blues. There aren't even any blue notes—the blue note being an anticommunity, unorthodox note. Maybe jazz was born in New Orleans, as the histories say, but it grew up elsewhere."

The Archive of New Orleans Jazz occupies a small, locked room on the third floor of the Howard-Tilton Memorial Library. Allen let me in, and handed me a sheet of paper headed "Statistical Summary of Holdings." The Archive, it revealed, possesses well over eleven thousand recordings, including twenty-four cylinders; thirty-nine piano rolls; almost nine thousand pieces of sheet music; fifteen hundred taped interviews; sixteen motion-picture reels; four thousand books, periodicals, catalogues, and microfilm rolls; and twelve thousand pieces of miscellany, among them posters, clippings, and photographs. Allen sat down next to a table cluttered with recording equipment, and fingered a pipe. "Bill Hogan, who's a professor of history here, got the ball rolling on all this," he said. "I'd talked to him in the late fifties about doing a thesis on recorded interviews with old jazz musicians. Bill Russell and I had already done a good many interviews on our own, but the cost was more than we could carry. Hogan knew the right people, and by 1958 we had a seventy-five-thousand-dollar grant from the Ford Foundation for starting the Archive. Russell was the first curator and I was his associate. The Foundation has given us over a hundred and fifty-six thousand dollars in all, but it's all gone, and now we're simply part of the library, which pays my salary. I took over in 1965. We can't afford to do much interviewing anymore, so now we're making digests of the tapes on hand. We used to make word-for-word transcriptions, but it was backbreaking—particularly with someone like Slow Drag Pavageau, the old bassist, who speaks an almost unbreakable code of Creole patois and consonantless English."

I remarked that Russell had been gloomy about the music in New Orleans.

Allen laughed. "Bill is always exercised over something, whether it's the Telephone Company or the deteriorating quality of Coca-Cola bottle caps," he said. "The number of brass bands *is* decreasing, and their personnels are often interchangeable. But there are new musicians coming up. I'm always meeting new faces. There may even be as many as twenty or thirty big bands—rock-and-roll and swing—which work occasionally in the city. Last week, I heard a marvellous band at Xavier University, and its best soloist, an alto saxophonist, is a *freshman*. And there is a scattering of modern groups. Ornette Coleman lived here a while back, before he got famous. Well, if you'll excuse me, I've got to prepare my weekly lecture. I have three or four students—doctors and the like—and I try to get musicians to talk to them. I've asked Tony Fougerat this week. Have you been to the New Orleans Jazz Museum, over in the Quarter? The director, Henry Clay Watson, may not know all that much about jazz, but he's a genuine, museum-trained museum man. Danny Barker and George Finola work there, too. Let's find some more non-tourist music tonight."

The museum is in a neat one-story brick building on Dumaine Street, and it is an appropriate setting for Watson, a short, precise, fluttery man who talks like an educated circus barker. "This is an institute of casual education," he told me. His hands were clasped across his stomach, and he moved steadily up and down on his toes. "We were founded in November of 1961 by the New Orleans Jazz Club, which still provides most of our support. Tulane is basically *oral* history survey. We are three-dimensional and *visual*. This is probably the smallest and most unique museum in the world. We have twenty to fifty times as much material in storage as is on display— *tons* of sheet music, beautiful William Sidney Mount prints, and the like. We have just acquired thirty full years of *Down Beat*. We are hunting desperately for storage area, and we may get a chance to move into an old bank building near the Royal Orleans Hotel. We authenticate every last piece of memorabilia that is given to us, and we—"

Watson was interrupted by a telephone call. I picked up a facsimile copy of the 1915 Blue Book, which the museum sells for five dollars. I remembered having read about the Blue Book in *Jazzmen*. It was a guide to Storyville, which was probably the only legal enclave of prostitution ever set up in this country, and it listed the names and addresses of the prostitutes (white, octoroon, and colored) and was sprinkled with rosy advertisements for specific "sporting palaces." I turned to the preface:

> This Directory and Guide of the Sporting District has been before the people on many occasions, and has proven its authority as to what is doing in the "Queer Zone."

Anyone who knows to-day from yesterday will say that the Blue Book is the right book for the right people.

### Why New Orleans Should
### Have This Directory

Because it is the only district of its kind in the States set aside for the fast women by the law.

Because it puts the stranger on a proper and safe path as to where he may go and be free from "Holdups," and other games usually practised upon the stranger.

It regulates the women so that they may live in one district to themselves instead of being scattered over the city and filling our thoroughfares with street walkers.

It also gives the names of women entertainers employed in the Dance Halls and Cabarets in the District.

An advertisement for "Miss Grace Lloyd" read:

Of all the landladies of the Tenderloin, there are few better known or admired than Grace Lloyd. Grace, as she is commonly called by all who know her, is a woman of very rare attainments and comes of that good old English stock from across the waters.

Grace is regarded as an all-round jolly good fellow, saying nothing about her beauty. She regards life as life and not as a money-making space of time.

Grace also has the distinction of keeping one of the quietest and most elaborately furnished establishments in the city, where an array of beautiful women and good times reign supreme.

Miss Lloyd recently went to enormous expense renovating her establishment, which had been almost totally destroyed by fire.

A visit will teach more than the pen can describe.

(When I got back to my motel, I totted up the number of girls in the Blue Book. There were nine octoroons, two hundred and fifty-four Negroes, and four hundred and sixty-four whites.)

Watson was still talking on the phone, so I wandered around the museum. A giant "Family Tree of Jazz" occupies one wall, and on another is an exhaustive chart tracing the origins of jazz from Spain in 758 A.D. to Dizzy Gillespie and Charlie Parker. A partition in the center of the room has five wall telephones which, when they are dialed, offer recorded lectures and illustrative music. The rest of the room is filled with display cases containing such authenticated memorabilia as a pair of Bix Beiderbecke's cufflinks, contributed by Hoagy Carmichael; one of Beiderbecke's cornets; the bugle that

Louis Armstrong played in the Colored Waifs' Home when he was thirteen, and a chunk of the flagpole that stood in front of the home; Armstrong's first cornet, with a mouthpiece notched by its owner to prevent it from slipping; the head of a bass drum belonging to Ray Bauduc when he was with Bob Crosby's Bob Cats; one of Sidney Bechet's soprano saxophones; the guitar that Johnny St. Cyr used with Jelly Roll Morton's Red Hot Peppers; and a clarinet owned by Larry Shields, of the Original Dixieland Jazz Band.

"It's good to see a New York face again," a quiet voice said. It was Danny Barker.

We shook hands, and I asked him how he was feeling.

"I've got the old diabetes, you know, and I haven't been so well. I took a whole lot of tests at the hospital yesterday, and my wife made me stay home last night. She hid my banjo so I *couldn't* play."

I suggested that we have lunch in the Rib Room of the Royal Orleans. When we left the museum, Watson, who was now showing a visitor a copy of the Blue Book, unclasped his hands and waved them.

At the Rib Room, we got a table immediately. I caught only one untoward look, and it came from an old man with a napkin tucked under his chin—a vicious squint that may have been nearsightedness. Barker ordered trout amandine. "I've been Jim Crowed in New York as long as I can remember, but I can be slippery here—move around," Barker said. "At one time, if I'd walked in here the customers would have been spilling their water, the waiters mumbling, and the headwaiter stumbling. Now everything's cool. I came back down here because there wasn't any work in New York. At least there's some action here, and I have over a hundred relatives. My autobiography—there's enough for *two* books—is all ready to go. I just need a publisher. It's been turned down by so many that I think I'll get some cheap paper and mimeograph machines, and get all those relatives to crank the handles." Barker smiled and leaned back. "In the winter, there is terrific party-giving here. We have the molasses king, the cotton king, the lumber king. Man, you can make two bills a night. The caterers are Negroes, and they and the musicians are tight. The musicians have their own table and they can eat and drink. And I work off and on at the Southland Jazz Club."

I asked Barker what he knew of Bunk Johnson.

"Bunk was considered the equal, or better, of King Oliver and Manuel Perez and Freddie Keppard. He was also a great ladies' man and a boozer, and it got him in trouble. Lee Collins, the trumpet player, told me once of some trouble Bunk got in. The Jefferson City Buzzards were an Irish Channel marching club whose members were stevedores, firemen, and policemen, and they loved to ball in the Irish fashion. They were all six-foot Irishmen from County Cork and Galway Bay, and they had some fracases. It was the custom in those days for a committee from the club to decide on the music it wanted for a particular dance or outing. So the committee went to Spannol's, the bar where Bunk hung out, and gave him a deposit to play with his marching band at an all-day parade. This must have been around 1914 and or 1915. Came the day, the Buzzards marched without a band, because Bunk didn't show up. So they sent word to Spannol's to tell Bunk he had blowed everything up and that they were going to catch him and put him in a coffee sack and throw him in the Mississippi. Although Bunk said he didn't get any deposit, he sent word back that he was willing to repay it, but the bread of friendship was beyond repair. Bunk was advised to leave town while the anger of the Jefferson City Buzzards subsided, and he went out to New Iberia, Louisiana, and from there he travelled all over the Orient and the world. It was in New Iberia that Bill Russell found him with no teeth and no horn in 1942 and brought him back to play again."

Barker took a bite of his trout. "But there were other trumpet players besides Bunk," he went on. "Buddy Petit, who never recorded, was the diminished-note king. Louis Armstrong plays a lot of his stuff. Petit was acknowledged by all New Orleans musicians as being one of the supergreats. And Chris Kelly was a good blues player. All these musicians played for different types of people. In fact, there was a caste system within the Negroes themselves. The Catholics liked Creole music, which was refined, and the Protestants were closer to blues shouting and spirituals and screaming to the skies and the Lord. In the downtown section, below Canal Street, Chris Kelly would be their boy. Kelly would never be allowed uptown, with all the skintight squeezing and hugging that happened when he played. All the bands had particular sections of society they entertained—high yallers, mulattoes, *comme il faut*, or blue bloods—and particular halls where they played. You'd find Kelly at Perseverance Hall, Petit at Economy Hall, and Sam Morgan at the France Amis. These halls were the homes of the benevolent societies and social clubs, of which there were once a hundred and fifty. The benevolent societies were like Blue Cross. If you wanted to form one, you got a dozen or so people together and went to see the doctor, the druggist, the undertaker. You got sick, needed medicine, or died, it was all paid for out of your dues. And there were yearly bonkeys, or banquets, for the members. Now there are only forty or so societies and social clubs left. The music at the old functions was always easy and freeflowing. It never excited you. Now it has become—in Preservation Hall and such—show business. You sit up there before an audience and you got these eyes on you all the time. You can't even scratch yourself on the bandstand. Most of the musicians playing in these clubs are old men—half blind, half sick. They're hamfat musicians. In the old days, the rough musicians kept pieces of ham fat in their pockets to grease the slides of their trombones or the valves of their trumpets. For every good musician, there was a hamfat. It looks like the hamfats didn't dissipate as much as the good musicians, because this town is full of them, and they're being exploited by smooth operators."

Barker put down his fork and pushed his empty plate away. He took a sip of coffee.

"But I've had the pleasure of playing beautiful music with beautiful people in my life. Now it's just a matter of the buck."

Allen took me on a dizzying tour that night. Our first stop was the front parlor of a Reverend Williams' house, in the uptown section, where a small band was rehearsing for a special church service. I recognized the Englishman Keith Smith, Earl Humphrey on trombone, and Andrew Morgan on tenor saxophone. A young Swede, Lars Edegran, was on piano, and there were a guitarist and a bassist. It was sweet, quiet ensemble music, and it sent the Reverend Williams' wife, seated in a rocker on the front porch, into violent motion and fervent singing. We stopped at the Golliwog Lounge to hear Armand Hug, another white New Orleans musician who has earned a reputation by staying at home. He looks like George Brent and plays like Jess Stacy. We stopped at the big, modern International Longshoremen's Association Hall, where a large rock-and-roll band made up of young musicians was pumping away impressively for a formal Negro subdeb cotillion. We stopped at the Haven, a small Negro bar. There was no dancing, but the band, made up of a trumpeter (who resembled Bill Coleman), a country-club tenor saxophonist, and rhythm, had some of the nonchalance of Tony Fougerat's group. And we stopped at Pepe's, a tourist spot in the Quarter, where there was a modern quartet led by the drummer Henry (Pickle) Jackson and including an alto saxophonist, an electric guitar, and a bass. Jackson was fascinating. He looks older than Paul Barbarin, but he plays flawless bebop drums.

"Hello and good morning," Allen said on the telephone the next day. "We're lucky—which isn't quite the right word under the circumstances—because I've just found out there's a funeral this afternoon in Walkertown, in Marrero. That's about eight miles out on the other side of the river, and there will be two bands—the Young Tuxedo and the Olympia. Betty Rankin, who is the associate curator at the Archive now, is taking us out."

On the other side of the river, the three of us drove between low, woolly clouds and flat country anchored by shopping centers and small factories. "The country funeral with brass bands is rapidly vanishing," Allen said. Mrs. Rankin, who is large and cheerful, nodded, and he went on, "The well-to-do and middle-class Negroes have begun to look down on it. They consider it Uncle Tom. It's too bad. There is no ritual like it anywhere in the world— dirge music on the way to the cemetery, and swinging music on the way back. They show death respect and then rejoice in life. Turn left just ahead, onto Ames Boulevard, Betty, and then left again, onto Second Street."

Walkertown is a dirt-poor Negro hamlet. Its one-story wooden houses are set on stilts, and the front yards are shabby. There are almost no trees. The dusty white streets, made of crushed clamshells, are flanked by open drainage ditches with planks for bridges. Mrs. Rankin pulled up near the Morning Star Baptist Church, a long wooden building with a mock-Spanish steeple. An enormous ear-trumpet loudspeaker was fastened to the front wall of the steeple, and air-conditioners jutted out of most of the windows.

Several musicians were milling around in front of the church. One of them strolled past and, seeing Allen, leaned into the car and said, "Hey, you brought yourself! How you feeling?"

It began to rain, and a second musician appeared. It was Kid Thomas. "Man, it rains at a funeral, it means it's washing away the dead man's sins. A really big sinner, it rains like hell." He smiled, showing a lot of gold teeth.

"There will be a lot of repeats from the Sunday parade," Allen said. "Andrew Morgan and Chester Jones and Jerry Green from the Onward, and Earl Humphrey, Papa Glass, Peter Bocage, and Milton Batiste from the Eureka. And Keith Smith, too."

The rain stopped, and we got out of the car. A thin female voice, singing a hymn, came out of the loudspeaker. A static-filled silence followed, and then a man spoke. A series of moans and screams grew louder and louder behind his words.

"The bereaved women generally try to outscream one another," Mrs. Rankin said. "I once went to a funeral where the deceased had a legal and a non-legal wife, and they screamed at each other for fifteen minutes. It was quite a show."

The church door opened, and two women in black and white, their faces wet and contorted, hobbled out on the arms of several men. A file of men wearing Odd Fellows' ceremonial aprons and neckpieces followed. The Young Tuxedo Band and the Olympia Band played a slow "Just a Closer Walk with Thee." Then the Olympia marched past the church and turned into Ames Boulevard, with the Young Tuxedo about fifty feet behind. A dozen Odd Fellows walked between them. The snare drum was muffled and the beat as slow as Big Ben's. "Saviour Lead Me," by the Olympia, was followed by the Young Tuxedo's "What a Friend We Have in Jesus." Dead, soft drumbeats separated the numbers. The second line ambled along quietly at one side of the road, and a long string of limousines nosed the Young Tuxedo. The procession moved between a housing development and a farmyard full of charging guinea hens, between a power station and a field of cows, and after a mile or so it halted at a wooden bridge over a deep ditch. On the other side, a dirt road disappeared into a patch of woods. The Young Tuxedo marched across the bridge, followed by the hearse, which moved cautiously, filling the bridge. The cemetery began on the left of the dirt road, and was a bedraggled sea of small stones, briars, wooden crosses, and long grass. Refuse had been dumped as fill on the other side of the road. A tunnel of trees dripped and whispered. The Young Tuxedo played "Saviour Lead Me" at the grave, and after the service the mourners walked slowly back to the boulevard. The Young Tuxedo suddenly started "When the Saints Go Marching In." The second line materialized in front. The music was thin and loose, compared with the New Orleans parade, and twice as brave. The sun came out, burnishing one of the tubas. The Olympia began a fast "Just a Closer Walk with Thee." In the second line, a fat man dressed in a tight blue suit and a small fedora threw back his head, switched his hips, and strutted through a crowd of leaping, delighted children. The two tear-drenched women from the church danced arm in arm. An old woman flopped heavily in circles, like a turkey with an injured wing, and was joined by an old man, who pumped his knees and trembled his hands. The returning limousines roared past, leaving big white dust devils. The Young Tuxedo played "Bye and Bye." The road was filled with dancers, and when the rain started again there were little screams. I looked down, and half a dozen tiny pistonlike children were sharing my umbrella. Their turned-up faces were split by smiles, and their cheeks were covered with rain.

We moved into Third Street and stopped in front of the house belonging to the head of the Odd Fellows. The old woman danced into a front yard across the street and onto the porch. Both bands, packed into a circle, played "Lord, Lord, Lord." It was a glorious five minutes. Twenty instruments rose and fell in broken, successive waves. The rain let up, and the music ended, stunning us all. The dancers ran down, and I could hear cars on Ames Boulevard. A thin middle-aged man in a cowboy hat said, "That was my papa was buried today. Fifty years he was an Odd Fellow."

Mrs. Rankin and Allen and I walked back to the car. "I don't believe I've been to a finer country funeral," she said.

"I share your feelings," Allen replied.

## Newport 1966

*July 1st*

The Newport Jazz Festival, which is twelve, continues to put on weight. Festival Field, set on a slope overlooking Newport Harbor where fishermen once dried their nets, has been enlarged from twelve thousand seats to eighteen thousand. These seats, stretching almost as far as the eye can see, cover nine acres and have been enclosed in an eight-foot-high cedar stockade. There is a huge new stage supported by a forty-five-ton galaxy of steel girders, and there are a couple of new two-story Japanese-style buildings—one an administration building complete with a conference room, and the other a performers' building, connected to the rear of the stage by a fifty-foot bridge. The musicians, who once had to change and wait in gusty, musty tents, appear pleased. A press building has been promised before the end of the season.

The first concert, given tonight, was a mixed grill. The Dave Brubeck quartet, which, despite the ministrations of Joe Morello and the elegant aesthetics of Paul Desmond, grows paler and paler. And a rock-and-roll singer called Little Esther revealed that she owes the late Dinah Washing-

ton everything except her tendency to sing flat. But Jimmy Smith, an
organist accompanied by electric guitar and drums, sounded like the
ocean, while the Newport Jazz Festival All-Stars (Ruby Braff, Bud Freeman, Gerry Mulligan, George Wein, Jack Lesberg, and Buddy Rich)
offered some fine, unstudied lyricism, particularly in "Rose Room" and "I
Never Knew." Braff played as if he might never play again; each solo had a
thousand good notes, a dozen leaping intervals, run upon graceful run, and
a beseeching passion.

I wonder if anything this weekend will match the climax of the evening—
two numbers by the Archie Shepp quintet, which had Roswell Rudd on
trombone, Charlie Haden on bass, Howard Johnson on tuba, and Beaver
Harris on drums. Shepp is a complete avant-gardist and a merciless parodist—attributes perfectly accented by his clothes, which consisted of a First
World War officer's jacket, tan Glen-plaid pants, a knitted cap, and tinted
Ben Franklin spectacles. His best number was that great rarity, a genuinely
funny piece of music. It began with slow, mournful, organlike chords,
changed to a wild, rocking Sousa-like march, drifted into a mocking treatment of Duke Ellington's "Prelude to a Kiss," in which Rudd gave Lawrence
Brown his lumps and Shepp gave Johnny Hodges his, returned to more hair-
raising Sousa, more simpering Ellington, and so forth. The tempo went up
and down and around, and there were brilliant ensemble clashes and some
superb solos. Johnson is an eloquent tuba player, and Rudd proved again
that he is an extraordinary trombonist who, like any consummate rebel, has
one foot planted in the past and the other in the future.

At a party given after the concert for the musicians, Rudd and Shepp and
Johnson went at it again. Gerry Mulligan, who would sit in with a treeful of
cicadas, joined them, got caught in the maelstrom, and went under.

### July 2nd

Newport generally enjoys hustling fogs and cool, keen winds, but the windless sun this afternoon in Festival
Field made it inadvisable to sit down on the folding metal chairs without blow-
ing on them first. The "new thing" was again on deck. Bill Dixon, a trumpeter,
presented a dull five-part dirge that was danced to by Judith Dunn, who
resembled a melting ice-cream cone. Charles Lloyd, a tenor saxophonist who
admires both John Coltrane and Sonny Rollins, was sturdier, and during a
quasi-gospel number his pianist, Keith Jarrett, put together a solo full of loose,
fresh chords and held-breath rhythms that was a masterpiece. Horace Silver,
who seemed Edwardian in contrast, was followed by Coltrane, whose group
included the tenor saxophonist Pharoah Sanders, another "new-thing" adherent. Sanders' solo in the first number soon turned into a series of thunderous
elephant shrieks, which went on and on and on. When I mentioned to a friend
that Sanders' solo appeared to have little in common with music, he replied,
"Exactly. It's not music and it isn't meant to be. It's simply sound, and has to

be judged as such. It's like which crosstown street in New York sounds best at noon on a weekday."

Thelonious Monk was perfunctory at tonight's concert, as were Stan Getz and the Mel Lewis–Thad Jones big band. But Nina Simone, also on hand, was hypnotic. She sang a couple of social-protest songs, "I Loves You, Porgy," and some blues made of grits and greens.

### July 3rd

We have been in the fiery furnace again all day, and tonight even the moon looked beat. The evening was taken up mainly by Duke Ellington and Ella Fitzgerald. The Ellington band coursed through a dozen numbers, most notably a "Take the 'A' Train" done partly in waltz tempo; a lullaby medley of "Black and Tan Fantasy," "Creole Love Call," and "The Mooche"; Harry Carney's long meditation on "La Plus Belle Africaine"; and "Rockin' in Rhythm," which over the years has become a perfect orchestral display piece. Fitzgerald, towing her own drummer (Ed Thigpen) and pianist (Jimmy Jones), joined the band, and they did a dozen more numbers, among them a swashbuckling "Sweet Georgia Brown"; a scat-sung version of "How High the Moon," in which snatches of "Mop Mop," "A Hard Day's Night," and "Smoke Gets in Your Eyes" blew by; and a fast "Cottontail" topped by some exhilarating four-bar breaks between Fitzgerald and Paul Gonsalves.

The Teddy Wilson trio, which had Gene Taylor on bass and Buddy Rich on drums, opened the concert, and in a medium-fast "Somebody Loves Me" Buddy Rich began his solo with rolls nailed down by rimshots, which gradually fell into a staccato pattern. Then he broke into double time, spreading his rolls-and-rimshots over his tom-toms; inserted some offbeat undertow figures; exploded all over his set again; sank back to the original tempo while slipping in double-time accents with his foot pedal; fired a fusillade of rimshots; and built up to a super crescendo.

Woody Herman rambled down Memory Lane this afternoon. His band, fifteen or sixteen strong, broke out such old anthems as "Apple Honey" and "The Woodchopper's Ball," played some of its current book, and then welcomed back three alumni and a ringer—Stan Getz, Zoot Sims, Al Cohn, and Gerry Mulligan. The emotion generated by the reunion suggested old Yale bucks warbling "The Whiffenpoof Song." Herman's regular band, which is young, plays with precision and might, and its chief tenor saxophonist, Sal Nistico, should be heard.

### July 4th

It's Louis Armstrong's sixty-sixth birthday, and the event was duly commemorated this afternoon by Bobby Hackett in "Struttin' with Some Barbecue." Hackett also played matchless versions of "I Got It Bad and That Ain't Good" and "Green Dolphin Street," and a marvellous duet with Dizzy Gillespie in " 'S Wonderful." Before that, Red Allen, hobbled by a hand-me-down rhythm section, worked his way through three remarkable numbers, and, before that, Kenny Dorham, Thad Jones, and Howard McGhee celebrated bebop, with McGhee taking the honors.

The wind finally swung into the north tonight, provoking Miles Davis into playing four surprisingly intense numbers. His tenor saxophonist, Wayne Shorter, demonstrated that he has been listening to Ornette Coleman, while his drummer, Tony Williams, kept up a steady swamping rush of cymbals. Dizzy Gillespie fashioned six fine numbers, but he didn't dance, mug, sing, or joke. He seemed to have left four-fifths of himself at home. The festival was brought to a close by Count Basie and his band, which includes Jimmy Rushing, who was in rough voice, and Roy Eldridge, who, having recently joined Basie, sounded like the new boy in school.

Archie Shepp is the winner and champion.

## Monterey 1966

*September 16th*

I came to the Monterey Jazz Festival, which began tonight, by way of Los Angeles, where I poked around in the ruins of West Coast Jazz, a movement that flourished in that city in the fifties. Los Angeles is not the sort of place you'd expect a night creature like jazz to flourish in. The sky is immense and blinding, and the city is immense and blinding. As a result West Coast Jazz, which got going in the early fifties, was almost diaphanous. Sired largely by the 1949 Gil Evans–Miles Davis–Gerry Mulligan Capitol recordings, it was cool and manicured. It was a blond music, which had, as Bud Shank, one of its founders and survivors, told me, a "soft, intellectual" quality. Its founders, who also included Shorty Rogers, Jimmy Giuffre, Art Pepper, Carson Smith, and Shelly Manne, were graduates of the finishing schools of Stan Kenton and/or Woody Herman as well as assiduous music students who admired Bartók and Stravinsky. They were supported by several jazz clubs and, more important, by recordings, which seemed at the time to be released at the rate of two or three a week. "It got so any new bass player or drummer who came on the scene was signed up for his own LP," Shank said. The movement even fostered its own unofficial recording firms—Contemporary and Pacific Jazz. It reached an apogee in some recordings by Manne and Giuffre and Rogers in which free improvisation and free rhythms were toyed with, and then, according to Shank, two things happened. "New York struck back with hard bop, and so damned many recordings were made the market flooded." West Coast Jazz expired in the late fifties, and its members drifted into the movie and television studios, where most of them continue as staff musicians, contentedly amassing

Porsches, horses, swimming pools, and thirty-foot ketches. The principal jazz clubs in Los Angeles—Shelly's Manne-Hole in Hollywood, and the Lighthouse in Hermosa Beach—now house either out-of-town musicians or such non-studio West Coast performers as John Handy, Charles Lloyd, and Bola Sete. The rest of the jazz in the city is limited to the Neophonic Orchestra, a large Stan Kenton Third Stream group which gives half a dozen concerts a year, and an experimental big band organized by the trumpeter Don Ellis which has been holding forth on Monday nights during the past year in a bar called Bonesville. Los Angeles, like New York, has its share of starving jazz musicians, but they appear to be mostly Negroes who, Shank says, are not proficient enough to work in the studios. "The Negro saxophonists just play saxophone," he told me, "and the trumpeters trumpet. In the studios, saxophonists have to double on everything from flute to oboe, and the trumpeters have to play in three or four styles. So, in spite of all the screaming and crying, it's not racial. Benny Carter has grown rich in the studios, and so have other Negroes."

The concert tonight was taken up by desultory performances by three of the movers and founders of West Coast Jazz—Evans, Mulligan, and Dave Brubeck, the last of whom presided over a miniature West Coast movement in San Francisco in the late forties. Evans appeared with a twelve-piece band, recruited on both coasts and including Mulligan, Elvin Jones, Johnny Coles (trumpet), and Howard Johnson (tuba). It had reportedly been rehearsing for a week, but little went right. The solos were weak, the brass and reed sections faltered, and the rhythm section communed with itself. Even the amplification system was awry. Evans' music, with its butterfly sonorities and tricky rhythm turns, demands perfection. Brubeck's quartet seemed to be visibly coming apart. Joe Morello and Gene Wright, at stage left, huddled together throughout the performance, Brubeck pumped away at stage center, and Paul Desmond, usually an articulate and flourishing improviser, shaped manicured sounds at stage right. It is disheartening that Brubeck, as safe as I.B.M. for over a decade, hasn't seen fit to experiment by adding new instruments and new blood.

The evening freshened considerably when Vi Redd, a blunt, funny singer and alto saxophonist, came onstage. Miss Redd, who worked with the exotic organ-and-vocal-trio group Earl Hines brought to New York a couple of years ago, sings in the hard, glancing fashion of the early Dinah Washington and plays like a backwoods Charlie Parker. Count Basie, minus Roy Eldridge, who once mysteriously said he *never* goes to California, marched through a dozen numbers, most of which suggested that he should strip down, as he did in 1950, to a first-rate small band built chiefly around his piano—one of the splendors of the age.

*September 17th*

Bola Sete, the Brazilian guitarist, appeared midway tonight with Sebastian Neto on bass and Paulinho on drums. Sete plays unamplified guitar, achieving a richness and clarity of tone that shame all amplified guitarists. He uses a great many chords, connecting them with short single-note passages, and he invariably plays softly. His style is free of the histrionics of the flamencan guitarists and of the neon drone of most contemporary jazz guitarists. Sete's bassist and drummer work beautifully with him, and in the last of half a dozen numbers, all done in South American rhythms, the group became indivisible. It turned into a delicate, rippling rhythm machine that moved gradually over tambourines, tuned bells, and gourds, to a marvellous drum solo by Paulinho. He used a *cuica* (a drumlike instrument with variable pitch) and sticks, which flickered quietly and effortlessly back and forth between his tuned bells, his tom-toms, the domes of his cymbals, and the rims of his drums, and he brought to mind—so gentle and fresh were his movements—the offhand displays Sid Catlett warmed himself and his audiences up with.

The tenor saxophonist Booker Ervin preceded Sete. Ervin invariably plays with considerable fervor, but somewhere between his imagination and the sounds that emerge from his horn a peculiar transformation takes place. Everything turns to wood. Wooden notes follow wooden smears that follow wooden runs, and one soon falls into a bamboo dream. Evans was on hand again and sounded brighter in his mother-of-pearl way, and there were run-downs by a singer named Carol Sloane, by Cannonball Adderley and his brother Nat, and by a quasi–"new-thing" tenor saxophonist named Joe Henderson. By this time it was midnight, and I wondered if Newportitis had begun to afflict Monterey, a festival long celebrated for its tidiness and economy.

When the curtain opened this afternoon, Jon Hendricks, the singer and people's poet, was seated before a dozen small children. He proceeded to read them a poem, written in couplets by himself, that was a loose history of the Negro in America, and every now and then he paused to allow the performers stationed behind him to sing and/or play. These included Big Mama Willie Mae Thornton, Muddy Waters, Shaky Horton (a harmonica player), Memphis Slim, the Paul Butterfield Blues Band, and a rock-and-roll group called Jefferson Airplane. Hendricks spoke repeatedly of the "children," by which he meant the Negro people and the squirming semicircle before him, and of the "un-Civil War," and then gave an imitation of a slave auctioneer. But the performers finally broke into the clear. Muddy Waters and Memphis Slim were in excellent voice (Memphis Slim sang one of his aching, tempoless blues), and Big Mama Thornton, an unheralded blues singer who rarely wanders from Oakland, where she lives, was empyrean. She is a giant woman who wears short hair and ankle-length skirts, and she moves with the grace that only certain outsized people seem to possess. She can move from a whisper to a shout in one bar, and she knows Billie Holiday's trick of wandering along behind the beat and then pouncing on it by jamming five or six words together in one sustained note. She sang a dozen numbers, most of them blues, and their power and invention and grace stayed with the listener well into the evening. Jefferson Airplane and the Paul Butterfield Band were surprises. Jefferson Airplane consists of two singers, two guitarists, a bassist, and a drummer. They sang and played two good blues, but it was too bad that their solo female member, Signe Anderson, wasn't given a number to herself. She has a strong, affecting voice which was rarely audible. The Butterfield group includes two Negroes and four whites (electric harmonica, two electric guitars, electric organ, electric bass, and drums) who worked their way through three numbers, the last of which was a ten-minute collective free-for-all blues that had much in common with some of the "new-thing" scrambles. The electronic din was terrific, but the music it amplified stayed afloat.

## *September 18th*

It has been made plain this weekend that electronic instruments are, for better or worse, here to stay (an electric saxophone is now on the market, and John Coltrane and Benny Carter have each bought one), and it has been proved that popular music is again moving toward jazz for sustenance and direction. More news was offered this afternoon: The four-four beat is practically dead. More than half the groups we have heard have used odd time signatures, and this afternoon Don Ellis and his twenty-piece band played five numbers that were in five-eight, five-four, twenty-seven–sixteen, seven-eight, and nine-four. The countdown alone on the twenty-seven–sixteen number took about a minute, and all through the number lips moved and heads nodded. The results here and elsewhere were mixed; melodic content was often sacrificed for rhythmic complexity. Nonetheless, the band plays with fire and precision, thanks to Ellis, who is a demonic conductor. One could *see* him pulling difficult chords out of the brass and reed sections. Equally startling was Steve Bohannon, a nineteen-year-old drummer who plays with exceptional invention and authority. Ellis himself plays a special four-valve trumpet, which enables him to reach quarter tones more easily. He tends, accordingly, to quarter-tone it all over the scale, and at times he resembled an avant-garde Al Hirt. One observer summed up the band this way: "Man, it's just the Stan Kenton band of today. You remember, everybody thought what Kenton was doing in the forties was so strange? Well, they got used to it. And the same thing will happen with Ellis. People will be dancing to him in twenty-seven–sixteen, and with their eyes closed, too."

Tonight was, with one exception, anticlimactic. Randy Weston, a blurred Thelonious Monk pianist, played for an hour and twenty-five minutes, in company with Ray Copeland, an earnest bebop trumpeter, Cecil Payne, another bebop holdover, and Booker Ervin. Denny Zeitlin was fast and empty, and Carmen McRae demonstrated again that she is probably the most skilled—albeit mannered and brittle—popular singer alive. The Ellington band, in satisfactory form, closed the weekend and accompanied Bunny Briggs in "David Danced Before the Lord with All His Might" and "Honeysuckle Rose." Briggs executed spinning, stomping offbeat steps; he raced from one side of the stage to the other, his feet clicking a thousand to the yard; he slid through huge, funny half-time strides and sudden running tiptoe steps; and, for good measure, he did the Frug and the Watusi. Even Johnny Hodges, who had spent an hour stonily contemplating the middle distance, watched.

*My dismissal of Paul Desmond was inexcusable; he was an elegant, thinking improviser, and as such, almost unique.*

# 1967

## The Burning Bush

John Hammond's "Spirituals to Swing—1967," given at Carnegie Hall, was a multivoiced celebration. The living celebrated themselves. (Only seven of the forty-odd performers had appeared in the first "Spirituals to Swing" concerts in the late thirties, but in the main they provided the best music.) The living celebrated the dead. (Among the large and attentive crowd of ghosts from the earlier concerts were Sidney Bechet, James P. Johnson, Charlie Christian, Lester Young, Herschel Evans, Hot Lips Page, Albert Ammons, and Fletcher Henderson.) Hammond quite rightly celebrated himself. (Without his ministrations we probably would not have been blessed by Billie Holiday and Count Basie and Teddy Wilson and Christian.) And it was a fine celebration of the blues; aside from several standards and a couple of gospel numbers, the entire program was blues.

George Benson, a young guitarist and Hammond's newest protégé, has a brilliantine tone, and he is apt to use ten notes where one or none would do, but he plays with a conviction and an occasional wildness that have been missing from the guitar since the days of Jimmy Shirley. Marion Williams, long the ballast of the Clara Ward Singers, came on next, accompanied by Marion Franklin on piano, Milt Hinton, and Jo Jones. She can growl, trill, shout, and drop, between eighth notes, from the top of her range to the bottom. And she can writhe and sashay and wink. It's a good show, and once in a while—as at the end of "Nobody Knows the Trouble I've Seen," when she rocketed in mid-syllable from an electric trill to a booming growl—it's a great one.

Then a small band made up of Buck Clayton, Buddy Tate, Edmond Hall, Count Basie, Hinton, and Jones ambled through—with Tate in the lead—a medium blues that discussed swinging, emotion honesty, and beauty. Basie floated off the stage on a wreath of smiles and was replaced by Ray Bryant, and Joe Turner appeared. Turner's voice is big and flattish and hard and almost vibratoless, and he applied it to his words as if it were a trowel. His lyrics have no wrinkles and no edges. And he has a matchless sense of rhythm and cadence, sometimes moseying along behind the beat and sometimes squeezing ten or so words into a single quick phrase. He opened with a medium blues and it was immediately clear that he was in perfect voice. His next number was unbelievable. He began, *a cappella*, with a ringing, iron rush ("Iliveacrossthestreetfromajukejoint"), then suddenly slipped into a slow, slow walk ("and all night we play the blues"). The verses went by, Clayton took two superlative choruses, and then Turner thundered the words—with the band in full, mounting voice behind—"I want the sun to rise, the wind to blow . . ." It was the Voice coming from the burning bush, and Turner, allowing the audience to get its face on straight again, next rolled through an easy blues, one whole rocking chorus of which was taken up simply by the word "Yes," uttered offbeat every couple of bars. Only masters can simultaneously proffer sentimentality and emotion, and that's exactly what Turner and his old friend Pete Johnson did in "Roll 'Em Pete." Johnson, who has been ill and in seclusion for the past decade, was propped up in a chair at the keyboard, and, energized by Turner and the soloists, he took three choruses in the treble while Bryant handled the bass. Clayton and Tate and Hall were admirable accompanists throughout, and Clayton demonstrated in each number that his obbligatos, which he has lent to everyone from Billie Holiday to Paul Robeson, are among the graces of the age—muted, they call from far away; open-horn, they insist like warm sunlight.

John Handy unluckily got caught with his sextet (violin, cello, guitar, bass, and drums) between Turner and Big Mama Willie Mae Thornton. Accompanied by Clayton et al., she sang five blues that had all the mountainous intensity of Turner's blues. She reached some sort of celestial point in her third number, which was done in a nearly motionless tempo, by starting, "I got a sweet little angel, and I love the way he spreads his wings." The words were softly walked out, and by the time she had repeated the line, raising her voice and her volume slightly, a spell had fallen.

The end of the evening had every right to be anticlimactic. Count Basie and his big band, augmented once again by Harry Edison, played three numbers, including a funny nonsense blues sung by Richard Boone, and were joined by Clayton, Hall, Tate, Turner, and Jo Jones, all of them backed by Basie on the organ, which he causes to tremble and sigh and whisper.

## Small Band

**D**uke Ellington's unique five-week stand at the Rainbow Grill is a sorrowing one. Not long before the engagement Billy Strayhorn, Ellington's indivisible alter ego since 1939, died, and certainly part of Ellington went with him. (Ellington continues to speak of Strayhorn in the present tense; his not being at bandside seems simply to mean that he is at home for the evening.) Nonetheless, the Rainbow Grill stint is immensely heartening, for it proves that the older Ellington gets (he is now sixty-eight) the more adventuresome and creative he becomes. During the past several years he has fashioned a program of "religious" music, which he has played successfully in churches all over the Western world. He has finished and recorded (with Strayhorn's great help) his notable "Far East Suite." He has charmingly reconditioned various popular songs of the moment, and he has done a series of subtle and ingenious parodies of such as Paul Whiteman, Stan Kenton, Woody Herman, and Wayne King that suggest that parody is simply imperfection perfected. And now he has settled down at the Rainbow Grill in a workshop jam-session way with an eight-piece group taken from the big band for what may be the longest engagement for dancing he has played in New York or anywhere else since the forties. Old numbers are being streamlined and regalvanized before one's eyes, and new numbers are being shaped and weighed.

The cream of the big band is on hand, and it includes Cat Anderson, Johnny Hodges, Paul Gonsalves, Lawrence Brown, Harry Carney, John Lamb (bass), and a new drummer, Steve Little. It has the depth and timbre and revolving colors of the bigger group, but it is also looser and more intense, and the soloists have more space and time to roam in. Hodges and Carney are playing with exceptional beauty. (Carney frequently uses his bass clarinet, on which he sounds like wind moaning across the mouth of a chimney.) Anderson, who is generally restricted to high-note grandstanding, is revealing a subtlety and skill that challenge Cootie Williams and Rex Stewart. Brown is less industrial than usual, and Gonsalves is ticking perfectly. At least a dozen of the numbers I heard were classic Ellington. These included a "C-Jam Blues" that was better than the celebrated 1942 recording (Anderson shivered and shook his way out of his solo and Carney began his with a great, sashaying break); a "Sunny Side of the Street" in which Hodges left fat, dying notes all over the bandstand while the band played organ chords and a double-time figure that explained his intensity; an easy, rocking "Rosetta"; and a "Happy-Go-Lucky Local" that came to a climax in a roaring, unison stop-time passage by the whole band. Most of the new numbers were handsome medium-tempo blues, one of which, "Sky Blue Suit," ended with Anderson composing muted poems to himself while the band slid gently through the final chorus. And of course there was Ellington, playing his leavening piano, smiling, signing autographs, hugging old friends, playing requests ranging from "I Can't Get Started" to "Something to Live For," and doing his funny monologue about finger-popping on the afterbeat while the band delicately hummed "Things Ain't What They Used to Be." It was the essence of Ellington—a silly, funning exterior designed, in this instance, to counteract Strayhorn's death. To miss Ellington at the Rainbow Grill would be like turning off one's radio just as Lindbergh was about to land.

## All Work and No Play

The antediluvian practice of calling on entertainers to perform seven nights a week has had mixed effects on jazz musicians, who, of all performing artists, most need replenishment. It has provided young musicians with essential on-the-job training, and it has, through sheer exposure, put the music in front of what has almost always been a tin-eared public. But in the main the weak have collapsed by the wayside or have turned to drugs or alcohol, and the strong, with rare exceptions, have become self-parodists or by-rote performers. A reform has clearly been needed, and the reform began to take do-it-yourself shape four or five years ago when Sonny Rollins, dissatisfied with the effect of the treadmill on his playing, went into temporary retirement. Ornette Coleman followed not long after, and others have done it since. (Needless to say, some of these furloughs are brought about by a lack of work, but all of them depend on generous friends and/or breadwinning wives.) Coleman, in particular, appears now only in occasional concerts, and the results have been beneficial. He has had the time to take up new instruments (trumpet, violin, and musette), and he has had the time to compose. More important, his playing, freed of the old tyranny, has grown steadily.

This was apparent when Coleman, in company with a quartet (David Izenzon and Charlie Haden on bass and Charles Moffett on drums) and the Philadelphia Woodwind Quintet, gave a concert at the Village Theatre. The sum of the evening was more impressive than its parts. Coleman demonstrated that he has continued to compress his alto-saxophone style without sacrificing its fire and fluency. (When he first came to New York, seven or so years ago, he was cornucopic; he had a million notes in his head, and he must have purged himself of most of them the first year. It was a bewildering experience for his listeners, but in the process he learned the great secret of selectivity.) Time and again at the concert he slipped into almost inaudible passages ("The Little Symphony," "Love and Sex"), and throughout he revealed complete control. He delved comfortably into the middle and low registers of the trumpet for the first time ("Just for You"), and on the violin ("A Capella for Four Wise Men") he curbed the histrionic tendencies he often shows. He got a tone on the musette that moved pleasantly back and forth between a conch and a bagpipe ("Buddha Blues"). Coleman's group is a model of collective interplay. Haden, playing pizzicato, and Izenzon, playing arco (they swapped roles in "Atavism"), worked simultaneously, while Moffett issued a steady persiflage of melodic counter-rhythms. New Orleans jazz has withered, but its greatest gift to music—the improvised ensemble—haunts everything from rock-and-roll to the "new thing."

The Philadelphia Woodwind Quintet played a Villa-Lobos piece and a short, tentative exercise by S. A. Chambers. Then, at the end of the concert, Coleman joined it in a new composition of his own, "Forms and Sounds." The form, straight from the church, was call-and-response; Coleman played a dozen or so brief cadenzas on the trumpet, each of which was answered by the quintet. And the sounds consisted of Coleman's squirting, high-note phrases and the wood-and-leaf textures of the quintet. The piece, though, suggested a series of parentheses strung out side by side, and it was disappointing that Coleman played *with* the quintet only in its final passage.

Perhaps Coleman will find his way toward appearing more often. His feet remain firmly in the old blues and his head is full of celestial things.

# 1968

## One-Man Band

By releasing "Art Tatum: Piano Starts Here"—four of the solos on the record constitute Tatum's first recording session, in 1933, and the rest are from a concert given in Los Angeles in 1949—Columbia reminds us how astonishing Tatum was. He died in 1956 at the age of forty-six, and he was astonishing from the time of his recording début, when he was just twenty-two, until his death. No one ever knew exactly what he was or what to do with him. He was said to be the greatest jazz pianist who ever lived and he was said to be not a jazz pianist at all. He was admired by classical pianists, by George Gershwin, by jazz musicians, and by dazzled laymen. People poked fun at his ornate style and his interpolations in his solos of "Rhapsody in Blue" and "Stars and Stripes Forever," and then wept at his next brilliance. He is still mentioned with awe and he is still put down, he is thought old-fashioned and ahead of his time, and nobody has decided yet what kind of pianist he was.

Tatum sprang from virgin soil. In the manner of all great innovators, he looked carefully around him and behind him before he jumped, learning Fats Waller's stride techniques and his respect for touch and precision, Earl Hines' single-note melodic lines and maelstrom arrhythmic breaks, and from God knows where a technique that few pianists of any sort have matched. Then he jumped, and his odd career began. He put together a small band, and it was soon clear that the context suffocated him. He was already a one-man band who helplessly welled up and swamped his sidemen. So he went out on his own and became a sensation. He converted the Fifty-second Street clubs where he often played into small, jammed temples. When the reverence most audiences accorded him was marred by drunks, he simply dropped his hands from the keyboard in mid-number and waited, his body motionless, until an almost audible quiet fell, then resumed playing. In the early forties Tatum put together a trio with Tiny Grimes on guitar (Everett Barksdale eventually replaced him) and Slam Stewart on bass. It had its moments, particularly in the ensemble interplay between the three musicians, but in the main Tatum sounded hobbled, and he again went out on his own, remaining successful and solitary until he died.

Tatum apparently had no desire to compose on paper, so he composed when he played. He did this by building baroque castles out of his arpeggios and chords and arrhythmic whirlpools, and by using a sly, oblique wit that made listeners know exactly what he thought of the tune. Like most of the other Eastern pianists (Hines, Mary Lou Williams, the stride men), he never took the blues seriously. He loved to parody boogie-woogie and his rare straight blues came through broadly smiling. Tatum's style was notable for its touch, its speed and accuracy, and its harmonic and rhythmic imagination. Each note—no matter how fast the tempo—was light and complete and resonant. Vast lower-register chords were unblurred, and his highest notes were polished silver. His speed and precision were almost shocking. Flawless sixteenth-note runs poured up and down the keyboard, each note perfectly accented, and the chords and figures in the left hand sometimes sounded two-handed. Such virtuosity can be an end in itself, and Tatum was delighted to let it be in his up-tempo flag-wavers, when he spectacularly became a high-wire artist. Tatum's bedrock sense of rhythm enabled him to play out-of-tempo interludes or whole choruses that doubled the impact of the implied beat, and his harmonic sense—his strange, multiplied chords, still largely unmatched by his followers, his laying on of two and three and four melodic levels at once—was orchestral.

Tatum would begin a medium-tempo number by playing, or playing with, the melody in ad-lib tempo for the first sixteen bars, rushing at and away from the melody, breaking his phrases with almost coy pauses, and then dancing on again. He would slip into a four-four tempo in the bridge with straight Fats Waller chords, using loose tenths in the left hand, and, near the end of the bridge, he would disappear into an arpeggio that climbed, descended, and reclimbed the keyboard, coming to an end in the middle of the final eight bars, where he would resume his ad-lib ministrations. He would start the second chorus in tempo, drop into sharp, on-the-beat single notes—*this* was Tatum the jazz musician, the no-nonsense improviser—and, for fear of letting such gravity get out-of-hand, abruptly shy away into another extended run, which would dissolve into an arrhythmic passage compounded of circular, bucking chords that lasted for the entire bridge. They would be followed by a snatch of stride-piano oompah bass, which rocked back and forth against chopping offbeat chords in the right hand. The final chorus would be a reprise of the first chorus and would often end in a ha-ha flatted chord that left the tune and the listener hanging in air.

All of Tatum is on the Columbia release. The four early numbers reveal him still in the process of putting together his flying machine. The wind-

whipped arpeggios are already there, but, though resplendent, they are disconnected and largely meaningless. Fats Waller is much in evidence, and so is
Earl Hines. The harmonies are still ahead of their time. But Tatum is a perfect whole in the 1949 Los Angeles concert. Almost every number has passages to ponder over—the runs being poured back and forth between the two
hands in "Someone to Watch Over Me"; a "Yesterdays" that is a complete
rebuilding of the tune, from the first note to the last; a tidal-wave, up-tempo
"I Know That You Know"; a delicate and (so rare for Tatum) fond version of
"Willow Weep for Me"; an incredibly light and deft takeoff of boogie-woogie
in "Tatum Pole Boogie"; and a "Man I Love" with an arpeggio, lasting some
eight bars, that no other pianist would dare.

# Newport 1967

*June 30th*

Tonight was touted as a history of jazz, but it turned out to be a parade of pianists made up of Willie the
Lion Smith, Earl Hines, Count Basie, Thelonious Monk, and John Lewis.
(The concert also turned out to be in the horn-of-plenty Newport Jazz Festival tradition; there were no fewer than ten groups, and the concert lasted
over five hours. The departing crowd, bent and shuffling, resembled a mass
of Stepin Fetchits.) Hines was the guidon. After a good solo rendition of
"You Can Depend on Me," he was joined by Ruby Braff for a couple of surprisingly successful duets. The two men, both self-preoccupied ornamental-
ists, had never played together before, but they got off a graceful "These
Foolish Things" and a fast, intent "Rosetta." Hines' solos were full of arrhythmic whirlpools and upper-register, single-note jubilations, and Braff managed to move in apposite parallels. Willie the Lion, got up in his summer
uniform (straw skimmer, white jacket, and cigar), played a vigorous if brief
"Carolina Shout" and then teamed up for three numbers with Don Ewell, a
disciple of Jelly Roll Morton and Fats Waller. Smith, who gives the deceptive impression when he plays that he is stretched out on a chaise longue, is
almost always unpredictable, and tonight was no exception. He produced
booming, irregular chord patterns and rifle-shot single notes, while Ewell, a
correct but swinging pianist, was an admirable foil. Basie backed Buddy Tate
and Buck Clayton in two sensuous numbers and then headed up his own car-
tel, but he was, lamentably, visible only in short solos and behind soloists.
(When will someone get Basie into a recording studio with a first-rate
rhythm section and let him loose—an event that hasn't taken place for over
twenty years?) An all-star reunion of former bebop kings—Dizzy Gillespie,
James Moody, Milt Jackson, Thelonious Monk, Percy Heath, and Max
Roach—was disappointing, save for Monk. Stewing enjoyably in his own
inexhaustible juices, he was imperturbable, particularly in "How High the

Moon," in which he took an excellent solo and supplied Gillespie with a stream of jarring chords that suggested a sheriff peppering the ground around an outlaw's feet. John Lewis brought up the rear with the Modern Jazz Quartet, demonstrating again that there are few pianists—tonight's diamonds included—who put as much grace and thought into each chorus.

The evening had other pleasures. The Newport Jazz Festival All-Stars (Ruby Braff, Pee Wee Russell, Bud Freeman, George Wein, Jack Lesberg, and Don Lamond) offered, among other numbers, a slow "Sugar" in which Russell, more sotto-voce than usual, fashioned—or perhaps was fashioned by—a four-bar phrase made up of incredibly juggled notes, and a slow "Summertime" in which Budd Johnson, sitting in on soprano saxophone, wailed and pirouetted à la Sidney Bechet. The concert was closed by the Albert Ayler quintet, a "new-thing" group that includes Ayler (a saxophonist), his brother (a trumpeter), and the drummer Milford Graves. Most of their efforts were expended on an occasionally funny parody of what sounded like a Salvation Army hymn and of fragments of "There's No Place Like Home" and "Eeny-Meeny-Miney-Mo."

### July 1st

The weather is getting restless. It is still cool, but fog has been doing the mazurka up and down Narragansett Bay all afternoon, and tonight it circled once about the town and fell asleep. So did much of tonight's concert. The John Handy Quintet (vibraphone, guitar, bass, drums, and the leader's alto saxophone) plodded through two endless numbers, one a musical attempt at "what it took to get James Meredith into the University of Mississippi" and the other a Spanish-tinged "new-thing" number called "Señor Nancy." Nina Simone, a Juilliard-trained pianist and singer who relishes a mean country blues, got hung up in a couple of interminable laments about loose men and fast women, and Dizzy Gillespie, appearing with his quintet, did four by-rote numbers. But the oddest disappointment was the new and revolutionary Gary Burton Quartet, which has Larry Coryell on guitar, Steve Swallow on bass, Stu Martin on drums, and the leader on vibraphone. Burton's group is working toward a distillate compounded of rock-and-roll and jazz, but these important explorations were only fitfully apparent. Coryell and Burton played an intricate duet using a variety of rhythms, and in a slow blues Coryell hit on one of those seemingly stumbling but perfectly executed phrases—several barely audible behind-the-beat single notes followed by silence and a leaping, brilliant run—that Charlie Parker coined. At twelve o'clock Buddy Rich appeared with his big band, and the pumpkin turned into a golden coach. Rich started with a medium blues, soared through Bill Holman's ingenious arrangement of the McCartney-Lennon "Norwegian Wood," and went on to a display number, the "Bugle Call Rag." His solo was a wonder. It incorporated a section in which his left hand moved at a thousand rpm's on his snare while his right hand floated casually back and forth between his tom-toms; a long, diminuendo roll that sank to barely audible knitting-needle clicking on his snare rims; and a Big Bertha climax. No sooner was the number over than Rich, bowing and sweating, launched into what appeared to be an introductory twelve-bar solo in medium tempo, reared back and said, "What'll we play?" It was a throwaway gag, but it was also an incredible little solo, a perfect solo. Gillespie ambled onstage and blew a dozen choruses of blues with the band, and for the final number, an eleven-minute version of "West Side Story," he climbed into the trumpet section, whispered to the other trumpeters, yawned, peered elaborately at the sheet music, and ogled and shouted at Rich, who, his hands windmills in a high wind, never batted an eye.

The afternoon concert was labelled "The Five Faces of Jazz," and it was devoted to Middle Eastern music, pseudo-ragas, Afro-Cuban funk, the *bossa nova*, and "Norwegian Wood." The participants included Herbie Mann, the Hungarian guitarist Gabor Szabo, Luis Enrique of Brazil, and such ringers as Gillespie and the German trombonist Albert Mangelsdorff.

### July 2nd

More fog, accompanied by snappy winds and low, pressing clouds. The afternoon concert began with half a dozen selections by Nobuo Hara and his Sharps and Flats, an eighteen-piece Japanese band. Swathed in smiles, the group was a formidable cross between late Jimmie Lunceford and early Stan Kenton, and its soloists suggested J. J. Johnson, Art Farmer, and Clifford Brown, plus Gene Krupa laced with Louis Bellson. In three numbers the band accompanied Housan Yamamoto, who played a large wooden flute called the shakuhachi. He gets a husky, pleasing tone on his instrument and a direct, lyrical quality not unlike that of Joe Marsala. The main event was a vibraphone workshop—Bobby Hutcherson, Gary Burton, Red Norvo, Milt Jackson, and Lionel Hampton. Burton sent up a ghostly unaccompanied ballad that was all willows and Debussy; Norvo produced a creditable "I Love You" (Cole Porter's) and then went into "I Surrender, Dear." He ended with a funny "Ida," for which he turned off his resonator and, using heavy mallets, clumped around the keyboard like a slow-motion tap-dancer. At odd intervals he shot out his right elbow—clearly a prearranged signal for Roy Haynes, his drummer, to play a rimshot. Haynes misfired as often as not, and it was good hamming. The rest was predictable. Hampton unloaded his customary two-by-fours. Hutcherson jammed a hundred notes into each measure, and Jackson kept his flowing lyric cool. All five vibraphonists got together for a closing blues; then the rain, floating around the rafters for the past twenty-four hours, came, blending its sound perfectly with the heavy work onstage.

The rain was still needling in low and hard and cold at eight, when the evening began. As it turned out, we could have all stayed home. Bill Evans, along with Eddie Gomez (bass) and Philly Joe Jones, swam steadily toward his own surface but never reached it; Max Roach and his quintet struck off hard-bop clichés; Woody Herman's big band dipped into the gospel bag, the blues bag, and the flag-waver bag; Miles Davis, wearing a dinner jacket and an untied bow tie, spent more time offstage than on; and the Blues Project, a heavily amplified five-piece group that has been moving from rock-and-roll toward jazz, was allowed just two numbers before being unplugged.

*July 3rd*

With a couple of exceptions, tonight was a continuation of last night. (The rain, coming in tropical explosions, continued all morning and then subsided into fog.) The Dave Brubeck Quartet showed more candlepower than has been its wont in recent years, and Sarah Vaughan wandered through eight follow-me-if-you-can numbers. The evening and the festival were closed by Lionel Hampton and a big band made up largely of Hampton alumni, among them Milt Buckner, Joe Newman, Frank Foster, Benny Powell, Jerome Richardson, and Snooky Young. The alumni, however, spent most of the dozen numbers sitting on their instruments while Hampton labored at the vibraphone, the drums, and the piano. In "Flying Home," though, Illinois Jacquet, who had played well earlier in the evening, went through his celebrated calisthenics, and it was like hearing Francis Scott Key sing "The Star-Spangled Banner." The other successful numbers in the concert were done by Red Norvo, Ruby Braff, and the Wein-Lesberg-Lamond rhythm section. Norvo floated earnestly over his vibraphone, playing excellent tag in his exchanges with Braff and Lamond, and looked—with his bearded, benign, expectant way of continually lifting his head from his instrument and searching the audience—like God watching out for the Devil.

The afternoon was given over almost wholly to big bands. Don Ellis's nineteen-piece group, outfitted with an eight-man rhythm section (three bassists, four drummers, and a pianist) and a mass of electronic equipment, played five absorbing numbers. There were fugues and passacaglias, raga-like passages, time signatures of five-four, three-and-a-half–four, and seven-four, a sterling parody of "Bill Bailey, Won't You Please Come Home?" and electronic effects that sounded like echoing caves. The concert ended with an extravaganza called the Milford (Massachusetts) Youth Band. It is, as far as I know, the largest jazz band in history, for it boasts sixteen saxophones, eleven clarinets, five trombones, twelve trumpets, a bass, four woodwinds, a French horn, drums, and three percussion. The band ranges in age from eleven to eighteen and includes nine girls. It played a recent Basie number, Benny Goodman and Artie Shaw, a blues, a Kentonish avant-garde number, a ballad, and a Near Eastern number, and played them almost as well as any current big band. The soloists were nearly as good. Best of all were the glorious passages in which the brass section, eighteen strong, opened up.

# Return Engagement

**W**here, for a few blessed hours, can one hear such celestial cleansing art as "Mood Indigo," "It Don't Mean a Thing," "Solitude," "Black and Tan Fantasy," "Sophisticated Lady," and "Rockin' in Rhythm" played by their composer and seven members of his brilliant atelier? At the Rainbow Grill, a handsome, Captain Nemo ship floating some nine hundred feet above the city, where Duke Ellington, in company with Cat Anderson, Johnny Hodges, Harry Carney, Paul Gonsalves. Lawrence Brown, the bassist Jeff Castleman, and the drummer Rufus Jones, is proving that he remains, in his seventieth year, the unacknowledged but undeniable Master of American music. When Ellington appeared last summer at the Rainbow Grill for the first time, it was a triumph. The band rivalled the Ellington small bands of the thirties and forties, new materials were broken out nightly, and Ellington himself, despite the death a short while before of Billy Strayhorn, was ebullient and gracious. But on the first night I went up to the Rainbow Grill last week, Strayhorn's passing seemed to have caught up with Ellington. "When I got a copy the other day of the new album we did of Billy's tunes," he said, "I couldn't even look at it, let alone listen to it. I just threw it on the bed." When the dog feels down, the tail stops wagging, and that night Ellington and the band were quiescent. New materials were not in evidence, a lot of medleys were trundled out, and there were half a dozen perfunctory vocals by Trish Turner and Tony Watkins. But, as in every Ellington performance, there were corrective moments: Ellington's crystal chime notes behind Harry Carney's bass clarinet on "Creole Love Call"; the classic Hodges "On the Sunny Side of the Street"; Cat Anderson's loving parody of Louis Armstrong on "Me and You"; Paul Gonsalves's two choruses on "Body and Soul," one very slow and full of his labyrinthine Charlie Parker–Ben Webster rushes, and one in triple time, where he managed to stay just *ahead* of the beat; and Strayhorn's last blues, "The Intimacy of the Blues," which had two singing choruses apiece from Hodges and Anderson and Gonsalves.

One of the extraordinary things about Ellington and his men is their ability, in the face of a nonstop, year-in-and-year-out schedule, to continually pull surprises out of their hats. When I went back to the Rainbow Grill the next night Ellington looked his customary forty and from the beginning— Cat Anderson's plaintive, barely audible muted solo, backed only by the bassist, on "Black and Tan Fantasy"—the band shone and jumped. It rocked behind Hodges on "I Got It Bad," with Carney providing mother-earth, basso-profoundo hums. It rocked behind Trish Turner on "Sonny" and "Look at Me," and it shouted on "Happy-Go-Lucky Local," while Gonsalves, his shoulders hunched and his face screwed prune-tight, played perhaps a dozen freighted, impassioned choruses. (Gonsalves is one of the few great cumulative improvisers.) A loose, careening "C-Jam Blues" had star-

tling breaks by Anderson and Gonsalves and Carney, and there was a rough
but right "Main Stem," one of Ellington's most complex and beautiful blues.
Hodges smoothed the deep suède of Billy Strayhorn's "Passion Flower," and
at the beginning on the second set Ellington, seated in semi-darkness by
himself, played Strayhorn's "Lotus Blossom." (He has said it is the tune
Strayhorn most liked to hear him play.) He played it to himself, and of
course he played it for Strayhorn, who surely heard.

## Coltrane

The late John Coltrane had become a messiah by the time of his death (he was just forty), in part because of
the extraordinary adulation he received. He won all the awards, popular
and critical; he was even elected to the *down beat* Hall of Fame, a usually
posthumous gallery. He recorded frequently and with apparent complete
freedom, and he worked steadily. He was placed in the forefront of the
avant-garde, and he was the cause of unbelievable amounts of eulogistic
prose. He was copied slavishly by younger saxophonists. Yet his messiahship
was partly his own doing, for in his last years his music became increasingly
"religious." One album was called "A Love Supreme," the love being for
God, and among the titles in another album, "Meditations," were "The
Father and the Son and the Holy Ghost," "Compassion," "Love," "Conse-
quences," and "Serenity." And he talked increasingly to his liner-note writers of uplifting people through his music, of inspiring them "to realize more
and more of their capacities for living meaningful lives." But attempts to
write program music succeed only in the mind of the composer or performer. One man's requiem is another man's polka.

Getting through the reverential cities of Troy that Coltrane vanished
under is only the beginning of getting at Coltrane himself. He wasn't even
easy to *listen* to. He had a blank, aggressive tone, and in his moments of
frenzy, which were frequent, he repeated series of manic shrieks, wails, and
screams that hurt the ear and stopped the mind. (His apologists were fond of
pointing out that none of us really know what *music* should or should not
sound like, but instinct, which can instantly isolate ugliness or beauty,
knows better.) And he never stood still long enough to be heard properly.
More and more, newness for the sake of itself became his very art. In the late
fifties he ran the chords, playing endless thirty-second notes. (Until then, he
had been a hard-bop saxophonist who had come up through rhythm-and-
blues bands and groups led by Johnny Hodges and Dizzy Gillespie.) In the
early sixties he shifted to modal improvising, to the scalar intricacies of Ravi
Shankar. Not even his instrument was sufficient, so he took up the soprano
saxophone and the bass clarinet and the flute, and he experimented in his
groups with odd instrumentations. In addition, he tampered with form and

harmony and rhythm. In a recording called "Ascension," he brought together two trumpeters, five saxophonists, two bassists, a pianist, and a drummer, and they played a racking nonstop thirty-eight-minute piece that alternated between jittery solos and demonic free-form ensembles. Moreover, he believed that long-windedness is not the soul of boredom, for sometimes one number lasted an hour and sometimes his solos went on for forty-five minutes. But every once in a while his restlessness passed and he came to a halt, stopped preaching, stopped screeching, and played a straightforward slow ballad or medium-tempo blues, and one suddenly understood what Coltrane was—the essence of good, old-fashioned lyricism. Such statements can be found in his best recording, "Crescent," and they are, in the singular manner of all great jazz improvisers, more human than musical. His tone deepens and yields, and he uses long, heavy phrases pulled along by a questing vibrato. His rhythmic placements are surprising, and so are his notes; it is magniloquent improvising. But born poets like Coltrane sometimes misjudge the size of their gifts, and in trying to further them, to ennoble them, they fall over into sentimentality or the maniacal. Coltrane did both, and it is ironic that these lapses, which were mistakenly considered to be musical reflections of our inchoate times, drew his heaviest acclaim. People said they heard the dark night of the Negro in Coltrane's wildest music, but what they really heard was a heroic and unique lyrical voice at the mercy of its own power.

*For further ruminations on Coltrane see page 825.*

## Which Ellington Are You?

The Duke Ellington who gave a concert of "sacred" music recently at the Cathedral of St. John the Divine seemed to have little in common with the straight-ahead Duke Ellington who led an exhilarating contingent from his big band last summer at the Rainbow Grill. It was even hard to believe that this new Ellington was related to the Ellington who gave his first church concert in Grace Cathedral in San Francisco in September of 1965. That Ellington appeared to be on to something. The concert had its overblown, quasi-holy sides (chanting choirs, solemn vocalists, a Formica piety), but it was exciting to hear the band in full stride in a *cathedral*—not so much because of the building's sacredness but because the band filled its architectural and acoustical grandeur. Moreover, the band was kept in the fore, and in at least one number, "David Danced Before the Lord with All His Might," it achieved a grandstanding majesty—Bunny Briggs dancing, Louis Bellson soloing, and the band shouting, all at once. But Ellington's new program of sacred music, which was given its première at St. John's, is altogether different. Every once in a while Ellington, who tends to view life with a pastoral, prismatic cheer, allows himself to be pressured into taking himself too seriously, and that's apparently what happened the other night.

At first, the concert seemed like a put-on, as Alice Babs, a flawless soprano from Sweden, sang this Ellington lyric:

Heaven, my dream,
Heaven, divine,
Heaven, supreme,
Heaven combines
Every sweet and pretty thing
Life would love to bring.
Heavenly Heaven to be
Is just the ultimate degree.

But after half the fourteen or fifteen numbers had been got through, it became clear that Ellington was in Sunday earnest. These numbers sported just about every "serious" church-music device. Two sizable choirs sang and chanted together and separately or backed a singer named Jimmy McPhail; the cathedral's organist offered a "dialogue" that was all crescendo and no diminuendo; Ellington played a syrupy hymn, accompanied only by bowed bass; and the lyrics, all by Ellington, went on and on in a confectionary way about God and the Golden Rule and Salvation. In the final number, "Praise God and Dance," the band and the vocalists and the choirs, blending hosannas, were surrounded by two batteries of dancers who, after crashing imaginary cymbals together and jitterbugging around, leaped down the main aisle and out of sight. It wouldn't have been surprising at this point if the Ark in life-size Styrofoam had floated out of the shadows.

The band, reduced most of the evening to accompaniment, kept its stately cool. Harry Carney had the opening number to himself, offering a gentle solo with one of those marvellous bent phrases that force melodic beauty to its limits. Johnny Hodges and Paul Gonsalves and Russell Procope (on clarinet) were given brief bits, and the two drummers on hand, Steve Little and Sam Woodyard, traded solos that at least had some godlike thunder in them. But best of all was "The Shepherd," a blues built around Cootie Williams' muted and open horn. Williams' once tricky, curving agility with a mute has slowed, which is just what a Grand Canyon like St. John's calls for, and when he let loose a couple of burning growls and a heavy-winged open-horn passage it suddenly seemed that the seventy-five hundred people in the cathedral were in the right place at the right moment.

## Small Print

One of the persistent beliefs in jazz is that the byways of America are peopled with unknown geniuses who, exposed, would astonish us all. But the world of jazz is small, it has an almost telephonic grapevine, and touring musicians who at one time or another play most of the general-store towns have notably curious, open ears. Another belief is that jazz contains a sizable population of excellent but underrated musicians who, because of mischance, the winds of faddism, or retiring personalities, exist in a permanent twilight, and this is true. Their names are legion, and a few of them are John Collins, Buddy Tate, Emmett Berry, Joe Thomas, Jimmy Rowles, and Benny Morton. Of these men, Morton, with his delicate, evasive style and self-effacing manner, is in some ways the most underappreciated.

A handsome, immaculately tailored man with a dreaming, affable face, Morton is sixty-one and was born in New York City. He joined Fletcher Henderson when he was nineteen and fell under the spell of Jimmy Harrison, who, along with Jack Teagarden, converted jazz trombone from a sidesplitter into a musical instrument. Morton worked with Henderson off and on until the early thirties and, after a five-year stint with Don Redman, went with greatest of the Basie bands. He joined the Café Society Uptown-Downtown troupe in the early forties, and eventually became a member of Teddy Wilson's Uptown band. In the mid-forties he made a lot of imperishable recordings, among them a twelve-inch 78-rpm Blue Note, "Conversing in Blue," on which he and Barney Bigard and Ben Webster fashioned a closing chorus that, in its curving, whispering lyricism, is one of the glories of jazz. Then he went underground, and he has since subsisted in the studios, in Broadway pit bands, and even in the Radio City Music Hall orchestra. A week or so ago Morton suddenly surfaced at a concert given at the Half Note by a group called the Jazz Giants, and in a recording made in Canada recently by the same group on the Sackville label.

Morton's style remains exactly what it was thirty years ago. It is an inward, private style, as if he and his instrument were in constant shuttered colloquy. His tone is quiet and even, and he uses none of the glissandi and whoops invented by Dickie Wells and carried on by J. C. Higginbotham and Vic Dickenson. But his solos, instead of sounding restrained, have a deliberate, uphill air, and they rely for the affecting moments not on smears or burred tones but on elegance and logic. He is, in large part, a melodic embellisher who will either shadow the written melody for whole choruses at a time or launch into short-phrased, seemingly inverted improvisations (always capped by a searching vibrato) that tint and heighten the original melody. He is a contradictory legato performer who in a slow tune will lag behind the beat for half a chorus and then slip into an earnest, jogging double time, and who in a fast number will play winding, half-time phrases that alternate with direct, on-the-beat variations. Morton plays in small print, and it is not until the end of his solo—with its repeated, slightly varied phrases, long-held single notes and abrupt, almost bouncing on-the-beat notes—that its ordered, mannerly design can be seen completely and clearly. Many jazz improvisers lurch from peak to peak, which tends to obscure the empty valleys, but Morton moves on a wide-open plain.

Morton has found himself in motley bands before, and the Jazz Giants is one of the oddest. Wild Bill Davison is on cornet, the late Edmond Hall's brother Herbie is on clarinet, Claude Hopkins is on piano, Arvell Shaw is on bass, and Buzzy Drootin is on drums. Morton, though he is the only member of the band who does not have his own display number, is the cement between these opposites, both in ensembles, where he plays discreet secondary solos, and in his actual solos. He was indispensable at the Half Note (particularly in "Them There Eyes" and "Bill Bailey"), and also in the Sackville recording ("Them There Eyes" again, and "I Would Do Anything for You," in which he takes a masterly solo).

## Newport 1968

*July 4th*

I t is the festival's fourteenth birthday, and not its announced fifteenth, since the 1961 concerts were a popular-music replacement erected on the ruins of the 1960 festival, which was sundered by the Newport riot. All that happened tonight, though, was a wild, crazy-legs cadenza by the pianist Joe Zawinul near the end of Cannonball Adderley's "Maria." It sounded like Bartók on a tear, and it was delivered with just the right touch of ham. For the rest of its time the Adderley group rummaged in its blues-gospel-funk-rock bag—"soul soap" music, as a friend appositely christened it—and later Nina Simone rummaged in hers. We also heard Mongo Santamaria, a conga drummer who leads a proficient Latin blues band; the guitarists Jim Hall and Barney Kessel, who played separately and together, the first declaiming for the introverts of the world and the second for the extroverts; and Gary Burton's group (Larry Coryell, Steve Swallow, Roy Haynes), which, disavowing its earlier revolutionary tendencies, shimmered like moonlight.

*July 5th*

The afternoon was sunny and limned by haze, and the evening fog made the trees around the Festival field look like low, gray-green clouds. The fog was also onstage and in the eyes of the beholders, for tonight we rambled down Memory Lane. The Basie band played itself for a couple of numbers and then—in a game that persisted throughout the evening and was called "I Can Play Your Music, Too"—

offered Jimmy Lunceford's arrangements of "Cheatin' on Me" and "For Dancers Only." Joe Thomas, Lunceford's tenor saxophonist and singer (not to be confused with the trumpeter of that name), was brought from Kansas City for the two numbers. He is a genuine jazz singer and he remains—though he is now an undertaker—one of the best graduates of Coleman Hawkins' academy. Basie was replaced by Woody Herman, who played two Goodman arrangements, backed Jack Leonard singing Tommy Dorsey's "Marie" (the brass section swooped through Bunny Berigan's solo), did Glenn Miller's "In the Mood," accompanied Erskine Hawkins in "Tuxedo Junction" and "Tippin' In" (Hawkins had a swinging, interesting band, but his banshee trumpet playing is no better now than it was twenty-five years ago), accompanied Bob Eberle in Jimmy Dorsey's "Amapola," "Tangerine," and "Green Eyes," and closed with Artie Shaw's "Nightmare" and "Summit Ridge Drive." Charlie Barnet led the Ellington band (with Nat Pierce on piano) in seven Barnet numbers ("Skyliner," "Pompton Turnpike," "East Side, West Side," and so forth). Since Barnet's main inspiration was the Ellington band, it was two mirrors staring at one another. Then Ellington himself appeared and played "Take the 'A' Train," "Passion Flower," "Sophisticated Lady," "Things Ain't What They Used to Be," and four slightly less shopworn numbers. Nostalgia Promenade was capped by a reconstituted Dizzy Gillespie big band using Gil Fuller arrangements.

The afternoon concert was notable for Rufus Harley playing a bagpipe in a pleasant tune called "Windy" (he somehow supplied all the notes that have been missing from the instrument since it was invented); a great Dizzy Gillespie open-horn solo in "Swing Low, Sweet Cadillac" (he had his quintet with him), which began with soft bouffant phrases and ended with shouts linked by Mad Hatter runs; and four numbers by the Elvin Jones trio (Joe Farrell, flute and tenor saxophone, and Jimmy Garrison, bass), including a standing-ovation bass solo in "Risa" and a long, pagoda-structured drum solo in "Kayiko's Birthday March."

The master-of-ceremonies scorecard is filling up. It already lists George Wein, Father Norman O'Connor, John Hammond, George Simon, Alan Grant, Billy Taylor, and André Baruch. A choral number arranged for them by Gil Fuller would be suitable before the weekend is out.

### July 6th

This afternoon, Montego Joe, another conga drummer, brought on another Latin blues band, and it played with a rocking precision epitomized by the solos of its tenor saxophonist, Bobby Brown, who combined the late John Coltrane's adventurousness with a loafing, old-fashioned lyricism. Tal Farlow, who has only recently emerged from a long semi-retirement, demonstrated—along with Johnny Knapp, Junie Booth, and Mousie Alexander—that inactivity is a two-edged sword. His ideas were fresh and sure and flowing, but his execution seemed stiff. Knapp, a many-handed pianist who recalls the lower-register ebullience of the late Eddie Costa, offset Farlow's tightness, and so did Booth, a good, limber Charlie Mingus bassist. Then Sonny Criss, a forty-year-old alto saxophonist and Charlie Parker offshoot, played four numbers with Billy Taylor, Booth, and Alexander. "Willow Weep for Me" included declamatory Parker-like phrases, long rests, and whispering runs. Its dynamics were extraordinary and its structure was flawless. It was the sort of performance that crystallizes everything, that makes time stop and wait. The remainder of the afternoon was a jumble. Benny Carter came on with Duke Ellington, Johnny Hodges, Jeff Castleman (bass), and Rufus Jones (drums), and the set got off on the left foot when Ellington facetiously introduced Carter as the man a symphony musician would consult about jazz and a jazzman would consult about the symphony. During the six tunes, Carter was given just three solos, and, although Carter is one of our most esteemed composer-arrangers, the tunes were all by Ellington or Billy Strayhorn. Backstage observers reported that after the performance Carter, a man of remarkably even humor, was shaken. The eighteen-piece University of Illinois Jazz Band, finishing up the afternoon, played with an aplomb and conviction which ironically suggested that when a form of jazz can be executed so well by the very young it has been exhausted.

The evening began well. Alex Welsh, a cornettist and the leader of a fine seven-piece English swing band, backed Bud Freeman, Pee Wee Russell (whose "Pee Wee's Blues" and "Love Is Just Around the Corner" were subtle and fresh and affecting), Ruby Braff, and Joe Venuti, who, at sixty-eight, managed "Body and Soul" and "Sweet Georgia Brown" much as he might have forty years ago. Then Joan Crawford, appearing on behalf of Pepsi-Cola for not altogether clear reasons, introduced Duke Ellington. "Hi, I'm Joan Crawford, and I can't tell you how wonderful it is to be with all my friends on this magnificent evening." She continued with a fruity eulogy to Ellington. When a genial heckler shouted something, she stopped, yelled "Shut up! You just shut up," and finished her script in a shaking voice. Ellington, possibly feeling a little maladroit after the afternoon, kissed Miss Crawford, played nine hand-me-downs and refused to end his set. (He finally left the stage, after Woody Herman, appearing from the wings, attempted to dance with him, whereupon George Wein announced the intermission, leaving the band sitting there with its mouth open.) The evening was rung down by Hugh Masekela, a South African Harry James, and by Dionne Warwick, a homogenized gospel singer.

*July 7th*

The afternoon was given over to Ray Charles, and it ranked with those celebrated Newport afternoon concerts of gospel singing (1957) and tap-dancing (1962). The evening was unavoidably anticlimactic. (Wouldn't it be better, since Sunday night is a gray and tapering time anyway, to simply have one Sunday concert, starting around three and ending at eight?) Ramsey Lewis, a tall, heavy-handed pianist, passed out three or four helpings of soul soap, and was followed by an odd, ethereal vocal trio from California called the Sound of Feeling and made up of a singer-pianist, Gary David, and the twins Alyce and Rhae Andrece. The group concentrates on impossible harmonies, the notes that exist in the cracks of the piano keyboard, and such metres as seven-four. There were Bergian sounds and spook sounds and Paul Verlaine set to music, but few sounds of feeling. It was chilly and expert, and it prompted a man sitting nearby to observe that it was "not very conducive to audience participation." Roland Kirk, a one-man reed section who seems to carry huge bags of sound around with him, sweated and swung and stomped through six numbers, sometimes playing his instruments separately and sometimes all at once. His clowning has yet to conceal the fact that he is a consummate musician. Don Ellis' infallible nineteen-piece Los Angeles band closed the festival with a number in thirteen-four, a country-and-Western in seven-four, an ingenious reworking of Charlie Parker's "K.C. Blues," and an electrophonic number that summoned up other galaxies.

The Charles concert began, as is now customary, with a dozen numbers by his fine big band, his vocal quartet (the Raelets), and a singer and dancer named Billy Preston. The Master, dressed in an olive velvet jacket, came on after the intermission, and before his first number was over his presence— Billie Holiday had the same thing and Mahalia Jackson has it—seized Festival Field; he could have done "The Beer Barrel Polka" and "Moon of Manakoora" without losing an ounce of attention. In the course of seventeen numbers, he sang his anthem, "Georgia on My Mind," getting off a "Now I said, Georgia" in a high soft moan, and backing himself all the while on piano with digging blues figures. He sang "Marie" in a bright, funny way, recalling his "Alexander's Ragtime Band," and the Beatles' "Yesterday" and "Eleanor Rigby," turning them into altogether new numbers. He sang a slow, swaying "Let's Go Get Stoned," he swung "You Are My Sunshine," and he ended with a long, layer-upon-layer version of "What'd I Say" that swung so hard it made the audience leap to its feet.

# 1969

## Pee Wee and Anita

Word has come that Pee Wee Russell died yesterday in Alexandria, Virginia, at the age of sixty-two. He was a shy man trapped in a sausage body and a clown's face. He sidled rather than walked, and his deep voice seemed to back out of him, producing long, subterranean utterances that were either unintelligible or very funny.

And when he tried to escape into alcohol he became mortally trapped. His style—the chalumeau phrases, the leaps over the abyss, the unique *why?* tone, the use of notes that less imaginative musicians had discarded as untoward—was, paradoxically, his final snare and his glory. People laughed at it. It was considered eccentric, and because eccentricity, the kindest form of defiance, baffles people, they laugh. But those who didn't laugh understood that Russell had discovered some of the secrets of life and that his improvisations were generally successful attempts to tell those secrets in a new, funny, gentle way. To be sure, he never revealed anything outright, probably because he enjoyed making his listeners work as hard as he did. And when, late in life, he took up painting, the results were a visual extension of his aural circumlocutions. Russell embossed his sound on the world and his wife knew it when she told me, to his delight, that his playing embarrassed her.

Jazz singers tend to have jerry-built voices, an intuitive rhythmic intelligence, a loose sense of intonation, and a freedom with melismatics that blows two-syllable words up into five and deflates three-syllable ones to a vowel. These characteristics are kept in balance by the one gift they all share—emotion and the ability to transmit it. Anita O'Day, who opened at the Half Note last night, is the uncommon reverse. She is a jazz singer by calculation and design. Each husky, sand-blown note is placed exactly behind, on, or in front of the beat, the syllables are expanded or contracted with millimetric care, she wavers her pitch for effect. She steers the listener's ear every inch of the way and she also transfixes his eye. Each inflection, beat, and tone is underlined with a movement: ankles delicately crossed and uncrossed, a rotating left shoulder, a punctuating akimbo elbow, a slow turn, ending with her head jutted forward and her hands horizontal at her sides, or her head in sudden profile and her legs planted jauntily apart. But the total effect can be unsettling. Again and again her perfections bring her to the edge of self-parody, and one longs for the slight slip, the disguised faltering that would make the human being inside the mannerisms and motions and invariably beautiful clothes real. Roy Eldridge and his quintet shared the bill with Miss O'Day, and in "Let Me Off Uptown," their old grandstanding duet from the Gene Krupa days, they got together to see if they could raise some goose pimples. They did.

# Dancing

One of the least necessary misfortunes of the past twenty years has been the almost unnoticed disappearance of jazz dancing. It was a comic, graceful, ingenious art, but it went out the back door just as television, its potentially perfect medium, was coming in the front. But thanks to the heroic efforts of the late Marshall Stearns we've had brilliant glimpses in the past decade of such tap-dancers as Bunny

Briggs and Baby Laurence, Groundhog, Honi Coles and Cholly Atkins, Pete Nugent, and Chuck Green, as well as of the marvellous Savoy Ballroom dancers—Al Minns and Leon James, who appeared this afternoon at Town Hall. It was a genial, dishevelled affair. The wrong accompanying recordings were played, numbers petered out before they got started, Minns' and James' comments backed and filled, and an eight-child "Company," made up of Minns' and James' children, provided brave, cluttered counterpoint. But there were exhilarating moments, when the two men— Minns is heavyset air and James a needle—did a cakewalk full of high knees and akimbo arms and supercilious looks; a dance called "Peckin'," in which they henned and roostered around the stage, their heads darting rapidly back and forth, their knees bent and knocking, their arms drunken wings; a soft-shoe composed of shooting legs and swimming arms; a Lindy Hop in which Minns picked up James and swung him around as though he were a child; and (Minns only) a celebration of Snakehips Tucker, whose slippery undulations suggested spaghetti sliding off a fork. An hour-long Minns-and-James television show, with live music and a brisk, brief commentary, would be consummate.

Tap-dancing isn't "the art of walking raised to a baroque magnificence" (the *Times*, April 15th), any more than a cathedral is a glorified rock, but it is jazz music exhilaratingly translated from the abstract into concrete human form. The offspring of the marriage of jazz and the old clog dances, tap-dancing has long been hounded by irony. When it was a staple in vaudeville, it was taken for granted as just another example of those picturesque gifts Negroes are born to. It was fun to watch, and taking lessons at the age of eight was the thing to do. Then, twenty years ago, it went underground, and almost automatically it became an art whose proponents were celebrated by being offered jobs as bellhops and elevator men. But this art survives, and every so often it surfaces. For the past four or five Monday nights, ten or so dancers have been gathering at the Bert Wheeler Theatre in the Hotel Dixie on West Forty-third Street. Present tonight were Chuck Green (around whom the evening is loosely built), Lon Chaney, Big Rhythm Red, Sandman Sims, Raymond Kaalund, Bert and Sandra Gibson, Letitia Jay (who is the show's "coördinator"), and two younger dancers, Jimmy Slyde and Jerry Ames. It was a funny, jumbled evening. Miss Jay and Sandra Gibson lumbered on and off the stage, Derby Wilson (a retired dancer) told vaudeville jokes ("I just saw a cross-eyed woman tell a knock-kneed man to go straight home"), Green reminisced, and the accompanists—a pianist and drummer, augmented midway by the trombonist Matthew Gee—often operated on their own rhythmic frequency. In the first half of the evening, Kaalund, wearing a rumpled felt hat pulled down over his ears, did a drunken, barely audible soft-shoe. His shoulders, his stomach, and his feet all went in different directions, and he looked as if he were dancing against a high wind. Sandman Sims placed a low, small circular platform on the stage and, sprinkling sand on it, did the Sand, his body bent and his feet scraping slowly around and around and producing sounds that fell somewhere between wire brushes and a steam engine starting up on wet tracks. The second half of the program was a simulated "cutting" contest in which Chaney, Sims, Rhythm Red, Ames, Green, Slyde, Gibson, and Kaalund each took several solo choruses, some accompanied and some not. Chaney began with the Paddle and Roll, which was full of heavy Baby Laurence steps, terrific kicks, and two-ton slides. He was followed by Kaalund, simultaneously dancing and skipping rope. Ames, who is a Donald O'Connor–Gene Kelly type of dancer, floated back and forth across the stage, throwing in flamencan steps and ballroom-dancing spins. Rhythm Red, an enormous, graceful man, was followed by Gibson, who did complex "wing" steps, and by Sims, whose legs at one point resembled calipers being quickly opened and closed. Jimmy Slyde has learned from Bunny Briggs and Baby Laurence, and he whipped around the stage like lightning, demonstrating great speed but no real style. Then Chuck Green, a tall, Lincolnlike man, pulled the rug deftly and simply out from under his colleagues with two slow, staccato choruses of blues; each step was crystal-clear, his rhythms were locked perfectly in place, and his movements were airlike.

At best, music is the most elusive art. It resides only in the ear—you can't touch it or smell it or look at it. Yet most people attending a musical performance unwittingly and perversely try to listen by watching, as if the notes coming from a horn might suddenly appear in comforting schools of half notes and eighth notes. Since the eyes and the ears tend to compete endlessly anyway, visual concentration overrules the ear, and that is what happened to this listener this morning when "Camera Three" offered a twenty-six-minute film about Jeremy Steig, the extraordinary flutist and painter.

The film, called *Jeremy*, was produced, directed, and edited by Joel Freedman, who also happens to be a cellist. It was put together over the past year and a half, and it is an attempt, in conservative *cinéma vérité*, to be a fly on the wall in Steig's life. Steig dances and plays by himself on a beach, horses around in the water with David Amram, plays a duet with Amram, plays a duet with Freedman, paints one of his marvellous satyr-choked murals while Freedman plays, and plays with his own group, the Satyrs (Adrian Guillery, Warren Bernhardt, Eddie Gomez, Bob McDonald). In many of the sequences, Steig is bare-chested and in underpants or bathing trunks—an excellent instance of naturalness giving the impression of affection. There are, when one shuts one's eyes, ghostly patches of music. Steig and Gomez play a little blues, and there are the duets, some of them only bars long, a broken-off free improvisation by the Satyrs, and bits and pieces of Steig playing *a cappella*. How fine it would have been to have one sustained number in which the camera was focussed blindly on a bare wall while Steig, who is an extremely adventurous jazz flutist, was given a chance to stretch out on his instrument and show why the film was made at all.

## Coleman

Coleman Hawkins died yesterday at the age of sixty-four. Hawkins invented the jazz saxophone, and, more than that, he spent forty years tinkering with his invention—remodelling it, streamlining it, polishing it. Most artists, of whatever kind, find a style that sustains them for life, even when sheer use turns it to self-parody. But Hawkins, instinctively detesting commercialism, changed his style every ten or fifteen years. He began—in the twenties, with Fletcher Henderson—as a nervous, serio-comic performer who spent notes by the thousand. This adolescent choppiness subsided, and he became a classic Romantic with a big-breasted tone and an Echo Mountain vibrato. Then his style lost weight, revealing a fluent, tough, muscled attack—the attack that produced his seminal 1939 recording of "Body and Soul." He passed into his fourth and final phase ten years ago, and it was unsettling. The best of his earlier modes was still there, but there was a new element—a naked, hellfire crying-out that suggested he had finally discovered what life is and didn't like what he saw. Hawkins' musical adventurousness—which kept musicians twenty years younger running—was simply a by-product of his unstemmable creativity. He spent most of his life *improvising*, which means that he altruistically gave part of himself away night after night, month after month, year after year. A sculptor can touch his work, a painter can stare at his finished canvas, but improvisation—except when it is recorded—is borne away the second it is uttered. Hawkins' generosity changed jazz, and jazz has changed Western music. One example will do. Harry Carney, the baritone saxophonist, has since 1927 been the rock that Duke Ellington has built his band on, and the Ellington band remains revolutionary and incomparable. Carney idolized Hawkins.

Hawkins' majesty was quietly embodied in his person. He was a handsome, straight-backed, medium-sized man who dressed impeccably and spoke distinctly in a low voice. Even in his later years, eroded by alcohol and the demands of his profession, he was seignorial. He offset his frail, stooped appearance by growing a patriarchal beard. He courted no one, but he had friends, and Roy Eldridge, the trumpeter, was perhaps the closest. "Coleman was a first-class cat all the way down the line," Eldridge said last night. "He was the old school. He never travelled economy, and, of course, he was like a genius on his horn. I guess I knew him as well as anybody. I got my first job—for twelve dollars a week, in 1927—through him, by copying his solo, note for note, off Fletcher Henderson's record of 'Stampede.' And I was the first person near him after he came back from five years in Europe in 1939. I had a Lincoln and he had a Cadillac, and we followed each other to gigs—

double things like that. He was a person people were afraid to talk to. If anything went wrong on a job, they wouldn't go to him, they'd always come to me. He was proud, but he wasn't cold, and he had a sense of humor. He just stayed away from cats he didn't like. People said he didn't like Lester Young, who was supposed to be his great rival. Man, I remember Coleman and I sat up all one night with Lester in the fifties, when we were with Jazz at the Philharmonic, trying to find out why Lester was up so tight. We never did. The last five years, Coleman was sick, and he just about quit eating. All he had eyes for, when he ate at all, was Chinese food, like Lester. But I'd call him in the evening and tell him what I was cooking. I'd tell him such-and-such, and he'd say, 'That sounds pretty good. I'll have to go out and get me some.' The next day I'd call again, and he'd forgotten everything. Coleman always had money, and he always spent it the right way. He'd have a Leica and a Steinway and three-hundred-dollar suits, but before anything else he always laid out six hundred dollars a month to take care of his rent and his wife and children. I often wondered if he had a little income of his own, but I never knew, because money was one thing we didn't discuss. Just a while ago I went out with Coleman when he wanted to look at a Rolls-Royce to buy, and I said to him, 'You'd look ridiculous riding around in that.' So he bought a Chrysler Imperial. Eight thousand in cash. I don't think he got to put more than a thousand miles on it."

## Back Again

Tonight Charles Mingus appeared at the Village Vanguard with a quintet and ended a self-imposed two-year retirement. The reports of Mingus that circulated during his retirement were fleeting and characteristic. He had a brush with the police in the Village when he refused to leave the roof of a parked car from which he was photographing a hippie demonstration. He was sometimes seen, in all his Orson Welles bulk, pedalling around the same area on a bicycle. He was evicted from his loft, and the proceedings became the subject of a *cinéma-vérité* documentary. His return has been equally in character, for Mingus, though the most commanding bassist and bandleader in jazz, is an oblique man. Once in a while during his retirement he'd drop into the Vanguard to listen to the music, and several weeks ago Max Gordon, the club's heroic owner, casually asked him when he was going to come out and play again. No definite response. A few days later Mingus left a note for Gordon with his telephone number. Gordon called, and Mingus said he wasn't sure. A week before the opening Mingus said yes and began rehearsing.

Mingus is propelled by his own winds. He can sit and talk gently of the outrages and stupidities of life; he can verbally lash an audience from the bandstand for half an hour at a time; he can publicly fire and rehire a sideman during an evening; he can play with butterfly delicacy and alarming fury; he can be thin and good-looking and attractively fat; he can arrive on a bandstand with a satchel containing an axe (Mingus humor: musicians occasionally refer to their instruments as "axes") and then, seated on his customary stool, drink a glass of milk. Tonight he was moving at a still-different speed. He looked like a seventy-year-old philosopher summoned to his alma mater for an honorary degree. He spoke to the audience quietly and briefly, he corrected his musicians politely, he smiled a lot, he played like Chopin serenading George Sand, and his expression was placid and benign. (It was also unfailingly alert; Mingus invariably gives the impression that the he *sees* every sound and texture and smell within reach.) The music was equally gracious. Some of his music—in particular his free-for-all ensembles—is demonic, but almost everything tonight was legato and lyrical and loping. There were a lot of ballads and medium-tempo blues, and only with Mingus' "Pithecanthropus Erectus," his reworking of Cole Porter's "Get Out of Town," did the group manifest some of Mingus' old steam. Mingus, a roll of adhesive tape at the ready, was apparently suffering from Soft Finger, the occupational ailment of out-of-practice bassists, and he took just one complete solo—on "In a Sentimental Mood." He pulled back on the beat, inserted dazzling runs, slipped in and out of double time, and, with his tone and timbre, gave Ellington's tune a pleased, delighted air. With the exception of the tenor-saxophonist Billie Robinson, the Vanguard group is made up of graduates of the Mingus seminary, and consists of Bill Hardman on trumpet, Charlie McPherson on alto saxophone, and Dannie Richmond on drums. McPherson is a fine Charlie Parker adherent, and Hardman plays with a staccato brilliance that seems in constant defiance of the legato upholstery that his model, Dizzy Gillespie, sometimes rests on. It was a quiet but unfailingly absorbing musicale.

Once seen and heard, Mingus hangs around in the mind, so I went back to see him tonight, partly to exorcise him, and partly to test the old legend that jazz soloists spend night after night pouring out fresh improvisations. When I arrived Mingus and his musicians were sitting on a banquette to the right of the bandstand, as if, in a curiously affecting way, they were awaiting an interview with a king—the king, of course, being the audience itself. Mingus still seemed swathed in peace. When he sat down on his stool and readied himself for the first number, a well-dressed drunk in the audience said something chummily condescending to him. Mingus pushed his bass at the man and said, "Here, you play, man." Then he turned his back, began playing, and spent the rest of the set looking stonily into the middle distance. The music spoke for him. "So Long, Eric," a tribute to the late Eric Dolphy, was the first number, as it was last night, but it sounded like a different tune. It was relaxed and even sloppy last night. Tonight it was angry and loud and expert. Richmond laid down a wall-to-wall carpet of Elvin Jones sounds, Hardman was quick and brilliant, as were Robinson and McPherson, and Richmond took the sort of head-knocking solo that Max Roach sometimes delivers when he is thinking about white men. "Pithecanthropus Erectus" appeared again as the second number, and it was an exhilarating tumult. Mingus, his fingers heavily taped and obviously hurting, shifted to the piano, where, with spare dissonant chords and hard offbeat single notes, he pushed the ensembles into savage free-for-alls that were broken by tough solos backed by equally tough riffs and organ chords. The number cleared the air (the drunk, his face floating and blank, looked as if he had been hung by his collar on a coat hook), and it prepared the way for an Ellington medley. Mingus took a solo, but it was cautious and almost inaudible. The set ended and the drunk left, and at the beginning of the next set Mingus the wise and imperturbable returned. Surprisingly, the group played a pair of venerable bebop numbers, "Good Bait" and "Koko." McPherson picked his way handsomely through "Just Friends," and there was a swarming version of Mingus' "Fables of Faubus," his acid memorial to the former governor.

## The Duke's Party

Last week, on April 29th, Duke Ellington was given his due by his country. The White House threw a black-tie seventieth-birthday party for him, and President Nixon presented him with the government's highest civilian award, the Presidential Medal of Freedom.

I arrived at the White House with my wife via the southwest gate at a quarter to ten. There was a chill in the air, and it was drizzling. We were ushered swiftly through a handsome oval reception room into a small room full of cabinets displaying the china used by various Presidents. Earl Hines, sipping champagne as he stood with his back to the Canton china used by George Washington, was watching a Navy Band trio made up of a drummer, a saxophonist, and an accordionist. "That's the damnedest accordion I ever heard," he said. "It sounds like a *guitar*. It's just luck I'm here, and I'm very happy about it. Duke and I have been *very* close friends for a *long* time. I just finished an engagement at Blues Alley here, and tomorrow I'm off for South America." Willie the Lion Smith, in his traditional garb of derby, horn-rimmed glasses, and cigar, drifted by looking like a well-slept owl, and Gerry Mulligan and Clark Terry, who were carrying their horns, began to play with the trio. Gunther Schuller, a fervent Ellington admirer came in, followed by George Wein. Marian McPartland was talking with Leonard Feather, the jazz critic, in a corner. The music was booming, and the guests had overflowed into an enormous arched hallway. Soon the aides wafted us upstairs and into the Great Hall where a receiving line had formed. The President, the Duke, Mrs. Nixon, and Ruth Ellington, the Duke's sister, were receiving the guests near the door of the Blue Room, and across from them a contingent from the Marine Band was playing. I hadn't seen Ellington since last fall, when I spent three days on the road with him and the band in the Deep South, and the contrast between the two situations was startling. The three days were typical of the nonstop, no-vacations life that Ellington has led for forty-six years. On a Monday night he played a sacred-music concert at South Carolina State College in Orangeburg. On Tuesday Harry Carney, his baritone saxophonist and sometime chauffeur, drove him (and me) two hundred and twenty-five miles to Fort Valley, Georgia, where, ten minutes after our arrival, at eight o'clock, he started giving a concert at Fort Valley State College. Immediately after it was over, we piled back into the car and drove four hundred miles to Vicksburg, where he was scheduled to give a Wednesday-night concert. The Fort Valley–Vicksburg jaunt is unforgettable. Carney drove very fast over mile after mile of two-lane concrete roads. It was pitch-black, and the headlights seemed to bounce off the darkness. Ellington dozed a little and then said "Lights." Carney, maintaining his speed, switched on the overhead light, and the road all but disappeared from view. Ellington, dressed in his usual long-haul costume of an old sweater, rumpled pants, and a black bandanna tied around his head, pulled a thick sheet of papers out of a small bag he takes everywhere and began to write. (The bag is shaped like a doctor's bag and was given him by Billy Strayhorn to hold the pills and other medicines he is never without.) Ten minutes later, Ellington said "OK," after Carney turned the light off. A similar work period took place every twenty minutes or so for the next three hours, and then we stopped for scrambled eggs and grits in a little town in Alabama. We were treated courteously, but nobody recognized Ellington. An hour or so later we stopped for gas, and Ellington called New York and talked with his doctor and longtime friend Arthur Logan about some ailment that was bothering him. It was four o'clock. I fell asleep, and woke up in another gas station, near Jackson, Mississippi. The sun was coming up. Carney had got out of the car to pay for the gas, and the attendant, a white man in his fifties, asked him, "Hey, is that Duke Ellington?" Carney nodded, and the man came up to Ellington's window. Ellington rolled it down and shook hands and said, "How's it going?" The attendant said, "*Are* you Duke Ellington?" Ellington nodded. "Wow! I've been listening to your records all my life. This is a great honor." Ellington rolled up the window and we drove off. "And I almost made it safely to the border," he said.

And here he was in the White House, in a tuxedo and a white ruffled shirt, standing next to the President and still nodding and smiling and shaking hands. When I reached the President in the receiving line, I told him he was doing a noble thing giving such a party, and he uttered a perfect "Pshaw!" Ellington looked at me blankly, and I told him my name. He gave his Mona Lisa smile and said, "And I was afraid *you* wouldn't remember my name." After being greeted by Mrs. Nixon, who looked frail and bemused, and by Miss Ellington, who was almost invisible under a huge wig, my wife and I were ushered into the East Room, where several hundred chairs had been set up. Television and newsreel cameramen were packed into a

screened-off area in the back of the room. (The *Times* reported that this was
the first time the White House had ever allowed such an event to be covered
by television cameras.) A ten-piece band was waiting on a dais in the front of
the room, and it was a sterling group, made up of Hank Jones, Jim Hall, Milt
Hinton, Louis Bellson, Bill Berry, Clark Terry, Urbie Green, J. J. Johnson,
Gerry Mulligan, and Paul Desmond. Vice-President Agnew was standing
between the band and the audience, beaming and looking like a maître d'.
When the room was full, the President and Mrs. Nixon, followed by Ellington and his sister, entered, and everyone stood. I can't resist such fillets of
melodrama, and I got a lump in my throat. The President, moving in a
quick, wooden way, jumped up on a platform in front of the bandstand and,
in his deepest rain-barrel voice, said something to this effect: "Sit down,
please, ladies and gentlemen. This is a very unusual and special evening in
this great room. Before the entertainment begins, we have a presentation to
make. I was looking at this name on here and it says 'Edward Kennedy' "—
he paused—" 'Ellington.' " Laughter. "For the first time during this Administration I have the honor of presenting the Presidential Medal of Freedom."
Ellington, standing pensively beside Mr. Nixon, was reading the citation
over his right shoulder. "In the royalty of American music, no man swings
more or stands higher than the Duke." The President handed Ellington the
medal. Everyone stood, and the applause was thunderous. "Thank you, Mr.
President," Ellington said, and, taking Mr. Nixon by both arms, he conferred *his* celebrated award—the classic French greeting of left cheek against
left cheek, right against right, left against left, and right against right. The
President blushed and took a seat in the front row. Ellington said thank
you again and listed the four freedoms that Billy Strayhorn had lived his
life by—freedom from hate, freedom from self-pity, freedom from fear of
possibly doing something that might help someone else more than it
would him, and freedom from "the kind of pride that could make a man
feel that he is better than his brother." Ellington sat down between Mrs.
Agnew and his sister, and the President jumped back up on the platform
and said, laughing, "One thing has been left out of the program—'Happy
Birthday.' Please don't go away while I try and play it, and everybody sing,
please, in the key of G."

Everybody sang, and then the band went to work. The music, which
lasted an hour and a half, was exceptional. Some two dozen numbers were
played, and almost all were by Ellington and/or Billy Strayhorn. The high
points included Gerry Mulligan's "Sophisticated Lady"; a duet by Terry and
Berry in "Just Squeeze Me"; a gorgeous Urbie Green solo in "I Got It Bad
and That Ain't Good"; a long, stamping "In a Mellow Tone"; an ingenious
medium-tempo version of Ellington's ordinarily dreamy "Prelude to a Kiss,"
arranged by Mulligan; three exhilarating choruses of "Perdido," by Earl
Hines; and a caroming Louis Bellson drum solo in "Caravan." Then Willis

Conover, who had arranged the musical festivities, introduced the musicians. Ellington stood up, bowed, and sat down after each name. The President darted back to the platform and said, "I think we all ought to hear from one more pianist." He pulled Ellington from his chair, and the Duke took the microphone. "It's the greatest compliment to be asked to follow this orchestra. I shall pick a name—gentle, graceful—something like Pat." He sat down at the piano and improvised a slow, Debussylike melody that brought the room to dead silence. Shouts of applause followed, and Mr. Nixon announced that if everyone would move into the Great Hall for refreshments, the East Room would be cleared for a jam session and dancing.

The lobby was full of celebrities—Mr. and Mrs. Richard Rodgers, Mr. and Mrs. Otto Preminger, Geoffrey Holder and his wife, Carmen de Lavallade, Mr. and Mrs. Harold Arlen, Daniel Patrick Moynihan, Mahalia Jackson, the Reverend and Mrs. John Yaryan (he was one of the sponsors of Ellington's first sacred-music concert, in Grace Cathedral in San Francisco in 1965), Dr. and Mrs. Logan, Mr. and Mrs. Cab Calloway, and Mr. and Mrs. Billy Eckstine.

Ellington himself moved easily from cluster to cluster, and when he got near us my wife said to him, "I was so glad you kissed President Nixon." "I think he liked that," Ellington replied. "I always kiss all my friends. So now he belongs." I asked him why he was wearing such a conservative shirt, and he said, "The man who was supposed to bring my pleated blue satin shirt lost it or forgot it, or something, and I had to go out and buy this and these studs and cufflinks."

A roar of music burst out of the East Room. Lou Rawls was shouting the blues, and he was followed by Eckstine and Joe Williams. Half the accompanying band was made up of the all-stars, complemented by Dizzy Gillespie, and half by members of the Marine Band who looked as if they were in Valhalla. The chairs had been pushed back and dancing began. Geoffrey Holder, an enormous man in a black velvet outfit with satin trim, leaped around with Miss de Lavallade, and Ellington danced in turn with Mrs. Logan, his sister, and Mrs. Yaryan. He did a peppy foxtrot. George Wein sat in on piano and was followed by Ellington. Then Ellington and Willie the Lion Smith (Smith tutored Ellington forty-five years ago) played a duet, and so did the Lion and Marian McPartland. Harold Taylor, the former president of Sarah Lawrence College, sat in on clarinet. Ellington danced some more, looking fresh and happy and very young (he was due to fly to Oklahoma City for a gig the next morning at eight), and then he went over to Dr. Logan, who was sitting in the front row. The Doctor took his pulse and pushed Ellington back on the dance floor. The Nixons had gone to bed shortly after midnight, but the East Room rocked on until well after two.

I said good night to Ellington near the front door of the White House.

He embraced me and my wife, and then, as if it had been her party, paid her the kind of compliment women take with them to their graves: "I'm so glad you could come. You looked so beautiful, and you brought such dignity to my party." He waved, and we went out.

As such evenings go, it was pretty fine. In fact only one thing was really wrong: the band, excepting Harry Carney, wasn't there. That magnificent assemblage is Ellington's voice, his right hand, his palette, his instrument, and not to have it present left a hole in the evening. But the next time I see the Duke I'll ask him about it, and he'll have the right answer. He always does.

## Newport 1969

*July 3rd*

Just after dinner, old Thunder, riding Lightning and leading Rain, careered up Narragansett Bay, and the fifteenth Newport Jazz Festival was off. The storm was the most compelling spectacle of the evening, for the concert resembled one of those saltless concoctions that were tossed together at Town Hall or Carnegie Hall in the fifties and early sixties to lure the college kids home on vacation. Anita O'Day, dressed in a spanking, long-jacketed linen suit, evoked her 1958 appearance at Newport, when, with her beautifully honed mannerisms, she had wowed everybody in a performance that lasted just twenty minutes. She evoked it, but, mysteriously, that was all. She sang as well, she looked as well, she moved as well—and nothing happened. Phil Woods and his European Rhythm Machine, made up of the alto saxophonist, a Swiss pianist, a French bassist, and a Swiss drummer, got the same reaction. Perhaps it was Woods. At his best he is an impassioned Charlie Parker adherent, but tonight he sounded unsettled and down. The group's single fine number had little to do with how it was played; it was the tune itself—"Ad Infinitum," a sad, lovely, long-lined melody by the "new-thing" pianist-composer Carla Bley. Young-Holt Unlimited, a soul-soap group whose leaders once worked with Ramsey Lewis, funked around, and there was one of Sun Ra and His Space Arkestra's cosmic Halloween parties. The band, carting hundreds of instruments onstage and dressed in hugoolie robes and tall elf hats, played an enormous number that included punctuating organ shrieks by Sun Ra, a neat parody of a Duke Ellington dreamboat number, some group singing reminiscent of the Modernaires, a passage in which everyone whaled away at a percussion instrument, and a shouting finale paced by Sun Ra striding regally across the stage with a couple of spiky sun symbols. But the evening closed hopefully. Bill Evans, accompanied by the brilliant Eddie Gomez on bass and Marty Morrell on drums, played three delicate ballads and was joined for two more numbers by Jeremy Steig. He developed long, tight, intense solos, with Evans celebrating him every note of the way, and it was a graceful performance.

*July 4th*

There had been an ominous, stifling atmosphere in Newport on the day of the 1960 riot. The town was choking. Hundreds of cars loaded with boozy teen-agers blocked the narrow streets, and the sidewalks and parks were jammed with even more kids, most of them barefoot and carrying cans of beer. Despite their blurred, rumpled appearance, they didn't look like potential rioters. Their oxford shirts and madras shorts were not inexpensive, and they were quiet. There were just too many of them. But that same night, ten thousand strong and full of beer courage, they stormed the already packed Freebody Park where the Festival was being held, and it took the police, fending off rocks and beer cans and finally resorting to tear gas, a couple of hours to send them packing. The boomerang result, of course, was that the Festival was shut down and didn't reopen for two years.

This afternoon Newport suddenly took on the same teeming, hothouse atmosphere. Even back streets were bumper to bumper, and almost every road was flanked by straggling Indian files of kids carrying packs and blankets and wine bottles. They are very different from their 1960 predecessors, most of whom probably spent today manicuring their lawns and minding their children. Their hair is long and tangled, their clothes are de-rigueur freakish (the boys shirtless or in tank tops and hip-hugging jeans, and the girls in bell-bottoms, with their shirttails knotted together just below their free breasts), and they look dirty. By the time the evening concert began, the situation around the Festival grounds was claustrophobic. There were kids as far as the eye could see: an army of them was camped on a bluff back of the Festival stage, another army was stretched out on the spacious slope that rings the opposite side of the grounds, and they were ten deep outside the walls and gates of the field. You could have sliced the dust in the air. There were twenty-two thousand people inside the s.r.o. grounds and probably an equal number outside. The reason for this crush was simple. The concert was to be given over largely to rock groups, and half a dozen or more are scheduled for Saturday and Sunday. The children had come, pilgrims all, to worship their music, their symbol, their weapon. They had come to hear Jeff Beck and Steve Marcus and Jethro Tull and Ten Years After, and to hear Blood, Sweat, and Tears and the only jazz group of the evening—Roland Kirk, who told them where much of their music had come from, and then, in his clowning, ferocious, multi-instrumented way, demonstrated how that source should sound. They loved it. The savage breast was soothed, and there was no riot.

An odd coincidence: In 1960 there were two jazz festivals in Newport—

the doomed Establishment one, and a small, exciting affair that had been hastily organized by Charlie Mingus and Max Roach and that included Coleman Hawkins and Roy Eldridge, Ornette Coleman, Jo Jones, and Baby Laurence. Today posters appeared on trees and fences announcing that Mingus and the trumpeter Lee Morgan would hold an "underground" jazz festival on Friday and Saturday nights at Cliff Walk Manor, the hotel where the first rump festival had taken place. I stopped in on the way back to my hotel to see if Mingus would pull another champion out of his hat. He didn't. It was a night-club gig, notable only for an irresistible merengué played by Morgan (there was no dancing) and for Mingus's work. But ghosts of 1960 were there—Mingus and Roach playing a brilliant fifteen-minute duet, Baby Laurence cannonading all over the the bandstand, Coleman Hawkins, and Roy Eldridge in consummate tandem, and a thinner, wilder Mingus passing a derby hat in the audience.

An interesting Canadian rock group, the Lighthouse, beefed up with horns and strings and snatches of improvisation, opened the concert this afternoon. It was followed by a helter-skelter "jam session" played by fifteen musicians, including Jimmy Owens and Howard McGhee, Benny Green, Buddy Tate and Brew Moore and Cecil Payne, the West Coast pianist Hampton Hawes, Ray Nance (violin), and the impeccable, winning Slam Stewart. A vocalist named Eddie Jefferson sang an embarrassing eulogy of Coleman Hawkins. Sometimes the living are harder on the dead than they are on each other.

*July 5th*

The kids came down from their rocks and rills this afternoon, and Festival Field, which was frequently almost empty at afternoon concerts in years past, was packed. They heard John Mayall, who was introduced as the thirty-five-year-old father of English rock and who was absorbing chiefly because of his derivations, which include Leadbelly and Muddy Waters and the old Jimmy Giuffre trio. And they heard the Mothers of Invention, whose musical-satirical roots go back to Spike Jones and Borrah Minnevitch and his Harmonica Rascals, and whose put-ons are paralleled by Charlie Mingus and Archie Shepp. But they also heard the Newport All-Stars and Miles Davis—an experience meant to explain George Wein's decision to hold what is turning out to be a jazz-and-rock festival: Take a couple of slices of rock and spread them with meaty jazz, and the kids are painlessly educated. But the jazz we have heard so far has been so vapid that it has turned into the Silvercup bread and the rock has become the pepperoni. At any rate, Davis was in striving form. Accompanied by piano, bass, and drums, he played a vast number consisting of short trumpet statements—some languorous and melancholy, some shrill and hard, and some unfinished staircases—surrounded by piano and bass and drum solos. The All-Stars opened the concert. On hand were Ruby

Braff, Red Norvo, Tal Farlow, Larry Ridley, Jack Dejohnette, and Wein himself on piano. Farlow and Norvo were excellent throughout, but the group hung together just once—in a slow blues memorable for Braff's declamations and for a one-chorus double-time duet between Norvo and Dejohnette.

The human swarm was almost as dense tonight as it was last night, but the atmosphere was less tense. And there was another difference. Sly and the Family Stone, a largely Negro rock group, was scheduled, and the audience had become half black and half white. Gerry Mulligan, with the Dave Brubeck trio, started things off. His humor and eloquence and long, deep lines were intact, and even Brubeck sounded crisp and authoritative. Art Blakey and his quintet delivered four motionless numbers, and then Gary Burton, who has been trudging around for the past couple of years between jazz and rock, brought on his quartet (Jerry Hahn, guitar; Larry Ridley, bass; Bill Goodwin, drums), and the two musics fused. The rhythms were largely rocklike, each number was collective (jazz and rock), and there were plenty of solos. Hahn has a spare, unfashionable style that depends as much on silence as on sound. His choice of notes is unexpected and his placement of them equally unexpected, and he bends enough of them in just the right way to bring the goose pimples out. Burton has given up his ringing, shushing attack for a Red Norvo clarity, and he played one number that was unaccompanied, and it sounded like a many-layered elaboration of "Beyond the Blue Horizon." The whole solo had a staccato, elbows-out effect, but the beat, though always there, was never directly stated. There was no lagging, there were no missteps. Nothing was missing and nothing was redundant. It was a perfect piece of music.

Then several astonishing things happened, and they happened so fast it is difficult to remember their exact order. Sly and the Family Stone were setting up their twenty or so two-ton speakers and amplifiers when a heavy, battering-ram thumping began outside the fence to the right of the bandstand. The booming stopped; a huge pole appeared above the fence, waved drunkenly about, and disappeared. Then fireworks, shot from the bluff behind the bandstand, bombarded the audience. It suddenly started raining, and the smell of smoke became unmistakable (the hordes outside, it turns out, had set fire to the grass behind the performers' quarters). George Wein rushed onstage and shouted at Sly Stone, asking him, for God's sake, to start playing. He did, and the dam, bulging for two days, broke. Kids, black and white, came pouring through a huge hole they had made in the fence separating the main area of the field from the box seats and the press section. They came like Visigoths, smashing the box railings and turning over chairs and forcing the occupants to flee. They poured into the press photographers' pit in front of the bandstand, filled it, and climbed up on the stage. Police and security guards ran onstage and there was a five-minute melee, with kids scrambling up, reaching the stage, and being tossed back into the pit. The only thing missing was the boiling oil. Sly and the Family Stone roared away, and then Stone, using lots of "like"s and "man"s and "uptight"s, persuaded the massed kids to sit down. All at once some sort of catharsis was achieved, and everything subsided. There were rumors that Wein would close up shop after Sly and the Family Stone finished, but, wisely, he didn't. The World's Greatest Jazz Band unenviably appeared next, and to its credit it had the kids dancing by the time it was halfway through its third tune, "Harper Valley P.T.A." The band accompanied Maxine Sullivan in four numbers, and she got through, too, and then Stephane Grappelli, the old Hot Club of France fiddler, played three delicate selections. When O. C. Smith, the singer, appeared, the battle was done. The kids had begun filing out singly and in small groups as Grappelli started. Some of them looked turned-on, some were unmistakably drunk, but most of them, wet and dirty and scrawny, just looked pooped.

*July 6th*

Last night's avalanche was not surprising and not new. Children overran the stage at the Paramount when Benny Goodman came to town, Frank Sinatra was attacked by his most ardent admirers, and there was the Beatles frenzy. The trouble with such adoration, aside from bruised bodies and smashed property, is that, paradoxically, it is antimusical. It's hard to listen to Beethoven or Thelonious Monk or Jethro Tull while you are doing the hundred-yard dash to a stage where the crush of people makes listening impossible anyway. To be sure, some rock—with its handmaidens pot and acid, with its vaudeville exterior, with its sternum-shattering volume, and with its unintelligible lyrics—is not meant to be listened to. Beneath its crashing political-social surface (where is the proletarian novel now?), it is designed to provoke a Kubla Khan euphoria. But jazz demands the same quiet attention and openness as poetry, which it resembles. So George Wein is unwittingly staging a war between the rock non-listeners and the jazz listeners. And nobody listens in wartime.

This afternoon an entirely different phenomenon appeared—James Brown, the meteoric singer and dancer. Brown is venerated by Negro teenagers, and they figuratively took over the field. He danced and sang at *them*, and, massed twenty-deep behind the press-section fence, they relished every word and gesture and step. The whites present seemed transparent. He has a heavy, attractive voice and he is a good, fluid dancer. His voice and dancing are indivisible. In slow ballads his voice is flicked by continual serpentine motions, and when he tears into a fast blues his dancing propels his singing, which may be compressed into one slamming word a chorus—a guttural "baybeee" or drawn-out "ymmyeh." He brandishes the microphone like a rapier, he does the splits, he falls down on his knees in mock exhaustion. He screeches into the microphone, whips around to one of his three drummers, chops his hand for a thundering rimshot, goes stock-still, and is abruptly off again. His ten-piece band never stops, and now and then four comely girls dance and sway about the stage—waterlilies on a blowing pond.

Brown's locomotive show cleared the air, and tonight was, by and large, a pleasure. B. B. King, the fine Chicago blues singer and guitarist—if he had Muddy Waters' or Joe Turner's voice, he would be nonpareil—sang half a dozen numbers and gave way to his white counterpart, the newcomer Johnny Winter. King, dressed in a plain suit, sang quietly and affectingly, while Winter, a tall, spidery man in long white hair and pipestem pants and a leather jacket, storked up and down in front of a battleship-sized bank of electronic equipment, shouting unintelligible blues and playing bad blues guitar. King and Winter were followed by routine displays by the Herbie Hancock sextet (polished hard-bop) and the Willie Bobo sextet (polished Latin funk), and then Buddy Rich came onstage with his big band and played four numbers, the last of them his bravura "West Side Story." It was closed with a long tidal-wave, three-ring, twenty-one-gun, now-damn-it, you-listen drum solo. The Festival, which had just ended, finally began.

## Richard Gibson (1)

Richard Gibson is a hefty, shrewd, funny, well-to-do forty-three-year-old former investments wizard and a philanthropic lover of jazz whose chief business in the spring of 1969 is trying to get the so-called World's Greatest Jazz Band of Yank Lawson and Bob Haggart on its artistic and financial feet. He and Lawson and Haggart are the "owners" of the band, which is set up on a cooperative basis. It included, as of tonight, Lawson and Billy Butterfield, trumpets; Bob Wilber, soprano saxophone and clarinet; Zoot Sims, subbing for Bud Freeman on tenor saxophone; Lou McGarity and Carl Fontana, trombones; Ralph Sutton, piano; Haggart, bass; and Gus Johnson, Jr., drums. The band is winding up a long stand at the Downbeat, at Forty-second Street and Lexington Avenue, and late in 1968 it was formally launched during a five-week stay at the Riverboat. Gibson has underwritten a significant amount of the band's costs at both places, and in the next couple of years he is prepared to sink an even more significant amount into the vision of which the band is only a part. "It's an absolute necessity that this band succeed," he says. "I can't build on a loss. But I'm a natural moneymaker. There's no way for me to succeed and not make money, and there's no way for me to make money and not succeed. Once the band turns the corner, some of its profits will spill on me. But first I want these jazz musicians to make some money. Jazz has failed too many times, for the wrong reasons." Gibson's vision includes the eventual formation of two totally different bands, as well as a plan that he refuses to disclose at the moment. "Look what happened when Walt Disney announced his *Alice in Wonderland*," he says. "Somebody else beat him to it, and his version was, I think, the only movie he ever lost money on." Gibson is convinced that if his vision crystallizes, the course of jazz will be changed.

Not surprisingly, the World's Greatest Jazz Band isn't, but it is, within its pepped-up Bob Crosby scope, very good. The arrangements are all by Haggart, and they are a fluid mixture of written and improvised ensembles, solos, and, refreshingly, improvised duets. The materials include old numbers ("Come Back, Sweet Papa," "Fidgety Feet"), swing standards ("Avalon," "After You've Gone"), and the up-to-date ("Sunny," "Mrs. Robinson," "Ode to Billie Joe"). The band has the shout and texture of a big band and the agility of a small band. When I first heard it a couple of weeks ago it was having a raggedy night: Butterfield didn't solo at all, Freeman and McGarity chugged, and the ensemble work was *bleu*. Tonight was totally different, and the presence of Sims may have had a lot to do with it. His brimming, long-lined eloquence was everywhere, and he was particularly rewarding in "Mrs. Robinson." Butterfield, who is a trumpeters' trumpeter, was in good, fussy form, and Fontana was superior. But perhaps the most inspirational news about the W.G.J.B. is Bob Wilber, who in the past year has developed an impassioned and original style on the soprano saxophone that comes close to matching the melodic affluence of his old teacher, Sidney Bechet. Most good jazz musicians start faltering at forty; Wilber stopped faltering at forty. The Gibson package at the Downbeat has other surprises. Also on hand are Maxine Sullivan, elfin and gray-haired and beautiful and in perfect, miniature Billie Holiday voice, and Joe Venuti, the wild, irrepressible seventy-year-old violinist whom Gibson tracked down a year or two ago after a long search. (Venuti stories are legion, and one of the best that Gibson tells has to do with a drummer who walked out on Venuti one night years ago. In revenge, Venuti filled the drums left behind with sand and shipped them to the drummer collect. The bass drum alone weighed six hundred pounds.) Most impresarios who have marketed jazz have been businessmen disguised as aficionados. Gibson is both.

## Richard Gibson (2)

I arrived in Denver on a Thursday afternoon in mid-September of 1969 to attend the preliminaries of Richard Gibson's seventh annual subscription jazz party, which begins on Friday at five-thirty in Aspen and ends on Sunday at six. All the news about the party that has filtered East in recent years has been good. A highly considered musician who has played it four times has said that the music "ranges from the excellent to the exceptional." Moreover, in the process of hiring his musicians for this year's party, Gibson has brought out of near-oblivion not only Joe Venuti and Maxine Sullivan but also Ernie Caceres, a fine and long-underrated baritone saxophonist, and Cliff Leeman, a former big-band drummer with an effortless, metronomic beat. Most important, Gibson persuaded Red Norvo to appear at the party in 1968, when Norvo, deeply troubled by hearing problems, had decided to quit music. Norvo and the rest of Gibson's reclamations have been working ever since.

Gibson met me at the airport. He is a fast-moving, fast-talking, enveloping man who is given to superlatives and laughter, and who favors sneakers and open-neck shirts. We take a car to his house in Denver, and he talks about the party: "I gave my first jazz party in 1963. My wife, Maddie, and I were sitting around our living room one night having a drink, and she asked me if I missed New York, where we lived until eight or so years ago. I said all I missed were the ocean and jazz. I couldn't do a damned thing about the ocean, but maybe I could do something about jazz, and so the idea of the party sprang full-panoplied that night. We wrote letters to everybody we knew in Colorado, and at first the response was poor but I brought in ten musicians from New York and we held the first party, with about two hundred guests, over a September weekend in the old Hotel Jerome in Aspen. We charged fifty dollars a couple. The next year, we had eighteen musicians and two hundred and seventy-five guests, and we charged eighty-five a couple, but the party didn't really catch on until the following year, when we had twenty-three musicians and over three hundred guests. It was awesome how bereft Colorado was of jazz. Most Coloradians had never heard, let alone seen, a jazz musician. We kept the party in Aspen four years, and when the Jerome was shut down for legal reasons we moved to Vail, a new ski resort about a hundred miles away. Now the place we played in in Vail is padlocked and we're going back to the Jerome. Even though I charge a hundred dollars a couple now, I lose several thousand a year on the party, but that's my privilege. It's meant to be strictly a *players'* party, and the audience is there only as a necessity, as a kind of warming mirror for the musicians. Aspen is a perfect place, and I'm hung up on it. It's away from everything, and it has wit, beauty, imagination. The people who live there are very individualistic. It provides the ambience for what I want, which is an isolated experience—an experience that is intense and extraordinary and that when it is over takes on a did-it-really-happen? dream quality for all the participants. The musicians—I simply choose the ones I know and like—react accordingly. Nobody loafs, because they sense that it is something special, that it's their party. Yet they have *time* to have a hangover or a bellyache or to waste a set. I decide who plays with whom in each set, and generally the musicians don't know who will be on the stand until they get up there. Marvellous surprises result. And the audience reacts in turn. Few people leave the room during the music, they are quiet, almost nobody gets drunk, and when the party ends, on Sunday, they scream for more. This year we'll have about five hundred people, including paying guests, guests of the party, and thirty-three musicians. Roughly half the guests are coming from Colorado and the rest from Sweden and Rome and Mexico and Toronto and from a good twenty or thirty states, including Hawaii, and I'm bringing Phil Woods, the alto player, from Paris."

Gibson lives in an old section of Denver, on the sort of mean but opulent street that turn-of-the-century *nouveau-riche* Americans exulted in. The street is narrow and heavily guarded by tall Chinese elms, and both sides are lined by mud-colored brick-and-stone mansions set shoulder to shoulder and decked out with massive eaves and high stoops. The inside of Gibson's house, with its dark, hand-carved panelling, parquet floors, distant ceilings, and stone solarium, is equally formidable. But every room is filled with musicians when we get there, and they have a cheering, softening effect. Teddy Wilson, sitting at the kitchen table and drinking a beer, talks about the late Coleman Hawkins' love for the unexpected, the unplanned. Bob Wilber, in tennis clothes, trots through the foyer, which is piled with musical instruments. Phil Woods is in the living room telling Joe Venuti, who is just back from a round of golf, that a cop, mistaking him for a hippie because of his long hair and Mod dress, grabbed him backstage at this year's Newport Jazz Festival, and that Dick Gibson, standing nearby, grabbed the cop and in turn was grabbed by another cop. Al Cohn and Zoot Sims are upstairs playing a tumultuous game of pool. Maddie Gibson, slender and brown-haired and attractive, moves from room to room, and the four Gibson children, ranging in age from fourteen to six, are underfoot everywhere. There is a pot of beef stew on the stove, and liquor bottles forest a small pantry. Maddie Gibson announces that everyone has been invited to the Flanagans', at the opposite end of the block, for cocktails and a buffet supper, and around six-thirty the migration begins. Musicians pour out of the Gibson house and out of half a dozen other houses, where the Gibsons' neighbors are putting them up. Zoot Sims, whose flowing hair and gap-toothed smile and bowsprit features give him a kindly Rasputin look, runs down the front steps, grabs a child's bicycle from against a tree, and pedals furiously up and down the sidewalk, his knees up to his ears, his hair standing out behind. An onlooker snaps a picture of him from across the street, and waves to the Gibsons. The Flanagan mansion, a forty-two-room behemoth, is already filled with tailored, glacéed Denverites. Seven or eight musicians, among them Toots Thielemans, Dave McKenna, Larry Ridley, Gus Johnson, and Woods are playing at one end of an enormous living room. The party is loose-jointed. After supper Mrs. John Love, the Governor's wife, takes a chair in front of the band, and is immediately surrounded by acolytes. People stretch out on the floor, digging the music, and once in a while a child shoots down the bannister of the main stairs, sails into the living room, and collapses on the floor. Musicians wander in, play, and are replaced, but there aren't many sparks, and around eleven the music peters out. Gibson spreads the word that the bus for Aspen will leave from in front of his house at ten sharp the next morning.

The bus trip takes six hours, including a lunch stopover in Vail and it is hair-raising. It begins with a grammar-school-outing air. We have gone only a few blocks when Gus Johnson shouts, "Stop the bus! Stop the bus! I forgot my teethbrush!" which provokes loud hilarity. And just before we board, Joe Venuti, round and implacable and cement-voiced, poses straight-faced for photographs in a derby jammed so far down on his head it splays out his ears and pushes his glasses halfway down his nose. Laughing musicians are all over the sidewalk. Around eleven o'clock we begin the long climb to Loveland Pass, which is just under twelve thousand feet. We move at twenty miles an hour because of our load, and once we are above the timberline we wind endlessly along a narrow two-lane road, the mountains rearing up on our left and bottomless chasms falling away on our right. "They don't put any guardrails on this road because of the snow-plows," Teddy Wilson says offhandedly. "This way, they just push the snow off the edge." Gus Johnson moans, "Oh, man, why did I have to sit on *this* side?" and someone else shouts, "Don't look up! Don't look up!" Gibson, sitting near the front and verbally spurring the driver on, laughs and says, "Funny things happen on these weekends. Billy Butterfield, the trumpeter, can get very excited, and when he does he's apt to bite. He bit Zoot Sims one night in my living room in Denver, and Zoot said to me later, 'You know, Dick, I can't figure it out. When he bit me, it hurt like hell, but he didn't leave any marks. Do you think his teeth are made of rubber?' And once when we were flying back to Denver after the party with the musicians on Sunday night and bumping the hell all over the place, I noticed Cliff Leeman sitting there in the dark and rubbing Noxzema all over his face. He didn't know anybody was watching him. Then he took out a big alarm clock and set it and put it in front of him, and the moment the wheels touched ground it went off, and he said, 'Right on time,' wiped his face, and got up. There have been spooky times, too. A couple of years back, we took the bus home on Sunday, and when we got to Loveland Pass, which is just ahead, we were hit by a flash snowstorm. There had been an accident moments before in the pass, and it was completely blocked. I was terrified, but I don't think any of the musicians knew what was happening. There we were, with very little air to breathe and a lot of aging musicians, and I thought, 'God, what if we're trapped up here five or six hours, how many of these great old men will keel over?' It was the worst moment of my life. Well, they cleared the wreck in half an hour, and, miraculously, we were on our way."

We grind through Loveland Pass, escorted by a mountain bluebird, and roar down toward Vail. We heel the wrong way into hairpin turns ("She won't tip over," the driver says, turning all the way around and smiling. "She just feels that way"), flush beautiful black-billed magpies, and yaw and bounce over straight bumpy stretches, like a jet landing too fast on a poor field. I keep my imaginary brake pedal pressed flat on the floor. But we make it to the hotel at five, and on the dot of five-thirty the party begins.

A bandstand has been set up in a corner of the Jeromes' dining room, which is small and high-ceilinged and already filled with guests. The room is homogenized Victorian (red wallpaper, globe chandeliers, transparent scalloped drapes) and the audience homogenized Nixonian (blazers, frosted hair, tweeds). Hard-core jazz fans tend to be an absorbed, nervous lot, given to skinniness or fat, and there are sprinklings in the room. Gibson greets his guests briefly over a microphone and pulls the first set out of his hat—Bob Wilber, Lou McGarity, Yank Lawson, Bud Freeman, Dave McKenna, Bob Haggart, and Sol Gubin—and we are back at Nick's again. Teddy Wilson, accompanied by Jack Lesberg and Cliff Leeman, who gives a fascinating exhibition of faking on the fast tempos, pedals easily through the next set (all the sets, it turns out, are about half an hour long), and he is followed by a group made up of Clark Terry, Woods, Kai Winding, Sims, McKenna, Ridley, and Johnson. A neo-bebop head of steam is built up, and during the second number, a funny, swaying "Donkey Serenade," Sims plays the first of what is to be, during the weekend, an astonishing number of driving, beautiful solos. He begins in "Donkey Serenade" gently, like a good tutor beginning the morning's lessons, and works his way into an ascending five-note phrase, breaks it off, repeats the phrase, breaks it off again, repeats it, and then effortlessly finishes it with half a dozen perfect ascending notes which fall off into a fast, turning run. Ben Webster growls and flutter notes creep in, and Sims closes with a drawn-out wail. McKenna, a huge, lowering man who often constructs crashing, two-handed solos down in the dark lower registers, flies off Sims' catapult, and the set ends with a fast "Perdido" driven by Sims, Woods, and McKenna. Gibson spins his lottery wheel and out come Bobby Hackett, Peanuts Hucko, Al Cohn, Carl Fontana, Ralph Sutton, Milt Hinton, and Morey Feld. The set is lighted largely by a silver Hackett solo, in "In a Mellow Tone," and the first concert is rounded out by a group consisting of Billy Butterfield, Matty Matlock, Caceres, Vic Dickenson, Lou Stein, Lesberg, and Johnson. Butterfield is irresistible in his solo and in the closing ensemble of "Swing That Music," and Caceres ambles easily around in a medium-tempo "Rose Room." It is eight o'clock, and dinner is a ravenous prospect.

The proceedings resume at ten o'clock in the Red Onion, a dark, rambling, low-ceilinged night club and restaurant three blocks from the Jerome. There are seven sets in all, starting with a Lawson-McGarity-Wilber-Freeman-Bucky Pizzarelli-Haggart-Sutton-Leeman group and ending with a Butterfield-Winding-Wilber-Caceres-Cohn-Thielemans-Hinton-Stein-Gubin group. After a time, I feel I'm watching a long freight slock slowly by, and it is a relief when originality and invention break through. This happens in "Lazy River," when Wilber, on soprano saxophone, plays two majestic choruses, and it happens again in "Now's the Time," when Thielemans, on amplified harmonica, lets loose chorus after swirling chorus, each full of good, odd notes and neo–Charlie Parker phrases. His exuberance strains his instrument to the point at which it loses identifiable tone, and the music, freed of instrumental limitations, suddenly seems absolutely pure. Sims, working with a Fontana-Cohn-Terry-Woods phalanx, gets off a champion solo in "Lester Leaps In," and Venuti, in company with Hucko and Norvo, plays a stamping "Sweet Georgia Brown." (By this time something awful has happened to the sound system, and Norvo's vibraharp becomes inextricably entwined with Stein's piano, producing a new, ear-shattering instrument, the vibrapiano.) Caceres, playing a lolling solo in "In a Mellow Tone," provides the evening's final stimulation. We have been treated today to six and a half hours of music, and almost ten hours are scheduled for tomorrow. But Gibson, hustling around and scribbling personnels on a thick sheaf of papers, appears tireless, and so does Maddie Gibson, who, ceaselessly nodding her head all evening, never drops a beat.

Gibson is right; Aspen has it. The air is thin and sweet and clear, and everything is unbelievably peaceful. We are in the lacuna between Aspen's summer cultural bustle and the skiing season. There are no traffic lights, and the wide, empty streets line away and disappear at the foot of the mountains. The buildings, low and well-spaced, look as if they have sprouted from the ground, and they range from weird, almost geometric sandstone or brick structures put up in the eighteen-eighties and nineties to new no-nonsense condominiums. (Aspen has successively been a gold-mining town, a ghost town, a silver-mining town, a ghost town, a cattle town, a ghost town, and a ski resort. Aspen will probably never be destitute again, for its skiing is now widely regarded as the best in the country.) Mountains ring the town, which is eight thousand feet up, and they lean back, letting in a nonstop Wagnerian show of mint-white clouds, black thunderheads, and topless blue skies. There are hippies around, and a few ten-gallons, but dogs seem to run the place. They're of every size and description, and they lounge on the corners, crisscross the streets, block doorways, snooze on bar floors, and wait in heaps in their owners' parked jeeps. Like most politicians, they ignore each other but bark a lot.

The music starts Saturday at quarter to one. The dining room is jammed, so I find a seat at the back of a bleacherlike platform set up in the lobby. The acoustics are surrealistic. Most of the music that squeezes out of the dining-room door is lost in the lobby, which is almost as high as the main concourse of Grand Central and is full of jabbering musicians. Butterfield, Matlock, Sims, Fontana, Dick Hyman, Ridley, and Leeman take the stand, and Butterfield and Sims are faultless, in a down, searching way, in "Willow Weep for Me." In the next set, Gibson's mix-'em-up tactics pay off. He puts Wilber and Caceres together with a rhythm section. The tonal similarities and differences of the two horns are fascinating, and the two men, clearly digging one another, play intense duet ensembles ("Poor Butterfly," "Rosetta"), rubbing along contrapuntally, letting an octave or two of air in between them, harmonizing briefly, and throwing off pleasant dissonances. Their solos form an unbroken flow of ideas and seem the work of one man, and they close with a slow, affecting "New Orleans." A Lawson–McGarity–Freeman–Hucko Nicksieland set jounces by, and Teddy Wilson, backed by Hinton and Bert Dahlander, a longtime associate of Wilson who now lives hereabouts, slides through half a dozen Gershwin tunes. I lose most of it in the hubbub, but manage to catch a medium-slow wire-brush solo by Dahlander that is full of easy staccato patterns and humming cymbals. Cohn joins Wilson for a couple of numbers, and there is a good set by Hackett, Matlock, and Dickenson, who is funny on a fast "Sweet Georgia Brown" and sinuous and moody on an unfamiliar ballad. (Most unfamiliar ballads have open-ended titles like "Here We Are Now" or "Tomorrow Will Be" or "If You Only Could.") It is four o'clock, and the ninth set has Sims and Fontana and rhythm. (Zoot is fond of Fontana, who is a brilliant trombonist. Yesterday, after lunch in Vail, Sims was wandering back to the bus ten or so feet behind Fontana, and, passing a parked jeep without a cap on its gas tank, he leaned over and called into the pipe, "Hello, Carl.") The set equals the Wilber-Caceres duet. There is a fast "Man I Love," with good solos by all, Fontana picks his way delicately through "The Shadow of Your Smile," and Sims plays an aching "Gee Baby, Ain't I Good to You?" The World's Greatest Jazz Band (Lawson, Butterfield, Wilber, Freeman, McGarity, Fontana, Sutton, Haggart, Johnson) closes the afternoon, and Butterfield and Lawson play a fine growling-and-moaning duet in "St. James Infirmary." The festivities are to resume at nine-thirty at the Onion.

Gibson's whim tonight is black tie, and everybody looks like a swell, Aspen being basically a gum-boot-and-lumberjacket town. Five sets step by, and it is puzzling why Gibson keeps them so short. The party, he says, belongs to the musicians, but when musicians hit a groove they like to stretch out—an indulgence generally forbidden in night clubs and at festivals and in recording studios. The five sets are notable only for two Wilber choruses on "Crazy Rhythm," for Sutton's solo rendition of a rare Bix Beiderbecke piano piece, "In the Dark," and for Fontana's playing with Winding and rhythm. Fontana is gentle, meticulous, lyrical, and subtle on all three numbers, and Winding, a bravura performer, must feel superfluous. Then the remarkable Venuti, accompanied by Hinton, Stein, and Feld, comes on. He is a first-class violinist who carries off his technique with humor and imagination (one celebrated device: he unhooks the frog on his bow, puts the bow stick beneath the violin and the bow hairs across the strings, and rehooks the frog, which enables him to play all four strings at once). His ideas never cease, and he swings unbelievably hard for a musician who came up in the twenties and early thirties, when jazz was still finding its rhythmic legs. He warms up with a fast "I Want to Be Happy," and in a blues he uses his four-strings technique, producing all sorts of dark, marvellous chords. Then Sims unexpectedly appears from backstage. Venuti roars into "I Found a New Baby," carrying the melody while Sims plays close counterpoint. Each man solos with exhilarating fervor, and the two go into a long series of four-bar exchanges in which Sims plays astonishingly hot and funny parodic figures. The final ensemble, jammed as hard as any collective improvised passage ever played, is unique, for the two instruments are so close tonally and melodically and rhythmically that they sound like one instrument split in half and at war with itself. The number ends, and Ira Gitler, an editor of *down beat*, appropriately shouts "Jazz ecstasy!" Sims retires, Venuti and McGarity play a polite duet, and Venuti, just before unpacking "I Got Rhythm," calls out, "Where's Zootie? Where's my Zootie?" Sims reappears, and the two just about match their first performance. We cool off for the rest of the evening with the World's Greatest Jazz Band; a Norvo-Hucko set, which is drowned by Morey Feld's flashy, unsteady drumming ("His girlfriend was in the audience," a musician explains the next day); and a good, funny version of Dizzy Gillespie's "Ow!" by Terry, Woods, Wilber, and Caceres. The Venuti-Sims explosion neatly imposes form on the weekend: two days to reach the peak, and one to get back down.

I have seen something yesterday and today that I have never seen before. At the end of nearly every set, the musicians smile and shake hands with each other.

After breakfast on Sunday, I run into Gibson in the lobby. He is wearing the guest badges for all seven jazz parties on the left side of his shirt, and he looks like a five-star general. We sit down, and I ask him to tell me about himself. "Well, I was born in Mobile, Alabama, and I was an only child. My father, a strange, witty, secret man, left when I was three to work in a brokerage house in New York, and my mother left not long after to be one of the early supervisors of hostesses for what was to become American Airlines. So I was raised largely by my maternal grandparents. At seventeen I joined the Marines, was wounded, and was out in a year. Public Law 16 enabled me to go right through the University of Alabama, where I got a degree in psychology and played left end on the football team. Then I hung around, taught a little creative writing, coached football, and ran the university's white-rat lab. One day I looked in the mirror—I guess I was twenty-four—and asked myself what the hell I was doing, and a week later I was in New York, beating the streets for a job. I ended up a space salesman for *Town & Country*, and went on the *Herald Tribune*, where I became the financial manager. That led to a vice-presidency with the Lehman Corporation. The last couple of years there got to be meaningless; I made a lot of money but spent every cent, and the commuting was an endless nettle. One two-degrees-below-zero morning I was waiting for the eight-two or whatever it was at the Larchmont station, and a railroad man came ambling down the tracks and said, 'It ain't coming today.' Well, *it* had run off the tracks in Stamford or somewhere. I thought, 'Somebody is trying to tell me something.' I went home and called my office and said I wasn't coming in, and the next day I quit. I searched the country, looking for both the best investment-banking firm and the best place to live, and Boettcher & Company and Denver won, both of which led to my involvement with the Water Pik. A Denver friend told me about this contraption a man had invented and was manufacturing in the basement of a bungalow in Fort Collins, which is sixty miles north of Denver, and that he was looking for financial backing. I knew enough about investment banking to know that you never loan money to inventors, but I drove up for a look. Four people were turning out several hundred of these strange boxes a year, and the place looked like Santa Claus's workshop gone wild. They gave me one, and I put it on a closet shelf and forgot about it. Well, it turned out that my gums were in bad shape and I was in grave danger of losing my front teeth. I came across the Water Pik one Saturday afternoon and started using it twice a day. When I went to my dentist five or six weeks later, he was astounded. My gums were perfect and my teeth saved. I found a president, Al Kuske, who is probably the finest businessman in the country, for the company, raised some money, and eventually quit Boettcher and became an executive vice-president of Water Pik. Everything went so well that the whole works was sold two years ago to a conglomerate for twenty-three million dollars. Now, at last, I'm doing exactly what I want to do, and I'm consumed with it. My life is devoted to getting the World's Greatest Jazz Band on its feet, and to related, even more important matters, and there's nothing surprising about this, because the single, constant, gathering thread in my life has been my love for jazz. In fact, my addiction, predilection, immersion in jazz precedes my memory. There was a colored settlement around the corner from where I was raised, and I can't recall the first time I went over there. Maybe it was 1930. The houses didn't have electricity, and I can still remember the smell of the candles."

Maddie Gibson appears, and her party badges are pinned across the front of her waist. She takes Gibson away on urgent business. The final session is to start at quarter to one at the Red Onion. A musician outside the Onion door says, "Man, I don't know if I'll make this next year. It's *too* much music. After the first half hour, the audience starts listening with its eyes, and even the musicians go off to the bar or take a walk when they're not up there." There are ten sets, but the shadows of Venuti and Sims are everywhere, and the few bright spots are provided by Wilber in "Beale Street Blues," by a handsome Hackett-Dickenson set and a driving Sims-Cohn set, and by a lucid, calm Woods in "Here's That Rainy Day." Norvo, badgered by one thing and another all weekend, finally comes into his own with an exquisite, ad-lib version of "The Girl from Ipanema." The fifteen musicians still on the premises climb up on the stand for the last number and boom their way through "The Saints Go Marching In." The crowd screams for more, and the party is done.

The musicians' bus, half empty now, leaves the Jerome on Monday around ten-thirty, but I fly back to Denver over the Rockies in a little two-engine Cessna. We spend most of the flight in a snowstorm, stirred from below by peaks, and we get up to seventeen thousand feet. The oxygen mask feels good. Then we slide out of the soup and down over brown, sunny plains and into Denver, back from Shangri-La.

# THE SEVENTIES

# 1970

## Big Bands

**A** paradox: the big-band era is supposedly gone, but there are more good big jazz bands around than ever before. These include, in addition to the Ellington, Basie, and Herman Institutes, the newer Don Ellis and Buddy Rich bands, Ray Charles's generally overlooked big groups, the so-called "rehearsal" bands of Thad Jones–Mel Lewis, Clark Terry, Duke Pearson, Frank Foster, and Bill Berry, the television-network studio bands (most of whose members moonlight in the rehearsal bands), and some of the college "stage" bands (the awesome University of Illinois band, for one). Ellington and Basie have largely maintained their standards; the rest are in every way superior to the nostalgia-ridden progenitors. They are more schooled, they are freer and sounder rhythmically, their arrangements are more imaginative, and their soloists are rarely less than excellent. They are what first-rate big jazz bands should be: exciting, delicate continuums of fine soloists and inspired ensembles. The big jazz-oriented bands of the thirties and forties (Ellington and Basie excepted) formed a conservative closed-circuit operation (a lot of the pioneering jazz musicians of the time, such as Art Tatum and Coleman Hawkins and Roy Eldridge, made up a parallel movement, and the two rarely converged), while the present big jazz bands are open, adventurous aggregations that use the best available soloists, the best of what the jazz revolutionaries are up to, the best arrangers, and the best of variants like rock, the *bossa nova*, and country-and-Western. That many of these bands do not work steadily is (except economically, of course) a blessing: as non-profit, self-pleasing groups, they are free of one-nighters, fads, and commercialism—the three bugbears of the old big bands.

The Thad Jones–Mel Lewis band at the Village Vanguard recently confirmed all this. But it was a surprise, too, for the Vanguard, where the band has been appearing on Monday nights since its formation over four years ago, was packed with the sort of alert, with-it people one found there when Mort Sahl and Nichols and May first came to town. The Thad Jones–Mel Lewis group is expert and roistering. Its arrangements, replete with handsome voicings and harmonies, are pretty much overrun by the soloists. Pepper Adams, the baritone saxophonist, went on for chorus after chorus in a nervous, I've-got-to-get-this-out fashion in an up-tempo number, "Once Around," and so did Roland Hanna, who constructed a brilliant piano solo made up of difficult simultaneously ascending and descending chords. Richard Davis, the bassist, took over Bob Brookmeyer's arrangement of Fats Waller's "Willow Tree" and, as is his way, was both sensational and stone-cold. Unfortunately, Jones was heard but briefly, and Mickey Roker, Mel

Lewis' replacement for the evening, foundered in the sheer mass of the band's sound.

Sy Oliver, the principal arranger for Jimmy Lunceford and Tommy Dorsey between 1933 and the late forties, is holding a retrospective of his work at the Downbeat with the help of a nine-piece group that includes two trumpets, two trombones, two reeds, and three rhythm. The Lunceford band, which flourished between 1930 and 1947, the year Lunceford died, has long been regarded as one of the four or five great big bands. As such, it resembles certain works of the imagination that, raised to false eminence, eventually appear invulnerable. To be sure, the Lunceford band was remarkably precise (its personnel changed very little during its best days, and its saxophone section often rehearsed, voluntarily, for hours at a time), some of its arrangements were ingenious (Oliver's "Organ Grinder's Swing"), it had humor and flavor, it was danceable, and it was a good show band. But it was not a great jazz band. (Compare it to Ellington and Basie, or even to Cab Calloway, Andy Kirk, and Benny Carter.) It used static two-beat rhythms, or a four-four beat that tended to sag or stampede. It was an arranger's band, an ensemble band, which favored florid saxophone writing (contrast Ellington's, Carter's, and Mary Lou Williams'), brass-bound trombone and trumpet figures, and section work that resembled thunderheads shouldering through the sky. Its novelty numbers, often built around a vocal trio, moved between parody and the maudlin, suggesting that the Lunceford band was the first and only all-black Mickey Mouse band. Its up-tempo instrumentals were windy and unswinging. And the band's soloists, in the cramped spaces granted them, were rarely better than mediocre. (Compare their astonishing counterparts in the Ellington and Basie bands.) Sy Oliver had a lot to do with all this, and later he had a lot to do with the metallic, Germanic quality of the Tommy Dorsey band, which became the white counterpart of the Lunceford band.

The band Oliver has at the Downbeat is a remarkable replica of the Lunceford band. It is precise, funny, maudlin, clever, and unswinging. The arrangements are stripped-down versions of the originals, and such numbers as "Margie," "Four or Five Times," "Yes Indeed!" "Cheatin' on Me," and "Ain't She Sweet" are full of soupy saxophones, bruiting trombones, and sticky rhythm. But there is an interloper in the band—a young tenor saxophonist, Bobby Jones, who, every time he soloed tonight, converted the group into a jazz band. A close student of Zoot Sims, he was particularly memorable in a long two-beat version of "Stardust"; using high notes, tumbling arpeggios, and big-bellied melodic bursts, he managed the old Chaplin trick of being both funny and moving.

Late in the evening, my head full of cute muted trumpets (another Oliver trademark) and toy-soldier rhythms, I went over to the Roosevelt Grill for the final moments of Bobby Hackett's quintet (Vic Dickenson, Dave McKenna, Jack Lesberg, Cliff Leeman), which will soon be dissolved when

Dickenson replaces Kai Winding in the World's Greatest Jazz Band (which will give the group *three* worthy soloists) and the rare Benny Morton replaces Dickenson in Hackett's group. Hackett and Dickenson together are the Jack Sprats of jazz. Hackett is cool, golden, and mathematical, and Dickenson is hot, shaggy, and funny, and between them they encompass most of what is worth knowing about jazz.

Bill Berry's new rehearsal band will be appearing at the Roosevelt Grill for a few more Sunday afternoons. Roughly half the band is made up of the Merv Griffin studio band, and present this afternoon, along with Berry, a brilliant trumpeter, were the equally brilliant trombonist Bill Watrous, Richie Kamuca on tenor saxophone, George Dorsey on alto saxophone (he is also in Sy Oliver's Downbeat band), Dave Frishberg on piano, and Jake Hanna, who was subbing for the drummer, Sol Gubin. The band's arrangements, which generally reflect Ellington or latter-day Basie, are by Al Cohn, John Bunch, Berry, Billy Byers, and Roger Pemberton. It is a light, precise, aggressive band, and its soloists are often stunning. Watrous is spectacular. He is a multi-noted performer in the manner of J. J. Johnson, but there is nothing predictable or glacéed in his work. He uses high notes, wild smears, intense, jumbling Dickie Wells phrases, and he can juggle the beat any way he chooses. Frishberg, an eclectic pianist whose style is completely his own, has been lurking superbly around New York for years, and he was exceptional this afternoon. And so was Berry, whose long solo in "Stella by Starlight" was a marvel of construction, lyricism, and invention. But most commanding of all was Hanna, who drove the Woody Herman band in the early sixties. His time is impeccable, as are his taste and sense of dynamics, and he has the airborne, propelling beat that only drummers like Dave Tough and Sid Catlett had. (Part of this is due to his having refreshingly resurrected the Chinese cymbal.) I doubt that Berry's band would be the same without him.

# Duo

Jim Hall and Eddie Gomez opened tonight in a new place at Tenth Avenue and Fifty-first Street called the Guitar. It turns out to be a small neighborhood bar that has been attractively refurbished by a black lawyer named Fred Hayes. There are no microphones, but you can hear, as well as see, from anywhere in the house. One of the wonders of jazz is how musicians of sympathetic bent who may never have played together can, without rehearsals and with little verbal communication, sit down and produce rich and indivisible music, which is exactly what happened tonight. In most of the numbers Hall started with an a-cappella chorus, soft and out-of-rhythm, and shifted into four-four time. Gomez entered from below, playing a countermelody and gradually increasing his volume. The two instruments then wove intricately around one another for a couple of choruses, building considerable rhythmic tension. Then Hall soloed, while Gomez "walked" behind him. Hall backed a Gomez solo with quiet, on-the-beat chords or with pushing off-beat puffs. In the final ensemble the two men sank into the marrow of the melody, turning around and around inside it, and then surfaced easily and brightly in the last four bars. Hall has always been a light, clean guitarist who has shied away from the multi-noted garrulity of most of his colleagues, but for a long time there was a studied, almost static quality to his playing. His phrases tended to come out in lumps, and he did not always swing. Now he flows continually. His phrases are still short and lucid, but they are full of sudden, intense figures that catch one unawares, they swing evenly and confidently, and they are invariably affecting. Gomez, who is just twenty-six, often plays his notes a fraction below pitch, with a sliding sound, and he plays with a steady passion that in at least one number, "Body and Soul," became almost frenzied. The two men fashioned a rarity—a *totally* improvised music, grounded in easy, impeccable musicianship.

## Mexican Bankroll

Johnny Hodges died yesterday at the age of sixty-three. (Ironically, he was stricken not on the road, where he spent most of his life, but in a dentist's chair in New York.) For thirty-eight years he sat stone-faced in the front row of the Ellington band, his eyes hooded, his parrot nose pointed straight ahead, or, if he was tired, which he was most of the time, with his eyes closed and his head resting on his right hand. Then, when Ellington called on him to solo, he would get up slowly (it seemed to take forever, though he was only about five and a half feet tall), roll like a sailor to the front of the stage, give Ellington a quick, ferocious look for having disturbed him, and start to play. And out would come one of the most lyrical and eloquent sounds of the century. His style, buffeted by several musical revolutions and by the brief ascendancy of Charlie Parker, never changed. His slow ballads, often written by the late Billy Strayhorn, were full of feline sotto-voce phrases, silken pauses, and those celebrated and astonishing glissandos, which fell dangerously but perfectly through a couple of octaves like a diver sailing off a hundred-foot cliff. When he played the blues, which he loved, he suddenly stepped out of this finery and became a rocking, down-home performer. He was one of the pillars as well as one of the pinnacles of the Ellington band, which will never sound quite the same again, and no one knew where his genius came from. Hodges, who, when he talked at all, talked about baseball and Westerns, never let on, even to his oldest friend, Harry Carney, who once said, "Johnny and I grew up on the same street in Dorchester, Mass., and we saw each other just about every day. We exchanged records and we'd copy choruses from Fletcher Henderson and Sidney Bechet and the Hot Five. Then he left home, and when he came back, a year or so later, he was a big-timer. He had a Mexican bankroll—that's a big bill on the outside that covers a roll of ones—and Bechet had given him one of his soprano saxophones. But he picked up his playing on his own. He could always play; I guess it was a natural gift."

## The Duke

I recently spent a good part of a day following Duke Ellington around the city. New York *is* Ellington's home (he keeps an apartment on West End Avenue), but he is here only a couple of times a year, and when he is, his schedule tends to be even heavier than it is on the road.

I met him around three-thirty in the afternoon at the National Recording Studios at Fifty-sixth and Fifth, where he was to record part of the music for a ballet commissioned by the American Ballet Theatre. The ballet is called "The River," and will be given its première at the New York State Theatre at Lincoln Center on the twenty-fifth of June. He greeted me with his French two-kisses-on-each-cheek and said, "What time did I call you last night?"

"Around twelve-thirty," I replied.

"I didn't get to bed until ten this morning, what with working on the ballet. I'm tired, babe, tired."

But he looked extremely well, and even his working clothes—an old blue sweater, rumpled gray slacks, and blue suède shoes—looked good. He went immediately into the recording booth, which, like most of the places Ellington goes, was crowded with relatives, friends, and hangers-on. Present were Stanley Dance, the critic and one of Ellington's right-hand men; Michael James, Ellington's nephew and an aide; Joe Morgen, his press agent; an admirer of thirty-five years' standing named Edmund Anderson; and a couple of admiring women. Ellington examined some sheet music and went out into the studio. He spoke to several members of the band and got loud laughs in response and, standing in the center of the studio, said, just before the first take, "We're going to get lucky on this one. Derum, derum, derum! One, two, three, four!" Rufus Jones started a rapid machine-gun beat on his snare drum, which was echoed on a glockenspiel and on timpani. The band came in, and the piece, called "The Falls," turned out to be unlike anything I had heard Ellington do. But then nothing new of his is quite like anything he has done before. The section passages of "The Falls" are brief but dense and booting, there are solo parts by Paul Gonsalves, and there are heavy, dissonant full-band chords. And all this is done against the furious *rat-tat-tat-tat* of the snare, the glockenspiel, and the timpani. It is exciting, tight crescendo music, and it reminded me of early Stravinsky, except that it was unmistakably a jazz composition. Ellington conducted (Wild Bill Davis sat in on piano), using the traditional upside-down-T-square motions in a slow, wooden way, as if he were swimming through molasses. All the while he chewed on something and rocked his head from side to side.

While the piece was played back, he sat in the recording booth with his head bowed, his eyes closed, and a hand on each knee. He looked up when it was over. "A waterfall—you can always *see* the top and you can always *hear* the bottom," he said. "So you've got the top and the bottom, and you can put anything you want in between."

He returned to the studio, and Anderson said, "Last November, I shot some film of the band in Paris. Afterward I told Johnny Hodges, who in all the thirty-five years I knew him never said more than two words, 'I got some great footage of you tonight.' He shouted at me, 'Not tonight! Not tonight! My eyes looked so bad!' Which was all the more amazing when you consider that on the stand Hodges kept his eyes closed most of the time."

Ellington led the band through six or seven more takes until he got the right one, and after a break he went to work on a part of the ballet called "The Mother." It is slow and ruminative, and includes a lovely flute solo by Norris Turney. Again, there were several takes and the session ended at six-thirty. Ellington made some phone calls, kissed several women hello and goodbye, and, surrounded by Morgen, Dance, and a friend who was driving for Ellington, a broad-shouldered Greek named Chris Stamatiou, left the studios for the City Center to talk with Alvin Ailey, who is choreographing "The River."

Down on Fifth Avenue, Ellington asked Stamatiou where his car was, and Stamatiou said in a garage around the corner. Ellington asked him how far it was to the City Center, and he said a block or so—an easy walk. "You mean you want me to *walk* a block? Well, I might as well, but it'll be the longest walk I've had in years," Ellington said. He started west on Fifty-sixth Street, moving in the determined, stiff way of older men with tired feet. He got a lot of double takes, and whenever he passed a garage or a restaurant with its complement of New York early-evening sidewalk loungers, he was greeted with, "Hey, Duke!" or "Mr. *Ellington*!" Each time, he looked interested and said, "How you been?" or "How's everything?" and shook hands as if he were greeting friends he hadn't seen in twenty-five years. He went in the back door of the City Center and up to the sixth floor, where he sat down abruptly with Ailey at a small table by the elevator door. They talked for twenty minutes, and then went down to wait for Stamatiou and the car. They continued talking, but the car didn't come, and after fifteen minutes Dance called the garage and found out that the car had broken down. Ellington kissed Ailey goodbye, and we got into a cab and headed downtown. It was about seven-thirty.

"We're going to the Half Note," Dance said. "Hugues Panassié's son Louis is in the country making some sort of film on jazz, and he asked Duke if he would mind coming down to the Half Note to be in a short sequence."

Ellington, who sat next to the taxi-driver, a young, bearded man, pulled a bright scarf out of his pocket and knotted it around his head turban-fashion. The driver, peering at Ellington out of the corner of his eye, missed a crucial right-hand turn at Dominick Street, and the Holland Tunnel appeared.

Ellington asked Morgen if he knew where the hell they were going, and Morgen said he had seen the Dominick Street turn just after we passed it. The driver made a hundred-and-eighty-degree swing in front of the Tunnel and stopped a moment later at the Half Note. Ellington took off his scarf and got out.

Inside, Ellington gave Panassié, an engaging man in his thirties, the *de-rigueur* greeting and asked him what to do. Panassié said he would like him to sit at the bar for a few minutes and answer a couple of questions. Mike Canterino, one of the owners of the Half Note, gave Ellington a Coke, and, bathed in blinding light, he sat down on a bar stool. "You know, I'm not really dressed for this sort of thing, but let me light a cigarette, so I'll look sophisticated," he said. He knocked over the Coke and said, "Oh, my! I'm the only nuisance I know who *knows* he's a nuisance!" The cameras rolled, and Ellington, looking as if he were in his living room with a few friends, spoke intimately about Panassié's father ("He serves the same muse I do"), and went on, "I don't think any music should be called jazz. I don't believe in categories. Years ago, uptown, I tried to get the cats to call it American Negro music or Afro-American music, because jazz just isn't right. Louis Armstrong plays Louis Armstrong music, Art Tatum plays Art Tatum music, Dizzy Gillespie plays Dizzy Gillespie music, and if it sounds good, that's all you need."

At about eight o'clock the klieg lights went off, and Panassié thanked Ellington warmly. Ellington and Dance walked to Sixth Avenue to find a cab, and on the way Ellington kept hitching up his trousers, which were secured by an old belt buckled at one side. "When I got that degree in Indianapolis last week, I had this same problem," he told Dance. "I was wearing a gown and all, and when I went out on the stage my pants started slipping, and I had to pull them up right through the gown. I don't know whether it's this stomach I've got that's causing the trouble or whether it's just that my bottom is getting smaller."

At Sixth Avenue a young black policeman greeted Ellington: "Hey, Duke. You waiting for the 'A' train?" Ellington said he was waiting for a cab, but asked if there was an 'A' train somewhere around to get back uptown in. A cab arrived, and Ellington gave the Central Park South address of his sister Ruth's apartment.

Ruth Ellington's apartment, which looks out over the Park, is mostly off-white, and the windows are hung with heavy glass-beaded curtains. There are a couple of big glass-topped tables, and in a corner is a small bar. She greeted her brother warmly, and he slumped into a chair, stretched his legs out straight, and threw his head back on a cushion. He closed his eyes. Ruth Ellington, who wore a big blond wig, a yellow blouse, and purple slacks, asked him if he wanted some Chinese food. He said no, he was just going home to bed. Stamatiou appeared and, leaning over Ellington, apologized about the car. Ellington grunted and waved one hand. A man in a white coat brought him a Coke, putting it down carefully on a paper coaster that showed a bass drum with a caricature of Ellington's head on it and the word "Duke" beneath. I asked Ellington about the ballet.

He opened his eyes halfway, took a sip of Coke, and lit a cigarette. His eyes closed again. "I'd been thinking about it for a while, and a year or so ago I was lying on a hotel bed in Vancouver and Alvin Ailey was with me and the story just came out," he said. "The river starts out like a spring and he's like a newborn baby, tumbling and spitting, and one day, attracted by a puddle, he starts to run. He scurries and scampers and wants to get to the marsh, and, after being followed by a big bubble, he does, and at the end of the run he goes into the meander. Then he skips and dances and runs until he's exhausted, and he lies down by the lake—all horizontal lines, ripples, reflections, God-made and untouched. Then he goes over the falls and down into the whirlpool, the vortex of violence, and out of the whirlpool into the main track of the river. He widens, becomes broader, loses his adolescence, and, down at the delta, passes between two cities. Like all cities on the opposite sides of deltas, you can find certain things in one and not in the other, and vice versa, so we call the cities the Neo-Hip-Hot-Cool Kiddies' Community and the Village of the Virgins. The river passes between them and romps into the mother—Her Majesty the Sea—and, of course, is no longer a river. But this is the climax, the heavenly anticipation of rebirth, for the sea will be drawn up into the sky for rain and down into wells and into springs and become the river again. So we call the river an optimist. We'll be able to play the ballet in any church or temple, because the optimist is a believer."

He took another drink of Coke, and after a while I asked him about Johnny Hodges.

"All I have to say is in the eulogy I wrote. Pastor John Gensel read it at the graveside. Hey, Stanley, have you got a copy of the Johnny Hodges eulogy?"

Dance rummaged around in his briefcase and handed me a double-spaced typewritten sheet. The eulogy began, "Never the world's greatest, most highly animated showman or stage personality . . . but a tone so beautiful it sometimes brought tears to the eyes. This was Johnny Hodges. This *is* Johnny Hodges. Because of this great loss, our band will never sound the same." It ended, "I am glad and thankful that I had the privilege of presenting Johnny Hodges for forty years, night after night. I imagine that I have been much envied, but thanks to God, and may God bless this beautiful giant in his own identity. God bless Johnny Hodges."

Dance said, "Hey, Duke, you're on television now, with Orson Welles on the David Frost show."

Ellington opened his eyes, heaved himself to his feet, and moved rapidly out of the room, saying, "Oh, he's one of my favorite people—Orson Welles."

# Newport 1970

*July 10th*

Newport, as Henry James discovered, can make a philosopher of anyone. Its contrasts do it: airborne eighteenth-century houses within calling distance of bloated eighteen-nineties mansions; CinemaScope skies, capable of simultaneously displaying a line squall and a clear three-quarter moon; a rocky, blowing coast and acres of asphalt parking lots; oceanic meadows and jumbled backstreets; and those venerable opposites—Trinity Church and Touro Synagogue. But Newport has not made a philosopher of George Wein, the Festival's producer. For sixteen years the Festival has continued to put on weight, with its increasing number of acts (many musicians resent this assembly-line programming and, economics willing, have forsworn the Festival), its longer and longer concerts, its gaggle of MCs, and its do-nothing groups. And yet every once in a while the thin man trapped inside this fat man escapes. He certainly did tonight. The evening was designed as a celebration of Louis Armstrong's seventieth birthday, but it was a lot more than that. The ten-strong Eureka Brass Band from New Orleans opened the evening. Its members had room to roam around the stage as if they were marching, and the acoustics suggested the group's glorious reverberations when it parades through the narrow streets in the French Quarter. Cap'n John Handy, the irrepressible seventy-year-old alto saxophonist, who seems to have absorbed everyone from Sidney Bechet to Charlie Parker, was on hand, and there were a snare drummer (Cié Frazier) and a bass drummer (Booker T. Glass) who between them managed sliding boomlay-boom patterns that any bebop drummer would admire. Bobby Hackett brought on his faultless quintet (Benny Morton, Dave McKenna, Jack Lesberg, Oliver Jackson), and it was a delight to hear Hackett's Armstrong-Beiderbecke bells alongside Morton's climbing, worrying melodies. Then a beguiling group called the New Orleans Ragtime Orchestra appeared. It was put together earlier this year by Lars Edegran, the Swedish pianist who has been working in New Orleans for the past four or five years, and it consists of trumpet, clarinet, trombone, violin (William Russell, the New Orleans jazz scholar), and the leader's piano, bass, and drums. It is a facsimile, right down to the arrangements, of the ragtime band led by John Robichaux in New Orleans before the First World War. It is a warm, gentle ensemble music (there are no solos) that moves along in waltz time or two-four time and accomplishes that spooky trick of making one feel nostalgic for an era and place and way of life one has never known. Particularly memorable among the numbers played were "St. Louis Tickle" (1904) and "Creole Belles" (1900). The Ragtime Orchestra was followed by six sterling trumpeters who in various ways were brought into being by Armstrong—Joe Newman, Hackett, Jimmy Owens, Wild Bill

Davison, Ray Nance, and Dizzy Gillespie. ("Louis Armstrong's station in the history of jazz is unimpeachable," Gillespie announced before playing, "and I would like to thank him for my livelihood.") Each, in top form, played two numbers, backed by McKenna, Larry Ridley, and Jackson, and the finest moments were offered by Gillespie in a slow, languorous "Ain't Misbehavin' " and in "I'm Confessin'," in which he sang an affectionate mock-parody of Armstrong; by Hackett's "Thanks a Million"; by both of Davison's numbers; and by Owens' superb "Nobody Knows the Trouble I've Seen," in which he played the tune in the low register, unobstrusively changing a note here and an accent there, which resulted in a first-rate piece of improvisation that sounded like straight melody. After Nance's second number Armstrong himself appeared and sang three numbers, accompanied by the rhythm section and Hackett's glancing obbligatos. Armstrong is still recuperating from a nearly fatal illness and he is not allowed to play his trumpet for more than an hour a day. But he looks fit and composed, and he was in excellent voice. The ovation was tumultuous, as was fitting for the man who invented jazz singing.

After the intermission the Preservation Hall Jazz Band, made up of the nucleus of the Eureka Brass Band, played five stirring numbers, then gave way to Mahalia Jackson. The last time I heard her, three years ago, she had lost a great deal of weight and her enormous voice had dwindled to a magisterial whisper. Now she has regained most of that weight, and with it her voice. Her first six numbers were stunning, and when she got to "Just a Closer Walk with Thee" she became almost savage. Her statuesque stage presence is celebrated, but in "A Closer Walk" she charged back and forth, growled, danced, shouted, and clapped her hands, and when Armstrong joined her she almost swallowed him. Yet when the two of them began "When the Saints Come Marching In," the results were empyrean.

### July 11th

This afternoon's concert started at noon and ended fifteen hours later, at six o'clock. The first three sets were in "workshop" form, and they involved two violinists, four trumpeters, and four drummers who played and then answered questions, most of which went like "Are you planning any more albums?" or "Did you go to music school?" Of the violinists, Jean-Luc Ponty and Mike White, Ponty was by far the more impressive. A classically trained player, he has the tone and technique that most jazz violinists lack, and his reading of the old "Yesterdays" was, with its John Coltrane colorings, rich and assured. The trumpeters (Owens, Gillespie, Newman, and Nance) played onstage while the drummers (Philly Joe Jones, Elvin Jones, Jo Jones, and Chico Hamilton) played at the back of the field, and after the trumpeters' first number, a good "Sunny," I went over to hear the drummers. They were, with the exception of Philly Joe Jones, who was neat and forceful, in a desultory, self-absorbed mood. Jo Jones appeared baffled, Chico Hamilton was stiff, and Elvin Jones was inconclusive. The trumpeters were followed onstage by a Rocklike Japanese quartet led by Sadao Watanabe, who was introduced as the Charlie Parker of Japan. Elvin Jones' quartet and Chico Hamilton's quartet went by, and so did a quintet led by Gary Burton. Keith Jarrett was on piano with Burton, and in the first number he played a fascinating, out-of-tempo solo that touched on Debussy and Schubert and Bill Evans. By this time it was five o'clock and my battery was low. Still another group was scheduled, but I went back to my hotel to recharge and watch the swallows relish the evening.

The thin man got out for a while tonight, and it was exhilarating. Kenny Burrell, accompanied by Ridley and Lenny McBrowne, opened the proceedings, and then acted as a rhythm section for Dexter Gordon, the forty-seven-year-old tenor saxophonist who has spent most of the past decade in Europe. Absence sometimes jams the memory and I had forgotten how persuasive Gordon was in the early fifties when, combining elements from the styles of Coleman Hawkins and Lester Young and Charlie Parker, he constructed the model later admired by Sonny Rollins and John Coltrane, who in turn brought along almost every tenor saxophonist who has appeared in the last fifteen years. Gordon has the ironwood tone that is now commonplace among tenor saxophonists, and an equally familiar amelodic way of phrasing that is made up of pitching runs, espaliered blocks of notes, and chameleon rhythms. There are few open places in his solos, which with their cathedral-like intricacy and weight, are difficult to absorb at one hearing. He is a musician's musician who goes after the mind and not the emotions. He was, according to the hair-raising illogic that governs most of the programming at the Newport Festivals, allowed only two numbers, but they were just about perfect. The second one, "Darn That Dream," was closed with a winding coda that recalled some of the weighty proclamations Coleman Hawkins liked to end his slow ballads with. The violinists, augmented by Ray Nance, reappeared, and Nance played an unabashedly soaring blues and a "Summertime" that was so intense it leaned on the listener. Dizzy Gillespie's new group played five predigested numbers, and then accompanied Don Byas, the fifty-seven-year-old master tenor saxophonist, who, like Gordon, has long been based in Europe. Byas, who is one of the most proficient admirers of Hawkins' operatic side (Hawkins was myriad; mere facets of his style often provided entire foundations for other players), was also allowed just two numbers, but they were spacious enough to reveal his curving melodic lines, his yearning Southwestern tone, and his ability to swing very hard. He also demonstrated that innate, dowagerlike assurance and poise that seems unique to the best of the musicians who came up in the thirties. Next, Nina Simone, who has become more interested in the message in her songs than in the singing of them, posed here and there about the stage, and made way for a blessedly short set by Herbie Mann, a flutist who is also good at posturing. The evening was closed by the Ike and Tina Turner Revue, a funny, churning ensemble that consists of a nine-piece band led by Ike Turner, who plays guitar; the Ikettes, a female trio that dances and sings; and Tina

Turner, who is beautiful and a fine shouter. The materials were gospel-soul-funk-blues, and I lost track of them when I got to watching one of the Ikettes, a tall, angular girl who liked to turn left when her compatriots turned right and who kept her mouth in a steady O, either because she was out of breath or because she had forgotten all her lyrics.

### July 12th

There are always one or two please-the-people-and-make-a-buck concerts at the Newport Festival, and tonight was one of them. Eddie Harris, a fashionably hard tenor saxophonist, started things, and then backed a young composer named Gene McDaniels who sang a couple of his own songs. He is a sharp, eloquent lyricist, and the best of his songs, "The Silent Majority" (pronounced "majoaratee"), had, among other necessary things, a couplet about the silent majoaratee "gathering around the hanging tree." Les McCann, the pasha of soul-soap music, came on, and was followed by Leon Thomas, the singer and yodeller. Thomas should attempt "The Star-Spangled Banner"; the results might be definitive. More soul soap, this time from the Adderley Brothers, and then Buddy Rich appeared. He looked gray and tired and his band sounded the same. He did, though, get off a series of hair-raising four-bar breaks on a medium blues. Ella Fitzgerald finished the program, and she provided proof that a singer's weight is to the voice what yeast is to bread. She has slimmed down and so has her voice. It has the high, bobby-sox quality of her "Tisket-a-Tasket" days, and it made her songs, which ranged from "Satin Doll" to "Raindrops Keep Falling," sound piping.

Roberta Flack, a singer-pianist in her late twenties, is a handsome, poised performer, who has a rich, steady contralto, gospel phrasing, and an electrifying sense of dynamics. Her first five numbers this afternoon were roomy and subdued, and then she let loose on "Reverend Lee," a funny affecting song by Gene McDaniels about God sorely tempting a preacher. Her handling of the words "Reverend Lee," repeated a dozen times during the song, was magic. Each time they came out differently, but in the best version she made the two words into ten, jamming some syllables together, separating others, and all the while granting almost each letter a different note. Then Bill Cosby brought on his twelve-piece Badfoot Brown and the Bunions Bradford Marching and Funeral Band. It is made up largely of Los Angeles musicians and includes a tenor saxophonist, a trombonist, two Fender bassists, three guitarists, two pianists, an organist, and two drummers. In the first two numbers the band accompanied Shuggie Otis, a sixteen-year-old blues guitarist and the son of Johnny Otis. He played a slow blues and a medium blues. The first was full of yearning and misery and pain (he is a motionless performer who smiles steadily, and the contrast between his coolness and the passion pouring out of his guitar was startling), and the second was a celebration of cheerfulness and good feeling. Then the Bunions

Bradford came on and for forty-five minutes played one number, apparently arranged by Cosby, that was, comic and ingenious and swinging. Most of the instruments were electronic, and the piece, which was blues-based, included samplings of just about everything good that has been invented in the past decade and a half by the "new-thing" school, by Charlie Mingus, by the Modern Jazz Quartet, by John Coltrane, by Miles Davis, and by the best rock groups. The tempo went up and down, there were dozens of slamming breaks, there were improvised duets, mountainous organ-chord climaxes, snatches of wild blues shouting (by the organist, Stu Gardner), a walking-bass passage, and a section in which the organist sang and played a rheumy, *a cappella* "White Christmas," which was startlingly interrupted several times by drum duets. Cosby conducted the piece with such intensity and precision that one had the impression that he was *playing* the band.

## All Dressed Up and No Place to Go

I received a telephone call not long ago from an Al St. Clair inviting me to the fifth annual Mobile Jazz Festival. St. Clair, who lives in Mobile and is a member of the festival committee, says that he has read a piece I have written on the gloomy state of jazz and that I might be cheered by the festival, which is devoted wholly to high-school and college jazz bands. The festival is small, nonprofit, and run on a competitive basis by a handful of young jazz-minded Mobilians. This year twelve high-school bands will compete, as well as fourteen big and small college groups from nine states, most of them Southern. The judges will include Thad Jones (cornet), Larry Ridley (bass), and three Mobilians—Mundell Lowe (guitar) and the brothers Al and Urbie Green (piano and trombone). St. Clair says that the music has been imposing in past years, and should be even better this year. I accept.

My trip a few days later, on a Thursday, is par for the course. We are an hour late taking off (no plane), and when we stop in Atlanta the end of the left wing slams into a parked food truck. The truck jumps several feet, and a foot-ball-sized hole is opened in the wing. We are transferred to another airline and another plane, on which I run into Jones and Ridley. Jones, who is tall, thickset, and funny, is a C.B.S. staff man in New York as well as co-leader of the Thad Jones–Mel Lewis big band, and Ridley, who is younger, smaller, and equally funny, has played a college gig with George Wein's band the night before in Maine and has been travelling ever since. A cloudburst keeps us on the runway for an hour, and we arrive in Mobile four hours late. St. Clair, a patient, quiet man, meets us (he has kept tabs on us, mysteriously, by "calling the computer" in Atlanta) and drives us to the Admiral Semmes Hotel, where the judges meet briefly and are given mimeographed sheets on which they are to grade the categories of Selection, Rhythm, Interpretation, Blend, Precision, and Dynamics. They are also to choose three big-band winners and three small-band winners, and they decide this year to disregard appearances and "presentation," on the basis that the music is what matters. A sliced-turkey-and-baked-potato dinner is held in the hotel for the festival committee, the judges, and the directors of the college bands. I sit between Lowe and Lee Fortier, the director of the Southeastern Louisiana College band. Lowe, who is in his late forties, is gracious and easygoing and lives in Los Angeles, where he is a freelance composer and arranger. He gave up on New York five years ago, he says, and doesn't understand why he hasn't lived in California all his life. He and Fortier, who is about the same age, appear to have known each other in the old days when Fortier was a trumpeter with Woody Herman and Hal McIntyre. Fortier is earnest and fast-talking. "I still play an occasional gig," he says. "I subbed for Al Hirt at his place in New Orleans three years ago, but those days on the road are gone for me. I have two daughters and a son and I've put down my roots. I've got a bachelor of music and a master of music from L.S.U., and I'm the musical director at Broadmoor High, which is in Baton Rouge. I started the first high-school stage band in Louisiana nine years ago, and before that I had an all-parish band. I also direct the stage band at Southeastern, which is over in Hammond. The kids I teach in high school have good taste, and they're very choosy. They have to join the concert band first, and we draw the stage band from that. They listen to jazz and they like good rock. I remember one of them bringing me a record by Blood, Sweat, and Tears before the group was anyways known nationally, and saying, 'What do you think of *this?*' I play a lot of jazz for them—Buddy Rich, the Thad Jones–Mel Lewis band, Don Ellis, Woody, and the old Basie band. And Charlie Parker and Clifford Brown and Coltrane. I play the old Basie records for time. That's the kids' biggest hang-up—time—and I'm a nut on the subject. And I recommend Jerry Coker's fine paperback, *Improvising Jazz.* Most of the emphasis in the stage band is on ensemble, but every once in a while a bunch of us sit around with our horns and get some blues going. I write some chords on the blackboard and we go around from instrument to instrument and change key and go around again, and they learn a little about improvising. The kids love the stage band. I could call a rehearsal any time of day or night and they'd be there. And when they graduate they come to me and say, 'Man, I hate to leave high school,' because they may be going to study medicine or engineering at a college where there isn't any stage band. It isn't easy for those that decide to stay in music. It's mostly studio work after college, or teaching, but maybe rock will be the way out. Last year a bunch of the kids had a rock band with four or five horns and solos and they really had something going."

By eight o'clock we are in the new Municipal Theatre, which has fine acoustics. James Brown is holding forth next door in the Municipal Auditorium, and there are two basketball games on television tonight. Brown and basketball are big in Mobile, and the house is only half full. The judges are seated in a transverse aisle at a table with student lamps. They have their heads together and are laughing. Their faces are lit from below and they look like cowpunchers around a fire. The Glassboro Lab Band from New Jersey opens the proceedings, which are devoted to the first half of the college groups. It is nineteen strong, and weak in the knees rhythmically, but it has a good pianist and an interesting bass trombonist. The Ray Fransen Quintet from Loyola is made up of trumpet, alto saxophone, guitar, bass and the leader on drums. The bass player is black—the first for the evening. The group plays Eddie Harris's "Cryin' Blues" in a tight, swinging, Horace Silver way. Fransen is an excellent drummer, and his soloists are commendable post-bop performers. The University of Alabama Stage Band has thirty pieces, and it includes one Negro (on organ) and four girls. It is a show band with almost no solos, and it too has rhythmic problems. The Butler-Farmer-Jackson Pack—alto, tenor, and baritone saxophones, trombone, piano, bass, and drums—is out of Southern University and is all black. The saxophonists reveal admiration for John Coltrane, and the group moves capably, in the manner of the Herbie Hancock sextet. The Morehead State University Stage Band from Kentucky is surprising. The drummer is tough and sounds like the old Don Lamond, and there is a wild alto saxophonist and flutist named Brad Jones. In a complicated number, "Concertino," a trombone, a trumpet, and an alto saxophone move to one side of the stage, where they solo and play ensemble figures, and are answered by the rest of the band. The gimmick works. The Louisiana State University–New Orleans Combo is led by Ben Smalley, a trumpeter and flügelhornist, and has piano, bass, and drums. Smalley, who is diminutive, plays with a sweet, florid precision. The group does "Here's That Rainy Day," "On the Trail," and a Brubeck number. Smalley would have little trouble in any New York or Los Angeles studio. The evening is closed by the University of Southern Mississippi Jazz Lab Band. It hustles, and in one number three soloists play at once, and in another, four French horns appear and the saxophone section doubles on a total of twenty instruments. Like the two groups just ahead of it, it is all white.

After the concert, St. Clair drives me to a party at Bill Lagman's house. Live oaks, mossy and thick-trunked, clasp hands across the streets, and the antebellum houses sit back on their plots, their big, elegant windows staring through porches and columns. They are 1830 New England houses, grown fat in an easy climate. Lagman, St. Clair tells me, has led a dance band for thirty years in Mobile and is on the festival committee. A year or two ago his musical faithfulness was rewarded with the Mr. Mobile Music Award. The guests are mainly involved with the festival. A fine buffet offers shrimps *rémoulades*. After a while Mundell Lowe, Thad Jones, and Al Green gather in a small room off the kitchen, where there is an upright piano. Lowe has his guitar and Jones his cornet, and Green, a constantly smiling man who taught his extraordinary younger brother, Urbie, sits down at the piano. A local bassist appears. It is the best possible way to hear jazz, and the music is easy and affecting. Jones plays with startling freshness, and Green is a good late-swing pianist. Lowe, who does not perform much anymore, settles slowly into his instrument, and the muscles around his mouth reflect his pleasure. There are blues and ballads, and Lagman gets out his trumpet and joins in. He has the gentle, old-lady tone of the old New Orleans trumpeters, and the constrast between him and Jones, who has a brilliant tone and a nervous, punching attack, is marvellous. I wish that the kids could be there.

I have a late breakfast on Friday with Chuck Suber, the publisher of *down beat*. He is an intense, unassuming man in his late forties, and he has spent a good deal of the past fifteen years travelling the country and helping to put the high-school and college stage-band movement on its feet. He hands me a six-page brochure he has written, *How to Organize a School Jazz Festival-Clinic*. It is terse and enthusiastic and exhaustive. He talks in much the same way: "Generally, the first music teachers in the public schools in this century were Sousa men, displaced when concerts in the parks and such began to give way after the First World War to the Model T and the movies. The next wave of teachers was made up in large part of dance-band men displaced after the Second World War, when the big bands began to disappear. Gene Hall, an inspired leader and teacher, organized the first college stage-band course in 1947 at North Texas State. He coined the euphemism 'stage band' simply because the terms 'jazz band' and 'dance band' were not acceptable in academic circles. Concurrently, jazz musicians were studying at Westlake College of Music on the Coast, and in Boston at the Berklee School of Music, which has now become a four-year college with an enrollment of nine hundred and fifty. The first high-school stage-band festival was held in Brownwood, Texas, in 1952. There were nine or ten bands. I was there, and it excited me tremendously. Gradually, Gene Hall graduates began fanning out—getting jobs in high schools and colleges, starting stage bands, fighting for recognition—and their students did the same thing. The Farmingdale High School Dance Band from Long Island, with Marshall Brown as its director, appeared at Newport in 1957, and became the first high-school jazz band to gain national recognition. In fact, it was something of a sensation. The next year the International Youth Band, which had kids from all over Europe and the U.S.A., was another Newport success. By 1960 Stan Kenton was hiring sidemen from North Texas State, and the thing had mushroomed. Fifteen or sixteen thousand high schools of all kinds now have stage-band courses, and there are sixty-two regional high-school festivals, some of them with as many as a hundred and twenty-six competing groups. Six colleges offer majors in jazz, or the equivalent of it, and four hundred and fifty colleges have accredited jazz courses. There is also a loose federation of a dozen or so college festivals, held, among other places, in Hamden, Connecticut, and Notre Dame, Little Rock, the University of Utah, San Francisco Valley College, and here in Mobile. Each sends a winning big band, combo, and vocalist to the National Collegiate Festival. The first such festival was held in Miami Beach in 1967, and the fourth one will be given in Urbana, Illinois, in May.

"The great problem, of course, is where will these kids find work after college? Some will try and make it on the road and some will wind up in the studios, but most of them will probably go into teaching, which of course results in a kind of closed-circuit, self-perpetuating system. Another problem is with the blacks. Integration has been slow, and many of the black schools, still hung up on the Negro-middle-class distaste for jazz, have nobody to organize and teach stage bands. But the whole program, despite the cul-de-sac conditions in jazz these days, is well worth it. It teaches the kids about a great, unique form of music. It teaches them a little about improvisation. Most important, it teaches them a valuable form of self-expression in an increasingly repressive and unoriginal society."

Suber is a judge at the high-school competition this afternoon. It starts at one-thirty in the Municipal Theatre. A dozen bands are scheduled. All are from Alabama, with the exception of the Starliners from Bowie, Maryland, and the Holy Cross Stage Band from New Orleans. It is only the second time the Mobile Festival has included a high-school competition. The house, which is nearly full, is made up largely of the relatives and friends of the musicians. Giggling and squirming are constant, and now and then a row of kids, uprooted by winds of enthusiasm, rises, flows down an aisle, and subsides in another row—pigeons suddenly clouding the air and settling fifty feet away. Solos, numbers, and sets are cheered wildly, and when each band finishes, its members file into the audience and sit in a clump. Feeling relieved and possibly heroic, with the eyes of a grateful audience riveted on them, they whisper and elbow one another. If the succeeding band sounds uncertain, the whispering becomes a steady counterpoint, but if the new group is obviously superior they grow still, amateurs digging old pros. Some of the bands are out of tune, some sag rhythmically, and many are marching bands in disguise. They play Neal Hefti, Marshall Brown, Stan Kenton, Blood, Sweat, and Tears, and the Beatles. The afternoon is a toss-up between the Holy Cross Stage Band and the Murphy High Band from Mobile. Both play the Beatles' irresistible "Hey Jude," but Murphy High, warmed by the bosom of local pride, brings the house to a boil. The last group is unbelievably old-fashioned ("That Old Black Magic," "I'll Be Around"), and provides a calming anticlimax.

I fall into an ironic reverie, remembering the music scene in my high school in the early forties. We had a band, or, rather, we had two bands—a ten-piece "big" one, which played dreary stock arrangements of the "Johnson Rag" and "Stardust," and a splinter Dixieland group. But it was an underground operation. We had no teacher or director. We were allowed to use a rehearsal room in the basement of the school chapel only when it was not occupied by the longhairs or the marching band. We provided our own arrangements, our own instruments, and even our own *raison d'être*, by giving illicit, well-attended jam sessions in the chapel basement. (During them, the resident music teacher, high-domed and wearing trousers invariably six inches too short, would poke his head in, and if he didn't throw us out, would smirk and slam the door.) Most of the musicians were terrible, but the exceptions were memorable. There was a flashy Gene Krupa drummer, a bass player with the power of Wellman Braud and the precision of Jimmy Blanton, and a musing, gentle cornetist who could play all of Bix Beiderbecke. There was also a tenor saxophonist from Maine who, though he couldn't speak two coherent sentences, played exactly like Lester Young. But those were champion times. We *were* Krupas and Blantons and Youngs, and since jazz had reached one of its peaks, our idols were almost always within visible reach. Now jazz has grown lean and withdrawn, but every backwoods high school has a *Good Housekeeping*–approved jazz band with school-supplied instruments, arrangements, practice halls, and teachers. A huge army of potential professionals, all dressed up and no place to go.

Another dinner is given before this evening's concert, at which the remaining college groups will play. The festival committee and the judges attend the dinner, and the judges are presented with miniature silver tankards. After dinner, St. Clair takes me through the Municipal Auditorium on the way to the theatre. It is almost the size of the Houston Astrodome and is packed with dining Shriners. The music tonight at the festival is, by and large, several notches above last night's. The Jacksonville State University Band plays Buddy Rich's version of the Beatles' "Norwegian Wood," and there is a fine, bursting trombone solo in "Summertime." The next group, a quintet from the University of Florida, is made up of semi-ringers, for its members are graduate students. They pump sternly through a couple of free-for-all "new-thing" numbers and sound like an Archie Shepp ensemble minus the humor. The Loyola University Jazz Lab Band, which I have heard about for several years, plays four swinging, precise numbers, one of them Don Ellis's difficult "In a Turkish Bath." It has a Negro bassist. Ray Fransen is on drums, and he makes everything cook. It is the best band we have heard yet. Some comic relief follows. The University Debs, hailing from Ball State University in Indiana and made up of eight very assorted girls accompanied by a rhythm section, yoohoo their way through a milky gospel number, some soft rock, and an imitation blues. The Louisiana State University Jazz Lab Band, which boasts the second black performer of the evening, is built mainly around the trumpet and flügelhorn of Ben Smalley. A nine-piece group, the Texas Southern University Contemporary Jazz Ensemble, has two whites and seven blacks, and is the first really integrated band at the festival. It is expert. It plays one long three-part number that suggests George Russell. The last band of the evening, Lee Fortier's Southeastern Louisiana College Stage Band, is every bit as good as a Woody Herman Band, and three of its numbers, arranged and/or written by an alumnus, Joe Cacibaudia, are fascinating. They are full of satisfying, teeth-grinding harmonies, a variety of rhythms, and subtle dynamics.

The competition is over, and the judges retire to a dressing room to choose the winners. There is a good deal of badinage, some of it salty. The University Debs are awarded a special prize, since they are in a class by themselves. Not surprisingly, Morehead, Loyola, and Southeastern sweep the big bands, while Ray Fransen's Loyola group, the University of Florida Quintet (the grad students), and Texas Southern (the integrated group) take the small-band honors. Suber and his compeers have already named the Holy Cross band the winner of the afternoon. Tomorrow night all eight winners will give a display program.

Off to another party with St. Clair, this one at a doctor's house, where a Dixieland band made up of local businessmen is to perform. The living room is built around an indoor garden with small trees, and the music is paunchy and purple-faced. A stocky man in his late thirties tells me that he acts as the group's bandboy. He says the band doesn't take itself seriously. I note the standing microphones in front of the band, the bank of recording equipment beside it, the stacks of tape, and the glistening instruments. Thad Jones sits in against his will—a cheetah pursued by hippos. Suber and I talk of the times when his father, who was head of Local 802 in New York, took him to the Savoy Ballroom to hear Chick Webb.

On Saturday morning I learn that someone got brutish with Thad Jones at the end of last night's party, and that, on top of that, his horn has been stolen from his hotel room. It is not the horn but the mouthpiece that matters. A trumpeter builds his chops around his mouthpiece, and adjusting to a new one is like starting a new career. I wander over to the theatre, where rehearsals are in progress, to talk with Ray Fransen, who seems the most confident and gifted musician in the festival. I notice that Mobile, like all old Southern towns, comes in warring parts. I'm in the middle of town, but I pass a sagging antebellum house and a field-size lot full of knee-high grass and gap-toothed shrubbery. Beyond the house I can see the twelve-story Admiral Semmes and the thirty-three-story First National Bank Building. The celebrated Mobile azaleas are in bloom, but the sour, noxious odor that rolled over the town yesterday, compliments of Mobile's two paper mills, still hangs in the air. Blacks seem to make it all right in the public places, but there haven't been many at the parties, and a member of the festival committee has told me that when the leaders of N.O.W., a civil-rights group, were invited to the festival, one of them told him that they would attend, so long as they didn't get "rained on" in the Municipal Theatre.

I find Fransen backstage. He is compact and round-faced and bearded. He is also articulate, outspoken, and out of step with his generation, for he has a strong sense of tradition. "I was born in New Orleans, and I've lived there all my life. No one in my family plays an instrument, but I was always exposed to music—to Cole Porter and Gershwin and even Art Tatum. When I was a kid I was real fat and introverted, and I used to stay home and listen to the old people's radio station, WWL. My father's a Nicaraguan. He's a dentist and damned good, and I guess it was he who, if he didn't lead me into music, allowed me into it. He loves music as art and he loves manual dexterity. I started lessons on drums six years ago, and on the side I played in rock groups. Both experiences dragged me. I went the whole rudimental route in the drum class, but drum rudiments are just like scales—a means to an end and not an end. I got tired of rock drumming quick; I didn't want to blow my eardrums out. Anyway, that's changing. The rock musicians are stretching out their numbers and getting into solos and other instruments than guitars. I consider myself a percussionist. I've learned most of the percussion instruments, including timpani and vibes. I'm going to do graduate work in ethnomusicology, but my prime interest is in being a performer. I'm not interested in amassing a fortune, but rather than prostitute myself musically, I'd sell shoes. Fortunately, with my background, I could probably get a job in a symphonic organization or in jazz or with certain rock groups. The reason the kids ignore jazz is partly because they associate it with parents, with a different era. It's supposed to be acquainted with brothels, and brothels are out. But when they *do* listen, they hear the excitement. I took my quintet into a small beer lounge on campus a while back, and at first nothing happened. Then it caught on and now the place is packed. But the kids are denying roots. They only want what's now. They say, 'I don't want to study Dixieland,' but I say, 'Man, you don't have to *study* it, just know what it is.' The past is there for a cat to take what he needs from it. Paul Desmond listened to Lester Young, and Gil Evans to Brahms, and they wouldn't be what they are if they hadn't. I listen and steal from everybody—Gene Krupa and Sidney Catlett and Chick Webb—and recently I've been listening to Joe Morello and Buddy Rich and Grady Tate. That's the drag about my generation—tossing everything out and replacing it with nothing. It's ridiculous. Everybody hates what's going on, but nobody has any solutions."

There aren't many surprises at tonight's performance. A lot of new material is brought out, though, including numbers by Charlie Mingus, Luis Bonfa, and Clifford Brown, and the Ball State Debs have new hairdos. Everyone plays well. For some reason, the trophies are handed out after the theatre has emptied, but it is good to see the three hundred or so kids cheering the winners and keeping their disappointments to themselves. The judges make the awards—all except Thad Jones, who flew home earlier today.

# 1971

## Miss Bessie

**M**unificence can be its own reward, but munificence that unexpectedly turns a profit is even better. Such is the case with Columbia's meticulous Bessie Smith reissue project, which is now over half-finished and which has suddenly become a best-seller. Since last summer, ninety-five of the magisterial singer's recordings have been brought out in three lavish two-LP sets, and there are two volumes, of sixty-four recordings, still to come. The five volumes will include almost everything she recorded. The exceptions are twenty unissued sides whose masters Columbia now cannot find, two not wholly certifiable sides made for another label at the outset of her career and mysteriously credited to the singer Rosa Henderson, and the soundtrack of Dudley Murphy's invaluable 1929 two-reeler, *St. Louis Blues*, in which, backed by a choir and a medium-sized band, she sings the Handy blues. (This version of "St. Louis Blues" has long been put down by Bessie Smith admirers, who have grumbled about the choir's getting in the way of her voice and about the film itself, which they consider disrespectful and tacky. But the massed sounds of the choir and band act as a fitting catapult for her voice, which *was* of operatic proportions, and the picture, at once silly and stark, is the sole record we have of what Bessie Smith looked like in action. Murphy, who went on to do his famous *The Emperor Jones*, was, like Carl Van Vechten, part of the Black Renaissance movement. Murphy wrote the scenario, which has to do with a black pimp who takes all Bessie's money and jilts her, and he made the film in three days in the summer of 1928 in a studio on Fourteenth Street.)

Bessie Smith's whole life tended to be an irony. She performed almost entirely before black audiences, and the occasions were so utterly black and foreign to whites that when Carl Van Vechten recalled a concert she did in Newark in 1925 he sounded like a nineteenth-century explorer describing a newly discovered Stone Age people:

> She was very large, and she wore a crimson satin robe, sweeping up from her trim ankles, and embroidered in multicolored sequins in designs. Her face was beautiful with the rich ripe beauty of southern darkness, a deep bronze brown, matching the bronze of her bare arms. Walking slowly to the footlights, she began her strange rhythmic rites in a voice full of shouting and moaning and praying and suffering, a wild, rough, Ethiopian voice, harsh and volcanic, but seductive and sensuous, too, released between rouged lips and the whites of teeth, the singer swaying lightly to the beat, as is the Negro custom.

Now, inspired partly by the expressive words, partly by the stumbling strain of the accompaniment, partly by the powerfully magnetic personality of this elemental conjure woman with her plangent African voice, quivering with passion and pain, sounding as if it had been developed at the sources of the Nile, the black and blue-black crowd, notable for the absence of mulattoes, burst into hysterical, semi-religious shrieks of sorrow and lamentation. Amens rent the air.

Her recordings were made exclusively for black people, and in time Columbia even put "race records" on her labels. She worked on black vaudeville circuits (principally the Theatre Owners and Bookers Association, whose initials commonly stood among black performers for Tough On Black Asses), and she travelled in her own railroad car, which amounted to a high-class portable ghetto. Her life and death were chronicled only by the black press. Her life was an astonishing feat of magic: she was wealthy, famous, and inordinately gifted, yet she remained almost completely invisible to the white world.

One of five or more children, she was born in poverty in Chattanooga sometime in the nineties. Her father died shortly after her birth and her mother died when she was nine. By the time she was in her teens, she had performed—probably as a dancer and clown and singer—in local amateur shows, and she had worked tent shows with Ma Rainey, the great blues singer. It is not certain how often she appeared with Ma Rainey, but it is clear from the recordings of both of them that Ma Rainey, who was ten years older, taught her a good deal, even though Bessie Smith refused to acknowledge it later on. Bessie Smith continued working tent shows, but in 1923, after a couple of false starts on other labels, she made her first successful record, for Columbia. The next five or so years were meteoric. She divided her time between T.O.B.A. tours and Columbia recording sessions in New York. She made a great deal of money and became a mountainous presence in the black world. But she and her husband, a Philadelphia policeman whom she married in 1923 and parted from in 1929, ran through her money (for a time it had been carefully watched over by Frank Walker, a Columbia official, and she had even bought a house in Philadelphia), and she began drinking heavily. And fashions were changing. Radio and movies had created a demand for more sophisticated singing, and by the late twenties her record sales had dropped precipitously. By the early thirties, she had fallen into semi-obscurity. Then she appears to have pulled things together, and in 1937, the year she died, she was planning a recording session, she was back on the road doing tent shows and theatres, and it has been suggested that she was thinking of acting (see the course of Ethel Waters' career).

Her death was nightmarish, and until the facts were dug up by two enterprising reporters—Sally Grimes, who published a story about Bessie Smith's death two years ago in *Esquire*, and Chris Albertson, who has just completed what should be the first reliable and thorough biography of Bessie Smith—it

had been widely believed that she died after being badly injured in an automobile accident near Clarksdale, Mississippi, and after being refused admittance to a white hospital. Grimes and Albertson reconstruct what happened
this way: Bessie Smith was travelling South with her common-law husband
and manager, Richard Morgan, from Memphis to Darling, Mississippi,
where she was to do a show. It was around four on a Sunday morning in September and there was no moon, but the stars were out. Ten miles north of
Clarksdale, he ran into the back of a mail truck pulling out onto the road.
(Rented mail trucks were used to deliver the Memphis Sunday papers.) The
top was ripped off the car and it turned over. Minutes later, Dr. Hugh
Smith, a surgeon who now practices in Memphis and who was going fishing
with a friend, pulled up. They moved Bessie Smith from the middle of the
road onto a grassy shoulder. (Smith didn't learn who she was until later.)
Her right arm was almost severed at the elbow, and she had internal injuries.
Another car, failing to see Smith's, piled into it, and two more people were
hurt. A couple of ambulances arrived forty-five minutes later, and Bessie
Smith was apparently taken to the G. T. Thomas Hospital, in Clarksdale.
(The hospital no longer exists.) The ambulance driver who took her recalls
that she died en route, but Albertson has found her death certificate, and it
says that she died at the hospital just before noon and that her arm had been
amputated: "Bessie Smith didn't have a chance," Smith told Grimes. "I have
no way of knowing the course of that ambulance, but I'll still say this, it
wouldn't have made any difference if she'd been hurt with her injuries on the
front steps of the University Hospital in Memphis. In 1937, with no blood
bank and a lot of new techniques that weren't available then, she didn't have
a prayer to survive. And it's quite probable that even in this day and time she
wouldn't have made it."

To judge by her photographs and the glimpses of her in "St. Louis Blues,"
Bessie Smith was a stunning woman. She was five foot nine and generally
weighed around two hundred. Both Zutty Singleton and Ethel Waters
remember that she was not Bessie but Miss Bessie. She had a broad face, a
high forehead, and a brilliant smile. Her fingers were long and graceful. She
favored furs and boas and wigs and long, flowing robes. Around 1933, Red
Norvo and Mildred Bailey frequently had dinner with her and Morgan, in
Harlem or at the Norvos' house, in Forest Hills, and Norvo remembers her
being "meek, humble, even-tempered, retiring," and not in the least Uncle
Tom. Norvo also remembers that once when Bessie came to dinner, Mildred
Bailey, who was close to Bessie's size, said "Say, Bessie, I have this dress that's
got too big for me, and I wondered if you'd like it"—followed by uproarious
laughter from the two women. Mezz Mezzrow, the clarinettist, recalls meeting her one night in a Chicago club: "When I told her how long I'd been listening to her records, how wonderful I thought they were . . . she was very
modest—she just smiled, showing those great big dimples of hers, and fid-
geted around, and I asked her would she do 'Cemetery Blues' for me, and

she busted out laughing. 'Boy,' she said, 'what you studyin' 'bout a cemetery for? You ought to be out in the park with some pretty chick.' Every time I saw her from then on, Bessie kept kidding me about the kinky waves in my hair; she'd stroke my head once or twice and say, 'You ain't had you hair fried, is you, Boy? Where'd you get them pretty waves? I get seasick every time I look at them.' " Bessie Smith was also, in the show-business way, excessively generous, to the point, indeed, of virtually not being able to hold on to money. But drinking transformed her. Sidney Bechet, who worked with her in the early twenties, wrote, "Bessie could be plenty tough; she could really handle her own. She always drank plenty and she could hold it, but sometimes, after she'd been drinking a while, she'd get like there was no pleasing her. She had this trouble in her, this thing that wouldn't let her rest, a meanness that came and took her over." The singer Ida Cox put the two Bessies together: "Bessie Smith was an old old friend and everybody loved her, which was why they was so shocked when she died in that accident. Of course, she *did* have enemies. Who don't? She was a very high-tempered person, and she didn't take anything from anybody. But she was a good girl, on the whole." She was, as Van Vechten points out, a majestic and hypnotic performer. She never used a microphone, but her voice filled the largest hall, and she moved around onstage with the special grace of very large people. But the way she looked is not completely lost to us, for, in that eerie way jazz musicians sometimes have of carrying on the images of revered predecessors, she lives on in the royal presence of Mahalia Jackson, who was a child when she heard her but who distinctly resembles her physically, as a performer, and as a singer.

There is no substitute for listening to a performer in the flesh, but the magnitude of Bessie Smith's voice is more than suggested in her recordings. It is, in some of her later and technically better ones, *there*. Her voice unquestionably had operatic possibilities, and in another time and place she might have become a diva. She had a heavy, almost ominous contralto, a "cast-iron" voice, as Berton Roueché felicitously put it. But her voice was not dense or inflexible like Paul Robeson's. It had a spacious, easy sound that one can almost walk into. It was warm, bearish, and utterly commanding. Even more striking was the way she moved this massive instrument around, for she had, within her limits, a flawless technique. She landed with both feet on every note, she had exact pitch, her bent notes stopped precisely where she wanted them to, her vibrato was controlled and effortless, and she had perfect diction. She also had a superb sense of rhythm, and she could move her phrases anywhere around the beat she wanted, and in doing so she became the first modern jazz performer—a performer of considerable influence on everyone from Louis Armstrong to Billie Holiday. One difficulty she never surmounted was not of her making. The power of her delivery often diminished her materials. Her style never changed during the ten years she recorded. (Her attack varied, of course, for she sang pop tunes, gospel-type songs, off-color songs, and novelty numbers as well as blues.) Indeed, she probably had another ten or twenty years left within her, and she knew it, for she had said she would not retire until 1960.

Columbia has done a herculean job on the Bessie Smith reissues. It has been able to find only fifty-seven intact Bessie Smith masters in its vaults, so decent prints of the hundred and three remaining sides, some of them in circulation for forty-seven years, have been searched out and borrowed from collectors. The records have been subjected to a new remastering process developed by Larry Hillyer, a Columbia engineer, and the results are a wonder. The pre-electrical recordings (electrical recording came in in 1925) have an uncanny presence and clarity, and the electrical recordings are even better. There is more than enough gold scattered through the three albums, even though one simply has to get used to the Sunday-school pianists and whinnying clarinettists she was generally offered as accompanists. They seem not to have bothered her much, and they are more than compensated for when she is accompanied by Fletcher Henderson and Joe Smith and Charlie Green, or by James P. Johnson, who was the most sympathetic accompanist she ever had. Of particular interest in the first album are "Black Mountain Blues," "Hustlin' Dan," and a couple of pseudo-gospel numbers in which she is backed by James P. and a bumbling vocal group. The second album includes the classic moaning, subterranean rendition of "Nobody Knows You When You're Down and Out," recorded in 1929, and the perfect "Dirty No Gooder's Blues." Charlie Green and Joe Smith and Henderson are on hand in the third album, and there are a dozen delights, among them "Weeping Willow Blues," "House Rent Blues," "Spider Man Blues," "Ticket Agent Ease Your Window Down," and the celebrated and funny six-minute "Empty Bed Blues," with its lumbering double-entendre lyrics. (Note also, in this album, the photograph of Bessie Smith, probably taken just after her career began to boom. She is wearing a dark, expensive silk dress, her hair is swept back, and she is fingering a long loop of pearls. Her head is slightly and beseechingly tilted. The veiled, inward-looking expression in her eyes is almost unendurable, and so is her sheer beauty.) But the best moments in the three albums take place during her last recording date, under the direction of John Hammond. It includes "Do Your Duty," "Gimme a Pigfoot," "Take Me for a Buggy Ride," and "Down in the Dumps." (Bobby Short has kept "Pigfoot" alive by singing it rousingly well at the Café Carlyle.) Hammond put together the best band that ever worked behind her—Frankie Newton (trumpet), Chu Berry (tenor saxophone), Benny Goodman, Jack Teagarden, Buck Washington (piano), Bobby Johnson (guitar), and Billy Taylor (bass)—and it shows in her singing. She swings, her voice is limber and free (though she sometimes seems a little short of breath), and there is a steady exuberance. The band is used behind her much as similar all-star groups were used in the Billie Holiday 1935–38 sessions, which Hammond also supervised. It plays loose ensembles or organ chords under her ("Buggy Ride"), the horns provide obbligatos ("Down in the Dumps," in which Teagarden and Newton, working with her in the first and last choruses, respectively, become startling alter-voices), and there are ample solos. (Newton, using tremulous bent notes and easy legato intervals, is particularly fine in "Do Your Duty" and "Pigfoot.") Hammond recently talked about the recording session: "I was twenty-two, and it was a marvellously productive year for me. I was driven. It was the year I covered the Scottsboro case and made Bessie Smith's last record date. I had found her in a gin mill in Philly, where she was a singing hostess. She was very broke and she was very excited about doing the date even though I told her there wouldn't be much money in it—two hundred for her and two hundred for the band, all of which I paid myself. I got that band together out of left field, and it was a mixed one, which was still a rarity then. Chu and Frankie and Teagarden had never worked together before, nor had they ever worked with Bessie. In fact, some of them had never even *seen* her. Buck Washington, of the old vaudeville team of Buck and Bubbles, couldn't read, and he wasn't the greatest choice on piano, but James P. Johnson, who would have been perfect, was out of town. I had to use a guitar because she wouldn't let me use a drum. The session was scheduled for ten in the morning—it was probably the only morning record date she ever had, and probably the only one where there was no liquor—and the four numbers were finished by one-thirty. All the songs, which she chose herself, were by Coot Grant and Sox Wilson. We had just one engineer and an old R.C.A. mike, which she stood at least two feet from. She wore a plain dark dress, and I would guess she weighed about one hundred and eighty at the time. She was an absolutely direct black woman. No Tomming, not a shade of the phony to her. The session was held in a small studio at 55 Fifth Avenue. Ethel Waters was in the building that day, and she and Bessie loathed each other, so I made very sure they didn't meet. Benny Goodman, who was then the Columbia house clarinettist, is only on one track because he had to leave for a Ben Selvin record date in the next studio. At the end of the session, the musicians all thanked me, and that doesn't happen very often."

# Newport 1971

*July 2nd*

Tonight's concert was old-fashioned and trudging. The newest Stan Kenton band, minus its ill leader, appeared, and it resembled every other Stan Kenton band. The arrangements by Ken Hanna and Bill Holman and Johnny Richards were rigid and cumbersome. The trumpets, five strong, screamed or played pastel muted figures; the trombones, also five strong, hummed heavy hymns; the saxophones frolicked in between. A new young drummer, John Von Ohlen, carried on with tremendous verve and precision, but to little avail. The music suggested the Chrysler Building translated into sound. The Buddy Rich band, which often seems like a diminutive Kenton group, moved through six made–in–Hong Kong numbers that were lighted by a tantalizing interlude played by Rich's new pianist, Bob Petersen—gospel chords and easy runs and good off-notes, all done with an immaculate touch. Rich's final number was given over to one of his unique and miraculous drum solos. It was played at double time, the original tempo, and half time, and it included a blinding single-stroke roll, a left-hand figure that few drummers could play with both hands, figure-eight patterns all over the set, breathless tickings on his snare rims, and a cymbal-roaring finale. Because of Rich's ubiquity in recent years, it is all too easy to take him for granted.

Last winter, Duke Ellington gave an odd and addled concert in New York. The band played unevenly and without appetite, the selection of numbers was lackluster, and the evening was closed by two surprising spectacles. In the first, Paul Gonsalves came down off the stage and soloed in the audience—a ham routine that was considered hot stuff at Jimmy Ryan's thirty years ago. And in the finale, a pseudo-rock piece called "One More Time," the whole band lined up stage front and played an endless series of riffs while Ellington's vocalists bounced around and sang. And Ellington did it again tonight. Two of his numbers, "Afro-Eurasian Eclipse" and selections from the new "Brava Toga Suite," were played out of tune and out of cadence; Cootie Williams lumbered through "Take the 'A' Train" (Ray Nance, whom the number was originally built around, remained in the trumpet section); there was a number from the "New Orleans Suite," and then the band went into "One More Time." The audience, made up of the hip and the faithful, looked on in disbelief, and Ellington looked at the disbelief with disbelief; when the number was over, he uncharacteristically turned on his heel and walked off the stage without a word.

Roberta Flack closed the evening. She has a rich and beautifully controlled contralto, but she is weighed down by much of her present material. She sings too many message songs and too many dirgelike ballads. But it is another matter when the tempo goes up and she tackles numbers like "Reverend Lee" and "To Love Somebody." In the latter, she gave an extraordinary demonstration of melodic embellishment by repeating the theme words, strung to a gently descending pattern of notes, at least a dozen times, singing them differently each time: "you don't know what it's like—to love somebody," "you don't *know* what it's like to love somebody," "you don't know—what it's like—to *love* somebody."

The kids, who came in armies two years ago to hear the rock groups at the Festival, are, mysteriously, back. They are camped by the thousands on the hillside above Festival Field and on the bluff behind the bandstand, and the air smells of pot. But the mood is not claustrophobic and ominous, as it was from the start that other weekend.

*July 3rd*

Eubie Blake, the eighty-eight-year-old composer and pianist, started things off this afternoon, and he was a delight. He played a ragtime piece, his fingers Jack-be-nimble, and he jazzed up "The Merry Widow Waltz." He played a Cole Porter number and he did his own "Memories of You" and "I'm Just Wild About Harry." He did them all as he would have done them seventy years ago, and they had a cheerful, innocent, take-me-out-to-the-ballgame air. Willie the Lion Smith, a crackling seventy-three, followed with four supreme numbers, including a novelty piece called "Hot Ginger and Dynamite," which he sang very well. Both Blake's and Smith's styles cry out for drum accompaniment (wire brushes and no foot pedal), and it was too bad somebody didn't sit in. Charlie Mingus's sextet (Lonnie Hillyer, Charlie McPherson, John Foster, Bobby Jones, and Virgil Day) got off four striving numbers, among them "Pithecanthropus Erectus" and his funny, rinky-dink parody of "Cocktails for Two." Hillyer's Mickey Mouse trumpet was faultless, and so was Jones' spaghetti-leg Ted Lewis clarinet. Freddie Hubbard, exploring that curious and lifeless extension of bebop known as hard bop, was interminable, and so was the New York Bass Violin Choir. Formed a year or so ago, the group consists of seven bassists (Milt Hinton, Ron Carter, Richard Davis, Sam Jones, Michael Fleming, Lisle Atkinson, and the leader, Bill Lee), a vocalist (A. Grace Lee Mims), a pianist, and a drummer. They played a fifty-minute folk operetta that had to do with life in Snow Hills, Alabama. Lee, who wrote the piece, narrated, sang, and pantomimed, Mims sang, and the fiddles provided accompaniment and contrapuntal sections, most of them bowed. Some of Lee's talking was funny and even affecting, but he and Mims are dreary singers and the music lacked melodic spine. It was the sort of effort that avant-garde high-school seniors sometimes get off as a graduation-day special.

Tonight the kids had bonfires going on the hill, and the roads around Festival Field were choked with bluejeans and bare feet. It's clear now why they are here: no other big festivals are scheduled anywhere this weekend, and they want to hear Aretha Franklin, who's on tomorrow afternoon.

Chase, a new group made up of four trumpets, guitar, organ, bass, drums, and a singer and led by Bill Chase, who once played lead trumpet for Woody Herman, turned out to be four blasting trumpets glued to a rock-rhythm section. The trumpet solos were mostly high-note and largely inaudible, and the singing was mediocre. Dave Brubeck and Gerry Mulligan, accompanied by Jack Six on bass and Alan Dawson on drums, took over, and in a medium blues Mulligan fashioned three husky, down-home stop-time choruses. Dionne Warwicke, who is the test pilot of the Burt Bacharach–Hal David combine, and who has added an "e" to her last name on the advice of her astrologist, sang a dozen Bacharach numbers. Either Bacharach, who has great style, has just one song, which he writes endless variations of, or Miss Warwick sings all songs exactly alike, for every number sounded the same.

Then, just after Miss Warwicke's last number, the trouble started. Ten minutes before, I had noticed kids dropping over the wooden wall at the back of the Field, but everything was still calm. When Miss Warwicke finished, George Wein walked rapidly to the front of the stage and made an emotional and frightening and ill-worded announcement to the effect that the audience was in danger (of what he didn't say), that we should file immediately and calmly from the Field, and that the concert had been shut down by order of the chief of police. Suddenly, three kids appeared in the aisle back of where I was sitting and shouted obscenities at Wein, and then I understood what Wein was trying to say: We were in for the same disruptive rumpus that took place two years ago when the kids smashed down fences and poured into the Field. The front of the Field, where the box-seat and press section are, was cleared but the crowd to the rear stayed put and roared its displeasure at having the concert stopped (Mary Lou Williams and a jam session led by the organist Jimmy Smith were still to come). Then the avalanche hit. Hundreds of kids poured through the boxes and the press section, smashing chairs and railings, and up onto the stage. (They had got only to the foot of the stage two years ago.) The lights onstage went out, but for more than an hour the kids sat there chanting, stamping thunderously in rhythm, shaking their fists, and yelling more obscenities. Gerry Mulligan's voice was heard briefly over the loudspeakers, telling the kids to cool it, and then Father Norman O'Connor, who had been the MC, made an impassioned plea, which seemed to have some result. The noise died slowly down, and by midnight, all passion spent, the brouhaha was over.

### July 4th

It was announced this morning that the authorities had decided to close the Festival down. The kids had, with classic effect, cut off their noses to spite their faces. They had also, as professed non-Establishment people, aborted a great non-Establishment music. After breakfast I went out to the Field. The front section was filled with splintered wood and garbage. The stage, constructed of immense steel girders, was intact, but a grand piano had lost its keyboard cover and some of the ivory on the low-register keys. I noticed a young, blond-haired, bearded man picking up garbage at the back of the stage, and I asked him what had happened last night. "The vibes were bad," he said affably. "On Friday night, they were beautiful. You couldn't walk twenty-five feet up on the hill without someone smiling at you. But things began going bad yesterday afternoon. The kids were calling the cops pigs and the cops got tired of it and started poking the kids with their nightsticks. I came down from the hill last evening and a cop yelled at me and stuck his stick in my gut, and it started then for me. Anyway, most of the kids on the hill were not really into jazz. They were here because of Aretha and because other people were here, and they were here because they've learned you can get a lot of nice things free, that you don't have to pay for everything, which is still a fad, not a philosophy. The kids who broke down the fence were malcontents and they were stoned, but you don't get stoned unless something is wrong in the first place." He pulled a couple of mimeographed sheets from his pocket and handed them to me. "Unlike two years ago, the kids were prepared this time," he said. The sheets were titled "Festival Street Sheet," and they had been issued by the Potemkin Bookshop in Newport. They told the kids where they could crash, not to hitchhike in front of cops, where there were bathrooms, when sunrise and sunset were, where to go for help on bad trips, where to swim and rent bikes, what to watch out for in the way of bad dope, and how to behave toward the natives:

> It's obvious that some people are making a lot of bread from your being here this weekend, and they could be treating you a lot better. But most of the people who live in this town aren't making money off this festival— they're just trying to survive a pretty confusing weekend. These people shouldn't be ripped-off or hassled—this means small stores, people's lawns, and people's feelings. Be cool to the people.

I walked to the back of the Field, and the word "malcontent" seemed mild. Five sizable sections of the ten-foot-high chain-link fence that encircles the Field had been flattened, and the inner wooden fence was full of jagged holes that looked as if they had been gnawed by huge rats. It was a prime instance of nature abhorring a vacuum. The kids camped on the hill, which was now covered with a snow of garbage, had looked down on the big empty spaces at the back of the Field and, souped-up by apple wine and drugs, decided they should be filled.

# 1972

## Finis

B ucky Pizzarelli and George Barnes have been playing rewarding guitar duets for almost a year in the tiny St. Regis Room—they sit on an eyebrow-size bandstand against one wall and share a single amplifier—and they have come to be known simply as "the guitarists." Barnes is a stiff, somewhat chunky player, who started in the thirties, before Charlie Christian, and Pizzarelli, younger, is a Christian graduate. But they are good foils. Pizzarelli provides excellent support on his bass string for Barnes' hopping, singsong solos, and Pizzarelli's lean, melodic lines scud along over Barnes' sharp two-and-four, two-and-four accompanying chords. Their ensembles, sometimes in unison and sometimes loosely improvised, are intricate and amusing. They appeared in fine form tonight, but after one set something went wrong. Between numbers, the two men muttered audibly at each other. Their playing began to go out of sync, and when their brief last set was over, they parted without a word or look. True Gilberts and Sullivans, they had, their manager said, gradually come to detest one another, and they were, as of tonight, splitting up. It was a rare, seriocomic occasion, for jazz musicians generally sheathe whatever hostilities they may have when they pick up their instruments. The guitarists' swan set was played not on their instruments but on each other.

Mahalia Jackson died yesterday, in Chicago, at the age of sixty. She was an unalterably majestic performer, no matter whether, at Newport in 1970, she was clowning around the stage with Louis Armstrong and shouting "When the Saints Go Marching In," or whether, at an Easter Sunday concert in 1967 at Philharmonic Hall, she was standing still as stone, her long, birdlike hands endlessly turning and smoothing and easing her words. Her curving contralto never lost its fullness or agility (she was recuperating from an illness when she did the Easter concert, and her voice had sunk to a whisper, but by the time of the Newport appearance she had regained her powers, and she gave one of her most stirring performances), and she remained, despite her godly materials, a great jazz singer. But more than Mahalia Jackson is gone, for she was the only mirror—in person and voice—that we had of her childhood idol, Bessie Smith.

## Teddy and the M.J.Q.

Teddy Wilson, who will be sixty this year, is a marvel, and we must not take him for granted. There are certain songs he has come to own over the years—"Stompin' at the Savoy," "Love for Sale," "I Only Have Eyes for You," "Sweet Lorraine," "Tea for Two"—and he played them tonight at the Cookery with ease and grace. The famous style was in place—the feathery arpeggios, the easy, floating left hand, the impeccable rhythmic sense, the intense clusters of notes that belie the cool mask he wears when he plays. If Tatum and Monk and Hines sometimes suggest painters, Wilson suggests a superb watercolorist, whose textures and colors and draftsmanship are an unfailing delight.

There have been, since jazz really got itself together fifty years ago, less than a dozen groups that, by building new houses with the best stones their predecessors left behind, have distinctly helped push the music forward. But one of them—the Modern Jazz Quartet—has done even more. It has unimpeachable taste and a self-charging musical imagination. It is sensitive but not precious, subtle but powerful, controlled but swinging, stirring but not sentimental. In recent years, the quartet (John Lewis, piano; Milt Jackson, vibraharp; Percy Heath, bass; and Connie Kay, drums) has appeared mostly in concert; the settings have a becoming dignity, but they tend to keep the group under glass. So a rare event is taking place, for the group—at its own request—is at the Village Van-guard. If the way it performed tonight is any indication, the gig will be not only a rare event but a high-water one. It played several fine new pieces, including "In Memoriam" (for a revered piano teacher), which turned out to be one of Lewis' most graceful melodic carvings since "Django" (also played). It played old gems like "England's Carol," "True Blues," "Home," "Bag's Groove," and "Pyramid," and it played tunes it rarely touches, among them Charlie Parker's "Confirmation," Thelonious Monk's " 'Round Mid-night," and "Willow Weep for Me." It tossed off about ten blues. Jackson went on chorus after chorus, with Lewis attentively paving the background with glistening medallions, and then Lewis went on and on. Heath was witty and ingenious, and time after time Kay developed that singular singing four-four beat that he learned so well from his master, Sidney Catlett. By one o'clock, the Vanguard seemed like a ship at sea—tossing and swinging and plunging—and the exultant atmosphere led its captain, Max Gordon, who is a master of the *sous mot*, to observe, "This place has a nice disarray tonight."

## New Coming

The slow, purposeful, painful game of hide-and-seek that Sonny Rollins, the masterly forty-two-year-old tenor saxophonist, has long played with his public appears to have finally ended. It began in 1959, when Rollins, who had become the most famous and influential tenor saxophonist since Coleman Hawkins and Lester Young, abruptly retired. He returned two years later, and was greeted with hosannas and a ninety-thousand-dollar Victor recording contract. But the scene had changed. The vacuum created by his absence had been filled by two revolutionary admirers—Ornette Coleman and John Coltrane. The three men jostled briefly for position, but Coleman himself began stepping in and out of little self-imposed oblivions, and Rollins' bonus-baby Victor records were not his best work. Coltrane, who had already built a com-manding style out of borrowings from Coleman and Rollins, surged into the lead, which he held firmly until his death, in 1967. No one, though, abhorred the vacuum Coltrane had left: Coleman remained out of sight, and in 1969 Rollins again disappeared. Then, recently, he surfaced like a whale at the Village Vanguard with a new quartet. He talked tonight between sets about his second return: "I had got into a very disillusioned attitude by 1969, a despondent attitude. The first time I dropped out, it was to write and study. This time it was disillusionment with the music scene. I started playing again in public last summer, at a festival in Norway, and it was a nice, inauspicious way to begin. I'm going to make my little contribu-tion, whatever it might be. There'll be no more hiatuses for me from now until the end, which isn't that far away when I consider the time I have left.

Time. It's a dimension I don't understand at all. I look in the mirror and study myself and I see that my face is changing, that it's aging, but inside I'm still little old me."

Rollins' new Coming at the Vanguard has been exhilarating. His style—volcanic, acerb, funny, wildly inventive—is intact; indeed, his playing, shorn of the extraneous "new-thing" hooliganisms that he tacked on to it in the sixties, is more imposing than ever. (Rollins has also consolidated himself. He emerged from his first retirement with a shaved head and a goatee, and he looked like a genie. Now he wears a normal head of hair, shades, and a modest beard.) Rollins did a singular thing in the fifties: He bent together the best elements of Coleman Hawkins and Charlie Parker. He extracted the muscle from Hawkins' tone, lopped off Hawkins' famous vibrato, and sharpened Hawkins' method of melodic playing by parodying it. He learned Parker's teeming disregard of bar lines, Parker's way with rhythm (the oddly placed notes, the silences, the avalanches of sixteenth notes), and Parker's trick of mixing surreal melodic passages with bursts of improvisation. And over all this he superimposed a witty garrulity that made his immensely long solos seem, paradoxically, like endless strings of epigrams.

Rollins played just two sets tonight, and each one had just three tunes. But each set went on for an hour and a half, and some of the tunes lasted fifty minutes. It was an extraordinary display of energy, an all-at-once attempt to loose three years of dammed-up brilliance. Rollins' very first number turned out to be untoppable. It started out at a breakneck tempo as Charlie Parker's "52nd Street Theme," and it ended in half tempo, fifty minutes later, as "Three Little Words." His twenty-minute solo bridged the two parts, and it was a furious creation, full of twisted fragments of melody, rough staccato passages shoulder to shoulder with serene behind-the-beat ones, mad Parker runs, and vinegary interpolations of melodies like "Moonlight in Vermont." Rollins' pianist, Al Dailey, who has absorbed both Art Tatum and Bud Powell, soloed well, and he was followed by Rollins' fine, sound bassist, Larry Ridley. Then the rhythm section fell silent, and Rollins went softly into one of his celebrated ten-minute cadenzas. It became encyclopedic and demonic. There were splinters of "Three Little Words," "Humoresque," and Chopin's "Funeral March," chaise-longue legato meditations, and sprinting double-time sections. The rest of the evening—a couple of ballads: "Easy to Remember" and "In a Sentimental Mood"; a couple of blues: "Sonnymoon" and "Blue Monk"; and a merengue—was anticlimactic Rollins but par for anyone else. Almost as phenomenal tonight as Rollins was his new and young drummer, David Lee. Rollins' nonstop methods have felled countless drummers, but Lee, beautifully under every Rollins phrase, demonstrated perfect time, dynamics, and a refreshing sense of taste.

When Earl Hines came East from Oakland eight years ago to give his celebrated concerts at the Little Theatre, he was in precarious condition. He had lost favor in much of the jazz world, both because he had been out of sight and mind and because jazz itself had changed in the decade since he had gone West. Always a supremely confident musician and showman, he had fallen prey to self-doubt; he was, in fact, thinking of quitting music altogether and going into shopkeeping with his wife. But his longtime friend and amanuensis, the English critic Stanley Dance, kept after him by long-distance telephone and set up the concerts; and the concerts themselves deservedly received a rousing response. Within a year or so, Hines' life had turned completely around. He had made half a dozen recordings, he had had a triumphant European tour, and he had appeared at the Newport and Monterey Festivals—occasions that have not always signified musical conquests but that nonetheless are always News. Suddenly, he was everywhere: in night clubs, on television, at festivals, on record after record, at Duke Ellington's seventieth-birthday White House party. But the excitement at having one of the great masters of jazz back in currency tended to obscure the fact that he was *playing* harder than he ever had and that year by year his style was growing denser and more complex and more exhilarating. No less than five unaccompanied solo recordings recently released—"Hines '65," "Earl Hines Plays Duke Ellington," "Earl Hines at Home," "My Tribute to Louis," and "Quintessential Recording Session: Earl Hines"—document this brilliant growth. Indeed, the "Quintessential" album, supervised by Marian McPartland, is extraordinary.

For a long time, the revolutionary style that Hines first exhibited in the late twenties in Chicago was hidden under Louis Armstrong's bushel. Hines' "trumpet-style" piano, as it was called, was said to be derived almost wholly from Armstrong's playing. But it is now clear that Hines and Armstrong borrowed from each other, and that Hines' style, a fusion of his own genius and what he had absorbed in Pittsburgh, where he grew up, was pretty well formed when he got to Chicago. Unlike such Eastern stride pianists as James P. Johnson and Willie the Lion Smith and Fats Waller, who were still oom-pahing their way out of the intricate straitjacket of ragtime, Hines used tenths or sudden single-note stabs in his left hand and a mixture of chords and long, single-note lines in his right hand. The stride pianists were locked in seesaw rhythms, but Hines did anything he chose with the beat. He would break up passages with double-time or out-of-tempo explosions, all the while implying a metronomic beat. And he covered these inventions with subtle decorations. He often ended his phrases with little tremolos that had the graceful effect of a vibrato on a vibratoless instrument, and he had a continually undulating sense of dynamics. He would accent the central notes of certain phrases, back away for a measure or two, then underline several more notes.

Then, over the next twenty years, a variety of things happened to Hines. He became the leader of a succession of good big bands, and his playing, though "featured," took a secondary place. (He once said, "I never considered myself a piano soloist anyway, so I was happy to just take my little eight bars and get off. It's the public that's pushed me out and made me a soloist.")

At the same time, a group of masterly admirers began appearing—among them Art Tatum and Teddy Wilson and Mary Lou Williams and Nat Cole and Erroll Garner—and the great originator, obscured by these attentive encircling saplings, no longer seemed as startling and fresh. Even the handful of piano solos he recorded in the thirties and forties sounded discursive and mechanical, as did the random small-band recordings he made throughout the fifties.

Hines will be sixty-seven this year, and his style has become involuted, rococo, and subtle to the point of elusiveness. It unfolds in orchestral layers, and it demands intense listening. Despite the sheer mass of notes he now uses, his playing is never fatty. Hines may go along like this in a medium-tempo blues: He will play the first two choruses softly and out of tempo, unreeling placid chords that safely hold the kernel of the melody. By the third chorus, he will have slid into a steady but implied beat and raised his volume. Then, using steady tenths in his left hand, he will stamp out a whole chorus of right-hand chords in between beats. He will vault into the upper register in the next chorus and wind through irregularly placed notes, while his left hand plays descending, on-the-beat chords that pass through a forest of harmonic changes. (There are so many push-me, pull-you contrasts going on in such a chorus that it is impossible to grasp it one time through.) In the next chorus—bang!—up goes the volume again, and Hines breaks into a crazy-legged double-time-and-a-half run that may make several sweeps up and down the keyboard and that are punctuated by offbeat single notes in the left hand. Then he will throw in several fast descending two-fingered glissandos, go into an arrhythmic swirl of chords and short, broken runs, and, as abruptly as he began it all, ease into an interlude of relaxed chords and poling single notes. But these choruses, which may be followed by eight or ten more before Hines has finished what he has to say, are irresistible in other ways. Each is a complete creation in itself, and yet each is lashed tightly to the next. Hines' sudden changes in dynamics, tempo, and texture are dramatic but not melodramatic; the ham lurking in the middle distance never gets any closer. And Hines is a perfervid pianist; he gives the impression that he has shut himself up completely within his instrument, that he is issuing his chords and runs and glisses not merely through its keyboard and hammers and strings but directly from its soul.

Most of the Hines records at hand are full of these beauties. The main exception is "Hines '65." It was made in London when Hines was still reconstituting himself, and it has a static, I-wish-I-could-get-going quality. There are traces of the mechanical mid-period Hines and strong suggestions of what is to come, but the crossing-over is not yet complete. The four other records, made within the past two years or so, are the new Hines. "Earl Hines at Home" is of particular interest, for it was recorded in his living room on a fantastic Steinway built in 1904 and given to him by an editor of the *San Francisco Chronicle*. The instrument has the wise, seasoned sound of first-rate pianos, and it is obvious that Hines relishes every tone. Listen to his slow reading of "You'll Never Know." Hines makes a stately rhapsody out of it, padding around richly and comfortably in the lower registers—a series of distant booms—and then leaping into the highest octave, where the notes are round and alabaster. Hines is again at a superior Steinway in the "My Tribute to Louis" album. He was meditating on his old colleague, for there are two affecting versions of "When It's Sleepy Time Down South"— the first, bravura and rumbling, and the second wistful and sad. There is a scattershot "Struttin' with Some Barbecue," and a wild, springing "A Kiss to Build a Dream On." The "Hines Plays Ellington" album is, barring two selections, an interesting instance of an improviser's being buffaloed by Ellington's sheer melodic strength as a composer. In "Sophisticated Lady," "Warm Valley," and "Come Sunday," Hines attempts to turn the melodies into his own channels. But they won't move, and he ends up encasing them in flourishes and embellishments—like ranch houses engulfed in ginger-bread trimmings. "C-Jam Blues" and "Mood Indigo" are different. Both are free, plunging Hines; listen, in particular, to the opening and closing sec-tions of "Mood Indigo," in which he coasts along out of tempo, developing a set of chords whose philosophical harmonies Ellington himself would admire. The "Quintessential Recording Session" album is precisely that. Hines reworks all eight of the tunes he set down on his famous 1928 Q.R.S. sides, and unlike the revisions of their early work that elderly authors indulge in (Henry James' eccentric New York edition of his novels), each one of these is a masterpiece. Note how he drifts sidewise into "A Monday Date," and how, through a gradually rising volume and more and more com-plex figures, he eventually constructs a castle of sound; how, in the opening section of "Chimes in Blues," he plays a series of delicate out-of-tempo chords; how the very fast "Chicago High Life" nonetheless gives the effect of slow motion; and how the harmonies in "Off Time Blues" flex and unflex, changing back and forth from triads to cumbrous flatted ninths. The record-ing, with its knotted intensity, its imaginative brilliance, and its richness and control, appears to be a climactic achievement. But Hines may fool us again.

Jimmy Rushing, the great blues singer, died yesterday, at the age of sixty-eight. He was a short, joyous, nimble, invincible fat man who shouted the blues as if he were wearing kid gloves and carrying a swagger stick. His diction was faultless; in fact, it had an elo-cutionary quality, for his vowels were broad and sumptuous, his "b"s each weighed a pound, and he loved to roll his "r"s. His lyrics had a pearl-gray, to-the-manor-born cast to them. His voice—light, tenorlike, sometimes straining—was not much, but it was hand-polished and it could be, despite his dandyish style, extraordinarily affecting, as in the mourning, deep-blue "How Long Blues" he recorded in memory of his friend Hot Lips Page. But most of the time Rushing's blues were elegant, lifting celebrations of life, and he sang them that way—his voice finally almost threadbare—until the day he died.

## A Sweet, Thin, Easygoing Person

**N**ot much is known about Charlie Christian's background. He was born in Dallas, in 1918 or 1919, and was raised in Oklahoma City. His father, a blind guitarist and singer, apparently taught him the guitar, and as a child Christian was a member, along with his father and two brothers, of a strolling group that gave sidewalk musicales in white districts. He started professionally as a bassist with the Alphonso Trent band well before he was twenty, and in the next several years he jobbed around the West, possibly getting as far east as St. Louis and as far north as Bismarck, in North Dakota, where he was heard, with astonishment, by the teen-aged Mary Osborne, who later became an ardent Christian disciple. He had heard Lester Young as early as 1929, but his own playing seems to have sprung whole from the rich soil of the Southwest. Then, in 1939, word about Christian got to John Hammond, the remarkable discoverer and shepherd of jazz talent. Hammond, on his way to the West Coast, looked up Christian, and, at Hammond's behest, Benny Goodman hired him. He stayed with Goodman just under two years, but the clarinettist treasured Christian as much as the celebrated master egotist was able to treasure any of his sidemen, and we are indebted to him for the thirty-odd records he allowed Christian to solo on. Christian's solos were never more than two choruses long, but it doesn't matter; his intense originality was in every bar he played. A handful of photographs survive, too, all but one showing a slight, dapper, serious young man wearing rimless glasses and a keep-out! expression. The exception is remarkable. It must have been taken at a *Metronome* "all-star" recording in 1940. Christian, seated next to Gene Krupa, is wearing a top-heavy high-crowned felt hat on the back of his head, an open double-breasted jacket, and a sports shirt, and he looks like a child in adults' clothing. But he doesn't have his glasses on, and his face, lean and flat and tight, is startlingly old. And there are Mary Lou Williams' recent recollections: "I think I was the one really got him to join Benny Goodman. I used to jam with Charlie in a little club in Oklahoma City when we passed through town with Andy Kirk's band, and one night in 1939 I asked him if he was going to take the Goodman job. I don't think he wanted to leave Oklahoma City, and I don't think his family wanted him to leave, either—maybe because they already knew about his sickness. All he said was 'Mary, I'll join if you'll join, too.' There *was* some talk about my going with Goodman, but I told him go ahead anyway, and he did. Later, whenever I was in New York with Kirk, I'd look Charlie up and we'd go to a basement room in the Dewey Square Hotel, usually around ten in the morning, and sometimes we'd jam, just the two of us, until eleven at night. It smelled down there and the rats ran over our feet and only ten keys on the piano played, but we didn't pay any attention. All those little figures that later became the famous riff numbers that Goodman recorded would come out, and after we'd played a couple of hours he'd put down his pick and play classical guitar and things like 'Rhapsody in Blue.' It was beautiful. He wasn't a swellheaded person at all. He was very sweet and easygoing—a sweet, thin, easygoing person. Fact, I only saw him mad once. At one of our sessions, he said, 'Mary, can't you call Benny and tell him to stay out of my solos? He keeps coming in in the middle of them, and I think if he doesn't quit I'm going back to Oklahoma.' Of course, he never did. The last time we played together, he must already have been quite sickly, because the only thing he wanted to eat was ice cream." What else survives of Christian? Such matters as his inveterate, debilitating, all-night jamming uptown with such other remarkable juveniles as Dizzy Gillespie, Charlie Parker, and Thelonious Monk; his tuberculosis, which hospitalized him permanently in 1941; and his death—a moth extinguished by his own flame—in a Staten Island hospital on March 2, 1942.

Christian was not the first great jazz guitarist. He was preceded, in the mid-thirties, by the masterly Belgian eccentric Django Reinhardt. Christian knew Reinhardt's work, and, the legend goes, could play some of his solos note for note, but that is as far as the admiration went. He applauded vigorously, then went his own way. (One wonders what Reinhardt thought of Christian's recordings, if, indeed, he knew them at all. He never heard Christian in the flesh, for he visited this country only once, in 1946, and Christian never got to Europe. What a marvel they would have been in a duet—Washington and Lincoln breaking bread!) Reinhardt was mainly an acoustical guitarist, and Christian was the father of the electric guitar. He never indulged himself by playing too loud or by hiding under the shimmering surface of his instrument. Instead, he used it as it was meant to be used— as an electronic *key* to what is basically a soft and secret instrument. At the same time, he was the first guitarist to transcend the guitar; that is to say that, in the manner of all great jazz musicians, what he *played* became more important than the instrument itself. (Lesser musicians remain locked within their instruments.) His style was a model of clarity and design and order. It had the wastelessness and purpose of geometry, the flow and logic of Albers. But the laconic exterior was frequently ruffled, for Christian freely transmitted the emotions that drove him—those unfathomable, nameless emotions that compel all first-rate music—and he did it without ever disturbing the master plan each solo seemed to follow. He was a surpassing technician, and at the age of twenty he had already learned a seminal secret about jazz improvisation that few players ever know—the value of silence. He rounded his phrases, which ran anywhere from one to ten or more bars, with little rests— some of them a beat in length, some a whole measure. They had a pleasant shock effect, and they allowed the listener to catch up with what had gone before and to ready himself for what was to come. (One of the strangest things about Christian's legion of imitators is that almost to a man they have completely ignored this aspect of his style. Indeed, they play thousands and thousands of notes nonstop, as if sheer musical poundage would raise them to Christian's stature.)

Christian loved the blues, as do all Southwestern musicians, and several of his choruses went like this: He'd start with a descending two-note phrase, repeat it quickly two or three times, and pause. He then reversed the notes, added several others, went into a behind-the-beat legato passage, a drifting-with-the-current passage, and paused again, briefly, climbed into fast, on-the-beat eighth notes that surged up and down the scale, and ended in a rocking, offbeat chord. An ingenious riff popped out at the beginning of the next chorus, and he repeated it several times, achieving a concentrated, singsong effect. Then he abruptly broke out of the riff, passed through a silent clearing, fashioned a descending phrase full of odd notes, and kept compounding the phrase past the end of the second chorus and halfway into the third. He then went limp and legato again, and, remembering the riff, repeated it once, lightly, and made way for the next soloist, who almost invariably began with a paraphrase of Christian's last measure. Christian's rare recordings of slow ballads were tropical delights. He pushed the melody straight before him, allowing it to swell sumptuously here and sink easily there, then took the melody, and, in a passage resting on long-held notes, turned it gently inside out before returning to direct melodic ruminations. His ballads became sensuous slow-motion dreams that filled the listener's mind. Christian's imagination, no matter the tempo or the materials, seemed to have no limit.

But how fine that we do have a handful of recordings—made by amateurs in night clubs—in which Christian stretches out and sounds as if he could play a hundred straight choruses without repeating a phrase. Three of these on-the-spot treats are now available, for the first time, in a Columbia release, "Solo Flight: The Genius of Charlie Christian." They are extended versions of "I Got Rhythm," "Stardust," and "Tea for Two"—all of them recorded by a disc jockey in a club in Minneapolis in September of 1939. The first number, a fast one, has four Christian choruses (spliced from two different versions); the second has two slow, singing choruses; the last has three perfect statements. Also on hand are Jerry Jerome (a middling tenor saxophonist who was with Goodman at the time), a pianist named Frankie Hines, and the bassist Oscar Pettiford. Everything of Christian is here—the rests, the little riffs, the funny interpolations, the *listen!*, on-the-beat phrases, the way-out notes and chords that were to be part of the cornerstone of the bebop movement. The rest of the LP consists mostly of sides made with Benny Goodman—two of them with the big band and the rest with small groups. A third of the latter are alternate takes that have never been released before ("I've Found a New Baby," "Royal Garden Blues," "Wholly Cats," and "All Star

Strut" among them), and in "Breakfast Feud" four Christian choruses, three of them lifted from unissued takes, have been spliced. Also included are two long studio warm-up numbers, in which Christian, along with Georgie Auld, Cootie Williams, Johnny Guarnieri, Artie Bernstein, and Dave Tough, rambles around comfortably in the blues. (One of them, "Waitin' for Benny," has a relaxed and brilliant open horn Williams solo.) Not included, though, are the ten or so other Goodman-Christian efforts, and it's too bad; we would finally have had their complete œuvre at hand. Most of the small-band sides among the present recordings have long been considered classics, but they would not be so without Christian. Listen to the pre–Christian Goodman small-band records and to the ones Goodman made after Christian—who had barely said hello to the world—was gone.

## New Digs

*July 1st*

The Eighteenth Newport Jazz Festival, removed for sociological and economic reasons from the gentle slope above Newport Harbor where it resided for eleven years, began in Carnegie Hall at five o'clock this afternoon as the Newport Jazz Festival–New York. The Festival made Newport hum. It packed its narrow streets and roads with rivers of cars and people. It provided Newport kids with their one big whoopee of the year. It brought people out on their lawns in the evening to ogle the swells from New York and Illinois and Colorado. It filled the merchants' coffers. It caused hotels and motels to sprout. It even put the weather on the *qui vive*, so that we invariably had one spectacular each weekend—a smashing thunderstorm, a woolen fog, a hellish heat wave, or a cannonading rain. It made Newport, twice famous before—in Colonial days and at the turn of the century—famous again, and the town, despite the grumbling of its officials, who were indulging in the classic love-hate behavior that the residents of all New England resort towns display toward tourists, enjoyed that. So Newport hummed, but New York, stripped of the furniture of automobiles and pedestrians by a record Fourth of July exodus, looked naked and empty today. Even Carnegie Hall was less than half-full this afternoon, and I had the feeling at the outset of the concert that I was in the wrong place—that the real Festival was going on somewhere else, perhaps in Newport. But the first group, the Modern Jazz Quartet, set things right with six flawless numbers, among them a blues, "Valeria," that had a sorrowing, gentle melodic line, played sotto voce by Milt Jackson; John Lewis's "In Memoriam"; and a swinging, spinning "Bag's Groove." The high point of the quartet's performance came during Jackson's first solo chorus in "Bag's Groove," when Lewis pushed a simple ascending background figure so close to Jackson's melodic line it threatened to get entangled in his spokes. But it didn't; it merely boosted Jackson up and into several superlative choruses. Stan Getz then floated serenely by on a powerful rhythm section that served to introduce the heralded twenty-one-year-old Philadelphia bassist Stanley Clarke. He has an extraordinary technique (he does not pluck his strings but brushes his fingertips over them), he already realizes the dramatic value of silence, his ideas are vigorous, and he has a huge tone.

During the evening concert at Philharmonic Hall (for the first six days of the Festival, there will be a five o'clock concert and a repeat nine o'clock concert at both Carnegie and Philharmonic Halls), Billy Eckstine demonstrated that he still has his celebrated bass voice but that he no longer can get it to the right place at the right time; Sarah Vaughan practiced her arabesques; and the Giants of Jazz (Dizzy Gillespie, Kai Winding, Sonny Stitt, Thelonious Monk, Al McKibbon, and Art Blakey) came to life just once, and that was in Monk's solo in a fast blues, in which he kept repeating a complex and funny phrase, making it higher each time, until it simply trailed off the end of the keyboard and into thin air.

### July 2nd

The Festival began in earnest today. In addition to the double Carnegie and Philharmonic stands, we were offered a one P.M. affair at Carnegie Hall (the first of six this week at that hour and place) and a midnight dance in the main ballroom of the Commodore Hotel. The one o'clock concert included an indifferent performance by the J.P.J. Quartet (Budd Johnson, Dill Jones, Bill Pemberton, and Oliver Jackson); a surprisingly pale one by Mary Lou Williams, a devout Catholic who is so sensitive to her surroundings when she plays that she has been known to feel bad vibrations even when there were half a dozen vigilant priests in the audience; a predictably tumultuous, driving one by Rahsaan Roland Kirk, who, with his customary galaxy of instruments slung around his neck, resembles a walking pawnshop; and a classic solo performance by the pianist Cecil Taylor. Taylor, as is his wont, played just one number, but it lasted forty minutes. It was full of his usual devices—the slamming chords, the agitated staccato passages, the breathtaking arpeggios, the blizzard density—but it had two new qualities: lyricism and gentleness. Again and again he slipped into clear lagoons where shadows of melody glided just below the surface. The audience, a full house made up mostly of kids, was transfixed, and it rewarded Taylor with what may have been the first standing ovation of his fifteen-year career.

Big bands dominated the rest of the day. At the five o'clock Philharmonic concert, Bobby Rosengarden's group from the *Dick Cavett Show* appeared, and it was good to hear such an impeccable and swinging band stretch out and to hear its two best soloists—the high-voltage trombonist Bill Watrous and the fine reedman Eddie Daniels—at length. Billy Taylor's twelve-piece group, from the defunct *David Frost* talk show, was porous in comparison, and was dominated by its leader's effusive piano. The chomping, barrel-chested Thad Jones–Mel Lewis band closed the proceedings.

Count Basie's band opened the nine o'clock concert at Carnegie Hall with over a dozen brassy, expert numbers that contained vocals by Joe Williams and by Al Hibbler, who sang a hand-carved tribute to Jimmy Rushing. They also contained a couple of self-effacing delights—eight solo choruses by Basie in a medium blues, and the bells-and-flowers sound of Basie and his master guitarist, Freddie Green, behind Hibbler and behind Williams' "In the Evenin'." The next band was a surprise. Assembled for the Festival by Benny Carter, who wrote the arrangements and three of the numbers, it included eighteen alumni from the bands of Basie, Cab Calloway, Erskine Hawkins, Duke Ellington, and Carter—among them Buddy Tate, Benny Morton, Dickie Wells, Harry Edison, Taft Jordan, Teddy Wilson, Milt Hinton, and Jo Jones. The band played with precision and verve both in the ensembles and the solos, the most striking of which were taken by Edison, Morton, Wells, Wilson, and Carter himself, who fashioned a brocaded "I Can't Get Started." A trio from the band also accompanied Maxine Sullivan in five numbers, and everything about her—the pixie features, the tipped-up chin, the motionless stance (her right arm hanging loose and her left poised lightly at her waist), the tissue-paper voice—was in balance and proportion. Carter's arrangements were full of those long, creamy, supple saxophone passages, and the only flaw was a Jo Jones drum solo in the middle of "Sleep." The number was arranged as a graceful, fleeting dream—it hums along at a terrific speed—and Jones' contribution, though very good, broke it in half.

Count Basie's band and Sy Oliver's bouncy Jimmy Lunceford group presided at the dance. The ballroom is long and narrow and tacky, and chairs, instead of tables, were arranged around its edges. Basie's band was sluggish and Oliver's peppy, and one missed the easy, coasting, middle ground that the best big dance bands invariably developed in the course of an evening. But it was instructive to watch the faces of the scattering of kids on hand when the Lindy Hop broke out; they looked as if they were seeing a ritual dance from the court of King Tut.

### July 3rd

Don Burrows, a clarinettist and flutist from Australia, opened the one P.M. concert, and he was as affecting as anyone who played all day. The chief reason—he is only a fair clarinettist, in the mold of Tony Scott and Buddy De Franco—was his sheer pleasure at being where he was. Most foreign musicians regard the Newport Festival as the Summit, and it was clear that Burrows felt that way. Several of his numbers had a fascinating folk flavor—a Down Under funk—and all his solos,

including one on a tiny flute, were impassioned. Lee Konitz, an alto saxophonist who long ago skimmed the cream off the styles of Charlie Parker
and Lester Young, followed, and he was at his best in an ingenious reworking of Louis Armstrong's "Struttin' with Some Barbecue," in which he and
the trombonist Marshall Brown used Armstrong's opening and closing
statements from the Hot Five recording as their ensembles, and in which
Konitz took a masterly solo, complete with darting melodic lines and
superbly placed off notes.

During the five P.M. concert at Carnegie Hall, Elvin Jones, in company
with a couple of reedmen and a bassist, was unusually restrained, and Bill
Evans, supported by Eddie Gomez and Marty Morrell, played six inward-
looking numbers that nonetheless flashed with Evans' taste and inventiveness. The nine o'clock Lincoln Center concert was a King Kong production.
Stan Kenton erected half a dozen or so numbers, their tops lost in the clouds,
and then accompanied a brittle and unsure June Christy. Woody Herman's
newest band was as volcanic as Kenton's (whatever happened to that velvet
quality, that squeeze-me sound, which big bands used to offer in between
their flag-wavers?), but it was more up to date, for there were fancy time signatures and snatches of gospel and rock. Such Herman old grads as Zoot
Sims, Red Norvo, Flip Phillips, and Chubby Jackson were brought out at the
end of the evening, and all of them managed to swing without lifting a single
decibel.

The first of two midnight jam sessions at Radio City Music Hall was
carried out by three different groups, which included Bobby Hackett, Roy
Eldridge, Vic Dickenson, Norvo, and Teddy Wilson (first group); Stan
Getz, Max Roach, Kenny Burrell, Mary Lou Williams, Dizzy Gillespie, and
Milt Jackson (second group); and Herbie Hancock, Tony Williams, James
Moody, Dexter Gordon, Harry Edison, Zoot Sims, and Rahsaan Roland
Kirk (final group). It lasted three hours, and some lights were lit, notably by
Hackett, Eldridge, Wilson, Mary Lou Williams, Getz, Tony Williams,
Harry Edison, and Kirk, who completely dominated his group
by choosing the numbers, determining backgrounds riffs, and playing
immense solos. The sound in the hall was badly distorted. (It was discovered later that the microphones were hooked up to the wrong set of speakers.) But the hall itself—the inside of a giant armadillo—was a good spot for
such a free-for-all. Its vastness seemed to provoke the brave little groups
onstage, which looked from the upper balconies like shipwrecked crews,
and the full house responded with lots of standing ovations and enthusiastic
billows of cigarette and pot smoke. Radio City Music Hall jumped, but it
would have jumped even more with one addition—Count Basie on the
great organ.

*July 4th*

Charlie Mingus' big band performed at five o'clock at Philharmonic Hall, and it sounded far better than it did several months ago. Particularly impressive among the five numbers was Mingus' "Ecclusiastics," a slow, beautiful gospel-flavored piece arranged in a succession of huge ensemble chords, which were divided by solos, double-time passages, and brief cacophonic bursts. The number used a big band as it should be used: every instrument was essential, the massed sounds proved new melodic and harmonic points, and a majestic aura was achieved. The second half of the program was given over to the American première of Ornette Coleman's forty-minute concerto grosso "Skies of America." The solo parts were played by Coleman, Dewey Redman (tenor saxophone), Charlie Haden, and Ed Blackwell, and the written sections by the American Symphony Orchestra. The piece marked one of the few times that jazz and symphonic techniques have been successfully wedded. The composed sections sounded like Coleman improvisations, and the improvised parts were instantaneous Coleman compositions. The soloists and the orchestra continually fed one another. Coleman and Redman would work their way through a difficult contrapuntal section, and then Coleman, who played superbly, would solo, and after a time the orchestra would come in behind. Coleman would finish, the strings would state a theme (often lovely), and Redman would solo, with the orchestra backing him. Then everybody would lay out and Coleman would solo, his notes ringing in the void, and the orchestra would rush in again with widely spaced chords. And so it went, with Coleman conversing endlessly with himself in the many tongues and tones he made available on the stage. The composition was orchestrated by Coleman in a purposely thin, high-pitched fashion, and at first it was distracting. But perhaps Coleman is right. The alto saxophone is a lightweight instrument, and it would founder in the rich orchestral gravy of, say, Berlioz.

The evening concert at Carnegie Hall was notable for what didn't happen. Miles Davis, scheduled for both the afternoon and the evening, failed to appear. (He told the press that he wasn't being paid enough and that he had never agreed to do the concerts in the first place, but the real reason may well have been fear, for he has played little in recent months, and a trumpeter's chops, if not used, can deteriorate in a week.) Davis was replaced by the trumpeter Freddie Hubbard, who got off a vacuous set, and then Sonny Rollins came on with his quartet and pretended that he wasn't there, either. During his three numbers, he walked ceaselessly in and out of the wings, pausing occasionally as he passed along the back of the stage to deliver a short cadenza, to play one chorus of the melody of "In a Sentimental Mood," or to ruminate briefly on "There Will Never Be Another You." His sidemen—Al Dailey, Larry Ridley, and David Lee—played some of the longest solos of their careers, all the while peering anxiously over their shoulders.

*July 5th*

The halfway point of the Festival was marked today by two cheerful events—Dizzy Gillespie was awarded the Handel Medallion by the city, and Eddie Condon, in company with some of his old helpmeets (Lee Wiley, Wild Bill Davison, Georg Brunis, Max Kaminsky, Buzzy Drootin, Bobby Hackett, and Benny Morton), officiated at a fine evening concert at Carnegie Hall. Two bands, padded with such non-Condon musicians as Joe Thomas, J. C. Higginbotham, Barney Bigard, and Dick Hyman, played six spirited evergreens. They were memorable for Davison's swearing, hell-bent lead cornet, for Brunis' short solos, still intact, note for note, thirty-five years after he invented them, for Bigard's loop-the-loop flights, and for a magnificent four-bar break delivered late in the evening by Hackett. Lee Wiley, long in retirement, sang midway through the concert. Her style, a subtle concatenation of Billie Holiday and Mildred Bailey, remains absolutely on keel, and it was pointed up in almost every phrase throughout her dozen numbers by her accompanists, who included Hackett, Teddy Wilson, Bucky Pizzarelli, George Duvivier, and Don Lamond. Indeed, they unobtrusively provided the most gracious and inventive backing I have ever heard a singer receive. The World's Greatest Jazz Band rounded out the concert. Vic Dickenson and Yank Lawson played a duet in "Colonial Tavern," Bob Wilber and Bud Freeman went through their funny, acrobatic "Just One of Those Things," Billy Butterfield and Lawson did "Baby, Won't You Please Come Home," Butterfield played a gorgeous flügelhorn version of "She's Funny That Way," and Ralph Sutton got off an expert revitalization of Meade Lux Lewis's "Honky Tonk Train Blues."

Gato Barbieri, a young Argentine tenor saxophonist who spends much of his time on the fringes of the avant-garde, gave a typically puzzling performance at the midday concert. He has a sweet, throaty tone, and most of his solos are made up of sustained, singsong planes of sound. But every once in a while, as if embarrassed by such a pounding-heart approach, he breaks into giant shrieks and wails, destroying the structure and mood he has so carefully developed. (The virtuoso bassist Stanley Clarke reappeared in Barbieri's group and again demonstrated his gifts.) Eubie Blake, who will be ninety next February, brought his splendid time machine onstage and took us directly back to 1900 in five numbers, three of them new creations, including a willowy waltz written for his wife and titled "Valse Marian."

*July 6th*

Every culture worth its salt has its counterculture, and the Festival's is the so-called New York Musicians Jazz Festival, which started last Friday and will continue through next Monday. It is being held in churches and parks and studios and theaters around the city, and, despite its attempt to be rebellious, it appears to be merely an inevitable overflow from the Newport affair. In fact, some of the musicians in it (Sun Ra, Archie Shepp, Wilbur Ware, Bill Hardman, Milford Graves, Rashied Ali, Jimmy Garrison, and others) have appeared at earlier Newport festivals and/or will appear at this one. It's also interesting that many of the prominent members of the only real anti-Newport festival, given in Newport at the Cliff Walk Manor Hotel in 1960, have long since packed away their war paint and are ensconced in the Festival establishment, among them Max Roach, Charlie Mingus, Ornette Coleman, and Charlie Haden.

Dizzy Gillespie celebrated his new medal at one o'clock at Carnegie Hall by playing four first-rate numbers with his sextet, which has an irresistible, rocking rhythm section (Mickey Roker on drums, Big Black on conga drums, Gary King on bass, Al Gafa on guitar, and Mike Longo on piano); by introducing a passel of visitors from his home town, Cheraw, South Carolina— among them a former teacher, the mayor, and Gillespie's twin nephews, Wesley and Presley; by singing "Sometimes I Feel Like a Motherless Child" in his high, aching voice; by dancing and telling jokes; by playing several of his compositions with the New York All-City Choir, an admirable body conducted by another Cherawian, John Motley; and by taking a solo in his final number, "Manteca," that included a seven- or eight-measure run as brilliant as anything Gillespie or any other trumpeter has ever played.

Following desultory performances by the Cannonball Adderley Quintet and by Oscar Peterson, *tout seul*, Mahavishnu, a rock-jazz group made up of two Americans (the violinist Jerry Goodman and the drummer Billy Cobham), a Czech (the pianist Jan Hammer), and an Englishman (the guitarist John McLaughlin), held forth at the five P.M. Carnegie Hall concert. It operated at well above the hundred-decibel level, and it was curious to hear improvisation so highly magnified. It was like walking through a garden full of Maillol nudes. At nine o'clock, in Lincoln Center, several New Orleans bands were joined by Harold Dejan and the Olympia Brass Band, as well as by the country-blues singer Robert Pete Williams and by a solo pianist, Bob Greene. Williams, not the most agile of the backwater singers resurrected in recent years, moaned and cracked his way through several blues. But Greene was startling. He is a Jelly Roll Morton scholar, and he played four Morton tunes, including "Tiger Rag," a piece derived from an old quadrille, which he delivered straight before jazzing it up. He has mastered all the nuances of Morton's style, and, if one closed one's eyes, it was Morton himself onstage. The New Orleans bands did not fare as well, but they rarely do outside their habitat. They have become dependent on the trappings and the moods of the French Quarter, and exhibiting them separately is like plunking a good 1710 banister-back chair down in a Scandinavian room. There was one exception, though. Ellyna Tatum, the New Orleans singer and street dancer, sang "Just a Closer Walk with Thee" with the Olympia Brass Band and then danced behind the band as it marched through the audience. She has no bones or joints, and her dancing is one long, uninterrupted fluid motion. Her elbows fly in and out, as if she were pumping a bellows, her legs bend slowly and then shoot her upright, her trunk undulates continuously, and her head whips wildly back and forth. She is a supreme free-form dancer, and it is too bad that she wasn't let loose onstage, where more of the audience could see her.

George Wein's second Radio City Music Hall jam session took place tonight. Two different groups, made up of Elvin Jones, Gerry Mulligan, Nat Adderley, Sonny Stitt, Jimmy Smith, and Gary Burton, played buoyantly and well. Then the third and final group, which consisted of, among others, Buddy Tate, Charlie Mingus, Milt Buckner, Cat Anderson, Jimmy Owens, and Charlie McPherson, swept through a good fast blues before settling into a slow blues that had two remarkable solos. The first was by the young trumpeter Owens, and it was a series of stately choruses, each more intense and daring than the last, and the second was by Mingus, who played heavy, arching notes, endless weird runs that skirted the edge of tonality, deep double-stops, broken, deliberately staggered connective passages, and double-time flights that moved faster than the ear.

*July 7th*

The one o'clock concert was an interminable demonstration of the new abstract jazz. It is made up mainly of free rhythms, deafening volumes, electrified soloists who may play at length two or three times in one number, wild ensembles, little discernible thematic material and little discernible form, and percussionists who work from tables laden with bells, bones, gourds, gongs, and the like. And it is resolutely humorless. Only Archie Shepp's group appeared to enjoy itself. During one long number, he shouted rudely while his trombonist soloed, a poem was read to thunderous accompaniment, and a little girl in a white party dress sang in a flat voice and was backed up by a fat trumpeter in a floor-length blue gown. Shepp has always been an avant-garde dresser, and I wonder if his costume today was a bellwether one, for he was wearing a rumpled business suit and a plain white shirt with an open collar.

The double concerts at Carnegie and Philharmonic Halls have ended, and tonight, at seven, the Festival moved to Yankee Stadium. It was a mistake. The audience was small and the acoustics were terrible, it rained, and Nina Simone got laryngitis and didn't show up. The audience sat along the third-base line, and the musicians played in a small covered bandstand over behind second base. But jazz musicians have a way of breasting perversity, and one at least sensed good performances by Dave Brubeck, who had Paul Desmond and Gerry Mulligan with him; by B. B. King; and by Ray Charles, who turned in hi-jinks renditions of "Take Me Out to the Ball Game" and "Indian Love Call."

*July 8th*

Yesterday, the *Times* ran a recent picture of the bandstand at Festival Field in Newport. It was standing knee-deep in grass, and it looked desolate and forlorn. It made me homesick, and tonight, instead of going back up to Yankee Stadium, where a predictable concert by Roberta Flack, Lou Rawls, Les McCann, and the Giants of Jazz was scheduled, I went to the New York Cultural Center to see the Bert Stern documentary *Jazz on a Summer's Day*, which was shot during the 1958 Festival. There were fine, if mud-colored, glimpses of Anita O'Day, Jimmy Giuffre, Bob Brookmeyer, Louis Armstrong, Jack Teagarden, Thelonious Monk, Big Maybelle, Mahalia Jackson, Buck Clayton, and Dinah Washington. They all played and sang well (especially Giuffre and Brookmeyer), Newport looked wonderful, and the movie should have cheered me up, but all it did was remind me that Teagarden and Armstrong and Mahalia and Dinah Washington and Big Maybelle are dead, and that Buck Clayton is suffering from an apparently incurable case of trumpeter's block, a weak lip.

The last of the one o'clock Carnegie Hall concerts was built around Duke Ellington and Bobby Short. The program, some fourteen or fifteen numbers long, was pretty much *de rigueur*, but it was performed beautifully (Cootie Williams, in "C-Jam Blues," "Take the 'A' Train," and "Satin Doll," played with that great primitive ferocity he now has), and it included a ballad, "Happy Reunion," played fervently by Paul Gonsalves, and a reworking of "Harlem," a "tone parallel," as Ellington calls it, written twenty years ago. It opened with a primeval trumpet call by Williams, went through several complex ensemble passages, taken at different tempos and enclosing brief solos, and ended with a long conversation between bass clarinet, alto saxophone, and two regular clarinets. The instruments, played by Harry Carney, Norris Turney, Harold Ashby, and Russell Procope, were truly people talking in the evening on a Harlem street corner, just as other parts of the piece suggested beautiful women strutting down Seventh Avenue or people *shouting* out of windows to passersby. The work has a denseness and tension that have largely disappeared from Ellington's composing, and it was a treat to hear it again. Near the end of the program, Bobby Short, thin as a pole and sporting a log-sized mustache, sang five songs associated with Ivie Anderson—three with the band and two at the piano—and they *did* summon up Miss Anderson, particularly "I Got It Bad and That Ain't Good," which Short sang with unerring plaintiveness and delicacy. Ellington closed the afternoon by bringing out a remarkable and beautiful Rumanian soprano named Aura, who hummed and scatted "Mood Indigo," pushing her voice up almost beyond hearing and never missing a note or losing pitch. The concert was the best swatch of Ellingtonia we have had in a long time.

*July 9th*

This Festival—so long, so multifarious, so overproduced—ended in an anticlimactic fashion, which was suitable, for it left its excellences standing clearly in the mind. A gospel program was held at nine A.M. in Radio City Music Hall, and because there were seven groups and just two hours for them to perform in (way had to be made for the regular twelve o'clock show), no one could do much more than warm up. Gospel music is not just lyrical; it is a music of possession and frenzy, which take time. But it was a pleasure to finally hear the Birmingham singer Dorothy Love Coates. She has a fine contralto and a spacious, magisterial way of phrasing; she is ready for Mahalia's shoes.

Later in the day, I at last got to see *Miss Truth*, which had been playing all week at the Carnegie Recital Hall. It is a drama with music and dance based on the life of a slave, Sojourner Truth, who was born in Ulster County, New York, in 1797, and who, after she gained freedom, became an activist and feminist. Written, composed, and acted in by Glory Van Scott, it is a charming and funny curiosity that particularly delighted the children in the audience.

# Big Joe

I t is time someone made a study of the effects of environment and climate on jazz. Herewith some notes: New Orleans jazz, nurtured in that easy, moist city, was a legato, flowing music propelled by the undemanding two-four beat. The instrumentalists had spacious tones and generous vibratos, and the music was largely collective, which suggested casualness and bonhomie. (New Orleans musicians are apt to greet one another by saying, "How you be? I see you brought yourself today.") When New Orleans jazz moved to Chicago, in the twenties, it tightened up. Arrangements were increasingly used, and so was the four-four beat. Soloists, by nature godlike and antisocial, came to the fore, and collective music waned. The legato attack gave way to an on-the-beat one, and even to staccato phrasing. The first generation of Chicago-born musicians carried these changes further by converting the music of their New Orleans models into a wild, winds-of-Chicago attack, full of breaks and surprising dynamics. (Some of the fastest jazz records ever made have come out of Chicago.) When New York took over as the capital of jazz, in the early thirties, it affected the music the way it affects everything: It made it grow up. Corners were smoothed, vibratos controlled, and tempos modulated. Rhythm sections began to swing for the first time, and the music became more and more subtle. Duke Ellington's music became New York music, and as he went so went the musical community—until the arrival, that is, of a kind of jazz that had been bypassed in the New Orleans–Chicago–New York trek. It was the music of the Southwest, and of Kansas City in particular, and when it was brought to town, in the late thirties, by Count Basie and Jo Jones and Charlie Christian and Lester Young, it turned everything around.

Not much was known about Kansas City jazz in New York; it had been geographically isolated and it had not been widely recorded. Indeed, its importance in the shaping of jazz was not fully understood until recently. Its irresistible and original characteristics seemed to imply endless spaces and crazy weather and the howdy openness of Southwesterners. It was laconic and at the same time highly charged. It swung very hard, but in a look-Ma, no-hands fashion. It was a face-to-face music, yet it often implied more than it said. It had a unique, mysterioso quality—a longing for distant hills and deep woods. The Southwestern horn players had big tones, and they transmitted emotion generously and in a variety of ways. Consider the opposite approaches of the Southwest's two most famous tenor saxophonists, Lester Young and Herschel Evans. Young, with his light, almost colorless tone, used laissez-faire melodic lines that tipped their hats to the melody, that applauded it with soft hands. He was gracious and accommodating and oblique. But Evans had a heavy, keening tone, a rich-soil tone, and his phrases, which were short and annunciatory, were continually shaded by bent notes and sad November inflections. Evans mourned the world in every chorus. The Southwestern musicians were also indefatigable, for they had been weaned on the legendary nonstop Kansas City jam sessions, which thrived in a city that literally never closed. (These sessions sometimes went around the clock, and they virtually wore out whole rhythm sections.) Kansas City jazz was a blues-soaked music. Blue notes and husky timbres infused every type of song, and the blues themselves were enriched in a way not known in jazz before. They were either light and happy—but never tongue-in-cheek, in the manner of many Eastern musicians—or brooding and majestic. There are countless instances of these approaches in the work of Basie and Joe Turner and Young and Buck Clayton, and now we have still another in "John Hammond's Spirituals to Swing: Thirtieth Anniversary Concert (1967)." The three best numbers in the album are blues performed by Turner, who, backed by several of his old Kansas City colleagues, is in superlative form.

In many ways, Turner, who is now sixty-one, is the epitome of Kansas City music. More than that, he encompasses all blues singing, from Blind Lemon Jefferson to B. B. King. When one listens to Turner, it is immediately clear that *this* is the way the blues should be sung, *this* is what his countless predecessors and contemporaries have been striving for. Everything about Turner is outsize and seignorial. He is well over six feet and heavily assembled, and he has a big head and mountain-encircling arms. His voice matches. It is deep and muscular and booming; it is a bear hug of a voice. But Turner never spends it all; one has the impression that he is using only two-thirds of his powers, that if he wanted he could blow the house down. He is also a master of inflection and dynamics and rhythmic control. He can amble thunderingly along behind the beat, ride it lightly, or push it mercilessly. And he has a rich dramatic sense. When his lyrics are concerned with diurnal, domestic matters, he sings in a gray, offhand way—he sometimes gives the effect of almost yawning—but when he delivers a line like, "But I want the sun to rise, the wind to blow," his voice becomes huge and commanding. The sun *rises*, the wind *blows*. When the lyrics are funny, his voice is mocking and implacable, as in this reverberating, almost frightening stanza:

> Don't the moon look pretty shining
>     down through the trees,
> Don't the moon look pretty shining
>     down through the trees,
>     . . . my baby look good walking
>     out on her knees.

Turner will go at a slow blues this way: He spreads out the first phrase behind the beat, and he uses just two notes (Turner is not a melismatic singer)—one for the first and last words of the phrase, and one for its middle section. Then he pauses a full measure, goes on to his second phrase, pauses again, briefly, and completes the line. He repeats the line, with slight melodic variations, subtracting one of the pauses and rearranging the lyrics in an almost sleight-of-hand way, as in:

> That one record, particular baby [pause],
>     *always* sticks in my mind,
> That one little song, particular darlin',
>     always sticks in my mind.

In the third line of the stanza he raises his volume and moves up slightly on the scale, then swoops abruptly down. He jams the first eight words of the first line of the next stanza together, and finishes the line by planting the remaining words six inches apart. The second and third lines are gap-toothed all the way through. Two more stanzas pass, and then, his words demanding intensity, he italicizes them and even repeats them, hammering away at the beat and at the inevitable woman he is imploring. He subsides again, and in the final stanza he goes up on the mountaintop. His voice rings, he inserts an iron blue note, and suddenly the hall he is singing in is filled with trumpeting winds. He repeats a key phrase in this stanza at the close of the third line, in the manner of announcing a victory, and then, as is his wont, lets loose a booming Bronx cheer to tell us that it is time to set foot on earth again. Turner's diction at slow tempos is intelligible in a drawling, backhanded fashion, but in a fast blues he doesn't have time for niceties. He flattens his words, and they become planes of sound that climb and fall and bend away, and it doesn't really matter what he is singing about. He has become a joyous, shouting, hornlike wash of melody and rhythm and emotion.

The album was recorded at a concert given five years ago in Carnegie Hall to celebrate the two great, pioneering concerts that John Hammond engineered there in the late thirties. On hand, along with Turner, are the gospel singer Marion Williams, the guitarist George Benson, the alto saxophonist John Handy, the blues singer Big Mama Thornton, and Count Basie's band. Big Mama Thornton is the only performer who comes close to matching Turner. She shrieks and yodels and moans and shouts with great authority, but there is a hysterical, overweening quality in her singing (the blues tend to melt away when they are pressed so hard), and I suspect that the surroundings unnerved her. Turner is extraordinary. Listen to the way he crowds his words together at the opening of the second stanza of his single slow blues, "I'm Going Away to Wear You Off My Mind," the way he beseeches his baby at the start of the fourth stanza, and the way, in the final stanza, with his accompaniment lifting behind him mightily, he turns into Zeus. His two other blues, "Roll 'Em Pete" and "Blues for John," are medium-fast, and they are brilliant exercises in hill-and-dale non-articulation. His accompaniment in "Blues for John" is handled in a slapdash way by the Basie band, but in "Roll 'Em Pete" and "I'm Going Away to Wear You Off My Mind" he is backed by a remarkable group made up of Buck Clayton (his lip still healthy), Buddy Tate, Edmond Hall, Ray Bryant, Milt Hinton, and Jo Jones. (Pete Johnson, who had been retired for years and who died not long after the concert, was added in "Roll 'Em Pete," and it was a misty moment when he went onstage. He and Turner had come to New York to appear at Hammond's first "Spirituals to Swing" concert, and before that they had worked together for years in the Sunset Café, in Kansas City. Johnson had led the house band, and Turner had been a singing bartender who occasionally stepped out on the sidewalk and shouted a blues that could be heard five blocks away.) Clayton is unbelievable throughout. His two solo choruses in "I'm Going Away to Wear" are celestial, and so are his obbligatos, particularly in the final majestic stanza, where he becomes a hallelujah alter-voice to Turner. Hall (*he* died not long after, too) and Tate and Jones and Bryant are admirable as well. They must have known, from the moment Turner started to sing, that magnificence was abroad that night.

## Jeru

For twenty years, Gerry Mulligan, the forty-five-year-old baritone saxophonist, arranger, and composer, has been celebrated for his forward-looking arranging and composing and for the unusual instrumentations of his various groups, but these innovations, though witty and graceful, have rarely been startling, and sometimes they have seemed inconclusive. And he has been celebrated as a player, but he has failed to dim the luster of Harry Carney or the impassioned caperings of the late Serge Chaloff. He has also become a celebrated Person, and this has been apt. He is a tall, thin, mordant, nervous, funny Irishman with red hair, a boyish smile, and a commanding presence. And he has nurtured his image carefully. When it was seemly, he was a bonelike figure who wore a crewcut and madras jackets; now, in his mod clothes, long hair, and huge, fiery beard, he looks like a patriarch. But Mulligan's pervasive presence and occasional musical rockets have long obscured the fact that he is an inspired and often ingenious conservationist who has spent his career pursuing and reshaping the traditional beauties of jazz. His arranging and composing are excellent and illuminating recastings of Count Basie and Duke Ellington and Gil Evans, and his playing is a finely carved set of variations on the best of such forebears as Lester Young and Coleman Hawkins.

Mulligan came to the fore as a member of the famous and beautiful nonet assembled by Miles Davis in 1948. The group recorded twelve 78-rpm sides in 1949 and 1950, and Mulligan, in addition to playing in all of them, arranged and/or composed four of the numbers. They were remarkable records for several reasons. The most complex small-band efforts yet made, they employed an unorthodox instrumentation (trumpet, trombone, French horn, tuba, alto and baritone saxophones, and a guitarless rhythm section) and the equally unorthodox visions of the arranger Gil Evans (B. A., Duke Ellington U., circa 1940) to distill and control the melodic and harmonic inventions of bebop. They also set the rhythmic discoveries of bop in perspective for the first time, and they put together, for an unforgettable group musical think, such future movers and shapers as Davis, Evans, Lee Konitz, J. J. Johnson, John Lewis, Max Roach, Gunther Schuller, and Mulligan, all of whom have brought tablets down from the mount. And the records provided the chief inspiration for the cool jazz that flourished in Los Angeles in the fifties. But the nonet, a prophet without honor, got little work, and in 1950 it disbanded. Mulligan wandered west, ending up in 1951 in Los Angeles, where, after some scuffling, he hit on his first and probably best-known group—a pianoless quartet made up of his horn, a trumpet, a bass, and drums. It was an attractive group, and it made Mulligan famous. Most of what it played consisted of a pair of melodic lines that moved seemingly at will through a carefully preserved silence broken only by the discreet sounds of the bass and drums (almost always wirebrushed). The ensembles were in unison or in a gentle counterpoint, and when one horn soloed the other noodled around in the background. It was a witty, agreeable music that asked little of the listener.

In 1953, Mulligan fleshed out his quartet with trumpet, trombone, French horn, tuba, alto saxophone, and another baritone saxophone—pretty much the makeup of the Miles Davis group—and made eight sides. They nod continually in the direction of the Davis sides, and there is some fine, dense ensemble writing by Mulligan, particularly in "A Ballad" and "Simbah." Then Mulligan temporarily set aside his quartet (it was never out of sight long, for it reappeared, with a trumpet or trombone as Mulligan's alterhorn, many times during the next decade), and in 1955 put together the best group he ever had. It was a sextet, and it was made up of trumpet, tenor saxophone, trombone, Mulligan, bass, and drums. It took up where his quartet left off, and it was a refreshing attempt to restore the collective ensemble to jazz in a time when the music, lured on by the apparently limitless time of the LP recording, consisted of little more than endless solos enclosed by dull unison ensembles. A typical Mulligan number went this way: The theme was stated by the horns, in unison or in harmony; solos followed, often backed by organ chords or by Ellington counter-melodic lines; a light, Basie walking-bass interlude came next; then the horns closed ranks for a long collective passage, partly written and partly improvised. When everything jelled, these ensemble passages, which drew indirectly on the collective efforts of King Oliver's Creole Jazz Band as well as on some of the pioneering small-band sides done in the thirties by the bass saxophonist Adrian Rollini, were enormously exciting. But Mulligan is an impatient man, and when the group failed to take hold he abandoned it and returned to his quartet. In 1960, casting back again to the Miles Davis sides, he organized a thirteen-piece "concert band." It included, at various times, Bob Brookmeyer, Clark Terry, Zoot Sims, and Mel Lewis, and it foreshadowed such current bands as those led by Terry and by Lewis and Thad Jones. It was an immaculately drilled band, but it was bland and it rarely swung. And Mulligan wrote very little for it, preferring to use such neophyte arrangers as the late Gary McFarland. The band lasted a couple of years, and then Mulligan, apparently closing the door for good on his adventurous years, entered his present now-you-see-me, now-you-don't period—one he has spent as solo performer at countless jazz festivals and concerts, as sideman with Dave Brubeck and Charlie Mingus, and as companion and husband to the actress Sandy Dennis, whom he married in 1965. It is a period that is pretty well summed-up in the first record Mulligan has made under his own name in seven years—"Gerry Mulligan: The Age of Steam." On hand are nine horns—among them Harry Edison, Bud Shank, and Bob Brookmeyer—and a large rhythm section made up of piano, guitar, bass, drums, and the percussionist Emil Richards. All eight numbers were written and arranged by Mulligan, and they are full of ghosts from the Davis days, the quartet days, the sextet days, and the concert-band days. Indeed, most of the numbers seem sketches for long-ago-finished oils. This is true even of "Grand Tour," a striking and original composition that abruptly ends in midsentence. A brooding, melancholy, arhythmic lullaby-hymn, in which Mulligan and Shank and Brookmeyer move along on different levels, stating and restating its plainsong melody, it is a mysterious and affecting piece that is quite unlike anything Mulligan or anyone else has recorded in jazz, and it is a pity that he did not carry it to the conclusion it suggests within itself—a further elaboration of its sorrowing melody, capped by a gradually intensifying polyphony.

So it is good to go back to Mulligan's "Jeru," an album recorded in 1962 and reissued a year or two ago, for it offers, in a direct, uncluttered way, the Mulligan who will probably outlast all the other Mulligans—the baritone saxophonist. His style was fully formed when he was twenty, and it has changed little since. (There is, though, a peculiar chameleon side to Mulligan's playing, for when he works with musicians he admires enormously he tends to take on their coloration. This happened most noticeably in a series of duets he recorded ten years ago with Ben Webster and Johnny Hodges and Thelonious Monk. The last one turned out to be disastrous, for the rhythmic approaches of Mulligan and Monk are very different, and Mulligan played as if he were Monk's partner in a three-legged race.) His style, like that of every baritone saxophonist, is continually challenged by his instrument, which, with its sheer size and weight and its bulky tone, threatens to engulf all comers. But he has met the challenge well. His tone is light, but his bottom notes have a suitable dropped-boulder effect. He moves around the horn with ease, and he almost invariably has enough energy left over to apply the icing of lyricism. His solos tend to be perfectly structured—indeed, form sometimes subdues content—and he rarely jars the listener, the way a Dickie Wells or a Pee Wee Russell does. The unexpected turns in Mulligan's improvisations appear in proportion to the level of intensity he reaches, and when he becomes red hot—he has always swung—he swaggers back and forth between octave notes and uses surprising high notes, smears, or intervals. In "Jeru," this happens in "Get Out of Town," a tight little Cole Porter melody that he limbers up and eventually turns inside out, as well as in the eight perfect choruses of blues he plays in "Blue Boy," the third consisting of one unbroken melodic line and the fifth of those swaggering intervals, and in his two choruses on "Lonely Town," the first dreaming and the second a fully conceived alter-melody to Bernstein's tune. Mulligan's accompaniment, which is flawless, is handled by Ben Tucker on bass, Dave Bailey on drums, Alec Dorsey on conga drums, and Tommy Flanagan on piano. Mulligan, above all, loves to play. He has fooled around with the soprano saxophone in recent years. Once, after dinner at a country restaurant he had never been in before, he took out his soprano, sauntered unannounced into the packed bar, where a mediocre pianist and drummer were holding forth, and played for an hour with such fervor that there was not a sound in the room. When he finished, he sat down at the bar, laughed, had a drink, and listened attentively while a woman offered him seventy-five dollars to play for her party in an adjoining room—then broke up.

One wonders what might have happened to Mulligan if Serge Chaloff, who was three years his senior, had not died, in 1957. Possibly nothing, for Mulligan had replaced Chaloff in all the baritone saxophone polls by 1953, apparently bringing Chaloff's powerful five-year sway to a close. Born in Boston of classically trained professional musicians (his father was in the Boston Symphony and his mother taught at the New England Conservatory), Chaloff worked his way unobserved through every kind of big band (Tommy Reynolds, Shep Fields, Ina Ray Hutton, Jimmy Dorsey, Georgie Auld, Boyd Raeburn) and then, in 1947, became part of the celebrated Four Brothers saxophone section in Woody Herman's Second Herd—a section that included Herbie Steward, Stan Getz, and Zoot Sims. He left Herman in 1950, after making an indelible mark on the band—he was as resounding an ensemble player as Harry Carney—and spent most of the rest of his life in brilliant, painful decline in Boston, where he died of cancer at the age of thirty-three. Sadly, there were those among his colleagues who did not bemoan his premature passing, for he was a drug addict whose proselytizing ways with drugs reportedly damaged more people than just himself.

In 1944 or 1945, Chaloff, who had learned his instrument at the feet of Harry Carney and Jack Washington, came under the influence of Charlie Parker, and by the time he joined Herman he had fully transferred Parker's inventions to the baritone. But he was not a copyist. His magnificent tone gave Parker's ideas a new dimension, he dared runs and complex passages that not even Parker had thought of, and he developed a passion in his playing that remains unequaled by any other saxophonist. His ballads were sumptuous. He never strayed too far from the melody, and he stated his variations in a battery of voices—cupped, whispering phrases; sudden declarations; cramped, *sotto-voce* runs; stuttering asides and divalike codas, in which his vibrato moved up and down in slow motion. At fast tempos, Chaloff somehow made the baritone saxophone a slip of a thing. He used gliding half-time phrases (his tone feathery and light), quick, reconstituting pauses, and preaching, triplet-ridden announcements, those now-listen-congregation! bursts with which Parker loved to preface his solos.

Fortunately, Chaloff is with us again, on the just reissued "Serge Chaloff: Blue Serge," which he made a year before he died. He is accompanied with sensitivity by Sonny Clarke on piano, Leroy Vinnegar on bass, and Philly Joe Jones on drums. There are seven numbers, and there are good things in all of them—his soft easing into the melody of "A Handful of Stars" and his two contributions to the exchange of four-bar breaks near the end of the tune, both of them delivered in meteoric runs; the furious attack on the very fast "The Goof and I"; the full-palette treatment of "I've Got the World on a String"; and the thorough and beautiful reconditioning he gives "Thanks for the Memory." There are occasional weak moments in the album— "Stairway to the Stars" is too slow and tends to sag under the weight of Chaloff's heavy, whispering tones and threatening vibrato, and he misses notes here and there—but on the whole it remains a superior, perhaps even classic, testament.

It is fascinating to hear Mulligan's "Jeru" album and Chaloff's "Blue Serge" in succession. The two men are different champions. Mulligan is elegant, lucid, thoughtful, and inventive, while Chaloff is blowzy, wild, inchoate, and brilliant. It is too bad they never recorded a duet album.

# 1973

## Beautiful

Ellis Larkins, the shy, brilliant, semi-transparent pianist, started out life in clear view. He made his début as a classical pianist at the age of eight, in Baltimore, where he was born and grew up, and his début as a jazz pianist at the age of nineteen, in New York, where he now lives. The second début was at Café Society Uptown in 1942, and during the next ten years he slipped back and forth between there and the Blue Angel and the Village Vanguard as the leader of his own trio, as a sideman with the clarinettist Edmond Hall, and as an accompanist of such singers as Mildred Bailey, Anita Ellis, Jane Harvey, Maxine Sullivan, Eartha Kitt, Georgia Gibbs, and Harry Belafonte. Then, turning to teaching, vocal coaching, and occasional radio, TV, and recording dates, he disappeared. He came up for air in the late fifties, at the Village Gate, with the harmonica player Larry Adler, and he surfaced again in the sixties, as an accompanist for Joe Williams. And last year he began an unlimited engagement at Gregory's, a *boîte* on the noisy southwest corner of Sixty-third Street and First Avenue. But several things belie his presence at Gregory's: his elusive, feather-touch style; his sliver shape, which is further deemphasized by big glasses, a generous mustache, and invariably dark clothes; and his method of communication, which lies somewhere between the spoken word (not really spoken but cast forth at random, soft and half-articulated) and an ingenious and vigorous sign language.

Gregory's consists of a small bar separated from the street by a glassed-in gallery. Larkins, accompanied by his bassist, Al Hall, sits at a small upright midway between the bar and the gallery, and he is an island of serenity besieged on one side by the din of his admirers, who tend to be fervent and numerous, and on the other by the din of traffic. But none of this appears to bother him, for there he sits—his body a parenthesis and his long, tuning-fork fingers touching the keys so lightly they seem only to suggest the tones that emerge—and spins out his fragile, luminous solos, solos that have the oblique light of De La Tour's candlelight paintings. There are intimations in Larkins' style of Count Basie and Fats Waller and Art Tatum, but beyond these his playing appears to be his own. It is a style—delivered conspiratorially by hands never more than inches apart—that celebrates silence and space: when no note is needed, none is played. Its dynamics range from a whisper to a murmur. Larkins' mixture of chords and single-note figures is ingenious. At first hearing, he appears to issue little more than a neat legato parade of chords that occasionally catch up to and embrace the beat, and, indeed, he will play a whole chorus of blues by repeating a simple riff. But much of the time his chordal passages are varied by surprising, almost half-hidden single-note lines that are brilliant synopses of Tatum's arabesques. His solos continually revolve, displaying at one moment silken single notes and at the next angora chords, and they are kept slowly spinning by his loping, urgent way of swinging.

When I discovered that Larkins, in addition to his duties at Gregory's, was in the midst of recording seven largely solo LPs under the supervision of the producer Ernest Anderson (historic, pioneering jazz concerts in New York and Boston in the forties; publicity work of various kinds in England ever since), I went to Larkins' apartment, which is catercornered to Gregory's, to talk to him. Freely decoded, this is what he told me: "I was the second of six children, and my mother, who died just last year, did housework and played piano and sang [*opens mouth, as if singing*]. My father, who died in 1942, was a cook and caterer and janitor, and he played violin [*rapid violin-playing motions*] with the Baltimore City Colored Orchestra. He taught me piano until I was six, and he was strict [*piano-playing gestures with both hands, followed by two emphatic forefinger stabs at a piano standing against one wall of his living room*]. Then I studied with Joseph Privett, then with his teacher, Austin Conradi, and with Pasquale Tallarico, and finally with Gladys Mayo. I went to the Peabody Conservatory, in Baltimore, when I was fifteen, and at seventeen, after graduating from high school, got a scholarship to Juilliard, which I attended for three years [*holds up three fingers*]. I had to give a little dissertation before I graduated, but I knew I couldn't get up there and talk. I was standing on a corner of Madison Avenue, on my way to the event, when what I'd do came to me [*hits his right temple with his right hand*]: demonstrate the similarities between the melodic lines of Bach and boogie-woogie. The teacher told me afterward that he knew that I'd made up the whole thing on the spot [*pulls an object out of the air and shapes it into a ball*] but that I'd done it very well. My touch on the piano is probably God-given [*looks up at the ceiling*], just as being able to improvise is. If you play a well-constructed tune, you go along with it, you ride with it, but if it leaks, you patch it and remake it. It's like improving a house by decorating it and adding wings and windows and such [*painting and hammering gestures with both hands*]. My idols in classical music were Chopin and Mozart and some Beethoven, and I still play them for my own pleasure. My idols in jazz were Fats Waller and Teddy Wilson and Art Tatum and Earl Hines [*steady piano-playing motions*]. I'm enjoying Gregory's which I hope I can use as a home base. If it gets too noisy when I'm playing, I just stop and turn on the jukebox, which I've had stocked with records by Nellie Lutcher, Ellington, Basie, and Charlie Barnet. The kids—twenty-one, and even younger—are coming in, and they're listening [*cups right ear*]. Ernie Anderson gives me complete freedom at the recording sessions, and I don't have any idea [*shrugs shoulders and holds out hands, palms up*] what I'm going to play before I sit down at the piano. We're finishing up LP number three tonight, at the studio over on West Forty-eighth. At seven. Come by [*beckoning motions with both hands*]."

Larkins was already there when I arrived. He greeted me in the control room by holding one finger in the air, cocking his head, and saying, "Don't tell me where we've met," and laughed—a prolonged, almost inaudible sigh. Larkins' wife, Crystal, introduced herself, and so did Ernest Anderson, who is white-haired, trim, and bespectacled. "I'm doing this project simply because I want to register some of the great neglected players before it's too late," he told us. He and Larkins went over a list of the tunes Larkins had already recorded, and Crystal Larkins, a short, forthright woman, told us that she and Larkins had known each other since they were seven, that he had accompanied her singing when they were eight, and that they had been married only a year, owing to previous marriages on both sides. Al Hall, who played with Larkins in the Café Society days, arrived, and was followed by another C.S. alumnus, the trumpeter Joe Thomas, and his wife, the singer Babe Matthews. Larkins went into the recording studio by himself, played some chords, so that the engineer could get his balance, and immediately started a slow version of "Who Can I Turn To?" He slipped into the control room when the take was finished, and the tape was played back. The first chorus went by, and Larkins made an abrupt stop signal with his right hand and said, "That's it." He returned to the studio, and Anderson said, "He's done just about everything in one take, but he did make two of Mercer Ellington's 'Things Ain't What They Used to Be,' and they're so beautiful and so utterly different that I'm going to use them both." Al Hall joined Larkins in the studio, and they did "The Lady's in Love." Larkins reappeared, and said to Joe Thomas, "Well, you brought your horn. Want to do 'Little Girl'?"

Thomas looked puzzled. " 'I Want a Little Girl'?" he asked. "I don't think I know that. Anyway, what key would you play it in?"

Larkins made flat, conciliatory motions with his hands, and said, "I'll play it with Al and then you come in and we'll do something else."

" 'Talk of the Town'?" Thomas said.

Larkins made the O.K. Ballantine sign with his right hand. He and Hall played "I Want a Little Girl," and he and Thomas and Hall did "It's the Talk of the Town" and "Blue Moon."

"I think I can translate what just happened," Anderson said. "Thomas didn't *want* to play 'Little Girl,' which, of course, he knows like the back of his hand. He wanted to play something that every other trumpet player hasn't recorded. Ellis got the message right away."

By this time, the control room was bulging. Billy Moore, a guitarist, who had been Larkins' first boss at Café Society Uptown, arrived with his wife, and after them came a songwriter and a singer named Emme Kemp. A small bar set up on one side of the control room was being supervised by a raggedy-mustached man in a tweed overcoat and a fur hat, identified only as

Freddy. Because of the reflection of the crowd in the glass that separates the studio and the control room, Larkins had become less and less visible. But his music was forcefully and elegantly present. "Sentimental Journey," "Rose Room," a ballad with lyrics by Crystal Larkins, and two takes of "Sweet Sue," went by. Joe Thomas, a stocky, heavy-voiced man, let loose six "Beautiful!"s and an "I *hear* you!" during "Sweet Sue." It was nearly ten o'clock, and Larkins, who hadn't been visible at all during the last two numbers, closed the session with "Solitude." I found him outside the recording studio afterward, and thanked him and said I would stop by Gregory's soon. He nodded, and clapped his hands soundlessly.

*For whatever sad reasons, Anderson's recordings of Larkins never surfaced, and he has since died.*

## The J.C.O.A.

B y the time the label "avant-garde" is applied to a pioneer movement, its work is mainly done. All that remains is consolidation, embellishment, and dissemination. This last calls forth imitators, students, and other admirers, who absorb much of the luster of their model. In time, a new avant-garde appears, and the preceding movement, which helped feed it, becomes respected and part of the mainstream, its middle-aged paunch keeping it afloat and in the eye of history. The present avant-garde in jazz is almost ready for the mainstream. It appeared fifteen or sixteen years ago, with the emergence of Cecil Taylor, who was soon followed by Ornette Coleman, Elvin Jones, John Coltrane, and that hybrid called third-stream music. All contributed bits and pieces to it. Jones moved away from the regular four-four beat and experimented with complex polyrhythms. Coleman and Coltrane abandoned chordal improvisation, replacing it with an improvisation based on motifs, on clusters of notes, on certain tones, or on a particular *feeling*. The conventional chorus and the measure were discarded. Taylor's approach was similar, but it was heavily infused with twentieth-century "classical" harmonies. The third stream was a compositional attempt to blend these rhythmic and improvisational departures with classical forms and instrumentations. A second *vague* of musicians and composers came along in the early sixties. It included Paul and Carla Bley, Pharoah Sanders, Roswell Rudd, Eric Dolphy, Mike Mantler, Milford Graves, Don Cherry, Albert Ayler, John Tchicai, and Archie Shepp. (Sun Ra, who was much older and had been banging his own avant-garde pots for a long time, also became a part of it.) In 1964, a nucleus of this group of musicians formed the Jazz Composer's Guild and the Jazz Composer's Guild Orchestra. The orchestra gave a series of groundswell concerts in Judson Hall late that year, and even poked its strange head into the sunlight at the 1965 Newport Festival. But the Guild, suffering from the internal scrimmaging that is one of the customary diversions of visionaries, fell apart, and on its ruins Carla Bley and Mantler built the Jazz Composer's Orchestra Association and *its* attendant orchestra. It is still going strong. Indeed, it has become a glistening little nonprofit institution that has its own record label, J.C.O.A., and one of J. P. Marquand's sons, Timothy, as its president. Two or three times a year it gives a series of free in-the-round concerts in New York, at which works in progress by various composers are played, and it has released two big, ambitious boxed albums—"The Jazz Composer's Orchestra" and "Escalator Over the Hill: A Chronotransduction by Carla Bley and Paul Haines." (The Association does things with style. Both albums are handsome and glossy and have well-designed booklets full of futuristic poetry and good photographs. Even the press releases are written studiously.) The J.C.O.A. had nothing to do with producing a third album, "Charlie Haden: Liberation Music Orchestra," which has been released by another label, but many of the orchestra's members appear in it.

They have a good time in disguise. The reeds include Perry Robinson, Gato Barbieri, and Dewey Redman, the brasses Cherry, Mantler, Rudd, Bob Northern, and Howard Johnson, the rhythm section Carla Bley, Sam Brown, Haden, Paul Motian, and Andrew Cyrille. The album has political overtones, but they are only frosting on the music, which is made up of four songs from the Spanish Civil War, three Bley pieces, Ornette Coleman's "War Orphans," two compositions by Haden (one a "re-creation" of some of the oppressive shenanigans indulged in on the rostrum during the 1968 Democratic Convention, and the other a memorial to Che Guevara), and "We Shall Overcome." The Spanish Civil War songs are lumped into one long piece, which proceeds roughly like this: There is an oompah opening ensemble and brief solos by Cherry and Rudd; Brown plays a long flamencan guitar passage, and Haden follows with a stirring single-note solo, and then shifts into guitarlike flamencan chords; the brass section floats in over a two-note ground bass, and Rudd plays a mock-ponderous solo in half time; the ensemble enters and the whole piece slows down; Barbieri plays a romantic melody and gradually works himself into a squealing frenzy—one of the unfortunate hallmarks of J.C.O.A. reedmen—and the piece goes out. The rhythms change continually, and there are brief cacophonic ensemble bursts, patches of straight, warm melody, and an overall feeling of fun and games. The second side is notable for Haden's marvelous flamencan thrumming in "Song for Che," for Carla Bley's quiet, lyrical piano in Coleman's piece, and for the grinding collective passages in Haden's salute to the Democratic Convention. Best of all, though, is the one-chorus version of "We Shall Overcome." The orchestra dips the melody in heavy, thick harmonies while Rudd improvises above, throwing in an utterly rending bent note halfway through. The version recalls the wonderful single-chorus ensemble rendition of "Abide with Me" that Thelonious Monk recorded in the late fifties with Coleman Hawkins and John Coltrane.

The first J.C.O.A. album comprises five compositions by Mantler—four "Communications" (Nos. 8 through 11) and "Preview." They are concertos that are built around the soloists—Cherry and Barbieri, Larry Coryell, Rudd, Sanders, and Taylor. The orchestra, twenty-odd strong throughout, includes many of the musicians in the "Liberation Music" album, together with such luminaries as Jimmy Knepper, Randy Brecker, Lloyd Michels, Steve Marcus, and Lew Tabackin. There are five bassists for each number, among them Steve Swallow, Eddie Gomez, Ron Carter, and Richard Davis. Mantler's compositions have an oppressive monochromatic density, but in general they set the soloists off adequately. As always, there are no fixed rhythms, and the forms seem aimless, for the pieces simply swell and subside, swell and subside, until they are done. (One wishes that the J.C.O.A. composers would occasionally resort to a regular sounded beat and that they would even use some of the older soloists around. The effect would be like coming on a "gee whizz" in a George Higgins novel.) Taylor pounds, slides, spins, skates, and scrambles his way all over the keyboard for the thirty-three minutes of "Communications No. 11," but Rudd is more impressive in "Communications No. 10," which is less than half as long. He is far and away the most inventive of the new trombonists, and he is a highly knowledgeable revolutionary, who came up through conservative musical ranks (Eli's Chosen Six and Eddie Condon). A decade ago, his style was apoplectic, and made up of elephant shrieks, roars, blats, and thousand-note runs. But always visible were his origins, in particular the playing of Dickie Wells and J. C. Higginbotham. They are in even stronger evidence now, for Rudd seems to have discarded the more frenzied aspects of his style. In "Communications No. 10" he plays a couple of passages that are fine tributes to the great, undersung Higginbotham, and the rest of the way he never goes much over the boiling point.

"Escalator Over the Hill" is a very different kettle. It is a sort of opera, in that there is instrumental music, a libretto, singing, recitative, narration, and choruses. (I don't know what to make of Carla Bley's Greco-Latin subtitle— "A Chronotransduction." "Chrono," of course, has to do with time and "transduction," according to the infallible American Heritage Dictionary, is "the transfer of genetic material from one bacterial cell to another by a bacteriophage." That last word is defined as "a submicroscopic, usually viral, organism that destroys bacteria." Wouldn't something like "I've Got You Under My Skin" have been easier?) But here the resemblance to opera ends, for there is no story beyond the fact that the first part of "Escalator" is set in an old hotel somewhere in the Western world and the second in a desert in India. Paul Haines' libretto is in Dada verse that goes like this:

> GINGER: Nurses dyeing their hair
>     Don't care
>     If the horse is locked

> The house still there.
> It doesn't seem
> To matter to them
> The traces
> Of horses
> And pineapple
> And cheese
> So many ingredients
> In the soup
> His Friends
> (*on their sides*):
> No room for a spoon.

There are also marginalia in the libretto that do not appear in the perform-ance, and these are often in the form of inside-out epigrams:

> Two skins better than one
> No skin better than none.

The singing is largely by Carla Bley, Jeanne Lee, Linda Ronstadt, and Jack Bruce, the last of whom was once with Cream. The narration is by Viva and others, the recitative by a host of people, and the intermittent music by a small rock group and elements from the J.C.O.A. There are good solos here and there by Cherry, Rudd, and Barbieri. The tone of the album is satiric, for there are take-offs of a society band and of a Broadway musical, and there are patches of funny electronic music. But the most impressive things in "Escalator" are Carla Bley's melodies, which are often quite beautiful. She has demonstrated this lyric talent before, and it's too bad that she has to bury it under such brouhaha.

# Eubie

The Ragtime revival continues, and at its head is Eubie Blake. Indeed, we are being inundated with Blakeiana. The flood began four years ago when Columbia released "The Eighty-six Years of Eubie Blake," a collection of thirty rags, marches, and blues, most of them by Blake. Although he had been in semi-retirement for more than thirty years, his playing on the record is rumbustious and attrac-tive. Then he was at festivals, on television, in solo concerts, in night clubs, and in recording studios. And now three new albums—"Eubie Blake, Fea-turing Ivan Harold Browning," "Eubie Blake: Rags to Classics," and "Eubie Blake and His Friends Edith Wilson and Ivan Harold Browning"—have been issued. In the first, he plays six loosely structured rags, five of them his own, and then, in eight numbers, accompanies Ivan Browning, a member of

the Four Harmony Kings, who appeared in Blake and Noble Sissle's celebrated all-black 1921 Broadway show, *Shuffle Along*. Browning is eighty-
two, but his singing, which is affectingly of its period, remains clear and
steady. Blake plays thirteen remarkably varied numbers on the second
record. He wrote eight of them, and these include a new waltz (his first published tune, "Charleston Rag," was written in 1899); rags, one of them also
new; a fine ballad, "You're Lucky to Me"; and several études, one of which,
written in 1923 and called "Rain Drops," suggests Debussy's short piano
pieces. The third record has five more Blake-accompanied Browning efforts
and three by Edith Wilson, a jazz-oriented singer of the twenties who
worked with Blake in one of the later editions of "Shuffle Along." Again,
there are more Blake piano solos, among them "Memphis Blues," his new
"Eubie Dubie," written with the pianist Johnny Guarnieri, and his ballad "I
Can't Get You Out of My Mind," done for a 1937 W.P.A. show called *Swing
It*. But Blake has also been supervising Blake reissues. "Eubie Blake: Blues
and Rags" and "Eubie Blake: 1921" contain twenty-two transcriptions of the
thirty known piano rolls that he set down between 1917 and 1921. These are
largely pop tunes, but the playing is vigorous and even audacious, particularly on the rolls that were not fancied up by their publishers before they
were issued. The last of the reissues, "Sissle and Blake: Early Rare Recordings," contains fourteen records that Sissle and Blake, who were known in
vaudeville as the Dixie Duo, made between 1920 and 1927. They are charming, peppy, and innocent. Then, on the crest of this efflux, comes a cheerful
book, *Reminiscing with Sissle and Blake* (Viking), by Robert Kimball (who,
with Brendan Gill, compiled *Cole*) and the pianist-composer William Bol-
com. It consists of sketches of Sissle's and Blake's lives, along with countless
photographs and reproductions of sheet music, newspaper reviews, ads,
posters, programs, and the like. Blake's earlier world now seems almost
antediluvian. The only child of former slaves (his father was secretly taught
the Spencerian hand by his owner's daughter), he grew up in Baltimore and
at fifteen was playing piano in a local bawdy house—a way of life that sustained him until 1915, when he teamed up with Noble Sissle, who was
already a lyric writer and singer. His theatrical career began with *Shuffle
Along* and lasted into the thirties, and by 1940 his first life was over. The
book, though, sidesteps several curious things about Blake: that he should
find himself the guidon of the ragtime resurgence when he was neither a
full-time ragtime performer nor even a pure one (he generally took liberties
with his materials), that he had so little to do with the great black music—
jazz—that was marshalling its forces everywhere about him when he was at
his peak, and that the predominant feeling in both his composing and his
playing has always been more white than black.

What ragtime was really about is demonstrated in a new and beautiful recording, "Scott Joplin: The Red Back
Book." It was instigated by the Joplin scholar Vera Brodsky Lawrence and

carried through by Gunther Schuller. Eight of Joplin's marvelous rags are played by a twelve-piece ensemble made up of trumpet, trombone, clarinet, flute or piccolo, tuba, piano, drums, two violins, viola, cello, and bass. (Two of the rags are also done as solos by the ensemble's exceptional pianist, Myron Romanul.) The instrumentation and arrangements are taken from "Fifteen Standard High Class Rags," a collection of stock arrangements made for dancing, parades, band concerts, and the like by E. J. Stark, D. S. De Lisle, and various unknown hands in the early years of the century and generally known as "The Red Back Book." Schuller has conducted the group, which is made up of New England Conservatory students, and the impeccably played results are a unique and graceful chamber music. The group, blessed with a knowledge of jazz which its turn-of-the-century predecessors rarely had, swings irresistibly, and delights abound: the intricate, superbly orchestrated "The Rag Time Dance"; Romanul's feathery solo version of "The Entertainer," and the way he and the ensemble work in unison in the opening strain of "Rag Time Dance"; the crystalline Charles Lewis trumpet solos, with their alarming intervals, in "Easy Winners," "Sun Flower Slow Drag," and "Maple Leaf Rag"; the piccolo solo in the first strain of "The Entertainer," backed by billowing oompah piano figures; and the sedate, subtle, gliding "Maple Leaf Rag."

## Duo, Nellie, and Marian

Jim Hall and Ron Carter have played as a guitar-and-bass duo for several years, and they work together like a team of pickpockets. They shadow each other's flights, echo them, celebrate them, and even anticipate them. But their first record, made late last summer at a brilliant concert given at the Playboy Club, has only just been brought out as "Alone Together: Jim Hall–Ron Carter Duo." Of the eight numbers, five are standards and the rest are originals by Sonny Rollins, Carter, and Hall. The standards are in ad-lib or slow-to-medium tempos, and they are languorous and ingeniously arranged. "Softly as in a Morning Sunrise" consists mostly of a string of ad-lib, *a cappella* eight-bar exchanges, with some Dick McDonough chords from Hall. In the title song, Carter states the melody, using quavering, miragelike notes, makes way for a luminous Hall solo that starts several beats late with a gliding two-note phrase, and returns for a solo while Hall brushes in chords in the background. "I'll Remember April" has a complex contrapuntal ensemble, a fine medium-tempo Hall solo, and a long, walking Wilbur Ware statement by Carter that is full of retards and sidestepping notes. The originals are chancy and sometimes breathtaking. Carter's "Receipt, Please" is a complex rising-and-falling melodic line with several smart key modulations, and Hall's "Whose Blues" is a fragile blues with strange fur-bearing chords planted in the last four bars of its melody. This is generous music. One can first study the rhythmic patterns in a number, then its melodic surprises, then its harmonic weights, then its textural shadings, then its wholeness and unity. And then go back and do them all over again.

Barney Josephson first brought Nellie Lutcher, the helter-skelter singer, composer, and pianist, from the West Coast to Café Society Downtown in the mid-forties, and she became an immediate success. Now he has brought her East again to the Cookery, after a long period of semi-obscurity, and she may well be off again. It's easy to see why. She effortlessly works both sides of the tracks. She is—with her striking, high-cheekboned face and her long, scuttling, dancing, crablike fingers—a funny and magnetic entertainer. But she is also, under all her explosive nonsense, a fine pianist and jazz singer. She grew up near Lake Charles, Louisiana, and when she was fifteen played in a band that included Bunk Johnson. At the same time, she listened to Earl Hines' radio broadcasts from the Grand Terrace, in Chicago. These country-mouse-and-city-mouse experiences remain side by side in her work and allow her, in a number like "Lake Charles Boogie," to play in a jangling, down-home, bedspring style, and, in a number like "The Lady's in Love with You," to deliver expert Hines arpeggios and rhythmic bursts. She has a light, glancing voice which gives the impression of forever slipping off its notes, and she is a master of melismatics: a six-noted Lutcher syllable is commonplace. Her diction is as casual as Jack Teagarden's, and when she tires of making sense out of her words she slides into whole choruses of scat singing beflagged with falsetto hums, mumbles, and cries. She sang all her own old hits tonight—"Fine Brown Frame" (an apt and laconic description of Big Sid Catlett, with whom she stepped out in the forties), "Hurry On Down to My House," and "Real Gone Guy"—and they were funny and good. But the best things she did were the fillers, which included a blindingly fast "Perdido" (her accompanists, Skeeter Best on guitar and Morris Edwards on bass, floated out behind her like coattails); a medium-slow "St. Louis Blues," in which each beat had a Bessie Smith gravity and presence; a rocking, singsong "Bill Bailey, Won't You Please Come Home"; and a fast "Alexander's Ragtime Band," which rattled around the room like hail on a tin roof.

There was a time in jazz when a good many of its appreciators spent more time classifying, stratifying, and categorizing their idols than they did listening to them. The guidelines they set out were as rigid as two-by-fours. Thus, it was decreed, Zutty Singleton played only with the likes of James P. Johnson or Pee Wee Russell or Sidney Bechet, and when he popped up on an early Dizzy Gillespie–Charlie Parker record his admirers were incredulous. But economic needs and the grim reaper have done their work, and no one even blinks now at the sort of group that Marian McPartland has brought into the Royal Box. It includes a member of the Kansas City school (Buddy Tate), the Chicago school (Jimmy McPartland), and the New York school (Marian McPartland), as well as two young eclectics, the bassist Rusty Gilder and the drummer Jackie Williams. The range of their material tonight was equally generous. Among other things, they played "You Turned the Tables on Me," "The Girl From Ipanema," "What's New," " 'Round Midnight," and "St. Louis Blues," and they played them with aplomb. It was not Chicago music or Kansas City music or New York music but lyrical, first-rate jazz. (Needless to say, this non-classifiable music *has* been categorized, and is frequently referred to as "mainstream" music.) Jimmy McPartland, who has been having embouchure troubles of late, played well, and it was a pleasure to hear Bix Beiderbecke's ghost rise up behind every solo. Marian McPartland, long accustomed to the format of a trio, was tight and sharp; she said what she had to say in a chorus or two, and there was none of the cloud-gazing she sometimes engages in. Tate played his customary tenor saxophone, but he also played alto, baritone, clarinet, and flute, lending each of them his lyricism and drive and drama.

## God

The greatest hurdle facing the makers of jazz recordings—both the producers and the performers of them, as well as the new breed of producer-performers—is how to judge on the instant what is good, what is right. Judging a performance of written music involves certain objective criteria, but judging improvised music is largely subjective. One listens in a solo for the mystical balance of technique and inspiration, of relaxation and tension, for the coupling of timing and energy that is swinging. Beyond that, it is a question of mood, digestion, and the fit of one's shoes—all of which explains why music that sounds glorious in a recording studio can mysteriously sound gelid on the record, and why a seemingly humdrum session can ultimately produce a superlative record. Yet a surprising number of musicians record easily and well throughout their careers. One, it has long seemed, was Art Tatum, who appeared equally brilliant and assured whether he recorded in a studio or on the concert stage. Now a new and extraordinary recording—"Art Tatum: God Is in the House"—proves that this wasn't so; that, indeed, as legend has had it, there were two Tatums. One was the virtuoso who moved with consummate ease through a world owned and run by whites, and the other was the secret genius who went uptown after his regular hours and played unbelievable music for his own pleasure in small black clubs for black audiences. (Not enough has been made of the fact that there is a great difference in the way many black musicians perform before white audiences and before black ones.) Musicians who heard Tatum in such circumstances have repeatedly touted this aspect of his playing, but it was difficult to believe them. How could there have been another and even better Tatum? Well, there was, and he is on every track of the record. The recording was done in acetate on a

portable recording machine in 1940 and 1941 by a Columbia student named
Jerry Newman. Three of the sides were made in his apartment and the
remaining ten in Harlem after-hours clubs—the Gee-Haw Stables,
Reuben's, and Clark Monroe's Uptown House. They make it clear that
Newman, who is now dead, was a master reporter; he was steadfastly self-
effacing and he invariably seemed to be in the right place at the right time.
(Some of his Harlem field recordings of Charlie Christian were issued over
twenty years ago, but nothing else has appeared until now. The liner notes
of the new album do not tell us where Newman's trove has been all these
years, why it has unexpectedly become available, or how much more exists.)
The numbers recorded in Newman's flat open the album, and, though
rather short, they forecast the wonders to come. The longest, "Georgia on
My Mind," is taken at a strong medium tempo and has two shattering passages—an abrupt arrhythmic one and a long, racing double-time line. The
Tatum who played for whites often confined himself, in a strange combination of the put-on and simply showing off, to breathtaking but empty semisymphonic displays, but the Tatum of "Georgia on My Mind" is altogether
different. He is a driving, aggressive jazz pianist whose flights of virtuosity
are completely in proportion to the whole piece. The same is true of "Sweet
Lorraine," "Fine and Dandy," and "Begin the Beguine," all of them done at
Reuben's and all of them packed with ferocity and inventiveness. Reuben
Harris, the proprietor, accompanies Tatum using whiskbrooms on a piece of
newspaper, and there is a steady flow of idle, delighted audience chatter. And
the piano Tatum plays is classically out of tune, but he surmounts this obsta-
cle with such ease that the instrument sounds, in the flashier passages, like a
Steinway grand. (The quality of the recording throughout the album is
remarkably good.) The next five sides were made at the Gee-Haw Stables.
There is a bravura, funny "Mighty Lak a Rose"; a gorgeous, rococo "Body
and Soul"; a rampaging "There'll Be Some Changes Made," with a vocal by
Ollie Potter, whose off-key singing only serves to spur Tatum on; and a couple of slow blues, in which Tatum sings. The album rises to its climax in two
long final tracks, done at Clark Monroe's Uptown House with Frankie
Newton and Ebenezer Paul (bass) sitting in. Newton, with his easy, barefoot
approach, is a perfect foil for Tatum, and the tunes—"Lady Be Good" and
"Sweet Georgia Brown"—are fine contrapuntal displays. ("Sweet Georgia
Brown" is fascinating for another reason. Tatum's first solo choruses, with
their weird notes and displaced rhythms, are an obvious parody of the
adventurous melodic lines that Charlie Parker and Dizzy Gillespie were
beginning to evolve. Pioneer beboppers often jammed at Monroe's, and perhaps some of them were in the house that night.) Newton plays a riff while
Tatum slips into an engulfing left-hand tremolo; Newton looses a tricky
descending figure, which Tatum immediately parodies; Newton starts to
float along far behind the beat and Tatum races into a double-time arpeggio;

Newton fashions a high, annunciatory figure and Tatum rumbles around in the lowest registers.

God's Tatum!

## Newport 1973

*June 29th*

The 1973 Newport Jazz Festival—New York began in a tureen of mist and rain and puddles in the Wollman Rink at seven minutes to noon, which may be the first time in the history of jazz that an event has started early. Gerry Mulligan pushed an eighteen-piece pickup band through six of his recent compositions, and it hummed and rolled and swung. The best soloists were Bob Brookmeyer, Jimmy Owens, Tom Scott (a wild West Coast saxophonist), and Mulligan himself, who was particularly moving in a slow version of "Waltzing Matilda." The Newport Ensemble, with George Wein (piano), Roland Prince (guitar), James Spaulding (flute and alto saxophone), Larry Ridley (bass), and Al Harewood (drums), was a puzzling outgrowth of Wein's various Newport Festival All-Stars, which were given to pleasant middle-of-the-road musings. It played two Minguslike numbers that included startling, impressionistic Wein solos. Long embedded in the Fats Waller–Teddy Wilson school, Wein sounded as if he had spent the winter boning up with Lennie Tristano.

A sea of bald pates, bifocals, and paunches flowed into Carnegie Hall early this evening to hear the Benny Goodman Quintet (Teddy Wilson, Lionel Hampton, Gene Krupa, and Slam Stewart). The music itself was mediocre (one exception: Teddy Wilson's solo in "Body and Soul"), but it was full of ghosts. Phrases first carved by Jimmie Noone, and even Pee Wee Russell, kept surfacing in Goodman's solos; and in Krupa's brief statements one heard the straight-ahead, marching rimshots-and-rolls that Zutty Singleton perfected in the twenties. Earl Hines stood dimly behind Wilson, and even Hampton, and Stewart's bowing summoned up Jimmy Blanton. Between numbers, Goodman himself seemed to be listening to these voices, for, seated on a stool, he would hook one foot on a rung, rest his clarinet on his knee, and gaze for long moments into space before finally turning to his musicians and telling them where to go next. A new group, composed of Ruby Braff (cornet), George Barnes (guitar), Wayne Wright (rhythm guitar), and John Giuffrida (bass), opened the concert, and in a lyrical fashion it, too, summoned up the past, by sounding remarkably like some of the small-band records that Django Reinhardt made with American musicians in Paris in 1937.

On to Philharmonic Hall at ten o'clock to hear a reprise of a blues con-

cert first given at six. The concert, by and large, was a shambles. But Muddy
Waters, with his great, sad, broad face and his slow, heavy, summer-mind
voice, sang four mighty blues, and so did Big Mama Willie Mae Thornton.
She has lost considerable weight since her last appearance in New York six
years ago and, with her stringy gray thatch, her immense hands, and her
wandering, beanpole legs, she looked like a huge shorebird. But she hasn't
lost her booming voice, and she shivered the timbers when she exploded in
her first number with "*Earlyonemorning*, my baby left me in my back door
cryin'." B. B. King acted as the MC, and when his turn came to play he
launched a monologue about Big Mama and how fine it was to be in this fine
hall with so many fine blues singers, and he went on so long there was no
time left for him to sing.


*June 30th*

I had an uncle who lived in a Victorian house where the rooms seemed to follow one another aimlessly
around, and he used to say that the only way to improve the place would be
to tear it down and start again. The same could be said of Philharmonic
Hall. Despite the endless acoustical tinkering that has gone on since it was
built, its sounds remain inexact and confusing. High notes screech, pianos
sound as if they had false teeth, and low tones breathe heavily. And the confusion is compounded by amplified instruments turned to peak volume.
Such aural indecencies plagued the seven-thirty concert this evening, and
perhaps even influenced the players themselves. Sonny Rollins, stunning in a
white suit and clearly immersed in his image, did little until his sensational
cadenza in his final number, "There Is No Greater Love." Mary Lou
Williams did not fare much better, and neither did Gil Evans, who, leading
a fifteen-piece band, played four long numbers decorated with gongs,
chimes, rattles, and taped wind sounds, and with interminable solos by Billy
Harper (tenor saxophone) and Howard Johnson (tuba). Keith Jarrett ended
the evening with an unaccompanied piano solo. It had spacious tremolos;
Tatum runs; snatches of gospel, Charles Ives, and George Gershwin; rubato
and double-time passages; and so forth—all based on the still-fashionable
notion in jazz that if a soloist goes on long enough the flower will inevitably
bloom.

The second Wollman concert seized the day. It was taken up by guitarists,
who, famous for their melodic garrulity, must have plucked a million notes.
But an impressive number were well considered. George Barnes went
through three fine numbers, the best of them a tough, medium-tempo blues
that was unfortunately marred by a blown-out amplifier. Chuck Wayne and
Joe Puma fashioned three unaccompanied duets, notable for their closing
contrapuntal ensemble in "There Will Never Be Another You," in which the
two kept passing and repassing one another, and for Wayne's fleetness and
Puma's grave deliberation in "L'il Darlin'." George Benson, backed by a

rhythm section, showed just where the thin line between invention and virtuosity lies. Much of his first number flashed and sang, and then he stepped over the line, and his remaining solos, though mercurial, were locked in and mechanical. Following was a brilliant performance by Jim Hall and Tal Farlow, accompanied on Fender bass by the exceptional Jay Leonhart. Farlow has not played much in recent years, and he creaked a little, but this unintentionally set off Hall, who, with his beautiful choice of notes, his silences, and his invariable rightness, gives the impression of ceaselessly surveying his melodic domain before picking his next note. His solo in "Prelude to a Kiss" was of the highest order, and after a single-note passage in "Summertime" he slipped into a succession of soft, blurred chords that seemed to have their faces pressed against the melody. There were two other rewards: Leonhart's quiet, radarlike accompaniment throughout, and his brief, remarkable solo in "St. Thomas," in which, using carefully spaced notes, he turned the melody over and over, each time infinitesimally altering it by adding a beat or dropping a note a tone or two. The rest of the concert included Pat Martino, Larry Coryell, and Roy Buchanan, who slid loudly into electronic swamp.

## July 1st

At six o'clock in Carnegie Hall, Ray Charles and James Baldwin gave the first of two run-throughs of their musical-dramatic collaboration "The Hallelujah Chorus—The Life and Times of Ray Charles." Both men were born poor, black, and gifted, but beyond that they have little in common. Charles remains a canny, tough, pinewoods primitive, and Baldwin is a delicate urban visionary; trying to weld their alien souls didn't make sense. What there was of the production went like this: Charles and his big band played a couple of slow numbers, one of them graced with two choruses of Charles' piano, and then Baldwin, at a lectern on the side of the stage, gave a brief "testimony service" about the tribulations of black people in this country. Baldwin moved to a stool set in the curve of Charles' piano and asked him simplistic questions (one fine, unrehearsed Charles response: "I came to earth with my music like any other necessary organ"), and after each one, Charles played. A couple of meaningless dramatic interludes involving Cicely Tyson, David Baldwin, and David Moses followed (one was taken from James Baldwin's short story "Sonny's Blues"), and Baldwin and Charles resumed their interchange. But by then a strange and moving thing had begun to happen. Apparently, Baldwin had suggested to Charles that he abandon his regular show, with its pop tunes, gospel numbers, and country-and-Western songs, and concentrate on his old blues. Charles did, and the results, in blues after blues, were superb.

The Duke Ellington concert at ten in Philharmonic Hall was a mishmash of bad taste (the trumpeter Money Johnson parroting Louis Armstrong in "Basin Street Blues" and "Hello, Dolly!"), beauty (the tonal elegance of the

clarinet trio, piano, and muted trumpet in "Creole Love Call," and Harry
Carney's mother-earth statement in "La Plus Belle Africaine"), and virtuosity (five vocals by the winsome and extraordinary Swedish soprano Alice
Babs). During the intermission, a colleague passed on a broadsheet
announcing the publication by Rutgers University of a new semiannual jazz
magazine, *Journal of Jazz Studies*, in which such aesthetic delights as these
will appear: "Authenticity and Originality in Jazz: Toward a Paradigm in the
Sociology of Music"; "It Ain't the Blues: Billie Holiday, Sidney J. Furie, and
Kitsch"; and "Institution Participation, Social Stratification, and Psychological Boundaries of Montreal Jazzmen."

## *July 2nd*

This afternoon Professor Longhair, a semi-legendary singer and barrelhouse pianist from New Orleans, started
the Wollman concert with eight numbers, and it was good to hear the ante-
diluvian turns of Jimmy Yancey and Pinetop Smith and Champion Jack
Dupree in his playing. He is one of the last repositories of this sort of rolling,
heavy-weave piano, and it will be a sad day when it is finally gone. Baby Laurence brought on his troupe of tap-dancers (John T. McPhee, Buster Brown,
L. D. Jackson, and Chuck Green), and they were accompanied by Jo Jones
and Milt Buckner (on organ). Laurence gave a breathtaking performance,
full of galloping offbeats and lightning sweeps across the stage, but it was too
bad he and Jones didn't exchange breaks. There is nothing more exhilarating
than drummers and tap-dancers attempting to outwit each other, and Jones
has a genius for such badinage. Mechanical performances by Charlie Mingus' new quintet of three of his best numbers—"Goodbye Pork Pie Hat,"
"Fables of Faubus," and "Pithecanthropus Erectus"—proved again that his
melodies, so original and lyrical and stark, shouldn't be entrusted to the
weak in spirit. The afternoon went out with Don Cherry, who sat cross-
legged on the stage and, surrounded by women and children and a small
galaxy of musicians, played occasional pleasant melodic bursts on his pocket
trumpet that were interlarded with sleigh bells, a screeching saxophone, and
a conch.

## *July 3rd*

An invaluable, if erratic, concert was given early this evening at Philharmonic Hall. It was a celebration of
American songwriting loosely based on Alec Wilder's classic study, *American
Popular Song*. Nine or so soloists, groups, and singers offered about forty
songs by Irving Berlin, Fats Waller, Eubie Blake, Cole Porter, Duke Elling-
ton, Harold Arlen, George Gershwin, Jimmy Van Heusen, Richard
Rodgers, and Wilder. Berlin was treated well by a group consisting of Jimmy
McPartland, Herbie Hall, Vic Dickenson, Art Hodes, Al Hall, and Al Hare-
wood. Indeed, one of their numbers was a lilting, exact reading by Herbie

Hall of "A Pretty Girl Is Like a Melody." Few jazz musicians pay such gentle, intelligent homage to those who provide most of their fuel. Earl Hines shot through four Waller tunes, the best of them a rampaging "Honeysuckle Rose." Teddi King and Ellis Larkins handled Cole Porter well, but Rahsaan Roland Kirk, accompanied by Marian McPartland, Larry Ridley, and Harewood, did an odd thing to Ellington and Billy Strayhorn: He made luminous songs like "Mood Indigo," "Black Butterfly," and "Satin Doll" sound brooding and savage. Barbara Carroll struggled somewhat with the complexities of "Blues in the Night," which has a steplike, fifty-eight-measure chorus, but she surfaced neatly in "Come Rain or Come Shine," and then went on to accompany Sylvia Syms, who did wonders with Arlen's difficult "Out of This World." For some reason, the four numbers from "Porgy and Bess" done by the Modern Jazz Quartet caused them to frieze. But the two final composers got choice treatment. Mabel Mercer, a little harried in voice and manner, sang Rodgers and Hart's "My Romance," "It Never Entered My Mind," "He Was Too Good to Me," and "I Wish I Were in Love Again." She was joined by Stan Getz, who provided support, and then soloed in a rare hymnlike manner. Gerry Mulligan rounded out the evening with praise for Alec Wilder's "It's So Peaceful in the Country," "While We're Young," and "I'll Be Around." He played the melody of each tune first, not touching a hair on its head, improvised a couple of choruses, and returned briefly to the melody. Even Wilder, who was in the audience and is given to intemperate language when performers change or miss his notes, was pleased. ("Not *one* of his notes was an enemy," he said.)

All Marian McPartland's banners were rippling at the beginning of this afternoon's Wollman concert, and she set down six exuberant numbers from her current repertory. The Modern Jazz Quartet stayed largely within the confines of the blues in its six selections, and there were joyous moments from John Lewis ("Monterey Mist") and Milt Jackson (his surprising accents in "True Blues" and the fast, glistening curve of notes with which he started his solo in "Bag's Groove").

*July 4th*

A counter-festival, the New York Musicians Five Borough Jazz Festival, is going on all over the city this week, and it is being played, in the main, by little-known musicians and by aging avant-garde or hard-bop players. George Wein has incorporated a good number of its musicians into the Newport Festival this year at six concerts at Alice Tully Hall. I went early this evening, and it was a dampening experience. Three groups—led by the tenor saxophonist Paul Jeffrey, the pianist Walter Bishop, Jr., and the trumpeter Tommy Turrentine—played endlessly in an area somewhere between hard bop and early avant-garde, and the only rewarding music was some smart drumming by Thelonious Monk, Jr.

It is not really clear why anyone wants to re-create jazz that was improvised and fresh fifty and more years ago; the results are no different from an expert Vermeer copy. But much of the ten o'clock Philharmonic Hall concert was taken up with such resurrections. Turk Murphy brought his King Oliver–Jelly Roll Morton band from the West Coast and managed, as always, to sound the way jazz might have if it had existed in mid-Victorian times. Wally Rose played five rags, demonstrating poor time and weak phrasing. Bob Greene played two eerily perfect Jelly Roll Morton piano solos, and was joined for five Morton instrumentals by Danny Barker and Tommy Benford (both played with Morton) and Herbie Hall, who again stole the honors. The Preservation Hall Band closed the evening. Its re-creations are deceptive, for they are attempts to recapture what its players never had in the first place.

*July 5th*

The stage at the Wollman Rink at one o'clock this afternoon was filled with percussion instruments—massive gongs, small gongs, chimes, bells of every size and description, drums and more drums, xylophone-type instruments, and vibraphones. Here and there were thick golden stands of saxophones, ranging from a tiny soprano to a massive bass. Five musicians, two with painted faces and one in a red hardhat and dirty coveralls, threaded their way onstage, a gong was struck, and the Art Ensemble of Chicago began its première New York performance. Its only number, which was entertaining for a third of the forty-five minutes it lasted, consisted of a sounding stream, single- and multi-layered, that flowed up and down through crescendos and diminuendos, some of which had a hocus-pocus majesty. In one, a bass clarinet played a tattered melody while assorted gongs were struck, the bass saxophonist made *Queen Mary* sounds, and a muted trumpet played. It took twenty minutes to clear the stage after the Art Ensemble had finished, and the steady shuffling, scraping, clicking, and bonging were, to all intents and purposes, the group's second number. The Art Ensemble never stopped calling attention to how its music was made, so it kept one on the outside looking in. The next group had the reverse effect. Made up of Sam Rivers (tenor saxophone, flute, and piano). Richard Davis (bass), and Norman Connors (drums), it created a cantankerous vortex that in time enfolded one almost completely. Indeed, when its one long excursion was over, the immediate feeling was of having just eased out of a pair of tight shoes.

There were accompanists for Ella Fitzgerald all over Carnegie Hall early this evening, and they included a re-creation of the Chick Webb band (six members were alumni); Ellis Larkins, whose tapestried backgrounds almost smoothed some surprisingly unsteady Fitzgerald singing (she overstepped phrases and even got blown about by her vibrato); and a small group (Roy Eldridge, Eddie Lockjaw Davis, Al Grey, Tommy Flanagan, Joe Pass, Keeter

Betts, and Freddie Waits) that was first allowed to jam seven ballads and up-tempo standards. Eldridge was the winner. He is sixty-two but in "Stardust" he put it together again: the steam-whistle effects, the red-banner flights, the stepping middle-register passages, and the coursing melodic lines.

*July 6th*

George Wein has become Broadway-minded. We have had the American popular-song production, the Ray Charles–James Baldwin production, and the Ella Fitzgerald production. And tonight at Carnegie Hall we were offered one called *Jazz Cabaret.* Tables with checked cloths had been set up onstage, and their occupants were served drinks throughout the concert, which began with yet another re-creation—the Cab Calloway band of the late thirties and early forties. But it was more than a re-creation, for better than half its members—among them Dizzy Gillespie, Doc Cheatham, Tyree Glenn, Quentin Jackson, Walter (Foots) Thomas, Danny Barker, Milt Hinton, and Cozy Cole—were alumni. We were about to hear the Cab Calloway band in the flesh again! But it never really happened. The band started with that old splendid coasting Charlie Christian riff, "A Smo-o-oth One," and suddenly Honi Coles and the Copasetics, a troupe of five good tap-dancers, flew onstage for three numbers. Nellie Lutcher sang five of her jangling, hooting tunes, and gave way to Louis Jordan, the funny, adept alto saxophonist and singer. He rolled through three songs, accompanied by a quartet from the band, and in one of them, a blues, he gave Doc Cheatham three choruses, which were exquisite. Ah, the band again and a number featuring Dizzy Gillespie! But then Esther Phillips, a raucous soul singer, towed an organist and drummer onstage and sang five interminable numbers, while the band sat soundless behind her. Now Calloway himself appeared, and there was hope: This fine assemblage would at last play its heart out. But I'd forgotten how much space Calloway used to hog on his records, and he did it again tonight. When his last vocal was over, the lights went up, and there the band sat, all warmed up and no place to go.

The second jam session at the Music Hall was no more a jam session than the one earlier in the week or the two given there last year. There were, in effect, six night-club sets: a group that included, among others, Red Rodney, Art Farmer, and Bill Watrous; a quartet with Bill Evans, Gary Burton, Eddie Gomez, and Marty Morrell; a trio with Jeremy Steig, Gomez, and Morrell; a big group involving Dizzy Gillespie, Jon Faddis, Stan Getz, Art Blakey, and Cecil Payne; Anita O'Day, accompanied by Jimmy Rowles, Larry Ridley, and Oliver Jackson; and another large group, which included Jackson, Milt Hinton, Larry Coryell, Earl Hines, Louis Jordan, and Sonny Stitt. Inevitably, there were moments. Rowles got off an exemplary chorus in "I Can't Get Started." Gary Burton was Corbusier. Faddis ran down some of Gillespie's well-tested circumlocutions. And Hines provided some largesse accompaniment. But why not put a first-rate group onstage and just let them go, as in the old Kansas City jam session? When the pianist tires, replace him. When the drummer weakens, bring on another. Such an organic affair might also make one forget the surroundings, which again blocked the suspension of disbelief.

A jazz festival should be a catalyst that brings musicians together who ordinarily pass in the night. That ideal was realized this afternoon in Alice Tully Hall at a youth concert organized by Marian McPartland and the music-educator and former drummer Clem De Rosa. The first three groups were coached by the trumpeter Joe Newman, the bassist Paul West, and the composer Eddie Bonnemere. Then De Rosa's local seventeen-piece All City High School Jazz Orchestra appeared, and wonders began. After its warmup number, the band went into Dee Barton's ingenious and extremely difficult arrangement of "Here's That Rainy Day." The first chorus is scored for four trombones, in unison and harmony, and they wafted through it. And so did the whole band in the rest of the arrangement, which is full of introverted harmonies and tricky voicings. Sonny Stitt, who had been invited to sit in, dived into the old riff blues "Jumping with Symphony Sid." The band, with De Rosa's remarkable seventeen-year-old son on drums, immediately settled in behind him, playing riffs and old Basie-band hums, and Stitt took off. He played a dozen choruses (on tenor saxophone), and they were intricate and soaring. Then he picked up his alto saxophone and played a slow "Lover Man," and, still smoking, he returned to his tenor and played a consummate version of "I Got Rhythm" in three tempos, the first of them slow and swaying.

# Cinderella Man

I t took a long time for Artie Shaw to subside. He became a Presence on the American landscape in 1938 when his first Victor release—Jerry Grey's arrangement of Cole Porter's "Begin the Beguine"—sold a million copies. Nothing could have been more surprising. Shaw, who was twenty-eight, was just another big-band leader; the tune, a Porter oddity with a hundred-and-eight-bar chorus, had not gone much of anywhere in its three-year existence, and Victor, which had been against recording it in the first place, pushed the A-side of the record, a bouncy version of "Indian Love Call." (Alec Wilder writes of "Begin the Beguine" in *American Popular Song*: It is a "maverick, an unprecedented experiment, and one which, to this day, after hearing it hundreds of times, I cannot sing or whistle or play from start to finish without the printed music. . . . I suppose it conjures up for the listener all sorts of romantic memories embodying the ultimate tropical evening and the most dramatic dance floors ever imagined. . . . [But] along about the sixtieth measure I find myself muttering another title, 'End the Beguine.' " Yet the song was unquenchable. In 1944, when Eddie Heywood recorded his elegant, stylized piano version, it became the only hit, barring Billie Holiday's "Strange Fruit," that Commodore Records ever had, and a decade after that it was still a high-school glee-club staple.)

The public began buying practically everything Shaw recorded ("Back Bay Shuffle," "Nightmare," "Deep Purple," "Traffic Jam"), and Shaw, who had been scuffling since he was fifteen, found himself hilariously netting as much as thirty thousand dollars a week. Then, late in 1939, he pulled the first and most celebrated of his disappearing acts by walking off the bandstand of the old Pennsylvania Hotel's Café Rouge in mid-evening and going to Mexico. It was seemingly suicidal. But less than three months later, Shaw had put together a new band, combining an oboe, a flute, a bass clarinet, a French horn, and a fifteen man string section, and its first recording, a Mexican ditty called "Frenesi," became another sizzling success, or "$ucce$$," as Shaw spells it in his autobiography, *The Trouble with Cinderella*. "Frenesi" was joined by "Temptation," "Stardust," "Concerto for Clarinet," "Dancing in the Dark," and "Moonglow," and the land was swimming in Shaw's music. He also made news in 1940 by marrying Lana Turner (who was followed in the next six years by Jerome Kern's daughter, Ava Gardner, and Kathleen Winsor), and in 1941 he made more by hiring a black musician, the rough-and-ready trumpeter Hot Lips Page. (It was the fashion for white leaders to hire black trumpeters. Benny Goodman had his Cootie Williams and Gene Krupa his Roy Eldridge. Shaw, though, had long been a racial pioneer. In 1937, he hired Billie Holiday and kept her with the band, through a lot of heavy weather, for a year and a half. Shaw appears in her autobiography as one of her few knights: "There aren't many people who fought harder than Artie against the vicious people in the music business or the crummy side of second-class citizenship which eats the guts of so many musicians. He didn't win. But he didn't lose either. . . . And people still talk about him as if he were nuts because there were things more important to him than a million damn bucks a year.") In 1942, Shaw put together what was widely regarded as the best of the service bands, and after the war he hired Roy Eldridge and assembled his last good big band. The great days of big bands were over, though, and Shaw knew it. He began ducking in and out of music, and in 1952, as if to ring the curtain down, he published his autobiography. It was well received as a piece of scorching confessional writing. Purged, Shaw quit music forever in 1954, and moved to Spain, where he remained until 1960, when he settled, sumptuously, in Connecticut. There is little resemblance between the handsome, wavy-haired Lothario of the thirties and forties and the present Shaw, who balances his near-baldness with a huge mustache and ferocious eyebrows.

Shaw belittles the musical side of his $ucce$$ in his book, but he did have the best of the big white bands. What, after all, were the others like? Glenn Miller's band, with its bosomy reed voicings and high-heeled rhythm section, had a feminine air, as did Harry James' band, which was dominated by his divalike trumpet. Jimmy Dorsey's band was bland and buttery, while his brother's veered back and forth between *Walpurgisnacht* and moonsville. Bob Crosby's Dixieland band was enmeshed in the spidery wood-blocks-and-cowbells drumming of Ray Bauduc, and Charlie Spivak's suggested angel food. Jan Savitt and Glen Gray operated well-oiled pumps, and so did Benny Goodman, except for that brief, green time in the summer of 1941 when he had Cootie Williams and Mel Powell and Charlie Christian and Sid Catlett. Claude Thornhill's band, though, was a beautiful loner; he used French horns and the damask arrangements of Gil Evans, who achieved textures and voicings that were as choice as Duke Ellington's.

Each of Shaw's bands had a different face. The "Begin the Beguine" outfit was tight and springy; it was a snappy Ford coupe. The "Frenesi" band, with its bouffant strings and walk-along tempos, was gentle and subtle, and it had an unmistakable jazz persuasion. It was also a peerless *dance* band. The 1945 band, with Roy Eldridge, was the closest Shaw came to an out-and-out jazz group. It was a disciplined, swinging, straight-ahead band. Yet it was Shaw's clarinet playing, always admired more widely by musicians than Goodman's, that gave his bands their final stamp. He had an innocent, delicate, impeccably tailored style. His tone was not robust. In the low register, he was soft and convincing, but he lacked the velvet spaces of Goodman and Edmond Hall and Pee Wee Russell, and when he went into the top register, which he often did, he sounded thin and synthetic. His solos, whether embellishments of the melody or full improvisations, were faultlessly structured. He had a way of playing the melody that invariably suggested that *this* is the way it should sound. And he was right. If the melody had any excess weight he eliminated a note here, a note there. If it was on the skinny side he added flourishes or moved down to the chalameau register, which tends to make every note sound wise. He impressed his melodic approach so thoroughly on certain tunes that when they surface anew one automatically hears Shaw's rendition. *Vide* "Moonglow" and "Stardust" and "Dancing in the Dark." Shaw's improvising was canny and agile. He used a great many notes, complex little runs that were almost asides, an on-the-beat attack, almost no vibrato, and soaring ascensions into the upper register. And he demonstrated considerable emotion on an instrument that resists emotion.

Several editions of Shaw's band are on three reissues—"Free for All: Artie Shaw and His Orchestra," "This is Artie Shaw," and "Artie Shaw Featuring Roy Eldridge." The first album has sixteen numbers, set down in 1937 by Shaw's second band (the first, garlanded with strings, had been formed the year before, but the public wasn't ready for such heresy). It was an eager group that is summed up pretty well in the five-and-a-half-minute "Blues March," which—Shaw expected—is a funny and rather touching instance of white boys trying to play those low-down Negro blues. The second album has twenty sides, made between 1938 and 1941, and it covers Shaw's banner years. It starts with "Begin the Beguine," goes through "Back Bay Shuffle,"

"Deep Purple," "Frenesi," "Tempetation," "Stardust," and "Moonglow," and ends with an odd date that Shaw did for Lena Horne, who is also backed by Henry Allen, Benny Carter, and J. C. Higginbotham. There are three sides by Shaw's first Gramercy Five, whose harpsichord caused a lot of deep thinking among the faithful. The LP also has the only vocal—and it is a marvelous one—that Billie Holiday recorded with the band; at least, it is the only one ever released. The side is again singular in that it was recorded at the session which produced "Begin the Beguine." The album with Roy Eldridge was done in 1944 and 1945, and the arrangements are fresh and modern. There are nine big-band sides and seven by the second edition of the Gramercy Five, and all but one (a vocal by Eldridge) are graced by the trumpeter. He had an electric effect on a big band. He was unmistakably there in the ensemble passages, and his solos, even if they were only eight bars long, had a lyricism and drive that caused lights to go on all over. Shaw's musical life, to all intents and purposes, ended with this band, and perhaps it's just as well. He always had good timing.

## Big Ben

**W**ord has come, in the benighted form of a notice buried at the foot of the *Times'* obituary page, that Ben Webster has died in Copenhagen at the age of sixty-four. But this passing reference is not altogether surprising, for Webster spent most of his mature years in semi-obscurity or in the shadow of his two great colleagues, Coleman Hawkins and Lester Young. (Weary of racism, the lack of steady work, and his second-banana status, he emigrated to Europe in the mid-sixties and never returned.) It had become increasingly clear by the late fifties, though, that Webster was at last pulling even with Young and Hawkins, whose styles had come loose in their final years. There were even heretical whispers to the effect that the two colossi of the tenor saxophone were not Young and Hawkins but Young and Webster. Young's easy majesty was unassailable, these dissidents claimed, but Hawkins' was not, for although his enormous authority never waned he eventually became the prisoner of the very innovations that had shaped every saxophonist—barring Young and Bud Freeman—of his generation. He began to seem locked into his endless chord progressions, his unbroken flow of notes, and his almost tyrannical rhythms. Webster, in contrast, had become a huge-toned, airborne marvel. His early style, formed in the bands of Bennie Moten, Andy Kirk, Fletcher Henderson, and Cab Calloway, stemmed directly from Hawkins, but it went through a subtle reshaping during the three years he spent with Duke Ellington in the early forties. He fell under the lyrical sway of Johnny Hodges, and this released a poetic outpouring that continued the rest of his life. But it was an intensely disciplined poetry. Unlike most jazz musicians, Webster had an elastic and governing sense of dynamics. He generally started a solo softly, sliding under his first notes and continuing throughout the chorus in a glancing, flickering fashion. A silken tension immediately took hold. He gradually raised his volume in his second chorus, and, depending on his mood (he was a man of temper, one of whose nicknames was "the Brute"), turned on an abrasive growl or moved through proclamatory phrases that carried into his final chorus and then gave way to the musings he had begun with. He was most celebrated for his slow ballads, and rightly; they were profound melodic embellishments. Using an enormous tone, a breathy, enveloping vibrato, and terrific glissandos, he constructed castles of sound that were romantic but never sentimental, luxuriant but tasteful, yearning but free of self-pity.

Webster, with his parrot nose, hooded eyes, and prowlike front, was a formidable-looking man. (His hats, though, were a tipoff to his astringent humor. They were too small, and he wore them brims up, on the back of his head. There is a looming photograph of him by Fred Seligo, taken low and from the front, in which he is in complete, featureless silhouette. But the massive shape, crowned with its ridiculous pillbox, is unmistakable.) One recalls Webster in many different weathers, and among the sunniest was his brief stay at the Three Deuces, on West Fifty-second Street, not long after he left Ellington. He was in a quartet led by Sidney Catlett and including John Simmons and Marlowe Morris. He would stand motionless beside the equally formidable Catlett, his back straight, his instrument slightly raised, and, his eyes closed, deliver one of his whisper-to-shout-to-whisper solos, turn expressionlessly to watch Morris and Simmons solo, and, facing front again, matter-of-factly exchange racing, four-bar breaks with Catlett, then softly restate the melody. The number done, he would open his eyes and peer deadpan over the assembled heads out front. The Brute, in his great eloquence, had spoken.

# Gene

Ben Webster and now, also at the age of sixty-four, Gene Krupa. Although he lived for a long time, his life had a fleeting quality. Between 1936 and 1942, he was, as a sideman with Benny Goodman and as the leader of his own big band, a famous man. Indeed, he was the first jazz musician to become a matinée idol. A small, good-looking man who played drums melodramatically—hunched over and gum-chewing, his black hair a wild flag—his image was in every eye and his name in every household. It was front-page news when he went to jail, briefly, on a drug-connected charge, and it was big news when he left Goodman in 1938 to form his own group. He became, particularly for those who grew up in the Depression, a phoenix rising. Then, in the next decade, everything went awry. He was overtaken by his admirer Buddy Rich and by the new complexities of bebop; and the big bands, which had formed his backdrop, faded out. On top of that, jazz students, peering through the tatters of his radiance, decided that the true pioneers of jazz drumming during Krupa's halcyon days had been Jo Jones and Chick Webb and Sid Catlett. Krupa's reputation never fully recovered from these reverses, but his contributions as a consolidating pioneer were genuine and invaluable. He absorbed in Chicago in the twenties those two founts of drumming—Baby Dodds and Zutty Singleton; he listened to Cuba Austin and Chick Webb in New York in the thirties, and he put together a streamlined composite of their styles. By simply playing with enormous dash and style, he brought jazz drumming up from the cellar it had been in since New Orleans days. He was, as well, the first drummer to solo at any length, and he has been indirectly blamed for the sins of other and lesser drum soloists ever since. (There have been, to be sure, very few good drum soloists. Among the best have been Rich, Jo Jones, Elvin Jones, Max Roach, Joe Morello, Krupa, Webb, and Catlett, the last of whom was the fairest of them all. Those who decry drum soloists should remember that there have been only a handful of great improvisers on any instrument.) Such adventurers as Catlett and Jo Jones certainly listened to Krupa in his ongoing days, and learned from him, and the reverse was true, too. Drummers, a high-flying breed, are as pleased to plunder as they are to be plundered.

## From Morton to Waller to James P.

Dick Wellstood, the forty-seven-year-old pianist, has no verifiable style of his own, but he has filled this lacuna with an extraordinary pianistic gallery. He can *be*, in whole or in part, Scott Joplin, Jelly Roll Morton, James P. Johnson, Zez Confrey, Fats Waller, Earl Hines, Joe Sullivan, Jess Stacy, Art Tatum, Wesley Wallace, Pete Johnson, Art Hodes, Hank Duncan, Luckey Roberts, Jimmy Yancey, and even Bill Evans. But he is not just an eclectic; he is a pianistic actor who slips inside other men's styles and brings them, with the help of his own considerable improvisational energies, startlingly to life. He did this tonight, time and again, at Michael's Pub, where he is leading a trio with Kenny Davern on soprano saxophone and clarinet and Cliff Leeman on drums. He saluted Fats Waller with "Keepin' Out of Mischief Now," with the rarely heard "Viper's Drag," and with "Handful of Keys." He executed a brilliant reading of James P. Johnson's "Carolina Shout," which, with its contrary left-hand patterns, is the stride pianist's supreme test, and he offered an exact version of Johnson's lacy "Snowy Morning Blues." He did Morton's beautiful "Sweet Substitute," filling the closing chorus with tremolos. He made Joplin's "Maple Leaf Rag" and Hines' "Rosetta" swing. He fashioned a Joe Sullivan dirge out of "Brother, Can You Spare a Dime," and he put Pete Johnson in charge of a cycling "Memphis Blues." Davern has listened to Sidney Bechet and Pee Wee Russell, while Leeman constantly recalls Dave Tough. But Leeman does more than that, for he has a talent that has almost vanished from jazz drumming—the fashioning of explosive four-bar breaks. Their split-second dynamics, varied textures, and unexpected accents are those of Sid Catlett. A typical break rushes by like this: a quick silence, a ringing offbeat rim shot, another lightning silence, two eighth notes on the bass drum, a triplet on the sock cymbal, and a couple of concluding rim shots, preceded by an offbeat on a tom-tom. It is rare, epigrammatic drumming.

## One Man's Meat

The Smithsonian has established a Division of Performing Arts, and within it a Jazz Program, which is headed up by Martin Williams. Williams is the American counterpart of the French jazz *philosophe* André Hodeir. During the twenty-odd years he has been writing about jazz, he has produced a number of books, among them two critical anthologies (one of them taken from the defunct monthly *Jazz Review*, which he helped found and edit), a primer on the music, a biographical-critical look at New Orleans jazz, a collection of his incidental essays, a collection of short, summing-it-all-up essays on the great jazz figures, and monographs on King Oliver and Jelly Roll Morton. Along the way, he has developed an uncluttered vision of jazz which has been notable for its lack of faddism, its firmness with the second-rate, and its sound, semi-musicological approach. One does not always agree with his enthusiasms and assessments, nor does one always admire his prose; the rustle of the academician's card file is often audible in it. Now, in his role at the Smithsonian, he has produced a brand-new history in six LPs called "The Smithsonian Collection of Classic Jazz." It consists of eighty-four recordings (some are excerpts) taken from the vaults of seventeen companies and stretching from a 1916 Scott Joplin piano roll to a 1966 Cecil Taylor. There is also a pleasantly designed forty-eight-page booklet by Williams which contains a history of the music, technical explanations of rhythm, form, and improvisation, a capsule guide to each record, and such thoughtful addenda as a jazz bibliography and a list of the principal jazz-record shops here and abroad. The collection fills a void. There have been similar endeavors before, but they have been pirated and abortive or else assembled by recording companies from their own necessarily incomplete catalogues. Williams has made it possible for the first time to survey in one sweep the main pinnacles of the music. Here are some of the principal beauties: Robert Johnson's spooky, deep-night blues, "Hellhound on My Trail," which starts, "I got to keep movin', blues fallin' down like hail / I can't keep no money with a hellhound on my trail"; Bessie Smith's majestic "St. Louis Blues"; three of Jelly Roll Morton's 1926 Red Hot Peppers sides, which mark the high point of New Orleans jazz; Sidney Bechet's mourning five-minute clarinet blues, "Blue Horizon," set down in 1944; the extraordinary Louis Armstrong–Earl Hines 1928 duet, "Weather Bird"; Armstrong's "West End Blues," and his two seminal solos, one muted and the other open-horn, in his 1930 "Sweethearts on Parade"; Red Allen's marvelous avant-garde statement on Fletcher Henderson's "Wrappin' It Up"; a graceful 1927 Fats Waller piano solo, "I Ain't Got Nobody" (listen, in particular, to the last couple of measures, when, in the highest register, he drifts into a slow-motion passage that gives the impression he is leaning on air); Meade Lux Lewis's choice "Honky Tonk Train"; Teddy Wilson's lovely solo in the Benny Goodman Trio version of "Body and Soul"; two superb Coleman Hawkins selections—the 1939 "Body and Soul" and the multi-layered 1943 "The Man I Love," made with Eddie Heywood, Oscar Pettiford, and Shelly Manne; two Billie Holidays, from 1937 and 1941, and two Art Tatum solos, from 1949 and 1956; Roy Eldridge's great "Rockin' Chair," recorded with Gene Krupa's band in 1941; three Count Basie numbers from his classic late-thirties days; and two Benny Goodman sextets, with extensive Charlie Christian solos. There are, as well, eight Duke Ellington numbers, the best made in 1940 and 1941 ("Harlem Air Shaft," "Concerto for Cootie," "In a Mellotone," "Ko-Ko," and "Blue Serge"); an encompassing duet, recorded at a New York concert in 1945 by Don Byas and Slam Stewart; eight numbers by Dizzy Gillespie and/or Charlie Parker, the finest being Parker's great slow blues ("Parker's Mood") and his two unbelievable 1947 versions of "Embraceable You"; six Thelonious Monks from the forties and fifties, of which his sly piano solo, "I Should Care," and the nine choruses of medium blues excerpted from Miles Davis' "Bag's Groove" are the cream; Miles Davis' brooding paraphrase of "Summertime," posed against one of Gil Evans' richest draperies; Sonny Rollins' ten or so choruses of blues on his 1956 "Blue 7"; a resplendent 1960 version of John Lewis's "Django," by the Modern Jazz Quartet; and an excerpt from Ornette Coleman's thirty-six minutes of free improvisation for double quartets made up of trumpet, reed, bass, and drums.

But these beauties are occasionally flecked with dross. Why bother with Fletcher Henderson's stodgy 1926 "The Stampede," even if it is an example of nonswinging jazz? And why include a middling Ella Fitzgerald and *two* of Sarah Vaughan's parabolas, and omit Mildred Bailey and Ivie Anderson altogether? Again, when there are so many exciting Lionel Hampton small-band sides ("Ring Dem Bells," "Haven't Named It Yet," "Hollywood Shuffle"), why include the so-so "When Lights Are Low"? Puzzling, too, is the presence of one of Ellington's pioneer extended pieces, "Creole Rhapsody"; it remains static and dull. Equally puzzling is Erroll Garner's "Fantasy on 'Frankie and Johnny,' " done in 1947, when he hadn't got himself together. Finally, are *eight* Ellingtons and *six* Thelonious Monks and *three* Ornette Colemans necessary in a limited survey of this kind?

At the outset of Williams' booklet, he carefully points out that the collection is by no means comprehensive, that much good material has been omitted, etc. But this hedging doesn't excuse the token inclusion of such masters as Sid Catlett, Ben Webster, Dickie Wells, and Charlie Mingus (the Mingus included is one of his least impressive rabble-rousers) and the complete absence of, among others, the Original Dixieland Jazz Band, any of the Metronome All-Star bands (what good illustrative catchalls they are!), Jack Teagarden, Pee Wee Russell, Bobby Hackett, Dave Tough, J. C. Higginbotham, Frankie Newton, Bill Coleman, Edmond Hall, Joe Turner, and Ray Charles, the last two of whom are surely, in their own ways, nonpareil. And this is to say nothing of the big bands of Benny Goodman, Woody Herman, Benny Carter (his 1933 one), and Andy Kirk. Secondary figures are sometimes more instructive than their big brothers.

## Entrepreneur

Eddie Condon (1905–73) was an idea in human form. The idea was simple and revolutionary: that jazz music is a complete way of life, encompassing both the prankish and the celestial, the Georg Brunises and the Louis Armstrongs. The human form was equally unadorned: A short, smooth, tightly packed man who, with his flat hair combed precisely just off center, his small, symmetrical face, and his flawless bow ties, had an unremittingly pumiced appearance. (In his later years, alcohol and its attendant miseries made him baggy and ghostly.) But Condon was more than just his own idea. He steadfastly celebrated it with his tongue, which was sharp, witty, and original. He seemed driven by propellers of persiflage.

On the French jazz critic Hugues Panassié, who came to America in 1938 to supervise some recordings by American musicians:

I don't see why we need a Frenchman to come over here and tell us how to play American music. I wouldn't think of going to France and telling him how to jump on a grape.

On Stan Kenton:

Every Kenton record sounds to me as though Stan signed on three hundred men for the date and they were all on time. Music of his school ought to be played close to elephants and listened to by clowns.

To a modish lady at a party:

Madam, is that a hat or a threat you're wearing?

His introductory remarks to the sparse audience at his first Town Hall concert, in 1942:

Lady and gentleman.

Throughout most of the forties Condon seemed to be all over jazz. He organized record dates, some of which have taken on a classic stamp. With the help of his energetic admirer Ernie Anderson, he instituted his long series of Saturday-afternoon Town Hall concerts, which were broadcast as well. He officiated at public jam sessions. He put together an autobiography, *We Called It Music*, with Thomas Sugrue. He opened his own jazz club in the Village. He ran pioneering jazz television programs. And for a time he and Richard Gehman did a record-review column for the *Journal-American* that was pure Condon froth. All the while, he battered away at the color bar by enlivening his own floating school of musicians (Max Kaminsky, Brad Gowans, Joe Bushkin, Joe Sullivan, George Wettling, Dave Tough, Pee Wee Russell, Georg Brunis, Bud Freeman, Wild Bill Davison) with such great black figures as Fats Waller, Red Allen, James P. Johnson, Sid Catlett, Rex Stewart, Sidney Bechet, Benny Morton, Vic Dickenson, Edmond Hall, Hot Lips Page, and Louis Armstrong. But there was a worm in the rose, and by the early fifties the music Condon had touted so long—a basically white and self-limiting version of the black music its practitioners had heard when they were kids in Chicago in the twenties—was just about worked out. The inventions of Charlie Parker and Dizzy Gillespie had become outgoing and unbridled, while Condon's music had begun to feed on itself.

Condon's tenure as the mouthpiece of jazz was a mammoth houseparty. There were no yesterdays, todays, or tomorrows. There was only tonight. From nine in the evening until five or six in the morning, one drank, played, listened, gabbed, laughed, and kicked the gong around. Very few of the children who grew up at this marathon knew their fathers. A good deal of the mad esprit that shaped those years has now been caught in *Eddie Condon's Scrapbook of Jazz*, and in two albums of reissues—"Eddie Condon & Bud Freeman" and "Eddie Condon's World of Jazz." The book, assembled by Condon and Hank O'Neal not long before Condon's death, contains hundreds of photographs, interspersed with letters, record labels, concert programs, drawings (the marvelous one done by Will Cotton in 1945 for the Profile of Condon written for *The New Yorker* by Rogers Whitaker), newspaper and magazine clippings, posters, ads, sheet music, and swatches of text by Condon, his wife, Phyllis, George Avakian, and others. The photographs are often invaluable. Among the best are Condon, a shining sixteen, with Hollis Peavey and his Jazz Bandits; Pee Wee Russell and Bobby Hackett at Nick's, both of them looking dewy and newborn; a Sunday-afternoon jam session at the old Jimmy Ryan's, in which Condon, Zutty Singleton, Joe Sullivan,

Sidney Bechet, Hot Lips Page, Sandy Williams, Max Kaminsky, Russell, and several unidentifiable musicians are roaring through the invariable Ryan's finale, "Bugle Call Rag"; Sidney Bechet, leaning against a piano, and Sid Catlett, enthroned at a snare drum, jamming backstage; Artie Shaw, Duke Ellington, and an unbelievably tiny Chick Webb playing at a party; that fine, short-lived 1944 band of Davison, Rod Cless, Williams, James P., and Kaiser Marshall; and Condon the impresario, hobnobbing with Yul Brynner, Johnny Mercer, Bing Crosby, Dimitri Mitropoulos, Joseph Szigeti, and Rita Hayworth. One wonders, though, why many of the pictures of Condon in his last years were included; they reveal that the party was indeed over.

The Columbia album, designed as a companion to the book, contains twenty-seven numbers recorded between 1927 and 1954. They are meant to illuminate the musical world that Condon moved through, and many do. Among these are Louis Armstrong's regal 1931 "Just a Gigolo," with its subtle opening muted solo; two of the wild-eyed Rhythmaker sides done in 1932 by Red Allen, Russell, and Singleton ("Shine on Your Shoes" and "Yellow Dog Blues"); a good 1936 Bunny Berigan ("That Foolish Feeling"); a number from Condon's first recording date ("Sugar"), made in 1927, with Jimmy McPartland, Frank Teschemacher, Bud Freeman, Joe Sullivan, and Gene Krupa, that is notable for the closing ensemble, which, with its accidental mélange of keys, may be the first atonal passage in jazz; a previously unissued take of Freeman's excited 1933 "The Eel"; and one of the extended numbers ("Blues My Naughty Sweetie Gives to Me") recorded in 1954 for George Avakian by two driving Condon bands working in tandem. Some of the nonsense on the rest of the record is pretty funny—in particular, vocals by Condon ("Indiana"), Johnny Mercer, Bing Crosby, and one Danny Stewart, who sings "Marie" in Hawaiian. Condon, a good rhythm guitarist, is on just nine sides.

The Atlantic album consists of twenty-four sides made for Commodore in 1938 and 1939. The first twelve are by three Condon bands. There are Pee Wee Russell's long, languorous, breaking-ground solo in "Love Is Just Around the Corner" (his rhythmic and melodic departures here are still singular); Hackett's already immaculate work in a slow "Jada"; Russell, Hackett, Jack Teagarden, and Jess Stacy in "Embraceable You," "Diane," and the pell-mell "Meet Me Tonight in Dreamland"; the great, kicking drumming of Dave Tough in the opening choruses of "Tappin' the Commodore Till" (one of the few times Tough comes through clearly on records); and Russell's shaded, falling-away solo in "Sunday." The remainder of the album is given over almost wholly to a Bud Freeman trio that involves Stacy and George Wettling. Stacy is a marvel, notably in "You Took Advantage of Me," "Three's No Crowd," "Blue Room," and "I Don't Believe It." He manages to slide under Wettling's heavy, footling drumming, and his ingenious accompanying makes Freeman's jouncing solos sound inspired.

# 1974

## Gallic View

Hard on the heels of Martin Williams' "The Smithsonian Collection of Classic Jazz" has come Columbia's huge survey of the music. It consists of no fewer than thirty-one albums (the Smithsonian's has six), which contain almost four hundred and fifty numbers (the Smithsonian's has eighty-six), ranging from kindergarten efforts in the early twenties by Louis Armstrong and Duke Ellington and Sidney Bechet to the work in the sixties of Armstrong and Miles Davis and George Benson. This omnibus goes under the strange title of "Aimez-Vous le Jazz," or "Do You Like Jazz," for it was apparently prepared in France by Henri Renaud. It is a highly uneven, non-comprehensive collection, and the packaging is minimal. The album covers are heavy glossed paper and the sporadic liner notes are inconclusive. And the sound is come-as-you-are (several of the rarer numbers have been transferred directly from scratched, cracked 78s). The discographical aspects are a maze. Some of the material had gone out of print. Some that had been reissued had again vanished. Some had never been reissued. And some had never been bought out at all. (This refers only to American releases, and does not take into account the frenzied pirating now going on here.) Among the more familiar efforts are Art Tatum's superlative 1949 California concert (Volume 2); sixteen Charlie Christian–Benny Goodman numbers, one of which ("The Sheik of Araby") has never been reissued (Volume 3); the guitarist George Benson's first Columbia record (Volume 19); seven of King Oliver's 1923 sides (Volume 21); two Miles Davis albums from the fifties and sixties (Volumes 1 and 17); and two volumes of live Benny Goodman trio and quartet numbers (Volumes 7 and 15). Far less familiar are four selections done by Sidney Bechet in 1938 with the baritone saxophonist Ernie Caceres, who provides a rooting alter-voice to Bechet's soaring (Volume 4); Duke Ellington's "Liberian Suite" and "A Tone Parallel to Harlem" (Volume 6); eleven of Teddy Wilson's earliest piano solos, done between 1935 and 1937 and never reissued before (Volume 8); sixteen 1939–41 Cab Calloway big-band numbers, also never reissued, that are resplendent for some early I-*think*-I-know-where-I'm-going Dizzy Gillespie solos, Chu Berry's runneth-over tenor saxophone, and Cozy Cole's hip schoolmarm drumming (Volume 10); the historic numbers Armstrong and Bechet made in 1924 and 1925 (Volume 14), a collaboration that, unfortunately, was tried only once more, in 1940;

spirited Fats Waller stews from 1922, 1929, and 1931–32 and including four more of the above-mentioned Red Allen–Pee Wee Russell Rhythmaker sides; several bumptious numbers by a Ted Lewis band that included Muggsy Spanier, Benny Goodman, and Bud Freeman and three rolling selections with Jack Teagarden (Volume 18); sixteen Duke Ellington big- and small-band sides from 1947 and 1951, among them "Three Cent Stomp" (winner of the Pun of the Year Award in '47) and a rocking blues, "Hy'a Sue" (Volume 20); fourteen 1929 and 1930 numbers by the Luis Russell band, which had Red Allen and J. C. Higginbotham and possibly the first genuinely swinging rhythm section in jazz (Volume 22); three brilliant early Gil Evans arrangements, done in the late forties for Claude Thornhill's unique big band (Volume 27); thirty-two Ellington tunes from the middle to the late twenties, among them both takes of the affecting, mysterious "Black and Tan fantasy," in which the avant-garde Jabbo Smith replaced Bubber Miley (Volume 29); and no fewer than four LPs (Volumes 23, 25, 26, and 28) of Louis Armstrong in the twenties, accompanying such singers as Maggie Jones, Nolan Welsh, Clara Smith, Sippie Wallace, Hociel Thomas, Bertha Chippie Hill, Blanche Calloway, Victoria Spivey, and Lillie Delk Christian, the last of whom not even Armstrong, who is herculean throughout, can heft.

Some of the most precious material in the Columbia collection has been assembled in three LPs. The first offers four tantalizing glimpses of Django Reinhardt, jamming in Paris in 1945 with such Americans as Joe Shulman, Ray McKinley, and Mel Powell (Volume 12). The second, given over to Coleman Hawkins, includes all the Chocolate Dandies sides made in 1930 with Jimmy Harrison, Benny Carter, and Bobby Stark, the ten graceful numbers Hawkins and Red Allen recorded in 1933, and the two fine, winging ones Hawkins did in 1941 with Count Basie's big band (Volume 31). The third LP is fascinating. On it are alternate takes of three Basie small-band classics—the 1936 "Shoe Shine Boy" and the 1939 "Dickie's Dream" and "Lester Leaps In." They are easily as rewarding as the takes first released. Also on this LP are six of the oddest records ever made. Lee Castle is on trumpet, Lester Young on tenor saxophone and clarinet, Glenn Hardman on organ, Freddie Greene on guitar, and Jo Jones on drums. Hardman is a two-ton cocktail-lounge organist, but his colleagues envelop him like a school of fish, allowing us to concentrate on their glistening beauties. Young is extraordinary on both his instruments, and his two choruses on tenor in the slow blues match anything he recorded (Volume 24).

## Son

**B**rooks Kerr has gradually been assembling a band at Churchill's, and it is all but complete. It has strange bedfellows. Paul Quinichette (ex-Basie) is on tenor saxophone, Matthew Gee (ex-Basie and ex-Ellington) on trombone, Franc Williams (ex-Ellington) on flugelhorn, and Sam Woodyard (idem) on drums. Quinichette (pronounced "Quinishay") has long held a day job, and it is a pleasure to hear him again. Because of his speaking similarity to Lester Young, he was nicknamed Vice-Pres when he appeared in the fifties. But Quinichette grew up in the territory bands of the Southwest, and the special quality that infuses the playing of so many Southwestern musicians presses steadily to the fore. The skin is Young but the stuffing is Herschel Evans and Buddy Tate. That was noticeable this afternoon at Churchill's when Quinichette delivered Evans' anthem, "Blue and Sentimental." His tone was somber, and there were blue notes, low-register booms, and abrupt high exclamations. It was the sort of naked lyrical performance that Young could never have lowered his cool for. It was equally fine to hear Woodyard, who has been out West for a long time. He is a deceptive drummer. When he was with Ellington, his gangling looseness gave the impression that he might fall off his drum stool or commit some musical atrocity. But his insouciance hides a subtle drive and precision. His foot-pedal work is sparing and clean, as are his fills on the snare drum, and his cymbal work pushes. He listens, and he has immaculate time. Williams was also a surprise. He is not known for his solo work, but he has a pure tone and a gentle, quiet, Shorty Baker attack, which was especially impressive in "Solitude." Gee is a good if somewhat congested trombonist who recalls Bennie Green, and he had an excellent turn in "Sophisticated Lady," played in honor of Harry Carney, who dropped by to check on everyone's deportment. Brooks Kerr kept everything together—the son leading his spiritual fathers.

## True Blue

**M**ary Lou Williams has been filling in at the Café Carlyle for Bobby Short, and seeing her in such genteel surroundings is like being served steak at a garden party. She has been playing with great strength and invention in the past couple of years, and she was again tonight. She was also, I suspect, bowing to her surroundings, for she chose straightaway tunes she does not ordinarily play—"The Man I Love," "My Funny Valentine," "Temptation," "Love for Sale," and "The Surrey With the Fringe on Top." But after obeisance to the melody, each of them took on a driving blues quality, and it was business as usual.

## Repertory

**N**o matter how diluted or coarsened or aged some of the music may be, one can still hear in the flesh almost every style of jazz—ragtime, stride piano, boogie-woogie, blues shouting, New Orleans jazz, Kansas City jazz, Chicago jazz, Dixieland, big- and small-band swing, bebop, hard bop, and the various Babelean experiments of the last fifteen years. But recently there has been a distinct and subtle change in the provenance of jazz: It is no longer, except for the music of its rapidly diminishing originators, a folk art. Its underground, wayward, untutored, father-to-son customs have almost vanished. The music is now courted by academics, by governments, and by institutions, and it, in turn, is courting them. Jazz musicians play comfortably in concert halls and museums and palaces. They apply successfully for grants, get degrees in jazz, and hold down chairs of music in colleges. The Smithsonian Institution has assembled the first intelligent and comprehensive recorded history of jazz. Most of the nominations for the brand-new hall of fame established by the National Academy of Recording Arts and Sciences are jazz records. Duke Ellington is a member of the National Institute of Arts and Letters, and he and other jazz musicians have begun amassing honorary degrees. The first number of the *Journal of Jazz Studies*, published by the Rutgers Institute of Jazz Studies, and designed to meet "the need for a multi-disciplinary and inter-disciplinary publication for scholarly articles about jazz and related musics," is out. A large, if quirky, selection of jazzmen is listed in the latest *Who's Who in America*. (Some who are in: Count Basie, Bob Brookmeyer, Ornette Coleman, Jim Hall, Freddie Hubbard, Percy Humphrey, Elvin Jones, John Lewis, and John Tchicai. Some who are not: Jo Jones, Milt Hinton, Hank and Thad Jones, and Zutty Singleton.) But the most recent episode in this headlong rush of jazz and the Establishment toward one another is the appearance this winter of no fewer than two jazz repertory companies—the National Jazz Ensemble, founded and directed by the bassist Chuck Israels, and the New York Jazz Repertory Company, founded and headed up by George Wein. They make it official: Jazz has a Past.

Repertory companies, devoted until now to formal music, drama, and dancing, have long been considered ongoing and beneficial. They provide paid, on-the-job training, they delight audiences by giving them delusions of critical grandeur, and they keep worthy works alive. But such companies are by nature interpretive, whereas jazz is largely an improvisatory music—which raises all sorts of troublesome questions: How should a jazz repertory company re-create, say, Jelly Roll Morton's 1926 "Grandpa's Spells"? Transcribe the entire recording, thus precluding any improvising? Transcribe the ensembles and allow new solos? Or simply let loose musicians still conversant with Morton's style? Should the company play Ellington when Ellington can still play himself supremely well? How should it treat great recorded solos? Transcribe them or improvise on them? Should it fool with material that is readily available in night clubs or on records? Should it commission fresh works? And here is a genuine puzzle—how should it bring to life one of the great recorded performances by Frankie Newton, Sidney Bechet, J. C. Higginbotham, and Sidney Catlett, when most of its beauties flowed from the musicians' unique, inimitable timbres and attacks? To date, the two companies have each given two concerts, and they have raised as many questions as they have answered.

The National Jazz Ensemble, based in Alice Tully Hall, is the Little Brother of the two. It has a single, sixteen-piece orchestra, limited funds, and a schedule of four concerts this season. The New York Jazz Repertory Company, based in Carnegie Hall, is a behemoth in comparison. Its many orchestras are drawn from almost a hundred musicians of every persuasion, it is amply funded, and it will give fifteen concerts this season. But Little Brother, by opening its series on November 21, got off the mark first. The concert, by turns, was charming, ingenious, dull, exciting, and esoteric. Its twelve pieces were by Louis Armstrong, Ellington, Charlie Christian, Charlie Parker, John Carisi, Thelonious Monk, Israels, Bill Evans, and Miles Davis. The band included, to name a few, Randy Brecker and Lew Soloff on trumpet, Garnett Brown on trombone, Jim Buffington on French horn, George Barrow and Sal Nistico on tenor saxophone, Benny Aronov on piano, Pat Martino on guitar, Herb Bushler on bass, and Bill Goodwin on drums. Israels conducted and occasionally played. The first number, which lasted less than a minute, very nearly topped everything that came after. It was a transcription of the thirty-two-bar solo Louis Armstrong took in his 1927 Hot Five recording of "Struttin' with Some Barbecue." The few rough spots in the solo had been ironed out, and the band, playing the solo in unison, soared. One of Armstrong's most adventurous early solos became a new, lyrical, almost avant-garde statement that had a sculptured, larger-than-life quality. And this became even clearer when the number was repeated at the close of the evening. The next selection was a mistake. It was a thinly voiced, somewhat stiff reading of Ellington's complex, sashaying "Rockin' in Rhythm." Since every Ellington composition comes in three interlocking parts—the melody, its orchestration, and the band's rendition—any other version is necessarily incomplete. Moreover, "Rockin' in Rhythm" is very much a part of Ellington's current repertory. In the next number, Charlie Christian's "Seven Come Eleven," the band caught a good deal of the flow of Christian's melodic lines, as well as the smooth bicycling of the Goodman sextet, but Martino's solo—he gets a jangling, five-and-ten sound—was obtrusive. Then came an apt study, carried forward by a trumpet and an alto saxophone, of the ensemble figure that Charlie Parker wrote in his "Confirmation." Israels made it plain that not enough has been done about Parker's ensemble lines, which, in their complexity, daring, and originality, sometimes exceeded the solos they enclosed. (It should be pointed out, though, that the original recordings of "Seven Come Eleven" and "Confirmation" *are* available.) Israels' notions of what a jazz repertory orchestra should do took unmistakable shape in John Carisi's "Israel." The tune was first recorded by the Miles Davis Nonet in 1949. Israels, however, used the arrangement Carisi devised in the fifties for

Gerry Mulligan's big band and interpolated a transcription, played by his trumpet section, of Davis's solo in the Nonet version. It worked, even though the long solos that were added tended to weaken the over-all design of the piece. The big-band arrangement written by the late Hall Overton in 1959 of Monk's "Little Rootie Tootie" followed, and it included a transcription of Monk's solo from his early trio recording of the tune. The first half of the concert was closed by Israels' own three-part variation on "Stella by Starlight." This had written and improvised solos, and sections that recalled the "Rhapsody in Blue" and "L'Histoire du Soldat."

Bill Evans sat in for the second part of the evening and reaffirmed the curious fact that he is far more relaxed as a sideman than as a leader. His unflaggingly brilliant solos were full of leap-frogging Bud Powell runs, short, intense phrases clustered around one or two sharply struck notes, and rich chordal fillings. When he is in such superb shape, he is the premier pianist of his generation. Israels' boxes-within-boxes devices were also in full view. "Nardis Variations" was an orchestration of a 1963 Evans trio recording, and on it Evans erected a whole new solo. And in the densest effort of the evening, Miles Davis's "All Blues," Israels, according to the program, "transcribed the melody as Davis played it on the record, and then orchestrated Evans' accompaniment to Davis' improvised solo, fleshing it out so that Evans [could] use it as a springboard for a new piano solo." Henry James would have relished such intricate footwork.

The National Jazz Ensemble's second concert, given late in January, was largely an extension of the first. "Lester Leaps In" incorporated an ensemble transcription of Lester Young's original 1939 solo. Horace Silver's "Moonray," written in 1958, was a salute to Silver's trumpet-and-tenor-saxophone ensemble, which was padded out here and there by the whole band and broken up by Randy Brecker and Sal Nistico solos. Miles Davis' "Solar" was a variation, both improvised and written, on Davis' original recorded solo. Ornette Coleman's "Tears Inside" was given similar treatment, but it failed to pin down the singular texture and timbres of the Coleman–Don Cherry version. The rest of the evening included, among other things, a new Herb Pomeroy piece, "Jolly Chocolate," which was an Ellington stew salted with Charlie Mingus polyrhythms; Charlie Parker's "Bloomdido," in which sections of a transcription of Parker's solo were dropped in between new solos; and "Dolphin Dance" and "Maiden Voyage," by Herbie Hancock, which served as miniature concertos for their composer, who sat in.

So Israels' approach to a jazz repertory orchestra appears set. His tastes are catholic ("Struttin' with Some Barbecue" was played again that night), but he specially favors the music he grew up with (he is thirty-seven, and his idols include Parker, Clifford Brown, Davis, Bill Evans, with whom he worked for five years, and John Coltrane). He rejoices in improvisation, and he celebrates it intelligently with his transcriptions and adept orchestrations. And he enjoys intellectual catch-me-if-you-can musical games. His band for the most part serves him well. It is primarily an ensemble group, whose soloists, though sometimes long-winded, are largely icing on the cake. The band does not always swing, but some of the mazes Israels takes it through discourage such refinements.

Four days earlier, Big Brother puffed into Carnegie Hall for its first concert, breathed heavily for three hours, and brought forth a mouse. The concert was in three lengthy parts. In the first, a seventeen-piece band, which included Zoot Sims, Budd Johnson, Eddie Bert, Joe Newman, Jon Faddis, Jimmy Lyon, George Barnes, and Panama Francis, played eleven of Sy Oliver's arrangements for the old Jimmie Lunceford band. (Oliver is one of the musical directors of the New York Jazz Repertory Company. The others are Billy Taylor, Gil Evans, and Stanley Cowell.) The Lunceford band had a show-biz streak, and this trait was emphasized as we bounced through "Ain't She Sweet," "By the River Sainte Marie," "Margie," "My Blue Heaven," "Cheatin' on Me," "Annie Laurie," "Organ Grinder's Swing," and " 'Tain't What You Do." But the Lunceford band had a serious, driving side, too, and such redoubtable numbers as "Yard Dog Mazurka," "Battle Axe," "Chocolate," "Impromptu," and "Uptown Blues" should have been aired. How fine it would have been to hear the slow, stark "Uptown Blues," and to have had its solos by Willie Smith and Snookie Young scored, respectively, for the reed and trumpet sections! But this N.Y.J.R.C. orchestra, which, ironically, played Oliver's arrangements better than Lunceford did, was doubly wasted. It ignored Lunceford's better half and it played material that Oliver's own band has used all over town for the past several years.

There was more waste in the second section of the evening, which was devoted to material that Gil Evans has been parading in night clubs. A curious thing has happened to Evans in the past couple of years. His best work is still ahead of its time, yet he has been trying to keep up with what he has already passed. That is, he has loaded down his sumptuous orchestrations with a synthesizer, rock rhythms, amplifiers, interminable solos, and a congested percussion section. The results suggest Jacob Marley's famous trip up Scrooge's stairs. The last section of the concert centered on a heavy-duty five-part piece, "Collection Suite," that was written, arranged, and conducted by the trumpeter Charles Tolliver and played by a thirty-piece group—a big band plus a four-man percussion group, a tuba, and eight strings.

The next N.Y.J.R.C. concert was as inscrutable as the first. Dizzy Gillespie brought a seventeen-piece band onstage for an announced program of his big-band pieces from the forties, and one looked forward to such eminences as "Ow!," "Two Bass Hit," "Things to Come," "Ool-Ya-Koo," and "Woody 'n' You." Instead, the band played his lovely but later "Con Alma," and then settled into a grim, twenty-minute Gillespie composition, "The Burning Spear," which was arranged by Chico O'Farrill and is full of busily changing tempos, ostinato figures, and a discordant "free" ensemble passage.

A twenty-two-piece band conducted by Billy Taylor completed the evening with two Oliver Nelson compositions, "Soundpiece for Jazz Orchestra" (1964) and "Jazzhattan Suite" (1967). Both are reminiscent of the "modern" soundtrack music that Neal Hefti, Henry Mancini, André Previn, Lalo Schifrin, and others have been turning out for Hollywood—a blues-tinged, brassy, baritone-bound, rhythmically bombastic music. These men have swept away the Dimitri Tiomkins, but, in their own way, they have become as insistent and as static. But there was a saving moment, and it came in "Jazzhattan Suite." Jimmy Knepper, using a plunger mute, took several blues choruses, which offered an abundance of his curiously revolving phrases, his surprisingly placed notes, and his dense, unique tone. The sound throughout the evening was unsettling. Microphones were used only for the soloists (but not for pianists and guitarists), while the various sections, sounded as if they were in the next county.

So Israels is already on his special, intelligent way, but Big Brother needs retooling. In the meantime, here are some suggestions for music to be studied, re-created, or distilled by the two companies: the 1940-41 Cab Calloway band, a surprising number of whose alumni are still playing; a big-band program of Benny Carter tunes and/or arrangements; a John Carisi retrospective; the Miles Davis Nonet; the Gerry Mulligan sextet; the John Kirby band; and transcriptions of such great solos as Louis Armstrong's in "Basin Street Blues" (1933), Bix Beiderbecke's in "I'm Coming Virginia," Charlie Parker's in his first "Embraceable You," and Don Byas in Count Basie's 1942 small-band version of "St. Louis Blues."

## Editor

Count Basie himself does not know exactly where his style came from. Asked about its origins a while ago, he sent up a cloud of defensive, deep-voiced "um"s and "ah"s, and then said, "Honest truth, I don't know. If my playing is different, I didn't try for it or anything like that. I stumbled on it. I do know that in the earlier years I always loved Fats Waller's playing, and that Fats and the other guys had such fast right hands there was no use for me to try and compete with them. Another thing that helped was my rhythm section with Jo Jones and Walter Page and Freddie Greene. They gave me so much freedom. I could run in between what Page and Freddie were doing. I didn't think a lot of execution on my part meant anything with them there. It would have just cluttered it up. My greatest kick was having fun with the rhythm section and setting things up for the band. Of course, I've always listened to the pianists who play a whole lot of notes. Like Tatum, who was impossible. If he'd stayed up nine years playing, I'd have stayed up nine years to listen to him. Oscar Peterson is kind of ridiculous, too, and so is Phineas Newborn. But for me, simplicity has always seemed right."

This simplicity evolved between the late twenties, when Basie was still a Waller pianist, and the mid-thirties, when his unique telegraphic style began to appear on recordings. And he has refined it and refined it until he can now play an eloquent chorus of the blues with just three or four notes sounded a dozen times. But his piano is remarkable for another reason. Most improvisers feed chords and melody and rhythm into their creative hopper, where these musical ingredients are instantaneously transformed into brand-new melodic lines that are flashed to the musician's fingers and lips. Basie, though, goes through one more step. Before his melodic lines reach his fingers, they are exactingly edited, so we hear only what he considers the ultimate parts of his original invention. Thus we get four notes of what might have been a twenty-note run, a single note from a triad, silence where a connective passage might have been, and a trill instead of a flatted ninth. But Basie's original melodic lines are always implied, and one can hear them running along in the distance—a train behind low hills. Basie, who edits not only his notes but the length of his solos, will go at several choruses of a slow blues like this: He will start with an ascending four-note figure in the right hand, pause, drop in an offbeat single note, pause again (this time for a couple of measures), play a two-note octave phrase, pause, and finish the first chorus with a fragment of melody sounded in the highest register. More silence eases by, and then it is suddenly broken by three or four heavy descending chords in the left hand, these capped by a simple right-hand chord, which he holds for over a measure. He pauses again, then starts a riff, breaks it off after he has played it twice, and inserts several offbeat notes, which are echoed by left-hand oompahs, and we go into the third chorus. Four or five single notes, spaced a beat apart, walk down through the middle register, and then there is a long pause, which ends in a rich, right-hand chord that is repeated as Basie goes into a stride bass, raises his volume, and—bang!—brings in the band. The rhythm section, of course, has been flowing steadily along—a quiet stream supporting Basie's boat.

When the solo is over, one realizes its perfections and relishes again the fact that Basie has probably not ever played a wrong note, a wrong accent, or a cliché. One also realizes that the offhandedness of the solo, delivered as if he were leaning against a post and idly kicking at the dust, accomplishes the opposite effect: It has swung hard, for he is a master of concealing tension with relaxation, of making climaxes seem like releases. And one realizes how eloquent the solo has been, how the precise, inspired placing of a single minor note accomplishes everything that a horn player's slur or bent note does. The solo, too, has been full of Basie's humor, which, learned so well from Waller, never fails him. It is the humor of surprise, of picking singular notes and chords and placing them where no one else would dare. Basie also learned the organ from Waller, and it is a pity he does not play it more often. He goes at it the way he goes at the piano, but with even more care, for he constantly amends the *instrument*. He suppresses its bombastic side by making it whisper and sigh and flutter, by making it muse. His organ accompaniment is particularly attractive. It sounds like wind blowing through a window screen, and it provides a cushion that makes average soloists seem better than they are and first-rate soloists seem perfect.

Basie is a short, slow, shy man who really feels that his playing is not all that much, and as a result he has recorded only about a dozen solo (with rhythm) numbers in his forty-five-year career. But he has recorded a fairly large number of revealing small-band sides, and there are eleven of them in "Count Basie, Super Chief," which has, in all, twenty-eight numbers made by Basie or Basie-affiliated musicians between 1936 and 1942. Ten of the numbers, among them both air checks and studio sessions, have not been issued before, and an almost equal number are being re-issued for the first time. There are wonders in addition to Basie all through the album—Jess Stacy's short, way-out solo in "Life Goes to a Party," which is under Harry James' name and involves a group made up, with the exception of the leader and Stacy, of Basie personnel; the dancing, staccato muted solo Harry Edison plays near the end of the entire band's "Miss Thing"; Jack Washington's fine pre–Gerry Mulligan noodling behind Edison, once more muted, in "Somebody Stole My Gal"; and the Don Byas solo in "St. Louis Blues," which proves again that a first-rate recorded solo is surprising no matter how many times you hear it. The rest of the cake is Basie's. Listen to the way he plays plain old Waller stride piano in "Shoe Shine Boy," and then to the almost avant-garde accompaniment, full of strange notes and accents, he gives Jimmy Rushing in "Evenin'," Helen Humes in "Where Shall I Go," and Edison in "Miss Thing."

Basie is nonpareil not only as accompanist but as band pianist. He *leads* his band with the piano—he rarely gives any visual signal aside from a nod or a look—and he does it with extraordinary variety. In slow tunes, he noodles along behind his soloists, making jokes and cryptic musical comments about what they are playing, and he decorates ensemble passages with approving garlands of notes. In fast numbers, he moves down into the lowest registers and issues rocking, invincible chords that have literally made his audiences and even his musicians shout. Listen to him all the way through the four wonderful small-band sides made in Chicago in 1939 and never before brought out because of the poor quality of their recording. They include "I Ain't Got Nobody," an unusually fast "Love Me or Leave Me," which has a full and extremely busy Basie chorus, "Going to Chicago Blues," and "Live and Love Tonight"—the last two played on organ in his best wind-in-the-willows way. And listen to the only solo track in the album, "Café Society Blues," in which he is accompanied by Greene, Page, and Jones. It denies completely Basie's assumption that he should not make solo records. His playing is robust and cheerful, and he beefs up his telegraphy here and there with fat chords, passages of stride piano, and rolling boogie-woogie. He

plays more notes than is his wont, and he sounds relieved at doing it. All
aphorists occasionally babble.

## Dancer

Agreat drummer dances sitting down. A great tap-dancer drums standing up. But the only instrument a
tap-dancer has is himself, so he is a special—and fragile—breed. Such
was Baby Laurence, who died earlier this week in New York, at the age of
fifty-three. Laurence was born (in Baltimore, as Laurence Donald Jackson)
twenty years too late. Tap-dancing, which evolved in this country over the
course of a hundred years from the ring shout, jigs and clogs, the soft-shoe,
and the buck-and-wing, reached its apogee in the twenties and thirties,
and went out of fashion when vaudeville was overrun by the movies. Laurence nonetheless patched together a career. He started at twelve, as a
singer, when such child stars as Buddy Rich and Jackie Coogan were international darlings, but by his late teens he had turned formidably to dancing. He came to the fore on Fifty-second Street, around 1940, with a
singing-and-dancing act that sang Jimmy Lunceford arrangements in six-
part harmony, and then he went out as a single, hoofing mainly in the
Midwest. In the forties and fifties, he danced with Duke Ellington, Count
Basie, and Woody Herman, and occasionally surfaced at small clubs in
Harlem. After a long illness, he materialized again, at the Showplace, on
West Fourth Street, in the winter of 1960. He danced at the small Max
Roach–Charlie Mingus rump festival in Newport that summer, and in
1962 he graced an abortive jazz festival sponsored by the government in
Washington. A few months later, he appeared with sensational effect at the
Newport Jazz Festival, along with such dancers as Pete Nugent, Honi
Coles, and Bunny Briggs. (The first time Briggs watched Laurence dance,
in the thirties, he paid him the tap-dancer's highest compliment: "I saw a
fellow dance," he told his mother, "and his feet never touched the floor.")
Then he drifted into an oblivion that finally ended in 1969, when word
came that he was back in Baltimore, had a day job, and was dancing weekends in a restaurant in a shopping center in Gaithersburg, Maryland. It was
a sad gig. Laurence, backed by an excellent trio led by the drummer Eddie
Phyfe, who was also, willy-nilly, Laurence's guardian-manager-employer,
danced a couple of times a night on a swaying plywood platform set up in
the center of a big, dark room. He was in raw shape, and his steps were
heavy and uncertain. The stolid Maryland burghers, sawing at their New
York Cut sirloins, paid him little heed. But Laurence finished strong: Early
in 1973 he suddenly reappeared in New York, and during the year he
headed up those successful Sunday-afternoon tap-dancing sessions at the
Jazz Museum, took in students, danced at the Palace with Josephine Baker,

did some television, and gave his triumphant performance at the Newport–
New York Jazz Festival.

He was a strange little man. His arms and legs were pipes, his face was
scarred, and he had hooded eyes. In the wrong light, he looked sinister, and,
indeed, orphaned at thirteen and later hemmed in by drugs and alcohol and
financial troubles, he tended to be devious and self-pitying. Yet his dancing
belied all that. In many ways, he was more a drummer than a dancer. He did
little with the top half of his torso; holding his head upright, he either let his
arms flap at his sides or crooked them. But his legs and feet were speed and
thunder and surprise. Unlike many tap-dancers, who rely on certain change-
less patterns, Laurence constantly improvised. His sound was not the serene
clickety-tick-tick of Bill Robinson or Chuck Green; it was a succession of
explosions, machine-gun rattles, and jarring thumps. There were no frills to
his dancing. He would start a thirty-two-bar chorus with light heel-and-toe
figures, drop in a heavy, off-beat heel accent with one foot and echo it with
the other, go up on his toes, and then release a double-time splatter of heel
beats, resume the heel-and-toe steps, breaking them frequently with ominous flat-footed offbeats, spin completely around, and start crossing and
recrossing his feet, letting off sprays of rapid toe beats each time his feet
touched wood. Laurence tended to work in a small area. (Briggs often skitters
thirty or forty feet across a stage, like a stone skipping over water), but next
he might move in a large circle, each toe stuttering alternately on the floor as
he moved, and, the circle complete, abruptly begin violent knee-pumping,
followed by toe-to-heel explosions that might last ten seconds before giving
way to a terrific double-time burst, a leap into the air, and a deep bow.

## Bix

George Gershwin—celebrated during his life, hurrahed in countless books since, and cheered widely last
year on the seventy-fifth anniversary of his birth—has long been
regarded as the premier American musical whiz-kid of the twenties and early
thirties. Even that ivied rococo snob Sir Osbert Sitwell was impressed:

In these years, too, William [Walton] became friends with George
Gershwin, the Jazz Phoenix. Though Gershwin was not an intimate
friend of mine, I knew him and liked him, and he would usually come to
have luncheon with us when he visited London. He possessed a fine racial
appearance: nobody could have mistaken him for anyone but a Jew. Tall
and vigorous, his clearly cut face with its handsome ram's head, the features prominent, but, as it were, streamlined, indicated will power, character, and talent. I have always understood that he was the son of
immigrants from Russia or Germany, and was brought up in the poorest
quarter of New York: but his manners were notably excellent, his voice

was pleasant, and though the force of his personality was plain in his whole air, he was modest in bearing, and I never noticed in him a trace of the arrogance with which he has been credited.

But the sands have been shifting, and it is now clear that Gershwin was but one of four unique American musicians at that time, the rest being Louis Armstrong, Duke Ellington, and Bix Beiderbecke. Of the four, Beiderbecke has been the least understood, and for good reasons. Gershwin, Armstrong, and Ellington each realized the American dream, but Beiderbecke died a penniless alcoholic, at the age of twenty-eight, in 1931. He was, save among musicians, who revered him, virtually unknown during his life, having been praised just twice in print. He rebelled against his German-American heritage, and was felt by his sanctimonious family to have betrayed them. And despite his recordings, few of which accurately capture his playing, his fragile beauties vanished with him.

Two new books should at last put him in perspective. The first, *Remembering Bix*, is a remarkable, unashamedly idolatrous memoir by the painter and writer Ralph Berton, and the second, *Bix: Man and Legend*, by Richard M. Sudhalter and Philip R. Evans, which has been in preparation for seventeen years, is a huge, slow-beating, almost daily record of Beiderbecke's life. Berton's book, like all zealous works, is highly uneven. The prose sometimes comes unglued:

> Soon [the new society] would level the enchanted tower in which [Beiderbecke] still remained stuck like a fly in amber, becalmed in the void of his middle-class mudflat.

The first hundred pages are a plodding and largely superfluous account of his life and times. And Berton's argument that Beiderbecke, who was awestruck by Stravinsky and Ravel and Debussy, was single-handedly struggling toward a new and unimagined American music seems silly. Beiderbecke, like George Gershwin, who was heading in the same compositional direction from the opposite side of the tracks (listen to the similarities between Beiderbecke's piano pieces and Gershwin's Piano Preludes), was simply ahead of his time; there are countless musicians now who play both jazz and formal music. But the rest of the book is acute and affecting. It is, in the main, a reconstruction of the months in 1924 when Berton, a precocious thirteen-year-old, was hanging around Beiderbecke, whom he had met through his brother, the drummer Vic Berton. Beiderbecke emerges as a classic American bucolic (he was from Davenport, Iowa) who happened to be possessed by music. He rarely bathed or changed his clothes; he was absent-minded; he was a fine natural athlete; he had, like many other diffident people, a laconic sense of humor; he had little will power, and already drank an alarming amount; he loved the possibly unique American pastime of horsing around;

and he was wowed by learning and sophistication. But there was no foolishness in the musician. His ear was sharp and retentive, his tone summoned up bells and harvest moons, his improvisations were daring and unique, he was unfailingly inventive, and he was a brutal self-critic. The Sudhalter-Evans book fills out Beiderbecke's misshapen life by chronicling almost every day of his highly productive stay with Paul Whiteman in the late twenties (long thought by the mythmakers to have been a frustrating period for Beiderbecke); his nervous relations with his family (he discovered late in his life that all the recordings he had made with Whiteman and others and mailed proudly home had been stored unopened on a closet shelf); his unfailing kindness to lesser musicians; his restless relations with women; his admiration for Louis Armstrong; and his miserable, needless death. Neither book explains why such a frail vessel contained so much lyricism and originality. But some questions have no answer.

# R.I.P.

Duke Ellington had no interest in posterity. Nor, except for his lifelong reverence for his mother, who died in the thirties, did he care about the past. (He played his old numbers, his "Mood Indigo"s and "Black and Tan Fantasy"s, only because he was grateful for having admirers to request them.) He was obsessed by the moment, and he sank visibly into whatever he was doing: composing at his piano in his West End Avenue apartment at four A.M. (he was rarely there more than a month or two a year); gravely answering silly questions at a midnight press conference after a concert at a small college when he had spent the previous night driving four hundred and fifty miles and would leave early that morning for another engagement; playing for the thousandth time the opening piano solo of "Rockin' in Rhythm," his face bemused and his seesawing right shoulder pumping fresh notes out; eating his customary steak in a small, dingy dressing room at the Rainbow Grill while his tired back was kneaded; calling his New York physician, the late Dr. Arthur C. Logan, from a roadside phone in the middle of Alabama just before dawn about his current ache or cramp (he was a full-time hypochondriac); carefully breaking several packets of sugar into his inevitable Coca-Cola (he gave up drinking, at which he declared himself an undefeated champion, in the forties); or telling a reporter, when he was asked in 1965 how he felt about being denied a special citation by the Pulitzer Prize advisory board, "Fate's being kind to me. Fate doesn't want me to be too famous too young." He considered his newest composition his best, his newest blue ruffled shirt his best.

During his fifty-year career, Ellington wrote and recorded thousands of compositions (some of the best watermarked by his brilliant alter ego, Billy Strayhorn), maintained and shepherded his consummate and inordinately expensive orchestra fifty-two weeks a year (it was his palette, his sounding board, his heart), and repeatedly took his music up and down the world. Like Jane Austen, he ignored wars, politics, fashion, and economics; music alone propelled him. He did not regard his music as jazz, nor did he like the word; perhaps he found it limiting, or perhaps, being a conservative man under his celebrated cool, he found it cheap. Nonetheless, we yaw without handles. His music *was* based squarely on the rhythms and harmonies and structures of jazz. He simply put these familiar components together in a new way. He rebuilt the old harmonies. He scored conventional instruments in mysterious voicings. He hired better-than-average jazz musicians and encouraged them to perfect previously unknown timbres and tones and effects. (Although he made several stars, he tended to avoid hiring stars, for there is only one sun in every firmament.) He used standard devices, such as a soloist playing against a reed background, but he made the background urgent and lyrical. He used improvisation, but in a private, guarded way: His soloists' materials were already semi-improvisations composed by Ellington in their own styles. And he daringly translated into his music much of what he saw and heard—trains and airshafts and twilight and urban hustle and tap-dancers and splendid New York nights. He saw music everywhere, and he spent his life getting it into notes on paper and teaching his musicians to play them as he had first heard them in his head.

The last ten years of his life were crowded and sometimes confusing. In his middle sixties, he suddenly became an Honored Person. The doctorates, medals, citations, keys to cities, and inductions into distinguished bodies had swelled into an avalanche by the time he died. This outpouring made it appear that he had been appreciated all his life. But he hadn't been. When he was at the height of his powers, between 1939 and 1942, during that magical period when he wrote and recorded with the best band he ever had some forty imperishable concerti, among them "Main Stem," "Jack the Bear," "Ko-Ko," "Blue Serge," "Never No Lament," "What Am I Here For?," "Sepia Panorama," "Bojangles," "Harlem Air Shaft," "Portrait of Bert Williams," and "Jumpin' Punkins," practically no one, outside of musicians, was aware of his momentous doings. But an unavoidable amount of Ellingtonia eventually accumulated, and in the mid-fifties he at last settled into focus. In reaction, he redoubled his efforts, though his best work appeared to have largely been done. A final absorption—composing his "sacred music" and playing it in churches and temples—came to mean more to him (he had read and reread the Bible) than anything he had done earlier, and in at least one exuberant number, "David Danced Before the Lord with All His Might," in which Bunny Briggs danced while the drummer Louis Bellson soloed and several choirs and the band shouted behind, one could understand why.

Ellington himself was as myriad as his music. It is doubtful whether more than a handful of people knew him well, for he did not have the time or the patience to probe the human condition. Indeed, he had, to an almost immodest degree, all the means for graciously keeping the world at bay. These included a beautiful smile, a dapper, Technicolor way with clothes, a courtly manner that became eloquent when he laid on one of his eighteenth-century compliments, a deep, sonorous voice, a limpid and elegant control of language (spoken, that is; his written words sometimes had a purple quality strangely at odds with the rest of him), a handsome mien, and a Nabokovian mastery of parry and thrust. This comes through forcefully in the last chapter of his autobiography, *Music Is My Mistress*. The chapter is set in the form of questions and answers. Thus:

Q: Can you keep from writing music? Do you write in spite of yourself?
A: I don't know how strong the chains, cells, and bars are. I've never tried to escape.
Q: You must get extraordinarily exhausted on your travels. How do you recharge or revitalize?
A: One must always conserve the agreeable or positive. It is not expedient to try to like or enjoy the negative.
Q: Is the blues a song of sorrow?
A: No, it is a song of romantic failure.

But there was another, earthier Ellington behind this façade, an Ellington who had little tolerance for stupidity (it wasted time) and none at all for greed and avarice, particularly if they impinged on artistic matters. Once, when he was traveling in his car in deep night from one job to another with Harry Carney, his baritone saxophonist, friend, and driver of almost fifty years, he went into a monologue on the evils of the recording industry. His voice darkened and became guttural, epithets flashed by, and he handed down harsh and angry indictments.

One Ellington irony is that most of what he gave us is gone. The great, buoyant band is rudderless, and of his music we have only his surviving compositions and his recordings, the latter several removes from the real thing. And we have our flimsy recollections: Ellington eating at three in the morning at Jilly's and wondering whether the trombonist Vic Dickenson still had his "three tones"; Ellington sitting backstage after an appearance at the Monterey Jazz Festival and listening attentively to an audition by a female singer he had never seen before and probably would never see again (such audiences, when he granted them, had an unmistakably royal air); Ellington fielding one of Johnny Hodges' malicious onstage looks with a warm smile; Ellington effortlessly and unwittingly upstaging his host at his seventieth-birthday party at the White House, and turning what in retrospect seems a politically motivated event into a grand evening; and Ellington on the road with Harry Carney:

ELLINGTON (*eating a chocolate bar*): After a while, you eat in self-defense. It gets so you hoard little pieces of food against the time when there isn't going to be any.

CARNEY: I've still got that fried chicken I bought in Orangeburg yesterday in the back.

Ellington (*laughing*): That's going to taste real good tomorrow, Harry.

And, again, after he and Carney had arrived in a town for a concert five minutes before curtain time and left town five minutes after the last number:

ELLINGTON: If I'm in any place too long, I start taking on the local accent.

Carney once reminisced: "In the early days, when we traveled through the South we'd go by train. We had two Pullmans—one for the band and one for our trunks and instruments. We generally slept on the train, but if for some reason we couldn't, we went to a colored hotel or to somebody's house in the colored section—maybe a schoolteacher's or a doctor's or a minister's—and we ate there, too. Of course, all the places we played down there, they were happy to hear the band. The drag was they'd be screaming and applauding and afterward you'd have to go back across the tracks. One jump I'll never forget. In 1933, we jumped from Paris, France, to Dallas, Texas, for a six-week theater tour. In Europe, we were royalty; in Texas, we were back in the colored section. It was some adjustment, but we were young and could take it." Ellington not only took it—he characteristically transfigured it.

Ellington's life was an unending attempt to get that next musical brick in place. So, day by day, month by month, year by year, he slowly built (he composed literally everywhere he went) a unique, intensely American music in the form of operas, shows (Broadway and television), suites, songs, concerti, fantasies, tone poems, and religious music. (He once pointed out that, like all the musicians of his generation, he was conditioned by the three-minute length of the old 78-rpm record, with the result that his more ambitious pieces often gave the impression of being mosaics made up of short sections.) But, no matter what form it took, it all bore his unmistakable stamp. Ellington had a singular and lofty vision of life, and his music steadily reflected it. The music was compounded of joyousness, sly humor (there were a lot of *sotto-voce* black jokes in it), an unquenchable love of beauty (natural and human), an illuminating intelligence, deep warmth, and a pioneer directness. Ellington was a supreme melodist but not a songwriter in the way of Richard Rodgers or Irving Berlin, and it was generally a surprise when one of his compositions became popular. A well-known example was "Concerto for Cootie," which turned into "Do Nothin' Till You Hear from Me." His music became a complete, free-floating organism, and when one heard Ellington music in Ellington arrangements played by the Ellington band, it was—good performance or bad—an unparalleled experience.

## Youth

On the night of June 16, 1927, a skinny, audacious seventeen-year-old saxophonist and clarinettist named Harry Carney joined Duke Ellington, Bubber Miley, Tricky Sam Nanton, Rudy Jackson, Wellman Braud, Freddy Guy, and Sonny Greer on the bandstand at Nuttings-on-the-Charles, a ballroom in Waltham, Massachusetts, and began an unrivaled stint with Ellington that lasted forty-seven straight years, that lasted, indeed, until yesterday, when Carney died, at the age of sixty-four. (After Ellington's death, Carney continued with the band, which was taken over by Ellington's son, Mercer.) One of Carney's nicknames was Youth, and his boundless stamina and pleased, persistently unworn face made it appear he would last forever. But, in fact, he died of sheer wear and tear ("The way the band never stops," he once said, "it sometimes seems that the year has at least four hundred days"). And he died, too, of bereavement, for the two men had an extraordinary relationship. They spent more time together than most married people—on bandstands, at rehearsals and recording dates, on trains, ships, and planes, and, since the late forties, driving from gig to gig in Carney's car, with Carney at the wheel and Ellington beside him, snoozing or writing music or "navigating." Carney regarded Ellington as part father, part older brother, and Ellington treated Carney with affectionate jocularity. Carney responded with laughter or feigned insult, but he lost his cool whenever Ellington, who had his share of perversity, kept him waiting in the car too long after a gig. Carney revered his baritone saxophone. It became an extension of him: When he wasn't playing it he was carrying it or cleaning it or fitting it out with a new reed. Carney patterned his playing on Coleman Hawkins early in his life, and he was not an innovator in the conventional sense. He was, however, probably the first estimable jazz musician to be hypnotized by tone, by sound. "I was always crazy about tone," he said. "All my teachers instilled that in me. It was always tone. Practice sustaining tones and you develop ear pitch, you strengthen your lip muscles, you develop diaphragm breathing, breathing from the stomach. Take a note and sustain it from pianissimo to double forte and try to keep it from pianissimo to double forte and try to keep it form varying pitch. And do it with and without a vibrato. That way, you eventually develop an exact tone center." Carney developed not only an exact tone center but a sound on his instrument that no other baritone saxophonist has matched. And it was one of the most beautiful musical sounds ever devised. Carney became the foundation of the Ellington band. He made Ellington's minor inventions sound noble and his noble inventions sound celestial. "Sophisticated Lady" is still with us because of the way Carney, who came to own it, played it. For all his great staying powers, Carney inclined toward fragility. He said one cool fall day, "I can't change into turtlenecks and scarves when the weather turns and then change back, if it warms up, without getting a cold. The same is true of putting on a hat the first time. And I can't take a bath without getting a cold unless I go straight to bed after. But eventually I found out from our travels around the world that human beings can make wonderful adjustments to climatic change. If I were just starting out, though, I'd probably suffer, but having done it so long it doesn't bother me." And it didn't. Carney probably missed only a couple of weeks at work during the half century he served his two masters.

## Still Jumping

Ellington's best sidemen became indispensable to him, and he, in turn, became indispensable to them. Few who wandered out on their own made much of a mark, and most of them eventually came back. But Sonny Greer didn't, and the band never really recovered. Greer left in 1951, after thirty years, and none of his replacements—not even the whizzbang Louis Bellson—matched him, because he had virtually grown up with the band and was an organic, root part of it. He knew what kind of backing Johnny Hodges and Cootie Williams and Tricky Sam liked, and he could tell pretty much which way their solos were going, so he could be there waiting at every turn. He knew which cymbals sounded right behind the trombones and what kind of rimshot would send Ben Webster on his way. He knew which rest to fill with a couple of thundering quarter notes on his tom-toms. Greer spoiled Ellington's horn men; they were always surprised when other drummers failed them and they had to stand on their own. Greer had class and a trim sense of melodrama. Enshrined above and behind the band in his gold-and-silver forest of chimes and cymbals and gongs and timpani, he performed an endless in-place ballet, twirling his sticks in the air, snapping his head smartly from side to side, alternating mysterious hooded expressions with diamond smiles, and reaching out to tap a cymbal as if he were knighting it. He was not much of a technician, nor was he much of a soloist, but he could make the Ellington band lilt and rock. His brushwork, which had a wall-to-wall effect, was superb, and he shared Harry Carney's frenzy over tone. He got a unique sound out of a set of drums. It was precise and metallic, yet it had a loose, flexible sound, an unhurrying sound. Happily, Greer has emerged from a long spell of retirement and is visible five nights a week at Gregory's in a trio led by Brooks Kerr and including Russell Procope on both alto saxophone and his Barney Bigard clarinet. Greer is in his mid-seventies and is roughly the shape and size of one of his drumsticks, but he is still dapper and stylish and snappy. Tonight, Kerr stocked a set with "Scattin' at the Kit Kat," "Jeep's Blues," "Jumpin' Punkins" (Greer's old specialty), "Mood Indigo," "I Got It Bad," "Don't

You Know I Care or Don't You Care to Know?," and "Jump for Joy."
Greer's sounds and motions—the popping eyes, the mock lunges, the imperious chin, the fly-swatting wrists—suggested that he was once again up
there behind the band, making it sound like the savviest musical organization around, which, during much of his tenure, it was.

## Farewell

After several farewell performances in this country and abroad, the Modern Jazz Quartet gave its closing-
out, all-sales-final concert tonight in Avery Fisher Hall. The group's
previous farewell concert was given in Sydney, Australia, on July 16, and it
was, as far as the group was concerned, just that. Then it was pointed out to
them recently by Harold Leventhal, who produced tonight's concert, that
since the quartet had started in New York it should finish in New York, and
the men reluctantly agreed. Several days before the concert, John Lewis
talked about the dissolution of the quartet, which had been together steadily
for twenty years (it played its first gig in 1952, though) and had not had a
personnel change for nineteen, which may be a record for longevity in
Western music, give or take the Budapest String Quartet and the Trio de
Trieste. Lewis said, "An enormous amount of fatigue had set in. We hadn't
had any vacation in three years, and the road was getting to us. We were
becoming too old for all those five A.M.'s at airports. And Milt Jackson was
getting restless. So we had a meeting in April, before we left for a tour of
Japan, and we agreed to break up. There was never any question of hiring
replacements, and we couldn't have a quartet with only two or three people.
So there was nothing for it but to agree. I think there were some little regrets
among the members toward the end, but I can't be sure. I didn't feel that
way myself. As a group, the quartet had surpassed many goals set by other
groups, and it had surpassed most of the goals it had set for itself. It's hard to
evaluate the group's contributions over-all, but specifically it's not. There's
no other vibraharpist in the world like Milt. He's the most brilliant. What
Connie Kay did was never that new, but it was *always* platinum. And Percy
Heath developed so tremendously. He developed the most of us all. I enjoy
listening to myself as a pianist, and if I had only been the piano player in the
group and not had to conduct rehearsals and write and arrange music I
would have enjoyed playing much more. My wife, Mirjana, plays quartet
records now when I'm in, and I see for the first time how good the group
played. But we were so busy we never thought of *how* we were doing it. We
had the luxury of playing together for so long that everyone always knew
what everyone else was going to do. When the quartet was together, we were
always wound up musically, and now we're trying to get used to being
unwound. I still have the feeling I'm about to go out on the road again, and

I think all the time about how much I can get done here before I do. All four of us are big gossips, and I think we miss our rehearsals, where we used to socialize. So we've taken to calling each other on the phone to talk, and there has even been some visiting. But I think we were right to break up when we did. When we started rehearsing for this concert we hadn't played together for over four months, and I expected, I wanted, our playing together again to feel strange and new. But it didn't."

When the quartet started out, it gave the impression—largely because of its occasional use of such devices as rondos and fugues—that it had egghead leanings. But it became clear soon enough that the group, instead of being revolutionary, had taken on the great task of distilling and conserving the best of what was going on around it and the best of what had gone before. It also revealed a strong distaste for musical cant, and it immediately countered through its own example all the dreary practices that had begun to appear in jazz (the long, windy solos, the insane tempos, the showoff rhythms, and the vacuous ensembles). By 1960, Lewis' graceful songs and the way the quartet played them had brought a new lyricism into jazz, as well as an unprecedented degree of elegance and precision. The quartet seemed to do everything right. It dressed beautifully, comported itself onstage with dignity and sangfroid, and played consummately. And the higher its standards became the harder it swung. But unalterable excellence tends to unnerve even the most appreciative, and the longer the quartet was around the more it was said that it didn't swing, that it was effete, that it played too much fancy music, that it was lightweight—that, in short, it was a bore. But the quartet managed nothing less than preserving, enhancing, and carrying forward the lyrical and emotional heart of jazz, just as Ellington and Basie and Armstrong had done before. And it did this with an intelligence and style and wit that made its appearances occasions for recharging and restoring the spirit.

The concert tonight was like no other Modern Jazz Quartet concert I can recall. It was loose and a little wild. The solos were longer than usual, and they had a singular urgency. The exchanges and counterpoint between Lewis and Jackson had gaiety and density and excitement. Kay was supercharged and (for him) quite loud, and Jackson was breathtaking throughout. Heath took a couple of extended solos, and his ensemble playing (almost inaudible the first half of the evening) was without flaw. Every facet of the quartet was on view—a host of blues, a waltz, a Spanish piece, "Summertime," a North African piece, "God Rest Ye Merry Gentlemen," a couple of program pieces, " 'Round Midnight," and a "Night in Tunisia" with a Jackson break that lifted his birdlike self right off the floor.

The members of the quartet are commoners again. John Lewis is teaching a couple of courses at City College, and will record on his own for Columbia. Jackson is working as a single. Kay has been recording with Paul

Desmond. And Heath, in between gigs with his brother Jimmy, has been fishing down at Montauk. During its last year, he reports, the quartet grossed more money than it ever had before. You can't quit any cooler than that.

## Choice

A classic singer, Anita Ellis, has come out of hiding after twelve years (two of them spent rehearsing) and is appearing with the uncanny Ellis Larkins at the Bird Cage, in Michael's Pub. She is quietly famous on two counts: She once dubbed in the singing voices of Rita Hayworth and Vera Ellen, and she is regarded by her admirers, one of whom is Eileen Farrell, as possibly the best singer of her kind alive, albeit one of the shyest and least confident. She keeps her hands desperately clasped in front of her when she sings, and in between numbers she sometimes tells her listeners what agony it is to stand in front of them and perform. Yet she is remarkably forceful and dramatic. She has a handsome, wide-cheeked face and a halo of short, dark hair, and the way she moves her head, opens and closes her eyes, and aims her chin gives just the right emphasis to each word. She is a skilled technician, whose intervals are elegantly and even joyously maneuvered, and her pitch sails down the center of each note. Her sense of dynamics allows her to move with utter assurance from a high, wiry phrase in "Porgy" to a dying shout. Her songs are hand-chosen—such standbys as "Porgy" and "Prelude to a Kiss" and "Someone to Watch Over Me," as well as such out-of-the-way numbers as Harold Arlen's "Riding on the Moon" and "I Wonder What Became of Me," Frank Loesser's "Spring Will Be a Little Late This Year," Willard Robison's "The Four Walls and One Dirty Window Blues," and a Henry Souvaine–Johnny Mercer song from the early thirties called "Wouldja for a Big Red Apple?"

Anita Ellis in the Bird Cage is a special New York experience, once common in the city. The room is small and high-ceilinged and filled with plants, and it has glass walls that let in the night city and that seem, too, to let in the old loves and worlds and times that she tells us about so beautifully.

Ellis Larkins is accompanying Anita Ellis with such humor and imagination and sympathy that he is, in truth, a collaborator.

# 1975

## Lady

The next several days will be spent celebrating Mabel Mercer's seventy-fifth birthday, which falls on February three and will be marked by a party on the St. Regis Roof. This afternoon, Alec Wilder talked about her. He has known her since she settled here in 1941, he has written many songs for her ("It's So Peaceful in the Country" is one), and he has come to think of her as an indispensable mother-sister-aunt figure. "I can't, I'm not sorry to say, go to Mabel's birthday party," he said. "That sort of event is just too much for me, and anyway I'm due on Grand Cayman Island in a couple of days. But I've written Mabel a letter putting it on the line, telling her *exactly* what she means to me. And I've sent her a plant, one that's in bloom now and that she can put in the ground later at her place near Chatham, upstate. When I first met her, at Tony's, on West Fifty-second Street, it was instant acceptance on my part, which is very rare, since meeting strangers has always been a threat to me. Indeed, she soon had complete control over me. I could be obstreperous in my drinking days, and if I came into Tony's noisy or wobbly, she'd give me one look and I'd find myself reproved and behaving correctly. It wasn't an angry or disapproving look; it was just a very elegant *look*. Or if I came in depressed she'd sense it immediately and sing a whole set of my songs. And I'd find myself cheered up. But then Mabel is a healer. I've gone up to visit her in the country a perfect wreck and in two days felt marvelous. It isn't that she does anything, that there is any laying on of hands or such. She just putters around her house, and cooks, and feeds her animals. But there is some quality, some corrective force, in her very presence. Little by little, she's improved her place. She's managed to pay off the mortgage, and when she's had a few extra pennies she's added a bathroom or a porch. So when she can't sing at all anymore she'll have her house to live in, and that's a blessing. Even better would be if some of her rich admirers—and she's had dozens—got together and set up an anonymous trust fund. But, knowing the rich—or, rather, *not* knowing the rich, despite decades of trying—that's highly unlikely.

"Mabel's singing isn't like any singing I've ever heard before. It isn't jazz singing and it isn't pop singing and it isn't classical singing. It's wholly original. Sometimes, over the years, she's sung songs I haven't particularly cared for, but I've always found myself listening. She invariably involves you: You catch her enthusiasm for certain lines she sings, and you listen for certain of her technical devices, like her changing of values on particular notes each time she sings the same song. From the very first, there was a strong feeling of normality in the rooms Mabel sang in. You'd look up and down and see an extraordinary cross-section—college professors, polite-society types, lawyers, Ivy League kids, singers and musicians, people like Dave Garroway, who'd come bag and baggage straight from the station or airport. She'd hold whatever room she was in in her hand, and do it with sheer dignity. She never said anything when she started a set or when it was over. She sat down and sang and got out. If there was talking or laughing, she stopped singing. She didn't look at anyone, she didn't say anything. She just stopped and waited. And when the racket subsided she started to sing again.

"In those days, we laughed a lot. We even laughed at *outré* things, as long as they had style. Mabel has a genuine sense of humor: not only does she laugh at jokes but she laughs at herself. She used to sing 'Porgy' a lot, and one night I noticed that, even with her marvelous diction, the words 'I've got my man' were coming out sounding like 'My goat my man.' When I told her, instead of asking me to go jump, as most singers would have, she laughed so hard she almost fell on the floor."

I was assigned at Mabel Mercer's birthday party to a table built for ten but seating sixteen. (Four hundred people bought tickets at twenty-five dollars a head, plus liquor.) Elbows perforce were pinioned, and the roast beef with potatoes and string beans was served in flying-wedge fashion. But it took a long time for the food to arrive, and before it did a white-haired, pink-faced Mabel Mercer admirer who attends all her openings and who was seated on my left passed me a note, which read:

> This reminds me of a dinner party on the *Poseidon*, except in the movie I seem to recall they got something to eat. Soon we will be sinking fast; the starboard lifeboats are being manned; the ship's orchestra is playing "Up a Lazy River." At 10:19 P.M., goodbye all. Vincent Astor, who used to own this hotel, would never have permitted this. Nor would he have allowed us to sit here and inhale Earl Wilson's cigar smoke (he's sitting behind us).

A short time later, Mabel Mercer arrived, and after the standing ovation a long-faced man sitting on my other side introduced himself—or re-introduced himself, for he, too, was an indefatigable Ellington follower—as Edmund Anderson and told me the following, which is the sort of almost useless information that Boswell kept track of and rightly so: that the St. Regis Roof opened in 1936, that it was given its Viennese look by the designer Joseph Urban, who had worked for Ziegfeld, that it was first called the Viennese Roof as a result, and that on the night it opened Jacques Frey and his orchestra were dressed in Viennese costumes and powdered wigs. At ten-forty-five, Donald Smith, who helped organize the birthday party, announced that the festivities would start in eight minutes. But they didn't, so Anderson went on to say that in 1938 he and Vernon Duke put on a concert on the Viennese Roof that was played by six musicians from Duke Ellington's band and fourteen musicians from the New York Philharmonic. It was called a High-Low Concert, the High being the longhair music and the Low the Ellington. Tickets were only five dollars, he added, but nobody came.

Forty-two minutes after Smith's announcement, the city gave Mabel Mercer an award, and the evening officially began. Sylvia Syms and Cy Coleman sang his "The Best Is Yet to Come." Sylvia Syms was in superb voice. Jimmie Daniels, who is in his seventies, delivered "What Is This Thing Called Love?" and was followed by Thelma Carpenter, who belted out "I Can't Give You Anything but Love." Mary Lou Williams did a long, multi-tempoed "My Funny Valentine." Ruth Warrick performed, and

Bobby Short did Cole Porter's "Looking at You." George Wein intoned "Thanks a Million," and Hugh Shannon got off a splendid "Down in the Depths on the Ninetieth Floor." Marian Seldes read Alec Wilder's letter to Mabel Mercer and messages from Leonard Bernstein and "Francis Albert," who sent two giant balloons in his stead. Ronny Whyte and Travis Hudson wound up the guest performances, and the manager of the hotel announced that the St. Regis Room, where Mabel Mercer has sung these past years, would henceforth be known as the Mabel Mercer Room. Mabel Mercer, resplendent in a gold-and-brown brocade gown that she made herself, came forward from her table, some of whose occupants were Mr. and Mrs. Roy Wilkins; Will Craik, a neighbor in the country; her two sisters; the singer Helen Merrill; and Charles Bourgeois, who has done more than anyone else to preserve whatever elegance is left in New York nightlife. She cut a giant cake surmounted by a replica of the chair she sits in when she performs, and then she sat down in her real chair and started to sing, and it was a wonderful time. Her voice suddenly had wings, and by the time she reached her fourteenth song, a vibrant and affecting version of Stephen Sondheim's remarkable "Send in the Clowns," the audience was rapt. She sang Alec Wilder's "While We're Young," and she closed with a rollicking "They All Fall in Love." The ovation was very long, and throughout she kept laughing and ducking her head and waving.

I talked with Mabel Mercer the next afternoon, and the setting could not have been bettered by Oliver Smith, who, indeed, was at the party, along with such other notables as Alexis Smith, Arlene Francis, Hermione Gingold, and Anita Ellis. It was a friend's sixteenth-floor apartment, which looks out over the Hudson and is on the floor below the adjoining penthouses occupied in the thirties by George and Ira Gershwin. Miss Mercer was rehearsing with her accompanist, Jimmy Lyon, for her opening tonight in the Mabel Mercer Room and after she had done half a dozen songs she rested on a sofa. "The party was an honor, of course," she said. "I've happened into a lot of people's lives, and they came to say hello. And I love to have my friends love me. But I couldn't wait until it was over; the whole thing embarrassed me so. It's incredible, ridiculous to be seventy-five. It's a dream. When I was young, we used to think anyone who was that age was—well, senile. But I feel marvelous, I feel just the way I've felt all my life, give or take some arthritis pains. Heavens! I thought I'd be rusting away somewhere by this time. There are good things about getting so old: You can make mistakes and no one blames you, because they don't listen to the trills and tra-las the way they used to. So the thrush—remember when they called singers thrushes?—is croaking her way through. Even though what I do has become almost a form of reciting, every once in a while the voice comes back and surprises me, and I think, Oh, God, I didn't know I still had that!

"Nightlife is very different now from what it was in the old days. It was far more lavish then, both on the Continent and over here. Flowers and champagne flowed from the audience to the performers. And it had terrific friendliness. The same people came to Tony's night after night, and, of course, we worked until four in the morning. Sometimes the place would empty out completely at two, and then suddenly at three they'd come piling in and we'd be jammed for the last show. Then we'd go on to an after-hours place, many of which were quite respectable, with food and a decent piano. People would get up and perform. Performers love to perform for other performers. They know what you're doing, and they're the best audience you can have.

"Retire? Nonsense! How would I pay my taxes and make improvements on my house? If I stopped singing, everything would probably stop and I wouldn't be able to watch the trees grow that I'm always planting up in the country. Years ago, I collected acacia seeds in Central Park and planted them at the house, and now the trees are enormous. And I've planted Christmas trees. The first few years, I could reach up and put a star on top, and the next few years I'd get a faceful of snow when I tried, and now I'd have to jump up to the sky to reach their tops. If I don't get to see the next century in, it would be nice to sit on a cloud and watch what's going on."

*Singers revered Mabel Mercer for her diction and her phrasing and her poise, for her complete performing. Among many others, Frank Sinatra worshipped her and so did Billie Holiday.*

# More Repertory

A couple of things had become clear by the time the New York Jazz Repertory Company and the National Jazz Ensemble wound up their first seasons last year. One was that there appeared to be no single way to reproduce the jazz of the past—that, indeed, practically anything went as long as the spirit and some of the letter of the original remained intact. The other was something of a surprise. The two companies found themselves engaged in a remedial task they had not really envisioned—that of dispelling the ignorance most Americans have about their own best music. People tend to get locked into the music they grow up on; whatever comes later is threatening and foreign, and whatever came before is quaint. This insularity was particularly true of the first rock generation, which, with unwise fervor, slammed the door on the past. But jazz musicians like Miles Davis and Buddy Rich and Joe Zawinul and Gil Evans have chipped away at the kids' armor, and, from all reports, they are beginning to pay attention. They have even had the welcome and disconcerting experience of listening to a 1927 Louis Armstrong Hot Seven for the first time and discovering that all "new" musics have to be broken in. Which is exactly where the repertory orchestras fit. By playing Jelly Roll Morton and Armstrong and early Ellington freshly and intelligently, they lift the music from the tombs of the twenties and thirties recordings. What had sounded ancient and strange so long on the old 78 rpm's becomes brand-new again.

The New York Jazz Repertory Company started its second season last fall, but Chuck Israels' National Jazz Ensemble, ensconced this year at the New School, gave its first concert last week and its second tonight. The band is again sixteen strong, and there are more new faces than old. Among these are Jimmy Knepper and the towering, venerable lead trumpeter Jimmy Maxwell; two estimable young trumpeters, Danny Hayes and Tom Harrell; and Greg Herbert, an alto saxophonist who is building absorbing superstructures on Charlie Parker's foundation. Back again are the pianist Benny Aronov, the drummer Bill Goodwin, and the tenor saxophonist Sal Nistico. Last year, Israels opened several concerts with an ingenious, unison transcription for full band of Louis Armstrong's solo on his 1927 "Struttin' with Some Barbecue." He did so last week, but two choruses had been added—the contrapuntal interpretation of Armstrong's record by Lee Konitz and Marshall Brown, and a close approximation, delivered with gusto by Maxwell, of Armstrong's closing solo in his 1938 big-band version of the tune. From there we jumped twenty-five years to Hall Overton's arrangement of Thelonious Monk's "I Mean You." It was valuable for Herbert's well-constructed solo and for Danny Hayes' very long one. His frequent runs somewhat resemble Dizzy Gillespie's, but beyond that he has his own big tone and a fine sense of design and order. Herbie Hancock's pastel arrangement of his "Dolphin Dance" was repeated from last year, as was "Lester Leaps In," which was carried forward with fervor by Nistico and the tenor saxophonist Dennis Anderson. Both numbers had exemplary solos from Aronov. There were more original flourishes from Hayes on Dave Berger's "Twelve Tone Blues," and Knepper and Nistico were brilliant on "Donna Lee," Charlie Parker's wizard rebuilding of "Indiana." There were worthy re-creations of Ellington's "Rockin' in Rhythm," which was done last year, too, and of his 1929 arrangement of "Hot Feet," as well as of Count Basie's 1938 "Every Tub," in which Maxwell applauded Harry Edison's swaggering, ballooning bridge. "Sweet Emma," a gospel blues by Nat Adderley that was arranged by Bob Freedman in the manner of Ray Charles' small band of the fifties, had good solos by Hayes, Nistico, and Aronov. Folded into the evening about midway were four numbers built around Jim Hall, who was a guest. First came a sparkling "St. Thomas," done with the rhythm section, then Hall's big-band arrangements of "It's Easy to Remember" and his own blues "Careful," and, last and most important, an *a cappella* solo by Hall on his new custom-built acoustic guitar. The solo was played without a microphone and was a long chordal meditation somewhat in the style of the pianist Keith Jarrett. In Hall's hands, the instrument was shimmering and delicate, and its sound appeared to reach every recess in the place.

The concert tonight got off to an uneven start. The first number was Ellington's "Harlem Air Shaft," an organic, multilayered blues (with a bridge), in which the solos grow like branches from the dense ensemble. It is a kaleidoscopic little concerto, and the original recording starts at a deceptive amble, which is abruptly upset a third of the way through by three explosive "Bugle Call Rag" saxophone-section breaks, which are virtually catapulted from the ensemble by Sonny Greer's driving, crescendo snare drumming, and are then followed by Cootie Williams' three climatic trumpet statements. For some reason, drummer Bill Goodwin sat on his sticks during the breaks, which were capped bravely by Maxwell/Williams, and all the air went out of the piece. Horace Silver's "Room 608" had teeming warm-up solos by Aronov and Harrell and Nistico, but Gil Evans' arrangement of "Moon Dreams," done in the late forties for Miles Davis' Nonet, never got around its narcissism. A light, speedy version of Dizzy Gillespie's "Con Alma" was played by Greg Herbert and Danny Hayes, who both *think* when they solo. Then the saxophone section, abetted by the rhythm section (just barely; the rhythm section never quite fell into place tonight), worked its way through Lee Konitz's "Subconscious-Lee," an I-can-do-it-better-than-Charlie-Parker reworking of "What Is This Thing Called Love?" The first half of the concert was closed by three numbers constructed around Roy Eldridge, who was in measured, elder-statesman fettle. He did his old Artie Shaw display number, "Little Jazz," a long and beautiful slow reading of "Body and Soul" that was enlivened by the band's playing a transcription of the startling double-time passage he recorded on the same tune in 1938 with Chu Berry and Sid Catlett, and a scrambling version of Louis Armstrong's very fast rendition of "Chinatown."

The second part of the evening was made up principally of two avant-grade compositions. The first, a Tom Pierson arrangement of Wayne Shorter's 1967 "Nefertiti," was commissioned by Israels and highly praised by him—an unfailing way to put an audience on the *qui vive*. It was, Israels explained, full of tensions, and he was right. It is a nervous, impassioned, declamatory number, in which Nistico soloed at great length at both fast and slow speeds while the rest of the band contributed a variety of contrapuntal figures. The other modernistic effort was by Israels, and it was far more accessible. Called "Skipping Tune," because of the intervals in its attractive melody, it is based on a harmless trick: The soloists are restricted in their improvisations to the major and Lydian scales. The rest of the evening was taken up by Aronov and the ensemble trading Bix Beiderbecke's Gallicisms in a gentle and effective rendering of his piano piece "In a Mist"; a somewhat flip version of Jelly Roll Morton's "Black Bottom Stomp"; and, as encores, two repeats from last week—"Hot Feet" and "Struttin' with Some Barbecue."

It is plain, with the début of the National Jazz Ensemble, that New York's two jazz repertory companies are again pursuing their subjects in very different ways. The New York Jazz Repertory Company is offering in-depth, one-subject concerts, which have included studies of Louis Armstrong, Count Basie, Miles Davis, Jelly Roll Morton, George Russell, and Bix Beiderbecke. These have been pasted together ingeniously out of original recordings, film clips, appropriate alumni, and the usual re-creations and transcriptions. This, in effect, is a graduate-seminar approach, while the National Jazz Ensemble is using the undergraduate survey approach. (An obviously oversimplified comparison: Some of the N.J.E.'s pieces are extremely complex and some of the N.Y.J.R.C.'s pieces are kindergarten stuff.) Thus, the National Jazz Ensemble's two concerts have already refashioned Jelly Roll Morton, Louis Armstrong, early and classic Duke Ellington, classic Count Basie, bebop, hard bop, Thelonious Monk, Gil Evans, Miles Davis, and the arranging and composing of such young musicians as Dave Berger and Tom Pierson. Such a survey has unfailing appeal, and it was obvious at both concerts: Someone was invariably pleased by something— Ellington's dicty 1929 rhythms, Thelonious Monk's wrought-iron melodic lines, Gil Evans' sweeping harmonic robes. On the other hand, the New York Jazz Repertory Company seminars are, except to older, more knowledgeable jazz students, immediately forbidding. If a potential ticket buyer has never heard Morton or Beiderbecke or George Russell, the prospect of an entire evening of Morton or Beiderbecke or Russell may scare him away. For all their dissimilarities, the two repertory companies are in nonsensical competition. They subsist on some of the same findings; they are producing basically the same music, albeit in different packages; and they are aiming at the same audiences. A suggestion: Let the two companies, short of merging, organize their scheduling so that the National Jazz Ensemble's survey course takes up the first half of next season and the New York Jazz Repertory Company's seminar course finishes it out.

## Three Pianists

Piano players are doubly blessed. Unlike fiddle and wind players, they don't wear out (Artur Rubinstein, Earl Hines, Eubie Blake), and they play an endlessly variegated instrument. The piano, especially in jazz, can be anything. It can be a full band or a consummate solo instrument. It can be a guitar or a bank of percussionists. It can rhapsodize as fulsomely as a string section or release single-note melodic lines that course like the wind. It can define the bones of harmonic thought. It can uniquely support and point up the human voice. It can, in its lowest registers, produce mysteries and majesties only a tuba can rival. It can even produce, when cleverly manipulated, notes that technically do not exist— blue notes and interstitial notes, those elusive non-notes jazz musicians invented. Yet the piano is a comparatively easy instrument, and as a result there's scarcely been room for all the jazz piano players. This overcrowding had been particularly discouraging for those special and delicate pianists whom Count Basie once called the "poets of the piano." Everything about them tends to be delicate—their attack, their touch, the construction of their solos, their very careers, which are often thwarted by a lack of recognition, by timidity, by poor timing, or by the discovery that there are easier ways to make a living. Consider Walter Norris. His name has been in the air in New York for years, but the only place he has worked any length of time is that non-place the Playboy Club. He was mentioned briefly in Leonard Feather's *Encyclopedia of Jazz* (born in 1931, in Little Rock; went to Los Angeles and worked with Stan Getz, Zoot Sims), but he is not in the most recent edition. There is a full-page photograph of him—thin, dark, gesticulating—in a documentary book about West Coast jazz by William Claxton, but no text. He played on Ornette Coleman's first recording, but few people remember. He has been with the Thad Jones–Mel Lewis band a year, but it plays here only one night a week when it is not on the road. But Norris' turn has come. A while ago, he told Bradley Cunningham, the sheltering and sagacious owner of Bradley's, that he is now "ready" to come out by himself. So he opened tonight at Bradley's, with the bassist George Mraz, for a week. He has clearly listened to Art Tatum, but he has also listened to Bud Powell and Teddy Wilson and Debussy and Ravel. His touch is even and light. His arpeggios whip and coil, have logic and continuity; his double-time dashes are parenthetical and light up what they interrupt; his long single-note passages continually pause and breathe; no tempo rattles the clarity of his articulation, which has a private, singing quality. He is an adventuresome and oblique pianist who likes to start his numbers with inside-out phrases, who likes to bang the heads of his harmonies together. His slow ballads are singular; they continually tap at the hull of the melody, testing its soundness, cheering its beauties. Tonight, Norris made "Falling in Love with Love" sound lean and swinging, and he tested every inch of "Everything Happens to Me." "Cherokee" has always had a Hi-ho-Silver quality, but he made it soar rather than race. He made "Maple Leaf Rag," which can be immovable, swing from within. He played a medium-tempo blues that had a swinging, waltzlike quality. And he got "Lover Man" out of the swoon Billie Holiday left it in thirty years ago.

Cecil Taylor packing them into the Five Spot for three solid weeks! Cecil Taylor playing *encores* to get off the stand! Cecil Taylor—iconoclast, super-avant-gardist, mysterioso pianist—a matinée idol! Incredible but true. When Taylor first came up, the thought of such acclaim would have caused jigging hilarity. There was nothing accessible or even specially attractive about his music. It operated completely on its terms; to join in, the listener did the work. Little has changed about Taylor. He is still tiny and muscular and solemn, and he still performs like a wrecking crew. He stabs and pounds and hammers the keyboard. His enormous glissandos skid heavily. He plays staccato arpeggios so fast they become ribbons of sound. His arms are blurred pistons, and he rocks in wild irregular circles. He comes very close to making visual music. And so his new popularity is suddenly understandable. His music, though totally dissimilar in content and construction, has all along been a forerunner of electronic music, of hard rock, and so has his way of performing it. The music around him has simply caught up to Taylor, and everything he does is now apposite. One can easily imagine turning on to Taylor, drifting down through his polyrhythms and dense harmonic tongues, through his massive chords and thundering arpeggios. Taylor's first number tonight at the Five Spot was the first set, and it lasted almost an hour and twenty minutes. It was vintage Taylor and it consisted of several immense Taylor solos spelled by somewhat shorter statements by the alto saxophonist Jimmy Lyons, an indefatigable cohort of Taylor's and an eclectic who spins out variations on the thoughts of John Coltrane and Ornette Coleman and Eric Dolphy. Perhaps Taylor's instrument no longer matters. He has become obsessed with blocks of sound, with sequoias of sound, and if he could not produce on the piano what he hears in his head, he would do it by other means. He would gather about him whales and jets and cascades, and make them sing and roar and crash. And we'd listen.

In 1953 and 1954, Norman Granz got Art Tatum into a recording studio for three or four sessions and told him to play whatever he wanted at whatever tempo he liked for whatever length of time. Tatum forthwith produced almost two hundred numbers, and a veritable selected works of Art Tatum was released. The albums have long been out of print, but Granz, after a fifteen-year hiatus in his activities in this country, is making records again, and one of his first acts has been to reissue one hundred and twenty-one of the Tatum solos in a thirteen-volume set called "The Tatum Solo Masterpieces."

There is nothing startling or major here. The albums simply contain Tatum piano solos that range from two minutes to almost seven minutes in length and that average around four minutes. The material is familiar and includes retreads of such Tatum display pieces as "Humoresque" and "Elegy" and "Danny Boy" as well as such Tatum-owned ballads as "Willow Weep for Me," "Moonglow," "Stompin' at the Savoy," "Begin the Beguine," and "Love for Sale." The albums take over nine hours to listen to, and if one dives in for a couple of hours at a time, several disconcerting things become clear about Tatum as he is here. He seems to have lost his sense of proportion and design. Many of the numbers move in fits and starts and have lumps and gaps and irregularities. A statement of the melody is interrupted (and so virtually destroyed) by one of Tatum's celebrated, out-of-tempo Earl Hines whirlpools. A passage of driving, on-the-beat improvisation suddenly dissolves into arpeggios and glissandos and grandstanding harmonies. A number abruptly ends after two choruses or rambles on indefinitely. (Compare the flawless pointillism of Teddy Wilson, who is so often wrongly thought of as a lesser Tatum.) Tatum never had much taste, and it is all but gone here. He gives straight rhapsodic treatments to

"Deep Purple" and "Night and Day" and "Without a Song"—which have cried out since the day they were written for a little derring-do and deviltry from their interpreters. And he attempts to take apart and rebuild such melodic edifices as "Willow Weep for Me" and "The Man I Love," the last of which turns into the only bad Tatum performance I can recall. Finally, his clichés become unavoidable for the first time. Here is the glissando that leads coyly into an in-tempo passage; the swirling, meaningless, befogging arpeggios, a Sargasso Sea of arpeggios; the busy ad-lib passage in which he keeps rushing up to and backing off from the beat. He rarely surprises us rhythmically or dynamically or with his improvisations, which tend to conceal rather than enhance. One must blame Granz for putting this flawed Tatum before the public and then magnifying him. He got to Tatum just three years before his death, when the great engines were beginning to run down. He also recorded him in the wrong way, for Tatum was a born showoff who was not particularly happy by himself in a recording studio. And Granz asked too much of him: better thirty beauties than over a hundred flawed effusions.

But there *are* stunning numbers in the set. "Come Rain or Come Shine" is Tatum near his best. It has a marvelous ad-lib chorus, full of reverent and exquisite harmonies, improvised passages that are serious and graceful extensions of Arlen's tune, and a climax that oddly celebrates two moods—cheerfulness and fleeting gloom. "Tea for Two" is a joyous parody that moves at top speed and has an in-tempo, out-of-tempo section that is a rococo masterpiece. "Blue Lou" is short, stripped-down, and full of business. "Please Be Kind" has a chorus in which the rhythm sways from side to side in slow motion. "I'm Comin' Virginia" is wild and irreverent and crowded with extraordinary harmonies. "Isn't It Romantic" has a double-time explosion, and "Aunt Hagar's Blues" is a merciless ribbing of the blues, a form that Tatum invariably poked fun at. And "Jitterbug Waltz" is ingenious simply for the off-center way that Tatum places his notes during his statement of the melody.

Norman Granz set out to build himself a monument in his Tatum solo recordings. His introductory note to the recordings reads: "The most important and satisfying work I ever had was the Tatum project—imagine! Having Art Tatum all to myself, an audience of one, doing almost two hundred songs for me."

# Newport 1975

*June 27th*

The first day of the twenty-first Newport Jazz Festival (and the fourth Newport Jazz Festival—New York) consisted of a repeat of the Bix Beiderbecke concert given on April 3 by the

New York Jazz Repertory Company and a jam session by a dozen members of the company's orchestra. These last included Patti Bown and Billy Taylor (piano), Chris White and Lisle Atkinson (bass), Alphonse Mouzon and Freddie Waits (drums), Zoot Sims, Eddie Daniels, and Cecil Payne (saxophone), Jimmy Owens, Chet Baker, Charles Sullivan, and Waymond Reed (trumpet), and Garnett Brown and John Gordon (trombone). The session, held in Carnegie Hall at eleven-thirty tonight, was discursive and showy. Payne and Daniels offered more notes than the ear could hold, and so did Brown and Atkinson, whose solos had a look-at-me quality. But there were corrective efforts. The drummers, alternately and in tandem, were often funny, Chet Baker took a light-boned solo on "Softly as in a Morning Sunrise," and Patti Bown was a mischievous wonder. She is an intense performer whose constant motions suggest an almost spent top, and whose accompaniment forms a secondary, self-effacing solo—a set of cheering and cautionary notes that push and steer the soloist. Her own improvisations are hardswinging précis of longer, more elaborate statements that she edits in her head. In her solo on "Oleo," she managed to suggest a parody of stride piano, limning and applauding its outlines and rhythms without ever quite stating them.

The Beiderbecke celebration, offered earlier in the evening at Carnegie, was widely overpraised its first time around. Two bands, representing the Wolverines and Jean Goldkette, caught much of the gentleness and clarity of his playing, but they ignored the driving, almost demonic side that in-person observers have testified to and that appears in his recording of "Barnacle Bill the Sailor." Jimmy McPartland, John Glasel, Franc Williams, and Warren Vaché handled his solos, in unison or separately, and only Vaché was truly on the mark. He can play Beiderbecke note for note, but he makes the notes sound as if he had invented them. There were other unexpected benefits. The bassist and tubist, Vince Giordano, played Adrian Rollini's formidable bass-saxophone parts in "Since My Best Gal Turned Me Down," "At the Jazz Band Ball," "Goose Pimples," and "Royal Garden Blues" with a booting looseness, and he also appeared in two numbers in which Joe Venuti, Zoot Sims, and Bucky Pizzarelli re-created Venuti's old recording group The Blue Four. This new group, which only indirectly had to do with Beiderbecke, played "China Boy" and a blues, and it had a texture (just about gone in jazz) and drive and joy that were unmatched during the evening. Dill Jones and Marian McPartland wandered through three of Beiderbecke's curious, circular piano pieces, and for half the evening Bill Rank and Speigle Willcox, Goldkette alumni, joined in. The tempos were much too slow in "Goose Pimples," "Way Down Yonder in New Orleans," and "I'm Comin' Virginia."

*June 28th*

Gospel singing is jazz gussied up and dressed in the clothes of the Lamb. Gospel singers use jazz phrasing and rhythms and inflections, and they often use them outrageously. They bend notes almost in two, they growl like bears, they jam six syllables into a single note, and they play hob with the beat. And jazz musicians brought up on church music have returned the compliment by dipping into these marvelous excesses. (Ray Charles is built on church music.) But everybody borrows from gospel now, for the music has moved well out into the secular (and white) world in the last couple of decades, and is even performed in night clubs and on days other than Sunday. The gospel program put together by Tony Heilbut for the early Carnegie Hall concert tonight was almost all first-rate. A film that showed us part of Mahalia Jackson's spectacular (and final) Newport performance in 1970 was shot mainly from below, and it had the surrealistic effect of making her head seem truly in the heavens. Two of Mahalia's teachers followed—Sallie Martin, who is seventy-nine and still sings in an enormous, looming contralto, and Thomas A. Dorsey, who is seventy-six and began as an accompanist for Ma Rainey. One of Mahalia's best disciples, Dorothy Love Coates, sang four numbers. But the evening belonged to a sixty-year-old singer named Claude Jeter, who was born in Montgomery, Alabama, and now lives in New York. Jeter is an astonishing gospel singer. Most gospel singers favor white and weight, but Jeter is thin and owlish and bespectacled, and he wears close-cropped hair and dark business suits. He sings mainly in falsetto now—a rich falsetto in the area of a countertenor. He begins a passage quietly and on the beat, pauses a beat, and abruptly shouts the next syllable, bending it half an octave and growling in a way that summons up the millennium-announcing days of Cootie Williams. Then, silent and still, he quickly searches the audience for the effects of such shocking music, and slips into his next phrase. His sense of time is ecstatic: It rivals Billie Holiday's, and it explains a great deal about Ray Charles'. He sang the "Battle Hymn of the Republic" slowly, and after he had broken his cries over us again and again, the possessed were on their feet and shouting, and the hall was rocking. And his two other numbers were equally commanding. The remainder of the evening was given over to the J. C. White Singers, who have helped Max Roach with some of his onstage sociological treatises; a good quartet, the Sensational Nightingales; and Marion Williams, who began with the late Clara Ward.

Mr. Suave (Benny Carter) and Mrs. Sexy (Maria Muldaur) gave the second concert at Carnegie tonight. They appeared for the first time in New York late last fall, and caused talk on both sides of the popular-music fence. What was Muldaur, a thirty-two-year-old pop-rock-country singer, doing with a *jazz* band, and what was Carter, a sixty-seven-year-old monument of the music, doing accompanying Muldaur? Carter says Muldaur has tremendous potential, and Muldaur says she loves working with Pop Carter, no matter what his age. (Actually, Carter is carrying forward a minor and honorable tradition in jazz. Countless first-rate jazzmen have helped of-the-moment singers by playing behind them and have gone unscathed.) Carter began the concert by leading a ten-piece New York pickup band that included Danny Stiles, Hank Jones, Frank Wess, Bucky Pizzarelli, and Grady Tate through four instrumentals. "Doozie" had fine solos by Stiles and Pizzarelli. Hank Jones offered a slow, crystal "The Very Thought of You," and Carter played luxurious versions of "Green Dolphin Street" and "The Shadow of Your Smile." None of his primness was evident, and his celebrated style—the stepping, descending patterns, the bowing melodic figures, the cool sense of time—moved past with ease and grace.

Muldaur gave the second half of the concert. She came onstage with her ringlets and small, pretty child's face and began scaling an unending series of bumps out into the hall. One's immediate reaction was that she should be spanked and sent to bed. But she's too old for that, and too old for the way she sings. She has a light voice, a cork voice, and an intuitive, little-girl way of phrasing. One hears Mildred Bailey, and once in a while there is an attractive cracked quality in her voice, but the rest is raggedy and waifish. She puts on a good visual show, though, and it was painless to watch her bump and wiggle through "Lover Man" and "Squeeze Me" and "Gee, Baby Ain't I Good to You" and "It Don't Mean a Thing if It Ain't Got That Swing." But it was far better to train the radar on Carter's arrangements behind her. Their sumptuous harmonies and roomy saxophone figures were beautiful.

### June 30th

Yesterday, four members of Bob Crosby's Bobcats were reunited on several ferryboat rides up the Hudson, and during the evening, at Carnegie Hall, the big bands of Buddy Rich and Harry James formed booming parentheses around the Ruby Braff-George Barnes quartet. The four old Bobcats were brother Bob, Yank Lawson, Eddie Miller, and Bob Haggart, and the four supporting non-Bobcats were Chuck Folds (piano), Johnny Mince (clarinet), George Masso (trombone), and Ron Traxler (drums). Miller has spent little time in the East. He is a missing link who belongs somewhere between Lester Young and Bud Freeman. He has Young's balsa tone and Freeman's homemade rhythmic attack. But his ballads are singular. He got off two during the one-o'clock boat ride—"Sophisticated Lady" and "Dream"—and they were crooning marvels. He keeps his vibrato down, he hugs the melody, and he moves steadily along just this side of bathos.

Buddy Rich opened the concert last night with eight blasters and a heavy, subaqueous drum solo, and it was closed by Harry James, who, in the evening of his career, is turning into a crazy-kid trumpet player. His solos on several blues had a nerviness and swagger one used to hear in a seventeen-year-old third trumpeter who had just come on the band. The Braff-Barnes quartet is a complex of high invention, precision, and big egoes, and when it is in balance there is no better group in jazz. But last night Braff was down (his runs didn't jell and his timing seemed slack), and Barnes was up (his seesaw rhythms were in abeyance and his melodic lines were relaxed and spacious).

Tonight, we were offered four organists at Carnegie (Don Lewis, Jack McDuff, Rhoda Scott, Larry Young) and two bands at the Roseland Ballroom. The organ concert was a commercial for the Hammond Organ people, who subsidized it, and the dance was part concert, part dance. The concert was given by Miyami and his New Herd, a billowing, derivative Japanese band that played both American standards and Japanese folk material. An explanatory narrative was read before each number, which was like returning your neighbor's lawnmower with a note telling him how to work it. Count Basie, surrounded by his customary glistening bottleworks, provided the excellent dance music.

*July 1st*

The Festival went into gear today, and we had, as we will have through Saturday, two concerts at seven-thirty and two at eleven-thirty. The first concert at Avery Fisher was the annual celebration of American popular song, and it went askew during the beginning set, or what there was of it. Zoot Sims and Jim Hall were scheduled to play George Gershwin, and they did get through "Embraceable You," "Someone to Watch Over Me," and "The Man I Love." Then, having taken up their allotted twenty minutes, they left the stage. It was the waiter removing your mousse when your head is turned. The two men are strikingly sympathetic musically, and their mutual aesthetic composure had just begun to show in "The Man I Love." Hall and Sims reshaped it and reshaped it again, and the results were superb. The audience was already leaning into their next number, a certain masterpiece—and they were gone. The misdeed was unwittingly compounded by Cy Coleman, who cheerfully played and sang twice as many numbers, and by Helen Humes, who delivered six Fats Wallers and a blues sweetly and well. Johnny Hartman, struggling with his intonation, celebrated Duke Ellington by singing two Ellingtons, one Billy Strayhorn, one Kurt Weill, a blues, and "On a Clear Day." Chet Baker, in company with a five-piece group, played three Rodgers and Hart songs in an overly jazzy way. But Margaret Whiting, serene and statuesque, brought the proceedings to a lyrical close with more than half a dozen Harold Arlen songs. She is a very good singer—a straight, knowledgeable, lilting singer— and she gave Arlen his due.

The second concert at Avery Fisher was taken up by Miles Davis, and there was little that was new in his first number and set, which lasted close to an hour. Davis went electric years ago, and he was surrounded onstage by amplifiers and electronic instruments. He played several solos, muted and open, electrified and not, and everything was as of old—the clams, the beseeching tone, the melodic, free-time passages, the seeming disjointed-ness, and the incessant effort to get through to whatever it is musically that he has been trying to get through to for the past twenty years. By the time I arrived at Carnegie to hear the program of solo pianists, Harold Mabern, Bernard Peiffer, and Barry Harris had slipped by and Dorothy Donegan, got up in a tight silver lamé gown that gave her a striped-bass effect, was giving "Tea for Two" what for. She was followed by Roland Hanna, Cedar Wal-ton, John Lewis, and Eubie Blake.

### *July 2nd*

Chuck Mangione and Gato Barbieri split the early concert at Avery Fisher tonight. Both have had vague avant-garde reputations, but now they've become the Glenn Miller and Artie Shaw of the present. Mangione wears funny clothes—a red felt hat, a short shirt that reveals his belly button, and leather pants. He writes attractive melodies, and plays them in a lush way. Barbieri wears funny clothes, too: a white suit and a black, wide-brimmed gangster hat. He uses a continually rasping tone and long-held, slowly revolving notes, and once in a while he peppers his music with chants or gaucho shouts.

Stan Getz and various associates, past and present, gave the late concert at Avery Fisher. Charlie Byrd, on acoustical guitar, set down four numbers, the best of them "Top Hat, White Tie, and Tails" and "Undecided." Jimmy Rowles, preserved in his own amber, played three slow ruminations ("Poor Butterfly," "Prelude to a Kiss," and "My Buddy"), in which each note had trouble getting free of the preceding one, and was joined by Getz for three slightly jauntier efforts. Gary Burton, equipped with four mallets and his shimmering vibraharp, erected twin towers of sound, which were full of alu-minum chords, brilliant circular phrases, and washing, ad-lib rhythms. Their motion was perpendicular. Getz reappeared, and he and Burton played a couple of hands of "Here's That Rainy Day." Getz brought on his present group (Al Dailey on piano, Clint Houston on bass, Billy Hart on drums) for two numbers, and then Heloisa Gilberto, the new wife of João Gilberto, did a Gilberto and "Joost Wan ov Dose Tings." Mabel Mercer, battling Getz's somewhat strident obbligatos, sang four perfect numbers. The masters of ceremonies were Marian McPartland and Alec Wilder, who, seated at a table at stage right, looked as if they were stuck in the library on a lovely Saturday afternoon.

### *July 3rd*

Pedaling backward, the day went like this: Cleo Laine and Johnny Dankworth gave the late concert at Avery Fisher. Dankworth, who would have made a good second alto saxophonist with Alvino Rey, played eight numbers with a New York pickup band

(Danny Stiles, Frank Wess, Jimmy Nottingham, etc.) and then accompanied Cleo Laine, who opened her sample box and offered us e. e. cummings, Spike Milligan, Shakespeare, Bessie Smith, "My Bill," a blues, and "On a Clear Day." A quartet named Oregon started the early concert at Avery Fisher, and its members took turns on guitar, piano, trumpet, sitar, tabla, violin, French and English horn, oboe, conga drums, bass, triangle, flute, and bass clarinet. Their music is Western "classical" streaked with East Indian music. They were followed by Keith Jarrett, who played four of his magical, rolling gospel-and-blues numbers. First, as is his wont, he stood, then he crouched, and finally he sat down like this:

Thelonious Monk, for so long seemingly imperishable, has been in semi-retirement, but he brought on a quartet made up of Paul Jeffrey on tenor saxophone, Larry Ridley on bass, and Thelonious, Jr., on drums. Monk himself has worn away, and so has his playing. He is thin and gray, and he sounded as he did thirty-five years ago. All the eccentricities have vanished, leaving a straight, modern-sounding chord-based pianist. Gone are the stringy runs, the spasmodic rhythms, the splayed chords, and the nervous humor. It was almost as if Monk were telling us that he had been putting us on all these years and that he had finally tired of the joke.

The day started with a bang. Zoot Sims appeared with a quintet at the last of the free noonday concerts that have been given this week on the northwest corner of Sixth Avenue and Fifty-first Street. The group included a revivified Jimmy Rowles, the trumpeter Marky Markowitz, the bassist Major Holley, and Mike DiPasqua on drums. Sims was buoyant, and so was Markowitz, an old big-band trumpeter who plays with a wasteless assurance and frequent nods in the direction of Rex Stewart and Roy Eldridge.

*July 4th*

On the occasion of the hundred-and-ninety-ninth anniversary of Independence, George Wein decided to open his own Hall of Fame, and here are the first lucky entrants: Bobby Hackett, Jabbo Smith, Barney Bigard, Vic Dickenson, Joe Venuti, Red Norvo, Teddy Wilson, Earl Hines, Milt Hinton, and Jo Jones. All were at Avery Fisher to play the early concert, and all were presented with plaques by John Hammond, who in turn was presented with one by George Wein. Two dozen numbers were played, and the proceedings, unlike most all-star ragbags, were orderly and intelligent. Of particular note: a clip from the "Sound of Jazz" in which a band made up of Stewart and Red Allen, Pee Wee Russell, Vic Dickenson, Coleman Hawkins, Milt Hinton, and Jo Jones played "Rosetta;" two live Dickenson solos on his own "I'll Cry" and "Constantly"; beautiful Norvo versions of "I Surrender Dear" and "Tea for Two" (Norvo, stationed off to one side of the stage, said later he felt as if he were playing in a sidecar); Earl Hines doing his own "Monday Date" and "Blues in Thirds"; three superior Teddy Wilson solos, with matching Jones brushwork; a willowy Bobby Hackett "Body and Soul," with superlative accompanying Jones high-hat (old man Jo was in superb form all evening); a burning Joe Venuti "Sweet Georgia Brown"; and a witty duet by Hinton and Jones. Unfortunately, Jabbo Smith didn't play. He appeared onstage during an ensemble and made the motions, but nothing came out. He was reportedly overcome with emotion. Never mind; better to leave undisturbed those dazzling solos he recorded in the late twenties and early thirties.

Over to Carnegie Hall at eleven-thirty to catch Sylvia Syms, who was jammed into a Lionel Hampton parade. She was accompanied by Mike Abene on piano, Randy Brecker, Jay Leonhart, and Panama Francis, and the best of her six songs were "As Long As I Live" and "More Than You Know." Then back to Avery Fisher to see if Sonny Rollins would shake off the queer paralysis that stage appearances seem to induce in him. He didn't. He played very little during his six numbers, and he used a husky Gato Barbieri tone and an odd mode of repeated notes and phrases. When the audience applauded, he rocked back and forth near the microphone and uttered strings of "Thankyouthankyouthankyou." But Rollins' idiosyncracies have never fooled anyone; he remains the wizard of living saxophonists.

### July 5th

There will be three more Hudson River ferryboat rides tomorrow and a big soul-soap bash out at Nassau Coliseum. So, for all intents and purposes, today is the last day of the Festival. The seven-thirty Avery Fisher concert began with a dark horse named Tania Maria. She is a small-faced, strongly built Brazilian singer and pianist, and she was accompanied by Helio on bass and Boto on drums. She sings in Portuguese, and none of her five songs was familiar, but it didn't matter. She has an urgent, precise hammering voice, and her singing is unbelievably close. There are no spaces, no chinks, no chances for her phrases to stand back and be admired. Her piano playing moves parallel to her singing and then fuses with it when she scat-sings. Where did this marvelous, fiery jazz come from? One hears in it suggestions of Carmen McRae and Ella Fitzgerald and Anita O'Day, but little else. Were the Brazilians singing and playing such music a hundred years ago? Did jazz really come up the Amazon?

After Tania Maria, I went over to Carnegie to catch Woody Herman's current Thundering Herd. It was like all the Thundering Herds he's had in the last fifteen years—young (three members had just been plucked from that extraordinary musical orchard, North Texas State), strident, forceful, and good. Stan Kenton occupied the second half of the program. Vast and tired and grandeur-ridden, he sat through most of the set while his boys Wagnered their way through "My Funny Valentine" and "All The Things You Are," a show-off blues, and some Latin edifices built around Candido, the rubbery conga drummer. The second concert at Carnegie started with Bill Watrous and his Manhattan Wildlife Refuge, and during the four numbers I heard Watrous demonstrated again that he is doomed for the rest of his life to try and domesticate a virtuosity that enables him to do anything on the trombone that comes into his mind and do it perfectly.

Sarah Vaughan was in residence at Avery Fisher for the late show, and during her second half she joked with Percy Heath, her bassist for the night, sang "Moonlight in Vermont" and "Poor Butterfly" and "Mean to Me" and a dozen other songs, rocketed time and again from her lowest register to her highest and from her highest to her lowest, gave lesson after lesson in melodic calligraphy, swallowed whole sets of lyrics alive, and stamped the word "rococo" on every one of our foreheads.

Earlier in the day, James T. Maher, the distinguished observer of American music, said that he was weary of the prolixity and density of so much contemporary jazz. It was becoming Brahmsian, and it reminded him of years ago, when, suddenly tiring of listening to symphonic music, he had turned with relief and pleasure to chamber music, where he could breathe again. He said that much the same thing had happened at the Hall of Fame concert. He also wondered where the plethora of notes jazz musicians play these days end up and whether the space there is unlimited.

# Zutty

By 1940, the pursuit of American primitivism in this country was well under way (collecting folk art, collecting black jazz musicians, recording Appalachian folksingers, writing dialect novels), and one of its choicest finds was the drummer Zutty Singleton, who died this July, at the age of seventy-seven. Between the late thirties and the early forties, Singleton, steadily visible at Nick's or the Village Vanguard or Jimmy Ryan's, was one of the mascots of the Brooks Brothers set. He played its private parties, and he played the Sunday-afternoon jam sessions at Ryan's, where the tapping of white buck shoes was thunderous. In the late thirties, he played a session on the St. Regis Roof that was broadcast to Britain, which was ecstatically told by the announcer, Alistair Cooke, that Singleton was the "greatest colored drummer alive." Singleton was an ingratiating performer. His ceaseless motions were puppetlike. His head rolled from side to side and his eyelids fluttered like butterflies. His arms seesawed, and he lunged to the right or the left for a choked-cymbal stroke or a tom-tom beat. He played with a cheerful mock ardor, and the instant he finished a number his broad smile came out like the sun. What chiefly held his admirers were his snare-drum rolls, which were beautiful. They flowed like cream on marble, and he used them everywhere—for background figures with the afterbeat emphasized, for press rolls in slow tempos, and in his solos, which often consisted of an unbroken roll that rose and fell, that shouted and whispered. For all that, Singleton was a patchy drummer who had barely enough technique to get by. He never learned to use a high-hat properly, his time was often unsteady, and his solos were predictable. His style came to a standstill around 1930, and it would have been unkind to compare him, ten years later, with such contemporaries as Sid Catlett and Jo Jones and Chick Webb. But Singleton was a fountainhead. He presided over drumming in Chicago during the late twenties and early thirties, when he worked with Louis Armstrong and Earl Hines, and from out of his shadow came drummers like Catlett and Gene Krupa and Lionel Hampton. He was a short, round, beamish man, an ingenuous, pleased country boy whose beginnings now seem Arcadian: "I was born in Bunkie, Louisiana," he once said. "My grandmother worked for a Dr. Hayes there, and when my mother was seventeen my grandmother summoned her up from New Orleans, where she was living with an aunt. My mother used to go to the local grocery store, which was owned by a man named E. E. Singleton. It looked like they got together, and that's how I appeared. He must have been in his thirties. I saw him just twice. He came to our house one night when I was six. He'd been hunting, and he had a lot of game. The other time, Viny Monroe, who'd been my midwife, came by and said, 'Come on, boy, I'm going to take you by your daddy's store.' She did, and those were the two times I saw him. Of course, the house we lived in he bought for my mother."

## Halie

Paradox crisscrossed much of Mahalia Jackson's life. She became famous in her last fifteen years by singing black religious music before white secular audiences. She was a great jazz singer who never sang jazz. (One wonders whether she *really* believed that, particularly when the spirit was on her and she stomped up and down the stage, swinging unbelievably hard.) She was a black hero to many whites and a "white" traitor to many blacks. She was a conspicuously charitable woman who never lost her New Orleans "evil." And now, she is the subject of a miasmic, six-hundred-page biography, *Just Mahalia, Baby*, which was put together by a New Orleans newspaperwoman named Laurraine Goreau. The author hung around Mahalia for twelve or thirteen years, and she must have jotted down the comings and goings—even from room to room in Mahalia's Chicago house—of every person who came in contact with her. The result is

a giant engagement calendar swarming with people who are not always introduced and who do not always have surnames. Once in a while, Mahalia's own
voice comes through, and we think, That must have been the way she talked,
the way she was—as in this passage about a transatlantic crossing:

> Even though the water made me sick, quite sick, I would find myself all
> day watching the sea, and the way the water would run. It never ran the
> same way; sometimes it was like this, and sometimes like that—sometimes
> like this—and like that. It keeps you interested all day long, watching
> which way the sea going turn—whether it's going spread out, or whether
> it's going drop; all these different forms that it takes. And the sounds it
> makes. There really is a song of the sea.

But much of the time the book drifts in and out of a synthetic voice that is a
queer attempt to make it seem as if Mahalia were talking about herself in the
third person. Hence:

> Right into running revival at Salem all week. Never mind tired—she
> promised God. Good she could tell Mildred to bring her singers one
> night. Let her be a part. Oooh, it's a small bed this week for Halie: Can't
> invite Rev. Bentley all the way from Philadelphia to preach and not give
> him the best, her queen-size; she sure wasn't going take Minnis's bed; got
> Laurraines in Sigma's or she wouldn't mind being in the little girl's. Any-
> way, Laurraines need to be there 'cause that's the closet where Allen keep
> the stationery and Laurraines writing the important people for her in
> India. Halie was ashamed to let it run this long. So *much!* But it was good
> to have people fill up some this space.

An outline of Mahalia's life eventually materializes. She was born illegitimate and poor in New Orleans in 1912. Her mother, Charity Clark, was a
minister's daughter, who died when Mahalia was five. Her father, Johnny
Jackson, was also a preacher, whose attentions warmed in direct proportion
to her fame. She was raised by an overbearing aunt, and when she was fifteen
she moved to Chicago with another aunt. During the next twenty years, she
worked her way up through the doctrinaire, jealous gospel world, changing
the music as she went along. She freed it rhythmically, and she made commonplace such devices as blue notes and growls and abrasive shouts. By
1950, she had had her first hit record, and she was on her way. One suspects
that she was never at peace for long. She was married twice—to an inveterate gambler and to a blowhard jazz musician—and divorced twice. She
became encrusted with hangers-on and bullies and sycophants. Her weight
weakened her health, and she was frequently bedridden during the last seven
or eight years of her life. But by the time she died she was no longer just a
gospel singer. She was a black American star, but Goreau doesn't tell us

whether, in reaching that eminence, she considered herself to have risen or fallen.

## Five Important Recordings

It is rare when a recording of a jazz concert bears out what one thought one heard. Generally, the concert turns out to be neither as good nor as bad as it seemed. But the recording of the swan-song concert given by the Modern Jazz Quartet at Avery Fisher last November—"The Last Concert: The Modern Jazz Quartet" is an exception. It *was* a classic evening. The recording also proves that the group was no longer the impeccable machine it had come to be. Indeed, the concert was not so much a celebration of what the group had achieved during its twenty years as it was a celebration of the new freedom of its four members, and this shows in almost every one of the fourteen numbers on the album, which is an edited version of the original three-hour concert. The group's counterpoint is pretty much intact ("The Golden Striker," "Summertime"), but the solos, once so carefully balanced with the ensembles, are long and almost aggressive. Listen to Milt Jackson in "The Cylinder" and "Summertime," and especially in "What's New?" and "Django." It's as if he were consciously knocking the stuffing out of "Django," which came to be an M.J.Q. hymn. And listen to Lewis's ascending opening phrase in his solo in "Summertime" and, midway, to its clusters of high notes. And to his statement in "Skating in Central Park." Even Percy Heath gets off two notable solos ("Blues in A Minor," "Bags' Groove"), and throughout Connie Kay swings with an almost thundering precision.

Not long before the late Ben Webster left for Europe, in 1964 (for good, as it sadly turned out), he got together with his old friend Milt Hinton at Hinton's house, in Queens, and the two men made some music. Luckily, Hinton turned on his tape machine, and four of the numbers they played have been brought out on one side of "Here Swings the Judge: Milt Hinton and Friends." Two of the numbers—Webster playing vigorous amateur stride piano—are indulgences, but the other two are invaluable. The first is a very slow version of "Sophisticated Lady," in which Webster plays the melody—a beautifully embellished, subtly altered melody—for one chorus, gives way to a chorus of Hinton, and returns for a chorus of serene and majestic improvisation. Webster never played better, and one reason was the sheer space at hand. There was no one to get in his way—no drummer, no pianist—and he soars. And the same is true of the second selection—a short, graceful "All the Things You Are." What a pity the two men didn't make a whole album!

During the forties, Lester Young made several dozen recordings for a small West Coast label, Aladdin, and a good proportion have been brought together in "Lester Young: The Aladdin Sessions." His long and tortuous disintegration had begun, but he was still in superior form, particularly in such ballads as "These Foolish Things," "It's Only a Paper Moon," "You're Driving Me Crazy," "She's Funny That Way," "Sunny Side of the Street," and "I'm Confessin'." Young doesn't bother with stating the melody. He launches immediately into his improvisations, and they are such complete reworkings that sometimes it is impossible to tell what he is playing. He literally creates new and fascinating compositions out of the composer's chords. The album reminds us of how much his squadron of imitators learned from him, and, at the same time, how little.

Jim Hall's first new record in a couple of years, "Jim Hall: Concierto," is a subtle, highly lyrical effort in which he is joined by Chet Baker, Paul Desmond (in just two numbers), Roland Hanna, Ron Carter, and the drummer Steve Gadd. There is a long, fast, inquiring version of "You'd Be So Nice To Come Home To" that is notable for Hall's spare solo, a brief bit of counterpoint between Desmond and Baker, and the first in the album of what turn out to be four first-class Baker solos. Baker has spent much of his career stepping on his own feet and obscuring the fact that, somewhat in Miles Davis's earlier mode, he is an intelligent, affecting player whose solos are often models of design and inflection and phrasing. They have a latter-day Beiderbecke quality. The second side is a fresh and eloquent study of Joaquin Rodrigo's mournful "Concierto de Aranjuez," which has been examined before by Miles Davis and the Modern Jazz Quartet. All hands (except the drummer) take forty-two-bar solos, and Baker and Desmond are excellent. And so is Hall, but his guitar is not favorably recorded. He uses a lot of low, reverberative notes, and they get entangled with the bass player, who is over-recorded, and with the pianist; who, though he plays well, is totally unneeded.

Anthony Braxton is a thirty-year-old saxophonist, clarinettist, and flutist from Chicago who, through no fault of his own, is being hailed as the new messiah, the new Charlie Parker-John Coltrane-Ornette Coleman. But Parker and Coltrane and Coleman were not nearly as wild-eyed as they first appeared; indeed, they turned out to be two-thirds conservative, one-third rebel, and Braxton is no exception. He is an orderly musician, and he has taken the best of Coleman and Eric Dolphy and Miles Davis and Benny Carter and Paul Desmond and added his own curious, almost arithmetical way of phrasing. Braxton's music is small and confidential. It lacks Parker's ferocity and declamatory tone, Coleman's heedlessness, and Coltrane's zealotry. Now he has made his second record on a label of consequence— "Anthony Braxton: Five Pieces 1975." There are four musicians (Braxton, trumpeter Kenny Wheeler, bassist Dave Holland, and drummer Barry Altshul), and the album consists of a straightforward and altogether admirable reading of "You Stepped Out of a Dream" and four of Braxton's politely shocking creations. These are identified only by mysterious formulas. Thus, the first number on Side 2 is

489 M
70 - 2 — (TH - B)

M

All four numbers bear a melodic likeness to Coleman's compositions, but they are arranged in a far more calculated manner. In "489 M" there is a long unison statement of the melody, and then Braxton improvises in quick succession on alto and sopranino saxophones, clarinet, flute, and bass clarinet. He plays straight and he moans and wails and makes monster sounds, but in an unagitated way. The third number on Side 1 has a devious, irregular stop-time background and a long section of solos, in which Braxton makes kissing sounds on his alto and Wheeler suggests Rex Stewart. Holland is fashionably huge-toned and lightning-fingered, and Altshul produces a soft, bonsai array of clicks, silken cymbal sounds, and tap-tapping snare-drum and tom-tom beats.

# 1976

## Cool

Until the mid-thirties, the only reference works jazz had were the data banks that its most assiduous record collectors carried around as heads. Then the first discographies appeared, and, after the war, were followed by more discographies and a still unabated flood of encyclopedias, histories, picture books, glossaries, bio-discographies, and, lately, fullfledged biographies. Two of the most recent reference works are *Jazz Talk*, by Robert S. Gold, and Brian Rust's *The American Dance Band Discography, 1917–1942*. Gold's work is a slightly revised edition of his *A Jazz Lexicon*, first published in 1957. It is, though far from complete and sometimes inaccurate, a fascinating look into the spoken language that black jazz musicians have invented to protect themselves from the white world, and from their own square brethren. This inventiveness is not surprising, for most jazz musicians tend, as informal court fools, to be very funny people, whose humor ranges from excellent workday hyperbole to the caperings of Dizzy Gillespie and Joe Venuti. Their comic inspirations also take the form of reverse exaggeration (something marvelous becomes "a mess" or "terrible"), synecdoche, and sheer poetic transformations (to travel is to "broom"). This language changes almost from day to day, and for good reason: since colloquial language rises (and formal language sinks), it is constantly being tapped by the world it is supposed to shut out. Some of the expressions, long since turned to clichés, that have come directly from jazz are:

| | |
|---|---|
| cop-out | -ville (as in splitsville) |
| corny | uptight |
| hangup | kicks |
| the scene | square |
| shades | way out |
| to dig | to have a ball |
| groovy | freebee |
| to split | cool |

Jazz musicians have smoked marijuana since the twenties, and they have created endless euphemisms:

| | |
|---|---|
| charge | pot |
| weed | vonce |
| Mary Jane | tea |
| muggles | stash |
| mootah | grass |
| boo | reefer |
| hemp | stuff |
| gage | roach |
| panatela | |

Some of their inventions were never picked up by the straight world and have become obsolete:

spots (written musical notes)
woodpile (xylophone)
hides (drums)
mice (violins)
dommy (apartment)
a fat man (a five-dollar bill)
a solid sender (a good record or performer)
a rug-cutter (a dancer)
reet (all right; yes)
bruz (brother)
hincty (suspicious)
a lane (a square)
to lay some iron (to tap-dance)

These are still inviolate and often choice:

to cop a nod (to sleep)
a crumbcrusher (a baby)
a fox (a girl)

to feel a draft (to sense hostility)
hame (an unpleasant job, after the actual word)
to make snakes (to have technical facility)
to woodshed (to practice)
a hawkins, or hawk (a cold winter wind)
to jump salty (to turn unpleasant or hostile)

So how many people would understand this: "Two things make me jump salty, man—when I feel a draft from a fox and when I take a hame"?

Brian Rust's dance-band discography comes in two big stubby volumes, and is over two thousand pages long. Rust has untangled the recording histories—dates and places, matrix numbers, labels, personnel, pseudonyms—of almost twenty-four hundred white dance bands (he has covered the black bands in another book, and has omitted Glenn Miller and Benny Goodman, each of whom already has his own definitive book), or presumably every dance band that recorded between the First and Second World Wars. Almost useless information is irresistible, and Rust's volumes are full of it. One learns that Bobby Hackett joined Horace Heidt in December of 1939 and left by July of 1941, and that during his tenure he worked behind such vocalists as Art Carney and Gordon MacRae and just missed Mary Martin, who recorded the "Pound Your Table Polka" on April 8, 1942. One can follow Joe Venuti through his early labyrinthine recording career—from 1924 to midway into the Depression. Here is a chonology of the bands he recorded with (some names are pseudonyms for Sam Lanin and Ben Selvin, who ran dance-band cartels, and whose groups must have recorded every day in the late twenties and early thirties):

Jean Goldkette
Roger Wolfe Kahn
Deauville Dozen
Irwin Abrams and His Knickerbocker Grill Orch.
Broadway Bell-Hops
Frankie Trumbauer
Paul Whiteman
Napoleon's Emperors
University Orch.
Ipana Troubadours
Smith Ballew
Chester Leighton and His Sophomores
Rudy Marlow
Dick Robertson
The Cavaliers
Jerry Fenwyck
Phil Spitalny

Rudy Vallée and His Connecticut Yankees
Steve Washington
Victor Young
Adrian Rollini
Dorsey Brothers
Freddie Rich's Radio Orch.
Russ Morgan

And one finds that Jerry Colonna, the pop-eyed Hollywood buffoon, played trombone briefly with Joe Herlihy and His Orchestra, and in June and July of 1927 recorded three numbers—"Cornfed," "State and Madison," and "Lighthouse Blues"—on the Edison Diamond Disc label before moving on to greater things.

## Unique

Eddie Costa was a small, wiry, intense pianist and vibraphonist, who was born in Atlas, Pennsylvania, in 1930, and was killed in an automobile accident on the West Side Highway in the summer of 1962. Costa worked with, among others, Joe Venuti and Tal Farlow and Woody Herman, and he reached a high mark in the mid-fifties, when he was in a trio that was led by Farlow and included Vinnie Burke on bass. Before it broke up, the group was recorded commercially but it was also recorded at its leisure in the apartment of Ed Fuerst, a record collector, American-song authority, and one-time road manager for George Shearing. The invaluable results of Fuerst's alertness have been issued as "Tal Farlow: Fuerst Set." Costa played with overwhelming percussiveness. Each improvisation resembled an excellent drum solo in its rhythmic intensity, pattern of beats, and elements of surprise. Costa liked to use octave chords in the left hand and single-note lines in the right, and he liked to thunder endlessly down in the lowest registers of the piano. At such times, he played chords in both hands and with stunning effect. He would let loose a staccato passage and then an impossible two-handed arpeggio, or he would deliver on-the-beat or offbeat chords—seesawing them, making them into sixteenth notes, somehow slurring them, and developing great drive and momentum. But Costa had a good sense of structure, for he dropped in frequent rests (he had clearly listened to Basie), and after a prolonged period of subterranean rampaging he would float up a register or two on the keyboard for several breathing, lightheaded choruses. There are four numbers on the album, and Costa is in fine form on "Jordu," which lasts almost fifteen minutes, and in which he plays low-register anvil music—offbeat chords, skidding chords, pitching chords. And listen to the double-time chordal dashes in his long solo on the pleasant "Out of Nowhere." Farlow is in prime condition throughout (he went into semiretirement two years later), and he takes an exceptional solo on "Opus De Funk."

# Jimmy Rowles

I t has become plain in the three years since Jimmy Rowles emerged from his hibernation on the West Coast that, regardless of style or category or age, he is the most prepossessing jazz pianist we have. There are many reasons: the very way he addresses a piano (some pianists sit down at the keyboard as if they were depositing an invaluable work of art on the piano bench), without hesitation, announcements, or one of those radar, room-circling who's-here? glances; his originality, which draws largely on Art Tatum; his imaginativeness and variety, which enable him to play long, muscular studies of slow ballads or fast, driving blues that swing and swarm and swell; his technique, which is used only to say what he has in his head; his harmonic sense, which leads him to plumb the songs he plays as well as to add new levels that turn them into formidable structures; his unfailing taste; his humor, which is evident in his choice of songs, in his tempos and rhythms, and in interpolations from other songs; and his improvisational abilities, which are spelled out in endless ways—the short, bent runs, the funny, falling-away passages, some of them almost slithery, the chords that have a single-note spareness. Tonight, at Bradley's, he gave us a soft "Looking at You," Tom Satterfield's "Restless," a brazen, chattering "Brazil," an impressionistic "Skylark," a jumping "Dancers in Love," "My Funny Valentine" as a dirge, a casual, hats-off "Sweet Lorraine," Billy Strayhorn's "U.M.M.G.," complete with some Oriental closing figures, and an attractive waltz that sounded like Willard Robison.

Rowles is also highly visible in a fascinating recording. "A Day in the Life of Billie Holiday," in which Billie talks, laughs, garbles, and sings her way through a rehearsal held in Los Angeles with Rowles and the bassist Artie Shapiro not long before she died. Her voice is almost leaden, but her intonation is fine, and on some of the numbers she is stunning—a fragment of "I Must Have That Man," a swinging "Everything Happens to Me," a lazing "Jeepers Creepers," a dreaming "Prelude to a Kiss," and two versions of "Please Don't Talk about Me When I'm Gone." In between, she swears, kids Rowles, and reminisces about such things as the audition she had in a Harlem club at thirteen and was laughed out of because she had no idea what a key was. Rowles plays sparkling piano behind her and gets off such a beauty at the beginning of the last bridge of "Everything Happens to Me" that Billie throws in a fast, parenthetical "There ya go!" Her laugh, which is all through the record, has a wild, scimitar quality, very bright and a little dangerous.

# Gone

R ay Nance—cornetist, violinist, singer, dancer, high-jinks person—died a few days ago at the age of sixty-two. Nance was with Duke Ellington from 1940 until 1963, and he was the epitome of what Ellington needed in his soloists. He was never a star. He was a singular stylist: any two Nance notes immediately identified him. He played with considerable emotion, particularly on the blues. His cornet solos were short, and he was not much of an improviser, but his fretting vibrato and feminine, beseeching tone made them invariably affecting. His solos preached and exulted. He was a good jazz singer, with an easy rhythmic baritone. His violin was often used for Billy Strayhorn's ballads, and it fitted their sheer textures. Nance liked to horse around and do funny dances, and, along with most of the musicians of his generation, he liked to drink. He worked where and when he could after he left Ellington, and most of the time he still played well. His cornet playing summoned up his idol, Louis Armstrong; it also displayed an ardent, unplaned beauty that has almost gone out of the music.

The Ruby Braff–George Barnes Quartet disappeared before it ever fully appeared. The group was formed in 1972 and dissolved in 1975. (In addition to the co-leaders, it consisted of Wayne Wright on rhythm guitar and John Giuffrida on bass; they were ultimately replaced by Vinnie Corrao and Michael Moore.) It worked less than half the time it lasted, and, as far as New York was concerned, it didn't seem to exist at all, for, outside of random concerts, it played here only five weeks— three at the Rainbow Grill, where it shared billing with a singer named Damita Jo, and two at Buddy's Place, on Second Avenue. Yet the Braff-Barnes Quartet was one of the best small jazz groups ever put together. It was disciplined, it invariably swung, and it did superior songs. The sound was a treble-bass blend reminiscent of the classic Rex Stewart–Barney Bigard– Django Reinhardt–Billy Taylor pickup group of 1939. It was lyrical *and* funky. The quartet had an electric in-person presence, and always played at the top of its gifts—no loafing, no padding, no windiness. Most jazz groups are monochromatic, but Braff-Barnes ceaselessly changed color. Braff's dynamics have never been more agile. Within four bars, he would move from a low-register whisper to a barely tapped high note to a full, middle-register cello tone. Barnes stretched his dynamic sense to its limits, too. Dreaming, barely voiced notes gave way to wild high-register *twang*s that sounded like a clarinet, and these gave way to soft, wind-harp chords. All the while, whether the two were soloing, playing in unbreakable unison, or fashioning elbowing counterpoint, there was the *whirr whirr whirr* of the rhythm guitar and the steady poling of the bass. Luckily, the group was decently recorded, and perhaps its truest record—with Wright and Moore—was done at a concert in the spring of 1974: "The Ruby Braff–George Barnes Quartet: Live at the New School." There are some true-blue moments—the two long, low Braff notes on "Solitude" that are indistinguishable from cello notes; the sliding, unearthly sotto voce way that Braff begins his solo on "Sunny Side of the Street" (it summons up Louis Armstrong's supreme solo on his 1930 "Sweethearts on Parade"); Barnes's ringing high notes on "Sugar"; Braff's tough, swinging solo on "Struttin' with Some Barbecue"; and the big-band ensemble effect the quartet achieves on "Rockin' in Rhythm."

## Unsung

**A** pair of musicians who should not be forgotten, and who are fortunately celebrated in new reissues: Charlie Shavers, trumpeter, composer, and arranger (1917–71), and Leo Watson, tiple, drums, trombone, and vocals (1898–1950).

Shavers was a highly gifted musician. A skilled arranger (he did most of the tight, polite arrangements for the John Kirby band, from 1937 to 1944), he wrote "Undecided," long beloved by jazz musicians, and he was a whirlwind trumpeter. He came up with Tiny Bradshaw and Lucky Millinder, and after he left Kirby he worked on and off for eleven years with Tommy Dorsey. He gigged away the rest of his life—with Jazz at the Philharmonic, as an accompanist to singers, and abroad. His death came two days after Louis Armstrong's, and went almost unnoticed. Shavers was short and roundish, and he had a cheerful, compulsive look. His music buffeted him, and he was in constant motion. When he was picking his way through a particularly dangerous arpeggio, he would lift his right foot and, completing the figure, slam the foot down and follow through by pointing his trumpet at the floor and hunching his shoulders. Shavers was the first virtuoso jazz trumpeter. He relished his powers. He had a big tone, a rococo attack—often spelled out in excited runs that matched Art Tatum's and Charlie Parker's—and he liked to fool around in the highest register. The showoff quality in many of his solos was fully intended (he carried to perfection what Harry James only began in his display pieces, and he paralleled in a less advanced harmonic way Dizzy Gillespie's tarantellas, which, indeed, he may have inspired), but every once in a while he set his fireworks aside and played with simpleness and lyricism. A reissue, "The Finest of Charlie Shavers," was made late in the fifties, and it provides Shavers with the setting every jazz horn player dreams of—large and bosomy string section. He plays ten ballads and is in relatively calm form. He lolls against the strings, letting loose broad lower-register figures, quick high notes, gentle double-time figures, and Rex Stewart half-valved notes. He embellishes and polishes each song until it gleams. Shavers the improviser is fully visible, though, on seven tracks of "Sidney Bechet: Master Musician." These were made in 1941, while Shavers was with John Kirby. He is very hot on "Twelfth Street Rag" and on "Limehouse Blues," but on "I'm Coming Virginia," "Mood Indigo," and a blues, "Texas Moaner," he is sorrowing and elegiac. Listen to the way he repeats a two-note Louis Armstrong figure at the beginning of his solo on "Texas Moaner" and then caps it with the proper blaring high note, and to "Mood Indigo," where he discovers, both in his melodic statement and in his solo, a rending blueness.

In his special way, Leo Watson was a genius. He was little known during his life, which was madcap and short. Much of his career was spent in a swinging novelty group called the Spirits of Rhythm, which flourished in the thirties and forties and was made up of various combinations of tiples, guitars, bass, and drums. Although he played the tiple (a stringed instrument between the guitar and the ukulele), trombone, and drums, he was primarily a scat singer. Scat singers are human horns who improvise often wordless, sometimes onomatopoeic songs, and the best of them have included Ella Fitzgerald, Anita O'Day, Betty Carter, Mel Tormé, and Louis Armstrong, who is said to have accidentally invented the form in 1926 when he was recording "Heebie Jeebies" and dropped the music. But Watson was the greatest of them all. His vocals contained long phrases of quickly revolving vowels that were interrupted feverishly with words used in a sly nonsense fashion. He had a wild sense of time, and in the late thirties he got off passages that predated Charlie Parker and Dizzy Gillespie by five years. His voice was harum-scarum. He growled, blared, whined, chanted, shouted, crooned. The recording that has brought Watson out of oblivion—"Pre-Bop"—was made in 1946 and contains his last record date. Four tracks were made—"Sonny Boy," "Tight and Gay," "The Snake Pit," and "Jingle Bells"—and with him are Vic Dickenson, Leonard Feather, who was the A&R man as well as the pianist, the bassist Vivien Garry, and the drummer Harold (Doc) West. The first three numbers are vintage Watson, but "Jingle Bells" suggests "Finnegans Wake." It begins in a slow tempo with ricky-ticky piano and Dickenson growling his way through the melody. Then West abruptly doubles the tempo, and Watson is off. Here, in rough transcription, is what he does:

> babadeladabaaaaaaaaaohhhhhhhhhhhhhhhhhdela
>    (*pause*)
> bells of the wedding of the wedding cake
> cut the cake, cut the cake, cut the beyyaaaaaaaaaa-yehbedoooo
> ooooooloayyyyy bebop deyaeeeeeeeeayo
> jingle bells, jingle bells (*growls*)
> snowbirds of Chicago (*pause*) Chicago Chicago
>    (*singing the melody*)
> ayeyiyiayeyiyibelopdeooooooooyaaaaaaaaaa bebop
> East Side West Side all around the town (*singing the melody*)
> all the birds of snow of Chicago (*legato, then his voice falls away and into*)
> aeyohhhhhhhhhhhhhhhhhhh deum
> (*Vic Dickenson solos, and Watson returns*)
> didge-ye-everhear didge-ye-everhear didge-ye-everhear didge-ye-ever-
>    hear
> Alexander's Ragtime Band? Band playing (*pause*)
> de-bing de-bing de-bing de-bing de-bing de-bing

the big bass drum de-bing bong bing
aaaaayaeeeeeeeeh (*and smoothly into a wordless closing duet with Dickenson*).

## Brother Ray

Billie Holiday was an urban woman who sang urban (however silly) songs. Her successor, Ray Charles, raised on church music in the lonesome Southern backwoods, is a primitive of the highest order, a shaman, a magic man, a hypnotist. He improvises constantly, and he will use any vocal weapon—melismatics, yodels, growls, crooning, falsetto, whispers, shouts, chanting, blue notes, grace notes, retards. It no longer matters whether he sings blues or country-and-Western or standards or "Eleanor Rigby" or "America"; it only matters how he sings. One waits for the shout that falls in a beat to a whisper, the flashing falsetto, the pine-sap diction, the pained hoarseness, the guttural asides, the spidery staccato sprays of notes, the polysyllabic explosions, the faster-than-the-ear dynamics. Charles does not display his feelings; he gives them to his audience, experiencing catharsis and offering sublimity. His music courses through him, making him rock from side to side, making his hands spring from the keyboard and sculpt air, making his feet dance. He is a prism constantly refracting his music. Charles shies away from New York, and that made his two Carnegie Hall concerts tonight a treat. During the first, he gave us a miniature Charles retrospective. He sang the blues; "Busted," in which he manages to convince you he is destitute when you know he has a million dollars in the bank; "Georgia on My Mind," a masterly lullaby whose first word, sung sotto voce and behind the beat as "Chor-ja," takes you immediately into shuttered rooms and long-ago afternoons; the delicate, teacup "Am I Blue?" and the chanting "I Can't Stop Loving You"; the hurrying "You Are My Sunshine" and the fast, rocking "What'd I Say?"

## Bags

Milt Jackson is an improviser of the rank of Coleman Hawkins and Charlie Parker and Teddy Wilson, and his years with the Modern Jazz Quartet suggested what might have happened if Joyce had joined the Bloomsbury group. The Quartet must have been a strain on Jackson. It confined his improvisational afflatus, imposed on him materials—some of them rather artificial and arch—that he would not otherwise have played, and demanded arduous and delicate ensemble work. He is a prolix, free-floating performer, and learning how to fit into the M.J.Q. must have taught him a good deal about self-editing, a skill few jazz musicians learn. Jackson has rid himself of the M.J.Q., but he is still at the mercy of another burden—the very instrument he plays. The vibraphone is an electrified marimba, a streamlined xylophone, a four-legged metal piano.

It has attracted some extraordinary musicians, but none has managed to circumvent entirely its neon tone, its hippy vibrato, and its science-fiction timbres. (Red Norvo has come closest; he approaches the clarity and tone of a piano.) Like the organ, the vibraphone constantly calls attention to itself. Its players must extract their solos from the instrument, and Jackson has become remarkably adept. He arrived at his preeminence in a roundabout way. He fell first under the stomping sway of Lionel Hampton (both Hampton's vibraphone and his mercurial two-finger piano playing, the latter having had more influence than has been acknowledged), and was then warmed by the suns of Charlie Parker, Dizzy Gillespie, and Bud Powell. The result is a performer of great fluidity and lyricism. Jackson's solos tumble and spill. They are full of hammered repeated notes (Hampton's piano), arpeggios, sudden rests followed by surprisingly accented behind-the-beat single notes, double-time dashes, legato chords, and a surpassing inventiveness. Since the dissolution of the M.J.Q., Jackson's solos go on and on, shouting and whooping, and listening to him is an ecstatic business. Much of his new quality has been caught on "The Big 3: Milt Jackson–Joe Pass–Ray Brown." There are two strolling ballads, Jobim's "Wave" and Django Reinhardt's lovely "Nuages." There is a fast "You Stepped Out of a Dream," in which Jackson starts his solo with a funny, jiggling, sidestepping passage that finally swings into his usual flow. And there is a gentle slow blues, "Blues for Sammy," in which he takes four choruses that both grieve and celebrate. The combination on the record of vibraphone and guitar and string bass works well. There are clearings in the ensembles, and each solo is well attended to by the two other players. It is a polite and brilliant coming-out party for Jackson.

## The Murphia

The inestimable cornetist-trumpeter Bobby Hackett died yesterday, at sixty-one, on Cape Cod, where he had moved five years ago. Hackett played his first engagement on the Cape at the Megansett Tea Room, in North Falmouth, almost forty-five years ago, and he played his last one at the Wequassett Inn, in East Harwich, this past Saturday. It had been his notion, after he finally settled on the Cape, to have his own club, where, except for occasional essential traveling, he would play most of the year, and where once a week his friends, professional and amateur, would be encouraged to sit in, for he believed there was little point in making music if it wasn't fun. But his club never came to pass, and he spent most of his time travelling all over the world to make enough money to live in a place he loved but really didn't live in at all. His whole life was that way—an endless parade of small disappointments, missed chances, broken promises, poor advice. He became a master scuffler, who endlessly patched and spliced and repainted, and somehow kept his modest ship afloat. Whenever one ran into him, he would be full of cheerful talk about new projects, but six or eight months later the projects had collapsed or vanished. Thus, his own record label, Hyannisport, only issued two records during its four-year life, and his ideal band (with his old friend Vic Dickenson and the pianist Dave McKenna, whom he considered nonpareil) only lasted a season. It was the same years ago when he missed the job of dubbing the sound-track for Kirk Douglas in "Young Man with a Horn" (Harry James did it, for a figure that increased every time Hackett told the story), and when he reportedly took a flat fee instead of royalties after making his famous mood recordings for Jackie Gleason. Indeed, money appeared to conscientiously skirt him. (One of his most fervent admirers said of him despairingly, "Bobby couldn't stand success. Ever since he was a kid, he was bent on self-destruction.") The wonder is that Hackett survived as well as he did. His playing threw angelic shadows, whether he was sailing through "Struttin' with Some Barbecue" or subtly recasting the melody of "What's New?" His tone was light and supple. His vibrato was reserved, and he had an impeccable rhythmic sense. He avoided the high and low registers, concentrating on the sunny middle octave. His solos had a prefigured design, a Greek Revival rightness. The excellence of his improvisations gave his solos a seeming sameness, but they were in fact full of fresh phrases and new turns. They also had a subtle wit, just as he did. He was small and trim, and had a small, laughing beaked face and glossy gangster hair. He sometimes wore a dime-size mustache, and he kept his eyes at a squint, as if what he saw out there should only be absorbed in small amounts. His voice was low, and he had a legato Providence accent. He prefaced almost everything with a long-breathed "Yehhh." He used it for both stoic and comic effect. Here are some of his *mots*:

On being asked how he liked his new bathtublike 1950 Hudson car: "Yehhh. I got to like it. I bought it."

On receiving no applause after completing a discreet dinner set in a noisy club: "Yehhh. I guess that was too confidential."

On a well-known virtuoso trombonist with whom he sometimes played: "Yehhh. Imagine his chops and my brains."

On seeing a couple of business associates of Irish extraction approaching on a Hyannis street: "Yehhh. Here come the Murphia."

When his work allowed him to stay on the Cape, one saw him everywhere—at Heinie Greer's celebrated Labor Day bash in Dennis, where Hackett, genuinely enjoying himself, would often be the only professional; at a concert held in a damp sway backed hall in Provincetown; at a Chatham resort hotel, playing dance music for gazelles and hippos; at the Columns in West Dennis, where he and Dave McKenna did memorable duets; at the Olde Inn in Orleans, when he'd sit in on Sunday afternoons with Marie Marcus and trade fours with his friend Jim Blackmore, a Cape heating engineer, who played one of Hackett's cornets, drove him to most of his gigs, and, like the rest of us, cherished him.

## Mr. Carter

**B**enny Carter, the elegant instrumentalist-composer-arranger, has begun edging back toward jazz, which he set aside for the Hollywood studios in the late forties. He has been sampling festivals, making records, teaching at Princeton, and accompanying Peggy Lee and the saucy Maria Muldaur, and now he has taken an engagement at Michael's Pub, his first such appearance in New York since 1942, when he had a group at the Famous Door that included the greenhorn Dizzy Gillespie. Carter was born in New York in 1907, and attended Wilberforce University. In 1932, after stints with Duke Ellington, Fletcher Henderson, Chick Webb, and McKinney's Cotton Pickers, he formed his own band, hiring such neophytes as Sid Catlett, Teddy Wilson, Ben Webster, Chu Berry, Russell Procope, and J. C. Higginbotham. But it was a bad time for big bands, and by 1935 Carter had gone abroad, where he worked as a BBC staff arranger. He put together another big band in New York in 1938, gave that up, organized several small groups, gave them up, and in the mid-forties moved to the Coast, where he assembled a final big band. The thirties were Carter's decade. He perfected his alto-saxophone style as well as his trumpet and clarinet playing. His arranging bloomed, as did his special abilities as a graceful and admired bandleader. (It was always a mark of distinction to be hired by Carter.) By the end of the thirties, he had developed an extraordinary persona. For a long time jazz was played by roustabouts and primitives. Carter was one of the first jazz musicians to go to college, and he wasn't expected to moan and shout and wear his blue notes on his sleeve. He was expected to keep his emotional cards close to his chest, and he did. He dressed flawlessly. His speech, possibly burnished by his B.B.C. stay, was orotund. And he was a handsome man, with intelligent, questing eyes and hundred-watt teeth. He was a gentleman who, we were reminded when he picked up one of his horns, also played music. To be sure, Carter was the most admired alto saxophonist of the thirties, but that was hardly surprising. Johnny Hodges didn't draw himself to his full height until 1940, and such colleagues as Charlie Holmes, Willie Smith, Tab Smith, Hilton Jefferson, and Pete Brown, though absorbing in their various ways, were not first-rank—which became startlingly clear when Charlie Parker exploded several years later. Carter looks almost exactly as he did thirty years ago, and his considerable gifts remain unimpaired. The arrangements he played last year with Muldaur had his customary uncluttered harmonies, his svelte saxophone writing, and his untroubled sense of space and structure. His alto-saxophone playing has grown even statelier. The joyous, declamatory tone has broadened, and the melodic lines have become longer and more complex. Tonight at Michael's Pub (his accompanists are Ray Bryant, Milt Hinton, and Grady Tate), he played custom versions of "Three Little Words," "Mean to Me," "Body and Soul," and "Honeysuckle Rose." His saxophone solos gave the effect of skywriting: each hung complete in the air before being blown away by the succeeding soloist. But the best part of tonight was Carter's trumpet playing. He doesn't take the instrument as seriously, and so his playing is freer. He works in stone on the alto and in wood on the trumpet. His phrases are short and judicious, he prefers a legato attack, and his lyricism is unstudied and airy. He has not played trumpet much lately, and one had the impression of ideas highballing helplessly past unheard, but he should soon be in good shape.

## Folly

The Sauter-Finegan band was put together in 1952 by the arrangers Eddie Sauter and Bill Finegan both for kicks and to show off their ingenious wares, and at the time it seemed overripe and somewhat precious. It was a hybrid group that had a six-man rhythm section and an odd instrumentation, which consisted of a tuba, a harp, and a reed section that doubled on piccolo, oboe, English horn, flute, kazoo, recorder, clarinet, and bass clarinet. Voicings like these were common: flute, two clarinets, two baritone saxophones; two flutes, two clarinets, baritone saxophone; and clarinet, bass clarinet, flute, two piccolos. The rhythm section gave off the sound of gongs, vibraphones, chimes, big bass drums, tympani, gourds, wood-blocks, sleigh bells, birdcalls, tambourines, and bongos. The band was a sound factory, capable of producing everything from a Bronx cheer to a hummingbird. It was Sauter and Finegan's folly, and it was no surprise when the aggregation finally sank of its own glittering weight. But this afternoon the band was brought brilliantly back to life at the Ninety-second Street Y. by Harvey Estrin, who was in the original S-F band, and the Y's Studio Orchestra, and it was a pleasure to discover that it had more substance and lyricism than one had thought. The concert made it clear that some of the Sauter-Finegan arrangements are easily up-to-date. The voicings are choice and change continually within each piece. The various sections do not bounce off one another but intertwine or run parallel. Sometimes Sauter and Finegan split up the sections vertically, putting half the reeds with half the brass, and, by adding soloists, they sometimes produce half a dozen or more voices at once. The texture of the arrangements is often elegant but rarely has the mandarin effect of Gil Evans, and the rhythm section, despite its resemblance to a henhouse at midnight, is not nearly as cluttered as it once seemed. The Y's Studio Orchestra, which came into being this year, is made up of New York musicians, some of whom are students and some professionals, and who range in age from fifteen to the forties. It played Sauter and Finegan's material with even more dash and aplomb than the original band. One did not get much sense of the abilities of its soloists, outside of the startling trumpet work of Charles Miller. Sauter and Finegan are arrangers, and they assembled an arranger's band.

## Big Little Band

In the late thirties, big bands, which had been prevalent in American popular music for over a decade, remembered that they had grown out of small bands, and, as a salute to their origins, many of them formed excellent small bands-within-bands. All these, lest they grow presumptuous, were given rib-tickling names. Tommy Dorsey had his Clambake Seven, Chick Webb his Little Chicks, Artie Shaw his Gramercy Five, Bob Crosby his Bobcats, Woody Herman his Wood-choppers (derived not from Herman's nickname, a corruption of Wood-row, but from the band's famous jump blues "Woodchoppers's Ball," recorded in 1939), Dolly Dawn her Dawn Patrol, and Count Basie his Kansas City Seven. (Mundane old Benny Goodman, mindful that he might one day frequent the conservatory, simply had his trios, quartets, quintets, sextets, and septets.) But small working bands (as opposed to groups put together only for recording) also proliferated on their own in the late thir-ties, and perhaps the most famous was the John Kirby sextet, which flour-ished from 1938 until 1941, when its original personnel (Charlie Shavers on trumpet, Buster Bailey on clarinet, Russell Procope on alto saxophone, Billy Kyle on piano, Kirby on bass, and O'Neil Spencer on drums) began to change. With the exception of Procope, the Kirby band had passed through that invaluable Harlem kindergarten the Mills Blue Rhythm Band, which foundered in 1937. In the mode of the time, the Kirby band was completely streamlined. It had no edges or bulges, and it invariably pointed into the wind. It was witty and relaxed, and it swung. The band mainly used unison scoring, which gave it a single, direct voice. It was a treble band, made up of high-pitched instruments—muted trumpet, clarinet, alto saxophone. And it was an ensemble band—its soloists jumped in and got out, and their various timbres barely ruffled its silken surface. (A startling exception: Charlie Shaver's *whap* open-horn solo on the group's Vocalion recording of "Royal Garden Blues.") In a typical medium Kirby number, Billy Kyle started by playing a close variation on the melody for sixteen bars while the band sup-plied organ chords behind him. The band took over the melody on the bridge, and Kyle, the band again sailing along behind him, finished the cho-rus. The second chorus was introduced by an ad-lib four-bar unison flourish, and then the ensemble, shifting into harmony, played a sixteen-bar variation of the melody, gave way to an eight-bar Bailey solo, and resumed its varia-tion of the tune. Shavers, still muted, soloed for sixteen bars at the start of the third chorus. Kyle took the bridge, this time without any organ chords, and the band played a mock Dixieland ensemble for the final eight bars. Of the band's four principal soloists (Kirby and Spencer rarely came forward), only Shavers and Kyle were first-rate. (Bailey had a reputation for being as schooled and fluid as Benny Goodman—they had the same teacher in Chicago—but his playing was academic and piping. Procope was simply a good workaday alto player.) Shavers was only nineteen when he joined the band, but his leaping baroque style was already in place. Kyle also dazzled. He had grown out of Earl Hines, and he used whipping single-note lines that were dotted with finely accented on-the-beat notes. Kyle soloing at a fast tempo with the band humming along behind him was a V-8 miracle. The Kirby band was not perfect. Its tight, gleaming style precluded much texture or surprise, and it had a weakness, then shared by many jazz groups, for jazzing the classics. Doing variations on Tchaikovsky and Haydn and Grieg and Chopin was thought to be funny, and even somewhat heretical. It put those holier-than-thou longhairs in their place.

Columbia recorded the Kirby band at its height but hasn't put out a Kirby reissue for twenty-five years. A new release on another label, "The John Kirby Sextet" (Classic Jazz), gives a good notion of the band. Of the twenty-four numbers in the album, thirteen were made in 1941, when the original band was intact, and the rest were done in 1943 and 1944, when the personnel still included Shavers, Bailey, and Kirby as well as such newcomers as George Johnson on alto saxophone, Budd Johnson on tenor saxophone, and possibly Specs Powell on drums and Clyde Hart on piano. (The liner notes give no indication that the later tracks have different personnel, nor do they give the origins of the tracks. Are they studio transcriptions, air checks, Muzak, or V-discs? Whichever, the recording quality is adequate.) The early material is the best and is notable for sly and witty versions of the "Original Dixieland One Step" and "Bugle Call Rag" (here called "Bugler's Dilemma"), a long version of the group's slow blues, "Blues Petite," and exceptional Kyle on "Close Shave," "Move Over," and "Old Fashioned Love." And listen to O'Neil Spencer on the 1941 sides. He was a classy brush drummer, and he had perfect time.

# Newport 1976

*June 25th*

The first concert of the fifth Newport Jazz Festival—New York, given at seven-thirty in Carnegie Hall by Tony Bennett (accompanied by a thirty-odd-piece orchestra led by Torrie Zito) and the Bill Evans trio, was professional, succinct, and often inspired. The promotional matter was misleading, for it suggested that Bennett would sing with Evans, the two having made a successful duet album during the past year. Bennett sang the first number, a jumpy "My Foolish Heart," with Evans, and they did two closing songs, but that was all. In between, Evans was joined by Eddie Gomez and Eliot Zigmund (drums) for six rather spirited numbers. Evans doesn't tell his listeners what he is playing, which is doubly rude: the composer is erased and the audience is made to feel unworthy of such information. It's like a minister neglecting to reveal his chapter and verse. But there was a possible "Spring Is Here" (Rodgers and Hart), two definites—"Up with the Lark" (Kern and Robin) and "Some Day My Prince Will Come" (Frank Churchill)—and three blanks. Evans played almost aggressively. He got loose from his habitual middle octave and produced some scintillating upper-register figures, and he piled up a series of encyclopedic descending chords during a fast number made chiefly of eight-bar exchanges. He came close to emerging from the inner-directed improvisational fortress he sequesters himself in these days. Gomez is one of the young brilliants on his instrument, and Zigmund is fashionably busy and circular. Bennett, buoyed by Zito's exceptional arrangements—Benny Carter saxophone figures, single-instrument backing, deft, floating string passages— sang over a dozen songs, among them "Just in Time," Fred Astaire's skimpy "Life Is Beautiful," " 'S Wonderful," "There'll Be Some Changes Made," "What Is This Thing Called Love?" and three Ellington numbers. He used dynamics and tempo changes, he belted and he sang sotto voce, and he missed very few notes. But he needs a new dance teacher. His onstage assortment of spins, one-arm akimbos, salutes, marching steps, and waffling hands sends up so much visual persiflage it camouflages his singing.

*June 26th*

For a long time in the sixties, Charles Mingus was rudderless. But, having been encouraged in recent years by a Guggenheim Fellowship, the publication of his funny, scurrilous autobiography, a university teaching job, and his realization that he is a seminal bassist, he has taken on direction again. At the first Carnegie Hall concert tonight, he was the roaring Mingus of the fifties and early sixties. He had with him two of the best musicians who worked for him then—Dannie Richmond (drums) and Jimmy Knepper (trombone)—and he played two of his best older pieces, "Good-bye Pork Pie Hat" and "Fables of Faubus." (The rest of his group was made up of Ricky Ford on tenor saxophone, Jack Walrath on trumpet, and Danny Mixon on piano.) He also played two new compositions—the short, fast "Remember Rockefeller at Attica" (sometimes the musical content of Mingus's jabs at politicians has less satirical edge than their titles), and a long lyrical piece, "Sue's Changes," which has a lilting, descending melody, tempo changes (double time, accelerando, decelerando), and brief, cacophonic ensembles. Mingus delivered short, fountainhead solos, but the best statements were by Knepper. He is an improviser of the greatest subtlety and invention. His phrases, set in a soft, scarfed tone, keep turning away from where you think they are going, and move in an intricate, organic fashion. Each phrase develops from the previous one, and each is stocked with surprises. They are also replete with the warming shadows and forms of those two masters Dickie Wells and J. C. Higginbotham.

Cobham/Duke, a jazz-rock group made up of Billy Cobham (drums), George Duke (piano), John Scofield (guitar), and Alphonso Johnson (bass), gave the late concert at Carnegie Hall. They play look-at-me music. On the left side of the stage were Cobham's drums, an orchard of sound perhaps six feet high and twelve feet across, which included a dozen or so bass drums, tom-toms, and snare drums (most of them transparent and lit from beneath), seven or eight cymbals, and two bent-knee megaphones attached to the front of the set and feeding into microphones. The right side of the stage was filled with Duke's workshop, a towering collection of electronic keyboards and synthesizers. Johnson and Scofield, anchored by their amplifiers and delivering occasional solos, stood guard at either flank. Despite the electronic din, the music was old-fashioned and straight-forward (Duke even sang a falsetto ballad), and it was played with endless laughs and brilliant smiles, suggesting that it was what it looked like—a joke.

### June 27th

As Confucius said: He who lives in the past walks backward into the future. Today, we had repertory in the afternoon, repertory in the evening, and repertory at midnight (all in Carnegie Hall). Taken chronologically, it began with Duke Ellington in 1927 and ended with John Coltrane in 1967. The Ellington repertory, the first of four to be given this week, consisted of twenty-two numbers from the twenties played by a New York Jazz Repertory Company group that was made up of, among others, Doc Cheatham, Dick Sudhalter, and Joe Newman (trumpets), Eddie Bert (trombone), Bob Wilber (reeds), Milt Hinton (bass), Panama Francis (drums), and Dick Hyman (piano), who was also the musical director. There were such monuments as "Rockin' in Rhythm," "The Mooche," and "Mood Indigo," "Creole Love Call," and "Black and Tan Fantasy" as well as the rarely heard "Harlem River Quiver," "Jungle Nights in Harlem," "Blues I Love To Sing," "Doin' the Voom Voom," and "Stevedore Stomp." The band acquitted itself pretty well. The trombonists had trouble reproducing Tricky Sam Nanton, and Norris Turney's Johnny Hodges was pale. There were constant rhythmic problems. The Ellington band of the twenties hadn't begun to swing, and it is almost impossible for present-day musicians to mimic vanished rhythmic ineptitudes. The tempo went up and down, and at times the rhythmic pulse died altogether. But the trumpets, joined midway by Cootie Williams, were excellent, and so was Bob Wilber. It was eerie how he made Barney Bigard's fifty-year-old improvisations sound like his own, how he often gave them more feeling and éclat than Bigard himself had.

The afternoon concert was twenty-five years farther along. The George Coleman septet, which included Harold Mabern (piano) and Frank Strozier (alto saxophone), re-created the hard bop of the early fifties, with its long solos and stout oaken ensembles. Another septet, led by the trumpeter Ted Curson, who graduated over a decade ago from the Charles Mingus Finishing School and then departed for a long European stay, played Mingus-type music of the fifties and early sixties. The concert was closed by a quintet led by Anthony Braxton, who recalled Stravinsky, the Dave Brubeck Octet, and some of the mid-fifties experiments of Shelly Manne and Shorty Rogers and Jimmy Giuffre. Braxton's pieces depend a good deal on his ceaseless reed doubling. This afternoon, he played alto, soprano, and bass saxophones and clarinet and contrabass clarinet. His bass saxophone is an eight-foot-high mastodon; if it were an inch higher Braxton would have had to stand on a stool to reach the mouthpiece.

The Coltrane program started becomingly but turned to sand. Elvin Jones' quartet played Coltrane's "A Love Supreme," and Jones revealed again that he is a master of polyrhythms and of the old business of keeping perfect time and listening to the people he accompanies. McCoy Tyner's sextet offered one number that was enlivened by his percussionist's leaping-salmon motions and by some Tyner staccato arpeggios. Then another N.Y.J.R.C. orchestra, with Jones and Tyner sitting in, did Andrew White's hodgepodge tribute to Coltrane. White himself, a tall man with coat-hanger shoulders and short pipestem pants, raced through a couple of Coltrane's solos, but the arranged passages for the band had little to do with the dark, impassioned strivings of Coltrane, who by the time of his death had passed from musician to messiah.

## June 28th

The pianist Keith Jarrett may become messianic if he persists in the course he took tonight at the late Carnegie concert. He appeared with the Norwegian saxophonist Jan Garbarek, who is making his first visit, and the bassist Charlie Haden and a large string orchestra. Jarrett played two of his own concerti grossi, each lasting over forty minutes. Both pieces were crowded, and some of those in the press were Chopin, Ornette Coleman, Alberto Arpeggio, Rachmaninoff, the blues, Tchaikovsky, Dmitri Tiomkin, gospel music, George Russell, and Cecil Taylor. In one passage, the strings went into a crescendo seesaw passage while Jarrett, a figure of ecstasy who often half stands and half sits, played jubilant chords, and we knew that the baby had been born and the mother would be all right. In another, with the strings humming and Jarrett throwing off legato, canoeing figures, the rains came at last and the crops were saved. Chopin didn't improvise, but Jarrett repeatedly showed us how he might have sounded if he had. Now and then it came off, particularly in short solos and in the passages, either in unison or in counterpoint, that he worked out with Garbarek.

## June 29th

The second Ellington retrospective, given in Carnegie Hall, dealt with the thirties, the preparatory time for Ellington's 1940–42 period, when he and the band became an indivisible masterwork. In the thirties, Ellington wrote the beautiful melodies that paralleled popular songs and included "Mood Indigo," "Sophisticated Lady," "Solitude," "In a Sentimental Mood," "Prelude to a Kiss," and "I Let a Song Go Out of My Heart." He wrote his first longer works—"Reminiscing in Tempo" and "Diminuendo and Crescendo in Blue." And he wrote the first of the innumerable miniature concerti that he furnished for his best soloists during the next forty years—"Echoes of Harlem," "Boy Meets Horn," and "Clarinet Lament." At the same time, the personnel of the band became almost fixed, and it revolved around the nucleus of Cootie Williams, Rex Stewart, Lawrence Brown, Tricky Sam Nanton, Juan Tizol, Barney Bigard, Johnny Hodges. Harry Carney, and Sonny Greer. When Jimmy Blanton and Ben Webster joined at the end of the decade, the varsity was complete. The thirties were also the time when the band began to swing. Tonight, a N.Y.J.R.C. orchestra that included Jimmy Maxwell, Bernie Privin, Dick Vance, and Cootie Williams (trumpets), Jack Gale (trombone), Bob Wilber, Kenny Davern (baritone saxophone), Lawrence Lucie (guitar), and Bobby Rosengarden (drums) played twenty-nine numbers, and the best were "Slippery Horn" and "I'm Checkin' Out, Goom Bye," for their reed writing; "Boy Meets Horn," the oblique and funny Rex Stewart vehicle; "Echoes of Harlem," in which Williams excelled; "Drop Me Off in Harlem"; and good loose versions of "Stompy Jones," "Portrait of the Lion," and "Ring Dem Bells." Jimmy Maxwell's Cootie Williams was fine, and Bob Wilber's Hodges and Bigard were again first-class. Jack Gale came close to Tricky Sam, and Kenny Davern to Harry Carney—at least in the section work. Davern's solos kept sliding away from Carney's massive tonal center. Yet how well the various Ellington soloists were recaptured was only of passing interest. What matters in the present Ellington retrospective is that many of his older works, their scores long since lost, are being transcribed from the records and put down once and for all on paper. Herewith some of the heroic ears who transcribed what we heard tonight: Keith Nichols, Bob Wilber, Alan Cohen, Brian Priestley, David Hutson, Sy Johnson, David Berger, Fred Norman, Jon Charles, and Dick Vance. Many of the same people also arranged the compositions. That is, they have—when many different versions of the same piece exist—worked out a final representative score.

*June 30th*

The third Ellington program, given early tonight at Carnegie, was half retrospective, half prospective. The program began with a N.Y.J.R.C. orchestra giving the first complete public performance of "Black, Brown and Beige" since its première in 1943, and then offered the Duke Ellington Orchestra, conducted by Mercer Ellington. It was Ellington's oblique Jane Austen way to write "Black, Brown and Beige"—which he subtitled "A Tone Parallel to the History of the American Negro"—at such a time; he knew that the war was a white war and that the real conflict, the one that had been going on in this country since the seven-teenth century, was between blacks and whites. "Black, Brown and Beige" was Ellington's first "long" work, but it is, like all such Ellington compositions, a collection of short, intertwining program pieces. The most famous, "Come Sunday," has become recognized as a beautiful hymn, and it was sung with distinction tonight by Carrie Smith. "The Blues," almost as well known, is at once applause for and an affectionate sideswipe at a form he often treated with mocking respect, and it was sung by Joya Sherrill. The rest of the work is made up of marchlike pieces, a waltz, dances, and a mood piece. "Black, Brown and Beige" is primarily an ensemble work and is full of Ellington's unique voicings. The singer in "Come Sunday" is supported by pizzicato violin, bowed bass, and muted trombone, and earlier in the same piece the melody is stated by bowed violin, muted trumpet, and open-horn trombone. "Emancipation Celebration" has a plunger-muted trumpet and a plunger-muted trombone playing together and contrapuntally, and "The Blues" has a figure by three muted trombones. Although self-conscious and stiff in places, "Black, Brown, and Beige" is Ellington at the top of his bent. The perform-ance tonight caps still another musical-archaeological triumph. All that Alan Cohen and Brian Priestley, who did the transcribing, had to work with were fragments of the original score, poor recordings made at the original concert and slightly later in Boston, and the recording of various parts of the work (it has never been properly recorded in its entirety) which Ellington himself made throughout the years.

Pop, as Mercer Ellington calls his father, would have been both delighted and bewildered by what his son has wrought. When Ellington died, his band was almost moribund. The incessant travelling and incessant repetition of materials had driven some of its older members to the edge and had caused the younger ones to fall into accidie. Mercer Ellington has only Harold Minerve, Alvin Batiste, and Chuck Connors from the old band, and he has filled the rest of his seats with young musicians. He has also raised the deci-bel level about fifteen points and installed a drummer, Rocky White, who believes that power is rhythm. Tonight, the band played a *fast* "Sophisticated Lady," "Gong" and "Tang" from the "Afro-Eurasian Eclipse," "Caravan," "In My Solitude," "Harlem Air Shaft," "In a Sentimental Mood," and Ellington's last multi-part work, "The Three Black Kings," which has a funny gospel section, a form that Ellington mysteriously skirted. The band's prolonged roar obliterated Ellington's wit, subtlety, and delicacy, but he would have marvelled at such pep.

### July 2nd

The cool pastel music extracted in New York in the late forties from the inventions of Charlie Parker and Dizzy Gillespie by such as Lennie Tristano and Lee Konitz and Stan Getz and Chet Baker and Gerry Mulligan eventually withered in southern California in the late fifties. At its peak, it formed little academies, and one of the best known was run by Tristano, an autocratic blind pianist who had taken his chief impetus from Art Tatum. He gathered about him young players like Konitz and Warne Marsh, and they developed a music whose intricate Charlie Parker–like ensembles were as important as the solos. It was breathless, darting music, and tonight, at the late Carnegie concert, it was brought back by Konitz and Marsh and the rhythm section of Eddie Gomez and Eliot Zigmund. (Tristano, long a self-appointed maestro, retired from public view years ago and refuses to come out again.) They played two of their oldies, "Wow" and "Subconscious-Lee," and they also did "Body and Soul" and a couple of originals. The best thing about their performance was the ensembles, which were not set unison efforts but improvised counterpoint, and became dense and daring. Marsh is another of the white Lester Young tenor saxophonists, and Konitz absorbed both Young and Charlie Parker.

Buddy Rich's big band took up the last half of the concert, and it gave a relatively subdued performance. It played ballads, a medium blues, a couple of harmless flag-wavers, and Rich's set piece "West Side Story," in which he delivered a long solo that was closed with a delicate and succinct lesson on how to play a true single-stroke roll. Here he is just before his solo:

*July 4th*

Two things were wrong before a note had been played at the highly anticipated fourth Ellington program, held in Carnegie Hall and dealing with his 1940–42 period. The N.Y.J.R.C. group for the evening had as its drummer David Lee, who is a gifted newcomer but has little conception of the drumming of thirty-five years ago. And its musical director was Joe Newman, who came up through Lionel Hampton and Basie and is not celebrated for his knowledge of Ellingtoniana, either as a player or as a leader. (Dick Hyman or Bob Wilber would, of course, have been just right.) Lee depended on a slogging snare-drum afterbeat—a device that Sonny Greer used crisply and with discretion. And he bungled the three great breaks in "Harlem Air Shaft," simply playing right through the final one. (Would it have been so difficult for him to learn from the original recording how Greer drove Cootie Williams with his stampeding, double-time snare-drum figures?) Beyond that, Newman almost invariably chose tempos that were too slow. These numbers never recovered—"Chelsea Bridge," "Daydream," "Raincheck," "Subtle Slough," "Blue Goose," "Across the Track Blues," "Warm Valley," and "Main Stem." Selden Powell botched Barney Bigard's solo in "Across the Track Blues," and Lee did the same for Greer in "Jumpin' Punkins." There was no definition, no—*now!*— at the brilliant, leaping start of "Jump for Joy," nor was there any in a laggardly "Jack the Bear." To be sure, the beauties of Ellington's voicings came through again and again, and Jimmy Maxwell and Butter Jackson handled Cootie Williams and Tricky Sam Nanton with dispatch. Ellington's 1940–42 period is one of the high marks of American music, and to re-create it for a generation that has perhaps never heard it before demands taste and intelligence.

## Pure Melody

I t took the bass fiddle forty years to move beyond being a timekeeper, a purveyor of quarter notes, a plugger of chinks in the rhythm section. The first bassist to break this bondage, to dare to improvise on his instrument (pizzicato and arco), was Jimmy Blanton, who was born in Chattanooga around 1920 and died of tuberculosis in California in 1942. Blanton was discovered by Duke Ellington late in 1939 and stayed with the band until late 1941, when he could no longer play. In that brief time, Ellington starred Blanton and his instrument in concerti like "Jack the Bear" and "Bojangles" as well as in the highly unconventional duets that he recorded with Blanton—"Pitter Panther Patter," "Mr. J. B. Blues," "Sophisticated Lady," and "Body and Soul." Ellington must also have made sure that Blanton was properly recorded, whether he soloed or not, for his big tone and easy, generous melodic lines move like rivers through every record they did together. Ellington handled Blanton's arrival in his customary things-will-work-themselves-out way. He writes of Blanton in his autobiography, *Music Is My Mistress*:

> He was a sensation. . . . We had to have him . . . although our bass man at the time [and for the previous four years] was Billy Taylor, one of the ace foundation-and-beat men on the instrument. So there I was with two basses! It went along fine until we got to Boston, where we were playing the Southland Cafe. Right in the middle of a set, Billy Taylor packed up his bass and said, "I'm not going to stand up here next to that young boy playing all that bass and be embarrassed." He left the stand, left us with Jimmy Blanton, and went on out the front door.

Despite Blanton's enormous tone, each note was complete and clear. His phrasing was spare, and his silences were as important as his notes. He adopted a hornlike approach to his instrument—that is, he no longer just "walked" four beats to the bar but also played little melodies—and suddenly the jazz orchestra had a new melodic voice. Blanton's accompanying was forceful; he pushed the band and its soloists by playing a fraction ahead of the beat. His measured hurrying had a beneficial effect on the Ellington band. Sonny Greer tended to play behind the beat, and a tension was created between Greer and Blanton which lifted the band and made it swing. Blanton was felt far beyond the band. Bass soloists appeared everywhere, and within the decade a whole class had assembled, among them Oscar Pettiford, Wilbur Ware, Red Callender, Charles Mingus, Slam Stewart, George Duvivier, Milt Hinton, and John Simmons. (Blanton, of course, had been preceded by a host of strong bassists, known largely as accompanists, who included Billy Taylor, Hayes Alvis, Artie Bernstein, Israel Crosby, John Kirby, Pops Foster, and Wellman Braud.) Ray Brown and the undersung Red Mitchell followed, and they were succeeded by an outpouring of bassists that continues to this day. Among these are Richard Davis, Scott La Faro, Paul Chambers, Gary Peacock, Charlie Haden, Steve Swallow, Ron Carter, Eddie Gomez, Jay Leonhart, Lisle Atkinson, George Mraz, Buster Williams, Dave Holland, and Michael Moore.

The stringed bass—the Fender bass is an electronic aberration—has become the dominant instrument of the decade. Stringed bassists, put off by the effortless BOOM BOOM BOOM of the Fender bass, have taken to amplifying their instruments, but they haven't learned how to handle electricity any better than electric guitarists, who had a thirty-five-year start. Almost without exception, they turn the volume up too high. The fibrous, twanging tones of the bass reverberate disastrously, and that causes the drummer and the horns to play louder, while the pianist, locked in by an invariably weak microphone and the decibel ceiling of the piano, disappears. The new bassists have become hypnotized by technique. They play dazzling runs, hammering double-stops, and engulfing guitarlike chords (the influence of

Ravi Shankar), and they fool around ceaselessly with pitch, playing just under or just over the note, which gives them a sour, freakish sound. Their solos tend to be full of bravado and swagger and, more often than not, hoodwink audiences in the way that drum solos did when they were a novelty in the thirties. A resounding eighth-note run is good for a hand, and a couple of fast triplets will bring down the house. Their accompaniment consists of counter-melodies whose off-pitch notes and singsong, hand-over-hand attack detract rather than balance, distort rather than emphasize.

But several of the new bassists have avoided this narcissism, and perhaps the best is Michael Moore. Moore came to New York eight years ago from Cincinnati, where he was born and attended the conservatory, and he has listened to La Faro, Swallow, Peacock, Stewart, Brown, and Mitchell—the tradition of Jimmy Blanton. Moore has a half-moon smile and a Sunday-school mien, and he plays with great fervor. He hovers lightly over his instrument, closes his eyes, and slams the door of concentration. His virtuosity is subordinate to his invention. He has perfected what Blanton, and then Pettiford and Mingus and Mitchell, set out to do—improvise melodies of whatever length on the pizzicato bass. (Bowed bass is extremely difficult, and few jazz bassists have mastered it. Slam Stewart, who hums in octave unison with what he plays, is adept, but many others have been intimidated by intonation problems; by the very awkwardness of bowing the bass, and by the instrument's grave and almost immobile tonal qualities. Symphonic bassists are no better off, but for a different reason. Although they play a great deal in ensembles, the literature for solo bass, like that for solo tuba, has only begun to be written.) Without resorting to double-stops or guitar flourishes or tonal jokes, Moore constructs lyrical passages of the highest order. The new bassists, in attempting to transcend their instrument, make it obtrude; Moore lifts his listeners into the realm of pure melody, where one is conscious not of notes being plucked but only of new songs. Moore has an unfailing and always surprising rhythmic sense; he catches you by starting phrases in odd places and by suddenly doubling his time. Where another bassist would use a connective triplet or an arpeggio, Moore rests. Each solo gleams and multiplies, and each is important, in the way that Sid Catlett's and Sonny Rollins' and Jim Hall's are. You sit very still when Moore plays.

Moore is appearing at the Bemelmans Bar with Marian McPartland once or twice a week, and tonight turned out to be a brilliant and perhaps unwitting tussle. McPartland was in remarkable form; her runs were sheet steel, her single-note rhythmic passages cantered, and her harmonies were layered and tropical. Moore's accompaniment was model (if relentless), his solos (slightly louder than usual) were songs, and after a time intense competition took place. McPartland would solo, shaping a closing passage in which her chords revealed level after harmonic level, and Moore would come back with a four-bar arpeggio, a cluster of chattering staccato notes, and, before his next flash, a disarming legato melody. Eventually, they developed a stream of counterpoint that tilted only slightly when one or the other came to the fore.

## Front Runner

**Z**oot Sims' head juts forward, his shoulders are stooped, he has a small paunch, and his legs are bent from so many years of hefting a tenor saxophone. But there is nothing decrepit about him. His eyes are watchful, his porcupine hair crackles, and his wit cooks. (He once described his difficult compeer and sometime rival Stan Getz as "a nice bunch of guys.") And he is playing with a vigor and inspiration that have brought him to the front of the great movement of saxophonists founded by Lester Young. Sims is a cheerful man who likes to play Ping-Pong, garden, make meat sauce, and laugh, but he is surprisingly diffident. Not long ago, he talked briefly of himself: "I was born in 1925 in Inglewood, California, which is south of Los Angeles, right by the airport. It was all lemon groves and Japanese gardens then. I was the youngest of six boys and one girl. My mother and father were in vaudeville, and they were known as Pete and Kate. He was from Missouri and she was from Arkansas. My mother never forgot a joke or a lyric, and she performed at the drop of a hat right up until she had a stroke a couple of years ago. My father died in 1950. He spent his last years on the road, scuffling, and he never sent any money home. It was out of sight, out of mind for him. But there was never any falling out among us. When he came for a visit, everybody forgave him, including my mother. I don't know how we made it. The gas and water were always being turned off, and we moved a lot. One move got me off the ground, though, because we had to go to a new school where they were recruiting kids for their band. They gave me a clarinet and my brother Ray a tuba and my brother Bobby drums. I was about ten. I liked the clarinet fine, even though it made my teeth vibrate, which is why I don't play with a biting grip today. Most sax players bite through their mouthpiece; mine hardly has a mark on it. I played clarinet three years, until my mother bought me a Conn tenor on time. I kept it through my Woody Herman days in the late forties, and I finally sold it for twenty-five dollars. I never had any lessons. I learned by listening to Coleman Hawkins and Roy Eldridge and Chu Berry, and later to Lester Young and Ben Webster and Don Byas. My mind was elsewhere in school, which I quit after one year of high. When I was fifteen or sixteen, I worked in an L.A. band led by Ken Baker. He put these supposedly funny nicknames on the front of his music stands—Scoot, Voot, Zoot— and I ended up behind the Zoot stand, and it stuck. Then, instead of joining Paul Whiteman, who invited me, I went with Bobby Sherwood. It was like a family, and Sherwood was a father image to a lot of us. Sonny Dunham was next, and after him it was Teddy Powell. I spent nine weeks on the Island

Queen, a riverboat out of Cincinnati that had a calliope player who knew 'Don't Get Around Much Anymore.' In 1943, I joined Benny Goodman, and he had Jess Stacy and Bill Harris. I got along fine with Benny, and I still do, even though when I asked for a raise on a one-night gig a little while ago he said, 'Zoot, you hurt my feelings.' In 1944, Sid Catlett asked me to take Ben Webster's place in his quartet after Ben got sick, and we played the Streets of Paris, in Hollywood. I got drafted and ended up in the Army Air Forces later that year and fought the Battle of the South. I was stationed in Huntsville, Valdosta, Biloxi, Phoenix, Tucson, and San Antonio, where I played every night in a little black club. I got out in 1946 and rejoined Benny, and then I went with Woody Herman and became one of the Four Brothers, with Herbie Steward and Stan Getz and Serge Chaloff. I loved that band. We were all young and had the same ideas. I'd always worried about what other guys were thinking in all the bands I'd been in, and in Woody's I found out: they were thinking the same thing I was."

Sims' stay with Herman put him more or less on the map, despite the presence of Getz, whose Keatsian chorus on Herman's 1948 recording of "Early Autumn" made him famous. During the fifties and sixties, Sims worked in Gerry Mulligan's experimental sextet and in his staid "concert" band, and he teamed up with Al Cohn in a duo that still functions. Now he roams the world as a leader and sometimes as a sideman, and slowly he has built a stainless reputation as a swinging tenor saxophonist. But Sims's eminence has become unshakable only in the past several years—perhaps since the historic set at Richard Gibson's 1969 jazz party in Aspen when Sims, teamed with Joe Venuti, whom Gibson had just brought out of semiretirement, played an "I Found a New Baby" with such concentration and swing and ferocity that the event has become a Pinnacle of Jazz. (Sims' and Venuti's performance was not recorded, and they have been fruitlessly corralled into recording studios three times since in hopes they would repeat their miracle.) Sims, as he suggests, is a compound of Coleman Hawkins, Don Byas, Lester Young, and Ben Webster. Most of the white tenor saxophonists who stamped themselves "Lester Young" in the forties—Getz, Cohn, Steward, Jimmy Giuffre, Buddy Savitt, Bob Cooper, Bill Perkins, Allan Eager, Brew Moore—worshipped Young's seeming languor and ignored his muscle. Sims was an exception, and his early style had a tough, bounding quality that has gradually been softened by Ben Webster's rhapsodic approach to melody. But Sims' early style has stuck in his listeners' heads, and he is praised too much as a "swinger" and not enough as a lyrical player. (Sims is deceptive. When his fount of invention is low, he simply turns into a rhythm machine: his phrases rock, his tone grows heated, and his notes swarm. He is swinging, but that's all.) He should be studied at slow tempos, and particularly on the blues, where he is apt to coin phrases of such lyricism and tenderness and grace that one goes back to them again and again for sustenance and to quell disbelief. These phrases, generally only a bar or two in length, have a beseeching quality, and rightly so. They have never been heard before and, unless they are recorded, are likely never to be heard again. But several instances of this eloquence have been caught on five new recordings. These are "Nirvana: Zoot Sims/Bucky Pizzarelli with Special Guest Buddy Rich"; "Zoots Sims and Friend"; and three releases on a Norman Granz label—"Zoot Sims and the Gershwin Brothers," "Basie and Zoot," and "Zoot Sims: Soprano Sax." Pay heed to the beginning of Sims's third chorus on the slow "Blues for Nat Cole" ("Basie and Zoot"), in which he plays a high, crooning phrase, and to the bold total improvisation launching his solo on "Mean to Me." And listen to the falsetto that states the melody on "Gee Baby, Ain't I Good to You" ("Nirvana") and to the opening of his melodic embellishments on "Wrap Your Troubles in Dreams" ("Zoot Sims: Soprano Sax"). There are other felicities in addition to Sim's lyricism: Basie's rollicking stride piano on "Honeysuckle Rose," and his breeze-in-the-elm organ on "I Surrender, Dear"; and much of the "Nirvana" album, which has some delicate Buddy Rich drumming, beautiful husky Sims on "A Summer Thing," and four Sims-Pizzarelli duets (of which there are eight more on "Zoot Sims and Friend"). The album given over to Sims's soprano, an instrument added to his stockroom several years ago, is surprising. He stays in the lower register and avoids much of the soprano's piping tendencies. He also stays pretty much in tune. The Gershwin album is of note only because it is a superb example of Sims' swinging hard and becomingly (he is accompanied by Oscar Peterson, Joe Pass, George Mraz, and Grady Tate) and saying almost nothing.

# Dexter

It wasn't easy to be an aspiring saxophonist in the early forties. There had been few choices until then about which way to go. Tenor saxophonists followed Coleman Hawkins or his best disciples (Chu Berry, Herschel Evans, Ben Webster, Illinois Jacquet, and Don Byas), and alto saxophonists studied Benny Carter or Johnny Hodges and checked out Pete Brown, Willie Smith, and Tab Smith. Then Lester Young appeared. Hawkins had championed an enormous cordovan tone, improvising on chords, and a foursquare rhythmic approach. Young, having learned a good deal not from Hawkins but, of all things, from three white saxophonists—Jimmy Dorsey, Frank Trumbauer, Bud Freeman—championed nothing. Indeed, his playing was almost anti-playing. His tone was light—it suggested soundless laughter—and he advanced a form of melodic improvising that, with its casual, long-held notes and easy selectivity, matched the new coolness of Billie Holiday and Teddy Wilson. No sooner had Young been absorbed than Charlie Parker appeared. Parker's tone fell between Hawkins and Young, and so did his improvisations. He worked with chords and melody, and eventually, as in his celebrated recordings of "Embraceable You," he passed through improvisation to the verge of a new *music*. Young had sidled into view, but Parker exploded. No one had ever heard such arpeggios on a reed instrument, such passionate, preaching blues playing, such avalanches of eighth notes. Faced with the totally dissimilar and equally attractive approaches of Young and Parker, what was a budding saxophonist to do? Tenor saxophonists followed Young and alto saxophonists Parker; adventurous tenor players also listened to Parker and adventurous alto players to Young. But a handful of saxophone players attempted to borrow a cup of this from Young and a cup of that from Parker, and to find a way between them. The most important was the tenor saxophonist Dexter Gordon, who is now fifty-three. Gordon's tone is hard and calculated, and resembles Parker's at its most careless, as do his occasional rhythmically congested clusters of notes. But Young has the upper hand in Gordon's work. Here, transmogrified, are the long-held notes, the horizontal improvisations, the vibratoless attack, and the way of biting his notes that Young developed in the forties.

Gordon came out of California, worked his way across the country and through New York, and disappeared into Europe permanently in the early sixties. He has become shadowy, and even legendary, and his current quick American tour is being greeted with reverence. Tonight the Village Vanguard resembled the night in 1961 when Sonny Rollins returned from his first and most famous retirement. Every handclap was a genuflection. Gordon's appearance doesn't discourage adulation. He is six and a half feet tall and has a long, Lincoln face. When he finishes a solo, he visibly withdraws from the world of improvisation by grimacing and baring his teeth, and he meets the applause by turning his saxophone on its side and offering it to the audience with both hands, like the country guitarist Ernest Tubb, who turns the back of his guitar to the audience at the end of his performances, revealing thereon the word "Thanks." Gordon's playing is an extension of his stature. His sound is big and his notes are big. He locks together giant cubes of sound in his solos, piling one on another until he has constructed a gleaming amphitheatre. He builds these edifices in a determined, almost harsh fashion, rarely missing a note, and finishes each phrase so that it has a clear, sharp edge. He plays few arpeggios, and the only vibrato he allows himself is slow and broad and dramatic. There is a lot of musical and physical ritual in Gordon's onstage work, and it tends to obscure the fact that he is a transitional figure who in the fifties helped to invent a tenor-saxophone style that has come to be called hard bop, and who helped get John Coltrane and Sonny Rollins going. Gordon's accompanists, all of them able and sometimes inspired, included Ronnie Matthews on piano, Stafford James on bass, and Louis Hayes on drums.

# Pops

E ach generation throws off its own cultural hybrids. These tend to be pretentious, expert, topically ingenious, addictive, and—when their novelty wears off—of some artistic merit. The most recent in jazz has been the Stan Kenton band. Its immediate predecessor, the Paul Whiteman orchestra, thrived for a decade and slowly subsided five years before Kenton's arrival, in 1941. The two groups had a good deal in common. Both were bombastic, well drilled, aurally hypnotic, and eccentric. Kenton believed that he was changing the course of jazz, and perhaps of American music itself, when what he was principally doing was providing dozens of jazz musicians with a unique finishing school, many of whose graduates would end up pumping away in Hollywood studios. His "innovations," as he called them, were overblown and humorless variations of earlier big bands, Jimmy Lunceford's in particular, and of the driest atonal music. Whiteman also attempted to be a cultural pivot, but in a far subtler way. He built a dance band into a first-rate orchestra of nearly thirty pieces, capable of playing symphonic music, light classical music, dance music, and big-band jazz. He didn't altogether satisfy the various musical communities—the classical boys found him "jazzy" and the jazz people found him starchy and unswinging—but he changed American music. He commissioned George Gershwin's "Rhapsody in Blue," and got Gershwin off to a start as a "serious" composer, to say nothing of helping to bring into being the best piece of music ever written about New York. He hired arrangers like Bill Challis and Tom Satterfield, who evolved pioneering harmonic patterns and instrumental combinations that were almost certainly studied by Duke Ellington and Don Redman and Benny Carter. And he gave a leg up to jazz soloists by exposing within the stately confines of his band Jack Teagarden, Mildred Bailey, Bing Crosby, Frank Trumbauer, Bix Beiderbecke, and Tommy and Jimmy Dorsey.

Gershwin has been thoroughly considered in the past five years and has reached an apogee with the uncut production of "Porgy and Bess" (he still needs a good, literate biographer, though), and now it is Whiteman's turn. Richard Sudhalter, the thirty-eight-year-old cornetist, Beiderbecke biographer, and jazz archivist, began reactivating Whiteman in England two years ago, with his New Paul Whiteman Orchestra, and he continued tonight at Carnegie Hall, with a concert called "Paul Whiteman Rediscovered." There were twenty-five musicians and six singers, and they performed "Rhapsody in Blue" and a couple of dozen of Whiteman's jazz-oriented numbers, among them "Sugar," "China Boy," "Changes," "Mississippi Mud," "Oh Miss Hannah," and "Happy Feet." Nine arrangements were by Challis and the rest by Satterfield, Lennie Hayton, Matty Malneck, and Ferde Grofé. The evening contained surprises. The "Rhapsody" heard was the original 1924 version done by Whiteman at its Aeolian Hall première, and it had an attractive leanness and directness. Three of the other numbers—"Singin' the Blues," "Runnin' Wild," and "Hallelujah"—were never recorded by Whiteman. The reed scoring during the evening was often astonishing: three alto saxophones on "Singin' the Blues"; four clarinets and a baritone saxophone on "Runnin' Wild"; and *two* baritone saxophones and a *bass* saxophone on "Changes." The band was admirable—the reed section had to double and redouble every four bars—and so were the soloists. Johnny Mince played Trumbauer with a jiggling intensity, and the old virtuoso Al Gallodoro did Jimmy Dorsey's circus alto-saxophone number "Oodles of Noodles" with a creamy brilliance that demonstrated what a beautiful instrument the alto saxophone is when played properly. Sudhalter handled Beiderbecke's solos with a combination of Beiderbecke's tone and logic and his own more modern phrasing and rhythmic attack. Larry Carr handled the Bing Crosby vocals with plenty of glottal stops, and the Rhythm Boys and the Whiteman Trio were done by Keith Nichols, Norman Fields, Bob Lenn, Art Lambert, and George MacDonald, who, sedate and furbished-looking, was with Whiteman in the early thirties. An unavoidable distraction: on numbers like "From Monday On" and "Happy Feet" the band tended to swing far harder than the original band could or would have. Most jazz musicians in the twenties hadn't learned to swing that way, and even if they had, Whiteman would have considered such abandon indecorous.

# 1977

## Erroll

Erroll Garner last appeared in New York at the Maisonette Room of the St. Regis in May of 1974. His playing was effulgent, and he looked as he always had—a short, gleaming, funny, cooking man, his black hair a mirror, his great parrot nose pointed into the winds of his invention. He rocked and grunted and hummed at the keyboard, and his astonishing hands—he could span thirteen notes—went like jackhammers. The ad-lib whirlpool introductions to his numbers, sometimes eight bars and more, seemed to have spread and deepened, to be complete manic compositions, and his four-four improvisations were joyous and intense. Not long after the Maisonette gig, Garner fell ill with pneumonia, complicated by emphysema, and, never having fully recovered, he died yesterday at the age of fifty-three.

Garner was an anachronism, for he was a true folk musician, who belonged with the great jazz primitives of the twenties and thirties. He was self-taught, he never learned to read music, and, like all masterly folk artists, he developed a style of such originality and presence that it became nearly autonomous. One bar was enough to identify him, and his style was so per-

suasive, and pervasive, that he influenced older pianists (Earl Hines), pianists
of his own generation (Oscar Peterson, George Shearing, Red Garland), and
pianists of the next generation (Cecil Taylor). Garner never finished high
school, and he was untroubled by the lapses of confidence and invention
which academic training often instills. Indeed, he was embarrassingly confident and inventive. The critic and record producer George Avakian
describes a Garner recording session for Columbia in 1953 "Erroll rattled
off thirteen numbers, averaging over six minutes each . . . with no rehearsal
and no re-takes. Even with a half-hour pause for coffee, we were finished
twenty-seven minutes ahead of the three hours of normal studio time—but
Erroll had recorded over eighty minutes of music instead of the usual ten or
twelve, and . . . his performance . . . could not have been improved upon. He
asked to hear playbacks on two of the numbers, but only listened to a chorus
or so of each, before he waved his hand." And Garner appeared equally at
ease in night clubs and on concert stages. He became the first wholly successful solo jazz performer. (Although he often appeared with a bassist and a
drummer, they were extraneous.) This was startling and brave, but it was
unfortunate, too, for his rare collaborations with horn players were
enthralling. In the fifties, Garner had been almost underfoot; in the seventies, he seemed to have receded from view. So this dazzling, unique performer was all but lost to a generation. Mary Lou Williams has said of
Garner, "Erroll came from my home town of Pittsburgh, and I first heard
him there in a little joint when he was fifteen or sixteen. One of my nieces
went to Westinghouse High School with him, and she'd told me about him.
He was like Art Tatum—all over the keyboard. He started coming to New
York, which scared him at first, in the late thirties or early forties, and he was
always in my house. When I was at Café Society Downtown, I'd get home at
four in the morning and Erroll would arrive at five and start playing my
piano. One time, I took him to a symphony, and he loved what he heard so
much that he rolled on the floor when he got back to my place, and then he
sat down and played the whole thing. He had that kind of ear. Another time,
he was playing here and he shouted suddenly, 'I got it! I got it!' What had
happened was he'd found that bum-bum-bum-bum four-beats-to-the-bar
left hand that he used the rest of his life. I tried to teach him to read once,
but it didn't work. After a while, he said, 'Ooooooh, Mary. I can't cut that,'
and he never learned. I also tried to get him to slow down and forget about
Art Tatum when he was starting out, and he did. Nobody influenced his
playing after that, and his style was completely his own, just like his fingering, which was built on a love of the piano keys. Partly, he worked his style
out so that he would never need bass and drums, which he didn't and partly
so that he could reach the public easily, which he did. But the style he played
in your house was wild and totally different. Erroll liked to laugh. He was so
comical you'd have to break down. He didn't like statics or arguments. If you
asked him about another musician, he always had a nice word. He never said

anything disagreeable about anybody. He was like a little boy, like a jolly kid of seven or eight playing baseball. And he was like Art Tatum, because he liked to hang out and play any raggedy old piano in any club or in anybody's house. He influenced a lot of piano players, and I think a lot of musicians were jealous of him for his success and all the money he made on songs he wrote, like 'Misty.' But Erroll didn't have time to let that bother him. He was too busy writing his songs in his head and playing the piano."

## Heretic

The run became fashionable in jazz in the forties. Propounded by Art Tatum and Charlie Parker and Dizzy Gillespie, the teeming run, ascending or descending, was taken up by every pianist, guitarist, trumpeter, and saxophonist. Some players used so many notes their solos resembled enormous glissandos. The individual note was sacrificed for babble, and silence, which allows music to breathe, vanished. Jazz began to sound harebrained. For a time, the trombone, alone among jazz instruments, resisted such baroque behavior. One of the most vulnerable of instruments, because of its technical oddities, its edgeless tone, and its lyrical propensities, the trombone had been a musical clown before being turned in the thirties into a poetic voice by Dicky Wells and J. C. Higginbotham and Lawrence Brown. But the young trombonists of the forties, envious of Parker's cascades, decided that the only way to get into the Bebop Club was to be a virtuoso. So they adopted a cool, nasal tone, stuffed their phrases with notes, and ran up and down their registers as if they were pianists or saxophonists. The grandeur of Wells and Higginbotham gave way to the cul-de-sac skating of J. J. Johnson, and then of Jimmy Cleveland, Urbie Green, Carl Fontana, and Bill Watrous. The new trombone virtuosity obscured the fact that the proper next step after Wells and Brown and Higginbotham *had* been taken. This was done quietly in the fifties by the brilliant and still largely unappreciated Jimmy Knepper.

A tall, diffident man with a small, closed face, Knepper was born in Los Angeles in 1927 and was playing the trombone by the time he was nine. He had some college training, and passed through the big bands of Charlie Barnet, Charlie Spivak, Claude Thornhill, Woody Herman, and Stan Kenton, and played in small groups with Charlie Parker and Gene Roland and Art Pepper. In 1957, he joined the first, and in many ways the most important, of Charles Mingus's seminars, and it was immediately clear that he had absorbed Higginbotham and Wells and Brown as well as the rhythmic and harmonic advances of Parker and Gillespie. Knepper had, and has, none of the dandyism of J. J. Johnson and his followers, nor does he blare or whine or shout. He has a loose, warm tone and a way of easing out his notes—even his occasional arpeggios—with an over-the-shoulder offhandedness. He seems to lounge when he plays. But his serenity is deceptive, for he is a subtle and complex trombonist. He is an epigrammatist of a high order. His phrases, choice and balanced and to the point, are smoothly linked so that entire solo choruses form an uninterrupted melodic line. His gentle tone resembles Lawrence Brown's, but he also shares Dicky Wells' delight in the inherent heresies of his instrument. Knepper's low notes are sometimes rude, his high notes wild. Plain in every phrase are the practices of Parker and Gillespie: the eighth notes, the ninth chords, the short, meteoric runs that start a split second late, the quirky bittersweet notes. Parker loved to open his blues solos with quick, shocking phrases, and Knepper will do the same. He will fashion a six- or seven-note announcement, its notes spread unevenly over an octave, so that they seem to bob and weave as they go by, and then pause, repeat the phrase, but with most of its notes altered a tone or half a tone, pause briefly again, and swing into an ascending passage topped with a small, high yell, followed by two low closing notes. He will start the second chorus with a double-time variation of his first-chorus announcement, pass through a low-curving note that ends in congested eighth notes, and, after a brief connecting slur, start a blue note, cut it off, drop in a couple of triplets, and plane into his third and final chorus with a series of ascending and descending notes, which he carries, with infinitesimal breaks, to the end of the chorus. His volume has risen and fallen almost imperceptibly all through the solo, and one realizes only at the end the urgency propelling each phrase. Some soloists wait for their notes; Knepper pursues his. The best improvisers of Knepper's generation are delicate and thoughtful, and demand close attention. Knepper's solos are propositions of musical beauty, not face-to-face pronouncements, and if you turn your ear they're gone.

Knepper's career has been evanescent, but he has been appearing every Wednesday and Thursday at Stryker's, where he is playing with Lee Konitz's Nonet. The group uses ensemble devices ranging from complex Lennie Tristano unison passages to mock-Dixieland tuttis, and it has a good, plunging full-voiced attack. The best thing about the group, aside from Konitz's marvellous fusion of Lester Young and Charlie Parker, is Knepper, who solos a lot and is wholly relaxed. He was especially commanding tonight on his own blues, "Birth of a Nation," on Konitz's arrangement of "Without a Song," and on a Tristano melodic line that, used as an opener, caught everyone with cold chops and sounded like an old Archie Shepp bee.

## Poet, Singer, Dancer

One of the incidental acts of the avant-garde in the sixties was the rediscovery of the soprano saxophone, a difficult instrument (pitch problems, mostly) that fell into disuse after Sidney Bechet's death, in 1959. John Coltrane is generally credited with

bringing it back, but he probably took it up because of Steve Lacy, a modernist who began playing it while Bechet was still alive. In 1967, Lacy moved
to Europe, and now—a forty-two-year-old with a delicate, almost transparent handsomeness—he has returned for a short visit, and appearances downtown at The Kitchen, Environ, and Ali's Alley, where he played tonight.

Before Lacy went abroad, he gave an interview that was printed in *The
Jazz Review*. Lacy said:

> [Music] can be regarded as excited speech, imitation of the sounds of
> nature, an abstract set of symbols, a baring of emotions, an illustration of
> interpersonal relationships, an intellectual game, a device for inducing
> reverie, a mating call, a series of dramatic events, an articulation of time
> and/or space, an athletic contest. . . . A jazz musician is a combination
> orator, dialectician, mathematician, athlete, entertainer, poet, singer,
> dancer, diplomat, educator, student, comedian, artist, seducer. . . . and
> general all-around good fellow.

Lacy practices what he preaches. His playing tonight was excited, bucolic,
abstract, emotional, intellectual, seductive, dramatic, and spatial. It demonstrated that the jazz avant-garde is refining itself. The relentless roars and
screams and shrieks of the sixties—purposeful rude black jungle noises—
have been muted and clarified, or simply discarded. The avant-garde has
brought back some of the old verities of jazz in new dress: lyricism, form,
the domestic emotions. Like the trombonist Roswell Rudd, Lacy came up
in Dixieland and swing bands and then passed through the nimbuses of
Cecil Taylor and Thelonious Monk. Lacy has a full tone, his pitch is
steady, and he is facile. (Staying in tune doesn't mean much in Lacy's
music, because keys and tonal centers have all but vanished. However, one
can judge pretty well after a time whether or not a musician is playing what
he wants to play.) Most of the first number consisted of long stretches of
semi-atonal ensemble, in which Lacy and the alto saxophonist Steve Potts
played rough unison or antiphonal figures. The second piece had a steplike
theme, and Lacy soloed ruminatively and at length. He began in the middle
register and then moved up, revealing a sweet tone, and passed into a series
of falsetto figures, sprinkled with squeaks and trills. The third number
opened as if the two horns were warming up, and for a minute or so one
didn't realize that they had begun. After a windy alto solo, Lacy put forth
his musical credo. We heard dogs, birds, anguished abstractions, throat-
clearings, squeals, blips, and quacks. His work has a double effect. Its surface is resolutely amusical in the conventional sense. It offers a series of
semi-abstract sounds, repetitive circular rhythms, and obscure thematic
materials. It is a self-centered music that sometimes seems to move wholly
through shrouded inner landscapes. Yet Lacy plays with a fervency that

carries within it the lyricism and daring we sensed when Armstrong and Parker and Taylor first arrived.

## Anthony Braxton

**G**rass will never grow on Anthony Braxton. Tonight, the clarinettist, saxophonist, and elaborate, revolving composer-arranger appeared in a concert at Town Hall in the new ingenuously egoistic mode: by himself. He came on after an hour and five minutes by the Revolutionary Ensemble, which was in a fragmented, doubling mood, and he blew six nameless alto-saxophone "numbers," each differentiated from the last only by texture, dynamics, and levels of intensity. One febrile number was based on two notes, short and long. Another had a gliding melody knotted with staccato dissonances. Still another was subtoned. Braxton toyed with breath, exuding notes that remained zephyrs or that crystallized briefly before becoming breath again. It was an intense piece, and suggested a man trying to move a piano silently through a sleeping house. The last number started as a formal exercise full of trills and high, bowing notes and turned into a parade of squeaks, quacks, grindings, clicks, grunts, and shrieks. Here and there, Braxton sounded exactly like Benny Carter. He displayed the same thoroughbred tone, the same slightly stiff rhythmic approach, the same high-collared intensity, but he did it without any of the conventional musical devices (keys, harmony, time).

Braxton has been turning out albums, too. The most recent are "Anthony Braxton: Duets 1976 with Muhal Richard Abrams" and "Anthony Braxton: Creative Orchestra Music 1976." The duets are lyrical, spiky, conventional, disturbing, and funny. "Miss Ann," by Eric Dolphy, "Nickie," by Braxton and Abrams, and Scott Joplin's "Maple Leaf Rag" are nearly straight readings, with Braxton playing the melody on clarinet and alto saxophone and Abrams pumping chords.

But

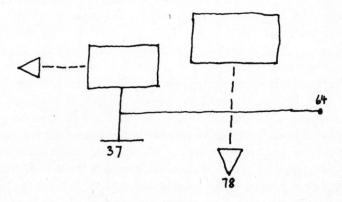

and

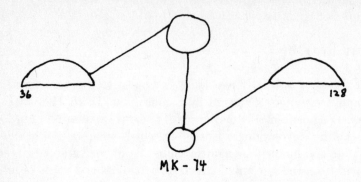

(as Braxton likes to designate his pieces) are jagged exercises, full of Cecil Taylor musings by Abrams, Braxton's Benny Goodman–toned clarinet, and carpenter noises.

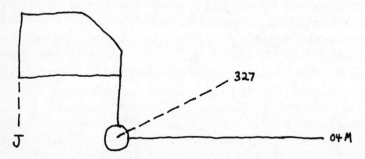

is taken up for the most part with a single note repeated five times: one one one one-one. Braxton plays the figure on his contrabass saxophone, which has a palatial bottom range that he barely taps, and Abrams is in unison. Braxton improvises while Abrams continues the figure. Abrams solos, using long melodic lines that keep running off the edge of his solo, and Braxton huffs in the cellar. Little bits of melody appended at either end of the piece offer some relief, but the rest of it recalls the boogie-woogie "train" pieces minus their lyricism.

There are six numbers in the "Creature Orchestra" album, all titled with Braxton's geometric devices, and they are done by slightly different big bands, which include such avant-gardists as Dave Holland, Kenny Wheeler, George Lewis, Roscoe Mitchell, Leo Smith, Abrams, and Warren Smith as well as such older-styled men as Seldon Powell, Cecil Bridgewater, Jack Jeffers, and Jon Faddis. Fletcher Henderson's concept of the big band as an augmented New Orleans ensemble of trumpet-clarinet-trombone-rhythm playing syncopated riffs and antiphonal passages broken by short solos lingers on, but Braxton is doing some serious tinkering. (So is the tenor saxophonist Sam Rivers, who likes ensembles in which the sections war har-

monically while sliding back and forth in overlapping layers, and likes double—or simultaneous—improvisation, an attractive practice that has frightened improvisational egos for decades.) On the second track of the first side,
Braxton breaks the band up and sends it wandering, but we always know
pretty much where everyone is from the periodic gongs, bass pluckings,
bells, cymbals, mosquito sounds, synthesizers, and wind sounds. On the last
track of the same side, the band plays a medium-tempo march that goes
awry about a third through. The rhythm disintegrates, the key center slides
away, a piccolo trumpet solos, and ostinato figures chase each other. There
is a stop-time section; then a clarinet and an alto saxophone improvise
together and are followed by a trombone that sounds like Kid Ory. The
clarinet reappears against a background riff, and the piece shifts back into a
straight march, with Faddis soloing above the ensemble. The best effort on
the second side of the album was apparently inspired by Duke Ellington. It
is latter-day Ellington seen in a distorting glass. The sections are quavery
and discordant, and the rhythmic emphases stagger. A contrabass-saxo-
phone solo pitted against an ostinato piano figure echoes, however surrealis-
tically, Harry Carney and Ellington's duet on "La Plus Belle Africaine," and
a good rangy Kenny Wheeler trumpet solo soars appropriately over Braxton's kindly, lumbering Ellington devices. Good parody is an exercise in
waspishness. But it is also a way of saying goodbye with affection and humor.

## Bach Lunch

Two superior pianists grew in Art Tatum's garden in the late forties. They were the Canadian Oscar Peterson
and the Englishman George Shearing. Peterson developed a technique,
which eventually became his very style, just as Buddy Rich's had become his.
Peterson exploded into his solos from his opening melodic choruses. The
"virtuoso" sign flashed incessantly, and it hid the fact that the chief content
if his solos was packed into their first eight or ten bars; what came after was
largely ornamentation and hyperbole. Shearing took a subtler course. He
put together a succession of exceptionally smooth quintets, made up of
vibraphone, guitar, bass, and drums, and he continually stepped back for his
sidemen or melted into the creamy ensembles. After a time, one listened to
the quintet rather than to Shearing, compelling though his bits of icing
were. Peterson, framed only by his various loose trios, swelled, while Shearing, embedded in a suave collective of first-class musicians, receded.

Shearing, who is at the Café Carlyle with the bassist Victor Gaskin, was
born blind, and he has developed agile defenses. Among them is a sense of
humor that includes practical jokes, nonsense, and puns. He explained
tonight at the Café that Bach, of whom he is exceedingly fond, had twenty
children, and Mrs. Bach, in order to circumvent having so many children
home from school for lunch, had invented the "Bach lunch." Later, he

announced that he had grown tired of song titles with the word "love" in them, and had taken to mentally substituting the word "lunch," which resulted in such pleasant turns as "Lunch Walked In," "Feel Like Making Lunch," and "Lunch Is Everywhere." He is a tough, delicate, intelligent man, and during the silent minute when he sizes up his audience from the piano just before his first set one can almost hear his senses moving through the room. Such a man would not be apt to lay his piano playing on. Indeed, his style, quintet or not, is elusive. He came to attention in the mid-forties, when no fewer than five pianists held the stage—Art Tatum, Teddy Wilson, Nat Cole, Erroll Garner, and Bud Powell—and he is forever tipping his hat to them, whether in a clump of Garner chords, a sixteen-bar Nat Cole melodic line, or a Tatum arpeggio complete with at least two keyboard sweeps. Shearing has a rich, harmonic sense, and his single-note melodic lines are crisp and exhilarating. His touch is feathery, bright, gentle. And he has one possibly unique quality. Jazz improvisers tend to re-create their materials in their own image. A classic example is Coleman Hawkins's 1939 record of "Body and Soul." Before Hawkins, it was simply a torch song left over from 1930. But Hawkins filled it with his special urgency and eloquence. He blew the song tight, and one can no longer hear it without also hearing Hawkins's version in the background. Shearing, his improvisations notwithstanding, finishes what a song's composer set out to do. Tonight, he played John Lewis's "Django" so that its stubborn, complex melodic structure took on—for the first time in memory—a melancholy, lullaby quality. He made "Django" an evening meditation on the great guitarist. He did the same thing for Garner's "Misty." It became a cheerful ballad, and three-dimensional Garner—not a parody but a distillation. One was surprised to look up midway and discover not Garner but Shearing, with his big, swinging face, his dark glasses collecting the light, his chin plunging down-right, down-right, down-right.

## Mary vs. Cecil

The Hines tradition, in the person of Mary Lou Williams, and the avant-garde, in the person of Cecil Taylor, collided in Carnegie Hall tonight, and it was no contest. That the two pianists agreed to play together at all was surprising. It was Wyeth versus Picasso, James Gould Cozzens versus Nathalie Sarraute, John Henry Belter versus Charles Eames. Mary Lou Williams explained in a program note how this came to pass:

> I was booked to England . . . in 1969. During that time I went to Ronny Scott's in London and heard Cecil Taylor play. I asked Andrew Cyrille, Cecil's drummer . . . to introduce me to Cecil. This, of course, he did. I felt great warmth from him . . . Later when I was working in the Cookery in New York, Cecil came to hear me practically every night. To my sur-

prise he mentioned the inspiration I gave him to create. One night I said to him "let's do a concert together" and he agreed. And he gave me the beautiful title "Embraced."

The reports during the weeks before the concert declared that the two were rehearsing together and that all was harmonious. Mary Lou Williams is sixty-six and has been playing professionally for fifty years. She has displayed a hard, modern single-note attack since the forties, when she had considerable mother-hen influence on the young beboppers. She has not changed, except that she can, when she's of a mind, play rather far out, demonstrating advanced harmonies and almost atonal single-note lines. Cecil Taylor is forty-four, and his career is twenty years old. But he is an omnipotent, unwavering one-man avant-gardist, whose style engulfs. His arpeggios are made not of single notes but of chords played consecutively in both hands. He plays at staggering speeds and with an opaque intensity. His selections may last more than an hour, yet he never falters. He grew up in an Ellington-oriented household and reportedly once resembled Erroll Garner and Thelonious Monk; occasionally one catches glimpses of them in his playing. If he were to look back and Mary Lou Williams were to look forward they might meet.

Here is the concert: The two pianists come onstage at the same time. She is in an elegant navy-blue gown, and he is in white—a white watch cap, a white shirt, and white pants. He also wears dark glasses. They sit down facing one another at grand pianos whose snouts dovetail at center stage. He plays a low left-hand figure at once, and works his way quietly up the keyboard. She follows him with her left hand. He fashions light, sharp chords in the right hand, she returns to the bass, and the two voices back and fill nicely. Anticipation sharpens. He indulges in some mock stride in the left hand. A passage of offbeat chords follows from both. She offers blues figures in her right hand while he clumps up and down the keyboard. The volume rises, and he bends lower and lower. They keep glancing up at one another. Suddenly he explodes, loosing one of his descending chordal arpeggios—his hands blurred humps. She looks startled and drops her hands, and he fires another arpeggio, and pauses. She plays a tentative, lyrical single-note passage in her right hand. He grows more strident. She again takes her hands from the keyboard, then unreels a batch of tremolos, a gentle riff that lasts for a chorus, some flatted notes, and four bars of stride. She falls quiet and he erupts. The bassist Bob Cranshaw and the drummer Mickey Roker unexpectedly appear, looking as if they had the wrong address. They move between free time and a regular beat, but they seem to have come to her aid, and, emboldened, she throws more blues figures at the feet of some ascending Taylor chords, and the two arrive at a coda, which he plays. The intermission lasts almost half an hour. The first twenty minutes after their return are civilized. Taylor softly states an eight-note theme, Mary Lou Williams plays soft counterfigures, and a spell circles down. He moves through pools of Debussy and Ravel, and she adds quiet, affirming chords. But it does not last. Taylor's chords thicken and his arpeggios quicken. She seems to lose heart and looks as if she were sitting by the wayside watching a noisy parade. Taylor dominates the next forty minutes. He lays out just once, but when he returns Cranshaw and Roker do, too, and the music comes to a circus climax. Taylor leaves the stage immediately—not to return—and Mary Lou Williams plays a couple of numbers with the rhythm section. Her playing is certain and inventive, and the house digs in ravenously.

## Wizard

Albert Murray—novelist, sociologist, polemicist—is a subtle and original thinker on black matters who, as he demonstrated in "South to a Very Old Place," abhors black cant as much as, or possibly more than, white cant. He has a good ear for black dialects, and he is a skilled writer. But his new book, *Stomping the Blues*, is almost unreadable. It is several books: an appreciation, strenuously inflated to a celebration, of jazz (particularly of the blues and of music played for dancing, or what Murray calls the "Saturday Night Function"); an arch apologia for the music which would have had heft thirty years ago; and an argument that the blues and jazz belong wholly to the black man. Murray's language betrays him: "But blues performances are based on a mastery of a very specific technology of stylization by one means or another nonetheless. And besides, effective make-believe is the whole point of all the aesthetic technique and all the rehearsals from the outset. Nor does the authenticity of any performance of blues music depend upon the musician being true to his own private feelings. It depends upon his "idiomatic ease and consistency." If a musician is not true to his own feelings, that is immediately apparent. If he does not feel what he is playing, he is pretending, and what he is playing is not authentic. Performing the blues with "idiomatic ease and consistency" produces imitation blues. Jazz has stood easily on its own for a couple of decades. It has become the American classical music and needs no apologists. Nor can it be regarded any longer as a black music. Listen to the guitarist Jim Hall: "I've always felt that the music started out as black but that it's as much mine now as anyone else's. I haven't stolen the music from anybody—I just bring something different to it." And consider the admissions in recent years by such black musicians as Lester Young and Rex Stewart and Duke Ellington and Anthony Braxton of the effect that white musicians have had on their work. The opening section of the book is a facetious disquisition on the blues: what they are and how they can be at least temporarily forestalled by listening to blues music. But when blues music—especially the Kansas City variety that Murray reveres—performs this inestimable service, what *are* the emotions it releases? What *are* those mysterious, bittersweet wellings-up that no other music evokes? Murray doesn't say.

*Murray mentions just one white musician in this strange, ill-conceived book. So it was not surprising when he turned up in the nineties as the unseen Wizard behind the at first all-black Jazz at Lincoln Center—and as a teacher and prop of its figurehead, Wynton Marsalis.*

## Tatumesque

A dam Makowicz (pronounced Makovitch), the highly touted thirty-six-year-old Polish pianist, opened at the Cookery tonight. He is a slight, good-looking man, with a small beard, a wide smile, and self-hypnotic pianistic concentration. Barney Josephson, the owner of the Cookery, introduced Makowicz, saying that this was the first time in all his years as an impresario that he had announced an act but that he could not help himself, since he found the pianist so moving. John Hammond, who was in the audience and who helped bring Makowicz over, reacted with such ecstasy to Makowicz's playing that each note appeared to be a personal gift. The applause brimmed and spilled over time and again. Makowicz has a dazzling technique and an unembarrassed passion for Art Tatum. His passion, though, is very nearly parodic, for he has mastered all Tatum's mannerisms—the encircling runs, the bursts of stride, the plethora of notes—and he uses them fulsomely. Each number swirls and races and plunges, and each is a baroque performance that sounds much like the preceding selection. But he lacks Tatum's touch and shocking harmonic sense. Instead of improvising on his materials (a mixture of old-fashioned standards and his own quirky compositions), he endlessly philosophizes on Tatum. Perhaps the reaction to Makowicz at the Cookery was caused by the sudden realization by those present of just how much they miss Tatum.

## The A.A.C.M.

*May 18th*

T he Association for the Advancement of Creative Musicians, a black musical self-help group, was organized in Chicago in 1965 by a thirty-four-year-old pianist and composer named Muhal Richard Abrams. Before long, it included the reedmen Joseph Jarman, Roscoe Mitchell, Kalaparusha, and Anthony Braxton, the trumpeters Lester Bowie and Leo Smith, the drummer Steve McCall, and the violinist Leroy Jenkins. It has continued to grow, and now numbers around a hundred and fifty. It is at once a music school, a finishing school, and a singular avant-garde movement. It came into being because of racial dissatisfactions, because its founding members were tired of the gray musical landscape of the early sixties, and because they had no place to play or be heard in Chicago. If no one else would listen, they would listen to each other, and grow from mutual esteem. In due course, various groups issued from under the wing of the A.A.C.M., among them the Art Ensemble of Chicago, the Creative Construction Company, Air, the Revolutionary Ensemble, and the countless Anthony Braxton combinations. But the A.A.C.M., like its spiritual ancestors of fifty years ago, has been slow to leave Chicago, and it did not venture to New York until 1970, when the Creative Construction Company gave a concert in a Greenwich Village church. Its provincialism is weakening. The Art Ensemble has spent a couple of years in Europe, and even appeared at the Newport Jazz Festival in 1973. The Revolutionary Ensemble is based in New York and turns up with reasonable frequency, as does Anthony Braxton, who has become well known in the past couple of years and was the first A.A.C.M. member to sign with a commercial label. But the first real invasion of New York by the A.A.C.M. began four days ago, when WKCR, Columbia's ingenious student radio station, initiated a week-long festival of A.A.C.M. music, which is being delivered in two parts: a ninety-hour non-stop broadcast of over a hundred A.A.C.M. recordings, unreleased tapes, and interviews; and four concerts, which start tomorrow night and will continue through four nights at Wollman Auditorium, on the Columbia campus. The broadcast, which ended today, was intelligent, thorough, and persuasive. Every principal recording by A.A.C.M. members was played (alphabetically and chronologically), and the music was beautiful, infuriating, savage, surrealistic, boring, and often highly original. It is primarily a "free" music, and there is a great dependence on instrumental variety. Most A.A.C.M. members play several instruments. Pocket trumpets, regular trumpets, and flugelhorns are common, as are bassoons, various tubas, and soprano saxophones, and there are percussion instruments from everywhere in the world. The recordings in the broadcast were spelled here and there by extensive interviews with A.A.C.M. figures, and here is a sampling, in paraphrase:

The A.A.C.M. has expanded the science of options for the music.

Keeping "the shout" in the music is what it's all about.

The A.A.C.M. sound? If you take all the sounds of all the A.A.C.M. musicians and put them together, that's the A.A.C.M. sound, but I don't think anyone's heard that yet.

Composition is as important as improvisation.

We are opposed to the word *jazz*. *Jazz* means nigger music.

In our meetings, we argue, fuss, get things straightened out orally.

Sometimes I take eight hundred pounds of instruments with me on a gig.

The A.A.C.M. introduces the musician to his complete self, and he joins for life.

The A.A.C.M. doesn't consider a creative musician an entertainer; his purpose is to enlighten—himself first and then the audience.

You take new musical steps and you refresh the public.

The broadcast revealed a determination to bring into being a new and durable music—a hard-nosed utopian music, without racial stigmata, without clichés, and without commercialism.

## May 19th

The origins of the A.A.C.M.'s music are reasonably clear. Paramount is the revolution set in motion in New York in the sixties by Ornette Coleman, John Coltrane, Eric Dolphy, Archie Shepp, and Cecil Taylor, and by the Jazz Composer's Guild, which was formed a year before the A.A.C.M. (The Guild, as far as I know, was never mentioned during the WKCR interviews, which is odd, but perhaps it was because of sheer Chicago hubris or because the Guild eventually became dominated by whites.) One also hears the methods and voices of Sun Ra and bebop and hard-bop, which many of the older A.A.C.M. members grew up with, and the receding sounds of Ben Webster, Coleman Hawkins, Fats Waller, James P. Johnson, Cootie Williams, and King Oliver. There are classical influences, too—Stockhausen, Boulez, Schoenberg, Berg, and John Cage. Revolutions aren't hatched in vacuums.

The first concert at Wollman began tonight with the Ajaramu Ensemble, which consisted of two trap drummers (Thurman Barker and Ajaramu), a reedman who doubled on percussion (Wallace McMillan), a conga drummer (Kahil-El-Zabar), a bassist (Felix Blackman), and a singing pianist (Amina Claudine Myers, an important presence in the A.A.C.M. firmament). Ajaramu started by himself and in time was joined by McMillan, and then by Amina Claudine Myers, who did some vocalise. Zabar, Barker, and Blackman appeared, and there was a lot of reed doubling. After a half hour—the conga drummer sailing, the trap drummers circling, Myers wailing and pounding, the reedman doubling—a sizable tumult was going. The volume fluctuated, and, just as a listener sensed the finale, someone had an afterthought and they were off again. The next group was a duo, made up of the trombonist and tubist George Lewis and the tenor and sopranino saxophonist, clarinettist, flutist, piccolo player, and bass clarinettist Douglas Ewart. Their music never stopped evolving, and frequently it sparkled. Ewart acted chiefly as a backstop off which Lewis, a tall, champing, cherub-faced twenty-two-year-old dressed in giant overalls, bounced an endless array of growls, glisses, slurs, harrumphs, cries, tremolos, roars, and whispers. Although the two musicians appeared to be reading, they played with a freshness and spontaneity that seemed improvised. The closing group was an all-star trio—a Charlie Parker/Dizzy Gillespie/Bud Powell group—that included Anthony Braxton, Leroy Jenkins, and Leo Smith, and it, too, appeared to read everything. The last of its three numbers had soft lyrical passages in which the voices talked away a summer's afternoon; agitato passages full of staccato alto saxophone and trumpet bursts; and a couple of Braxton clarinet statements, wherein he demonstrated a flawless tone and technique. But there was not enough of Jenkins's violin. The trio had a contrapuntal clarity that opened all sorts of musical rooms, some of them familiar and some only glimpsed before.

*May 20th*

The second concert began tonight with the Third Wave Sextet (odd echoes of the third stream and the *nouvelle vague*) which included Barker, Blackman, and Zabar as well as Ewart, the reedman Edward Wilkerson, and the pianist Adegoke Steve Colson. All are in their twenties or early thirties. Incense burned, and in the last number Zabar spent a good deal of time chanting, "Cree-a-tore, help us," pitching the first word somewhere around middle C and the next two a couple of tones lower. Aside from what appeared to be an attempt in the second number to get two complex rhythms going at once, the music was fairly safe. The last number had a regular beat, and there was a good deal of improvisation. Ewart showed again that he is a first-rate musician and a good and intense improviser, especially on tenor saxophone and bass clarinet. Kalaparusha came next. Born Maurice McIntyre, he appears to be in his forties, and he admires Charles Parker, Dexter Gordon, Sonny Rollins, and such marble-toned players as J. R. Monterose and Johnny Griffin. His first four numbers were done a cappella on alto and tenor saxophones and included a couple of standards and the bebop blues "Disorder at the Border"; then he was joined by bass and drums. Kalaparusha is a fox. His saxophone solos, which were vibratoless and bold and straightforward, were framed by interludes in which he read verses about creativity and music and life and played some purposely inept acoustic guitar. His nonsense was a relief; the A.A.C.M. music has been largely humorless. Air, the final group, had Fred Hopkins on bass, Steve McCall on drums, and Henry Threadgill on reeds and hubcaps. Hopkins was thunderously amplified, McCall's bearded face passed through hypnotic contortions, and Threadgill produced pleasing steel-drum sounds on his hubcaps. It was the freest group we have heard. There were long solos, and everything was improvised. It suggested the feckless, churning ensembles of Ornette Coleman at the Five Spot in 1960.

*May 21st*

The A.A.C.M. has a galactic sense of time. Its concerts begin forty to fifty minutes late, and intermissions last half an hour. The musicians wander on and off the stage in slow motion. Their solos are often Coltranean in length, and their numbers—in order not to mistakenly lock out a soloist before he is done—sometimes last a couple of hours. Consider the final group tonight, a septet led by Muhal Richard Abrams. It included Barker and McMillan and some newcomers—the bassists Leonard Jones and Brian Smith, the baritone saxophonist Mwata Bowden, and the trumpeter Frank Gordon. It played just one number: After a marching-band ensemble, the horns and bassists went offstage, leaving Abrams and Barker. Abrams played an immense solo, full of knotted chords and florid Luckey Roberts right-hand passages. The bassists and horns returned for an impassioned passage, backed by Abrams banging the keys with the palms of his hands. Abrams and the horns exited, and the drummer and bassists went through a long seesawing conversation. Gordon appeared, stuck a mute in his bell, and played some Miles Davis, accompanied only by the bassists. He switched to flügelhorn and played a blues. Then McMillan charged on, playing his tenor at top volume, and was eventually driven off by Bowden. The bassists and drummer appeared and reappeared, but along the way the bassists soloed and so did the drummer, who kept leading up to and backing off from a steady four-four barrage. Everyone assembled for an ostinato unison figure, and the music subsided with a string of tinkles and hums and pings. An hour and fifty minutes had elapsed. Most A.A.C.M. members belong to the first LP generation, and they think in twenty- or thirty- or forty-minute blocks. The 78-rpm generations were conditioned to three- and five-minute limits, which forced them into improvisational compactness.

George Lewis had preceded Abrams's septet with a champion solo performance. He hereby assumes the avant-garde trombone crown long worn by Roswell Rudd and the virtuoso trombone crowns of Albert Mangelsdorff and Bill Watrous. Lewis gives the impression that there are two or three of him onstage at once. He moves a lot: his right arm, or slide arm, flaps up and down, like a duck taking off; winds of emotion shake him; he tick-tocks his head. And his attack is constantly changing. No sooner has he completed one virtuoso bit of business than he is off on the next. These included four consecutive—almost overlapping—ascending arpeggios played in sixty-fourth notes and in different keys; a muted passage in which he seemed to play two melodic lines at once; an open horn passage in which, after having sprayed water into his mouthpiece, he sounded like an echo chamber; another muted passage (this time using a plunger mute), in which he mumbled gibberish through his instrument, all the while using his slide and seeming to blow out the words; and his runs and glisses and roars, done with relish and enormous humor. Lewis could easily have made the Ed Sullivan show. But, for all his cavorting, he is a serious musician. Several times during the heaviest chuckling he sneaked in legato melodic passages and whispering blues figures that were startling and beautiful.

The opening group, led by Amina Claudine Myers, was the A.A.C.M. at its weakest. The ensemble included two doubling reedmen (Ewart and

McMillan), two percussionists (Ajaramu and Kahil-El-Zabar), and a bassist (Leonard Jones). Their one number lasted an hour and ten minutes, and had long percussion passages, long reed solos, and some Myers singing (gospel-like) and piano playing (gospel, with bop petticoats).

*May 22nd*

What has come to be the A.A.C.M. repertory company (Thurman Barker, Brian Smith, Kahil-El-Zabar, Wallace McMillan, Adegoke Steve Colson) started the concert tonight as the Colson-McMillan Ensemble. It played with the earnest, youthful long-windedness that it had manifested in its earlier appearances. The numbers clocked twenty, twenty-five, and thirty-five minutes, and proved, despite the group's avant-garde patina, to be the same old hard-bop of the fifties and early sixties. It is the predecessor of the popular electronic salads of Herbie Hancock and Chick Corea and Freddie Hubbard. The A.A.C.M. brand could be equally popular, with its vocals, unison flutes, larruping timbres, and myriad percussion sections.

The festival was closed by the A.A.C.M. Orchestra, which has grown out of the experimental big band that Muhal Richard Abrams first assembled in Chicago in the early sixties. Tonight, it included eight reeds, two trumpets, two trombones, four percussionists, three bassists, three pianists, and three singers. The single number lasted an hour and a half. Everybody has been trying to figure out how to replace the old six-brass, five-reed, four-rhythm big band that wore out sometime in the forties. Mingus has put forward contrapuntal ensembles, and this has worked with ten or twelve pieces, but he has never shown us where to go from there. Gil Evans envisions the big band as a radiant sunset, and he pins down its colors with French horns and tubas and woodwinds. The Jazz Composers Orchestra makes large granitic sounds. Sam Rivers offers sliding sections that sometimes overlap and some-times collide, and he uses multiple soloists. All these inventors have one thing in common: the *group* takes precedence over the materials. The A.A.C.M. big band does it the other way around. Abrams presents his band with a series of ideas—rhythmic, melodic, harmonic, humorous—which suggests the kaleidoscopic images in "Yellow Submarine": sounds keep evolving and changing shape and color. The band may resemble a small group or a giant rhythm section or an old swing band or John Philip Sousa. Some of the chameleon images we heard tonight were Amina Claudine Myers's singing backed only by Martin Alexander's trombone, and Bernard Mixon's by bassoon, clarinet, and alto saxophone; John Jackson's bursting Dizzy Gillespie trumpet improvisation spelled out over a tightly muted Frank Gordon counter–trumpet line; a dense, almost turgid reed figure played against rolling drums; George Lewis's tuba accompanied by Brian Smith on pizzicato bass and Kahil-El-Zabar on gourd. Then, after half an hour or so, the band abruptly fell silent and everyone leaned back and started talking, as if they had been told to take five. It was massed vocal counterpoint. This lasted a minute, and ended as sharply as it had begun, with an abrasive ensemble figure that melted into a conga solo. An oboist and a soprano saxophonist joined Lewis's tuba while the band rested, and a baritone saxophone, an alto saxophone, and a bassoon began an angry discourse that dissolved into two voices and two flutes in unison. The second hour was announced by a splintering ensemble figure sandwiched between piercing trumpet sounds and a galloping rhythm section. This changed into a marching-band section with goose-stepping rhythms. An Ellington dream passage—all reeds, with an alto saxophone improvising on top—filled the air, and the marching band resumed. George Lewis got his chance, accompanied by a hefty ensemble figure, and he made the best of it. He played at an outrageous volume, and he used a thousand notes, his slide arm flailing. Then the band did some reverse showing off. To prove to all the squares and doubters out there that it, too, could play that old-fashioned jazz music, it switched into a medium-tempo blues, complete with a Mixon blues vocal and straightforward solos by George Lewis, Amina Claudine Myers, and Kalaparusha, who delivered a fine, pushing tenor-saxophone solo. The band swung and rocked, and, school being out, so did the audience. Then Abrams, who was conducting, decided that the point had been made. He leaned far into his reed section and made a rapid faucet-turning-off motion with his right hand. The band shifted into a chaotic collective roar, and crashed into silence.

Fortunately, the four A.A.C.M. concerts were underwritten by grants: the total attendance was probably about four hundred. But such events are carried by the wind, and in due course take hold.

# Newport 1977

*June 24th*

A perfect G above high C, a flawless arpeggio, a fusillade of one-hundred-and-twenty-eighth-note drumbeats, a trumpetlike tuba solo—all are virtuoso achievements whose flash and wizardry we rank with tall buildings and long bridges. Consider Sarah Vaughan, who opened the sixth Newport Jazz Festival–New York at Carnegie Hall tonight with her trio (Carl Schroeder on piano, Walter Booker on bass, and Jimmy Cobb on drums). It was her fourth straight appearance at the festival, but the wonders and eccentricities of her style remain wondrous and eccentric. Like Art Tatum, she falls between jazz and formal music. Her voice, which has four octaves and equals that of many operatic sopranos, comes in unequal parts: a rich middle section, a little-girl high register, and a sometimes vulgar, echoing bottom range. She uses her voice like a horn, and is a first-rate improviser, whose long, turning phrases rival those of Milt Jackson and Ruby Braff and Lucky Thompson. When she began, thirty years ago, she was a daring singer; now she is a virtuoso player, whose songs are merely catapults. Her arabesques engulf her lyrics, which become merely suggestive, no more intelligible than moos. Her ending tonight to a fast "The Man I Love" went like this: "I'm dreaming of the maaaaaaaaaaa Iiii looooooooowhooooooh." The keystone of her perform- ance was an ad-lib a cappella "Summertime," which she summed up in a thousand notes; Gershwin's lullaby was in there somewhere among the eight-bar phrases, the ruined lyrics, and the dense grace notes. She also did a lot of scat singing, by herself and with Clark Terry and Dizzy Gillespie, the latter of whom arrived onstage, unannounced. At one point, when Terry and Gillespie and Vaughan were all going at once, you could scarcely see the trees for the rococonuts.

*June 25th*

The singer Betty Carter, who opened the midnight concert at Carnegie Hall tonight, makes Sarah Vaughan sound like Kate Smith. She first sang with Lionel Hampton's big band in the late forties, and, proclaiming Billie Holiday her major influence, she has been a fanatic jazz singer ever since. Lithe and smiling, she pours around the stage, freezing here and there in Martha Graham positions, as if she were attempting to make her melodic lines three-dimensional. These melodic lines are surrealistic. She starts many of her phrases with the dying notes that Billie Holiday locked herself into in the early forties, and then she works tortuously through purposely off-pitch improvisations, full of jolting intervals and sour harmony. She is hard going, not because she is different and surprising but because she invariably seems to take the per- verse melodic turn. She pulverizes her lyrics, and when a "skylark" or a "spring can really hang you up" comes through clearly, it is a road sign glimpsed in the fog. Betty Carter is a better scat singer than Sarah Vaughan. She uses rests and sudden, rhythmic starts and stops, and she gives her consonants and vowels coloration. She must have studied Leo Watson.

*June 26th*

More singing, this time of a classic nature. Mel Tormé has grown into a big-voiced singer with a way of flaw- lessly shading and adjusting his attack. He also writes some of his songs and all of his arrangements, conducts his accompanying band, and plays drums and piano. He is a generalissimo onstage, and during his performance at Carnegie Hall tonight (among other songs, he did "Send In the Clowns," "Carioca," "Lulu's Back in Town," "Gloomy Sunday," "Mountain Green- ery," "Misty," "Blues in the Night," "Lady Be Good," and "When the World Was Young") he conducted Herb Pomeroy's band (which accompa- nied him) with one hand and his back; summoned Gerry Mulligan onstage by first smothering him with superlatives (superegos handle superegos best);

supplied a piano accompaniment to Mulligan's baritone-saxophone solo in "Misty" (Mulligan played better during his several numbers with Tormé than he did earlier with his own group); and dared to make a fast swinger of "Send In the Clowns."

*June 27th*

Double Image and the Revolutionary Ensemble were on hand tonight at Alice Tully Hall. Double Image is made up of two vibraphonists—David Friedman and David Samuels—the bassist Harvie Swartz, and the drummer Mike DiPasqua. All six numbers were originals, and all were short and full of double improvisation, instrument switching, and sudden starts and stops. Because of the group's collective treble tone, it resembled the Modern Jazz Quartet. More often, though, it had a floating, aluminum quality, and one expected it to take off—supported by vibraphone wings and driven by bass and drums—and fly easily and swiftly through the high-ceilinged hall. The Revolutionary Ensemble was less elusive. The Ensemble's subtlety, humor, and audacity make it one of the most inventive of the avant-garde groups, and tonight it raised another bold banner by playing without amplification. This gave it a pure, huddled sound that forced the audience to lean mentally forward. The rewards were plentiful: Sirone's long open-horn trombone solo, played against Cooper's one-two mallet beats on his tomtoms; an Oriental piece played by Jenkins on a small xylophone, backed by Cooper's sticks on gourds and Sirone's arco bass; all three on recorders and tin whistles and piccolos (birds during false dawn); Jenkins's violin against more of Cooper's softly thundering mallets; and the fine collective turmoil of their last number.

A flood of proficient, inventive alto saxophonists came along after Charlie Parker and Lester Young in the early fifties, and chief among them were Lee Konitz, Phil Woods, Sonny Criss, Sonny Stitt, Jackie McLean, Lennie Niehaus, Bud Shank, Herb Geller, Art Pepper, and the late Paul Desmond. Pepper worked for Stan Kenton in the forties and fifties, and then put in a couple of long stints in prison for drug violations. These vicissitudes have made him something of a legend, and he was added to the program at Tully tonight not because he fitted in stylistically but because he was making his first visit to New York in a very long time and there was no other spot for him. Despite his obvious nervousness, he played with conviction and passion. He was perhaps best in his own ballad, "My Laurie," done at a variety of tempos, and in a very fast "Caravan." Pepper began as a Parker admirer but has added John Coltrane, so that his playing now has a split-level effect. His solos first rise and fall through Parker patterns and then shift into Coltrane shrieks and yells. He was ably accompanied by Gene Perla on bass, Joe LaBarbera on drums, and Onaje Allan Gumbs on piano. Gumbs took several spacious solos; he has heavy hands and a tumultuous, swinging attack.

*June 28th*

George Wein appeared before the early event at Carnegie Hall tonight to announce that the idea for what we were about to hear—a string of great jazz soloists unencumbered by accompaniment—had been stolen from a concert given not long ago in Berlin. But Wein need only have looked to the New York jazz lofts, where unaccompanied soloists are common. And anyway, all the instruments at tonight's concert, with the exception of the violin, were percussion and rhythm instruments, which have long been accustomed to standing on their own. John Lewis led the parade with three of his own tunes and Thelonious Monk's " 'Round Midnight." Lewis does not have a notable left hand and he rarely performs without bass and drums. He wandered in Debussy circles, and when he moved into a regular beat it was in a tentative way. Gary Burton has been building abstract solos for years, but he did even better when he brought out his friend Steve Swallow, on Fender bass, for duets. They developed some excellent counterpoint, and Swallow, using his instrument with discretion, demonstrated again that he is one of the founders of present-day bass playing. Indeed, he easily edged his forebear Charles Mingus, who appeared with the pianist Robert Neloms for two brief numbers: a slow arco Ellington hymn, in which Mingus played flat, and a pizzicato "I Can't Get Started," in which he got a bamboo sound—probably the fault of his amplifier. Art Blakey delivered two drum solos; Buddy Rich or Max Roach would have been better. Joe Pass is the preternatural guitar soloist, and his four ballads shone with Tatum figures and rich harmonic imagining. Joe Venuti closed the procession, and it didn't sound easy for him; his style has leaned on rhythm sections for fifty years. But he got by with a pinch of this and a pinch of that. Then the soloists formed what amounted to a rhythm section plus vibraphone and violin and played "C-Jam Blues." Lewis, borne by Mingus and Blakey, played eight rocking choruses, outclassing everyone and making the old complaints about his unswinging stiffness even more incomprehensible.

*June 29th*

Toshiko Akiyoshi, the Manchurian-born Japanese pianist, and Lew Tabackin, the American reedman, formed the T.A.–L.T. big band four years ago in Los Angeles, and it appeared tonight at Avery Fisher Hall. (Sixteen strong, it is made up largely of young West Coast studio musicians.) Tabackin is the principal soloist, and Toshiko, his wife, leads and does the handsome arrangements, which incorporate *nō* songs, fancy section writing (the section as a soloist, in the Benny Carter manner), unusual voicings (flutes pitted against a bass trombone), and, more often than not, a rhythmic attack that suggests the early Woody Herman Herds. Tabackin first appeared in New York ten or twelve years ago, and it was soon clear that he was out of the ordinary. He had the complaining tone of the hard-bop saxophonists, but he also revealed an affection for Ben Webster and Paul Gonsalves, and for Sonny Rollins. Tonight he played at length at a variety of tempos, and each statement was exceptional. His respect for Webster and Gonsalves and Rollins is undiminished, and his tone has softened and widened.

It was a surprise to arrive at Carnegie after the Toshiko-Tabackin and find that the concert of four solo pianists already in progress was unamplified. There sat two concert grands on an otherwise empty stage. Teddy Wilson and Adam Makowicz had finished, but George Shearing had just settled down for what appeared to be his patented all-purpose night-club-and-concert program—"Dream Dancing" and "Greensleeves," done in a variety of styles; "Happy Days Are Here Again," done as a lament; "Lullaby of Birdland," done as Tatum and Bach; "Misty," done as a rhapsody and as Garner would have played it; and "Let It Snow," possibly done as a comment on the backstage air-conditioning. Shearing's playing was mischievous and perfect. Every note rolled easily through the hall, and the same was true of Earl Hines's sound, which followed. The Master did "I Cover the Waterfront," a long "My Monday Date," "I Feel Pretty," and "Jitterbug Waltz," and he showed off all the devices he invented fifty years ago—the little vibratolike tremolos, the arrhythmic escapades, the glittering treble figures, the elevator left hand. As is his wont now, he enclosed them in clouds of Jamesian pianistic syntax, entirely appropriate to the most august of American jazz pianists.

## June 30th

Eighteen years have passed since Ornette Coleman set off his revolution. Louis Armstrong fired the first revolution, in the mid-twenties, and it is instructive to compare what had happened to him a couple of decades later. His playing had grown somewhat lackluster, and he had been forced temporarily out of favor by bebop. Armstrong, bewildered and diminished-looking in photographs taken at the time, had been the king of jazz only ten years before and he must often have wondered what had happened. Coleman has suffered vicissitudes, but they have been largely self-imposed. He is a poor businessman and, like Sonny Rollins, he has hidden himself away for long periods. The improvisational, structural, and thematic freedoms he introduced are still being experimented with—by the A.A.C.M. in Chicago and here, by American expatriate musicians, by Europeans and Japanese, by the downtown loft musicians, and, most important, by Coleman himself. Despite, or perhaps because of, his various voluntary exiles, he is more famous than ever before, and he is playing with greater invention and discipline. Nonetheless, he must have been surprised by the full house at Avery Fisher tonight, for it wasn't long ago that he had difficulty filling half of Town Hall. He must have been surprised, too, that perhaps a third of those present were about five years old in 1960; they had come to hear a legend. What they did hear was brilliant and very real—or at least the first half was. Coleman surrounded himself with seven musicians (Don Cherry on trumpet, Dewey Redman on tenor saxophone, James Blood Ulmer on guitar, David Izenzon and Buster Williams on bass, and Ed Blackwell and Billy Higgins on drums), three of them (Cherry, Blackwell, and Higgins) carryovers from the old Five Spot days. They played five Coleman numbers, and each was a surging display of what he has wrought. "Name Brain" was short, and had brief jammed ensembles and solos by Cherry on pocket trumpet and by Coleman. Eighteen years ago, Cherry was a beanpole whose pants were a foot too short, and his playing had a flailing, uphill quality. Tonight, wearing a gold-threaded blue pantaloon suit, his bony face aged and secret, he played with emotion and fluidity. His solo in "Sound Amoeba," full of bent notes and long pauses, was of the highest lyrical order. Coleman was once a torrential player who believed in drowning his listeners. But his solo in "Name Brain" was played in a legato half-time. He moved through Benny Carter ascending-and-descending steps, and he stayed in the middle register. He used easy repetitive figures, and loose blue notes. His playing was the same in a long, harrowing lament called "The Black House," in the fast "Raceface," and in "Sound Amoeba," in which a long written ensemble was followed by eight to-the-point *a cappella* solos. Nearly as effective was "Mr. and Mrs. Dream." This consisted almost wholly of ensemble, whose gradually increasing intensity became almost unbearable, provoking Coleman, who was clearly seized by what they had just played, to say to the audience, "We'll take a little breather so that the dream doesn't wake up." In the second half of the concert, Coleman brought together two highly amplified guitarists, an electric bassist, and two drummers, one of them his son. They played loud modified rock, and Coleman just about disappeared from hearing. It is puzzling that Coleman, who has been working on this electronic group two years, considers it his highest achievement.

### July 1st

Count Basie, recovered from his heart attack and looking fresh and fit, appeared tonight at Carnegie Hall with his band, and in under two hours played a dozen or so instrumentals (among them vehicles for the tenor saxophonists Eric Dixon, Jimmy Forrest, and Eddie Lockjaw Davis, the trombonist Al Grey, and himself), and then provided accompaniment for Joe Williams (who sang "Every Day," "Goin' to Chicago," "Blues in My Heart," Jon Hendricks's "Evolution of the Blues," "In the Evenin'," and "Rocks in My Bed"), all the while piloting his ship from the keyboard with an occasional raised finger, an almost imperceptible nod, a sudden widely opened eye, a left-hand chord, a lifted chin, a smile, and playing background and solo piano that is the quintessence of swinging and taste and good cheer, even when almost nothing happens around it, as was the case tonight.

### July 2nd

The New York Jazz Repertory Company swung into action tonight at Carnegie with brief retrospectives of Roy Eldridge and Earl Hines. Eldridge declined to be present at his portion of the evening, and one reason certainly must have been a reluctance to hear others re-create solos that he himself can no longer play. And what majestic, scarifying solos they are! Joe Newman, Jon Faddis, and Jimmy Maxwell played the transcriptions together with precision and great rhythmic drive, and they included "Wabash Stomp" and "Heckler's Hop" (1937), his celebrated rampage on Gene Krupa's 1941 "Let Me Off Uptown," and his sedate "Little Jazz," made in 1945 with Artie Shaw.

Hines presided at the piano during his half of the concert, and he was accompanied by a hand that included, in addition to Maxwell, Newman, and Faddis, Bernie Privin and Doc Cheatham, trumpets; Eddie Bert, Janice Robinson, and Eph Resnick, trombones; Budd Johnson, Bob Wilber, Norris Turney, Frank Foster, and Cecil Payne, reeds; Carmen Mastren, guitar; George Duvivier, bass; and Bobby Rosengarden, drums. We heard "West End Blues" and "Weather Bird" from his Armstrong Chicago days and "My Monday Date" and "Apex Blues" from his Jimmy Noone Chicago days, and we heard big-band re-creations from the thirties and forties of such numbers as "G. T. Stomp," "Deep Forest," "Number 19," and "Father Steps In." But best of all were two piano solos with rhythm—"Rosetta" and "Blues in Thirds." In the last, Hines played three quick, irregularly spaced ascending chordal explosions and, a chorus later, four bell-struck single notes, placed just behind the best and scattered around middle C. He received a standing ovation, which caused one observer to say, "While they were standing and clapping, I was down on my knees praising God."

## Reissues

Though it is a deliquescent music, jazz has long behaved as if it were immortal, flinging its improvised beauties to the unattending air and prematurely consuming some of its most gifted adherents. Only the recording machine prevented it from remaining a provincial Southern music that in due course would probably have petered out. But recordings have never been perfect. The early acoustic ones made jazz piping and toylike—music for a Teddy bear's party. And current recordings are of such microscopic intensity that the mechanics of music-making—the clank of valves, the scrape of bows, the intake of breath—

often overshadow the music. Other shortcomings are the Arctic properties of recording studios; the habit that recording companies have of rarely keeping their goods in print long enough for people to find out they exist; the unbelievably decrepit record-distribution system (frontier women had an easier time ordering Paris gowns); and the Reissue Problem, which is aggravated by greed, whim, and a lack of foresight and taste.

Jazz began to be widely recorded in the twenties, and the first reissues appeared in the mid-thirties. They were doubly welcome, for they restored Bessie Smiths and Louis Armstrongs that had become rare and expensive, and they were generally reprinted with full discographical information, correcting the heedless taciturnity of the original labels, which offered only the names of the featured performer and the composer of the song. (Bessie Smith's original Columbia recording of "The St. Louis Blues" lists the composer, W. C. Handy, and "Organ and Cornet Accomp."—the "cornet accomp." being by Louis Armstrong.) Reissues came out on single 78 rpm's or in stout pasteboard albums that held from four to six ten-inch records and eventually included photographs and pioneer liner notes. In the early fifties, reissues were transferred to ten-inch and then twelve-inch LPs, and now transfers are being effected to tape. But it is only in recent years that recording companies have begun to reissue valuable jazz material properly: chronologically; in complete recording sessions; and with one or more alternate takes, which allow the listener to follow the musicians' thinking and inspiration (or lack of it). RCA, which used to start and abandon new reissue programs every other year (the Camden label, label "X," the Collectors Issue series, the Vintage Series), has reactivated its Bluebird label and is bringing out, complete, its Benny Goodman, Glenn Miller, Tommy Dorsey, Fletcher Henderson, and Fats Waller. And it has reissued for the first time all the small-band sides that Lionel Hampton made for Victor between 1937 and 1941, thus erasing more than twenty years of mistreatment it had subjected Hampton collectors to. This privation began in 1954, when the company put out a twelve-inch LP called "Hot Mallets." Nothing was right about it. It had twelve three-minute numbers instead of the sixteen that LPs could hold, the selections were erratic, and no more than two numbers from any one session were used (generally four were made). Two years later, Jazztone, a mail-order record club, leased twelve equally scatter-shot titles from RCA and sent them out as "Lionel Hampton's All-Star Groups." The following year, Camden reissued twelve Hamptons on "Jivin' the Vibes." One had been previously reissued, and there were no complete sessions. In 1959, another Camden, "Open House," appeared with twelve numbers, five of them repeats, and in 1961 Hampton was restored to the RCA Victor label with twelve titles on an album called "Swing Classics." Six of these titles were repeats, but the celebrated "Sunny Side of the Street" with Johnny Hodges and the classic "Haven't Named It Yet" with Red Allen, J. C. Higginbotham, Charlie Christian, and Sid Catlett were reissued for the first time. A decade passed. The silence was finally broken by the Vintage Series' "Lionel Hampton, Volume I," which had the first four Hampton sessions complete and in order. But Volume II never materialized, and silence fell again until the release of Hampton's collected works. (Between 1954 and 1971, six Hampton albums were issued, but they included only fifty-four of the ninety-one Hampton sides.)

Herewith some Arista and RCA reissues, with the Hampton set first:

"THE COMPLETE LIONEL HAMPTON" (Bluebird)

Hampton was both a curiosity and a strong musical force in the late thirties. He was born in Louisville, in 1913, and raised in Chicago, where, as a neophyte drummer, he (along with Sidney Catlett) fell under the influence of the Chicago band instructor Major N. Clark Smith and of such drummers as Zutty Singleton, Jimmy Bertrand, and Jimmy McHendricks. In 1927, he went to California and worked with Les Hite, Louis Armstrong, Buck Clayton, and Herschel Evans. He stumbled onto the vibraphone in 1930 and recorded on it with Hite and Armstrong, although he was still a drummer. (He had also picked up enough piano to be a good Earl Hines emulator.) In 1936, he took a band into the Paradise Club in Los Angeles. One night, Benny Goodman sat in, and he invited Hampton to record with the Goodman trio on vibraphone, and soon after to join the band, where he stayed until 1940. Hampton captured the public fancy immediately. He was the second black that Goodman had hired, and he was ambidextrous and a showman. He hummed and grunted, he threw his drumsticks in the air and danced on his drums, and he played lightning two-finger piano. (The regular pianist took care of the left-hand part.) Hampton's vibraphone style was loose and swinging, and had come in part from Hines and Armstrong and Coleman Hawkins. Hampton used a lot of loud pedal, he played on or near the beat, and he made his solos and those around him *go*. His drumming, in the fashion of the times, was frantic. He soloed mainly on fast tempos and crowded his beats tightly together. His speed was deceptive, and it made him sound like a virtuoso and hid his gifted, hard-pressing amateurism. His piano playing, though, has never received due consideration. He borrowed his two-finger attack from the vibraphone, and used it with passion and clarity. He carried off tremolos and staccato passages that no ordinary pianist could manage, and it is entirely possible that Charlie Parker and Dizzy Gillespie studied Hampton's pouring figures. Hampton played with joy: he knocked himself out and he mesmerized his musicians and his audiences.

Hampton was enough of a sensation to be asked by Victor in 1937 to lead a series of small-band recordings designed to compete with the Teddy Wilson–Billie Holiday series under way at Brunswick and to be an extension of Benny Goodman's Victor trio and quartet recordings. He took his first group (nine Goodman sidemen) into a New York studio in February of 1937, and his last one (eight sidemen from his fledgling big band) into a Chicago studio in April of 1941. He drew his personnel mainly from available big bands (he recorded in New York, Chicago, and Hollywood), and he often mixed styles and schools. He blended an Ellington horn section (Cootie Williams, Lawrence Brown, Johnny Hodges) with a rhythm section (Allan Reuss, John Kirby, Cozy Cole) drawn from Goodman, the Mills Blue Rhythm Band, and Stuff Smith's group. He combined musicians from Goodman, Basie, and the John Kirby band, and musicians from Louis Armstrong, Goodman, and Roy Eldridge. On one date, he assembled the whole spectrum of 1939 jazz, with Benny Carter, Edmond Hall, Coleman Hawkins, Joe Sullivan, Freddie Green, Artie Bernstein, and Zutty Singleton. On another, he played all-star, by inviting Carter, Ben Webster, Hawkins, and Chu Berry, who were accompanied by a Benny Goodman–Cab Calloway rhythm section. One of his most successful sessions was drawn entirely from the Earl Hines band of 1938. The records were not haphazard. Most have head arrangements, some have almost sumptuous scores (Benny Carter as arranger), and even those that are largely jammed have their own order and logic. Not surprisingly, the records are built around Hampton as vibraphonist, pianist, drummer, and vocalist, but ample solo space is reserved for his guests. As a result, many of the Hampton records are among the longest of their time—several in the album run close to three and a half minutes. The delights in the album include all the accompanying and all the solo work of Jess Stacy and Clyde Hart, who were Hampton's principal pianists during his first two years of recording (the records are uncommonly well made, and Hart's accompaniment to Hampton's vocal on "I'm Confessin'" is brilliantly clear); the ease and irresistible swing of the Hart–Charlie Christian–Artie Bernstein–Catlett rhythm section on "Haven't Named It Yet" and "I'm on My Way from You," which has one of Red Allen's most lyrical trumpet solos; Coleman Hawkins's pressing solo on "Singin' the Blues"; Cootie Williams's tearing crescendo growl solo and Sonny Greer's fine snicketing four-bar drum break on "Ring Dem Bells"; the duet by Lawrence Brown and Harry Carney on "Memories of You"; "Rock Hill Special," with its oblivious, plunging Hampton piano; the stampeding "Gin for Christmas," a reworking of "Bugle Call Rag" in which Hampton's drumming and Ziggy Elman's bar-mitzvah trumpet produce go-man-go shouts during the last chorus; and Nat Cole's lovely piano solo on "Blue (Because of You)."

The best of the recordings were done between 1937 and 1939. After that, Hampton was busy getting his own big band going, and the novelty had worn off. The best are also surprisingly and resolutely old-fashioned. If Teddy Wilson and Billie Holiday (abetted by Lester Young and Jo Jones and Buck Clayton) were pointing in new directions on their Brunswick dates, Hampton was working strictly within the New Orleans-dominated tradition of Zutty Singleton and Louis Armstrong. There is a hot, heavy atmosphere on a lot of the recordings, and the rhythm sections are almost always foursquare and relentless. (Compare any of the 1938 Hamptons with the Young–Clayton–Walter Page–Jo Jones Kansas City Six sides from the same year: the Hamptons barge, and the Kansas City Sixes fly.) But Hampton's Victor recordings provided a brilliant climax for a form of jazz that would soon be set aside by Young and Charlie Parker.

"THE RED NORVO TRIO WITH TAL FARLOW AND CHARLES MINGUS" (Savoy)
A pointillistic distinction: It was apparently Red Norvo, and not Lionel Hampton, as the histories have long claimed, who first played the vibraphone in jazz. Norvo played it in 1928, soon after the Deagan company invented its Vibra-Harp, but he did not switch to it full time until the forties, preferring the small, neat sound of the xylophone. Even if Norvo had chosen to stay with the vibraphone, it is doubtful whether he would have eclipsed Hampton's omnipresence. Norvo was too subtle and too light on his feet to be a founding father. Instead, he was an ingenious musical designer who invented a succession of streamlined groups, each far enough ahead of its time to be copied and then obscured by its imitators. In the mid-thirties, he put together the first working non-Dixieland small band. It was a soft, swinging octet that used the honeyed arrangements of Eddie Sauter. It was the first working group to have a full-time jazz singer: Mildred Bailey. Norvo led various quicksilver groups in the forties, and was in one of Benny Goodman's best small bands. He starred with Woody Herman's First Herd in 1946, from which he extracted a chamber group for some recordings that were harmonically advanced versions of his group of ten years before. Then, in 1949, he organized a daring trio that certainly must have passed within the hearing of John Lewis and Milt Jackson when they were toying with the notion of the Modern Jazz Quartet.

Its best edition had Tal Farlow on guitar and Charles Mingus on bass. Like all innovators, Norvo preferred malleable unknowns to stars. He found Farlow in a small New York club, and Mingus in Los Angeles. Norvo stepped off into space with the trio. What, he wondered, should a vibraphonist do behind a guitar solo, and what should a guitarist do behind a vibraphone solo, and how should either or both accompany bass solos— what, in short, should be done to keep the trio from simply unravelling? Keep soft and busy, he discovered. When Farlow soloed, Norvo supplied little islands of chords or suggestive runs, and when Norvo soloed, Farlow either kept time or played dreaming, behind-the-beat accents. Norvo and Farlow took turns shimmering behind Mingus's solos, and Mingus provided constant mushrooming support. The ensembles were generally set variations on the melody played in counterpoint or unison and were boppish in nature. Unlike most of the bebop groups, the Norvo trio did not dress other people's chords up with its own titles but used undisguised standards ("Night and Day," "Cheek to Cheek," "This Can't Be Love") and such fash-

ionable creations of the time as "Swedish Pastry" and "Godchild." The
Savoy reissue is taken from material recorded in 1950 and 1951, and it
makes several things clear. The Norvo trio preferred lightning tempos. It
was self-charging: Farlow seems to activate Norvo, who plays some
admirable solos ("Night and Day" and the three takes of "Godchild"), and
Mingus stirs both and, in turn, produces some of his best recorded solos.
The trio had a hot delicacy, and it seemed to spin its music out of the air
around it.

"THE COMPLETE FLETCHER HENDERSON, 1927–1936" (Bluebird)
All thirty-four of the numbers, good and bad, that Fletcher Henderson
recorded for Victor. The bad ones, presumably made to mollify nervous
A&R men during the early part of the Depression, have titles like "My
Sweet Tooth Says I Wanna (But My Wisdom Tooth Says No)." "Malinda's
Wedding Day," and "I Wanna Count Sheep (Till the Cows Come Home)"
and whiny vocals by Ikey Robinson, George Bias, Dick Robertson, John
Dickens, and Harlan Lattimore. The good ones, done between 1934 and
1936 by the last creditable Henderson band, are a crowd of solos by Roy
Eldridge, Coleman Hawkins, Red Allen, and Chu Berry, many of them
exceptional and all of them cushioned by Henderson's easygoing arrangements. Hawkins, not yet a chordal locomotive, was continually experimenting with time, delaying the beat, playing wild double-time passages, and in
general searching for the limits of four-four time. He was also trying on
different-sized tones. He displayed a hard tone, a heavy tone, a rolling tone.
He was the most closely attended musician in jazz, and each innovation
seemed to spawn a new style. Here, on "Hocus Pocus," are the origins of
Herschel Evans; on "Strangers" one hears the mold for Chu Berry. Henderson's bands, so unsuccessful commercially, were equipment-supply houses
for the rest of jazz. Eldridge's work sent Dizzy Gillespie on his way, and
Berry's (having tipped its hat to Hawkins) helped form Don Byas. Sidney
Catlett's drumming on the 1936 "Riffin'" must have been the model for
Alvin Burroughs in the 1938 "Down Home Jump" and "Rock Hill Special"
on the Hampton album. And, of course, Henderson's arrangements had a
good deal to do with Benny Goodman's ascension in 1935. Playing with
Henderson was the sine qua non of the big-band world. The scattering of
photographs in the album reflects this: everyone looks easy, elegant, refined.
Henderson sits at the wheel of a beautiful roadster, a snappy fedora pulled
down over his right eye, his expression bemused. Another picture shows his
1927 brass team in tuxedos and patent-leather shoes, and still another has
John Kirby and Walter Johnson in linen suits. There are a lot of white shoes,
and the poses are cool. It has been said repeatedly that the Henderson band
was never properly caught on records, and this must be true. Its recordings

tend to imply more than they state. But Eldridge, at least, is still at large, and
his power and snapping excitement are what the band was about.


"DON BYAS: SAVOY JAM PARTY" (Savoy)
Coleman Hawkins's influence didn't cease in the thirties. His offshoots had
offshoots, so that his genealogy, reaching down to the present, looks roughly
like this:

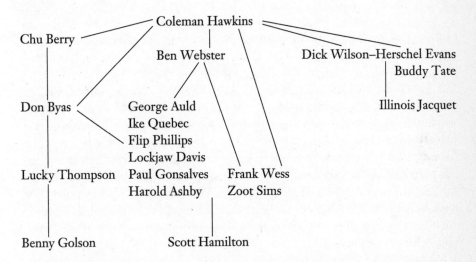

One of the most powerful of Hawkins' admirers was Don Byas, who died
in 1972 in Holland. Byas was born in 1912 in Muskogee, Oklahoma, and in
the thirties he became part of the same California scene as Lionel Hampton
and Buck Clayton. He arrived in New York in the late thirties, and landed a
job with Count Basie in 1941. He stayed with Basie three years and then
gigged around Fifty-second Street until 1946, when he moved to Europe for
good. Byas set down some momentous solos during his New York years. He
announced his presence by taking two choruses on Basie's record of "Harvard
Blues" which remain among the great blues statements. His tone outswells
Hawkins's, and the solo has a unique and insinuating legato quality. The following year, he just about matched himself on Basie's small-band recordings
of "Sugar Blues" and "St. Louis Blues." Then, in 1945, he recorded a furioso
work of art. He and the bassist Slam Stewart played an impromptu breakneck
"I Got Rhythm" to open a Town Hall concert, and Byas took nine choruses
that—volcanic, vortical, almost vicious—held the place of honor in Baroque
Hall until the arrival of Sonny Rollins, fifteen years later. (Byas's feat can be
heard in the "Smithsonian Collection of Classic Jazz.")
　　Byas's style was voluptuous. He put bones in Chu Berry's attack, and he
taught himself to think faster than any jazz improviser had before. His tone

was big enough to house all the notes he played, and he was a master of dynamics. He had a broad vibrato and liked big intervals and high, almost split notes that resembled adolescent voice breaks. His New York flowering coincided with the emergence of bebop, and he fitted in very well. In 1944, he was a member, with Dizzy Gillespie, George Wallington, Oscar Pettiford, and Max Roach, of the first bebop band on Fifty-second Street. He was a master of the jet tempos the boppers liked, he understood their harmonic stratagems sometimes better than they did, and he liked to completely alter the materials he improvised on. But Byas never mastered the irregular, suspended rhythms of bebop. He was locked in Coleman Hawkins's four-four box, and perhaps, being a man of ego, that helped send him off to Europe, where Hawkins's style was revered. Byas recorded around a hundred titles in New York, and thirty-two are on the Savoy reissue. The best of his colleagues are Charlie Shavers, another encyclopedist; Clyde Hart, Byas's buddy, whose death in 1945 may have been another reason for his departure; Slam Stewart; and Emmett Berry. "Riffin' and Jivin'," "Don's Idea" (two takes), "Bass C-Jam" (two takes), "How High The Moon," and "Cherokee" are superior up-tempo Byas. About half the numbers are ballads of various speeds: here is Byas the voluptuary, the heart-render, the worshipper of softness. Byas came back to this country just once—in 1970, when he appeared at the Newport Jazz Festival. He played well, but the response was lukewarm. His beautiful, unabashed romanticism had gone out of fashion.

# Breeding

John Hammond's autobiography, *John Hammond on Record,* is the reverse of what one expected. It is frank and buoyant about his family and background, and low-voiced and defensive about his place in jazz music and civil liberties. Moreover, the book, written in collaboration with Irving Townsend, is delivered in a style-less, store-bought monotone that is the direct opposite of Hammond's ebullient, superlative-spattered self.

Hammond was born in 1910 in a Vanderbilt mansion on East Ninety-first Street, which still looks down on Andrew Carnegie's Georgian house across the way. The mansion had, Hammond tells us, six stories and two cellars, a ballroom seating two hundred and fifty, two elevators, and a staff of sixteen. It also had gleaming parquet floors, eighteen-foot ceilings, and immense marble fireplaces. But Hammond, already a closet liberal, took pains when he was at St. Bernard's, a nearby boys' private school, to enter the house by a circuitous back route, so that no one would know where he lived. His father came from the Midwest and was the son of a Union general. He became a wealthy banker, railroad man, and lawyer, but the boss was Hammond's mother, Emily Vanderbilt Sloane, a great-granddaughter of

Commodore Cornelius Vanderbilt, and an enormously wealthy woman. She still engages Hammond. He says of her:

> She was both fascinated and repelled by the high society which was her natural station, and she soon fashioned her own way of living with it. It was not possible for her to rebel politically as a young girl, and she knew little of politics anyway. But through religion she could rebel socially. She would not flaunt wealth as her mother did. Instead she would impose, first upon herself and later upon her family, a code of moral behavior and responsibility which would serve as an example to her small world of the duties of the blessed. She was a beautiful woman, tall for her time, and with the erect bearing the nineteenth century required of elegant ladies. There was no arrogance in it, simply evidence of good breeding. Vanity was lavished only on her hair and ankles. She had her hair—a woman's "crowning glory"—cared for regularly by the only Jewish woman she knew, Mrs. Block, whom she described as a Hebrew. She cared little for clothes, never wore a dab of powder in her life, and would not allow lipstick to be brought into her house. Her only formal education was private tutoring by Miss Spence; her parents did not approve her mixing with even the uncommon herd in private schools. Like all Vanderbilt women, with the exception of my sister Adele, she did not go to college.

She never drank or smoked. She did not approve of Democrats, and her knowledge of racial minorities was limited to fantasies. "I want you to know that everybody is born alike," she told Hammond. "But with Negroes their skulls harden when they are twelve. There *is* a difference." She played the piano, recited poetry and the Bible, and believed in an afterlife. She did not dance or swim, and was physically inhibited—unlike her mother, Emily Thorne Vanderbilt, who was "extremely proud of her bosom and very daring for her day about revealing it." Hammond's mother was a soft touch and a philanthropist, who toward the end of her life (she lived to be ninety-six) became so involved with Moral Re-Armament that he and his sisters feared for the family fortunes and were forced to intercede.

Hammond switched to Browning from St. Bernard's, and until he went away to Hotchkiss he "lived the life of a coddled little rich boy, tolerant like my mother of weaknesses and sins in others, intolerant of any fall from grace in myself, ignorant as Mother was of the world beyond our island of social and financial equals, except to realize that there were people out there who were not like us. I shared her religious fervor, her prejudices, and her saintly resolve to set an example for others, then to forgive them when they failed to measure up to it. Like her, I was already the reformer, fired with her energy, certain in the right, oblivious to physical infirmities [his mother had become a Christian Scientist] which all right-minded flesh could overcome, an inheritor of the guilt and therefore the obligations of wealth." Hotchkiss, in the persons of its headmaster and a senior English teacher, both the sort of provincial Puritan liberals who have aerated New England prep schools for seventy years, turned Hammond around. He entered Yale in the fall of 1929 but within two years had dropped out, because of two attacks of hepatitis and an already consuming interest in jazz and black people. (He recovered from his second bout of hepatitis at the Millionaires' Club in Georgia, where he would bring the *Chicago Defender*, the *Baltimore Afro-American*, and the *Pittsburgh Courier* into the dining room, to the astonishment of the black waiters.) In September of 1931, he produced his first recording, for Columbia, with the pianist Garland Wilson, and shortly afterward he moved from Ninety-first Street to an apartment on Sullivan Street.

By this time, Hammond was well grounded musically. He had taken up the violin at eight (he later switched to viola), and had been exposed to improvised music at twelve, when he heard Paul Specht's Georgians in London. He had already started reading *Variety* and collecting records, and soon he was sneaking out to shows. Hotchkiss let him come to New York to pursue his violin lessons, after which he got into the habit of dropping in at the Alhambra Theatre or the Club Saratoga or Smalls Paradise in Harlem to hear the likes of Bessie Smith, Duke Ellington, Sidney De Paris, Red Allen. J. C. Higginbotham, and Bill Coleman, and he continued these adventures while he was at Yale. Before long, he had become an impresario out of sheer pluck, and as the thirties went on his accomplishments grew dazzling. He "discovered," helped discover, or furthered the careers of Count Basie, Billie Holiday, Charlie Christian, Teddy Wilson, Meade Lux Lewis, Pete Johnson, Albert Ammons, Chu Berry, Benny Carter, Benny Goodman (who married Hammond's sister Alice), Red Allen, Jo Jones, Lionel Hampton, Helen Humes. Lena Horne, Fletcher Henderson, Gene Krupa, Israel Crosby, and more. He made bellwether recordings, for Columbia and its affiliated labels, with Henderson, Holiday, Goodman, Bessie Smith, Wilson, Mildred Bailey, and Basie. He broke the color line repeatedly by putting together mixed bands for in-person appearances, radio broadcasts, and recordings. (Hammond covered the Scottsboro trials in the early thirties for *The Nation*, and he joined the board of directors of the N.A.A.C.P. in 1935. He was never entirely happy with the organization, feeling that it was too conservative, and he resigned in 1967.) He also put on the two invaluable "Spirituals to Swing" concerts at Carnegie Hall in 1938 and 1939, and had recordings of them released on the Vanguard label in 1959. Hammond had a quiet time in the forties, but in the fifties he engineered a superb series of recordings for Vanguard and Columbia around Buck Clayton, Vic Dickenson, Ellis Larkins, Ruby Braff, Jimmy Rushing, Mel Powell, and Jo Jones. And he has not been idle since, for he has also shepherded Mahalia Jackson, Bob Dylan, Aretha Franklin, Leonard Cohen, and Bruce Springsteen. Hammond's various emprises have sometimes obscured his larger accomplishments. He helped clear the way for desegregation. He showed

Americans that they had for their delectation an amazing new music that was largely the invention and the glory of American blacks. He changed the course of Western music by championing Basie and Holiday and Goodman, to say nothing of enabling them to have solid careers when they might not have had any. He got America swinging.

Hammond seems somewhat dazed by all this himself, for he puts little energy into recounting his exploits. He mentions hearing Lester Young when Young was with a faltering King Oliver in 1933, but he doesn't say where or how or what. He mentions making Bessie Smith's last records, but again gives us almost no details. He does reveal, slowly and unwittingly, that he does not understand (or sometimes even like) those musicians who have not needed his help or have rejected it. He favors Fletcher Henderson's Joe Smith over Louis Armstrong, which is like rating Utrillo over Picasso. He doesn't like Frank Sinatra, and he has mixed feelings about Duke Ellington, who kept him at arm's length. His attitudes toward Mildred Bailey and Red Norvo, who were sometimes his guidons, are oddly ambivalent. (He accuses Mildred Bailey of being jealous of Billie Holiday!) Some of his musical opinions are refractory, too. He declares that Coleman Hawkins reached his peak in 1933, when Hawkins, dispensing styles right and left, was just slipping into gear. He dismisses the admirable violinist Claude Williams, and he puffs the lachrymose, romantic Chu Berry. And, in a queer passage, he refuses to accept the new and seemingly watertight version of Bessie Smith's death advanced by Chris Albertson in "Bessie."

Hammond the enthusiast sums himself up: "It will always be difficult for me to sit still, to wait for a moment or a day before setting out to discover the world all over again. I am an early riser, among the first to buy each day's *Times*, and my daily armful of new magazines is as much my trademark as my crewcut. Since I first discovered Mr. Epstein's newsstand at Ninety-first Street and Madison Avenue I have never missed an issue of any periodical with something to say. This compulsion to see, to read, to hear everything as soon as possible, is as strong now as it ever was, and to be the first to know—or, certainly, never the last—is vitally important to me."

# Umbrellas of Sound

The pianist and composer Herbie Nichols died in 1963 at the age of forty-four. He was gifted, elusive, bedevilled. He made his living in Dixieland bands when, in truth, he compared favorably with Thelonious Monk and Bud Powell. Almost his entire mature recorded output was done between May of 1955 and November of 1957, when he set down thirty-two titles for the Blue Note and Bethlehem labels. The critics made much of the recordings, and for a time Nichols was petted and admired, but this didn't change the shape of his career. Perhaps it was too late. Bebop already sounded conventional, even old-fashioned, and hard-bop was full of pianists who at first hearing played rings around him. Then Ornette Coleman arrived and slammed the door on the forties and fifties. Nichols died in obscurity, but he has recently begun to flourish in memoirs and reissues. Bethlehem has brought out its 1957 LP as "Herbie Nichols," and Blue Note has put together its four Nichols sessions as "Herbie Nichols: The Third World." The Blue Note reissue has a fine memoir by the trombonist Roswell Rudd, who studied with Nichols in 1960. And the short chapter on Nichols in A. B. Spellman's *Four Lives in the Bebop Business*—that wayward, fascinating, critical-political set of biographical studies (Cecil Taylor, Ornette Coleman, and Jackie McLean are the other subjects)—is available again in a Schocken paperback, which has been inexplicably retitled *Black Music: Four Lives*. Nichols was born in New York of West Indian parents, and he was a kind, proud, bemused, very tall man with intellectual learnings. He had roamed widely in the literature of classical piano, and he knew every jazz style. It is not clear from reading Rudd and Spellman why his career was such a botch. He frequently exchanged ideas with Monk, he worked for Lucky Thompson and Sonny Stitt and Archie Shepp, he showed his songs to Mary Lou Williams, who used some of them. But nothing happened, and he kept finding himself on the bandstand with Wilbur De Paris and Big Nick Nicholas.

Whether they admit it or not, most jazz improvisers are caught within the space created by the composer of the tune they are playing. Nichols, though, created his own space. All but four of the numbers on the reissues are his, and he doesn't burrow into them, as improvisers are wont to do, but constantly enlarges them. He likes his melodies, and he keeps returning to them, so that by the end of the performance they seem twice as imposing. His style owes its squiggly runs to Ellington and Monk, its broken phrase-endings to Bud Powell, and most of its harmonic content to Monk. And Monk governs many of his songs. When Nichols plays, there are no rests or bare places or patches of blue sky. His music is dense and vertical. The right hand moves through stop-and-go single-note melodic lines that fall on the beat or run ahead into arpeggios or glisses, or into chords that quickly dissolve into fresh single-note lines. All the while, the left hand clucks and fusses. It plays offbeat chords and single notes, stridelike rhythms, and echoes of the right hand. At first, it is difficult to tell whether Nichols's technique was faulty or he purposely played in such a haphazard, fluctuating way. He misses notes, lets the final notes of phrases die, and allows runs to come out faded and almost inaudible while the succeeding phrase trumpets and blares. But Nichols knew exactly what he was doing. Indeed, his self-knowledge and pianistic abilities were so acute that his playing has a calculated, almost cold cast to it. It asserts and proclaims, and maybe this quality put off some of Nichols's colleagues, most of whom took their talents for granted.

Nichols was a pianist of considerable originality who fashioned attractive umbrellas of sound, and it is easy to dip into the reissues anywhere. His minor-key songs, often arranged in descending chords ("The Spinning Song," "House Party Starting"), are almost catchy, and so are some of his fast numbers ("Terpsichore," "Brass Rings"). Nichols's best solos dance, and to such an extent that they would work well for many modern choreographers. He uses three alternating bassists (Al McKibbon, Teddy Kotick, George Duvivier) and three drummers (Art Blakey, Max Roach, Dannie Richmond), and it is interesting that none of the six have ever played better on records. Nichols said that he would have loved to be a drummer (the tonal effects of drums fascinated him, and he felt that they formed a central part of any performance), and there is an enfolding percussiveness about his playing which clearly surprised and challenged his accompanists. Red Norvo once pointed out that many musicians end up playing the wrong instrument. Perhaps Nichols was one.

# 1978

## Selfishness Is Essential

**D**uke Ellington's Boswell turns out to be Stanley Dance, a sixty-seven-year-old English jazz chronicler and aide-de-camp, who by dint of sempiternal doggedness has put together what amounts to a three-volume biography. With the publication of *Duke Ellington in Person*, written with Ellington's son Mercer, it is now complete. The first volume, *The World of Duke Ellington*, was brought out in 1970. It consists of a couple of interviews with Ellington, a transcription of an Ellington press conference, interviews with twenty-six sidemen and three alter egos (Tom Whaley, Ellington's copyist; Mercer Ellington; and Billy Strayhorn), and Dance's own accounts of a Latin-American tour, Ellington's seventieth-birthday party at the White House, the first two Sacred Concerts, and Ellington preparing for a Monterey Jazz Festival. The second volume, Ellington's limpid and funny autobiography, *Music Is My Mistress*, was published in 1973, a year before he died. Except for an extended final chapter of questions and answers compiled by Dance, the book was written by Ellington himself. Mercer describes the process: "Stanley had expected that it would be done with a tape recorder, following the same method they had used for articles, so he was surprised to find that Pop intended to write it himself. The manuscript that eventually materialized was . . . written on hotel stationery, table napkins, and menus from all over the world. Stanley became so familiar with the handwriting that he could often decipher it when Pop could not." In *Duke Ellington in Person*, Dance taped Mercer, and edited the results. All three books, like Ellington himself in his last twenty years, are somewhat helter-skelter. They are sometimes inconclusive, patchy, and—considering their subject—unaccountably flat. There are countless photographs in the three volumes, but little sense of Ellington in the flesh—of his umbrous, polished voice; his gracious laugh; his accent, which was universal and aristocratic; his long, handsome, beautifully lived-in face; his careful, philosopher's gait; his locked concentration when he worked; his quick searching of the middle distance before zeroing in with a mot: "Selfishness can be a virtue. Selfishness is essential to survival, and without survival we cannot protect those whom we love more than ourselves." But the three books help. With his wit and elegance and cool and originality, Ellington was one of the most oblique and elusive of all twentieth-century masters. Toby Hardwick, who was in Ellington's first band, got a glimpse before Ellington slammed the door: "The amazing thing about him is that the language, the slant, everything . . . didn't rub off from someone else, and it wasn't a legacy either. He went inside himself to find it. He's an *only*, that's for sure."

Ellington was a combination of romantic and realist—or perhaps he was a realist who learned early that it is easier to pass as the opposite. His prose reflects this. Others might write in black and white, but Ellington wrote in color. Yet underneath was a sharp vision of life. An excursion on night life in *Music Is My Mistress* begins with typical Ellington sumptuousness, but soon it narrows: "Night Life is cut out of a very luxurious, royal-blue bolt of velvet. It sparkles with jewels, and it sparkles in tingling and tinkling tones. . . . Night Life seems to have been born with all of its people in it, the people who had never been babies, but were born *grown*. . . . Some of them were wonderful people, and some were just hangers-on of a sort. . . . There were a few hustlers, who depended upon finding suckers for survival. And there were some who were too wise to hustle, who only wanted to have enough money to be able to afford to be a sucker."

He expands on the celebrated announcement he made when he was informed that he had almost won a citation from the Pulitzer Prize committee, and ends with a genial, begloved sarcasm. The entry has its own page, and he calls it "Acclaim":

The Pulitzer Prize music committee recommended me for a special award in 1965. When the full Pulitzer committee turned down their recommendation, Winthrop Sargeant and Ronald Eyer resigned.

Since I am not too chronically masochistic, I found no pleasure in all the suffering that was being endured. I realized that it could have been most distressing and distracting as I tried to qualify my first reaction: "Fate is being very kind to me; Fate doesn't want me to be too famous too young."

Let's say it had happened. I would have been famous, then rich, then fat and stagnant. And then? What do you do with your beautiful, young, freckled mind? How, when, and where do you get your music supplement, the deadline that drives you to complete that composition, the necessity to hear the music instead of sitting around polishing your laurels, counting your money, and waiting for the brainwashers to decide what rinse or tint is the thing this season in your tonal climate?

When he has nothing but good tidings to impart, he relaxes, and becomes almost spare and supple: "To me, the people of London are the most civilized in the world. Their civilization is based on the recognition that all people are imperfect, and due allowances should be and are made for their imperfections. I have never experienced quite such a sense of *balance* elsewhere." The opening paragraph of his autobiography is a fairy tale, a put-on, and probably the truth: "Once upon a time a beautiful young lady and a very handsome young man fell in love and got married. They were a wonderful, compatible couple, and God blessed their marriage with a fine baby boy (eight pounds, eight ounces). They loved their little boy very much. They raised him, nurtured him, coddled him, and spoiled him. They raised him in the palm of the hand and gave him everything they thought he wanted. Finally, when he was about seven or eight, they let his feet touch the ground."

Like all working romantics, Ellington was highly superstitious. He believed, Mercer tells us, that windows had to be shut in thunderstorms lest a draft bring the lightning in; that giving people shoes meant they might walk away from him; that it was bad luck to bring peanuts or newspapers backstage or to arrive there whistling; that thirteen was a lucky number; and that the color brown was bad luck, because he had on a brown suit the day his mother died. (The dust jacket of his autobiography was originally brown but was changed to blue at his horrified insistence.)

Mercer's book is unsparing but fair. He says that Ellington had a sadomasochistic streak that caused him to hurt others when he most needed them. He also affirms Toby Hardwick's early judgment: "*He likes to manipulate*. It's a little quirk all his own. He thinks no one has the slightest idea about this. He likes to manipulate people around him, and gets the biggest kick when he wins. It's not like using someone, it's more like a game." Another game that Mercer discovered was Ellington's inviting him to his motel room on the pretext of looking at a new arrangement or checking a faulty ledger when all he wanted was company. This fear of showing weakness eventually hardened into a genuine toughness.

Ellington's reputation as a composer has lately been under revision, and *Duke Ellington in Person* will hasten the process. He was more of a primitive than most people knew. Mercer writes:

So far as learning to read music was concerned, he was never exactly avid. . . . There were many people in those days, of course, who went to schools . . . so that they would be recognized as being "able to do it"—

being able to read—and they would have considered it cheating to play a record and copy what was on it—and do it just by ear. Ellington sat down and did that time and again. He'd gradually figure out what somebody had done, listen to the beat, and analyze the whole thing. How he ever learned the value and time you'd give a note so that you could represent it on paper, I don't know, but he was able to do this without tutors or formal training. He finally wound up knowing how to write music.

Most primitives are trapped in their only invention—their style. But this was never true of Ellington. Mercer says, "Formal training, to him, implied adhering to the rules and a lack of creativity. He didn't like the rules in anything. To discard a rule was a source of inspiration . . . because he immediately saw the way to make it work in reverse. One whole composition was dedicated to making the seventh chord rise instead of resolve downward. It was a number that never gained much recognition, but I remember his telling me how he had gotten away with it and how nobody had ever thought it sounded bad." Feeling his way early in his career, Ellington got in the habit of listening closely to what was played around him and of asking his musicians for suggestions. This attentiveness became a collective method of composing, which never completely left him, and which in his later, prize-ridden years he perhaps would not have readily acknowledged. Ellington's sidemen repeatedly mention this method in *The World of Duke Ellington*:

> SONNY GREER: "We'd just talk things over and make suggestions on the interpretation."
> HARRY CARNEY: "He was always a great compiler, and one of the guys' ideas would suggest something else to him."
> BARNEY BIGARD: "When I played a solo, or Johnny Hodges played a solo, he'd be listening, and if you made a passage that he liked, he'd write it down and build a tune on it."

Mercer Ellington says that this method sometimes caused grief. "In the past, [Johnny Hodges] had sold his rights to songs for $100 or $200, just as Fats Waller and Ellington had done when they were young and gullible,. When Pop turned some of these songs into hits, Rab [Hodges] wanted the deal changed, and when he was refused he became unhappy. That explains why he would sometimes turn toward the piano onstage and mime counting money."

Ellington was more than a composer. Like a great film director, he was a catalyst, a synthesizer. He had the divine gift of impelling his musicians to offer him their best, which he would put toward the musical vision he had in mind. Hodges or Bigard or Ben Webster would give him eight or twelve beautiful bars and those would pass through his head and come out as "Mood Indigo" or "Sophisticated Lady." (Mercer Ellington says little about

Billy Strayhorn, who, a kind of second son, remains a mystery. It is conceivable that without Ellington pushing him Strayhorn would have been a minor, if greatly gifted, composer. But those songs directly credited to him certainly equal Ellington's, and in some instances come close to surpassing them.) The Ellington afflatus was dangerous. It drained his musicians, and at the same time, because so many of his tunes were written specifically for them, it spoiled them. When longtime sidemen left, they either dropped into obscurity or, thirsting for the Master's attention, returned to the fold.

An Ellington tune played in an Ellington arrangement by the Ellington band was unique. Mercer describes this eloquently: "[Ellington] sought a sensuality in the way his music was expressed; there was always an emotion attached to the sound. Or I might say that he was always very conscious of the need to make the listener *feel* experiences with the sound, almost as though he were creating apparitions within the music."

## Ladies

Two pianists from the pianistic river that flows through New York:
Joanne Brackeen is tall and shy and bespectacled, and she has four teenage children. Her hair is fuzzy, and she wears long, thin flowered dresses. She was born in Venture, California, which is between Oxnard and Santa Barbara, and the principal pianist she heard around home was Frankie Carle. Then she discovered Art Tatum and Bud Powell, and not long after that in Los Angles she discovered Ornette Coleman, still unknown here in New York. John Coltrane, whose influence is yet to be reckoned, came next. She took lessons from a famous local pianist named Sam Saxe, who also got his best students good jobs. She worked for Dexter Gordon and Charles Lloyd on the Coast, and since then she has been with Stan Getz and Art Blakey and Joe Henderson as well as on her own. She has lately joined the elect at Bradley's, where she now is playing. She is a brilliant, close-textured pianist. Her solos have the insistence and intensity of Coltrane, who before becoming long-winded and extra-musical played as if he wished to inhabit not only each tune but each listener. Brackeen's intensity takes her into every number in the same Coltrane way. (Her repertory is humdrum, but it doesn't matter. Her choice of songs provides sufficient inspiration, form, and melodic support.) Her attack is basically single-noted. She likes arpeggios that run along just this side of full slides, and she gives their notes slightly more value than they would ordinarily have, which makes each tooth flash as the smile goes by. She breaks her single-note figures in odd places, like Powell and Coleman, and she will resume with double-time patterns or an open cluster that dissolves into one of her highly detailed arpeggios. Her chordal passages are somewhat forbidding: they tend to be cold and without resolve. (Every pianist should study Jimmy Rowles's wooded, graceful har-

monic progressions.) Her left hand is strong and variously arranged, and she is not overly romantic. In a slow ballad ("Days of Wine and Roses," "These Foolish Things"), she will move to the edge of the swamp where Keith Jarrett and McCoy Tyner and Chick Corea disport in slow motion, but she stops there to watch.

Jazz musicians often worked behind vaudeville performers in the twenties and thirties, and sometimes they joined in. Drummers danced and threw their sticks into the air, clarinettists and trumpeters made silly noises, and pianists wore gloves and played standing up. These antics lasted into the forties, when jazz musicians, suddenly self-conscious about being called artists and/or about the possibility of being taken as Uncle Toms, pulled down a scrim between themselves and their listeners. But a few of the vaudeville musicians survive, and one is Dorothy Donegan, who is at Jimmy Weston's with the bassist Arvell Shaw and the drummer Ray Mosca. She is a medium-sized Rubens, with a court jester's face, and everything she plays is translated into action. She rocks back and forth and from side to side. She forms her feet into a giant wedge and stomps it. Her head rolls wildly, and her face is possessed by fearful middle-distance stares, a whorl-like mouth, and bowsprit lips. She bangs her eyes shut and hums demonically. This frenzy—a balletic music—obscures her playing, and that's too bad, for Donegan is a first-rate Tatum pianist. She has a rich, flying left hand and a right hand whose roller-coaster lines and ten-pound chords summon up Tatum's. She constructs mountains of sound on such foundations as "Tea for Two" and "The Man I Love," interlarding the layers with bits of "Rhapsody in Blue," boogie-woogie, stride basses, key changes, and loud-pedal chords, all the while playing at the speed of light. She has been showing off so long she probably doesn't remember what you are really supposed to do when you sit down at a keyboard.

## Fat Girl

For a time, the line of descent from the brilliant trumpeter Fats Navarro, who died in 1950, at twenty-six, kept breaking down. Navarro's banner was picked up almost immediately by Clifford Brown, another dazzling player, but Brown was killed in an automobile accident in 1956, also at twenty-six. Two years later, Booker Little appeared, but he died suddenly in 1961, when he was twenty-three. By the mid-sixties, Navarro seemed forgotten. But now his legacy, streamlined and brought up to date, has reappeared in Woody Shaw, who is thirty-four.

Navarro, who was of Cuban, Chinese, and black extraction, worked his way up through the bands of Snookum Russell, Andy Kirk, Billy Eckstine, and Lionel Hampton. Here is how Charles Mingus introduces him in his autobiography, *Beneath the Underdog:* "There was a man named Fats

Navarro who was born in Key West, Florida, in 1923. He was a jazz trumpet player, one of the best in the world. He and my boy [Mingus, that is] met for the first time on a cold winter night in 1947 in Grand Central Station in New York City. Lionel Hampton's band had just got off the train from Chicago and [the trumpeter] Benny Bailey gaily said good-bye and split: he was leaving for Paris, France. The guys all stood around in their overcoats by the clock, waiting for the new man joining the band. A big, fat fellow walked up carrying a trumpet case and asked in the oddest high squeaky voice 'This the Hampton crew?' and [the trombonist] Britt Woodman intro-duced Fats Navarro." Mingus adored Navarro, and he makes him into a self-destroying angel (Navarro died of tuberculosis and heroin addiction) as well as a Mingus mouthpiece who detests white men, bookers, managers, club owners, audiences, and all the impedimenta that weigh down black jazz musicians. Navarro is given several Mingus diatribes. One goes:

> Mingus, I still ain't as scared to die as I am to go home to see my mother and family in Florida. You should see all the churches we got out in Key West. The white man's got 'em too. I heard 'em praying once when I was little in some kind of weird tongue. I later found out it was Latin. Imag-ine! Nigger-hating Southern white man that can't hardly read or write English sitting up in a church looking holy with his big red turkey neck, speaking in Latin!

Navarro was a gentle, becoming man who apparently brought out the perverse in his celebrators, most of whom imbued him with evil spirits. Ross Russell, the Charlie Parker hagiographer and bebop critic, converts Navarro into a combination of Sydney Greenstreet and a well-known A&R man of the time in his novel *The Sound*. The hero of the book, based closely on Parker, is a benighted, drug-ridden trumpet player named Red Travers, and Navarro, who is given his real nickname, Fat Girl, is an unnervingly omnis-cient record collector who also happens to be a pusher:

> Red was accompanied by a great butterball of a man with drooping mus-taches and a Charlie Chan face called Fat Girl . . . Fat Girl had large, liq-uid eyes that swam under beautifully modeled lids and lashes. They reminded Bernie of the eyes in an eastern idol . . . His dress, manners and speech were the quintessence of hip, up-to-the-minute Harlem. "Gassed!" Fat Girl said. "Big eyes to hear you blow, man!"

The origins of Navarro's trumpet playing are not altogether clear. He is said to have idolized Charlie Shavers (who was a cousin), and perhaps this accounts for his fondness for eighth notes, delivered in non-stop up-and-down patterns. If he listened to Shavers, he must have heard Buster Bailey and Billy Kyle, who were in John Kirby's band with Shavers and were equally rococo and multi-noted. And Charlie Parker and Dizzy Gillespie surely turned Navarro from improvising on standard chords to improvising on augmented ones. But after wandering among these masters Navarro sought his own way. Bebop had a harum-scarum quality, a fondness for odd notes, broken rhythms, and jet speeds. Its soloists started and stopped in strange places; rushes of notes would be followed by silence or half-speed phrases: blasts would subside into whispers, and whispers would suddenly become shouts; solos would last far longer than their players' invention warranted; tempos would be so fast they'd freeze the soloist or make him gibber. None of this perturbed Navarro. He understood that the frenetic quality of much bebop derived partly from the ineptness of some of its players and partly from the exuberance its superior players felt at having new chords and freer rhythms to ride around in. So in his solos he clothed the genuine departures from swing inherent in bebop with logic and beauty. Set against the background of his often dishevelled peers, a Navarro solo was like an immaculate fairway flanked by ankle-deep rough. His solos compare extremely well with Dizzy Gillespie's most famous effusions of the time, but they got less attention from the public, because they lacked the italics and bold face that Gillespie always set himself up in. Gillespie liked to clown and blare and do the fandango up and down his registers. He liked to blow the grass flat and divide the waters. But the truth is that Navarro was the better trumpet player. He concentrated on his tone, which was full and even; on his chops, which were almost perfect (he rarely split or dropped notes, the way most bebop trumpeters did, Gillespie included); and on his sense of order, which gave his solos a Churchillian ring and flow. He stayed largely in the middle register, but his occasional ascensions were masterly. The notes, though high, were big and smooth, and there was none of Gillespie's occasional pinched quality. Sometimes Navarro's phrases lasted ten or twelve bars: they crossed meadows and stiles and copses before landing. But every so often he would insert a clump of whole notes that would have the effect of briefly throwing his solo into slow motion. He would punctuate these serene juxtapositions with silence, and shift back into his handsome parade of eighth notes.

Navarro can be profitably studied on "Fats Navarro: Fat Girl." There are twenty-eight tracks, made in 1946 and 1947, and the best are those with the pianist Tadd Dameron, a gifted and largely unsung bebop arranger and composer who brought order and inspiration to the recording sessions he participated in. Of interest as well is "Charlie Parker: One Night in Birdland"—a radio broadcast Navarro did at Birdland with Parker and others, supposedly a week before his death. But this seems hard to believe, for he is in sparkling, driving condition.

Clifford Brown, who was seven years younger than Navarro, rose quickly after Navarro's death. (In the year before he died, Navarro dwindled to about a hundred pounds. In his liner notes for "Fats Navarro," Dan Morgenstern tells of running into him in the subway in the summer of 1950 and finding him so depleted as to be almost unrecognizable.) By 1955, Brown, who was from Wilmington, Delaware, had become the most applauded young player in jazz. He had color and fire and great forward motion. His solos in outline resembled Navarro's, but they were delivered with greater intensity and they were more prolix. Brown raced and swam around his horn, as if he had intimations of his limited time and had to get as much said as possible. When he was killed, there was an uncommon rush of sentiment in the jazz world. (The tenor saxophonist and composer Benny Golson wrote a resonant dirge-ballad called "I Remember Clifford," which was widely recorded and continues to be played today.) Then Booker Little, out of Memphis and barely twenty, began to move to the fore, and Navarro and Brown were with us again. Little belonged somewhere between Navarro and Brown. He was a thoughtful player who seemed to release his notes unwillingly, as if he feared he would never find their like again, and he had a certain moroseness of tone and attack which suggested he had also studied Miles Davis. But Little had clarity and warmth and invention, and a distinct flair for composing and arranging.

Woody Shaw appeared in the mid-sixties. He worked with Eric Dolphy (as had Little), Horace Silver, Art Blakey, McCoy Tyner, Gil Evans, and the drummer Louis Hayes, and lately he has led his own group. He lists as influences Gillespie, Navarro, Brown, and Little, together with Freddie Hubbard, Lee Morgan, and Donald Byrd. Also audible are Ornette Coleman and Don Cherry. Shaw was a fancy player at first. But, with the help of the unique Dolphy, he began to realize that ceaselessly running the chords of a tune was a form of imprisonment, that chords were commands as well as signposts. He also realized that Dizzy Gillespie runs had become clichés, and another form of bondage. He expanded his sense of invention. He began using sizable intervals (all trumpeters should study Ruby Braff's, which resemble air pockets) and nests of legato notes where one could pause and rest. He shied away from the chord structure, throwing in bursts of notes that had little to do with their environment but fitted anyway. And he mixed everything up cleverly. He would open a chorus with a turning, half-time phrase, its notes played in an almost impressionistic way, pause, leap into his high register for two quick, jabbing notes, the second broken off purposely, sail into a fine, hilly Navarro-Brown passage, which ended in an old-fashioned, waving vibrato reminiscent of Frankie Newton's in the mid-thirties, and close out the solo with a couple of blistering, descending arpeggios and a final group of calm, legato notes. (Shaw has also made his first album, a sturdy effort called "Rosewood." "Rahsaan's Run" and "Theme for Maxine" are done by Shaw's current group, which includes Carter Jefferson on reeds, Onaje Allan Gumbs on piano, Clint Houston on bass, and Victor Lewis on drums. The four other titles are with an augmented and not necessarily superior band.)

For all his originality and energy, Shaw suffers two shortcomings that have afflicted almost every trumpeter since Fats Navarro and Clifford Brown. One is a sharp, shallow tone (compare the rich brassiness of Thad Jones, the velvet musings of Braff, and the impeccable, almost octagonal sound of Joe Wilder), and the other is a tendency to make everything he plays seem difficult to execute. When audiences are reminded of the effort it takes to please them, they grow restive. Audiences are interested in being entertained, a state of euphoria that should appear as effortlessly given as it is received.

## South Lawn

Calvin Coolidge and Herbert Hoover didn't invite Louis Armstrong to the White House, nor did F.D.R. ask Fletcher Henderson or Count Basie or Duke Ellington. Harry Truman had a classical singer in the family, and Dwight Eisenhower was not musical. Neither were the Kennedys, but they did swing, and in the spring of 1962 the Music Committee of the President's People-to-People Program sponsored an International Jazz Festival in Washington. It was given everywhere in the city but at the White House. Seven years and two Administrations later, the White House officially opened its gates to jazz by giving Duke Ellington the Presidential Medal of Freedom and a seventieth-birthday party. It was a joyous time. Richard Nixon, his Uriah Heep mask set aside, was almost buoyant, Ellington was serene and gracious, and the tributary music (by the likes of Jim Hall, Urbie Green, Paul Desmond, Hank Jones, Gerry Mulligan, Earl Hines, and Willie the Lion Smith) was excellent. Then, three days ago, the President and Mrs. Carter gave a "jazz concert" on the South Lawn of the White House.

The music began at five o'clock and ended just after dark. A buffet supper of jambalaya was accompanied by the Young Tuxedo Brass Band, from New Orleans. Just after six-thirty, President Carter jumped up on a bandstand that had been erected at the northwest corner of the lawn, and gave a capsule history of the music. He refreshingly pointed out that racism had slowed its acceptance, admired its freedom and self-discipline, told of first listening to it in the early forties, and closed by saying that "over the period of years the quality of jazz could not be constrained," which had a fine Faulknerian surge. The President spent most of the concert seated on the grass about fifteen feet from the front of the bandstand, and he listened closely. When he was particularly moved by a musician, he got quickly to his feet and congratulated him. He told the pianist McCoy Tyner that what he had just played was "beautiful," and after Cecil Taylor was finished he pursued him (Taylor's stage exits are phenomenally swift) across a corner of the bandstand and under a low-lying magnolia tree. He spoke with Lionel Hampton and Phyllis Condon, and with Charles Mingus, who was confined to a wheelchair.

The musicians were clearly impressed by Carter's appreciation, and after a time it seemed to affect the music itself.

Eubie Blake started the main part of the concert. Now ninety-five, he played two of his own numbers, "Boogie Woogie Beguine" and the famous "Memories of You." One has come to relish Blake for his unflagging turn-of-the-century spirit and for his two-foot hands, whose fingers stroke up and down the keyboard like trireme oars. With Dick Hyman, Doc Cheatham, and Milt Hinton accompanying her, Katharine Handy Lewis, the daughter of W. C. Handy, sang her father's "St. Louis Blues," and her sweet, faraway voice was cushioned by Cheatham's elegiac obbligatos. Mary Lou Williams did an eight-minute a cappella history of jazz piano playing which went somewhat awry—the little sea of sound she created was filled with waves of ragtime and boogie-woogie and blues and ballads and bebop, and they tended to break every which way. The first group to appear on the bandstand was made up of Clark Terry, Roy Eldridge, Benny Carter, Illinois Jacquet, Teddy Wilson, Hinton, and Jo Jones, and it played "In a Mellotone" and "Lady Be Good." Not much happened. Jones dragged the tempo, Carter was dicty, Terry was calligraphic, and Jacquet decorated the evening with his lustrous Southwestern tone. Bebop and hard bop, in the persons of Sonny Rollins, McCoy Tyner, Ron Carter, and Max Roach, did Rollins' "Sonnymoon for Two," and the concert came alive. Rollins played a brilliant, compressed solo, full of vertical melodies, repetitions, and quotations, and Roach matched him with staccato snare-drum figures—super-double-time figures, executed at teeth-gritting speed. A group of stylistic first cousins, which included Dizzy Gillespie, Dexter Gordon, George Benson, Herbie Hancock, Ron Carter, and Tony Williams, did ebullient versions of "I'll Remember April" and "Caravan." Williams equalled Roach's staccato ruminations, and Gordon refloated Lester Young. Then Ornette Coleman, accompanied only by his son Denardo, on drums, played two of his own compositions back to back, and his tone and boldness and invention were like proclamations. His songs were classic Coleman—long, sorrowing, descending melodic lines, enlivened here and there by double-time passages—and his improvisations would have carried even further without Denardo's heavy drumming. Cecil Taylor came next, and President Carter, his back curved and his arms clasped around his raised knees, was transfixed. Taylor was dazzling and brief. He got off several of his almost staccato arpeggios, a lyrical passage, and some jackhammer chords. The last scheduled group was a mixed grill consisting of Lionel Hampton, Stan Getz, Zoot Sims, George Benson, Chick Corea, Ray Brown, and Louis Bellson. It did "How High the Moon," and Zoot Sims, playing two excellent choruses, brought the evening to a climax. Getz did two choruses of "Lush Life," and it was a case of the song (Billy Strayhorn) and the musician fitting perfectly: "Lush Life" prodded Getz and Getz filled in its sinuous outlines.

Then President Carter returned to the stage and declared that jazz was "just as much a part of the great things of the nation as the White House itself or the Capitol Building down the street," and asked for more music. Hampton set off "Flyin' Home," and Jacquet played his old solo. Pearl Bailey rose out of the audience in response to a request from Mrs. Carter, and sang a couple of songs. The darkness had about touched ground when Dizzy Gillespie and Max Roach reappeared for a stamping, funny duet, with Roach using only his high-hat cymbals. The President and George Wein were watching side by side next to the bandstand, and Wein looked as if his mother, who was in the audience, had neglected to tell him that there would be no need for him to turn to stone if he ever found himself cheek by jowl with a President of the United States. Gillespie, dropping several "Your Majesty"s, asked Carter if he would sing the old bop tune "Salt Peanuts." It isn't easy. The singer, at a fast tempo, is obliged to chant a dozen "Salt peanuts." "Salt" is one note; "pea–," also one note, jumps an octave; and "nuts," one note, too, drops back three tones. Carter brought it off. Gillespie then asked him if he would care to go on the road with his group, and the President said. "I might have to after tonight."

The scenery and furnishings for such occasions matter. The South Lawn, with its hummocks and dells, is a beautiful piece of geography. The crowd, numbering around a thousand, sat on the grass or at picnic tables set up diagonally to the bandstand. When the concert began, the sun, coming in over the old State Department Building, was merciless. But it obliged and went down, making way for a pale-blue sky and a lemon moon. Honeysuckle replaced the air, and swallows rocketed between the trees. After the music, the President, surrounded by family and friends, walked back to the White House at roughly the speed of a slow blues.

# Newport 1978

*June 23rd*

This is the seventh year of the Newport Jazz Festival in New York, the fifth straight year that Sarah Vaughan has sung at the festival, and the second straight year that she has starred at its opening. She did so in Carnegie Hall tonight, and all four octaves were in order—particularly her quasi-baritone, an area roomy enough to hold a dance in. Her vibrato was sumptuous, and her intervals, ascending and descending, were chasmal. She did a fast "I'll Remember April," a slow "I Fall in Love Too Easily," Tadd Dameron's "If You Could See Me Now," a Gershwin medley, and Duke Ellington's "I Got It Bad and That Ain't Good," wherein she sang "I'm not made of woooooooooood-ah." Audiences now react to Sarah Vaughan the way they do to drummers. She is a virtuoso, a high-wire act, an eighth wonder. Her accompanists of these many years are Carl Schroeder on piano, Walter Booker on bass, and Jimmy Cobb on drums.

*June 24th*

Ella Fitzgerald recorded "A Tisket, A Tasket" with Chick Webb forty years ago. Some of her lower tones have more resonance now, and her middle register has thickened, but her voice is still a teenager's—light, pure, boxy, emotionless. She and Billie Holiday started in the thirties as born singers. Both had almost unnervingly natural attacks, but by the mid-forties Holiday was decorating her singing with mannered bent notes and a long-gowned solemnity, and Fitzgerald got increasingly "jazzy" until she was doing little besides scat singing. This jazz-like attack became fixed in the fifties, and, despite her recorded voyages into Gershwin and Kern and Porter, she has never shaken loose from it and moved on. She still tends to pump up certain phrases with anticipatory sylla-bles, as in Cole Porter's "Dream Dancing," which she sang tonight at Carnegie Hall as "drehehehumeum dancing." She inserts falsetto notes, needlessly big intervals, and ski-jump glisses; she often resembles a lesser Sarah Vaughan. She seemed edgy tonight. Her intonation was off, she never quite swung, and some of her songs were poorly chosen or were sung at odd tempos. She included "Satin Doll," with its silly lyrics, and "Ain't Misbe-havin'." She did "I Cried for You" at a *very* fast tempo, and "That's My Desire," a song forever associated with Velma Middleton and Louis Arm-strong. In between, she scatted, a forlorn cement that failed to hold her per-formance together.

But there was a surprise at the concert. Fitzgerald's accompanists were Tommy Flanagan on piano, Keter Betts on bass, and Jimmy Smith on drums, and they were given fifty minutes to themselves. Flanagan belongs with Jimmy Rowles and Ellis Larkins and Dave McKenna. He has humor, a zephyr touch, an oblique and original harmonic sense, and unwearying invention. His great facility makes what he does sound too easy—the tricky, quiet, single-note melodic lines that often abruptly slow to a walk just before they end; the loose, echoing tenths in his left hand; the nimble parallel chords; the love of melody; and the multilayered improvisations he builds on a tune like "Body and Soul," which he played tonight. He also played a medium-tempo blues; "Good Bait"; a bossa nova; Thelonious Monk's "Fri-day the Thirteenth," into which he let a lot of light and air; and "All the Things You Are."

Is it possible, decade after decade, to appreciate a music that isn't fully comprehensible, that is boring and exhilarating, overweening and lyrical, ponderous and fleet—the music, in short, of Cecil Taylor? Yes. One simply relishes Taylor's stamina and technique, his willful and joyous obscuran-tism, and the immense bath of sound—the omnisound—he engulfs us in.

At the late concert at Carnegie tonight, he brought along Jimmy Lyons on alto saxophone, Ramsey Amin on violin, Raphé Malik on trumpet, Sirone on bass, and Steve McCall on drums. They played a single one-hour number with opening and closing ensembles that sounded like free dirges, and there were extensive solos for the violin and horns, punctuated by Taylor solos. He was flamboyant and triumphant. He played glisses, Niagara arpeggios, chords struck with his fist, impenetrable low-register figures (not helped by muddy amplification), and a long and lovely passage of improvised Debussy.

### June 26th

Wild Bill Davison, at seventy-two, is the same batch of mannerisms, tics, and poor jokes that he was almost forty years ago, when he first arrived in New York. He puts his cornet just to the left of the center of his lips, aims it at third base, and beetles his brows. At the close of each pivotal phrase, he removes the horn and shakes it. He wiggles the pinkie of his right, or fingering, hand with each vibrato. He still wears his hair flat and parted slightly off center (it lines up perfectly with his embouchure), his blue eyes still snap, and his face is as smooth as a honeydew. He is probably the best Chicago-style lead trumpeter-cornettist who ever lived, and he is a fiery and lyrical soloist. He uses a hoarse tone, he plays right on top of the beat or ridiculously far behind it, and he is concise to the point of being aphoristic. He is a consummate melodic improviser, and the delight in following one of his solos is guessing when he will suddenly fall behind the beat into a soft legato phrase, when he will insert an upper-register shout, when he will drop an octave. One can hear where Ruby Braff and a host of lesser players came from, and one can hear the parts of Louis Armstrong and Bix Beiderbecke and King Oliver that Davison came from. He is in the middle of his annual two-week stint at Eddie Condon's. He did easy versions of "Keepin' Out of Mischief Now" and "I Can't Believe That You're in Love with Me," a fast "All of Me," a rolling "You Took Advantage of Me," and a fast "When You're Smiling."

### June 27th

Between 1930 and 1945, most jazz improvisers played the songs of George Gershwin, Harold Arlen, Irving Berlin, Richard Rodgers, and their like, and in the forties the Gershwins' "I Got Rhythm," disguised in an immense variety of bebop hats, seemed to be their *only* song. Before that, they had written much of their material, and since the early fifties they have resumed the practice. Every so often, George Wein likes to pay tribute to American song at the festival, as he did tonight at Carnegie. Alberta Hunter, accompanied by Gerald Cook and Al Hall, sang six of her own numbers, and confirmed the suspicion that several hearings are more than enough to admire her pipes, pep, and perseverance.

(She is eighty-three now.) Dick Hyman (on the Carnegie Hall electric organ) and Ruby Braff did three Fats Waller songs—"How Can You Face Me?," "Ain't Misbehavin'," and "Honeysuckle Rose." The contrast between Braff's cello tone and the rainbow shades that Hyman got from his various keyboards was subtle and rich. Braff was full of delicate, glancing notes as well as his familiar basso-profundo excursions. Hyman's touch called up Waller's own playing, so the old fox was doubly celebrated. Irene Kral brought along her Anita O'Day–Carmen McRae patterns and imposed them on three Cole Porters ("Experiment," "Easy to Love," "Ev'ry Time We Say Goodbye"). And Stan Getz, in company with the superior pianist Al Dailey, did three Alec Wilder songs ("I'll Be Around," "Ellen," and "The Winter of My Discontent") and Thad Jones' "A Child Is Born," which has Wilder lyrics. Getz played each song straight before embellishing it, and Dailey worked up a series of harmonic adventures in "Ellen." The final set was a celebration of Harry Warren, Arlen, Berlin, Arthur Schwartz, and Eubie Blake, done by Mel Tormé, who doubled on piano; Gerry Mulligan, who also sang; and Jimmy Rowles. They were backed by George Duvivier and Oliver Jackson. The group had rehearsed—to the point where it could easily go out on the road. Tormé sang Arlen's "Get Happy," and Rowles sang Warren's "I Wish I Knew." Tormé sang Arlen's "Let's Take a Walk Around the Block," and Mulligan sang Schwartz's and Larry Hart's very early "And Fall Asleep with a Smile." Mulligan, who has a cheerful, attractive voice, also sang Schwartz's "By Myself," while Tormé sang highly effective obbligatos behind him. Jimmy Rowles played a handsome version of Warren's "You're My Everything," and Tormé did Arlen's "On the Swing Shift" and "Accentuate the Positive." There was an Irving Berlin medley in which Tormé did "How About Me?," Mulligan played "Easter Parade," Rowles played, "Remember," and Tormé sang "Alexander's Ragtime Band." Tormé, summoning up Ben Webster, closed with a beautiful version of Blake's "Memories of You."

*June 29th*

Tormé was back tonight—at Avery Fisher, with its exasperating, furry sound—and again he lifted the proceedings. He was accompanied by Buddy Rich's big band, which went through its customary maneuvers and then fell back for a Rich gallimaufry, complete with a whisper-to-crescendo snare drum roll, ricky-ticking on the drum rims, elephant tomtoms, and straight-ahead, pavement-pounding Chick Webb snare figures. Dizzy Gillespie came aboard for a long, sensational solo. He sent up flares; fashioned a gentle, careering passage of half-valved notes that were almost subliminal; and loosed plumb runs. Tormé warmed up with Count Basie's "Down for Double" and with "You Are the Sunshine of My Life," and brought Stan Getz on for "Here's That Rainy Day." Getz is the last of the romantic saxophonists, and when he plays ballads one just wishes that he wouldn't keep peering out longingly between the notes. Tormé joined him, and the supper-club Tormé of the other night had been replaced by the Las Vegas Tormé. It was the same singer, but in italics—the daring phrasing and dynamics, the hand-wrought substitute notes, the cantorial voice. He sang Toots Thielemans's "Bluesette," and in "I Can't Get Started" he and Gillespie did obbligatos for one another. He sang Harold Arlen's "Blues in the Night," using a five-story Gothic arrangement by Marty Paich, in which the tempo changed continually. Tormé likes to top himself, so he did a whipping improvisation on Ella Fitzgerald's famous scat version of "Lady Be Good."

Meanwhile, over at Carnegie Hall, the Trapp family of jazz, the Brubecks, were bouncing through "Blue Rondo à la Turk," a ballad called "Tea for Jane," and a peculiar tribute to Fats Waller that began with blues and boogie-woogie, neither of them forms that Waller was particularly at home with. Darius Brubeck played several skillfully turned single-note melodic lines on his electronic keyboards, but his brothers (Chris on bass and Danny on drums) were stolid. Brubeck *père* busied himself at his piano with his old impossible task of trying to re-create the lyrical freight he hears within him.

### June 30th

Chick Corea, once a Latin-band pianist and now, at thirty-seven, the operator of a small musical empire, gave two concerts at Avery Fisher Hall tonight, and both were sold out. Corea's music, whether in his compositions or in the way he chooses to play them, is soft and romantic and elusive. It hovers on the edge of jazz, of classical music, of rock. It is melodic and pretty, and it often feigns complexity, so as not to insult its audiences. Woody Herman's band played Corea's "Suite for Hot Band" and it had blues effects, brass-band effects and lots of solos. Corea and Gary Burton played a couple of duets, in which their instruments (vibraharp and acoustic piano) clipped and twined. Then a thirteen-piece ensemble with strings, rhythm section, horns, and the singer Gayle Moran went through five long pieces. There were lots of flute solos and ostinato passages, and Moran sang and vocalized in a lunging soprano. In the last two numbers, Corea, on acoustic piano, was joined by Herbie Hancock on the Yamaha electric piano. Corea and Hancock toured for two months last winter, and their duets, on acoustic piano, were full of Lisztian rhapsody, flash, and empathy.

At a midnight concert in Carnegie Hall, Sam Rivers offered a quintet, made up of Ted Dunbar on guitar, Mike Nock on piano and synthesizer, Dave Holland on bass, and Bobby Battle on drums, and a big band, made up of four trumpets, two trombones, five saxophones, a tuba, a bass, and drums, and including Ricky Ford, Hamiet Bluiett, and Chico Freeman on reeds, Jack Walrath on trumpet, Holland, and Barry Altschul on drums. The quintet played the conservative half of "The Hong Kong Suite," which consists of eight ten-minute sections, four of them traditional jazz and four avant-garde. For nearly an hour, Rivers and his cohorts issued an uninterrupted series of melodic reflections on the small-band jazz of the forties and fifties. The tempos and time signatures changed constantly; there were quiet, studied solos by Rivers and Dunbar and Nock; and the music circled and circled but never came to rest. The big band was another matter.

Rivers arranged his musicians in a loose, three-sided box centered on the tubist, the bassist, and the drummer, while he played and conducted at its open end. They did an hour-long piece called "Evocation." It had a lot of "free" figures played separately by the sections in long, heavily accented melodic lines or all at once in thick, cacophonic ensembles. Soloists, one or two at a time, passed between the sections, and were rarely more than functional. Rivers is a possessed musician (after a time, he resembled a puppet, spinning just above the ground among his musicians, his back now toward us, now toward them), but for all his efforts "Evocation" never took off. Nor did it have any of the humor of an avant-gardist like Archie Shepp, who is aware that parody both blesses and buries what has come before.

## Neo

When the tenor saxophonist Scott Hamilton came down to New York two years ago from Providence, where he was born in 1954, it was as if Ben Webster and Flip Phillips had returned in one. Hamilton's big, surprising tone was that of Webster, and his attack and phrasing incorporated Flip Phillips. But he was not a copyist; the accidents of his upbringing had largely given him his style. It was also clear that he was a good musician, that he was inventive and eloquent, and that his improvisations would move down his own paths as soon as he was ready to knock away the molds he had borrowed.

Hamilton is of medium height and shape and, given two or three more inches, could pass as the young Bix Beiderbecke. The tops of his ears fan out, and he wears a small mustache. His brown eyes turn down at their outer corners and are set wide apart. His hair is thick and dark and divided down the middle. He talks about himself easily, and without pose or apology.

"My father, whose name is Robert, is a painter who teaches at the Rhodes Island School of Design," he said the other day. "In two years, he'll be sixty-five and can retire, and I don't know what will happen. Now he paints a thousand pictures and puts them in closets, and then, to make room for new paintings, he has a burning, which he did in a field in Maine a while ago. He's had shows in Boston and some critical success, but he's apprehensive about New York. I think he likes being a big fish in a small pond. He's short, and he's got a beard and a sense of humor, and we get along fine. My mother is younger, and she's an artist, too—mostly in fabrics. And I have a younger

sister who's at R.I.S.D. I don't know what she does, and when I see her I
always forget to ask.

"I took piano lessons when I was five, but that didn't last, and when I was
eight I studied clarinet, which didn't last, either. I played harmonica professionally with local blues groups at fourteen, and I didn't take up the tenor
until I was seventeen and in my last year in high school. My clarinet background helped, and I had listened to jazz records since I was nine or ten. My
father had a lot of 78s, and we split his collection. Half were in my room and
half in his studio. When I was eleven, I listened to the Beatles, but then I
went back to jazz and listened to Lester Young and Coleman Hawkins and
Ben Webster. Unfortunately, I missed seeing them all. Hawkins played in
Providence once near the end of his life, when I was thirteen or fourteen, but
I didn't get there, and, of course, Webster went to Europe in the mid-sixties,
and Lester died when I was four. Just to have got a little piece of any of them
would have been enough. I started playing tenor with a blues band that had
a Muddy Waters singer. I sounded terrible, but I knew the notes, and it was
the best training just to jump in and play. In a while, I worked with organ
trios in black Elks clubs in and around Providence, and I worked a place in
Cambridge where they packed guns and stayed open until ten in the morning. Then I formed a group with a guitarist named Fred Bates—the Hamilton–Bates Blue Flames. We had a bass player and the drummer Chuck
Riggs, who's with me now. We drove an old Ford van, which wobbled all
over the highway, and we went up and down New England–Vermont and
New Hampshire in winter, and Nantucket and Martha's Vineyard and Block
Island in summer. No one wanted a jazz band then. The people who hired us
thought *everybody* was a rock group, and when we started playing they were
surprised. But they didn't throw anything at us, and, one way or another, we
made a living. Block Island was where I met Arnett Cobb, the great Texas
tenor player. He'd driven two thousand miles from Houston because he'd
been told that Block Island was the Las Vegas of the East, and he didn't
know what to make of it when he got there—no laundromat, so he had to
wash his clothes in the sink; not enough electric power to run the organ he'd
brought; and an out-of-tune piano. But he got through it, and he let me sit
in all the time. Fred Bates married and Chris Flory came in on guitar, and we
still work together a lot. I think I decided to move to New York when they
raised my rent in Providence to twenty dollars a week. I'd played with Roy
Eldridge in Boston, and he encouraged me in every way. In fact, I'd be
nowhere without him. The first job I had here was a Tuesday night with the
house band at Eddie Condon's. Right after, I went into Michael's Pub for six
weeks with Billy Butterfield, and on the basis of that I figured I could make
it. I've worked steadily since, and for a guy who just walked in I've been
lucky. A lot of gigs have been on the road, but I don't mind. Hotel rooms are
beginning to feel more like home than the place I have on West Fifty-fifth
Street, which is practically bare.

"As opposed to some musicians, I have poor concentration. When I play, I try to relax and *not* think. My best ideas come out of a blank, out of an abstraction. Roy Eldridge says when he plays he tries to imagine he's inside a bubble, and I like that. Some musicians see chords and colors and all sorts of images in their heads when they improvise, but I have no bent toward such things. I work in terms of chords. I have a good harmonic ear, but I have to struggle to remember melodies. I learn a new ballad by putting on a Frank Sinatra or Tony Bennett record. My tone goes on and off, but it's more automatic now than it was two years ago. I figure that what's going to happen to my style will happen without me, so I'm just letting my playing take place. I can feel it changing from month to month. It's more original than when I first came to New York. Maybe within five years I'll be able to tell it's me when I listen to one of my records."

Hamilton's style comes in two parts. At fast tempos, he often recalls Flip Phillips. Despite his demurrers, he makes the melody float when he states it. He does this by skimming the written notes in such a way that the melody seems to create itself. He plays softly, and he uses a short, gentle vibrato. When he improvises, he alternates long notes with tight, turning, Paul Gonsalves runs. He indulges in occasional high notes and booting honks, but he never falters. At slow tempos, Ben Webster comes to the fore. His vibrato widens, his tone thickens, silences appear, and he recaptures Webster's hymnlike power. His sound surrounds the ear. All this is clear at Crawdaddy, where Hamilton is appearing with Dick Katz on piano and Chuck Riggs on drums. He has a good repertory, and two sets went like this the other night: a medium "The Very Thought of You," a slightly faster "What Is This Thing Called Love?," a medium "You're Getting to Be a Habit with Me." He did a very fast "It Don't Mean a Thing If It Ain't Got That Swing," a slow "Don't Blame Me," a medium "It's You Or No One," and a fast "The Man I Love." The singer Barbara Lea sat in with great effect on "The Lady Is a Tramp" and "Someone to Watch Over Me," and Hamilton continued with a medium "Broadway," a very slow "Lotus Blossom," and a sailing "Limehouse Blues." John Bunch was standing in for Katz that night, and splendidly, and Riggs stayed largely with his wire brushes, which he uses with precision. (He should perhaps study Sid Catlett's way of invincibly *padding* along on the snare drum with brushes.)

Hawkins and Webster and Young were gone or moved away or were worn out too soon, and Hamilton is a superior replenishing presence. More important, he is an antidote, a corrective, to the flat, hard, toneless way of playing the tenor saxophone that has been fashionable for almost twenty years.

## Tommy

The jazz nascence that took place in Detroit and its environs in the forties and early fifties produced four remarkable pianists—Hank Jones (b. 1918), Barry Harris (b. 1929), Tommy Flanagan (b. 1930), and Roland Hanna (b. 1932). All have leaned on each other and on generally shared idols. Jones and Flanagan admired Fats Waller, Art Tatum, Teddy Wilson, Nat Cole, and Bud Powell. Flanagan also learned from Jones, and Jones in later years probably listened to Flanagan. Harris admired Powell and Flanagan, while Hanna admired Flanagan and Erroll Garner. All four remained more or less hidden from the public until recent years: Jones as an accompanist for Ella Fitzgerald and as a studio musician; Flanagan as an accompanist for Tony Bennett and Fitzgerald; and Hanna and Harris as industrious sidemen. Jones, who is just six years younger than Teddy Wilson, is their doyen. His touch is pearled, and his improvisations are spun out of willowy single-note melodic lines that reflect Wilson's fluidity and Powell's harmonic advances. His single notes are polite and his harmonies cast soft light. Homogeneity itself is his style. Harris must have passed through Jones's benign influence, but when he was a teenager he fell under the spell of Powell and Charlie Parker, for he constantly applauds their wheeling, irregular, slightly acidulous melodic lines. Harris's phrase endings tend to wilt and fall away, as if they were being blown out of hearing, and the rest of his attack, lacking dynamics and silence, often drones. Bebop players equated silence with weakness. Hanna is a buoyant, resplendent pianist. He uses a great many chords and baroque melodic lines, and he likes to keep coming to climaxes. His melodic surges continually ascend and descend, and as each breasts a hill Hanna celebrates with a crescendo. Jones, Harris, and Flanagan are cool players, but Hanna toils at his large, domed structures. Flanagan plays with nicely controlled passion and with considerable wit. He sparkles like his old idol Nat Cole. He shares Wilson's delicacy and logic and Tatum's touch and technique, and he clearly admires Powell's circuitous melodic inventions. He ranks with the other Wilson-Tatum-Cole disciples—Jimmy Rowles and Dave McKenna and Ellis Larkins—but he is more consistent. It is rare to come away from hearing Flanagan without something new and ingenious.

Flanagan looks Edwardian. He is of medium size, and is mostly bald, with a hedge of whitish hair at the back of his head. A luxuriant mustache and glasses balance the hair. He has a quick, diffident smile and a soft voice. He does not like to talk about himself, but when he does he fashions each sentence as if it were part of a solo. He is a shrewd, kind man who speaks well of many of the pianists around him—Herbie Hancock, McCoy Tyner, and Cecil Taylor, the last of whom "plays with beauty." Flanagan talked of his life and his playing. "I was born in Conant Gardens, on the northeast side of Detroit," he said. "I was the youngest of five boys and a girl. They still live in

Detroit, some of them in the house where we were born. My father was eighty-six when he died, last year. He came from near Marietta, Georgia, and he moved to Detroit just after the first war. He was a letter carrier for thirty-five years. He had great spirit and humor, and he showed us all the things of how to be a good person. Dad and I looked like each other. He was bald, and I lost my hair early, so we looked alike a long time. My mother passed away in 1959, shortly after I moved to New York for good. She came from Wrens, Georgia, and she was Indian-looking and only about five feet two. During the hard years of the Depression, she sold dresses for a mail-order company, and then made patchwork quilts from the samples of fabric the company sent her. She really encouraged me on the piano. She taught herself to play, and when she heard me imitating my older brother, Jay, who also plays piano, she gave me lessons. Later, I studied with Gladys Dillard, who's still teaching in Detroit. She taught me the correct pianistic attack—how to finger correctly and use the tips of my fingers. My mother was always interested. When I put on an Art Tatum record, she'd listen and say, 'Is that Art Tatum?' That made you feel good. I also listened to Fats Waller and Teddy Wilson, but Hank Jones, a more modern Wilson, made a lot of sense to me, and so did Bud Powell, whom I heard with Cootie Williams in Detroit. Powell was the kind of player who made you say right away, 'What? I never heard that before!' And there was Nat Cole. The meaning and the force and the swing—he had that appeal. The pulse, the driving voice of his piano. He made his notes bounce. My older brother introduced me on the scene, helped me get my feet. I had my first job in a club when I was in high school. I was too young to mingle between sets, so I'd go in the back and do my homework.

"For a long time, mostly when I was accompanying Ella Fitzgerald, I never thought I had enough technique for a soloist. But then I found I liked to put myself out there. I always feel after I solo that maybe I should have worked it out more first. I always hear so much space that I could have filled in. The piano takes care of itself when you play it, so I think in terms of horn lines a lot. Also, if I have my eyes closed I see the keyboard in my head and I see what I might want my hands to do. Improvising gives you a great sense of freedom. When you find that out—that you're making your own song—you can go on endlessly. Of course, you learn something each time you play the same song—particularly if you play it in a different key. That sharpens your wit, makes you play better, keeps you away from the clichés."

Many improvisers lead the listener directly to the heart of their work. "Listen to how this arpeggio falls and to how these ninth chords enfold the melody," they seem to say. But Flanagan dissembles and distracts. At first hearing, one gets an impression of immense busyness, of the air being filled with fluctuating chords and melodic lines, of someone playing for himself. Flanagan seems to be shielding himself with his music the way a philosopher shields himself with abstraction. But what he is doing—working outward from within his materials, rather than the far

more common reverse—soon becomes clear. He often states the melody
with dissonant, levering chords played offbeat or staccato. Never decorative,
they are fresh and manipulative, and reveal both a respect for the melody and
an intense desire to alter it. He breaks the chordal flow with single notes on
the bridge of the first chorus, and fashions variations of his opening chords
for the final eight bars. Then he slides into full improvisation, with his single-note patterns, which come in non-stop Art Tatum arpeggios, done with
a salute and a smile (Flanagan loves to put patches of other pianists' playing
in his solos, so that one comes upon Teddy Wilson runs and Thelonious
Monk seesawings and George Shearing sotto voce grace notes); his ascending runs that break off, regroup, break off, regroup; his interval-filled
descending figures that suggest someone going downstairs three steps at a
time; his charging rhythmic phrases whose accented first notes make the
succeeding notes *snap*, double-time phrases that race ahead to clear the way,
and legato phrases that form sauntering rear guards. First-rate improvisation suggests that if one looked at the sheet music one would find the notes
the soloist has just played. That's what Flanagan does.

Having at last quit Ella Fitzgerald, Flanagan has decided to go out on his
own, and this is fine news, for his work with the singer generally prevented
him from appearing in New York more than once a year. (What finally
drove him to his decision was two days last summer in which, on tour with
Fitzgerald, he went from Provence to Newcastle upon Tyne to Provence to
Wolf Trap, Virginia.) Unlike many jazz musicians, Flanagan comes through
equally well in person and on records. In recent years, he has made four
recordings on which he is the leader, and all of them have surprises. The
albums are "Eclypso," made with George Mraz on bass and Elvin Jones on
drums; "Tommy Flanagan 3," done with Keter Betts on bass and Bobby
Durham on drums; "The Tommy Flanagan Tokyo Recital," done with
Betts and Durham; and "Something Borrowed, Something Blue," made with
Betts and with Jimmie Smith on drums. Flanagan is in fine form in the first
album, but he tends to rein himself in in favor of his sidemen, who are given
generous space. "Something Borrowed, Something Blue" is a peculiar effort.
Flanagan plays electric piano on two numbers, and Thelonious Monk's "Friday the 13th" is spiffed up with a ground bass, a back beat, and shuffle
rhythms. The title song, with its attractive descending melody, is Flanagan's,
and it implies that he should write more music. The "Tokyo Recital" album
is exceptional, even though the bass and drums are overrecorded. It has a
seven-minute "Caravan" surrounded by strong dissonant chords; a "Chelsea
Bridge" full of ascending arpeggios and Debussy single notes; and a "Take
the 'A' Train" that closes with a series of wild, witty four-bar exchanges with
Durham. (The record is made up largely of Strayhorn tunes, and also
includes "The Intimacy of the Blues," "Something to Live For," "All Day
Long," and "Daydream.") The "Flanagan 3" record, done at the Montreux

Festival, is also worthwhile, especially for a loose, stretching performance of "Easy Living," which Flanagan likes to play. When he settles into tempo, he gets off a rising-falling upper-register run that holds the light like a blue sky.

## Dance

Live recordings offer us the workaday musician, complete with clams and clichés. They also offer surprise and beauty of a kind often forestalled by the celebrated chills of the recording studio. This is certainly true of the invaluable "Duke Ellington at Fargo, 1940, Live"—a recording that has long been available in pirated form and now, having been cleared with Ellington's estate, is issued legally for the first time. It is an almost complete documentation—taken down on a portable acetate recorder by two local enthusiasts named Jack Towers and Dick Burris—of a dance played on November 7, 1940, at the Crystal Ballroom in Fargo, North Dakota, by just about the best of all Ellington bands. (Thirty-five of the forty numbers recorded have been preserved in the album. The omitted selections, with one exception, either are musically negligible or have irremediable sound problems.)

Countless live recordings have appeared in recent years, and most are from radio broadcasts or from concerts or night clubs. Few have been done at dances, which jazz musicians love, because they can see their music reflected in the bodies of the dancers: the better the music the better the dancing, and the better the dancing the better the music. Nor do many of the recorded dances follow the course of the evening from the cold-lip, off-pitch beginnings at eight o'clock to the relaxed, often bleary doings at one. Catching the Ellington band on this particular night was extraordinary luck. It was a time of upheaval: Cootie Williams, an anchor of the band since 1929, had left to join Benny Goodman five days before, and his replacement, Ray Nance, had just reported for duty. The band had changed very little in the previous decade. Otto Hardwick had departed and returned, Rex Stewart and Lawrence Brown had been added, Artie Whetsol had been replaced by Wallace Jones, and late in 1939 Ben Webster and Jimmy Blanton had joined. By this time, the Ellington band members could dream one another's dreams and predict, within reason, one another's solos. With the exception of Webster, Brown, Carney, Blanton, and Johnny Hodges, the 1940 band was a collection of inspired primitives, who were exactly what Ellington wanted. None were first-rate improvisers (Barney Bigard and Tricky Sam Nanton—Bigard blessed with an unbelievably liquid Albert-system clarinet tone, and Nanton with an eerie "talking" muted style—played endless variations on the same solo), and all had choice musical tricks and peculiarities that Ellington loved to work with. These included Stewart's half-valve effects on cornet, Williams's and Nanton's plunger-mute sounds,

Hodges's and Harry Carney's tones, and Sonny Greer's charging, intuitive drumming.

The dance at the Crystal Ballroom began shortly after eight with a short set played without the leader. This included a brisk version of "It's Glory," a rambling "The Mooche," and a jumping but truncated "The Sheik of Araby." The album begins with "The Mooche" ("Glory" and "Araby" are omitted without much loss), which has statements from Hodges, Tricky Sam, and Stewart. At nine o'clock, the radio station KVOX broadcast nine numbers, among them a "Ko-Ko" which is perhaps even better than the studio version done eight months before ("Ko-Ko" remains the most sophisticated and ingenious large-ensemble blues ever written); a "Pussy Willow" in which Nance takes his first, tremulous, but instantly recognizable solo, and which has an exhilarating moment when, after a humming three-note saxophone figure played four times, the last with Carney sliding under to give it bottom, Ellington yells, Greer lets loose an oceanic roll, and the full band roars in; a "Harlem Air Shaft" wherein Rex Stewart takes over Cootie Williams's three brief rampant passages but fails to give them Williams's urgency and power; and a couple of moony vocals by Herb Jeffries and Ivie Anderson during which one can practically hear the dancers' feet. (One *can* hear Freddy Guy's guitar and Greer's brushes. The sound in the album is, almost without fail, good, and by the time we reach a steam-heated version of "Rockin' in Rhythm," which must have been played around eleven-thirty, it is close to studio quality.) After the broadcast, the band relaxes and we are given a loose "Bojangles," complete with two excellent choruses of Ben Webster; a fine "You Took Advantage of Me," called "On the Air," with leaping Hodges, who is equally good on "Never No Lament" (eventually "Don't Get Around Much Anymore"); and a leisurely, five-minute "Sepia Panorama" that has two more startling Webster choruses. The only disappointment in this part of the album is the omission of "The Sidewalks of New York," which has first-rate Jimmy Blanton and a long, muted, across-the-bay Rex Stewart solo backed by one of Ellington's beautiful singing reed figures. The evening was two-thirds over, and the band had found its groove. Rocking rundowns of "Cotton Tail" (taken very fast), "Conga Brava," and the slow "Across the Track Blues" (the title refers to the feelings that the Ellington band members suffered when, after playing to cheering white audiences, they were forced to sleep in the black section of town) are followed by a jammed "Honeysuckle Rose," in which Ray Nance takes his first violin solo with the band, and "Wham," in which he scat-sings in the manner of Leo Watson. Then we come to the peak of the evening—a slow, four-minute "Star Dust" that is given over to three choruses by Ben Webster. It was Webster's reply to Coleman Hawkins' "Body and Soul," set down the year before, and it was a formidable one. (It pleased Webster so much that he took a copy of it with him wherever he went for the rest of his life.) A medium-tempo "Rose of the

Rio Grande," with Ivie Anderson singing and Lawrence Brown in limousine form, follows, and the evening closes with a whooping "St. Louis Blues" that has an Anderson vocal, good Tricky Sam, and six champing choruses of Webster. Sonny Greer was Webster's co-star that night—whacking a cowbell on annunciatory offbeats, using a great pushing afterbeat, punctuating trombone solos with timpani beats, and sloshing everyone with his cymbals. Greer has long been pushed aside as a drummer, but he was, with Sid Catlett and Jo Jones, the best of the big-band drummers.

# 1979

## His Work

In *The Fred Astaire & Ginger Rogers Book,* Arlene Croce suggests that Astaire is "his own form of theatre." That is, he is—as a dancer, a singer, an actor—wholly original, and so incomparable. His dancing was a blend of balletic outlines, ballroom dancing, and polyglot jazz steps. The tap-dancer Bill Robinson called him an "eccentric" dancer, and another tap-dancer, Cholly Atkins, said, "He used balletic turns but came out of them with a jazz kick and slide." Astaire was something of a surrealist in his movie dancing. He danced on clouds and up the wall and across the ceiling, and his grace was such that, though his feet might be making a clatter, he gave the impression of being soundless, of not touching the ground at all. No one has paid much attention to his singing until recent years, but it balanced his dancing. Singers revere Astaire. Anita Ellis, who worked with him in two films in the early fifties, has said, "He was his work. He was a perfectionist. On the set, every inch of every step was worked out, and when he sang I always felt that he eased up and became calmer, that his singing was a nice place for him to be." Sylvia Syms has said, "What he lacked vocally he made up in immaculateness. He invented lyrical economy. His singing was the shortest distance between two points. He danced words. He carried the grace of his dancing over into his singing. The songwriters appreciated him because he was musically pure and they knew he wouldn't confuse anybody. No matter what he sang, it always had movement. He was never interrupted by having a matinée-idol face, and his own songs—the songs he wrote—always remind me of soft-shoe." The singer Barbara Lea has said of him, "He belonged with the incidental singers, like Johnny Mercer. He wasn't trying to sell anything but the song, which he got across with precision, clarity, and humor. There wasn't any ego trip involved. He had no intention of astounding you. Of course, he had great materials to work with. The composers who wrote for him wrote light rhythm songs, because he was a dancer, and a circular thing took effect. Their songs probably made him even more that way, which made them produce more of the same sort of songs, and so on. Another important element of Astaire's singing was that he always sang as a character in a show or movie—not as himself, like a night-club performer. That gave him protection from himself, from any temptation to whoop himself up." (Astaire worked once in a night club, in the twenties, and disliked it.)

For all the clarity and order of Astaire's singing, its origins are mysterious. (He does not say very much about his singing in his autobiography, *Steps in Time*. Nor, for that matter, does he say much about his dancing.) He came up through vaudeville and the early Broadway and London musical in the teens and twenties. "Popular" singing was still semi-European, and was in the hands of the light-operatic troubadours and the early crooners. Vibrato lingered in the corners of every singing style, and tenors were much admired. Singers used a crying quality (bent notes, even sob effects) in their torch songs, and all aspired to a polish that was supposed to mirror emotion. The singers of the time, with few exceptions, got in the way of the first-rate songs already being written by Jerome Kern, Irving Berlin, and George Gershwin, and their recordings have aged poorly. But by the late twenties Astaire was already on the side of the angels—the angels being Ethel Waters and Bing Crosby and Louis Armstrong. He must have heard their recordings, and it has been said that he was influenced by the prolific South African singer Al Bowlly. Astaire seems to have put his singing together early, for he is quickly recognizable on the "Lady, Be Good!" recordings that he made in 1926 with George Gershwin on piano. The ease and sense of swinging that he lacked then came to him by the time he went to Hollywood, seven years later.

As Sylvia Syms suggests, the rhythmic intensity and brilliance that governed Astaire's legs and feet certainly controlled his singing. He has a light baritone, and his timbre is smooth. It is an angular, tidy, pure-cotton voice with little vibrato. (It had more in the twenties.) It arose from necessity, and it is tough and adaptable. He can sing anything from "A Fine Romance" to a nonsense dialect song like "I Love Louisa." His long notes may waver and he sometimes lands near his notes instead of on them, but he makes every song fresh and full-faced, as if each were important news. His singing is also self-effacing. There doesn't seem to be anything between the words and the listener: the lyrics pass directly from the sheet music to the ear.

Astaire has not made a great many recordings. The most ambitious were done in 1952, when Norman Granz persuaded him to go into a Los Angeles studio, where he set down thirty-four vocal numbers and three tap-dances. He was accompanied by Oscar Peterson on piano, Barney Kessel on guitar, Ray Brown on bass, Alvin Stoller on drums, and, in all but nine numbers, Flip Phillips on tenor saxophone and Charlie Shavers on trumpet. The notion of recording Astaire with jazz musicians was a good one, and it is a pleasure to hear him unfettered by visual images and a large orchestra. He sings his old standards—including "Steppin Out with My Baby," "A Needle in a Haystack," "They All Laughed," "A Fine Romance," "I Concentrate on

You," "I Love Louisa," and his own fine "I'm Building Up to an Awful Let-Down" and "Not My Girl." The three tap dances are done with the rhythm section, at tempos ranging from medium to very fast, and they are good, exciting Astaire tapping—often offbeat, legato, and full of his typical sailing-through-the-air open spaces.

## Oil and Water

Jazz began as a collective music played by spasm bands and marching bands and bands put together for picnics and dances and boat rides. Its early practitioners, untutored and certain only of the melodies they played and the aural space they had to fill, leaned together, and their solos were limited to short breaks and occasional statements of melody. This lovely polyphonic music thrived at least twenty-five years, and then, with the arrival in the mid-twenties of such technically accomplished players as Sidney Bechet and Louis Armstrong and the Harlem stride pianists, was set aside, to be briefly renovated in various shapes and sizes by Charles Mingus and Gerry Mulligan and Archie Shepp. By the nineteen-fifties, jazz had become a solo music. The ensemble had shrunk to a skimpy unison melodic line, and soloists, encouraged by the new LP recordings and by the jam-session philosophy abroad at the time, became meandering and long-winded. The soloist as an entity arrived in the sixties with John Coltrane's mammoth excursions and Cecil Taylor's unaccompanied one-hour deluges. Now concerts and recordings and night-club appearances by one-man bands like Leroy Jenkins and Anthony Braxton and George Lewis are commonplace. But what a lonely and illusory music! Only the human voice can stand alone as a musical instrument. (The piano, of course, is multi-voiced.) All others, ironically, strive to sound like groups by resorting to enlarging devices such as double-stops and trick-tonguing and overblowing. Jim Hall, our paramount guitarist and a consummate impro-viser, has reduced his musical environment, but only as far as a duo—a combination he has practiced with constant success for a decade. There is little that two instruments cannot do together. They can fashion counterpoint, which hones and brightens their voices. They can pit their timbres and set up invigorating cross-rhythms. They can subtly comment on each other in their accompaniment. And they can play in unison or in harmony, or play dissonantly and give the impression of many voices. Hall has worked most often with bassists (Ron Carter, Michael Moore, Jay Leonhart, Jack Six, Red Mitchell), and recently he was recorded with Mitchell at Sweet Basil. The results have just been released as "Jim Hall/Red Mitchell." There are two blues ("Big Blues" and "Osaka Express"), both by Hall, a Mitchell original ("Beautiful"), a Hall original ("Waltz New," based on "Some Day My Prince Will Come"), a Bart Howard ("Fly Me to the Moon"), and a Hall-Mitchell arrangement of a Mexican folk song ("Blue Dove"). Exceptional things happen: the slow, almost collapsed "Beautiful," which is notable for the gradual way Hall moves into his solo and for the circular figures he plays following Mitchell's solo; the legato single notes which Hall delivers after a heavy chorded passage in "Waltz New"; his John Lewis single notes on "Big Blues," and the six loose sotto-voce choruses that he and Mitchell fall into just before its final ensemble; and the swaying "Osaka Express."

Hall likes musical surprises, and has appeared at Hopper's with his old friend and compeer the valve-trombonist Bob Brookmeyer. Brookmeyer, who was much in evidence during the fifties and sixties, went West to the studios ten years ago, and has only recently returned. He is forty-nine and came out of Kanasa City, and he grew up in the shade of Jack Teagarden, Vic Dickenson, Bill Harris, Brad Gowans, and J. J. Johnson. His style has not changed. He long ago developed a brass-tongued loquacity that has more in common with such virtuosos as Bill Watrous and Urbie Green than with Teagarden and Harris. He affects a smoky tone, Dicky Wells smears and shouts, a placid vibrato, and brief falsetto leaps. He plays with lyrical glibness, and his phrasing and aim are unerring. He is, in Well's way, often funny. It is odd to find him and Hall working together, for they are almost wholly dissimilar. Hall is spare, elusive, soft, and reluctant to part with his beauties, while Brookmeyer always plays as if he were attending a convention. At Hopper's, the two musicians seemed to be playing in adjacent rooms with the door open. Their ensembles did not blend into a double-edged voice but remained a trombone and a guitar playing simultaneously. Brookmeyer's volume forced Hall to play louder than usual, and he almost never backed Hall's solos (organ chords, melody, riffs—all would have been proper), which took on a lorn, voyaging air. And Brookmeyer's and Hall's rhythmic centers were different. Brookmeyer plays in a pummelling, sometimes staccato on-the-beat style, and Hall often favors easy, downstream phrasing. Oil and water, the two men filled the room with powerful improvisations, and we heard rich, turning versions of "Begin the Beguine," an Andy La Verne original called "Exactly Alike," "Baubles, Bangles, and Beads," "Embraceable You," John Lewis's "Skating in Central Park," and a medium-tempo blues, in which Hall got off a solo full of surprised notes.

## A Burning Desire

**W**hen Louis Armstrong began his spectacular rise in Chicago in the twenties, the generosity and invention and originality of his playing provided source material for a thousand admirers. One of the most gifted is the seventy-three-year-old trumpeter Adolphus (Doc) Cheatham, who before reaching his present glory led a largely subterranean career as a lead trumpeter and sometimes soloist. He was born in Nashville, where he worked behind Bessie Smith and Ma Rainey and Clara Smith, and he moved to Chicago when he was twenty-one. He had a lean time until he joined Sam Wooding in 1928 and went to Europe. A few years later, he was with McKinney's Cotton Pickers, and a year after that he began a seven-year stay with Cab Calloway. Brief jobs with Teddy Wilson's and Benny Carter's big bands followed, and he was hired by Eddie Heywood, whose small band included the trombonist Vic Dickenson. It worked at Café Society Downtown, and was famous for its tight ensembles and spirited solos and for Heywood's Earl Hines piano. Then Cheatham suffered a collapse. "I never was a very strong person," he once told Stanley Dance, "and when I was young I was very thin. Travelling on the road a lot, and just living on sandwiches, was more than I could take." When he recovered, he started teaching. Some of his students were Latins, and that led to a fifteen-year stint of playing in Latin bands (Machito, Perez Prado, Marcelino Guerra, Ricardo Ray). He also doubled with Wilbur de Paris and Benny Goodman.

"I went to Chicago in 1926," he said the other night at Crawdaddy where he is appearing with a trio (Chuck Folds and Jackie Williams). "And I heard all the many marvellous musicians who were there—Louis Armstrong, who was the first to really solo on the trumpet, and Tommy Ladnier, who was next to Armstrong, to my way of thinking. I heard King Oliver, who was a gutbucket player, and Freddie Keppard, who had a military style and was so powerful he blew his mute right out of his trumpet and across the stage one night. He was so full of jazz nobody could hold him. And Jelly Roll Morton was around. I liked him, but I guess nobody else did. He was a braggadocio sort of fellow. He would tell you *he* was the pioneer of jazz, and you couldn't dispute him. He had a hard time in Chicago, and he almost starved when he went to New York, in 1928. Of course, that was fifty years ago. In that time, I've learned some confidence, and that's what my playing is based on—experience, and knowing thoroughly the melody and chords of the tunes I play. Tommy Ladnier taught me to always listen to the bass, and then everything would fall into place. It's also important to have the right men with you. They can lead you up the right path, or they can mislead you and break your heart if they don't know what they're doing. I learned from Louis Armstrong how to treat a chorus—not to overdo anything, not to waste notes, to keep things as trim as possible. When you improvise, you have a kind of picture in your mind. If you play a love song, perhaps you see a pretty girl, and if you play a buck-dance sort of number you put yourself in the character of what you are playing, like an actor. Duke Ellington's 'Ring Dem Bells' leaves you in a happy frame, and the blues—the real blues—is such a sad thing it fills you with sorrow."

Cheatham laughed. "Sorrow is what filled my father when I became a musician. His parents were descendants of the Indians who settled in what is now Cheatham Country, near Nashville. He was a barber who owned a three-story building that also had a tailor shop and baths, and his trade was white. His brothers were doctors and his sisters teachers. My mother was part Cherokee, and she came from Atlanta, Georgia. She was a schoolteacher way back in the eighteen-hundreds, and she was very beautiful and highly educated. She became a laboratory assistant at a medical college in Nashville. I had just one brother, and he was a dentist. My father didn't want me to be a musician because mostly what you saw in Nashville were circus musicians, and it seems like they drank all the time. He finally gave in when he realized it wouldn't be any use to stand in my way. So I was the sort of black sheep of the family. But when you take up an instrument you become addicted to it. You get a burning desire to play and play. Maybe that's why I never drank whiskey. I already had my addiction."

Cheatham is spare and elegant and ageless. His face is narrow, his eyes are heavy-lidded, and his nose is geometric and patrician. He talks in a confabulatory way, and he punctuates his memories of musicians by frequently saying, "They come and they go. They come and they go." When he plays, he points his horn toward the heavens and holds his arms level, as if he were about to take flight. His attack is lyrical and jaunty. (Armstrong has not been Cheatham's only influence. He has also admired Johnny Dunn and Louis Panico and Joe Smith and the late Shorty Baker.) He has a gentle tone and a discreet vibrato. His soles are a succession of lines, steps, curves, parabolas, angles, and elevations. They move with the logic and precision of composition, yet they have the spark and spontaneity of improvisation. Cheatham's rhythmic underpinnings have a bony clarity and emphasis: *all* his notes seem to stand out. Most brass players his age barely have the wind and lip to speak and eat, but he is continually adventurous. He loves big intervals, and he rarely lands on less than one foot. He successfully tries little ascensions that reach toward high C. His phrasing crosses bar lines with ease, and he constructs melodic lines that run for ten or twelve measures. There is little he cannot play. His ballads are round-limbed and placid, and his blues, though courteous, are melancholy, and even mean. His up-tempo numbers leap and jump. He is a wizard with mutes—particularly the plunger mute, which he handles with such force and subtlety and surprise that he sometimes matches Cootie Williams. And this daring, inexhaustible player never falters. He plays and plays, solo after solo, evening after evening, and each time he is fresh and affecting.

In the course of two languorous sets at Crawdaddy, he played "Gee, Baby, Ain't I Good to You?"; a fast, glancing "Just Friends" that suggested his old friend Bill Coleman; a slow "Jelly Roll Blues" with a muted solo that had an inner-mind intensity; a ruminating "Dear Old Southland," in which he sang in his plaintive, piping way; an ad-lib "Just a Closer Walk with Thee," a hymn that he converted into a lullaby; and two displays of his plunger-mute work in a brooding "St. Louis Blues" and a smoking "Summertime." When he executed a diminuendo-crescendo growl with his plunger mute in "Summertime," the sound exploded.

# A Giacometti Sound

In the mid-fifties, a young English advertising man named Jeff Atterton began a transatlantic correspondence with the clarinettist Pee Wee Russell, which lasted until Atterton moved to New York, in 1959. Most jazz musicians care little for writing letters, but Russell had a singular prod—his rare and highly literate wife, Mary. She would sit Russell down and, equipped with a quart of ale, he would talk; she would simultaneously edit and type, and out would come vintage Russell. He was not an accessible man. He was shy, fearful, self-depreciating, and even furtive, and strangers were lucky to get two half-swallowed sentences. But Russell had a strong ego, and Atterton's attentive letters clearly stirred him—so much that some of his answers offer the best looks we will probably ever have into his precarious, lyrical self. Here are some excerpts. Russell was a born dissembler:

> Mary, who knows how to spell cat, explained about Boswell and Johnson to me. You didn't expect me to know, did you? I've been approached several times by guys who want to write my biography but I can't figure out why a publisher would be interested. I haven't done anything except spend my life with a horn stuck in my face. My personal life may have been more stormy than the average office clerk but almost everybody's life is more stormy than that. And why would anybody want to read about it. . . . If I ever want to read about myself I could always find some publication that says—Charles Ellsworth Russell, Jr., b. March 27th in Maplewood, Missouri . . .

Russell knew he was good, but he spent much of his life either being paranoid or perversely denying his worth:

> I had a couple of little set backs that made me feel lousy for a while but I got over it. After one or two sleepless nights. I had a record date set. Modern musicians and strings. It fell through at the last minute. The modern kids are beginning to discover me. Mary says she always expected it. She told me that before it happened. She says I'm more modern than any of them because she never understood what . . . I am doing. I wanted that date. . . .

He had a sharp sense of hyperbole, the mainspring of humor:

> I'm a weary Indian. Home a week and I'm still beat. Fall River was awful. No hotel. I stayed in a motel. The motel was okay but no place to eat. I wish you could have seen me trudging a mile down the road to a bean

wagon. And the joint itself was a prohibition type place. Semi-hoodlums who told me how to play. Bass, piano, drums and saxophone. I don't want to criticize the musicians but I didn't know what they were doing and they didn't know what I was doing. The night one of the inch brow owners told me not to lean against the piano when I'm on the stand was too much. I snarled at him and scared him to death. . . .

I have a record date on the 18th and 19th. I'm going to use Bud Freeman and Nat Pierce. Ruby [Russell's close friend the cornettist Ruby Braff] doesn't work as a side man but he will for me. I hated . . . to ask him, but I got real strong and did and all he asked me was what time does he show. It's for a small company so they'll probably put the album out before it's made. There isn't any waiting around like the big companies. . . .

Alcohol nearly killed Russell in 1950, and for the rest of his life he struggled to keep it at bay. Eating properly was one way:

I'll tell you how I got fat. I drink at least two quarts of beer every day. I never got drunk on beer in my life. I drink an eggnog every day. . . . And I have a glass of milk with every meal. I eat breakfast and dinner and I have a sandwich or crackers and cheese late at night when I'm watching TV. When I'm away from home I lose weight. I don't eat and forget to take my daily vitamin pill. And I drink too much whiskey. But when I'm home I'm a healthy guy. Try my diet. I've gained most of my weight around my middle. But, what the hell. I'm a middle aged guy and it's time I got fat. . . .

And on death:

Josh's funeral was a pretty sad deal. [Josh Billings, a sometime drummer from Chicago, died in 1957.] Not too many guys. Condon said a few words. In good taste, incidentally. Josh didn't have any family. The hearse went off alone with no one to follow it. . . . Until then I didn't give a damn what happens to me after I'm through but right then and there I made Mary promise that I'll have a lot of people around when it happens and they're all to get drunk and say what a great guy I am. No matter what they think of me. . . .

Russell's decennial has been marked by four reissues. Two are of permanent interest—"Salute to Newport: Featuring Pee Wee Russell" and "Jazz Reunion: Pee Wee Russell, Coleman Hawkins." They reaffirm what many of Russell's admirers knew when he died—that he was the most original of all jazz clarinettists, a unique improviser. Vicissitude had forced him to earn much of his living with the Chicago-Eddie Condon school of jazz, but he didn't belong in it. This was made unalterably clear in the mid-sixties by a late-blooming series of recordings in which he worked comfortably with non-Condon musicians (one date was with Earl Hines, Elvin Jones, and a batch of Ellington sidemen) and with materials by Thelonious Monk, John Coltrane, Ornette Coleman, Ellington, Billy Strayhorn, Willard Robison, and Tadd Dameron. There were three incomparable things about Russell's attack: his tone, which was subtle and homemade, and unlike a standard clarinet sound; his rhythmic sense, which enabled him to escape the four-four prison that most swing musicians were caught in; and his daring, which drove him to try—and almost always get away with—passages of such wild-ness and complexity that no clarinettist reading them in transcription would be able to play them. Russell loved the chalumeau register, and he loved the blues. His blues were an examination of the proposition that there must be a way to make sadness bearable and beautiful. He would start a solo with half a dozen low, breathy staccato notes jammed together, repeat them and pause, rise almost an octave to a flickering, half-sounded note, and, before this ascension had registered on the ear, drop back to more staccato breathiness and into a dodging, undulating stretch of notes that had a Giacometti sound. He would for the first time bow in the direc-tion of the beat by constructing a four- or six-bar on-the-beat melody, and then sneak back down to the cellar for some asides, subtones, and almost palpable breaths. The first chorus done, he would grow less and less knot-ted. He would move slowly up the scale, growing louder, until in the last chorus he would reach C above middle C with a banners-unfurled declara-tiveness. He managed in these solos to make the listener forget that he was hearing a clarinet. (Benny Goodman's playing was the opposite: This is how you play the *clarinet*, it seemed to say. Russell didn't object; he loved Goodman.) Instead, the listener became wholly caught up by the *sound* of Pee Wee Russell—by a strange, solitary voice that had never been heard in jazz before.

That voice can be heard with remarkable strength and clarity on the reis-sues. The "Salute to Newport" album has twenty numbers, a dozen of them recorded in 1959 with Vic Dickenson, Bud Freeman, Buck Clayton, and Dick Cary. Russell rarely wrote music, but all the selections are his and, as if out of embarrassment, they have such elliptical titles as "Oh No," "Oh Yes," "But Why," and "This Is It." Only one of the numbers lasts more than four minutes, and five last under three minutes, so Russell has little chance to stretch out, although he is superb on "Dreamin' and Schemin' " and "Are You Here?" The remaining sides on the "Newport" album were done three and a half years later by a George Wein group that included—in addition to Russell and Bud Freeman—Ruby Braff and Marshall Brown. (Brown helped Russell, in 1962 and 1965, to record his meditations on Coltrane and Ornette Coleman and Tadd Dameron.) There is an excellent Russell slow blues, "The Bends Blues," but he is spectacular on a medium-tempo "Keepin' Out

of Mischief Now." He solos immediately after Braff, who is at his most
baroque—runs within runs; big intervals; juicy, low, tomato notes—and
Russell is at his (purposely) sparest. His solo seems to occur in a place of his
own invention. It has no tempo, no recognizable melody, no immediately
obvious underlying chord structure. It is a surrealist solo that turns and lazes
and muses, listening to itself and moving gradually across an open, endless
part of Russell's mind.

Much of "Jazz Reunion" is on the same level. The recording has Coleman Hawkins, Emmett Berry, Bob Brookmeyer, Nat Pierce, Milt Hinton,
and Jo Jones—what Russell considered fast company. There are six
extended numbers, including a Russell blues, two Ellington numbers, a Russell original, and James P. Johnson's "If I Could Be with You One Hour
Tonight"—a tune that Russell and Hawkins, in company with Glenn Miller
and Gene Krupa, recorded in 1929 as the famous "One Hour." Russell
never worked harder than he did on "Jazz Reunion": witness the five-chorus
edifice of melancholy and triumph that he constructed on the slow blues
"Mariooch."

## Small Label

**M**ilt Gabler, the founder of Commodore Records, was born in New York in 1911, the eldest of six children
of a New York mother (Susie) and an Austrian father (Julius). He went
to Stuyvesant High School, and summered at Silver Beach, in Throg's Neck.
His father owned a hardware store on Third Avenue, near Forty-second
Street, and a radio shop on Forty-second Street, which was called the Commodore out of respect for the hotel across the street. Gabler started at the
hardware store, then switched to the radio shop, where he began stocking
phonograph records. In the mid-thirties, the jazz bug having bitten him, he
and Marshall Stearns invented the United Hot Clubs of America, which
leased rare, out-of-print records from various companies and reissued them
on its own U.H.C.A. label. A company that put out nothing but jazz
records—albeit old ones—was a novelty, and so was its practice of listing on
its labels the personnel, instrumentation, and date and place of recording.
Gabler, a man of high standards, was not particularly pleased with the
offhanded way the big companies were treating jazz. So he decided, late in
1937, to form his own recording company. He held his first session on January 17, 1938, the day after Benny Goodman's Carnegie Hall concert. The
group—of quasi-Chicago persuasion—was the prototype of what became
the backbone of Gabler's catalogue. It was made up of Bobby Hackett, Pee
Wee Russell, Georg Brunis, and Eddie Condon, all of whom were working
at Nick's in Greenwich Village; Jess Stacy, who was with Goodman; the bass
player Artie Shapiro (Joe Marsala), Bud Freeman (Tommy Dorsey), and
George Wettling (Red Norvo). Only Freeman and Wettling had been

directly connected with the Chicago style of playing, although Stacy and Russell had passed through its fringes. It was a gabby, winging-it hand-me-down of King Oliver's Creole Jazz Band and the white New Orleans Rhythm Kings: loose ensembles, often played in a give-'em-hell diminu-endo-crescendo fashion; a string of solos, sometimes launched by a brief ensemble burst or by a break, and often underscored with organ chords played by the horns, which recalled glee-club humming; and an occasional drum solo or closing four-bar drum break. Unlike a surprising number of early white jazz fans, Gabler brought a wide intelligence and a good ear to the music. (There were few black jazz "fans." Jazz, instrumental and vocal, was not an alien, collectible form to black listeners but an everyday past of their lives.) Gilbert Millstein, in a Profile of Gabler published in *The New Yorker*, quotes an anonymous musician on Gabler's skills as an A&R. man:

"There's a ray comes out of him," the musician said. "You can't help doing something the way he wants. Here is this guy can't read a note of music and he practically tells you what register you're going to play in just by the position of your head."

Gabler's early catalogue is imposing, and includes Billie Holiday's "Strange Fruit," and her great blues "Fine and Mellow," and "Yesterdays," and the stately "I Gotta Right To Sing the Blues"; a good number of Chicago-type sides, many the best of their kind; twenty or so piano solos and band sides by Jelly Roll Morton, who was still full of music; a dozen sides by Buck Clayton and Lester Young and Jo Jones, and as many by Roy Eldridge and Benny Carter and Chu Berry and Coleman Hawkins and Sid Catlett, all of them the avant-garde of jazz; and a session with Fats Waller that belongs with the cream of his recordings.

In 1941, Gabler began working full time for Decca, and he eventually became its chief A&R. man. He has said, "It didn't matter who I had recorded for Decca during the week—Louis Armstrong, Peggy Lee—or how far I had flown to do it. I couldn't wait to go into the studio on Saturday and make my Commodores. I had to get all those musicians down, I had to preserve them, and I did nothing but enjoy doing it. It's as vivid as yesterday. The only regret I have is that I bypassed Charlie Parker and Dizzy Gillespie when they first appeared on Fifty-second Street. I'd like to have their music in my catalogue now." Gabler continued making Commodore records regularly until around 1948, and he wound everything up in 1951. (His father's radio shop, which became the famous Commodore Music Shop, moved a few feet east and then across the street, not far from its namesake, where it closed in 1958.) What Gabler did was preserve—in the face of the dreary, devouring big bands—the very heart of jazz: its small bands. He inspired Blue Note and Keynote Records, which followed his courageous ways, and the host of fly-by-night labels that documented the new music of Parker and

Gillespie. And he is indirectly responsible for the countless independent labels that support the music now. But Gabler's catalogue hasn't been completely in print since the mid-fifties, when the LP arrived and chaos began. Gabler himself reissued some material on LP, and quit. A record club brought out more, and went out of business. Gabler leased masters to labels here and abroad, which reissued them higgledy-piggledy, often as collections of tenor saxophonists or clarinettists or pianists but rarely chronologically and in complete sessions. The last coherent attempt to reissue the catalogue in this country was undertaken by Atlantic seven years ago, but that fell by the way, too.

Now Gabler has decided to bring out his entire oeuvre, session by session and including the alternate takes. There are ten LPs in the first batch of reissues, which are being distributed by Columbia, and not all of them are knockouts. Eleven Bud Freeman trio sides (with Jess Stacy and George Wettling) are as monotonous and jouncy as ever—despite Stacy, who repeatedly attempts to aerate the proceedings with his laughing tremolos and swimming way of swinging. The four famous Mel Powell–Benny Goodman sides ("When Did You Leave Heaven?," "Blue Skies," "Mood at Twilight," and "The World Is waiting for the Sunrise") open an LP, but the rest is filled out with three undistinguished Mel Powell big-band sides and four frumpy Joe Bushkin–Bill Harris–Zoot Sims selections. Another LP is given over to four Jack Teagarden numbers (with Ernie Caceres on clarinet. Max Kaminsky, Norma Teagarden on piano, and George Wettling) and four sweating Max Kaminsky sides (with Rod Cless on clarinet and Frank Orchard on trombone). The rest of the reissues are full of delights. A Jelly Roll Morton LP contains twelve piano solos, five of them with his naked, melancholy vocals. There is a Lester Young–Buck Clayton LP on which Young plays a lot of his skinny, lissome clarinet, and the rhythm section (Freddie Green, Walter Page, Jo Jones) moves in an area no rhythm section had moved in before. These are classic sides, and as flexible and graceful as they were forty years ago. A Coleman Hawkins LP includes the 1940 Chocolate Dandies session, with Roy Eldridge, Benny Carter, and Sid Catlett, and in addition to its familiar beauties there is an alternate take of "I Can't Believe That You're in Love with Me," done at a slower tempo than the one originally released. It rocks and sways, and Eldridge takes a fascinating solo—sure, lyrical, biting. A Wild Bill Davison reissue has all the first-rate sessions he did in November of 1943, and they roar and champ and steam. Davison liked to pick up the melody and hurl it down the ensemble, making his cohorts tumble after. The champion of the ten albums is given over in part to the quartet that Sid Catlett had on Fifty-second Street in 1943 and 1944: Ben Webster, who is the leader of the record date; Marlowe Morris on piano; and John Simmons on bass. There are two takes of everything, excluding "Just a Riff," and they are particularly valuable for Webster and for Catlett's brilliant solos on the two "Sleep"s and his just-like-that two-bar breaks on the two "Linger Awhile"s.

## Soul Soap

**K**eith Jarrett, the thirty-four-year-old Pennsylvania pianist, composer, and musical phenomenon, has his own pedestal. His admirers, who are legion, have put it up, and they haven't stinted. They have made it possible for him to be paid over ten thousand dollars for a one-and-a-half-hour solo concert, and for his record label (ECM) to issue a ten-LP album ("Sun Bear Concerts") that sells for seventy-five dollars. They sit in worshipful silence at the outset of his concerts while he lectures them on comportment, and after he has played they show a brimming fervor. Jarrett doesn't look like a matinée idol. He is of medium height and almost skinny. He affects an Afro hairdo, which crowns a set of triangles—a small, wedgelike face with a sharp nose and jack-o'-lantern eyes. But he is a Dionysian performer. His music possesses him, and he goes through a continuous dance at the keyboard which forms a hypnotic visual counterpoint to his music. He rarely sits on the piano bench. He half crouches, sometimes slipping so low that when he occasionally throws his arms in the air it appears he is about to catch the lip of the keyboard to keep from plunging into the abyss. He rotates his shoulders and rocks back and forth. He twists his head, jerks it, ducks it, and throws it back. His face passes through demonic contortions. All the while, he hums in unison falsetto or issues loud ecstatic "ohhhhh"s—missiles of emotion that both applaud his efforts and warn the audience that it is in the presence of important doings. These doings cannot be classified except by saying that he plays an improvised piano music that anthologizes much of the Western (classical and jazz) and Oriental music of the past couple of centuries. A Jarrett performance may reflect and refract Bill Evans, Indian ragas, Ray Bryant, Stephen Foster, Chopin, Dave Brubeck, Cecil Taylor, Beethoven, Art Tatum, Debussy, Bud Powell, Brahms, the blues, Rachmaninoff, Gospel music, Bach, Horace Silver, Lennie Tristano, flamenco music, folk songs, the "Warsaw Concerto," McCoy Tyner, George Gershwin, the "Bolero," boogie-woogie, and Liszt. These structures have grown encyclopedic. One of them may last three-quarters of an hour, and may go something like this: Jarrett begins with a ground bass and open Debussy chords. He pedals slowly along in this mode, then shifts into another ground bass and develops a repeated single-note figure in the right hand, which becomes flamencan before it rises into the upper registers and evaporates. A third ground bass materializes (repetition is the backbone of his playing), and he begins hitting hard, offbeat right-hand chords. He repeats these maddeningly for a minute or so and, suddenly stopping, switches to a passage of soul soap with a rolling bass and dense Ray Bryant right-hand chords. The Debussy opening passes in review again and is transformed into a Bill Evans ballad, which eventually closes with parallel Bach runs. A waltz rounds the corner (despite Jarrett's varying rhythms, there are no rhythmic surprises in his work), and he plays very softly, just at the threshold of sound. He keeps whispering this waltzing softness until the listener falls under a spell. But Jarrett is a masterly melo-dramatist, who knows precisely when to shift scenes. The waltz fades away, and he lunges into a crowd of dissonant chords, letting them grind against one another until all that remains is a lullaby left hand, which supports a Rach-maninoff melody in the right hand. This is spun out languorously in widely spaced single notes in the highest register—notes that are struck like chimes in an intense, slow-motion legato. He grows softer and softer, over a period of minutes, and the notes, now in the far distance, stop. There is a long pause—for his audiences have learned that they must not tread on his skirts—and the roar begins.

The "Sun Bear" album consists of ten such edifices, built at five concerts given between November 5 and November 18, 1976, at Kyōto, Ōsaka, Nagoya, Tokyo, and Sapporo. Jarrett will probably never surpass them, even though they surpass the celebrated Köln concert of a year and a half before. Their texture and movement, their dynamics and occasional virtu-osity are dazzling, and so are the lyrical patches that turn up, particularly in the second part of the Kyōto concert and the first part of the Nagoya. These patches sound like improvisations on such numbers as "Summertime" and "I Loves You, Porgy" or like reworkings of a yearning ascending-descending blues motif that appears again and again in his work. They light up the fail-ings in the musical landscape around them. Despite Jarrett's outward prolix-ity and his poetic flashes, the emotional content of his work is on a level with that of Thomas Wolfe and Judy Garland and Cecil B. De Mille. The playing is bravura and self-indulgent, like a dandy constantly changing clothes. It shouts and day-dreams. It is an improvised music that feeds on itself.

Jarrett began as a jazz pianist in the early sixties, working with Art Blakey and Tony Scott and Charles Lloyd. He caused a small sensation when he appeared with Lloyd at the Newport Jazz Festival in 1966. Lloyd let Jarrett loose on one number, and he played a long, complex rhapsody that seemed startling and highly original. Only Cecil Taylor and Dave Brubeck played that sort of Wagnerian chordal piano. Jarrett's oceanic solo concerts have carried him a considerable dis-tance from his origins, and, perhaps to redress this, he has begun working again in selected jazz clubs with a quartet. (Jan Garbarek is on tenor saxo-phone, Jon Christensen on drums, and Palle Danielsson on bass.) In New York, he chose the Village Vanguard, because its owner, Max Gordon, was the only one who would hire his trio in the sixties. He told Gordon that he would charge him just a thousand dollars a night but that Gordon could ask no more than six dollars and fifty cents at the door—presumably to allow the faithful to encamp without undue economic anxiety. Gordon agreed (he also agreed to have the piano tuned twice a night), and Jarrett played at the Vanguard for five days. Gordon can handle something under three hundred people a night, and by opening day he was sold out for the week and had turned away at least a thousand reservations. There weren't many surprises in the music except that it had a distinct jazz flavor. Each number had ensembles, a sounded beat, and solos. Garbarek took a couple of lengthy solos, but the rest of the time he provided chordal backdrops or was silent while Christensen and Danielsson pumped away behind Jarrett, who shaped solo after solo, each full of Bach and Monk and Beethoven and Copland and Coleman and Evans and Debussy and Gershwin. At the same time, he undulated like sea grass, moved his shoulders as if he were inching across no man's land, made serpentine motions with his neck and head, and fired off countless booming "ohhhhh"s. In between piano solos, he secreted himself behind a pillar at one side of the bandstand and played the timbales with ferocious abandon. The room was awash with awe at the end of the long first set, and the line of waiting acolytes stretched up the steps and down Seventh Avenue.

## Late Mingus

Charles Mingus spent most of his life at the barricades, but his chief weapons were words. In time, his life was awash with words. He wrote an immense autobiography, out of which Nel King quarried *Beneath the Underdog*. When he was at the top of his combative powers in the late fifties and early sixties, he published long, angry letters in magazines, and dictated smoking liner notes for his albums. Sometimes his verbal fervor elbowed clarity aside, as in this disquisition on the beat, from a 1963 liner note:

> You don't play the beat where it is. You draw a picture away from the beat right up to its core with different notes of different sounds of the drum instruments so continuously that the core is always there for an open mind. While you make it live now and then you go inside the beat, dead center, and split the core to the sides and shatter the illusion so there is no shakiness ever. If one tries to stay inside dead center or directly on top of the beat or on the bottom, the beat is too rigid on the outside where it is heard. The stiffness should only be felt inside the imaginary center of the exact tempo's core.

He was a voluminous talker, and his words came out in light, fast, irregular clumps, like the phrases in his bass playing. Sometimes his words went by so fast there was no time for them to reveal their meaning. He occasionally lectured night-club audiences ten minutes at a stretch, issuing a mixture of invective, musical pedagogy, autobiography, and homemade philosophy. These broadsides had a cathartic effect on Mingus, and they stunned his listeners. But once in a while words failed him. Max Gordon, the inventor and shepherd of the Village Vanguard, has described what happened when they did:

> He'd start a set, then stop. "Try that again," he'd cry. Often, when he was several minutes into a number, his hand would go up. "Hold it," he'd shout. He seldom let a number play [unbroken] to the end . . .
>
> Mingus knew what he wanted; he had written the piece, and by God he wanted to hear it the way he wrote it.
>
> One night, in the middle of one of his compositions . . . he leaned his bass fiddle against the piano, threw his hands up in despair, walked over to Jimmy Knepper, the trombonist, and hit him a thundering blow in his solar plexus. Jimmy went down, and the set was over.

Mingus's physical explosions were indiscriminate. He went after his audience, his sidemen, and the people who hired him. Gordon recalls another night:

> Jazz musicians have the privilege of a cash draw every night. It says so in the contract, and is sacrosanct even when there is no contract. At closing one night, Mingus came around for the usual draw. Unfortunately, the Vanguard didn't have enough cash on hand. Mingus, raging, walked behind the bar, selected several unopened bottles of Scotch, and vowed he'd turn them into cash somewhere to take care of the needs of his men. But it was 4 A.M. and bars were closed, so he smashed a couple of bottles on the floor, grabbed a kitchen knife, which he held threateningly in front of me, and, still unmollified, stood on a chair and punched his fist through a light fixture. He knocked the fixture askew but the bulb inside stayed lit. I have never had the thing fixed. . . . The "Mingus light" I call it. You can see it if you ask a waiter.

Mingus's music was a distillation of Duke Ellington, gospel music, Charlie Parker, the blues, Jimmy Blanton, New Orleans polyphony, and fast small-band swing music. It was another weapon, another way of talking. At its best, it was a concatenation of voices, now solo, now in duet, now in quintet or octet—all shouting, laughing, exulting, announcing. It was not always meant to be intelligible; each voice was directed at and dependent on the others. Despite its boisterousness and bulk, it kept turning inward, the better for each voice to hear the others. Mingus's music (his compositions and his improvisations, together with the improvisations of his sidemen, which he rigorously patrolled) had no style in the conventional sense of such composer-bandleader-performers as Duke Ellington and John Kirby. Ellington was Mingus's principal inspiration. He taught Mingus to use multiple themes and original voicings and "talking" instruments. He probably also helped shape Mingus's gift for writing lyrical blues-directed melodies and for finding musicians who were almost invariably adaptable to his needs. (Mingus's bass playing, an intense elaboration of Ellington's bassists Jimmy Blanton and Oscar Pettiford, was more annunciatory than melodic. It had great vigor and virtuosity, and it was always recognizable, because of its mixture of eighth notes, silences, and tremolos, and its "vocal" attack and resonant tone.) Perhaps the reason Mingus's music had no style was that it never stood still long enough. Mingus was constantly experimenting, and his music, which ranged from long-limbed love songs to raging dissonances, had few boundaries. Jazz rhythms—the accents and multi-noted cascades of bebop notwithstanding—had changed little since the thirties, when jazzmen first learned to swing, and this bothered him. He used accelerando and decelerando. He used breaks and stop-times. He wrote passages that had no sounded beat, and he superimposed tricky, sliding double-time rhythms on plodding four-four time. He doubled tempos and halved them, tripled them and halved them. So intent was he on rhythmic surprise and perfection that he fashioned a drummer, Dannie Richmond, in his own image. When Mingus found him, Richmond was twenty-one and had played drums only a few months. (He'd been a tenor saxophonist.) Mingus taught him unswerving time, the melodic possibilities of drums, and how to make a drum solo fit its environment. When Richmond came aboard for good, in 1957, Mingus's music changed permanently.

Mingus's fascination with time and the beat came in large part from his instrument, but it is not altogether clear where his love of counterpoint came from. Certainly he learned from Ellington, whose music was a steady vying of voices, and he probably learned from his work with the fleet, thickly plotted trio that Red Norvo had in the early fifties. (Mingus often said that all his discoveries were made in the forties, when he lived on the West Coast.) Mingus liked to float six or seven horns at once. He would sketch their general courses, and as they gathered steam he'd urge them on with shouts and with his locomotive bass. Sometimes he let two or three voices tangle and forced the rest into the comfort of riffs, and sometimes he let them all fall into cacophony—presaging the "free" ensembles of Sam Rivers and the Art Ensemble of Chicago. These experiments suggested the texture and excitement of the old New Orleans ensembles, but, unfortunately, Mingus never carried them through, either in his small-band efforts or in the big bands he toyed with in the sixties and seventies. Mingus's influence has already been wide (though rarely acknowledged), and is visible among such bassists as Scott La Faro and Steve Swallow and Gary Peacock, and among the avant-garde; his music also preserved the old beauties of jazz handed down by Lester Young and Charlie Parker. This wasn't any trouble for Mingus: he simply set himself to music.

We are in the midst of a Mingus celebration. Two recent Carnegie Hall concerts have been devoted to his music (which is just as incomplete without him as Ellington's music is without him,) and there are four recent Mingus albums, three of them reissues. The new album, "Me Myself an Eye," was made less than a year before his death in January 1979, and he does not play on it. It bears his mark, but in general it is shallow and overblown. The four numbers, two of them reworkings of old Mingus efforts, are played by twenty-five piece bands, and little is added by the extra avoirdupois. The longest selection lasts a half hour and is called "Three Worlds of Drums." There are several series of drum solos, played by Joe Chambers, Dannie Richmond, and Steve Gadd; a couple of huge ensemble expostulations; a parade of solos (Jack Walrath, Randy Brecker, George Mraz, George Coleman, Eddie Gomez, Mike Brecker, and Larry Coryell); and, in the last three or four minutes, a beautiful, enfolding flamencan melody, played by the brass, which resolves into a dirge, backed by deep, descending organ chords. The least valuable of the reissues, "Nostalgia in Times Square," brings together fourteen numbers that Mingus recorded at several different sessions in 1959. Four have never been released before, and the rest restore various ensemble and solo deletions. But not much happens. "Boogie Stop Shuffle" has rhythmic intensity, and "Open Letter to Duke" has one of Mingus's lingering, lazing melodic lines. Mingus and Jimmy Knepper take striking solos on "Pussy Cat Dues," and "Song with Orange" has a fine Mingus blues melody. For whatever reasons, Mingus was not happy at Columbia, and his best work at this time was done with Atlantic and with Candid. Atlantic has assembled a three-record set, "Passions of a Man," which covers the years from 1956 to 1977. Much of Mingus's most attractive work is on it: the Gospel-blues pieces "Wednesday Night Prayer Meeting" and "Cryin' Blues" (but where is "Moanin' "?); the cool, melodic "Pithecanthropus Erectus," "Reincarnation of a Lovebird," and "Sue's Changes"; the multi-rhythmic "Tonight at Noon" and "Haitian Fight Song"; and a surprise from 1974—a five-and-a-half-minute slow blues called "Canon," in which a good blues melody is handed back and forth, in largely unembellished canon form, between two horns, a piano, and Mingus's bass. The Candid reissue is "Mingus Presents Mingus," and it was made in 1960, with the working band he had then— Ted Curson, Eric Dolphy, and Dannie Richmond. The four men had developed a telepathic understanding, a joint imaginativeness. The album includes "What Love" and "All the Things You Could Be by Now If Sigmund Freud's Wife Was Your Mother," which are reworkings of "What Is This Thing Called Love?" and "All the Things You Are"; "Original Faubus Fables"; and the twelve-minute "Folk Forms, No. 1." This last is one of the most remarkable of all Mingus's recordings. It begins with Mingus playing a simple blueslike figure. He is joined by Richmond, in ad-lib time. Dolphy enters (on alto saxophone), and is almost immediately followed by Curson, who is muted. The horns converse, the rhythm slips into four-four time and is interrupted by breaks and out-of-tempo passages. Dolphy and Richmond drop out, and Mingus backs Curson. Richmond and Dolphy return, and all four men swim around and around and come to a stop. Mingus solos without backing, and Richmond reappears, pulling the horns after him. There is another stop, and Dolphy solos against broken rhythms, and the four take up their ruminations again. After a third stop, Richmond solos and he and Mingus go into a kicking, jumping, unbelievably swinging duet. Mingus falls silent, allowing Richmond to finish his solo, and there is a stop. Mingus solos briefly, and all converse intently until the rhythm slows, Dolphy moans, and they go out. It should be said that near the end of "What Love" Mingus and Dolphy (on bass clarinet) have a long and different kind of "conversation" on their instruments—apparently about Dolphy's intention of quitting the band.

## Hodges, Again

Hearing the Duke Ellington band live during its last ten years was like attending a sporting event. For the most part, the contestants were not the leader versus the orchestra (though that was sometimes the case) or members of the orchestra versus members of the orchestra (also occasionally true) but the leader and his orchestra versus the audience. The object of the game for the performers was to distract the audience so that it wouldn't notice how weary they were of much that they had to play or how badly they might play it, and the object for the audience was to get past the massed personalities onstage to the unique, exultant Ellington timbres and textures. Ellington had all kinds of weapons—his elegant verbiage, his celestial, his put-ons (the "I love you madly"s, the finger-popping exercise). So did the band. Johnny Hodges feigned sleep or stony boredom. Cootie Williams strutted. Lawrence Brown oozed hauteur. Ray Nance clowned. Paul Gonsalves looked subaqueous. And there were hypnotic rituals, like the trumpet-clarinet-trombone trios that assembled solemnly at midstage to play "Mood Indigo" and "Black and Tan Fantasy." Eventually, we got through these divertissements, only to realize that when Ellington and the band were gone, the jig would be up—without them we would be reduced to memory, and to recordings. But recordings, like good portrait photographs, take on their own life: sheer availability gives them bulk and vigor, and in time they come close to supplanting their originals. Nor did we know that Ellington recorded constantly, and that a great deal of what he set down was unreleased. So the flood of new Ellington recordings that have appeared during the past few years has been surprising and welcome—in particular, three small-band sessions done in New

York and Hollywood in 1959 and 1960, and released as "The Smooth One: Johnny Hodges" and "Duke Ellington: Unknown Session."

Hodges is the star of three tracks on the second album and of all the tracks on the first. It's increasingly clear that he was at the center of the Ellington firmament. His sound, style, and steadfastness (he missed only four years between 1928, when he joined the band, and 1970, when he died) were essential to Ellington's thinking and music, and so were his compositional gifts. Hodges's balance of emotion and coolness, intensity and ease, poetry and matter-of-factness became the badge of the band. He was also a key to its curious origins. (Mercer Ellington ponders them in his book about his father.) The Ellington band was always considered a New York creation, but for a long time it was a New Orleans band in disguise. During the twenties and thirties, it used such New Orleans musicians as Wellman Braud (bass), Lonnie Johnson (guitar), and Sidney Bechet and Barney Bigard. It used muted techniques brought forward by King Oliver, and many of its brass players reflected Louis Armstrong. Harry Carney admired Coleman Hawkins, who, in turn, admired Armstrong. The drummer Tommy Benford remembers Hodges in Harlem in the twenties:

> One Monday, at the Hoofer's Club, a kid named Johnny Hodges sat in, and Willie the Lion Smith, who had the band, hired him on the spot. He didn't sound like anybody. But later Sidney Bechet put together a band and it had Hodges and me, and we went into Herman's Inn. The first night, Hodges, who had been playing clarinet and alto, picked up Bechet's soprano and played it, and Bechet about went crazy. After that, Sidney encouraged Hodges on the soprano, and he even gave him one, which Hodges still had when he died.

Hodges transposed Bechet's methods to the alto saxophone and streamlined them. He eliminated Bechet's operatic vibrato and his tendency to run the scales. He bottled Bechet's urgency and served it in cool, choice doses. He skirted Bechet's funky tendencies—his growls and squeaks and odd, bubbling sounds. But he kept Bechet's pouring country tone, his impeccable sense of time, and his rhapsodic approach to slow materials. The result was two Hodges styles—one fast and one slow. The fast style, used largely on the blues, consisted of adroit embellishments suspended from a supply of rif-flike four- or five-note phrases that Hodges stockpiled through the years. He would issue two or three of these figures in each solo (his solos rarely lasted more than three choruses) and connect them with silences, quick backstairs runs, blue notes, and chugging single notes. He had a strong sense of dynamics, and would play his first chorus in gossiping whispers. Then, using a loud three-note proclamation, he would start his next chorus, drop back to a whisper for two bars, and go up to a shout again and finish the solo. His blues solos (like the novels of Ivy Compton-Burnett) came to sound almost exactly alike. But this was deceptive, for he arranged his materials with ingenuity and imagination (as Compton-Burnett did). He also had a deep well of blues emotion, and was a legato player who unfailingly swung. His blues solos were elegant, rocking chants, but his slow ballad numbers seemed to be the work of a different musician. Around 1940, Ellington and/or Billy Strayhorn began writing a series of ballads for Hodges ("Warm Valley," "Day Dream," "Passion Flower," "Mood to Be Wooed"), and Hodges made them into a new kind of music. It was unashamedly romantic, but it was played with such intensity and perfection that it transcended sentimentality. Hodges moved through a set of curves in these solos. He would slide into almost every note, and use curving ascending or descending glisses, each of them delivered with on-pitch precision. Hodges did not play nearly enough medium-tempo standard songs. The ones he did play were often classic (his "Sunny Side of the Street"), and gave the impression that he was lobbing the melody back and forth from hand to hand. He was a master of paraphrase. When he played a melody "straight," he would alter a note here and a note there, subtract or add beats, and fashion an alter-melody that praised and complemented the original. He was a mysterious, shrewd, monosyllabic man, short and oval. In the autobiography *Music Is My Mistress*, Ellington says of Hodges, "His tonal charisma is difficult to describe, but he always referred to it as 'the kitchen.' If someone else played something in his style, he would say: 'All right, come out of the kitchen.' "

## Five Important Recordings

S ince Jimmy Rowles settled in New York in 1974, he has been recorded many times—on his own and with such as Zoot Sims, Charles Mingus, Stan Getz, Stéphane Grappelli, and Lee Konitz—but nothing has come out quite right. He has sounded bland or dispirited or uninventive; or if he appeared in promising form he hasn't been allowed to stretch out. It had begun to look as if Rowles's style would never be caught, as if we would be doomed to follow him from night club to night club (his most natural habitat), collecting a brilliant arpeggio here and a brilliant coda there, only to find, two or three days later, that they had faded and were gone. But "Al Cohn and Jimmy Rowles: Heavy Love" and "Jimmy Rowles: We Could Make Such Beautiful Music Together" go a long way toward laying the fear that Rowles would never be properly recorded.

The first is a swashbuckling, eloquent, free-as-you-go duet by Rowles and his old friend the tenor saxophonist Al Cohn. (Liner notes on jazz albums are looking up. David A. Himmelstein describes Cohn's provenance this way: "Out of Lesterville, a Dexter runabout, with four brother-doors and chicken liver wheels," which means that Cohn admires Lester Young and resembles Dexter Gordon, that he was one of the famous Woody Herman saxophonists known as the Four Brothers, and that he plays with a cantorial lyricism.) Cohn and Rowles do five standards and one blues, largely in medium tempo, and they are never apart, even when they solo. Cohn's sound echoes in the mind when Rowles is alone, and when Cohn solos Rowles pulls all his accompanist stops. He supplies off-beat chords, broken chords, seesawing chords, thump-thump-thump on-the-beat chords, and crabbed single-note lines that make Cohn glint. He anticipates Cohn, duplicates him, and mischievously parodies him. Rowles's solos are often special—particularly the single-note excursions on "Them There Eyes" and "Sweet and Lovely," and his second chorus on "Taking a Chance on Love," in which he plays a series of ascending staccato notes, striking some of them two or three times to achieve a nervous stuttering effect.

On the second record, Rowles leads a trio that has George Mraz on bass and Leroy Williams on drums. The best number is a five-minute "Stars and Stripes Forever" done as a bossa nova. Rowles plays the melody in lagging single notes, improvises, and then goes into a heavy, full-orchestra section, all horns blaring, and returns to his lagging single notes, finishing with a coda made up of part of "Taps." There is also an elegant "We Could Make Such Beautiful Music," and a "Here's That Rainy Day" where, in the total-improvisation way of Lester Young, he leaves every note of the melody unturned. He does a funny version of Erroll Garner's "Shake It, but Don't Break It," and closes the record with overly long readings of "I Can't Get Started" and "In the Still of the Night."

The twelve sides on "Billie Holiday: Swing Brother, Swing" were recorded between 1935 and 1939, and eleven have never before been released in this country on LP The generally anemic accompaniment (the musicians are taken from Benny Goodman, Jimmy Lunceford, Chick Webb, Fletcher Henderson, Red Norvo, Stuff Smith, and Bobby Hackett's band at Nick's) probably helps explain why they have been out of print so long. So do the songs. With the exception of "They Can't Take That Away from Me" and the good but forgotten "I Don't Know If I'm Coming or Going," "I Wish I Had You," and "You're Gonna See a Lot of Me," the material is Tin Pan Alley strudel: "Life Begins When You're in Love," "The Moon Looks Down and Laughs," "Forget If You Can," "You're So Desirable," and "Hello, My Darling." But Billie Holiday treats each song as if it were prime Gershwin or Rodgers. She carefully unfolds the lyrics and holds them up for us to see. She hand-paints each melody, concealing the nonsense and the clichés. She does her incomparable legato act, loafing along behind the beat, her shoulders hunched in mock surprise, her fingers spread in the idling air, then catches up in the last chorus, the last eight, the last measure. Teddy Wilson is on eight sides, and Claude Thornhill, who was a better pianist than he has ever been given credit for, is on three. Listen to his things-to-come solos on "The Moon Looks Down and Laughs" and "Forget If You Can."

Red Norvo has an uncanny way of making classic recordings, and "Red & Ross" is one. It was recorded at Donte's, in North Hollywood, and on hand with Norvo are Ross Tompkins on piano, John Williams (not to be confused with the older Johnny Williams) on bass, and Jake Hanna on drums. Nightclub recordings are often baggy and self-indulgent, but "Red & Ross" is tight and graceful and swinging. At least one intensely pleasing thing happens on each of the six long tracks. On "Whisper Not," played as a piano solo, Tompkins settles into his improvisation with a sudden descending, skipping double-time run that is breathtaking. "The One I Love," taken at a fast tempo, has another exhilarating Tompkins solo, and near its end bass and drums lay out while Norvo and Tompkins play counterpoint—a bramble of voices moving complexly and daringly. The two repeat their attractive act even more tellingly on "All of Me." "How About You?" has half a dozen eight-bar breaks by Hanna, whose admiration for Sid Catlett has worked handsomely for him. On "It Might As Well Be Spring," Norvo and Hanna, using brushes on his cymbals, play a glancing, airborne duet. "Everything Happens to Me" is very different from the rest of the album. It is slow and is given over largely to Norvo, who makes it into a melancholy hymn.

"The Bob Brookmeyer Small Band" is a continuous and often beautiful celebration of melodic improvisation, carried out by the leader on valve trombone, Jack Wilkins on guitar, and Michael Moore on bass, with the excellent Joe LaBarbera on drums. The recording, which has presence and clarity, was done at Sandy's Jazz Revival, a night club in Beverly, Massachusetts, and it is made up of fifteen numbers, ten of them standards and the rest originals or reworkings of standards by Brookmeyer, Andy Laverne, and Art Koenig. Melodic improvisation—as opposed to abstract improvisation—comes in several weights. The lightest is embellishment. The player alters the melody subtly, as if he were translating it into another language, by adding grace notes, subtracting notes, rearranging rhythms, and applying his particular timbres. Variation is a fussier form of embellishment. Sometimes the melody vanishes altogether and the player becomes as important as the melody itself. Total improvisation, the rarest of the lot, is just that: the player, using either the melody or the chords of the tune as bedrock, builds a new and more complex melody. If the original song is a winter tree, total improvisation is a July tree.

Brookmeyer is a master of all three forms of improvisation, but he concentrates here on the first and last. His masterly embellishments are evident on "Sweet and Lovely," "Some Day My Prince Will Come," and "You'd Be So Nice To Come Home To." The total improviser does his vanishing trick on "Smoke Gets in Your Eyes," "Body and Soul," and "I Can't Get Started." His rebuilding of the three is complete; there is no way of knowing what the original melody is without being told. Brookmeyer is a brilliant but puzzling musician who won't let the listener alone. He plays him to death. He is a lyricist, but he buries his poems in notes, smears, arpeggios, in a kind of anti-sissy bravado. It is instructive to compare Brookmeyer with Jimmy Knepper. Both are middle-aged, second-generation beboppers, but Knepper has become an aphorist while Brookmeyer is still an explainer. Wilkins, in his thirties, is a superlative guitarist who, like Jim Hall, is not hemmed in by his instrument. He likes to get off figures that suggest pianists or saxophonists or trumpeters. He uses a full tone and he prefers the upper registers and he has a good sense of dynamics. He is a wild melodist. He will throw a handful of notes into the high register, make them ring, fill the space after them with silence, and dive into his lowest register, touching each octave as he falls past. Then he will ascend and strike more urgent bells, and go into driving Django Reinhardt chords, which give way to more silence and curling, meditative middle-register single notes. His rhythmic attack accents his melodic freshness and independence. He shadows his notes, rides in front of them, and dots their "i"s. He and Michael Moore work together well. Moore's improvisations, often done in *his* high registers, are pure and lofty. Moore plays over half a dozen solos on the album, and all are superior. The album marks the first time that Moore has been heard properly and at length on records.

Air is made up of Henry Threadgill on reeds and hubkaphone, Fred Hopkins on bass, and Steve McCall on drums. Like the Art Ensemble of Chicago, Air relies on subtle racial humor and on collective abstract improvisation. Its wheels throw off showers of timbres and textures: Threadgill plays baritone saxophone, making Queen Mary honks, while Hopkins plays wild arco figures and McCall bounces from tomtom to tomtom; Threadgill plays flute and Hopkins supplies delicate pizzicato runs while McCall moves through his cymbals with wire brushes; Threadgill plays his hubkaphone, which consists of a dozen or so hubcaps strung out on a kind of drying rack, and Hopkins and McCall go into Afro-Cuban rhythms. "Open Air Suit" and "Lore" were made in studios, and "Montreux Suisse" was recorded at the Montreux Jazz Festival. Threadgill plays flute, and alto, tenor, and baritone saxophones on the first, which has four studied pieces. They are described this way on the back of the album: " 'Open Air Suit' was cut and designed for Air as a five piece suit. Whereby from a customed viewpoint Air was considered, however it was conceived as something that Air would have to fit itself up to or rather into. As a piece each person had to play a hand on the basis of what they had in their hand, secondly on the basis of what was possibly open. Remembering at all times never to photograph one's entire position or game plan prematurely." "Lore" is a conservative investigation of Jelly Roll Morton ("Buddy Bolden's Blues" and "King Porter Stomp") and Scott Joplin ("The Ragtime Dance"), and the approach is either gently parodic or *almost* straightforward (Threadgill does some fine embellishing), so that one doesn't know whether to laugh at the old-timey music or weep at its suggested beauty. The group is firmly on its own ground in the festival recording. "Let's All Go Down to the Footwash" has an Ornette Coleman melody, and "Abra" is an abstract blues. The fifteen-minute "Suisse Air" is largely Threadgill bonk-bonking on his hubkaphone, with Hopkins and McCall supplying a lot of Afro-Cuban rattling. It achieves considerable momentum but near the end is blown to bits when Threadgill picks up his baritone.

# THE EIGHTIES

# 1980

## Addict

In Henry Mayhew's great nineteenth-century oral history *London Poor,* a boy with "long and rather fair hair" speaks of the rigors of his childhood:

> I'm a native of Wisbeach, in Cambridgeshire, and am sixteen. My father was a shoe-maker, and my mother died when I was five years old, and my father married again. I was sent to school, and can read and write well. My father and step-mother were kind enough to me. I was apprenticed to a tailor three years ago, but I wasn't long with him; I runned away. I think it was three months I was with him when I first runned away . . . I stopped in lodging-houses until my money was gone, and then I slept anywhere—under the hedges, or anywhere . . . I had to beg my way back . . . but was very awkward at first. I lived on turnips mainly. My reason for running off was because my master ill-used me so; he beat me, and kept me from my meals, and made me sit up working late at nights for a punishment.

And here, a hundred and twenty years later, in the autobiography *Straight Life,* is the alto saxophonist Art Pepper speaking of his childhood:

> One time when my father had been at sea for quite a while he came home and found the house locked and me sitting on the front porch, freezing cold and hungry. She [Pepper's mother] was out somewhere. She didn't know he was coming. He was drunk. He broke the door down and took me inside and cooked me some food. She finally came home, drunk, and he cussed her out. We went to bed. I had a little crib in the corner, and my dad wanted to get into bed with me. He didn't want to sleep with her. She kept pulling on him, but he pushed her away and called her names. He started beating her up. He broke her nose. He broke a couple of ribs. Blood poured all over the floor. I remember the next day I was scrubbing up blood, trying to get the blood up for ages.

Most of Mayhew's four-volume work consists of interviews he conducted with London street people—prostitutes, beggars, flower girls, pick-pockets, sweeps, peddlers. Pepper's book is largely a self-interview. He is a drug addict, and seven years ago, after he had finished three years in Synanon, he began talking his life into a tape recorder as an act of catharsis and stabilization, and this letting loose continued for several years. There is a plethora of tape-recorded books—books set down in a false prose, whose authors have sidestepped the hard, distillative act of writing. But "Straight Life" demonstrates again and again that Pepper has the ear and memory and interpretative lyricism of a first-rate novelist. He describes what happened to the tenor saxophonist John Coltrane:

He got on that treadmill and ran himself ragged trying to be new and to change. It destroyed him. It was too wearing, too draining. And he became frustrated and worried. Then he started hurting, getting pains, and he got scared. He got these pains in his back, and he got terrified. He was afraid of doctors, afraid of hospitals, afraid of audiences, afraid of bandstands. He lost his teeth. He was afraid that his sound wasn't strong enough, afraid that the new, young black kids wouldn't think he was the greatest thing that ever lived anymore. And the pains got worse and worse: they got so bad he couldn't stand the pain. So they carried him to a hospital but he was too far gone. He had cirrhosis, and he died that night.

Here is the sort of subterranean soul Mayhew might have relished:

I looked around the club and saw this guy there, Blinky, that I knew. He was a short, squat guy with a square face, blue eyes; he squinted all the time; when he walked he bounced; and he was always going "Tchk! Tchk!"—moving his head in jerky little motions like he was playing the drums. Sometimes when he walked he even looked like a drum set: you could see the sock cymbal bouncing up and down and the foot pedal going and the cymbals shaking and his eyes would be moving. But it wasn't his eyes; it was that his whole body kind of blinked.

Pepper was born in 1925, in Gardena, California. His father was a tall, tough, handsome merchant seaman and labor organizer, and his mother, raised by an aunt and uncle, never knew her parents. Pepper's parents were twenty-nine and fifteen when they were married, and he was born with rickets and jaundice. There was little to the marriage. Pepper's father was at sea, and his mother was irresponsible and dissolute, and the relationship soon broke up. Pepper was sent to his paternal grandmother in the California countryside when he was five. He was a lorn, fearful child. "I'd wander around alone, and it seemed that the wind was always blowing and I was always cold," he recalls. "I was afraid of everything. Clouds scared me: it was as if they were living things that were going to harm me. Lightning and thunder frightened me beyond words. But when it was beautiful and sunny out my feelings were even more horrible because there was nothing in it for me." His grandmother was a cold German woman, who had her own sorrows, and when his father, who paid her to raise the child, visited between sea trips, Pepper was caught in a cross fire:

My grandmother cooked a lot of vegetables, things I couldn't stand—spinach, cauliflower, beets, parsnips. And [my father would] come and sit across from me in this little wooden breakfast nook, and my grandmother would tell me to eat this stuff, and I wouldn't eat it, couldn't eat it. He'd say, "Eat it!" My grandmother would say, "Don't be a baby!" He'd say, "Eat it! You gotta eat it to grow up and be strong!" That made me feel like a real weakling, so I'd put it in my mouth and then gag at the table and vomit into my plate. And my dad was able, in one motion, to unbuckle his belt and pull it out of the rungs, and he'd hit me across the table with the belt. It got to the point where I couldn't eat anything at all like that without gagging, and he'd just keep hitting at me and hitting the wooden wall behind me.

Pepper took up the clarinet at nine, and his father would sit him in bars in San Pedro and make him play "Nola" and "The Music Goes 'Round and 'Round" while his friends nodded approvingly and said, "That's Art's boy. He plays nice music." Pepper switched to the alto saxophone when he was twelve, and by the time he was seventeen he was married and working for Stan Kenton. He was in the Army from 1944 to 1946, and then spent five more years with Kenton and made his name as an original and graceful alto saxophonist. But his true career, the weight and heat of this book, began in 1950, when he became addicted to heroin. He was already an alcoholic, and he had long popped pills and smoked pot. None of these gave him surcease from the demons of loneliness and self-hatred. The heroin did—particularly the first time he tried it: "I could feel it start in my stomach. From the whole inside of my body I felt the tranquility . . . Sheila [a singer] said, 'Look at yourself in the mirror! Look in the mirror!' And that's what I'd always done: I'd stood and looked at myself in the mirror and I'd talk to myself and say how rotten I was . . . I thought, 'Oh, no! I don't want to do that! I don't want to spoil this feeling that's coming up in me.' . . . But she kept saying, 'Look at yourself! Look how beautiful you are!' . . . I looked in the mirror and I looked like an angel." In 1953, Pepper was arrested and sent to jail for possession of narcotics. During the next thirteen years, he spent more time in jail than out of it. He did five years in San Quentin, and his descriptions of life there are relentless and brilliant.

Pepper hit bottom just before he put himself in Synanon. He was an alcoholic and a junkie, and his career as a musician was in abeyance. His girlfriend had thrown him out, and he found himself, aged forty-four, sitting on his mother's porch, surrounded by his few belongings, and drinking brandy in the midday sun:

My mother had changed a lot over the years. She had found God. She had accepted Christ as her personal savior, and she'd stopped drinking and smoking . . . She said, "What happened? Where's Christine?" I said, "Christine's gone. She's gone. She's finished. She's gone. She left me here." My mother said, "Oh, Junior, you can't stay here! You know that. We've tried that before. It won't work." I said, "Don't get upset. Don't start flipping out, ma! I know it isn't going to work. I'm not asking to stay with you. I'm not going to stay with you. I know you don't want me to stay with you. You'd rather have me lay in the gutter and die than have me stay with you!" She said, "You don't have to talk like that." I said, "Well, it's true, isn't it?" She said, "Oh Junior, *please!*"

Pepper has married again, and he is playing and recording. He is in a methadone program. He has no illusions. ("And that's what I will die as—a junkie.") Nor does he have any remorse or self-pity. He has lived the inverse of the straight life, and he has lived it as well as he knows how. He does not rail against the laws that treat addicted human beings as criminals: the straight world has *its* hangups. He is an eloquent and gifted man.

## Newport 1980

*June 27th*

When the Whitney Museum put on its "Flowering of American Folk Art" show, in 1974, it acknowledged the help of Philip Morris, Inc., in small print on the copyright page of the catalogue. Here is how George Wein is acknowledging the help given the Newport Jazz Festival this year by the Brown & Williamson Tobacco Corporation: the Newport Jazz Festival-New York has become the Kool Newport Jazz Festival. (This offers all sorts of possibilities—the Lark Metropolitan Opera, the Tareyton New York Philharmonic, the Winston American Ballet Theater.) The twenty-sixth edition of the festival got under way at seven o'clock in Carnegie Hall with a four-hour concert in honor of Charlie Parker who died in 1955, at the age of thirty-four. The pianist Joe Albany played a rhapsodic blues and gave way to a group led by Jay McShann, who had hired Parker when Parker was eighteen. Although McShann's group had Howard McGhee, Clark Terry, Charlie Rouse, Budd Johnson, and Cecil Payne, the chief pleasures were his blues piano and Gus Johnson's Sid Catlett drumming. A souped-up version of Parker's "Yardbird Suite" was sung by Bob Dorough and played by the alto saxophonists James Moody, Lou Donaldson, and Lee Konitz, backed by John Lewis, Percy Heath, and Oliver Jackson. Konitz's fleet, winding solo was full of fine secrets. Lewis and Heath did an exquisite duet on Parker's "Billie's Bounce," and the saxophonists returned for a look-out-I'm-passing "Cherokee." Max Roach gave a spiel about Parker and played a drum solo. Dizzy Gillespie and Dexter Gordon were fleshed out by Al Haig, Chuck Wayne, Slam Stewart, and the drummer Eddie Gladden. Gordon wandered through the gloaming, and Gillespie used his kitchen silver. Jimmy

Raney, constructing a lot of fast, searching interior melodic figures, lifted a group led by Stan Getz. Barry Harris and Tommy Flanagan, the yin and yang of Detroit pianists, played two numbers, and Harris was aggressive, and even sparkling. Then Flanagan, Gus Johnson, and the bassist Gene Taylor, together with Gerry Mulligan, Zoot Sims, Al Cohn, and Jimmy Knepper, played Parker's "Ornithology" and a ballad-and-blues medley. Flanagan, full of feints, double-time dashes, and upper-register diamonds, fashioned two first-rate choruses on "Ornithology," and was matched by Knepper. On the medley, Flanagan rolled out a beautiful ballad, and Knepper, thin and tall and looking as if he might waft away, suddenly came forth with "Parker's Mood." It was a shouting, stuttering blues, and the sermon Parker meant it to be. The final group—Curtis Fuller, Jimmy Heath, Red Rodney, and Billy Mitchell, with a rhythm section of Walter Davis, George Duvivier, and Philly Joe Jones—slid down bebop mountain and came to rest on the boulders of hard-bop valley.

*June 28th*

At five-thirty in Carnegie Recital Hall, Dardanelle sang and played a dozen or so songs, among them "It Could Happen to You," "Spring Can Really Hang You Up the Most," "Out of This World," "It's All Right with Me," and "In the Evening." By demonstrating in her small, sweet, perfect, birdlike way just how to perform good American songs, she shamed almost all the twenty or so instrumentalists and singers gathered in Carnegie Hall tonight to celebrate Fred Astaire. (How do you celebrate Fred Astaire? Copy his dancing? Copy his singing? Copy his acting? Or, as was done tonight, perform the songs he helped make famous? Each is a poor second.) Mel Tormé began the evening at the piano, singing his own lyrics to "They Can't Take That Away from Me." Ruby Braff, aided by John Bunch, George Duvivier, and Connie Kay, did "My One and Only" and "I'm Putting All My Eggs in One Basket," and they were joined by Clark Terry for a polyphonic "Dancing in the Dark." Braff departed, and Terry did "It's Like Looking for a Needle in a Haystack" and was joined by Lee Konitz for a polyphonic "All of You." Terry departed, and Konitz played "Isn't This a Lovely Day" and "I Concentrate on You." Stan Getz did "I'm Old-Fashioned" and "Easter Parade" and departed, forgetting to announce Sylvia Syms—an oversight that would have cost him his head in other days. She sang five numbers, and sounded troubled. Her vibrato got loose and her voice kept catching the wrong lights. George Shearing, accompanied by Brian Torff, played "Waltz in Swing Time," "You Were Never Lovelier," and "Puttin' On the Ritz," and sang "Change Partners." His singing has a dusty, old-dad air. The ten final songs of the evening were done by Tormé and Gerry Mulligan, who were first brought together at the festival three years ago. Tormé sang awhile; Mulligan sang to Tormé's piano accompaniment; Tormé and Mulligan sang; Tormé sang while Mulligan played and hummed organ chords; Mulligan played. Tormé sang well, but without the fervor he has shown in his recent New York outings, and Mulligan carried his own weight.

### June 30th

Al Cooper's Savoy Sultans, made up of two trumpets, three saxophones, and four rhythm, was the house band at the Savoy Ballroom in Harlem from 1937 to 1945. It was a jump band—a rhythm machine that had one purpose: to make the customers dance their heads off. It did, and it generated such steam that it demolished all the alternating bands. (Earl Hines said, "The Sultans could swing you into bad health.") It was a primitive group, which played blues and the pop tunes of the day. The section work was offhand, the ensembles were riffs, the soloists were competent reproductions of Roy Eldridge and Coleman Hawkins. There were a lot of hustling black jump bands then (Sabby Lewis, Erskine Hawkins, the Mills Blue Rhythm Band), but none of their recordings capture what they sounded like in front of dancers. They were driving and free and exultant. They were showing off for the dancers, and the dancers, in return, showed off for them. It was a fervent, ritualistic relationship that made the music as close to visual as music can be. The drummer Panama Francis has resurrected the Sultans in the last year or so, and tonight he brought the band into Roseland. He had Franc Williams and Irving Stokes on trumpet, Bill Easley and Howard Johnson on alto saxophones, George Kelly, who was a member of the original Sultans, on tenor saxophone, Red Richards on piano, John Smith on guitar, and Bill Pemberton on bass. They played two sets of standards, riff blues, ballads, and old Sultan arrangements, and caused consternation and delight. Francis, a somewhat heavy Chick Webb drummer overlaid with Sid Catlett traceries, played like a madman. He pushed and roared, and one could almost see the music catapulting off the bandstand, lifting the meanest dancer, exalting the best.

The other end of the jazz rainbow appeared this afternoon at Carnegie Recital Hall. Leroy Jenkins, the elfin forty-eight-year-old violinist, violist, composer, gave a solo concert in which he played seven of his compositions. Jenkins's music occupies an unclear area. It is impossible to tell what is written and what is improvised, what is "classical" and what is jazz, what is serious and what is not. This is how "Hipnosis" went: Jenkins played two long trills, an octave apart, then produced a high, somewhat flat (conscious or not?) mosquito sound, went back to the trills, repeated the mosquito sound slightly differently, did a variation of the trills, and restated the mosquito sound. He interposed a short melodic figure, which he pored over several times, and returned to the trills and the mosquito sounds, and the piece ended. It was five minutes long. One composition had blues overtones, and one was built around a fairly direct folk-music motif, but the rest gave the impression they were scrims concealing a music in Jenkins's mind which he does not yet choose to expose. There was no sounded beat and very little of an implied one.

## July 1st

Tonight at Town Hall, the jazz-film collector David Chertok showed twenty-six selections, from feature films, soundies, documentaries, and television. It was an eerie ride. Jazz recordings are blind but jazz films see, and there again were Art Tatum, Erroll Garner, Louis Armstrong, John Coltrane. Sidney Bechet, Ben Webster, Nat Cole, Billie Holiday, and Don Byas. These windows into the past showed Armstrong and Velma Middleton doing an outrageous ham-bone version of "That's My Desire"; Bechet skirling through "St. Louis Blues," backed by a straining French band; Don Byas, largely in shadow, playing a sumptuous "Don't Blame Me"; and Ben Webster, a smoke-haloed presence, clapping perfunctorily in a Danish night club after a windy Dexter Gordon performance, then turning to order another drink. Some of Chertok's clips were very funny, among them an unbelievably busy shipboard swimming-pool scene that included Bert Lahr, Red Skelton, Tommy Dorsey and his band, Eleanor Powell, and Buddy Rich; an eccentric dance done in blackface in 1929 by James Barton, his body vibrating one moment from head to foot, his legs spaghetti the next, his arms whirligigs the next; and Sammy Davis, Jr., strutting at age seven before a beautiful, overreacting Ethel Waters.

## July 2nd

Almost nothing was right about "Blues Is a Woman," a celebration of female blues singing held at Avery Fisher tonight. Somewhere along the line, the event got mixed up with feminism, and that would have made Ma Rainey and Bessie Smith and Chippie Hill hoot. The concert was presented in the form of a history that purported to show that female blues singing continues intact. But the great women blues singers flourished in the twenties and early thirties, and have since been replaced by the women gospel singers. The handful of women blues singers who have appeared since the thirties are anachronisms: Helen Humes, Julia Lee, Dinah Washington, Big Mama Thornton. The singers chosen for the concert included Linda Hopkins, Sippie Wallace, Big Mama Thornton, Beulah Bryant, Koko Taylor, Nell Carter, and Adelaide Hall. Hopkins can summon up Bessie Smith, but her stage manner is kittenish. Sippie Wallace, never a commanding blues singer, is in her eighties, and Beulah Bryant, who has a heavy, immovable voice, is in her sixties. Mama Thornton seemed subdued, and Koko Taylor, though full of growls and gospel turns, was mechanical. Nell Carter, with her sharp, elbowing voice and comic dancing, is a Broadway person, as is Adelaide Hall. The accompaniment was supplied by Jay McShann, Little Brother Montgomery, and a band made up of Doc Cheatham, Vic Dickenson, Kenny Davern, Dick Hyman, Bill Pemberton, and Panama Francis. Cheatham's and Dickenson's obbligatos shone.

The new romantic eclecticism has been on view the past couple of afternoons at Carnegie Recital Hall. Yesterday, Hilton Ruiz, who is twenty-eight, played four numbers in which he revealed his fondness for McCoy Tyner, Thelonious Monk, James P. Johnson, Albert Ammons, Cecil Taylor, and Bill Evans. He likes to soften his edges with rhapsody, and he avoids a sounded beat. This afternoon, Mitchel Forman, who is twenty-four, revealed in the course of nine numbers that he is the thinking man's Keith Jarrett: he is less maudlin and more delicate. Martial Solal, the formidable French Art Tatum admirer, was added after Forman. He was witty and tough and abstract. Each number was an explosive display of arpeggios, glisses, left-hand thunder, and locked-chording, carried out with great clarity. He made Forman sound like tea being poured.

### July 3rd

The first half of "Swinging Taps," a program held at Avery Fisher tonight and given over in part to tap-dancing, was exhilarating. The little renaissance of tap-dancing begun in the early sixties by the late Marshall Stearns (the stunning afternoon of tap-dancing he organized for the 1962 Newport Jazz Festival; the equally stunning appearance at the Village Gate in 1964 of the legendary dancer Groundhog) has probably reached its height. The number of first-rate dancers is low (Chuck Green, Sandman Sims, Honi Coles, Bunny Briggs) and is not likely to be replenished. The competitive, charged, echoing backroom environment that the great dancers knew is gone. Tonight, the Widespread Depression Orchestra played half a dozen numbers, several of them with Bob Wilber, who did his unimpeachable Johnny Hodges. Then the band began "Caravan," and there was Chuck Green—a square, flapping scarecrow moving in half time, his head bent forward in concentration, his arms loose. He danced in the space of a card table, and his simplicity and elegance were flawless. Green's dancing is designed to be heard; he is a snare-drum dancer. Abetted by two perfectly placed and pitched floor microphones, he filled the hall with crystalline clicking and rattling, with square, loping four-four rhythms from the late thirties. On "Take the A Train," he inserted some sharp double-time patterns and some oily slide steps. He dedicated his final number to his model, John W. Bubbles. Green has got heavier and slower in the past ten years, but his dancing remains precise and gleaming. Sandman Sims, who followed, is a flash dancer. He uses most of the stage, and he is fond of hitting his heels together, opening and closing his toes, dancing on one foot, and flinging his legs off to one side. He aims at our eyes. He closed with a couple of sand dances, using a three-by-four board covered with fine sand. The first was shuffling and subtle, and the second an ingenious improvisation on the sounds of a steam locomotive.

After the intermission, Benny Carter, joined by Doc Cheatham, Jimmy Maxwell, Budd Johnson, Curtis Fuller, the violinist Joe Kennedy, and a rhythm section of Ray Bryant, Major Holley, and Oliver Jackson, played four interminable numbers before settling down reluctantly to accompany Honi Coles and the Copasetics—Charles Cook, Buster Brown, Bubba Gaines, Brenda Bufalino, and Debbie Mitchell. They did four or five numbers, ending with "Bugle Call Rag," but they had had to wait too long for Carter to finish, and they lacked the intensity and rhythmic press of Green and Sims.

### July 4th

Max Roach has said that he learned a great deal from tap-dancers, and one can sometimes hear Baby Laurence figures in his more intricate snare-drum work. He also learned from Sid Catlett and Kenny Clarke, and they are distantly audible, too. Thirty-five years have passed since Roach, who is now fifty-five, was a neophyte, and during that time he has become the most influential modern drummer. He is spoken of as a "master," as the premier drummer of all time. He appeared at Carnegie Hall tonight with a quartet (Cecil Bridgewater on trumpet, Odean Pope on tenor saxophone, Calvin Hill on bass), and played six numbers. Two of the numbers were a cappella drum solos, and two numbers included drum solos. Roach's accompanying has changed little. He creates a "melodic" flow of broken-rhythm cymbal, snare, and bassdrum sounds. This melodic wash does not vary much (although its details are always shifting), and it has no subtlety or dynamics. (Roach has never got a good drum sound. His tightly muffled snare resembles a hatbox, and his tomtoms have no resonance.) In a short solo, he will begin with his cymbals, walking through them with both drumsticks, and then, with one hand, start a staccato series of strokes on the snare head and rims, shift both hands to the snare for a flurry of two-stroke-roll beats, make a kind of giant left-to-right triplet on his four tomtoms, double the tempo in cross-strokes between his snare and his two big right-hand tom-toms, all the while firing machine-gun bass-drum beats, walk back through his cymbals, and slow his bass drum down to a stop. Roach has what used to be called "fast wrists," and much of what he does is technically dazzling. But he doesn't swing. He leaves your feet flat on the ground, your head and hands still. What a mystery!

### July 5th

This afternoon at Carnegie Recital Hall, Jimmy Rowles wiped out all the pianists who had preceded him during the week. Rowles operates on a level of intelligence and wit and skill uncommon in jazz. Many jazz musicians spend their energy on technique or on disguising their lack of originality. But Rowles, from the first bar, comes face to face with what he has to do: transform the song before him into a new song, full of wit, style, subtlety, and fresh melody. And he immediately lifts the listener to his plane. Today, he played "Remember When," which drifted into his huge repertory from a 1934 Jimmy Lunceford record; his special commingling of Billy Strayhorn's "Isfahan" and "Blood Count"; Carl Perkins's "Groove Yard"; and Cole Porter's "Dream Dancing" and "Looking at You." He did six of his own tunes, including "The Lady in the Corner" and "Pygmy Lullaby." He did "Darn That Dream," "That's All," and "How Come You Do Me Like You Do," and he closed with "Jitterbug Waltz" and Strayhorn's "Lotus Blossom." "Pygmy Lullaby" was mournful and delicate, and "The Lady in the Corner" was funny and swinging. "Jitterbug Waltz" had an improvised section in which Rowles abandoned the melody for a series of blocklike inventions. "Lotus Blossom" was an intense aside. All of Rowles's harmonic ingenuity was on view, and in almost every tune he dropped in a quick, querying arpeggio just to make sure we were listening.

*July 6th*

The "new music" concerts given at Town Hall during the festival, by the Art Ensemble of Chicago, the Beaver Harris-Don Pullen group, Dollar Brand, James Blood Ulmer, Archie Shepp, the World Saxophone Quartet, Robert Kraft, and Carla Bley, have not, for the most part, been very new. (Nor were fringe figures like Ulmer, Brand, and Kraft apposite.) The Art Ensemble has been around over a decade, and so have Shepp and Bley and Harris-Pullen. With the exception of Carla Bley, none of them have changed much. When Bley played the festival in 1965, her music was dour and monochromatic. Last night, it was jumping and accessible and full of singing and funny lyrics, and she demonstrated that she has become something of a comedian. Dressed in high heels and a Ginger Rogers print dress, her blond frizzed hair a thatched roof, she conducted by dancing and weaving and laughing. Would that tonight's concert had been as nimble. Called "The New Music Remembers the Old Master—Duke Ellington," it was played by a fourteen-piece group that included Frank Gordon on trumpet, Byard Lancaster on reeds, Ricky Ford on tenor saxophone, and Pat Patrick on baritone. Two numbers were arranged and conducted by Oliver Lake, one by Julius Hemphill, one by Leroy Jenkins, and three by Muhal Richard Abrams. None of what these four did to Ellington—using free ensembles, long, sometimes disquieting solos, frequent tempo changes, sly harmonies, and multiple soloists—improved or changed him. But he would have appreciated the attention.

# 1981

## The New Red Norvo Trio

Red Norvo formed his famous trio of vibraphone, guitar, and bass in 1949, and kept it together for seven years. It included the guitarists Mundell Lowe, Tal Farlow, and Jimmy Raney, and the bassists Red Kelly, Red Mitchell, Clyde Lombardi, and Charles Mingus. Norvo once talked about its early days, at his home in California: "I got the idea for my trio after I'd moved out here. I figured a group with just vibes and guitar and bass could go into almost any place on the Coast, which would mean I could spend more time at home. Naturally, what happened was that our first booking was into Philly. We were playing opposite Slim Gaillard, who was swinging hard and making a lot of noise, and I felt naked. I wanted to know, what do you *do* behind a guitar solo with a vibraharp? Use two mallets? Four mallets? What? It was awful. But by the last couple of days it began to unfold for me a little. Then we went to New York, and one night I stopped in to eat at Billy Reed's Little Club, where they had this sissy group. The guitarist, whom I didn't know, played sixteen bars of something that spun my head. Mundell Lowe was on guitar with me, and he wanted to stay in New York, but he said he knew a guitarist who would be just right, and I told him I'd heard one who would be just right, too. I insisted Mundell hear my man and Mundell insisted I hear his man, and you know what happened—they turned out to be the same guy, Tal Farlow. I took the trio to Hawaii, and when we got back to the Haig, here in Los Angeles, my bass player wanted to leave, and one night Jimmy Rowles came in and asked me if I remembered the bass player I had used when we backed Billie Holiday in Frisco a while back. I said I did—Charlie Mingus. We called all around Frisco, and no one knew where he was, and finally we found him here—carrying mail. He wasn't playing at all, and he was big. I'd watch him sit down and eat a quart of ice cream . . . But he went down in weight with us, and by the time we opened [in New York] he was fine. He could play those jet tempos that most drummers can't touch, and he was a beautiful soloist."

The best of the small bands in jazz—among them the Creole Jazz Band, the Basie, Goodman, and Ellington groups, the John Kirby band, the Norvo trio, the Modern Jazz Quartet—have shared a loose density, an unbreakable collective sense, a lyrical bent. The Norvo group, made up of two stringed instruments and a hybrid percussion instrument, all with delicate timbres and all inclining toward the treble registers, went a little farther. Its music was closer to thought than to action, to spirit than to flesh. The trio stripped its music to the essentials of melody and rhythm and improvisation, almost eliminating the barriers between musician and listener. The music seemed to emanate from the listener himself. The trio played with great gentleness. Even when it hustled, it suggested rather than stated, pointed rather than pushed. Few of its numbers gave the impression of having a beginning, a middle, and an end. This was marvellous trickery, for each piece was meticulously structured. From the first note, the listener was caught, and he remained caught until the final note. The ensembles were in unison or in harmony and were generally elaborate variations on the melody. Guitar solos were backed by the bassist and by Norvo chords, played offbeat or behind the beat, and bass solos rested on on-the-beat guitar chords, which achieved a soft railroad click-click-click. The guitarist and bassist would give Norvo four-to-the-bar support, or the guitarist would circle him with admiring offbeat chords. Sometimes the closing ensemble repeated the opening one, and sometimes it offered a new variation on the melody. Being rhythmically perfect, the trio loved difficult tempos—the very fast, the serenely slow—and it rarely spent much time in between. It was great fun to watch, mostly because of Norvo, a fugitive from the vaudeville of the twenties, who likes to make O mouths, pop eyes, and assorted manic movements.

For years, people have been after Norvo to reorganize his trio, and at last he has. Tal Farlow, who has been in semi-retirement, is on guitar, and Steve Novosel, from Washington, D.C., is on bass. Norvo has taken the group into Michael's Pub. In many ways, the new trio is better than the old one. The old one was a meteor: it always got where it was going in the fastest, most direct way. The new trio meanders a little and favors easier tempos. The old trio, in spite of its gentleness, was all muscle, while the new one is unclenched and relaxed. Best, the new trio has discarded—or perhaps simply forgotten—the bebop finery of the old group, which, in the mode of the time, was decked out in Charlie Parker melodic lines, flatted ninth chords, and ensembles that were so tightly woven in the Parker manner that they were opaque. The new trio's ensembles are looser, the solos are longer, and Norvo and Farlow indulge in the sort of counterpoint that was once at the heart of jazz. (Norvo first began fooling with the device fifteen years ago, with the pianist Dave McKenna.) On opening night, during the middle sections of "All of Me" and "How About You?," Novosel lay out, and Farlow and Norvo, suspended in midair, developed exquisite melodic lines that at once pushed past and embraced one another—the great paradoxical magic of counterpoint. And on "How About You?" Novosel joined Norvo and Farlow after their chorus, and three voices floated through the room. Farlow was one of the first guitarists to be influenced by Charlie Parker, and in the forties he invariably used five notes where one would have done. Now silence appears, and stands on its own. His solos think and move in peaceful and deliberate ways. They are the poems of a middle-aged man. All Norvo need do is match the standard of beauty he established for himself forty years ago. And he does. Here are the ducking runs, the crystalline melodic pools, the winglike tremolos, the crowding, cheeky chords, the soothing momentum. There was much graceful music on opening night—in Norvo's and Farlow's contrapuntal excursions; in Norvo's kid-glove opening and closing choruses on "We'll Be Together Again," both done ad lib and a cappella; in his sunrise solo on "All of Me"; in his four-mallet figure behind Farlow on "The Jitterbug Waltz," a kind of shadowing ground figure; and in Farlow's fleeing, smiling solo on the fast "Fascinating Rhythm." Brilliance sometimes blinds; Norvo, Farlow, and Novosel light the way.

## Down the River

*Friday*

George Wein has sold his Newport soul to the Brown & Williamson tobacco company. The original Newport Jazz Festival has become, in its twenty-seventh year, the Kool Jazz Festival New York. Brown & Williamson will pay Wein an undisclosed amount over the next five years for having removed the name Newport (also the name of a rival mentholated cigarette, of course), and it will assume all advertising and promotional costs of the festival. (This all becomes a gallimaufry when we are also told that Wein, in order to protect his copyright on the name Newport Jazz Festival, will hold a two-concert Newport Jazz Festival in Newport in August.) Wein states in the program that his deal with Brown & Williamson will enable the festival to continue. More likely, it will help the festival to continue its self-competing giantism (this year hundreds of musicians will perform over ten days in fifty events at fourteen locations in New York and New Jersey, and some of the events will last twelve hours and involve simultaneous performances), its repetitiveness (a dozen events being held this year are variants of events given before), and its deepening unimaginativeness.

The festival began this afternoon in Carnegie Recital Hall with an unaccompanied concert by the pianist Cedar Walton. He played three standards, three Duke Ellington tunes, a couple of Bud Powell numbers, and some of his own material. Walton is a clear, robust, declarative pianist, who speaks with the tongues of Art Tatum, Powell, and Lennie Tristano. But this afternoon, without rhythmic support, he donned protective rhapsodic robes. His arpeggios rose and fell, and he kept breaking them in unexpected Bud Powell places. These ceaseless contrary motions caused Walton to slip and slide rhythmically, and they also hid the fact that, at his ease with a bassist in a night club, he is a joyous and swinging pianist.

Walton was better at the evening concert in Carnegie Hall. This was a celebration for the old drummer Art Blakey that was carried forward by Blakey's present group and by such alumni as Walton, Walter Davis, Johnny Griffin, Jackie McLean, Freddie Hubbard, Bill Hardman, Donald Byrd, and Curtis Fuller. It was hard-bop heaven again. (Blakey formed his first Jazz Messengers in 1954.) There were the dull unison ensembles, the interminable solos, and Blakey's toneless thunderclap drumming. But it was good to hear Hardman's hilly phrasing (so intense beside Hubbard's glassy vacuity), and to hear how far Griffin, who has lived in Europe for many years, has moved from where Don Byas stopped. The sound system nearly destroyed the evening. The piano sounded like china being unpacked and the ensembles like a hennery when a fox gets in.

*Saturday*

The pianist Joanne Brackeen, tall and narrow and stooped, appeared in Carnegie Recital Hall this afternoon in a blouse and skirt and an immense Virginia Woolf straw hat. She did half a dozen numbers, all of them unidentifiable but presumably hers, and they varied from silken Debussy barges to hardboiled Keith Jarrett fantasies. Rhythm and melody were implied. It was a mannered music also marked by Cecil Taylor avalanches and bellying McCoy Tyner chords. The straw hat seemed disembodied after a time, and it never stopped bobbing and swaying and tipping.

There was a long, loose history of Chicago jazz at Carnegie Hall this evening. A swing group led by the bass trumpeter Cy Touff and including Norman Murphy on trumpet, Franz Jackson on tenor saxophone, Marty Grosz on guitar, Truck Parham on bass, and Barrett Deems on drums played four easy, elated numbers. Touff's flat-faced playing contrasted nicely with Murphy's sweet, round tone and Jackson's Ben Webster lyricism. Next came a surprising duet by two members of the Association for the Advancement of Creative Musicians—the reedman Roscoe Mitchell, who works with the Art Ensemble of Chicago, and the trumpeter Hugh Regan. They did one ten-minute number, which was made up of long-held treble notes, some in unison and some in a freakish bagpipe harmony, broken here and there by scratching sounds, steamboat whistles, and bird tremolos. It was funny, needling, free music. There was booing, and several people fled the hall, their fingers in their ears. Time fell back thirty years for a bebop set by the trumpeter and reedman Ira Sullivan, who had Lee Konitz on alto saxophone, Chris Anderson on piano, Victor Sproles on bass, and Wilbur Campbell on drums. There was good ensemble lobbing by Sullivan and Konitz, and Campbell revealed that he is an alert, driving bebop drummer. Then back twenty more years, to around 1930. Art Hodes played a solo version of "St. Louis Blues," which moved from deep-blue left-hand chords to stride figures, and he and Parham accompanied Mama Yancey for three numbers. She is in her mid-eighties and came onstage in a wheelchair, but her dry, sad voice was intact. She sang "Trouble in Mind" and "Make Me a Pallet on the Floor," and Hodes was there at every turn with tremolos and low-register rumbles. He rocked the hall. The tenor saxophonist Von Freeman (father of the tenor saxophonist Chico Freeman) moved us up to the fifties with a hard-bop group that had Paul Serrano on trumpet, Sproles, and Campbell. Von Freeman is a curious saxophonist. He likes dying notes and notes that sound as if they were split, and his tone is reedy and diffuse. Sonny Rollins is always passing by. Then back to 1930 for good. Jimmy McPartland and Wild Bill Davison (together and separately), assisted by Frank Chace on clarinet, Jim Beebe on trombone, and a rhythm section of Hodes, Parham, Grosz, and Don DeMicheal on drums, went through seven Chicago anthems, including "Sugar," "Royal Garden Blues," "Big Butter and Egg Man," and "China Boy." McPartland hustled (he sang on one number), and Davison rooted and growled. The concert was produced by Harriet Choice, and the singer Joe Williams read a script she had prepared as if he were a Latin teacher intoning a first-year student's composition. At the very beginning of the evening, he also demonstrated the melismatic street cry he used as a kid when he hawked the Chicago *Defender*.

## Sunday

Duos are cheaper to hire than trios or quartets, and in the past ten or fifteen years they have become the most fashionable jazz ensemble. Their members have discovered that the form, which involves counterpoint, soloing, unison and harmonic playing, accompanying, and intense listening, is as challenging as any in jazz. They have also discovered that a successful duo must balance. The players must be equally gifted, they must relish each other's work, and their instruments must be complementary. Multi-noted instruments (guitar with guitar, piano with piano) work well, and so do different single-noted instruments (alto saxophone with tenor saxophone, trumpet with trombone), and one single-noted instrument (tenor saxophone) with one multi-noted instrument (guitar). But identical single-noted instruments (two trumpets, two trombones), hobbled by similar tones and timbres, do not. A program of duets—seven in all—was assembled by Dan Morgenstern at Carnegie Hall tonight, and only one really worked. This was made up of the guitarists Wayne Wright and Marty Grosz. Wright, a Django Reinhardt admirer, favors quavery single-note lines, while Grosz uses a chordal attack. They offset each other's solos, and they have worked together enough to have found each other's nooks and crannies. They did "It Don't Mean a Thing If It Ain't Got That Swing," Reinhardt's "Tears," "Goody Goody," and a three-part piece written down in the thirties by the guitarists Dick McDonough and Carl Kress. Red Rodney and Ira Sullivan played their trumpets and flügelhorns, Zoot Sims and Lee Konitz played their soprano saxophones, and Major Holley and Slam Stewart sang and played their basses. Herbie Hancock on acoustic piano and the bassist Ron Carter turned out to be Hancock accompanied by Carter. The same imbalance was true of the singer Carol Sloane and her pianist, Norman Simmons. The final group, made up of Milt Jackson and John Lewis, sounded exactly like what it was—the top half of the Modern Jazz Quartet. Herewith some foolproof duos for concerts to come: Zoot Sims and Bucky Pizzarelli; Jim Hall and Michael Moore; Red Norvo and

Dave McKenna; Dick Wellstood and Ralph Sutton; Ellis Larkins and Joe Wilder.

## Monday

We listen to jazz to be surprised. Tonight, at an all-star concert at Carnegie Hall, we waited a long time. Set after set went by, consisting of the likes of John Bunch, Eddie Bert, Al Grey, Kenny Burrell, Frank Foster, Dave Brubeck, Bobby Rosengarden, and Gerry Mulligan, and then it happened. Ellis Larkins, accompanied by the the bassist Billy Popp, played two unamplified blues—one slow and one in medium tempo. The first, Larkins' own "Happiness Boy Chaser," was an ingenious arrangement of right-hand riffs that circled over an ostinato bass, rose in a delicate crescendo, and subsided. The second, Mercer Ellington's "Things Ain't What They Used to Be," deepened the subtle blue mood established in the first number. Here were Larkins' zephyr touch, his rueful ease, his hidden, spinning arpeggios, his cumulative rhythm. He enthralled us, and nothing that followed (Dizzy Gillespie, Clark Terry, Machito, Cecil Payne, Benny Powell, Billy Taylor, Jimmy Rowles, Zoot Sims, Mel Tormé, Joe Albany, Kenny Davern) diminished his hold.

## Tuesday

Two groups played at Avery Fisher Hall tonight— the Red Norvo Trio, which was meant to be the crowd-quieter, and the Chick Corea Quartet, which was meant to be the main draw. But there was a dazzling turnaround. The evening, to all intents and purposes, ended with Norvo. He insisted that his group be heard without amplification, and its treble, lattice-work music could be heard everywhere. Norvo's trio, with Tal Farlow on guitar and Steve Novosel on bass, was reconstituted three weeks ago (he disbanded his first trio in 1956), and it is now close to perfection. The ensembles breathe, the accompanying is clair-voyant, Farlow has his chops back, and Novosel is braver. There were won-ders in every one of its ten numbers: Farlow's double-time solo on "Here's That Rainy Day"; Norvo's serene, belling, hymnlike a-cappella version of Bix Beiderbecke's "Candlelight"; Norvo and Farlow's twining but parallel counterpoint on "The One I Love" and "Fascinating Rhythm"; and all of Fats Waller's "Jitterbug Waltz," a tricky, irresistible tune that seems to force jazz musicians to surpass themselves.

Chick Corea changes his musical address every year or so. Having aban-doned Electronic Heights, in Fusion City, he introduced a group tonight that included a hard-bop tenor saxophonist (Joe Henderson), an aging avant-garde bassist (Gary Peacock), and a bebop drummer (Roy Haynes). And he himself played acoustic piano. The music, partly written, partly improvised, was romantic, motionless, and eclectic (tatters of free jazz, acres of hard bop). No one seemed to be who he was. Peacock, that lyrical speedster, had a barbarous sound and used a lot of whining notes. Haynes, a champion chatterer, sounded bored. And Corea never got much beyond several two-handed high-register glisses. But what else could he do? He, too, had been out front during Norvo's set.

*Wednesday*

It no longer matters whether Art Tatum was a great jazz pianist. He was a magnificent hybrid, caught somewhere between Vladimir Horowitz, on the classical side, and Lee Sims, on the popular side, and he changed the course of jazz with his rococo, million-noted, arpeggioed attack. Charlie Parker heard him as a young man, and so did Bud Powell and Lennie Tristano and Don Byas and John Coltrane. We are still swimming in his florid sea. Tonight, at Town Hall, the pianists Billy Taylor and Dick Hyman gave a joint lecture on Tatum, and they illustrated their remarks by performing separately and together and by bringing on such pianists as Jaki Byard, Dick Wellstood, Adam Makowicz, John Lewis, Ellis Larkins, and Barry Harris. They also sat in, separately, with the old Art Tatum Trio—Tiny Grimes on guitar and Slam Stewart on bass. The presence of some of their exemplars was puzzling. There is very little of Tatum in John Lewis, and Byard's Tatum is watery. Wellstood and Harris are a generation removed: Wellstood mirrors one of Tatum's idols, Fats Waller, and Harris one of Tatum's descendants, Bud Powell. The best of tonight's illustrators was Hyman himself. (Taylor is too diffuse, Larkins brings us mainly Tatum's touch, and Makowicz is close to an unintentional caricature.) Hyman's "Body and Soul" with the trio was faultless, and so was his solo reading of the Thad Jones-Alec Wilder "A Child Is Born." All that he lacks is Tatum's pneumatic touch and his ability to make you gasp. A series of duets—Byard and Lewis, Harris and Taylor, Wellstood and Hyman, Larkins and Makowicz—followed. The winners were Wellstood and Hyman with a stride version of "If Dreams Come True." They matched that look-out! quality that Tatum took on when he shifted into a stride bass at a fast tempo and blew the house down. There are only two film clips of Tatum in action; both were shown tonight. The first is a snippet from a "March of Time" newsreel, and the second is from a jam-session sequence in a feature film called "The Fabulous Dorseys." But one hears and sees more in it of Charlie Barnet and Ziggy Elman and Ray Bauduc than of Tatum.

*Thursday*

The lack of decent movie footage on early jazz music was due to racism and ignorance. (How would Samuel Goldwyn have known in 1933 that Louis Armstrong was playing the most lyrical and original music in the United States when Olin Downes, the *Times'* music critic, didn't know either?) Bessie Smith and Charlie Parker appear only once on film, and the brief glimpses we have of Bix Beiderbecke and Chick Webb are useless. There is no known footage of Fletcher Henderson, King Oliver, Jelly Roll Morton, or Charlie Christian. What does exist from the twenties and thirties and forties (television has done far better than Hollywood) is almost accidental: generally hoked-up "jam sessions" from feature films (one has Wingy Manone on trumpet, Joe Venuti on violin, Les Paul on guitar, Jess Stacy on piano, and Abe Lyman on drums), newsreel clips, and cheap shorts made as fillers to be shown between the cartoon and the newsreel. (The first honest, serious attempt to capture jazz in the movies was Gjon Mili's 1944 "Jammin' the Blues.") The film collector David Chertok showed thirty-four of these oddities at Town Hall tonight, and all were of big bands. The earliest was from 1933 (Claude Hopkins playing "Careless Love" in a huge barbershop, with Edmond Hall on alto saxophone), and the most recent was from the late forties (Woody Herman's "Lemon Drop"). In between, we saw Charlie Barnet playing "Cherokee" in a field next to a tepee; Bob Crosby doing "Sugarfoot Stomp" in a baggage car; and Gene Krupa playing a frantic, yeah-man "Leave Us Leap." But we also saw the 1943 Duke Ellington band doing two numbers with Ben Webster, Tricky Sam Nanton, Ray Nance, and Johnny Hodges; Sidney De Paris, still in his Louis Armstrong shoes, soloing with Don Redman in 1934; the 1936 Jimmie Lunceford band doing "Nagasaki"; and a brief solo by Don Fagerquist on Les Brown's "I've Got My Love to Keep Me Warm." There was good singing along the way by Frank Sinatra, Helen Forrest, Peggy Lee, Billy Eckstine, Fran Warren, Helen O'Connell, Sister Rosetta Tharpe, and Louis Armstrong, who did "I Can't Give You Anything But Love" in a bartender's jacket.

## Friday

The late-afternoon piano concerts in Carnegie Recital Hall continue to be uneven. Ram Ramirez, who wrote "Lover Man" and plays composer's piano, did a Duke Ellington medley and a medley of songs associated with Billie Holiday, a couple of blues, some Gershwin, a tune by Richie Wyands, and "Lover Man." He is a loose-kneed swing pianist who has listened to Red Garland and Erroll Garner. Albert Dailey offered half a dozen harmonic castles, built of arpeggios, loud pedal, rubato, and portmanteau chords, and concealing in their dungeons such songs as "Emily" and "What Is This Thing Called Love?" Dorothy Donegan, a vaudevillian who plays Art Tatum piano, made her corkscrew faces and played her usual concatenation of "Tea for Two," "Rhapsody in Blue," and "The Man I Love," all the while using rubber tempos, interpolation, stride piano, and white water arpeggios. And this afternoon Ross Tompkins, who went West with the "Tonight Show" band ten years ago, followed in the ad-lib footsteps of Walton, Brackeen, and Dailey. He is a fine jazz pianist, and it's too bad that, on this rare trip East, he didn't show us that.

At an afternoon concert at the 1970 Newport Festival, Bill Cosby presented a Los Angeles band that he called Badfoot Brown and the Bunions Bradford Marching and Funeral Band. It was made up of a tenor saxophonist, a trombonist, two Fender bassists, three guitarists, two pianists, an organist, and two drummers. Its principal number lasted forty-five minutes and was a sly, blueslike survey of modern jazz, done up with endless breaks and tempo changes, duets, mountainous crescendos, and a vocal of "White Christmas" interrupted several times by drum solos. The piece swung massively, and it remains indelible. Tonight, Cosby brought B. B. King, Arnett Cobb, Nat Adderley, Jimmy Smith, and Mickey Roker into Carnegie Hall to play the blues. They played slow blues, medium blues, and fast blues, but the group never found its heart. Cosby himself delivered the best music—a parody of a blues singer who can't get off a word unless it has at least a dozen notes in it. A study in melismatic madness, it cut so close to the bone it shook up B. B. King.

### Saturday

All-female jazz events are voluntary acts of segregation and seeming admissions that only through numbers can women equal men in jazz. But women have long been equal to men in jazz. Men have dominated its instrumental side, but women have dominated its vocal side. A syllogism could even be fashioned: the human voice is the greatest instrument; women are the greatest jazz singers; therefore, women are the greatest jazz instrumentalists. Who has surpassed Billie Holiday's sense of rhythmic placement? Who has scaled the melodic peaks and plumbed the melodic depths of Sarah Vaughan? Who has matched the majesty of Bessie Smith? So "Women Blow Their Own Horns," a concert put together by Rosetta Reitz at Carnegie Hall tonight, was needless. And it was not an all-female event anyway—Melba Liston's band had three men, and Dizzy Gillespie and Clark Terry wandered on and off during the evening. The Willene Barton quintet began the concert, with two old-fashioned jump numbers and a slow "As Time Goes By." The leader, sawing her tenor saxophone up and down, appeared to be cutting her way through her music. Dorothy Donegan did a coherent "An Affair to Remember," then opened her "Tea for Two" box and let her flying arpeggios out. Melba Liston, who was in Dizzy Gillespie's big band in the fifties, played four numbers, two of them in the sort of barely moving tempos that dance bands used to sink into late at night. Britt Woodman, the old Ellington trombonist, was with her, along with a fine tenor saxophonist named Erica Lindsay. The rest of the evening was a kind of jam session, with Marian McPartland or Dorothy Donegan on piano, Mary Osborne on guitar, Jean Fineberg on tenor saxophone, Lucille Dixon on bass, and Barbara Merjan on drums. Gillespie and Terry leafed through their solos.

*Sunday*

Miles Davis, absent from jazz for the past five years or so, turned up for two shows at Avery Fisher Hall tonight with a reedman (Bill Evans), a rock guitarist (Mike Stern), a Fender bassist (Marcus Miller), a percussionist (Nino Cinellu), and a drummer (Al Foster) and, for the hour that the first show lasted, pretended he was in *Apocalypse Now*. Davis was dressed for the trip. He had on a fisherman's cap, a dark jacket, which he kept taking off, a singlet, gray pipestem pants, and clogs. It was night, and the darkness was broken by a searchlight that followed Davis as he stumped from side to side of the boat; sat on a stool in front of Foster's drums, his back to the audience; raised his fist and brought it down to turn the ship of sound in a new direction; played one of his brief solos (sixteen or twenty bars at the longest), his back bent almost double, so that the bell of his horn was inches from the floor; and sipped from a cup brought by a deckhand. The heavy-metal roar of guitar, bass, and drums was almost always present, and to make himself heard Davis had a small microphone fastened to his trumpet. His muted solos rose clearly above the din, and when he took out his mute and let loose an open-horn blast the crocodiles on the banks jumped. Davis played one non-stop number, which was unidentified and unidentifiable. Evans soloed on soprano and tenor saxophone, the guitarist soloed, and the percussionist soloed. The tempos changed ceaselessly, and so did the rhythm. Davis's chops are in good shape, but he played the same solo again and again. It went like this: an ascending shriek (Dizzy Gillespie, 1945) followed by a scurrying downward run; a second, lower shriek; silence; another run, broken off abruptly in the Bud Powell manner; silence; a three-note cluster, the last note flatted and held for a measure or two; silence; an upward run; and a closing six-note cluster. When the boat reached Kurtz's hideaway, Davis turned to the audience for the first time, and *waved*, as if to let us know that he is just one of us after all and that what we had been watching—it was a visual music—was only imaginary.

This afternoon, at the last of three concerts given during the week at the Guggenheim Museum, the drummer Louis Hayes appeared with Frank Strozier on alto saxophone, Harold Mabern on piano, and Jimmy Rowser on bass. Strozier came up from Memphis in the fifties with the late trumpeter Booker Little, the tenor saxophonist George Coleman, and Mabern, and he is one of the most original of Charlie Parker's second wave of admirers. The group played five numbers. The finest was a long, intense "My Funny Valentine." It had formidable opening and closing cadenzas by Strozier and an in-tempo solo, full of Parker runs, Stozier's peculiar high-register pipings, and his way of shaping a phrase—a descending six-note figure, say—and playing it over and over, each time with slight variations.

*Tuesday*

Having a jazz festival at all in New York is like shipping artichokes to Castroville. The thirty or more jazz night clubs in the city celebrate the music continuously. During the past year or so, we have heard Jabbo Smith, the Lee Konitz Nonet, Lee Konitz and Gil Evans in a duo, Art Hodes, the Red Norvo Trio, Ralph Sutton, the George Coleman Octet, Warne Marsh, and endless piano-and-bass duos. Now still another duo, made up of Dick Hyman and the California pianist Roger Kellaway, has turned up at Michael's Pub. Hyman and Kellaway first played as a duo at one of Dick Gibson's Colorado jazz parties. Hyman, with his long, pale face and white, flickering fingers, is an academic Art Tatum, while Kellaway, bearded and stubby-fingered, is an academic Oscar Peterson. (Both men are also gifted composers and arrangers.) They balance. Hyman's touch is light and self-effacing, while Kellaway digs in—sometimes he splats the upper register with his right elbow. Hyman suggests and Kellaway points, Hyman outlines and Kellaway itemizes. Hyman, got up tonight in a dark-blue blazer and tie, swayed from side to side at the keyboard, while Kellaway, in an electric-blue velvet jacket, light-colored trousers, and a yellow open-neck shirt, bent over tightly or, when he got off a good one, reared back. Duo pianists can be relentless, crowding the air and making an endlessly quarreling music. But Hyman and Kellaway step aside when the other takes off. On "Yesterdays," Kellaway played octave melodic lines in both hands and Hyman laid down drifting, applauding tremolos. Hyman unrolled into-the-wind arpeggios in "Get Happy" and Kellaway rocked around in his lowest register. They made rhythm machines out of "Get Happy" and an Albert Ammons boogie-woogie number and out of a slow "Just a Closer Walk with Thee." On a very fast "Blue Skies," they sat at the same keyboard and switched places every other chorus. Their hands advanced, bowed, retreated, advanced, bowed, retreated, and the sound was as thick as thunder. On a medium-tempo "Remembering You" (Kellaway's song, and the closing theme of "All in the Family"), they did two-handed octave figures and in the last chorus created brilliant counterpoint, their right hands making voices that wound around and around, never touching, never separating.

# New Bird

The lurid, secret, phantasmagoric shape of Charlie Parker's life has not made him easy to write about. He bulges out of the fiction he appears in, and is surrealistic in his two biographies. He was a legend when he was alive, and the legend has grown. He is now a demigod—a wizard primitive musician who is widely thought of as the greatest jazz improviser, a super-dropout who seemingly outwitted society by almost completely skirting it, a Gargantuan whose appetites destroyed him. The newest attempt to get him down in a book comes from France, and it is a surprising one. It is called *To Bird with Love* (Editions Wizlov), and consists largely of giant photographs—over two hundred and fifty of them—that have been assembled by Parker's widow, Chan, who lives in France, and by Francis Paudras, a French graphic artist. It is a monolithic book. There are blowups of Parker's head that are the same size as Parker's head. Indeed, all the pictures—they bleed off the page—give the impression of being life-size. (The book measures ten and a half inches by fifteen, weighs seven pounds, and has over four hundred pages.) Scattered among the pictures are reproductions of Parker ephemera and Parker's "papers": his driver's license, stamped with traffic violations; letters, cards, and notes; contracts and telegrams; a pawn ticket (a hundred dollars for his alto saxophone—dated seven weeks before his death). The book is arranged chronologically and becomes, as the images and papers accumulate, his life. But, alas, the book presupposes considerable knowledge of that life. Many photographs have no captions or information of any kind. Some have semi-poetic effusions supplied by Chan Parker: facing pictures of Parker with his arm around fellow-musicians are labelled "Those touched became profound by the passage," and a double-page spread of Parker's head is captioned "Exhale the melody exquisite, inhale a cry of anguish, a plea for acceptance and understanding."

Here, for the sake of reference, are the bones of Parker's life: He was born in 1920 in a suburb of Kansas City and raised by his mother, Addie Boyley, in the city proper. His father, a vaudevillian and Pullman chef, disappeared when he was eleven. Parker did well in grammar school, but then his life began to accelerate. By the time he was sixteen, he had dropped out of high school (he'd been a freshman for three years), he was married and had a child, he was a professional alto saxophonist and a member of the musicians' union. And he was on his way to becoming a drug addict. At seventeen, he went briefly to Chicago and New York, where he heard Art Tatum, whose teeming melodic lines became a permanent part of his musical furniture. He joined Jay McShann's Kansas City band when he was nineteen, and stayed with McShann off and on for three years. He rooted around in Harlem for a time after that, then went with Earl Hines' band and with Billy Eckstine's all-star bebop band. He made his first important recordings in 1944, and late in 1945 he went to Los Angeles with Dizzy Gillespie in a band that included Milt Jackson, Al Haig, and Ray Brown. (It was the first bebop band to cross the Rockies, and it had the same effect as the arrival of the Spaniards: the natives were incredulous.) But, constantly souped up with drugs and alcohol, he collapsed, and midway in 1946 he was committed to Camarillo State Hospital. In the biography *Bird Lives!*, Ross Russell quotes a doctor who took care of Parker:

A man living from moment to moment. A man living for the pleasure principle, music, food, sex, drugs, kicks, his personality arrested at an infantile level. A man with almost no feeling of guilt and only the small-

est, most atrophied nub of conscience. One of the army of psychopaths
supplying the populations of prisons and mental institution. Except for
his music, a potential member of that population. But with Charlie Parker
it is the music factor that makes all the difference. That's really the only
reason we're interested in him. The reason we're willing to stop our own
lives and clean up his messes. People like Charlie require somebody like
that . . .

Parker was released, in buoyant shape, in 1947, but by the time he reappeared in New York later that year he was down and out again. He went to
France in 1949 and to Scandinavia in 1950. During the last five years of his
life (he died March 12, 1955), he disintegrated steadily but continued to
work, sometimes brilliantly (the famous Massey Hall concert in Toronto in
1953, with Dizzy Gillespie, Bud Powell, Charles Mingus, and Max Roach).
His last job in New York, or anywhere, took place over the weekend of
March 4 and 5, 1955, at Birdland, with Kenny Dorham, Bud Powell, Mingus, and Art Blakey. On the second night, Powell got drunk, insulted
Parker, and walked off the bandstand. Parker shouted Powell's name endlessly through the microphone, but Powell refused to come back. The club
emptied, and Parker left and got drunk himself. Four days later, he set out
for an engagement at George Wein's Storyville, in Boston, and on the way
stopped off at the apartment of Baroness Pannonica de Koenigswarter, in
the Stanhope Hotel, on Fifth Avenue at Eighty-first Street. He had a
seizure, and three days later died there, aged thirty-four.

Some of the photographs in *To Bird with Love* are famous shots taken by
William Gottlieb and Gjon Mili and Robert Parent, but many appear to be
snapshots rescued from albums and drawers and wallets. Here is Parker
rehearsing in some hall with an experimental big band led by the arranger
Gene Roland and including Zoot Sims, Al Cohn, Jimmy Knepper, and
Eddie Bert; Parker in a double-breasted chalk-stripe suit standing ceremoni-
ously beside Duke Ellington; Parker on a Paris stage with Sidney Bechet,
Bernard Peiffer, and Don Byas; Parker's mother, worn, bemused, kindly;
Parker's childhood home, its windows gone, and surrounded by saplings and
overgrown shrubs; and a derelict three-story brick building in Kansas City
that once housed a night club called Subway, where Parker worked with Jay
McShann and Jesse Price when he was seventeen. Ross Russell quotes
McShann on Parker's already sneaky ways: "He was a strange kid, very
aggressive and wise. He liked to play practical jokes. And he was always bor-
rowing money, a couple of dollars that you'd never get back." The pictures
in the last hundred or so pages of the book are often dismal. Parker is overweight, his eyes are unfocussed, he looks beat and dejected. Most frightening
of all are three double-page photographs taken on the bandstand at Birdland
during Parker's final engagement there. In the first, a huge Parker leans over
to say something to Bud Powell, who, seated at the piano, has mad blank-

white eyes. In the second, Powell, still mad-looking, plays while Art Blakey stares angrily at him. In the last picture, Powell is out of sight, Mingus has vanished, and Parker, fat and sweating, plays backed by Blakey. All three pictures have a dark, hellish cast: demons are loose.

There are rare glimpses of a jazz musician's backstage life in *To Bird with Love*, particularly in a couple of exchanges of letters between irate nightclub managers and the musicians' union and between a defensive Parker and the musicians' union. Toward the end of his life, Parker often behaved poorly on the job or failed to show up at all. The manager of the Latin Quarter, in Montreal, writes to an officer of the musicians' union in New York:

Now for [the musicians'] appearance. When they arrived at the club, they looked anything but musicians, at least, those [we] have been in the habit of engaging. They were shabbily dressed, torn shirts, even on Mr. Parker's back; they were unshaven, dirty looking and not fit to be presented to any public.

Parker's answer to the union official is calm and even stately:

For explanation: It is an over night ride on a train from New York to Montreal, and the men who arrived in the early evening went immediately, as soon as they got off the train, to the Latin Quarter to ascertain what the requirements of the engagement were, and naturally, this being in the neighborhood of 7:30 in the evening, and we not scheduled to play until 10:00 o'clock, and having ridden all day on a very dirty train, all of us certainly admit we were definitely not dressed to make a professional appearance ... When we appeared ... at the prescribed time of 10:00 P.M., my entire band wore dark blue suits, were cleanly shaven, and were ready to perform in a professional manner.

Six months later, Parker apparently misbehaved at the Tiffany Club, in Los Angeles. The manager writes to the same long-suffering union official in New York:

Mr. Parker played four sets instead of five, consisting of 17–14–18–20 minutes each. During these short sessions, Mr. Parker played very little. He leaned on the piano and weaved from side to side, obviously intoxicated. His eyes were shut for three and four minutes at a time and he didn't play a note. He sweat profusely, and wiped his brow with his forefinger and thrust sweat to the floor, unbecoming to a performer. His stage behavior was the most deplorable I have ever witnessed. Patrons laughed and giggled and wondered what next.

Parker will have none of it:

> His comments about my behavior on the stage are purely a matter of personal opinion and conjecture. All I can say is that the people seemed satisfied with my performance and applauded the performance.

Parker, however, lost out; the union decreed that he pay the Tiffany Club five hundred dollars in damages.

## Duke Ellington

Refused admittance to the Broadway musical stage except for the short-lived *Beggar's Holiday*, done with John Latouche in 1946, Duke Ellington created his own musical theatre. This was not surprising, for he was, with his ornate courtesy, his cool, sharp humor, his sometimes arcane dress, and his tinted, mocking speech, intensely theatrical—and so was his often programmatic composing. *Jump for Joy*, produced in Los Angeles in 1941, and *My People*, produced in Chicago in 1963, were elaborate revues in which the music dominated the acts. (That is also the case in the current *Sophisticated Ladies*, despite the highly touted dancing and singing.) *A Drum Is a Woman* was a fantasy written in the mid-fifties for television. *The River* was an almost Bunyanesque allegory done for American Ballet Theatre in 1970. And his so-called Sacred Concerts were unique extravaganzas that were premièred at Grace Cathedral, San Francisco, in 1965, at the Cathedral of St. John the Divine, New York, in 1968, and at Westminster Abbey, in 1973, not long before he died. The Sacred Concerts came to seem to him the most important things he had written. "I am not concerned with what it costs," he wrote of the first Sacred Concert in his autobiography, *Music Is My Mistress*. "I want the best of everything possible. I want the best musicians, the best singers and coaches—amateurs or professionals—and I want them to give the best they have. I want all the help I can get and to say that I hope I am good enough to say because this is the performance of all performances—God willing." Ellington's Sacred Concerts never matched the dimensions of Berlioz's Requiem (four brass bands, full orchestra with sixteen kettledrums, a five-hundred-voice choir), but he did his best to fill the empyreal spaces of the cathedrals and churches and temples he worked in. His band was the base, and to it he added choirs, the cathedral organ, male and female vocal soloists, narration, and dancers, tap and ballet. The results were uneven. Some of the songs had the density and fervor of religious music. Others were romantic, and even lachrymose: they sentimentalized God, possibly making Him an adjunct of Ellington's revered mother. Some of the dancing was showy and superfluous, and so were some of the band instrumentals (long drum solos). The performers were erratic, and varied from the sublime (the Swedish soprano Alice Babs, the tap dancer Bunny Briggs, the band itself) to the melodramatic (the singers Jon Hendricks and Tony Watkins, and the dancer-choreographer Geoffrey Holder). But it was spectacular when everything came together.

This happened in the "David Danced Before the Lord" done at the Fifth Avenue Presbyterian Church in December of 1965. There, in full aural and visual flower, was Ellington's vision. The number, which was recorded during the concert, begins with a short, annunicatory band chord, and this is immediately followed by Briggs dancing fast, light steps. He continues by himself for sixteen measures, and drops into rangy half-time steps. (He dances throughout the number, which lasts six minutes.) The saxophones play the lovely steplike thirty-two-bar melody (originally "Come Sunday"), which, like a lullaby, covers less than an octave and a half and is built on sequential notes. It is played in half time to the dancing, and this sets up an exhilarating rhythmic tension. A choir chants the words over the band, which further enriches the rhythms, and in the next chorus the choir hums the melody while the band plays countermelodic figures—beautiful little flags of the sort that Ellington ran up again and again in his best work. The band falls silent, and the choir chants for a chorus, backed by Ellington and the rhythm section. (Don't forget the continuing rattling, clicking, stomping drone of Briggs' feet, and how, every once in a while, he throws in wild, off-beat, two-footed steps, which jar everything around him.) The choir rests, and Ellington and Briggs do a charging duet for a chorus. Then the choir hums the melody again, there's a pause, and Briggs gives an electrifying shout, which is answered by sixteen bars of ensemble band shouts. At the same time, the drummer (Louis Bellson) solos, the choir chants, and a clarinettist sails into the stratosphere. This mad five-tiered float careers along for eight bars, and Briggs dances out into the sun by himself for several easy measures, and the piece comes to rest with a final band chord.

Part of Ellington's third Sacred Concert was given a trial American run at Queens College in 1975, and recently it was announced that it would be played in its entirety at the Cathedral of St. John the Divine. But, for whatever reasons, the concert was limited to snippets from all three concerts, which were done by a troupe that included the Mercer Ellington band, the Byrne Camp Chorale, the soloists McHenry Boatwright, Alpha Brawner-Floyd, Anita Moore, Tony Bennett, and Phyllis Hyman, the tap dancer Honi Coles, an Alvin Ailey group, and Douglas Fairbanks, Jr., as narrator. (Fairbanks' Hollywood-English accent fitted Ellington's New York biblical words uncommonly well.) Nine numbers from the third Sacred Concert were played (about half of the whole), and they sounded much like the earlier concerts. But there were good moments: David Young's tenor-saxophone solo, backed by the chorale, in "The Brotherhood"; the chorale singing "Alleluia" softer and softer, accompanied only by a bass; and Joe

Temperley's a-cappella baritone-saxophone solo on "The Majesty of God" (Temperley's tone is strikingly close to Harry Carney's, but it lacks Carney's great *bottom*), and the succeeding quiet, ascending organ chords from the band. "David Danced Before the Lord" was among the ten numbers taken from the earlier concerts, but it was short and choppy. Coles never had a chance to get his momentum going, and the towering last chorus was omitted. Boatwright and Brawner-Floyd were lugubrious and often off pitch, while Hyman and Moore, who did gospel songs, and Bennett, who did a fine Ellington song called "Somebody Cares," swung.

It was strange not having Ellington there. He was at his best at his Sacred Concerts, and he somehow managed to make their disparate parts blend. In *Music Is My Mistress*, he unwittingly told us how: "As I travel from place to place . . . taking rhythm to the dancers, harmony to the romantic, melody to the nostalgic, gratitude to the listener . . . receiving praise, applause, and handshakes, and at the same time doing the thing I like to do, I feel that I am most fortunate because I know that God has blessed my timing, without which nothing could have happened." He left us his music, but he took the timing.

Ellington's Sacred Concerts were, in their way, sometimes ludicrously inflated imitations of the thirty or more masterpieces he set down between 1940 and 1942 for Victor Records. It is still not altogether clear why this exuberant flowering took place. The surrounding musical soil was sandy, and the Ellington band itself had been going through dry times. The rhythm section was inert, the arrangements often had a staccato, old-fashioned sound (toy-soldier muted trumpets, ornate saxophone writing), and the ensemble playing was imprecise. Even such fine numbers as "Riding on a Blue Note," "Blue Light," "Barney Goin' Easy," and "Portrait of the Lion" seemed inconclusive. In 1939, things began to stir. The composer and arranger Billy Strayhorn joined the band, and by the end of the year he began to take hold. Ellington left his old, tenacious manager, Irving Mills, and went with the William Morris agency. He also left Brunswick Records, whose sound was closed and soupy, and signed with Victor, whose sound was clear and open. The band made a heartening European tour (black jazz musicians were already going to Europe to be revitalized; indeed, they were often overwhelmed by applause and kindness), and the bassist Jimmy Blanton and the tenor saxophonist Ben Webster became part of the band. Blanton, who was just twenty-one, was the first modern bassist. He had a big tone and unshakable time, and he was the first bassist capable of "melodic" improvising. He woke the band up rhythmically. Webster was thirty, and he had been with Ellington briefly, as well as with Andy Kirk, Fletcher Henderson, Cab Calloway, Benny Carter, and Teddy Wilson. ("I always had a yen for Ben," Ellington says in his autobiography.) All the big black bands except Ellington's had tenor-saxophone stars. Basie had Lester Young and Herschel Evans; Andy Kirk had Dick Wilson;

Fletcher Henderson had Coleman Hawkins; Cab Calloway had Chu Berry. But Ellington's major saxophone soloist had been the alto and soprano saxophonist Johnny Hodges. Webster enriched the band tonally, and he brought it new intensity and emotion. In return, Ellington built "Cotton Tail" and "Just A-Settin' and A-Rockin' " around Webster, and gave him an invaluable opportunity to sit beside Hodges in the saxophone section and absorb him. Within a year or so, Webster, already on the verge of being first-rate, was the equal of Young and Hawkins. So the band was complete. On trumpets were Wallace Jones, Rex Stewart, and Cootie Williams (replaced late in 1940 by Ray Nance); on trombones Juan Tizol, Lawrence Brown, and Tricky Sam Nanton; on reeds Otto Hardwicke, Barney Bigard, Ben Webster, Johnny Hodges, and Harry Carney; and in the rhythm section Ellington on piano, Fred Guy on guitar, Jimmy Blanton on bass, and Sonny Greer on drums.

Ellington's 1940–42 masterpieces have strong jazz characteristics—improvised or partly improvised solos, jazz timbres (plunger mutes, growls, instrumental tonal peculiarities), and a regular sounded beat. They also have classical characteristics—fixed solos (originally improvised solos, which gradually became set), concertolike forms, and complex scoring, some of it rivalling Berlioz's. And they were entirely original in their instrumental combinations and in their odd, often surprising structures. Ellington used the twelve-bar blues and the thirty-two-bar a-a-b-a song form, but he decorated them with introductions and codas, with interludes and transitions, with key changes, with dissonance. Much of the time, his materials appeared to dictate his forms. "Sepia Panorama" has an "arch" form. The first chorus lasts twelve bars, the second chorus lasts sixteen bars, the third lasts eight, and the fourth twelve; the fifth chorus repeats the fourth chorus, the sixth repeats the third, the seventh repeats part of the second, and in the eighth we are back at the first chorus. "Concerto for Cootie" has an eight-bar introduction, and the first chorus is thirty-six bars long (two ten-bar sections and two eight-bar sections). A two-bar transition leads into the second chorus, which is sixteen bars. There is an eight-bar recapitulation of the first ten bars of the first chorus and an eight-bar coda. Ellington (and, increasingly, Strayhorn) wrote most of the materials. Ellington had considerable help from his sidemen, who would contribute a melody here and a bridge there, and who often groused about not getting more credit (to say nothing of royalties). He also reworked chestnuts like "Chloe" and "The Sidewalks of New York," and occasionally he built a new structure on old chords: "In a Mellotone" was based on "Rose Room," and "Cotton Tail" on "I Got Rhythm." He wrote several different kinds of pieces. There were programmatic or descriptive pieces, like "Just A-Settin' and A-Rockin'," "Harlem Airshaft," and "Dusk." There were tone poems, like "Blue Serge." There were rhythmic exercises, like "The Giddybug Gallop," "Ko-Ko," and "Jumpin' Punkins." There were plain old blues, like "Across the Track Blues" and "C Jam Blues." And there were miniature concertos, like "Concerto for Cootie" and "Jack the Bear."

How does one of these Concertos go? Here is "Ko-Ko," a minor blues and no relation of Charlie Parker's "Ko-Ko," made five years later. It starts *in medias res*. Sonny Greer gives a couple of quick timpani beats, and Carney goes immediately into a chuffing sustained note in his low register—his house-moving register—and is backed by the trombone section, possibly salted with one trumpet. The introduction lasts eight bars. In the first chorus, which is twelve bars, Juan Tizol plays an ingenious six-note figure that is pursued closely by the reed section in such a way that it sounds like a continuation of Tizol's figure. Tizol starts the sentence and the reeds finish it. In the next two choruses, twelve measures apiece, Tricky Sam Nanton, using a plunger mute, solos against offbeat muted trumpets and the reed section, which plays a sighing three-note figure. Greer punctuates on his tomtoms. In the fourth chorus, also twelve bars, the reeds repeat the figure they used in the first chorus, and the trumpet section supplies "ooh-wa"s. Ellington himself surfaces from behind, throwing runs and chords into the air. The twelve-bar fifth chorus is climactic. The trumpet section plays a repeated long-held note (one of the trumpets, probably Williams, uses a plunger mute) while the saxophone section, broken into two groups, plays accented figures and a melody parallel to the trumpets. The dissonance is almost overpowering. Then the reeds and trombones slide into an eight-bar interlude, pausing for several two-bar breaks by Blanton. In the seventh chorus, the trumpets again play long-held notes, and the saxophones play a countermelody. Carney returns in the final chorus with his very low chuffing note, backed by the trombones. The reeds climb abruptly into view and disappear into a closing full-band chord. The atmosphere of the number is rough and hustling. There are few treble sounds, and there is little delicacy. The piece bullies. It sets out to be abrasive *and* lyrical, and it succeeds. It is also almost completely an ensemble piece—a kind of concerto for orchestra.

All this is by way of saying that the Smithsonian Collection (the record label of the Smithsonian) is well along in its Ellington reissue project, begun six years ago. Four albums have been released—"Duke Ellington 1938," "Duke Ellington 1939," "Duke Ellington 1940," and now "Duke Ellington 1941." Each of the first two albums has thirty titles and two alternate takes, and although Ellington's strengths are evident, nothing prepares us for what happens at the start of the 1940 album. This includes twenty-eight selections and four alternate takes. At least seven numbers are mediocre, but weak Ellington was superior to almost everything else in popular music. The four duets that Ellington did with Jimmy Blanton (how fine for the young Blanton, how selfless of Ellington) are in the album, and there are two takes of "Mr. J. B. Blues." The 1941 album has twenty-four selections and eight alternates, and it has even more lacklustre material. Fourteen of the numbers are radio transcriptions made around the same time as the Victor sides, and they don't add much to our Ellington knowledge. How much better to have put in the ten or eleven classic sides—one is the surging "Main Stem"— Ellington made in 1942 before a union-imposed recording ban, which lasted into 1944, brought his great creative splurge to an end. But there are tracks from two "soundies," which were three-minute films made for jukeboxes equipped with tiny screens. The first is a furious (but truncated) "Cotton Tail" and the second is an easy "C-Jam Blues" notable for the longest drum solo (twelve bars) that Greer, an infrequent soloist, ever recorded with Ellington. He rarely used the muffling pads on his snare drum or tomtoms, and he kept his drumheads very tight. The result was a sharp, ringing tone. His solo is staccato and rocking. It crackles. It is played mostly on his snare drum, although he inserts one fast round-the-set explosion. The 1940 and 1941 albums include the rattling swing of "Jack the Bear," "A Portrait of Bert Williams," "In a Mellotone," and "Jumpin' Punkins," which has a lot of two-bar Greer breaks ; the tonal depths of "Dusk" and "Blue Serge"; the almost ecstatic shout by what sounds like the full band between Hodges' solos on "Never No Lament"; Cootie Williams' fury on "Harlem Airshaft" and his acidulous preaching on "Never No Lament"; all of Ben Webster's solos, and particularly his classic statement on "Blue Serge," with its growling near the end; and the sly, affecting work of Tricky Sam Nanton, who was in frequent evidence in 1940 and 1941.

## Reunion

The Modern Jazz Quartet—those who considered it delicate and marginal notwithstanding—was at the heart of jazz in the sixties. Its members grew up under the grand masters of swing (Count Basie, Duke Ellington, Roy Eldridge, Ben Webster, Coleman Hawkins, Lester Young, Art Tatum, Jimmy Blanton, Lionel Hampton, and Sidney Catlett). They also grew up alongside the founders of bebop (Charlie Parker, Dizzy Gillespie, Bud Powell, Thelonious Monk, and Kenny Clarke). The swing musicians taught them the beauties of straight melodic playing. They taught them chordal and melodic improvisation, rhythmic precision, musical taste, how to swing, and what the work ethic was. They taught them, without ever saying so, that jazz is an art, and that being a jazz musician can be ennobling. With the exception of Milt Jackson, the members of the quartet did not absorb as much from their bebop peers. They learned the new harmonic and rhythmic vocabulary of bebop, and they studied its exuberance and flashiness. They marvelled, as everyone did, at the improvisational depth and daring of Parker and Gillespie and, to a lesser extent, Bud Powell. But they eventually rejected bebop's garrulity, which was brought on in large part by the arrival of the LP recording, with its forty-five-minute time limit. (Lewis once said of the quartet's beginnings, "There were things wrong in the music around us that we all agreed on, and some of them were long, long solos and that formula on a tune of everybody playing the melody in the first chorus, followed by a string of solos, and then the melody again.") They also rejected its tonal harshness and its harmonic tyranny—the endless, competitive "running of the changes" that bebop improvisers loved. But Jackson embraced Parker and Gillespie and their principles. Lionel Hampton had taught him the fundamentals of swinging, and Jackson added Parker's and Gillespie's speed and fluidity. John Lewis never moved much beyond Basie and Webster and Young, and Percy Heath and Connie Kay never abandoned Blanton and Catlett. So the quartet had three feet in swing and one foot in bebop, and it was far more conservative than it seemed when it came up, in the early fifties. What gave it the deceptive glow of newness was its odd, largely accidental instrumentation (Lewis, Jackson, and Ray Brown, its original bassist, were part of Gillespie's big band before they decided to play on their own) and its use of Baroque devices and materials—the fugue, the rondo, and Lewis's "Italian" compositions. It was a swing group aerated by the imaginations of Parker and Gillespie—an up-to-date outgrowth of the Benny Goodman small groups, the King Cole Trio, and the Red Norvo Trio.

The quartet was not alone at the center of the music. It was flanked by Thelonious Monk (his compositions, his quartets, his brilliant pickup recordings for the Riverside label) and by Charles Mingus (his ceaseless experiments with instrumental combinations and with improvisational modes—in particular, collective improvising). But in 1973 this triumvirate began to disappear. Mingus, hampered by illness, became increasingly ineffectual, and Monk went into a mysterious retreat and stopped performing. Then, in 1974, the quartet, which had been in existence for twenty-two years, disbanded. It reassembled in 1976 for two brief Midwestern tours. A week or so ago, reassembled again, it capped a two-week tour of Japan and San Francisco with a concert in Avery Fisher Hall. The concert was a beauty, and Lewis made it clear, once and for all, that he is far from being Jackson's improvisational inferior. It was often said in the sixties that Jackson was wasted on the quartet. He *is* an exceptional improviser, who constantly circumvents the metallic properties of his instrument. He is a rhapsodic melodist who uses surging Charlie Parker lines that pitch up and down his keyboard. He has a strong sense of dynamics, and he has unlimited ideas. Lewis, on the other hand, is the soul of brevity. The unofficial leader of the quartet and its chief composer and arranger, he is probably the most undervalued pianist of his generation. He has said that, in the main, horn players, not pianists, shaped his style, and this must be true, for the only pianist clearly audible in his work is Count Basie. He uses few notes, and he plays with a relentless rhythmic intensity. He does this with repeated notes, with simple repeated riffs, with occasional legato tempo dips, and with monosyllabic on-the-beat single-note figures. He is as lyrical a player as Jackson, but he implies his lyricism, while Jackson broadcasts his.

Lewis was in rare condition at Avery Fisher Hall. There was none of the stiffness and pompous simplicity that sometimes affect his improvisations. Again and again, in such numbers as "Odds Against Tomorrow," "The Cylinder," "Billie's Bounce," and "Willow Weep for Me," he was full of ease and swing and freshness. (Jazz musicians have often pointed out that they play best when they are exhausted. The quartet, after its Japanese marathon, flew directly to San Francisco, where it gave two concerts in one day; then it took off for New York, and arrived at Avery Fisher from the airport.) Jackson never falls below excellence, and he poured out solo after passionate solo, especially in "What's New?," "'Round Midnight," "The Martyr," and "Willow Weep for Me." Lewis lent Jackson his customary sterling support, with offbeat chords, with applauding declarative figures, and with polite counterpoint. Neither Heath nor Kay solos much; their beauties lie in the self-effacing way they hold up Lewis and Jackson—in the velvet they provide for the jewels.

# 1982

## Monk

The pianist and composer Thelonious Monk, who died last week, at the age of sixty-four, was an utterly original man who liked to pretend he was an eccentric. Indeed, he used eccentricity as a shield to fend off a world that he frequently found alien, and even hostile. A tall, dark, bearish, inward-shining man, he wore odd hats and dark glasses with bamboo frames when he played. His body moved continuously. At the keyboard, he swayed back and forth and from side to side, his feet flapping on the floor. While his sidemen soloed, he stood by the piano and danced, turning in slow, genial circles, his elbows out like wings, his knees slightly bent, his fingers snapping on the after-beat. His motions celebrated what he and his musicians played: Watch, these are the shapes of my music. His compositions and his playing were of a piece. His improvisations were molten Monk compositions, and his compositions were frozen Monk improvisations. His medium- and up-tempo tunes are stop-and-go rhythmic structures. Their melodic lines, which often hinge on flatted notes, tend to be spare and direct, but they are written with strangely placed rests and unexpected accents. They move irregularly through sudden intervals and ritards and broken rhythms. His balladlike tunes are altogether different. They are art songs, which move slowly and three-dimensionally. They are carved sound. (Monk's song titles—"Crepuscule with Nellie," "Epistrophy," "Ruby, My Dear,"

"Well, You Needn't," "Rhythm-a-ning," "Hackensack"—are as striking as the songs themselves. But none beat his extraordinary name, Thelonious Sphere Monk, which surpasses such euphonies as Stringfellow Barr and Twyla Tharp.) His improvisations were attempts to disguise his love of melody. He clothed whatever he played with spindly runs, flatted notes, flatted chords, repeated single notes, yawning silences, and zigzag rhythms. Sometimes he pounded the keyboard with his right elbow. His style protected him not only from his love of melody but from his love of the older pianists he grew out of—Duke Ellington and the stride pianists. All peered out from inside his solos, but he let them escape only as parody.

Monk hid behind his music so well that we know little of him. He was brought from North Carolina when he was little, he eventually settled in the West Sixties, and he lived there until his building was torn down. He married the Nellie of his song title, and he had two children, one of whom became a drummer. He began appearing in New York night clubs around 1940, but he achieved little recognition until the late fifties. (He was often lumped with Charlie Parker and Dizzy Gillespie; however, he did not have much in common with them outside of certain harmonic inventions.) Part of the reason for Monk's slow blooming was his iconoclastic music, and part was the fact that he was unable to perform in New York night clubs from 1951 to 1957—the time when Charles Mingus and the Modern Jazz Quartet and Gerry Mulligan were becoming famous. (The police had lifted his cabaret card, because he had been found sitting in a car in which narcotics were concealed.) But when he returned to the scene, he suddenly seemed to be everywhere—on record after exceptional record, at concerts and festivals, at the old Five Spot and the Vanguard and the Jazz Gallery. He filled us with his noble, funny, generous music.

Then, in 1973, he vanished again. There were rumors that he was ill and had been taken in by his old friend and mentor the Baroness Nica de Koenigswarter, who lives in a big house in Weehawken, New Jersey. The rumors turned out to be true, and this is what the Baroness had to say about Monk before he died: "No doctor has put his finger on what is wrong with him, and he has had every medical test under the sun. He's not unhappy, and his mind works very well. He knows what is going on in the world, and I don't know how, because he doesn't read the newspapers and he only watches a little telly. He's withdrawn, that's all. It's as though he had gone into retreat. He takes walks several times a week, and Nellie comes over from New York almost every day to cook for him. He began to withdraw in 1973, and he hasn't touched the piano since 1976. He has one twenty or thirty feet from his bed, so to speak, but he never goes near it. When Barry Harris visits, he practices on it, and he'll ask Monk what the correct changes to 'Ruby, My Dear' are, and Monk will tell him. Charlie Rouse, his old tenor saxophonist, came to see him on his birthday the other day, but Monk isn't really interested in seeing anyone. The strange thing is he looks beautiful.

He has never *said* that he won't play the piano again. He suddenly went into this, so maybe he'll suddenly come out."

But Monk must have known he wouldn't. His last public appearance, at the Newport Jazz Festival of 1976, was painful. His playing was mechanical and uncertain, and, astonishingly, his great Gothic style had fallen away.

## Sonny Greer

The longer Duke Ellington's musicians stayed in his band, the younger they seemed to become. Perhaps this Fountain of Youth effect came about from their having to keep up with Ellington's voluminous composing, from their constantly having to cope with new music. Perhaps it stemmed from their inborn originality: many were great American primitive artists. Perhaps it could be explained by the mystique of elegance and excellence that bound them together. Sonny Greer, Johnny Hodges, Lawrence Brown, Cootie Williams, Harry Carney, Ray Nance, Russell Procope, Ellington himself—all invariably looked ten or twenty years younger than they were. This was particularly true of Greer, who, seemingly in his fifties, died a little while ago at the age of seventy-eight.

Greer had been a co-founder of the Ellington band, in the early twenties, and he remained Ellington's drummer and unofficial co-captain for almost thirty years. (Worn out by being on the road and by Ellington's relentless brass, he left the band in 1951 with a splinter group headed by Hodges and including Lawrence Brown. Hodges and Brown returned to the band permanently several years later, but Greer never went back.) Greer's appearance and his playing were inseparable, and they helped to established the band's high tone and cool assurance. He was a thin, handsome, dapper, concave man with a wide smile and a smooth cap of black hair. His eyes, which he often popped, matched his hair, and he had a drummer's long fingers. His rich, quick speech gave him an Ancient Mariner insistence. Greer came up in the vaudeville tradition, and he was a consummate showman. He encircled himself in the thirties and forties with a forest of white drums that included a snare drum, tomtoms, a bass drum, and timpani. These were lit by cymbals, chimes, and gongs, and decorated by temple blocks, wood blocks, and cowbells. He even had a vibraphone. Often dressed in white, he sat at the center of this gleaming array and, his trunk motionless, allowed his Shivalike arms to dart among his cymbals and drums. He would snap his head from side to side on the beat, his chin slightly lifted, and smile brilliantly. He would lunge at a cymbal or spin a stick into the air. He would loose a heavy mock frown. He was an incomparable accompanist, who would launch a Ben Webster tenor-saxophone solo by tapping a cowbell, fill an ensemble pause with a couple of eighth notes on a timpani, make his Chinese cymbal hiss beneath a Tricky Sam Nanton muted-trombone solo, place easy, clicking, pushing rimshots on the afterbeat behind a Rex Stewart cornet solo. He cooled the band when it grew frenzied, and heated it when it was too cool. He once described his methods: "I learned how to keep my drums crisp, to tune them so they had an even, clear sound. I knew about showmanship, about how audiences eat it up—that it ain't what you do but how you do it. Things like hitting three rimshots and opening and closing one side of my jacket in time. I always strove for finesse. I always tried to shade, and make everything sound beautiful. It was my job to keep the band in level time, to keep slow tempos from going down and fast tempos from going up. Those things meant more to me than solos, which I rarely took."

Greer was born William Alexander Greer, Jr., in Long Branch, New Jersey. His father was an electrician with the Pennsylvania Railroad, and his mother was a modiste. He had an older sister and a younger sister and brother. He didn't waste a minute of his childhood. He caddied, peddled fish, delivered newspapers, became a master pool player, and learned how to sing and play the drums. He said that he had learned most of his music from a tall, elegant drummer named Eugene (Peggy) Holland, who once played the Keith Theatre in Long Branch for two weeks with J. Rosamond Johnson. Ellington, sly and jocose, saw Greer's beginnings as a drummer somewhat different. He wrote in *Music Is My Mistress*, "Instead of following in his father's footsteps, Greer . . . [banged] on his mother's pots and pans, and he developed his own style of drumming from those banging beginnings . . . A natural supporting artist with his pots and pans, he kept time with horses trotting, people sweeping, and people digging ditches. He didn't indulge in such activities himself, but he kept time with those who did . . . and he dug the value of teamwork all the way back. By adding his own embellishments, he developed what was later to be his forte. Everything in his life, I think, has always been done in a happy way, even though not according to Hoyle." What Ellington meant at the end of his tribute was that Greer was an old-fashioned opportunist, who always had his eyes peeled, his tongue ready, his cue in hand. He developed a set of homilies that supported his view of life:

When you're getting ready to lie, don't smile.

Pool is like the violin—you've got to play an hour every day.

Bread cast upon the sea comes back buttered toast.

I always had an ambition to make money and not have money make me.

If there are three people going that way and only two people this way, then there must be more happening that way than this way, so I'm going that way, too.

> Retired people lie under a tree and play checkers, and first thing you
> know they're gone.

So Greer didn't retire. (He lived on the West Side, with his wife, Milli-
cent, a Cotton Club dancer he was married to for over fifty years. They had
a daughter and grandchildren, great grandchildren, and even great-great-
grandchildren.) From the mid-seventies on, he played dates with his friend
Brooks Kerr, and with the Ellington clarinettist and alto saxophonist Russell
Procope. After Procope died, Greer and Kerr kept going. He sat at his
drums in the same erect poised way he had when he was with Ellington, and
it was not hard (at Gregory's or the West End Café, or at some private
party) to summon up from Greer's playing alone the rest of the band.

## Dizzy Gillespie and Bill Coleman

Excerpts from three concerts given by Dizzy Gillespie and the Mitchell-Ruff Duo (Dwike Mitchell on piano,
Willie Ruff on bass and horn) during the past decade or so have been
released on an album as "Dizzy Gillespie—Live." The concerts were held at
Dartmouth in 1970, at Yale in 1974, and at Town Hall in 1980. The album
reveals that Gillespie, who will be sixty-five years old this fall, can still play
with fire. He pictured himself as an iron man in his recent autobiography,
and he appears to be right.

When Gillespie came up, in the mid-forties, his style was an intricate and
explosive composite of Roy Eldridge, Charlie Parker, Charlie Shavers, and
Art Tatum. It was dense and rococo. Each solo billowed, and each, with its
cascade of notes, got where it was going as fast as possible. Gillespie *ran*. He
liked to spell out on the piano the new augmented chords—for the benefit of
himself and other musicians—and he would then build his solos out of them,
using combinations of notes that only Charlie Parker had dared before. He
liked to knock down the bar lines, in the manner of Art Tatum, and let his
phrases tumble on for six or eight measures. He liked to shock. In a chorus of
medium-tempo blues, he might begin with a high-register blast, followed by
a resounding silence. He would then play a snatch of the melody in a soft,
vibratoless half time, and slide into a descending double-time run, pause,
and work out a climbing, zigzag figure. More silence, followed by a high
two-note yell, a run, and a low, slow closing whole note. All Gillespie's solos
offered hair-raising melodic flights and masterly rhythmic inventions. Half-
time passages slipped into on-the-beat figures, which gave way to double
time, which dropped to half-time, which then sped up to full time. His solos
swung, and it did not matter if in his haste he split notes, missed them, or
allowed his tone to shriek.

Gillespie's playing has slowed to a fast walk. His trademarks—staccato,
undulating connective phrases; upper-register excursions; serpentine runs;

fat, blinding opening notes—are intact, but he surrounds them with new effects. He uses more silence (sometimes three or four beats go by between phrases), and his playing is gentler and quieter; he no longer has to shout for attention, the way he did in the forties. His phrasing is simpler. Quarter notes do for eighth or sixteenth notes, and he registers them firmly in the air before moving on. Much of Gillespie's playing used to be almost subliminal; now it is fully visible. He reverts to the melody more than he once did, perhaps to make sure he is on course. He also, curiously enough, reverts to two trumpet players who have never been associated with him—Red Allen and Rex Stewart. He must have listened to them in the late thirties, and perhaps it has taken this long for what he heard to surface. He uses richly spaced, low-register Allen notes, and even reproduces the fluttering tremolo that Allen opens his solo with on "A Sheridan Square." He has also adopted Stewart's famous half-valved notes—an effect that is achieved by pressing a trumpet valve partway down and blowing a note that is slightly below the one sounded when the valve is released. It is a pleasing effect: the first note, squeezed and thin, becomes rounded as the valve rises. It is like passing through a low doorway into a high-ceilinged room. Aging brass players take a while to warm up, and when Gillespie is sufficiently heated he can get off passages of great brilliance and éclat. He is, after so many years, still king.

The album has twenty-one numbers. Four are by Mitchell and Ruff, one is a Mitchell piano solo, one is a funny, buck-dancing Gillespie solo on the Jew's harp, one is a Gillespie-Ruff duet, and the rest are by the three men. Both Mitchell, who is fifty-two, and Ruff, who is two years younger, have had musical training, and they are not the sort of chamber-jazz musicians Gillespie generally plays with. Ruff is a good Charlie Mingus bassist and a virtuoso horn player, and Mitchell is a florid, occasionally impassioned Art Tatum admirer who favors the loud pedal. They work well with Gillespie, partly out of admiration and partly because they stay out of his way. (Ruff plays horn with Gillespie on just three numbers, and the duets are tentative.) Gillespie, also unencumbered by a drummer, is free to fly, and he does. He produces half a dozen careful, muted choruses at the beginning of "Blues People," which is Charlie Parker's "Now's the Time," and returns at the close for five open-horn choruses, complete with a breakneck upper-register passage. He does the verse of "My Man," ad-lib, gracing the melody with added notes and new harmonies, and then jumps into a sparkling medium-tempo solo that at first suggests Charlie Shavers. "Lover Man" is taken out of tempo all the way through, and is a winding, complex melodic study. More than half the album is given over to the 1980 Town Hall concert. There is an ad-lib Gillespie rendition of "I Remember Clifford," and on his own "Ow!," based on the chords of "I Got Rhythm," he delivers an open-horn solo that crowds the listener to the ropes. On "Conception," the three men, starting off without any theme or tempo, wander around in their shirt-sleeves. Ruff plays horn, and he and Gillespie solo well and do some counterpoint; all three reach the finish line more or less together. A very slow version of "Mood Indigo" threatens to fall apart even before it gets going but is rescued midway through the first chorus when Gillespie, improvising on the second theme, goes into a sudden, left-hand open-horn descending passage. It fools with time. It is intense and casual and lyrical and surprising. It swings, and is altogether beautiful.

It is not too late to celebrate the elusive and magical trumpeter Bill Coleman, who died late last summer, at the age of seventy-seven. He lived with his Swiss wife in a small farm-house in the village of Cadeillan, in southwestern France. Born near Paris, Kentucky, he spent almost half his life in France, where, he said, no one ever called him "nigger." He first went abroad in 1933, with Lucky Millinder, and he went back again and again, until the Second World War drove him home. He was in constant demand here, and he worked with Teddy Wilson, Benny Carter, Fats Waller, John Kirby, Andy Kirk, Noble Sissle, and Sy Oliver. Between 1942 and 1944, he settled in New York, where he either led or appeared in trios with the pianists Ellis Larkins and Mary Lou Williams. He also turned up in Wilson's sextet at Café Society Uptown (Emmett Berry, Edmond Hall, Benny Morton, Johnny Williams, Sid Catlett), and at the Sunday-afternoon jam sessions at Jimmy Ryan's. In 1948, the war over and his racial patience exhausted, he went back to France for good.

Coleman's early recordings, made here and in France in the thirties with Fats Waller and Django Reinhardt and Dickie Wells, were always hard to come by, and the same is true of the scattered sessions he did in the forties, with Wells and Lester Young, with Mary Lou Williams, and with Nat Cole and Coleman Hawkins. So little of Coleman exists here that it might not be an exaggeration to say that scarcely two or three hundred people in America knew who he was when he died.

Like most players of his generation, he listened to Louis Armstrong. He also listened to the dulcet-toned Joe Smith, and to the heretical Jabbo Smith, who came to New York when Coleman did, in the late twenties. Coleman's playing, like Coleman himself, was never still. He preferred the middle registers, and he moved constantly from one end of them to the other. He played with a dancing lyricism, but he played with such delicacy that he gave the impression of shying away from his notes. He came at them from slightly below or above, sounded them, and was gone, his vibrato barely stirring the air. Few jazz improvisers know how to construct sequential solos, but Coleman's had a rare logic. He never lost the melodic thread he was weaving, and when he finished a solo there was nothing extraneous, nothing missing. It rested complete in the mind.

Coleman did well enough in France. He generally worked as much as he needed to, and he recorded frequently. He was made a Chevalier de l'Ordre National du Mérite, and he dictated his memoirs to his wife, who, failing to find an English or American publisher, translated them into French and had them published. He played almost to the time he died, and his playing didn't change much. It slowed down, it flattened out. Would that he had not been driven away. He was always missed.

## Good Tidings

Old and New Dreams, made up, at Lush Life, of Dewey Redman on tenor saxophone and musette, Don Cherry on pocket trumpet and piano, Charlie Haden on bass, and Ed Blackwell on drums, suggests the Hot Five without Louis Armstrong, the Red Hot Peppers without Jelly Roll Morton. Barring Redman it is the same quartet that Ornette Coleman had at the Five Spot Café in the winter of 1960. That group, more or less intact until Coleman disbanded it in 1962, was first reassembled, with Redman standing in for Coleman, on a 1976 recording called "Old and New Dreams" (after a Redman number in the album). The recording was acclaimed, and in 1978 the four men decided to become a working group. They wanted to celebrate Coleman's compositions, and they wanted, as Coleman protégés, to reinvestigate his old adventures and discoveries. (Redman grew up in Fort Worth with Coleman and has played with him frequently.) What made Coleman's Five Spot quartet so startling was its leader's passionate and unshakable belief in what he was doing (a new kind of improvisation, based on mood, melody, and certain tonal centers and rhythms) and the blazing, headlong way he and his musicians carried it out. They travelled fast across ground that only a few jazz musicians had seen, and that none had explored. The quartet, which had a hounding tension, was exhausting. The listener first had to clear away the verbiage that almost immediately engulfed it (brickbats or messianic superlatives). Then he had to learn *not* to listen for chords, conventional melody, keys, chorus structures, or expected rhythmic turns. He had to do some virgin listening. The group was not nearly as madcap as it seemed. Its improvisations were strongly attached to Coleman's muscular melodies, the rhythmic pulse was strong, if not always stated or steady, and the collective playing loosely resembled early New Orleans polyphony.

Old and New Dreams is aptly named; its music is a series of meditations, carried out with striking calm, on the old Coleman quartet. Redman is an earthy Coleman whose rhythm-and-blues origins show. Sometimes his solos wander and sometimes he plays with logic and great feeling. Cherry has changed. During his Five Spot days, he sounded shrill and inconclusive; his solos went against the grain of the music. Since then, he has broadened his technique, and he has experimented with the folk music of Europe, Africa, and India. He has replaced uncertainty and implication with a declarative ease. Haden was from the first a passionate impulsive player. He has avoided the current bass fads (sliding, sing-song notes, wooden tone, empty technical displays), and he has developed his melodic sense. He has become a hornlike voice in the group. Blackwell, a native of New Orleans, is a funny, melodic drummer. No matter what tempo he is playing, he sits behind his drums—his dark glasses halfway down his nose, his elbows loose, his shoulders rounded, his hands hayforks—as if he were ambling down a country road. He gets a lot of melodic continuity out of his snare and cymbals and tomtoms, and much of what he does as an accompanist and as a soloist is based on New Orleans marching-band drumming.

Most of the time at Lush Life, Old and New Dreams sounded like an adventurous edition of Art Blakey's Jazz Messengers. The melody was stated in unison or in rough counterpoint by the horns, there were long solos, and the melody was restated. There was little of the collective interplay of Coleman's quartet, and the solos were approachable and often highly melodic. Cherry alternated outpourings of notes with brief melodies, and his tone was sure and sweet. Redman steamed, and Haden and Blackwell developed immense, marching rhythms. It's a wonder they had the strength. The room was full, and there was little ventilation. The temperature on the bandstand must have been in the high eighties. Jazz musicians, more often than not, are still hired hands.

## Teddy Wilson

Teddy Wilson still presides when he sits at the piano. He will be seventy this year, but all is in place—the ramrod back, the flat hands, the square elbows held close to the sides, the slightly raised chin, the lowered eyes, and the compressed, almost imperceptibly moving lips (the only register of emotion in an otherwise masklike face). His figure, once thin as a stamp, has thickened, and his hawklike profile has become a series of arcs and spheres. His famous style—a delicate and subtle tracery of single-note melodic lines framed by discreet chords—now comes in two grades: preset and largely predictable (a reflection of the boredom with their own skills that occasionally afflicts all perfectionists), and, when he is stirred by a good audience or an aggressive rhythm section, resplendent and exciting. Wilson's musical life has been unassailable and invaluable. His faultless taste has informed the music wherever he has gone. The very excellence of his style, though rarely directly imitated, has seemed to force his most gifted admirers (Billy Kyle, Nat Cole, Mel Powell, Hank Jones, Lennie Tristano, Jimmy Rowles) into shaping almost equally exceptional styles. He has helped give the music, long heedless and untutored, an awareness of its own elegance and brilliance.

Wilson was one of the first black jazz musicians to come from an educated, middle-class background. He was born in Austin, Texas, and raised in Tuskegee, Alabama. His mother was a librarian at Tuskegee Institute, and his father was head of the English Department. Wilson attended Talledega College for a year, but in 1929 he went North to try his wings as a jazz pianist. He joined Speed Webb (Roy Eldridge, Vic Dickenson) and then replaced Art Tatum in Milton Senior's band in Toledo, Ohio. He worked in local Chicago bands and filled in for Earl Hines at the Grand Terrace Ballroom. In 1933, he travelled with Lous Armstrong's indifferent big band, and before the year was out he had been summoned to New York by Benny Carter. The Carter Band (J. C. Higginbotham, Wayman Carver, Sidney Catlett) collapsed in 1934, and Wilson went on to Willie Bryant (Cozy Cole, Ben Webster, Carter). Then his sun rose. At the behest of John Hammond, he began making a series of all-star small-band recordings for Brunswick, many of them with Billie Holiday. (By the time the series ended, in 1941, he had recorded close to a hundred titles.) He also sat in with Benny Goodman at a party at Red Norvo's house in Forest Hills; a few weeks later he was on the first of the Benny Goodman Trio records. He joined the Goodman band in 1936, and stayed three years. Jess Stacy was Goodman's regular pianist, so Goodman had Wilson appear only with the trio and, later, the quartet. It was a courageous time for Wilson. He was the first black musician to be attached to a big white jazz band—*the* big white jazz band, in fact. He was cheered on the bandstand but off the stand was relegated to "colored" hotels and boarding houses. In 1939, Wilson, encouraged by his sudden fame, put together his own big band. It was a clean, well-lighted group that included Shorty Baker, Doc Cheatham, Ben Webster, and J. C. Heard, but it lasted barely a year. It was done in by its sheer high-class professionalism and by the departure of Ben Webster, who joined Duke Ellington. From 1940 to 1944, Wilson led a superb sextet at Café Society Downtown and Café Society Uptown. By 1950, bebop was entrenched. Wilson, only thirty-eight, had passed through the most productive period of his life. Since then, he has pieced together a brave career from teaching, radio work, recordings, and endless travelling as a solo act.

Wilson's style has changed little since 1935. At first, it was a mixture of what he admired in Earl Hines (the single-note melodic attack, the little right-hand tremolos, the restless left hand), the stride pianists (the rhythmic precision and the love of melody), and Art Tatum (the touch, speed, arpeggios, and fearless harmonic sense). But he quickly worked out his own style, and what we have come to be so delighted by is its calm, riffling runs, some of them the shortest distance between two points and some with a tricky sidewise motion; the short declarative single-note phrases, the first measure often repeated once or twice to give a pleasant stuttering effect; the dashing double-time single-note bursts; the peppery, sometimes quite dissonant right-hand chords; the way he tosses the melody back and forth between his hands like a juggler; the left hand constantly moving from tenth chords (on and off the beat) to single-note accents and patches of stride; the love of the middle and upper registers. It is easy to listen to a Wilson solo and hear very little of it. His solos are worked out so quietly and fastidiously that they give the impression that they would rather not be heard at all—that they would prefer to stay safely inside their originator's head. There isn't much for the listener to hold on to. The colors are light, the textures silken. There are almost no dynamics; each note is struck perfectly and with the same force as the one before it. Nor is there any rhythmic commotion. Wilson's solos move along one-two-three-four, one-two-three-four, and have none of the legato fooling-with-time experiments of Red Allen and Lester Young and Billie Holiday. (Part of the appeal of the Wilson-Holiday Brunswicks is the contrast—not to say struggle—between his rhythmic rectitude and her alarming and irresistible rhythmic liberties. She sometimes sang entire vocals just outside the beat while Wilson, in his accompanying and in his solo, effortlessly gave her a reading of her exact location.) What finally makes Wilson's solos difficult to get near is their melodic logic. (It has been said that his playing is cold. This is not true. The emotion is simply gloved.) They form landscapes of sound—ordered, serene (even the fast tempos), polite, beautiful.

## King Again

It is hard now to understand why the Frank Sinatra who first appeared with Tommy Dorsey over forty years ago had such an electric effect. RCA has reissued, as "The Tommy Dorsey-Frank Sinatra Sessions," all eighty-three of the vocals that he did with Dorsey between February 1, 1940, and July 2, 1942, and they are, with a few celebrated exceptions, vapid and inert. Sinatra had broken with the bouncy, gingham style of Bing Crosby (although he seems to have listened to sleeker crooners, like Eddy Howard), and, by virtue of his simplicity and straightforwardness, he projected a kind of modernity. But his sense of phrasing was unfinished and his diction was unsteady—he tended to let his words drift away open-ended. There was a slight nasal quality to his singing, he was not always in tune, and he had little sense of dynamics. His vibrato sounded skinny. He has said that he modelled his singing on Dorsey's bland, stainless trombone playing, and his early singing does have the same creaminess, the same reluctance to rock the melodic boat. Of course, Dorsey, whose personality was the direct opposite of his playing, didn't make things easy for Sinatra. Fewer than a quarter of the songs Sinatra was asked to record are worth hearing more than once, and this was during the years when numbers such as "It Never Entered My Mind," "I Concentrate on You," "Blues in the Night," "The Nearness of You," "Bewitched," "How High the Moon," "It's So Peaceful in the Country," and "Soft as Spring" first came out. The tempos Dorsey chose were often so slow that the music sounded as if it might congeal, and the backgrounds, full of muted trumpets, high-pitched reeds, and dull rhythmic patterns, provided little support for the singer. The best things Sinatra recorded with Dorsey were done with the Pied Pipers. Four of these numbers—"I'll Never Smile Again," "Star Dust," "I Guess I'll Have to Dream the Rest," and "The One I Love"—still have a hymning, bas-relief quality.

It is equally difficult to connect the Sinatra of the Dorsey days with the Sinatra of "Trilogy," the surprising album he put out two years ago, and the Sinatra who recently gave ten concerts at Carnegie Hall. The vicissitudes of his career are well known: his being dumped by Columbia Records in the early fifties; his return to fame and fortune through Hollywood and Capitol Records in the fifties and sixties; his gradual vocal deterioration in the late sixties, and his retirement in 1971 (now referred to by Sinatra as a "vacation"); his often shaky comeback, begun in 1973; and the surpassing of his old strengths in "Trilogy," which contains several classic recordings—"It Had to Be You," "My Shining Hour," "More Than You Know," "Something," and "Love Me Tender." (The album also contains a section called "Reflections on the Future in Three Tenses." It is a fantasy, with words and music by Gordon Jenkins, in which Sinatra, narrating and singing and backed by a huge chorus and orchestra, takes a trip through space and prepares himself for old age and death. It's Sinatra with the sillies.)

Sinatra's new strengths were displayed in almost all the fourteen songs he did at his second Carnegie Hall concert. His voice, close to a tenor in his Dorsey days, has become a true baritone, and it has taken on timbre and resilience. He can growl and sound hoarse. He can shout. His vibrato is tight and controlled. He has a fine sense of dynamics. He has mentioned his admiration for Billie Holiday, and she seems at this late date to have subtly possessed him. He uses her exhilarating rhythmic devices and her sometimes staccato, rocking diction. Occasionally, his voice resembles the heavy, robed one she developed in the forties. Also evident are the definitive phrasing of Mabel Mercer and, in small pinches, the abandon of Ray Charles. The early Sinatra sang with veiled emotion; the present one was clearly moved by much of what he did at Carnegie Hall, and his transports were passed on to the audience. He did a slow, husky "Come Rain or Come Shine," using Billie Holiday's legato pacing, his face brimming with emotion. He did an ad-lib "When Your Lover Has Gone," backed by organ chords, and a rocking "The Lady Is a Tramp." He did another classic "It Had to Be You," a pushing "I Won't Dance," and an easy ad-lib "As Time Goes By." All his showmanship was in place. There were the searchlight blue eyes that give the impression they are looking into every pair of eyes in the hall; the ineffable cool and skill that make his singing appear effortless; the flashing smiles that dispel the emotion of the last song and prepare the way for the next one; the fluid stage motions, even including the seemingly ostentatious sipping of a glass of red wine.

## Bunny Berigan

**L**ouis Armstrong was the first sunburst in jazz—the light a thousand young trumpeters reflected. But two other trumpeters, both less imitable than Armstrong and both suffering from short, damaged careers, were also closely attended. One was Jabbo Smith, and the other was Bix Beiderbecke. These two had an equally evanescent admirer—Bunny Berigan. Out of fashion most of the forty years since his death, Berigan was once revered as a kind of Beiderbecke replacement. But he successfully absorbed both players (along with Armstrong, of course) and constructed his own passionate style.

Born in 1908 in Hilbert, Wisconsin, of a musical Irish-German family, Berigan took up the violin at six, switched to the trumpet at eleven, and had his first professional job when he was thirteen. He never finished high school, and was a full-time musician at eighteen. He moved to New York in 1928, got to know Rex Stewart and the Dorsey brothers, and in 1930 was hired by Hal Kemp. During the next four years, he did studio work, made a great many recordings, and worked for Paul Whiteman. He got married and had children and became a disastrous drinker. In 1935, he joined Benny Goodman. Jess Stacy was on piano, and he once said of Berigan: "I worked with Berigan in the Goodman band in 1935—in fact, travelled across the country with him in Goodman's old Pontiac. He dressed conservatively, and, with his little mustache and his widow's peak and his glasses, he looked like a college professor. He was a wonderful man and an electrifying trumpet player, and he didn't have a conceited bone in his body. He was always kind of not satisfied with his playing. After he took a solo, he'd say, 'I started out great but I ended up in a cloud of shit.' His drinking was awful. We'd stop every hundred miles to get him another bottle of Old Quaker, or some such. Of course, business was so bad until we got to the Coast that it was a panic band, and that didn't help him. We played a dance in Michigan and thirty-five people came—all of them musicians. In Denver, we had to play dime-a-dance music, with a waltz every third number. Berigan used to complain about Goodman all the time. Berigan was playing lead trumpet and hot solos, and, finally, every night about eleven, after those difficult Fletcher Henderson arrangements and all the solos, he'd say, 'This is impossible,' and take the last drink—the law-of-diminishing-returns drink—and wipe himself out. We roomed together in Denver, and, what with his drinking and the altitude, he'd wake up at night, his throat dry, thinking he couldn't breathe. He'd tell me, 'I'm dying, I'm dying,' so I'd soak some towels in cold water and wrap them around his head, and that would ease him and he'd go back to sleep saying, 'You saved my life, Jess.' I don't know why, but Berigan left the Goodman band while we were at the Palomar in Los Angeles, just after we caught on, and came back to New York, where he had his own little group at the Famous Door, on Fifty-second Street. On the way back from the Coast, Goodman had a long, successful run in Chicago, and when we hit New York we were the top—the biggest thing in American music. I've always wondered if Berigan regretted leaving the band when he did. But he never let on."

Berigan was at his peak during the next couple of years. He recorded with Billie Holiday and Mildred Bailey, and with Tommy Dorsey, Artie Shaw,

Johnny Hodges, Fats Waller, and Teddy Wilson. He sat in on a Louis Armstrong date, and one Sunday afternoon he backed Bessie Smith at the Famous Door. In 1937, he put together his own big band. It was spirited and swinging. (George Auld, George Wettling, Sonny Lee, Dave Tough, Buddy Rich, Joe Bushkin, and Allan Reuss passed through.) But Berigan was a poor businessman, and in 1939 he went bankrupt. His health had deteriorated. He worked briefly for Tommy Dorsey, and put a couple of temporary bands together. He died at the age of thirty-three, in 1942.

One side of Berigan's style was romantic, melodramatic, and garrulous. It had a kind of Irish cast. The other side was blue, emotional, down, funky. He would fool around in his lowest register, playing heavy, resonant notes—gravestone notes. He would play blue note after blue note. Both sides of his style would appear in a single solo. He might start two choruses of the blues in his down style. He would stay in his low register, growling and circling like a bear. (Only Ruby Braff and Charlie Shavers got the same sound down there.) He would use four or five notes, shaping them into short, reiterated phrases. At the start of his second chorus, he would suddenly jump to a high C or D, go into a flashy descending run, and wing through a couple of large intervals. His vibrato would become noticeable, and his tone would open up. He might dip into his low register at the end of the solo, but he'd finish with a ringing Irish high C. Berigan's execution was almost flawless. He was a daring and advanced improviser, who fooled with offbeat and behind-the-beat rhythms and with all sorts of tonal effects. Yet his melodic lines were logical and graceful. There was an outsize quality to all Berigan's playing; he was a three-man trumpet section pressed into one. He dominated every group he was in: on Benny Goodman's recordings of "Sometimes I'm Happy" and "King Porter Stomp" and on Tommy Dorsey's of "Marie" and "Song of India" his famous solos stand like oaks on a plain. Only Red Allen and Roy Eldridge achieved a similar majesty in their big-band work. (Louis Armstrong's big-band majesty was ready-made; he was often the only soloist.)

Berigan has been brought forward again by a Time-Life "Giants of Jazz" album and by Volume I of the RCA "The Complete Bunny Berigan," which will collect all eighty-nine of the recordings he made with his big band. The Time-Life album contains forty numbers made between 1930 and 1939. The first, a Hal Kemp "Them There Eyes," reveals Berigan as Louis Armstrong, and the last, an all-star "Blue Lou," as himself. Many of the finest numbers in the album were recorded in the mid-thirties with small pickup groups. (Omitted, though, are "Bughouse" and "Blues in E-Flat," done with Red Norvo and Chu Berry, and "Honeysuckle Rose" and "Blues," done with Fats Waller and Tommy Dorsey.) Of particular note are Berigan's long melodic lines on the two Gene Gifford numbers; the three Bud Freeman selections, especially "Keep Smiling at Trouble," where he moves readily back and forth between the two parts of his style; the growls and low, fat sorrowing notes on "Blues," made with his own group; and the rocking, irresistible way he plays the melody in the first chorus of Irving Berlin's "Let Yourself Go," backed by organ chords and a strong Dave Tough afterbeat. Tough and Berigan galvanized each other. In the Time-Life album, Tough also appears on Dorsey's "Marie" and "Song of India," set down on one January day in 1937. Berigan's solos in both those numbers possess the eternal resilience that all improvisation aims at but rarely reaches. This quality shines through Berigan's celebrated miniature trumpet concerto "I Can't Get Started." The number, lasting roughly five minutes, begins with a bravura twelve-bar trumpet cadenza played over sustained band chords. Berigan sings a chorus in his pleasant, piping voice. A second, nine-bar cadenza follows, and he launches triumphantly into the melody, ending with a celestial E-flat.

The RCA reissue has thirty-one numbers. The best are "I Can't Get Started," "The Prisoner's Song," "Caravan," "Study in Brown," "Frankie and Johnny," "Mahogany Hall Stomp," and "Swanee River." The rest of the album is given over to songs like "The Lady from Fifth Avenue" and "All Dark People Are Light on Their Feet." Whatever the material, Berigan is everywhere, playing lead trumpet, soloing, filling the air with his serene and muscular poetry.

*It is entirely possible that much of Berigan's work came directly from the first ten or so bars of both takes of Louis Armstrong's astonishing, slowly turning, low-register solos on "Some of These Days," made in 1929 with a small pick-up group. And the solos certainly long ago sank into Ruby Braff.*

# Otis Ferguson

Jazz did not attract a steady group of commentators in America until the mid-thirties, when it was almost forty years old. This group, which included apologists, enthusiasts, hagiographers, and critics, grew steadily, and by the early forties it was made up of such as George Simon, Charles Edward Smith, John Hammond, Marshall Stearns, George Avakian, Wilder Hobson, Dave Dexter, Jr., George Hoefer, Frederic Ramsey, Winthrop Sargeant, William Russell, Leonard Feather, Helen Oakley, Barry Ulanov, George Frazier, and Otis Ferguson. (For all his faulty exuberance, the father of these writers was the French critic Hugues Panassié, who in 1934 had published his *Le Jazz Hot*, the first book of unalloyed jazz criticism.) Ferguson stood out from the pack. He approached his subject with detachment and style and poetic overtones, granting it understanding and honor instead of zealotry and huzzahs. He was among the first to applaud the musicians' own musical intelligence and the first to write about the music with some regularity in a general-interest national magazine; nineteen of his jazz pieces appeared in *The New Republic* between 1936 and 1941. But in 1943 he was killed in action in Italy, and by the fifties he had become a cult, a kind of lesser James Agee—revered and out of print. So it is fine to have *The Otis Ferguson Reader*, which brings together all thirty-five of his jazz pieces, twelve of them previously unpublished. (It also includes some of his film criticism, pieces on the circus and on radio, autobiography, a poem that was printed in *The New Yorker*, and book reviews, one of them a surprisingly tough piece on Edmund Wilson's "The Boys in the Back Room," which had itself been published in *The New Republic* eight months before.) The book has been edited by Robert Wilson and Dorothy Chamberlain, Ferguson's former wife, and there is a helpful memoir by Malcolm Cowley, who worked with Ferguson at *The New Republic*.

Ferguson was born in 1907 in Worcester, Massachusetts. He spent four years in the Navy in his late teens, then finished high school, and was graduated from Clark University in 1933. He joined *The New Republic* the following year. Already an ambitious writer, he liked to think of himself as being on the side of the common man. His friend Jess Stacy has said of him, "The most I saw of Otis was when I was with Benny Goodman at the Pennsylvania Hotel in 1937. He was about five foot nine, and a down-to-earth guy. He liked me, I liked him, and we hung out together. We'd go to Kelly's Bar on Thirty-fourth Street between sets, and after work we'd go to the Hickory House and have a steak and listen to Joe Marsala. Then we'd walk over to my apartment, in Tudor City—it was on the twenty-second floor—and look at the boats on the river. We'd hoist a few and talk about music and listen to Walter Gieseking and Debussy and Ravel. He loved to hear those things. If we got loaded, we'd badmouth Benny and throw darts at a picture of him I had. Otis realized the importance of the piano in a big band, and when he came to hear us he'd sit practically under the piano on the bandstand, which annoyed the hell out of Benny, which pleased us."

The war between the poet and the Philistine permeated Ferguson's writing. He was influenced by Mencken and Hemingway, but he disguised his literary pretensions with slang and pseudo toughness. He speaks of Lionel Hampton as "this boy Lionel" (not intended as a racial slur) and of Benny Goodman's musicians as "hard-boiled, cynical bozos." He did not often bring the lyrical and the slangy sides of his style successfully together; his prose would lean precariously one way or the other. Sometimes he was silly, in the Carl Sandburg manner: "Jazz was the country where [Bix Beiderbecke] grew up, the fine high thing, the sun coming up to fill the world through the morning." Sometimes he slipped into a melodramatic gargle: "And, in the measure of his chorus, [Jack Teagarden] always uses the savage velvet of a good trombone, the beat of jazz and lilt of the phrases to arrive at something that is terrific on a leash or sad, or gorgeous, or enchanting with echoes of a better day." When the poet took over, he approached a mystical density: "I recommend for your pleasure and for posterity the 'Blues' . . . as being perfect in the collective feeling and very high and strange in the interludes of Norvo and Wilson, whose instruments come up through the pattern with the renewing sweetness of fresh-water springs." But once in a while everything worked, as in this passage from a previously unpublished piece on Bix Beiderbecke: "You will know him by the little ringing shout he can get into a struck note; by the way each note seems to draw the others after it like a string of cars, giving the positive effect of speed even in his artful lags and deliberation, a sort of reckless and gay roll; and by the way, starting on the ground, he will throw a phrase straight up like a rope in the air, where it seems to hang after he has passed along, shaking gently." And Ferguson could be sharp. On John Hammond: "He is to be respected and thanked, but not safely followed as a mentor." On jazz: "The best improvisation is a tune woven around the other tune, the original, an implied counterpoint but standing by itself." On the old rhythm sections: "The iron of the banjo chords."

The world of jazz was a different place in the mid-thirties. Despite the efforts of John Hammond and Benny Goodman, few jazz bands, of whatever size, were integrated. Black audiences were not welcome in downtown clubs, which were inhabited largely by white bands, and white audiences were no longer as free in the uptown clubs, which tended toward black bands. (Barney Josephson's Café Society, which opened in Greenwich Village in 1938, was the first night club to offer mixed bands to mixed audiences.) White jazz was easier for a white man to come by in the flesh, and this availability is reflected in Ferguson's output. His liberalism is clear, but he writes largely about white jazz musicians—his celebrated pieces on Beiderbecke, Jess Stacy, and Goodman, and his less well known ones on Ziggy Elman, Jack Teagarden, and Red Norvo. He sometimes seemed to have blinders on. In 1941, he wrote that Billy Butterfield was "the only really exciting new [trumpeter] to be heard in ten years"—a statement that eliminates Red Allen and Roy Eldridge and even Louis Armstrong. And what of Bunny Berigan? And where, in all these pieces, are Dicky Wells, Benny Morton, Art Tatum, Lester Young, Ben Webster, Harry Edison, Frankie Newton, Sidney Catlett, and Billie Holiday? He does have a thoughtful piece on Ellington, though, and a good one on Teddy Wilson (published here for the first time), and one of his last articles for *The New Republic* is an appreciation of the Spirits of Rhythm, which included the guitarist Teddy Bunn and the mad scat singer Leo Watson.

# Making Do

*Friday*

There will be twenty Kool Jazz Festivals in the United States this year, including the New York edition, which began late this afternoon with a solo recital by Art Hodes. It was held in the Forum Room of the New York Sheraton, a mirrored cave with raspberry trimmings and stalactite chandeliers. (Carnegie Recital Hall, the usual center for these events, is being renovated.) Hodes played seventeen numbers, and they included his mixture of stride pieces ("Grandpa's Spells," "Snowy Mornin' Blues"), blues, standards ("Am I Blue," "Sweet Georgia Brown," "Georgia"), and oddities ("Maryland! My Maryland!," "Battle Hymn of the Republic"). He used a lot of tremolo and two-handed staccato effects, but his playing lacked the elasticity and depth of his night-club performances. Concert-hall situations still make old speakeasy performers jumpy.

The evening came in two different parts. Max Roach brought his quartet (Odean Pope on tenor saxophone, Cecil Bridgewater on trumpet, Calvin Hill on bass), plus a string quartet, into Avery Fisher Hall, and they played three compositions that were a mixture of recycled bebop, bad Hindemith, and sheer Roachian pomp. The strings did little for Roach's drumming or for Pope and Bridgewater, neither of them a prepossessing soloist. The second half of the concert was given over to Freddie Hubbard, McCoy Tyner, Ron Carter, and Elvin Jones. Hubbard was lyrical in his overblown way, Tyner suggested ocean motion and Carter a royal palm, and Jones' multilayered, multi-colored drumming was superb.

The second part of the evening was played at Carnegie Hall by the Stan Getz quartet (Jim McNeely on piano, Marc Johnson on bass, Victor Lewis on drums) and a Benny Goodman group (Teddy Wilson, Lionel Hampton, Phil Flanigan on bass, and Panama Francis on drums). Getz's seven selections (among them "The Night Has a Thousand Eyes," Bud Powell's "Tempus Fugit," and Billy Strayhorn's "Blood Count" and "We'll Be Together Again") reaffirmed the fact that it was partly his reimagining of Lester Young, and not exclusively Young himself, that shook up so many young white tenor saxophonists forty years ago. Another reaffirmation: Getz, in the long ago, listened hard to Johnny Hodges and Don Byas. Goodman and friends did ten numbers, and the best were the medium-tempo "Someday Sweetheart," "It Had to Be You," and "Don't Be That Way." The flagwavers were short of breath. Goodman gave half a dozen instances of his old flair and brilliance. Hampton played percussively rather than melodically. Wilson was impeccable: each solo climbed and sank, sank and climbed; his touch was golden, his evenness justice itself.

### Saturday

Good minions make good empires. In recent years, George Wein has hired others to produce his programs, and tonight at Avery Fisher Hall the American impresario George Schutz and the German critic Joachim-Ernst Berendt put together a three-hour concert called "Jazz and World Music." It was played by forty or so musicians from India, Brazil, Germany, Turkey, Senegal, England, Japan, and the United States. The American flutist Paul Horn, using taped flutes and electronic echo-effects, played movie music with an India tinge—

Deborah Kerr and Jean Simmons in the foothills of the Himalayas. Rainbow, made up of L. Subramaniam on violin, Ashish Kahn on sarod (a sitarlike instrument with twenty-five strings), Pranesh Kahn on tabla, and the American alto saxophonist John Handy, sounded like an Indian bebop group. The ensembles resembled unkempt unison bop figures, and there were solos based partly on Indian scales. Handy, a perfervid, big-toned descendant of Charlie Parker, was in good form, but it was too bad the group didn't allow itself more free collective interplay. Codona, the third group, consists of Don Cherry on pocket trumpet and doussn'gouni (a Malian guitar that looks like a giant tomato with a hoe stuck into it handle first), Collin Walcott on sitar and tabla, and Nana Vasconcelos on percussion. We heard Cherry on trumpet backed by sitar and conga drum; Walcott on sitar backed by maracas; Cherry on trumpet backed by tabla; Cherry on some sort of piccolo backed by maracas and cymbals. An American Indian tenor saxophonist named Jim Pepper did some chanting with Codona and played a John Coltrane saxophone solo. The final group of the evening, Karl Berger's Music Universe, was thirty strong, and on hand were Randy Brecker, Ed Blackwell, Leroy Jenkins, Collin Walcott, and Lee Konitz. Berger, a German-born composer and vibraphonist, conducted the two immense numbers, which, though melodically simple (the second was built around a four-note folk motif), were dressed up in constantly changing rhythms and instrumental combinations. There was also a parade of soloists, the best of whom was Konitz. He was accompanied at first by bass and drums; then he went on alone. He played a long, witty melody, a kind of very long song, that was beautiful. The rest of the two numbers had ensemble dissonances, singing and chanting, dancing, and the avant-garde big-band clutter that has become familiar during the past ten years in the works of Sam Rivers and Muhal Richard Abrams.

## Sunday

Alec Wilder would not have been altogether displeased by the concert given in his honor at Carnegie Hall this afternoon: he always knew that beauty is rare, and that praise well given is even rarer. He would have threatened not to come but at the last would have appeared backstage or out front, dressed in his summer uniform—a rumpled linen jacket, gray trousers, moccasins. He would have roared in disbelief at the huge drawing of his head fastened to a baffle at one side of the stage, and the length of the concert would have made him restless. He would have been annoyed by some of the liberties taken with his music, and he might have disagreed with some of the selections. He might also have been mystified by the evening's refusal to swing—to get up off its somewhat sanctimonious rusty-dusty and go. But many things would have pleased him: the amount and variety of his music that was performed (about two dozen songs, including "Baggage Room Blues," "A Long Night," "Who Can I Turn To?," "Lovers and Losers," "Mimosa and Me," and "Blackberry

Winter"; two woodwind-octet numbers; the third and fourth movements of Suite No. 1 for Horn, Tuba, and Piano; all of the Jazz Suite for Four Horns; and all of the Suite for Baritone Sax, Horn, and Wind Quintet, written for Gerry Mulligan); the complex, tough chords that Marian McPartland used at the beginning of her solo on "Jazz Waltz for a Friend," written for her; the adept octet performances (by Walter Levinsky, Wally Kane, Raymond Beckenstein, Dennis Anderson, Don Stewart, Kenny Werner, Paul Meyers, and Edwin Schuller) of "Such a Tender Night" and "Kindergarten Flower Pageant"; the quality and strength of Mabel Mercer's voice on "Did You Ever Cross Over to Sneden's"; the snap that Gunther Schuller, conducting, got out of the horns in the Jazz Suite for Four Horns; Jackie Cain's straight, sad "Remember My Child"; Stan Getz's reverential, equally mournful "Where Do You Go (When It Starts to Rain)?"; and the stately readings, one muted and one open-horn, by the trumpeter Joe Wilder of "Trouble Is a Man" and "Blackberry Winter." Most of all, he would have relished the fact that the concert belonged as much to its performers as to him. He once said, "Players tend to like what I write; composers don't. Composers think of performers as necessary evils . . . But I consider the written music only a guide. The notes suggest, they tell only part of the story. I'll take half the credit, and all the rest goes to the performer. Performers! Those great, beautiful people are my saviors." Loonis McGlohon produced the program.

Praising the living is even harder work. Tonight, in Carnegie Hall, at "Buddy Rich: A Retrospective" (produced by the jazz writer Burt Korall), the drummer was lionized not so much for his drumming as for his show-business attributes. There were photographs of him as a child star, as a teen-age whiz in Joe Marsala's band, and as Tommy Dorsey's twenty-two-year-old wunderkind. He and Mel Tormé, who was the master of ceremonies, bantered, and there was a funny bit of slapstick between Rich and a Zildjian from the Zildjian cymbal factory, who was trying to give him an award. He did a short tap dance with Honi Coles, and he played number after mechanical number with the band. He also played one long solo, and it seemed—aside from brief passages near its end involving his cymbals and his drum rims—labored. What we did not hear was the tasty performer who surfaces in small-group situations—particularly in duos and trios and quartets. Once, at the old Newport festival, Rich opened a concert by sitting in with Teddy Wilson. On "Somebody Loves Me," he accompanied with great delicacy on wire brushes, then took a long-legged, spidery solo with his sticks which told more about his powers than anything tonight.

*Monday*

Including occasional non-jazz events in a jazz festival rubs the listeners' fur the wrong way, but gives them valuable perspective. Early this evening, at Alice Tully Hall, Eileen Farrell and Mabel Mercer rendered thirty songs in such a way that words and music became a continuum: words were music, music words. Seated regally side by side, they seemed, in their ease and artlessness, to be at the very center of music—a pair of goddesses telling us what all songs should sound like. Ten numbers were done as duets, and each singer did about ten numbers alone—Eileen Farrell standing or seated, Mabel Mercer always seated. Eileen Farrell kept her voice within the bounds of her songs, allowing herself to soar only in "Over the Rainbow." Mabel Mercer sang two of her songs and did the rest parlando, and near the end of the concert she read A. A. Milne's "Vespers" and Edna St. Vincent–Millay's "The Ballad of the Harp-Weaver," her voice both bleak and revelatory at the ballad's close:

There sat my mother
With the harp against her shoulder,
Looking nineteen,
And not a day older,

A smile about her lips,
And a light about her head,
And her hands in the harp-strings
Frozen dead.

And piled up beside her
And toppling to the skies,
Were the clothes of a king's son,
Just my size.

Eileen Farrell spoke at the beginning of the evening of how, as a music student in the early forties, she first heard Mabel Mercer sing, and of how Mabel Mercer had been a part of her life ever since.

### Tuesday

We had the avant-garde at five and nine at Avery Fisher this evening, but the old guard, brought in to restore law and order at the end of the nine-o'clock concert, was routed. The first concert had two groups—an octet led by the tenor saxophonist David Murray (commonly of the World Saxophone Quartet), and a septet led by the reedman Henry Threadgill (commonly of Air). Murray's group included Bobby Bradford on cornet, John Purcell on alto saxophone, Craig Harris on trombone, John Hicks on piano, and Steven McCall (also of Air) on drums. Its music was surprisingly conservative. The opening and closing ensembles were played either freely or in a slightly out-of-focus unison, the tempos were distinct, and the soloists rested on organ chords or brief riffs. The soloists summoned up Albert Ayler and Ornette Coleman and Roswell Rudd and Cecil Taylor. It was good to hear Bradford, who worked with Coleman almost thirty years ago in Los Angeles, and who plays with a pleasant lyrical edge. Threadgill's group, made up of Harris, Olu Dara on cornet, Brian Smith and Fred Hopkins (Air) on bass, and Pheeroan Aklaff and John Betsch on drums, was more adventurous. After two brief ensemble numbers, it went into a half-hour fanfare that sounded roughly like this: the drummers began with smooth snare-drum rolls; the horns offered a martial figure, and then parodied it; one bassist, playing arco, did a unison figure with the trombonist, and the trumpeter played a mournful figure backed by chords from the trombonist and the alto saxophonist; the drummers rose up slowly behind a succession of brief solos, finally reaching a climax, which gave way to short horn punctuations and a sudden, slamming end.

The World Saxophone Quartet opened the second concert. In addition to David Murray, it has Oliver Lake and Julius Hemphill on alto saxophones and Hamiet Bluiett on baritone saxophone. The group has grown more sedate since its first festival appearance, three years ago, when it indulged in funny Stepin Fetchit stage business and heavy parodying of such as Duke Ellington and Guy Lombardo. The parody remains, and so does the avant-garde fretwork of scrambled ensembles, animal-noise solos, and weak key centers, but the quartet has become hooked on rich reed sounds. It doubles constantly, and tonight we heard these combinations: bass clarinet, two soprano saxophones, and alto clarinet; two tenor saxophones, a soprano, and a baritone; three flutes and a bass clarinet; tenor, soprano, alto, and baritone saxophones; and three tenor saxophones and a baritone. The group delivers these instrumentations in a swashbuckling, aggressive way. Perhaps it is telling us how much it digs those old, statuesque sounds—those old sounds it also loves to parody—of Harry Carney and Ben Webster and Coleman Hawkins and Johnny Hodges.

The second half of the concert was taken up by four reedmen who, however slyly and glancingly, had been parodied by the World Saxophone Quartet. They were Stan Getz, Zoot Sims, Al Cohn, and Jimmy Giuffre, and they were meant to be a recreation of one of Woody Herman's late-forties Four Brothers saxophone sections. (Getz, Sims, Herbie Steward, and Serge Chaloff formed the first one.) But they seemed fatigued by the idea, and the only freshness came from ballad solos by Getz and Sims. The rhythm section consisted of Ben Aronov on piano, Frank Tate on bass, and Shelly Manne on drums. Manne was so busy tatting and sewing and knitting back there that sometimes the brothers couldn't get a sound in edgewise.

*Wednesday*

There was a meandering, bucolic quality to "Salute to Pres," at Carnegie Hall tonight. It might even have pleased Lester Young, a reflective, poetic country man. (He died in 1959, at the age of forty-nine.) The evening began with a showing of Gjon Mili's

1944 short "Jammin' the Blues," in which Young, abetted by Harry Edison, Illinois Jacquet, Sid Catlett, and Jo Jones, plays a couple of blues, his round, convex Oriental face turned by Mili's closeups and moody lighting into a huge moon. Then Ira Gitlet, a producer of the concert and its master of ceremonies, read a tatterdemalion poem he had written about Young. The last stanza goes:

> He was a cat who was really laid-back
> His audience was always soulfully paid-back
> He floated like a butterfly and stung like a bee
> Long before the coming of Muhammad Ali.

Gitler went on to read a history of Young's life taken from some of his old liner notes and printed like a score in the festival program. Now and then, he paused and there was music—first by a big band that included Harry Edison, Jimmy Maxwell, Vic Dickenson, Eddie Bert, Allen Eager, Al Cohn, Budd Johnson, John Lewis, Bucky Pizzarelli, Milt Hinton, and Oliver Jackson. It played "Every Tub," "Jive at Five," "Jumpin' at the Woodside," and "Broadway," and was joined midway by Zoot Sims and Stan Getz. The band also did "Lester Leaps In," but it was sandwiched between two recordings—Count Basie"s 1936 "Evenin'," which was Young's first record date, and "Countless Blues," a 1938 small-band session on which Young plays clarinet. The big band departed for the evening, leaving its rhythm section, and Sims and Johnson did a soprano-saxophone duet on "I Want a Little Girl." A six-saxophone version of "Tickle-Toe" followed (Cohn, Sims, Eager, Getz, Johnson, Buddy Tate). The famous Holiday-Young sequence from the "Sound of Jazz" television show came next, and the concert wandered into a different pasture. A group made up of Edison, Tate, Dickenson, Pizzarelli, Hinton, Teddy Wilson, and Roy Haynes played three numbers that had nothing to do with Young, and Teddy Wilson did two piano solos, backed by Hinton and Jo Jones. (The rhythmic tussling in the three small-band numbers was fascinating. Wilson plays directly on the beat; Haynes scatters accents everywhere; and Edison, Dickenson, and Tate like to play behind the beat.) Young reappeared during the concert's last five numbers. These were an exceptional "These Foolish Things" by Sims and an equally fine "Polka Dots and Moonbeams" by Getz; small-band versions of "D. B. Blues" and "Jumpin' with Symphony Sid", and a 1943 Young recording of "I Got Rhythm," done on the Signature label with Bill Coleman, Dicky Wells, Ellis Larkins, and Jo Jones, and notable not for Young's uninspired solos but for Wells' two whooping, triumphant choruses.

The celebration by themselves of sixteen supposedly young and unknown musicians at Carnegie Hall earlier in the evening was overcrowded and inconclusive. At least eight of the musicians are not unknown, and some are far from striplings. These were Chico Freeman on tenor saxophone, Wynton Marsalis on trumpet, James Newton on flute, John Purcell on alto saxophone, Craig Harris on trombone, Jay Hoggard on vibraphone, Anthony Davis on piano, and Hamiet Bluiett. It was difficult to judge most of the truly unknown players in their allotted time. These were Ronnie Burrage on drums, Kevin Eubanks on guitar, John Blake on violin, Daniel Ponce on percussion, Bobby McFerrin on vocals, Paquito D'Rivera on alto saxophone, Abdul Wadud on cello, and Avery Sharpe on bass. But the fact that most of them are romantics came through clearly. Their compositions dream, and their improvisations are lush and close. They have startling techniques, but they also seem to understand the emotional freight that the great jazz performers have carried forward from generation to generation. The bias of most of the sixteen is toward the recent avant-garde; absent from the proceedings were such equally gifted but more conservative young players as the pianists Fred Hersch and Lee Ann Ledgerwood and the guitarists Emily Remler and Howard Alden. And where was Wynton Marsalis's brother Branford, a tenor saxophonist and possibly a more interesting player than the smooth, cool Wynton?

## Friday

The Swiss pianist and composer George Gruntz and the American poet and playwright Amiri Baraka have written a jazz opera called *Money*, and about a third of it was given its world première tonight at the La Mama Annex. (The entire opera, in eleven scenes and using eighty performers, last four hours.) The music, played by a fourteen-piece onstage band that included Gruntz (conducting and playing piano), Chico Freeman, Frank Gordon (trumpet), Howard Johnson (tuba), Janice Robinson (trombone), Cecil McBee (bass), and Billy Hart (drums), is attractive and swinging, and Gruntz uses it imaginatively: the recitative and songs (none reach the level of arias) are backed with organ chords and by soloists, playing singly or together, and by various rhythmic combinations. The band is a constant and welcome presence. But Baraka's libretto is embarrassing. It deals with the romantic affairs and careers of a black singer (Vea Williams) and a black saxophonist (Chico Freeman), and a rich white American (Sheila Jordan) and a Russian diplomat (Kenneth Bell). Castro comes to power, Malcolm X is murdered, and there are bitter mentions of Ike and McCarthy and busing and freedom marches. There is too much recitative. Why not allow the singers to improvise their delivery, even improvise some of the lines? Why not allow the instrumentalists and singers to improvise together? Why not start again?

## Saturday

Bob Wilber's new group, The Bechet Legacy, is an attempt to perpetuate the music of the New Orleans clarinettist and soprano saxophonist. Using Mike Camico on trumpet, Mark

Shane on piano, Mike Peters on guitar and banjo, Reggie Johnson on bass, and Butch Miles on drums, Wilber plays loose adaptations of Sidney Bechet recordings, and, with his unique ability to get inside the musical skin of musicians like Bechet and Johnny Hodges and Johnny Dodds, he does them very well. He curbs Bechet's headlong vibrato and keeps his melodic trajectories closer to earth. He is more polite. Bechet the soprano saxophonist dominated every ensemble he played in, either forcing trumpet players to blow themselves purple or simply sweeping them aside. The Bechet Legacy gave a concert this afternoon in the Guggenheim auditorium, and, with Chuck Riggs sitting in for Miles, played "Cake Walking Babies from Home," "Kansas City Man Blues," "Roses of Picardy," "China Boy," "Blues in Thirds," "Love for Sale," "Summertime," and "Oh, Lady Be Good!" Wilber also did half a dozen of Bechet's own songs, all of them inward and minor-sounding. Riggs' foot-pedal work was heavy, and so were his unimaginative snaredrum figures, both in his accompanying and in his solos. He should have remembered what Sid Catlett did two-thirds of the way through Bechet's recording of "Summertime"—shifted from wire brushes to a carpet of press rolls with his sticks. It lifted the recording from a good one to a magisterial one.

The singer Sylvia Sims suggested to George Wein last winter that he include in the festival a concert of songs by American women. Wein agreed, and we heard the ramshackle results at Avery Fisher tonight. Sylvia Syms, Carmen McRae, Carrie Smith, Bill Henderson, and Chris Connor sang the songs, Zoot Sims and Dizzy Gillespie improvised on them, and Mike Renzi (piano), Jay Leonhart (bass), and Shelly Manne accompanied. (Only about half of the women songwriters were identified, and we were never told whether they had done the music or the lyrics or both. Nearly all the songs are collaborations, but in the attributions below just the women involved are mentioned.) Carmen McRae remains locked within her mannerisms (the forced melismatics, the steplike phrasing, the dull, brassy voice). One of her five songs was unidentified, two were undistinguished, one was "Some Other Spring" (music by Irene Wilson Kitchings), and the last was Billie Holiday's "Billie's Blues." Zoot Sims played "Fine and Dandy" (music by Kay Swift), "I'm in the Mood for Love" (lyrics by Dorothy Fields), and an unidentified ballad. Carrie Smith's five numbers included "That Ole Devil Called Love" (music and lyrics by Doris Fisher) and Bessie Smith's "Back Water Blues." Bill Henderson, suffering from Avery Fisher nerves, didn't stop oversinging until his final number. "If They Could See Me Now" (lyrics by Dorothy Fields). Chris Connor is one of Anita O'Day's progeny, and she sang two songs by Peggy Lee, Ann Ronnell's "Willow Weep for Me," and songs by Bertha Scott and Dorothy Fields. Dizzy Gillespie did "Lullaby of the Leaves" (music by Bernice Petkere) and "The Way You Look Tonight" and "On the Sunny Side of the Street" (both with lyrics by Dorothy Fields). With the time almost gone, Sylvia Syms came on for "You

Oughta Be in Pictures" (music by Dana Suesse) and "Them There Eyes" (music and lyrics by Doris Tauber), and everyone joined hands for a loose-wigged "How High the Moon" (lyrics by Nancy Hamilton).

### Sunday

Mediocrity burns slowly, so it took a long time to get through the Lionel Hampton concert at Carnegie Hall tonight. Hampton's seventeen-piece big band did eight numbers, among them a semisymphonic "Moonglow" and a Japanese folk song. Then it was jam-session time. Hampton played some blues with Freddie Hubbard, Clark Terry, Al Grey, Phil Woods, Sonny Stitt, Arnett Cobb, Roland Hanna, Milt Hinton, and the drummer George Kawaguchi, and some ballads with Teddy Wilson, Dizzy Gillespie, and Stan Getz, plus the Hampton big-band rhythm section. The last number was an eight-cylinder "Flyin' Home."

# 1983

## Old Wine, New Bottles

A new preservation movement, made up of young neo-swing musicians, came into being in the mid-seventies, and it is growing steadily. Already in its ranks are the guitarists Howard Alden and Chris Flory, the bassist Phil Flanigan, the saxophonists Scott Hamilton, Chuck Wilson, and Loren Schoenberg, the clarinettist Chuck Hedges, the drummers Butch Miles, Chuck Riggs, and Fred Stoll, the trombonist Dan Barrett, and the trumpeter Warren Vaché. These musicians have in a way moved beyond their predecessors; they contain the past and the present. They hold in balance the love of melody and tonal quality of the old swing musicians and an awareness of the harmonic expansions and rhythmic freedoms that have taken place in jazz in the past twenty years. Of all these players, one of the most impressive is Vaché.

He is a stocky, medium-sized man with brown hair, a brown mustache, and deep-brown eyes. He plays with intense concentration, but he is cool, and he has a sharp tongue. He lives in Rahway, New Jersey, not far from where he grew up. He recently talked about himself: "I was born in Rahway on February 21, 1951. My father is a bass player, and he still has a band that works around Rahway, but he made his living as a salesman when I was growing up. He was born in Brooklyn and was raised around Camden. My mother was born and raised in Brooklyn. I have one brother, Allan, who's two years younger. He plays very good clarinet with the Happy Jazz Band, in San Antonio, Texas. I started on the piano when I was seven, and switched to the trumpet at nine. I studied first with Jim Fitzpatrick, in Plainfield. He'd been with Hal Kemp. After that, I studied all through school and through Montclair State College. I even have a degree that will enable me to warp the musical minds of small children, should I ever wish to. It was the trumpeter Pee Wee Irwin who kept me in college. My dad discovered in the late sixties that Pee Wee and Chris Griffin had a music school not far from us, and he introduced me to Pee Wee, and it was love at first sight. He was one of the most underestimated musicians of all time. No one knows what a good trumpeter that man was. Anyway, I'd stop in and see him three or four times a week, and he'd teach me by example. He told me to get Charlier's 'Études,' and I did. I'd practice and get nowhere near where I was supposed to be. One time, I played an étude for him and he listened and said, 'Well, that's not quite right.' He didn't have his reading glasses with him, so he played the étude from memory—perfectly. My early jobs were with Dixieland bands, which were all over the place. I had a job with Billy Maxted, who fired me after a week, and with Dick Hyman's band—the one that accompanied Twyla Tharp in 1977. I was in the house band at Condon's for a while, and I had a trio at Crawdaddy. I travel with the Concord All Stars a couple of times a year, but most of the time I just gig around. I'd like to find work in New York with the trio, but a lot of the places that would be right— like Bradley's and the Knickerbocker and Zinno—have no-horns zoning restrictions. I used to listen to Roy Eldridge at Ryans when I was at Condon's—he was awesome. And I'd drop in on Buck Clayton when he was at Crawdaddy. I liked to listen to the notes he *didn't* play. As far as I'm concerned, the best trumpeter walking now is Ruby Braff. The taste and intelligence! Ruby is inventing a new language. The hardest thing about any brass instrument is the sheer physical effort it takes to play softly and subtly. You can bull your way through the trumpet, and it will sound that way. But to play it right you have to lean all your muscle and emotion into it. Like Ruby. My dad had a large collection of swing-music records, and that was always in my ear. But I've never made a conscious decision about which way to go as a player. I was a Miles Davis freak in high school, and I listened to Fats Navarro and Clifford Brown. I think it came down to content. There is a lot of content—emotional and human—in the older music, in Bobby Hackett and Lester Young. If we're still being moved by Beethoven why shouldn't we still be moved by Bobby and Pres?"

There are ghosts of Clayton and Braff and Irwin in Vaché's playing, and, to a lesser extent, ghosts of Charlie Shavers and Roy Eldridge and Joe Wilder. But the heart of his work is his own. Many of the old swing trumpeters were laconic players. They didn't waste notes, because the fewer the notes used, the lighter the technical burdens. But Vaché is of the baroque persuasion. He is always looking for ways to stem the torrent of notes that besiege his imagination. In recent years, he has begun to succeed, and most of his solos are logical and ordered; there may still be extra phrases, but there are rarely extra notes. He has not, however, controlled his tendency to lark around in the upper register, where he sounds peaked and strained. He will start a solo by coming in just over the trees, using an oblique tone and a fragmentary opening phrase. His tone will slowly broaden, and he will go into an ascending phrase—a don't-mind-me-phrase—repeat it an octave higher, and pause. Suddenly he will dart into a complex double-time figure, racing down his horn three steps at a time, come to rest on a trill, move into a rifflike four- or five-note figure, repeat it, and leap back up his horn and into the upper register, spraying eighth notes right and left. Vaché is one of the rare players who love the challenge of a song's bridge, of passing without injury through those eight-bar thickets. This time, he pauses, then lays back and delivers it in a studied, pulled-in rhythmic float. He will start the last eight bars of his solo in his upper register, go down into his middle register, pull his volume over his ears, and vanish whence he came. Vaché has picked up all the old tricks of his trade. He can play fine wa-wa plunger-muted trumpet, he can growl like Buck Clayton and half-valve like Rex Stewart, and he can make his tone swell on slow ballads. There is nothing academic or precious about his playing. He is, in a lesser way, as fresh and surprising as Red Allen and Roy Eldridge were in the thirties. Vaché is showing us that the sort of improvisation in which a player takes a melody and a set of chords and fashions from them a new, parallel melody that heightens the original and stands on its own is far from exhausted.

## Earl Hines and Peck Kelley

Earl Hines, who died last spring, at the age of seventy-nine, was a bravura performer. Solidly built, with a big, square face and big, square hands, he moved constantly at the keyboard, swaying back and forth and feinting from side to side, his elbows pumping and his legs out like ski poles. He had a blacksmith's touch (he could untune a freshly tuned piano in twenty minutes), and he issued a steady, overlaying stream of grunts and exclamations. His face moved between joy and pain. He kept his eyes half shut, his gleaming teeth clenched, his lower lip in a permanent, breathing pout. No one knows exactly where his cornucopic style came from. For a long time, it was said that he had taken it from Louis Armstrong when the two first worked together in Chicago in the twenties—that he played "trumpet-style" piano. But Hines' playing seems to have been pretty much formed by the time he arrived in Chicago, in 1924. (He disavowed Armstrong's influence, and ordinarily this could be discounted, since many jazz musicians are devious about who their early models are. Hines, though, was not a devious man.) What took place between Hines and Armstrong takes place between any gifted young collaborators—intense mutual admiration. In his right hand he used single-note melodic passages, octave chords, winding arpeggios, and gentle, quick phrase-ending tremolos, which were like little vibratos. (Hines eventually discarded these tremolos, but they can still be heard in the playing of Jess Stacy, one of his earliest admirers.) His left hand was made up of tenths, offbeat chords, patches of oompah, and sudden single notes. Sometimes a single-note melodic line was carried from his right hand to his left and back. Hines liked to shake things up. He would break the tempo unexpectedly and fashion wild arrhythmic passages, in which he might scatter right-hand chords all over the upper keyboard, opposing them in the left hand with bucking, irregular single notes. The effect was more intense than counter-point, because the two bodies of sound warred. These rhythmic squalls passed as abruptly as they came, leaving the water as unhurried and blue as before. Hines had other dramatic devices. He would fling clusters of notes out of his high register, filling the air with needles of sound. Or he would go into an octave tremolo in his right hand and keep it going for ten or twenty choruses, and then, the audience exhausted and waiting for his hand to fall off, he would stop, smile brilliantly, and retire the number with a modest sotto-voce coda. The pianist Dick Wellstood once wrote aptly of Hines:

> For all the complexity in his playing, Hines exercises fairly simple har-monic vocabulary, and in any event his peculiar stuttering rhythmic sense gives his phrasing such force as to make harmonic analysis almost mean-ingless. The dissonances he uses are more the result of his fascination with the overtone of the piano than of any concern with elaborate har-monic substitutions. Accented single notes making the upper strings ring, or open fifths or octaves sounded a tone or semi-tone apart (either will do) at opposite ends of the keyboard are to him among the most beautiful of sounds. His is the music of change, based on the rhythms of the body in a graceful way unique to the older jazz players.

Hines invented a new way to play jazz piano. Before him, the music had been dominated by stride pianists (James P. Johnson, Willie the Lion Smith, Luckey Roberts, Fats Waller and by blues pianists (Pine Top Smith, Jimmy Yancey, Cripple Clarence Lofton, Charlie Spand). The stride pianists had taken ragtime piano and put a four-four engine in it, and the blues pianists had invented a deceptively simple, almost onomatopoeic music full of weather and trains and unrequited love. Hines moved into the uncharted territory between these attacks and became the first modern jazz pianist. His playing, framed by his hot big band, was broadcast almost nightly in the thir-ties from the Grand Terrace ballroom in Chicago, and it permeated the country—particularly the Midwest and the Southwest. Not many young pianists escaped his influence. Here are some who learned from him, directly or indirectly: Joe Sullivan, Teddy Wilson, Nat Cole, Mary Lou Williams, Count Basie, Jess Stacy, Mel Powell, Nellie Lutcher, Billy Kyle, Dave Bow-man, Garnet Clark, Gene Schroeder, Clyde Hart, Countess Johnson, Eddie

Heywood, Erroll Garner, Dick Wellstood, Art Tatum, and Lennie Tristano. And Hines' blood, thinning but unmistakable, can be followed down through Bud Powell and Bill Evans to Fred Hersch.

Few long careers ascend steadily, and Hines' was no exception. After the adventurous days of the twenties, he put together his big band, and it lasted twenty years. It was both a cushion for his playing and a school for exceptional young musicians and singers, among them Budd Johnson, Omer Simeon, Darnell Howard, Alvin Burroughs, Ray Nance, Trummy Young, Freddie Webster, Benny Harris, Bennie Green, Shadow Wilson, Charlie Parker, Dizzy Gillespie, Ivie Anderson, Billy Eckstine, and Sarah Vaughan. Hines had talent-scout ears. Then, in 1948, having been a general for almost as long as he could remember, he stepped back into the ranks and became a sideman with Louis Armstrong's All Stars, which included Barney Bigard, Jack Teagarden, and Sidney Catlett. He stayed four uneasy years, then settled on the West Coast, where he worked in assorted Dixieland bands. By the early sixties, he had fallen into despair and confusion, and he was ready to quit music and open a shop with his wife. But his old friend Stanley Dance, the English jazz critic, kept after him, and in the winter of 1964 Hines came East for the first time in ten years and gave two concerts at the Little Theatre, on West Forty-fourth Street. The reviews and the ensuing publicity got his wheels going again, and within a year or so he was working steadily, often as a soloist, and he went on working, from one end of the world to the other, almost to the day he died. Most jazz musicians find a style and stay within it, safe and unchanging. But after Hines' renaissance his playing gradually became more prolix, and his old one-chorus solos grew into Jamesian exercises. Each chorus became an elaboration of the previous chorus, and two or three notes did the work of one. Hines seemed to want to engulf his listeners. But he could still knock you out with an upper-register explosion or with three or four stuttering notes at the start of a bridge.

Hines' philosophy was rigorous and old-fashioned. He was one of the last of the great jazz showmen. He believed that a performer's primary task is to please his audience. He once said with satisfaction, "I never considered myself a piano soloist. I was happy just to take my little eight bars and get off. It's the public that's pushed me out and made me a soloist." (This was not strictly true, of course. He was an exceptional, even a radical, jazz soloist by the time he was twenty-two—long before he had any public to speak of.) He kept fit, dressed well, smiled a lot, spoke graciously to his audiences, and invariably played as hard as he knew how. (Flat-stomached and muscular his whole life, Hines used to throw a medicine ball with Joe Louis in the thirties, and he often did exercises to strengthen his fingers.) He didn't believe in taking his troubles onstage or in burdening others. "The greatest thing to draw wrinkles in a man's face is worry," he said in the sixties after his fortunes had changed. "Why should I be unhappy and pull down my face and drag my feet and make everybody around me feel that way, too? By being what you are, something always comes up. Sunshine always opens out."

Peck Kelley, the legendary Texas pianist, who died in his eighties in 1981, turns out to have been another Earl Hines admirer. Kelley became a legend because he was praised by the likes of John Hammond, Jack Teagarden, Pee Wee Russell, and Harry James, because he refused all entreaties to leave Texas (he was born in Houston); and because he refused to make records. He was a Texas recluse who died, as far as we Yankees knew, preserved in silence. Not so. On two successive Sunday afternoons in June of 1957, Dick Shannon, a Benny Goodman clarinetist and a longtime Kelley admirer, persuaded the pianist to go down to the studios of radio station KPRC, in Houston, and play a little on what was said to be the best piano in town. He also persuaded Kelley to play with the tapes running. Kelley enjoyed the sessions, and he even enjoyed listening to the tapes in later years, but he refused to have them released. His playing at all into a tape recorder, though, set him going in the direction of the public arena, and Milt Gabler, of Commodore Records, has finished the trip for him. Gabler has released fourteen numbers from those two afternoons as "Peck Kelley Jam." (Also on hand were two guitarists, a bassist, and a drummer.) The album reveals Kelley as technically adroit, harmonically rich, inclined to rhapsody, and rather staid. He sounds as if he had listened to the old radio pianist Lee Sims in the twenties, to Earl Hines in the thirties, and to Art Tatum (who grew up on Sims and Hines) in the forties. Beyond that, he doesn't swing much, and when a number goes on too long he runs out of improvisional gas. But if Kelley sounded in the twenties and thirties the way he sounds here it would have been a surprise to run across him in some Houston or Galveston tonk. Discovering a professional in an unlikely place automatically makes him seem twice as large as life.

## Whiz Kid

Jazz never lets up on its practitioners. It asks that they get up before an audience (perhaps a jaded one or an ignorant one) five or six nights a week and for several hours spin music out of their heads (perhaps in a noisy night club or in a half-filled concert hall with bad acoustics) which swings, is well played, and has never been heard before. And it asks that they do these things, as often as not, without adequate pay, without adequate rest or decent food (if they are on the road, as they are most of the time), without dressing rooms or tuned pianos, and without due praise. Some musicians meet these demands by constructing solos out of prefabricated patterns and figures. Some use the same solos over and over. Some plagiarize or parody themselves. Some grow obtuse and listless and uncaring. Some take drugs and alcohol. A few perform brilliantly as long as their strength lasts. As a result, the music is constantly searching for fine new players. When, every five or ten years, it finds one, he is often treated like a messiah, and this tends to strain his invention, turn his head, and subject him to the jealousy of his peers, and even of his elders. That is what happened to Ornette Coleman when he appeared in New York, in the fall of 1959. Still a raggedy Texas country boy, he arrived almost unknown from the West, and, laying his unorthodox, hellbent Charlie Parker style before enshrining hordes at the old Five Spot, he became the toast of the jazz world. (He was also ridiculed by such aging revolutionaries as Charles Mingus and Miles Davis; aging revolutionaries often become more inflexible than those they originally displaced.) Coleman took this adulatory roar to heart. By 1962, he had gone underground, because night-club owners and entrepreneurs and recording executives would not grant him the respect he felt he was owed, and would not pay him what he felt he was worth. And he has rarely come out since. So will success spoil Wynton Marsalis, the dazzling twenty-one-year-old trumpeter from New Orleans? For the past couple of years, Marsalis, a double enfant terrible, who plays jazz and classical trumpet with equal ease, has been bathed in acclaim. When he was seventeen, he was allowed into the Berkshire Music Center, at Tanglewood, a year early and won an award for being the outstanding brass player. A year later, he was wowing them at Juilliard, and CBS signed him to a recording contract as a jazz and classical player. Art Blakey hired him and Herbie Hancock hired him, and the last year he was chosen best trumpet player in the *down beat* readers' poll, trouncing Miles Davis by almost five hundred votes. He also made a resounding début at the Kool Jazz festival in New York. But all this tohubohu seems to have left him unmoved. The voice that comes through in the handful of interviews he has given to *down beat* and Columbia Records is steady, self-critical, and wry.

On classical music: "I studied classical music because so many black musicians were scared of this big monster on the other side of the mountain . . . I wanted to know what it was that scared everybody so bad. I went into it and found out it wasn't anything but some more music . . . I think—I *know*—it's harder to be a good jazz musician at an early age than a classical one. In jazz, to be a good performer means to be an individual, which you don't have to be in classical music."

On his own excellence: "It was funny being [at Tanglewood] because I could always tell how shocked they were that a black kid my age could play *their* music so well. In fact, because I was a kid and they didn't know until things progressed how good I was, I had to sit there on many a night listening to these other guys messing up parts I could have played correctly. But I remember how much I shocked Gunther Schuller . . . when he found out I could play jazz. You see, I knew they couldn't believe that a seventeen-year-old who could play the hell out of classical music also knew a lot about jazz."

On his image: "I do not entertain and I will not entertain. I'm a musician. When you see me on the bandstand, I'm always going to look sharp. How can you get respect from an audience when you come on the bandstand looking like a bum? You're in the wrong before you play a note."

On his jazz playing: "So far as being a jazz musician, I have a lot to learn. My playing isn't spontaneous enough. I play too many eighth notes. It's not open enough."

On tradition: "The key is . . . to take what is already there and sound like an *extension* of that . . . Music has a tradition that you have to understand before you can move to the next step."

Marsalis is dapper and of medium build, he has a round face and wears round wire-framed spectacles. He was born October 18, 1961. His older brother, Branford, is a gifted post-Coltrane saxophonist, and his younger brother, Jason, is a trombonist who has not yet come out. Their father, Ellis Marsalis, is a late-bop pianist and teacher. Wynton Marsalis took up the trumpet when he was twelve and was playing first trumpet in the New Orleans Civic Orchesta by the time he was in high school. Marian McPartland heard him around then. "I heard Wynton five or six years ago when I had a trio at the Hyatt Regency in New Orleans," she said recently. "We did a concert in the ballroom for school kids, and Wynton and Branford brought their band and played. I was flabbergasted. I think they were about fifteen years old, and they were so together it was unbelievable. I give clinics for kids all over the country, and I hear a lot of people with great potential. But Wynton seemed fully grown from the first. His mother says he has always been a little man, that he was never a little boy. He's going from strength to strength. I don't know any kids who have the ambition he has. He has already listened a great deal and absorbed a great deal, and he obviously will continue to. Much of what he hears will be taken in, and what comes out in the next five or so years should be unlike anything we have heard before."

When Marsalis was at Juilliard, he played with the Brooklyn Philharmonia and in the pit band of "Sweeney Todd." His style was well defined three years ago. Unlike most of the new trumpeters of the past twenty-five years, it does not rest in the shade of Dizzy Gillespie. It belongs to the line established by Gillespie's peer Fats Navarro—a line that has been brought down to the present by Clifford Brown, Booker Little, and Woody Shaw. But Marsalis has big ears. By his own word and from the evidence of his playing, he has also listened to Louis Armstrong, Don Cherry, Miles Davis, Clark Terry, Freddie Hubbard, and Rex Stewart. All these trumpeters color his style, which is still inseparable from his formidable technique. Indeed, much of his energy goes into trying to control that technique, into trying to keep it from carrying him out of sight around the next corner. He has an acute sense of dynamics, and moves easily from murmurings to blares. His tone is round. He can play with or without a vibrato. He can growl, trill, half-valve, and use any sort of mute. He has complete possession of all his registers. And how he moves through them! His descending arpeggios are sometimes so crowded they almost flatten into glissandos. He loves yawning intervals, and will play a quick three-note phrase, drop an octave without missing a beat, and repeat the three-note phrase, producing an echo that suggests he is two trumpeters instead of one. He will start a downward run and suddenly break it, sound a single note an octave higher, resume the arpeggio exactly where he left off, break it for another upward octave leap, and finish the run. Despite the great number of notes he plays, he understands the value of silence, the dramatic effect of isolating single notes and meteoric passages with stillness. He also knows the value of surprise. He will cap several easy single notes with silence, then drop in a double-time phrase jammed with strange notes strangely placed. He will rocket in and out of his high register, leaving little stabs of sound behind. He will stroll unexpectedly through his low register, sounding big, dark, blank-faced notes. Marsalis is not yet complete. Technique, rather than melodic logic, still governs his improvising, and the emotional content of his playing remains hidden and skittish. (It is interesting to compare the work of Jimmy Blanton, Charlie Christian, and Clifford Brown when they were Marsalis's age. They had already balanced technique and emotion.) And ballads stump Marsalis. The old songs must be played from inside; the player has to breathe them. But Marsalis, overblowing, remains outside.

## "The Sound of Jazz"

The confusion about the soundtrack of "The Sound of Jazz," the celebrated hour-long program broadcast live on CBS television on December 8, 1957, began a minute or so before the program ended, when an announcer said, "Columbia Records has cut a long-playing record of today's program, which will be called 'The Sound of Jazz.' It'll be released early next year." A Columbia recording by that name and bearing the CBS television logotype was issued early in 1958, but it was not the soundtrack of the show. It was a recording made on December 4th in Columbia's Thirtieth Street studio as a kind of rehearsal for the television production. It included many of the musicians who did appear on December 8th, and except for one number the materials were the same. Columbia probably made the recording as a precaution: a live jazz television program lasting a full hour (then, as it is now, the basic unit of television time was the minute) and built around thirty-odd (unpredictable) jazz musicians might easily turn into a shambles. It didn't. The soundtrack, which is at last available in its entirety—as "The Real Sound of Jazz," on Pumpkin Records—is superior to the Columbia record in almost every way, sound included.

"The Sound of Jazz" has long been an underground classic, and a lot of cotton wool has accumulated around it. So here, allowing for vagaries of memory, is how the program came to be. In the spring of 1957, Robert Goldman asked me if I would be interested in helping put together a show on jazz for John Houseman's new "Seven Lively Arts" series, scheduled to be broadcast on CBS in the winter of 1957–58. I submitted an outline, and it was accepted. I invited Nat Hentoff to join me as co-advisor, and we began discussing personnel and what should be played. Our wish was to offer the best jazz there was in the simplest and most direct way—no history, no apologetics, no furbelows. But John Crosby, the television columnist of the *Herald Tribune*, had been hired as master of ceremonies for the "Seven Lively Arts," and we feared that he would do just what we wanted to avoid—talk about the music. We suggested listing the musicians and the tunes on tel-ops (now common practice), but Crosby was under contract for the whole series, and that was that. Crosby, it turned out, pretty much agreed with us, and what he did say was to the point. For the brilliant visual side of the show, CBS chose the late Robert Herridge as the producer and Jack Smight as the director. The excitement of the camera-work and of Smight's picture selection—he had five cameramen—has never been equalled on any program of this kind.

Here is the form the program finally took: A big band, built around the nucleus of the old Count Basie band, was the first group to be heard, and it included Roy Eldridge, Doc Cheatham, Joe Newman, Joe Wilder, and Emmett Berry on trumpets; Earle Warren, Ben Webster, Coleman Hawkins, and Gerry Mulligan on reeds; Vic Dickenson, Benny Morton, and Dicky Wells on trombones; and a rhythm section of Basie, Freddie Green, Eddie Jones, and Jo Jones. This utopian band, which Basie seemed immensely pleased to front, played a fast blues, "Open All Night," written and arranged by Nat Pierce, who did all the arranging on the show. Then a smaller band, made up of Red Allen and Rex Stewart on trumpet and cornet, Pee Wee Russell on clarinet, Hawkins, Dickenson, Pierce, Danny Barker on guitar, Milt Hinton on bass, and Jo Jones, did the old Jelly Roll Morton–Louis Armstrong "Wild Man Blues" and Earl Hines' "Rosetta." The group was a distillation of the various historic associations, on recordings, of Allen and Russell, of Allen and Hawkins, and of Stewart and Hawkins, with Dickenson's adaptability holding everything together. The rhythm section was all-purpose and somewhat in the Basie mode. Thelonious Monk, accompanied by Ahmed Abdul-Malik on bass and Osie Johnson on drums, did his "Blue Monk." The big band returned for a slow blues, "I Left My Baby," with Jimmy Rushing on the vocal, and for a fast thirty-two-bar number by Lester Young called "Dickie's Dream." Billie Holiday sang her blues "Fine and Mellow," accompanied by Mal Waldron on piano and by Eldridge, Cheatham, Young, Hawkins, Webster, Mulligan, Dickenson, Barker, Hinton, and Osie Johnson. The Jimmy Giuffre Three, with Giuffre on reeds, Jim Hall on guitar, and Jim Atlas on bass, did Giuffre's "The Train and the River," and the show was closed by a slow blues, in which Giuffre and Pee Wee Russell played a duet, accompanied by Barker, Hinton, and Jo Jones. Crosby introduced each group, and there were pre-recorded statements about the blues from Red Allen, Rushing, Billie Holiday, and Guiffre. (I found these intrusive, but Hentoff and Herridge liked them.) The show was held in a big, bare two-story studio at Ninth Avenue and Fifty-sixth Street, and the musicians were told to wear what they wanted. Many wore hats, as jazz musicians are wont to do at recording sessions. Some had on suits and ties, some were in sports shirts and tweed jackets. Monk wore a cap and dark glasses with bamboo side pieces. Billie Holiday arrived with an evening gown she had got specially for the show, and was upset when she found that we wanted her in what she was wearing—a pony tail, a short-sleeved white sweater, and plaid pants. There was cigarette smoke in the air, and there were cables on the floor. A ladder leaned against a wall. Television cameras moved like skaters, sometimes photographing each other. The musicians were allowed to move around: Basie ended up watching Monk, and later Billie Holiday went over and stood beside Basie.

The atmosphere at the Columbia recording session was similar. Many of the musicians had not been together in a long time, and a rare early-December blizzard, which began just before the session and left as much as a foot of snow on the ground, intensified everything. It also caused problems. Our plan had been to reunite the All-American rhythm section of Basie, Freddie Green, Walter Page on bass, and Jo Jones, but Page called and said that he was sick and that, anyway, he couldn't find a cab. (He didn't make the television show, either, and he died two weeks later.) Eddie Jones, Basie's current bassist, replaced him. Thelonious Monk didn't turn up, and that is why Mal Waldron recorded a four-minute piano solo, aptly titled "Nervous." There were various other differences between the recording and the show. Frank Rehak took Benny Morton's place on the recording, because Morton was busy. Harry Carney, a man of infinite graciousness, filled in for Gerry Mulligan, a man of infinite ego, because Mulligan insisted he be paid double scale, and was refused. Doc Cheatham solos on the Columbia session but only plays obbligatos behind Billie Holiday on the television show; he had asked to be excused from all soloing, claiming that it would ruin his lip for his regular gig with a Latin band. Lester Young provides obbligatos behind Jimmy Rushing on "I Left My Baby" on the Columbia record, and he also solos twice. He was particularly ethereal that day, walking on his toes and talking incomprehensibly, and most of the musicians avoided him. But he was intractable on Sunday during the first of the two run-throughs that preceded the television show. He refused to read his parts, and he soloed poorly. He was removed from the big-band reed section and was replaced by Ben Webster, and his only solo is his famous twelve bars on "Fine and Mellow"—famous because this sequence has been used so many times on other television shows and because of Billie Holiday's expression as she listens to her old friend, an expression somewhere between laughter and tears. Billie Holiday came close to not being on the show. A week or so before, word of her difficulties with drugs and the law had reached the upper levels at CBS, and it was suggested that she be replaced by someone wholesome, like Ella Fitzgerald. We refused, and were backed by Herridge, and she stayed.

It is astonishing how good the music is on "The Real Sound of Jazz." Billie Holiday and Red Allen and Jimmy Rushing are in fine voice. The big-band ensembles are generally dazzling. The solos are almost always first-rate. (Giuffre is dull, and Roy Eldridge is overexcited.) Listen to Dickenson's boiling, shouting statement on "Dickie's Dream," wisely taken at a slightly slower tempo than on the Columbia record, and to his easy, rocking solo on "Wild Man Blues." And listen to Rex Stewart, sly and cool, on "Wild Man" (he had recently emerged from a long semi-retirement) and to the way Jo Jones frames its breaks—suspending time, shaping melody, italicizing emotion. Some of the music on the show has not weathered well. Monk, surprisingly, sounds hurried and the Giuffre trio, which was extremely popular at the time, is thin and synthetic. And Pee Wee Russell swallows Giuffre in their duet. CBS never ran the program again, but it was shown at the Museum of Modern Art in the sixties, and there is now a copy at the Museum of Broadcasting.

## Fauntleroy and the Brute

Ben Webster was born in Kansas City, Missouri, on March 27, 1909. He was an only child, and, like many black musicians of his time, was raised by women—his mother, whom he called Mame, and a grandmother or great-aunt, whom he called Mom. Both were schoolteachers, and they created a genteel home, in which Webster, according to the bassist Milt Hinton, invariably "behaved like a Little Lord Fauntleroy." That was the angelic Webster. The other Webster, called the Brute by musicians in later years, hung out on the streets of Kansas City and became a womanizer, an expert pool player, and a dangerous drinker. His old friend Jimmy Rowles has said of Webster, "When Ben was sober, he was the sweetest, gentlest, nicest man in the world. When he was juiced, he was out of his head. Very few people could handle him. He was about four feet across in the shoulders, and he'd start throwing that left hand and he'd break things. I think he was eighty-sixed in every bar in Los Angeles. And he would not allow anyone to take the Lord's name in vain. He once threw Don Byas the length of a White Rose bar in New York because Byas was at a table saying Lord this and God that. Ben lived with his mother and grandmother in Los Angeles in the fifties, and when I'd pick him up for some golf or a record date his grandmother would say, 'Now, Benjamin, you fix up that back yard before you go, please, and, Jimmy, you sit down on that davenport and wait until he's finished.' Ben became a revered figure in Europe, but he was always lonesome there. He'd call on the phone from Copenhagen, where he lived, and play stride piano and talk, and he'd stay on for a couple of hours."

Webster played piano and violin before the tenor saxophone, and the piano was the unrequited love of his life. His mother encouraged him, and he learned from the blues pianist Pete Johnson, who lived across the street. In the late twenties, Webster worked as a pianist in small territory bands; then Buddy Johnson persuaded him to take up the saxophone, and gave him his first lessons. He spent three months in the Young family band, and had more lessons from Lester Young's father. (He also helped pull Lester out of the Rio Grande, and many years later he pulled someone out of the Hudson.) He joined Eugene Coy's Black Aces as a saxophonist, and during the thirties he passed through the big bands of Blanche Calloway, Bennie Moten, Andy Kirk, Fletcher Henderson, Benny Carter, Willie Bryant, Duke Ellington, Cab Calloway, and Teddy Wilson. Early in 1940, he rejoined Ellington, and he stayed three triumphant years. (He married in 1942, but it didn't stick.) Except for a brief return visit with Ellington in 1948, Webster scuffled the rest of his life. He played with countless pickup groups. (He turned up at the Metropole in 1964 with Buck Clayton, Max Kaminsky, Pee Wee Russell, J. C. Higginbotham, and Bud Freeman.) He made occasional records with Jimmy Rowles and Harry Edison. He appeared with Coleman Hawkins and Lester Young on the "Sound of Jazz" and was the strongest of the three. He drank more and more, and grew huge. He settled in Europe in 1964, and he died there in 1973.

Two of Webster's friends talk about his last years. The first is Milt Hinton: "By the early sixties, Ben's mother and grandmother were dead, and he had moved back East and was just floating around hotels in New York, so I had him come out and stay at my house in Queens. I'd buy a case of beer, and we'd go down in my basement and play, just the two of us. Or else, if I was at work, he'd just sit and drink beer and listen to tapes. At the time, Barry Galbraith, Hank Jones, and Osie Johnson and I were known as 'the New York rhythm section,' and we'd make as many as three recording sessions a day, at forty-one dollars and twenty-five cents per—which wasn't bad, because a hundred dollars went a long way then. Ben would get calls to make some of these sessions, but he'd ask for triple scale, and the producers always turned him down. But he had been with Duke Ellington, you see—he was a star, and that was it. Finally, my wife, Mona, told Ben that he had a God-given talent and it was a shame he wasn't using it. That surprised him, I think, and when he got an offer to go and play in Europe he took it, and, of course, he never came back. I saw him a few times over there, but his behavior had deteriorated, and after a while I avoided him."

The other friend is the trumpeter Doc Cheatham: "There was something Ben always wanted, but I never figured out what it was. It kept him unhappy all the time. He could be so nice on some people and so rough on others. I don't think any of that affected his playing, except I used to hear a sense of worry in his ballads. The last time I saw him was in England in 1967. He came to see me, and he had these great big bottles of stout, one in each pocket. All that drinking and something always on his mind. I don't think Ben wanted to live. He wanted to destroy himself, and he did."

Webster had two different styles. The first—a thin, angry-sounding extension of Coleman Hawkins—lasted from the early thirties until he joined Duke Ellington. His second style began to emerge during his first year with the band, and had become fully grown by the time he left. It grew in Johnny Hodges' hothouse—an influence that Webster was quick to acknowledge. (He once told a Danish radio interviewer, "That's what I tried to do—play Johnny on tenor.") And it must also have been shaped by Harry Carney's sound. Webster's tone grew bigger and bigger, he became a master of dynamics, and he developed an attack that took something from the heavily ornamented melodies of Coleman Hawkins and from Hodges' monosyllabic blues preaching. He became a supreme blues player and a supreme ballad player. He would start a medium-slow blues solo very softly with a weaving five-note phrase, pause, play a high, barely audible blue note, and duck back to his opening phrase, still as soft as first sunlight. He would harden his tone slightly at the start of his next chorus, issue an annunciatory phrase, repeat it, insert a defiant tremolo, and end the chorus with a dizzying, three-steps-at-a-time descending figure. He would increase his volume even more in his final chorus, and sometimes he would revert to his old style. His tone would grow hard, he would growl and crowd his notes, he would shake his phrases as if he had them clamped in his teeth. These blues solos were jazz improvisation as autobiography. Webster's ballads were very different. They were romantic and yearning. They were majestic but never pompous, passionate but never sentimental. A Webster ballad came in three parts. First, a heavy, robed statement of the melody, in which he moved along behind the beat, shifting a note here, adding a note there—a kind of combing and patting into place of the composer's song. Then an intense one-chorus improvisation, which converted the melody into a new Webster song. And then a half-chorus restatement of the original. As the years went by, Webster's ballads became more and more fervent, and in the late fifties and early sixties he would close certain phrase endings by allowing his vibrato to melt into pure undulating breath—dramatically offering, before the breath expired, the ghost of his sound. Webster's appearance matched his playing. He was of medium height, and had wide wooden-soldier shoulders and a barrel chest. He had an eagle nose and prominent eyes and a strong chin, which he raised slightly when he played. His saxophone was kept shieldlike in front of him, and he rarely moved. His badge was a small fedora, worn on the back of his head, its brim up. Seen in silhouette, it looked like a halo.

# 1984

## Michel Petrucciani and Paul Whiteman

Jazz was once a spare, monosyllabic music. Improvisers thought in terms of individual notes, of bar lines, and of the twelve-bar (blues) or thirty-two-bar (standard) chorus. They grew up within the three-minute limitations of the ten-inch 78-rpm. recording, and they appreciated being given an eight-or-sixteen-or twenty-four-bar solo. (Sometimes a slow number lasted only two choruses.) Such compression often resulted in beauty and high emotion. King Oliver and his protégé Louis Armstrong were wasteless players, and so was Bix Beiderbecke. They were joined in the thirties by Red Allen and Benny Carter and J. C. Higginbotham, by Lester Young and Ben Webster and Sidney Catlett and Jimmy Blanton. Some improvisers developed telegraphic styles—what they didn't play meant as much as what they did play. These included Count Basie, Joe Thomas, Emmett Berry, Bobby Hackett, and Johnny Hodges. Then Art Tatum took hold. His travelling arpeggios, harmonic towers, virtuoso technique, and tireless desire to dazzle suggested that jazz could be a baroque music. Charlie Parker studied Tatum, Dizzy Gillespie studied Parker, Bud Powell studied all three, and by the time their countless students come forward jazz had become baroque. Improvisers filled their solos with runs and with sixteenth and thirty-second notes. New multi-noted chords bloomed like orchids. Soloists, encouraged by the twenty-five minutes to a side of the new LP recording, became garrulous. Few ever knew what they wanted to say, because they had so much time to decide. By the sixties, soloists were going on for forty-five minutes, for an hour, for an hour and a quarter. Listening to John Coltrane and Cecil Taylor became an unselfish act: you gave up an hour of your life each time one of them soloed. During recent years, this floridity has struck pianists particularly hard. In the manner of the great nineteenth-century rhapsodists, they envision their pianos as theatres. Consider their forefather, Dave Brubeck, carrying his immense Wagnerian solos from campus to campus in the fifties. Also Oscar Peterson, Chick Corea, Herbie Hancock, McCoy Tyner, Roger Kellaway, and Keith Jarrett. At first, the tiny, twenty-one-year-old French pianist Michel Petrucciani seemed the newest member of this group. He likes to show off his technique. He likes to rhapsodize and to wander through ad-lib meadows. He likes the loud pedal. But much of this is adolescent fat, for the more one hears Petrucciani the clearer it becomes that the improvisational horses he is driven by are tough and original.

He was born in Orange, and grew up in Montélimar, not far from Avignon. His father is Sicilian and his mother French, and he has two brothers. All the men are musicians. He settled in Big Sur a couple of years ago, and did his American apprenticeship with the tenor saxophonist Charles Lloyd.

Petrucciani first appeared in New York at the Kool Jazz Festival in 1983, and he made his New York night-club début recently at the Village Vanguard. The girdling presence of a bassist (the Swede Palle Danielsson) and a drummer (Eliot Zigmund) helped bring his passionate style into focus. He has listened widely. He says that Bill Evans was "a god on earth," and he admires Debussy, Ravel, Bach, and Bartók—the idols of most big-eared jazz musicians. Evans is at the heart of his work, and there are passing allusions to Lennie Tristano, Erroll Garner, Thelonius Monk, Tatum, and Tyner. He has a strong touch. His hands are not large (he suffers from a bone ailment, and is just three feet tall), but they are steel. Petrucciani is a complete improviser, in the manner of Lester Young and Charlie Parker. He often plays his own compositions, and he rarely states their melodies. This can be confusing, since American listeners love the pleasant game of ferreting out an improviser's sources. Even when he does a standard, he disguises it, keeping his melodic flags in the far distance. Like most young improvisers, he has a great deal to say, and sometimes he tries to say it all at once. Chords are piled on chords, arpeggios surge and vanish and surge again, complex single-note figures collide in the middle registers. He is an avid new reader telling you the entire plot of his first Dickens. But the next number will be open and uncrowded and breathing. He will play well-spaced single notes, placing them carefully around the beat and shaping them into beautiful new melodies. He will construct a ladder of octave chords, cap it with a two-handed tremolo, go into a short, double-time run, and return to his single notes, three or four of which he will repeat over and over, changing them slightly each time. He may use an ascending staccato pattern, his hand rocking rapidly up the keyboard, or he may rumble around in the cellar the way Eddie Costa used to. The piano has no vibrato, its timbres are limited, blue notes can be only hinted at, there is no way to play a Johnny Hodges dying glissando. But the sheer vivacity of Petrucciani's attack carries him through these obstacles, as does his use of certain emotion-producing devices: dynamics, placement of notes behind the beat on fast tempos or ahead of the beat on slow ones, large intervals, tremolos, and sudden forays into the highest register.

Paul Whiteman gave his first and most famous "Experiment in Modern Music" concert at Aeolian Hall on February 12, 1924. This past February, sixty years to the day, the conductor Maurice Peress and a twenty-one-piece orchestra offered a polished and imaginative re-creation of much of the original. (Praise should go to the percussionist Herbert Harris, who managed to find a way between swinging too hard and sounding stuffy; to the pianist Dick Hyman; and to Peress himself.) Whiteman gave the concert to enhance the reputation of his already celebrated orchestra, then ensconced at the Palais Royal, a night club at Broadway and Forty-eighth Street. He wanted the orchestra to be thought of not as a dance band but as the classiest, most accomplished musical ensemble in the world. Which is why at Aeolian Hall it played everything from a tongue-in-cheek Original Dixieland Jazz Band number to Irving Berlin and Zez Confrey to Victor Herbert and Edward Elgar, and why Whiteman invited Galli-Curci, Mary Garden, Leopold Godowsky, Fritz Kreisler, Rachmaninoff, and every New York journalist from Gilbert Seldes to Heywood Broun. But the actual reasons Whiteman offered for holding the concert are mystifying. His manager Hugh C. Ernst wrote in the original program reproduced for the Peress concert:

> The experiment is to be purely educational. Mr. Whiteman intends to point out, with the assistance of his orchestra and associates, the tremendous strides which have been made in popular music from the day of the discordant Jazz, which sprang into existence about ten years ago from nowhere in particular, to the really melodious music of today, which—for no good reason—is still called Jazz.

Whiteman had probably heard little jazz beyond the stylized, imitative galloping of the Original Dixieland Jazz Band. Few jazz recordings had been made, and the best of them—by Clarence Williams, Kid Ory, the Creole Jazz Band, and James P. Johnson—were not well known. And almost no jazz was available in the flesh in New York—Fletcher Henderson, with Louis Armstrong in his trumpet section, would not arrive at the Roseland Ballroom on Broadway until the fall of 1924. (Whiteman, his fadometer always working, soon learned about the music. Three years later, his orchestra was filled with jazz musicians.) We remember the Aeolian Hall concert because it included the première of George Gershwin's "Rhapsody in Blue," a piece commissioned by Whiteman, who liked to hand out such largesse. (Later on, he favored Aaron Copland, Duke Ellington, and David Diamond.) Peress dug up the original score, arranged for only a dozen or so instruments, and the piece—unwittingly such a stunning evocation of New York—sounded bony and exciting and newborn, and far more moving than any of the countless overweight renditions long taken as the original.

## Like a Lilt

It has been almost fifty years since Count Basie, who died this spring, at the age of seventy-nine, brought his unknown band east from Kansas City and changed the course of Jazz. (Basie was not by nature an innovator; most of the inventions embodied by the Kansas City band were accidental or necessary.) Although Basie's musical changes were not always imitable, they were freely offered. One was his rhythm section, which included him on piano, Freddie Green on guitar, Walter Page on bass, and Jo Jones on drums. Jazz rhythm sections had long been insistent, metallic, and inflexible; Basie's was double-jointed and oblique. It swung with one hand behind its back. Page played an easy four-four beat (and the right notes), Green clocked the chords and made butterfly sounds in the background, Jones connected Page and Green with his swimming high-hat, and Basie added metaphor, impetus, humor, brevity, and direction. No one has explained how the Basie rhythm section evolved, and probably no one will. Even Jo Jones, a man of many words, was stumped when he talked about it with the critic Stanley Dance: "It became a wedding. Instead of one and three [the beats sounded] and two and four, it became one, two, three, four, and then it was like a lilt." Another Basie gift was Lester Young. He had a light tone, a legato, horizontal attack, and a way of improvising that extracted and distilled whatever poetic content the original song had—and if it had none he supplied it. Young was unearthly. He floated just above the Basie band, never touching it yet never losing touch with it. His playing primed the young Charlie Parker and brought into being a teeming school of alto and tenor saxophonists, many of whom are still at large. Basie's last gift was his piano playing, which, in a sense, he never offered at all. For fifty years, he pooh-poohed it, all the while slowly emptying it of standard pianistic content, as if he hoped to make it vanish altogether. By the seventies, a Basie solo chorus might consist of only ten notes. But his playing—epigrammatic, swinging, flawless, witty—became cherished and famous. More often than he imagined, while the band played, the soloists soloed, and the singers sang his listeners waited for his next two or three choruses of blues, his next four-bar introduction, his next eight-bar bridge, and they were rarely disappointed. Despite his outward cool, Basie had unmistakable inner fires. He always got off in his solos a legato phrase or a cluster of blue notes that quickened the heart. And he was a supreme accompanist, with an alert, highly skilled harmonic sense. He'd place several perfect single notes behind a trumpet soloist, or a stairway of descending, marching chords under an ensemble passage, and his band flew.

The first part of Basie's long, commanding career ended in the early forties, when the Kansas City band began to harden, presaging the monolithic Basie machines of the fifties, sixties, and seventies. (What a bench that first band had—Buck Clayton, Harry Edison, Dicky Wells, Benny Morton, Vic Dickenson, Lester Young, Herschel Evans, Buddy Tate, Don Byas, Jack Washington, and the All-American Rhythm Section). By 1950, the days of the big dance bands were over, and Basie broke up his band. He put together a leaping small group that included Clark Terry, Buddy De Franco, Wardell Grey, Charlie Rouse, Serge Chaloff, Gus Johnson, and Buddy Rich. But no leader of a big band, accustomed to being wrapped in sound, can sit still long in a small band. It's like going back to the Matterhorn after Everest. In 1951, Basie assembled a big show band, a concert band. He hired the best arrangers and good but rarely distinguished soloists (arrangers had been necessary evils in the Kansas City band), and within a year or so he had a Jaguar of a band that could roar, whisper, and turn on a dime. The personnel changed slowly during the next thirty years (Basie always paid well), but the band never changed. When it did play for dancing, particularly in a confined space, it rippled and glistened with reserve power.

Basie was born an only child in Red Bank, New Jersey. He was intensely private, and parried all personal questions. But he was what he seemed to be—a shy, funny, monosyllabic man who liked to eat, laugh, and lead a big, swinging band. Short and well padded, he sat at the keyboard slightly ajar, directing the band with a succession of nods, pointed fingers, smiles, and stares. Once, when he was asked where his celebrated pianistic style came from, he said, in his deep, easy voice, "Honest truth, I don't know. If my playing is different, I didn't try for it or anything like that. I stumbled on it. . . . Another thing that helped was my rhythm section. . . . I could run in between what Page and Freddie were doing. I didn't think a lot of execution on my part meant anything with them there. It would have just cluttered it up." So, no hyperbole, no sham, no put-on—just as in his music, which was always honest, even when it began, in later years, to resemble limousines and skyscrapers.

# Morton Monologue

J elly Roll Morton (1890?–1941) never quite got a handle on his life. Born in New Orleans, he was by trade a pianist, a singer, a composer, an arranger, and a bandleader, but he spent many of his first thirty-five years as a pool shark, a pimp, a minstrel, a promoter, and a nomad. When he did turn to music full time, in the mid-twenties in Chicago, it was too late. The sixteen classic small-band sides he recorded for Victor celebrated an ensemble jazz that had been in its prime ten years before. And when he moved to New York, in the late twenties, the big swing bands were at the ready, and jazz had become a music of soloists. The young New York musicians who hung out at the Rhythm Club, at 132nd Street, baited Morton, calling him corny and out of date. Like many gifted people, Morton was restless and insecure, and he hid behind a big mouth. He countered by claiming that everything New York musicians were doing he'd done first, that he was the greatest jazz pianist in the world. But in 1930 his Victor recording contract ran out. Morton, a practiced scuffler, tried the cosmetics business and played when he could. In the mid-thirties, he took a band on the road, coming to rest in Washington, D.C., at a seedy second-floor night club on U Street called the Jungle Inn. A record collector named Kenneth Hulsizer visited the Jungle Inn often in 1936, and he reported in the English magazine *Jazz Music* that neither Morton's playing nor his mouth had weakened. Hulsizer said he had "never heard Morton say a good word for another piano player." Morton put down Fats Waller ("All that singing and hollerin' he does. I originated that . . . He just copied me"), Duke Ellington

("He ain't no piano player . . . He's got [Barney] Bigard, a good New Orleans boy, sitting right beside him all the time, telling him what to do. Take Bigard away and Ellington ain't nowhere"), and Earl Hines ("He was flashy. Flashy but not solid. He tried to play more piano than he knew how"). Morton's boasting was part hyperbole, part conviction. It also had truth in it: Morton did record the first comic jazz vocal, and Bigard did help shape the Ellington band. Morton seemed more overbearing than he was, because he never stopped talking. Using this loquacity as a framework, Samuel Charters, a poet, novelist, translator, and jazz and blues historian, has written a funny and moving novella, *Jelly Roll Morton's Last Night at the Jungle Inn* (Marion Boyars). In it Morton sits down with a fan like Hulsizer after his last night of work at the Washington club (by the time he went back to New York, in 1938, Morton, out of fashion a decade, had begun to attract a coterie) and delivers an uninterrupted monologue on his life and work. It is a free improvisation on the musical autobiography Morton tape-recorded for the folklorist Alan Lomax at the Library of Congress in the spring of 1938. (Parts of this trove of Americana have been available from time to time on commercial recordings, and parts are transcribed in Lomax's biography of Morton, *Mister Jelly Roll*.) Charters has soaked himself in the Library of Congress material, and his Morton seems very close to the Master himself. Here are the humor, the bombast, and the intelligence. And here, just beneath the skin of the book, are the weariness and disappointment and bewilderment. The tone of Morton's voice is right, and so are his languorous speech rhythms. (He stammered when agitated, though.) The book begins:

> I certainly want to thank you for coming around to the club here to listen to my music. An artist always appreciates it when folks come around and it's very, very nice when they want to sit down like this and talk and have a little drink. This is very lovely whiskey and I certainly appreciate you leaving the bottle on the table here. Of course there have been a lot of parties, people coming to hear me play and bringing their friends and booking agents and managers and so forth and so on. It always is that way when you have something to offer the people and I always have had something to offer which they couldn't get from nobody else. If it's jazz music you're thinking about, when you come to see Jelly Roll Morton you don't need to go no further because I'm the one that invented it. I am the one that started it all. Of course you know that. When you come here the first time and we sat talking I told you all about that and I know you were listening because you got a pair of ears and you don't use them just to keep your hat off the end of your nose.

Compare these passages from Charters' novel and Lomax's biography. First, Charters:

Of course the music was right there, in us. Negroes had been making up music for so long we had everything there inside us. We just didn't know how to get it out, and it never was any kind of music that you could write down all of it on paper. You could get some of it, and I myself was considered one of the best when it came to getting down the true sound of jazz on paper, but if you took a blues or one of those type of number there was no way you could put it down in notes.

And Morton speaking to Lomax:

When you have your plenty rhythm with your plenty swing, it becomes beautiful. To start with, you can't make crescendos and diminuendos when one is playing triple forte. You got to be able to come down in order to go up. If a glass of water is full, you can't fill it any more; but if you have a half a glass, you have the opportunity to put more water in it. Jazz music is based on the same principles.

The novel drifts from episode to episode. Morton tells us of a dive outside Pensacola named Boodie's Place and of its huge bouncer, Skinny Walter; of country honky-tonks divided down the middle, with whites on one side and blacks on the other; of the bloody Robert Charles riots in New Orleans in 1900, set off when a black man shot two white policemen; of New Orleans whorehouses, where he played as a young man; of a love affair in Tijuana with a beautiful girl named Rose; of his meteoric passage through New York before the First World War; of his time in Chicago and his hilarious affair with his landlady, a country woman named Mildred; and, briefly, of his sad days in New York in the thirties.

Several of the best comic passages have to do with racial matters. In one, Morton explains that many blacks were convinced that the white man had brought on the Depression just to put the black man, who was on the rise, back down again. Here is another: "When you got onto the train you'd meet up with your old friend Jim Crow again and he'd say to you, no, you don't want to sit down in the car here that's nice and clean and has a washroom at the end of it. I have a special car just for you. Now it's not so clean, maybe, and some of the people in it are kind of rough, but that's where you and me are going to sit. Now you could say, no Mister Crow, I don't like the looks of this place, but he'd just shake his head and take you by the arm and you'd go sit down where Jim Crow put you." And here is Morton attempting to finagle his way into Mildred's room in the middle of the night:

So I said in a low voice, you don't know what kind of money a guy like me makes on a job when there's plenty people listening and giving you tips for their request numbers. Of course she got very interested when I said money, but she came back at me, what you talking about, what kind of money. It's just one kind of money that I ever heard of. What is this special kind that you got?

That kind of stumped me on account of I had just came in from the street, but I said back at her after a minute had gone by, sweetheart, I got dollar bills here that go so high up in their numbers that they don't just print the President's head on it. They got his whole body standing there in a new suit of clothes.

Morton scuffled when he got back to New York; then it looked as if his fortunes had turned. He recorded over thirty numbers—his first of consequence in nine years. He appeared at Nick's, in Greenwich Village, with an all-star band, he was offered a job on Fifty-second Street, he was on the radio. But, attracted by rumors that his late godmother may have had some diamonds, he hooked together his two big old cars and drove to California, where he died six months later. This time, he was too early. The New Orleans revival was under way, and by the mid-forties such compatriots as Bunk Johnson and Kid Ory and Zutty Singleton were becoming famous. Morton, working his mouth, would probably have been the most famous of all.

## The Blue Notes

Alfred Lion and Francis Wolff, the visionary German immigrants and ardent jazz-record collectors who founded Blue Note Records in New York in 1939, created a classic catalogue of recordings during the first five or so years of the company's existence. The two men worked exclusively and unfashionably with black musicians, and they mixed them up in unique and joyous ways. They put the New Orleans clarinettist Edmond Hall with the Chicago boogie-woogie pianist Meade Lux Lewis (on celeste) and added the fleet young avant-garde Oklahoma City guitarist Charlie Christian (on acoustic guitar) and the bassist Israel Crosby. The four numbers they made are airy and spacious and delicate. Lion and Wolff combined the trumpeter Frankie Newton with the trombonist J. C. Higginbotham, and on one date they added Sidney Bechet. The rhythm sections included either Lewis or his Chicago peer Albert Ammons, the bassist Johnny Williams, and Sidney Catlett. Lion and Wolff put Bechet with Lewis, the guitarist Teddy Bunn, Williams, and Catlett, and Bechet made a surpassing four-minute "Summertime," which became something of a best-seller. They let Ammons and Lewis loose on twelve-inch 78-rpms for the first time, giving them the room to find their imaginative limits. They even allowed Lewis to record a slow blues, "The Blues," which lasted twenty-five minutes and filled five 78-rpm sides. (They also let him do four twelve-inch sides on harpsichord. It was not a fortunate meeting: both Lewis and the instrument sounded put upon and helpless.) Blue

Note's last great early outpouring took place between 1943 and 1945 and included Sidney De Paris, Hall, Vic Dickenson, Benny Morton, Harry Carney, James P. Johnson, and Catlett.

Some of these recordings were reissued thirty years ago on ten-inch LPs. After Blue Note was sold to Liberty Records, in 1965, some were released chaotically on twelve-inch LPs. All have long been out of print, and it has seemed in recent years as if Lion and Wolff's early records might vanish. But a record producer and jazz writer named Michael Cuscuna and a former recording executive named Charlie Lourie have started Mosaic Records, and they intend to reissue most of the early Blue Note recordings (as well as material from other labels) by leasing them from whoever owns the labels, packaging them in limited editions, and selling them by mail. Their first reissue of the early Blue Notes collects all the solo work the boogie-woogie pianists Meade Lux Lewis and Albert Ammons did for the label between 1939 and 1944. Called "The Complete Blue Note Recordings of Albert Ammons and Meade Lux Lewis," the set contains thirty-four sides, only twelve of which have been reissued before and eight of which have never come out at all.

Boogie-woogie is blues piano music. The left hand plays a variety of basses—two and three-note four-four basses, complex four-note eight-to-the-bar basses, octave "walking" basses, and basses that are a mixture. Most are ostinato, but some are interrupted by odd climbing or descending single-note figures. The main function of the left hand is to provide an insistent rhythmic impetus that sets off the right hand. The right hand uses a lot of dotted eighth or sixteenth notes, heavy, often hammering chords, riffs, floating offbeat chords (sometimes placed just behind the offbeat), tremolos, and single notes spaced out four or five to a chorus. The result is a sort of counterpoint, in which there is a lot of dissonance—and a lot of consonant poetry. At its best, boogie-woogie was a powerful, primitive blues music—a strange outpouring of the black South and Southwest around the time of the First World War. The oddest thing about this music was that it became a fad in this country between 1938 and the early forties. But the music was too limited, too ingrown to withstand such exposure, and the craze almost destroyed it. The craze also destroyed its chief practitioners, all of them worn musically threadbare long before they died.

By the time they made their first Blue Note recordings, Ammons and Lewis, nurtured by Pinetop Smith and Jimmy Yancey, were quite different from one another. (In 1928, Smith, Ammons, and Lewis lived in the same rooming house in Chicago.) Ammons was a loose, swinging pianist. His left hand rocked ("Boogie Woogie Blues"), and his right hand was a constantly revolving array of tremolos, glinting upper-register figures, and brief single-note melodic lines. "Suitcase Blues" (after Hersal Thomas's recording) and "Bass Goin' Crazy" are jumping. They are full of billows and wind. Lewis was probably the better pianist, but he had a hard, narrow quality. (None of the boogie-woogie pianists were highly accomplished; their techniques generally allowed them to play what was in their heads, and missed notes and uneven chorus lengths were ignored in the hustle.) Ammons worked in oils; Lewis did etchings. Lewis's onomatopoeic train pieces ("Honky Tonk Train Blues," "Chicago Flyer," "Six Wheel Chaser," "Bass on Top") are thundering wonders, but they have a mechanical quality—they *are* machines. This quality comes through in the celebrated twenty-five-minute "The Blues." Done in a medium slow tempo, it is a meditation on the blues spelled out in offbeat chords, low-register single notes, and occasional tremolos, accompanied by a gentle four-four single-note left hand. It is absorbing to compare Lewis's long blues with any of the slow blues that Art Hodes has been setting down in recent years. Lewis's work does not have the "down" feeling, the blue intensity, the deep melancholy of Hodes, who grew up in the same place and time as Lewis and Ammons and is probably—though he is rarely given his due—the greatest of blues pianists. (Lion and Wolff recorded Hodes in the mid-forties.)

Mosaic Records' second and third batch of reissues of the early Blue Notes is made up of "The Complete Recordings of the Port of Harlem Jazzmen" and "The Complete Blue Note Forties Recordings of Ike Quebec and John Hardee." The first album has just one LP and consists of ten numbers—five set down on April 7, 1939, by Frankie Newton, J. C. Higginbotham, Albert Ammons, Teddy Bunn, Johnny Williams, and Sidney Catlett, and five set down two months later by the same group plus Sidney Bechet and with Meade Lux Lewis replacing Ammons. The Quebec and Hardee album, on four LPs, has forty-nine tracks, fourteen of them previously unreleased. They were done with eight different small groups between 1944 and 1946, and among those on hand are Tiny Grimes, Catlett, John Simmons, Marlowe Morris, the late Trummy Young, Milt Hinton, Oscar Pettiford, Buck Clayton, Keg Johnson, John Collins, and J. C. Heard.

An extraordinary number of good jazz recordings were made in 1939. These include Count Basie's "Dickie's Dreams," Duke Ellington's "Tootin' Through the Roof," the Benny Goodman Sextet's "Soft Winds," Lionel Hampton's "Haven't Named It Yet," Erskine Hawkins' "Tuxedo Junction," John Kirby's "Royal Garden Blues," Jack Jenney's "Star Dust," Woody Herman's "Woodchopper's Ball," Andy Kirk's "Big Jim Blues," Glenn Miller's "In the Mood," Jelly Roll Morton's "Mamie's Blues," Jimmie Lunceford's "Uptown Blues," Muggsy Spanier's "Relaxin' at the Touro," Coleman Hawkins' "Body and Soul," Billie Holiday's "Fine and Mellow," and Rex Stewart's "Solid Old Man." But none of these dim the Port of Harlem recordings. Made at the height of the big bands, which depended largely on monochromatic ensembles interrupted by brief solos, the Port of Harlem recordings were given over almost completely to improvised solos. They also concentrated on the blues, slow and medium. They were not designed for the giddy, the loose-wigged, the jitterbug. Lion wanted his musicians to go down into the instrumental blues further than anyone had gone before, and that's pretty much what they did.

The personnel on both dates was drawn from the new Café Society Downtown (Ammons, Lewis, Newton, Williams), from Louis Armstrong's big band (Higginbotham, Catlett), and from the Spirits of Rhythm (Bunn). Bechet, of course, had his own groups. It was a daring combination. Newton was a gentle, lyrical trumpeter, a legato performer who liked to drift down his solos, and Higginbotham was an eloquent trombonist who liked to shout and exult. Bechet took his own musical world with him wherever he went, and it didn't matter to him if it fitted or not. The pianists were solo boogie-woogie players, not much used to working with ensembles, and the rhythm section was modern but adaptable. (Catlett purposely plays old-fashioned, down-home drums, using press rolls and on-the-beat rimshots as well as beautiful tongue-in-cheek Baby Dodds ricky-ticky on his bass-drum rim; compare his dashing, driving ultra-modern work just six months later with Hampton on "Haven't Named It Yet.") "Daybreak Blues," from the first session, is built around Newton, who, instead of playing blue notes and smears, constructs a lovely melody in his first solo. (He does this again in the opening of "Port of Harlem Blues.") Higginbotham is equally melodic in "Wearyland Blues," which is built around him, and in "Port of Harlem Blues" the two men commune, establishing a musing quietness that carries through the ensemble at the end. The tempo goes up slightly in "Mighty Blues," which has two clarion Higginbotham choruses. (The Blue Notes are among the best and most consistent records Higginbotham made.) "Rockin' the Blues," the last number of the session, is a stomping boogie-woogie band number that Catlett carries in the palm of his hand.

The second session, with Bechet, has a different feeling. The first two numbers are again set around Newton ("After Hours Blues") and Higginbotham ("Basin Street Blues"), and are notable for Higginbotham's four-bar breaks—especially the next to the last. Newton and Higginbotham rest on "Summertime," which is a Bechet extravaganza. The remaining two sides are by the whole band, and they are soaring slow blues that come to a fiery conclusion in the jammed closing ensemble of "Pounding Heart Blues." The original Port of Harlem 78-r.p.m.s sounded as if they had been recorded in a closet, and the first three numbers on the Mosaic reissue still do; the rest have been opened up, although there is a disturbing cavern effect here and there. (Eight of the ten numbers were done on twelve-inch discs—a rarity for the time, and certainly a contribution to their looseness and sense of space.) But the sound doesn't matter. The dignity and beauty and simplicity of the music pass directly from the players into the listener.

The tenor saxophonist Ike Quebec was born in 1918 and died in 1963. He became known in the mid-forties through his Blue Note records and as a member of Cab Calloway's band, and he had a brief return to favor in the late fifties when he again recorded for Blue Note. A member of the Coleman

Hawkins-Ben Webster school, he had a big, rough tone and a big vibrato, and he took up a lot of room when he played. He tended to dominate his recordings, both because of his sound and because of his attack, which was direct and emotional. He dominated his listeners, too: whole solos stay in the mind forty years later, as do various short passages, such as the devastating three-note phrase with which he opens his solo on "Mad About You." Unlike Hawkins, who was not particularly comfortable with the blues and preferred the harmonic ladders of the thirty-two-bar song, Quebec was at ease with both the blues and standard songs. He grafted blues emotions onto his slow ballads, and he brought the lyrical urgency of ballad playing to his blues. There are five different Quebec sessions on the Mosaic reissue, and they range from quintets to septets. There are good numbers in each session: "She's Funny That Way" and the great "Blue Harlem" from the first; "If I Had You" and "Mad About You" from the second; "Dolores" and "The Day You Came Along" from the third ("The Day You Came Along" has never been released before); the master of "I Found a New Baby" and both takes of "I Surrender Dear" from the fourth; and "Basically Blue" and the first take of "Someone to Watch Over Me" from the last. Listen to Buck Clayton on "I Found a New Baby" (he is uncertain on the alternate take) and to Keg Johnson on the master of "I Surrender Dear." He was the tenor saxophonist Budd Johnson's older brother, and he was a complex and original soloist.

John Hardee was a Texas tenor saxophonist who was born in the same year as Quebec and died last spring. He enjoyed a small success in New York in the late forties, then went back to Texas for good. He did three dates for Blue Note, and they reveal his big Southwestern tone and his sure sense of swing, but they also show that he was an uncertain improviser, whose melodic lines lacked logic and continuity. Sid Catlett is on drums on the first two sessions, and he makes Hardee work.

With the release of "The Complete Edmond Hall/James P. Johnson/Sidney De Paris/Vic Dickenson Blue Note Sessions" and "The Complete Blue Note Recordings of Sidney Bechet," Mosaic Records has nearly finished its rescue and restoration of the best of the early Blue Notes. The first of the two new reissues has sixty-six selections, on six LPs, many of which are by a kind of repertory company consisting of De Paris, Hall, Ben Webster, Dickenson, Johnson, Jimmy Shirley, and Sidney Catlett. Hall leads one of the repertory-company sessions, and he also leads three other, very different sessions, which include Charlie Christian, Red Norvo, Teddy Wilson, Benny Morton, Harry Carney, Carl Kress, and Catlett. There are also eight James P. Johnson solos and a Vic Dickenson date. The Bechet set has seventy-four selections, on six LPs, recorded by Bechet with the Port of Harlem Seven, a trio with Josh White, his own quartet, and assorted bands made up of De Paris, Dickenson, Max Kaminsky, Art Hodes, Sandy Williams, Wild Bill Davison, Albert Nicholas, and Jonah Jones.

Four of the eleven groupings on the first album are by the repertory company, and the first three are as fresh as they were forty years ago. (The fourth suffers from the absence of Catlett, who is replaced by the plodding Arthur Trappier—not "Al," as he is called in the personnel listings.) The versions set down of "High Society," "Royal Garden Blues," "After You've Gone," "Everybody Loves My Baby," and "Ballin' the Jack" have never been surpassed, and "After You've Gone" is one of the great jazz recordings. There are also five lilting medium-slow blues. The music on these recordings is not classifiable. It may have been designed by Alfred Lion to mesh with the New Orleans revival then under way, but it has little to do with New Orleans music. Edmond Hall was born not far from New Orleans, but he came up in big and small swing bands, as did Webster, De Paris, Dickenson, and Catlett. James P. Johnson, of course, was one of the pioneer stride pianists, and he helped build the bridge from ragtime to jazz. (He doesn't actually fit very well here. Someone a little sleeker—a Joe Bushkin or Eddie Heywood or Kenny Kersey—would have been better.) The ensembles are loosely arranged or jammed, but they are not in the New Orleans or Chicago mold. The voices do not strive or jar or jostle; they coast and converse, they cast no shadows. The solos they enclose are often exceptional, and they are often supported by riffs or organ chords. It is an amiable, cool New York music of a kind now gone—and it should be studied by such modern archeologists as David Murray and Henry Threadgill. The brilliant "After You've Gone" is, like the soaring "Sweet Sue" done eleven years earlier by Red Allen, Dicky Wells, Benny Carter, and Coleman Hawkins, simply a string of solos. But they are so good and fit so tightly that the number gives the impression it is going faster and faster when it is actually moving easily and steadily and with grand momentum toward its triumphant final chorus: Sidney De Paris paraphrasing the melody over organ chords and Catlett's lifting half-open high-hat. (Listen all through these numbers for the rhythmic hide-and-seek Catlett plays with De Paris and Dickenson, who rarely played as well with other drummers, and to his tongue-in-cheek Dixieland drumming on "Ballin' the Jack.")

One of Edmond Hall's four sessions is quite famous. It includes Hall, Charlie Christian on acoustical guitar (the only recordings he made with an umamplified instrument), Israel Crosby on bass, and Meade Lux Lewis on celeste, a chichi forerunner of the electric piano. Hall, with his cordovan Albert-system clarinet sound and his growls and stilted rhythmic sense, represented the old school, as did Lewis; Christian, then with Benny Goodman, belonged with early modernists like Lester Young and Thelonious Monk; and Crosby, reading the future, often played melodic rather than rhythmic bass. Despite Crosby's big low register, it was a treble group, full of piping and tintinnabulation. It also never quite swung, and it is still not clear why. Perhaps Hall was ill at ease. (He liked a strong Catlett-style flow under him.) Perhaps Crosby's melodic ruminations got in the way. Perhaps Lewis, a tractor-trailer driver, felt he had been put at the wheel of a Morris Minor.

Perhaps Christian did find Hall and Lewis archaic. The remaining Hall
dates swing and are free of pretension. One has no drummer and includes
Red Norvo, Teddy Wilson, Carl Kress, and Johnny Williams, and the other
has a rhythm section made up of Don Frye, Everett Barksdale, Junior
Raglin, and Catlett, and a horn section of Hall, Benny Morton, and Harry
Carney. The first session is cheerful and cool (Norvo and Wilson, true
stylemates, are in excellent form), and the second has great melodic
beauty—attend to both takes of "It's Been So Long" and "I Can't Believe
That You're in Love with Me." The album has one other blessing—a 1951
Vic Dickenson date on which the trombonist plays four numbers backed by
Bill Doggett on organ, John Collins on guitar, and Jo Jones on drums. Dickenson does two good medium-tempo numbers and two classic slow numbers—sly, satiric readings of "Tenderly" and "I'm Gettin' Sentimental Over
You." Tommy Dorsey made this last famous as his theme song, but, never
able to improvise, he always played it smooth and straight. Dickenson performs it with a cunning smoothness, then steps off into an improvisation full
of smears and asides and whispers that gently twit Dorsey's silkiness and the
tune itself. And there are three choice solos by Collins, a fine guitarist who
worked for Art Tatum and Nat Cole.

Although Sidney Bechet's New Orleans style never changed, he regarded himself as a modern musician who
liked to travel in fast musical company—thus the sides made for Victor in
1940 and 1941 with Red Allen, De Paris, Rex Stewart, Charlie Shavers, Higginbotham, Dickenson, Sandy Williams, Earl Hines, Kenny Clarke, and
Catlett. But, for whatever reasons, many of the seventy-odd numbers he
recorded for Blue Note during the next fourteen years were made with inferior musicians. There were exceptions. The De Paris-Vic Dickenson session
of 1944 contains the Bechet slow blues "Blue Horizon," played on clarinet
and full of antediluvian melancholy, and it also has a lovely "Muskrat Ramble." A date done a month later with Max Kaminsky has some high-spirited
ensembles—particularly those in which Bechet, again playing clarinet,
moves through his own hollowed-out space between the trumpet and the
trombone ("High Society" and "Salty Dog"). A 1945 session with Wild Bill
Davison swings (despite the ponderous rhythm section), and there is a serene
series of duets done the next year with the New Orleans clarinettist Albert
Nicholas. The final session on the album, done in 1953, during Bechet's last
visit to this country (he had settled in France), is with fast company. Jonah
Jones is on trumpet, and there is a streamlined rhythm section built around
the fine, little-known pianist Buddy Weed. Jones is majestic throughout and
Weed sparkles, and Bechet responds to them both.

Mosaic has reissued the last of the early Blue Notes under the title "The Benny Morton and Jimmy Hamilton
Blue Note Swingtets." Included are four numbers apiece by Benny Morton's
All-Stars (Morton, Barney Bigard, Ben Webster, Sammy Benskin on piano,

Israel Crosby, and Eddie Dougherty on drums), Jimmy Hamilton and the Duke's Men (Hamilton, Ray Nance, Henderson Chambers on trombone, Otto Hardwicke on alto saxophone, Jimmy Jones on piano, Oscar Pettiford on bass, and Sidney Catlett), and the Sammy Benskin Trio (Benskin, Billy Taylor on bass, and Specs Powell on drums). Although none of the three sessions are first-rate, there is fine work throughout. These include Morton's rare bravura open-horn blues chorus on the slow "Conversing in Blue," and the closing ensemble, in which the horns nod and whisper and consult; the same group's flying, lissome "Limehouse Blues"; Catlett's ringing, relentless let's-get-this-going accompaniment all through Hamilton's boppish "Slapstick"; and Benskin's light, pleasant Marlowe Morris solos on his trio numbers. Despite its weaknesses (overarranging on the Hamilton date, Bigard's clichés), the album nicely closes Mosaic's invaluable early Blue Note reissues.

## Vic

André Hodeir, the French critic and composer, once wrote that a jazz musician's musical life ends at forty— that thereafter he becomes repetitious and increasingly weary, whether for psychological or physical reasons. But Hodeir laid down his infamous dictum thirty years ago, when jazz was barely sixty years old and the first generation of truly accomplished jazzmen had only begun passing into middle age. Since then, the list of aging musicians who have defied Hodeir's Law by playing with freshness and invention, by even playing with deepening inspiration, has steadily increased. A partial accounting: Milt Jackson, Jimmy Knepper, Count Basie, Bobby Hackett, Benny Carter, Marian McPartland, Jim Hall, Johnny Hodges, Charlie Rouse, Buck Clayton, Buddy Rich, Doc Cheatham, Teddy Wilson, Ornette Coleman, Red Allen, Warne Marsh, Zoot Sims, Buddy De Franco, Art Farmer, Red Norvo, John Lewis, Edmond Hall, Cecil Taylor, Art Tatum, Charles Mingus, Ben Webster, Thelonious Monk, Lee Konitz, Jo Jones, Joe Venuti, Dizzy Gillespie, Art Hodes, Erroll Garner, and Vic Dickenson. Of all these marvels, Dickenson, who died a month ago, at the age of seventy-eight, seemed almost ageless. As the years went by, he never looked any older, and his playing never diminished. Keeping his cool was essential to him—it was a matter of pride—and perhaps that insulated him. The only thing that visibly gave out was his feet, and their failure left him in his last decade with a slow, leaning-tower gait. He had a tall, narrow frame and a tall, narrow head. His arms and hands and legs were long and thin. The expression in his eyes flickered between humor and hurt, and his smile went to one side. He was a laconic man who said he had become a musician because "I know I wouldn't have been a good doctor, and I wouldn't have been a good cook. I know I wouldn't have been a good janitor, and I don't have the patience to be a good teacher. I'd slap them on the finger all the time, and the last thing I ever want to do is mess up my cool." He always liked a drink, and he made his drinks evenly spaced signposts that ran through his days and nights; before he took his first one of the day, he'd say, "Ding ding," a placative phrase borrowed from his friend Lester Young. Dickenson enhanced every group he played with, in the way that the expert and unassuming hold life together. You knew that his solos would be witty and inventive. You knew that each one would give you—in a laughing smear, in the way he sidled up to a melody, in a tight, swinging *speaking* phrase—some music to take home with you. You knew that he did not merely play the trombone but used it, with his soft tone and gloved attack, to appraise what went on around him, to express his bemused, amused view of the world.

Dickenson's life was his music. He had come up, as was customary in his time, through the big bands (Blanche Calloway, Claude Hopkins, Benny Carter, Count Basie), and he did not find them congenial. He did not like the drudgery of section work, and he was put off by the generally skimpy solo space. He first made his mark in the early forties in Eddie Heywood's smooth sextet. Heywood had the sense to let Dickenson stretch out, and he would do lazy-daddy parodies of songs like "You Made Me Love You," pulling their lachrymose melodies out of shape and advancing the notion that music could be funny without being clownish. Dickenson worked with Doc Cheatham in Heywood's band, and Cheatham recently said of his friend, "Vic was always helping people, getting them jobs, looking out for them. He helped me correct several things—little melodies I was doing wrong. There wasn't anything he didn't know about music. Sometimes I'd call him on the telephone just to stick him. I'd sing him some obscure tune I'd found, and he'd name it right off. You had to work with him a long time to appreciate him, because he didn't talk much. That was the only thing wrong with him. He'd answer your question, that's all. He could do anything—make biscuits, things like that. Once, when we were working for George Wein in Boston, my wife and I lived with him in this tenement, wood, on the third floor, a terrible firetrap, and one morning just after Vic had finished making biscuits and we were sitting down to eat, the firemen came running up the stairs and said the building next door was on fire and we'd better get out. Well, Vic told the firemen, 'We'll get out after we eat our ham and eggs and biscuits,' and we did. My first child was born while we lived there, and Vic never charged us any rent or anything." From the late forties on, Dickenson was usually in New York, playing in this or that small band, occasionally leading his own group, and filling his nights and ours with countless solos, each newborn and affecting. He wrote songs, too, and he gave them melodies that sounded like his improvisations. He also gave them special titles—"What Have You Done with the Key to Your Heart?," "Constantly," "I'll Try." He was chagrined that none of them ever caught on.

Bobby Hackett became the centerpiece of Dickenson's musical life in the fifties. The tall and the short of it, they complemented each other perfectly, and worked together every chance they got. (Hackett died in 1976.) Hackett was the logician and Dickenson the humanist. Hackett had bells in his sound and Dickenson voices. Hackett rhymed and Dickenson was in free verse. Dickenson, who was nine years older, laughed a lot with Hackett, who was on a constant, funny low boil, and he revered Hackett's "beautiful, perfect playing." When they were on the road together, they would retire to their hotel room after work, and Hackett would play his guitar (Glenn Miller had hired him as a guitarist), and Dickenson would sing in his nasal, upturned voice. In 1969, Dickenson and Hackett were invited to play at one of Dick Gibson's September jazz parties in Aspen, Colorado, and Hackett, who was a diabetic and was not supposed to drink, fell off the wagon the night before. He and Dickenson sat together the next morning on the bus to Aspen, and Hackett looked ashen and transparent. He slept most of the way, his head back, his mouth open. He did not move when the bus stopped for lunch in Vail, but Dickenson got off and came back with some soup and a sandwich and made Hackett sit up and eat. By the time the bus reached Aspen that afternoon, Hackett was restored and ready. Dickenson said he never got over missing Hackett after his death. Nor would Hackett have got over missing Dickenson, had things worked that way. Nor will we.

# 1985

## Classic Jazz Quartet; David Murray's Octet; and Zoot Sims and Al Cohn

Dick Wellstood, Joe Muranyi, Marty Grosz, and Dick Sudhalter have formed a group, and it had its first full run in the middle of January at Hanratty's. Muranyi, a gusty, ongoing man who held down the clarinet chair in the Louis Armstrong All-Stars for five years, talked about the origins of the group: "We first played together at a party Hayes Kavanagh gave at his place in Westchester in the summer of 1983. He's a lawyer and a jazz fan, and he gave the party to raise money for an East Berlin Dixieland band that was on its way to a festival on the Coast. It was an eating-hot-dogs-in-the-sun kind of affair, and we played one set and liked each other very much. We talked about doing it again sometime, but nothing happened for six or eight months. Then we did some one-nighters, and a New Orleans promotion at Lord & Taylor—making gumbo on the third floor, that sort of thing—and Grosz and I went out for coffee and a hamburger and we both said 'Hey!' and that established it. We realized we had a bird in hand. We started writing material and rehearsing, and we made a record for George Buck's Audiophile label. We did Garrison Keillor's radio show. The group's a true cooperative. Everybody can yell at everybody else, and everybody writes for it. Grosz and Sud are fast, and

Wellstood and I are slow. The band gives us a venue for our music, and as a musical entity it can do anything—it has sweep. Sud is involved with the twenties, with Bix and Whiteman, and Grosz is into the thirties and swing, and Wellstood can be quite moderne. Nothing in our repertory suffers from a lack of attention. If anything, we analyze everything too much. Grosz came up with a name—the Bourgeois Scum—but we settled on the Classic Jazz Quartet. The group has no one personality, because it is made up of all of our personalities, which are very different. I think of Wellstood as gruff and tough, which is both genuine and a front. Sud is Mr. Prissy, and Grosz is an out-and-out comedian. Sud is the most compelled of all of us. Wellstood and Grosz and I have been around longer and are sluggards by comparison. I think we want to get on the concert and festival circuit, and we should be able to handle everything in New York from Condon's to the Carlyle."

The group is what one expected—fresh, tight, swinging, and witty. It's a summation and a reworking of the best small-band jazz from the twenties to the early fifties. (Bebop is still beyond its ken, if not altogether beyond its powers.) On opening night, the group recalled the Bechet-Spanier Big Four, the John Kirby Sextet, the Spirits of Rhythm, the Delta Four, Woody Herman's Woodchoppers (mid-forties version), the Gerry Mulligan Quartet, Joe Marsala's Delta Four, and Joe Venuti's Blue Four. The ensembles are in unison or in harmony, and sometimes they are jammed. Wellstood and Grosz occasionally mix in harmonically, and Muranyi moves between clarinet and soprano saxophone, and Sudhalter between open horn and a variety of mutes. Solos are backed by piano and guitar, by just piano or guitar, by riffs and Ellington chords, by group singing (as in the Gerry Mulligan Quartet), and by nothing—a cappella soloists are let loose over the abyss whole choruses at a time. These devices change constantly, and sometimes a little nervously, mockingbird fashion. Grosz is a good Fats Waller singer, and the quartet sings Paul Whiteman's "Mississippi Mud" in German. (Muranyi, who is of Hungarian descent, says he has little German but is boning up on it. He has also begun writing an account of his years with Louis Armstrong. The opening sentence goes, "I first met Louis Armstrong in the Bronx.") The repertory, so far, tends to be precious, and even campy. Sudhalter and Grosz like to resurrect songs of the twenties and thirties, so we get Harry Warren's "Cryin' for the Carolines"; James P. Johnson's "Porter's Love Song to a Chambermaid"; DeSylva and Brown's "Turn On the Heat"; "My Gal Sal"; Jimmy Durante's "Inka Dinka Do"; "A Cabin in the Pines"; and McHugh and Fields' "Freeze and Melt." (Refurbishings of such excellent ancients as "That's a Plenty" and "Sweet Substitute" would not be amiss, and neither would reworkings of such contemporary pieces as John Lewis's "2 Degrees East, 3 Degrees West," Thelonious Monk's "Blue Monk," and Benny Golson's "Whisper Not.") Wellstood's accompanying opening night rocked the group and gave it the bottom its generally treble sound needs. Grosz is a strong rhythm guitarist and a good chordal soloist. The horns set each other off well. Sudhalter is an elegant, if sometimes brittle, Beiderbecke admirer, and Muranyi soars and shouts in his Jimmy Noone–Sidney Bechet way.

David Murray's Octet, now five years old, more or less takes up where Wellstood and company stop. It is investigating and redefining the jazz of the fifties and sixties and seventies, with occasional trips back into the forties, and even the thirties. It is part of the avant-garde, if the avant-garde in jazz is avant anymore, having reached the great age of twenty-five. Like Air and the World Saxophone Quartet, of which Murray is also a member, the octet has been examining its roots. One hears John Coltrane and Albert Ayler and Archie Shepp and Ornette Coleman, but one also hears Ellington and Charles Mingus and Paul Gonsalves and Sonny Rollins and J. C. Higginbotham and Cootie Williams. Indeed, the octet rests largely on Mingus and Ellington; its chief differences are a fondness for playing outside the key system, a tendency to overblow (a prevalent sin among musical pioneers trying to prove themselves), and avoidance of a four-four beat. In its semitonal way, Murray's music has a cacophonous edge—a grating quality that is close to the sound of some of the earliest jazz performers, who sounded that way because they didn't know enough to sound any other way. It is an uphill sound, but once the ear gets used to it, it becomes less rebellious; the ear likes to balance opposing sounds, just as the mind likes to hold opposing thoughts. Murray writes and arranges all his materials. He often keeps two or more themes going at once, he uses Ellington backgrounds, and he finishes pieces with what appear to be free-for-all ensembles. He admires Mingus's tempo changes, his textural variety, and his tumultuous approach to music. Very little daylight filters through Murray's arrangements, and sometimes the music is impenetrable. Murray is a good, and even eloquent, melodic composer ("Home" and "Lovers"), and he is a player who moves from Gonsalves runs to Ayler animal noises to Coltrane squeals to fat Buddy Tate notes. The octet was at Sweet Basil in January, and on hand were John Purcell on reeds, the trumpeters Hugh Regan and Olu Dara, the trombonist Craig Harris, the pianist Adegoke Steve Colson, the bassist Wilbur Morris, and the drummer Steve McCall. (The hand of the Association for the Advancement of Creative Musicians still lies heavy on the avant-garde.) Dara has an imposing tone, and Harris likes J. C. Higginbotham. It would be enlightening to hear the octet and the Classic Jazz Quartet on the same bill—the octet moving and bruising, the quartet laughing and scratching.

Zoot Sims and Al Cohn have been working as a duo and in countless other combinations for nearly thirty years. Both admired Lester Young when they were starting out and have since become adjoining branches on Young's mighty tree. Both are emotional players, with Sims being the less heated. They have larger tones than Young; sometimes they match the big-house sounds of Coleman Hawkins and Ben Webster. They also like high, bent notes—alto-saxophone notes—that suggest Stan Getz, who came up with them and may have influenced them, or been influenced by them, or been influenced by still another Young student, Herbie Steward, who may have influenced all three of them: such matters are now lost in the fogs of jazz time. Sims and Cohn breathe each other's air, and could probably, if the need arose, take each other's solos. They did a week at the Blue Note early in January, and they also gave a concert at the Church of the Heavenly Rest, using as accompanist Dave McKenna, a pianist whose left hand encompasses guitar, bass, and drums. McKenna began the concert with a loping "I Can't Believe That You're in Love with Me," following it with a fast, cleansing "Please Don't Talk About Me When I'm Gone," and an "Alice Blue Gown" in which he doubled and halved the tempo and skidded into a little accelerando. Sims joined McKenna and reached his customary high lyricism on a slow "My Old Flame," then surpassed himself on a very slow "Willow Weep for Me." He went backstage, and Cohn did four voluptuous selections—a fast "Them There Eyes," a slow "Embraceable You," a fast blues, and a slow "When your Lover Has Gone." By this time, McKenna—almost fossilized by a steady job as a solo pianist at the Copley Plaza, in Boston—had caught fire and, his great hawk face loose with emotion, played an exhilarating solo on "Them There Eyes" and chomping, tilting guitar accompaniment on "When Your Lover Has Gone." It was time for Sims to join Cohn, but Gerry Mulligan, who loves to sit in, came on with his baritone saxophone, and played a beguiling "Georgia." Sims and Cohn reappeared, and the three horns sailed through "Broadway" and "It's a Wonderful World," using riffs in their ensembles and unwittingly making one long for Mulligan's mid-fifties sextet, in which the four horms developed an improvised collective music that hadn't been heard before and hasn't been heard since.

## The Mulligan Sextet and Paul Gonsalves

Gerry Mulligan's sextet lasted only from the middle of 1955 until the end of 1956, and it filled a lacuna in Mulligan's career between his pianoless quartets of the early fifties and the big band he put together in 1960. The sextet included Jon Eardley or Don Ferrara on trumpet, Zoot Sims on tenor saxophone, Bob Brookmeyer on piano and valve trombone, Mulligan on piano and baritone saxophone, Peck Morrison or Bill Crow on bass, and Dave Bailey on drums. Brookmeyer and Eardley had worked in Mulligan quartets, and Sims and Mulligan had played together off and on in New York and on the Coast. Morrison and Bailey sat in at a Mulligan rehearsal, were admired, and became part of the sextet. It is not clear where the idea of the sextet came from. Certainly Mulligan's quartet, which was formed in 1952 and was dependent on the mannerly, counterpoint of Mulligan and the trumpeter Chet Baker, contributed to it. And Mulligan must have listened to the ser-

pentine melodic lines that Lee Konitz and Warne Marsh were working out
with Lennie Tristano, and to the early contrapuntal investigations of the
Modern Jazz Quartet and Dave Brubeck. He may also have had in mind the
old Adrian Rollini groups, which he relished. The result was a partly written, partly jammed music built on unison or free-flowing ensembles, solos
backed by organ chords or Ellington melodic fragments, and a clear,
uncluttered rhythmic pulse, not unlike Tristano's metronomic timekeeping. It was a dense, swinging music, and when the four horns took off at the
end of a number for several choruses of collective soloing (far less staccato
and far more melodic than the soloing of the ordinary Dixieland or New
Orleans ensemble) audiences found themselves shouting and jumping. But
Mulligan was heady and restless at the time, and because the public
response was limited, or there weren't enough jobs, or he wanted to get on
with other things, he dissolved the group.

Fortunately, the sextet went into the Mercury recording studios five
times, and the results give a loose idea of what it sounded like. Three LPs,
made from thirty-four numbers set down (including alternate takes), were
released in the fifties, and have long been out of print. PolyGram has reissued
the best of them, "Mainstream of Jazz: Gerry Mulligan and His Sextet," and
it has also issued, on "Mainstream of Jazz: Gerry Mulligan and His Sextet,"
Volumes II and III, fourteen numbers never released before. The original
"Mainstream of Jazz" remains a superior album. On "Ain't It the Truth,"
"Igloo," "Lollypop," and "Blue at the Roots," there are good jammed ensembles, and on the first number Mulligan and Sims play a long and successful
duet—a fresh approach that doesn't turn up anywhere else on the records.
The two "Blues" in Volume II have some ensemble jamming, and so does
"Demanton," which is based on "Sweet Georgia Brown." There are more
glimpses of the group's collective work on "Broadway," in Volume III. The
ardor and ease of Brookmeyer and Sims held the sextet together, and countered Eardley's stiffness and weak lip and Mulligan's tendency to keep trying
to make indelible emotional statements. (Don Ferrara appears only on four
numbers, all done at the group's last recording session and included in the
original "Mainstream of Jazz" album.) The longer the sextet went on, the
hotter and more inventive it became. It's too bad Mulligan let it go.

The tenor saxophonist Paul Gonsalves joined Duke Ellington in 1950, at the age of thirty, and stayed until his
death, in May of 1974, nine days before Ellington himself died. Gonsalves
became famous in 1956, when Ellington, closing the third Newport Jazz Festival, let him loose in his "Diminuendo in Blue" and "Crescendo in Blue,"
and Gonsalves, driven by a rocking, hypnotic Sam Woodyard beat, played
twenty-seven choruses, which lifted the crowd to near-pandemonium and
gave Ellington, who had been somewhat sluggish for several years, a boost
that helped carry him through the rest of his career. It was a bravura performance that Gonsalves was forced to ape again and again (he once played

sixty-six choruses), even though such flag-waving was contrary to everything he and Ellington stood for. Gonsalves, who was a flowing distillation of Coleman Hawkins, Ben Webster, Don Byas, and Charlie Parker, was most comfortable at medium and slow tempos. This is clear on a new and strange Ellington record, "Duke Ellington and His Orchestra: Featuring Paul Gonsalves" (Fantasy). It was made in New York on the afternoon of May 1, 1962, and all eight numbers are given over to Gonsalves. The session had apparently long been in Ellington's mind, and that is odd, because he had never allotted so much space to one of his soloists, and he never would again. So here is Gonsalves playing all the way through "C Jam Blues," with its many breaks, through "Take the A Train," through "Happy-Go-Lucky Local," and through "Caravan." Four of the eight tunes are fast or have fast sections, three are medium, and one is slow—a languorous reading of Ben Webster's famous vehicle "Just A-Sittin' and A-Rockin'," in which Gonsalves plays a chorus of embellishments and a chorus of improvisation. "Caravan," in medium tempo, has a passage of the sort that jazz fans wait for in the way baseball fans wait for inside-the-park home runs, triple plays, and umpires reversing themselves. Gonsalves plays around the melody for the first sixteen bars, and at the bridge he shifts into another dimension. He goes into a kind of half time, and invents a beautiful, full-blown song that has nothing to do with "Caravan" but floats serenely over it, a complete composition. It lasts just eight bars, and has the ethereal air of Jess Stacy's famous 1938 solo on Benny Goodman's "Sing, Sing, Sing." The Ellington band eventually had the same effect on Gonsalves that it had on most of its star soloists; few broke away, and those who did generally came back, cowed by the outside world. Ellington should have urged his stars to continue doing small-band sessions under their own leadership, as they had done so frequently in the thirties and forties. These recordings at least made them feel they owned their own skins. They also produced some imperishable music. Ellington's nod toward Gonsalves' gifts on that May afternoon twenty-three years ago was gracious but double-edged: it benefitted the master as well as the servant.

## Cootie Williams and Jo Jones

Within two weeks, near the end of the summer, Cootie Williams and Jo Jones died. Williams was seventy-five and Jo Jones seventy-three.

Cootie Williams spent twenty-three years with Duke Ellington. His first stint lasted from 1929 until 1940 and his second from 1962 until Ellington's death. He became the first Ellington star. Williams was celebrated for his use of the plunger mute, and no one ever equalled him, despite the beauties of such Ellington colleagues as Rex Stewart and Ray Nance. Bubber Miley, Williams' predecessor in the Ellington band, had picked up the technique from King Oliver, who pioneered it, and had passed it on to the trombonist

Tricky Sam Nanton, who taught Williams. It is a curious technique—as specialized and delicate and arduous as lacemaking or truffle hunting. The trumpeter places a small metal mute in the bell of his horn and, with his free hand, manipulates a plumber's rubber plunger over the bell to achieve wa-was, trains-across-the-bayou moans, whinnyings, whoops, growls, and all manner of intricate quasi-human vowel sounds. Some of these effects are done partly with the lip, and all depend on lung power. Williams' open-horn playing was stately; he was an ebullient Louis Armstrong admirer, and he had an enormous sound. But when he took up his mutes he became shadowy and keening, he spoke in unearthly tongues. Williams' plunger-mute work was particularly effective on the blues. He would start a chorus tightly muted, and play a three-note phrase made up of a short note, a higher long note, and a short note that fell between the first and second notes. It was a secret sound that passed directly into the inner ear. He would repeat this phrase, making it louder and holding the second note a fraction longer, then go into a simple ascending phrase, opening and closing the plunger to achieve wa-was, which would be soft and would fall just behind the beat. He'd end the phrase with the plunger slightly ajar, and deliver a dying blue note. Next, he would start a growling sotto-voce note, gradually increase his volume, and slowly open his plunger. When the growling became almost unendurable, he would abruptly cut it off. Using large intervals, he would lapse into laughing sounds, moving the mute rapidly from side to side, slip in a tricky double-time phrase, and close the chorus with another tightly muted note. The agility of these effects was startling, but Williams never lost track of what he was doing. The strange and beautiful sounds he made were always fastened to handsome underlying melodic statements.

Benny Goodman lured Williams away from Ellington in 1940, and he stayed a year. Although he loved the band, it was not a profitable musical time for him. Ellington's backgrounds had supplied him with handsome melodies against which to shine, but he sounded naked and somewhat primitive with Goodman—perhaps because of Eddie Sauter's fussy arrangements. During the next twenty years or so, he had a successful big band and a durable small band, which played at the Savoy Ballroom. He liked to hire young revolutionaries, and he helped bring along Bud Powell and Thelonious Monk. His plunger-mute work eventually fell into abeyance, and when he rejoined Ellington it had lost its swiftness and surprise. His open-horn work was still majestic; on a blues like "The Shepherd," he talked of wind and darkness. Williams was medium-sized and straight-backed and barrel-chested. He had a dark, granitic face, and he looked like an emperor up in the trumpet section. (The drummer Elvin Jones once said of his own brief stay with the Ellington band, "I guess I didn't connect with the anchormen, because they complained about my playing to Duke. I don't know whether Cootie, who kept giving me the fisheye, wanted me to call him Mr. Williams and shine his shoes or what.") But he became highly animated when he moved front and center to solo. His face twisted with effort, his eyes closed, he would slowly lift his shoulders, drop them, and lift them again, lean to the right or left, and, when he paused to let someone else take eight bars, execute little dances and talk to himself. At the end of his solo, he'd bring his horn down smartly to his side, do an about-face, and march back to his chair. Williams made little of his consummate skills. He once said, "I laughed out loud at first when I heard those weird wa-wa-wa jungle sounds. Then it seemed to me since I'd been hired to take Bubber Miley's place, I better learn to play the mute like him. I never heard Bubber in person, so I learned from Tricky Sam Nanton. Duke didn't tell me I had to learn, I just did, and it didn't take very long."

Jo Jones took the clutter out of jazz drumming. As part of the Count Basie rhythm section of the late thirties and early forties, he helped demilitarize jazz rhythms. He brought the high hat forward, using it to propel ensembles and soloists, and, by playing irregular figures on it, to give the impression he was sliding back and forth under the band, like a sheepdog rounding up its charges. He made the beat even more fluid by continually changing his ride-cymbal patterns and by dropping in offbeats on his bass drum. His snare-drum accents did not frame and tint what he heard—they exploded. Sidney Catlett used his snare accents to parse the solos he backed; Jones' accents were italics and exclamation points. Jones' wire-brush playing was clean and spare and ringing. His wire-brush solos danced and jubilated. But his solos with sticks tended to be agitated and abrupt. He disguised this by evolving a master solo based on one developed in the forties by Catlett. He was, like most of the older drummers, a great showman, an unabashed showoff. He twirled his sticks and crossed his arms when he played and made windmill patterns. He was a handsome man, and he smiled continually. When he wasn't playing, he talked. Primed by a single question, he would deliver several hours of uninterrupted stream-of-consciousness. He tended in these monologues to be arch and a bit of a blowhard. He called the musicians he mentioned Mr., and he made his listeners feel they were paying court. Toward the end of his life, his delicate style thickened, and occasionally he parodied himself or had unsteady time. But the next night everything would fall into place, and he would play with his old buoyancy, and, with a rimshot or an exhilarating high-hat fill, suddenly take your breath away.

# Peakèd

*Friday*

The avant-garde concerts that Verna Gillis has produced during the past five years for the Kool Jazz Festival, which began today, have been moved from Irving Plaza to St. Peter's

Church. The first of four concerts was opened tonight by Walt Dickerson, a fifty-four-year-old vibraphonist from Philadelphia. Dickerson, who hasn't played much in New York in recent years, arrived here in 1960, was heralded as the most important vibraphonist since Milt Jackson, and moved on to Europe. He plays softly, using small rubber mallets instead of felt ones, and he covers the instrument with sixteenth notes, delivered at the speed of a sandpiper's legs and isolated by silences or pools of reverberating Milt Jackson notes. He did what appeared to be one forty-five-minute piece, divided into short sections. The cumulative effect was miniaturist and skittery. He was accompanied by the bassist Doug Christner, who played unison and harmonic lines or laid out and watched the notes swarm.

The singer Carmen Lundy, accompanied by Harry Whittaker on piano, Curtis Lundy on bass, and Victor Lewis on drums, took up the second half of the concert. She sang a dozen or so numbers by Jobim, Stevie Wonder, Cole Porter, George Benson, and Jerome Kern, and she was hindered throughout by poor acoustics. (That man's beseeching sounds tend to evaporate as they rise in His churches is one of God's meanest jokes.) The drummer and bassist overpowered her, and even when they rested she blared or echoed. It was nonetheless clear that she is a good singer. She has a strong contralto and sure pitch, and her distortions of melody and lyrics (she falls somewhere between Betty Carter and Sarah Vaughan) seemed to be exactly what she wanted them to be.

Marian McPartland gave the first of the Festival's one-hour solo piano concerts in Carnegie Recital Hall late this afternoon. Her program included Duke Ellington's tricky, funny "The Clothèd Woman," a blues, a John Coltrane number, Johnny Mandel's fine "Emily," her own "Ambience," Alec Wilder's "I'll Be Around," "I Hear a Rhapsody," Ahmad Jamal's pretty, steplike "Without You," Bob Haggart's elegant blues "My Inspiration," Cole Porter's "From This Moment On," and "Royal Garden Blues." But almost every selection was submerged in thick chords and deep bass figures—these last resembling Dave McKenna's left-hand drone. Whenever a single-note melodic line came into view, it would be caught from behind by a chordal wave. Presenting jazz pianists alone, as pure and elevated as it may seem, rarely works. Without rhythmic support and guidance, they tend to turn into rhapsodists.

*Saturday*

The principal difference between Carla Bley's and Archie Shepp's avant-garde ensembles of twenty years ago and David Murray's big band (his octet plus three) is that Murray has replaced the satiric pokes Bley and Shepp took at earlier jazz with admiration, and even with reverence. Time and again, one hears in his compositions and arrangements his respect for Sidney Bechet and Duke Ellington and Charles Mingus, and hears in his own playing his respect for Ben Webster and Paul Gonsalves. Murray, who is just thirty (he looks like Ben Webster at the same age), grew up on Cecil Taylor and Ornette Coleman and Albert Ayler, and their harmonic and rhythmic and improvisational investigations overlay his music. They tint his vision of what Bechet and Ellington and Mingus were. He loves Ellington's harmony and odd instrumental combinations—particularly as they evolved in his last versions of, say, "Caravan," which became more and more acidulous harmonically. (Hear Murray's "Terror.") He uses Mingus's accelerando and decelerando, and his "free" ensembles, in which the instrumental voices sound as if they were arguing amiably. (Hear Murray's "Train Whistle.") He borrows the stampeding quality at the heart of much of Bechet's music in the thirties and forties. (Hear Murray's "Bechet's Stomps," in which, however, he mistakenly uses two-beat rhythms; Bechet was a four-to-the-bar man.) All this was on view tonight at Town Hall, where Murray's big band gave its first concert. In the band were Murray on tenor saxophone and bass clarinet, Baikida Carroll and Olu Dara on trumpet and cornet, Steve Coleman and John Purcell on alto saxophone, flute, and clarinet, Craig Harris on trombone, Bob Stewart on tuba, Vincent Chancy on horn, John Hicks on piano, Fred Hopkins on bass, and Marvin (Smitty) Smith on drums. Six of the eight numbers were by Murray and the rest by Lawrence (Butch) Morris, who conducted. Morris has great freedom. He decides when to bring in the background figures, what combinations they will play in and for how long, and what the background dynamics will be. This fluid "arranging" makes each version of a Murray piece different from the last, and is akin to the old "head" arrangements used by the big bands of the thirties and forties. The most impressive soloists were Harris, Olu Dara, who has a singing tone, and Murray, who plays passionately but has not yet successfully bridged the gap between his Albert Ayler squeals and his Paul Gonsalves hymns. Purcell, Chancy, and Stewart were not far behind. Some of the soloists—Murray included—went on too long, and strained the group's collective fabric.

George Wallington, one of the early bebop pianists, came out of a long Florida retirement to appear in Carnegie Recital Hall this afternoon. Bop pianists especially need rhythmic undergirding; one of the first things they did in the forties was to turn over the rhythmic duties of the left hand to their bassists and drummers. To compensate, Wallington used thunderous left-hand chords, which obliterated his lively right-hand Bud Powell figures. Worse, he played only his own original songs and didn't tell us what he was doing. Jazz fans relish the shock of melodic recognition, and when it doesn't come they grow disoriented and gloomy.

*Sunday*

Dave Frishberg, the skinny, promising house pianist at the old Half Note twenty years ago, has long since become Dave Frishberg the successful pianist-songwriter-singer. This Frishberg writes funny lyrics, usually with a topical or autobiographical bent, which descend from Gilbert, Porter, Hart, Mercer, and Burrows and are clothed in modest melodies, themselves often funny. Frishberg's most famous songs are probably "I'm Hip" (done with Bob Dorough), "Peel Me a Grape," "Van Lingle Mungo," "Sweet Kentucky Ham," "The Wheelers and Dealers," and "My Attorney Bernie," and they deal with life as it once was and life as it is among the pacesetters. Frishberg has a vibratoless voice, and no one sings him better. This afternoon at Carnegie Recital Hall he did more than a dozen numbers, including "I'm Hip" ("I'm too much. I'm a gas! I am anything but middle-class") and "My Attorney Bernie," and also "Zanzibar," "Blizzard of Lies" (a list of the endless deceptions we practice on each other every day: "We'll send someone right out. Now this won't hurt a bit. He's in a meeting now. The coat's a perfect fit"), "The Dear Departed Past" ("Tomorrow wasn't built to last"), and "Do You Miss New York?" ("And do you ever run into that guy who used to be you?"). Frishberg is a fine two-handed pianist who has a way of making everything he plays fresh and valuable. Witness this afternoon his affecting medium-tempo version of Ellington's "The Mooche."

## Monday

George Wein likes to build amorphous concerts around departed jazz musicians, and tonight he gave us the dazzling, disordered Bud Powell, who died, aged forty-one, almost twenty years ago. Powell distilled his style from Art Tatum and Billy Kyle and from Charlie Parker and Dizzy Gillespie. It consisted of abrupt single-note melodic lines in the right hand and insistent, often monotonous offbeat chords and single notes in the left hand. His playing was deceptive. At fast tempos, which he loved, his galvanizing melodic lines gave the impression of great heat, even though they concealed a coldness, an inertness. At slow tempos, he sometimes verged on the lackadaisical. But Powell influenced nearly every jazz pianist who grew up in the forties and early fifties, and, filtered through Bill Evans, he can still be heard everywhere. The concert tonight, held at Town Hall and arranged by Ira Gitler, was built around the pianists Walter Davis, Jr., Tommy Flanagan, George Wallington, Barry Harris, and Walter Bishop, Jr., all followers of the Master. Davis appeared with the tenor saxophonist Jimmy Heath, Ron Carter, and the drummer Art Taylor; Flanagan with George Mraz and Taylor; Wallington (amazingly) again by himself; Harris with the bassist Marc Johnson and the drummer Leroy Williams; and Bishop with Jon Faddis, Heath, the alto saxophonist Jackie McLean, the baritone saxophonist Cecil Payne, Johnson, and Roy Haynes. Davis aped Powell in a colorless, insistent way. Wallington muddied him. Bishop was matter-of-fact. Flanagan, who also listened to Nat Cole and Hank Jones when he was coming up, was seraphic. And Harris, a sometimes stolid pianist, celebrated Powell with a laid-back lyricism. (Bebop pianists stayed on top of the beat.) Harris, in fact, took the evening. He did an easy, clear-eyed version of Powell's "Celia," a medley of Powell tunes (Powell had a distinct gift for composing), and a lovely "Tea for Two," done just as Powell might have but couldn't have, because he lacked Harris's warmth and reverential hindsight. In the middle of the evening, we were shown forty minutes from an unedited documentary film about Powell which was shot in France and Denmark in the fifties by Francis Paudras. We saw Powell playing in night clubs in Copenhagen and Paris, often with Kenny Clarke and the bassist Pierre Michelot; Powell endlessly walking in a city and near a waterfront; Powell playing with Charles Mingus; and Powell and Thelonious Monk, their arms around each other. The occasional glimpses of Powell in repose, his eyes hooded and empty, his face stone, were chilling.

## Wednesday

Most jazz musicians don't put it all together until they are around thirty. Then their technique catches up with their inspiration or their inspiration catches up with their technique, they digest early models and influences and find their own voices, and they learn to swing. This axiom has been repeatedly tested by the young wizards, most of them in their early twenties, who have poured into New York in the past ten years, including George Lewis, Anthony Braxton, Scott Hamilton, Howard Alden, the Marsalis brothers, Michel Petrucciani, Terence Blanchard, Donald Harrison, Fred Hersch, and David Murray. These musicians already have more technique, musical awareness, and historical sense than their predecessors ever had. This is true of the spectacular New Orleans contingent, many of whom appeared in Carnegie Hall tonight for a concert called "Young New Orleans." The trumpeter Terence Blanchard and the alto saxophonist Donald Harrison came on first, with Mulgrew Miller on piano, Phil Bowler on bass, and Ralph Peterson, Jr., on drums. They played five long hard-bop numbers. Blanchard, who looks about fourteen, has a sweet tone and is out of Miles Davis and Art Farmer, and Harrison has listened to Coltrane and Ornette Coleman and Charlie Parker. Miller plays long, ropy single-note lines, and Peterson did not leave an accent unturned. The group's emotional level is low, and it never quite swung. It was followed by Kent Jordan, a flutist, who got off one smooth up-tempo number. He gave way to the Dirty Dozen Brass Band, a kind of marching band made up of two trumpets, a trombone, a tenor saxophone, a baritone saxophone, a snare drum, and a bass drum. It plays Monk and Ellington and Herbie Hancock and also old numbers like "Lil' Liza Jane" and "St. James Infirmary." It uses a lot of riffs, and its soloists tend to be edgy and staccato. The snare drummer, Jenell Marshall, who also serves as leader, is not as strong as he should be (a deeper snare drum and rimshots would help), and the group's refusal to jam any of its ensembles repeatedly leaves it at the edge of high merriment.

The second half of the evening was given over to the twenty-three-year-old grand master Wynton Marsalis, accompanied by Marcus Roberts on piano, Charnett Moffett on bass, and Jeffrey Watts on drums. He played two unidentified fast numbers, two ballads ("Lazy Afternoon" and "Dear Old Southland"), and "St. James Infirmary," and the glassy brilliance so evident when he first appeared a couple of years ago had softened. Miles Davis is still clear in his playing, but tonight there was a lot of Rex Stewart, and even some Harry James. Marsalis played six or seven choruses of medium-tempo blues in his last number, and they made it clear that he has begun to let his emotions mingle with his technique.

*Thursday*

Microscopic Septet and Curlew occupied the second of Verna Gillis's avant-garde concerts at St. Peter's Church tonight. The Septet, which opened the evening, is made up of Joel Forrester on piano and Phillip Johnston on soprano saxophone (they are co-leaders, and write and arrange most of their material), Don Davis on alto saxophone, Paul Shapiro on tenor saxophone, Dave Sewelson on baritone saxophone, David Hofstra on bass, and Richard Dworkin on drums. The Septet has been together, jobs allowing, for seven years, and reflects the *nouvelle cuisine* that flavors so much modern jazz. The Septet has been affected by Duke Ellington (in its voicings and in the work of Johnston and Davis, who suggest various sides of Johnny Hodges) and by the satiric doings of Carla Bley and Archie Shepp. It likes old blues riffs, free Ornette Coleman jamming, Charles Mingus tempo changes, and a steady four-four beat. It makes whinnying sounds and Queen Mary roars—devices that go back at least to the Original Dixieland Jazz Band. The group smiles a lot. This is distracting, for it is not clear whether its members are laughing at themselves, at their materials, or at us. Or at all three.

Curlew is composed of George Cartwright on tenor saxophone, Fred Frith on electric bass and violin, Tom Cora on cello, and Pippin Barnett on drums. It is a fast-walking, light-weight version of the Art Ensemble of Chicago and of various Ornette Coleman groups. It plays dissonant bird-sound ensembles, has Milford Graves drumming, some of it electronic, and is as solemn as the Microscopic Septet is jokey.

*Friday*

It must be difficult for Ray Charles to maintain the emotional level demanded by his way of singing. But he almost always does, and when he doesn't the façade stays in place, the sounds are right, the mood is at least approximate. Tonight, at Avery Fisher Hall, he sang ten songs, backed by his big band and by the Raelettes, and was resplendent. He did his anthems ("Busted," "I Can't Stop Loving You," "Georgia," and "What'd I Say"), and he did "Oh, What a Beautiful Mornin',"

"Some Enchanted Evening," and "How Long Has This Been Going On?," the last of which he converted into a cuckold's lament. He talk-sang through most of "Busted," and he did "Georgia" so slowly you could count its spokes. He also suspended a beautiful falsetto over it. He made his renditions of "Oh, What a Beautiful Mornin' " and "Some Enchanted Evening" instances of funk ennobling bunk. And in "I Can't Help Loving You" he sang a jumble of melismatic notes in the first chorus which were so crowded and rich they gave off heat.

When Roland Hanna, that small, regal, expert pianist, appeared in Carnegie Recital Hall at the 1979 Festival, he leaned on his rhapsodic side. He also played a lot of his own compositions. He did both again there this afternoon. Five of the eight songs were his, and notable were the stately "After Paris," dedicated to Coleman Hawkins, and the larking "Century Rag," dedicated to Eubie Blake. Hanna sits straight and stock-still for some moments before each number, as if he were marshalling the notes he is about to play.

### Saturday

In recent years, the Festival has broadened its scope to include certain downtown jazz clubs. Fat Tuesday's is one, and Phil Woods' quintet was there tonight. Woods, one of the best of Charlie Parker's descendants, has long had a quartet, with Hal Galper on piano, Steve Gilmore on bass, and Bill Goodwin on drums, but he has now added the trumpeter Tom Harrell, an exceptional player who suggests Fats Navarro. Tall and thin, Harrell stands onstage absolutely motionless, his head bowed and his eyes closed, his shoulders bent, and his trumpet hanging at his knees from crossed hands. When he plays, he raises his head, holds his trumpet straight in front of him, bends his knees slightly, and undulates slowly. He has a good tone, and uses almost no vibrato, giving his slow ballads a flat, ribbonlike quality. At medium and fast tempos, he shapes silvery melodic lines that move along just below his upper register and are interrupted by rests and by nice staccato single notes. His agile Dizzy Gillespie runs are connective rather than for show. He never lets up, and he never loses his improvisational thread. His solos think. He was superior tonight, particularly on his own "Gratitude" and on a number called "Round About." Woods, who is primarily an alto saxophonist, played clarinet on a couple of numbers. He should play it more often; he sounds like Benny Carter.

Bradley's is not officially part of the Festival, but it is only a little south of Fat Tuesday's, and Tommy Flanagan and George Mraz were there tonight. Bradley Cunningham has instituted a policy of silence while the music is playing—a revolutionary move in a temple of noise. It worked tonight, and it seemed to have a sensational effect on Flanagan. He played with a knockabout invention and passion. He slammed into the beginning of each improvisation and into his reprises after the bass solo. His single-note lines surged, his chords gleamed, the wind was constantly at his back. Flanagan's first two sets were reminiscent of the exhilarating night at Bradley's when Zoot Sims, armed only with Sidney, his soprano saxophone, took on Stan Getz for half a dozen numbers (they were accompanied by Jimmy Rowles and Horace Silver), and won.

## Mingus at Work

Late in the afternoon of September 18, 1965, at the Monterey Jazz Festival, after three hours of music by Gil Fuller's big band, by the pianist Denny Zeitlin, and by the alto saxophonist John Handy, Charles Mingus brought onstage a new octet, made up of three trumpets (Lonnie Hillyer, Hobart Dotson, Jimmy Owens), a French horn (Julius Watkins), a tuba (Howard Johnson), an alto saxophone (Charles McPherson), drums (Dannie Richmond), and himself on bass and piano, and in the next half hour or so played four numbers, the last of them a parody of "When the Saints Go Marching In," and left the stage. It was a puzzling performance. The music was spiritless and unevenly played, and the set had an abortive air. It looked at the time as if Mingus was out of sorts because the preceding band, a quintet led by John Handy, a former Mingus sideman, had given a fiery, perhaps untoppable set. It turns out, with the release of "Charles Mingus: Music Written for Monterey, 1965: Not Heard . . . Played in Its Entirety at U.C.L.A.," that Mingus's lacklustre behavior had nothing to do with Handy. The album, recorded at a U.C.L.A. concert a week later, includes the eight numbers Mingus had planned for Monterey. It also offers two solutions to the Mingus Monterey mystery. One is given in the liner notes, in a paraphrase of something written by Jimmy Lyons, the festival's producer and founder, in a kind of history of the festival published five or six years ago as "Dizzy, Duke, the Count and Me." The passage in the book goes like this:

> The following year we brought [Mingus] back. But there was a screw-up with some records he recorded himself and wanted to sell at Monterey. You had to buy them through him. He said the records were never shipped out here. That's when I had to get on my knees.
>
> He was wearing a bowler hat, dark suit. He got me on stage and said to his band, "I think I'll just take the money and pay you guys off and this ofay bastard is standing here and he's going to make me play when he hasn't done what he was supposed to be doing." He looked at me and said, "You want me to play?"
>
> I said, "Of course, it's in your contract. I've given you half the money."
>
> "Okay, you get down on your hands and knees and beg me."
>
> I got down on my knees.

Mingus offers the second solution. In his opening remarks in the album, he says, "We're going to play the music we planned to play [at Monterey]. But for some reason—this is not an apology—we only had twenty minutes. No one knows who the guy was with the red beard—Jesus, Buddha, Moses, Muhammad, somebody, but he say get off. They can't find him. Neither can I." The truth may lie somewhere between. The concert was already three hours old and people had started to leave, which wouldn't have pleased Mingus much; Mingus, never patient, was probably exasperated at having to wait so long; and maybe some records that he wished to sell *hadn't* arrived. In any case, we now know what we missed on that hot, blue afternoon, and we also have, in the East Coasting album, an invaluable account of Mingus at work. Mingus had the U.C.L.A. concert recorded, and he released it on his label a year later. (Only two hundred copies were pressed.) It included not only all the music (except for an "I Can't Get Started") but also his introductions, his admonishments to the band, an aside to the "New York jazz critics," jokes, philosophy, and his recitation of one of his song-poems. Mingus was a natural man. He never adjusted to a situation; the situation adjusted to him. So here he is working hard in front of a college audience—a musical magician, a tireless agitator, a brilliant seer. This is how the album goes:

After his introduction, Mingus and his tubist, Howard Johnson, start an eighteen-minute number called "Meditation on Inner Peace." It is one of Mingus's "conversation" pieces. That is, at various points the soloists, instead of constructing abstract musical improvisations, "talk" to one another through their instruments, making sounds that resemble questions, exclamations, laughter, expressions of sympathy, and the like. Mingus begins arco over Johnson's two-beat ground bass. Jimmy Owens and Mingus play contrapuntally. Owens drops out, and Mingus plays solo double-stops. McPherson enters, and he and Mingus "talk." Dannie Richmond reinforces Johnson's two-beat bass. Julius Watkins and Mingus talk. Mingus plays by himself, then talks with one of the trumpeters. The trumpeter starts playing high notes, the band comes in behind, and things become agitated. The ground bass gets faster and faster. The band goes into one of Mingus's semitonal collective scrambles, and falls away as the ground bass slows down to a walk. There are more trumpet shouts, Richmond sets off some round-the-set explosions, Mingus plays some piano chords, and the piece ends. Mingus introduces his sidemen, and announces "Once Upon a Time, There Was a Holding Corporation Called Old America." He talks to the band, and they go into a mournful melody and stop. Mingus plays the melody on the piano, and the band starts and stops again, and he sends half the band "to the back room to figure this thing out," keeping Hillyer, Richmond, and McPherson. These three plus Mingus begin "Ode to Bird and Dizzy," a fast mixture of solos and quotes from such famous bebop numbers as "Salt Peanuts," "A Night in Tunisia," and "Hot House."

McPherson solos while Mingus and Richmond trade four- and two-bar breaks behind him (a unique accompanying device), and Hillyer solos. Mingus and Richmond move forward together in an exhilarating way, and Richmond solos. The number ends at an unmanageable speed. The full band plays an ad-lib dirge that was done at Monterey—"They Trespass the Land of the Sacred Sioux." It lasts eight minutes, and is arranged around a lovely Mingus melody and solos by Owens and McPherson. "The Arts of Tatum and Freddy Webster" follows. What it has to do with Art Tatum and Webster is not clear; it is still another dirge, and it is taken up with some lush Hobart Dotson trumpet and by several tempo changes. More rich Mingus melody is offered in the second (and successful) attempt at "Once Upon a Time, There Was a Holding Corporation Called Old America"—a somewhat disjointed eleven-minute piece full of Mingus shouting, wild French horn, and trumpet solos. Mingus offers some of his vest pocket philosophizing before the number starts: "I feel pretty free here [in America]," he tells the audience. "I don't feel confined, or anything like that. . . . You're only confined by your own self and what you wanted to do and didn't do when you was a little boy or a big boy, and all of a sudden you find yourself trapped by yourself, but you blame it on other people. It's a pretty way of thinking." Then Mingus does a rough, not very convincing parody of "Twelfth Street Rag" (not "Muscrat Ramble," as it is called on the album), and breaks for an intermission, first taking care of business by summoning (presumably) the student in charge of the concert: "Peter James Thompson, I'd like to see you in the back. Peter, we have a little matter to work out financially." A pleasant, eight-minute medium-tempo number, with two strains, called "Don't Be Afraid, Because This Clown's Afraid, Too" opens the final section of the concert, and is followed by "Don't Let It Happen Here," a Mingus recitation-with-music that goes in part:

One day, they came and they took the Communists, and I said nothing, because I was not a Communist.

Then one day, they came and they took the people of the Jewish faith, and I said nothing because I had no faith left.

One day they came and they took the unionists, and I said nothing, because I was not a unionist.

One day they burned the Catholic churches, and I said nothing, because I was born a Protestant.

Then one day they came and they took me, and I couldn't say nothing because I was as guilty as they were for not speaking out and saying that all men have a right to freedom on any land.

The liner notes of the album include reproductions of documents explaining how the master tapes of the U.C.L.A. concert, stored with Capi-

tol Records in New York in the sixties, were destroyed in 1971 when the
New York studio was closed. If Mingus wasn't bedevilling himself, someone
else was bedevilling him.

# 1986

## Basie Slips By

In the late thirties and early forties, the two greatest big bands in jazz were led by Count Basie and Duke
Ellington. They remain without equal. They also remain antithetical.
Basie and Ellington grew up in the shadow of ragtime and of such stride
pianists as James P. Johnson, Willie the Lion Smith, and Fats Waller, but by
the late thirties Basie had begun the self-editing that would result in his telegraphic style, and Ellington had turned to a harmonic attack rich enough
to foster Thelonious Monk and Cecil Taylor. The Basie band had grown
out of the Southwest bands of Walter Page and Bennie Moten. (When it was
brought to New York from Kansas City by John Hammond in 1936, it was
enlarged from nine to fourteen pieces by its booker, Willard Alexander.)
The Ellington band was a New York band with a New Orleans bias and had
grown organically out of the heart and mind of its leader. The musical pecking order within the Basie band was soloist, arranger, composer. In the
Ellington band, it was the reverse. The Basie band swung from the beginning, but the Ellington band swung consistently only after the arrival, in
1939, of the bassist Jimmy Blanton. Basie was microphone-shy, and conducted from his piano bench. Ellington loved the microphone and was an
outsized presence onstage, sometimes playing, sometimes conducting on his
feet, sometimes shouting, always moving. Basie was short, genial, shy, and
laconic. Ellington was tall, smooth, gracious, and outgoing. It is not surprising that Ellington himself wrote most of his life story, in *Music Is My Mistress*. (Stanley Dance helped him pull the book together.) Nor is it surprising
that Basie decided to tell his story to the writer Albert Murray—a task that
was completed before Basie's death. The book has now been published as
*Good Morning Blues*.

What is surprising about Basie's book is its length and heft. His taciturnity was celebrated, and in *Good Morning Blues* he tells us, "I never did have
a lot of words. Hell, I still don't have but so many right now." So the book's
four hundred closely printed pages immediately raise expectations—maybe
this secret little man, this wizard pianist and bandleader, is at last going to let
us in on how he has done what he had done so well and for so long. The best
and longest part of the book takes Basie to the age of thirty-seven. (He died
at seventy-nine.) There are glimpses of growing up black and poor in fashionable Red Bank, New Jersey, in the years before the First World War.

Basie's mother, who was from Virginia, took in washing and did some free-lance cooking. His father, also from Virginia, was a caretaker and a gardener. (Did either of them ever work for the family of Edmund Wilson, who was growing up safe and well-to-do on the other side of the tracks? Basie probably never read Wilson, and Wilson probably never heard Basie. They did, however, come to form the bookends of mid-twentieth-century American culture.) Music consumed Basie early, and he never got any farther than junior high. ("I used to stay in one grade so long it was shameful.") He wanted to be a drummer but changed his mind after he heard his friend Sonny Greer, who lived in nearby Long Branch. He took some piano lessons and listened to such stride pianists as Willie Gant and Donald Lambert. He gigged around the Jersey shore, and in 1924 he took off for New York. He ran into Greer, met Duke Ellington and Willie the Lion, and signed up with a vaudeville act called Katie Krippen and Her Kiddies. They travelled by train, and the experience produced one of the few lyrical patches in the book: "I have always been crazy about trains. I love the way they sound, whether they are close up or far away. I like the way the bell claps and also all the little ways they do things with the whistle. And I also like the way they feel when you are riding them and hearing them from the inside." After a year on the road, Basie settled briefly in Harlem. Fats Waller gave him some pointers on the organ, and he worked with the trombonist Jimmy Harrison. He wanted to be an entertainer rather than a full-time pianist, and his uncertain pianistic skills lost him two jobs—to the stride pianist Joe Turner and to Claude Hopkins. He went back on the road in 1926 with a singer and dancer named Gonzelle White. "She must have been in her late twenties or early thirties," Basie told Murray. "She was very light-skinned, and she had curly red hair and was very well put together. She was not a large woman. She was the kind of small, nice-looking woman that you think of as being very cute. And, of course, she always wore fine, stylish clothes and costumes, and she also sported a diamond in one of her front teeth." He heard Earl Hines in Chicago, and he met Hot Lips Page and Jimmy Rushing in Tulsa. Page and Rushing were with Walter Page and His Blue Devils, who mesmerized Basie. The book has some funny passages in it. One night after Basie had joined the band, Lips Page lent Basie one of his three suits:

> I didn't know what I was getting myself into. I couldn't get rid of him. Everywhere I went he was right there with me, saying, "Don't lean on that."
>
> Or he'd say, "Hey man, that chair is kinda dirty."
>
> "Hey, Basie, watch it sitting down." . . . That was one of the most uncomfortable evenings I've ever had in my life.

The Blue Devils ran out of work, and Basie went to Kansas City and played organ for the movies at the Eblon Theatre. He finally heard the famous

Bennie Moten band, and was as taken with it as he had been with the Blue Devils. He knew that Moten was the band's pianist, but, he tells us, "I have always been a conniver and began saying to myself, I got to see how I can connive my way into that band." He did it—by collaborating on some arrangements with Eddie Durham, Moten's trombonist and guitarist. He became the group's leader briefly in the early thirties, and when it disbanded he took over a group at the Reno Club in Kansas City. He brought in former members of the Blue Devils and the Bennie Moten band, and in due course had the nine-piece group that John Hammond heard over station W9XBY and eventually sent on its way.

By the mid-forties, the Basie band had begun to lose its heat, its easy, left-handed drive, its misterioso quality. The deep blueness of "Song of the Islands" and "Goin' to Chicago" and "Nobody Knows" gave way to such strident Art Deco numbers as "Avenue C" and "The Mad Boogie." The band was becoming the sleek leviathan that Basie would perfect in the fifties. The book itself becomes mechanical at this point. There are endless itineraries, lists of recording dates and personnel changes, show-business encomiums to left and right, and pleased accounts of playing for American Presidents and English royalty. (Murray has done a lot of legwork on the logistical details of Basie's bands—down to what forgotten movie was accompanying a Basie show—and he has put it all into Basie's mouth, not always comfortably.) It becomes clear that Basie has slipped genially by again without saying much of anything. He tells us at the outset that there will be no intimate revelations, but we learn that he liked to play the horses, that he liked to drink and womanize, that he could be scheming, that he was married twice and had a daughter, and that he spent a lot of time in the "doghouse." But we don't learn what we wanted to learn—where his exquisite, pearl-by-pearl piano style came from, how it felt to lead and to play with such extraordinary sidemen as Lester Young and Herschel Evans and Buck Clayton and Dicky Wells and Jo Jones, how such a fun-loving man happened to conceal the vein of melancholy that was so clear and poignant in his blues piano solos. The reader wants Murray to *make* Basie talk about his music. If he did try, maybe Basie, who had perfected the art of self-denigration, just laughed, winked, and shook his cool head.

## American Jazz Orchestra and the Leaders

A new repertory group, the American Jazz Orchestra, has been brought into being by the critic Gary Giddins. John Lewis is its musical director, and Cooper Union, where it recently gave its first concert, is its sponsor and base. The notion of trying to preserve and reproduce an improvised music was first sanctified during the winter of 1973–1974, when the National Jazz Ensemble, headed by the bassist and composer Chuck Israels, gave five concerts at Alice Tully Hall, and the New

York Jazz Repertory Company, headed by Sy Oliver, Billy Taylor, Gil Evans, and Stanley Cowell, gave fifteen concerts at Carnegie Hall. (There were earlier repertory attempts: the neo–New Orleans music of the early forties; the re-creation of the Fletcher Henderson band, with many of its original members, at the Great South Bay Jazz Festival in 1957; the Red Allen, Count Basie, and Billie Holiday segments of "The Sound of Jazz," given later that year; and Duke Ellington's constant refurbishings of his own old beauties.) The National Jazz Ensemble, using sixteen pieces and imaginative arrangements, favored the small-band music of the forties, fifties, and sixties, but it took as its theme a near-showstopper from 1927—a unison transcription, played by the entire band, of Louis Armstrong's solo on his Hot Five version of "Struttin' with Some Barbecue." The New York Jazz Repertory Company, using a pool of a hundred or so musicians, did everyone from Bix Beiderbecke to John Coltrane, often with elephantine results. Both groups lasted several seasons and died from public apathy and a lack of funds. But jazz repertory has continued in one form or another. Dick Hyman and Bob Wilber have re-created the music of King Oliver, Jelly Roll Morton, Sidney Bechet, James P. Johnson, and Duke Ellington, and Vince Giordano has done various dance bands of the twenties, thirties, and forties. Harvey Estrin has brought the Sauter-Finegan band back to life in several concerts at the 92nd Street Y. Lee Konitz has assembled a nonet that bears a close resemblance to the Miles Davis group of 1949. Panama Francis has resurrected the Savoy Sultans, and Paul Whiteman has been done by Dick Sudhalter and Maurice Peress. The Classic Jazz Quartet is, in its way, a repertory group that gets inside the small-band music of the twenties and thirties. And Sphere and Dameronia have revived Thelonious Monk and Tadd Dameron. But Gary Giddins feels that the time has come to institutionalize such homegrown attempts. He recently wrote in the *Village Voice*:

> The next step, it seemed to me, was to create permanently housed jazz ensembles under the auspices of arts centers. They would have to be every bit as stable, secure, and accomplished as the orchestras that conserve nineteenth-century European music in practically every major city in the United States. Under the batons of great conductors (a relatively new line of work in jazz), such orchestras would not only reclaim and refurbish seventy years of indigenous music, but provide a stream of commissions to contemporary composers.

But the problem of how to re-create an improvised music has never been completely solved. Many solutions have been put forward. Recordings have been transcribed note for note and played either note for note or with new solos. Old solos have been transcribed and scored for reed or brass sections, then incorporated into old arrangements. Old solos have been used as the basis of new improvisations. But what of these stubborn questions: Why reproduce, say, Jelly Roll Morton's 1926 "Doctor Jazz" when the original recording is available and clear? Is it more informative and enjoyable for an untutored audience to hear the number imitated in the flesh than to hear the original record on decent sound equipment—particularly since audiences tend to listen with their eyes instead of their ears? How do young musicians re-create music originally played in a combustible, semi-intuitive manner? How do they get inside the music rhythmically? (Tone and timbre can be matched with relative ease.) And what of the fact that many old recordings failed to capture their subjects faithfully, whether because of poor sound, misguided supervision, time limitations, or nervous musicians? These recordings may be fixed in our ears, but they are nonetheless false. A theatrical repertory company works from a true text; a jazz repertory company works from old, often unreliable recordings, improvisation frozen by time, and an array of unorthodox attacks and timbres. Poets, not copyists, are needed for such work.

The American Jazz Orchestra concert, given in the Great Hall at Cooper Union, didn't solve any problems, but it inadvertently advanced one that didn't exist in 1973. The National Jazz Ensemble and the New York Jazz Repertory Company had on tap many musicians who had played the original music or known it first hand. It was going home for Budd Johnson to do an Earl Hines concert, for Joe Venuti to do the Blue Four, for Cozy Cole to do Cab Calloway, for Taft Jordan to do Chick Webb, for Ray Nance to do Duke Ellington. Most of these musicians have died, and Giddins and Lewis have had to call in musicians who came up in bebop or hard-bop days (Hank Jones, Dick Katz, Jimmy Heath, Eddie Bert, Jack Jeffers, Jimmy Knepper, Ted Curson, Major Holley, Charli Persip), or even more recently (Jon Faddis, Randy Brecker, Marvin Stamm, Craig Harris, John Purcell, Hamiet Bluiett). The program included Fletcher Henderson ("Big John Special," "Wrappin' It Up," "King Porter Stomp"), Duke Ellington ("Cottontail," "Concerto for Cootie," "Jack the Bear," "Harlem"), Jimmie Lunceford ("For Dancers Only," "Lunceford Special," "Yard Dog Mazurka"), Count Basie ("Taxi War Dance," "Jive at Five," "Every Tub," "One O'Clock Jump"), and Dizzy Gillespie ("Confirmation" and Slide Hampton's "Fantasy on 'Shaw 'Nuff' and 'Anthropology' "). There was tentativeness everywhere. Charli Persip never took hold (there are few things more tonic than a big band in full shout, with a Sid Catlett or a Sonny Greer or a Jake Hanna in command), and John Lewis's tempos tended to be too slow. The ensemble passages didn't have much snap; there was very little *swinging*. The fresh solos were often better than the re-created ones (Loren Shoenberg's Lester Young on "Taxi War Dance" was an exception, and so was Virgil Jones' open-horn section of "Concerto for Cootie"), and notable among them were Jimmy Knepper's two triumphant choruses on Hampton's "Fantasy," Hamiet

Bluiett's swaggering on "Jive at Five," and, on the Hampton, Dizzy Gillespie's soft, slippered exchanges with Jon Faddis, who, as in his wont, overblew. Probably the most successful piece of the evening was Ellington's "Harlem," a twelve-minute tone poem commissioned by the NBC Symphony in 1950. Maurice Peress conducted with verve, and the band responded. Gary Giddins made onstage comments about the music between sections, and, though to the point, they recalled the days when jazz was armored in apologetics. Let us hope that future concerts will enlist such magical reproducers of old music as Dick Hyman, Howard Alden, Vince Giordano, Dick Sudhalter, and Dick Wellstood, and also Bob Wilber and Scott Hamilton, both of whom would have added a great deal to the Ellington the other night. Let us hope, too, that newly commissioned pieces will be carefully weighed; many of the new pieces done in the past by repertory groups have turned out to be all wind and motion.

The Leaders is a six-piece all-star band formed a couple of years ago for the purpose of touring European jazz festivals, and it made its first New York appearance at Sweet Basil. It included Lester Bowie, replacing Don Cherry on trumpet; Arthur Blythe on alto saxophone; Chico Freeman on tenor saxophone; Kirk Lightsey on piano; Cecil McBee on bass; and Famoudou Don Moye on drums. The group falls somewhere between hard bop and the avant-garde of the sixties and seventies. (Most of its members are in their forties.) It has been marked by the rhythmic practices of Charlie Mingus and by the parodic and eclectic tendencies of the Association of the Advancement of Creative Musicians. Bowie and Moye are early members of the Art Ensemble of Chicago, which came out of the A.A.C.M., as did Chico Freeman; Lightsey has played for Dexter Gordon and been an accompanist to singers; McBee has worked with everyone from Miles Davis to Sam Rivers to Freeman; and Blythe is an adaptable and excitable post-Coltrane player. The group didn't do much at an early set late in the week. There were three long numbers, and the disappointingly brief ensembles were in vague unison or in free form. The rest of the time was occupied by solos. Freeman is the most impressive member of the group. He has something of Paul Gonslaves' inner-directed flow (but none of his sly subtlety), and he has a sure, rich sound. Bowie likes to anthologize other trumpeters' licks (Cootie Williams, Dizzy Gillespie, Miles Davis), and he is not above making neighing sounds. Blythe gives the impression that he is flying over his materials. Moye is a good melodic drummer, but he is overbearing, and that caused Lightsey and McBee to shout in order to be heard. The group's closing number, a short parody of "Blueberry Hill," had a thunderous afterbeat, and it swung harder than anything that had come before. The parodied strikes back!

## The Big Bands

**G**unther Schuller and Martin Williams have put together for the Smithsonian Collection a recorded history of the big jazz bands, called "Big Band Jazz." Stretching from 1924 to 1955, it contains two Paul Whitemans, five Fletcher Hendersons, two McKinney's Cotton Pickers, one Luis Russell, one Jesse Stone, one The Missourians, one Casa Loma Orchestra, two Bennie Motens, four Earl Hineses, four Chick Webbs, five Jimmie Luncefords, five Benny Goodmans, one Andy Kirk, four Tommy Dorseys, six Count Basies, two Charlie Barnets, three Artie Shaws, three Glenn Millers, two Harry Jameses, one Benny Carter, two Erskine Hawkinses, seven Duke Ellingtons, one Louis Armstrong, two Lionel Hamptons, four Woody Hermans, one Billy Eckstine, two Boyd Raeburns, two Dizzy Gillespies, two Claude Thornhills, one Elliot Lawrence, and one Stan Kenton. It does not contain anything by the Mills' Blue Rhythm Band, Bob Crosby, Les Brown, Gene Krupa, Jay McShann, Lucky Millinder, Teddy Wilson, Red Norvo, Teddy Powell, Bob Chester, Jimmy Dorsey, Sabby Lewis, Hal McIntyre, Jack Teagarden, Spike Hughes, the Metronome All-Star bands, Cootie Williams, Cab Calloway, the Sauter-Finegan band, Georgie Auld, or the Savoy Sultans. To judge simply by what has been left out and by the number of selections granted certain of the bands, it is clear that "Big Band Jazz" is an eccentric and even capricious anthology. Taken as a whole, though, it is a testament to a body of jazz music that was rarely as good as it should have been yet was often better than the mass-production standards that governed it.

Ragtime, early in the century, was the first nationwide popular-music fad in this country, and the big bands, which flourished from around 1930 to 1950, were the second. (Popular singers came next, then rock.) The big bands grew indirectly out of the New Orleans ensemble of trumpet, clarinet, trombone, piano, guitar, bass, and drums. (By big bands I mean big bands with a jazz inclination, and not such sweet, Mickey Mouse bands as Guy Lombardo, Wayne King, Russ Morgan, and Sammy Kaye.) They swelled from around ten pieces in the twenties to twenty and sometimes thirty in the forties, and eventually they included four or five trumpets, three or four trombones, five reeds, and a rhythm section of piano, guitar, bass, and drums. String sections of various sizes came and went. Because such a number of instruments could not play polyphonically in the New Orleans manner, arrangers came into being. They wrote figures for the various sections to play, leaving space here and there for improvised solos. These figures were riffs (short, repeated phrases); rhythmic punctuations, especially for the brass; organ chords played by any or all of the sections; and straight-out melodies or melodic fragments. In the early big-band days the sections worked in a kind of call-and-answer pattern: the reeds would play a riff and the trumpets would answer with a wa-wa phrase, the trombones would state

a melody for eight bars and the reeds would answer with an eight-bar variation of that melody. There wasn't much harmonic adventurousness. Unison
and octave-unison voicings were common, and the reed sections, generally
made up until the late thirties of two alto saxophones and two tenor saxophones (with everybody doubling on clarinet), had a Goody Two Shoes
sound. Fletcher Henderson perfected this foursquare mode of arranging,
and it became prevalent and lasted into the forties. But in the late thirties
such experimental arrangers and arranger-leaders as Duke Ellington, Benny
Carter, Sy Oliver, and Mary Lou Williams began to be felt. They made the
big bands they wrote for sound like small bands. They added new voicings
and new harmonies, they pointed up the timbres of their soloists and made
them an organic part of their surroundings, they eliminated blare and pomp,
they put color and texture in their background figures, they loosened the
staid nineteen-thirties rhythmic underpinnings. Each had his own voice.
Mary Lou Williams was lean and poetic. She might use only three or four
instruments in ensemble passages, and when she used her full resources the
band resembled an octet. Like Carter and Ellington, she added the dimension of mood to many of her arrangements. Some were misterioso, some
were melancholy, some were silken. Benny Carter's bands never sounded
big, either. He wrote long, complex melodies for his reed section, and he pitted biting brass figures against them to keep them from cloying. He was a
master of dynamics, and his own exemplary improvisations on alto saxophone, trumpet, and clarinet lifted his arrangements. Sy Oliver had a gift for
catchy melodies. He also had a sure sense of dynamics and a love of rhythmic
excitement. It took iron drummers like Jimmy Crawford and Buddy Rich to
weather the rhythmic jolts in his arrangements. He had, like Ellington and
Williams, a gift for mood. Ellington turned the big jazz band into a work of
art. He collected idiosyncratic soloists and wrote miniature concertos
around them. These were notable for their voicings (he often combined
instruments from the different sections), for the stream of beautiful sub-
melodies that floated through the background of every arrangement, for the
band's soaring sound when he pressed all his instruments into one voice.
Ellington moved from the big-band medium into his own sphere. One more
gifted experimental arranger appeared in the forties—Gil Evans. He learned
from Ellington, and he favored an instrumental palette that included horns
and tubas. He was a romantic, and his sounds were rich and stately. The
leaves were always turning in Evans' music. There were hundreds of big
bands in the thirties and early forties, but there were also many small groups.
Some were contained within the big bands, and would come forth once or
twice an evening to show off the big group's star soloists. Some were working groups, and were generally found in night clubs. If the big bands were
novels, the small bands were short stories.

The big bands were inescapable. Not only did they endlessly crisscross
the country but many were heard every night on network radio between

eleven and one. They were, of course, dance bands, and hearing them in the flesh could be an exhilarating experience—the intensity of the sound, the timbres of both the sections and the soloists, the rhythmic momentum, the excitement of never knowing what a musician would play when he stood up to solo. (Some bandleaders ordered their stars to repeat note for note the solos they had recorded, particularly if the records were hits.) In turn, people packed twenty deep in front of a bandstand could make a soloist do exultant things. There were three kinds of big bands: the young, heedless, swinging ones (Erskine Hawkins, Bennie Moten, the 1945 Woody Herman); the great commercial bands (Tommy Dorsey, Artie Shaw, Benny Goodman, Glenn Miller, Lionel Hampton, Jimmie Lunceford); and the iconoclastic bands (Duke Ellington, Count Basie, Andy Kirk, Benny Carter, Claude Thornhill). The Smithsonian album is a mixture of all three.

Here is what happens on two numbers in the album. The first is Jimmie Lunceford's 1936 recording of Sy Oliver's "Organ Grinder's Swing." It is a subtle and ingenious set of variations, taken at a medium-slow tempo, on the old eight-bar children's refrain "I like coffee, I like tea, I like the girls, and the girls like me." The melody is played in unison the first time through by muted trumpet, muted trombone, and clarinet (Ellington's "Mood Indigo" trio), accompanied only by temple blocks. There is an eight-bar bridge, in which a baritone saxophone states a variation of the melody while Sy Oliver growls on muted trumpet. The theme is restated by a celeste, accompanied again by the temple blocks. A four-bar clarinet interlude gives way to an eight-bar open-horn trumpet solo by Paul Webster, with saxophone chords behind. Then Oliver, again muted and growling, solos against pushing, off-beat saxophone chords, and the eight-bar theme reappears, played this time by the baritone saxophone, the growling Oliver rampant behind.

The second number is Duke Ellington's 1941 version of Billy Strayhorn's "Just A-Sittin' and A-Rockin'." It consists largely of an eloquent dialogue between Ben Webster and the band, with afterthoughts by Tricky Sam Nanton and Barney Bigard. Ellington and Jimmy Blanton share the four-bar introduction, and Webster states the four-note, two-bar melody and is answered by the band. Over the course of two thirty-two-bar choruses, he plays this theme twenty-four times, each time slightly differently, and is immediately answered by the band. He is a Lewis Carroll figure trying again and again to get his way, and being told with every nuance authority can think of, "We shall see." Ray Nance takes the bridge in the first chorus and Webster in the second. Webster finishes his queries, and Nanton and Bigard divide the last chorus. Nanton solos while the band plays Webster's theme, and Bigard picks the melody up and finishes. Ellington and Blanton close with a four-bar coda. A simple, daring, elegant piece of work.

The other choice numbers in the album include Jimmie Lunceford's "Uptown Blues," with Snooky Young's lordly trumpet solo; Ellington's "Take the 'A' Train," "A Gypsy Without a Song," "The 'C' Jam Blues,"

"Perdido," and the charging "Main Stem"; Mary Lou Williams' bony, sad "Big Jim Blues," played by Andy Kirk; Count Basie's "Sent for You Yesterday" and "9:20 Special," the last chorus of which is graced by a visiting Coleman Hawkins, who is backed by Jo Jones rimshots and those stepping-into-the-cellar Basie left-hand chords; Erskine Hawkins' "Tuxedo Junction" and "Midnight Stroll," both full of light, cool motion; Woody Herman's soaring "Apple Honey"; and Claude Thornhill's humming "Donna Lee" and "Robbins Nest." There are also a generous and welcome number of selections by the big commercial bands, among them Glenn Miller's "In the Mood" and "A String of Pearls" which rests on Bobby Hackett's indestructible one chorus cornet solo; Tommy Dorsey's "Well, Git It!," "On the Sunny Side of the Street," and "Opus No. One"; Artie Shaw's "Star Dust" and "Begin the Beguine"; and Charlie Barnet's "Skyliner."

There would have been room in the Smithsonian album for a good many of the omitted bands if the selections by Ellington, Basie, Lunceford, Herman, Goodman, Hines, Henderson, and Webb had been pared down—excellence makes its point quickly. Leaving out such mediocre—even poor—material as Louis Armstrong's "Leap Frog," Lionel Hampton's "Till Tom Special," Harry James' "The Mole" and "Friar Rock," Luis Russell's "Ol' Man River," and Glenn Miller's "I Got Rhythm" would have made even more room. And do we need to wade through all of "Sing, Sing, Sing" *again*, particularly when Andy Kirk and Benny Carter are given just one number apiece? The text of the handsome album booklet is by Schuller and Williams, and it is a good primer on big-band jazz. The photographs are plentiful and excellent. Some of the solo credits are incomplete, and we are not told, among other things, that Sy Oliver's "Well, Git It!" is a reworking of the old "Bugle Call Rag."

## B.G.—and Big Sid

B enny Goodman sometimes gave the impression that he would live forever. Like most prolific virtuosos, he was difficult to keep in focus. He made a pass at retiring when he was forty, but he kept reappearing with a new group or a new recording. He was the first important jazz musician to play classical music—a seeming trespass that caused bewilderment and concern among the faithful of both persuasions. His image gradually changed from severity (rimless glasses, patent-leather hair, business suits) to geniality (horn-rims, tousled hair, tweed jackets). He disappeared into his own legend, which decreed that he was a monster—a penny-pinching, thoughtless martinet, who bullied his sidemen and hogged the solo space. It was often said after he reached fifty that his abilities had declined. Yet, however uneven he may occasionally have sounded (he was plagued by depressions and back problems), he played almost as well at the end of his career as he had at the beginning.

But Benny died in June, at the age of seventy-seven, and perhaps it is time to tally the results. There were a lot of Benny Goodmans: the pioneer jazz virtuoso who made the clarinet as important a solo instrument as the trumpet was in the thirties; the unwitting and perhaps unwilling musical evangelist who, in 1935, introduced the young of this country to their own great native music, aerating their Depression lives and making them dance like Shakers; the tough Chicago boy who married a Vanderbilt; and the second-generation Russian Jew who became one of the most famous of the many Russian Jews who have graced American music for the greater part of this century.

Goodman was the ninth of twelve children. His father worked in the stockyards, and his mother was illiterate. He studied with the classical clarinetist Franz Schoepp, who also taught Jimmy Noone and Buster Bailey. He joined the musicians' union when he was thirteen and Ben Pollack's band when he was sixteen. He worked for Pollack on and off from 1925 to 1929, in company with Glenn Miller, Jack Teagarden, Bud Freeman, and Jimmy McPartland. From 1929 to 1934, when he formed his first big band, he scuffled in New York, playing in Broadway pit bands and doing radio shows, and recording with everyone from Bessie Smith to Enrique Madriguera and Ruth Etting. In 1934, his band became one of three bands chosen to play on a weekly three-hour NBC program called "Let's Dance." "If anyone were to ask what was the biggest thing that has ever happened to me," Goodman once said, "landing a place on that show was it." A year later, at the behest of his booker, Willard Alexander, he took his band on the road. They played Pittsburgh, Milwaukee, Denver, Salt Lake City, and San Francisco without much success. But when they got to Sweet's Ballroom, in Oakland, the NBC show had begun to take effect, and there were lines around the block, and it was the same at the Palomar, in Los Angeles, where they were held over for a month. They stopped at the Congress Hotel, in Chicago, on their way east, and stayed six months. They had the country jumping. Back in New York, they had a long engagement at the Hotel Pennsylvania, then went west again to do the Palomar and make a movie. They were at the Pennsylvania in the fall of 1936, and during the winter they made their uproarious appearance at the Paramount Theatre; the audiences, thoroughly worked over by Goodman's recordings and almost daily radio broadcasts, danced in the aisles, stood on their seats, and sometimes stayed through all five shows. In January of 1938, Goodman reached an apogee when, still the unwitting ground-breaker, he gave his famous Carnegie Hall concert. (It was a press agent's idea.) With the exception of Jess Stacy's "Sing, Sing, Sing" solo, the evening was not musically prepossessing, but the concert gave jazz a stature it had not had before.

By this time, the band included the trumpeters Ziggy Elman and Harry James, the pianist Jess Stacy, the drummer Gene Krupa, and the small-group specialists—the pianist Teddy Wilson and the vibraphonist, drummer, and singer Lionel Hampton. The personnel of Goodman's bands rarely remained fixed for more than a week. He constantly fired musicians, or they quit, offended by his capricious behavior. He had a particularly hard time with drummers. Here is an incomplete list of the drummers, stars and journeymen, who passed through his bands between the mid-thirties and the mid-forties: Sammy Weiss, Gene Krupa, Lionel Hampton, Dave Tough, Buddy Schutz, Nick Fatool, Harry Jaeger, Jo Jones, J. C. Heard, Sidney Catlett, Ralph Collier, Alvin Stoller, Howard Davis, Morey Feld, Buddy Rich, Louis Bellson, Lou Fromm, Tom Romersa, Don Lamond, and Cozy Cole. Duke Ellington used Sonny Greer from the mid-twenties to 1951.

For whatever reasons—perhaps it was an unconscious wish to keep the competition down within his band—Goodman never hired any first-rate trombonists or tenor saxophonists in the thirties. (Goodman could be inscrutable. In 1938, he borrowed Lester Young from Count Basie for a recording date, and in the course of six numbers gave Young just one eight-bar solo.)This most famous of the Goodman bands was sandwiched between the frenetic trumpet playing of Elman and James and the heavy, here-we-go-down-the-pike drumming of Gene Krupa, with Goodman as its main soloist. The band never had the subtlety of Basie and Ellington and Andy Kirk. It was a very white band, and relied on bravado and muscle. It tended to shout when it played "Bugle Call Rag" and "King Porter Stomp," and to breathe heavily in slow ballads.

Goodman's next and most important band was altogether different. It began to take shape in the late thirties, after James and Krupa departed and Goodman switched from Victor to Columbia. He hired the lead trumpeter Jimmy Maxwell and, in the next year or two, the trumpeters Cootie Williams (from Ellington) and Billy Butterfield (from Artie Shaw), the guitarist Charlie Christian, the trombonist Lou McGarity, the pianist Mel Powell, and, in 1941, the bassist John Simmons and the drummer Sid Catlett. But this graceful band didn't last long. Christian fell ill and died, Simmons and Williams left, Catlett was fired, Billy Butterfield went with Les Brown, and Mel Powell was drafted. The musicians'-union recording ban, which went into effect in the summer of 1942 and lasted almost two years, was the final stroke. Toying occasionally with bebop, which he never liked much, Goodman had a series of middling bands in the late forties. He had, by then, made close to a hundred recordings with his small groups, many of them among the finest of all jazz records. Then, crippled by the popularity of singers and by a thirty-percent wartime entertainment tax, the big bands began to fail, and in 1948 Goodman gave up his band. The most successful part of his career was over; it had lasted just thirteen years. For the rest of his life, he put together a seemingly endless succession of big and small bands for State Department tours, for night-club gigs and television shows, for recording sessions, and even for a fortieth-anniversary celebration of his Carnegie Hall concert. This reconstituted evening remains vivid only because he had three pianists shuttling on- and offstage (Jimmy Rowles, John Bunch, Mary Lou Williams), a girl singer he had first heard a week or so before, and a finale in which he sat down and soloed with his feet up on one end of Lionel Hampton's vibraphone.

Goodman played a demanding instrument with almost unfailing beauty for fifty years—an extraordinary stretch, unmatched by any other jazz musician. Buddy DeFranco once explained why the clarinet is hard to play: "The clarinet's three registers—chalumeau, middle, and altissimo—are built in twelfths. If you press the octave key on a saxophone, you go up or down an octave, but on a clarinet you go twelve tones—from, say, low F to middle C. Saxophones have pads over the air holes. When you press a key, the pad closes the hole and you get a note. Clarinets have seven tone holes and no pads, and you have to close them with the ends of your fingers. So you have to have absolute finger control. If any air escapes, you get a terrible squeak or no note at all. Going from the middle register of the clarinet to the altissimo is very awkward because the fingering changes completely. That's the reason so many clarinetists seem to lose control when they go into the top register, why they tend to shriek." Goodman had a full, even tone in all three registers. But it never got in the way of his playing. It never came first, as it often did in the work of Pee Wee Russell and Edmond Hall and Irving Fazola. He was a melodic improviser, and his attack—the snapping runs, the quick, almost epigrammatic melodies, the carefully screened emotion, the rhythmic surefootedness—invariably implied that he knew where his solo would land long before it got there. Goodman's style changed little. In the thirties and the early forties, he would occasionally growl and carry on, but later he abandoned such emotional yawing and became almost academic. After he married gentry and became a Connecticut gentleman, his playing always had a press.

Sidney Catlett joined Benny Goodman early in June of 1941 and was fired in October. His place was taken by a mediocre drummer named Ralph Collier. When Goodman was asked many years later why he had done something similar to Toscanini's firing Vladimir Horowitz, he said, "It's always been one of my enigmas—drummers." The band appeared that summer at the Steel Pier, in Atlantic City, at the Hotel Sherman, in Chicago, and at Frank Dailey's Meadowbrook, in Cedar Grove, New Jersey. It broadcast almost every night, and it went into the recording studios in Chicago and New York seven or eight times. From all indications, Catlett, who suddenly found himself in the challenging and auspicious position of being the first black drummer ever hired full time by a white big band, behaved with his customary tact, taste, and brilliance.

Here is what Mel Powell, now a classical composer and professor of music, said of Catlett the other day: "I always thought that this giant of a man had no peer as a percussionist. After all, he was playing on nothing but a set of traps—a snare drum, a couple of tom-toms, a bass drum, and some cymbals. Yet he invariably sounded as if he were playing delicately tuned drums.

Where he hit his snare with his stick, how hard he hit it, where and how he hit his cymbals and tom-toms—all these things transformed ordinary sounds into pitches that matched and enhanced what he heard around him. His sensitivity and delicacy of ear were extraordinary. So was his time. He'd nail the band into the tempo with such power *and* gentleness that one night I was absolutely transported by what he was doing. Watching him lift and carry us, I took my hands off the keyboard and missed the beginning of a solo. I don't think I have ever been more awed by a musical performance. Sid's personality reflected his playing. He was lovable and loving. He was gentle. He was compassionate and concerned. He was also vulnerable. I saw tears in his eyes the night he was told, just after he'd joined the band, that his uniform wasn't ready yet, that he'd have to play in his street clothes, and so—to him—look unfinished. He had a wonderful sense of humor, and, among other things, he liked to take off black stereotypes. He had never flown—in fact, he had carefully avoided flying. But the only way to get to a gig we had in Canada was by plane. Sid asked to sit next to me, and when they were starting to rev the engines one of the boys in the band called out, 'Hey! What's that weird noise in the engines?' Sid turned to me and rolled his eyes and said, 'Oh, merciful God!' It was flawless Stepin Fetchit—and it almost hid his fear. I have never been able to figure out why Benny fired Sid. All that comes to mind is that Benny was not a follower and neither was Sid. But Benny was the boss."

Catlett had spent his career in the big black bands of Benny Carter, Rex Stewart, Fletcher Henderson, Don Redman, and Louis Armstrong, and the job with Goodman put him squarely before the white public. It also put him in tacit competition with the celebrated Gene Krupa, who had left Goodman three years earlier to start his own big band. Catlett was thirty-one years old and at the height of his powers. Goodman's dismissal must have stunned him, but it didn't derail him. He returned briefly to Louis Armstrong's unpressed big band and then went with Teddy Wilson's masterly sextet at Café Society Uptown. He was the only drummer at the Metropolitan Opera House concert in January of 1944. (Those present were winners of an *Esquire* jazz poll, and they included Armstrong, Art Tatum, Billie Holiday, Red Norvo, Mildred Bailey, Teddy Wilson, Jack Teagarden, Coleman Hawkins, Roy Eldridge, Lionel Hampton, and Oscar Pettiford.) He had his own small groups in the mid-forties, and he recorded with everyone from Eddie Condon to Duke Ellington to Lester Young to Dizzy Gillespie. In 1946, he became an original member of Louis Armstrong's All Stars. A heart attack in 1949 slowed him down—but not enough—and he died on Easter Sunday in 1951.

Catlett sounds relatively subdued on the eighteen or so studio recordings that he made with Goodman. Recording engineers, still using jumpy pre-tape equipment, were wary of drummers, and often placed them at the back of the studio. And Goodman, the perfectionist, tended to frown on any sort of inspirational waywardness when he recorded. But now, with the release of

"Benny and Sid 'Roll 'Em'," it is at last clear how Catlett really sounded with Goodman. He drove the band (and Goodman) almost unmercifully, and he demonstrated once and for all how to play big-band drums. The recording consists of twenty-five air checks (one is made up of snippets of "Roll 'Em" taken from four different broadcasts) recorded between July 12 and October 8, 1941. The broadcasts were recorded by a Denver fan and by the New York collector Jerry Newman. The record was produced by Jerry Valburn, who, with the help of Jack Towers and John T. Gill, has very nearly restored the recordings to what they must have sounded like on a decent radio. The selections include old Goodman material ("Sing, Sing, Sing" and "Ida"), numbers made popular by other bands ("Flying Home," "Tuesday at Ten," "Concerto for Cootie," "One O'clock Jump"), and tunes that Goodman either had recently recorded or was getting ready to record ("A Smooth One," "Benny Rides Again," "The Count," "The Earl," "Pound Ridge," "Clarinet à la King," and "Roll 'Em"). The Goodman band was primarily an ensemble group with one principal soloist—its leader. Other soloists (in order of space given them) were Cootie Williams, Lou McGarity, Vido Musso, Billy Butterfield, and Catlett, who was mainly allotted two-and four-bar breaks. Catlett, though never obtrusive, is everywhere—almost tilting the band on the first "The Earl" and the first "Benny Rides Again"; using luxurious press rolls behind Williams on a languorous, dreaming "Concerto for Cootie"; using three perfectly placed tomtom beats on the final bridge of "The Birth of the Blues"; driving Goodman very hard with his tomtoms on a fast "Sing, Sing, Sing"; and dropping, like mots, his immaculate and unique rim shots. Catlett clearly had a strange effect on Goodman, who solos at great length throughout the recording. The precise, parsed Goodman of the studio recordings is nowhere to be heard. This Goodman is wild and woolly, and even experimental (the first chorus of "Pound Ridge"). Sometimes, perhaps driven beyond his powers, he is forced and empty. Catlett was over-qualified.

## From Joplin to Goodman, and Slightly Beyond

*Tuesday*

The 92nd Street Y's second annual mini-festival Jazz in July began tonight in Kaufmann Concert Hall. The advance material has been somewhat overwrought. A concert built around three clarinettists is called "Licorice Shticks," and an evening of jazz-influenced classical music is "Blazing Fiddles: Symphonic Flirtations with Jazz." The concert tonight involved ragtime and the pianist Max Morath, who was the master of ceremonies. Morath is a ragtime historian who likes to make jokes about the music, and whenever he was onstage there was a feeling that someone would run out and hold up a laugh card. But the music survived the gags, thanks to the pianist-bandleader-composer Dick Hyman, who is the artistic director of the festival and also played tonight, and to the tubist Harvey Phillips, who conducted the first-rate eighteen-piece 92nd Street Ragtime Concert Band. (Its members, tuned to the general jocularity, had on bow ties and red silk vests.) Included in the band were the trumpeter Joe Wilder, the trombonists Wayne André and George Masso, the clarinet-tist Phil Bodner, the banjoist and guitarist Howard Alden, and the drummer Ron Traxler. The best numbers were James Scott's "Grace and Beauty," Joseph Lamb's "Ragtime Nightingale," Scott Joplin's "Maple Leaf Rag," and Adaline Shepherd's "Pickles and Peppers," which brought much merri-ment from Morath over the fact that it was used as a campaign tune by William Jennings Bryan when he lost the Presidential election to William Howard Taft. The evening wandered chronologically. Hyman and the band played orchestrations of Jelly Roll Morton's "Grandpa's Spells" and "The Pearls," which revealed how close Morton's music was to ragtime, and Hyman played a solo version of Morton's numbing "Finger Buster," a dis-play piece Morton used to cow competitors with. Phillips also did the "Trombone Blues," a "Walkaround" played by circus bands when acts were being changed. He closed the evening with a ringing "Stars and Stripes For-ever," after which the musicians waved tiny American flags and looked sheepish. Earlier, the singer Carrie Smith, who likes to re-create Bessie Smith, did half a dozen red-hot-mama numbers, including "After You've Gone," "Ja-Da," and "Beale Street blues."

The Y festival, it should be pointed out, is self-limiting. Dick Hyman told Jon Pareles in today's *Times*, "Until bebop . . . jazz still played by the rules of songs. It was improvisations on themes people knew, and people could pick up on them, even if they had never thought songs could be done this way. In the newer music, you don't quite know what's going on until you learn the new language—it's a different repertory, a different length of solos and a dif-ferent goal in performance. . . . Not to be too blunt, but the music takes itself too seriously now. . . . What this festival is not about is music that is somber, perplexing, hostile or boring. It's a festival of hot jazz." In short, a paean to old practices, old principles, old joys.

*Wednesday*

Dick Hyman put together a model jazz concert tonight. Here is how the first half went: The house band for the evening—Joe Wilder, the tenor saxophonists Buddy Tate and Al Cohn, the trombonist Al Grey, the pianists Derek Smith and Hyman, the bassist Milt Hinton, and the drummer Butch Miles—played a medium-tempo "Perdido." Wilder and Cohn disappeared, and Grey and Tate did a fast "Tangerine." Carrie Smith, backed by Hyman, Hinton, Miles, Wilder, and Cohn, sang "You've Changed" and an Alberta Hunter blues. Hinton played an unaccompanied solo on "Jericho." Tate offered "Polka Dots and

Moonbeams," and Hyman and Smith did unaccompanied duets on "Gravy Waltz," a gospel-like number by the bassist Ray Brown, and on Jerome Kern's "All the Things You Are." Grey appeared with the rhythm section for a very slow "Summertime." This half of the concert was closed by Tate and Cohn, who hustled through a fast Count Basie number and were joined in the last chorus by Wilder and Grey.

The rest of the evening had even more variety. The tap dancers Honi Coles, Bubber Gaines, and Charles (Cookie) Cook did half a dozen numbers. Then Joe Wilder, on flugelhorn, played two a-cappella choruses of "Willow Weep for Me." Cohn and Derek Smith each had a solo excursion, and Carrie Smith returned for the last three numbers of the concert, in company with the whole band, both pianists presiding.

## Thursday

Vince Giordano and his various bands have been expertly reproducing the jazz of the twenties and thirties for over ten years, and tonight they gave another exhibition of how to do jazz repertory. In the course of fifteen numbers, the band re-created Bix Beiderbecke as he was with the Wolverines, with Jean Goldkette, with Frankie Trumbauer, with Paul Whiteman, and with his own groups. The band included two trumpets, trombone, three reeds, piano, banjo, guitar, drums, violin, a singer, and the leader on string bass, tuba, bass saxophone, and a Bing Crosby vocal, and it swung without being quaint (a common fault among the pioneer repertory groups of ten or fifteen years ago) or too free (young repertory musicians are apt to unconsciously use rhythmic devices unknown in the twenties and thirties). The ensembles, with their intricate saxophone writing and staccato brass, were never stilted, and neither were the solos. Bill Challis's complex, multilayered arrangements ("Clarinet Marmalade," "Lonely Melody," " 'Taint So Honey, 'Taint So") never faltered, and Fud Livingston's 1927 arrangement of his "Humpty Dumpy" was a revelation—its fresh, winding harmonies and voicings presaged the Ellington of the thirties. Beiderbecke's solos were played by Randy Sandke, a trumpeter who has digested the styles of the twenties, thirties, and forties. Beiderbecke has been widely imitated, and among his most persuasive admirers have been Jimmy McPartland, Red Nichols, and the early Bobby Hackett. At first, Sandke's tone was not quite belling enough, and he played too far behind the beat. But halfway through he began punching out his notes and making his tone linger. Dick Hyman played Beiderbecke's "In a Mist" with the seeming casualness that Beiderbecke himself, a come-as-you-are pianist, might have displayed.

During the second part of the evening, Hyman and the violinist Stan Kurtis redid three of the small-band numbers that Joe Venuti recorded in the late twenties and early thirties—"The Wild Dog," "Four String Joe," "Satan's Holiday." Kurtis caught Venuti's sound and came close to his insuperable swing, and all that was missing was the guitar and the bass saxophone that Venuti used on some of his original recordings. The ten final numbers of the concert were given over to a Jelly Roll Morton band, made up of Warren Vaché, on cornet; Phil Bodner; Jack Gale on trombone; Hyman; Major Holley on bass and tuba; Marty Grosz on banjo; and Ron Traxler. They played two of the famous 1926 Red Hot Pepper numbers, and the rest were taken from the often underrated dates Morton did after he moved from Chicago to New York in 1928. Vaché did well with Ward Pinkett's acidic trumpet, and Gale was masterly in recapturing the trombonist Geechy Fields. Bodner, doing Omer Simeon and Albert Nicholas, was uncanny—he poured and mooned and was tonally perfect.

## Tuesday

Jocularity reigned again tonight. We were offered a program of stride piano playing, and the pianists on hand—Dick Wellstood, Dick Hyman, Mike Lipskin, Ralph Sutton, Judy Carmichael, and Jay McShann—played not only as soloists and in duets but in a round robin and six strong at three pianos. (McShann did not really belong. He is a Kansas City blues pianist, and his duets with Sutton were a jarring mixture of Eastern stride and Western blues.) Wellstood and Hyman fashioned two blithe and crowded duets, the second of which, Jerome Kern's "Who," was full of echoes of the version done in 1939 on Bluebird by Frankie Newton, Pete Brown, and James P. Johnson. Mike Lipskin, who studied with Willie the Lion Smith, did four solo numbers (with Butch Miles playing over-fancy wire brushes on a snare drum set upstage front), and got the ho-ho tone of the evening going by making jokes and singing two off-key Fats Waller-type vocals that sounded more like parodies than like the tributes they were meant to be. The round robin, with Lipskin, Wellstood, and Hyman, followed. Wellstood played a fine solo rendition of "Lulu's Back in Town," and Hyman matched him with a solo "Jeepers Creepers." The Classic Jazz Quartet came on for just three numbers. These included "Happy Feet," Fats Waller's "How Can You Face Me," and the Boswell Sisters' "It's the Girl," done without a vocal. Sutton and McShann did "Lady, Be Good," and Sutton, who moves readily between ironbound stride numbers and Debussy ballads, performed by himself, and McShann sang and played a solo blues. Judy Carmichael, a young stride pianist from California, did four numbers and demonstrated a strong left hand and a mechanical, striving right hand. All the pianists appeared in the jam-session finale, and so did the Classic Jazz Quartet.

Two notes: Almost no amplification has been used during the festival (Kaufmann Hall may be the best small auditorium in New York City), and it is marvellous to hear music without distortion of any kind. We have been treated to what is well on its way toward vanishing—unadulterated human music.

Milt Hinton has taken close to thirty thousand photographs of his colleagues during his fifty-year career, and forty-five of his pictures are on display in the gallery adjacent to Kaufmann Hall. Hinton took his pictures at
rehearsals, in recording studios, onstage and backstage, on the bus, and on
the street—probably out of a need to try and slow down the fluid, evanescent
life around him. In one picture, the clarinettist Scoville Browne and the
bassists Jimmy Blanton and Al Lucas stand in front of the Hotel Braddock in
Harlem in 1940, with the twenty-two-year-old Blanton, who was already on
his brilliant way (he died two years later), in snappy chest-high, chalk-striped
trousers and a straw hat. In another, Dizzy Gillespie and Charles Mingus are
laughing uproariously at a beer stand at the 1971 Newport Jazz Festival. In
another, taken in 1967, Gene Krupa is at his drums, the handsome, flamboyant youth still visible in the middle-aged man. Again, Willie the Lion Smith
and Eubie Blake sit silently side by side, the Lion in his derby and cigar and
Blake with his oarlike hands in his lap. And, finally, Tyree Glenn and Chu
Berry, Hinton's old mates in the Cab Calloway band of the early forties,
stand in their overcoats beneath a sign reading "Hamburgers. Hot Dogs.
Lunches. For Colored Only."

*Wednesday*

"Licorice Shticks" was begun by Kenny Davern, accompanied by Milt Hinton, Howard Alden, Dick Hyman,
and Butch Miles. Davern came up in the early sixties, during the last days of
the Condon gang, and he has worked frequently with Dick Wellstood and
Bob Wilber. Emotion governs his style. He did a medium-tempo "Linger
Awhile," a very slow, almost creepy "Summertime," and a medium "Wrap
Your Troubles in Dreams," and was joined by the Belgian harmonica player
and composer Toots Thielemans for a slow blues, which was distinguished
by Alden's solo—particularly his ringing third chorus. Davern closed with a
jigging "Jazz Me Blues." Peanuts Hucko, a veteran of the big bands, the
Condon gang, the studios, and the Louis Armstrong All Stars, is possibly the
best of Benny Goodman's imitators, and he did three gleaming Goodman
numbers, the last (with Thielemans) an excited, pressing version of Goodman's old flag-waver "The World Is Waiting for the Sunrise." The festival
poked its nose carefully into modern times in the person of the clarinettist
Eddie Daniels, a Juilliard graduate who worked in the sixties and seventies
with the Thad Jones–Mel Lewis band and is stylistically in the mode of
Sonny Rollins and John Coltrane. He played three partly written, rather
monotonous numbers that moved between jazz and classical music ("Alone
Together," Gershwin's Second Prelude, and a C.P.E. Bach solfeggietto),
and a very fast "I Want to Be Happy," on which he and Milt Hinton played
a duet. In the evening's last number, the three clarinettists plus Thielemans
did a rummaging, rampaging "Sheik of Araby."

*Thursday*

It is strange that jazz and classical music got in each other's hair for so long—the one sneering at the old bore and the other at the messy upstart. Improvisation was part of European formal music well into the nineteenth century, and virtuosity has long been one of its guidons. And jazz musicians were quick to absorb European harmonic methods and forms. European composers were beguiled by jazz rhythms, and jazz musicians readily admired the pastels of Debussy and Ravel. Whether classical composers were much influenced by jazz when it first became widespread has never been clear, and it wasn't any clearer after tonight's attractive concert, the last of the festival. A twenty-nine-piece orchestra, under the direction of Maurice Peress, played seven formal compositions (one was an excerpt) supposedly influenced by jazz. Five were written in the twenties, when jazz began to take hold, one in the thirties, and one just ten years ago. The most impressive of the early pieces were George Antheil's "A Jazz Symphony" (1925) and James P. Johnson's "Yamekraw: A Negro Rhapsody" (1927). Antheil's composition boils with Stravinsky dissonances and has the staccato weight of Soviet industrial music. There are jazz touches—a sounded regular beat, a wa-wa trumpet solo over a ground bass, and crashing piano interludes (played by Ivan Davis) that predict the Cecil Taylor of forty years later. The composition ends, however, with a heady, swirling waltz—the lady of the house sweeping out the poker players at one in the morning. Johnson's piece, probably written in reaction to Gershwin's "Rhapsody in Blue" (the first formal piece to truly reflect jazz), is genteel and primitive and sentimental. There is a stride-piano passage (Dick Hyman was on piano) and a flash of boogie-woogie and several choruses of the blues, swathed in strings. It is a timid, inert piece. Bohuslav Martinu's short "Le Jazz" (1928) resembles a Paul Whiteman orchestration of the period, and a suite from Darius Milhaud's ballet "La Création du Monde" (1923) resembled Debussy and had a long, melancholy alto-saxophone solo (played smoothly by Jack Kripl) that had a peculiar and oblique jazz feeling—almost akin to one of Charles Mingus's meditations. Hyman appeared in his own "Ragtime Fantasy," for piano and orchestra (1976), a sedate and polished reflection of that elegant music which came to life in a rattling Baby Dodds-style drum passage and in direct ragtime allusions by the pianist. The most unusual selection of the evening was John Alden Carpenter's "Krazy Kat," in which the orchestra played melodic string passages while George Herriman's "Krazy Kat" cartoons were shown on a screen at the back of the stage and a narration was read by June Le Bell. (The narration and the music worked at cross-purposes.) It was good to see Herriman's surreal drawings blown up, but the music had little or nothing to do with jazz. The program was closed by Gershwin's " 'I Got Rhythm' Variations" (1934). The orchestra and the piano (played by Ivan Davis) exchanged fragmented variations on Gershwin's famous song (where would bebop have been without it?), and there were suggestions—they resound all through Gershwin's later orchestral works—of "Rhapsody in Blue."

# 1987

## The Keynotes

Supervising jazz recordings in the days of the 78-r.p.m. recording was delicate and demanding. The A&R (artists and repertoire) man, as the recording director is called, was responsible for choosing congenial musicians, for getting them into the studio on time, for helping them pick apposite material, for somehow softening the frigid atmosphere of most recording studios, for making the musicians' improvisations fit the three- or five-minute time limit of the 78 without deflating them, and, most difficult of all, for deciding immediately just how good a take was. One of the sharpest of the old A&R men was Harry Lim, a Dutch-Javanese jazz fan and organizer of jam sessions in Chicago and New York, who, in the mid-forties, supervised fifty or so small-band sessions for the Keynote label, nearly a third of which are among the best of all jazz recordings. (Keynote, begun in 1940 by Eric Bernay as a left-wing folk-music operation, became in Lim's hands the equal of such other pioneer independent jazz labels as Milt Gabler's Comodore and Alfred Lion's Blue Note.) All but two or three of Lim's classic sessions were done in 1944, when he was in his mid-twenties. Small-band swing had suddenly risen to a kind of pre-bebop climax, and recording companies were frenetically attempting to fill the vacuum left by the just ended recording ban. Lim directed no fewer than twenty-one sessions between the end of 1943 and the end of 1944, five of them in a two-week burst in late spring. He had an unerring and daring sense of whom to record and in what combinations. He put Lester Young, who was in loose, superlative form, with the sparkling, chameleon pianist Johnny Guarnieri (who could paraphrase Teddy Wilson, Count Basie, and Fats Waller), the humming bassist Slam Stewart, and Big Sid Catlett. He put three trumpeters (Roy Eldridge, Joe Thomas, Emmett Berry), four trombonists (Benny Morton, Vic Dickenson, Bill Harris, Claude Jones), and four saxophonists (Coleman Hawkins, Tab Smith, Don Byas, Harry Carney) with rhythm sections. He put Coleman Hawkins and Teddy Wilson together four times (both were at their most commanding), and mixed them, on two of the sessions, with either Roy Eldridge or Buck Clayton. He put Joe Thomas with the ex-Lunceford trombonist Trummy Young and with the still imperious Earl Hines. He turned eight times to Thomas, mixing him also with the huge, jumping alto saxophonist Pete Brown, with Red Norvo and Vic Dickenson, and with Jack Teagarden and the pianist Herman Chittison. He used small groups from the big bands of Cab Calloway,

Count Basie, Duke Ellington, and Woody Herman. The Basie session turned out to be the best small-band date the pianist ever made. Lim went West and recorded Nat Cole and Benny Carter. He recorded George Barnes' sleek sextet in Chicago and the New Orleans clarinetist Irving Fazola.

Very little that Lim did in 1944 went wrong, but early in 1945 he began to change direction. Always attentive to little-known players, he became obsessed by them. He recorded saxophonists like Herbie Haymer and Babe Russin and Corky Corcoran, and trumpeters like Clyde Hurley and Manny Klein and Dick Cathcart. He used pianists like Bernie Leighton and Tommy Todd and Skitch Henderson. He made his first second-rate recordings. There were notable exceptions: the Nat Cole date; a couple of sessions with the trombonist Bill Harris; Joe Thomas's elegant "Black Butterfly" session; and Lennie Tristano's first recording date under his own name. In 1946, the label got into financial difficulties, and the next year Lim quit, leaving his invaluable masters behind. Keynote was bought by Mercury Records, which in time was absorbed by Phonogram, which became PolyGram. Mercury reissued some of the Keynotes in the fifties, and some came out on the Trip label in the seventies. Then, for a long time, nothing happened, and it began to seem that the great early Keynotes, like the great early Blue Notes, had disappeared.

But now the Japanese jazz expert Kioshi Koyama, working in conjunction with PolyGram and with the Japanese branch of Phonogram, has brought forth the entire Keynote catalogue in a boxed set of twenty-one LPs, as "The Complete Keynote Collection." The reissue includes almost three hundred and fifty performances, a third of them alternate takes and previously unreleased masters. The first twelve LPs, which go through 1944, are essential, and the bright spots carry most of the remainder. Here are four classic numbers from the early sessions. The first is the fast blues "Afternoon of a Basie-ite," recorded on December 28, 1943, by the Lester Young Quartet. Johnny Guarnieri, doing his Basie, plays three choruses, backed by tight, pushing Catlett high-hat. (High-hat of this kind is invariably associated with Jo Jones, but Catlett recorded some in 1933, when Jones was still to be heard from.) Young takes five choruses, using every swinging trick he knew: honks; lazy nasal figures; marvellous short, tucking runs; half-time swoops. Catlett backs him with a panoply of snare and bass-drum accents that the early bebop drummers must have listened to. Slam Stewart appears for two choruses, and on the first of the two takes of the number Guarnieri spices Stewart's solo with some wild upper-register figures. Catlett solos for one chorus, using his high hat and snare on the first take and mainly snare figures on the second. Both solos crackle and jump. Young returns for two more choruses, and the number ends. Young and Catlett recorded together only twice, which is a pity. They worked like birds and air.

The second number, recorded a month later, is "Fiesta in Brass," by Little Jazz and His Trumpet Ensemble—Eldridge, Thomas, and Emmett

Berry, joined by Guarnieri, Israel Crosby on bass, and Cozy Cole on drums. It is a study in brass textures. Eldridge, though muted, is rough-toned and hurrying; Berry is querulous but patient; the gentle Thomas soars and ponders. The number is a medium blues, and consists of identical opening-and-closing unison annunciatory ensembles enclosing two-chorus solos by Guarnieri, again doing his Basie, and Eldridge, Thomas, and Berry. Thomas, with his ballooning tone and his exquisite choice of notes, takes the honors.

The third and fourth numbers are part of the Joe Thomas–Trummy Young–Coleman Hawkins–Earl Hines date, on February 22, 1944. Sam Coslow's "Just One More Chance" is built around Hawkins, who plays a chorus of embellished melody (backed by lovely ascending organ chords), gives way to a chorus of Earl Hines (with a bridge by the guitarist Teddy Walters), and returns for a closing twenty-four bars of improvisation. There are two takes, and both match the best of Hawkins' recorded ballads. He sounds as though he had finally decided to wipe out all those impinging Lester Youngs and Ben Websters and Don Byases with one majestic, obliterating number. His tone is enormous, his vibrato surging. He plays with power and delicacy and lyricism. "Thru' for the Night" is the fourth number. Its attractive melody, written by Trummy Young, is based on "Honeysuckle Rose." The band does the melody in a swinging, medium-slow tempo, with Hines providing icing. Then, cushioned on a repeat of the melody, he splits a chorus with Walters. Hines' solo is full of tremolos and glisses and runs, topped by upper-register diamonds. His dynamics are the breezes presaging a storm. Thomas takes an empyrean half chorus, and Trummy Young, very delicate and nasal, takes the other half. Hawkins plays twenty-four resounding bars, and there are eight measures of closing ensemble.

## Traps, the Drum Wonder

When Buddy Rich first recorded his "West Side Story" medley, late in 1966, his solo, surrounded by eight minutes of instrumental framework, lasted just under two minutes. When he made what turned out to be his final recording of the number, in April of 1985—Rich died early this spring, at the age of sixty-nine—he took two solos, the first four minutes long, and the second six minutes long. His life—though dogged by chronic heart trouble, by financial difficulties, by a wild temper, and by a boundless ego—seemed, like his solos, to gain momentum. The pianist Mel Powell appeared with Rich on a jazz cruise in the fall of 1986. "He was playing superbly," Powell said recently. "He was relaxed, and not in a show-business mood. He sounded sturdy but subtle. Working with just small groups and without any pressures must have been a joy to him. He didn't much want to take solos, and when I gave him the signal for four-bar exchanges he barely agreed. His playing demonstrated what it might have been like throughout his career if he had been able more often to play in such convivial, low-key situations. Working with big bands was a kind of theatre that he both loved and loathed and never got free of. He looked marvellous on the cruise. His hair was whitish, but he had a Palm Springs tan, and there wasn't a wrinkle in his face. We had a kidding relationship, and when I asked him how he managed to keep so well he said, 'By staying on the road,' which is indeed where he spent most of his life."

Rich was born in Brooklyn, and he had two sisters and a brother. His parents were in vaudeville. He once described his mother as "a singer and a heavy-made woman and very pretty," and he went on to say, "My father was a soft-shoe dancer and a blackface comedian. He was strong and nice-looking and had a great sense of humor. But when you stepped out of line you got a shot in the mouth and that straightened you out." Rich's parents brought him into their act when he was a toddler, and at the age of seven he travelled around the world as Traps, the Drum Wonder. For a time, in the early thirties, he was making a thousand dollars a week singing, dancing, and drumming, and was the second-highest-paid child star, after Jackie Coogan. But in 1936, to his father's chagrin, he turned his back on vaudeville. The clarinettist Joe Marsala hired him, and, two years later, gave him the space on "Jim Jam Stomp" for his first recorded drum solo, a seventeen-second explosion—on snare, snare rims, woodblock, cowbell, and bass drum—that must have turned heads. In 1938, Rich took a job with Bunny Berigan's big band, then he moved on to Artie Shaw and, later, to Tommy Dorsey. He formed his own big band in the mid-forties, but that was a shaky time for big hands, and it went under. During the next twenty years, he patched together a career with Jazz at the Philharmonic, with Harry James' and Les Brown's big bands, and with various small groups. He formed another big band in 1966, and he kept it off and on until he died.

New York was full of great drummers when Rich came up. He listened to Tony Briglia with the Casa Loma band, to O'Neil Spencer, to Dave Tough, to Lester Young's brother Lee, to Sidney Catlett, to Gene Krupa, to the singer and drummer Leo Watson, and, above all, to Chick Webb, the tiny, amazing hunchbacked drummer from Baltimore. (With the exception of Catlett, who was well over six feet, all the master swing drummers were small. Napoleons of Noise, a contemporary dubbed them.) Webb's driving, on-the-beat snare-drum figures reappeared again and again in Rich's solos. Though totally untrained, Rich became a virtuoso and, like most virtuosos, he became a captive of his technique. His technique was his style, for he had no style in the conventional sense. He could play what amounted to a single-stroke roll with one hand, and he could very nearly do the same thing with one foot, on the pedal of his bass drum. He could move between his tom-toms and his snare drum and his cymbals with such speed that he gave the impression he was playing simultaneously on three different parts of his set. His long solos were not rhythmic investigations as much as avalanches—he wanted to bury his listeners with his brilliance, with crushing rolls and rimshots, with round-the-set rocketry and bass-drum thunder. Occasionally, he relented. He would take a funny wire-brush solo, or fool around a long time on his cymbals. That's what he does through much of his second solo in his 1985 "West Side Story" recording. He begins with a hard right-and-left Chick Webb figure on his snare, and switches to his cymbals (he was using four, plus his high-hat), making breeze noises, chime sounds, all the while growing softer and softer. Then he moves to his snare rims for a ticking mile-a-minute roll, carries the roll to his closed high-hat, inserts a couple of offbeat rimshots on his snare and a tom-tom, drops some jolting bass-drum bombs, returns to his cymbals, rolls again on his rims, and settles onto his snare for some brokenfield figures, interspersed with cymbal splashes and bass-drum accents. He closes with one of his great showoff feats: a single-stroke roll, gradually slowed down to alternate individual strokes, then just as gradually speeded up until it returns to a full, creamy roll. He mixes in his cymbals and his bass drum and, sharply increasing the volume on his snare drum, brings the solo to a climax.

Rich did not get a particularly attractive timbre on his drums—they always sounded gray and matter-of-fact. Nor did he have much taste. He kept excellent time behind whomever he was accompanying, but how he did his accompanying—whether to back a trombonist with a ride cymbal or a high hat, say—didn't seem to matter to him. Instead of carrying a band from within, in the subtle, insinuating manner of Webb and Tough and Catlett, he pushed it before him, like a man throwing someone out of his house. And it was never certain—except in his sometimes exhilarating four- and eight-bar breaks—that he could swing. He had a metronomic quality—an inability to move his time back and forth within a beat. There are several passages in the two long solos that Catlett took during Louis Armstrong's Symphony Hall concert in 1947 ("Satchmo at Symphony Hall") which are so rhythmically infectious they make you dance. Rich never did that; he wowed you but rarely moved you.

Rich was compact and slightly below medium height. He had close-cropped hair, battered-handsome looks, and what he would have described as a Charlie Glamour smile—although, dead serious on the stand, he did not often show it when he played. He was a sharp dresser, and he liked to drive fast. He was sardonic and unpredictable, and he affected a slightly belligerent air. He had a caustic show-biz wit; when he didn't strain, he could hold his own with Johnny Carson. As a bandleader, he was something of a martinet. He was not a blowhard, but he did not have any false modesty. He once said, "I'm told I'm not humble, but who is? I remember being interviewed by a college kid once, and he said 'Mr. Rich, who is the greatest drummer in the world?' and I said 'I am.' He laughed, and said 'No, really, Mr. Rich, who do you consider the greatest drummer alive?' I said 'Me. It's a fact.' He couldn't get over it. But why go through that humble bit? Look at Ted Williams—straight ahead, no tipping of his cap when he belted one out of the park."

Rich demonstrated where he was headed when he was with Artie Shaw's band. Shaw said of him not long ago, "When Buddy came in the band, in 1939, he couldn't read music—and, for that matter, I don't think he could read any better at the end of his life. I told him that some of our arrangements were pretty complex. He asked me if he could sit out front a couple of nights and learn the arrangements. He did, and said he was ready, and he was—amazingly so. He was an amusing, ebullient kid, and sometimes he'd get so excited when he was playing that he'd yell and rush the beat. Near the end of the year he was with the band, he began going off on his own in his playing, doing things that were good for him but not for the band. I sat him down and told him what he had begun doing, and not long after we parted amicably. He went with Tommy Dorsey, which was just right, because Tommy had a big show band. The vitality and exuberance that poured out of Buddy were endless."

Virtuosos share one nightmare. "When I think that I can't play the way I want to play," Rich once said, "I'll hang up my sticks. That'll be it. There'd be nothing more horrible than to hear some guy say, 'Poor Buddy Rich, he doesn't have it anymore.' " He needn't have worried.

## John Hammond and Dick Wellstood

With his customary princely aplomb, John Hammond wrote in his autobiography, *John Hammond on Record*, "Death has never frightened me. I have led a full life, one I have enjoyed, and when it ends it ends." It did early this summer, when he was in his seventy-seventh year. Although he was slowed by repeated heart attacks, Hammond never stopped going. He explained in his autobiography what drove him: "It will always be difficult for me to sit still, to wait a moment or a day before setting out to discover the world all over again. I am an early riser, among the first to buy each day's *Times*, and my daily armful of new magazines is as much my trademark as my crewcut . . . This compulsion to see, to read, to hear everything as soon as possible is as strong now as it ever was, and to be the first to know—or, certainly, never the last—is vitally important to me. To allow the events of a single day to reach me second hand, to miss my morning call at the newsstand, to drive without the car radio turned on, to pass by a marquee announcing a show or a movie or a jazz player unknown to me will never be possible. I try to be careful, but I cannot stop."

Hammond was a great discoverer and champion of American musical talent. His most adventurous and influential years lasted from early in the Depression to the first of the recording bans in the forties. Here are some of the things he did during that exhilarating time: took a *mixed* band (Frankie Newton, Benny Carter, Pee Wee Russell, Fats Waller, Eddie Condon, Artie Bernstein, and Zutty Singleton) to the staid Mt. Kisco Golf and tennis Club for a 1932 Saturday-night dance; recorded such relatively unknown masters as Fletcher Henderson, Carter, Coleman Hawkins, Red Allen, Chu Berry,

Roy Eldridge, Dicky Wells, Teddy Wilson, Sidney Catlett, Benny Goodman, Red Norvo, Artie Shaw, Bud Freeman, and the boogie-woogie pianists
Meade Lux Lewis, Albert Ammons, and Peter Johnson; drove down to Kentucky (in the indomitable Hudson he used in scouring the country for talent)
to help Malcolm Cowley, Quincy Howe, Edmund Wilson, and Waldo Frank
hand out food to striking coal miners in a time when strikers and their sup-
porters were often beaten up, or even killed; tracked down an out-of-fashion
Bessie Smith in Philadelphia, brought her to New York, and gave her her last
recording session, a glorious affair in which the great singer, still in fine voice,
was backed by Newton, Goodman, Berry, and Jack Teagarden; covered two
of the Scottsboro trials in Decatur, Alabama, for *The Nation*, and joined the
board of the N.A.A.C.P. (Hammond was one of the most incisive civil liber-
tarians of his time); supervised many of the incomparable recordings Billie
Holiday made between 1935 and 1941, got the Benny Goodman band on its
feet and helped record the first Goodman Trio sides (Goodman, Teddy Wilson, Gene Krupa); put Harry James in a recording studio with Wilson,
Norvo, and the bassist John Simmons for a classic six-minute slow blues that
covered both sides of a ten-inch 78-rpm record, anticipating the spacious pastures of the LP recording; brought the Count Basie band out of Kansas City
and sent Basie on his way; gave Lester Young and Charlie Christian their first
recording dates (Young with Basie, and Christian with Goodman), débuts
that changed forever the way the tenor saxophone and the electric guitar were
played; and, in 1938 and 1939, presented the two "Spirituals to Swing" concerts at Carnegie Hall, in which he offered to the world the gospel singers sister Rosetta Tharpe and Mitchell's Christian Singers, the blues singers Sonny
Terry, Big Bill Broonzy, Ida Cox, Joe Turner, and Jimmy Rushing, the
pianists Ammons, Johnson, and Lewis, the Count Basie band, the Benny
Goodman Sextet and the Kansas City Six (in which he put Charlie Christian
and Lester Young side by side), and a kind of New Orleans band made up of
Tommy Ladnier, Sidney Bechet, and James P. Johnson. And all the while,
when he had the chance, he was tooling around in his Hudson in the Midwest
or the Deep South, searching for genius.

Hammond was distracted in the forties. He was drafted into the Army,
where he fought racial battles with various redneck superiors, and he had
personal problems. But he came storming back in the fifties with a series of
often brilliant recordings built around Vic Dickenson, Mel Powell, Ellis
Larkins, Jimmy Rushing, Jo Jones, Emmett Berry, Buck Clayton, Ruby
Braff, and Count Basie. The records, done for Vanguard and Columbia,
were distinguished not only for their music but for their natural sound and
for their pioneering use of the LP's extended time. A surprisingly different
Hammond appeared in the recording studios in the sixties and seventies. He
was still Hammond the Discoverer, but the discoveries—Aretha Franklin,
Bob Dylan, Paul Winter, Denny Zeitlin, George Benson, Bruce Springsteen—had a pop flavor. The old purist had begun doctoring his soup.

Hammond had an American patrician background and American patrician looks. His mother, Emily Vanderbilt Sloane, was a great-granddaughter of the Commodore, and his father, John Henry Hammond, was the son of a Union general. Hammond's mother was imperious, religious, philanthropic, energetic, asocial, and a de-rigueur racist. She was also extremely wealthy. His father, about whom he says comparatively little in his autobiography, did not have money but became a successful banker, lawyer, and railroad man. He was far more flexible than his wife, and, Hammond suggests, had the makings of a closet liberal. Hammond had four older sisters, one of whom, the rebellious Alice, managed to marry both a British M.P. and Benny Goodman. Hammond grew up in a lordly mansion on East Ninety-first Street, and, after Hotchkiss and a brief stint at Yale, moved to Sullivan Street, in the Village and began making jazz recordings. (He started out with a private income of twelve thousand a year, much of which went to needy musicians, to pay for recording sessions no one else would pay for, and to civil-rights causes.)

Hammond changed very little over the years. He was around six feet tall. He had a high forehead, an elegant, slightly hooked nose, and a blistering constant smile. His effusive graciousness made it seem as if he were always holding court. He had an onrushing way of talking, made up of bursts of superlatives connected by deep hums. He tended to use his listeners as sounding boards. The trumpeter Ruby Braff, whom Hammond began boosting in the mid-fifties, likes to tell of a telephone conversation he once had with Hammond:

"Hello, Ruby, This is John. How are you?"
"Well, I'm in bed with pneumonia and I feel awful."
"Wonderful, Ruby. Now, what I called about . . ."

Hammond's image was boyish. He wore Ivy League clothes, but in a careless, teen-age way, and he invariably affected a crewcut. And he drove a car with abandon, throwing more looks at his passengers than at the road.

But this image was deceptive. The writer and critic James T. Maher has said this about Hammond: "I always loved John's enthusiasm. It was constantly reinforcing. He could get so cranked up about some new musician—once, it was this 'perfectly extraordinary' Yugoslavian trumpet player—that resisting him was like standing up to a tidal wave. He had an angelic enthusiasm, which found improbable perfections. John's nervous energy was such that no sooner had he arrived somewhere with some new intelligence than his foot was out the door—you caught him on the wing. He laughed a great deal, but he was not a witty man. Alec Wilder, who knew him well, could never resist putting him on. Once, John told a girl singer he was recording that the title of Alec's song 'Who Can I Turn To?' was ungrammatical, that it should be '*Whom* Can I Turn To?' News travels fast in the jazz world, and when Alec ran into John a few days later he asked him if he had seen the new Broadway hit musical 'Better Foot Forward.' John didn't get the joke. He was, I suppose, the ultimate connoisseur—one who comes to think that he knows more than the objects of his veneration. He became rather infamous for telling people how and what to play. And in the days when he was still a sort of adviser to the Goodman band he became known as 'John the undertaker.' Whenever he appeared at a rehearsal or a recording session, the musicians knew that one of them would probably be replaced by his newest enthusiasm. His 'discoveries' became graven in stone in his mind—perhaps because he was over-interviewed when he was young. It seems fairly certain, to cite an example, that Red Norvo and Mildred Bailey took John to Harlem to hear the young Billie Holiday rather than John having found her himself. But he was unique and a good man—a patrician bad boy who turned left and became both a realist and a romantic."

Like most enthusiasts, Hammond sometimes missed the mark. He never understood the majestic complexities of Louis Armstrong and Duke Ellington—possibly, it has been suggested, because neither man ever sought his help. (He rated the Fletcher Henderson trumpeter Joe Smith higher than Armstrong.) He felt that Coleman Hawkins stopped developing in 1933, when Hawkins had just begun the supernal ascent that he would not complete until the late forties. He did not consider Benny Carter's compact, lyrical trumpet playing first-rate. Bebop never reached him, and he was rarely interested in white musicians. And many of his enthusiasms of the sixties and seventies have proved less than stunning.

Hammond's autobiography was perverse. It was warm and expressive about his family, and defensive and oblique about music and his life as a civil libertarian. But there are patches of eloquence, and one of them serves him well: "I still would change the world if I could, convince a nonbeliever that my way is right, argue a cause and make friends out of enemies. I am still the reformer, the impatient protester, the sometimes-intolerant champion of tolerance. Best of all, I still expect to hear, if not today then tomorrow, a voice or a sound I have never heard before, with something to say which has never been said before. And when that happens I will know what to do."

Not long after eight o'clock on the evening of July 21st, Dick Hyman and Dick Wellstood opened the 92nd Street Y's "Jazz in July" festival by sitting at two grand pianos in Kaufmann Hall and playing three intricate, charging stride-piano duets. Hyman, with his slender, delicate attack, provided the tracery, and Wellstood, with his Germanic sound, provided the thunder. They backed the singer Carrie Smith for three numbers, and Wellstood joined Vince Giordano & the Nighthawks for a set of early Benny Goodman music. Then, got up in an unaccustomed tuxedo, he went off to the Bemelmans Bar in the Carlyle Hotel, where he was spelling Barbara Carroll. (Wellstood said that although he was born in Greenwich he was born in "clam-digging Greenwich, not backcountry Greenwich," and wearing a tuxedo at the Carlyle made him feel easier with the swells who came to hear him. Three days later, he died suddenly, of heart failure, in Palo Alto, where he had gone for a weekend Jazz gathering. He was fifty-nine.

Wellstood is not mentioned in John Hammond's autobiography. He was white, and it is likely that Hammond regarded him merely as a skilled copyist, an assiduous re-creator of Fats Waller and James P. Johnson. But Wellstood was a great deal more. He regarded himself as "a contemporary musician who uses tools that are out of fashion," and he was right. In the last decade or so of his life he moved forward stylistically, folding bits and pieces of Count Basie and Thelonious Monk and Bill Evans and Cedar Walton into his playing, and broadening his repertory to include Monk and the Beatles and Wayne Shorter. He also gained self-confidence, eventually deciding that he had become "quite excellent" and wondering why he didn't work steadily. Wellstood was witty, sardonic, acute, and matter-of-fact. (He claimed that he liked working in a cha-cha band as much as he liked playing jazz.) In the fifties, he went to law school during the day and played at night, and passed his bar exam. (He finally joined a law firm several years ago, and practiced for ten claustrophobic months before returning to the piano.) He was a good, piquant writer. (From a set of liner notes for a Donald Lambert album: "In a world full of pianists who can rattle off fast oom-pahs or Chick Corea solo transcriptions or the Elliott Carter Sonata, there are perhaps only a dozen who can play stride convincingly at any length and with the proper energy.") He thought things out. (He once said, "Audiences are rarely on the same wavelength as performers. In fact, two very different things are going on at once. The musician is wondering how to get from the second eight bars into the bridge, and the audience is in pursuit of emotional energy. The musician is struggling, and the audience is making up dreamlike opinions about the music that may have nothing at all to do with what the musician is thinking or doing musically. If audiences knew what humdrum, daylight things most musicians think when they play, they'd probably never come.")

Wellstood was a bearish, tousled, guttural man. He had a shy smile, which embraced him as much as his listeners, and laughing eyes, cleverly hidden behind glasses. Over the years, he became an endearing figure, onstage and off—a description that might have either pleased or horrified him, depending on how ferocious he felt he should be that day.

## Ellington Slips By

I t is not likely that anyone will write a good biography of Duke Ellington. Like many prominent blacks in his day, he developed a subtle and largely impenetrable series of disguises. These included his orotund conversation, often delivered in the form of put-ons, which ranged from mock unctuousness to high flattery (to a female guest at the close of the seventieth-birthday party given him at the White House: "I'm so glad you could come. You looked so beautiful, and you brought such dignity to my party"), the amused expressions that flickered across his seignorial (sometimes masklike) face; his Technicolor written efforts (as in his autobiography, *Music Is My Mistress*); his double-entendre song titles ("Warm Valley" and "T.T. on Toast"); his almost foppish way of dressing (six-inch trouser cuffs, ruffled shirts); and the Ellington band itself, which was the secret and spacious house in which—blinds drawn—he spent so many nourishing years. Eventually, all these camouflages became automatic, and it was increasingly difficult to tell where they stopped and Ellington began. Of the half-dozen or so biographical efforts that have been published since his death, in 1974, only *Duke Ellington in Person*, a sharp, pained memoir by Ellington's son, Mercer, penetrates any of the Ellington veils. (Mercer Ellington's book was done with Stanley Dance, who also helped the Duke assemble his autobiography.) Certainly James Lincoln Collier's new book, *Duke Ellington*, built squarely on Mercer Ellington's effort, doesn't bring us much closer to the Master. Collier trots through the now standard résumé of Ellington's life: his genteel, middle-class upbringing in Washington, D.C., his lifelong devotion to his mother, his playboy ways and early-and-only marriage, his prolonged love affairs, his more or less accidental entry into music as a pianist, his first fame as a bandleader at the Cotton Club, his manipulation of and slyness with people, his consuming hypochondria, and his gradual acceptance of the belief that he was an important composer, with the concomitant need to hear every new piece performed by his band, which it sometimes seemed he kept in existence just for that purpose.

What Collier principally wants to get across is that Ellington was *not* the great American composer, as many have claimed—that, indeed, he was not a composer at all in the conventional sense. Collier points out that many of Ellington's best-known numbers were written partly by Ellington and partly by members of his band, in what proportions we may never know. Oftentimes, Ellington arrangements did not exist on paper but were worked out in recording studios and committed to memory by the band. (Many of the Ellington numbers played by repertory groups use arrangements that have been transcribed, note by note, from Ellington recordings.) Sometimes Ellington harmonized and orchestrated his pieces, and sometimes these essential tasks were done by others. Collier suggests that Ellington was, above all, a synthesizer, who saw to it that all the requisite parts of a big-band jazz number—the song, its orchestration, the proper soloists, the tempo— were aligned and ready to go. Collier compares Ellington's methods to those of a master chef: "The chef does not chop all the vegetables himself or make the sauce with his own hands. But he plans the menus, trains the assistants, supervises them, tastes everything, adjusts the spices, orders another five minutes in the oven for the lamb. And in the end we credit him with the result. So it was with Duke Ellington: wherever he got the ingredients, it was with his artistic vision that shaped the final product."

But it wasn't as simple as that. Ellington's greatest numbers, written and recorded between 1940 and 1942, were fluid and ongoing collective improvisations that began with the invention of a melody and ended by shaping the section work that surrounded and supported the soloists. Some of these group improvisations were never finished; Ellington tinkered with them off and on for thirty years. The results, when everything fell into place, were masterpieces of "composed" improvisation, unmatched in American music.

Collier moves swiftly through the last thirty years of Ellington's musical life (he seems to get struck forever in the years around 1930), dismissing most of Ellington's concert pieces, secular and sacred, and passing lightly over the hundreds of short, workday numbers turned out between the longer ones. This is too bad. Despite their episodic nature, some of the concert pieces have merit, and much close listening needs to be done to the late short numbers. (What of the two dozen or so funny and ingenious parodies he recorded of the theme songs of other bandleaders?) Collier is troubling in other ways. He likes to insult his readers' intelligence (Washington, D.C., is "a short distance from Baltimore"), and he is often careless with facts (John Hammond did not organize Benny Goodman's 1938 Carnegie Hall concert, and Ellington's "Controversial Suite," a kind of parody of Dixieland and Kenton music, was being played several years before 1951). And he gives us slow, unenlightening musical analyses of such Ellington classics as "Ko-Ko" and "Harlem Airshaft"—numbers long since taken apart and put together again by Ellington musicologists. He likes to call Ellington's sidemen "virtuosos," thereby revealing that he does not understand the unique and fragile home-brewed nature of many of the musicians who inhabited Ellington's band. At the same time, he scants certain Ellington musicians. He dismisses Sonny Greer outright, claiming that Greer did not drive the band but played alongside it. Greer *was* a homegrown drummer and a showoff, as many drummers of his generation were, but he swung, he had decent time, and he had great style. He got a wake-up, morning tone out of his drums, and he was a first-rate cymbal player. He had much to do with establishing and preserving the Ellington *sound*. Greer was with the band thirty years, and it was never the same after he left. Collier is also off the mark about Ray Nance, a gifted violinist and jazz singer, and a trumpeter of knotted, complex emotions, who had a way of playing slow blues that made you sit very still.

Collier fails to grasp Ellington's polarities. At one end was the pure humor that aerated much of his music (Collier tends to take Ellington far too seriously), and at the other end the ghostliness, so beautifully described in Mercer Ellington's book: "[Ellington] sought a sensuality in the way his music was expressed; there was always an emotion attached to the sound. Or I might say that he was always very conscious of the need to make the listener *feel* experiences with the sound, almost as though he were creating apparitions within the music."

Jazz musicians write good books—not as-told-to or tape-recorded books but books they write themselves. These include Ellington's *Music Is My Mistress;* Charles Mingus's ribald memoir, *Beneath the Underdog;* Danny Barker's salty *A Life in Jazz,* finally published last year; Rex Stewart's portraits of his peers, *Jazz Masters of the Thirties;* Artie Shaw's epigraph-laden *The Trouble with Cinderella;* and Max Gordon's *Live at the Village Vanguard,* Max being as close to a jazz musician as you can get without actually playing an instrument. (Max's instrument is the Vanguard.) And now Marian McPartland, the English-born Renaissance person (pianist, composer, record-label owner, teacher, and radio producer and personality), has put out a collection of descriptive and biographical sketches, *All in Good Time.* The book contains, among other things, portraits, written between 1960 and 1983 for music magazines, of Paul Desmond, the bassists Ron McClure and Eddie Gomez, Mary Lou Williams, Bill Evans, Benny Goodman, and Alec Wilder. McPartland keeps herself out of the way much of the time (although she is a born self-publicizer, an ability few jazz musicians have and all need), and is nowhere in sight in her highly effective chapter on Desmond, a witty man, who tells her, "I'm glad [Ornette Coleman] is such an individualist. I like the firmness of thought and purpose that goes into what he's doing, even though I don't always like to listen to it. It's like living in a house where everything's painted red." She is equally good on her old friend Alec Wilder, who wrote music for her and marvelled at her improvisations. ("God! That would have taken me a week to write and she played it in five seconds!") She says in a postscript to the piece that Wilder's "greatest gift and the most lasting one of all was his music." I'm not sure that Wilder's greatest gift wasn't his complex, brilliant, echoing self.

# 1988

## Cruising

*Saturday*

Jazz festivals of various sorts were held in Australia and France in the forties, but the first permanent festival took place in mid-July of 1954 on the grounds of the small, rickety, fashionable tennis Casino in Newport, Rhode Island. By the late fifties, the Newport Jazz Festival, as it was called, had become a fixture, and its countless spinoffs cover the earth. But many of them, including the various permutations of the Newfort Festival itself, have grown faddish and overweight. Jazz flourishes in small, heedless situations. It also depends on its entrepreneurs. Two of the most imaginative (and least well-known) are Hank O'Neal and his wife, Shelly Shier. For the past five years, they have run a series of mini-festivals on the S. S. Norway, which cruises year-round between Miami and the Virgin Islands. The O'Neals invite about fifty musicians (and their families) for one-or two-week stints, and the musicians play in two comfortable cabaretlike rooms and in an eight-hundred seat theatre. The programs are varied and loosely shaped. There are one-hour afternoon recitals, and evening jam sessions that stretch into the morning hours. The sets are easygoing and uncrowded, and the musicians are arranged in congenial, non-competitive groups. The audiences never have to travel more than a couple of football fields to get to the music, and there are no tickets or cover charges or minimums or hassles about seats. The audiences also have two simultaneous (and very different) events to choose from each evening.

The Norway sailed at four-thirty this afternoon, and after two days of open sea it will stop for day visits at St. Marten, St. Thomas, and Great Stirrup Cay, returning to Miami early next Saturday—a round trip of over two thousand miles. The music began at nine o'clock in the Club Internationale, a plush, high-ceilinged room filled with sofas and overstuffed chairs. A small bandstand and a small dance floor are at one end, and a bar is at the other. Life-size plaster statues of Bacchus and Triton are set in niches at the bandstand end. A group made up of Buddy Tate on tenor saxophone, Al Grey on trombone and bass trumpet, Jay McShann on piano, Major Holley on bass, and Oliver Jackson on drums did six numbers, most of them blues. It was good shake-down music. Grey, a slender man with a smile slightly wider than his face, played an agile bass-trumpet solo on "Days of Wine and Roses" and got off some heavy muted wa-wa trombone on "St. James Infirmary." Tate, as always, slid up and down his special emotional slopes. The Tate-Grey group alternated with the tenor saxophonist Don Menza, the pianist Roland Hanna, the bassist Milt Hinton, and the drummer Louis Bellson. Menza is a hard-blowing player who works largely on the West Coast. He has a shouldering attack and a perfervid sound. Hanna is a beautiful player whose improvisations emerge in bursts—a train passing under a series of bridges. This fitfulness fell away in "Satin Doll," and he got off a sweeping single-note line. It is a comfort to hear Bellson, a taut, precise drummer in the Buddy Rich mold. He has a dry, almost baked tone, and his breaks and solos are flawlessly designed.

The Checkers Cabaret, a low-ceilinged red-and-black room with a long bar and a spacious dance floor, will be offering big bands during the week, and tonight we heard Panama Francis and the Savoy Sultans. The original Sultans, one of the house bands at the Savoy Ballroom in the late thirties and early forties, had two purposes—to play for dancing and to swing ferociously. They used a lot of riffs broken by short solos, and they blew whole bands away. Francis resurrected the Sultans in the late seventies, and although his personnel has changed, his straight, hot Chick Webb drumming keeps everything at a boil.

## Sunday

This morning a marvellous Caribbean cloud show was mounted on the eastern horizon, with white thunderheads standing to the left, a frieze of sheeplike black clouds moving swiftly between the thunderheads and the ship, impenetrable deep-gray rain clouds directly opposite, and slim silvery ball-gown clouds to the right. The entire show was sandwiched by a high cobalt-blue sky and the royal blue of this tropical ocean.

The *Norway*, originally the *France*, is something of a white elephant. Her keel was laid in 1957, the first year that more people crossed the Atlantic by air than by sea. She was, and is, the largest of all passenger ships: she is one thousand and thirty-five feet long, and she weighs over seventy thousand tons. The *France's* essential, tourist-class passengers began to desert her for the air in the early seventies, and the French government, which had been subsidizing her, abandoned her, and she was tied up indefinitely at the Quai de l'Oubli in Le Havre. In 1979, the Norwegian Caribbean Lines bought her, and she was converted from a fast, indoor North Atlantic ship into a sedate, outdoor Caribbean ship. Her famous silhouette, with its two huge winged stacks (*grandes cheminiées à ailerons*), was left intact except for a couple of touches of giantism: two one-story-high signs, reading "NORWAY," were installed between the stacks, and a pair of enormous tenders, ninety feet long and capable of holding four hundred passengers apiece, were installed on the foredeck, between dinosaurlike davits. So the France-Norway has been given a second chance, even though she draws too much water (thirty-four feet) for the harbors she visits and is a little grand for the small seas she sails.

At two o'clock, there was a parade of pianists in the Club Internationale. Roland Hanna did three numbers—a dramatic (yet oblique) "Love for Sale," a slow Debussy ballad, and a blues. The Chicago pianist Eddie Higgins played two Clare Fischer pieces and a Jobim, and he was inconclusive. Art Hodes, looking frozen in such fast company, got himself through "Tennessee Waltz," "Summertime," and "It Ain't Necessarily So," and a jumpy reading of "St. Louis Blues." Jay McShann did three blues, was followed by the Japanese pianist Makoto Ozone, a brittle player in the florid, Corea-Hancock mold. His four numbers, including a "Someday My Prince Will Come," left little to the imagination. Mel Powell wound up the recital with two disappointingly brief numbers. He also served as the master of ceremonies, and he was at his mock-professorial best, filling the room with his big laugh and rumbling mots, and coating all the pianists who preceded him with buttery compliments.

Late in the afternoon, a program called "Meet the Stars" was held in the Checkers Cabaret. Six of the bandleaders on board talked about themselves, then answered questions from the audience. On hand were Cab Calloway,

Panama Francis, Benny Carter, Buck Clayton, Jay McShann, and Erskine
Hawkins. Calloway tended to hog the proceedings, ending his perorations
with "I've had a wonderful career, and you [the audience] made it possible.
So the money's there. I'm pretty well heeled. I enjoy it." Panama Francis,
who once worked for Calloway, added this observation, which is shared by
other Calloway alumni: "You hit on time. You quit on time. You got your
money on time." The leaders were asked to divulge their ages, and, considering their vitality and unflagging abilities, their revelations were buoying.
Calloway is seventy-nine, Francis sixty-nine, Carter eighty, Clayton seventy-six, McShann seventy-eight, and Hawkins seventy-three.

The vibraphonist Gary Burton appeared at nine in the Club Internationale with his Berklee Ensemble, which consists of Makoto Ozone (a graduate of Berklee College, in Boston) and four Berklee students—the alto
saxophonist Doug Yates, the tenor saxophonist Donnie McCaslin, the
bassist Gildas Boclé, and the drummer Marty Richards. Burton is a rococo
vibraphonist who uses four mallets and floods every number with notes. His
figures behind the other soloists let no one rest, melodically or harmonically,
and the result was a dissonant, vertical music. The group played a Chick
Corea, a John Scofield blues, Victor Young's "Beautiful Love," and Billy
Strayhorn's "Isfahan." The alternating group in the Club had Flip Phillips
on tenor saxophone, Kenny Davern on clarinet, Roland Hanna, Howard
Alden on guitar, Milt Hinton, and the drummer Chuck Riggs. The materials ("Sometimes I'm Happy," "Cotton Tail," "Sweet Georgia Brown") have
been played so often and so affectionately by jazz musicians that they seem
to swing by themselves. Phillips, an amalgam of Ben Webster, Don Byas,
and Lester Young, was particularly acute, and right behind were Hanna and
Alden, a Red Norvo graduate and post-Charlie Christian guitarist with a
lovely tone, an advanced harmonic sense, and an infallible sense of structure.
The comedian and singer Martha Raye is on board, and halfway through the
group's celebration she sat in and sang "I Remember April," "The Man I
Love," and "The Sunny Side of the Street." She has a reputation among
older jazz musicians as a good, swinging singer, and in the thirties she used
to sit in up in Harlem. Even so, she was a surprise. Her singing verged on the
surrealist extravagances of Betty Carter and Leo Watson.

The Chicago-style cornettist Wild Bill Davison, who is as snappy and
tart as he was forty years ago (he is eighty-two), was sitting out front during
the Burton set, and, deep in his jowls, was listening to Burton's quite modern
alto player with the same blank intensity that Winston Churchill must have
given the paintings of Francis Bacon.

*Monday*

Eight A.M. again. The ship moving gently over gray water, through gray fog, and under gray rain. The horizon
was about three hundred yards away, and there was rain overhead on the

Oslo Deck (the boat deck). Fifteen minutes later, the horizon retreated several miles, the rain stopped, and the water turned its customary resounding royal blue. There were small whitecaps, and they broke into Queen Anne's lace. The ship took on speed, slowly passing in the far northeast a black Martin Johnson Heade storm.

There was a jam session in the Saga Theatre after lunch. Buck Clayton conducted loosely, and present were the trumpeter Eddie Allen, Al Grey, Kenny Davern, the Danish violinist Svend Asmussen, Roland Hanna, Milt Hinton, Howard Alden, and Oliver Jackson or Louis Bellson. "Jumpin' at the Woodside," "Moten Swing," a ballad medley, and "Lester Leaps In" went by. Hanna and Asmussen turned up bright things on "Woodside," and Alden played another closely reasoned statement on "Lester Leaps In." (Clayton led a series of studio jam sessions for Columbia Records in the fifties, and they are classic recordings. He had with him Trummy Young, Coleman Hawkins, Jo Jones, Billy Kyle, Urbie Green, Lem Davis, and Julian Dash—to say nothing of his own eloquent playing. Clayton's last flowering as a player took place in the sixties, but his teeth and gums and other health problems were already bothering him, and by the mid-seventies he had all but retired. He made several attempts at comebacks in New York, and they were encouraging. His lip was weak, but his warmth and lyricism were intact, and it seemed that it would be only a matter of weeks before he was in top form again. But he did not play again, and eventually word came that he was hopelessly discouraged and would play no more.)

In the fifties and early sixties, Buddy Tate led a Count Basie-type band at the Savoy Ballroom and the Celebrity Club, on 125th Street. Tonight, he took a new Celebrity Club band into Checkers, and it had the Basie trumpeter Harry Edison, the Ellington alto saxophonist Norris Turney, Al Grey, Jay McShann, Major Holley, and Oliver Jackson. Edison, who often plays the trumpet the way Basie played the piano, was at his languorous best in "Things Ain't What They Used to Be," and Tate took a lonesome, blue clarinet solo in "Hootie's Blues."

Two groups appeared in the Club Internationale tonight. One was a maroon velvet quartet made up of Benny Carter, Makoto Ozone, the bassist George Mraz, and Marty Richards. Among their numbers were "Green Dolphin Street," "Honeysuckle Rose," "Lover Man," "You'd Be So Nice to Come Home To," and "Secret Love." Mraz excelled in "You'd Be So Nice," and Carter constructed solo after perfect solo, and even played trumpet on two numbers. Carter, heaped with awards and medals and honorary degrees in recent years, shows no age or swelling of the psyche. The brilliant teeth shine, lighting his impeccable manners and dress. His alto-saxophone playing is as gracious and obliging as ever, and he has returned to his trumpet.

The other group was led by Wild Bill Davison. With him were Kenny Davern, Eddie Higgins, Howard Alden, the bassist Bob Haggart, and Chuck Riggs. Wild Bill likes to rampage, but tonight, tiring by his second set, he slowed down and was lyrical in "Do You Know What It Means to Miss New Orleans," "Love Is Just Around the Corner," and Fats Waller's lovely lullaby "Blue Turning Gray Over You."

## Tuesday

Chip Hoehler is the bandmaster of the *Norway,* and he has a pool of thirty-nine musicians who play dance music, music to swim to, cocktail music, music for shows, country-and-Western music, and big-band jazz. Born in New York in 1941, Hoehler is a cool, compact man who came up through Marshall Brown's Newport Youth Band in the late fifties (he is a trombonist) and through the road bands of Charlie Spivak and Warren Covington. He had his own band in the Bahamas for eleven years and put together his present aggregation in 1979. He has several excellent soloists in his jazz band: Fred Norman on piano; a Paul Gonsalves tenor saxophonist, Larry Spivak; the trumpeter Tom Swayze; and the alto saxophonist John Lux. Hoehler's jazz band has the rare ability to jump into the skins of other bands. Tonight, in the Checkers Cabaret, it became the old Erskine Hawkins band, which flourished in Harlem in the late thirties and early forties. Primarily a dance band, it used a relaxed mixture of riffs, call-and-response patterns, organ chords, and wa-wa brass figures. Its secret was playing a fraction behind the beat; this gave it a rubato swing, a knee-action motion. It had three good soloists: the trumpeter Dud Bascomb; his brother Paul, a tenor saxophonist; and Julian Dash, another tenor saxophonist. Hawkins himself played harum-scarum trumpet, and you were never sure what you would hear—a Harry James style, a Rex Stewart style, a Snooky Young style. He has led a hotel band in the Catskills for twenty-five years, and has retained all his eccentric verve. (Many of the old big bands linger on, but in strange and parlous ways. Some are "ghost" bands—those once led by Glenn Miller and Tommy Dorsey and Count Basie and Duke Ellington—and some, like Erskine Hawkins', go on in the outlands and are still led by their originators.) Hoehler's men caught much of the quality of the original band, and they were particularly apt in "Weary Blues," "Tuxedo Junction" (one of Hawkins' big hits, later made bigger by Glenn Miller), "Gin Mill Special," and "After Hours," Avery Parrish's classic hymn to the slow blues.

Hoehler's band rested, then did a set of Buck Clayton's originals and arrangements, with Clayton conducting. Clayton fell into an acedia after he stopped playing, but lately he has been doing a great deal of big-band writing. Ten of his numbers were played tonight, and they demonstrated that he has somehow transposed his trumpet playing into his writing. His melodies are occasionally irresistible ("Yorkville," "Beaujolais," "Nancy's Fancy"), and his arrangements are graceful enlargements. His saxophone writing winds around like Benny Carter's, his trumpets shout. Finest of all tonight was a long slow blues, called "Homeless." Each soloist takes two choruses, the first backed by the rhythm section and the second by lovely counter-melodies or organ chords. It is one of the rare instances in which a piece of program music works as music and as metaphor. Clayton, as thin as a pin and as dapper and handsome as ever, conducts by not conducting. He cups his hands like jai alai racquets, faces them toward the floor, and moves them almost imperceptibly up and down. Or he holds his hands flat, palms up, and raises them an inch or two to signify more steam. When he wants a certain soloist, he points a crooked finger at him and lifts his chin just above the horizon.

### Wednesday

Hank O'Neal created a stir last year by persuading Mel Powell to come on a cruise and play jazz in public for the first time in thirty years. This afternoon, Powell, who is scheduled to appear tonight, rehearsed in Checkers with Benny Carter, Howard Alden, Milt Hinton, and Louis Bellson. They rolled through "Stompin' at the Savoy," a slow "Makin' Whoopee," Eubie Blake's "You're Lucky to Me," and "What Is This Thing Called love?," and between times Powell was ornate and witty. The quintet's appearance in Checkers tonight was frequently brilliant. Powell got off some Hindemith chords on the bridge of his first chorus on "Stompin' at the Savoy" and some Milton Babbitt chords on the bridge of his second chorus on "What Is This Thing Called Love?" Carter was a marsh hawk in flight throughout, and Bellson was crisp and luminous. Alden played with great invention, and stands a good chance of being voted M.V.P. at the end of the week.

The evening ended in the Club Internationale with a good set by Kenny Davern, Svend Asmussen, Alden, Bob Haggart, and Chuck Riggs and a middling one by Carter, Tommy Flanagan, Hinton, and Bellson. There was some nice counterpoint in the first between Davern and Asmussen, who swings in a curved, willowy way, but the Flanagan-Carter-Hinton-Bellson group never seemed to reach its proper propulsiveness.

Mel Powell was sitting outside Checkers before his rehearsal this afternoon and said that he had a cold—his first "since Muggsy Spanier."

Walking is wonderful on the *Norway*. Seen broadside, she is slightly swaybacked, so no matter which end you start at on the International Deck (enclosed) and the Oslo Deck (open), which contain the longest unobstructed stretches on board, you get a downhill start. If you walk in the direction the ship is going, you really fly.

### Thursday

A tour of the engine room this morning. The temperature sometimes reaches a hundred and thirty degrees and the noise a hundred and thirty decibels. It is an astonishing concatenation of pipes (some like hoses, some like Roman columns), boilers (the two main ones, painted silver, tower out of sight), drive shafts (they are two hundred and fifty feet long and at least two feet thick), turbines, valves, tanks, pumps, stairways, grid passageways, and torpedo-size fire extinguishers. It is about eight hundred feet long and seven stories high. A feast for Demuth and Sheeler and Crawford; a fantasy for Coleridge and Kafka and Cocteau! After an hour of more or less steady descent (some of the railings on the ladderlike stairways were too hot to hold), we ascended in an elevator to the International Deck, which was freezing and very quiet.

Gary Burton and Makoto Ozone played an hour duet in the Club I. this afternoon. They did two Chick Coreas, two Ozones, a Steve Swallow, and a couple of standards. Burton uses a lot of resonator and Ozone a lot of loud pedal, so they shimmered, sometimes in harmony, sometimes in counterpoint, sometimes in unison.

A pleasant approximation of the first concert last Saturday took place tonight in the Club I., and included Buddy Tate, Norris Turney, Al Grey, Jay McShann, Major Holley, and Oliver Jackson. Jackson uses drumsticks the size of logs, but he showed verve and imagination and kept the proceedings moving. Wild Bill Davison led the alternating band, and said just before he went on the bandstand, "Drinking almost killed me and quitting drinking almost killed me, too. One morning after my wife, Anne, made me stop, I was having breakfast at home in Santa Barbara and I heard birds singing outside for the first time. I told Anne, 'I hear birds singing,' and she said, 'Bill, those birds have been singing at breakfast as long as I can remember.' "

According to John Maxtone-Graham, the elegant historian of ocean liners, the custom of being invited to have dinner at the captain's table began in the nineteenth century when immigrant passengers, required to feed themselves, ran out of food and were given free company rations. The free rations at the Captain's dinner tonight included marinated and smoked salmon, cream-of-ratatouille soup, sliced beef tenderloin with morels, duchesse potatoes, snow peas, chayote and bean sprouts, chocolate mousse, and coffee and cognac. The wines were from California—a Chardonnay from Château St. Jean and a cabernet from Clos du Val. The ship had begun rolling noticeably by ten-thirty, and the captain, making a jest, said we were going through "a little hurricane."

Time stopped a couple of days ago. It is difficult to remember what day it is, and appointments don't seem terribly important. The music moves in slow motion, no matter the tempo.

*Friday*

We went through the captain's little hurricane all night, with the ship doing a lot of thrashing about. Clouds had moved back in by morning, and the seas were heavy and white-haired—too heavy, it turned out, for us to stop at Great Stirrup Cay, a big sandbar a hundred and fifty miles east of Miami which the Norwegian Caribbean Lines owns and which is used for swimming and picnicking. There was a good deal of grumbling, so Hank O'Neal put together a jam session in the Club I. It began around two o'clock, and present were Benny Carter, Don Menza, Gary Burton, George Mraz, and Oliver Jackson. They played half a dozen numbers and were joined along the way by Flip Phillips, the trumpeter Ed Allen, and one of Chip Hoehler's tenor saxophonists. Carter—dressed in wrap-around shades, a raspberry shirt, black pants, and white shoes—played trumpet. His solos on a couple of medium blues and on "Stompin' at the Savoy" and "Body and Soul" were spare, delicate, and singing. Panama Francis sat in and played with an even four-four Sid Catlett beat. Burton took a beautiful ad-lib, a-cappella solo on "Body and Soul," and elsewhere supplied a billowing field of background chords for his compeers.

There is a small observation deck directly over the bridge and just forward of the mast, and it's a good place to get some air. Tonight, wind—a combination of the easterlies and the ship's motion—was so strong it was impossible to stand there for more than ten seconds. It was a malevolent wind, and would have flicked us overboard, given the chance.

*Saturday*

The ship docked in Miami at 6 A.M. on a placid, sunny sea. The musicians went ashore around ten o'clock, and were surprised to feel the concrete pier rock gently under their feet. Wild Bill Davison was sitting on a bag waiting for a taxi, and he said, "Now she wants me to quit smoking."

## Jimmy Knepper, Peggy, and the Duke

For the past couple of years, Bradley Cunningham, of Bradley's, on University Place, has been adding a horn player to his customary Sunday-night piano-and-bass duo. One Sunday not long ago, Bradley—at the behest of Sue Mingus, the widow of Charles Mingus and the manager of the Mingus ghost band, Mingus Dynasty—hired the master trombonist Jimmy Knepper, a former Mingus sideman and the leader of the Dynasty. He was accompanied by the pianist Kenny Barron and the bassist Buster Williams, both Bradley's regulars. Barron, a heavy, percussive player, pushed Knepper, a lyricist and thinker, in most of the right places. And Williams, one of the fashionably florid, bamboo-toned bassists, kept his accompanying more or less in the background and the length of his solos within sight.

Knepper is tall and thin and laconic. (He said at Bradley's that he's been losing a pound a year and if he lives long enough—he is sixty—he will disappear.) He has a small face, afterthought hair, and long, trombone arms. He wears glasses and looks like the class brain. Knepper came up at the end of the big-band era and during the early years of bebop, and one can hear in his work considerations of J. C. Higginbotham and Dicky Wells and Lawrence Brown, and also the melodic lines and expanded harmonies of Charlie Parker. He is one of the few musicians of his generation who successfully combine the rhythmic tensions of swing and the rococo melodies of bebop. He is an original. He has a casual trombone tone, neither voluptuous nor nasal, and he avoids the bag of tricks that the instrument sometimes induces—growls, smears, shrieks, roars. He is a limitless improviser. Many improvisers rely on patterns they hit upon early in their careers: they play variations on their own frozen variations. They make it easy for the listener, who comes to count on these set phrases. But Knepper, in his oblique way, constantly needles us. Each solo is full of fresh phrases, fresh rhythmic turns, and fresh melodic insights.

For all that—or perhaps because of it—Knepper has never got his due. He is one of those superior jazz musicians who, for whatever reason, rarely win polls, don't grow rich, never rock the boat. He isn't even easy to find. He doesn't make many records, and all his regular jobs—with the Mingus Dynasty, with Buck Clayton's new big band, with Loren Schoenberg's big band, with the American Jazz Orchestra—are part time. Hearing him at length at Bradley's was a choice event. He opened his first set with three easy choruses of "Stompin' at the Savoy" and then went into a fast "What Is This Thing Called Love?" He began his solo in the second number with a sixteen-bar phrase of such subtlety and dexterity that notes seemed to be hidden behind notes, and he ended the number with an eerie, rolling-back-the-beat legato passage. In a slow "Out of Nowhere" he was as smooth as Tommy Dorsey, and he used a lot of triplets and the sort of odd, outside-the-chord notes that Duke Ellington loved and that give improvised melody nubble and texture. Knepper closed his first set with a medium-tempo "Autumn in New York," in which he demonstrated his agility and his melodic invention (though Knepper doesn't really *demonstrate* anything; he simply does difficult things with ease).

Peggy Lee came back to the Ballroom this winter. Her voice and phrasing were as crafty as ever—lithe, laid-back, spacious, dark, rhythmically flawless. She likes to wear costumes when she sings, and this time she was a polar bear. She wore a white silk gown, a patterned white silk jacket trimmed with marabou feathers, a platinum fall, and large, round, tinted rhinestone glasses. She did her anthems—"Fever," "Is That All There Is?," "Johnny Guitar," and "Them There Eyes"—but she also did Duke Ellington's buoyant "Jump for Joy" and three blues. She sings the blues in the same sad, easy way as Billie Holiday. All of Peggy Lee's moves are miniature—a lop-sided smile, a low laugh, a floating hand—but all have purpose and weight. She makes her listeners feel cherished. Her singing lulls you, and it is easy to forget how daring it still is.

The American Jazz Orchestra completed its third season in the Great Hall at Cooper Union by giving an Ellington evening. The centerpiece of the concert was "Black, Brown and Beige," Ellington's first voyage into extended composition. The piece, which runs about fifty minutes, was written in late 1942 and early 1943. It had been played before in its entirety only three times: at a warmup session at the Rye (New York) High School on January 22nd, 1943; at Carnegie Hall the following night; and at Symphony Hall in Boston a week later. The New York newspaper reviewers gave it poor marks, and Ellington, dismayed, never played the piece again. But he recorded parts of it, and dipped into it from time to time ("Come Sunday," "The Blues") for special recordings and for his sacred concerts. The newspaper boys were right, but for the wrong reasons. Ellington was not working within the symphonic form, or within any kind of European form. He had written a piece which consisted of half a dozen or so episodic, semi-programmatic sketches mourning the travails and celebrating the triumphs of the American Negro. And he had written it not for a symphony orchestra but for his unique jazz-dance band. Considered in such terms, "Black, Brown and Beige" was a startling musical act. No other bandleaders until Woody Herman and Stan Kenton, several years later, pressed a dance band into such high-flown duty. The notion of a "Black, Brown and Beige" had been in Ellington's mind for at least ten years, and its completion was, among other things, a sociopolitical act: he was issuing a kind of musical Emancipation Proclamation—the title, indeed, of a section of the "Brown" movement.

Beside the small concertos Ellington set down between 1940 and 1942, "Black, Brown and Beige" seems pompous and overblown. The *sound* of music, like some of Berlioz, is more persuasive than the music itself. But the piece has beauties. One is the spiritual "Come Sunday," played at Carnegie Hall by Johnny Hodges as an ethereal alto-saxophone solo, full of godlike glissandi and sighing, almost lachrymose whole notes. If it is possible to make religious music cool and sweet, Hodges did it that night. (Fortunately, the concerts at Carnegie Hall and Symphony Hall were recorded, and the patched-together result can be heard on the Prestige label as "The Duke Ellington Carnegie Hall Concerts: January 1943.") Other, lesser beauties include an ad-lib *acappella* trumpet-section passage in "Black"; Harold Baker's lilting solo just after "Come Sunday"; and an odd, dissonant reed-and-trombone passage just after Rex Stewart's solo in the same section. Also to be noted throughout the piece is Ellington's revolutionary use of tempo. He shifts speeds constantly, sometimes even using accelerando and decelerando. He lapses into ad-lib again and again. He uses waltz time and jumpy six-eight. This is where Charles Mingus came from.

Maurice Peress conducted "Black, Brown and Beige" at Cooper Union, and it was a spirited and idiomatic performance. Mel Lewis captured many of Sonny Greer's effects, especially Greer's slogging afterbeat rim shots, and Loren Schoenberg moved handsomely between Ben Webster's style and his own. Norris Turney, who was with Ellington in the band's later years, approximated Hodges' solo, and Jimmy Knepper was admirable, even doing a little plunger-mute work. The first part of the evening was given over to interpretations of half a dozen or so of Ellington's short masterpieces, among them "Main Stem," "All Too Soon," "Bojangles," and an eighteen-minute version of "Mood Indigo" put together by Ellington in 1950. (There was also one number by Billy Strayhorn, whose best work equals and some-times surpasses Ellington's.) John Lewis, the music director of the American Jazz Orchestra, conducted this part of the concert and, as is his wont when he conducts, set some disastrously slow tempos. The "Mood Indigo," which had lovely things in it, went by like a swaybacked horse.

## Stéphane Grappelli and Warne Marsh

The eightieth-birthday celebration held in Carnegie Hall in April for Stéphane Grappelli involved the cellist Yo-Yo Ma, the singer Maureen McGovern, the Juilliard String Quartet, the harmonica player Toots Thielemans, the dancer and singer Harold Nicholas, the New York rhythm team of Mike Renzi, Jay Leonhart, and Grady Tate, and the pianists and composers Michel Legrand and Roger Kellaway, the last of whom doubled as musical director for the evening. Aside from an occasional Gallic touch (a couple of Legrand songs, the first movement of Debussy's String Quartet in G Minor), the concert had noth-ing to do with Grappelli until it was well into its second half. Then three things happened: Grappelli, appearing for the first time, did an easy "Sweet Lorraine" with Yo-Yo Ma, Kellaway, and the rhythm section; swam through a P. T. Barnum "Pennies from Heaven," in which he was teamed with Legrand and Kellaway, the string quartet, Yo-Yo Ma, Thielemans, Nicholas, and the rhythm section—all of them, at one point, sawing, blow-ing, tinkling, thumping, and plucking; and played several liquid, jumping numbers with his trio (Marc Fosset on guitar and Jon Burr on bass.) He has lost nothing: his melodic lines arch and float and skim. Grappelli believes that performers should dress dramatically onstage, and he was in one of his famous warring outfits—a light-colored, open-neck flowered shirt and Black Watch pants. You could hear him before he made a sound.

The tenor saxophonist Warne Marsh died late last year, at the age of sixty. He died in California, where he was born and raised. He had distinguished Hollywood antecedents. His father, Oliver H. T. Marsh, was a well-known cinematographer (*David Copperfield*, *A Tale of Two Cities*), and his aunt Mae Warne Marsh, after whom he was named, was a silent-film star. Marsh came up under the tutelage of the brilliant, relentless pianist and teacher Lennie Tristano, whom he considered nonpareil. His friend the alto saxophonist Gary Foster once said of him, "His sound on the tenor is completely untenorlike, just as Jimmy Knepper's sound on the trombone is completely untrombonelike. Both men seem to use their instruments simply as vessels to contain their notes. They could be playing any instrument." His tone was brown and thick, and he used almost no vibrato. His melodic lines were Proustian. He was an intellectual improviser, who played intensely complex melodic lines, which demanded complete concentration and offered no over-the-counter emotions. He was never a popular player: he never courted his audience when he performed. He disappeared inside his music. He was a shy, hidden, restless man who waited for the world to come to him and, when it did, returned the compliment in full. Marsh might have been a cult figure but wasn't. Cult figures often leak; Marsh was watertight.

# 1989

## Max

**M**ax Gordon had reached the great age of eighty-six when he died. He was still at the helm of his beloved Village Vanguard, which, at fifty-five, is probably the oldest night club in the world. Standing row upon row in the sizable space of his past were the extraordinary performers whose careers he had started or furthered— Woody Allen, Pearl Bailey, Bobby Short, Wally Cox, Comden and Green, Leadbelly, Nichols and May, Harry Belafonte, Judy Holliday, Barbra Streisand, Mort Sahl, Mildred Bailey, Lenny Bruce, the Weavers, Carol Sloane, Aretha Franklin, Josh White, and almost every jazz musician from Zutty Singleton to Albert Ayler.

Max backed into his life. He was brought to this country from Svir, Lithuania, in 1908, and in 1926 he moved to New York from Portland, Oregon, where his family settled. He studied law at Columbia, but he lasted only six weeks. Greenwich Village was full of poets and writers and painters, and, drawn by its ferment, he took a furnished room near Washington Square. Max's Village was made up of writers and vagabonds like Harry Kemp, Maxwell Bodenheim, Joe Gould, and John Rose Gildea—not the tony group that included Edmund Wilson, Elinor Wylie, Edna St. Vincent-Millay, and e. e. cummings. Kemp, who was big, loved Max, who was small. "Kemp lived on the dunes at Provincetown," Max said once, "and he helped start the Provincetown Playhouse. When he came back to town, he'd look for me in the coffeehouses and he'd shout, 'Max! Where are you? I have a new poem to read to you!' and crush me with an embrace."

For five years, Max worked at odd jobs, read at the Public Library, and hung out with the poets at the coffeehouses. In 1932, at the insistence of a friend named Ann Andreas, he opened his own place, the Village Fair Coffee House, on Sullivan Street. The poets came to drink, and declaim their poetry, but the club lasted only a year. ("Unbeknownst to me, one of the waitresses got caught trying to sell liquor to a cop in plain-clothes, so they put a cop on the premises every night, and there he sat in his uniform, and it put a pall on the place," Max explained.) In 1934, Max opened another place, on Charles Street, and called it the Village Vanguard, for a reason that he could never remember. In February of 1935, he moved a couple of blocks north, without skipping a night's work, to the Vanguard's present site, on Seventh Avenue between Eleventh Street and Waverly Place.

No architect would design a place like the Vanguard, which, in its accidental way, is a perfect union of form and content. A pie-shaped basement some sixty feet long, it has a small bandstand at its south end, or apex, and a small bar at the other end. A passageway behind the bar leads to a disused kitchen, which became Max's office, a dressing room, and a gathering place for jazz musicians. The walls of the main room were once covered with murals and are now covered largely with photographs. When someone asked Max who decorated the Vanguard, he replied, "It decorated itself." Max was married and had two daughters, but, in truth, he was married to the Vanguard. He once said, "This place has been like a love match to me. I've probably spent more time in it than anywhere else. I've even slept here, stretched out on a couple of tables. I've learned that if you're good to the Vanguard, the Vanguard will be good to you." He often spoke of the place as if it were flesh and blood. "The Vanguard has a life of its own. It's nice to people. It doesn't push them around. It doesn't make them feel it's trying to inveigle them into more drinks. It doesn't hustle. If people want a drink, they get it. If they don't, they don't." Max was revered by the people who worked for him, and although he had a sharp ear and eye, he never tried to shape his performers. If they met expectations, they were asked back. He said, in a resigned way, "I never got to know a lot of the people who appeared at the Vanguard. Maybe they were scared of me, maybe I was scared of them. Maybe they were like John Coltrane, who was always surrounded by worshippers. I loved his music, but I never said four words to him."

The Vanguard was not Max's only invention. From 1943 to 1963, he was co-owner, with Herbert Jacoby, of the Blue Angel, on East Fifty-fifth Street. Jacoby was a supercilious Frenchman who had started out in the Paris *boîtes*, and Max was, in his own cheerful estimation, a Village bumpkin. Once Max got his bearings in the rarefied atmosphere that Jacoby moved in, the two got on well enough, and eventually worked out a smooth system. They tried out new acts at the Vanguard and, if they went over, shipped them to the Blue Angel. Max often claimed he was not a businessman; what he really meant was he wasn't greedy. Whatever profits he made were the result of offering a pure product in decent surroundings at a reasonable

price. Ambition got the better of him only twice, with disastrous conse-
quences. In the late forties, he and Jacoby bought the faltering Café Society
Uptown from Barney Josephson and, at enormous expense, converted it
into the posh Le Directoire. After a deceptive early success, it foundered,
and they sold it back to Josephson, for five thousand dollars. In 1955, Max
and Michael Field, the cookbook writer and classical pianist, opened a fancy
ice-cream parlor, Maxfield's, near the Paris Theatre, on West Fifty-eighth
Street. It had tile floors, marble counters, red velvet walls, brass chandeliers,
homemade ice cream made with cream, and coffee brewed every twenty
minutes. The Bergdorf's crowd found it outrageously expensive, and the
after-theatre crowd stayed away because it didn't have a liquor license.

In the early sixties, the Vanguard, long neglected for Max's uptown
interests, nearly went under. Max had to sell his car and his house on Fire
Island. He borrowed ten thousand dollars ("One of the axioms of the night-
club business is you have to have somebody to lean on for money") and, by
dint of shrewd booking (quality jazz acts that might become popular; popular jazz acts that had quality), pulled the Vanguard through. Max was of two
minds about money. He knew it was essential, but he also knew how
ephemeral it was—which is probably what made him carry a comforting roll
of bills, bills that fluttered like leaves onto the table and the floor when he
pulled them out of his pocket to pay a restaurant check.

In the early seventies, he moved back to the Village from the Upper East
Side, and after that his life became simpler. He lived in a small apartment on
Lower Fifth Avenue, and he ate dinner at Joe's, on MacDougal Street, or at
Pirandello, just east of Washington Square. He went to the Vanguard twice
a day—in the afternoon to do his booking, take reservations, and replenish
his stock, and in the evening to watch the cash register, talk to friends, and
listen to the music. He'd sit at his desk in the back or at a table near the door:
an owlish man with receding white hair, heavy-rimmed glasses, and a big
cigar. Clothes puzzled Max. For much of the year, he wore a chamois shirt,
open at the neck, a corduroy suit, and, when he went out, a shapeless black
hat, pulled so low that only tendrils of white hair showed. He liked to talk, in
his casual, enunciatory way ("I feel all right. I feel pretty gude"), and he
loved to laugh. At a memorial service for Max, Katy Abel, the Vanguard's
longtime doorkeeper, reported that once two men appeared at the top of the
steps leading down to the club and started fencing with loaves of French
bread. She asked Max what to do, and he looked up the stairs and said, "Ask
them if they want some butter."

In a nonchalant way, Max eventually began to take himself as seriously as
he took the Vanguard. In 1980, he published a memoir, *Live at the Village
Vanguard*. He wrote it himself, page by page, over a period of seven years,
and it is a funny, literate book. Here is his caption for a photograph of the
singer Betty Carter at the Vanguard: "I happened to walk in on her last
show. It was late, it was February, the snow was on the ground; there was

nobody in the joint. And there she was, singing to a lot of empty chairs and tables. I could never get that picture out of my mind. She used to come around, looking for work. 'Let's wait and see,' I'd say. Then finally she said, 'You should hear me again, hear me somewhere else, hear me in a place other than the Vanguard.' So I went all the way up to Harlem to hear her at a place called Wells's. I heard her and put her to work. And today she's Betty Bebop, the greatest bebop singer of them all. And do you know what? I can't afford her anymore; she now sings in arenas and does concerts in college gymnasiums. But she comes down to see me. We sit in the kitchen and talk." He kept a pile of his books at the Vanguard, and he estimated he had sold two thousand copies. This is what he said about the techniques he used in the book: "I kept trying to find a way to get my ideas across, and I hit on dialogues, sometimes with real people, sometimes with people based on real people. Some of the dialogues are fictional, but it's fiction borrowed directly from life. Life fiction, you might call it."

Max was the last of the old-style New York jazz-club owners, who not only operated honest places but loved the music. Others, down through the years, have included Nick Rongetti (Nick's), Jimmy Ryan and Matty Walsh (Jimmy Ryans), Barney Josephson (Café Society Downtown and Café Society Uptown, the Cookery), Ralph Watkins (Kelly's Stable, Basin Street East, the Embers), Art D'Lugoff (the Village Gate), the Canterinos (the Half Note), the Termini brothers (the Five Spot), Gil Wiest (Michael's Pub), and Bradley Cunningham, (Bradley's). Josephson, who ran the Café Societies from 1938 to 1948 and the Cookery from 1971 to 1982, died last September, and Cunningham, who opened Bradley's in 1969, died in November. Barney, Bradley, and Max lived and worked within a three- or four-block area, but they didn't commingle much. Max sometimes ate dinner at Bradley's (Bradley was rarely there that early), and Bradley would turn up at the Vanguard when Max celebrated an anniversary of some sort. Barney, a stylish, elegant man, tended to stay on his own turf. They were of a kind in their different, rebel ways. New Yorkers aren't heavy mourners, but they have long memories.

# Mixed Blessings

**G**rove's Dictionary of Music and Musicians has embraced jazz. Grove first approached the music with some sort of seriousness in 1980, when the *New Grove Dictionary* included not only articles on jazz but almost two hundred entries on jazz musicians. It came even closer in 1986, in the *New Grove Dictionary of American Music*—more than four hundred entries on the music and its makers. Now the *New Grove Dictionary of Jazz* has arrived, and it attempts to encompass all the jazz literature that has accumulated since the mid-thirties, when Hugues Panassié published the first critical book on jazz (*Le Jazz Hot*),

Charles Delaunay published the first discography (*Hot Discography*), Louis Armstrong the first jazz autobiography (*Swing That Music*), Dorothy Baker the first jazz novel (*Young Man with a Horn*), and Otis Ferguson the first more or less regular jazz criticism in a national magazine (*The New Republic*).

Here are some of Jazz Grove's particulars. It comes in two volumes, each measuring eight and a half inches by eleven inches, and each just shy of seven hundred pages. There are two broad columns to a page, set in readable type on good stock (there is no indication of whether or not it is acid-free), and surrounded by generous gutters (there is no rule between the columns, and none is needed). Of the forty-five hundred entries, three thousand deal with individuals, and among them are musicians, composers, arrangers, record producers, editors, discographers, impresarios, and writers. The rest of the entries have to do with such subjects as jazz notation, the beat, bands of whatever size and disposition, harmony, improvisation, arrangements, recording, transcription, synthesizers, festivals (two hundred listings), night clubs (nine hundred listings), jazz libraries and archives, the instruments peculiar to jazz, record labels, jazz groups, jazz films, and jazz terms. Each entry on an individual gives his working name, his real name, his nickname, his date and place of birth (and death), a summary of his career, a selective discography and bibliography, and the repository of any oral history he may have done. Most of the musicians are American, but there are also hundreds of international players, ranging from the Turkish trumpeter Maffy Falay to the Argentine bassist Alfredo Remus to the Dutch reed player Jan Morks. The volumes contain a couple of hundred apt and often unfamiliar photographs, taken mainly from the collection of Frank Driggs, and there is a twenty-page bibliography in small type at the back of the second volume, just before a list of the names and origins of the dictionary's two hundred and fifty contributors, many of whom are unknown academics who are not always as hip as they might be. The relatively few well-known contributors include Danny Barker, Joachim Berendt, Edward Berger, Ran Blake, John Chilton, James Lincoln Collier, Frank Driggs, Leonard Feather, Mark Gridley, Lawrence Gushee, André Hodeir, Felicity Howlett, Michael James, Dan Morgenstern, Paul Oliver, Henry Pleasants, Lewis Porter, Brian Priestley, John Rockwell, Bill Russell, Gunther Schuller, Ernie Smith, Richard Sudhalter, J. R. Taylor, Michael Ullman, Martin Williams, and Valerie Wilmer. The largest number of entries are by Barry Kernfeld, who edited the dictionary and is a musicologist.

Chief among Jazz Grove's blessings is bringing under one cover the biographical entries that for so long have been buried in the six volumes of Leonard Feather and Ira Gitler's *Encyclopedia of Jazz*, in John Chilton's *Who's Who of Jazz*, in Roger Kinkle's *Complete Encyclopedia of Popular Music and Jazz*, and in Al Rose and Samuel Charters' directories of New Orleans jazz. It is fine, too to have the entries on films, night clubs, record labels (nothing is more fleeting in jazz), jazz festivals, and jazz archives and libraries; the essays on jazz (almost novella length), jazz forms, harmony, arranging, rhythm, and improvisation; and the histories of the instruments used in jazz, some of them almost invented by jazz musicians (the drum set, many of the saxophones, the vibraphone, the electric guitar).

In many ways, jazz has been a hand-me-down, word-of-mouth music, often unchronicled, unfilmed, and under-recorded, at least until recent times. Jazz Grove, in trying to get the specifics of this ephemeral music on paper, has made a good many mistakes, some of them wild, some of them minor. A selective list, in alphabetical order: Despite his occasional association with jazz players, the harmonica player Larry Adler is not a jazz musician. James Lincoln Collier, in his Louis Armstrong entry, scants the celestial Victors Armstrong recorded late in 1932 and early in 1933. Astonishing statement No. 1: Daniel Zager claims that Amiri Baraka (LeRoi Jones), an emotional, highly politicized writer, has had "a profound influence on jazz criticism." Gene Bertoncini and Michael Moore's beautiful, unclassifiable duo cannot in any sense be considered a "bop duo." Art Blakey did not learn how to use "his elbow on the tom-tom to alter the pitch" in Africa; he learned it from his master, Sidney Catlett, who used the device long before Blakey went abroad. Bob Brookmeyer was not the first important valve trombonist after Duke Ellington's Juan Tizol—Brad Gowans was. There is no mention in the Tina Brooks discography of the comprehensive Mosaic Blue Note reissue brought out several years ago. (The discographies following the biographical entries tend to be poorly chosen.) Nor is there any mention in Ray Charles' entry of his being a great jazz singer. Three things are wrong in this sentence from the long and comprehensive entry on drums: "Many drummers from the 1950s onwards—notably Sonny Greer, Chick Webb, Chico Hamilton, and Elvin Jones—have also employed timpani mallets." Webb died in 1939, Sid Catlett used mallets extensively in the early forties, and Greer and Jones have rarely, if ever, used them. The entry on Art Farmer does not place him in modern jazz or describe his original and exquisite style. Astonishing statement No. 2: James Lincoln Collier claims that "jazz usually takes place in the context of an actual or simulated jam session, which has some aspects of a ritual." Jam sessions, which have nearly died out, were manhood-testing rituals; they stood to one side of the nightly, almost blue-collar business of jazz as, first, a dance music and then as an art music. If Gus Johnson's "aggressive but fluid and dance-like style made him the best drummer (Count) Basie had after Jo Jones," then what about Shadow Wilson, Buddy Rich, and Sonny Payne? The sublime tap dancer Baby Laurence is no longer alive; he died in April of 1974. There is no mention that the recording director Harry Lim was responsible in 1944 on the Keynote label for some of the best jazz recordings ever made. Astonishing statement No. 3: Barry Kernfeld writes in his essay on Charles Mingus that "Mingus's accomplishments surpass in historic and stylistic breadth those of any other major figure in jazz." Including Louis Armstrong, Charlie Parker,

Thelonious Monk, and Mingus's acknowledged master, Duke Ellington? The New York night-club listings are far from complete. (See the priceless glossary of Harlem clubs in the booklet prepared in the early sixties by George Hoefer for the Columbia boxed set called "The Sound of Harlem"—a booklet nowhere mentioned in the bibliography. And where in the New York listings are such clubs as Pookie's Pub, Bourbon St., Buddy's Place, the Back Porch, Frank's Place, the Royal Box, Plaza 9, Hopper's, the Composer, the Limelight, the Roosevelt Grill, the Rainbow Grill, Shepheard's, and the Guitar?) We are never told what instrument the Chicago clarinettist and alto saxophonist Joe Poston played. This meaningless description appears in the entry on Mickey Roker: his drumming "draws upon the inherent impetus of the blues." Leonard Feather leaves out Leo Watson, Jelly Roll Morton, and Hot Lips Page in his essay on jazz singing. And in the brief paragraph accorded the trumpeter Joe Wilder nothing is said about his style or the fact that he was one of the first jazz musicians to function on both sides of the jazz-classical fence.

Three more quibbles: (1) Although the bibliography at the end of Volume II appears fairly complete, the bibliographies appended to many of the biographical entries are at best haphazard. (2) These figures have been unfairly omitted from Jazz Grove: the baritone saxophonist Gil Mellé; the pianist Dorothy Donegan; the drummers Victor Lewis and Baby Lovett; the tubist-bassist-bandleader Vince Giordano; the bassist Ray Drummond; the jazz singers Barbara Lea, Carol Sloane, Peggy Lee, Sylvia Sims, and Nellie Lutcher; the record producer Milt Gabler; and the night-club owners Barney Josephson and Max Gordon (mentioned in passing in the night-club listings). (3) In his preface Kernfeld declares that he has purposely left out gospel singing. Too bad. Such gospel singers as Mahalia Jackson, Marion Williams, Dorothy Love Coates, and Claude Jeter are, their idiom notwithstanding, among the greatest of jazz singers.

Many of Jazz Grove's short biographies are admirable. These stand out: J. Bradford Robinson's on Red Allen and on Buddy Bolden; Barry Kernfeld's on John Coltrane and on Freddie Hubbard; John Chilton's on Bobby Hackett; Michael James' on Warne Marsh; Bob Zieff's on Bobby Stark; Lawrence Gushee's on King Oliver and on New Orleans jazz; and Gunther Schuller's on Ornette Coleman.

James Lincoln Collier is a born revisionist. His latest effort is a ninety-five-page pamphlet, "The Reception of Jazz in America" (Institute for Studies in American Music, Brooklyn College), in which he attempts to demolish the old belief that jazz, neglected in its own country, was first appreciated by Europeans. Collier claims that Americans have always been knowledgeable about jazz and that they began to write intelligently about it in the twenties and early thirties, long before the Europeans knew what was happening. Two of the early American critics he advances for attention are familiar: the novelist and photographer Carl Van

Vechten and the blues specialist Abbe Niles. He pulls the third out of his hat—R. D. Darrell, long a critic of and handyman writer about classical music. Darrell, it turns out, wrote about jazz for small-circulation music magazines from the mid-twenties to the early thirties. Collier quotes Darrell persuasively on Ellington; he understood what he was hearing. Collier points out that in 1937 *Time* estimated that there were half a million "serious jazz fanciers" in this country. (Benny Goodman was riding high then and the swing craze had begun, so *Time*'s guess might have been somewhere near the mark. But such widespread jazz admiration has never been evident since. When two or three jazz fans find each other anywhere, they consider themselves a crowd.) Collier also argues that the belief in European clairvoyance was started by American leftists who wanted the American establishment to look reactionary. He claims that Hugues Panassié's *Hot Jazz*, which is generally credited with turning us on to jazz in this country is emotional, inaccurate, and irresponsible. (Panassié, of course, had not yet been to America, and had based his book on recordings.) But for all its ineptness Panassié's book had an enthusiasm and love for the music which jarred and excited the American young. (Gunther Schuller says that Panassié brought him to the music.) Collier is not convincing when he attempts to pooh-pooh the Swiss conductor Ernest Ansermet's astonishing description of Sidney Bechet, written in 1919, when jazz was largely sequestered in New Orleans. Nor does he explain why there have always been so many people in this country who cannot even tell you what jazz is.

## Mingus Regained

Charles Mingus's two-hour assemblage, "Epitaph," was given its première early in June at Alice Tully Hall by a thirty-piece jazz orchestra conducted by Gunther Schuller. It marks the first advance in the composition of large-scale jazz works since Duke Ellington's 1943 "Black, Brown and Beige," a fifty-minute piece that can now be considered an overture to Mingus's leviathan, which is full of Ellington devices and Ellington melodies.

Although money problems forced Mingus to work with small groups most of his life, his head was always full of big sounds. These took the form of works for large jazz bands, and they were realized perhaps half a dozen times either on recordings or at concerts. One of the concerts, given at Town Hall in 1962, with thirty all-star musicians on hand, was meant to be a summation of Mingus's work, but, as so often happened in his involuted life, it went wrong. The concert, moved forward five weeks at the behest of the company that was to record it, became a four-hour rehearsal, in which copyists were still at work onstage and almost nothing was played in its entirety. The most commanding music was Mingus's various harangues—to his musicians, to the recording technicians, and to the restive audience. But the concert has turned out to be the acorn from which "Epitaph" grew. More than half of the eight or so numbers played that night in 1962 appeared in different form at Alice Tully Hall. They became part, it is now clear, of a large work that Mingus completed sometime in the early seventies and set aside because he was convinced that, in the rock climate of the time, he would never be able to raise the money to have it properly performed. As Mingus the master ironist knew, its title would mean nothing unless he was dead and the piece was discovered and played.

"Epitaph" was turned up by the musicologist Andrew Homzy while he was cataloguing the bags and boxes of music Mingus left behind when he died, ten years ago. Homzy writes in the program notes, "Approximately twenty scores for a large jazz orchestra written on oversized, frayed, and yellowed paper were discovered in the collection. On some of these scores the title 'Epitaph' was written; on others, 'Epitaph' appeared as a subtitle for what at first looked like independent compositions. Significantly, all the measures on all of the scores were successively numbered. . . . Further study . . . led Gunther Schuller to the conclusion that Mingus's hope 'was to find improvisation and spontaneity and freedom, and at the same time compose a large extensive frame of reference. That's the problem . . . that in jazz has not yet been solved. Only Duke Ellington really tackled it. But Ellington was still writing songs and fashioning suites around them. ["Epitaph"] has nothing to do with thirty-two-bar-song forms. It is composition in the true sense.' " Homzy said just before the concert, "It's not the kind of piece where the themes are connected. It's more of an anthology, a panorama complete in itself. When I found the score, I felt the energy coming up from the pages, as if they had a life of their own. Friends have told me they had the same sensation when they looked at Mozart scores in Salzburg."

It took five months for twenty copyists and two computer programs to assemble a five-hundred-page score, containing over four thousand measures of music. It could not have been easy. Here are some of the instructions that Mingus left about how he wanted one of the parts, "Please Don't Come Back from the Moon," scored: "We usually extend the E-flat-minor-A-flat-seven sound together—more or less with arabic harmonies gradually sneaking in . . . the piano gives a two-bar cue and we're back at the top again . . . Perhaps the brass or other section could have a cue chord that one of the section men could conduct in for two or more bars. This cue can be used throughout the piece. Since there is no time bars after we reach the minor mode, I would like to have section or sections, 'pattern' riffs, that space themselves spasmodically, so the piece won't have that four-bar–eight-bar feeling. 'Like' the trumpet plays the melody on the E-flat–A-flat part in harmon mute close to a mike. . . . He begins with just rhythm—then little things sneak in on the third and fourth beat. Then out some bars—then in on the beat."

"Epitaph," as played at Alice Tully, contained nineteen sections, over half of them reworkings of pieces that Mingus had written and/or played from the late thirties to the early seventies. These included "Started Melody" (an improvisation on "I Can't Get Started," a song Mingus often played), "Moods in Mambo," "The Self-Portrait—The Chill of Death" (from 1939), "O. P. (Oscar Pettiford)," "Please Don't Come Back from the Moon," "Monk, Bunk and Vice Versa," "Peggy's Blue Skylight," "Better Get Hit in Your Soul," and "Noon Night." There were five balladlike sections, the mambo, four blues, two improvisations on standard tunes, and six uncategorizable sections, a couple of them over ten minutes long. In "Epitaph" Mingus uses every device known to jazz—and to him. The tempo doubles and is halved, decelerates and accelerates. There are accented and unaccented four-four beats, and two-four beats. There are lengthy sections without any sounded rhythm. There are ritards and places where the beat is at the very front of each note. There are riffs and ostinatos. There are breaks and stop-times and chase choruses. There are growl trumpet and growl trombone solos, pizzicato and arco bass solos, a bassoon solo, a recited poem, and chanting by the orchestra. There are all sorts of melodic interpolations—a bugle call, bits of "Tea for Two," an Ellington band call and echoes of Ellington's "Happy Go Lucky Local," a riff from the "One O'clock Jump." At the end of the final number, the entire orchestra improvises at once.

The harmonic pallet moves from huge unison chords to impenetrable dissonances. The great trombonist Jimmy Knepper, a longtime, long-suffering Mingus sideman and the present leader of Mingus Dynasty, the Mingus revival band, once said about Mingus as an orchestrator, "I never felt he was as great an orchestrator as some people made out. For instance, in 'Cumbia' he would use the trombone with the bassoon and the bass-clarinet. If you put them all together, it just sounds like mud. There are at least half a dozen places where Mingus has four or five ensemble voices going at once—mass counterpoint that is so dense that the ear can't take it all in.

The most complicated movements—the two parts of "Main Score," and "Main Score Reprise," "The Self-Portrait—The Chill of Death," and "The Children's Hour of Dream"—are in constant motion. No phrase lasts more than two or three measures. The music resembles the way Mingus talked—in fast, irregular, often slurred bursts. The wild, acidulous, melancholy "The Children's Hour of Dream" went like this: A heavy bass ensemble chord slid into a brief, sorrowing melody, echoed by a solo alto saxophone, then by a flute; a walking-bass ostinato began and was joined by stabbing offbeat chords, played by the brass; still other instruments (it was impossible to tell in what combinations) thickened the ostinato, and there were more offbeat stabs; a reed figure shot past; a trombone figure entered and was opposed by high, light trumpet sighs; timpani strokes introduced a melody for the brass, the reeds played a balancing melody, backed by a piano tremolo and a new, very fast ostinato, and muted trumpets floated above; a short, muttering trombone figure anchored an oboe; the ostinato slowed, and a muted trombone and a tenor saxophone soloed against swelling brass and drums. Then the drums went into a kind of "Saber Dance" rhythm, there were more of the earlier, giant offbeat chords, and the mournful opening melody rolled by again. Everything speeded up, and in quick succession we heard more brass; heavy, descending, steplike unison figures played by what sounded like the entire orchestra; the opening melody replayed with its alto-saxophone flourish, again the steplike unison figures, the opening melody with its flute flourish, and—bang!—it all ended. There had been no consistent beat, yet the timbres, the accents, the phrasing were jazzlike. "The Children's Hour of Dream" is part jazz, part Stravinsky modern, part Ellington, part Mingus—a new conglomerate.

The orchestra was made up of six trumpets, six trombones, three alto saxophones, two tenor saxophones, two baritone saxophones, a bassoon, a contrabass clarinet, a tuba, two pianos, two basses, a vibraphone, a guitar, drums, and percussion. Present, among many others, were John Handy, George Adams, and Jerome Richardson on reeds; Roland Hanna and John Hicks on pianos; Urbie Green, Britt Woodman, and Eddie Bert on trombones; Randy Brecker, Lew Soloff, Wynton Marsalis, and Joe Wilder on trumpets; and Victor Lewis on drums. The soloists, battling huge sounds on every side, were adept, and four in particular shone: the trumpeters Soloff and Brecker; Michael Rabinowitz, who played five lyrical choruses of the blues on his bassoon; and the canny Jerome Richardson, who began an alto-saxophone solo with half a dozen eerie, falsetto, strangely placed, descending bent notes that settled into a fine Charlie Parker-like chorus. The musicians, with only a week of rehearsals behind them, were, clams easily accepted, heroic. Columbia recorded the concert, and at the end, when two sections had to be redone, Gunther Schuller told the audience, "This music is so difficult—you have no idea."

# A Hostile Land

The big news in jazz during the strange, suspended summer of 1941 was that some of the best and most successful white bands had again begun to hire black musicians. Benny Goodman, who already had Charlie Christian and Cootie Williams, took on Sidney Catlett and John Simmons. Artie Shaw, who had once employed Billie Holiday, recorded four numbers with Red Allen, J. C. Higginbotham, the pianist Sonny White, and the guitarist Jimmy Shirley. Later in the summer, he hired Hot Lips Page. Perhaps the biggest news was that Gene Krupa, still rising as a leader, had brought in Roy Eldridge. (Krupa had previously used Leo Watson on several recordings.)

Eldridge, who was thirty, was little known outside jazz circles, where he was regarded with awe, but he was famous when he left Krupa, in 1943.

Aside from a spell with Fletcher Henderson's band, those two years were his first big-league experience. "Riding up on that stage at the Paramount Theatre with the Krupa band scared me to death," Eldridge once said. "The first three or four bars of my first solo, I'd shake like a leaf, and you could hear it. Then this light would surround me, and it would seem as if there wasn't any band there, and I'd go right through and be all right.

Eldridge played melodramatic fast solos with Krupa ("After You've Gone," "Twelfth Street Rag") and dramatic slow solos ("Rockin' Chair," "Georgia on My Mind"). He delivered hip, funny vocals ("Let Me Off Uptown," "Knock Me a Kiss"). And sometimes he sat in on drums while Krupa fronted the band. A short, bristling, jumping man with a two-hundred-watt smile and snapping eyes, Eldridge astonished the white audiences who flocked to hear him. He continued to wow them when he joined Artie Shaw, in 1944, and he wowed them throughout his career. His love-hate relationship with these audiences was the central paradox of his life. "Droves of people would ask him for his autograph at the end of the night," Shaw has said, "but later, on the bus, he wouldn't be able to get off and buy a hamburger with the guys in the band. He thought he was travelling through a hostile land, and he was right." The life of the great black soloists was a constant scuffle, compounded by racism. After a short European tour with Benny Goodman, in 1950, Eldridge stayed on in Paris almost a year— presumably to catch his racial breath—and when he came home he made a hair-raising début at the old Stuyvesant Casino. He then joined Norman Granz's Jazz at the Philharmonic, where he stayed for much of the fifties. He accompanied Ella Fitzgerald in the early sixties, flickered through Count Basie's band in 1966, and, after endless gigging, settled into Jimmy Ryans in 1970.

For a long time, Eldridge was said to be the link between Louis Armstrong and Dizzy Gillespie. But it has gradually become clear that although he stands between them, he was linked only to Gillespie, and was Gillespie's chief model. Eldridge had ferocious pride, and he would never admit that he had heard Armstrong any earlier than 1931 or 1932, when Armstrong, having passed through his first, rough-and-ready revolutionary phase, suddenly became a player who lived in his upper moonlit register. Eldridge must have studied this Armstrong, particularly his fondness for O altitudo notes, but he and Armstrong had very different natures: Armstrong went where the waters took him, while Eldridge invariably headed upstream. Armstrong was a melodic player who used silence and whole notes; Eldridge loved speed and lightning and noise. He told the jazz writer John Chilton, "I had this thing about playing as fast as I could all the time. I double-timed every ballad I did, and never held a long note." Eldridge listened closely to the wild men of the music. One of these was the breakneck trumpeter Jabbo Smith, who, presaging Dizzy Gillespie, stampeded the New York brass players in the late twenties before moving to the Midwest, where Eldridge had a run-in with him in

Milwaukee. "We met at a place called Rails," Eldridge said. "We played fast
and slow. The crowd thought I had cut Jabbo, and he didn't talk to me for
two weeks, but I didn't fool myself. I knew he had cut me." Another player
Eldridge studied and did combat with was the cornettist Rex Stewart, who
always went after notes that no one had played before. And Eldridge must
have listened to Red Allen when Allen was with Fletcher Henderson, in the
mid-thirties. Allen was a one-man avant-garde, who played "strange" notes
and had a revolutionary sense of time. He stretched regular four-four time to
make it accommodate his melodic inventions without losing the rhythmic
pulse. But Allen also had a dark, turning-away sound, and it was that elusive
quality which Eldridge absorbed. Of course, one of Eldridge's first and greatest admirations was the garrulous Coleman Hawkins of Fletcher Henderson's
1926 recording of "The Stampede." (Later, he and Hawkins became fast
friends, and worked, drove, and drank together until Hawkins' death, in 1969.)

The intensity and energy of Eldridge's mature style gave it a bas-relief
effect. His tone was heavy and irregular. His growling and rough low register often had an angry cast, and as he grew older it became even more plangent. You wondered, when you went to Jimmy Ryans in the seventies, how
he could get his massive style airborne yet again. There were two
Eldridges—fast and slow. The fast Eldridge was wild and even maniacal. He
might start a solo with an ascending shriek that was part run, part glissando.
Then he'd drop, in a dodging run, through three registers and play a low
long note, capped with a brief, hurried vibrato. He would leap to the top of
his middle register and issue five strutting staccato notes, placed slightly
behind the beat, and whistle back into his high register. He'd move rapidly
between two high notes the way most trumpeters move between middle C
and E, and pass through a two-octave interval and into a simple middle-
register figure. A pause, and he'd go down another octave, to his sad low register, and close the solo with a glancing high note. Eldridge was erratic.
Either his adventurousness would carry him off the deep end or he might
find himself in a situation that made him uncontrollably nervous—playing in
front of a congregation of his peers, as he had to do several times in 1957 on
the television show "The Sound of Jazz." Then he'd blare and show off and
play empty, gesticulating things. His best slow ballad numbers were
anthems. He would generally stay in his middle or low register and play ceremonial embellishments on the melody before moving into a full improvisation. This would involve sizable melodic fragments separated by frequent
rests and sounding like the original melody turned inside out. Eldridge's
slow ballads had a cathedral quality that no other jazz trumpeter—even the
1932 Armstrong—has surpassed.

Eldridge died last winter, at the age of seventy-eight. He had quit playing in 1979, when his health began to
deteriorate. "I don't miss the music anymore," he said several years after he
had stepped down. "I've had enough fun and praise and ovations to keep me.

I played fifty years, and that was long enough. Anyway, I found out the main doors were always locked. The color thing. I also found out I'd never get rich." For the last thirty or so years of his life, Eldridge lived, when he was off the road, in a small house in Queens, not far from the Nassau border. He lived with his wife, Vi, who had been a hostess at the old Savoy Ballroom, and whom he had married in 1936, and with his only child, Carole, a legal secretary. Very little in his house suggested what his life had been. In a small alcove off his living room he kept awards from the magazines *down beat* and *Esquire*, one from 1945 and one from 1946; a certificate of appreciation from Mayor John V. Lindsay; and a letter from President Jimmy Carter, thanking him for appearing at the jazz concert given on the South Lawn of the White House in June of 1978. Eldridge never changed much in appearance. His hair whitened and his glasses thickened, but his high, scrapy voice was full of pep and laughter. He would have been pleased by a summation of his work offered the other day by a fervent admirer: "Eldridge was a player of great magnitude."

## Goodbye, Michael

For the past seven years, one of the best open secrets of New York night life was the nearly year-round Sunday concerts given by the duo of Michael Moore (bass) and Gene Bertoncini (guitar) at Zinno, in Greenwich Village. But last spring Moore— some think he is the greatest living contrabassist of whatever kind—sold his house, in Bangor, Pennsylvania; had its contents packed in a forty-foot container; collected his portable bass and his wife, Meena, who is Indian, and their six-year-old son, Matthew; and moved to India, thereby leaving an irreparable hole in American music.

Moore talked about his move a few days before he left: "The packers came yesterday, but they didn't have enough boxes or tape, and one of them was drunk. Then, in the middle of it all, we had to close on the sale of the house. This all began one day at home when I was working on a piece I had written with Mick Goodrick, and I said that we should go and live in India and do nothing but sit and write music. I said it as a lark, but I had been to India with Meena to visit her family, and I knew how pleasant the hill stations are and how great the schools are. I had seen how far ahead of Matthew scholastically his Indian cousins were. Meena was born in London of Indian parents, but she was educated in Darjeeling, and I knew what a joke my own education was in comparison with hers. We had already been having trouble in Bangor. The officials decided to close our small local school and put all the kids—including Matthew—in a huge school an hour away by bus. We were very much opposed, and we got very much involved, and if we hadn't been perhaps we wouldn't have experienced the seamy things we did. Meena, not being white, became the center of the battle, and people threatened to burn us out. That made us think seriously for the first time about moving to India. Another thing was my career. I've been making a living mostly in night clubs as a bass player for over twenty years, and I'm tired of it. Anyway, I've never been that fond of performing. Being on a stage in front of people makes me nervous. I get *agita* in the stomach, as the Italians say. I was attracted to the bass in the first place because it was a background instrument—so what happened but I ended up playing mostly in duos and trios. I've also come to hate travelling. I don't intend to spend my sixties and seventies carting a bass up and down the country. I want to do more study-ing and writing. I've become a born-again Christian in the past seven or eight years, and I've been writing songs based on the Bible. I want to use my talents in a spiritual way, and writing spiritual songs comes easily to me. I clothe the words in the Bible with my melodies, which frees me from the thirty-two-bar standard-song box. I've written about thirty of these songs, and I'm hoping to get them published. I have also written a long piece for the bass, at the Eastman School, where I've been teaching summers. So I've gotten my feet wet in composition. I've always idealized the life of a painter and the writer and the composer. I've idealized the life of being alone in a room with nothing but yourself and your work.

"I've also been playing a lot of piano. I wouldn't feel comfortable yet about playing in public here, but over there I can work at it without embar-rassment. Accompanying pianists like Jimmy Rowles and Roger Kellaway and Tommy Flanagan taught me an incredible amount. I'd go home after working with them and try and incorporate in my piano what I had heard that night. A lot of the improvised music I like is endangered. It's gotten to the point where if you don't take care of it it'll go away, it'll disappear. At the same time, everything in jazz has gotten compartmentalized. You have to play a certain way to get anywhere. That freedom of the sixties and seventies is gone. Look at Jimmy Rowles. He's a timeless player, but there's no place for him. He should be playing in New York, where he's scarcely ever been, and he should be recorded every day. This is all part of the feeling I have that our values are out of whack in this country, that something is seriously wrong. So, at forty-five, I have to look elsewhere.

"I met Meena in 1981, in Edmonton. She owned part of a jazz club there, and she also managed it. She's a painter and a cordon-bleu chef. Her mother and brother live in Edmonton, and the rest of her family is in India. Her great-grandfather was one of the last rajas. She grew up in an extended fam-ily where the cousins are all like sisters and brothers. I like that family feel-ing. We're planning to rent a house in the Nilgiri Hills, the spice hills, south of Bangalore. There are four or five little towns up there, and we're leaning toward Kotagiri, which was a British hill station, seven thousand feet up. We're going to live on the money from the house, and I'm going to teach in a college nearby. I'll be out from under the constant financial pressure I've had here. I'm making just about the same money I was making ten years ago, and there was a nine-week period last summer when I didn't have any work at all. I've never been able to put together a retirement plan, and I don't have any medical insurance. Meena's family is excited that she is married to an American jazz musician. Artists are next to God in India. I've heard that the alto player Charlie Mariano is in Bombay, and I know that Maynard Ferguson lived in India for a while. He told me there are a lot of Indian jazz musicians. I loved the peaceful feeling I had when I was there.

"I feel bad about Gene. We've been playing together off and on for seventeen years. I had more trouble telling him I was leaving than telling my own parents. I told him that I had given him the best years of my life, and that even if the duo was to get busier it would mean a lot of travelling and being away from my family, and I didn't want that. Meena and I are homebodies. I told him that he'd be a lot freer now, that he'd have a chance to do all kinds of things he'd never done before. Gene's a worrier, and I told him he wouldn't have to worry about me anymore."

Michael Moore was born in Cincinnati, and came to the duo via the Cincinnati College–Conservatory of Music, the big band of Woody Herman, the Marian McPartland trio, and the Ruby Braff–George Barnes quartet. Gene Bertoncini, born in the Bronx in 1937, came to the duo via the architecture school of Notre Dame and the television bands of Merv Griffin and Skitch Henderson. Bertoncini and Moore first met in Salt Lake City twenty years ago, and played together soon after, in New York. Here is what Moore said about Bertoncini several years ago: "He never plays for himself, the way most guitarists do. He wants people to like his music, but without his having in any way to sell out. He's not fettered by what's hip. He hasn't listened widely in jazz. Sometimes when he solos, I don't hear any influences. It's all him. He has a great ear and perfect pitch and he can read anything. He does harmonic things I've never heard any other guitarist do. Improvisation used to be a means for him, but it has slowly become an end. What he's after is beautiful melody. He's a melodic improviser. He's moved by all good melody—that strain is in everything he does." And here is what Bertoncini said about Moore at the same time: "There is nothing about him as a player that I don't admire. Years ago, when I worked in the Philharmonic Café after concerts, Michael used to sit in and play the arco parts. I was bowled over by the warmth of his sound, and I still prefer him to any classical bassist. He is also a great pizzicato accompanist, and a brilliant improviser. I don't know anyone on any instrument who takes you on a melodic trip the way Michael does. I love to watch people responding to his solos. I consider him one of the great living jazz musicians. We've always thought of the music as being bigger than either of us. I've seen a dark side of Michael on occasion, but he cares about my feelings and I care about his."

Bertoncini does not overpraise Moore. His pizzicato solos, delivered more and more frequently in his upper registers, consist of ecstatic melodic lines, each line flowing into the next, and each bearing little flags of the original melody, which orient us and sharpen the freshness of the surrounding improvisations. These melodic flights have an urgency that no other bassist has matched, with the possible exception of the Charles Mingus of the early sixties. Mingus's solos had a bravura exuberance, a here's-how quality, while Moore's are dedicated to the proposition that beautiful melody can be wrested from even mediocre songs. Mingus bullied you; Moore takes you by the hand. Moore's pizzicato tone has the even, deep *string* sound of such earlier bassists as Jimmy Blanton and Oscar Pettiford and Mingus, and it is an antidote to the fashionable overamplified tone of most contemporary bassists. And Moore is an immaculate timekeeper. He chooses the right notes in every chord, and he lands at their center or just forward of their center in such a way that the time never sags or races. Somewhere along the line, Moore grew courageous about his arco playing, and he began to take almost as many arco solos as pizzicato solos. His bowed-tone is rich but delicately edged—it doesn't have the insistent, mahogany sound of, say, Gary Karr's—and, unlike that of most other arco players, it never goes flat. He rarely improvises with his bow; instead, he plays straight melody or choice melodic variations. These last are paeans to the almost impossible art of instantly making up beautiful melody.

Neither does Moore overpraise Bertoncini. He is an original jazz guitarist. Most of the guitarists who have appeared during the past forty years have been offshoots of Charlie Parker, or offshoots of his offshoots—handing down dazzling eight- or sixteen-note arabesques, showers of notes that give the listener no chance to pick and choose and breathe. They have also developed an interchangeable tone: electric, twangy, cheap—a neon sound. Bertoncini uses very little amplification, and comes as close as Jim Hall to a pure acoustic sound. His solos are constantly surprising, because they are free of licks. He is as much a celebrator of melody as Moore is. His solos, though less intense (guitar intensity is to bass intensity what a tenor is to a basso), are subtle investigations of the undersides of melody. (Moore works on top of his melodies.) His solos are full of short runs, placed unexpectedly; silences; dodging, behind-the-beat phrases; and easy connective passages. Bertoncini never belabors. He invites the listener in—just once—and if he hesitates goes on without him.

One of Moore and Bertoncini's last sets at Zinno took place a week before Moore left for India. The mournful news of his actual departure date had spread fast, and the little room at Zinno where they played—a wide hallway between the bar and the main dining room—was packed. Most professional musicians are hard, punctilious workers, and everything appeared to be business as usual. Moore, tall and trim, with his pleased, round burgher's face, was standing with his back to the left-hand wall of the room and holding his new portable "stick" bass, made specially for him by David Gage. Bertoncini, short, gray, handsome, with his guitarist's stoop and his sabre-like right thumbnail (he doesn't use a pick), was seated on a stool just in front of Moore. They opened with Denny Zeitlin's "Quiet Now," a blues with a bridge, and that was followed by Antonio Carlos Jobim's "Quiet Nights." Both numbers were warmups for a swinging "Sweet and Lovely," in which Bertoncini balanced runs with reining-in ritards. Alec Wilder's "Winter of My Discontent" was a bowed bass solo. It hummed and sang, moving elegantly through the thickly carpeted rooms where bowed basses live. Clare Fischer's "Pensativa" preceded a superb "My Funny Valentine" arco solo played partly against romantic Bertoncini chords. The duo ended the number with a chorus of counterpoint, the two instruments knocking heads, straining to get away from each other, embracing, arguing, harmonizing, creating a new, near-perfect music. A bossa nova had a lingering Bertoncini solo and a wild round of four-bar exchanges. The set ended appropriately, with a medium-tempo blues. Bertoncini soloed, and Moore issued a series of high melodies, each more radiant than the last.

Several weeks after Moore's departure, Bertoncini talked about his friend and colleague: "The nature of being a bass player is you have to have a lot of clients. You have to take a lot of work that isn't that great. Mike often had to play with musicians who were supposed to be good but who he didn't think *were* that good. He had a thing about pianists who played too many notes, who didn't play melodically or didn't keep good time. Sometimes he spoke of getting home after a gig and having a backache from working so hard to keep time. Years of schlepping a bass for not all that much money got to him. So did being treated just as any old bass player instead of as a major soloist, which he is. He would say to me that performing didn't mean that much, which was the opposite of the way he looked and acted on the stage. In fact, I never saw anyone who seemingly loved to play more than he did. He always denied it, but I think he revelled in people's attention. If he didn't get attention, it upset him. As a bass player, he got more acclaim than most. For him to say he was tired of it all doesn't make sense.

"The duo would have gone on forever. I think it was the best jazz duo, and we were on the verge. We were getting calls from festivals in Norway and Brazil and Canada. Three years ago, we did ten concerts, and the next year fifteen. This past year, we did more than twenty, and that doesn't count the Sundays at Zinno and the occasional night-club gigs and private parties. And there was always the possibility of working off and on with another musician—a horn player, say, like Chet Baker, whom we played with in a club in Annapolis.

"I started on my own as a guitarist, but I always had a duo in mind. I feel honored that Mike chose me as his partner. He seemed to respect me as a musician. I felt that my reputation as a musician was that much better for working with him. After a while, I guess I got to rely on him. There was no question we'd be safe, his playing was so dependable. The challenge for me is to go out there and grow. I just came back from a festival in Norway, and I used a Norwegian bass player, and it worked OK. Anyway, I can't imagine things working out in India for this great musical force. I can't imagine him hiding his gifts in a culture where he can't make that much of a musical contribution. His gift is needed here. Mike started reading the Bible several years ago, and he changed totally. He used to get angry and be critical about almost everything, but he gradually became a model of patience. I'd be concerned about a certain job situation, and I'd run it past him, and he'd say, 'Sure! Let's do it!' I think he prayed about his decision, and I feel good about that. It was nice to be around the high values in his life and in his music. He never played a note he didn't mean. He never joked with the music.

"But there was always something lurking in Mike—a weariness of the music business, of I don't know what. His living way out there, near the Delaware Water Gap, didn't help. Neither did the fact that he *always* had his answering service on. You have to be accessible in the music business."

Odysseys are never simple, and Moore's is not over. Word has come to Bertoncini in a roundabout way that Moore and his wife have left India and are living in England, where she is working and he is writing a string quartet. The only letter Bertoncini has got from Moore was written in India, and in it Moore said that a restaurant they had eaten in had a lot of flies but that the carbonara sauce wasn't bad.

*Moore has long since returned to New York, where he now lives. He and Bertoncini occasionally play together, and that is, as always, ecstatic. But they have mostly gone their own brilliant, utterly original ways, each shedding his particular light, each moving us that invaluable inch or two off center.*

## Miles

**M**iles Davis has led a bedevilled life. He was born in 1926 in Alton, Illinois, and raised in East St. Louis. He has an older sister, Dorothy, and a younger brother, Vernon. His father was a dentist who eventually retired to a two-hundred-acre farm he owned, in Millstadt, Illinois. His mother was beautiful and stylish and idle. He got on well with his father, but found his mother, whom he loved, possessive, peevish, and heavy-handed. He took up the trumpet at ten, and by the time he was in high school he had been given his second trumpet and had met his first idol, Clark Terry. He worked in a local band led by Eddy Randle, then, at eighteen, he suddenly accelerated. He had the first of two children by a woman whom he never married; he graduated from high school; he worked for two weeks in Billy Eckstine's legendary bebop band, with Charlie Parker, Dizzy Gillespie, and Art Blakey; he moved to New York and enrolled in Juilliard; and he began hanging out with Parker and Gillespie and Fats Navarro. A year later, his attractive aura already working, he was on one of the earliest and most famous bebop records ("Billie's Bounce," "Now's the Time"), with Parker, Gillespie, and Max Roach. And he appeared on Fifty-second Street with Parker and Coleman Hawkins. His style, though still hesitant, began to emerge.

In the late forties, inspired by Claude Thornhill's big band, he organized the nonet (among the players Lee Konitz, Gerry Mulligan, Kai Winding, John Lewis, Max Roach) that made the celebrated Capitol album "Birth of the Cool." The nonet's laid-back quality and calm, intricate, deep-red arrangements made it the most adventurous small band since the Ellington small bands and some of the Woody Herman Woodchopper sides of 1946. (The typical small bebop bands of the time were not ensemble groups, like the nonet. They used leaping, tongue-tying unison opening-and-closing collective passages, but the often long solos that came between carried the musical weight.) Davis also began taking drugs. He describes what happened in his new autobiography, *Miles*: "I lost my sense of discipline, lost my sense of control over my life, and started to drift. It wasn't like I didn't know what was happening to me. I did, but I didn't care anymore. I had such confidence in myself that even when I was losing control I really felt I had everything under control. But your mind can play tricks on you. I guess when I started to hang like I did, it surprised a lot of people who thought I had it all together. It also surprised me." (The book, done with a poet and teacher named Quincy Troupe, is petulant, outspoken, defensive, honeyed, error-filled, and impressionistic—and loaded to the gunwales with four-letter words. Davis uses them more as hammer blows than for their literal meanings, and they soon become a dull barrage, which, for whatever reasons, gradually abates as the book goes along.)

Davis takes pains to point out that he was not alone in his addiction. Many of the best young musicians of the late forties—black and white—became heroin addicts, and he needlessly names them. Here, in the late fifties, is Billie Holiday, one of the most famous victims of this devastating plague: "She was looking real bad by this time, worn out, worn down, and haggard around the face and all. Thin. Mouth sagging at both corners. She was scratching a lot." (There are other eloquent patches in the book, but it is difficult to tell whether they are Davis's or Troupe's doing. Listen to this description of the church music Davis heard early in his life: "We'd be walking on these dark country roads at night and all of a sudden this music would seem to come out of nowhere, out of them spooky-looking trees that everybody said ghosts lived in. Anyway, we'd be on the side of the road—whoever I was with, one of my uncles or my cousin James—and I remember somebody would be playing a guitar the way B. B. King plays. And I remember a man and a woman singing and talking about getting *down!* Shit, that music was something, especially that woman singing. But I think that kind of stuff stayed with me, you know what I mean? That *kind* of sound in music, that blues, church, back-road funk kind of thing, that southern, midwestern, rural sound and rhythm.") Davis began stealing and even pimping to support his heroin habit. He was busted on the West Coast. He was busted again when he went home, ostensibly to give up drugs. He quit heroin in 1953, backslid, and quit for good in 1954.

Almost immediately, his professional life turned around. He led two classic recording sessions in 1954. The first consisted simply of two blues, the medium-tempo "Walkin'" and the faster "Blue 'n' Boogie." Each took up one side of a ten-inch LP, and both were played by Davis, Lucky Thompson, J. J. Johnson, Horace Silver, Percy Heath, and Kenny Clarke. Davis's mature style—annunciatory, clipped, vibratoless, singing—dominated both numbers and both recordings. The second recording had three originals and one standard tune, and on hand were Thelonious Monk, Milt Jackson, Heath, and Clarke. (Davis, along with Charles Mingus and Duke Ellington, has always chosen musicians who can both obey and enrich his sometimes abstruse musical designs.) Davis was in a paradoxical mood. Although he loved Monk's playing, he made him lay out behind his solos on three of the numbers. Both recordings were hailed as bellwethers; actually, they marked an enlightened reshaping of the straight-ahead, uncluttered swing of Red Norvo and Count Basie and the trumpeter Joe Thomas. Davis and his men set aside the eccentricities and excesses of bebop (in whose house most of them had been raised) while retaining its broadened harmonic base. A year later, Davis appeared at the second Newport Jazz Festival with a pickup group consisting of Gerry Mulligan, Zoot Sims, Monk, Heath, and Connie Kay—all musicians he had worked with. He played three numbers—open-horn versions of "Hackensack" and "Now's the Time," and a muted, inner-ear " 'Round Midnight." His from-the-mountaintop, time-stopping open-horn solos made it clear that Davis, who had been struggling for much of the time since he came East, had arrived. Columbia Records agreed, and before the year was out had signed him to a contract he says was worth three hundred thousand dollars a year. (He stayed with Columbia until 1985, when he went to Warner Brothers Records.) Davis's comments in *Miles* on the Columbia signing are far from the it's-not-my-fault defensiveness of the artist who has had a windfall: "And yes, going with Columbia did mean more money, but what's wrong with getting paid for what you do and getting paid well? I never saw nothing in poverty and hard times and the blues. I never wanted that for myself. I saw what it really was when I was strung out on heroin, and I didn't want to see it again. As long as I could get what I needed from the white world on my own terms, without selling myself out to all of those people who would love to exploit me, then I was going to go for what I know is real."

Davis had entered his great period. He assembled the first of two working bands, and it included, at various times, John Coltrane, Cannonball Adderley, Red Garland, Bill Evans, Paul Chambers, and Philly Joe Jones. Davis, like Mingus, began experimenting with different kinds of improvisation, and he made the album "Kind of Blue," in which he gave his players modal sketches to work their variations on, and set them loose, one take per number. The results are cool, subtle, edgeless music. Davis was also busy in the

Columbia studios making three concerto albums—"Miles Ahead," "Porgy and Bess," and "Sketches of Spain"—in which, accompanied by a big band playing Gil Evans' velvet arrangements, he was the only soloist. (Would that Louis Armstrong had had such cosseting when he was at his height, in 1933!) Davis's second famous small working band arrived in the sixties and had Wayne Shorter, Herbie Hancock, Ron Carter, and Tony Williams. Its repertory moved between mooning, muted ballads and furious up-tempo numbers, in which Davis, always a middle-register player, ventured into the upper regions and used unaccustomed avalanches of notes.

Davis's life since the early sixties has been hill-and-dale. He has been married to and divorced from the dancer Frances Taylor and the actress Cicely Tyson. He has been plagued by medical problems, among them hip operations, a stroke, two broken ankles, pneumonia, and diabetes. From 1975 to 1980, he dropped out. He gave up playing and retired to his house, on West Seventy-seventh Street. Here, brutally, is what he did: "I just took a lot of cocaine (about $500 a day at one point) and fucked all the women I could get into my house. I was also addicted to pills, like Percodan and Seconal, and I was drinking a lot, Heinekens and cognac. . . . I didn't go out too often and when I did it was mostly to after-hours places up in Harlem where I just kept on getting high and living from day to day. . . . The house was filthy and real dark and gloomy, like a dungeon." George Butler, of Columbia Records, got Davis back on the track, and he began coming out again in 1981. Since then, he says, he has given up drugs and drinking. He has also given up his house, and now divides his time between Malibu and an apartment on Central Park South.

Although Davis has tinkered endlessly with his music (various types of improvising, odd time signatures, synthesizers, an electric trumpet), his playing, which resides at the still center of all these experiments, has changed little. He has never been much of a technician, and he has been clever enough to keep his style within his abilities. When he came East in the forties, he ignored his limitations, and his solos were sometimes a string of clams. He ignored them again when he had the Shorter-Williams band and began shooting wildly into the upper register, with nerve-racking results. Many people have influenced Davis—Louis Armstrong, Clark Terry, Shorty Baker, Fats Navarro Ahmad Jamal, Bobby Hackett, Gil Evans, Lester Young, Charlie Parker, and Dizzy Gillespie. Perhaps the heaviest hand on his playing was that of an early teacher who told him never to play with a vibrato, that he'd have plenty of time for a vibrato when he grew old and could no longer control his lip. His no-vibrato attack sometimes gives his playing an abrupt, telegraphic air, but he softens this by using a lot of rests and long notes. He also softens his attack with his tone. It is full, but it is not a brass tone, a trumpet tone. It is human sound compressed into trumpet sound. His solos in the Gil Evans "Sketches of Spain" album have a unique pleading, sorrowing quality. There have been many other players who have got a human sound—Johnny Hodges, Ben Webster, Red Allen, Pee Wee Russell—but their tonal qualities have never superseded the basic sound of their instruments. Davis has succeeded in making almost visible the emotions—longing, sadness, pity—that move just beneath his complex surface. But his eerie, buttonholding sound is not as common on his recent, synthesizer-controlled recordings, where electronics and odd time signatures dominate the surroundings, and cause him to sound removed and disjointed. The great Davis still resides in his recordings of thirty years ago.

Davis has become a business. On one of his Warner Brothers Records release, "Amandla," he lists his production coordinators, his tour manager, his business manager, and his personal manager. The cover of the album is a semi-abstract self-portrait. (Like such earlier worthies as Pee Wee Russell and George Wettling, Davis has taken up painting.) Beneath Davis's head are the bell of a trumpet and a globe, with the African continent thereon. Davis's eyes, looking into the middle distance, are cold and furious, as if he were tallying the various imponderables that have kept him from becoming the genius he believes himself to be.

# THE NINETIES AND BEYOND

# 1990

## Max and Kit

The 92nd Street Y, famous for its "Lyrics and Lyricists" series, its poetry readings, and its Schubertiade, hasn't paid a great deal of attention to jazz, and, perhaps because of that and to balance Dick Hyman's conservative "Jazz in July" concerts, it inaugurated late in January a three-day festival of modern jazz, called "Jazz in January." It was subtitled "The Worlds of Max Roach," and was organized by the drummer himself.

Roach, now sixty-six, made his mark in the mid-forties with Dizzy Gillespie, Charlie Parker, and Bud Powell. Working under the suns of Kenny Clarke and Sid Catlett, he has gradually evolved a revolutionary style that is melodic and multi-rhythmic. He no longer simply accompanies other instruments but plays melodically alongside them. His drumming has become largely abstract; he improvises rhythms in the ensembles and in his solos which may have no discernible pulse and nothing to do with the underlying beat. Instead of swinging, the way Catlett did, he fills his listeners' heads with a succession of timbres that reach from the treble of his cymbals to the subterranean movements of his bass drum. It is possible to marvel at Roach's complexities without tapping your foot once.

Roach is a polymath. In 1960, he and Charles Mingus put together a brilliant rump festival in Newport to protest George Wein's behemoth. Two years later, he made a tempestuous trio album with Mingus and Duke Ellington. (Ellington sailed serenely over the surrounding temperaments.) He has written, and performed in, several large pieces dedicated to anti-racist causes. He started a percussion group, called M'Boom, and his Double Quartet, which consists of trumpet, tenor saxophone, bass, drums, and a string quartet. He has recently recorded with such avant-gardists as Anthony Braxton, Archie Shepp, and Cecil Taylor. He is a professor of music at the University of Massachusetts, and he was awarded a MacArthur Foundation fellowship.

Roach made only cameo appearances at the first two "Jazz in January" concerts. Then, on the third night, he and the video artist Kit Fitzgerald filled Kaufmann Hall for an hour and a half with drums and pictures. Roach's drums were set up center stage on a dais, and behind the dais was a sizable movie screen. As Roach played, a mobile television cameraman shot him from every angle. The images appeared on a small monitor in front of Kit Fitzgerald, who sat behind a battery of television equipment at the foot of the stage. Using a computerized keyboard—a kind of video synthesizer—she improvised on what she saw on her monitor, and her improvisations were relayed to a projector behind the screen. Roach improvised on what was in his head, and Fitzgerald improvised on Roach. The images Fitzgerald created were never still, and were avant-garde "painting." You saw Rorschach blots; kaleidoscopic images; recollections, here and there, of the work of Morris Louis, Marsden Hartley, and Richard Diebenkorn; Roach's head and hands, frozen and in motion; drumsticks turning into descending stairs; drumsticks fracturing into hundreds of highly colored cubes; cymbals shining like moons, then melting into Daliesque watches; Roach enormous and Roach in the distance, ghostly and indistinct. Surprisingly, his sounds and Fitzgerald's pictures did not war, as the aural and the visual so often do. You heard what you saw, and saw what you heard. Roach's performance was broken into ten sections, and he started many with a deceptively simple rhythm on his high hat and bass drum. This might be made up of a high-hat whole note and two bass-drum quarter notes, and it would become an ostinato over which he would improvise his abstractions—a formidably difficult patting-your-head-and-rubbing-your-stomach exercise. As each section built, Roach used all his melodic devices: he rattled his sticks ferociously on his snare and tomtom rims; he got round booms with his mallets on his snare (its snares had been released) and on his tomtoms, and ocean swells on his cymbals; he used only wire brushes on a snare drum set up at stage right, and sticks on a high hat at stage left.

The memory of the first two "Jazz in January" concerts was nearly obliterated by the Roach-Fitzgerald duet. On the first night, the Uptown String Quartet—half of the Double Quartet—composed of Diane Monroe (violin, and a teacher at Swarthmore), Lesa Terry (violin, and member of the Broadway "Black and Blue" band), Eileen Folson (cello, and a former member of the New York Philharmonic), and Maxine Roach (viola, Max's daughter, and a graduate of Oberlin), played eleven numbers, including ragtime pieces, spirituals, a couple of blues, a semi-tonal piece, and a piece in which the group first strummed their instruments and then plucked them. Everyone soloed, and the quartet, despite some pitch lapses, had a nice ecumenical lilt.

The second night, the trumpeter Lester Bowie brought on his Brass Fantasy, which consists of four trumpets, a horn, two trombones, a tuba, drums, and percussion. Bowie, who is just shy of fifty, has been an avant-garde terror for twenty-five years. He is also a comedian. He wears a doctor's white coat onstage, and he likes to use his horn for blats, growls, squeals, and half-valve effects—sounds first floated by the Ellington cornettist Rex Stewart in the early forties. The Brass Fantasy did a kind of gospel blues, three songs associated with Billie Holiday ("God Bless the Child," "Strange Fruit," and "Good Morning Heartache"), a Whitney Houston ("Saving All My Love for You"), and a number called "The Emperor," in which the trombonist Steve Turre soloed on small and large conch shells, separately and then together, and achieved an alto, calling-over-the-flats sound. The band moved between glutinous dance-band harmonies and dissonant ensembles. Bowie's solos, barring melodic patches, were full of barnyard sounds. His doctor's coat used to be made of cotton, but he wore satin at the Y.

The afternoon before "Jazz in January," WNYC presented the first of this season's "New Sounds" concerts at Merkin Hall, and it served as a preamble to the Y festival. The jazz minimalist, reedman, and composer Jon Gibson had Martin Goldray on piano, Blue Gene Tyranny on synthesizer, and Bill Ruyle on percussion. Gibson has worked with Philip Glass, and his four pieces were filled with the Raymond Loewy effects of the minimalists—one-two-three melodies, ostinatos, repetition, and a dull glossiness. The Les Misérables Brass Band followed. Made up of two trumpets, horn, trombone, alto saxophone, baritone saxophone, tuba, drums, and percussion, it is an excited, hybrid group: it played a merengue, an East European march, David Byrne's "In the Future," a Pakistani meditation, and Jimi Hendrix's "Manic Depression." The phenomenal tubist Marcus Rojas danced while he played; the trumpeter Frank London, who is the leader, made Lester Bowie sounds; and the trombonist David Harris blew so hard he quivered. The Les Misérables band made Bowie's Brass Fantasy and the much touted Dirty Dozen, from New Orleans, seem peaked.

The concert was closed by the World Saxophone Quartet, which, when it started out, in the mid-seventies, liked to parody everyone. But it has grown sedate, and it spends much of its time celebrating its own sumptuous sound. (David Murray is still on tenor saxophone, Oliver Lake on alto, and Hamiet Bluiett on baritone, but the alto saxophonist Julius Hemphill has been replaced by Arthur Blythe.) The group, which seemed off center, played six unidentified numbers. Murray did a lullaby and Lake a long *a cappella* passage. There were bits of free ensemble, and some chocolate harmonies on a fast riff tune. In the fifth, and best, number Bluiett played Duke Ellington's "Sophisticated Lady," holding himself to the sort of reverential melodic embellishments and transcendent basso-profundo tones that Harry Carney used when Ellington featured him on the song. Carney loved to boost other baritone saxophonists, and Bluiett's performance would have pleased him.

## Imagining Music

For a long time, jazz fans were idolaters, who enshrined their Louis Armstrongs and Billie Holidays and Charlie Parkers. This defensive zealotry was particularly apparent when the music was still regarded as mean and primitive. Early jazz writers were even more protective. They made such troubled heroes as King Oliver (down and out in Savannah in 1938, aged sixty), Bix Beiderbecke (dead of drink in 1931, aged twenty-eight), and Bunk Johnson (toothless and hornless in New Iberia, Louisiana, aged forty-five) into tragic figures and wrote about them with an "O lost, and by the wind grieved, ghost" sentimentality. This sentimentality leaked into the first full-length jazz movies in the fifties, and it's still in evidence, despite such heavy lumber as *'Round Midnight* and *Bird*. (The best feature film about jazz is the little-known, low-budget *The Gig*, written and directed in the mid-eighties by the playwright Frank Gilroy. It deals with a group of white amateur musicians—and a black professional ringer—who play a summer gig in the Catskills, and it explains for the first time the blue-collar ethos of the average jazz musicians.) The same myth-making has also affected most of the fiction written about jazz since 1938, when Dorothy Baker published *Young Man with a Horn*, a pioneering, worshipful novel based on Beiderbecke.

But how *do* you write fiction (or poetry, for that matter) about painters and dancers and writers and musicians? The jazz fan's idol-making is common to all the arts. Perhaps there are three ways to write about a Picasso or Balanchine or Horowitz: ennoble him; reduce him to life-size; try to show him as the obsessed, gifted drudge most artists are. Laboriously spinning their works out of themselves, artists are desperate more often than exultant. They take no vacations: one invention leads to another, and the iron must never be allowed to cool. All camouflage themselves. Writers pretend to be inarticulate, painters speak in symbols or hyperbole, musicians gossip and tell jokes, dancers talk about their bodies and about food. There is an added difficulty in writing fiction about jazz: The music is ephemeral. A novelist can describe the "Appassionata" and tell you exactly how his pianist hero plays it, but a jazz novelist must describe a music that is gone the instant it is played. Nowhere else does invention turn into memory so quickly. (Playwrights have an edge in writing about jazz: plays are a performer's art, like jazz. Witness Jack Gelber's *The Connection* and August Wilson's *Ma Rainey's Black Bottom*; both even have onstage bands.)

Marcela Breton clearly kept these difficulties in mind when she put together the anthology of jazz short stories she calls *Hot and Cool*. There are nineteen stories, arranged in rough chronological order. The earliest, by Rudolph Fisher, a novelist of the Harlem Renaissance, was published in 1930, and the most recent, by Martin Gardner, in 1987. Five of the stories deal directly with jazz. Six are largely taken up by racial matters, and six are about drugs and drinking. One is about a jazz fan, and one is a love story. The quality of the stories varies a good deal. "Mending Wall," by Willard Marsh, is set in Mexico and reads like an inept translation from the Spanish. Fisher's story, "Common Meter," is an engaging antique that is full of dated black slang and anthropomorphic musical descriptions: "Clarinets wailed, saxophones moaned, trumpets wept wretchedly, trombones laughed bitterly, even the great bass horn sobbed dismally from the depths." In Ann Petry's "Solo on the Drums," a jilted drummer makes his "big bass drum growl," and in "The Screamers" LeRoi Jones, using an arty epigrammatic prose, converts the music into Message: "The repeated rhythmic figure, a screamed riff, pushed in its insistence past music. It was hatred and frustration, secrecy and despair. It spurted out of the diphthong culture, and reinforced the black cults of emotion. There was no compromise, no dreary sophistication, only the elegance of something that is too ugly to be described."

These various excesses are nicely balanced by Terry Southern and Richard Yates and Langston Hughes. Southern writes with great subtlety about a white jazz lover who unwittingly becomes, in a black musician's disparaging words, a "professional nigger lover." Yates tells us of a black pianist who enrages two white admirers by Uncle Tomming with an important night-club owner. Hughes, in his best jess-lissen style, deals with a rich white matron, Mrs. Ellsworth, who underwrites the classical training of a black woman pianist, Oceola Jones; in the end, Oceola marries and goes back to playing blues. ("Is this what I spent thousands of dollars to teach you?" Mrs. Ellsworth asks as Oceola makes "the bass notes throb like tom-toms deep in the earth.")

There are several funny stories in the book. In Peter De Vries' "Jam Today," which first appeared in *The New Yorker*, the narrator goes to a forties "platter party," at which each guest is asked to play his favorite 78-rpm record. The party turns out to be made up of moldy figs who believe that no good jazz has been played since 1930, but the narrator brings a Benny Goodman big-band record. Embarrassed, he breaks the record and stuffs it into his overcoat pocket, then discovers when he leaves that he has put it in his host's pocket. Martin Gardner's "The Devil and the Trombone" deals with a professor returning home from a wearying evening meeting who stops in at a church to rest his mind and listen to the organ music he hears inside. The organist, dressed in a white robe, has wings folded at his sides, and he is playing unearthly music. Out of the blackness behind him comes a tall, hairy figure with swarthy skin and a forked-tail, who begins playing raucous tailgate trombone. The two jam together, and their music is so empyrean that the professor finds he suddenly understands the meaning of life—when the music stops, and the angelic figure tells him to go back to his pew and wake himself up. Donald Barthelme's ingenious "The King of Jazz," which also appeared in *The New Yorker*, is about the perfervid way that jazz has progressed in its ninety years, today's heroes trampling on yesterday's myths. It also attempts to solve the problem of how to describe the music—a problem that many writers have attacked with a metaphor in each hand. He gives us thirteen hilarious examples of how to approximate the sounds of jazz. Here are four: "That sounds like polar bears crossing Arctic ice pans? That sounds like a herd of musk ox in full flight? That sounds like male walruses diving to the bottom of the sea? That sounds like fumaroles smoking on the slopes of Mt. Katmai?"

Toni Cade Bambara's "Medley" is a dialect story told by a black beautician who walks out on the bass player she lives with. She describes him:

Larry Landers looked more like a bass player than ole Mingus himself. Got these long arms that drape down over the bass like they were grown special for that purpose. Fine, strong hands with long fingers and muscular knuckles, the dimples deep black at the joints. His calluses so other-colored and hard, looked like Larry had swiped his grand-mother's tarnished thimbles to play with. He'd move in on that bass like he was going to hump it or something, slide up behind it as he lifted it from the rug, all slinky. He'd become one with the wood. Head dipped down sideways bobbing out the rhythm, feet tapping, legs jiggling, he'd look good. Thing about it, though, ole Larry couldn't play for shit.

Al Young's "Chicken Hawk's Dream" is short and nearly perfect. It begins: "Chicken Hawk stayed high pretty much all the time and he was nineteen years old limping down academic corridors trying to make it to twelfth grade." Chicken Hawk is a drug addict who lives in Detroit and dreams that he is walking around New York playing fantastic alto saxophone. He is so sure that the dream is true that he borrows a horn to practice on. But he can only make it squeak. He blames the horn, and drifts away with his friend Wine. Later, the narrator runs into Chicken Hawk on the street, and Chicken Hawk tells him that he is about to leave for New York to put together a band and make some records, as soon as he gets his horn out of hock.

Three stories in *Hot and Cool* move close to the heart of jazz. The longest, at sixty-three pages, is "The Pursuer," by the Argentine novelist Julio Cortázar. It was published in the late sixties, and is a thinly disguised account of the last months in the life of Charlie Parker, here called Johnny Carter. Cortázar moves inside Carter's complex, duplicitous, crazy head. Carter tells his Boswell, a critic named Bruno, about how he has been remembering his past: "It wasn't thinking, it seems to me I told you a lot of times, I never think; I'm like standing on a corner watching what I think go by, but I'm not thinking what I see. You dig?" Bruno decides not to alter the second edition of his biography of Carter, despite Carter's having told him that the book was fine except that he had been left out of it. Bruno explains with infuriating cool, "I decided not to touch the second edition, to go on putting Johnny forth as he was at bottom: a poor sonofabitch with barely mediocre intelligence, endowed like so many musicians, so many chess players and poets, with the gift of creating incredible things without the slightest consciousness (at most, the pride of a boxer who knows how strong he is) of the dimensions of his work."

Far more famous is James Baldwin's "Sonny's Blues," published in the late fifties. Baldwin was an exceptional essayist, but his fiction was often heated and clumsy. "Sonny's Blues" is about a drug addict who finds salvation—apparent salvation—by becoming a jazz pianist. The narrator, who is Sonny's straight older brother, goes to a club to hear him and, after the first set, sends a drink up to the bandstand for Sonny. (There are a number of gaffes in the stories, and this is one. Musicians rarely stay on the bandstand between sets.) Baldwin ends the story with a disastrous sentence: "For me, then, as they began to play again, [the drink] glowed and shook above my brother's head like the very cup of trembling."

In its handmade, assiduous way, Eudora Welty's "Powerhouse" may be the best fiction ever written about jazz. It first appeared in *The Atlantic*, in 1941, when she was a new writer, and it seems to be based on her having heard Fats Waller on the road in the South. (The central figure, Powerhouse, *is* Waller, and not "a pianist in the style of Albert Ammons and Meade Lux Lewis," as Marcela Breton claims in her introduction.) The story is an extraordinary mixture of surrealism and truth. It has a jittering comic surface, like Waller himself, that hides, as Waller's did, the heaviness and sadness most blacks carried around in this country fifty years ago—particularly if they were musicians from New York doing a string of one-night stands in the Deep South. The musicians play, have a beer at a nearby black café between sets, and play again. Here is some of Welty's exotic description of Waller: "You can't tell what he is. 'Nigger man'?—he looks more Asiatic, monkey, Jewish, Babylonian, Peruvian, fanatic, devil. He has pale gray eyes, heavy lids, maybe horny, like a lizard." Powerhouse tells his musicians that he has got a telegram from one Uranus Knockwood, saying that his wife is dead. He had talked to his wife on the telephone the night before, and she said she might jump out of the window. But no one knows who Uranus Knockwood is (a Welty conundrum, in which the despotic Greek god Uranus is guarded by Lady Luck), and the musicians begin to understand that perhaps Powerhouse is fantasizing and that his fantasy rests on the hope that expecting the worst might bring the opposite. Eudora Welty makes the reader see *and* hear Powerhouse. He is outsize in the story, but he is utterly human—a huge man, like Waller.

## Giants

Virtuosos do not fit easily into jazz. The music revolves around improvisation, and jazz improvisers need only enough technique to play what they hear in their heads. (The drummer Sidney Catlett never considered himself a virtuoso, but he got off certain dazzling snare and cymbal patterns that not even the virtuosic Buddy Rich could match. Catlett's technique was an extension of his imagination; impossible figures popped into his head and instantaneously became real.) Too much technique saps improvisation: it causes floridity and grandstanding, and it tricks audiences into believing that bombast is music. Jazz has harbored two undeniable virtuosos (Rich may have been a third), but no one else has ever known quite what to do with them. They are Sarah Vaughan, who died last spring at the age of sixty-six, and Art Tatum (1909–56), whose final recordings have been issued—with an hour of previously unreleased material—on six compact disks called "Art Tatum: The Complete Pablo Group Masterpieces."

Sarah Vaughan was born in Newark and joined Earl Hines' big band as a singer and second pianist when she was nineteen. She never had any formal training—she was a bebop baby. Charlie Parker and Dizzy Gillespie were in Hines' band, and so was the singer Billy Eckstine. Vaughan made her first recordings with Eckstine when he formed his own big band in 1944, and a year later she made a small-band record with Parker and Gillespie. By the end of the fifties, she had become a famous singer who moved easily between jazz and popular song. By the end of the sixties, she was a singer of operatic dimensions. She grew to diva proportions, and so did her voice. She had four octaves, each clear and spacious. She sang falsetto, and she could sound like a baritone. She could drop from soprano to baritone in the space of one word. Her low tones were cavernous and her high notes were silver peaks. She had several different vibratos, and when it pleased her she could sing without any vibrato at all. (Think of the Kate Smith singers of the thirties: their vibratos led them.)

In 1980, the composer, conductor, and critic Gunther Schuller introduced Vaughan at a recital she gave at the Smithsonian, and he said that she was "the greatest vocal artist of our century," a hosanna that he immediately complicated by adding that she was "the most *creative* vocal artist of our time." This was true. She was a wonderful embellisher and improviser, who never sang a song the same way twice. She remade her materials—generally, the songs of Rodgers and Hart, the Gershwins, Kern, Porter, and Arlen—in her own image. The cost to the songs was sometimes high. She altered melodic lines and harmonies, mislaid lyrics, and used so much melisma that the words became unintelligible. At her most unfettered, she became a horn singer. Yet her melodic lines were of such complexity and daring that no horn player could have played them. Ultimately, she became a kind of abstract singer, whose materials were inadequate for what she did but were all she had. She could, of course, also sing a song relatively straight. But the richness of her voice was always there, and, no matter how few melodic and harmonic alterations she made, this richness tended to overshadow the song, to lean over it, like a voluptuous woman reading a book.

Vaughan and Art Tatum revelled in their techniques. Vaughan liked to show off her intervals, her perfect pitch, her vibratos, and her range. Tatum liked to show off his touch, his startling speed, his two-handed runs, and his left hand, which could match his right. As Vaughan and Tatum grew older, they inevitably leaned more and more on their technical tricks. Vaughan shuttled between her registers, held notes so long they took on a life of their own, and pretended she was Joan Sutherland or Paul Robeson. Tatum released harmonic clouds, making his chords sound as if they had fifteen or twenty notes, and connected them with long runs—coils of sound that trapped the listener and freed Tatum of the burden of fresh improvisations. He gave the impression at such times that he was speeding luxuriously through the song; in reality, he was pedalling easily in place. Both Vaughan and Tatum were worshipped by their audiences and by their fellow-musicians—for their bravura effects and for their musicianship—and they wore their mantles with a pleased arrogance.

Tatum's career didn't last much more than twenty years. (Vaughan's lasted forty-five years, an impressive length of time for any singer, and more impressive still when one realizes that her voice was even more resilient and powerful at the end of her career than at the beginning.) Tatum was recorded only fitfully until the early fifties, when the jazz impresario Norman Granz had him set down about two hundred numbers, more than a hundred of them solo efforts and the rest with various instrumentalists. Granz got to Tatum when he was already showing signs of prolixity, but there are sufficient flashes of his old brilliance. This is particularly true of the group numbers, even though Tatum had spent most of his career as a solo pianist and found it difficult to squeeze himself into ensemble situations. He towered over musicians he was supposed to accompany, or else soloed so magnificently that he dwarfed everyone else.

Granz recorded Tatum with seven groups between 1954 and 1956. There were fourteen numbers with Benny Carter (on alto saxophone) and Louis Bellson; eight with Roy Eldridge, the bassist John Simmons, and the drummer Alvin Stoller; twenty-five with Lionel Hampton and Buddy Rich, augmented here and there by the trumpeter Harry Edison, the bassist Red Callender, and the guitarist Barney Kessel; ten with Callender and Jo Jones; eight with Buddy DeFranco, Callender, and the drummer Bill Douglass; and seven with the tenor saxophonist Ben Webster, Callender, and Douglass. Carter and Tatum got along well: Carter coasts easily over Tatum's polite waves, and Bellson is steady and swinging. Their best side is a medium-tempo "Blues in B Flat." In it, Tatum's four impassioned choruses amount to a short history of blues piano, and Carter's four come as close to being impassioned as he ever gets.

The Eldridge session doesn't quite work. The trumpeter, using a mute most of the time, buzzes along somewhere near Tatum, and his open horn is not as galvanic as it often was at this period. Tatum becomes irrepressible behind Eldridge's second chorus in "I Surrender Dear," when he looses an avalanche of notes that suggest a bad boy rolling down a hill in a barrel to get attention. Tatum, Hampton, and Rich recorded fifteen of their numbers at one session. Rich is heavy, and Hampton's vibes sound like nails being poured into a tin can. But Tatum has a good time. He drops some stride piano in behind Hampton on "Hallelujah," he solos behind Hampton's solo in "Body and Soul," and he reproduces Nat Cole's bridge from his trio recording of "What Is This Thing Called Love?" Harry Edison helps things along in the eight numbers he is in, but he is almost thrown in "Verve Blues" when Tatum plays some less than tonal tremolos behind him. The trio numbers with Red Callender and Jo Jones are just that—Tatum accompanied by bass and drums. Jones takes a couple of airy brush solos, and Tatum swings surprisingly hard in "Isn't It Romantic?" and "I Guess I'll Have to Change My Plan."

The Tatum-DeFranco-Douglas-Callender numbers are a lark. DeFranco, the most fluent of all jazz clarinettists, suits Tatum completely. They play tag, echo each other, parody each other, attempt to escape from each other, and turn each other's figures inside out. DeFranco once said of the session, "I was sick that day, but it wasn't an occasion I would have missed. It was a game between us of 'Can you top this?' He'd play some astonishing figure and laugh, or turn and make a face at me over one shoulder. Or he'd rest his right hand on his knee and play with just his left hand, making it sound like both hands. I think he could have outwitted Charlie Parker."

Tatum's date with Ben Webster was his last studio recording; he died two months after. It is an elegiac session. Webster, who idolized Tatum, plays with an enormous tone, and he doesn't growl, hit any clams, or coast. The two men rise up to meet each other, and in "Night and Day," "My Ideal," and "Where or When" they become one. Felicity Howlett, the Tatum wizard, has pointed out that Webster "considered 'Night and Day' to be his finest recorded performance." He is surely sitting on Tatum's right.

## The Commodores

**M**osiac Records, the jazz counterpart of the Library of America, decided several years ago to put out the huge Commodore catalogue (1938–54). Two volumes, each containing twenty-three LPs, have appeared, and the third and final volume, which will be somewhat smaller, is due soon.

Commodore was the first American all-jazz label. It was started by a shrewd, amiable, tireless jazz lover named Milt Gabler. Born in Harlem in 1911 of an American mother and an Austrian father, Gabler was taken into his father's radio shop after graduating from Stuyvesant High School; the shop was on Forty-second Street, opposite the Commodore Hotel. He had begun listening to jazz, and in due course he stocked jazz records. In the mid-thirties he started reissuing and selling out-of-print jazz records. The records were notable on two counts—they were the first jazz reissues, and they were the first recordings on which the personnel and the instrumentation were listed. Around the same time, Gabler began sitting in on recording sessions, and in 1937, dissatisfied with the way Victor, Columbia, and Decca were handling (or not handling) jazz musicians, he decided to make his own jazz records. The first session took place on January 17, 1938, the day, after Benny Goodman's Carnegie Hall concert. On hand were Bobby Hackett, Pee Wee Russell, George Brunies, and Eddie Condon, who were playing at Nick's, in the Village; Jess Stacy (who was with Goodman); Artie Shapiro (Joe Marsala); Bud Freeman (Tommy Dorsey); and

George Wettling (Red Norvo). Gabler produced his last Commodore session in 1950, and the last official Commodore record was made in 1954 by Leonard Feather and Danny Gabler, one of Milt's brothers. Gabler produced almost ninety Commodore dates, using over a hundred and fifty musicians and singers. Gilbert Millstein, in a Profile of Gabler published in the *The New Yorker*, quotes an anonymous musician. "There's a ray comes out of him," the musician said about Gabler. "You can't help doing something the way he wants. Here is this guy can't read a note of music and he practically tells you what register you're going to play in just by the position of your head."

Gabler's tastes were not encyclopedic. He is still hale, and he says in an interview in the booklet for Volume I of the Mosaic reissue that the first jazz record to knock him out was "There'll Be Some Changes Made" and "I've Found a New Baby," by the Chicago Rhythm Kings. The record was made in 1928, when Gabler was seventeen, and three of the Rhythm Kings—Muggsy Spanier, Joe Sullivan, and Eddie Condon—would record again and again for him. (The music that teenagers like penetrates their bones.) The Rhythm Kings played a polyphonic small-band music that became known as Chicago jazz. It had improvised opening and closing ensembles and short solos often backed by organlike hums. A four-bar drum break followed by four more bars of ensemble often served as a coda. Sometimes the closing ensemble was delivered in a diminuendo-crescendo fashion, which gave the number a rampaging air. Chicago jazz, originally patterned after New Orleans jazz, was played by white musicians. After most of them moved to New York, in the early thirties, they revolved around the witty, hustling Condon. Their music could be heard from the late thirties to the late sixties at Nick's at the various Eddie Condon clubs, and at both Jimmy Ryans.

Many of the sessions in the Commodore catalogue are given over to Chicago jazz. The rest are divided among the black swing musicians of the thirties and forties and fifties; such ancients as Jelly Roll Morton and Bunk Johnson; miscellaneous pickup groups; and solo pianists. (Gabler loved pianists, and he recorded—or reissued—solo sessions by Stacy, Joe Bushkin, Joe Sullivan, Willie the Lion Smith, Mel Powell, Teddy Wilson, and, again and again, the impenetrable George Zack.) Absent from the catalogue, though, is the whole bebop movement. There are no Charlie Parkers or Dizzy Gillespies, and Gabler is rueful about having missed them.

For all the Zacks, lacy Smiths, and plodding Chicago dates, there is brilliant music in the first two volumes of the Mosaic. (The second volume closes in 1945.) The best of the Chicago sides are the 1938 dates with Hackett, Jack Teagarden, and Max Kaminsky; the seventeen-minute 1940 "A Good Man Is Hard to Find" with Kaminsky, Spanier, Russell, and Stacy (originally spread out over four twelve-inch 78-rpm sides); and the 1943 "That's a Plenty" session with Wild Bill Davison, Russell, Brunies, and Wettling. "That's a Plenty" and "Panama," made at the same session, are probably the greatest Chicago-style recordings ever made. Davison was a champion lead cornettist and a driving, emotional soloist, and the two numbers stomp and fly. The momentum built up in the final ensemble of "That's a Plenty" is almost frightening. Russell is on a great many of the Chicago dates, and although he came to hate the music ("There's no room left in that music," he once said. "It tells you how to solo") he frequently plays with daring and originality. He teeters constantly on the edge of tonality, and he sometimes gets off patterns that would startle Ornette Coleman and Cecil Taylor. (He was once paired with Thelonious Monk at a Newport Jazz Festival concert, but when Russell soloed, Monk, puzzled or surprised, laid out.) His slow blues, particularly in the chalumeau register, are grieving and jubilant. Hackett is *juste* on most of his sides. And listen to Ernie Caceres, the unsung Texas baritone saxophonist, in the first take of Miff Mole's "Beale Street Blues." He begins his solo, in a "talking" fashion, in his high register, and he mostly stays there, making that ponderous instrument sound feathery and casual. Stacy sparkles in his half-dozen band dates. He plays a low, rocking figure behind Caceres in Hackett's "New Orleans" which gives the uncanny impression that he is backing Caceres on a second baritone saxophone.

Gabler's sessions with the swing musicians are full of beauties, too. Lester Young played his rare, lissome clarinet in all five numbers of the famous Kansas City Six date (Buck Clayton, Young, Eddie Durham, Freddie Green, Walter Page, Jo Jones), and six weeks later Gabler put Chu Berry (Cab Calloway's band) with Roy Eldridge (his own band) and Sidney Catlett (Louis Armstrong's big band). This was the first small-band record Catlett had done since 1933, and he makes Berry and Eldridge hum. Early in 1939, Billie Holiday set down her almost unbearable requiem "Strange Fruit" and her slow blues "Fine and Mellow." A year later, Gabler assembled Eldridge, Benny Carter, Coleman Hawkins, and Catlett for four numbers, including two complementary versions of "I Can't Believe That You're in Love with Me." The issued take is fast, and the alternate is in a rocking medium tempo. Both are classics. Early in 1942, Gabler recorded a superb Benny Goodman session, under Mel Powell's name. Present are Billy Butterfield, Goodman, George Berg, Powell, Al Morgan, and Kansas Fields. Goodman and Powell never swung harder than they do in "The World Is Waiting for the Sunrise." Late in 1943, Gabler mixed members of the Eddie Heywood Downtown Society Cafe band with members of Teddy Wilson's uptown band, and they did an indelible "The Man I Love" and a supreme, slow "Uptown Cafe Blues." And early in 1944 he recorded a Basie-oriented group including Lester Young and Dickie Wells, and the marvellous quartet Catlett had with Ben Webster, Marlowe Morris, and John Simmons.

Some of the miscellaneous recordings that turn up on the Mosaics were made for other labels and bought and released by Gabler. There are two creamy dates that were run by Leonard Feather—one with Hackett, Marsala, Pete Brown, and the stream-of-consciousness singer Leo Watson, and the other with Bill Coleman, Marsala, and Brown, accompanied only by bass and guitar. There is a handsome slow "Clarinet Blues" that features Stacy, Butterfield, Eddie Miller, and the honeyed clarinettist Irving Fazola. There are twenty-five Jelly Roll Morton numbers, made a year before Morton died. Twelve are rough-neck band sides, and the rest are piano solos, several with classic Morton vocals.

Mosaic does not do anything by halves. The surviving takes of each number are given, with the issued version presented first. Sometimes there are as many as four takes. Listening to them all is like reading a novel in which all the early drafts are included. In addition to the interviews with Gabler, the accompanying booklets contain complete discographies, fresh photographs, and indefatigable liner notes by Dan Morgenstern, who brings this hybrid form close to perfection.

# 1991

## Sidney Bechet

The soprano saxophonist and clarinettist Sidney Bechet was, in his primeval way, probably the most lyrical and dramatic of all American jazz musicians. He was born in New Orleans in 1897 and died in Paris in 1959. New Orleans at the beginning of the century had long been a hothouse of opera, classical concerts, and brass bands, and the clarinettists who were Bechet's models—Lorenzo Tio, Jr., George Baquet, and Big Eye Louis Nelson—had grown up within this tradition. They had ornate attacks and intense vibratos (most used the B-flat Albert-system clarinet, which has a plummy, Edwardian sound); they relished glissandos and crowds of notes; and they sailed like swallows over the thick collective ensembles of the early New Orleans jazz bands. Bechet, who was something of a prodigy, began as a clarinettist and cornettist (he is said to have been a brass-band cornettist of great power), but made the esoteric soprano saxophone his principal instrument after coming upon one in a London shop in 1920. His style on the soprano was almost operatic. He had a wide, rapid vibrato, a sumptuous, commanding sound, and a majestic, often highly emotional attack. (None of the soprano saxophonists he inspired—among them Johnny Hodges, Bob Wilber, Steve Lacy, John Coltrane, Zoot Sims, and Branford Marsalis—have matched his tone. Nor have they always managed to play this difficult instrument in tune, as Bechet did.) He was a rococo improviser, who used a lot of exclamatory effects like growls and sustained, sometimes piercing high notes. He made simple phrases sound ingenious by the way he placed and accented their notes. He

liked long notes, which snapped in the wind of his vibrato, and he liked
ascending and descending swoops and daring intervals. Rococo jazz players
often become trapped in their own swirls, but Bechet's melodic lines invariably moved forward; he was as powerful a rhythmic player as he was a
melodic player. When he stretched out, his solos seemed to gain momentum
(he had flawless time), to gather themselves together and gallop down the
final eight or sixteen bars. His clarinet playing was not as prepossessing as his
soprano. He got a thin, piping tone that was further diluted by his overwhelming vibrato. He sounded diminished on the clarinet. But when he
rooted around in his chalumeau register, which approximated the roominess
of his soprano, he would turn up outrageous blue notes and mourning sotto
voce asides.

Bechet doesn't fit anywhere stylistically. His vibrato always made him
sound old-fashioned, but he wasn't old-fashioned. Nor was he modern. He
created his own time and lived within it. He was a New Orleanian, but he
didn't have much in common with such New Orleans heavyweights as Louis
Armstrong and Red Allen. (He did seem akin to an older New Orleans musician—Jelly Roll Morton. They recorded together only once, but the results
are intimate and natural.) He was at ease with an extraordinary variety of
musicians. They ranged from Earl Hines to Sidney Catlett to Charlie
Shavers to the Ellington band, and on to the modernists Kenny Clarke and
Martial Solal. Yet he remained imperturbable and unchanged. He did not
like the other horns in his bands to upstage him. He would play duets with
them, and he gave them solo space, but he never let them dominate.

His life was equally untrammelled. The youngest son of ten children
born to relatively comfortable Creoles of color, he took up the clarinet at
seven or eight, and lost interest in school not long afterward. He became a
working musician even before his teens, and he began wandering, and wandered the rest of his life. By 1918, he was in Chicago with King Oliver and
Freddie Keppard, and a year later he was in London with Will Marion
Cook's Southern Syncopated Orchestra. The orchestra played in London's
Philharmonic Hall, and the Swiss conductor Ernest Ansermet went to hear
it several times and published an uncannily perceptive piece about it in the
Swiss *Revue Romande*. His comments on Bechet begin, "There is in the
Southern Syncopated Orchestra an extraordinary clarinet virtuoso who is, so
it seems, the first of his race to have composed perfectly formed blues on the
clarinet." And they end, "What a moving thing it is to meet this very black,
fat boy with white teeth and that narrow forehead, who is very glad one likes
what he does, but who can say nothing of his art, save that he follows his
'own way,' and then one thinks that this 'own way' is perhaps the highway
the whole world will swing along tomorrow." When the S.S.O.'s engagement ended, Bechet played in various English clubs and dance halls. A fan
named Harvey Astley heard him. "Bechet's playing with the Jazz Kings was
a sensation," he wrote many years later in the *Jazz Journal*. "Always arriving

late, with a bulge in his hip pocket, he set the band alight as soon as the first few notes had fallen like rain from his magic clarinet. . . . The bright spot of the evening was when Bechet sat down in the middle of the dance floor, legs crossed, tailor-fashion, and proceeded to give us solos on his soprano sax, usually starting off with the Prologue from *Pagliacci*."

In 1922, Bechet had some sort of contretemps with a prostitute in England, and he was deported. He returned to this country and appeared with Alberta Hunter in a show called "How Come" at the old Apollo Theatre, on West Forty-second Street. He worked briefly with Duke Ellington, who revered him, and he had a hand in starting the Club Basha in Harlem. Then he was hired to play onstage in the "Revue Nègre," which starred Josephine Baker and opened in Paris in 1925. The show travelled to Belgium and Germany, but collapsed when Baker was hired away by the Folies-Bergère. Bechet the wanderer took off for the Soviet Union with a band led by a trombonist named Withers. He had become increasingly wayward; he was late for performances of the Baker show, and sometimes he didn't turn up at all. He got into real trouble in Paris in 1928. One morning, around breakfast time, he and the banjoist Mike McKendrick got into an argument about a woman and began shooting at one another outside a café in Montmartre. Three people, including the pianist Glover Compton, were wounded (McKendrick and Bechet were unharmed). Bechet went to jail in Paris for almost a year and was barred from the country. Back to the United States, a stint with Noble Sissle, and several months with his red-hot six-piece band at the Savoy Ballroom. Then the Depression closed in, and Bechet, after making a pass at tailoring, considered becoming an undertaker. But he rejoined Sissle in 1934 and stayed until 1938, when he went into Nick's in Greenwich Village. His fame increased steadily during the next fifteen years, but he was a poor businessman, and he never stopped scuffling. He returned to France for a jazz festival in 1949, and settled there permanently in 1951. (The operators of the festival had somehow got Bechet's banishment lifted.) Although the French came to love Bechet and he died cosseted and celebrated, he never made life easy for himself, or for others. His white hair and round face gave him a kindly-uncle look, but he was a martinet on the stand, and he had a terrible temper. ("It was like working for Bismarck," the pianist Dick Wellstood once said.) And he could be sly and evasive and parsimonious. Like most New Orleans musicians, pride was his engine.

Some of Bechet's best recordings were made for Victor between 1932 and 1941. He recorded fifty-seven numbers for the label, and RCA has now released them all together for the first time on three CDs, as "Sidney Bechet: The Victor Sessions." At least half of the fourteen sessions in the set contain classics. "I've Found a New Baby" and "Shag," from the first Victor date, recorded in 1932 with the Savoy Ballroom band, are rampaging up-tempo numbers—ringing announcements that a new and irrepressible jazz improviser had arrived. (Bechet had made a couple of famous dates with Louis

Armstrong in 1924, but most of his earlier recordings were done with singers.) Six years later, the French jazz critic Hugues Panassié came to this country to produce some records, and the four he made with Bechet— "Really the Blues," "Ja-Da," "When You and I Were Young, Maggie," and "Weary Blues"—are easy, graceful small-band sides, despite the presence of the dreadful clarinettist Mezz Mezzrow. The Jelly Roll Morton date, recorded a year later with a pickup band that included the New Orleans clarinettist Albert Nicholas, the trumpeter Sidney De Paris, and the drummer Zutty Singleton, is peerless. Bechet's solos soar, De Paris growls, and the ensemble passages are dense and mysterious. De Paris reappears in "Wild Man Blues" and "Nobody Knows the Way I Feels Dis Mornin'," made in 1940, with Sandy Williams on trombone and Sid Catlett on drums. Both numbers are supreme dirges. (The "Shake It and Break It" from the same session that is included on the album is an interesting but inferior take. No mention is made of this substitution in the accompanying booklet, which is a garble. Nor are we told that the three numbers tacked onto the end of the album were not done for Victor but for V-disc, a Second World War label that was distributed exclusively to the troops.) Three months later, Bechet led one of the strangest dates he ever made. Present were the Ellington cornettist Rex Stewart and the great modernist pianist Earl Hines, along with two New Orleans veterans, the bassist John Lindsay and the drummer Baby Dodds. Hines is exceptional, particularly in "Save It, Pretty Mama," and Stewart, apparently piqued at not being the first choice on trumpet for the date, is nonetheless at his cantankerous best.

Two of Bechet's last Victor sessions had Charlie Shavers on trumpet; his facility and huge tone match Bechet's generous dimensions. There are a meditative slow blues "Texas Moaner," a medium-fast "Lady, Be Good," on which Catlett takes a stunning eight-bar solo, and a "Mood Indigo," where Shavers and Bechet (on clarinet) stay down in their lower registers and talk like old, concerned friends. There are countless recordings of "Mood Indigo," but none is more blue and beautiful.

Bechet had a freakish streak. In April of 1941, succumbing to the adulation that by then surrounded him, he made pioneering, multi-track, one-man-band versions of "The Sheik of Araby" and "Blues of Bechet," on which he played clarinet, soprano and tenor saxophones, and piano, bass, and drums. The effect, with its concentrated vibratos, is like being at a tea for aging divas.

## Rollins Rampant

The tenor saxophonist Sonny Rollins gave another of his Carnegie Hall concerts in April. With him were his regular band—Clifton Anderson on trombone, Mark Soskin on piano, Bob Cranshaw on bass, and Al Foster on drums—and two guests, the guitarist Jim Hall, who was a member of a Rollins quartet in the early sixties, and the sensational twenty-one-year-old trumpeter Roy Hargrove. Rollins, now sixty, has been praised ecstatically for much of his forty-year career. He has been called the greatest living tenor saxophonist, the greatest living improviser, and the greatest of all tenor saxophonists. Almost everything about him attracts attention. A tall, V-shaped, eagle-faced man, he has appeared over the years with a shaved head, a Mohawk, an Afro, and Vandykes of various heft. He wears brilliant-colored caftans, or crisp white double-breasted suits, and an occasional large hat. He moves constantly onstage, and for a time he liked to walk out into the audience and play in the manner of those cabaret singers of the thirties who sat at their patrons' tables and serenaded them. He is prone to moods and heavy self-examination. Sometimes, if he is out of sorts musically, he will wander in and out of the wings during a concert, and play perfunctorily. If he is really upset, he takes a sabbatical. The second, and most famous, of his sabbaticals lasted two years. During a later sabbatical, in the early seventies, Rollins went to India and played by himself in a cave. But no matter how many leaves he took, he always came back to Max Gordon's Village Vanguard, a kind of pedestal for him. On what may have been his last visit, he arrived with a rhythm section, four other saxophonists, and a white trumpet player he had heard on the Coast and was crazy about. The group played the first set, and Gordon tells what happened next in his autobiography, *Live at the Village Vanguard:*

> The men were in their places, ready to start the second set, waiting for Sonny. Where was Sonny? I went looking for him, in the kitchen, the men's room, on the sidewalk out front, and in the back—no Sonny. . . .
>
> "What the hell's happened to Sonny?" I whispered to Al Dailey at the piano.
>
> "Probably on his way back to India."
>
> "That's not funny, Al. . . ."
>
> And do you know what? Sonny never showed up for the second set. He vanished. And I haven't seen him since.
>
> I was about to lock up for the night. Al was there. He stayed with me to the end. "What d'you think, Al?" I asked him. "What really happened to Sonny?"
>
> "It's that blond trumpet player," said Al. "Like I told you, he sounded great in California but terrible in New York. Sonny couldn't take him."
>
> "Why didn't Sonny fire him? . . . How can a trumpet player sound great in California and terrible in New York?" I asked Al.
>
> "It's the vibes, man, the vibes!"
>
> "What vibes?"
>
> "Coltrane, Miles, Coleman Hawkins, Bill Evans, Mingus, and Sonny himself, cats who've played here and left their vibes here, man! . . . That blond cat didn't belong in this company. The vibes scared the hell out of him!"

Rollins' style reflects a complex, indefatigable attitude toward life, one which he once summed up for the critic Gary Giddins: "Don't ever shrink from the belief that you have to prove yourself every minute, because you do." His playing coalesced in the early fifties, and by 1956, when he recorded his serene, classic blues "Blue 7," with Tommy Flanagan, Doug Watkins on bass, and Max Roach, it had become magisterial. It was an ingenious mingling of the styles of Coleman Hawkins and Charlie Parker, overlaid with hints of Dexter Gordon and Don Byas. His tone was big and hard and aggressive, and he used no vibrato. His attack was clipped, even abrupt—more percussive than melodic. He placed his notes just so, between beats, or ahead of the beat. His phrasing suggested a boy crossing a stream on jumping stones.

The avant-gardists Ornette Coleman and John Coltrane had listened to Rollins in the fifties, and he began listening to them in the sixties. For much of that decade, he set aside his deceptively simple style, and experimented. He used nonmusical sounds, and he fiddled with strange scales and with atonality. When he went into the Village Vanguard in March of 1972, just after his Indian trip, he had changed again. He had become a whirlwind. His runs roared, and there were jarring staccato passages and furious double-time spurts. He seemed to be shouting and gesticulating on his horn, as if he were waving his audience into battle. On opening night, he played just two sets, but each lasted an hour and a half. A couple of the numbers went on for nearly an hour, with fifteen- or twenty-minute-long solos, topped, at the end, with ten-minute codas, complete compositions in themselves. He filled everything with spiky interpolations—Chopin's "Funeral March," "Three Little Words," "Humoresque," and "Moonlight in Vermont." He became encyclopedic: Coleman Hawkins hustled by, followed by Gordon and Parker and even Johnny Hodges. He pumped so much music into the Vanguard that night that it was difficult to breathe.

Rollins has cooled down since, but he has never stopped tinkering. He has used electrified groups and rock rhythms, and he has even crossed over into fusionland. But every so often his passions stir, and the old Rollins reappears, to prove again that he is one of the commanding generals. He is not always charitable about demonstrating his superiority; last year, he invited the tenor saxophonist Branford Marsalis, Wynton's older brother, to join him at Carnegie Hall, and blew him away. Before this year's guests came onstage, Rollins played a medium-tempo "Long Ago and Far Away," in which he gave a classic demonstration of what Gunther Schuller once labelled "thematic improvisation." Rollins played two bars of melody, dropped into a quick inside run, a double-time lunge, and a sotto-voce turn-around, stated the melody for two or three more bars, improvised again, offered more melody, and so forth. This kind of now-you-see-it, now-you-don't melodic improvisation makes the listener, constantly teased, work twice as hard. Rollins was dressed in a knee-length red tunic, black pants, shades, and a medium-sized beard, and all during the number he moved around the stage and plowed his horn up and down, up and down, like a whaler cutting through a heavy chop. He gave us more thematic improvisation in his next number, a merengue, and then rested and let his sidemen solo. (Why do rock-trained soundmen do such terrible things to ordinary acoustic instruments? Soskin's piano suggested a twanging Hawaiian guitar, and the sound seemed to be coming from somewhere above his head.) Roy Hargrove then joined Rollins for "Once in a While," an up-tempo Charlie Parker blues called "Big Foot," and a tune Rollins had named after him, "Young Roy." Hargrove is already complete. He has a strong, easy tone and a fluent, logical, swinging attack. He has sidestepped Dizzy Gillespie and Miles Davis and listened to Fats Navarro and Clifford Brown, while his occasional flashiness and constant forward motion bring to mind early Roy Eldridge.

Jim Hall appeared after the intermission, and he and Rollins did "Without a Song," "With a Song in My Heart," "Where Are You," "The Bridge," and Rollins' great merengue "St. Thomas." Rollins loves Hall's intense, secret harmonic trips, and Hall spent much of his time on the outer-most edge. He formed odd, circular single-note melodic lines, and kept interrupting them with stepping, offbeat chords. Hall's solos never hesitate; they always sound as though he had effortlessly translated into music exactly what he has heard in his head. Rollins had become heated by the time "St. Thomas" arrived and, carried away, he forgot to give Hall—Mr. Polite—a solo. Even Hargrove, back onstage, was forced aside as Rollins, alternately pumping up the melody and decorating it, filled the hall with a Village Vanguard frenzy. The roar when he finally finished was oceanic.

## Wynton Looks Back

*Tuesday*

The fifth annual Classical Jazz festival, sponsored by Lincoln Center and held in Alice Tully Hall, began tonight. (Lincoln Center has suddenly embraced jazz. In addition to Classical Jazz it will offer twenty-one concerts, lectures, and film programs during the next nine months.) The concert, called "At the Court of King Oliver," was a celebration of the great New Orleans cornetist and bandleader, whose Creole Jazz Band was the first consummate jazz band to make records. It worked in Chicago between 1922 and 1924, and included at its height Oliver on first cornet, Louis Armstrong on second cornet, Johnny Dodds on clarinet, Honoré Dutrey on trombone, Lil Hardin on piano, Bill Johnson on bass, and Baby Dodds on drums. The twenty-nine-year-old virtuoso trumpeter Wynton Marsalis, who is the director of the festival and is scheduled to play at all the concerts this week, appeared with a band made up from his own working group—Nicholas Payton and Greg Stafford on cornets, Fred Lonzo on trombone and slide-whistle, Michael White (the evening's director) on clarinet, Farid Barron on piano, Don Vappie on banjo, Wycliffe Gordon on tuba and string bass, and Herlin Riley on drums. (All but Barron and Gordon are, like Marsalis, from New Orleans.) The band played sixteen Creole Jazz Band numbers as well as two numbers by a 1926 Oliver band, two duets Oliver recorded in 1924 with Jelly Roll Morton, and two blues songs on which he had been an accompanist. (Thais Clarke sang.)

The Creole Jazz Band and Jelly Roll Morton's 1926 Red Hot Peppers were the last of the masterly New Orleans ensemble bands—they were, in fact, out of date by the time they made their records. The first jazz soloists—Armstrong working on his own, Sidney Bechet, Coleman Hawkins—were coming forward and would convert jazz into a soloists' music by 1930. The Creole Jazz Band played rags and blues and novelty songs. Its ensembles were partly arranged and partly jammed. It used a lot of two-bar breaks, some of them played in tricky duets by Oliver and Armstrong, and there were occasional short solos. This description of the Oliver band is, of course, based on its recordings, which give little indication of what the band was like in its natural habitat, the dance hall. Because of the limitations of acoustic recording, the musicians sound like tin soldiers playing tin drums. And they had to fit themselves into the three-minute-plus length of the ten-inch 78-rpm record. As a result, they stuck mainly to ensemble playing, in which mistakes would sink quickly to the bottom. (The Oliver-Armstrong duets had probably been memorized by then.) People who heard the band live in Chicago say that it was loose and freewheeling, with ample solo space for all. These listeners also mention the precision and power and swing of Oliver's playing—things that are only hinted at in the recordings. The pianist Jess Stacy remembered hearing the band at the Plantation Café: "The first time I ever went to hear Oliver, he was playing 'Ukulele Lady,' and he was playing the fool out of it, and he took five or six choruses in a row. He played sitting down, and he didn't play loud. He knew his instrument. He wasn't spearing for high notes; he stayed right in the middle register. His chord changes were pretty and his vibrato just right—none of that Italian belly vibrato. You could hear that both Louis and Bix had learned from him. In fact, Bix was nuts about him, and one of the things he liked was that Oliver played open horn a lot."

The Marsalis band pretty much followed the recordings, allowing the musicians to burst forth just once—near the end of the evening, in a raggedly, pushing "Dippermouth Blues." But, in the best repertory fashion, it somehow imagined how the Creole Jazz Band played in a club, and went at the music with great energy and lift. It made this intricate music *roll*. There were rough edges. Fred Lonzo's slide-whistle solos in "Sobbin' Blues" and

"Buddy's Habit" were flat (the eerie, elegant originals, unusually clear in the recordings, were played by either Armstrong or Baby Dodds), and Marsalis, flexing his famous technique, was overly decorative on Oliver's timeless three-chorus solo in "Dippermouth." And Marsalis and Michael White forgot that the Creole Jazz Band was primarily a dance band, and that good dance bands use a lot of dynamics. The Marsalis band played at one ringing volume, which would have dismayed Baby Dodds. "The Oliver band played for the comfort of the people," he told Larry Gara in "The Baby Dodds Story." "Not so they couldn't hear, or so they had to put their fingers in their ears. . . . Sometimes the band played so softly you could hardly hear it. . . . We played so soft that you could hear the people's feet dancing." And Herlin Riley, Marsalis's drummer, should have studied Dodds' oceanic press rolls. His own barely lapped at the shore.

*Wednesday*

None of these jazz singers appeared in "Two Divas of Jazz" tonight—Carol Woods, Roberta Flack, Helen Merrill, Barbara Lea, Carol Sloane, Betty Carter, Jackie Cain, Susannah McCorkle, Marlene VerPlanck, Sylvia Syms, Nancy Marano, Meredith D'Ambrosio, and Nancy Harrow. Instead, Shirley Horn, a cabaret singer and pianist, and Abbey Lincoln, a kind of pop singer, were chosen. Horn, a soft-voiced inward singer who fills small rooms easily, seemed in a concert hall to be wearing a hat that was too big for her. Her first five songs—Irving Berlin's "I Like It"; a blues; "Soothe Me," a song June Christy sang with Stan Kenton; Isham Jones' "It Had to Be You"; and the thirties ballad "Foolin' Myself"—were done with Wynton Marsalis, the harmonica player Toots Thielemans, and the tenor saxophonists Branford Marsalis and Buck Hill. Thielemans was lightsome and darting, and Horn's accompaniments on piano matched and sometimes surpassed the soloists. She is a flawless miniaturist, but she made one mistake: singing "Foolin' Myself." Billie Holiday has owned that song lock, stock, and barrel since she first sang it, in 1937.

Abbey Lincoln, accompanied by Cedar Walton on piano, David Williams on bass, and Billy Higgins on drums, did nine songs. Among them were a mawkish glimpse of Duke Ellington in Heaven, by Walton; "Brother, Can You Spare a Dime?"; "How High the Moon"; a Thad Jones song; and "Blue Monk"—unbelievably fitted out with lyrics. Lincoln kept doing look-at-me things. She walked back and forth in front of her accompanists when they soloed, flashed quick smiles at the audience, and slumped onto a stool and looked morose. Perhaps she was searching for her articulation, her phrasing, her sense of time, even her voice. The alto saxophonist Jackie McLean and Marsalis provided obbligatos and solos. McLean was out of tune, and Marsalis, possibly sensing the slough onstage, was bravura.

*Thursday*

Jazz is in a retrospective stage, but certain styles are gone forever. One is the blue, windblown music of Kansas City, best exemplified by the Basie band of the thirties and early forties. Recordings exist, and a few of the original Basie monoliths are still standing, among them Buddy Tate, Harry Edison, and Buck Clayton—the last no longer as a player but as a composer and arranger, who has transmuted his lyrical trumpet playing into his songs and orchestrations. But the heart and soul of the band, the famous All-American rhythm section—Basie, Freddie Green on guitar, Walter Page on bass, Jo Jones on drums—has departed, and none of its imitators can manage more than an inexact mirror image of that magic foursome. It made rhythm out of air, sliding under Lester Young and Dicky Wells and Clayton and lifting them skyward, and it presided over the Basie band's complex and delicate system of checks and balances. The muted Clayton piped beautifully in the distance, while the open-horn Edison came right at you; Young's pale-moon tone balanced Herschel Evans' earthbound sound; Basie was aphoristic, his soloists eloquent.

Tonight's program, "Kansas City Swing and Shout," was like a lithograph of a painting: the right shapes and colors were there, but there was no texture or depth or feeling. What might be thought of as the detritus of Kansas City music took up the first part of the concert. Claude (Fiddler) Williams, who was Basie's guitarist briefly in the late thirties, played six numbers on the violin with Ted Dunbar on guitar and Aaron Bell on bass, and demonstrated that his arabesques are not always in tune. Then the pianist Jay McShann, backed by Bell and Oliver Jackson on drums, did "Willow Weep for Me" and four blues, one of which he sang in his thin, bare voice. "Willow" started slow and down, as it should, but ended in a jarring jump tempo. McShann is a surprisingly adroit player harmonically, but his improvisations have long been set in stone.

There was some momentum in the second half of the evening. The Lincoln Center Jazz Orchestra—fifteen strong and including Wynton Marsalis; Britt Woodman on trombone; Norris Turney, Joe Temperley, Charles McPherson, Frank Wess, and Todd Williams on reeds; Roland Hanna on piano; and Kenny Washington on drums—played five Basie numbers, two Bennie Motens, an Andy Kirk, a Harlan Leonard, and two Jay McShanns. The tempos, set by David Berger, who conducted and had made the transcriptions from the original recordings, were just right, and Williams and Wess provided uncanny simulations of Herschel Evans and Lester Young. But the soloists were never allowed to stretch out, even in the infinitely expandable "One O'Clock Jump." Scholarly shadow play prevailed.

*Friday*

Ten or fifteen years ago, George Wein began filling his New York festival with "tribute" concerts. Some celebrated the living, but most honored the dead, and tended to be sentimental, unfocused, and overlong. They generally included a narrator who might offer an elegy; film clips; recordings (often the unintended high point of the evening); and live music, frequently by musicians who had worked with the departed. Tonight, Marsalis honored the tenor saxophonist John Coltrane in a program called "Coltrane Serenade," and did it with taste and dispatch. Coltrane died suddenly, at the age of forty, in 1967. Originally influenced by Coleman Hawkins and Charlie Parker, he became as influential as either of them. He also became, because of the sheer passionate weight of his improvisations, a mythic figure. This evening, eleven small groups performed sixteen Coltrane compositions in a manner that would have pleased that powerful, disturbing player. In the first half, nine numbers were played by various combinations of Wynton Marsalis, Wes Anderson on alto saxophone, Todd Williams, and Charles McPherson, all of them backed by the rhythm section of Marcus Roberts on piano, Christian McBride on bass, and Billy Higgins on drums. Roberts, who is blind, is in his twenties, and was classically trained. He suggests Cecil Taylor put through a Mouli grinder. He has Taylor's thunder touch and, like Taylor, often ends his solos with cloud banks of chords. But he starts them with single-note lines made up of dazzling, spiky runs and oddly placed notes. Taylor swings intellectually; Roberts jumps and rocks. Anderson, who is also in his twenties, looks something like Pete Brown (three hundred pounds) and sounds like Pete Brown (concise, swinging) with Charlie Parker icing. Williams, who caught Herschel Evans so well last night, turns out to be a fervent Coltrane admirer. He delivered a moving version of "Alabama," a Coltrane mood piece that recalls, in its density and dark overtones, Billie Holiday's "Strange Fruit." The longest number was the brilliant "Dahomey Dance." All the horns were present, and McBride, who is eighteen, was joined by another stripling bassist, Reginald Veal. Williams did his Coltrane, Marsalis got off some Harry James "Flight of the Bumblebee" passages, and Roberts rose up behind Anderson at the end of his solo like the moon coming over the mountain. Then the bassists soloed together, the one playing background notes and the other soloing mightily in the fashionable big-bamboo way.

The second half of the concert was altogether different. With the exception of McBride, who stayed put, youth was replaced by old Coltrane hands or by Coltrane's immediate descendants—the pianist McCoy Tyner, the drummer Roy Haynes, and the reedmen Joe Henderson and John Stubblefield. The volume went up, and solos stretched to the horizon. Tyner, who has been as influential as Coltrane, is an opaque, many-layered pianist who loves the loud pedal, and Henderson is a fluent, full-toned hard-bop tenor saxophonist who only occasionally looses a Coltrane shriek. Stubblefield played bass clarinet, and got off some deep-throated beauties in his final chorus of "India." Over the years, Haynes, one of the early chattering bebop drummers, has grown louder and louder; a couple of his rim shots all but stopped the music. Marsalis reappeared for "Transition," and did more Harry James, coloring it with the dirty tone James used when he wanted his listeners to know he could play jazz trumpet.

### Saturday

Duke Ellington liked to compose musical portraits of people he admired. They were not programmatic, but rhythmic and coloristic approximations; they went after flairs and accents and glints. Many of the best were done in the late thirties and early forties. Tonight, we were offered "Portraits by Ellington," played by the Lincoln Center Jazz Orchestra (eighteen strong this time, plus five guests). We heard Ellington's graceful 1928 "Black Beauty," a portrait of the singer Florence Mills (Ellington's various versions never matched the stark elegance of the recording made in the mid-forties by the trumpeter Joe Thomas); his great 1939–40 portraits of the pianist Willie the Lion Smith, the dancer Bill Robinson, the comedian Bert Williams, and a Harlem character called Jack the Bear; and his 1970 "New Orleans Suite," which celebrates Louis Armstrong, Sidney Bechet, the bassist Wellman Braud, and Mahalia Jackson. Also included were the "Liberian Suite," a series of five jangling, cheerful dances, written in 1947; a four-part "Portrait of Ella Fitzgerald," written a decade later, and notable for a long and exquisite trumpet solo by Emory Thompson and for a perfumed Ellington narration delivered by the singer Milt Grayson; and an inconclusive "Self-Portrait of the Bean," which Coleman Hawkins recorded with Ellington in the sixties. Dave Berger again did the transcriptions (particularly difficult with Ellington, who continually crossbred instruments in his arrangements) and again conducted with considerable verve.

The "New Orleans Suite," forty minutes long, took up most of the second half of the evening. For some reason, Berger had rearranged the suite's nine sections (sidestepping the evening's program, which follows the 1970 Atlantic recordings) so that the suite ended with the mechanical, riff-filled "Second Line" instead of with the "Portrait of Mahalia Jackson." Ellington, a master of perversity, made his Jackson portrait a sixteen-bar blues, a form that the great gospel singer had said she would never sing in public. (She is said to have sung the blues in private one evening at the Lenox School of Music in 1960.) Two days before the Jackson section was recorded, Johnny Hodges, Ellington's empyrean alto saxophonist, died, and the number turned into a double dirge. It consists of seven choruses. Four are played by solo flute over a melody carried by three clarinets, a tenor saxophone, and a bass clarinet; and three are played by a muted wah-wah trumpet, a tenor saxophone, and a wah-wah trombone, over a melody carried by reeds and trumpets. The piece moves at a stately walk, and is full of murmurs and asides and undertones. And it is full of pathos, a rare emotion in Ellington's music. (He considered sorrow a private matter.) "Portrait of Mahalia Jackson" belongs with his classic tone poems—"Mood Indigo," "The Mooche," "Blue Serge," and "Black and Tan Fantasy." The band played throughout the evening with a looseness and eloquence and occasional swagger that recalled the Ellington band at its most telling—when, on a long engagement somewhere, it didn't have to think about anything except music and that week's paycheck.

Wynton Marsalis has become a conservator in his Classical Jazz festivals. Bob Wilber, the clarinettist, alto saxophonist, and jazz scholar, once said, "All the museum work, the musical anthropology, that has been practiced in jazz has been done by middle-class whites. Why? Whites have gone back and exposed the roots of what began as a black music, while black musicians have almost exclusively practiced the cult of the hip. We have been the conservatives and they have been the revolutionaries." Ten years ago, most young black musicians had never heard King Oliver and Louis Armstrong; their sense of the history of jazz began with the Miles Davis of the early sixties. But Marsalis, solidly grounded in the past by his father, the pianist Ellis Marsalis, is attempting to teach a new generation of black musicians where they came from.

He's doing it in a disquieting way, though. It appears that he is reviving not only the older music but also the reverse racism popular among black musicians in the fifties and sixties. Just six of the fifty-four performers used this week at Lincoln Center were white. Blacks invented jazz, but nobody owns it.

# Lady Day

In June of 1937, Billie Holiday, backed lustrously by Buck Clayton, Lester Young, and Jo Jones, made an extraordinary recording of an inconsequential Tin Pan Alley tune called "Me, Myself and I." The lyric ends, "Me, myself and I are all in love with you." The song could be a description of Holiday herself, for she was at least three different people. The most famous was the tortured tabloid figure, who, desecrated and dying, was arrested in her hospital bed by New York police for possession of drugs. (This Holiday, now largely legendary, is very much with us—in movies, on the stage, and in novels, poems, biographies, and autobiographies, including her own hocus-pocus "Lady Sings the Blues.") The second Holiday was the singer, the statuesque presence, standing on the stage with a gardenia in her hair, her elbows bent at her sides, her left hand snapping silently on the afterbeat, her head titled back, almost visible music pouring out of her. (This Holiday can be heard, at various removes, in the singing of Frank Sinatra, Julie Wilson, Nancy Harrow, Peggy Lee, and Susannah McCorkle.) The third Billie Holiday was almost invisible. She was the insecure child who, less than twenty years younger than her ineffectual parents, never had the chance to grow up. Battered by racism, by hoody music-business people, and by a succession of manipulative lovers (she married twice), she hid behind a violent temper and a foul mouth, and searched most of her life for solace in drugs and drink. (This Holiday remains as elusive as ever.)

Billie Holiday was born in Philadelphia in April of 1915 to Sadie Fagan and Clarence Holiday, unmarried teenagers. She was raised in Baltimore, and she was a wild one. At ten, she was sent to a Catholic reformatory, the House of the Good Shepherd for Colored Girls, and at twelve she was a prostitute. When she was fourteen or fifteen, she moved to New York. She had been singing since she was thirteen, and several years after she moved north she was discovered in a Harlem club by Mildred Bailey and Red Norvo. Billie made her first important recordings in 1935, when she sang "I Wished On the Moon," "What a Little Moonlight Can Do," "Miss Brown to You," and "A Sunbonnet Blue" with a small pickup band that included Benny Goodman, Roy Eldridge, Ben Webster, Teddy Wilson, and Cozy Cole. She was already scratching out a living in such Harlem clubs as the Yeah Man, the Hot-Cha, Pod's and Jerry's, the Alhambra Grill, and Dickie Wells's Clam House. Her career was never smooth. She took her first downtown job at the Famous Door, on Fifty-second Street. Working opposite the roughneck white New Orleans trombonist George Brunies, she was told not to sit with the customers between sets—to stay out of sight. She lasted four days. Then she joined Fletcher Henderson at the Grand Terrace in Chicago; the manager, Ed Fox, shouted at her, told her she sang "too slow," and fired her after a single evening. She went back to Fifty-second Street, alternating at the Onyx Club with the violinist Stuff Smith. Smith became jealous of all the applause she got, and she was fired again. She retreated to Monroe's Uptown House, in Harlem, and, in 1937, joined Count Basie, leaving under mysterious circumstances after less than a year. Then, putting her head in the lion's mouth, she went with Artie Shaw, who fended off the bigots until Maria Kramer, the owner of the Hotel Lincoln, in New York, where Shaw had landed an important job, made her use the service entrance and the freight elevator, and she quit.

She was given a reprieve in 1939. Barney Josephson, the owner of the new and completely integrated Café Society Downtown, hired her, and she stayed for a (more or less) peaceable year. Josephson did not allow his performers to use marijuana at the club, and between shows Billie would sometimes get in a cab and go up to Central Park and smoke pot. "One night she came back and I could tell by her eyes that she was really high," Josephson once said. "She finished her first number and I guess she didn't like the way the audience reacted. Performers often wear just gowns and slippers, no underwear, and at the end of the song Billie turned her back to the audience, bent over, flipped up her gown, and walked off the floor." Billie worked on Fifty-second street in the forties, and it was there that she began wearing her famous gardenia. The singer Sylvia Syms claims that she was responsible for Billie's first putting the flower in her hair. She used to hang around Billie on the Street, and one night, at Kelly's Stable, Billie burned her hair with a curling iron just before she was to go onstage. Syms ran down the street to the Three Deuces and bought a gardenia from the hat-check girl, and Billie fastened it on the burned place. "I can remember her . . . at the Onyx Club," Syms has said, "coming down those little stairs in the back and the lights softening and the room becoming silent and her moving onto the stage and looking just like a panther."

In 1947, she was arrested for the possession of drugs, and her life began going downhill. She spent nine months in the federal women's reformatory in Alderson, West Virginia. The New York police revoked her cabaret card, and she was never again able to work legally in a New York night club. (Without a cabaret card, entertainers could not appear in any place where liquor was sold. The police supervised this cruel, archaic practice until the late sixties, when it finally ended.) She was allowed to give concerts in New York, and, of course, she could work in clubs elsewhere. She earned a considerable amount of money, but it slipped through her fingers or was stolen by hangers-on and dishonest managers. Drugs, then heavy drinking began to affect her voice. But the old lightsome Holiday would surface occasionally. She sang, startlingly, like the bluebird of 1937 on a European tour she made in 1954. She also sang well on the CBS television show "The Sound of Jazz" in 1957, and her sequence—she sat on a high stool, her hair in a ponytail—has been shown so often on television that it has become the image most people have of her. She died in 1959, at the age of forty-four. She had fifteen fifty-dollar bills strapped to one of her legs and seventy cents in the bank.

No one had ever sung like Billie Holiday when she first appeared. She was deceptive. She made her voice sound smaller, more little-girlish, than it actually was; it gave the impression of being completely homemade. (She took her rhythmic ideas from Louis Armstrong and her poise from Bessie Smith.) Her articulation was so clear that she seemed to speak her lyrics, and her vibrato let out just enough emotion. She had the uncanny ability to digest new songs at a recording session and sing them—improvise on them, really—as if she had known them for years. Billie was a rhythm machine. No jazz instrumentalist has had a more flexible sense of time, and it was infallible. In such recordings as "It's Too Hot for Words," "Foolin' Myself," "I Can't Pretend," "I Must Have That Man," "I Don't Know If I'm Coming or Going," "You're Just a No Account," and "A Sailboat in the Moonlight" she disconnects each song from its chump-chump-chump rhythm, and, for the two minutes or so that her vocal lasts, makes the song float along somewhere behind the beat, thereby setting up an irresistible, swinging tug-of-war between the original tempo and her version of it. This freeing effect was doubled when Lester Young accompanied her. They were twins rhythmically and tonally, and while she sang he would improvise a soft countermelody behind her— applauding her, caressing her, welding their voices. (Young died just four months before Billie; their voices in decline, faltering and bare, had remained much alike.) These passages—in "I'll Never Be the Same," "A Sailboat in the Moonlight," "Born to Love"—are incomparable lullabies.

In the late thirties, Billie began to take herself seriously. Her morose, indelible recording of "Strange Fruit" (done not for Columbia but for Commodore), a devastating song about lynching, became something of an event, and she began to be courted by liberals and lefties. Her voice grew heavier, she used dramatic dying notes, and her larking, daring quality diminished. She lost some of her rhythmic agility. She still sang very well—better, indeed, than anyone else—but the joy and the quickstepping intensity were less apparent. This new seriousness persisted through the forties and was underlined by the strings and bouncy big bands she was given as accompaniment. Then, around 1950, her voice took on a subtly dismaying hue. Her undertones and low notes began to sound almost burnt; they took on an acrid quality. By the mid-fifties, only the outlines of her original style were in place. Her voice came and went, just as Mabel Mercer's did in her last years, and she often used a gravelly parlando. She refused to let on that anything had changed, and this bravery gave her a confusing majesty.

# 1992

## Bird Lives

Charlie Parker, abetted in the late thirties and early forties by such elders as Art Tatum and Lester Young, and by such contemporaries as Dizzy Gillespie, Max Roach, Thelonious Monk, and Bud Powell, forever changed the face and form of jazz. Gillespie and Roach, the only survivors of this revolutionary wing, have become establishment superstars, but Parker, who died in 1955, still overshadows them. (Parker would have made merry with the fame of Gillespie and Roach. He once introduced Gillespie onstage as "my worthy constituent.") Although the public barely knew of Parker during his short, misshapen life, musicians revered him; he and Louis Armstrong are probably the most imitated jazz players. He was obsessed by his music, and he was obsessed by the pleasure principle—in his case, drugs, alcohol, and sex. The best part of his career lasted less than ten years; he was only thirty-five when he died. The furnishings and customs and rules of daily life meant little to him, and his famous, melodramatic death was fitting—he collapsed in the East Side apartment of the Baroness Pannonica de Koenigswarter, to the sound of a thunderclap. So was the immortalizing graffito, "Bird Lives," that appeared across the country almost immediately.

Parker has also been kept before us by Gary Giddins' elegant biographical essay "Celebrating Bird," by Clint Eastwood's cumbersome movie "Bird," and by a seemingly endless flow of recordings, many of them made, under adverse conditions, on primitive equipment by Parker followers. The newest Parker recordings of this kind have been issued by Mosaic, under the title "The Complete Dean Benedetti Recordings of Charlie Parker." They have been legendary for years, and though their release is not, as the liner notes claim, "a find on the level of the uncovering of King Tut's tomb," they are startling and valuable. The recordings were made in March, 1947, at the Hi-De-Ho Club, in Los Angeles; in March, 1948, at the Three Deuces, on Fifty-second Street, in New York; and in July, 1948, at the Onyx Club, also on Fifty-second Street. The album contains two hundred and seventy Parker items; some are only a few seconds long, and some last more than six minutes.

The legend of the Benedetti recordings went this way: Dean Benedetti was an obscure drug dealer who followed Charlie Parker everywhere he went and recorded on a wire recorder everything he played. Benedetti then died or disappeared, possibly in Europe, and the recordings vanished like the Holy Grail. The truth, as the jazzologists Phil Schaap and Bob Porter reveal in the Mosaic liner notes, is this: Dean Benedetti was born in Utah, of Italian parents, in 1922. He went to jail briefly in the mid-forties, in California, for possessing marijuana, but he was never a dealer. He became a saxophonist, and organized a good bebop band, which included the pianists Russ Freeman and Joe Albany and the trombonist Jimmy Knepper. He seems to have spent just fifteen nights recording Parker, although it's possible that there were other occasions. (And he never used a wire recorder.) Benedetti drifted out of music in the early fifties and moved to Italy, where he died of a muscle disease in 1957. He left his Parker trove to his older brother Rick. Eleven years ago, Rick Benedetti told Bob Porter that he had Dean Benedetti's recordings, and four years ago, after fruitless negotiations with other record labels, Benedetti sold them to Mosaic.

Parker was as close to being in mint condition as he would ever be when Benedetti recorded him at the Hi-De-Ho Club. He had recently been confined for six months in Camarillo State Hospital after setting fire to a bed in his hotel room in a drug-induced stupor. He hadn't played in the hospital, and when he started again his playing was fresh and strong. He was apparently free of drugs, although he was drinking. (The stories about Parker's ability to drink and still play well were widespread. Russ Freeman remembers him at an after-hours club in Los Angeles called Jack's Basket. "One night Bird was drinking heavily and Lucky Thompson was on the stand playing," Freeman told Bob Porter. "He was so drunk his head was lying on the table. Lucky finished and Bird [got up and] started to play. This is a man who was out of his brains, [but] he played like something from outer space. I just sat there with my mouth hanging open.")

Art Tatum and Roy Eldridge and Coleman Hawkins were the first rococo players in jazz. They rained runs and glisses and arpeggios, but they respected bar lines and the foursquare rhythms of Jo Jones and Sid Catlett. Parker sailed over the bar lines and loosened the old rhythmic ways. He started and ended phrases in weird places, inserted daring, luxurious silences in his melodic lines, and let his tone, which was casual and "human," fall where it might. Parker is often said to have been the greatest of jazz improvisers, and it is easy to understand why. The older melodic improvisers often substituted tricks for technique. Or they depended on timbre and slyness (Dicky Wells, Vic Dickenson), on epigrams and elegance (Count Basie, the trumpeter Joe Thomas), on emotional turbulence (Wild Bill Davison, Sidney Bechet), on melodrama (Roy Eldridge, Trummy Young), or on dynamics and melodic larking (Erroll Garner, Pee Wee Russell). Parker had unlimited, home grown technique, and he had great musical intelligence. You have to listen hard to his solos to get past his blunt, vibratoless tone, to grasp his almost mathematical progressions, and to keep up with his astonishing velocity. He could convert a standard like "Embraceable You" or "Star Dust" or "The Man I love" into a brand-new song of beauty and complexity. He never gave the listener emotional baths, but he came close on slow blues. He had grown up in Kansas City, where the blues were in the light and air, and he knew how—with whispers and asides and preaching phrases—to take his blues down as far as Bechet and Art Hodes and Buck Clayton took theirs.

The Benedetti recordings are not always easy to listen to. They were made on fragile metal-based disks and on early paper tape, and the recording conditions were rarely congenial. Hassled by waiters and club managers, Benedetti was forced to set up his machine in awkward places. At the Onyx, he worked in a cramped space beneath the bandstand, directly under Max Roach's drums, which rattle and roar, making Parker often sound as if he were playing in the next room. But the ear adjusts, as it does to the old pre-electric recordings from the twenties, and soon you are at the Hi-De-Ho and the Deuces and the Onyx. In a way, the Benedetti recordings are most remarkable for being *there*, for catching the roughness and boredom and jubilation of typical nightclub performances, for making it possible to hear the *work* that jazz musicians put into making their music. There are slightly under two hundred items from the Hi-De-Ho, and because Benedetti, single-minded and economical, turned off his machine when Parker was silent, what we hear is Parker, Parker, Parker. But there are glimpses of the rest of the band, which was excellent; it included Howard McGhee on trumpet, Hampton Hawes on piano, Addison Farmer on bass, and Roy Porter on drums. Parker plays a number of ballads that he never recorded in a studio. There was a vocalist at the Hi-De-Ho, and there may have been dancing, for these ballads—among them "I Don't Stand a Ghost of a Chance," "It's the Talk of the Town," "Prisoner of Love," "I Surrender, Dear," "The Very Thought of You," and "Body and Soul"—move in slow motion. But Parker never lets them collapse. He plays melodic variations, he disappears into complete improvisations, he slips in and out of double time. Many of the rest of the numbers are bebop pieces, which were often reworkings of standards: "Wee" was based on "I Got Rhythm," "Donna Lee" on "Indiana," "Ornithology" on "How High the Moon," "Hot House," on "What Is This Thing Called Love?," and "Groovin' High" on "Whispering." Parker sounds utterly relaxed at the Hi-De-Ho. He uses silence in his solos as if it were sound, and his tone is fuller than it had ever been. You can hear him thinking. And he doesn't gesticulate and show off as he would later in his career.

Many of the seventy or so items that Benedetti recorded a year later on Fifty-second Street are hampered by their poor sound. Parker was back on drugs, and, for that or other reasons, he sounds very different. (The famous band he had at both the Deuces and the Onyx included Miles Davis, Duke Jordan on piano, Tommy Potter on bass, and Max Roach on drums.) His tone is frequently harsh, he plays strange shouts and semi-shrieks, he falters here and there, and he uses old Parker licks. There are also patches of wild, headstrong brilliance. By that time, Benedetti was recording entire numbers. There are a couple of wonderful, long "How High the Moon"s, a blueslike "September Song," and, best of all, a "Well You Needn't" in which Thelonious Monk, who wrote the tune, sits in. He and Parker rarely played together, and it is a revelation to hear how composed and mannerly Parker is as he works his way through Monk's spiky, dictatorial background chords. Davis is far more fluent throughout than he was in studio recordings at that time, and Roach makes it clear that, at the age of twenty-four, he had it all together. He also, in contrast to his current cerebrations, swings hard.

The photographs in the Mosaic album booklet are fresh. There is one of an apple-cheeked, teen-age Jimmy Knepper, and two of Parker on Fifty-second Street in the mid-forties. He is with Ben Webster in one and with a tenor saxophonist named Fred Greenwell in the other. In both photographs Parker looks like a frightened rookie who has just been asked to play with the big boys.

## The Other Allen

Jazz was at its most heterogeneous in 1957. Its many schools, freed of the silly moldy-fig-versus-bebop skirmishes of the late forties, functioned side by side—supper in the Ark. You could hear the pioneers of New Orleans jazz, Chicago jazz, stride piano, boogie-woogie, and swing and, hard by, the ascendant originators of bebop and hard bop and cool jazz. Brilliant things kept happening. An unknown Cecil Taylor, presaging a new avant-garde, had just released his first album, and the forty-nine-year-old New Orleans trumpeter Henry (Red) Allen made an uncanny old-avant-garde record. Bobby Hackett's witty sextet, a cross between Miles Davis's "Birth of the Cool" nonet and Bud Freeman's "Summa Cum Laude" band, appeared at the fourth Newport Jazz Festival. So did Mahalia Jackson, thereby helping to move gospel singing out of the church and into the secular sun. The first of the two nearly perfect Great South Bay jazz festivals was held in a tent on Long Island, and it offered Charles Mingus and Jimmy Knepper, a Fletcher Henderson reunion band, Miles Davis and Sonny Rollins, the Lawson-Haggart Jazz Band, Horace Silver and Art Farmer, and Jimmy Rushing. John Coltrane briefly became a member of a Thelonious Monk quartet that had Wilbur Ware on bass and Shadow Wilson on drums (it was possibly the best of Monk's quartets), and it appeared with stunning effect at the Five Spot. The year ended with a bang. On December 8th, CBS television showed "The Sound of Jazz," a live, hour-long summing-up of the music which has become a permanent part of the history of jazz.

But nothing that happened in 1957 is more vivid than Red Allen's recording. Out of print for thirty years, it has been reissued on a Bluebird CD called "Henry 'Red' Allen: World on a String." (With Allen are Coleman Hawkins, Buster Bailey on clarinet, J. C. Higginbotham on trombone, Marty Napoleon on piano, Everett Barksdale on guitar, Lloyd Trotman on bass, and Cozy Cole on drums.) Although Allen had not made an important recording since the early forties, more than half of the eleven numbers on the Bluebird disk contain trumpet solos of such daring and beauty that they caused the young avant-garde trumpet player Don Ellis to say in *Down Beat*, "What other trumpet player plays such asymmetrical rhythms and manages to make them swing besides? What other trumpeter plays ideas that may begin as a whisper, rise to a brassy shout, and suddenly become a whisper again? . . . Who else has the amazing variety of tonal colors, bends, smears, half-valve effects, rips, glissandos, flutter-tonguing (a favorite on a high D), all combined with iron chops and complete control of even the softest, most subtle tone production?" Ellis went on to say that he considered Allen the most advanced trumpeter in New York—this at a time when Miles Davis and Ellis himself were in the forefront of the younger players.

Allen had a strange, self-defeating career. He had been an advanced, highly original player since his days in the thirties with Fletcher Henderson and the Mills Blue Rhythm Band. But, like many highly original people, he kept getting in his own way. In 1929, he had refused a job with Duke Ellington, who was just about to break loose. Then, in 1934, Allen turned down a job as the leader of the Blue Rhythm Band and joined instead as a sideman. A loose-jointed Harlem band, it included the trumpeter Harry

Edison, the alto saxophonist Tab Smith, and most of the musicians who would become the John Kirby Sextet. Three years later, he went with Louis Armstrong's ramshackle big band, and spent three years in Armstrong's trumpet section as a largely non-soloing player. It was as if Artie Shaw had joined Benny Goodman's reed section. In 1940, Allen formed his own fine, small swing band, but it gradually developed show-biz mannerisms. He kept the band together until the early fifties, and after gigging around New York took a group into the Metropole Café. He stayed there until a few years before he died, in 1967, at fifty-nine. The Metropole, on Seventh Avenue at Forty-seventh Street, was shaped like a railroad car. It had a long bar against its north wall and, behind the bar, a narrow platform, backed by mirrors. The musicians, sometimes fifteen strong, stood side by side on the platform and played, exhibits in a sideshow. Only the pianist and the drummer were allowed to sit down, and the musicians at one end of the lineup often could not hear what the musicians at the other end were playing. Allen became a star there. People with no musical leanings would go to hear him do numbers like "Ride, Red, Ride," his volcanic, flag-waving version of the old "Tiger Rag." He'd count off by shouting, "Wamp! Wamp!," sing the raucous vocal, usually with the audience joining in, let his racing sidemen solo, sing again, play a couple of garish, blaring choruses, and close with a shouted, many-syllabled "Nice!"

By the time Allen made his 1957 recording, the early, unique Allen had been all but forgotten. (Occasionally, he would play soft, ruminative ballads at the Metropole, but not many people listened, and he would quickly go into his next rampage.) After he moved away from Louis Armstrong's influence, in the early thirties, Allen sounded like no other trumpeter. He had a free-floating sense of time, his tone was lustrous and dark, he used a great many blue notes, and he liked long notes and notes at the edges of his chords. When he played ballads like "Heartbreak Blues" and "There's a House in Harlem for Sale," his solos exalted sorrow. His playing never lost its matter-of-fact New Orleans flavor. No matter how complex it got, it always had its hands on its knees.

The 1957 recording made it clear that Allen's old, beautiful style had not vanished: he may have been making a living as a vaudevillian, but he was secretly writing poetry. Both Allens—the exhibitionist and the poet—are on the record, and they set each other off nicely. "Ride, Red, Ride," " 'Swonderful," "St. James Infirmary," and "Ain't She Sweet" are Allen at the Metropole. But in most of the remaining numbers he lets the poet sing. Allen starts each of these numbers by gently paraphrasing the melody. He then steps aside and lets his sidemen solo. (Hawkins is masterly and complete, but Higginbotham is wild and sometimes hair-raising, and Bailey, as always, is fleet and empty. Cozy Cole, as heavy as a wrench, uses a relentless backbeat that nearly ruins a couple of numbers.) Allen's opening melodic paraphrasings are warmups for his solos; they are also classic demonstrations of how to sculpt melody—how to make it three-dimensional. In his solos, the melody, though always stirring nearby, is transmuted into a series of Jamesian extravagances that, were they transcribed, would be impossible to play. The solos, filled with clauses within clauses, move constantly—no phrase lasts more than three or four measures. He will start with a two-bar patch of melody, swoop up an octave, play a trill, drop an octave and a half and hold a low note for three bars—using no vibrato and making the note so wide and smooth you could stand on it—then slide up a glissando, give us another melodic fragment, dodge through a rising-and-falling stretch of eighth notes, cut loose a sudden high note, cap it abruptly, and fall back into the cellar. His tone throughout is largely soft and nudging and hoarse. But he is not showing age or wear; he is being confidential. He has secrets to tell. The emotion he achieves is sometimes unbearable. Gunther Schuller, sending the word down from Olympus, says at the close of a long section on Allen in his 1989 book "The Swing Era" that his two-chorus solo in "I Cover the Waterfront" is "one of the most magnificent extended trumpet solos of that or any other period." But close attention should also be given to "Love Is Just Around the Corner," "Love Me or Leave Me," and "Sweet Lorraine."

Allen appeared eight months later on "The Sound of Jazz," and more than held his own in fast company. And two years after that, on a pair of lowbrow LPs done with the ancient New Orleans trombonist Kid Ory, he nearly matched his 1957 playing. In 1966, just six months before he died, Allen and Pee Wee Russell went up to M.I.T. to give a concert. They had played together on "The Sound of Jazz," and they had made a series of stamping records in 1932 with a cheerful singer named Billy Banks. Neither of them was at ease in Cambridge. The hall was new and cold, the audience small, and the modern rhythm section introspective. But the old warriors played some beautiful things, and Allen, who acted as leader, was memorable in a long, restless solo on "Body and Soul."

Allen was a big, serene, gentle homebody. He lived in a fifth-floor walkup in the East Bronx with his wife, Pearlie May, his police dog, White Fang, and his school-age grandchildren, or "grands," Alcornette and Juretta. He had a hound-dog face, but when he laughed everything lifted and he looked almost buoyant. He liked black New Orleans coffee, hot peppers (swallowed straight), and an occasional taste. He knew that he had never got the acclaim he deserved, that he was considered a kind of second banana to Roy Eldridge, who learned from Allen but never admitted it. He didn't have much work the last few years of his life. Sometimes he'd play along with musical shows on his television or he'd go down to a place in the Village called the Dom and sit in with the modern clarinettist Tony Scott. One of the musicians who went to his funeral was Ornette Coleman, the new king of the avant-garde. That would have pleased Allen.

## Last Set

Sylvia Syms died suddenly in May of 1992, at the end of a set in the Oak Room of the Algonquin. She had changed her style a good deal in the previous ten years, as she realized that her age and her physical difficulties (the partial loss of a lung, emphysema, asthma, brittle bones, dental problems, faltering hearing) were affecting her singing. Her vibrato, always pronounced, had got out of hand, and she was having trouble maintaining a melodic line. So she had fashioned an attack that recalled the one Mabel Mercer adopted during her last years. (Syms used to listen to Mercer closely at the St. Regis.) She developed a swinging parlando, in which she pruned her vibrato, disguised her melodic lapses with brilliant dynamics, and placed her notes just so. Like her first model, Billie Holiday, she made herself into a rhythm machine. This revamping had a surprising effect. The emotion she poured into her songs seemed to double, and her voice, always an imperious contralto grew enormous. Even at her peak, in the sixties and seventies, she was never as famous as Holiday or Ella Fitzgerald. She had only one hit record, an up-tempo version of "I Could Have Danced All Night," made in the mid-fifties. But she claimed that it didn't bother her, and she once said, "I have no desire to be a superstar. I don't think I could stand the responsibility of having to prove myself every single day. If you don't make it, you have a ball trying. But I've made it. I don't know by whose standards, but I've made it by mine. So the only person I have to satisfy now as far as my singing is concerned is me."

She was born Sylvia Blagman, in Manhattan, of a Russian father and a New York mother, and was raised in Brooklyn. Her father detested her going into show business, and her autocratic mother, who died just shy of her ninety-fifth birthday, never took sides—a response far more wearing than direct criticism. She got into acting when Mae West asked her to join "Diamond Lil," and she had sporadic successes on and off Broadway in "South Pacific" (she was a superb Bloody Mary), "Camino Real," "Funny Girl," with Carol Lawrence, and "Dream Girl," with Judy Holliday. But singing was her life, and she worked in almost every notable room in the country. The tenor saxophonist and bandleader Loren Schoenberg used to drive her to Brooklyn to see her mother, and the minute they rolled away from the curb she'd say, "Give me a line," meaning a line of lyrics from a song he'd like her to sing. She'd sing the song and say, "Give me another line," and she'd sing that song, and so it went until they reached her mother's. Talking was also her life. She frequently said that she talked too much—onstage, during her two marriages, with managers and club owners—and that she had probably talked herself out of being famous. Short and round, she had a wide face, an ear-to-ear smile, and a big laugh. (When a friend told her that she had named her tiny, elegant Siberian cat after her, Sylvia laughed and said, "Is she fat?") She liked to give the impression that she was a tough broad. And, in truth, she was tough. But she was also selfless, shrewd, eloquent, funny, and highly intelligent. Singing or talking, she invariably filled your cup.

At the Algonquin, she had put together a tribute show called "Sylvia Syms Celebrates Sinatra." (Old friends, she and Sinatra had coffee together on the phone every day.) A set early in her second week included over a dozen songs associated with Sinatra, among them Harold Arlen and Johnny Mercer's "Blues in the Night" and "My Shining Hour," Cole Porter's "I Am Loved" and "Just One of Those Things," and Sammy Cahn and Jimmy Van Heusen's "All My Tomorrows." It was a fine act—her slow ballads never stalled, and her rhythm songs swung. (She was backed by the excellent duo of Russ Kassoff on piano and Steve La Spina on bass.) In her dressing room after the show, attended by the young singer Daryl Sherman (just as she herself had attended Billie Holiday on Fifty-second Street fifty years before), she spoke out, as she always did. She had unaccountably never worked at the Algonquin, and she said she needed publicity (the house was only half full that night). She wondered what had happened to a piece she had been led to believe would appear in the Sunday *Times*. She also wondered why she hadn't had any reviews. Her eyes were too bright as she spoke, and she seemed distraught. Three nights later, after finishing a flawless second set (Kassoff said she didn't give him the eye once), she went over to speak to Cy Coleman, who had come to hear her, and collapsed. It was, she had often said, exactly the way she wanted to go.

## The Heart, The Head, and The Pipes

If it were possible to chart a human life on a graph, Rosemary Clooney's would show two peaks, divided by a chasm. The line would begin rising in 1945, when, at the age of seventeen, she and her fourteen-year-old sister, Betty, were hired as singers by radio station WLW, in Cincinnati, and it would continue upward through 1947, after they had joined Tony Pastor's band. The line would reach its first peak in the early fifties, marking four exuberant, almost simultaneous events in Clooney's life—her marriage to the actor José Ferrer (*Moulin Rouge*, *Cyrano de Bergerac*); her famous hit record of "Come On-a My House"; her starring, with Bing Crosby and Danny Kaye, in the movie "White Christmas"; and her appearance on the cover of *Time* in February of 1953. The *Time* writer, clearly entranced, wrote "The Clooney voice is known to the trade as both 'barrelhouse' and blue, i.e., robust and fresh, with an undercurrent of seductiveness. It can spin out a slow tune with almost cello-like evenness, or take on a raucous bite in a fast rhythm. In a melancholy mood, it has a cinnamon flavor that tends to remind fans of happier days gone by—or soon to come."

In the early sixties, after the birth of her five children—three boys and two girls, born at the rate of one a year—the line would suddenly turn and drop. Clooney and Ferrer had separated, and she began taking pills. "I started taking pills to sleep," she said recently. "A lot of women took pills then—my mother took them. And everybody kidded about bennies—Benzedrine—and Miltown. I took downers—Seconal, Librium, Miltown, Nembutal, Doriden. Of course, if you take too many downers they have a reverse effect—you can't sleep at all." She and Ferrer were divorced in 1967. A year later, the line would reach the bottom of the graph: severely addicted, she had a breakdown. "I was dead behind the eyes," she continued. "The records I did then sound like they were made underwater. I misbehaved with everyone, onstage and off, and when my friend Bobby Kennedy was killed I cracked up. I was convinced that he was still alive, that his death was a cruel hoax. I went on a kind of self-destructive rampage, and it lasted until a priest I knew convinced me that it was God's wish that I sign myself into the psychiatric ward of Mt. Sinai Hospital in Los Angeles. I was there a month, and when I was released I started eight years of therapy, private and group. It was the worst time of my life. I was strapped financially. I had the expense of all that therapy, and word had got around among club owners that I was undependable. I was living with the five kids in Beverly Hills, in the house on North Roxbury that Joe had bought in 1953. My friend Jackie Rose from my early days in New York had taught me to cook, and I put in a garden. And I sold some of my jewelry. When I was well enough, I took any work I could get—usually in Holiday Inns on weekends."

The line would remain at the bottom of the graph until 1974, when Bing Crosby, who was concerned about Clooney, asked her to appear with him in a benefit concert at the Dorothy Chandler Pavilion, in L.A., celebrating his fiftieth year in show business. Several successful tours around the country and abroad with Crosby followed, and she became a founding member of a travelling show called 4 Girls 4, with Margaret Whiting, Helen O'Connell, and Rose Marie. Then the line would move steadily upward, and would reach its second peak in the late eighties. She had begun annual sold-out monthlong engagements at New York's Rainbow & Stars, possibly the most elegant night club in the country, and she was making yearly albums for Concord Records. Critics talked about the great warmth and assurance in her singing, about the "new plateau" it had reached. She found herself hobnobbing in the minds of her admirers with the likes of Crosby, Billie Holiday, Frank Sinatra, and Mabel Mercer.

Clooney, always attended by her friend the dancer and actor Dante DiPaolo, now works six or seven months of the year. The chief events in her professional life in 1992 have been her February stint at Rainbow & Stars; a brilliant concert early in March in the Baird Auditorium, at the Smithsonian; and the benefit concert—an annual event—she held in April at the Dorothy Chandler for the Betty Clooney Foundation which works with brain-damage survivors and is also a memorial to her sister, who died of an aneurysm in 1976. (In her private life this year, three of her children have been married, in quick succession, leaving her "weddinged out.")

On several of her days off, Clooney talked about her life. She began in a New York hotel room. Many singers, when they talk, turn their singing into parlando. But Clooney, the most laidback of performers, talks quickly, and laughs in a low, barrelling monotone. The speed of her talk suggests that she is afraid her words—as lyrics always threaten to do—might evaporate, or sink to the bottom. Her speaking voice, though it has become deeper, sounds much as it did in *White Christmas* and *Deep in My Heart*. (She has been in five movies.) Her classically arranged face, with its wide-set eyes, square-bridged nose, and secure chin, remains the same. But the rest of her, beseiged by the flanking attacks of childbirth and middle age, has expanded. She has become a Maillol, a mother earth, a diva. Born in Maysville, Kentucky, and brought up there and in Ohio, she is a Southern-Midwesterner; utterly natural, she is the same onstage as off. When she sings, she holds the microphone casually in her right hand, and, with large glasses perched halfway down her nose, a half smile on her face, carries on as if she were gossiping over the back fence. She moves lightly, her pretty ankles flashing.

"There was music all over our family," Clooney said. "My father was a good singer, and my Aunt Anne Guilfoyle sang with local bands. Betty and I sang around the house, we sang on the street, we sang everywhere. Our daddy would take us to a creek that joined the Ohio, and the three of us would sit on a bank and sing 'Five Foot Two, Eyes of Blue' and 'Home on the Range' and 'The Old Covered Bridge.' WLW, where Betty and I first worked, was the most powerful station in the Midwest, and it had a lot of musicians on the staff. The piano that Fats Waller had played in the thirties was still there, and you could see the rings his glasses had left. It was almost a shrine. When I was nineteen and Betty was sixteen, we auditioned for Tony Pastor's band. His singer, Virginia Maxey, was leaving. We got the job, but we needed a legal guardian to go with us when the band went on the road, so my Uncle George Guilfoyle, who'd just got back from the service, took us on. He was very watchful, very strict. Betty and I were paid a hundred and fifty dollars a week apiece, and all three of us lived on that and sent money home to Grandmother Guilfoyle. In those days, you could stay in the Chase Hotel in St. Louis for eight dollars a night. We travelled in a rented bus. Betty and I sat in the front, and Uncle George sat behind us. Our dresses were hung in the back of the bus with the band's uniforms. The band did a lot of one-nighters and often we'd make a three-hundred-mile jump after a gig, arriving around daybreak in the town we were working in that night. Danny Gregory the band manager, smoked these awful Italian cheroots and he loved hotel lobbies. When it was payday, he'd get up from his chair and say, 'The eagle flies today!' Danny's real name was Gregorio. The Pastor band was kind of an Italian band. Tony's name was Pestritto, and his boy singer, Tommy Lynn, was Tommy Leonetti. And there were other guys with Italian names. Tony played the tenor saxophone and sang—he was a good singer, who sang the way he played. He loved Ben Webster, and whenever we were in New York he hung out with Ben. Tony was also a good showman, a good clown. Betty and I sang in every possible combination—with each other, with Tommy Lynn, with Tony, with Tommy and Tony. And I sang by myself. It helped that I could sing in Virginia Maxey's keys. When I made my first record with the band—'I'm Sorry I Didn't Say I'm Sorry (When I Made You Cry Last Night)'—I was so scared that I sang in a whisper. A writer in *down beat*, or someplace, said it was a new style, so I tried to sing the same way on my next record, but it didn't work. We stayed with Tony about two years—until Betty decided to leave. I had a Columbia recording contract by then, and I went out on my own. For a while, I made less than I had with Tony. I lived in New York, but I worked in Philly and Detroit and Cleveland and I did a summer radio show with Tony Bennett. Then Mitch Miller came in as the A. & R. man at Columbia, and he gave me "Come On-a My House'—an Armenian song sung in an Italian accent by an Irish-German girl. I hated the song, but Mitch told me if I didn't do it I was through.

"The doors opened. Starting in the early fifties, I worked on and off with Bing Crosby in movies and television and on the radio. If he smiled on you, you were anointed, and it made life a lot easier. He was Mr. Cool. 'Hiya, partner,' he'd say. 'How're ya doin'?'—and keep moving. When we were making *White Christmas*, Irving Berlin came to the soundstage and began walking nervously up and down before Bing did his takes on the song. Bing went over to Berlin and put his hand on his shoulder, and said, 'Irving, why don't you go to my dressing room and sit down and relax, and I'll be right along. There's nothing I can do to hurt your song.' I visited Bing at Rising River, his fishing place up near the Oregon border, and I visited him at his place down in Baja California. We became quite open and personal, talking on and on after dinner. But in the late sixties and early seventies, when I was mostly out of commission, I didn't see him at all.

"Then, around Christmas of 1974, he asked me to do the benefit at the Dorothy Chandler Pavilion. I learned some new songs, but I was nervous, because I'd been out of the big time. Bing saw that I was afraid I'd forget my words, and he said, 'The audience is not here to hurt you, Rosie. If you walk out there with a piece of paper in your hand, nobody will shoot you.' We did several tours after that, and they put me back on my feet. In some ways, Bing was strange. He liked to eat dinner every night at six, then take a walk. He paid me a very small salary, but when I had all the kids with me in London he put us up at the Dorchester. The strangest thing about him was that he filled in all the swimming pools at his various places. He didn't desroy them—just had them filled in with dirt. I don't think he could handle illness or death very well. He never called me when I was sick, and he never called when

Betty died. I found our later that he would ask people who were in touch with me, 'How's Rosie? She all right?' "

Rosemary Clooney stopped talking, and Dante DiPaolo came into the room and handed her a batch of telephone messages. He is tall and handsome and graying, has laughing eyes, and looks constantly pleased. He sat down, and this exchange took place:

ROSEMARY: Dante's father was a coal miner in Colorado. He'd come over from Italy. In the mid-forties, he moved to California and became a labor boss.

DANTE: He was Cecil B. De Mille's favorite man on the set.

R.: As a kid, Dante could copy any dance he saw. When his mother took him to auditions in Hollywood, she dressed him in a top hat and tails, because she thought that was that you wore to auditions. She was a seamstress.

D.: I used to dance anywhere I could. A friend of the family would take me to these strip joints full of blue lights and fan dancers, and I'd ask the band to play "Dinah" or "Stars and Stripes Forever," and I'd do a buck-and-wing. I'd wear a sailor suit, and people would throw money. I got my first big break when I was thirteen, in 1939. I was a singing newsboy in *The Star Maker*, with Bing Crosby,

R.: I met Dante in 1953, when I was making *Here Come the Girls*, with Bob Hope.

D.: Nick Castle was in charge of the dancing, and he asked me to show Rosemary some steps. I was a chorus boy. I think we had lunch together, but fraternizing like that on the set was frowned upon.

R.: After I married Joe, Dante and I stayed in touch, but we drifted apart, and he married a French showgirl and went to Italy and made a dozen movies with titles like *Blood and Black Lace*. He had to use his eyebrows a lot. One day in 1973, I was driving home from a therapy session in my Corvette when this white 1956 T-bird pulled up beside me at a light, and the driver leaned out his window and said "Rosella," and smiled. That was Dante's nickname for me, and it *was* Dante. I told him to call me, and he wrote my number in the dust on his dashboard. We've been together ever since.

D.: You didn't say I was Shirley Maclaine's boyfriend in *Sweet Charity*.

R.: You were only on the screen three minutes, Dante, and you had shades on.

Dante laughed, and left the room.

Rosemary said, "Dante and I banter a lot—the kids used to call it the 'Rosemary-Dante Show'—but he's the most selfless man I ever met. I couldn't get along without him. We'll never get married. We've both done it once. He's my friend. He's fine, I'm fine."

Rosemary Clooney's Washington concert was exhilarating. Half her songs were from her *Rainbow & Stars* show ("Straighten Up and Fly Right," introduced by part of the acetate that was made at WLW the day she and Betty auditioned; "Sweet Kentucky Ham"; three Duke Ellington tunes; "More Than You Know"; "Hey There"; and "Thanks for the Memory"), and half were fresh ("Just Friends," "Tenderly," "Sentimental Journey," "They're Either Too Young or Too Old," and "I'll Be Seeing You," among others). She was backed by her jumping Rainbow & Stars band—Warren Vaché on cornet, Scott Hamilton on tenor saxophone, John Oddo on piano, David Finck on bass, and Joe Cocuzzo on drums. Before the last number, "The Best Is Yet to Come," Janet Solinger, an official of the Smithsonian, read a citation and presented her with a large medal, the James Smithson Bicentennial Medal. In return, Clooney gave the Smithsonian the gold recording of "Come On-a My House" struck after the record sold a milion copies.

In the car on the way to a Smithsonian supper at Bice, one of Washington's hot Italian restaurants, Clooney talked about singing. "Singing is the only thing I've done all my life," she said. "I've had lots of boyfriends, one husband, five children, small houses, big houses—but singing is the one constant. When I was little, I listened to the bands broadcasting from the ballrooms round the country every night, and that was my dream—to sing in the great ballrooms. I don't read music, but it has never seemed alien to me. My singing is almost automatic. I listened to everybody. My father was a Crosby fan, and Bing was important to me as a singer. So was Tony Bennett. He always sounded like Mildred Bailey to me. Ethel Waters was an influence, and I listened to Ella Fitzgerald and Doris Day and Helen O'Connell. You always felt the pulse in Doris's singing; she had a rhythm section in her voice. My songs are filtered through my sensibiities. They reflect what is going on in my life. Sometimes disastrously. When I was at the Royal Box in New York, my friend the pianist Buddy Cole died. I had worked a lot with him, and when I sang 'Tenderly' that night I started to cry, and had to stop."

When Clooney began recording for Columbia, she had a breathtaking voice. It was light and rich and unbelievably pure. She had an even, delicate vibrato, perfect time, and perfect pitch, and she swung. Her ballads lulled and insinuated, and her rhythm songs were joyous. Voices tend to sink and narrow with age, and Clooney's is no exception. She has become cautious—trimming her vibrato, shortening her long notes, easing her way between her intervals. But her voice still has its round sunniness, its embracing quality. Her friend the songwriter Alan Bergman has said of her, "Rosemary never overwhelms a song. She is always true to the melody. Singers should have it in three places—the heart, the head, and the pipes. Rosemary does."

Clooney still lives on North Roxbury. Dante is with her, his Thunderbird in the garage. The house, a big two-story Spanish stucco-and-red-tile, is two blocks from Sunset Boulevard and three from the Beverly Hills Hotel. When José Ferrer bought the house (from the singer Ginny Simms and her husband), Jack Benny lived across the street, Eddie Cantor was catercornered, Ira Gershwin was next door, and Jimmy

Stewart was down toward Sunset. Clooney's house was built in the twenties by the actor Monte Blue, who got started in D. W. Griffith's *Intolerance*. The house has baronial touches: a giant wooden front door now painted but possibly old, that has a Prohibition-era peephole door; a two-story entrance hall with a four-abreast staircase, a wrought-iron bannister, and a sizable chandelier; and a huge sunken living room, furnished with facing sofas the size of whaleboats. The largest of the five upstairs bedrooms is driven by a massive silvery dressing table, made for Clooney of mirrors and glass at Universal studios—something "fitting for a star," Ferrer said when he gave it to her. The back yard of the house is early Beverly Hills deluxe: there is a guesthouse on one side and a fifty-foot tiled pool on the other; the pool has its own cabaña, and beyond the pool is a tennis court. The house has ghosts. For ten months in 1936 and 1937, George and Ira Gershwin rented the house and filled it with their compeers: Jerome Kern, Fred Astaire, Irving Berlin, Igor Stravinsky, Yip Harburg, Harold Arlen, Lawrence Tibbett, Moss Hart, Paulette Goddard, Arnold Schoenberg. In an upstairs workroom, the Gershwins finished "A Foggy Day" and "Love Is Here to Stay," and George painted his intense, staring portrait of Schoenberg. And, notoriously, in 1934 the crooner Russ Columbo accidentally fired an antique duelling pistol, possibly in the same room, and was killed.

A couple of days after the Betty Clooney Foundation benefit (the Bob Hopes, Debby Boone, Barry Manilow, Bernadette Peters, Joe Williams, Joel Grey, Cleo Laine, Margaret Whiting, Dianne Reeves, the Four Tops, Tony Martin, Harry Crosby, Donna McKechnie, Marilynn Lovell, Alan Bergman, herself, and a big band conducted by Peter Matz), Rosemary Clooney sat in a corner of her den, which looks out on the back yard, and talked about her rootless childhood, about Billie Holiday, and about Joe Ferrer. "This room always makes me think of Billie," she said. "In the summer of 1956, Joe and I had a box next to Dinah Shore and her husband at some tennis matches, and Joe asked them if they'd like to have dinner and go hear Billie at a place on Hollywood Boulevard. I'd had various fleeting meetings with Billie, and I didn't think she liked me. There weren't many people at the club, but she sang with flashes of brilliance. You'd hear the sound of pain, then the pain would turn to laughter. When she finished, she stumbled getting off the stand, and came over to say hello. She looked at Dinah Shore and said to me, 'What are you doing sitting with this woman?' Joe was always quick on his feet, and he said, 'Billie, why don't you come to the house tomorrow afternoon and visit with Rosemary?' Someone drove her over, and we sat in here and drank gin and orange juice for hours. She talked about Tony Pastor and how he had helped her when she was sick. She talked about dressing rooms and their isolation, and how alone we girl singers were. She talked about looking in the mirror and how hard it was, because you might look so awful. The one thing she didn't talk about was singing. The room was blue with smoke, and I remember looking out at the California sunshine and thinking that we had made a den of iniquity out of the room. Just before she left, I asked her if she would like to be the godmother of my second child, Maria, who was about to be born, and she said yes, that it takes a bad woman to be a good godmother. It was the last time I saw her.

"My mother and father were unstable people. My father was a drinker, and my mother was more interested in selling ready-to-wear than she was in raising children. I don't thing Betty and I and our younger brother, Nicky, spent more than two weeks in the same house with them. We lived with one or the other, or with Grandmother Clooney or Grandmother Guilfoyle. Both my parents came from Maysville. Mother's name was Frances, and she was eight years younger than my father. She had dark hair and blue, blue eyes, and she was vivacious and theatrical. She had a large nose and a striking profile, like a face on a Roman coin. Watching her was like watching a movie. She was a high-powered salesperson, and it carried over into her personal life—she conned people and was manipulative. Betty was a lot more understanding of my mother than I was. We never really got on, even after Mother moved in with Joe and me. My father—his name was Andrew—had hazel eyes and black hair, and he played the ukulele and laughed all the time. He was a housepainter. His father was the mayor of Maysville, and when my father misbehaved my grandfather told them to lock him up for the night. Once, when he was drunk, my father walked right out a third-story window. A balcony broke his fall, and he wasn't hurt.

"We were Catholics in a Protestant town. The streets of Maysville were paved with bricks, and it was the hemp capital of Mason County. It also had one of the biggest loose-leaf-tobacco markets in the world. There were tobacco auctions in the fall, and the whole town would smell of tobacco. Grandfather Clooney had a jewelry shop, and he and Grandmother Clooney lived over it. In the Ohio River flood of 1937, the water came right up to the second floor. My father tried to get him to move his crystal and china, but he just stood in the door of his shop and said, 'It won't come any higher.' The shop was never the same, and neither was he. Grandmother Clooney was German, and she took morphine. She was a lacemaker, and she always smelled of violets. She and Grandmother Guilfoyle hardly knew one another; it was 'Mrs. Clooney' and 'Mrs. Guilfoyle.' Grandmother Guilfoyle had been a schoolteacher. She had nine children and was overweight. She cooked huge amounts of food. When the Pastor band came for dinner, she killed, dressed, and cooked twenty-two chickens. She fed all the tramps who stopped at the back door. Once, during the Depression, someone suggested that she stop using butter, and she was furious and said, 'I'm going to the river,' meaning that she was going to the Ohio and jump in. She didn't like genteel words. The comics were funny sheets, a closet was a press, and playing the piano was chording. I corrected her once, and it hurt her feelings. Sometimes, when there wasn't enough money, they turned off the gas and electric. But then she cooked over the grate in the fireplace, and we made out.

Jackie Rose, attractive and gray-haired, was visiting Clooney, and she poked her head in the living-room door and said that she had made chicken salad for lunch and was off to do some shopping on Rodeo Drive. She lives in Waitsfield, Vermont, and owns a country emporium called The Store. When she had gone, Clooney said that Jackie Rose and Joe Ferrer had taught her just about everything she knows.

"I met Joe in New York in 1951,' she went on. "Jackie and I were living in a tiny studio in the posh Hampshire House. The apartment belonged to her mother. I'd been going out with people like Dave Garroway. I remember him saying the night before he hosted the first *Today* show that he thought Pat Weaver, who was the head of NBC, was nuts, that the show would never work. I met Joe on the Robert Q. Lewis show. We saw each other at lunch with other people, then without other people. He was married but was getting separated, and he was sixteen years older than I was. He came from a wealthy family in Puerto Rico that had sugar-cane property. His father was a lawyer. He went to Princeton and did Triangle Club shows, and one summer he was a gofer at a theatre that Josh Logan ran in Suffern, New York. Joe was a jazz fan, and he played a little piano and was a great admirer of the bandleader Georgie Auld. Later, when each of our children was born he'd find Georgie and they'd celebrate.

"Things began to get more intense. He had a job in Europe, and he wanted me to go, but it was the tail end of the big studios, and Paramount, where I had a contract, let it be known that you didn't go to Europe by yourself with a married man. In 1953, we were married, in Durant, Oklahoma, not far from the Texas border. I had just finished *Red Garters*, and I joined him in Dallas, where he was doing *Kiss Me, Kate*. The screenwriter Ketti Frings stood up for us, and took the only pictures we have of the wedding. I went back to Hollywood to do *White Christmas*, and Joe did a season at the City Center with Jean Dalrymple. After he bought this house, we went to Europe. It was the best vacation I've ever had. We stayed at Claridge's in London for seven weeks, and I met Olivier and Gielgud and Emlyn Williams. We went on to Paris and down to the South of France and to Rome, where Bogart was making *The Barefoot Contessa*.

"In 1955, I began having children. It was quite a trick having kids year after year and keeping a career going. Miguel was first. He looks like Joe and is an actor. He played Albert in *Twin Peaks*. Maria came in 1956. She's beautiful—she has dark hair and looks like every picture I've ever seen of Joe's mother, who died when he was at Princeton. Maria is a designer, and she just got married. Gabriel was premature. He's a good painter and a good cook. He's married to Debby Boone, Pat's daughter, and they've done three children's books together. Monsita Teresa was born in 1958 and lives in Virginia Beach. Her husband is a vice-president of the Family cable-television channel, and they have three boys, so I now have seven grandchildren. Rafael was the last child, and he came in 1960. He's the only one who looks like me. He lives in New York and is very successful in voice-overs—Uncle Ben's Rice, Miller Beer, you name it. He married a lovely Italian girl.

"Joe was supportive of my work, but I think he was also envious. He constantly took singing lessons, because he marvelled at the ease with which I sang, and he wanted to be able to do the same thing. I gradually realized that one of my functions was to be a kind of once removed audience for him. He'd tell people on the phone in detail what he had done that day, or on a trip he'd just taken, and that was how I'd learn about what he had been doing. He was moved more by performances than by life itself. He could cry when an emotion was produced onstage, but not in actual life. I was having an affair myself when we broke up, so I wasn't blameless. But I'd known for a long time that he was conducting his life that way. He broke my heart in small increments.

"But Joe died in January, and the children are handling their grief. Maybe the reason I've been complimented so much on my singing in the past six months is that it reflects the stage I've reached. For the first time, I'm at ease in my life."

## The Real Jelly Roll

**P**oor Jelly Roll Morton! The indomitable, pioneering American composer, pianist, and bandleader is being commemorated on the centennial of his birth not with a postage stamp or a medal but with George C. Wolfe's spurious Broadway musical "Jelly's Last Jam." Help, though, has arrived at Michael's Pub, where the luminous New Orleans actor and playwright Vernel Bagneris (pronounced Bahnereez) and the virtuoso Norwegian pianist Morten Gunnar Larsen are putting on a brilliant two-man show called "Jelly Roll Morton: A Me-morial." But Wolfe's show first. It revolves around a black dancer named Jelly Roll Morton, who is a Scrooge in Creole clothing. (The musical repeatedly echoes "A Christmas Carol.") This Morton is a greedy, hypocritical bully, and also a light-skinned racist, who "denies the black soil from which the rhythm [of jazz] was born," and who, late in the evening, says angrily, "There ain't no coon stock in this Creole." Change the lead's name in "Jelly's Last Jam" to, say, Bill Robinson, and it becomes clear what the show really is—an experimental study, done within a traditional Broadway-musical framework, of the life and death of a black misanthrope. In short, a psychomusical.

Morton's real outlines, though, are constantly suggested onstage, and anyone who knows something about his life will find it impossible not to keep comparing his ghost with Wolfe's monster. Wolfe says that Morton was a Creole. Strictly speaking, he was a Creole of color, or a café au lait, as they were once called—a partial descendant of the original Creoles, who were French-speaking white aristocrats of the early nineteenth century. Wolfe changes Morton, one of the great jazz pianists, into a tap dancer— presumably because Gregory Hines, who plays Morton, is a star. And Wolfe makes Morton a contemptible racist, even though Morton invari- ably hired black musicians, and none ever suggested he was a bigot. (To be sure, Morton, acutely aware of his own worth, *was* arrogant, and some- times displayed the so-called New Orleans evil—a red-eyed paranoia that seized all New Orleans musicians when they imagined they had been slighted or insulted.)

But the worst of Wolfe's distortions in "Jelly's Last Jam" involve Mor- ton's music. Apparently believing that it was not "black" enough or emo- tional enough, he hired the arranger-composer, Luther Henderson to write a homogenized "modern" score. The result is a tasteless stew on which float largely unrecognizable bits and pieces of Morton compositions. Morton's greatest records, made in Chicago in 1926 and 1927, are elegant, driving examples of polyphonic jazz. They prefigure Duke Ellington, yet celebrate the old free-for-all New Orleans ensemble music. Balancing elation and sor- row, humor and pomp, the blues and ragtime, they are as "black" as jazz got at the time.

The real Jelly Roll Morton could have been the hero of a wonderful musical. He was funny, preposterous, wild, mischievous, and immensely gifted. Born around 1890 in New Orleans, Morton left home in his teens and spent most of his life on the road. He liked money, women, clothes, and comfort, and he was a swell and a tireless braggart. (Publicity agents did not exist then, of course; show-business people—particularly black ones—had to blow their own horns.) One afternoon in 1940, a year before he died, he went to a Hot Lips Page rehearsal in New York, and he asked Page what style his band was playing in. Page said Kansas City style, and Morton replied, "Kansas City style, Chicago style, New Orleans style, hell, they are all Jelly Roll style!" In a famous letter to *down beat*, written in the late thirties to counter an assertion made on a radio program that W. C. Handy invented jazz, he declared, "I guess I am one hundred years ahead of my time." Morton belongs in that curious American pantheon of tall-tale heroes, alongside Paul Bunyan and Davy Crockett and Johnny Appleseed.

In the spring of 1938, the folklorist Alan Lomax, alerted by Alistair Cooke to the fact that Morton was playing in Washington, invited him to the Library of Congress to talk about his life. Lomax set up a portable recording machine in the Coolidge Auditorium and sat Morton down at a grand piano and asked him questions. At intervals over the next few weeks, Morton talked and sang and played into Lomax's micro- phone, and the results form one of the great American autobiographies, or novels. Lomax fashioned a book out of the recordings, called "Mister Jelly Roll." Unaccountably, the Library has never issued the tapes, but independently produced sets have appeared from time to time. Vernel Bagneris and Morten Gunnar Larsen have based their show wholly on Morton's own words and music.

Larsen opens the evening at Michael's Pub with Morton's "Sporting House Rag," and Bagneris, standing in the dark at the back of the house, intones the opening words from the Library of Congress recordings: "As I can understand it, all my folks were in the city of New Orleans long before the Louisiana Purchase, and they came directly from the shores of France." Dressed in a natty royal-blue chalk-stripe suit and matching cap, Bagneris materializes onstage, looking uncannily like Morton, and establishes his hauteur by telling us that his family often took him to the opera, where he heard "Il Trovatore." Larsen plays an excerpt from the opera straight, then jazzes it up, Morton fashion, and we learn how Morton went about inventing jazz. Bagneris, who has a light baritone, then sings "Mister Jelly Lord," a funny self-tribute song by Morton ("The man's an angel with great big feet"), and begins a story about how Morton beat one Aaron Harris at pool, not knowing that Harris had killed eleven people, including his sister and brother-in-law. A lovely blues follows, and Bagneris sits down and smokes a cigarillo while Larsen plays Morton's "Pep." Bagneris sings "Winin' Boy" and, during a Larsen chorus, goes into the first of half a dozen casual, sinuous dances. They illustrate Morton's music. The old Harlem dancer Pepsi Bethel helped Bagneris with the choreography, and his steps, done on air and in a kind of slow motion, are full of bent knees, fast side shuffles, pecking motions, pedalling, spins, and hip undulations, and they echo such dances as the Chicken, the Shimmy, the Eagle Rock, the Jig Walk, the Suzy-Q, and the Shorty George.

By now, Bagneris *is* Morton and, his voice low and amused, he demonstrates how, on arriving in a new town, he would don a fancy suit and strut casually down the main street, collecting admiring female glances, retire, put on another dazzling suit, and repeat his walk, telling his admirers that he could change his suit several times a day for a month and never wear the same one twice. The songs and dances and stories slide beautifully by, and Bagneris ends the evening by reading Morton's obituary from *down beat* and by singing his mournful "Sweet Substitute," a touching example of Morton's occasional attempts to write pop songs. Midway in the show, Bagneris puts on a tattersall vest and tan trousers, and, while he's changing, Larsen plays Morton's astonishing "Fingerbreaker," a roaring up-tempo display piece with a rocketing left hand and shouldering right-hand chords. (Morton used the piece to blow away other pianists; it's not surprising that the Harlem stride pianists didn't care for him.) The piano never rests in Bagneris's show. We hear Morton's lacy, cluttered pieces; his direct, down blues; his volcanic fast numbers; and his rhythmic surprises, which trip you no matter how often you hear them.

Bagneris, in his early forties, is a classic anti-star—subtle, organically grown, more or less directionless, child-like, generous, and still surprised at his talents. In the past thirteen years, he has written four funny comedies with music, all of them close studies of various kinds of black lowlife. They include "One Mo' Time," set in a vaudeville theatre in New Orleans in 1926, and "Further Mo'," a sequel; "Staggerlee," a rhythm-and-blues musical that takes place in a small Southern town in the fifties; and his current Morton show. "One Mo' Time" opened at the Village Gate in 1979 and ran for three and a half years, spawning seven worldwide road companies, one of which played a year and a half in London. "Further Mo' " opened at the Gate in May of 1990 but lasted only five and a half months. ("It got better reviews than 'One Mo',' " Bagneris said recently. "But then the Gulf War thing broke out, and it went down the drain. In two weeks, the box-office fell from eighty per cent to twenty. There was no touring company. Nothing. It broke my heart.") "Staggerlee" ran six months at the Second Avenue Theatre, and helped bring Ruth Brown, then an out-of-fashion rhythm-and-blues singer, back into view, which led to her starring role on Broadway in "Black and Blue."

Bagneris is a one-man band. He not only writes his shows but often directs them, acts in them, sings in them, and dances in them. He moves from craft to craft with New Orleans ease, never allowing one to outweigh another. He also takes occasional side trips into other people's worlds— notably as the mournful Accordion Man in the 1981 movie version of Dennis Potter's "Pennies from Heaven," and as the African-American writer Jean Toomer in a PBS drama "A Marriage: Georgia O'Keeffe and Alfred Stieglitz."

First-rate talents often sprout from tangled roots. Bagneris is an exception. He has a loving, orderly family, he went to good schools, and, with the help of various grants, he attended Xavier University. After graduation, he taught English briefly in a high school, and then, impatient, began shuttling back and forth, money permitting, between New Orleans and the Mickery Theatre, in Amsterdam. There he absorbed the acting techniques of the Polish director and teacher Jerzy Grotowski. "He was somewhat like Stanislavsky in that he taught you how to build a character from inside yourself instead of just fabricating it," Bagneris has said. When he returned to New Orleans for good, in the early seventies, he founded the New Experience Players. It was the first integrated theatrical company in New Orleans, and it introduced Ionesco, Beckett, and Albee.

Bagneris was born on July 31, 1949. He was named after his first cousin the New Orleans drummer Vernel Fournier. His father's father, Nemour Bagneris, was from Hispaniola, and he jumped ship in New Orleans sometime around 1900. "He had black blood and blue eyes," Bagneris said recently, "but he fit into the Creole community—the Creoles of color, as they used to be called. He married a white French-woman, whose husband, also white, had died. She already had three children, and they had eight more, one of them my father. When he was growing up, he thought the oldest children were passing for white, and he hated them for it. Then he found out they *were* white. It cured him of making racial distinctions. My mother, Gloria Diaz, was born in New Orleans. Her family had been there forever.

"I was raised in the old Lafitte housing project, which was built by Huey Long. It's a drug-infested ghetto now, but it was a nice place then, full of poor people raising families. When I was still little, we moved to the first of several two-family houses in the Seventh Ward. It was known as the back o' town, and it was all Creole families and musicians. It didn't matter what your background was—it might be Spanish or Mexican or Italian or Moroccan. We were all people of color, people who couldn't be white. It was a giving society. If somebody went fishing, he'd dump a shitload of crabs and fish on your stoop. Or if somebody bought a cow he'd give you a slab of beef. My father worked in the post office for thirty years, and he waited on table. He also worked the balls during Mardi Gras, helping people into their costumes. I did that, too, when I was old enough. You'd make twenty-five or thirty dollars in tips. My father never let my mother work, so her energy went into housekeeping. She was a fantastic housekeeper. You'd go to the bathroom in the middle of the night, and when you came back your bed would be made."

In 1978, Bagneris put together an improvised piece that had to do with jazz and black vaudeville in the twenties. He asked his grandmother how black performers talked at the time, and he studied collections of vaudeville jokes and "coon" jokes. The Swedish clarinetist Orange Kellin, who lived in New Orleans, helped him dig up a couple of dozen vaudeville songs and blues, among them heavy double-entendres like "Kitchen Man" and "The Right Key but the Wrong Key-hole." He wrote a script and got hold of three black singers—Topsy Chapman, Thais Clark, and Sylvia (Kuumba) Williams. The production, called "One Mo' Time," was set in the twenties when the blues singers Bessie Smith and Ma Rainey were big stars on the T.O.B.A. circuit (the Theatre Owners' Booking Association, better known among black performs as Tough on Black Asses), and it deals with one night at the Lyric Theatre in New Orleans. Big Bertha Williams and Her Touring Company, several notches below Smith and Rainey, are on the bill, and we watch them footing it onstage and carrying on backstage. Ma Reed, one of the two enormous singers in the troupe, talks backstage with Papa Du (Bagneris), the group's manager:

MA REED: Speakin of hotels, we got one don't we?
PAPA DU: Well, not exactly.

Ma Reed: Not exactly?

Papa Du: Now look here Ma. I asked the man at the desk about the rates. He said it was five dollars for the first floor, four dollars for the second floor, and three dollars for the third floor. I was turnin to leave, he said "What's the matter, aren't our rates alright?" I said "Your rates is fine, your hotel just ain't high enough."

Ma Reed: Well, how come we always got to stay in places where hot an cold water means hot in the summer and cold in the winter? (*Laughs*)

Papa Du: Now, Ma, if you'd just quit all this singin' and dancin' routine and go git yourself married.

Ma Reed: Married? Oh no honey, not me.

Papa Du: And why not?

Ma Reed: Cause nobody don't want to marry me when I'm drunk an I sure as hell don't want to marry nobody when I'm sober. (*Laughs*)

"One Mo' Time" had been running for six months in New Orleans when Bagneris's friend Carl Colby asked him one night why he didn't *do* something with the show, and Bagneris said he thought he *was* doing something. Colby said he'd invite Jerry Wexler, the record producer, and Art D'Lugoff, the owner of the Village Gate, down from New York to see the show. It was already quite famous; nobody passing through missed it. On the night Wexler and D'Lugoff came, Odetta and Allen Ginsberg were in the audience, and so was James Baldwin. Eubie Blake had been there two nights before, and Tennessee Williams saw it five times. Wexler and D'Lugoff liked "One Mo' Time" so much that they took it to New York, and it opened at the Gate in October of 1979.

"My Morton show began to take shape in 1984—*before* 'Jelly's Last Jam,' in fact," Bagneris said the other day. "I have a whole history with Morton. In 1976, I played him in a raunchy movie called 'French Quarter,' which became a big drive-in hit. A year later, Louis Malle asked me to play Jelly in his 'Pretty Baby.' I was signed and ready and walking around the set with Malle when he heard about 'French Quarter.' The Paramount people panicked, and I was out. Morten Larsen and I had been fooling around with a Morton piece based on the Library of Congress recordings, and I wrote something and brought it to New York for a workshop, using Terry Waldo on piano. I invited Wexler and D'Lugoff and a few other people. Then I went to Martinique to dig their beguine music, which resembles our Creole music—what Jelly called the Spanish tinge. When I got back, I found that the word was out. The producer Pam Koslow had announced they were going to do a musical based on the life of Jelly Roll Morton, and that it would star Gregory Hines. The next I knew, Koslow called me in New Orleans and asked me if I'd like to write the book. I told her where I was coming from about Morton, and she said 'Can you write a tap ballet?' I said I wouldn't know how to write a tap ballet, and she said, 'Well, some kind of dance expression.' I said I wouldn't know how to do that, either, and pretty soon I heard they were talking to Samm-Art Williams. I was working on 'Staggerlee' by this time, and maybe a month later Margo Lion, another producer of the New York Jelly show, called and asked again if I'd be interested in being involved with the show. I said, No, I was at work on 'Staggerlee,' and she said, 'Can't you postpone it?' and I said no. Of course, what they were doing in New York eventually became 'Jelly's Last Jam.' Before Morten Larsen and I opened at Michael's Pub, I told George Wolfe, the director, out of courtesy, that I was going to do my little show at the Pub, that it didn't have anything to do with his show, and he thanked me for telling him. One night the whole cast of 'Jelly's Last Jam' came to the Pub to see the show. They loved it, and they were amazed at what Jelly was really like. George didn't come. By this time, Jelly's fans, who are very partisan, had made a lot of angry noise about George making him into a mean racist, and maybe he had got that mixed up in his mind with my show. I don't know.

"I suppose that one of the reasons I'm drawn to Morton is that he never let his color get in his way. His mouth did, but not his Creole background. I don't know how many auditions I've done only to find that I was either too light for a part or too dark. You think sometimes that every drop of black blood you have is a drop of poison, even if it's just one-thirty-second of you.

# 1993

## Nancy and Eddie

No more lyrical, subtle, and exhilarating jazz-cabaret group exists than the New York duo of Marano and Monteiro. But you have to look sharp to find them. Because of their unfashionable makeup—two voices, accompanied by Monteiro's encyclopedic accordion—they are still working the fringes: half a dozen or so one-night stands a year at J's on upper Broadway; four Sundays in a row at Zinno, in the Village; a single shot at the cabaret festival in Town Hall last fall; a concert, with two other groups, at the JVC jazz festival this summer; gigs in Edgewater and Montclair, New Jersey. The duo's music is so intimate and smooth and quick on its feet that it demands a small room and intense concentration. It also deserves two different kinds of hearing—in the flesh, where you can listen with your eyes, as most people do, and at home, where you can work your way slowly through the duo's exceptional new CD, "A Perfect Match."

Marano and Monteiro are Nancy Marano, a singer, pianist, arranger, and songwriter who teaches at the Manhattan School of Music and appears several nights a week by herself in Peacock Alley at the Waldorf, and Eddie

Monteiro, a virtuoso accordionist and singer who pieces out a living by playing weddings and private parties. They belong to a curious, idiosyncratic tradition in jazz—that of singing-and-playing duos, trios, quartets, and the like.
These groups, preceded by the New Orleans spasm bands of the teens and
twenties (homemade instruments, improvised lyrics), were often regarded as
novelties, because they used odd instrumentations and a lot of razzmatazz.
They took hold around 1930, and included the Mills Brothers, who became
increasingly homogenized; the peppy, swinging Sunshine Boys, made up of
Dan and Joe Mooney (Joe, singing and accompanying himself on accordion
and organ, later had his own smooth, indirectly lit groups); the famous
Boswell Sisters (Martha, Vet, and Connee), who, equally peppy and swinging, were also notable for tight harmony and shifting tempos (they even used
Charlie Mingus accelerando and decelerando), and for Connee's powerful
contralto (she, a white woman, had listened to Bessie Smith, and, turnabout,
Ella Fitzgerald listened to her); the Spirits of Rhythm, a jumping quintet
that numbered the extraordinary stream-of-consciousness scat singer Leo
Watson; and Slim (Gaillard) and Slam (Stewart), the fomer a scat singer who
invented an early form of hip-nonsense talk, and the latter a first-rate bassist
who hit upon a new sound—humming in octave unison with his bowed bass.
In the early sixties, the Swingle Singers, started in France by an American,
and consisting of four men and four women, fashioned a kind of twentieth-
century plainsong out of Bach and Purcell and Beethoven. (By now, these
groups no longer accompanied themselves but relied on traditional rhythm
sections.) And, over here, Lambert, Hendricks, and Ross (Dave Lambert,
Jon Hendricks, and Annie Ross) sang ingenious, bebop-infused copies of
recordings by Count Basie, Horace Silver, and Duke Ellington, fitting out
their melodic lines (ensemble and solo) with jivey lyrics by Hendricks. Then
the tradition stalled; most of the groups that followed L. H. & R. were, until
the arrival of Marano and Monteiro, neos or parodies of earlier groups.

Marano and Monteiro first met in the mid-seventies, but began working
together only six years ago—one night a week in a noisy television bar in
Orangeburg, New York. They recently talked about their lives. They talked
separately, but everything each said seemed to reflect or corroborate what
the other said, as if they were talking together. They both speak quickly,
Marano aiming in and Monteiro, a classic extrovert, aiming out.

MARANO: I grew up in Cliffside Park, New Jersey, a mile or two south of
the George Washington Bridge. My father is Italian and my mother Czech.
My father, Nick Marano, was a classically trained pianist, but he could play
anything. When he was nineteen, Vincent Lopez hired him for his band at
the Taft Hotel. He was on staff at WINS when radio stations had live music,
and he did jingles and Broadway rehearsals, and even opera rehearsals, and he
did club dates. Then he went out on his own. For a long time, he was the
pianist at the Paris in the Sky restaurant in the Hotel Suburban, in East
Orange. It was owned by Dorothy Kilgallen and Dick Kollmar, and that job

put my sister and me through the Manhattan School of Music. But the best thing about my father was that he made you *want* to please him. He insisted that my sister and I start off classically, and when we were ten and eleven he brought in a teacher from Juilliard, a man named Yehuda Guttman, to teach all of us, himself included, which for him meant brushing up on his Chopin.

MONTEIRO: Both my parents were Portuguese. They settled in the Portuguese colony in Newark, and I was born there. My father ran a bar in Newark, Jimmy's Roscommon House, which he took over from an Irishman. I never saw him when I was a kid, because all he did was work. My mother was a great seamstress who did piecework in a factory. She decided that her first kid—me—would play the accordion, and I started lessons when I was five with a taskmaster named Charlie Nunzio. My mother was mean about it. She used to tie me to a chair to make me practice. I learned transcriptions of classical pieces—Bach inventions and Liszt pieces with four-octave runs. I also listened to the popular accordionists—Art Van Damme and Leon Sash and Joe Mooney.

MARANO: I was a piano major at the Manhattan School, and I studied with Robert Goldsand. My sister, June, and I both teach there now—she's an opera coach, and I'm in the jazz division. I never studied formal singing. I always sang as a kid, but I didn't want a classical sound. I wanted a jazz sound. I listened to Ella's songbook albums and to Sarah Vaughan and Lena Horne. I listened to Peggy Lee's pitch and understatement and to Mel Tormé's records with Marty Paich. And I listened to the harmonies of the Hi-Los—and so did Eddie. Now I'm listening to Shirley Horn, who knows everything about space, silence. But I don't know what's going to happen to our music—where the young singers are going to come from. I do workshops every summer in Venice for the Manhattan School, and we get kids from all over Europe. They can sing Betty Carter and Bobby McFerrin note for note, but they have no idea what the melodies are that Carter and McFerrin base their singing on. And when you try and take them back to the originals they can't do them.

MONTEIRO: When I was thirteen or fourteen, maybe a little older, I heard the great Brazilian accordionist Sivuca, and it was like primitive man discovering fire. He accompanied Miriam Makeba and Harry Belafonte, and he sang along in unison with what he played, and that's where I learned the trick—not from Slam Stewart or Major Holley, although I did pick up some things later from Major. I went to the New York College of Music, which was eventually taken over by N.Y.U. They didn't know what to do with me when I applied: "An accordionist? We don't teach accordion." Well, I had perfect pitch, which I demonstrated, and I played a two-part Bach invention and the toughest part of Liszt's "Spanish Rhapsody," and they took me on as a theory major.

MARANO: I first met Eddie when we were doing a private party for Peter Duchin. I had started doing club dates after a one-year contract with Columbia

Records didn't lead anywhere and I didn't break into the jingle-singer world, which is what I wanted to do. You don't have much chance to sing creatively on club dates, and I think it was only after Eddie and I began working together that I really developed. He has an incredible gift. He approaches music from a gut point of view, almost from a childlike view. He's mischievous, and he loves surprises. I'll catch that look out of the corner of his eye when he alters a chord behind me or drops in a new rhythmic pattern. It's a did-she-hear-*that* look. We hear together harmonically and musically and personally. We don't argue. If I worry, he lightens me up. If he gets too wild, I quiet him. It's a marriage of sorts.

MONTEIRO: When I first heard Nancy, I thought, Well, here's another chirp. But I learned right away that she had an uncolored sound, a pure voice. I also discovered that I couldn't shake her, that I couldn't make her branch break if I injected any surprises into what I was doing. I like horsing around musically. Once, when we were on the stand at J's, three women at a front table were talking loudly about whether they were going to pay their bill with a check or cash, and when I went into my solo I worked in the words "No checks, just cash," and broke the place up. I love experimenting with harmony. Harmony is like a painter's palette. I don't want to work just in black-and-white. I want to use pink and blue and green. Nancy understands that, because she's as into harmony as I am. She also keeps me in line. She tells me how to dress, and she corrects the pronunciation I use when I sing: "That's not 'Woncha,' Eddie. It's 'Won't you.' "

Marano and Monteiro generally rehearse once a week. They usually meet in the living room of the apartment she and her seventeen-year-old daughter, Joanna, share in Fort Lee. (Monteiro lives with his wife and their thirteen-year-old son, E. J., in East Hanover, New Jersey.) They rehearsed late one morning a couple of days before their last appearance at J's, in February. The room was full of light and greenery and books and records. There was a sofa and a chair with huge, slablike cushions on one side of the room and a dining-room table under the windows on the other side. Marano, complaining of a bad back, which she said she woke with that morning, sat awkwardly on the sofa. She has the conventional Italian beauty of wide-set dark eyes, dark hair, and curves. Monteiro is blustery-handsome, with heavy eyebrows, a brush cut, and a small beard. He sat on a kitchen chair in front of the sofa, his accordion on his left knee (accordions weigh from twenty to thirty pounds) and rows of sheet music arranged on the floor. As Marano had explained a day or two earlier, the duo devours material. Some instrumental jazz groups play only three numbers in a fifty-minute set, but Marano and Monteiro's numbers rarely last more than five minutes, and in the course of two or three sets they'll perform thirty songs. And since a lot of their fans appear every time they play they constantly need new material. Marano chooses most of their songs. If Monteiro likes a new song, she sketches an arrangement, or they work it out together; if he doesn't, she puts it aside.

She balanced the sheet music of David Raksin's "The Bad and the Beautiful" on the edge of the sofa, where they could both see it. She sang the first sixteen bars, with Monteiro playing organ chords behind her, his eyebrows raised. Just before the bridge, he stopped, saying, "Hey man. I'm not crazy about it. In fact, I don't like it. I'd probably use nothing but strings behind you if we did it."

She replaced the Raksin with Benny Golson's classic minor-key "Whisper Not." They settled immediately into the concentration and tribal communication unique to jazz musicians. They used few words, seemed to predict each other's thought, and moved steadily forward, their frequent hesitations and pauses notwithstanding. They skipped glances off each other when one of them produced a good phrase, and they grunted and sighed and said "no"s and "yes"es without knowing they were saying anything. They were sitting in the room, but they were really inside the music, the door closed.

As Marano sang a chorus of "Whisper Not," Monteiro played offbeat chords behind her. He shifted into stop-time chords and they scatted in unison on the second chorus, and stopped just before the bridge.

"It's tight, intricate work, this thing," he said. "We won't change it much." He suddenly played eight bars of George Shearing's "Lullaby of Birdland," hoping he could fit it into the vicinity of the bridge. Sticking bits and pieces of other songs into the one he is doing cheers him.

"I don't see the purpose of 'Lullaby' right there," she said.

"But I don't want to disappoint George," he replied. Shearing frequently comes to hear them. "He told me his newest joke on the phone the other day. He and Ellie have been spending summers in the Cotswolds, in England, you know, and cows come right up to their cottage. George said he asked the cows which Duke Ellington song they liked best, and they 'Mooed Indigo.' "

She said, "Shearing's puns! I don't know how Ellie stands it."

They scatted the rest of the second chorus together, first in unison, then in counterpoint. "I wish the bridge were longer," she said. "It doesn't seem like eight bars."

Monteiro suddenly began to improvise, closing his eyes and humming a beautiful unison falsetto with what he was playing. When he reached the bridge, Marano came in and sang the final sixteen bars. They ended on an abrupt high note.

"Hey, you can't use such a high note for an ending, Eddie. A note like that shrinks your cords, and if we went into 'Autumn Nocturne' next, which starts on a low D, nothing would come out."

"O.K., you got it. You know, even with all this rehearsing, I feel like a boxer when we get up there on the stand in front of an audience. After the first number, I say to myself, 'Are you cut? Are you bleeding?' "

She nodded.

The rehearsal ended eight or nine songs later. Monteiro unstrapped his accordion and put it on the floor. He looked at a big tray of croissants and Danish that Marano had put out before they started. "Gee, I never saw those." Monteiro loves to eat, and is developing an impressive Eugene Pallette.

"Don't, Eddie. Sit down at the table. I'm bringing out a pasta salad."

Sarah Vaughan and Ella Fitzgerald and perhaps Mel Tormé move through the far background of Marano's singing, but she has her own strong, effortless alto. She is a true jazz singer. She plays hob with the beat. Her diction is immaculate. She is not afraid of timbre or of striving for certain dangerous effects. In her final chorus on the duo's recorded version of Duncan Lamont's marvellous lament "I Told You So," she uses Billie Holiday dirty tones, and she even breaks her voice—with devastating results. She has a big voice, but she handles it so deftly and coolly (she seems never to miss a note) that it has none of the smothering quality of, say, Sarah Vaughan's. (She sings the patter words in the middle of Jobim's "One Note Samba" so fast they become a verbal glissando.) She is a perfect foil for Monteiro's musical high jinks. When he alters a chord, or emphasizes a different syllable in a word, or changes quarter notes to eighth notes, she sails serenely past, aware and appreciative but unflappable. He sometimes speaks of the accordion, which he says goes back to China, as having a reputation that is a "nemesis," and so it has. But, much in the manner of the great tubist Harvey Phillips, who in the past thirty years has raised the tuba single-handed from a Falstaffian laughingstock to a canonized eloquence, Monteiro has made the accordion into a swinging virtuoso kaleidoscope. Adroitly mixing all his instrumental sounds (there are sixty-four, including organ, piano, pizzicato bass, flute, strings, and brass), he turns air into music that has never been heard before and that has nothing to do with the soapy, lachrymose accordions of a thousand polka bands. He can suggest, in a rarefied way, Dizzy Gillespie trumpets, Art Tatum runs, celestial choirs, stately big bands. His colors constantly revolve, and you have to move quickly to keep up. Even when he is accompanying Marano on a floating, ad-lib ballad, he turns his sounds over and over, inventing new emotions, filling the cracks that good music never tolerates.

Here is how Marano and Monteiro do Hoagy Carmichael and Johnny Mercer's "Skylark." Monteiro plays an eight-bar introduction, ad lib, using rich chords that seem to spill over, each into the next. He pauses for a resounding beat, and she goes into the famous and ingenious first line: "Skylark"—she sings "Oh-a-a Sky-lark"—"have you anything to say to me?" He plays whispering chords behind her. When, at the end of the first verse, she gets to the words "where someone's waiting to be kissed," he sings softly with her in unison, gently expanding the body of sound. He stops singing, keeps his organ chords going, and starts singing again when she reaches "a valley green with spring" and again at "a blossom-covered lane." She slides into the bridge over windlike chords, and he hums in unison to the chords, and she finishes the first chorus. He solos, using his keyboard for piano and organ effects and his voice for unison humming. He becomes a one-man choir. She returns on the bridge, and he scats softly behind her, then drops into a measure of surprising four-four pizzicato bass, and returns to the ad-lib tempo. Together, they sing the last line of the song, "So, if you see them anywhere, won't you lead me there?" They sing echo fashion. She ends with another melismatic "Skylark," and he, doing a Monteiro, suddenly changes keys, and locks up with a brusque G-major chord.

In a way, Marano and Monteiro began when Mabel Mercer first heard the unknown Monteiro. Though Mercer was never a jazz singer, she nonetheless influenced jazz singers (her just-so phrasing, her subtle rhythmic emphases, her Abba Eban diction), and she had a sharp, tuned jazz ear. Mercer was working at Cleo's on the West Side, and Monteiro was accompanying another singer on Mercer's off nights. She stopped in to hear the singer and was knocked out by Monteiro. She told her old friend Alec Wilder about him, and Wilder, equally wowed, invited him to appear on his National Public Radio show. The mysterious momentum that sweeps the gifted toward the place where they should be was set in motion. Monteiro and Marano had met shortly before the radio show (he sang and accompanied himself on the program, proving that as a solo singer he needed Marano to fill his sails), and not many years later they began working together. Marano and Monteiro are two voices intertwined with a sixty-four-piece orchestra. They are also musical questers. Monteiro explains: "Maybe what I like the most in life is anything a little dangerous: flying, motorcycle racing, car racing, scuba diving—I've done them all, including a plane crash, nothing broken. That and taking things apart to see what makes them work, which is what Nancy and I do. We take songs apart, find out what makes them tick, and put them back together, maybe better."

## First Lady of Song

For a time, early in their lives, Ella Fitzgerald, the most celebrated of female American popular singers, and Billie Holiday, the most celebrated of female American jazz singers, seemed like kissing cousins. Both were born poor and black into flimsy, fatherless families—Fitzgerald in Newport News, Virginia, on April 25, 1918, and Holiday in Philadelphia, on April 7, 1915. By 1930, they had moved to New York, Ella to Yonkers, and Billie to Manhattan. Both sang in their early teens, or before, but they were already facing in opposite directions. Ella had fallen under the sway of the white singers Connee Boswell and Dolly Dawn, while Billie had listened to Bessie Smith and Louis Armstrong. Ella, taking her singing for granted, watched the scandalous eccentric dancer Snake Hips Tucker and decided she wanted to be a dancer. When she was fifteen or sixteen, she entered an amateur contest at the Apollo Theatre as a dancer, but she lost her nerve at the last moment and instead sang the only two songs she knew—"Judy" and "The Object of My Affection." She won, entered other contests, and, after a brief zigzag time, was hired as a singer by the drummer Chick Webb, who became her protector and guardian. (Amateur contests were a kind of Depression escape hatch. Many urban theatres held amateur nights once a week, and there were weekly amateur contests on the radio.) On June 12, 1935, Ella made her recording début with Webb's band on the Decca label, singing "I'll Chase the Blues Away" and "Love and Kisses." She was seventeen years old.

Although Fitzgerald's extraordinarily resilient voice began to show wear in the mid-eighties, she gave a concert in New York as recently as 1992, and she has had the longest career of any American popular singer. Her career comes in three parts. The Webb years lasted until 1941. (She took over the band after Webb's death, in 1939.) From 1941 to 1955, she worked as a single, recording helter-skelter with everyone from the Ink Spots to Louis Jordan ("Stone Cold Dead in the Market"), Louis Armstrong, Bob Haggart ("Oh, Lady Be Good"), and Ellis Larkins. (She and Larkins, a masterly accompanist, made a ten-inch duo LP of Gershwin songs in the early fifties which is used in music schools as an example of how to sing a ballad.) Then, in 1956, she was taken over permanently by the entrepreneur and recording executive Norman Granz. Her career had pretty much come to a stop, and Granz, realizing that her abilities as a singer of classic American songs had been largely ignored, persuaded her to do her famous "Song Book" albums, and during the next decade she recorded often definitive versions of the work of Irving Berlin, the Gershwins, Harold Arlen, Duke Ellington, Jerome Kern, Johnny Mercer, Cole Porter, and Rodgers and Hart. In many ways, the Ellington "Song Book" is the best, particularly her version of Billy Strayhorn's "Lush Life," which she does ad lib, accompanied only by Oscar Peterson. The song itself is an uneasy combination of delicacy and crudeness, yet she threads her way through easily, using little improvisation and making the music float, a trick Ella at her most relaxed could always do. It's a classic performance.

Ella's style was complete by the time she broke up the Webb band. The little-girl voice that bounced along through her early records had grown nearly as much as it ever would, give or take a new low register, a loosening vibrato, and heavier timbres. The fact that her voice never became womanly, that both her slow, cushiony ballads and her leggy up-tempo scat numbers had a preternatural smoothness, made her seem ageless. (Her own life may or may not have been so effortless. She is intensely private, but we do know that she has been married twice, the second time to the bassist Ray Brown; has one child; and now lives in a Beverly Hills house.) What had happened in the Webb days was that the drummer had, through the sheer hypnotic power of his playing, unwittingly and permanently shaped her style: she still loves rhythm singing. For that reason, her lyrics, though carefully articulated, convey rhythm, not meaning and emotion. She is, of course, an impeccable singer, and her assimilable, almost square perfectionism has influenced countless other singers, among them Carol Sloane, Doris Day, Rosemary Clooney, Mel Tormé, and Maxine Sullivan, whose style grew directly out of Ella's very first Webb recording.

But Ella cannot sing the blues. She decorates them, she embellishes them, but she remains on the outside—which brings us back to Billie Holiday, a great blues singer and Ella's best reflector. The directions the two singers would go in became clear early in their careers. In 1938, Ella recorded a mock children's song, "A-Tisket, A-Tasket," and had her first big hit. A year later, Billie made "Strange Fruit," a "Guernica" about lynching, which was the closest thing to a hit *she* ever had. The jazz clarinettist Tony Scott once summed up the two performers this way: "A singer like Ella says, 'My man's left me,' and you think the guy went down the street for a loaf of bread or something. But when Lady says, 'My man's gone' . . . you can see the guy going down the street. His bags are packed and he ain't never coming back."

In reality, it was Billie who, by destroying herself, packed her bags and left, while Ella, now seventy-five, has gone on singing.


## Jumpin' at the White House

In the middle of June, 1978, President Jimmy Carter gave a serene and joyous jazz concert on the South Lawn of the White House. It began with the sun boiling in over the old Executive Office Building and ended, three hours later, under a cool yellow moon. Almost everyone who mattered played, from the Young Tuxedo Brass Band of New Orleans to Cecil Taylor and Ornette Coleman. But the concert was not a White House first. Nine years earlier, President Nixon celebrated Duke Ellington's seventieth birthday with a dinner followed by a concert and a dance. This past June, fifteen years to the day after the Carter concert, the White House again embraced the music. The celebration, prompted by the fortieth anniversary of the Newport Jazz Festival, came in two parts and lasted nearly four hours. The first part was taken up by the Smithsonian Jazz Masterworks Orchestra, nineteen strong and conducted alternately by Gunther Schuller and David Baker, and the second part by three small bands, with two solo pianists and several singers interspersed. The S.J.M.O., starting around six o'clock, held forth on the South Balcony of the White House, and the rest of the music, starting two hours later, took place inside a huge warehouse of a tent that had been set up on the South Lawn directly behind the White House. (President Carter's entire evening had been alfresco, with the audience seated at picnic tables or on the grass.) The Smithsonian band included the mellifluous trumpeter Joe Wilder; two old Ellington trombonists, Britt Woodman and Buster Cooper; and the ingenious Lester Young saxophonist Loren Schoenberg, and it offered upward of thirty big-band anthems, among them Charlie Barnet's "Cherokee" and "Skyliner," Tommy Dorsey's "Well, Git It," Count Basie's "Shiny Stockings," and Duke Ellingtons's "Rockin' in Rhythm" and "Main Stem." As it turned out, though, the band, sitting some thirty feet above the ground behind a substantial railing, was barely audible. The music either wafted into the nearby magnolia trees, or, piped into the tent, was reduced to Muzak. WETA-TV, the PBS outlet in Washington, had agreed to film the second part of the evening for an "In Performance at the White House" program, and apparently someone had decided that the S.J.M.O., if allowed to perform inside the tent, would only clutter up the bandstand. In fact, the bandstand stage seemed big enough to hold a symphony orchestra, and the band's paraphernalia could have been removed from the stand several times over during the half hour between its last number and the second part of the program. In effect, the best jazz repertory band in the country, playing what was often the best music of the concert, was used for seating music.

At precisely seven-fifty, the President and Mrs. Clinton appeared onstage in the tent—she in a black-and-tan animal-print top and wide-legged black pants, and he in a navy blazer, gray pants, and a purplish shirt open at the neck. Mrs. Clinton introduced the President by saying that there is "no bigger jazz fan in the county," and Clinton said that jazz was "America's classical music," a music of "struggle, but played in celebration." The Clintons sat down at adjoining tables immediately in front of the bandstand. (There were more than seventy tables in the tent, each seating ten people.) Wynton Marsalis brought out his septet and played his own thirteen-minute suite "Modern Vistas As Far As the Eye Can See," which had discordant Charles Mingus ensembles, Ellington harmonies, a lovely repeated descending figure, and a Marsalis solo full of Rex Stewart half-valving and guttural sounds. The second number, announced as an Ellington blues called "Play the Blues and Go," was strikingly similar to the sinuous, loose-limbed blues that Johnny Hodges used to write in his sleep. (At this point, the greenery outside was turning dusk-gray, and various helicopterlike insects had discovered that the tent, roughly the temperature of a brick factory, was open on the sides.) A young pianist from Santo Domingo named Michel Camilo played an ornate solo ballad that matched his flaming-orange suit. Rosemary Clooney, under orders to do just two numbers, sang "Love Is Here to Stay" and Dave Frishberg's funny, forlorn hymn to the loneliness of being on the road, "Sweet Kentucky Ham," and then, her voice just beginning to jell and the audience just beginning to get her into focus, left the stage. A somewhat ill-matched pickup group, led by Illinois Jacquet, and including Clark Terry on trumpet, Al Grey on trombone, Dewey Redman's son Joshua on saxophone, Dick Hyman on piano, Charlie Haden on bass, and Elvin Jones on drums, played a medium-tempo "I Got Rhythm" variant called "One More for Dizzy," on which Jacquet pasted his famous "Flyin' Home" solo, a classic example of a long-frozen improvisation that is nonetheless fluid and stirring every time he plays it. Not much else happened in the number until Elvin Jones, taming his style for the music at hand, took a slashing, startling eight-bar solo in the final chorus. In the group's second tune, a medium blues, Terry, playing sotto voce, got off a double-time figure that went by so fast it was back before it had left, and Jacquet moved his sumptuous Southwestern tone around like a dealer arranging bibelots.

Television lights had been blazing since the set began, and two or three handheld cameras swam relentlessly around the stage, seemingly peering into the musicians' ears, examining their cuticles, and counting their hairs. Dorothy Donegan, in a silver jacket and navy-blue pants covered with sequins, sat down at the piano and made a moue at the President, who, trans-fixed since the music began, gave his all-purpose half smile and tilted his head slightly to his left. For the next three or four dazzling minutes, Done-gan showed us a cross-section of a number whose layers were made up of "I Can't Get Started," some Rachmaninoff, "The Man I Love," and boogie-woogie. As she gained speed, her right leg began gyrating, and it looked as if she might jump up and do one of her tumultuous dances, but she contained herself, finishing with a blinding two-handed run.

Into each concert some acedia must fall, and Bobby McFerrin wound his way through two of his surrealistic vocal exercises, one solo and one with the pianist Herbie Hancock, who then accompanied Joe Henderson, a kind of secular John Coltrane, in what has become his "Body and Soul"—Billy Strayhorn's "Lush Life." Hancock stayed on to back the flaccid soprano sax-ophonist Grover Washington, Jr., who played a Hancock tune called "Just Enough," and both made way for the evening's final pickup group, a muscu-lar bebop assemblage that numbered Red Rodney and Jon Faddis; Jimmy Heath, Henderson, and Washington; and a rhythm section of John Lewis, Christian McBride, and Thelonious Monk, Jr. They played medium-tempo versions of Dizzy Gillespie's "A Night in Tunisia" and "Confirmation." John Lewis, soloing in both numbers, offset Faddis's crimson overblowing, and so did Rodney, in two beautifully structured solos.

Joe Williams joined the group for the finale, and sang "Every Day I Have the Blues" and Joe Turner's "Shake, Rattle and Roll." When Williams sang the words "I'd rather drink muddy water and sleep in a hollow log," he asked the audience to join in, and the President obliged. At the end of the second number, Clinton ran onto the stage, shook hands with everyone, and sum-moned all the earlier performers. He said something about jazz being a "music of inclusion, a music of democracy," and suddenly someone handed him a tenor saxophone. Miles Davis's waltz "All Blues" began, and Clinton, with Illinois Jacquet standing beside him, shepherd-fashion, took two fine choruses of the sort you might have heard on a Big Bill Broonzy record from the forties. (He is, however, a Zoot Sims fan. Not long ago, he wrote Louise Sims, Zoot's widow, saying, "I *loved* Zoot's music and would have been honored to have him play at my Inauguration.") Williams and McFerrin started singing, and Clinton joined Jacquet and Joe Henderson for some background riffs. The music gradually subsided, and Jacquet hugged the President. Clinton left the stage and joined Mrs. Clinton, and they were immediately swallowed by well-wishers.

## Celebrating the Duke

The worst thing about Duke Ellington's death, almost twenty years ago, was that he, of all people, turned out to be mortal. Because of the profound, ageless, ongoing joyousness and originality of his music, he appeared to have mortality beat. He never changed much, even in his seventies. His long, handsome, lived-in face got longer and more handsome. His hair became an indeterminate color. He affected a ponytail. And the celebrated bags under his eyes grew heavier. (They represented "an accumulation of virtue," he said.) But everything else remained the same: his wit and unflappability (on being asked early in his career how he felt about racial slurs: "I took the energy it takes to pout and wrote some blues"); his sly graciousness; his endless talent for putting on friend and foe alike; his deep, limber voice and princely dress. Best of all, he never stopped playing his subtle, unique piano and composing his American music and leading his surpassing band; he never stopped making his music seem to compliment his audiences for their perspicacity in coming to hear him.

Ellington invented a new music. It was not fully understood during his lifetime, and it is still not properly appreciated. He fashioned it out of what he heard and saw around him. He translated his senses into music, not in a diaphanous Debussy way but in a hands-on way. Wilfred Mellers, the English composer and critic, once wrote of Ellington, "His genius is to be equated with his ear, which is the servant of his experience." Largely self-taught, he used whatever tools came along: the improvisation and rhythms of jazz, which grew up with Ellington in the twenties; European harmony and atonality; the eight-and twelve-bar blues; and the thirty-two-bar American song. If his music was loosely programmatic, it was also, in his mind, political. In 1930, just seven years into his career, he told a New York reporter, "I am not playing jazz. I am trying to play the natural feelings of [the black] people." Nine years later, he wrote, in *down beat*, "Our music is always intended to be definitely and purely racial." Ellington never thought of music as abstract; when the band played a new Ellington piece it became almost palpable to him. He maintained his band for fifty years at enormous expense, because he could not live without hearing what he had written the night before.

Most of the big bands that surrounded Ellington in the thirties and forties came in two distinct parts—their leaders (Tommy Dorsey, Glenn Miller, Artie Shaw) and the dispensable hired help. But Ellington and his musicians were indivisible. He wrote specifically for his musicians, and they played what he had written specifically for him. They often amended or enlarged on his melodies at rehearsals or in the recording studio, and then he amended or enlarged on their changes. Ellington was a brilliant eccentric who attracted brilliant eccentrics. (One of the oddest things about this great musical sophisticate was his love of New Orleans jazz. He revered Sidney Bechet, and lured him into the band briefly in the twenties and thirties. He hired Barney Bigard and Wellman Braud, both from New Orleans, and he tried to hire Red Allen and Edmond Hall, both New Orleanians, too. Johnny Hodges learned how to play the soprano saxophone from Bechet, and Tricky Sam Nanton learned how to use a plunger mute from Bubber Miley, who had learned it from the New Orleans trumpeter King Oliver. Cootie Williams picked up the plunger from Nanton, and his open-horn playing constantly celebrated Louis Armstrong.) The greatest of Ellington's musicians developed timbres and tones and techniques—glorious tics, almost—that had never been heard before. Cootie Williams' plunger mute screamed and talked and moaned. Johnny Hodges used ethereal glissandos and a thick, pushing tone when he played the blues. Rex Stewart's half valvings were sounds heard through a swinging door. Lawrence Brown's solos were satin, and Harry Carney's low register was the voice of God.

Ellington's mysterious orchestrations were the heart of his music, and they became even more adventurous after the gifted arranger and composer Billy Strayhorn joined the band, in 1939. There were melodic figures carried by a muted trumpet, a muted trombone, and a clarinet; two clarinets and a bass clarinet, the last scored on top; two tenor saxophones, a clarinet, and a muted trombone playing eerie organ chords behind a Hodges or Ben Webster solo (some of the loveliest things Ellington wrote were background counter-melodies); a bass clarinet and an arco string bass, in unison and backed only by Ellington, snapping his fingers on the afterbeat; the trombone section sounding abrupt offbeat bursts, lightened—you couldn't be sure—by a clarinet or a muted trumpet, scored high. Ellington loved to baffle the critics. Some of them have studied the unearthly opening ensemble chorus of his 1931 recording of "The Mystery Song" for sixty years without figuring out the instrumentation. As André Previn once said to the critic Ralph J. Gleason after they had heard Ellington together, "You know, Stan Kenton can stand in front of a thousand fiddles and a thousand brass and make a dramatic gesture and every studio arranger can nod his head and say, 'Oh yes, that's done like this.' But Duke merely lifts his little finger, three horns make a sound, and I don't know what it is."

Ellington had briefly considered a career as a painter, and it is not an exaggeration to say that he was a colorist who painted with sound. His unison clarinets suggested chrome yellow, his open-horn trombones dark gray, his open-horn trumpets silver, his muted trumpets off-white. The entire band, playing a triumphant unison figure, blazed a deep red. Jazz was the engine of the band. (Ellington disliked the word "jazz"; he felt that it circumscribed his music.) There were improvised solos, often repeated night after night once they were recorded, and solos that Ellington wrote out that sounded improvised. He used every kind of jazz rhythm, and when he had the right drummer (Sonny Greer, Louie Bellson, Sam Woodyard) the band could swing hard. He was a master of the seemingly simple business of choosing the right tempo. He would set the precise stroll for a languorous Johnny Hodges number, the precise easy rock for a straightforward blues, the precise hustle for "Rockin' in Rhythm."

Ellington's most fervent admirers like to say that he is the greatest American composer. This suggests that he surpassed Charles Ives, Virgil Thomson, Aaron Copland, Elliott Carter, Samuel Barber, and the rest, to say nothing of such resident imports as Varése, Bartók, Schoenberg, Stravinsky, and Hindemith. But all of them were European apples, and Ellington was an exotic American orange. The Coplands and Thomsons used traditional European compositional methods and the usual "classical" instruments. Ellington was a miniaturist, bound by the thirty-two-bar song and the three-minute time limit of the 78-rpm record. And he never used French horns, English horns, oboes, bassoons, flutes, or fiddles—except, of course, for Ray Nance. He did try a "symphonic" piece, the famous forty-five-minute "Black, Brown, and Beige," premièred in 1943 at Carnegie Hall, but it was panned by the heavy-weight New York critics. Seven years later, he wrote a far more coherent long piece, the fourteen-minute "Harlem," full of thick, sliding instrumental voices laid over constantly shifting rhythms. He finally settled, midway in his career, for writing "suites." These consisted of several loosely related three-or four-minute pieces gathered under a title. Even his ambitious so-called sacred music, written during his sixties and seventies, was made up of short pieces, padded with sopranos, choirs, drum solos, and tap dancers—Ellington's take on the furbelows of religious music.

For a long time, it was customary to put Ellington's piano playing down. It was stiff, it was clunky, it didn't swing. He had been tutored by stride pianists like James P. Johnson and Willie the Lion Smith, but over the years, when no one was looking, he became, in his singular, peppery, sometimes outrageous fashion, a kind of avant-gardist, much admired by Thelonious Monk, and even by Cecil Taylor. He was a masterly accompanist. His single notes under the band gave the impression that he was balancing the entire ensemble on one finger, and when he mischievously dropped in jarring, almost atonal figures behind, say, Johnny Hodges you wondered if Hodges would make it to the end of his solo. In his later years, Ellington came out from behind the band and made several exceptional solo-piano records. He had an easy touch and far more technique than he let on. He wrote in *Music Is My Mistress*, his sequinned autobiography, "And would you believe that the great Art Tatum sometimes got up from the piano and asked *me* to play?"

Ellington spent the last thirty years of his life flying his band around the world to make enough money to keep it intact; he never had the time to become an institution. But the marble edifice is finished and the carving is being done above the door. The Smithsonian, through the offices of John Edward Hasse, its curator of American music, has bought Ellington's papers (a hundred thousand pages of music, seventy-eight scrapbooks) and will publish a series of Ellington arrangements, enabling repertory groups and college ensembles to play Ellington properly for the first time. (Many of his original scores simply wore out or were lost, and have never been available.) Hasse has assembled a ghostly Ellington exhibition that will travel around the country. On view are the rosary and cross he is said to have worn most of his life; the Presidential Medal of Freedom given him by President Nixon; full-sized cutout photographs of Jimmie Blanton, Tricky Sam Nanton, Ivie Anderson, Johnny Hodges, and Ellington himself; Barney Bigard's clarinet and Clark Terry's flugelhorn, and part of Sonny Greer's once majestic drum set; and an interactive television that shows Greer playing (or synching) the crackling twelve-bar solo he took in the 1941 short called "Jam Session."

Hasse has also published a new biography of the Duke, "Beyond Category: The Life and Genius of Duke Ellington," and the musicologist and Ellington scholar Mark Tucker has put together an anthology of writings by and about Ellington, called "The Duke Ellington Reader." Hasse's book is clear, methodical, and thorough—a biography of a career. The following description of Ellington at twenty-four, when he left Washington, D.C., for New York, is about as personal as Hasse gets. It's also an excellent instance of his three-hundred-and-sixty-degree approach: "Ellington had by now established his personality. He was tied strongly to his mother, secure, self confident, optimistic, prideful, aristocratic in demeanor, charming, well mannered, easy with people from all walks of life, religious, ambitious, clever, didactically oriented, street smart, shrewd in business, restive with categories, averse to writing while inclined toward oral communication, a stylish dresser, and a growing individualist." For all his ebullience and jiving around, Ellington was an intensely private man, and it is not likely that any biographer will get further inside his closely veiled self than Mercer Ellington (Duke's son and only child) and Stanley Dance did in Mercer's 1978 memoir, "Duke Ellington in Person." But Hasse at least corrects the messy, askew vision of Ellington put forward in James Lincoln Collier's 1987 biography, and he gives proper emphasis to some of the brilliant, often neglected recordings Ellington made in the fifties and sixties.

Tucker's book weighs in at five hundred and thirty-six dense pages, and it includes early interviews with Ellington, a surprisingly astute 1929 mention of Ellington by Abbé Niles ("There is more and better melody in one of the dances of this astounding Negro than in ten of the pallid tunes of the average operetta"), and R. D. Darrell's long and passionate critical essay, written in 1932, when Ellington was just getting it together and Americans weren't supposed to know anything about their new music. One of Darrell's closing paragraphs: "There is absolutely nothing in popular music, all too little in any music, that touches the uncannily twisted beauty, the acrid pungence of nostalgia which Ellington in his great moments achieves. I can compare it only with the tortured rapture of Roland Hayes' face and hands as he sings certain spirituals, an agonized ecstasy too profound, too piercing to be glimpsed without a sense of sacrilege that so naked a baring of the soul should be witnessed by others."

One of the best pieces in the book is the 1978 liner note (essay, really) done by Lawrence Gushee for a Smithsonian reissue of twenty-eight of the masterpieces Ellington recorded in 1940. He writes, "There is a strain of craziness in Ellington that is never pervasive, yet can often be heard in his piano accompaniment, in odd trombone phrases ending in mid-air, and in brief passages of polytonal or extremely dissonant harmony. They are there for the very attentive, but the ordinary listener can and does pass them by. The avant-garde calls this hedging; the successful performer, prudence." Also included are Richard O. Boyer's still valuable Profile of Ellington, done for *The New Yorker* in 1944; Irving Townsend's glimpse of Ellington at work in the recording studio, which was his hearth and home (Ellington's recordings take up almost two hundred closely printed pages in Tom Lord's new jazz discography); the Duke himself discussing food, critics, his music and life; and various excellent pieces by those inestimable Ellington chroniclers Helen and Stanley Dance—in particular Stanley Dance's moving funeral oration, delivered on May 27, 1974, at the Cathedral Church of St. John the Divine. (And find, before it vanishes, the often extraordinary two-volume set of Ellington small-band sides, "The Duke's Men," recorded in the thirties and recently reissued with liner notes by Helen Dance, who actually oversaw most of the sessions as probably the very first female A&R person. Listen, especially, to Johnny Hodges doing Sidney Bechet in "Wanderlust" and Cootie Williams growling and being disconsolate in "Jitterbug's Lullaby" and the exquisite background counter-melody behind Barney Bigard in "Chasin' Chippies.")

Ellington was born in Washington in 1899, of a genteel light-skinned mother and a worldly father of darker hue. He was a noble gent, and there were several of him: the elegant, funny, gracious Ellington, modelled on his urbane father, who got off mots like "Pretty can only get prettier, but beauty compounds itself"; the musical Ellington, speeding across Mississippi at three in the morning in Harry Carney's car and asking Carney if he'd mind turning on the overhead light so that he could write some music; the salacious Ellington, describing in detail a lady he had met after a concert with whom he would have liked to dally; the ultra-cool onstage Ellington, conducting his band with looks and nods from his piano, then getting up and snowing the audience with his smile and a couple of gently mocking "I love you madly"s; the angry, guttural Ellington, his head in a bandanna, privately cursing the moneymen who run the record business; the Ellington whose courage, racial blindness, and sheer persevering dignity complemented Martin Luther King's vision; and the childlike, wondering Ellington, always on the lookout for some new revelation to write a piece of music about. From his autobiography:

> I've seen the Northern Lights many times, but one night in Canada, when Harry Carney and I were en route from Three Rivers, Quebec, to North Bay, Ontario, on Route 17, we saw the greatest display of all.
>
> It seemed to us as though we were two short men standing behind two tall men at a magnified Radio City while a stage production was on. We could not see the players, only shadows and reflections of performers passing back and forth before a brilliantly lit backdrop. You could see the course of the prima donna, the prima ballerina, the heavy, and all the dancing and show girls, many of them in formation. It was the greatest stage production I've ever seen.

The majestic, dissonant, many-layered piece that came out of this experience is called "Northern Lights," and it is part of "The Queen's Suite." Ellington recorded the suite, at his own expense, in 1959, several months after he had met Queen Elizabeth in England. He had a single pressing made and, royalty to royalty, had it sent to the Queen, thereafter steadfastly refusing to have it released to the public. It was not issued until 1976, two years after his death.

By 1959, Ellington was in his last great creative push. In 1957 alone, he had recorded his Shakespearean suite, "Such Sweet Thunder," and his Ellington songbook with Ella Fitzgerald. He had also written and performed in his short opera for television, "A Drum Is a Woman." And he had taken the time to record a classic small-band number, "Where's the Music?" Between 1959 and the mid-sixties, he recorded three notable suites ("Suite Thursday," "Afro-Bossa," and "The Far East Suite") and another classic small-band number, "Blues in Blueprint"; did the all too brief soundtrack for Otto Preminger's "Anatomy of a Murder"; and devoted several superb albums to the work of other composers. These included witty, sensuous versions of "The Nutcracker Suite" and "Peer Gynt," both done as almost narcissistic Ellington tonal celebrations, rich reworkings of some of the hits of the day ("People," "Moon River," "I Want to Hold Your Hand," "Days of Wine and Roses"), and a dozen parodies of old big-band numbers. (His arrangement of Stan Kenton's "Artistry in Rhythm," full of pizzicato Ray Nance violin and Harry Carney bass clarinet, puts the huge, noisy Kenton oeuvre in hilarious perspective in slightly over three minutes.)

But all this was a kind of resurrection. In 1955, four years before "The Queen's Suite," Ellington had had a sinking spell; in fact, the word was that he had done his best work. The band placed fourth in the *down beat* readers' poll that year, and during the summer it was reduced to accompanying figure skaters at the Aquacade in Flushing Meadow Park. The following January, a critic in a Toledo paper called an Ellington performance a "carnival of uncouth and ugly sound." But out of such adversity salvation sprouts. Johnny Hodges rejoined the band in 1955, after a four-year sabbatical, and the resilient, swinging Sam Woodyard took over on drums. The saxophone section, now made up of Hodges, Russell Procope, Jimmy Hamilton, Paul Gonsalves, and Harry Carney, suddenly became the best he had ever had, and Clark Terry and Ray Nance were still in the trumpet section.

In July of 1956, Ellington played his first Newport jazz festival. The band was the last act on closing night and didn't get onstage until almost midnight. (Ellington: "What are we—the animal act, the acrobats?") It opened with a new three-part suite, probably written in Ellington's helter-skelter fashion the night before, then went into his 1937 blues "Diminuendo and Crescendo in Blue." Ellington soloed for several choruses, the ensemble played the "Diminuendo" section, Ellington returned briefly, and Paul Gonsalves, getting the nod, took off. (Ellington knew exactly what he was doing. Gonsalves had soloed at length on the "Diminuendo" one night at Birdland in 1951, stirring the audience to a frenzy.) Backed by a heavy, mesmerizing Woodyard afterbeat, Gonsalves went into a trance. By his tenth chorus, the crowd had begun to roar, and dancing had broken out in the aisles. Ellington himself was dancing and yelling onstage. By the twentieth chorus, the crowd was on the edge of pandemonium. George Wein, the festival's producer, shouted at Ellington, asking him to wind it up, and Ellington shouted back, "Don't be rude to the artists!" Gonsalves finally ran out of gas after his twenty-seventh chorus, and the band returned for the last section of the piece. Ellington settled the still roaring crowd with Johnny Hodges' "Jeep's Blues." The press coverage of the event was ecstatic, and six weeks later *Time* put Ellington on the cover. A perverse, canny, exhilarating show-biz stunt of the kind Ellington generally abhorred gave him enough momentum to carry him through the rest of his life. He once said, his face straight and his tie tied, "I was born in 1956 at the Newport festival." Most of us, flat-footed and earnest, would have said reborn.

# 1994

## King Louis

**W**ynton Marsalis, the thirty-two-year-old trumpet player, ideologue, and Pooh-Bah of the Lincoln Center jazz program, has praised Louis Armstrong so often ("I love him. He was king" and "It's unbelievable the level of majesty he reached") that he has helped make it official: Armstrong, who died in 1971, just short of his seventieth birthday, lives. (He lives in academia, too; the Louis Armstrong Archives have opened at Queens College.) Of course, Miles Davis and Dizzy Gillespie, who, in their different ways, made Marsalis possible, also loved Armstrong. Davis once said, "You can't play anything on the horn that Louis hasn't played—even modern." And Gillespie, who had a feeling for apothegms, said, "No him, no me." Even Bing Crosby, generally Mr. Cool, said that Armstrong was the "beginning and the end of music in America." Armstrong knocked out nonmusicians as well. Gerald Murphy, the painter and bon vivant, had a copy of "Weather Bird," Armstrong's stunning 1928 duet with Earl Hines, placed in the keel of the hundred-foot schooner he had built in the early thirties, and he named the boat Weatherbird. And Tallulah Bankhead stayed sane throughout a three-year run on Broadway of Noël Coward's "Private Lives" by playing Armstrong's 1927 recording of "Potato Head Blues" during every performance. Armstrong even wowed the longhairs. Virgil Thomson wrote in 1936, "His style of improvisation would seem to have combined the highest reaches of instrumental virtuosity with the most tensely disciplined melodic structure and the most spontaneous emotional expression."

By the end of his life, Armstrong had become as famous as Coca-Cola. He had also become the first black American superstar, and belonged in that uneasy American pantheon that includes Henry Ford, Lindbergh, Harriet Beecher Stowe, and F.D.R. But celebrity is often mindlessly conferred when the celebrated can no longer do what made him famous, or when what he invented has become buried and forgotten under accumulated applause. (How many of Judy Garland's fans, fervently cheering her quavery, wrecked singing in the late sixties, remembered the startling perfection of her 1939 "Over the Rainbow" in "The Wizard of Oz"?) Eventually, the Armstrong who had revolutionized American music in the late twenties and early thirties all but vanished inside his famous image. You knew when you went to see him that you'd hear "Indiana," "When It's Sleepy-Time Down South," "Mack the Knife," "Tiger Rag" ("One of them good ol' good ones"), "Hello, Dolly," and "My Bucket's Got a Hole in It." You knew there would be a lot of horsing around (his enormous singer Velma Middleton doing the splits) and mock hilarity (ribald jokes, blinding smiles, pop-eyed grimaces). You knew that Armstrong's invincible singing would sound as if it were coming from the center of the earth, but that his trumpet playing would sound stencilled and tired, as would much of the playing of his All Stars. You also knew, though, that you were listening to Louis *Armstrong*, and that you had better pay attention, because he might suddenly stop you with an impassioned "Sunny Side of the Street" like the one he got off late on the closing night of the 1958 Newport Jazz Festival.

What you should have known but probably didn't know when you heard him was that toward the end of his career he was senselessly overbooked and overworked. He told Richard Meryman in 1966, "This life I got is very rough and few can do it. Now I'll come off five months on the road, have maybe a week off, then right back out. We don't have no days off—feel like I spent nine thousand hours on buses, get off a bus, hop a plane, get in town just in time to play a gig, chops are cold, come off that stage too tired to raise an eyelash. Sometimes up at 5:30 the next morning to get to that next gig—just a whole lot of ringing and twisting and jumping and bumping and things." But Armstrong never rebelled. He was devoted to his manager, a former Chicago hoodlum named Joe Glaser, who was once described by the mild-mannered Max Gordon as "the most obscene, the most outrageous, and the toughest agent I've ever bought an act from." Armstrong regarded Glaser as his protector. "If you didn't have a white captain to back you in the old days—to put his hand on your shoulder—you was just a damn sad nigger," he said to Larry L. King in 1967. "If a Negro had the proper white man to reach the law and say, 'What the hell you mean locking up MY nigger?' then—quite naturally—the law would walk him free. Get in that jail *without* your white boss, and yonder comes the chain gang!" But Armstrong wouldn't have rebelled anyway. His music, no matter why, where, or how often he was asked to perform it, was his badge and his heart, and had been since Joe Oliver summoned him to Chicago from New Orleans in 1922 to play second cornet in his Creole Jazz Band. Oliver set Armstrong's life in motion, and Armstrong, in his gratitude, never paused.

Born in a back alley in New Orleans to a domestic and prostitute, Mayann Albert, and a shiftless laborer, Willie Armstrong, he had been a wild street kid, uneducated and directionless. In 1913, he was sent to the Colored Waifs' Home for Boys, where he picked up the rudiments of the cornet. He married for the first time in 1918 (he was married four times), and a year later he worked in Fate Marable's band on the riverboat S. S. Sydney. There he learned to read music, and was heard ecstatically when the boat docked at various places upriver by Bix Beiderbecke and Jess Stacy.

During the first half of Armstrong's career, he performed as a soloist in front of various-sized big bands. (The sixty and more Hot Five and Hot Seven records he made between 1925 and 1928 were simply studio sessions.) And from 1947 until he fell ill, in the late sixties, he led his All Stars, an ambiguous swing sextet that started out on a lofty musical level (Barney Bigard on clarinet, Jack Teagarden on trombone, Earl Hines on piano, Arvell Shaw on bass, and Sidney Catlett on drums) and went slowly downhill after the originals left. Soon after he arrived in Chicago, he had learned from watching the great dancer Bill (Bojangles) Robinson that playing his instrument was only part of what he was supposed to do in front of an audience; the rest was to *entertain*—to be comical and loose and sharp. (Armstrong was often accused by younger musicians of behaving onstage like an Uncle Tom, but there was nothing servile about him. Armstrong onstage was the same as Armstrong offstage—a tough, primitive, funny genius, full of high jinks and body jokes. He was also his own kind of racial activist, angrily quitting a State Department tour when Governor Faubus obstructed school integration in Arkansas.) In his way, Armstrong was an autodidact, and he loved to write, particularly letters. Here is part of his description of Robinson's act at a matinée in 1922 at the Erlanger Theatre. He wrote it in longhand a year or two before he died:

> I had Bill Johnson to take me to a matinee show one day so I could see this man whom I had heard and read about in my early days in N.O. And Bojangles came up to every expectations and opinions that I had of him before I saw him in person. . . . It was a long time before Bojangles could open his mouth. That's how popular he was and well liked by all who understood his greatness as a dancer and a showman. He waited after the thunderous applause had finished—and looked up into the booth and said to the man who controlled the lights—Bill said (to him) *Give* me a *light My* color. And *all* the lights *all* over the house *"went out."* And *me* sitting there when this happened with the whole audience just roaring with laughter . . . Then Bojangles went into his act. His every move was a beautiful picture . . . He imitated a *trombone* with his walking cane to his mouth. . . . He told a lot of funny jokes. . . . Then he went into his dance and finished by skating off of the stage with a silent sound and tempo. *Wow* what an artist. I was sold on him ever since.

Armstrong immediately shook things up in Chicago. He broke away from the shelter of the collective New Orleans ensemble and became the first jazz soloist. He unwittingly made the improvising soloist into a hero, and by the mid-thirties the landscape he had created was full of Benny Goodmans and Roy Eldridges and Art Tatums and Coleman Hawkinses. His tone filled out and became statuesque and instantly identifiable, and it never diminished. The missed or cracked notes that had dogged him in the early twenties vanished. He began putting his notes in unexpected places, creating irresistible surprises. These rhythmic jolts pointed the way for Billie Holiday and Lester Young and Red Allen, and echoes can still be heard in the playing of pianists like John Lewis and Dave McKenna and Tommy Flanagan. The solos and cadenzas he recorded in Chicago in 1928 on numbers like "Muggles," "Tight Like This," "Basin Street Blues," and "West End Blues" were so fresh and brilliant that a whole generation of musicians fell into line behind him. He also discovered, lamentably, that he could bring an audience to its feet by playing forty or fifty high C's in a row, and several times came close to permanently ruining his lip. At the same time, as if to balance this grandstanding, he occasionally moved down into his low register, with alarmingly beautiful results. Whenever he did this—in the first chorus of his solo on the 1929 "Knockin' a Jug"; on both takes of his second solo on "Some of These Days," made later the same year, and in his muted opening solos on "Sweethearts on Parade" and "All of Me," recorded in 1930 and 1932—he would slip into a slow-turning half-time as well, and you suddenly knew that here was the lyrical, moving, secret center of Louis Armstrong. He continued to share these secrets on perhaps a third of the thirty or so numbers he recorded for Victor between December of 1932 and the following April. His solos on "That's My Home," "Basin Street Blues," "I Gotta Right to Sing the Blues," "Hustlin' and Bustlin' for Baby," and "Laughin' Louie" radiated a breadth and majesty usually associated with classical music. They had long-held, vibratoless whole notes—planes of sound—arching blue notes, uncannily graceful upper-register figures, and rhythmic dislocations, all governed by a regal ease. Armstrong seemed, in effect, to be standing on a hilltop, declaring, for all who cared to listen, a new music.

Although Armstrong told the Belgian critic Robert Goffin around this time that he was "the rage of the nation," things began to go mysteriously wrong in his life. He went to Europe for the first time, and had severe lip problems and was called "barbaric." He had run-ins with a crooked manager and with the Mob in Chicago and New York. His second wife, Lil Hardin, sued for divorce, and his wife-to-be, Alpha, began spending his money. When he returned to the recording studios in October of 1935, he was a different Armstrong. The lyricism and majesty had been damped. His backup band, led by the pianist Luis Russell, was nondescript (it didn't come to life until Sidney Catlett joined in 1939), and he was forced, with Glaser already at the controls, to record a lot of third-rate material. In fact, Benny Goodman was the rage of the nation, and Armstrong, the great innovator, had slipped off to one side. And so it went for him right into the mid-forties, with bebop washing over jazz and the big bands starting to go under. But late in 1946 the phoenix stirred. One of Armstrong's old models, Bunk Johnson, dragged out of retirement by New Orleans revivalists, had come to New York and was creating a small uproar, and Armstrong, perhaps goaded by this New Orleans ghost, started appearing in the recording studios and at concerts with various small New Orleans-style bands. Some of the burnish reappeared in his playing, and the idea took hold at the management level that perhaps the time had come to dump his big band and put him with a small group modelled loosely on the old Hot Fives and Hot Sevens. The All

Stars were assembled, and they opened at Billy Berg's in Los Angeles in mid 1947, and would, in their many transmutations during the next twenty years, make both Glaser and Armstrong millionaires.

One part of Armstrong's arsenal never changed—his voice. People parodied his gravelly-guttural sound, but this was largely because they didn't know how to get through its bulk and weight to what was inside, to his *singing*. He was, in truth, a marvellous, lightsome singer. (It has often been said that his singing was a direct extension, a kind of mirror, of his playing. But his singing was more of a distillation of his trumpet work. He used the same rhythmic tricks, the improvisation, and the free emotion, but he eliminated the impurities in his playing—the high notes and the by-rote figures.) He never sang out of tune, or put his accents and notes in the wrong place. He knew how to articulate, and how to set each song, no matter how trifling, into focus. He could sing ballads and up-tempo songs and the blues. He could turn a novelty number like the 1932 "Hobo, You Can't Ride This Train" into something at once comic and swinging and moving. He invented jazz singing, providing a munificent lode for everyone from Bing Crosby and Louis Prima to Billie Holiday and Ella Fitzgerald. He demonstrated that four-four time was not a trap but a frame to work against. Listen to the split-second pause between "Louis" and "Dolly" near the beginning of the most famous recording he ever made.

In the mid-fifties, the record producers George Avakian and Milt Gabler, each in his own way, brought the old, florescent Armstrong briefly but brilliantly back to life. Avakian took the All Stars, made up by then of Barney Bigard on clarinet, Trummy Young on trombone, Billy Kyle on piano, Arvell Shaw on bass, and Barrett Deems on drums, into Columbia's studios, and they set down more than twenty numbers by W. C. Handy and Fats Waller, most notably a slow, luminous middle-register "Blue, Turning Gray Over You." A year later, Gabler, the founder of Commodore Records and a longtime A&R man at Decca Records, hit upon the notion of having the All Stars (one welcome change: Edmond Hall had replaced Bigard) re-create forty or so of Armstrong's classic recordings from the twenties and early thirties. With Glaser's consent, he scheduled three successive sessions in December of 1956 and four in January of 1957. Sy Oliver and Bob Haggart wrote arrangements that loosely followed the originals, and the outlines of Armstrong's old solos were sketched out on the lead sheets—for him to do with as he chose. A reed section was added on half the numbers, for supporting riffs and inspirational organ chords. The critic Leonard Feather supplied autobiographical segments for Armstrong to read between the numbers, and the whole was issued as "Satchmo: A Musical Autobiography of Louis Armstrong." Mosaic Records, the astute reissue house in Stamford, Connecticut, has brought out the "Autobiography" again, minus Feather's interpolations and with a long, searching Armstrong-as-hero essay by Dan Morgenstern. But Mosaic has academic tendencies, and has surrounded the "Autobiography" with all the generally undistinguished studio sessions made by the All Stars for Decca, calling the project "The Complete Decca Studio Recordings of Louis Armstrong and the All Stars."

Twenty numbers in the "Autobiography" are based on material Armstrong recorded in the late twenties and early thirties, and the rest on the earlier Hot Fives and Hot Sevens. There is an anemic feel to these last; it was not easy for polished musicians like Young and Kyle and Hall to go back thirty years and get inside the heads of primitive players like Johnny Dodds and Kid Ory. But "Gully Low Blues" captures the thick slow-blues atmosphere of the original, and "King of the Zulus" easily surpasses its predecessor. It is a medium-tempo blues with some nonsense talk in the middle and two Spanish-tinged stop-time sections, and Armstrong plays with a dark, feverish dexterity. He throws off blue notes, trills, little runs, double-time figures, and behind-the-beat pauses. The color and shape of his two solos eerily suggest what Joe Oliver must have sounded like in his prime. The remake of "Knockin' a Jug" is stunning. The original, recorded early one morning with three black musicians (Armstrong, Kaiser Marshall on sticks and brushes, and Happy Caldwell on tenor saxophone) and four white ones (Eddie Lang on guitar, Joe Sullivan on piano, Eddie Condon on guitar, and Jack Teagarden on trombone), is simply a string of blues solos, taken at a medium-slow tempo and capped by Armstrong's two majestic closing choruses. (It was one of the first mixed recording sessions, but no fear; personnel were not yet listed on 78-rpm record labels.) The new "Knockin' a Jug" follows the same pattern, with Barrett Deems (see Marshall on the original) playing a flawless press roll with his sticks on a wood block behind the opening and closing choruses. After Kyle's solo, the reed section, anchored by a baritone saxophone, comes in, and Armstrong takes his two choruses, starting lower than on the original and gradually working his way up through his middle register, using several rests along the way. Halfway into the first chorus, he suddenly dislocates the time, charging quickly and briefly ahead, then falling back (all in the space of a measure) to the four-four flow of the chorus. It is one of the handful of classic recorded slow-blues solos, and its melancholy is almost palpable—everything down and out in Armstrong's life compressed into twenty-four bars.

There are half a dozen other marvellous tracks in the "Autobiography," and they include a very slow "If I Could Be with You," with an astonishing, aching Armstrong vocal; an equally slow "Lazy River" that has a startling four-bar break made up of a climing glissando, and, just after, four rending repeated staccato notes; a long, leisurely "Sunny Side of the Street," with Armstrong's second vocal chorus restored; and a "Some of These Days," in which his second solo captures much of the secret, low, half-time wonder of his original 1929 solos.

After the "Autobiography" was finished, Armstrong settled back into the entertainment machine Joe Glaser built for him. But, as he told Richard

Meryman, he got home once in a while. Armstrong's friend the publicist Phoebe Jacobs remembered recently what it was like to visit him at his house in Queens. "It was wild," she said. "Sometimes when you arrived, he'd be playing along with a recording by Benny Goodman or Guy Lombardo, and taping it. Or singing along with Mahalia Jackson and taping that. And while you were talking, he'd tape you without telling you. But his real therapy was his writing. He'd say to me, 'You lick the envelopes and the stamps, I'll do the writing.' His libary was amazing. He had everything there was about black music, and he even had two books about Hitler. 'If you want to hate someone, Pops,' he'd say, 'you got to know why you hate him.'"

# 1995

## Harlem Morning

Around ten o'clock on a morning in mid-August of 1958, an extraordinary group of jazz musicians began gathering outside a row of brownstones on 126th Street, between Fifth and Madison Avenues. They had been invited by *Esquire* to have their picture taken for a special jazz issue, scheduled for January of 1959. Fifty-eight musicians turned up. They included New Orleans, New York, Chicago, Kansas City, and bebop musicians—the whole glorious jazz schmear as it existed in the late fifties in New York. There were megastars (Count Basie, Coleman Hawkins, Lester Young, Roy Eldridge, Dizzy Gillespie, and Gene Krupa); future stars (Gerry Mulligan, Thelonious Monk, Sonny Rollins, Charles Mingus, Art Farmer, Art Blakey, and Horace Silver); former Ellingtonians (Rex Stewart, Lawrence Brown, Tyree Glenn, Oscar Pettiford, and Sonny Greer) and former Basieites (Buck Clayton, Dicky Wells, Jimmy Rushing, Vic Dickenson, Jo Jones, and Emmett Berry); great teachers and shapers (Mary Lou Williams, Luckey Roberts, Willie the Lion Smith, Red Allen, and Zutty Singleton); indispensable journeymen (Milt Hinton, J. C. Higginbotham, Joe Thomas, Stuff Smith, Wilbur Ware, Chubby Jackson, Hank Jones, and J. C. Heard); an Eddie Condon contingent, minus its leader (Pee Wee Russell, Miff Mole, Bud Freeman, Max Kaminsky, and George Wettling); one American woman singer (Maxine Sullivan) and one English woman pianist (Marian McPartland); a ringer (an unknown musician from Buffalo named Bill Crump); and one messup (Willie the Lion), who, bored with waiting in the hot sun, had wandered off when the chosen shot was taken, leaving a noticeable gap next to Luckey Roberts. The youngest musician, at twenty-eight, was Eddie Locke, and the oldest, at seventy-one, was Roberts.

It had been the notion of Robert Benton, then the art director of *Esquire*, to include a batch of new photographs of jazz musicians for the January issue. He brought in Art Kane, a young hotshot freelance art director, and Kane suggested that a group photograph be taken in Harlem, the cradle of New York jazz. He also offered to take the picture himself, even though he'd had almost no experience as a photographer. The word went out on the jazz grapevine, and the musicians began trickling in on time, despite the heavy duty of being anywhere but in bed at ten in the morning. (Jazz musicians are night creatures; a musician at the shoot said he was astonished to discover that there were two ten o'clocks in each day.) Because they are peripatetic, jazz players sometimes don't run into one another for years at a time; as the crowd swelled, so did the milling, the pressing of the flesh, the hugs, and the how-ya-beens. Kane started shooting anyway. Milt Hinton, a fine amateur photographer, handed his wife, Mona, his 8-mm movie camera and told her to aim it and press the button. He himself began taking stills; so did a student of Willie the Lion's named Mike Lipskin. Eventually, the crowd formed a ragged line on the sidewalk between two high brownstone stoops. Then, with Kane pleading and shouting from across the street, part of the group, led by Red Allen, rose up onto the stoop in between, so that the assemblage resembled an upside-down "T." Count Basie, tired of standing, sat on the curb, and twelve kids, mostly from the neighborhood, sat next to him, forming an emphatic line under the picture. Some of the musicians were coatless and in sports shirts, but most wore ties and jackets. Some were even in dark suits, and seven had hats on. Except for a few nervous Young Turks like Johnny Griffin, Mingus, Sahib Shahab, and Rollins, everyone looked pleased and relaxed about being where he was. Dizzy Gillespie, standing at the far right with his legs crossed, is sticking his tongue out at his onetime idol, Roy Eldridge, who is directly in front of Gillespie and has turned his head awkwardly toward him. Gillespie the irrepressible had obviously just called, "Hey, Roy!"

Kane took a hundred and twenty exposures, and the final selection duly appeared as a double-page spread in *Esquire*. It caused a small sensation, and soon became a permanent part of jazz arcana. The image also stuck in the head of a pretty, witty, famous New York blonde named Jean Bach. Born in Chicago and raised in Milwaukee, Bach has been a passionate jazz fan since she was eighteen and began hanging out with Duke Ellington and Roy Eldridge. In 1941, she married an Eldridge imitator, Shorty Sherock, and spent seven tumultuous years travelling with Sherock's group. ("It was a strange band," she once said. "It had a floating Basie-type rhythm section and an Italianate trumpet section that played a little sharp and real loud.") Then she got a divorce, moved to New York, married a TV producer named Bob Bach, and, in time, began producing the Arlene Francis show on WOR radio. She retired in the eighties, and several years ago she began brooding about Art Kane's picture. The surprising result is a brilliant, funny documentary film called "A Great Day in Harlem." It's about the taking of the picture, and it's also about mortality, loyalty, talent, musical beauty, and the fact that jazz musicians tend to be the least pretentious artists on earth.

Jean Bach lives in Gertrude Vanderbilt Whitney's old studio on Washington Mews, and the other day she sat in her living room and talked about her film. "I kept asking myself how all these fabulous musicians had got together on somebody's brownstone stoop in Harlem to have their photograph taken. All I knew was that a man named Art Kane had taken it and that it had run in *Esquire*. I started asking musicians I'd run into who were in the picture how it had come about, and I'd generally get these hazy, gee-I-can't-remember-man answers. One day I noticed that only a dozen or so of the fifty-seven people in the picture were still with us, and the electric light went on. It was time for me to interview the survivors, and maybe film the interviews, for the record."

Bach talked to her friend Bill Harbach, who had made some short films, and he put her onto a film person named Kemper Peacock, who found her a cameraman named Steve Petropoulos. Before she knew it, she had fifty or sixty hours of interviews. She talked to Johnny Griffin and Art Farmer, both of whom live in Europe, at New York gigs, and she filmed Bud Freeman in a retirement place in Chicago. She finally caught up with the elusive Art Blakey in "his gorgeous West Side apartment." She shot Gerry Mulligan in his house in Connecticut, and she did several interviews in her living room, placing each musician in a different part of the room to fool the viewer. Sahib Shahab died two weeks after she talked to him, and Blakey three months later, and since then Freeman, Gillespie, Buck Clayton, and Max Kaminsky have gone. Then Milt Hinton told Bach's friend Charles Graham about Mona's 8-mm film, and she decided to somehow combine that footage, if it still existed, with the filmed interviews—in other words, to make a movie. Bach asked her friend Kathryn Altman—Robert Altman's wife—for advice, and she suggested that Bach get in touch with a producer named Matthew Seig, who works with Altman. Seig said yes, and when Mona Hinton's film was finally found, in Milt's basement in Queens, Seig told Bach that it was time to rent a studio and hire an editor. They hired Susan Peehl, who edited the fine 1993 Billie Holiday documentary "Lady Day: The Many Faces of Billie Holiday," and put her in a studio apartment over on Third Avenue, where she lived the picture night and day for the next year and a half. Seig also came up with the brilliant idea of using footage from the "Sound of Jazz" television show, which aired just six months before the Harlem shoot and included many of the same musicians.

Bach went on, "Then I discovered the joys of getting permissions from music publishers to use their music. There are twenty-three songs, or pieces of songs, in the picture, and to date they have cost well over a hundred thousand dollars. I realized early on that I couldn't swing all the costs myself, and I applied to every foundation that exists, and all I could hear was the sound of pocketbooks snapping shut across the country. I finally got a grant from a baby friend in Milwaukee. She and her husband have the Jane and Lloyd Pettit Foundation."

The film was finished last June. It has been shown in London and for a week on the Coast, and is therefore eligible for the Academy Awards, and it won a first prize at the Chicago Film Festival. "So far, I've only had one real demurrer," she said. "And it came from Artie Shaw. We're old friends, and when we had lunch on the Coast a little while ago I asked him what he thought of the picture, and he said, 'Jean, do you want me to be polite, or do you want me to be honest?' I said the latter, and he had all these niggling criticisms, and then I realized what was really bothering him. In the film, sweet Bud Freeman speculates that in a hundred years Pee Wee Russell might prove to be more highly thought of than Benny Goodman. What rankles Artie is that Freeman said *Goodman*. If he had said Shaw, Artie would have just laughed and said something like 'Oh, Pee Wee.' "

Susan Peehl's quicksilver editing of "A Great Day" mixes interviews (she sometimes cuts rapidly back and forth between two musicians talking about the same subject, to give the impression that they are conversing with each other), archival footage, sequences from the "Sound of Jazz," Mona Hinton's film, Hinton's and Mike Lipskin's stills, and more than a dozen of Art Kane's alternative shots. She mixes these last in such a way that the musicians move and talk and gesticulate: you are on 126th Street in 1958. She also gives us miniature portraits of Thelonious Monk playing and doing one of his impromptu dances, and of Lester Young in his famous black porkpie hat, his flat eyes peering out of his pale, flat face. Near the end of the film, there is a calm, and Art Farmer says, "We don't think about people not being here. If we think about Lester Young, we don't think, Well, Lester Young was here but he's not here anymore. Lester Young *is* here. Coleman Hawkins *is* here. Roy Eldridge *is* here. They are in us, and they will always be alive." Farmer has a dark, heavy voice, and he makes you shiver.

## The Young Guns

The trumpeter Wynton Marsalis, arrived in New York in 1979, aged seventeen, and joined Art Blakey's Jazz Messengers the following year. His immediate followers were the trumpeters Terence Blanchard and Wallace Roney, the alto saxophonist Donald Harrison, and the pianists Kenny Kirkland, Mulgrew Miller, and Marcus Roberts. But it soon became clear that these musicians were not a nouvelle vague. They were, in fact, conservatives bent on refurbishing a music—aptly called hard bop—that had grown out of bebop in the fifties and sixties, and eventually died of dullness. They were neo-hard-boppers, whose gods were John Coltrane and Miles Davis. By the early nineties, this invasion of twenty-year-olds had become a flood. It poured out of Marsalis's groups, out of the Berklee College of Music, in Boston, and out of a couple of informal schools of music run by the singer Betty Carter and by Art Blakey, both of them partial to hiring fresh young musicians. (Blakey, who died in 1990, once said, "The average man doesn't want to have to use his brain when he listens to music. Music should wash away the dust of his everyday life.") The flood continues to pour through the city, loosing a sashaying energy that rivals the perfervid early days of Coltrane and Coleman and Monk. The neo-hard-boppers turn up at Bradley's, the Iridium Room, Sweet Basil, the Time Cafe, and the Village Vanguard, and since they all seem to have recording contracts with major labels they also turn up with new CDs in hand. (Think of Parker and Gillespie in the mid-forties, shunned by the majors and grateful to be recorded by any two-bit label.) Here, in no particular order, is what some of the neos sound like.

Christian McBride: bass; born in Philadelphia in 1973; studied briefly at Juilliard. He is said to have appeared on seventy albums in the past couple of years, and has recently issued his own first album, "Gettin' to It". He displayed a big tone at the Vanguard in March, and boundless enthusiasm. His intonation is erratic when he plays arco. (He reveres the bassist Ron Carter, but he should study Michael Moore's incomparable arco work.) And he tends, when he solos pizzicato and attempts complex double-time figures, to lose the beat. Since the bass has become the chief timekeeper in jazz, such unsteadiness could be embarrassing.

Nicholas Payton: trumpet; born in New Orleans in 1973; studied with the pianist Ellis Marsalis, Wynton's father. He looks much like the Louis Armstrong of 1925 and plays with the same somewhat heedless vigor. He has no vibrato, and he uses all his registers. He likes half-valving and squeezed notes, and when he runs out of ideas he fires off trills and meaningless runs. He has listened to Miles and Clifford Brown and Freddie Hubbard. His first CD under his own name is "From This Moment . . ."

Cyrus Chestnut: piano; born in Baltimore in 1962; studied at the Peabody Conservatory, Berklee, and at Betty Carter College. A huge, round presence who suggests Lionel Hampton's Milt Buckner, he was seen at both the Iridium Room and the Regattabar, in Cambridge, in March. He is, primarily, a good showman, who likes heavy lower-register chords (reminiscent of Eddie Costa) and chordal explosions. He uses a lot of loud-pedal on slow ballads, and he has good dynamics. He can whip through lightning runs, and he often leans on repeated figures for melodramatic and rhythmic effect. Red Garland stands in his back-ground. Chestnut's newest album is "The Dark Before the Dawn."

Jacky Terrasson: piano; born in Berlin, of a French father and a black American mother, in 1965, and raised in Paris; has lived in the United States off and on for ten years, attending Berklee for a year and B.C.C. for eight months. Terrasson is a dazzling player, and an ingratiating showoff. He has a remarkable sense of dynamics, and he can move easily from a cool, medium-tempo single-note blues that fluctuates between two keys to a

dreaming ad-lib version of "What a Difference a Day Made." He constantly
jars you by putting his notes in unexpected places, and he uses silence to lyrical effect. Many of the neos write their own songs, and that is ambitious and
admirable, but it leaves the listener groping for handles: how do you judge
an improvisation based on unknown material? Seven of the eleven numbers
on Terrasson's only CD, "Jacky Terrasson", are standards, though. Terrasson is not walking into the future backward; he's an original.

Joshua Redman: tenor saxophone; born in Berkeley, California, in 1969;
graduated summa cum laude from Harvard and turned down Yale Law
School to become a full-time musician. Redman is handsome and articulate,
and he has become, willy-nilly, the matinée idol of the neos. Night after
night, the Village Vanguard heaved with adulation when he appeared there
in March. He is a skilled, straight-ahead post-Coltrane player, a kind of
miniature Sonny Rollins. He has a big tone, and he embosses his solos,
which are melodic and lilting, with occasional modish shrieks and grunts. He
also has a flair for writing catchy gospel and/or blues-flavored melodies that
recall the "funk" and "soul" tunes Horace Silver and Bobby Timmons tossed
off forty years ago. Redman is the son of Dewey Redman, the old avant-
garde tenor player. Young Redman says his father has had little or no influence on his playing, and, indeed, they have got to know each other only
recently. Redman's newest CD is "MoodSwing."

James Carter: soprano, alto, tenor, and baritone saxophones, bass clarinet, and flute; born in Detroit in 1969, and studied locally with Donald
Washington. Sometime in the fifties, tenor-saxophone playing changed
drastically: the sumptuousness and lyricism of Coleman Hawkins and Don
Byas were replaced by a hard, vibratoless tone and a bulling-ahead attack.
Emotion became masked, and the saxophone, long an embracing instrument, turned remote and blank-faced. Carter is a surprise. Not only is he
equally adept on his instruments (listen to the blues he plays on bass clarinet
on his "The Real Quietstorm" album), but he has clearly gone back and
studied Hawkins and Byas and Johnny Hodges. He has also studied Coltrane
and Eric Dolphy, and when he mixes them all together the results are over-
arching. He and Terrasson are the most headlong and adventurous of the
neos. Try the howling up-tempo eleven-minute "Take the 'A' Train" on the
new James Carter Quartet CD, "Jurassic Classics."

The original hard-bop players worked within iron frameworks. Their
instrumentation of trumpet, tenor or alto saxophone, piano, bass, and drums
rarely changed, and their ensembles, generally consisting of written unison
figures, enclosed often interminable solos—triggered in part by the seemingly eternal time limits of the still novel LP recording. The youngest of the
neos tend to work only with a rhythm section, and, of course, that allows
them even greater solo space. They are an ingenuous and sweet-natured lot.
Their CD booklets are filled with acknowledgments listing families, friends,
and lovers, and some even include God or "the Creator." (See the CDs of

Carter, Chestnut, Payton, and McBride.) The original hard-boppers were Tough Tonys in comparison. Many were strung out, and died from drug abuse and other misadventures. Their music was over-weening, while the music of their descendants is jejune, vulnerable, and romantic. It is not clear yet whether the neos are producing elegiac echoes or a prelude to the next jazz upheaval.

New female jazz singers seem to appear regularly, but for a long time the space behind Joe Williams (now seventy-six) and Mel Tormé (sixty-nine) and Ray Charles (sixty-four) has been empty. Then, a couple of years ago, the six-foot-four, thirty-six-year-old Kansas City singer Kevin Mahogany suddenly arrived in New York. There is little he cannot do. He has absorbed Billy Eckstine, Williams, Charles, Al Hibbler, Betty Carter, and Leo Watson. He can sing the blues, and he can sing ballads, italicizing their lyrics and burnishing their melodies. (He does not, in the old all-cream way of Eckstine and Williams, make you feel you are listening to a Ballad.) He can scat, endowing that threadbare form with the rhythmic push of Leo Watson and the high quirkiness of Betty Carter. He can sing Monk and Gillespie and John Lewis and Miles Davis (instrumentals with Lyrics pasted on), and he can sing soul songs and novelty songs. And he is a startling gospel singer, who shouts, hums, bends notes in two, growls, and locks every syllable to five or six notes. When he showed up at Bradley's, in April, accompanied by Norman Simmons on piano and Scott Colley on bass, he stood near the bar, loose as a goose, and sang a medium-tempo "Our Love Is Here to Stay," using a little scat and some seamless dynamics and rhythmic shifts; "The Girl from Ipanema," with a scatted coda; a driving "Route 66"; an almost motionless "My Foolish Heart"; Miles Davis's "All Blues," done with just Colley; and a fast, jumping "Take the 'A' Train." (It has become fashionable to roar through Billy Strayhorn's famous anthem, but the song doesn't seem comfortable being hustled down the street; it drags its handsome feet, and sounds disjointed.)

Mahogany has a baronial baritone and careful, telling dynamics: whispers explode into shouts, glissandos die into whispers, growls hurtle across the sky, long notes shiver the timbers. He has perfect pitch, and his vibrato, when he uses one, is tight and orderly. And, through his sly use of tonal and rhythmic exaggeration, Mahogany, like another giant Kansas City singer, Big Joe Turner, gives off a constant undercurrent of swinging mockery, as if he were telling us, "I mean every word I'm singing, man, but, you know, I'm cool."

# Giant Steps

John Coltrane was obsessed by music. He wanted to create a new music—a new medium, almost—and he pursued his vision by studying Indian music, Spanish music, and African music. He listened to every saxophonist from Don Byas and Johnny

Hodges to Parker and Dexter Gordon, from Sonny Stitt and Ornette Coleman to Sonny Rollins and John Gilmore. Byas, pillowy at slow tempos and demonic at fast tempos, moved to Europe after the Second World War. He once told the drummer Arthur Taylor, "Trane and I were tight. Every time he came to Europe, the first place he would go to, he would ask, 'Where is Don Byas?' Always went where I was playing, never said hello. . . . He would sit in the club all night long and never move. I wouldn't know he was there. I'd say to myself, That looks like Trane sitting back there. So when the set was over, I would go and ask, 'How long have you been here?' He'd say, 'I just came in.' "

Rhino Records has just released a seven-CD set, "The Heavyweight Champion: John Coltrane, The Complete Atlantic Recordings." Coltrane was with Atlantic from January of 1959 until May of 1961, and it was largely a transitional time for him: he had his first "hits" ("Giant Steps" and "My Favorite Things"); he took up the soprano saxophone, inspired by Sidney Bechet; and his new quartet began recording. With only six months of Coltrane's contract left, the Atlantic tracks began to take off. There are wondrous slow blues, like "Village Blues" (two takes), "Blues to Elvin," and "Blues to Bechet," this last notable for Jones's merciless foot-pedal work, snare accents, and flooding cymbals; a fractured, caroming "Summertime"; and two lovely ballads, "Central Park West" and "Every Time We Say Goodbye." In these sessions, devices he would use again and again come to the fore—vamps, ground basses, a kind of circular rhythm, and long duets with Elvin Jones.

Impulse! has brought out four releases taken from its archives: a three-CD set entitled "A John Coltrane Retrospective: The Impulse! Years" and reissues of the albums "A Love Supreme," "John Coltrane and Johnny Hartman," and "Ballads: The John Coltrane Quartet." The Impulse! CDs—true, mature Coltrane—begin a few days before his Atlantic contract ran out, and end several months before his death. The first number is a ten-minute inside-out version of "Greensleeves," which, compared with Coleman Hawkins's noble, impassioned recording, clearly suggests the distant ether that Coltrane was already breathing. The final number, "Offering," lasts more than eight minutes and is shaped like an arc. It begins with a misterioso Coltrane theme (he had a headful of them), locks into a furious cycle of circular arpeggios, double notes, and strangulated sounds—a surging mass seemingly played on an unknown celestial instrument—and ends with the same theme, delivered with deep, foghorn notes. Elsewhere on the "Retrospective" CDs, Coltrane uses more and more incantation, on numbers like "Alabama," "Spiritual," "Crescent," and "Dear Lord," and he also allows a disturbing aspect of his work to surface: he sometimes became so obsessed with getting all those notes out that he didn't swing. On the thirteen-minute "Spiritual," recorded live at the Village Vanguard in 1961, he plays a pleasant, almost motionless soprano-saxophone solo, then gives way to the ingenious Eric Dolphy on bass clarinet, and suddenly the number begins to move.

Coltrane tried to describe some of his methods in a *down beat* interview in 1960. "I was trying for a sweeping sound," he said. "I started experimenting because I was striving for more individual development. I even tried long, rapid lines that Ira Gitler termed 'sheets of sound' at that time. But actually, I was beginning to apply the three-on-one chord approach, and at that time the tendency was to play the entire scale of each chord. Therefore, they were usually played fast and sometimes sounded like glisses. I found there were a certain number of chord progressions to play in a given time, and sometimes what I played didn't work out in eighth notes, sixteenth notes, or triplets. I had to put the notes in uneven groups like fives and sevens in order to get them all in. I thought in groups of notes, not of one note at a time."

Very little in Coltrane's playing was accidental. In night clubs, he practiced before sets and between sets, and when he went into the recording studio he arrived an hour early and rehearsed everything he planned to play. The longtime Atlantic Records engineer Tom Dowd has said, "He would stand in a corner, face the wall, play, stop, change reeds, and start again. After a while, he would settle on the mouthpiece and reed that felt most comfortable to him, and then he would start to work on the 'runs' that he wanted to use during the session. I would watch him play the same passage over and over again, changing his breathing, his fingering, and experimenting with the most minute changes in his phrasing. . . . As the rest of the band members started to arrive, he would nod a greeting but never stop playing."

Visionairies rarely leave clear tracks. Coltrane was born poor in Hamlet, North Carolina, in 1926, and reared in High Point. His cousin and lifelong friend Mary Alexander was once asked whether his family had any notion that he would be an artist, and she gives a blunt answer that sums up a philosophy prevalent among Post-Reconstruction black Americans: "No, nobody thought anybody was going to be anything." Coltrane took up the alto saxophone, and after he moved to Philadelphia with his family, in 1943, he worked for King Kolax and the blues shouter Eddie (Cleanhead) Vinson. He had switched permanently to tenor by the time Dizzy Gillespie hired him, in the late forties; he had also started to drink and use drugs, and Gillespie finally had to let him go. In 1954, he joined Johnny Hodges, who was on the only sabbatical he ever took from Duke Ellington's band, and Hodges left a lasting, if subtle, mark on him.

A year later, Coltrane joined Miles Davis, who was just coming into his own, and it was then that his career really began. He recorded (unevenly) with Davis, but he was still messed up, and Davis fired him on more than one occasion. He nearly died of a drug overdose in San Francisco, and when he recovered he quit drinking and drugs and took up God, wavering only briefly thereafter. In 1959, Davis rehired him, and he was on the famous "Kind of Blue" album. Soon after, he left Davis, and, buoyant and full of strength, put together his celebrated quartet—McCoy Tyner on piano, Jimmy Garrison on bass, and Elvin Jones on drums—which stayed together for much of the rest of his life. It is not clear how much Coltrane's home life meant to him. He was married twice, first to Naima Grubbs and then to the pianist Alice McCloud, who bore him three sons. He died unexpectedly, of a liver ailment, in Huntington, Long Island, where he had just bought a house.

Music can only suggest. It can't be religious or political or patriotic or programmatic. But Coltrane's thirty-two-minute "A Love Supreme" is an ardent attempt, full of incantation and even vocal chanting, to thank God for his blessings, to present him with Coltrane's very soul. The six ballads he recorded with the exquisite singer Johnny Hartman and the eight ballads done with his quartet raise another thought about Coltrane. All these beautiful numbers are reverent, melodic interpretations, free of affectation and sentimentality. But do they represent the *real* Coltrane—the peaceful, lyrical, big-toned, God-loving Coltrane, the Coltrane who was never really comfortable belaboring us with unholy shrieks and double notes and chords piled on chords, like bales stacked in a warehouse?

After Coltrane, the hero of the Atlantic and Impulse! recordings is Elvin Jones, the greatest of all modern drummers. He holds Coltrane in his extraordinary hands in every number, pushing him gloriously in his longest solos, nipping at his heels in the slow numbers, perhaps in large part making him what he was. Jones once said of Coltrane: "He left me absolutely alone. He must have felt the way I played, understood the validity of it. There was never any rhythmic or melodic or harmonic conflicts. . . . I was never conscious of the length of Coltrane's solos, which sometimes lasted forty minutes. I was in the position of being able to follow his melodic line through all the modes he would weave in and out of, through all the patterns and the endless variations on variations. It was like listening to a concerto. The only thing that mattered was the completion of the cycle that he was in. I'd get so excited listening to him that I had all I could do to contain myself. There was a basic life force in Coltrane's solos, and when he came out of them you suddenly discovered you had learned a great deal."

Toward the end of his life, Coltrane, photographed incessantly, began to look messianic. His long, handsome, still face, usually in profile, was as serious as stone—he might have been posing for "The Thinker"—and when he turned toward the camera he looked right into your head. I still agree with much of an appraisal I wrote of Coltrane the year after his death. Here is part of it: "Born poets like Coltrane sometimes misjudge the size of their gifts, and in trying to further them, to ennoble them, they fall over into sentimentality or the maniacal. Coltrane did both, and it is ironic that these lapses, which were mistakenly considered to be musical reflections of our inchoate times, drew his heaviest acclaim. People said they heard the dark night of the Negro in Coltrane's wildest music, but what they really heard was a heroic and unique lyrical voice at the mercy of its own power."

On second thought, I would change "sentimentality" to "the romantic." Coltrane was never mushy.

# 1996

## Lovano the Great

For the past ten or fifteen years, jazz, like much of the rest of American culture, has been running in place. Instead of originators, there have been neo-swing musicians, neo-bebop-pers, neo–hard-boppers, neo-big bands, neo-avant-gardists, neo-stride pianists, neo–New Orleans players, and neo-Dixielanders. Among these, of course, are neo-Armstrongs, neo-Beiderbeckes, neo-Hacketts, neo-Davises, neo-Getzes, and neo-Coltranes. What is particularly nettlesome about this stasis is the neo-hard-bop tenor saxophonists. They continue, like their fore-bears, to play as if they were grappling with their listeners, and to flaunt overweening wooden tones. If the four great lyrical progenitors of the tenor saxophone—Coleman Hawkins, Lester Young, Ben Webster, and Don Byas—were poetic, the neo-hard-boppers are prosy and matter-of-fact. You need to go back every so often and listen to Hawkins's "Sweet Lorraine," to Webster's ballads with strings, to Young's "Back to the Land," and to Byas's "Harvard Blues" to make sure that such beauty of tone and melodic line really existed.

But a savior has been slowly materializing in the nineties—the tenor sax-ophonist and composer Joe Lovano. (He also effortlessly plays the soprano, alto, and C-melody saxophones, a variety of clarinets, and drums.) Born in Cleveland in 1952, the son of a local tenor saxophonist, Lovano attended the Berklee School of Music and passed through the Woody Herman band, the Thad Jones-Mel Lewis band, and Charlie Haden's Liberation Music Orchestra. He worked with the drummer Paul Motian and with the for-ward-looking guitarists John Scofield and Bill Frisell. And he listened. In the liner notes of "Tenor Legacy," the 1994 album he made with Joshua Red-man, he lists sixty or so saxophonists whom he has played with or studied, or both: among them are masters like Sonny Rollins and Dexter Gordon; old modernists like Steve Lacy, Phil Woods, Lee Konitz, Johnny Griffin, and Dewey Redman; Lester Youngites like Stan Getz, Zoot Sims, Al Cohn, and Jimmy Giuffre; and Young Turks like Redman, Branford Marsalis, and Kenny Garrett. Other models he has mentioned at one time or another include Charlie Parker, Sonny Stitt, Jackie McLean, John Coltrane, and Ornette Coleman. With so much in his hat, Lovano can move anywhere he

wants in jazz with consummate ease. He can play tonally and atonally. He
can play with a traditional rhythm section and with a "free" one. He can
be as hard as Coltrane and as soft as Parker. He can play *a cappella* solos and
he can fit into tightly organized situations. He can play romantic ballads
and he can improvise on themes by Charles Ives and William Grant Still.

In the words of the composer and conductor Gunther Schuller, Lovano
has a "sovereign command of his instrument(s)." He has a big tone, not
unlike the tones of Chu Berry and Don Byas, and he uses a vibrato, when it
is meet, at slow tempos. Most hard-bop tenor saxophonists are monochromatic, but Lovano has a daring and exhilarating sense of dynamics and tonal
color. He can play loud and suddenly become sotto voce. He will dodge
softly up and down his registers, fashioning delicate, sliding runs; mix them
with silences and with half-time phrases; and often end with two or three
descending notes, almost below hearing, that rend you.

But there are two Lovanos. One is the heedless, hard-driving Lovano who turns up at the Village Vanguard and
other clubs, either with one other horn and a rhythm section or with just a
rhythm section. This Lovano solos at great length; he pushes his solos
before him, keeping them airborne and swinging. He teaches and preaches,
often going up on his toes, his eyes tight shut. (He is hefty, and has a
Vandyke and receding hair.) This Lovano appears on a brand-new two-disk
Blue Note release, "Joe Lovano: Live at the Village Vanguard." The first
disk, made in March of 1994, has the brilliant iconoclast Tom Harrell on
trumpet and flügelhorn (he and Lovano, hand in glove, have recorded and
worked together countless times), Anthony Cox on bass, and Billy Hart on
drums. Many of the numbers flirt with atonality (five are by Lovano, one is
by Harrell, and one is by Vernon Duke), and the bass and drums play free,
circular time. There is is an introverted "I Can't Get Started," in which the
original melody occasionally passes by, masked, and Harrell, on flugelhorn,
showers us with dozens of beautifully struck notes. Harrell has a marked gift
for writing handsome, mournful melodies, and on his "Sail Away" both he
and Lovano are reverential.

On the second disk, made a little over a year ago, Lovano appears with
Mulgrew Miller on piano, Christian McBride on bass, and Lewis Nash on
drums. It's a blowing session. Lovano plays two Coltranes, "Lonnie's
Lament" and "26-2"; Monk's rarely heard "Reflections"; Charlie Parker's
"Little Willie Leaps"; and Charles Mingus's "Duke Ellington's Sound of
Love," done as a Lovano solo. Miller is a fashionably florid pianist, and
McBride keeps a tight rein on his time when he solos.

The other Lovano—the lyrical, moving Lovano—emerges when the
musical climate is the most controlled. This happens on three recent albums.
The first, newly released in this country, was recorded at a jazz festival in
Amiens in 1989 and is called "Joe Lovano Wind Ensemble: Worlds."
Lovano's old friends Bill Frisell and Paul Motian are present, and so are Tim

Hagans, on trumpet; Gary Valente, on trombone; and the Frenchman Henri Texier, on bass. The lyric soprano Judi Silvano, now Lovano's wife, appears on all of the seven connected numbers that make up "Worlds." Wonderful things happen throughout: the rampaging collective ensemble on the title track; Lovano's two-minute *a cappella* ad-lib solo at the start of "Tafabalewa Square" and Silvano's skirling solo over a drone background; and Kenny Werner's affecting ballad, "Two Hearts," in which Silvano sings the lyrics with Lovano echoing her, Lovano plays a soft, mercurial solo, and Silvano returns to the lyrics with Lovano again behind her.

The second album, "Mike Mainieri: An American Diary", is an oddity. On hand are Mainieri on vibraphone and marimbas, Lovano on his various reeds, Eddie Gomez on bass, and Peter Erskine on drums. The materials include Leonard Bernstein's "Somewhere," a Frank Zappa composition, a spiritual, a Scottish folk melody, and snippets from Aaron Copland, Roger Sessions, and Samuel Barber. Lovano is buoyant and even ardent on the spiritual and the folk air, but listen, in particular, to the little lullaby he slips in at the end of his opening solo on "Somewhere."

The third album is the already celebrated "Rush Hour," on Blue Note. Nine of the thirteen numbers were arranged and/or written by Gunther Schuller, and are Third Stream music. These are played by two different ensembles: one is made up of fifteen strings, flute, harp, guitar, two string basses, and drums; the other is made up of five reeds, two horns, trumpet, trombone, tuba, vibraphone, two string basses, electric guitar, and drums. The remaining numbers are marvellously idiosyncratic Lovano confections. He plays tenor and soprano saxophones, bass clarinet, and drums on one, and is joined by Judi Silvano. There is a Lovano-Silvano duet, a Lovano duet with himself on tenor saxophone and drums, and, at the end of the record, a stunning three-and-a-half-minute *a cappella* Lovano tenor solo on Billy Strayhorn's "Chelsea Bridge." The orchestral muscle on Schuller's "Headin' Out, Movin' In" and "Rush Hour on 23rd Street" sometimes threatens to flatten Lovano, but the rest of Schuller's arrangements are lyrical and supportive. They include three ballads: Ellington's "Prelude to a Kiss," Matt Dennis's "Angel Eyes," and Vernon Duke's "The Love I Long For"; a shadowy, secret version of Monk's "Crepuscule with Nellie"; an elbowing Mingus piece, "Peggy's Blue Skylight"; and the mournful "Lament for M," Schuller's tone poem for his late wife. About four and a half minutes into the last, Lovano plays several soft descending notes, backed by harp, that nearly make you weep.

# Tom Harrell

**T**he fads that have long swirled across jazz sometimes make the progress of unfashionable worthies so arduous that if and when they gain recognition they are middle-aged and out of steam. Older musicians, of course, generally know who these starvelings are, and go out of their way to use them on records and for gigs. At present, the best-known unknown is the brilliant forty-nine-year-old trumpeter, flügelhornist, and composer Tom Harrell, whom the alto saxophonist Phil Woods has called a "genius" and "the best musician I've encountered in forty years of playing music." Since the early seventies, Harrell has worked his way through Woody Herman's band, Horace Silver's group, the Woods quintet, Charlie Haden's Liberation Music Orchestra, and the Mel Lewis band. Finally, in the late eighties, he put together his own small group, and, perhaps more important, he began recording and doing dates with Joe Lovano. "Tom is thrilling to play with," Lovano said recently. "He's a poetic musician, and one of the most beautiful of all improvisers. He's a completely free player, an emotional player. Sometimes his chops can't handle all his ideas, and if he isn't executing right I've seen him put down his trumpet in the middle of a solo and pick up his flügelhorn. When we worked together with just bass and drums for a week at the Village Vanguard in 1994, we went beyond technique and form. The music became pure expression. At times, it seemed as if it might blow right past us. Once Tom hears a piece of music, he memorizes it. I think he can play all of Diz's and Parker's most famous solos."

What Harrell does in his solos is pay his almost imperceptible respects to the best of his predecessors. You may hear a flash of Clark Terry, a Navarro-like melodic line, some of Harry Edison's bravura coloring, a Clifford Brown cascade, a Miles Davis rumination. He improvises on his heritage, but he also tries to invent music that has never been heard before. Lovano has pointed out that there are two Harrells—a restrained studio Harrell and a hellbent night-club Harrell. (In much the same way, there are two Lovanos.) The studio Harrell likes to leave spaces between his phrases, and he likes to shift into lilting double-time passages on slow numbers. He often uses his flugelhorn in the studio; it has, of course, a bigger tone than the trumpet, a sound that trumpeters like to sink into. Listen to the studio Harrell on his two tracks on Jim Hall's recent "Dialogues" CD—in particular, "Skylark," in which Harrell plays a nearly straight chorus of melody and then improvises, gently turning Hoagy Carmichael's song into an urgent, complex lullaby. And listen to the sly and mysterious "I Can't Get Started" on Lovano's Village Vanguard CD, where Harrell, following an extraordinary Lovano solo, unreels ascending and descending ribbons of sixteenth notes that go on so long you fear he has become obsessed and may never stop. But he does, suddenly, gathering himself, and loosing several bent, italicized half-time phrases and three descending notes before racing up the next hill. Harrell *composes* his solos as he plays, and he makes his listeners work, as all first-rate improvisers do. If your mind wanders, though, you will be left standing there while the Harrellmobile vanishes over the horizon.

Harrell was born in Urbana, Illinois, in 1946, and grew up in Palo Alto, California. His father is a retired business psychologist, and his mother is a statistician. He has an older sister who is the principal of a school in Minnesota. He started playing music early—piano first, then trumpet—and by the time he was a teen-ager he was gigging around San Francisco. He had a rocky time in high school and college (Stanford), drinking and carrying on. He was, in short, a social maladroit, and once he even attempted suicide. When he was in his early twenties, it was determined that he was a schizophrenic, and he was put on a drug that has since enabled him to live a somewhat normal life. The drug has side effects. It gives him headaches and makes his muscles relax, causing him to shuffle when he walks, and to stand stock-still on the bandstand between his solos, with his head resting almost on his chest and his horn hanging from one hand. (He is six feet two inches tall, and bone thin.) A fluent talker when the vibes are right, he likes to let aphoristic thoughts float to the surface of his conversations. Thus:

Form is rhythm on a larger scale.

I like to use my mind to push the music forward.

It's nice to give your listeners the feeling they're in their homes when you play, to make even an amphitheatre feel like their living room.

In jazz, you can transcend your ego with the music.

The first music was made by birds and water and trees.

Harrell feels that improvisation and composing are the same thing, just carried out at different speeds. He is a striking composer, who works both tonally and atonally, and who has a genuine gift for mournful, minor-sounding melodies. "I tend to write in fragments," he has said. "I store these, then go back to them and put them together—like an architect. I like twelve-or sixteen-bar phrases, unconventional lengths. The arranger Russ Garcia once told me to sing before I write music." Lovano says of Harrell's composing, "Everything he writes has its own flavor. He writes for the moment, for the people he is recording or playing with. He'll use very complex harmonies and simple melodies, or complex bebop-type melodies and relaxed harmonies. But his tunes never crowd you."

RCA Victor has just signed Harrell to a contract, and his first album will be released next month. There are two groups on the album: his quintet, and the quintet expanded to a nonet, which includes—who else?—Joe Lovano. The Harrell scoring on a couple of the nonet numbers is so dense and full of

basso-profundo sounds that you can almost lean against them. The RCA
contract has cheered Harrell immeasurably. It reminds him of a time when,
still a kid, he sat in with Lee Morgan in San Francisco. "I guess he liked me,"
Harrell said the other day. "When I came off the bandstand, he told me,
'Hey, you're a motherfucker, and I'm not going to let you sit in anymore.' "
Harrell then doubled over with laughter, his head nearly touching the floor,
and let loose a soft, curving sound that would have fitted into any of his solos.

## The Wilder Side

The songwriter-composer Alec Wilder, who died in 1980, at the age of seventy-three, would have reacted to
Desmond Stone's judicious and unblinking biography, "Alec Wilder in
Spite of Himself," in the same way he reacted to the profile of him that I
wrote for The New Yorker in the early seventies—with private pleasure and
loud public outcries to the effect that his privacy had been destroyed and his
life ruined. He would have been secretly disconcerted, though, to discover
that Stone's book has arrived at a time when he is nearly unknown, except
among young classical musicians and those rare cabaret singers who have the
taste and skill to perform his songs.

Wilder, of course, created his own biography as he went along. He did
this by writing thousands of letters to his friends and acquaintances, in which
he discussed every aspect of his life—including such passions as nature, jazz
improvisation, trains, Harold Arlen, and writers like John Cheever, Peter De
Vries, and Sylvia Townsend Warner and such aversions as the hoi polloi,
garish dress, rock music, and fools; by writing, with James T. Maher, a consummate book, "American Popular Song," in which he evaluated, in a point-
edly personal way, eight hundred or so of the three hundred thousand
popular songs submitted for copyright in this country between 1900 and
1950; by publishing a revealing collection of faux letters, called "Letters I
Never Mailed"; and by creating a persona of such vividness and complexity
that it became his finest work.

This persona was strikingly housed. Wilder was tall and handsome, his
face was dramatically lined and worn, and his eyes were beacons. He had a
trombone voice, and he loved to laugh and swear and shout things like "No,
I don't believe it!" when he was surprised or pleased. He invariably wore a
sports jacket, a tie, gray flannels, and loafers. He kept his small mustache and
his coursing gray hair just so, and his distinguished profile at the ready; he
never shied away from photographers. But, as Stone points out almost
immediately, there were two distinct and totally dissimilar Wilders—the
witty, funny, lightsome, sober Wilder and the fearsome alcoholic, who when
he was in his cups insulted foes and friends alike so viciously that the apolo-
gies and roses the next day did not always work.

Wilder was a nomad, flitting endlessly over the surface of his turbulent and emotional life. He never owned anything beyond the contents of two or three suitcases, and he gave away all the countless books he bought and read. He never rented or owned an apartment or a house but spent roughly half the year in a small room at the Algonquin Hotel and the rest of his time in Key West, Nantucket, Cambridge, Maine, and Rochester, where he was born. He never married, which causes Stone to wonder, as many others did, whether he was gay. I suspect that, timid and fragile as he was (he once broke a leg jumping off a Fifth Avenue bus), he was a true neuter. Anyway, he kept falling in love with notable women, among them Judy Holliday, Peggy Lee, and the writer Jean Stafford.

Alec Wilder was born of a delicate Southern belle and a successful, rough-and-ready banker. The family was genteel and dysfunctional. Alec's father died when Alec was two, and his mother—cold and unresponsive by temperament—became an alcoholic, all but permanently closeted in her bedroom, with the shades drawn, suffering from "rheumatism." She moved the family to New York around the time of the First World War, and Alec—a classic sensitive, who hated sports and attracted bullies—went to St. Paul's school in Garden City, to Lawrenceville in New Jersey, and to the Collegiate School in New York. He detested the first two schools and graduated successfully from the third. Sometime in the late twenties, he went back to Rochester and studied privately at the Eastman School of Music, and became friends with Mitch Miller and Goddard Lieberson. He returned to New York in the mid-thirties and before long became a fixture of the city's musical life.

Stone gives us an excellent rundown on the enormous amount and variety of American music that Wilder wrote during the next fifty years—opera, orchestral works, film scores, ballet music, band music, musical-comedy scores, chamber music, solo and contrapuntal pieces for every instrument in the orchestra, Third Stream music, art songs, and popular songs. He was primarily an old-fashioned, unsentimental melodist, who called himself the "president of the derrière-garde," and whose formal pieces were often complex developments of his songs. The best of these songs (among them "I'll Be Around," "It's So Peaceful in the Country," "The Sounds Around the House," "Who Can I Turn To," "Blackberry Winter"), with their strange intervals and difficult, odd melodic turns, form a parallel oeuvre—brainier, more original—to the songs of Gershwin and Berlin and Rodgers and Arlen.

But until concerned hands took hold, in recent years, a good deal of Wilder's music floated around unpublished, unrecorded, unplayed, even unknown. He was seldom paid for his music, because he wrote much of it for friends and for instrumentalists he admired, and it remains a mystery how he managed to live as comfortably as he did. (Stone tells us that Wilder was broke at the end of his life, and that his old friend and admirer Frank Sinatra stood ready to bail him out.) Wilder passionately loved living, but he was also an obsessed, lifelong smoker and died of lung cancer. He once wrote in a letter that the dead "were not skeletons lying in boxes" but, rather, "were very faint shadows hovering above their graves." He is buried in a country graveyard outside Rochester, but surely, restless and insatiably curious as he was, he must occasionally get down to the Algonquin. The one unfailing stabilizer in his life was his sense of humor. He mailed me this letter late in 1972:

A smiling black man . . . has just introduced himself to me in the Algonquin lobby with such reverence and awe that my impulse was to turn my head to see who was standing behind me. No, he meant *me*! . . .

Here I was, momentarily leaving for Key West in a state of depression the depths of which bottomed all previous ones, convinced of the dementia of the Western World, unable to write any more music, disillusioned by the unresponsive behavior of my closest friends, as close to a nervous collapse as I had ever been—and what happens? A black man, with honest love in his eyes, tells me he reveres me!

So I assume that this is the ultimate irony, not unlike a novelist who has just swallowed a bottle of sleeping pills being told that he has won the Nobel Prize.

But no, it's worse. For as I leave the hotel with the irreverent, mindless bellman, I am aware of his mouth-splitting amusement. . . . Yet he explains nothing. So, as I get in the cab, I ask him what possibly could be so funny and he gaspingly tells me, "He thought you were Thornton."

## The Dean

The Jones Boys, as they were called in the fifties and sixties, included the pianist Hank Jones (born in 1918); the trumpeter, composer and bandleader Thad Jones (born in 1923, died in 1986); and the drummer Elvin Jones (born in 1927). These three are, of course, brothers, who rank with the most gifted, adventurous, and persuasive of all jazz musicians. Thad was the co-founder of the bellwether Thad Jones–Mel Lewis Orchestra, a fine composer ("A Child Is Born"; lyrics by Alec Wilder), and a formidable trumpet player who never got his due. Elvin perfected an extraordinary polyrhythmic attack during his years with John Coltrane, and has become the most widely imitated modern drummer. And Hank, who has been a kind of one-man foundation under jazz during the past fifty years (a Jazz at the Philharmonic mainstay, an accompanist for Ella Fitzgerald, a CBS staff musician, the pianist on a thousand record dates), is widely regarded as the dean of jazz pianists. One winter, for a short, delirious time, George Shearing was ensconced in the Café Carlyle while Hank Jones was across the hall in the Bemelmans Bar. The minute his first show was over, Shearing, a dazzling pianist himself, would speed across the hall on the arm of his wife, Ellie, and station himself at Jones's right elbow, and remain until it was time to go back to work. "Hank has been my mentor since 1947," Shearing said recently.

Jones first came to New York in 1944, to join Hot Lips Page's band, on Fifty-second Street. He was entering a land of pianistic giants and near-giants. Art Tatum was God, and nearby were Nat Cole, Teddy Wilson, and Marlowe Morris, and just coming up were Bud Powell, Al Haig, Erroll Garner, and Thelonious Monk. Jones listened, appropriating a little of Tatum, a little of Wilson and Cole, and a little of Powell and Garner. The result is a quiet, lyrical, attentive style, so subtle and technically assured as to be almost self-effacing; you have to lean forward to catch Jones properly. He will start two choruses of the blues with delicate single notes, placing them in surprising, jarring places, either because behind the beat or off to one side—a path over a rocky place—and then play several dissonant chords; return to single notes, this time letting them pour in Tatum runs, some going up, some down; slip in more chords; and close the solo with a chime sound. Unlike most modern pianists, Jones constantly uses his left hand, issuing a carpet of tenths, little offbeat clusters, and occasional patches of stride. Jones's solos *judge*, and they rest far above the florid, Gothic roil that many jazz pianists have fallen into in the past twenty years.

Jones is a crisp, compact, serious man who laughs a lot and invariably wears a tie and jacket. He likes to talk about improvisation, and here are some of the things he said recently: "You have to stay in shape, so I do scales and exercises three or four hours a day, and then I practice sight-reading. Of course, there is an extremely important prelude to improvising. Every tune you play has its correct tempo, and you have to find it. When you do, it practically plays itself. It's not what *you* think it should be, it's what the tune demands. Improvisation is instant composing. You try and conceive the totality in your mind of what you're going to do, and then flesh it out with an F-minor seventh, or G-flat minor, or augmented fourth. You're superimposing another line on the original composition, and you think about the chord pattern—not each chord—and you think about the melody. Music is colorless, but there are shades of music—brightness, sombreness, any kind of mood. It's difficult not to repeat certain figures and patterns. When you do, it means your concentration is not what it should be. Concentration is the difference between the great players and the players who are not great. Other pianists have told me that once in a rare while they play on a level they have never reached before, and this makes me wonder if there is a level of the subconscious that improvisers suddenly tap into. I remember once I was working with Coleman Hawkins and J. J. Johnson and Max Roach, and I was late. They were already on the bandstand, and that must have shocked me, because I reached a level that I've only reached a few times since."

Jones spends as much time as he can on a farm he bought some years ago in upstate New York, but he still appears in New York, tours abroad, and makes at least one CD a year. In the past five years he has recorded two stunning trio albums—"Essence," with Ray Drummond on bass and Billy Higgins on drums, and "Hank Jones: Upon Reflection," with George Mraz on bass and Elvin Jones on drums. The second album contains ten Thad Jones songs, and is full of marvellous Hank Jones single-note lines and wild, whomping Elvin Jones brushwork. (Elvin is so strong that he once hugged Zoot Sims and broke two of his ribs.) Jones has also recently made two solo albums, "Hank Jones: Live at Maybeck Recital Hall" and "Hank Jones: Handful of Keys" a celebration of Fats Waller, who occasionally passes through Jones's playing. (He had died just a year before Jones arrived in New York.) The Waller is rather noncommittal, but listen to the way Jones rebuilds "Oh, What a Beautiful Morning" and "Blue Monk" on the Maybeck Hall CD. Best of all, though, is Jones's recent "Steal Away: Charlie Haden and Hank Jones."

Haden, the sometime avant-garde bassist, had heard Jones's majestic 1977 recording of "It's Me, O Lord" in the Smithsonian "Jazz Piano" box, and he asked Jones if he would be interested in recording an album of spirituals and hymns with him, and Jones said yes. There are seventeen tunes, among them "It's Me, O Lord," "Nobody Knows the Trouble I've Seen," "Swing Low, Sweet Chariot," "I've Got a Robe, You Got a Robe," "We Shall Overcome," and "Amazing Grace." The album, as quiet as God's thoughts, is unique and irresistibly affecting. The two men work as one, in unison or in harmony, and the recording becomes a subtle meditation on the horrors of slavery as well as a celebration of the great songs that came to be the slaves' solace. This album is also a celebration of Jones's parents, both of whom were seven-days-a-week churchgoers. (Jones still feels uneasy about performing on Sunday.) Most of the numbers are played straight but with the harmonic and rhythmic inflections that separate jazz from the rest of music. On "Wade in the Water" and "Go Down, Moses," however, Jones improvises delicately, and on "We Shall Overcome" he pauses after a unison statement of the melody, Haden begins to "walk," and Jones suddenly lifts into four ringing choruses of the blues, his single-note lines sparkling and his chords belling. It's an electric moment.

## Love Match

Columbia has released "Miles Davis & Gil Evans: The Complete Columbia Studio Recordings," a reissue of the three famous Davis-Evans collaborations—"Miles Ahead," "Porgy and Bess," and "Sketches of Spain"—which were made between 1957 and 1960. There are six CDs; three contain the three original LPs, together with rehearsal takes and alternate takes. The three others include the strange "Quiet Nights" album and later fragmentary Davis-Evans get-togethers, along with still more takes, remakes, overdubbings, and related effluvia from the dozen or so sessions that were needed to make the original recordings. In addition, there is a two-hundred-page booklet composed of the original LP liner notes (George Avakian, André Hodeir, Charles Edward Smith, Nat Hentoff), an Avakian account of how the Davis-Evans collaborations came about, analyses and overviews by Bill Kirchner and Bob Belden, and page after page of annotations and microscopic discographical data by the inde-fatigable jazzologist Phil Schaap. Perhaps we once knew, and had forgotten, that these recordings, made on tape instead of the wax disks used for 78 rpms, were the beginning of the debatable practice of editing and splicing jazz recordings, a practice now much reduced. Schaap, for instance, tells us that "The Meaning of the Blues," in "Miles Ahead," is the only complete, unspliced take on that album. In short, the Davis-Evans albums in the Columbia box are composite jazz, pastiche jazz.

Davis and Evans were an unlikely pair. The trumpeter, born Miles Dewey Davis III, in 1926, was raised in an upper-class black family in East St. Louis. He came to New York in 1944, and, though still a tentative player, was soon appearing on Fifty-second Street with Charlie Parker and Cole-man Hawkins. Evans arrived in New York from California two years later to work as an arranger for Claude Thornhill. His background was mysterious. He was a late child, born in Toronto, in 1912, of Scotch-Irish stock. He once said that his father had been a gambler and that his mother, a tiny woman, "carried a mandolin with her." He also said, "She played folk music. I think they came from Calcutta. They were married in Australia. They moved to Jersey. Then they moved to Canada." His mother, a cook and nursemaid, brought him up in Saskatchewan, British Columbia, Montana, and Stockton, California.

When he arrived in the city, Evans immediately rented a big one-room apartment behind a Chinese laundry on West Fifty-fifth Street, and it became a come-as-you-are salon for such brilliant Young Turks of the time as Parker, Davis, Bud Powell, Gerry Mulligan, John Lewis, Lee Konitz, and Max Roach. Evans, already in his mid-thirties, became the hub of the Fifty-fifth Street salon, and certainly helped to bring into being the nonet that recorded the celebrated "Birth of the Cool" sides in 1949 and 1950. The nonet, made up mainly of salon members, including Davis, was in essence a miniature version of the revolutionary Thornhill band and the acorn out of which the Columbia Davis-Evans sessions grew.

Davis and Evans did not work together again for seven years. Davis went through the first of the drug-addicted times that plagued his life, and Evans drifted into freelance arranging, mostly for vocalists. In 1954, Davis, back on track, recorded two long knockout blues, "Walkin'," and "Blue 'n' Boo-gie," and a year later he made a sensational unscheduled appearance with an all-star pickup group at the Newport Jazz Festival. Because of this, George Avakian signed him for Columbia Records, and a year or so later he began thinking about Davis and Evans's collaboration on the nonet sides and about the luxuriant airborne arrangements that Evans had done for Thornhill. And he began thinking about Davis's stark lyricism on "Walkin' " and his startling Newport outing. Visions generally start as questions: Why not let Davis and Evans expand what they had begun in the "Birth of the Cool" sessions?

Here is what Evans once said about Davis and himself: "[Miles and I] happened to have the same kind of an ear for sound, a certain sound. I could appreciate his sound, and he could appreciate my sound in the orchestra. There was a certain emotional connection. . . . When he first started out, he didn't have the sound he had eventually. You fill it in. You breathe harder into it. You fill the horn up. . . . It was like it needed to have more flesh and blood to it. It was very stark at the beginning. . . . Later he had more of the melancholy cry that he wanted to get." (Some of the quotes used in this piece, and much of Evans's early background material, were gathered by Gene Lees for his *Jazzletter*.) In an interview done with Ben Sidran not long before his death, in 1988, Evans said of his arrangements, "They're all melancholy. That's one of my characteristics." Sidran replied, "Miles is the voice of melancholy," and Evans continued, "[His] sound is the thing that put us together."

The music Evans and Davis created is unique and largely unclassifiable. Columbia allowed Evans to put together an eighteen-piece band that included five trumpets, four trombones, two French horns, a tuba, two woodwinds, two saxophones, and bass and drums. It *is* an expansion of the Thornhill band, which Evans once described to Nat Hentoff this way: "The sound of the band was almost a reduction to an inactivity of music, to a stillness. Everything—melody, harmony, rhythm—was moving at minimum speed. The melody was very slow, static; the rhythm was nothing much faster than quarter notes and a minimum of syncopation. Everything was lowered to create a sound, and nothing was to be used to distract from that sound. The sound hung like a cloud."

But Davis and Evans's music is richer and deeper and more subtle. It seemed in the late fifties like a new music, a high-class concertized jazz that belonged in the echoing arena where Paul Whiteman had once held forth and where you could still hear the huge, glistening sarabandes of Stan Kenton. More than that, it was an ineffably cool music that caught the current *angst* of Camus and Kerouac and the dying Billie Holiday. It reached its sad hands out to the listening public and, at the same time, it wowed the critics. It is full of metaphor, this music, and it is almost visual. The brocade curtains of Debussy and Ravel, and even Berlioz, keep opening and closing in it, and there are glimpses of the Fauves and of the pleasingly warring interiors of early Vuillard. It is November music, but it is never bleak; the trees may be bare, but they are beautiful, baroque trees. Most important, it is autobiographical music. The emotions raised by Evans's scores—his flutes and clarinets sliding around his tuba, his flutes in the foreground and his horns and trombones in the far distance, his tuba balanced on his horns—and by Davis, who is, of course, the only soloist on all the albums, are almost embarrassingly intimate. Most of the emotions triggered by the best jazz are abstract: the hair stands up on your neck, and you shiver a little. But Davis, fed by Evans, is telling you, in his monosyllabic way and with his long, vibratoless notes, about his life, about how sad it has been, about how he pities himself. He is not telling you how hard it is to be black; he is telling you how hard it is to be Davis, and Evans, constantly underneath and around, never stops nodding, "Yes, yes. That's the way it is." So listen on the "Miles Ahead" album to "The Maids of Cadiz" and "My Ship" and "The Meaning of the Blues," and on "Porgy and Bess" to "Gone, Gone, Gone" and "Prayer (Oh Doctor Jesus)," which builds into an extraordinary chant. And, since so much Spanish music has a melancholy face, listen to all of "Sketches of Spain." To be sure, the music occasionally goes into tempo, the drummer plays an afterbeat on his snare rims, Davis grows heated, and we move into a politely swinging jazz drawing room. This happens in "Miles Ahead" and "Springsville" and "The Duke," in the first album, and, on "Porgy and Bess," on "Buzzard Song" and "Gone" and "Summertime" and "There's a Boat Dat's Leavin' Soon for New York." After all, the Davis-Evans music is closed and complete, with jazz ticking away far inside it. Pale versions of it still turn up on soundtracks, but it is a music of ecstasy, and Evans took it—harmonically, instrumentally, coloristically—as far as it could go.

For whatever reasons, Duke Ellington is rarely mentioned in connection with Evans. But Evans grew sidewise out of Ellington (and Billy Strayhorn), simply adding timbral depth and harmonic outbuildings with his woodwinds and horns and tubas—instruments that Ellington never felt the need of. The Davis-Evans Columbia albums were a kind of musical love match, and the two men behaved very differently on their own. Davis went on to lead a series of exhilarating small bands, and Evans made several albums on his own that are full of swing and drive and invention. (Both men, though, got lost in the jangling fog of electronic music in their last years.) Most impressive of Evans's non-Davis outings are two albums called "New Bottle, Old Wine" and "Great Jazz Standards." Evans remakes fifteen jazz classics in his own image, among them "St. Louis Blues," Jelly Roll Morton's "King Porter Stomp," Fats Waller's "Willow Tree," Lester Young's "Lester Leaps In," Thelonious Monk's " 'Round Midnight," John Lewis's "Django," and Don Redman's "Chant of the Weed." He uses Johnny Coles and Steve Lacy and Jimmy Cleveland as soloists, and he plays piano—real arranger's piano, loose and full of unexpected corners. Also impressive is "The Individualism of Gil Evans." In the somewhat ramshackle but *misterioso* "Hotel Me," he uses, consciously or unconsciously, the same descending four-note tremolo that is at the heart of Joe Marsala's eerie 1941 recording "Lower Register." Evans gives the tremolo to his trombones, and they never get it quite right, but it doesn't matter: the effect is much the same. There is also a meandering blues on the CD— Willie Dixon's "Spoonful." Thad Jones plays a long, dancing, singing trumpet solo on it that makes one wonder what the Columbia albums would have been like with Jones, a masterly player, in place of Davis, who, in effect, was less an expert instrumentalist than a storyteller and an impressionist—a "sound," as Evans so often put it.

# 1997

## Heir

The jazz drum set, having evolved slowly during the past sixty years, generally contains a snare drum, several tomtoms, a bass drum, a high hat, and two or three cymbals. But the thirty-one-year-old drummer Leon Parker began stripping his drums in the late eighties. "I wanted an instrument that was transportable, something I could get close to," he has said. "Also, I had gotten turned off by the huge sets the rock drummers use. Who needs ten cymbals and ten drums? I started experimenting. First, I took away the tomtoms, then the high hat, then the bass drum, then all but one cymbal. I used a three-inch snare drum, and I put top skins on both sides. When I worked with Kenny Barron, I used just a ride cymbal, that's all. It became my minimalist concept, and I was committed." Nowadays, his set usually consists of a three-inch snare; a floor tomtom tipped on its side and equipped with legs, a foot pedal, and a cowbell; and a thin, eighteen-inch, hand-hammered, flattop ride cymbal. He also uses wire brushes and amazingly light parade-size drumsticks.

Unwittingly, Parker the progressive has gone back to the drums used in the thirties and forties by the pioneer New Orleans drummer Baby Dodds— a snare, a bass drum, a cowbell, a wood block, and one cymbal. The alto saxophonist, clarinetist, and jazz scholar Bob Wilber worked with Dodds in the late forties, and he once said of him, "He was a percussionist more than a drummer. He thought of drums in terms of colors and how to mix them. He was fanatical about tuning his drums, and he'd be on the stand a half hour before show time, tightening and tapping, tightening and tapping. His time was superb, and his whole playing was heavy and low. The tonality was down where it didn't get in the way, as so much modern drumming does. He principally used his bass drum and powerful, accented press rolls on his snare drum, and he didn't have a high hat. But he had a ride cymbal, and he played it in a way that young drummers think they invented—just four beats to the bar, *ting-ting-ting-ting*, his head down low, and his right arm crooked like a dancer's over his head and the cymbal, and his whole body shimmying and shaking in time to the music. It was an unbelievable experience to have Baby behind you." The exceptional pianist Bill Charlap says much the same of Parker: "He gets many different colors, and he's got brilliant time. Many drummers just don't groove; they lack that intensity in their beat. But Leon's got real pop to his time. Wham! And his sense of intricate rhythms never gets in the way of his grooving."

Parker was born in White Plains, New York, into a "big, complicated" family made up of blacks, Native Americans, and, a ways back, whites. His father works in the town's post office, and his mother is a social worker in a local nursery school. He began "beating on things at the age of three," and by the time he was in his teens he was working informally with a drummer named Ray White. He was also a drummer in a black band that played for black people all over Westchester Country and into Connecticut. "We played every kind of music for weddings and dances and parties," Parker said recently. "We were there to make people happy. I loved it. It was where I got my foundation, the social connection." Parker didn't start coming to New York until he was eighteen, because, like many suburbanites, he was leery of the city. Fordham offered him a scholarship, but he decided he wanted to stay in music. At first, he hung around the alto saxophonist Arnie Lawrence, who was teaching at the New School. Then he started jamming at Augie's, on upper Broadway, with the alto saxophonist Jesse Davis and the pianist and organist Larry Goldings. ("I got him going on the organ," Parker has said of Goldings.) He met his wife, Lisa, at Augie's (they have a six-year-old daughter named Evandrea), and they went to Europe for eight months and performed on the street in France and Portugal and Spain. Lisa played an Indian flute and Parker an African drum, and they made things out of seashells and sold them. Back in New York, he appeared at the old Village Gate with Goldings and Charlap, with the bassists Sean Smith, Ed Howard, and Larry Grenadier, and with the pianist Bruce Barth. "I had my first group, Square Root, at the Gate with Sean Smith, Bill Charlap, and the alto saxophonist Allen Mezquida," Parker has said. "The bassist Harvie Swartz introduced me to Kenny Barron, and I worked with him, and Joshua Redman introduced me to his father, Dewey, and I played with him. I think a lot of the younger musicians engage in false worship. They should be studying the classic *living* players like Barron and Dewey Redman and Jimmy Heath and Tom Harrell and Roy Haynes. Roy Haynes is my man. I first heard him when I was eleven, and I knew that was it. He should be playing solo at Lincoln Center. He should be knighted and get one of those genius awards. He must wake up every day and just grow and grow."

Undistracted by the impulse to move constantly around a full drum set and dilute his rhythmic patterns, Parker concentrates on his snare and its rims, on his tomtom bass drum, and on his ride cymbal. He can be ferocious and as soft as silk. He uses rim shots (hitting the snare skin and the snare rim at the same time), which, lamentably, went out of fashion with Buddy Rich and Jo Jones, and he develops rhythmic combinations on his ride cymbal—*dot de-da, dot de-da, dot de-da, de-da de-da dot dot de-da*—that rise to shimmering crashes, then subside to whispers. He constantly mixes his wire brushes and his sticks, sometimes using a wire brush in his left hand and shushing it across his snare on two and four so that it sounds like a high hat, and a stick in his right hand for his ride-cymbal strokes and for occasional accents on his snare and his tomtom bass drum. Most drum solos, bereft of thought and logic and color, are simply displays of technique, random bursts of thunder and lightning. Parker's solos, relatively short, are improvisations on certain chosen patterns. He will start with heavy, irregularly spaced beats on his snare but with the snares released so that the drum becomes a tomtom. He will break these beats with an occasional rim shot, then slide onto his snare rims, issuing a fusillade of *tick-tick-tick-ticks*, all the while using half-time beats on his bass drum. He will go at his ride cymbal, holding his right-hand stick vertically and hitting its outer edge with light, skating beats, shift the stick onto the cymbal proper, and, rapidly clamping and releasing the cymbal with his left hand while steadily hitting it with his right-hand stick, create an ascending series of crashes and shimmers, drop a booming bass-drum beat, suddenly raise his sticks in the air over his head and hit them together wildly, and with a whacking rim shot end the solo.

Like Baby Dodds, Parker is also a percussionist. He will put aside his brushes and sticks, and use just his hands. He opens and closes his first CD, "Above and Below," with solos—the first eighteen seconds long and the second slightly over a minute—played on *himself* with his hands, clapping, slapping, pummelling, and they are the high points of the disk. On his new CD, "Belief," he plays straight jazz drums on only three tracks, and on the rest he uses shakers, conga drums, a wood block, bells, a frame drum, an ashiko drum, a dumbek, and handclaps. He also sings eerie, wordless songs, as does the percussionist and composer Natalie Cushman. And he rarely uses 4/4 time, but frequently works out variations on 6/8 time. The trumpeter and flugelhornist Tom Harrell, who appears with great effect on two tracks on "Belief," said this about Parker recently: "His grooves are amazing. I've heard him use 3/8 on his bass drum and 4/4 on his ride cymbal at the same time. His ride-cymbal beat makes incredible propulsive swing. It's a beautiful connection playing with Leon. It's hypnotic."

Parker has a bright-penny look. He also has a slight Napoleonic cast. He is small, genial, compact, bald, and a fast, persuasive talker who laughs explosively. "I was losing my hair," he said the other day, "and, since it's now fashionable for young men of color to be bald, I took the rest off. Anyway, perhaps I aspire to be a monk, an actor, a world-music messenger. My career has been a solitary journey. I want to be empowered to do what I feel about jazz. I'm broadening the audience for the music. I'm bringing kids into my arena, and they're listening. I stand up for the musical truth. I've always been ready for something, and now I'm starting to come into it."

One night, after hearing Parker at Bradley's, I asked him if he had ever heard Sid Catlett, the greatest of jazz drummers. (Catlett died, aged only forty-one, in 1951, just as the LP era was beginning. He would have continued to change jazz drumming, as his peer Jo Jones did.) Parker said that he hadn't heard Catlett; in fact, he had him mixed up in his head with Baby Dodds. I invited Parker to stop by my apartment the next day, and I played two famous Catlett solos for him. Recorded in the fall of 1947 at Symphony Hall, in Boston, when Catlett was with Louis Armstrong's All-Stars, these solos are wonders of melodic drumming, still fresh, still ahead of their time. Parker was wowed by them, particularly by the way Catlett mysteriously hits—left-right, right-left— one stick on the other on the snare head in a blinding succession of clicks; by his playing a simple beat on the rim of a tomtom that swings so hard you want to shout; and by his rumbelaying back and forth between his snare and his tomtom and making pure melody. Parker understood Catlett immediately.

## The Getz Gang

**W**hat a monstrous angel the tenor saxophonist Stan Getz was! Born in 1927, of Russian Jewish stock, he was driven by the extraordinary lyrical heat that marked so many of the Russian Jewish musicians who graced jazz in the thirties and forties. He became a professional when he was fifteen, and a year later he joined the insuperable trombonist Jack Teagarden, who taught him, among other things, to drink. By the time he was seventeen, he was an alcoholic, and not long afterward he started using heroin. (He did not conquer his addictions until he was nearly sixty.) He passed through the bands of Stan Kenton, Jimmy Dorsey, and Benny Goodman, the last of whom fired him for missing shows while he ran around New York trying to score. He married for the first time in 1946 and again in 1956, and he is known to have had more than five children. He went with Woody Herman's brilliant Second Herd in 1947, and became one of the famous Four Brothers saxophone section. (It has been estimated that roughly half of this Herman band was strung out.) Late in 1948, he recorded his short, uncannily beautiful solo on Ralph Burn's "Early Autumn" for Herman, and when the record was released he became an instant star. He left Herman in 1950, and for the next forty years he led innumerable small groups, all of them made up of first-rate, often unknown musicians.

Getz died in 1991, and his fame has been steadily diminishing. Reissues, along with recordings never before released, continue to appear, though, and there is a full-length biography, "Stan Getz: A Life in Jazz," by Donald L. Maggin. The book is both a hagiography and a litany of the endless woes that beset Getz: his alcoholism and his drug addiction, which landed him in jail for six months in 1954; his troubles with the I.R.S.; his painful inarticulateness; his two attempted suicides; his corrosive legal troubles with his second wife; his physical abusiveness; his massive ego; and his easy lasciviousness. There were many Getzes, and their schizoid tendencies prompted Zoot Sims's famous mot "Stan is a nice bunch of guys." Maggin is a fan; in buddy-buddy fashion, he refers to Getz as "Stan" throughout the book, and he writes of his playing, "He added to his gift for melody a wide range of sounds—whispers, cries, shouts, purrs, wails. And he always projected his notes with a personal timbre, a poignant ache that penetrated to the listener's marrow." Such statements celebrate but don't explain the mysteries of Getz's style.

He was the most persuasive of the throng of white tenor saxophonists who were influenced by Lester Young in the forties. But eventually the castles of sound that Getz built on Young's style had little to do with the no-nonsense, down-to-earth Young; these sounds were, in fact, startlingly new in jazz. Getz became a romantic, an idol, a kind of Liszt or Elvis Presley. The idolatry that surrounded him grew out of his dulcet, swooning ballads and his beseeching, let-me-in tone. (Of help, too, were his all-American, square-faced handsomeness, his electric-blue eyes, his compact build—he was a terrific swimmer—and his sharp clothes.) When he played a nearly tempoless version of "Thanks for the Memory," or "Summertime," or Jerome Kern's "Yesterdays," sighs arose, both from the music and from his listeners.

In time, Getz's style became closer to the playing of Young's stylistic opposites—the master saxophonists Coleman Hawkins, Ben Webster, and Johnny Hodges, all of whom had been setting down hymnlike ballads since the thirties. But there was a fundamental difference—an almost black-white thing—between these men and Getz. The older men were grounded in the blues; blue notes and blues figurations formed a subtle underpinning to everything they played. They had paid their dues, and they no longer needed to spell out in their solos what they had been through as black men and black musicians. Getz, on the other hand, was not a striking blues player, and his style was highly personal. It recalled the playing, in the fifties and sixties, of his friend and admirer Miles Davis. (The two men, in age less than a year apart, died within months and miles of each other, in California.) There was a self-pitying edge, an oh-me-oh-my sound in Getz and Davis, and one wonders whether their dependence on drugs caused this plaintiveness, or whether they used their music to air their various neuroses and private woes. Getz's singular tone grew partly out of the skewed emotional freight he carried with him most of his life and partly out of the fact that he had started on the alto saxophone. Although he soon switched to the tenor, he never mastered its full tonal possibilities. (Consider Hawkins and Webster.) In almost every solo, he would shoot into his upper register, and the sorrowing sounds would take over. These ascents gave his playing a feminine quality, and suggested that he was an alto saxophonist trapped inside a tenor saxophonist.

Getz was a superb musician. (He once said that the perfect tenor saxophonist would have "my technique, Al Cohn's ideas, and Zoot's time.") A lightning reader, he was never fazed, as many jazz musicians are, by new material. He had a photographic musical memory; once he had mastered a Woody Herman arrangement, he apparently never needed to look at it again. He was equally at ease in very fast tempos (an area that turns many otherwise excellent jazz musicians into automatons), in rocking middle speeds, and in ad-lib ballads. He could play straight melody without being florid or freezing (a failing of many post-Charlie Parker musicians), and he was a consummate melodic improviser, a maker of instant new melody. He relished challenges. In 1961, he commissioned the arranger and composer Eddie Sauter to write a piece for him, a springboard for his improvisation, and the result, called "Focus," was a seven-part, thirty-five-minute composition for small string orchestra. The longest part is slightly over six minutes, and the music in general floats back and forth between Hollywood and Bartók. Getz was shown the music and in one day recorded his often ingenious variations, the strings pumping away behind him. He considered "Focus" the best album he ever recorded, and he was right.

Maggin has put together a Getz CD to accompany his book, and it contains eleven selections, made between 1952 and 1991. It starts with "Night Rider," which is taken from "Focus," and is played in a kind of mock fast tempo, full of staccato, splintering Getz figures. "Corcovado" ("Quiet Nights of Quiet Stars"), done in 1963, with João and Astrud Gilberto, helped to start the bossa nova craze of the mid-sixties. (For a time, it made Getz a rich man.) Getz was an impeccable obbligato player, and he wraps sinuous supporting figures around Ella Fitzgerald in "You're Blasé" and around Abbey Lincoln in "I'm in Love." "Summertime" was set down in 1964, with the vibraphonist Gary Burton, and "Night and Day" in 1991, as a duet with the pianist Kenny Barron. The first is serene and melancholy, but the second, made at a concert in Copenhagen, sounds strained and mechanical, although it never falls below the high level that Getz invariably maintained. The prize on Maggin's CD is another duet, this one backed by a rhythm section, between Getz and the valve trombonist Bob Brookmeyer. The tune, "Who Could Care?," is Brookmeyer's, and the two dodge and weave and dance around each other, then back each other, insistent shadows.

The newest previously unreleased Getz CD, "Stan Getz: Yours and Mine," was recorded at a concert in Glasgow two years before he died. Four of the seven numbers are ballads, and they are full of spaces and unaccustomed low notes, which give the impression that Getz was at last sinking into the proper sounds of the tenor saxophone. The three others are medium- and up-tempo numbers, and again make it clear that he could do anything with rhythm.

The sweet, nagging beauty of Getz's ballad playing has gone largely out of fashion, and out of jazz. This is particularly noticeable in the playing of the young saxophonists. John Coltrane's influence—the guttural tone, the screams, the animal noises—remains pervasive. These saxophonists should listen to Getz. He may have worn his troubled Jewish heart on his sleeve, but, at his best, he could play rings around God.

## The Prince of Jazz

In 1983, when Wynton Marsalis was just twenty-two and was still a new and startling arrival, I wrote of him: "Marsalis is not yet complete. Technique, rather than melodic logic, still governs his improvising, and the emotional content of his playing remains hidden and skittish." Since then, setting aside Marsalis's playing for the moment, he has, of course, become a ubiquitous presence in New York. He is the artistic director of the Jazz at Lincoln Center program, and he is responsible for staffing and leading its jazz orchestra and for guiding its almost weekly events, which include lectures, films, discussion groups, concerts, recitals, and children's programs. He takes the band on U.S. and European tours, and he composes much of its music. Along the way, he talks to and plays for high-school kids around the country; he estimates that he has given a thousand of these clinics. He is also the unofficial head of the Young Turks who have been appearing in the past ten years, among them Christian McBride, Joshua Redman, Nicholas Payton, Wes Anderson, and Marcus Roberts. And he is the owner of a lucrative recording contract with Columbia Records, which, judging from the free-wheeling nature of the almost two dozen Marsalis CDs released since the eighties, gives him complete artistic freedom. Dapper, as well, and an easy autobiographer, Marsalis has become a man-about-town and the first C.E.O. in jazz. Such masters as Sidney Catlett and Roy Eldridge and Coleman Hawkins worked their courageous, mostly solitary ways through their musical lives, but Marsalis is nurtured and shepherded by the essayist and novelist Albert Murray and by the writer Stanley Crouch. In recent years, Crouch has written all the liner notes for Marsalis's albums; they tend to be very long, and they swim with fulsome encomia for Marsalis's playing and composing. Crouch has even knighted Marsalis, dubbing him not long ago "the prince of jazz."

If I believed fourteen years ago that Marsalis's playing was incomplete, it remains, measured against the great brass tradition of Louis Armstrong,

Eldridge, Red Allen, Fats Navarro, and Dizzy Gillespie, unfinished. Marsalis the trumpeter even prompted the idiosyncratic pianist Keith Jarrett to tell the *New York Times Magazine*, "I've never heard anything Wynton played sound like it meant anything at all. Wynton has no voice and no presence. His music sounds like a talented high-school trumpet player. . . . Behind his humble speech, there is an incredible arrogance." Marsalis's technique—he can also play classical trumpet with ease and beauty—has been duly celebrated, but it has hindered more than helped him. Virtuosity has always got in the way of jazz musicians. Marsalis almost always gives the impression that he is *outside* of what he is attempting to improvise on, that he is straining to get inside, to transform whatever he is playing (blues, generally) into something new and moving. He growls, uses a plunger mute, makes laughing sounds and hoarse sounds, lets loose crude Rex Stewart noises, and sews together all these effects with dizzying runs and seven-league intervals. But he fails to stir the feelings, to jar the heart.

Marsalis has told Stanley Crouch that "In my generation, we didn't know how to play the blues, couldn't improvise over chord changes, didn't know anything about swinging—and didn't care either. We interpreted all these musical skills as expressions of a bygone era that had no relevance to us. A serious misconception." Since leaving New Orleans, where he was born and raised (his father is the pianist and teacher Ellis Marsalis), Marsalis has spent more time rummaging in the attics of jazz than in its present. He has discovered Louis Armstrong and Harry Edison and Clark Terry and Rex Stewart, and he has taken Miles Davis as his master. At the same time, he has listened to the great jazz composers and to the great bands, in particular to Duke Ellington and Count Basie, as well as to George Gershwin and Charles Mingus and the early Ornette Coleman. He has stitched together a many-colored jazz coat for himself, its cloths and threads borrowed from these originators, and he wears it constantly.

In the past seven or eight years, the logorrheic tendency in Marsalis's teaching and lecturing has begun to infect his composing. At first, he wrote pleasant melodic lines, often anchored in the blues. Then he put together a yawning forty-minute suite, "Blue Interlude," which was followed by "Griot New York," a two-hour ballet score filled with Gershwin operatic touches, spirituals, Charlie Spivak trumpet, Debussy, boogie-woogie, John Kirby, hokey Dixieland, and Charles Mingus. The piece might work behind dancers; by itself, on the CD called *Citi Movement*, it is merely peppy and glib. But now Marsalis has written a three-hour jazz oratorio, *Blood on the Fields*. Carting a fourteen-piece Lincoln Center Jazz band, a solo violinist, and three singers with him, he has performed the piece up and down the country, and gave the penultimate U.S. performance late in February, 1997, at Avery Fisher Hall, several days before the troupe took off for a two-week European tour.

The oratorio consists of twenty-seven sections made up of a narration chanted and sung by Jon Hendricks, Cassandra Wilson, and Miles Griffith, and underpinned by the orchestra, which handles the choral sections à la Johnny Long and also has several interludes to itself. The story concerns two slaves, Jesse (Griffith), an African prince, and Leona (Wilson), an African "commoner." They are sold and they work in the fields, "liftin' and a totin'." Jesse, bent on trying to escape, visits a wise man, Juba (Hendricks), who warns him of the possible perils. Jesse ignores Juba, flees, is caught, and given forty lashes (good rim-shot drumming by Herlin Riley). Ten or fifteen episodes later, Jesse and Leona successfully escape together and head north. The narration falls somewhere between Carl Sandburg and Jerome Kern and suggests a play about slavery written by a precocious eight-grade class. (How could Marsalis, who grew up in a comfortable middle-class family in the nineteen sixties, believe that he could convincingly recreate the grinding cruelty and stink of slavery? He should study the early incredible crayon drawings of the black artist John Biggers.) Here is Jesse exulting before he and Leona escape:

> The sun is gonna shine
> Upon this land today
> He'll show his warm round face and smile
> He'll play the bluest blues high yellow style
> Sun is gon' shine.
> The sun is gonna shine
> Just like he do each day
> His light will be so bright and clear
>
> He'll warm those soulless hearts long cloaked in fear
> Sun is gon' shine

The singers, breaking into scat now and then, nearly made their materials swing. Hendricks, of course, is a master of fast patter, and Griffith, with his rich, wild baritone, was a surprise. Wilson's contralto was heavy and moving on a long slow blues, "Will the Sun Come Out?" (Marsalis is credited with having written the entire narration, but surely the hand of the ever-tending Crouch is visible.) Much of what the band played rested squarely on Duke Ellington, especially on his later, straining religious music. The saxophones and trombones used Ellington harmonics and the trumpets Ellington mutes. Herlin Riley has some of the jangling, swinging looseness of Sonny Greer (his press rolls were immaculate), and Gideon Feldstein, the baritone saxophonist, came close to the majesty of Harry Carney. Wycliffe Gordon, the trombonist, knows his Tricky Sam Nanton so well he almost parodies him, but his open-horn solos roared and stomped. The Lincoln Center band is a jivey, expert group.

Perhaps Marsalis will write a jazz opera, a jazz symphony, a concerto for jazz trumpet. Whatever, it will be adept mimicry, adept synthesis. So go out into the jazz fields and listen to such true contemporary voices as those of Kenny Barron and Roy Haynes and Tom Harrell, of Joe Lovano and Bill Charlap and Sean Smith, of Leon Parker and Brad Mehldau and Steve Wilson. They have long since run with the past, and are now spreading their own singular organic beauties.

Blood on the Fields was, astonishingly, awarded a Pulitzer Prize. Duke Ellington, the master of us all, was notoriously denied a Pulitzer in 1965, which caused him to say, "Fate is being kind to me. Fate doesn't want me to be famous too young." Marsalis, of course, is already what the Duke was afraid he might become. Fate, contrary to all indications, has not been kind to him.

# 1999

## The Natural

There is a secret emotional center in jazz which has sustained the music since it outgrew its early melodic and rhythmic gaucheries, in the late twenties. This center, a kind of aural elixir, reveals itself when an improvised phrase or an entire solo or even a complete number catches you by surprise. When these lyrical bursts happen in night clubs or at concerts, their afterimages inevitably fade. Caught on recordings, though, they last forever. So here, in no particular order, are some classic recorded beauties: the first twelve or so bars of Louis Armstrong's second solo on both takes of "Some of These Days," played in a revolving half time in his low register and unlike anything else he ever recorded (Columbia; 1929); the eerie, almost surrealistic melody that Paul Gonsalves fashions on the first bridge of a "Caravan" done with Duke Ellington (Fantasy; 1962); Charlie Parker's stunning two-chorus solo on "Funky Blues," replete with an opening now-listen preaching figure, a shivering, sotto-voce run at the start of the second chorus, and a dodging, ascending climatic figure (Verve; 1952); the cluster of soft, keening notes that Joe Lovano plays near the end of "Lament for M," a dirge by Gunther Schuller written in memory of his wife for "Rushhour" (Blue Note; 1995); the Sidney de Paris–Ben Webster–Vic Dickenson–James P. Johnson–Sid Catlett "After You've Gone," certainly as close to a flawless jazz recording as exists (Blue Note; 1944); and all of the remarkable pianist Bill Charlap's "Turnaround," an Ornette Coleman blues that he fills with huge, stuttering chords and sailing-along-the-tonal-edge single-note lines (Criss Cross; 1995).

Indeed, Charlap is a lyrical repository. At thirty-two, he is the best, but least well known, of a swarm of gifted pianists who have appeared in New York in the past decade. He has already filled much of the sizable space once occupied by Bill Evans, who still reverberates almost twenty years after his death. Unlike many of the younger pianists, whose tastes tend to be parochial, Charlap has absorbed every pianist worth listening to in the past fifty years, starting with Art Tatum, Teddy Wilson, Duke Ellington, Jimmy Rowles, Erroll Garner, Nat Cole, and Oscar Peterson, then moving through Bud Powell, Thelonious Monk, Hank Jones, Tommy Flanagan, and Bill Evans, and finishing with Herbie Hancock, Chick Corea, and Kenny Barron. His ballad numbers are unique. He may start with the verse of the song, played ad lib, then move into the melody chorus. He does not rhapsodize. Instead, he improvises immediately, rearranging the chords and the melody line, and using a relaxed, almost implied beat. He may pause for a split second at the end of this chorus and launch a nodding, swinging single-note solo chorus, made up of irregularly placed notes—some off the beat and some behind the beat—followed by connective runs, and note clusters. He closes with a brief, calming recap of the melody. His ballads are meditations on songs, homages to their composers and lyricists. He constantly reins in his up-tempo numbers. He has a formidable technique, but he never shows off, even though he will let loose epic runs, massive staccato chords, racing upper-register tintinnabulations, and, once in a while, some dazzling counterpoint, his hands pitted against each other. His sound shines; each note is rounded. Best of all, in almost every number, regardless of its speed, he leaves us a phrase, a group of irregular notes, an ardent bridge that shakes us.

Charlap has a narrow, handsome face, attentive eyes, and a direct, ready-to-laugh voice. He talks fast, and when he talks about his music he gradually accelerates. Here is what he said recently: "I don't ever remember not playing the piano. Everything was by ear at first, and I'd pick out everything I heard. When a teacher came to the house, I'd charm my way through the lesson. It was very painful and slow for me to learn to read music. The songs of Arlen, Gershwin, Porter, and Berlin were paramount in my house, so jazz is about vocalism for me. Even a drum is vocal. To me, there are three steps in improvisation. The first involves the player's concentration, his heavy thinking. In the second, he becomes almost blasé, and he lets his fingers do the walking. And in the third he is detached from what he is doing. He's moving the pawns of the music, yet he has become a listener, who's, like, sitting there and watching what he's doing. From this stage, you go on to experience that supreme feeling, that omnipotent feeling at the heart of improvising."

Charlap knocks out both his musical contemporaries and his musical elders, some of whom are almost twice his age. The matchless bassist Michael Moore made a tight duo album with Charlap in 1995, and has said of him, "So many players of Bill Charlap's generation haven't digested Jimmy Rowles, maybe haven't even heard of him, one of the greatest pianists. A lot of the young piano players today take themselves so seriously that sometimes their solos turn into complete piano concertos. They eat everything on the musical table and leave nothing for anyone else. But Bill goes right through each tune to the bone. He has a great imagination, and he has lightness and humor, even the pratfall kind of humor. We played a kind of Mafia Christmas party a while back, and when the guests sang the 'Twelve Days of Christmas' Bill played something totally different behind each person. He did Stockhausen behind a guy who couldn't carry a tune, and he played the 'St. Louis Blues' behind a woman who thought she could sing."

The guitarist Gene Bertoncini is another Charlap admirer. He was part of a spectacular trio that included Charlap and the bassist Sean Smith and drew S.R.O. crowds on a 1996 jazz cruise on the S.S. Norway. "What I admire, aside from his playing, is his incredible knowledge of songs," Bertoncini said recently. "Whenever I work with him, he'll say, 'Gene, have you heard this song from 1947, or this song from 1938?' So in that way, although he's only thirty-two, he's an old man."

Born on East Fifty-first Street, in New York, Charlap grew up in a musical and theatrical atmosphere. His mother is the singer Sandy Stewart, and his father, who died when Charlap was seven, was the songwriter Moose Charlap. Moose wrote most of the music, with Carolyn Leigh, for the Mary Martin "Peter Pan" that was on Broadway in the mid-fifties. And he wrote the music, with Eddie Lawrence, for a still lamented 1965 musical called "Kelly," which got terrific reviews in Philadelphia but was disastrously fiddled with at the last minute by its producers and closed in New York after one night. Lawrence has said, "Moose loved to laugh, and he loved to sing. He had a gravelly, wonderful voice—a rough kind of thing, like Aznavour. When he died, we were working on a musical about Paul Gauguin." Bill Charlap went to the Town School and to the High School for Performing Arts when it was still in a dilapidated building on West Forty-sixth Street. He spent a year or two at SUNY-Purchase, and he studied classical piano, but, he says, "My classical piano was not authentic. I was speaking classical piano with a jazz accent. A teacher I had asked me why I played everything with street rhythms." Gerry Mulligan hired Charlap in the late eighties, and he has since divided his time between his own trio and random gigs abroad and with the Phil Woods Quintet.

You have to search for Charlap in New York. He did four nights recently at the Knickerbocker Bar & Grill, on University Place, and the gig was hard work. Most people go there to eat and drink and talk, and the piano is almost in afterthought. It sits on the floor hard by a low wall that separates the huge main room from the thundering bar. Charlap's first number on his third night was a medium-tempo version of Kurt Weill's "Here I'll Stay." It was full of backpedalling chords, loose, almost atonal single-note lines, and a couple of mercurial arpeggios. The din in the place was palpable, but Charlap's passion for his music was immediately clear in his playing and in his bobbing, tightly masked face, which stayed a foot or so above the keyboard. Six people near the piano clapped at the end of the tune. His next number, Gerry Mulligan's "Curtains," got eight claps, and Irving Berlin's "The Best Thing for You" got ten. Cole Porter's "All Through the Night," played at an up tempo, was the last number in the set, and, when it began, a heavy, middle-aged, wool-wrapped Irish couple stood up in the bar to leave, stopped ten feet from the piano, and listened, their big Irish faces still and pleased. They clapped twice before they left, and there were twelve more claps from the main room. Charlap has said of the Knickerbocker, "It's a great place to practice when you're not working that night."

Find Charlap's newest CD, "All Through the Night," and listen carefully to the start of the second full chorus on Alec Wilder's "It's So Peaceful in the Country." Leaving a beautifully chorded and measured melody chorus, he steps off into a handful of unevenly spaced single notes, a firm 4/4 rhythm underneath, and the earth moves.

# 2000

## Seeing Music

The brilliant gypsy guitarist Django Reinhardt was born Jean Baptiste Reinhardt, near Liverchies, Belgium, on January, 23, 1910, and died of a stroke in Fontainebleau on May 16, 1953 after a pleasant day of fishing in the Seine. Between 1934, when he and the violinist and pianist Stéphane Grappelli formed the Quintet of the Hot Club of France, and the late forties when the electric guitar and bebop began closing in on him, he made hundreds of recordings, appeared in clubs and at concerts all over Europe and Britain, and became one of the most famous jazz musicians in the world. Charles Delaunny, the son of the unique Parisian geometric colorists Sonia and Robert Delaunay, created the first jazz discography and shepherded Django through much of his sometimes chaotic professional life. Delaunay said of Reinhardt in a visit to this country in the seventies: "There were two personalities in him. One was primitive. He never went to school and he couldn't stand a normal bed. He had to live in a gypsy caravan near a river, where he could fish and catch trout between the stones with his bare hands, and where he could put laces between the trees and catch rabbits. But Django also had nobility, even though he could be very mean to the musicians who worked for him."

Male Gypsies exist in a kind of timeless macho continuum in which appointments and obligations are largely meaningless. In 1946, Django, dreaming of visits with Hollywood stars, finally got to this country for a three-month tour. He travelled with the Duke Ellington band in its private railroad car, and they played in Cleveland, Chicago, Detroit, and Pittsburgh before a final Carnegie Hall concert. But on the evening of the concert, Django ran into the French boxer Marcel Cerdan, who was about to appear in a bout at Madison Square Garden and, slipping into Gypsy time, went to a bar with Cerdan to drink and talk about life and France. When he suddenly remembered where he was supposed to be, he jumped into a cab, and because he had almost no English, ended up somewhere on the East Side. He finally got to Carnegie Hall at eleven o'clock and played four numbers, backed by the band, and probably including a blues, a variation of "Tiger Rag," one of his own dreaming pieces, and "Honeysuckle Rose." The applause was reportedly thunderous. Ellington mentions Reinhardt in his autobiography, *Music Is My Mistress:* "Among those I think of as citizens of Paris was Django Reinhardt, a very dear friend of mine and one who I regard as among the few inimitables of our music. I had him on a concert tour with me in 1946, so I could enjoy him the more."

Delaunay supervised most of Django's recordings, and he described, on his visit here, what music meant to Reinhardt: "Life for Django was all music. He was full of constant enthusiasm when he played—shouting in the record studio when someone played something he liked, shouting when he played himself. . . . When he was accompanying in the bass register he sounded like brass, and in the treble like saxophones. He had a constant vision of music—a circle of music—in his head. I think he could see his music." Reinhardt's style had such presence and power and imagination that, in the manner of masters like Charlie Parker and Sidney Catlett and the Armstrong of the early thirties, he surpassed his very instrument. He created an almost disembodied, alternately delicate and roaring whorl of music. Charlie Christian, who flourished between 1939 and 1941, when Django was near the top of his powers, became the first consummate electrical guitarist and, following Lester Young's lead on tenor saxophone, fashioned long hornlike lines that had their own flawless logic and beauty. (Jim Hall, the paramount guitarist, still idolizes Christian, and Hall, in turn, is idolized by such contemporary guitarists as Pat Metheny. Reinhardt's utter originality largely confounds imitation.) But Reinhardt turned the songs he played inside out, decorating them with his winging vibrato, his pouring runs and glisses, his weaving and ducking single-note lines, and his sudden chordal tremolos and off-beat explosions. All these sounds were controlled by his adventurous rhythmic sense. Like Billie Holiday and Red Allen and Jimmy Rowles, he could leap ahead of the beat, or fall behind it, or ride it mercilessly. And this rhythmic sense was constantly colored by his dynamics, which moved back and forth between flutters and whispers, talking tones, and cascades and roars. Two peculiarities shaped Reinhardt's playing: he had enormous hands and the two smallest fingers on his left hand—his fret-board hand—were permanently bent at the second knuckle. (They had been burned in a fire in his caravan that injured him so badly that his other wounds never healed properly.) The huge hand made the crippled fingers nonetheless work: thus the mysterious chords and melodic lines that no one had ever heard before.

Reinhardt might start a medium-tempo ballad with three or four bars of slightly altered melody, played in single notes behind the beat, each phrase graced by his vibrato, pause for a beat, and go into a brief mock double-time, rest again, drop in an abrupt, massive chord and release a hissing upward run. Then he'd cut his volume in half and turn into the bridge with a delicate, fernlike single-note variation of the melody, letting his notes linger and bend and float on his vibrato. Just before the end of the bridge, he would loose another off-beat chord, let it shimmer for three or four beats, work through a humplike arpeggio, lower his volume again and return to a delicate single-note variation of the original melody, and come to a rest. Almost all his solos in the thirties and early forties have an exotic romanticism; the notes roll and echo with Eastern European and Spanish overtones. Armstrong and Ellington had taught him to swing and be cool, but he filtered them through his Gypsy mind.

The original Quintet of the Hot Club of France probably grew indirectly out of the violinist Joe Venuti's and the guitarist Eddie Lang's various string groups of the late twenties and early thirties. But its instrumentation of violin, solo guitar, two rhythm guitars, and bass was unique. From its beginning, it was a swinging, lithesome group, at ease with big-voiced uptempo numbers, delicate, twirling ballads, and direct, haunting blues. It certainly presaged Benny Goodman's small groups, Artie Shaw's Gramercy Fives, and even the Modern Jazz Quartet. Grappelli and Reinhardt experimented ceaselessly with the quintet on its recordings. They had one or two violins, they subtracted a rhythm guitar, there were violin and guitar duets, guitar and bass duets, and solo guitar numbers. Grappelli occasionally played piano (he loved Art Tatum), and later in the Quintet's life, if Grappelli was unavailable, one or sometimes two clarinets were added. The original Quintet (with some personnel changes) lasted from December 2, 1934, when it gave its first public performance in Paris, until September 3, 1939, when Britain and France declared war on Germany. The group had been touring England with great success, and Grappelli decided to stay in England, where he lived off and on for the rest of his life. Reinhardt and the rest of the Quintet took one of the last boats back to France, where they somehow survived and even flourished despite the Nazi interdiction on gypsies. (Django kept on the move, working in the south of France and in north Africa, disappearing occasionally into the Gypsy netherworld, and once even trying to get across the border into Switzerland.) Grappelli and Reinhardt were reunited in England in 1946, and they made their last recordings in Rome in 1949.

More than half of the hundred and nineteen numbers in a new Mosaic-album "The Complete Django Reinhardt and Quintet of the Hot Club of France Swing/HMV Sessions 1936-1948" are by the Quintet or its variations, and it is full of such-beauties as the space between Django's notes on "Solitude," and his rustling tremolos behind sweet Grappelli (who did not find his strength and great fervor until the later forties; after Reinhardt's death he played all over the world well into his nineties); his delicate, barely audible opening chorus on "When Day Is Done"; the astounding train piece, "Mystery Pacific," which has roaring staccato chords, played at a blinding tempo by three low-register guitars; his four exquisite choruses on "I'll See You in My Dreams," accompanied only by bass, and the wild elbowy, up-tempo "You Rascal You," again done just with a bass; and the strange off-notes in "Little White Lies," and the clarinettist Hubert Rostaing's lifting "organ" hum behind Reinhardt. American music was outlawed by the Nazis, so "Exactly Like You" became *Pour Vous,*" "Little White Lies" became *Petite Mensonges,*" and "Dark Eyes" became *Les Yeux Noirs.*"

In 1935, when the quintet was barely a year old, Django, already sought after, began sitting in on occasional recordings with American musicians, among them Coleman Hawkins, Benny Carter, Bill Coleman, Dicky Wells, Rex Stewart, Barney Bigard, Eddie South, and Larry Adler. (Fifty-seven of them are on a DRG album, "Django and his American Friends.") Reinhardt is given solo space on roughly half of the numbers, starting with the loose, joyous sides made by Coleman, Shad Collins, and Bill Dillard on trumpets, Wells on trombone, Dick Fullbright on bass, and Bill Beason on drums. He takes a floating blues chorus on "Bugle Call Rag," while the trumpets riff softly in the distance, and he delivers one of his great shouts near the end of "Between the Devil and the Deep Blue Sea." He has a full chorus on the classic slow blues "Hangin' Around Boudon," with Wells and Coleman backing him. He fashions one of his pre-bebop bebop solos on "Japanese Sandman." Bill Coleman reappears with a different group and Django solos on the slow "Big Boy Blues," backed only by the drummer playing a stark press roll with his sticks. Then the Hot Club Quintet accompanies the celebrated American harmonica player Larry Adler who, despite his massive ego, was not much of a jazz musician. He pushed the melodies of his songs into odd forced shapes, and he had a harsh sound. But Django counteracts him on "Body and Soul," on a strange, fast "Melancholy Baby," and on "I Got Rhythm," often working in his ringing low and middle registers.

In 1939, Rex Stewart, Barney BIgard, and the bassist Billy Taylor arrived in Paris with Duke Ellington, and set down five numbers with Reinhardt that remain timeless small-band performances. Stewart, dark and brooding, loved queer squeezed notes that he produced by pressing his valves halfway down, and Bigard, cheerful and circular, was the last of the rococo New

Orleans clarinettists. Django's solos are easy and gentle; he sounds as if he had grown up with Stewart and Bigard. Listen to the slow blues "Solid Old Man." Django solos twice with Bigard accompanying him—so the story goes—with whisk brooms on a suitcase. His opening solo has several silences and he uses only five or six notes, but his second solo is full of little announcements and complex hilly phrases. Stewart stays mainly in his low register, releasing a tremolo and a couple of tight half-valvings, and Bigard soars a little and finally lands down in his chalumeau register. Each of the other four numbers the quartet made has similar beauties.

Stéphane Grappelli knew Django as well as anyone in the world, and here is part of what he told me in 1974: "Ah! The troubles he gave me! I think now I would rather play with lesser musicians and have a peaceable time than with Djangoo and all his monkey business. One time, Djangoo and I were invited to the Elysée Palace by a high personality [probably Charles De Gaulle]. We were invited for *dinnair*, and after dessert we were expected to perform. Djangoo did not appear. After *dinnair*, the high personality was very polite, but I can tell he is waiting, so I say I think I know where Djangoo is when I don't know at all. The high personality calls a limousine and I go to Djangoo's flat in Montmartre. His guitar is in the corner, and I ask his wife where he is. She says maybe at th e *academie* playing billiards. He was a very good player of billiards, very *adroit*. He spent his infancy doing that and being in the streets. His living room was the street. *Alors*, I go to the *académie*, and when he sees me he turns red, yellow, white. In spite of his almost *double* stature of me, he was a little afraid. In the world of the gypsy, age count, although I am only two years older than him. Also, I could read, I was instructed. He have two days' *barbe* on his face and his slippers on, so I push him into the limousine and we go back to his flat to clean him up a little and get his guitar. Djangoo was like a chameleon; *à toute seconde* he could change keys. He was embarrassed about everything, but his *naturel* self came back, and when we arrived at the Elysée and the guard at the gate saluted the limousine, he stick up his chin and say. 'Ah! They recognize me!' "

And here is a very different Django. Phoebe Jacobs, who has spent much of her life smoothing the way for the likes of Duke Ellington and Benny Goodman and Louis Armstrong, met Django in 1951 when she was traveling in the south of France with Lucille Armstrong, Louis' wife, and Moustache, the huge Parisian club owner. "Django seemed nervous and over-anxious next to Moustache, even though it was probably because of who Lucille was," she said recently. "He patted Lucille's arm and behaved almost like he was smitten with her. And when he played for her, the tenderness that came out in his music was like a man stroking a woman's breast."

# 2001

## Louis, Miles, and the Duke

**A** conundrum: Only three per cent of the CDs sold last year were jazz recordings, yet an estimated fifty books on the subject were either published in 2000 or will be published next year. Perhaps all the critical reassessing, which has been gaining momentum in the past ten years, persuaded Ken Burns to make his newest and boldest docuthon, a nineteen-hour film called "Jazz," which will be shown in ten parts on PBS in January. He considers the film the completion of a cultural trilogy that began with "The Civil War" and continued with "Baseball." In the manner of his earlier epics, "Jazz" is both a history and a panorama of a unique improvisational American music that first surfaced in New Orleans around 1900 and is still producing gifted musicians.

The project wasn't easy. Not only has jazz developed with bewildering speed but it's kept changing names—New Orleans jazz, Chicago jazz, Dixieland, Kansas City jazz, swing, boogie-woogie, bebop, hard bop, cool jazz, the new thing, free jazz, and all the neos that have appeared in recent years. Burns has covered this chameleon subject in the only way possible, with an endless series of segments that move constantly back and forth in time. The film swarms with statistics. There are more than five hundred selections on the soundtrack (a lot of them snippets), and many underscore (or are blotted out by) fifty-seven talking heads. These include the trumpeter and C.E.O. of Jazz at Lincoln Center, Wynton Marsalis; the critics Gary Giddins, Nat Hentoff, and Stanley Crouch; the actor with the booming laugh, Ossie Davis; the *Times* cultural critic Margo Jefferson; Mercedes Ellington, the Duke's granddaughter; the sociologist and novelist Albert Murray; and such musicians and singers as Dave Brubeck, Arvell Shaw, Jon Hendricks, Artie Shaw, and Jimmy Rowles. A couple of dozen voices read Geoffrey Ward's straight-ahead script, and there is a host of advisers, among them Marsalis (Senior Creative Consultant), Crouch, and Murray—the so-called Holy Trinity, which governs Jazz at Lincoln Center and is clearly felt in "Jazz."

The film's chronology moves spasmodically. We get only to 1928 by the end of the third episode, and to 1939 by the end of the sixth. The seventh starts with Charlie Parker and Dizzy Gillespie, but they recede, and then take over much of the eighth, along with Miles Davis, Thelonious Monk, and Dave Brubeck. The ninth program, going from the fifties into the sixties, introduces John Coltrane and Ornette Coleman, and suddenly the pace quickens. Sonny Rollins, Clifford Brown, Sarah Vaughan, Art Blakey, and Horace Silver flash by and Miles Davis returns and is followed by Coltrane

and Coleman. The tenth and last episode gallops. There are glimpses of
Charles Mingus, Archie Shepp, the Art Ensemble of Chicago, and Cecil
Taylor, longer looks at Coltrane and Davis, and a montage of such newcom-
ers as Joshua Redman, James Carter, Dianne Reeves, Nicholas Payton,
Marsalis, and Gonzalo Rubalcaba. The series closes with quick farewell
salutes to the titans—among them Louis Armstrong, Ellington, Count
Basie, Monk, Davis, Dizzy Gillespie, Benny Goodman, and Ella Fitzgerald.

Audiences tend to listen to live music or music on film with their eyes, and that is what happens with "Jazz." In
fact, Burns begs us to look at his huge film, and if we happen to absorb some
of the music on the soundtrack so much the better. Burns was faced with a
familiar problem before he started the project. Very little jazz was filmed
before the thirties, so he was forced to use still photographs. He is, of course,
a master at making photographs look live—moving his camera slowly into
the picture for a closeup, scanning the picture from left to right or from bottom to top—and sometimes he cheats a little in, say, a crowd scene by adding
murmuring crowd sounds in the background. These photographs are offset
by the commentators (both Marsalis and Giddins appear scores of times) and
by a great many not always correlative filler shots, made up of New Orleans
street scenes, Mississippi riverboats, the Chicago lakefront, trains pounding
across the country (musicians on the road), winding into stations, and creeping across high bridges at night. And we see New York City, from Harlem
to the Battery, at every time of day and night and in every weather (some of
the night shots are strikingly reminiscent of Georgia O'Keeffe's New York
paintings), dancers in the Savoy ballroom (again and again), boxy cars driving cross-country on narrow pre-turnpike roads in the thirties, hoboes on a
freight train and lines of jobless men during the Depression, and several sick-
ening shots of lynchings, accompanied by Billie Holliday singing "Strange
Fruit." (Burns returns frequently to the racial slights most black musicians
endured, particularly while travelling in the South.)

Much of Burns's travelogue disappears when he starts using rare films of
jazz in the thirties and forties. We get wonderful glimpses of Benny Goodman's famous 1938 Carnegie Hall concert; a concert Louis Armstrong gave
in Copenhagen in 1933, his high notes ricocheting, his tempos blinding, and
later, in the fifties, Armstrong doing a funny duet with Perry Como, on television, his teeth, voice, trumpet, and high-fives overpowering; the Chick
Webb band at what appears to be the Savoy, with the tiny, amazing Webb
high above his drums; Fats Waller at the piano, leering and mugging; Bessie
Smith, standing at a bar and singing "St. Louis Blues" in Dudley Murphy's
invaluable 1929 short; the Jimmie Lunceford band waving its instruments
back and forth in unison; and the Glenn Miller band performing "I've Got a
Gal in Kalamazoo," with Tex Beneke and the Modernaires in creamy voice;
and a couple of tantalizingly brief shots of Art Tatum.

It soon becomes clear that the heroes of "Jazz" are Armstrong, Ellington,

Charlie Parker, Goodman, and Miles Davis. Armstrong and Ellington are, in effect, sainted. Armstrong is repeatedly called a genius, and Ellington the greatest American composer. Armstrong was the first great jazz soloist, but his most impassioned period lasted largely from 1928 to 1933. During that time, he made countless supreme recordings: the 1929 "Some of These Days," in which he goes down into his low register (where he spent little time during his career) and forever inspired the trumpeters Bunny Berigan and Ruby Braff; the soaring, almost operatic 1933 "Basin Street Blues"; and, of course, his extraordinary opening solo on the 1928 "West End Blues," an annunciatory improvisation unmatched in Western music. Overworked but incredibly conscientious, he spent much of the rest of his long career (he died in 1971) playing by rote. Then, suddenly, he'd knock you out again. This happened on two Columbia albums, "Louis Armstrong Plays W. C. Handy" (1954) and "Satch Plays Fats" (1955), and, two years later, on remakes for Decca of "King of the Zulus" and "Knockin' a Jug." Both match his most majestic work.

Ellington is treated in the same heroic, aerated way (Wynton Marsalis: "Duke Ellington knew how to take what could be and make it what is. He understood what it took to make something invisible visible"). It is, though, misleading to call him the greatest American composer. Ellington was a miniaturist who created a new American music full of New Orleans echoes, jazz rhythms, handmade harmonies, and fresh instrumental combinations. He was, like Berlioz, an orchestral genius. Ellington's most startling years lasted from 1940 to 1942, when he put together almost forty unique three-minute concertos built around members of the band ("Jack the Bear," "Day Dream," and "Cotton Tail" are on the soundtrack, along with "Take the 'A' Train," Billy Strayhorn's most famous contribution to the Ellington œuvre). During the next thirty years, he assembled many "suites," some of them of great beauty and originality. He never lost his poise and humor and flair. Burns includes a couple of interviews with Ellington, who is in the same top, leg-pulling form that he was in during the early seventies, when the English critic Stanley Dance asked him if the blues is "a song of sorrow" and he replied, "No, it is a song of romantic failure."

The film's portraits of Charlie Parker and Miles Davis and Benny Goodman are surprisingly blunt. Parker's slyness and selfishness and addictions to drugs and alcohol are made plain. And so are Goodman's bullying and self-centeredness and Davis's arrogance and cruelty to women and fellow-musicians, and even his public. But the amount of space and energy and musical adulation that is given to these five musicians in "Jazz" tends to throw the project out of balance. Many first-rate musicians are tapped only in passing or are ignored altogether. Those who are mentioned briefly, then left on the cutting-room floor, include Charles Mingus, a great bassist and a wildly original composer and bandleader; the Modern Jazz Quartet, for forty years the most lyrical and swinging of jazz chamber groups; and the seminal pianists Earl Hines, Bud Powell, and Bill Evans, who, taken together, invented modern jazz piano.

The essential musicians who are ignored completely include Big Sid Catlett, the greatest jazz drummer (he does a twelve-bar solo in a funny 1947 black feature film, "Boy! What a Girl," that would have fitted beautifully into "Jazz"); Nat Cole, who helped bring Hank Jones and Tommy Flanagan into being (neither of them makes the cut, either); and Erroll Garner, a true and brilliant primitive who left his pianistic prints all over jazz. There are more: Pee Wee Russell, an endlessly original and lyrical clarinettist; the trombonists Vic Dickenson and Jimmy Knepper, utterly different but both inimitable and ceaselessly inventive; Jim Hall, Charlie Christian's successor; and the cornettist Bobby Hackett, whose one-chorus solo on Glenn Miller's "A String of Pearls" belongs with Armstrong's baroque edifice on "West End Blues." (Hackett worshipped Armstrong, who, in turn, considered Hackett his "main man.")

The interviews are sometimes invaluable. Artie Shaw, his image Buddha-like, talks about playing the clarinet, the most difficult of all jazz instruments:

> Here's this clumsy series of keys on a piece of wood, and you're trying to manipulate them with the reed and the throat muscles and what they called an embouchure, and you're trying to make something happen that never happened before. You're trying to make a sound that no one ever got before, creating an emotion. You're trying to take . . . notes and make them come out in a way that moves you. If it moves you, it's going to move others. . . . Very rarely does it happen, and when it does you remember it for the rest of your life.

And here's the bassist Arvell Shaw, who worked with Louis Armstrong off and on from 1945 until Armstrong's death: "What he did, what he played, came from within. It came from his own heart—and from his mind. It wasn't anything contrived. It was him, it was Louis, what he was, the essence of his being. . . . He was a completely honest man musically and every other way that I knew about."

The soundtrack choices for the anointed in "Jazz" are sometimes puzzling. Louis Armstrong's 1931 "Stardust" is played five times, but we never hear his 1930 "Sweethearts on Parade," with its empyrean muted opening chorus, full of still tricky rhythmic jumps and pauses. We hear Artie Shaw's "Summertime" but not his "Stardust," which has a clarinet solo that he must still remember. We hear the tentative 1949 Miles Davis of "Venus de Milo" and "Boplicity" but not the tight, assured 1954 Davis of "Walkin'," a muscular, ringing Davis and the antithesis of the weepy Davis of the late nineteen-fifties Gil Evans collaborations (heard here). Charlie Parker was a consummate blues player, but "Parker's Mood" is not on the soundtrack, and neither are his two classic choruses on the 1952 "Funky Blues."

I don't know if the Burns film will make people tap their feet, or make them feel as if they were watching a film about ancient Egypt. I don't know if it will make them flock to record stores to buy jazz CDs, or make them put on the Rolling Stones. But I do know that "Jazz" is a big, noisy panorama, and that panoramas rarely have room for lyrical secrets. Jazz is full of the lyricism that sustains our love of the music. Here are some: the way Sid Catlett picks up the trumpeter Sidney De Paris and sends him sailing down the last chorus of "After You've Gone" (1943); the soft, unearthly start of the tenor saxophonist Ike Quebec's solo on "Mad About You" (1944); the almost sotto-voce blue note Benny Goodman gets off in the third chorus of "Pick-a-Rib, Part II" (1938); Red Allen's leaning-back trumpet solo on Lionel Hampton's "I'm on My Way from You" (1939). All of these are old lyrical secrets, to be sure. But new ones keep turning up in the works of Bill Charlap and Joe Lovano and Tom Harrell. And they turn up in Jean Bach's "A Great Day in Harlem," a peerless hour-long documentary about how Art Kane took a photograph for *Esquire* of fifty-seven jazz musicians gathered in front of a Harlem brownstone one day in the summer of 1958. The film also turns out to be a close look at how jazz musicians talk, move, play, and think. And, as such, it unwittingly prepared the way for Burns's "Jazz," then upstaged it.

## Big Ben

Aside from memories, all that remains of the unique and magisterial tenor saxophonist Ben Webster, who died in 1973, in Amsterdam, is his plain gravestone in Copenhagen ("Ben Webster 1909–1973"), where he lived during his last years; Ol Betsy, the so-christened tenor that he bought in 1938 and used the rest of his life (he left deathbed instructions that Ol Betsy was never to be played again, and it now resides at the Institute of Jazz Studies, at Rutgers); assorted CDs and a new, revivifying Mosaic reissue, "The Complete Verve Johnny Hodges Small Group Sessions 1956–1961," which includes ninety-five tracks, half of which Webster, then at his peak, sits in on; and Webster's first biography, "Ben Webster: His Life and Music" (Berkeley Hills), a scattershot but valuable effort by the Dutch writer Jeroen de Valk.

In 1964, Webster, who had never been to Europe, was offered a month-long gig at Ronnie Scott's club in London. He went, and he never came back, thus joining the dozens of black American jazz musicians who immigrated to Europe in the fifties and sixties. His life had all but dried up here. In 1963, his mother, Mayme, and his great-aunt Agnes Johnson, both beloved, had died in their nineties. They had reared him in Kansas City, where he was born, and had always taken him in when he needed to go home and retrench. (He was married once, briefly, in the forties.) And it had become increasingly difficult to find work. (So much so that in the early six-

ties he appeared at the Metropole, on Seventh Avenue, with a hybrid group
that included Pee Wee Russell, Buck Clayton, J. C. Higginbotham, and Bud
Freeman.) Caught between the Beatles on the right and the jazz avant-garde
of Ornette Coleman and John Coltrane on the left, Webster had slipped
totally out of fashion. There has long been a disturbing tendency among jazz
aficionados to regard each innovation in the music as "progress," a practice
that sends the musicians who have supposedly been supplanted into the
outer darkness.

When Webster arrived abroad, he discovered almost immediately that he
was relished not only in England but in Sweden and Norway and Denmark
and Holland, and in due course he settled in Amsterdam, where he was coddled by his landlady, a Mrs. Hartlooper. (Mayme and Agnes Johnson had
spoiled Webster so completely that he could not function properly without
some sort of loving caretaker.) In 1969, he moved to Copenhagen, where he
was shepherded by a nurse, Birgit Nordtorp. He worked almost steadily, but
his drinking, which had begun to accelerate in the forties, was getting in the
way. Like Bob and Ray's Captain Wolf Larsen, who was an angel when he
was sober and kicked his passengers down the galley stairs when he was
drunk, Webster, normally as sweet as cream, became so fractious when he
was drunk that he had long been known among American musicians as "the
Brute." The pianist Jimmy Rowles loved Webster, and said after his death,
"Benny Carter was the only man he'd listen to when he was like that. . . . Ben
used to say of Carter, 'There's a man who can bake a cake as light as a feather
and whip any man.' " Rowles also knew the good Webster. They hung out in
the fifties, when they lived and worked on the West Coast, and sometimes
they played golf. "We'd tee up," Rowles said, "and all these fancy types would
be waiting their turn, mumbling under their breath about that big black guy
who was holding them up. Ben would have one of his little hats on the back of
his head, and he'd stand before the ball, his big front sticking out, and talk to
himself: 'Now, Ben, do it just like when you were in the Masters. Keep your
head down, and not too many Wheaties.' And he'd take a terrific swing—
*pouf!*—and the ball would dribble ten feet. We only saw each other on the
tees and greens, but we laughed our way around the whole course."

For all his idiosyncrasies, Webster was a meticulous musician, and he
soon discovered a musical problem in Europe that had never existed at
home: many of the best European musicians he played with tended to be
amateurish; instead of supporting him, they ended up in his wake. These
problems eventually aggravated his drinking, and he began showing up at
concerts and clubs dead drunk, or missing important engagements altogether. Webster had broad shoulders, a fine beaked nose, and imperious
flanking bags under his eyes, and he radiated a powerful handsomeness. But
in his last years he gained an enormous amount of weight; his legs gave out
and he used a cane, and his playing became halting and even incoherent. Yet
he never lost his sweetness. De Valk quotes a young tenor saxophonist,

Jesper Thilo: "He lived alone, and he really liked it when someone came by. I went over to his flat a lot. We'd have a beer or something stronger, and talk about music. . . . I think he wanted the same role for himself that Coleman Hawkins had in New York. He wanted to help me with things he knew a lot about, like tone formation. He taught me a lot about embouchure, about how to develop a good sound."

Coleman Hawkins, Lester Young, and Ben Webster were the founding emperors of the jazz tenor saxophone. Hawkins more or less invented the instrument, Young reinvented it tonally and melodically (Hawkins sped through the chords, while Young floated above), and Webster developed an enormous lyrical sound and swinging directness—an easy, embracing quality—that touched you in a way that Hawkins and Young, for all their genius, rarely did. Webster had rummaged around in Hawkins's style for most of the thirties. Then, in 1940, he joined Duke Ellington and fell under the sway of the magical Johnny Hodges, who by example taught him about tone and emotion, about how to trap his listeners. When he left Ellington, in 1943, and joined Sid Catlett on Fifty-second Street, he had perfected his huge style.

It came in three speeds. He seemed to breathe rather than play his slow ballads; he'd start phrases with a whispering breath that would grow majestically into a full tone, then gradually melt back into breath—a kind of aural appearing-and-disappearing act. Webster's ballads were intimate and cajoling, but never sentimental. Everything tightened when he played the blues. The breathiness vanished, and his phrases became short and hard; he preached and badgered. His ballads insinuated, but his slow blues were in your face. Webster swung irresistibly in medium tempos. His blues moved at a run, and if he played a thirty-two-bar song he would alter the melody discreetly in the first chorus, then elbow the melody aside, replacing it with pure blocks of sound. Fast tempos sometimes got away from him. He'd coast through his first chorus and, either angry or perhaps hungover, start growling, an abrasive sound that would finally end a chorus or two later with a shuddering, out-of-my-way tremolo. But sometimes this abrasiveness worked, as in Webster's celebrated roaring solo on Ellington's "Cotton Tail." In the late forties, with Webster sailing along, jazz was struck by a cataclysm it still suffers from. Art Tatum and Charlie Parker began flooding the music with sixteenth notes and cascading, glissandolike runs and arpeggios, and they turned jazz into a baroque music. Webster became one of the last non-rococo players, a champion of quarter notes and whole notes. But the thousand-notes-a-chorus musicians who eventually surrounded him made his rich, wasteless lyricism sound monumental.

For whatever reason, most of Webster's music on the Mosaic album is blues of various speeds. Many of them are classics, in particular the five blues recorded in April of 1958 with Roy Eldridge, Vic Dickenson, Hodges, Billy Strayhorn (whose accompaniment is spiky and rueful), and Sam Woodyard, and the four blues set down by almost the same group several months later. "Not So Dukish" and "Preacher Blues," done in September of 1958 with an Ellington contingent, takes the blues even further down. Best of all, though, are the dozen lightsome, loving numbers that Hodges and Webster, the Master and the Disciple, recorded with a rhythm section in 1960, among them "Dual Highway," "Ifida," and "I'd Be There"—three instances of the secret language that jazz musicians often speak. Six of the Hodges-Webster duets have never been released before.

Webster, clean and sober, appears in a photograph in de Valk's biography, and Webster, drunk, appears in a picture in the Mosaic album booklet. The first photo from the biography, taken in 1968 in Amsterdam, shows Webster sitting on a beautiful bike, his left foot resting on the sidewalk. He is gesticulating with his left hand and talking to someone, and he is dressed elegantly in a dark tie, a dark shirt, and a dark suit with a white handkerchief in his breast pocket. He has one of his smallish fedoras on his head, and his shoes are shined. Both Hodges and Webster appear in the photograph in the album booklet, and it is terrifying. It was taken at a party in Chicago in 1955. Hodges is dressed in a tie and a sweater and a houndstooth jacket. He is holding a drink and gazing calmly to his right. Webster, at the left, looks wild and unkempt. His left arm is draped heavily around Hodges' shoulders, his tie is loose, and his shirt is open at the neck. He is looking in the same direction as Hodges, but his mouth is open, his eyes are squinted, and he looks like he is shouting and just about to push Hodges away and flatten the enemy.

The Webster who lived uneasily between these two Websters appears in de Valk's book, too. In 1971, Webster played a concert in Oslo attended by the Crown Prince of Norway. Afterward, the musicians were introduced to the Prince. Webster, whose stick legs were in poor shape, was the last to make it up to the royal box. Quoting the trumpet player Keith Smith, de Valk writes, "The other band leaders were through with their formal introductions . . . when the distinct sound of curses and groans grew uncomfortably nearer, echoing up the grand staircase. . . . Ben, having finally completed his ascent, staggered through the door. . . . The aide—almost speechless at the break in decorum—proceeded with his introductions: 'Your Royal Highness, this is Ben Webster.' The Crown Prince nodded regally, and the aide continued, 'Mr. Webster, may I present his Royal Highness the Crown Prince of Norway,' pointing Ben nervously in the right direction, at which point Ben lunged forward, slapped the Crown Prince on the back, yelling 'Ben Webster, King of the Tenors—pleased to meet you, Prince!' "

# Index

# Index